14th Conference of the European Chapter of the Association for Computational Linguistics 2014

(EACL 2014)

Gothenburg, Sweden
26-30 April 2014

ISBN: 978-1-63266-396-2

Printed from e-media with permission by:

Curran Associates, Inc.
57 Morehouse Lane
Red Hook, NY 12571

proceedings.com

Some format issues inherent in the e-media version may also appear in this print version.

Printed by Curran Associates, Inc. (2014)

Association for Computational Linguistics
209 N. Eighth Street
Stroudsburg, Pennsylvania 18360

Phone: 1-570-476-8006
Fax: 1-570-476-0860

acl@aclweb.org

Additional copies of this publication are available from:

Curran Associates, Inc.
57 Morehouse Lane
Red Hook, NY 12571 USA
Phone: 845-758-0400
Fax: 845-758-2634
Email: curran@proceedings.com
Web: www.proceedings.com

Table of Contents

Preface: General Chair

Welcome to EACL 2014, the 14th Conference of the European Chapter of the Association for Computational Linguistics! This is the largest EACL meeting ever: with eighty long papers, almost fifty short ones, thirteen student research papers, twenty-six demos, fourteen workshops and six tutorials, we expect to bring to Gothenburg up to five hundred participants, for a week of excellent science interspersed with entertaining social events.

It is hard to imagine how much work is involved in the preparation of such an event. It takes about three years, from the day the EACL board starts discussing the location and nominating the chairs, until the final details of the budget are resolved. The number of people involved is also huge, and I was fortunate to work with an excellent, dedicated and efficient team, to which I am enormously grateful.

The scientific program was very ably composed by the Program Committee Chairs, Sharon Goldwater and Stefan Riezler, presiding over a team of twenty-four area chairs. Given that this year we had long paper submissions, followed by a rebuttal period, followed by a very stressed short paper reviewing period, this meant *a lot* of work. Overall, Sharon and Stefan handled over five hundred submissions, or over 1,500 reviews! The result of this work is a balanced, high-quality scientific program that I'm sure we will all enjoy. The PC Chairs have also selected the three invited speakers, and we will have the pleasure of attending keynotes delivered by Simon King, Ulrike von Luxburg, and Dan Roth – a great choice of speakers!

The diverse workshop program was put together by the Workshop Chairs, Anja Belz and Reut Tsarfaty, under very strict deadlines due to the fact that as in previous years, workshops were coordinated with other ACL events (this year, ACL and EMNLP). Even in light of the competition, Anja and Reut negotiated a varied and attractive set of fourteen workshops which will keep us busy over the weekend prior to the main conference.

Also on that weekend are the six tutorials, selected from among several submissions by the Tutorial Chairs, Afra Alishahi and Marco Baroni. Again, the tutorials offer a set of diverse and timely topics, covering both core areas of NLP and tangential fields of research.

We included in the program a large number of demonstrations, selected by Marko Tadić and Bogdan Babych, the Demo Chairs. And an integral part of the scientific program is the Student Research Workshop, put together by the SRW Chairs, Desmond Elliott, Konstantina Garoufi, Douwe Kiela, and Ivan Vulić, whose work was supervised by the SRW Faculty Advisor, Sebastian Padó.

The Proceedings that you're reading now were compiled by the Publication Chairs, Gosse Bouma and Yannick Parmentier. Their responsibilities include the preparation of all the proceedings, including the main session, the SRW, the demo session, the workshop proceedings etc. – thousands of pages, all under very strict deadlines.

It has been a very special pleasure for me to work with an excellent local organization team. The Local Organization Chairs, Lars Borin and Aarne Ranta, were assisted by an extremely efficient team, Yvonne Adesam, Martin Kaså and Nina Tahmasebi. Their effort cannot be overestimated: from dealing with the two universities over issues of conference space and funding, through dealing with two professional conference organizers, to corresponding with authors, participants and of course all the other chairs. Add the stress involved in being in charge of a hefty budget that has to be balanced by the end of the conference, and you can only admire the relaxed way in which they took upon themselves this daunting task.

The local team included also Peter Ljunglöf, the Publicity Chair, to whom we should all be grateful for the beautiful web site of the conference and the timely e-mails, tweets and Facebook statuses. The Local Sponsorship Chairs, Sofie Johansson Kokkinakis and Staffan Larsson, worked together with the ACL

Sponsorship Chairs Jochen Leidner and Alessandro Moschitti, to obtain some much needed financial support. Sincere thanks are due to the various sponsors for their generous contribution.

The local team did a wonderful job organizing a social program this year. This includes a reception at the City Hall on Sunday, a catered poster and demo session on Monday, a conference dinner on Tuesday and of course, the famous Cortège at the very end of the conference. A perfect mix of business and pleasure.

I am grateful to all members of the EACL board for their advice and guidance, and in particular to past Chair Sien Moens, Chair Stephen Clark, Chair-elect Lluìs Màrquez and Treasurer Mike Rosner. Many thanks are also due to the ACL Treasurer Graeme Hirst and of course, as always, to the ACL Business Manager Priscilla Rasmussen, who was always there with her vast experience to clear up uncertainties and lend a helping hand.

Finally, let us not forget that this is all about *you*: authors, reviewers, demo presenters, workshop organizers and speakers, tutorial speakers and participants of the conference. Thank you for choosing to be part of EACL-2014, I wish you a very enjoyable conference!

Shuly Wintner, University of Haifa
General Chair
March 2014

Preface: Program Chairs

We are delighted to present you with this volume containing the papers accepted for presentation at the 14th Conference of the European Chapter of the Association for Computational Linguistics, held in Gothenburg, Sweden, from April 26 till April 30 2014.

EACL 2014 introduced a short paper (4 page) format in addition to the usual long paper (8 page) format, which led to the highest total number of submissions of any EACL. We received 317 valid long paper submissions and were able to accept 78 of these papers (an acceptance rate of 24.6%). 49 of the papers (15.4%) were accepted for oral presentation, and 31 (9.8%) for poster presentation. In addition, we received 199 valid short paper submissions and were able to accept 46 of these (an acceptance rate of 23.1%). 33 of the papers (16.6%) were accepted for oral presentation, and 13 (6.5%) for poster presentation. The EACL 2014 schedule also includes oral presentations from two papers published in the Transactions of the Association for Computational Linguistics, a new feature of this year's conference.

The introduction of short papers, handled in a second round of submissions, meant a somewhat higher workload for our program committee, and we are very grateful to our 24 area chairs for recruiting an excellent panel of 434 reviewers from all over the world, and to those reviewers for providing their feedback on the submissions. Each submission was reviewed by at least three reviewers (at least two for short papers), who were then encouraged to discuss any differences of opinion, taking into account the responses of the authors to their initial reviews. Based on the reviews, author response, and reviewer discussion, area chairs provided a ranking for papers in their area. Final selection was made by the program co-chairs after discussion with the area chairs and an independent check of reviews.

Each area chair was also asked to nominate the best long paper and best short paper from his or her area, or to decline to nominate any. Several papers were nominated, and of these the program co-chairs made the final decision on the Best Long Paper and Best Short Paper awards, which will be awarded in a plenary session at the conference.

In addition to the main conference program, EACL 2014 will feature the now traditional Student Research Workshop, 14 other workshops, 6 tutorials and a demo session with 26 presentations. We are also fortunate to have three excellent invited speakers: Dan Roth (University of Illinois at Urbana-Champaign), Ulrike von Luxburg (University of Hamburg), and Simon King (University of Edinburgh).

We would very much like to thank all of the other people who have helped us put together this year's conference. Most importantly, all of the authors who submitted their work to EACL, without whom we would have no conference at all! The number and quality of both long and short paper submissions in many different areas shows that we are maintaining and growing a broad and active community. We are greatly indebted to all the area chairs and reviewers for their hard work, which allowed us to choose from amongst the many high-quality submissions to put together a strong programme and provide useful feedback to authors. The START support team, and especially Rich Gerber, were of great help in swiftly answering all of our technical questions, and occasionally even knowing more about our job than we did! We thank the invited speakers for agreeing to present at EACL, and the publication chairs, Yannick Parmentier and Gosse Bouma, for putting this volume together. The local organizing committee (Lars Borin, Aarne Ranta, Yvonne Adesam, Martin Kaså, and Nina Tahmasebi) have been invaluable in arranging the logistics of the conference and coordinating with us on many organizational issues, and we are grateful to the publicity chair, Peter Ljunglöf, for ensuring up-to-date programme information on the conference web site. We thank also the Student Research Workshop chairs for smoothly coordinating with us on their schedule. Last but not least, we are indebted to the General Chair, Shuly Wintner, for his guidance and support throughout the whole process.

We hope you enjoy the conference!

Sharon Goldwater and Stefan Riezler
EACL 2014 Programme Chairs

General Chair:

Shuly Wintner, University of Haifa (Israel)

Program Chairs:

Sharon Goldwater, University of Edinburgh (UK)
Stefan Riezler, Heidelberg University (Germany)

Local Organizing Committee:

Lars Borin (chair), University of Gothenburg (Sweden)
Aarne Ranta (chair), University of Gothenburg and Chalmers University of Technology (Sweden)
Yvonne Adesam, University of Gothenburg (Sweden)
Martin Kaså, University of Gothenburg (Sweden)
Nina Tahmasebi, Chalmers University of Technology (Sweden)

Publication Chairs:

Gosse Bouma, University of Groningen (The Netherlands)
Yannick Parmentier, University of Orléans (France)

Workshop Chairs:

Anja Belz, University of Brighton (UK)
Reut Tsarfaty, Uppsala University (Sweden)

Tutorial Chairs:

Afra Alishahi, Tilburg University (The Netherlands)
Marco Baroni, University of Trento (Italy)

Demo Chair:

Marko Tadić, University of Zagreb (Croatia)
Bogdan Babych, University of Leeds (UK)

Student Research Workshop Chairs:

Desmond Elliott, University of Edinburgh (UK)
Konstantina Garoufi, University of Potsdam (Germany)
Douwe Kiela, University of Cambridge (UK)
Ivan Vulić, KU Leuven (Belgium)

Student Research Workshop Faculty advisor:

Sebastian Padó, Heidelberg University (Germany)

Sponsorship Chairs:

Jochen Leidner, Thomson-Reuters/Linguit Ltd. (Switzerland)

Alessandro Moschitti, University of Trento (Italy)
Sofie Johansson Kokkinakis, University of Gothenburg (Sweden)
Staffan Larsson, University of Gothenburg (Sweden)

Publicity Chair:

Peter Ljunglöf, University of Gothenburg and Chalmers University of Technology (Sweden)

Area Chairs:

Enrique Alfonseca, John Blitzer, Aoife Cahill, Vera Demberg, Chris Dyer, Jacob Eisenstein, Micha Elsner, Katrin Erk, Afsaneh Fazly, Katja Filippova, Alexander Fraser, Iryna Gurevych, Chin-Yew Lin, David McClosky, Yusuke Miyao, Hwee Tou Ng, Slav Petrov, Simone Paolo Ponzetto, Sebastian Riedel, Verena Rieser, Helmut Schmid, Izhak Shafran, Hiroya Takamura, Lucy Vanderwende

Reviewers:

Fadi Abu-Sheika, Meni Adler, Nitish Aggarwal, Lars Ahrenberg, Afra Alishahi, Yaser Al-Onaizan, Yasemin Altun, Waleed Ammar, Jacob Andreas, Ion Androutsopoulos, Gabor Angeli, Mihael Arcan, Yoav Artzi, Jordi Atserias Batalla, Michael Auli, Harald Baayen, Timothy Baldwin, David Bamman, Mohit Bansal, Marco Baroni, Loïc Barrault, Núria Bel, Kedar Bellare, Islam Beltagy, Luciana Benotti, Yinon Bentor, Jonathan Berant, Sabine Bergler, Raffaella bernardi, Klinton Bicknell, Chris Biemann, Arianna Bisazza, Yonatan Bisk, Roi Blanco, Michael Bloodgood, Phil Blunsom, Nathan Bodenstab, Branimir Boguraev, Bernd Bohnet, Gemma Boleda, Danushka Bollegala, Francis Bond, Kalina Bontcheva, Johan Bos, Houda Bouamor, Thorsten Brants, Chloé Braud, Fabienne Braune, Chris Brew, Ted Briscoe, Julian Brooke, Marco Brunello, Paul Buitelaar, Harry Bunt, Aljoscha Burchardt, David Burkett, Stephan Busemann, Bill Byrne, Nicoletta Calzolari, Ivan Cantador, Yunbo Cao, Giuseppe Carenini, Marine Carpuat, Xavier Carreras, John Carroll, Dave Carter, Francisco Casacuberta, Pablo Castells, Nathanael Chambers, Jason Chang, Ming-Wei Chang, David Chen, Hsin-Hsi Chen, Wenliang Chen, Chen Chen, Kehai Chen, Colin Cherry, Jackie Chi Kit Cheung, David Chiang, Christian Chiarcos, Kostadin Cholakov, Christos Christodoulopoulos, Jennifer Chu-Carroll, Cindy Chung, Massimiliano Ciaramita, Philipp Cimiano, Stephen Clark, Shay Cohen, Bonaventura Coppola, Marta R. Costa-jussà, Danilo Croce, Heriberto Cuayahuitl, Walter Daelemans, Cristian Danescu-Niculescu-Mizil, Dipanjan Das, Brian Davis, Munmun De Choudhury, Marie-Catherine de Marneffe, Gerard de Melo, Thierry Declerck, Michael Deisher, Steve DeNeefe, John DeNero, Pascal Denis, Michael Denkowski, Leon Derczynski, Marilena di Bari, Barbara Di Eugenio, Alberto Diaz, Michelangelo Diligenti, Markus Dreyer, Gregory Druck, Jinhua Du, Xiangyu Duan, Kevin Duh, Ewan Dunbar, Nadir Durrani, Marc Dymetman, Judith Eckle-Kohler, Koji Eguchi, Vladimir Eidelman, Andreas Eisele, David Elson, Angela Fahrni, James Fan, Richárd Farkas, Manaal Faruqui, Miriam Fernandez, Raquel Fernandez, Oliver Ferschke, João Filgueiras, Mark Fishel, Jeffrey Flanigan, Radu Florian, Mikel Forcada, Karën Fort, Eric Fosler-Lussier, Victoria Fossum, Jennifer Foster, Gil Francopoulo, Stefan L. Frank, Stella Frank, Francesca Frontini, Alona Fyshe, Michel Galley, Juri Ganitkevitch, Wenxuan Gao, Claire Gardent, Dan Garrette, Guillermo Garrido, Albert Gatt, Georgi Georgiev, Andrea Gesmundo, Arnab Ghoshal, George Giannakopoulos, Daniel Gildea, Kevin Gimpel, Jonathan Ginzburg, Yoav Goldberg, Julio Gonzalo, Spence Green, Edward Grefenstette, Camille Guinaudeau, Sonal Gupta, Francisco Guzman, Nizar Habash, Barry Haddow, John Hale, David Hall, Keith Hall, Greg Hanneman, Sanda Harabagiu, Christian Hardmeier, Matthias Hartung, mohammed hasanuzzaman, Katsuhiko Hayashi, Zhongjun He, Michael Heilman, James Henderson, John Henderson, Aurélie Herbelot, Ulf Hermjakob, Raquel Hervas, Graeme Hirst, Hieu Hoang, Johannes Hoffart, Mark Hopkins, Veronique Hoste, Fei Huang, Xiaojiang Huang, Xuanjing Huang, Rebecca Hwa, Nancy Ide, Gonzalo Iglesias, Diana Inkpen, Ann Irvine, Jagadeesh Jagarlamudi, Srinivasan

Janarthanam, Lifeng Jia, Richard Johansson, Doug Jones, Laura Kallmeyer, Jaap Kamps, Evangelos Kanoulas, Damianos Karakos, Graham Katz, Simon Keizer, Frank Keller, Shahram Khadivi, Adam Kilgarriff, Jin-Dong Kim, Seungyeon Kim, Katrin Kirchhoff, Philipp Koehn, Alexander Koller, Terry Koo, Anna Korhonen, Zornitsa Kozareva, Emiel Krahmer, Marco Kuhlmann, Roland Kuhn, Shankar Kumar, Jonathan Kummerfeld, Patrik Lambert, Phillippe Langlais, Guy Lapalme, Egoitz Laparra, Mirella Lapata, Staffan Larsson, Thomas Lavergne, Alon Lavie, Florian Laws, Lillian Lee, Junhui Li, lishuang li, Zhenghua Li, Maria Liakata, Chu-Cheng Lin, Krister Linden, Xiao Ling, Bing Liu, Jing Liu, Qun Liu, Yang Liu, Karen Livescu, Peter Ljunglöf, Elena Lloret, Adam Lopez, Annie Louis, Wei Lu, Yanjun Ma, Ji Ma, Klaus Macherey, Wolfgang Macherey, Bernardo Magnini, Inderjeet Mani, Chris Manning, Daniel Marcu, José B. Mariño, André F. T. Martins, Yuval Marton, Rebecca Mason, Yuji Matsumoto, Takuya Matsuzaki, Cettolo Mauro, Arne Mauser, Chandler May, Diana McCarthy, Ryan McDonald, Bob McMurray, Yashar Mehdad, Edgar Meij, Arul Menezes, Florian Metze, Christian M. Meyer, Jeffrey Micher, Bonan Min, Margaret Mitchell, Behrang Mohit, Karo Moilanen, Monica Monachini, Christof Monz, Raymond Mooney, Andrea Moro, Alessandro Moschitti, Thomas Mueller, Smaranda Muresan, Brian Murphy, Seung-Hoon Na, Tetsuji Nakagawa, Toshiaki Nakazawa, Preslav Nakov, Ramesh Nallapati, Vivi Nastase, Tetsuya Nasukawa, Roberto Navigli, Mark-Jan Nederhof, Sapna Negi, Matteo Negri, Ani Nenkova, Graham Neubig, Vincent Ng, Jian-Yun Nie, Jan Niehues, Joakim Nivre, Brendan O'Connor, Stephan Oepen, Kemal Oflazer, Naoaki Okazaki, Gozde Ozbal, Sebastian Padó, Martha Palmer, Patrick Pantel, Cecile Paris, Christopher Parisien, Rebecca J. Passonneau, Alexandre Passos, Siddharth Patwardhan, Michael Paul, Michael J. Paul, Adam Pauls, Sasa Petrovic, Daniele Pighin, Andrei Popescu-Belis, Maja Popović, Fred Popowich, Matt Post, Sameer Pradhan, John Prager, Stephen Pulman, Matthew Purver, Sampo Pyysalo, Behrang Qasemizadeh, Ariadna Quattoni, Chris Quirk, Altaf Rahman, Owen Rambow, Ari Rappoport, Sujith Ravi, Alexis Raykhel, Michaela Regneri, Roi Reichart, Ehud Reiter, Jason Riesa, German Rigau, Alan Ritter, Stephen Roller, Laurent Romary, Carolyn Rose, Michael Roth, Dana Rubinstein, Rachel Rudinger, Vasile Rus, Alexander M. Rush, Graham Russell, Delia Rusu, Kenji Sagae, Horacio Saggion, Kazi Saidul Hasan, Hassan Sajjad, Mark Sammons, Baskaran Sankaran, Felix Sasaki, Giorgio Satta, Hassan Sawaf, David Schlangen, Nathan Schneider, Björn Schuller, Sabine Schulte im Walde, Yohei Seki, Hendra Setiawan, Aliaksei Severyn, Serge Sharoff, Libin Shen, Shuming Shi, Hiroyuki Shindo, Ekaterina Shutova, Advaith Siddharthan, Carina Silberer, Mario J. Silva, Khalil Sima'an, Michel Simard, Kiril Simov, Serra Sinem Tekiroglu, Sameer Singh, Olivier Siohan, Gabriel Skantze, Nathaniel Smith, Stephen Soderland, Anders Søgaard, Thamar Solorio, Hagen Soltau, Swapna Somasundaran, Lucia Specia, Valentin Spitkovsky, Caroline Sporleder, Edward Stabler, Mark Steedman, Josef Steinberger, Georg Stemmer, Amanda Stent, Mark Stevenson, Matthew Stone, Veselin Stoyanov, Carlo Strapparava, Michael Strube, Sara Stymne, Keh-Yih Su, Katsuhito Sudoh, Weiwei Sun, Mihai Surdeanu, Jun Suzuki, Mary Swift, Stan Szpakowicz, Whitney Tabor, Partha Pratim Talukdar, Joel Tetreault, Simone Teufel, Stefan Thater, Mariët Theune, Blaise Thomson, Jörg Tiedemann, Christoph Tillmann, Kristina Toutanova, David Traum, Ming-Feng Tsai, Richard Tzong-Han Tsai, Ioannis Tsochantaridis, Yulia Tsvetkov, Dan Tufiş, Masao Utiyama, Tim Van de Cruys, Antal van den Bosch, Benjamin Van Durme, Josef van Genabith, Paola Velardi, David Vilar, Andreas Vlachos, Stephan Vogel, Clare Voss, Stephen Wan, Haifeng Wang, Kai Wang, ling wang, Wen Wang, Pidong Wang, Yu-Chun Wang, Taro Watanabe, Bonnie Webber, Jason Williams, Philip Williams, Colin Wilson, Travis Wolfe, Dekai Wu, Sander Wubben, Fei Xia, Deyi Xiong, Deyi Xiong, Peng Xu, Bishan Yang, Hui Yang, Muyun Yang, tae yano, Limin Yao, Dani Yogatama, François Yvon, Beñat Zapirain, Richard Zens, Torsten Zesch, Luke Zettlemoyer, Feifei Zhai, Hui Zhang, Joy Ying Zhang, Lei Zhang, Min Zhang, Yi Zhang, Yue Zhang, Meng Zhang, Liu Zhanyi, Shiqi Zhao, Tiejun Zhao, Xin Zhao, Xin Zhao, Muhua Zhu, Chengqing Zong

GOLD SPONSORS

Google™

معهد قطر لبحوث الحوسبة
Qatar Computing Research Institute
Member of Qatar Foundation عضو في مؤسسة قطر

SILVER SPONSOR

FINDWISE
SEARCH DRIVEN SOLUTIONS

BRONZE SPONSORS

facebook

Yandex

SUPPORTERS

W UNIVERSITY of WASHINGTON

UNIVERSITY OF GOTHENBURG — MASTER'S PROGRAMME IN LANGUAGE TECHNOLOGY

Talkamatic FREE DIALOGUE

EXHIBITORS

M&C MORGAN & CLAYPOOL PUBLISHERS

Springer

OTHER SPONSORS

UNIVERSITY OF GOTHENBURG

City of Gothenburg

SAS OFFICIAL AIRLINE A STAR ALLIANCE MEMBER

HOSTS

CLT
Centre for Language Technology
Gothenburg, Sweden

Improving Word Alignment Using Linguistic Code Switching Data

Fei Huang* and **Alexander Yates**
Temple University
Computer and Information Sciences
324 Wachman Hall
Philadelphia, PA 19122
{fei.huang,yates}@temple.edu

Abstract

Linguist Code Switching (LCS) is a situation where two or more languages show up in the context of a single conversation. For example, in English-Chinese code switching, there might be a sentence like "我们15分钟后有个meeting (We will have a meeting in 15 minutes)". Traditional machine translation (MT) systems treat LCS data as noise, or just as regular sentences. However, if LCS data is processed intelligently, it can provide a useful signal for training word alignment and MT models. Moreover, LCS data is from non-news sources which can enhance the diversity of training data for MT. In this paper, we first extract constraints from this code switching data and then incorporate them into a word alignment model training procedure. We also show that by using the code switching data, we can jointly train a word alignment model and a language model using co-training. Our techniques for incorporating LCS data improve by 2.64 in BLEU score over a baseline MT system trained using only standard sentence-aligned corpora.

1 Introduction

Many language users are competent in multiple languages, and they often use elements of multiple languages in conversations with other speakers with competence in the same set of languages. For example, native Mandarin speakers who also speak English might use English words in a Chinese sentence, like "你知道这个问题的solution吗？(Do you know the solution to this problem ?)". This phenomenon of mixing languages within a single utterance is known as Linguistic Code Switching (LCS). Examples of these utterances are common in communities of speakers with a shared competency in multiple languages, such as Web forums for Chinese emigrés to the United States. For example, more than 50% of the sentences we collected from a Web forum (MITBBS.com) contains both Chinese and English.

Traditional word alignment models take a sentence-level aligned corpus as input and generate word-level alignments for each pair of parallel sentences. Automatically-gathered LCS data typically contains no sentence-level alignments, but it still has some advantages for training word alignment models and machine translation (MT) systems which are worth exploring. First, because it contains multiple languages in the same sentence and still has a valid meaning, it will tell the relationship between the words from different languages to some extent. Second, most LCS data is formed during people's daily conversation, and thus it contains a diversity of topics that people care about, such as home furnishings, cars, entertainment, *etc*, that may not show up in standard parallel corpora. Moreover, LCS data is easily accessible from Web communities, such as MITBBS.com, Sina Weibo, Twitter, etc.

However, like most unedited natural language text on the Web, LCS data contains symbols like emotions, grammar and spelling mistakes, slang and strongly idiomatic usage, and a variety of other phenomena that are difficult to handle. LCS data with different language pairs may also need special handling. For instance, Sinha and Thakur (2005) focus on words in mixed English and Hindi texts where a single word contains elements from both languages; they propose techniques for translating such words into both pure English and pure Hindi. Our study focuses on Chinese-English LCS, where this is rarely a problem,

*The author is working at Raytheon BBN Technologies now

but for other language pairs, Sinha and Thakur's techniques may be required as preprocessing steps. Primarily, though, LCS data requires special-purpose algorithms to use it for word alignment, since it contains no explicit alignment labels.

In this paper, we investigate two approaches to using LCS data for machine translation. The first approach focuses exclusively on word alignment, and uses patterns extracted from LCS data to guide the EM training procedure for word alignment over a standard sentence-aligned parallel corpus. We focus on two types of patterns in the LCS data: first, English words are almost never correct translations for any Chinese word in the same LCS utterance. Second, for sentences that are mostly Chinese but with some English words, if we propose substitutes for the English words using a Chinese language model, those substitutes are often good translations of the English words. We incorporate these patterns into EM training via the posterior regularization framework (Ganchev et al., 2010).

Our second approach treats the alignment and language model as two different and complementary views of the data. We apply the co-training paradigm for semi-supervised learning to incorporate the LCS data into the training procedures for the alignment model and the language model. From the translation table of the alignment model, the training procedure finds candidate translations of the English words in the LCS data, and uses those to supplement the language model training data. From the language model, the training procedure identifies Chinese words that complete the Chinese sentence with high probability, and it uses the English word paired with these completion words as additional training points for translation probabilities. These models are trained repeatedly until they converge to similar predictions on the LCS data. In combination with a larger phrase-based MT system (Koehn et al., 2003), these two training procedures yield an MT system that achieves a BLEU score of 31.79 on an English-to-Chinese translation task, an improvement of 2.64 in BLEU score over a baseline MT system trained on only our parallel corpora.

The rest of this paper is organized as follows. The next section presents related work. Section 3 gives an overview of word alignment. Sections 4 and 5 detail our two algorithms. Section 6 presents our experiments and discusses results, and Section 7 concludes and discusses future work.

2 Related Work

There has been a lot of research on LCS from the theoretical and socio-linguistic communities (Nilep, 2006; De Fina, 2007). Computational research on LCS has studied how to identify the boundaries of an individual language within LCS data, or how to predict when an utterance will switch to another language (Chan et al., 2004; Solorio and Liu, 2008). Manandise and Gdaniec (2011) analyzed the effect on machine translation quality of LCS of Spanish-English and showed that LCS degrades the performance of the syntactic parser. Sinha and Thakur (2005) translate mixed Hindi and English (Hinglish) to pure Hindi and pure English by using two morphological analyzers from both Hindi and English. The difficulty in their problem is that Hindi and English are often mixed into a single word which uses only the English alphabet; approaches based only on the character set cannot tell these words apart from English words. Our current study is for a language pair (English-Chinese) where the words are easy to tell apart, but for MT using code-switching data for other language pairs (such as Hindi-English), we can leverage some of the techniques from their work to separate the tokens into source and target.

Like our proposed methods, other researchers have used co-training before for MT (Callison-Burch and Osborne, 2003). They use target strings in multiple languages as different views on translation. However, in our work, we treat the alignment model and language model as different views of LCS data.

In addition to co-training, various other semi-supervised approaches for MT and word alignment have been proposed, but these have relied on sentence alignments among multiple languages, rather than LCS data. Kay (2000) proposes using multiple target documents as a way of informing subsequent machine translations. Kumar et al. (2007) described a technique for word alignment in a multi-parallel sentence-aligned corpus and showed that this technique can be used to obtain higher quality bilingual word alignments. Other work like (Eisele, 2006) took the issue one step further that they used bilingual translation systems which share one or more common pivot languages to build systems which non-parallel corpus is used. Unlike the data in these techniques, LCS data requires no manual alignment effort and is freely available in large quantities.

Another line of research has attempted to improve word alignment models by incorporating manually-labeled word alignments in addition to sentence alignments. Callison-Burch et al. (2004) tried to give a higher weight on manually labeled data compared to the automatic alignments. Fraser and Marcu (2006) used a log-linear model with features from IBM models. They alternated the traditional Expectation Maximization algorithm which is applied on a large parallel corpus with a discriminative step aimed at increasing word-alignment quality on a small, manually word-aligned corpus. Ambati et al.(2010) tried to manually correct the alignments which are informative during the unsupervised training and applied them to an active learning model. However, labeled word alignment data is expensive to produce. Our approach is complementary, in that we use mixed data that has no word alignments, but still able to learn constraints on word alignments.

Our techniques make use of posterior regularization (PR) framework (Ganchev et al., 2010), which has previously been used for MT (Graca et al., 2008), but with very different constraints on EM training and different goals. (Graca et al., 2008) use PR to enforce the constraint that one word should not translate to many words, and that if a word s translates to a word t in one MT system, then a model for translation in the reverse direction should translate t to s. Both of these constraints apply to sentence-aligned training data directly, and complement the constraints that we extract from LCS data.

3 Statistical Word Alignment

Statistical word alignment (Brown et al., 1994) is the task identifying which words are translations of each other in a bilingual sentence corpus. It is primarily used for machine translation. The input to an alignment system is a sentence-level aligned bilingual corpus, which consists of pairs of sentences in two languages. One language is denoted as the target language, and the other language as the source language.

We now introduce the baseline model for word alignment and how we can incorporate the LCS data to improve the model. IBM Model 1 (Brown et al., 1994) and the HMM alignment model (Vogel et al., 1996) are cascaded to form the baseline model for alignment. These two models have a similar formulation $\mathcal{L} = P(t, a|s) = P(a)\prod_j P(t_j|s_{a_j})$ with a different distortion probability $P(a)$. s and t denote the source and target sentences. a is the alignment, and a_j is the index of the source language word that generates the target language word at position j. The HMM model assumes the alignments have a first-order Markov dependency, so that $P(a) = \prod_j P(a_j|a_j - a_{j-1})$. IBM Model 1 ignores the word position and uses a uniform distribution, so $P(a) = \prod_j P(a_j)$ where $P(a_j) = \frac{1}{|t|}$, where $|t|$ is the length of t.

Expectation Maximization (Dempster et al., 1977) is typically used to train the alignment model. It tries to maximize the marginal likelihood of the sentence-level aligned pairs. For the HMM alignment model, the forward-backward algorithm can be used the optimize the posterior probability of the hidden alignment a.

4 Learning Constraints for Word Alignments from LCS Data

We observed that most LCS sentences are predominantly in one language, which we call the *majority* language, with just a small number of words from another language, which we call the *minority* language. The grammar of each sentence appears to mirror the structure of the majority language. Speakers appear to be substituting primarily content words from the minority language, especially nouns and verbs, without changing the structure of the majority language. In this section, we explain two types of constraints we extract from the LCS data that can be helpful for guiding the training of a word alignment model, and we describe how we incorporate those constraints into a full training procedure.

4.1 Preventing bad alignments

After inspecting sentences in our LCS data, we found that the words from the target language occurring in the sentence are highly likely not to be the translation of the remaining source word. Figure 1 shows an example LCS sentence where the speaker has replaced the Chinese word “要求” with the corresponding English word “request”.

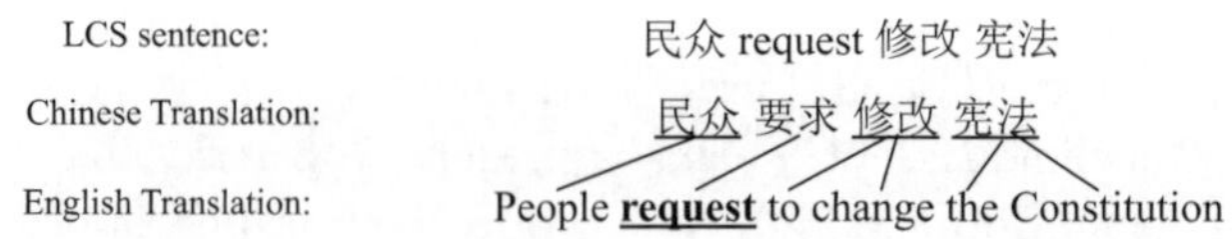

Figure 1: The upper sentence is the original LCS sentence. The bottom ones are its translation in pure Chinese and English. Underlined words are the original words in the LCS sentence.

In most LCS utterances, the minority language replaces or substitutes for words in the majority language, and thus it does not serve as a translation of any majority-language words in the sentence. If we can enforce that a word alignment model avoids pairing words that appear in the same LCS sentence, we can significantly narrow down the possible choices of the translation candidates during word alignment training.

Formally, let t^{LCS} be the set of target (Chinese) words and s^{LCS} be the source (English) words in the same sentence of the LCS data. According to our observation, each s_j^{LCS} in s^{LCS} should not be aligned with any word t_i^{LCS} in t^{LCS}. We call every target-source word pair (t_i^{LCS}, s_j^{LCS}) from LCS data a **blocked alignment**. For a set of word alignments WA $= \{(s_w, t_w)\}$ produced by a word alignment model, define

$$\phi_{\text{BA}} = \sum_{(s_w,t_w)\in \text{WA}} \mathbf{1}[(s_w, t_w) \in \text{BA}] \quad (1)$$

where BA is the set of blocked alignments extracted from the LCS data. We want to minimize ϕ_{BA}. Figure 2 shows a graphical illustration of this constraint.

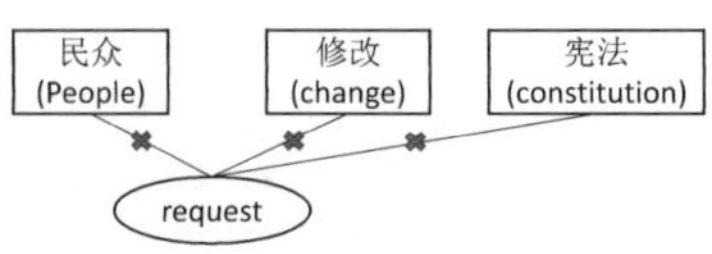

Figure 2: Illustration of the blocked alignment constraint.

4.2 Encouraging alignments with substitutes proposed by a language model

Another perspective of using the LCS data is that if we can find some target word set $t^{similar}$ from the target language which shares similar contexts as the source word s_j^{LCS} in the LCS data, then we can encourage s_j^{LCS} to be aligned with the each word $t_m^{similar}$ in $t^{similar}$. Figure 3 shows example phrases ("民众建议修改", "民众要求修改", "民众拒绝修改" etc) that appear in a Chinese language model and which share the same left context and right context as the word "request." Our second objective is to encourage minority language words like "request" to align with possible substitutes from the majority language's language model. If we see any of "建议, 要求, 拒绝" in the parallel corpus, we should encourage the word "request" to be aligned with them. We call this target-source word pair $(t_m^{similar}, s_j^{LCS})$ an **encouraged alignment**.

Formally, we define

$$\phi_{\text{EA}} = |C| - \sum_{(s_w,t_w)\in \text{WA}} \mathbf{1}[(s_w, t_w) \in \text{EA}] \quad (2)$$

where $|C|$ is the size of the parallel corpus and EA is the encouraged alignment set. We define this expression in such a way that if the optimization procedure minimizes it, it will increase the number of encouraged alignments.

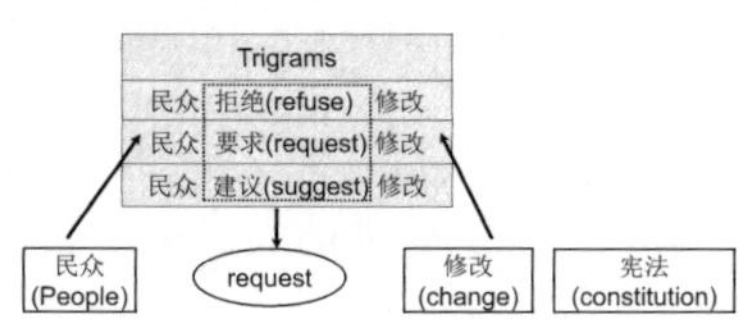

Figure 3: Illustration of the encouraged alignment constraint. The dotted rectangle shows the candidate translations of the English word from the tri-gram output from the language model

Algorithm 1 shows the algorithm of calculating $t^{similar}$. $(t_l^{LCS}, s_j^{LCS}, t_r^{LCS})$ is a (target, source, target)word tuple contained in the LCS data. l and r denote the left and right target words to the source word. We use the language model output from the target language. For each pair of contexts t_l and t_r for the source word, we find the exact match of this pair in the ngram. Then we extract the middle word as the candidates for $t^{similar}$. Here, we only use 3 grams in our experiments, but it is possible to extend this to 5grams, which might lead to further improvements. The EA constraint

Algorithm 1: finding $t^{similar}$

1: **Input:** s^{LCS},t^{LCS}, language model LM
2: Set $t^{similar}$=$\{\}$
3: Extract the 3 grams $(t_l, t_m, t_r) \in gram_3$ from LM
4: set $S = \{\}$
5: For j from 1 to size($gram_3$)
    if $(t_l^j, t_r^j) \in S$
        add t_m^j into $C_{t_l^j, t_r^j}$
    else
        put (t_l^j, t_r^j) into S
        set $C_{t_l^j, t_r^j} = \{\}$
6: Extract tuple $(t_l^{LCS}, s_j^{LCS}, t_r^{LCS})$
    if $(t_l^{LCS}, t_r^{LCS}) \in S$
        add $C_{t_l^{LCS}, t_r^{LCS}}$ into $t^{similar}$
7: **Output:** $t^{similar}$

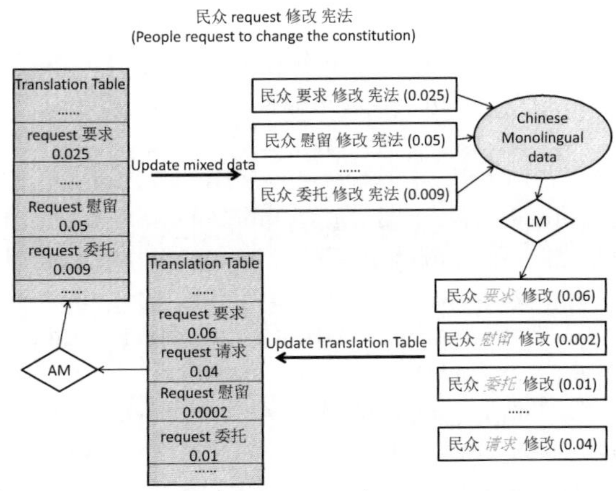

Figure 4: The framework of co-training in word alignment. AM represents alignment model and LM represents language model. Green italic words are the encouraged translation and red italic words are the discouraged translation.

is similar to a bilingual dictionary. However, in the bilingual dictionary, each source word might have several target translations (senses), so it might be ambiguous. The candidate translations used in EA are from language model (3 grams in this paper, but it can be extended to 5 grams), which will always match the contexts. Additionally, the bilingual dictionary contains the standard English/Chinese word pairs. But the LCS data is generated from people’s daily conversation; it reflects usage in a variety of domains, including colloquial and figurative usages that may not appear in a dictionary.

4.3 Constrained parameter estimation

We incorporate ϕ_{BA} and ϕ_{EA} into the EM training procedure for the alignment model using posterior regularization (PR) (Ganchev et al., 2010). Formally, let x be the sentence pairs s and t. During the E step, instead of using the posterior $p(a|x)$ to calculate the expected counts, the PR framework tries to find a distribution $q(a)$ which is close to $p(a|x)$, but which also minimizes the properties $\phi(\mathbf{a}, \mathbf{x})$:

$$\min_{q,\xi} [\mathbf{KL}(q(\mathbf{a})||\mathbf{p}(\mathbf{a}|\mathbf{x}, \theta)) + \sigma||\xi||] \quad (3)$$

$$\text{s.t. } \mathbf{E}_{\mathbf{a}\sim q}[\phi(\mathbf{a}, \mathbf{x})] \leq \xi \quad (4)$$

where KL is the Kullback-Leibler divergence, σ is a free parameter indicating how important the constraints are compared with the marginal log likelihood and ξ is a small violation allowed in the optimization. To impose multiple constraints, we define a norm $||\xi||_A = \sqrt{(\xi^t A \xi)}$, where A is a diagonal matrix whose diagonal entries A_{ii} are free parameters that provide weights on the different constraints. Since we only have two constraints here from LCS data, $A = \begin{pmatrix} 1 & 0 \\ 0 & \alpha \end{pmatrix}$ where α controls the relative importance of the two constraints.

To make the optimization task in the E-step more tractable, PR transforms it to a dual problem:

$$\max_{\lambda \geq 0, ||\lambda||_* \leq \sigma} -\log \sum_{\mathbf{a}} p(\mathbf{a}|\mathbf{x}, \theta) \exp\{-\lambda \cdot \phi(\mathbf{a}, \mathbf{x})\}$$

where $||\cdot||_*$ is the dual norm of $||\cdot||_A$. The gradient of this dual objective is $-\mathbf{E}_q[\phi(\mathbf{a}, \mathbf{x})]$. A projected subgradient descent algorithm is used to perform the optimization.

5 Co-training using the LCS data

The above approaches alter the translation and distortion probabilities in the alignment model. However, they leave the language model unchanged. We next investigate a technique that uses LCS data to re-estimate parameters for the language model as well as the alignment model simultaneously. Co-training (Blum and Mitchell, 1998) is a semi-supervised learning technique that requires two different views of the data. It assumes that each example can be described using two different feature sets which are conditionally independent. Also, each feature set of the data should be sufficient to make accurate prediction.

The schema fits perfectly into our problem. We can treat the alignment model and the language model as two different views of the LCS data.

We use the same example "民众request 修改宪法" to show how co-training works, shown in Figure 4. From the translation table generated by the alignment model, we can get a set of candidate translations of "request", such as "'要求","请求",etc. We can find the candidate with the highest probability as the translation. Similarly, from the language model, we can extract all the ngrams containing " 民众" and "修改" as the left and right words and pick the words in the middle such as " 建议, 要求, 拒绝" etc as the candidate translations. We can then use the candidate with the highest probability as the translation for "request". Thus both models can predict translations for the English (minority language) in this example. Each model's predictions can be used as supplemental training data for the other model.

Algorithm 2 shows the co-training algorithm for word alignment. At each iteration, a language model and an alignment model are trained. The language model is trained on a Chinese-only corpus plus a corpus of probabilistic LCS sentences where the source words are replaced with target candidates from the alignment model. The alignment model is retrained using a translation table which is updated according to the output word pairs from the language model output and the LCS data. In order to take the sentence probability into consideration, we modify the language model training procedure: when it counts the number of times each ngram appears, instead of adding 1, it adds the probability from the translation model for ngrams in the LCS data that contain predicted translations.

Algorithm 2: Co-training for word alignment and language modeling

---

1: **Input:** parallel data X_p, LCS data X_{LCS}, language model training data X_l
2: Initialize translation table tb for IBM1 model
3: For iteration from 1 to MAX
    $tb \leftarrow$ Train-IBM(X_p)
    $tb' \leftarrow$ Train-HMM($X_p|tb$)
4:     For each sentence x_i in X_{LCS}:
        For each source word s_j in x_i:
            1) find the translation t_j of s_j with with probability p_j from tb'
            2) replace s_j with t_j and update sentence's probability $p^s = p^s * p_j$
        $X_l^{new} \leftarrow X_l \cup x_i$
5:     LM $\leftarrow$ Train-LM(X_l^{new})
6:     Extract the tri-gram $gram_3$ from LM
7:     For each sentence x_i in X_{LCS}:
        run Algorithm 1: finding $t^{similar}$
8:     update tb' using (t_m, s_j) where
        $t_m \in t^{similar}$ and $s_j \in x_i$
9: **End For**
10: **Output:** word alignment for X_p and LM

---

6 Experiments and Results

6.1 Experimental Setup

We evaluated our LCS-driven training algorithms on an English-to-Chinese translation task. We use Moses (Koehn et al., 2003), a phrase-based translation system that learns from bilingual sentence-aligned corpora as the MT system. We supplement the baseline word alignment model in Moses with our LCS data, constrained training procedure, and co-training algorithm as well as IBM 3 model. Because IBM 3 model is a fertility based model which might also alleviate some of the problems caused by LCS data. To clarify, we use IBM1 model and HMM models in succession for the baseline. We trained the IBM1 model first and used the resulting parameters as the initial parameter values to train HMM model. Parameters for the final MT system are tuned with Minimum Error Rate Training (MERT) (Och, 2003). The tuning set for MERT is the NIST MT06 data set, which includes 1664 sentences. We test the system on NIST MT02 (878 sentences). To evaluate the word alignment results, we manually aligned 250 sentences from NIST MT02 data set. For simplicity, we only have two types of labels for evaluating word alignments: either two words are aligned together or not. (Previous evaluation metrics also consider a third label for "possible" alignments.) Out of the word-aligned data, we use 100 sentences as a development set and the rest as our testing set.

Our MT training corpus contains 2,636,692 sentence pairs from two parallel corpora: Hong Kong News (LDC2004T08) and Chinese English News Magazine Parallel Text (LDC2005T10). We use the Stanford Chinese segmenter to segment the Chinese data. We use a ngram model package called SRILM (Stolcke, 2002) to train the language model. Because our modified ngram counts contain factions, we used Witten-Bell smoothing(Witten and Bell, 1991) which supports fractional counts. The 3-gram language model is trained on the Xinhua section of the Chinese Gigaword corpus (LDC2003T09) as well as the Chinese side of the parallel corpora. We also removed the sentences in MT02 from the Gigaword corpus if there is any to avoid the biases.

We gather the LCS data from "MITBBS.com," a popular forum for Chinese people living in the United States. This forum is separated by discussion topic, and includes topics such as "Travel", "News", and "Living style". We extract data from 29 different topics. To clean up the LCS data, we get rid of HTML mark-up, and we remove patterns that are commonly repeated in forums, like "Re:" (for "reply" posts) and "[转载]" (for "repost"). We change all English letters written in Chinese font into English font. We stem the English words in both the parallel training data and the LCS data. After the cleaning step, we have 245,470 sentences in the LCS data. 120,922 of them actually contain both Chinese and English in the same sentence. 101,302 of them contain only Chinese, and we add these into the language model training data. We discard the sentences that only contain English.

6.2 Word Alignment Results

In order to incorporate the two constraints during the Posterior Regularization, we need to tune the parameters σ which controls the weights between the constraints and the marginal likelihood and α which controls the relative importance between two constraints on development data. We varied σ from 0.1 to 1000 and varied α over the set $\{0.01, 0.1, 1, 10, 100\}$. After testing the 25 different combinations of σ and α on the development data, we find that the setting with $\sigma = 100$ and $\alpha = 0.1$ achieves the best performance. During PR training, we trained the model 20 iterations for the dual optimization and 5 iterations for the modified EM.

Table 1 shows the word alignment results. We can see that incorporating the LCS data into our alignment model improves the performance. Our best co-training+PR$^+$ system outperforms the baseline by 8 points. Figure 5 shows an example of how BA is extracted from LCS data can help the word alignment performance. The upper figure shows that alignment by the baseline system. We can see that the word "badminton" is aligned incorrectly with word "陶菲克(Taufik)" . However, in the LCS data, we see that " 陶菲克(Taufik)" and "badminton" appear in the same sentence "陶菲克的badminton太厉害了(Taufik plays badminton so well)" and by adding the blocked constraint into the alignment model, it correctly learns that " 陶菲克(Taufik)" should be aligned with something else, and it finds "Taufik" at end. Table 2 shows some of the translations of "badminton" before and after incorporating the LCS data. We can see that it contains some wrong translations like "乒乓球室(pingpong room)","陶菲克(Taufik)"etc using baseline model. After using the LCS data as constraints and the co-training framework, these wrong alignments are eliminated and the translation "羽球(another way of expressing badminton)" get a higher probability. We found that IBM 3 model can also correct this specific case. However, our co-training+PR$^+$ system still outperforms it by 6 points.

System	F1
Baseline	0.68
IBM 3	0.70
PR+BA	0.71
PR+EA	0.70
PR$^+$	0.73
co-training	0.74
co-training+PR$^+$	0.76

Table 1: Word alignment results (PR$^+$ means PR+BA+EA).

Figure 6 shows an example of how EA is extracted from LCS data can help the word alignment. The solid lines show the alignment by the baseline model and we can see that the word "compiled" is not aligned with any Chinese word. After using the LCS data and the language model, we find that "集纳(compile)" shows up in the same context "书(book) 起来(up)"as "compile" along with "装订(staple)" and "订(staple)", therefore "(compile, 集纳)" will be an encouraged alignment. After adding the EA constraint, the model learns that "compile" should be aligned with "集纳".

6.3 Phrase-based machine translation

In this section, we investigated whether improved alignments can improve MT performance. We

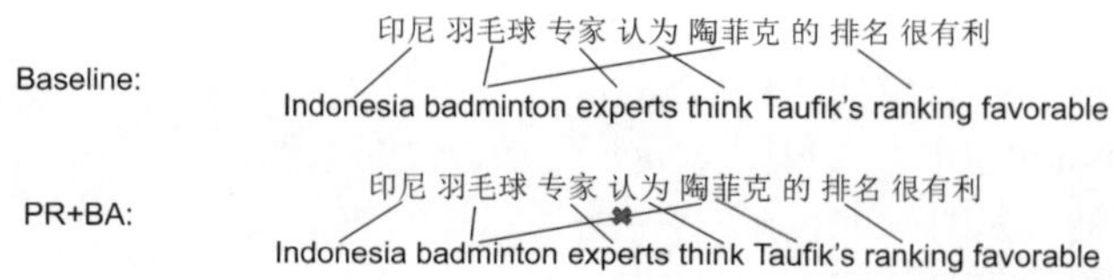

Figure 5: After incorporating the BA constraint from the LCS data, the word "Taufik(陶菲克)" is aligned correctly.

Baseline		PR+co-training	
Translation	Probability	Translation	Probability
羽毛球(badminton)	0.500	羽毛球(badminton)	0.500
乒乓球(pingpong)室(room)	0.500	羽球(two of the three characters in badminton)	0.430
打(play)羽毛(feather)	0.250	打(play)羽毛(feather)	0.326
羽毛球(shuttlecock)头(head)	0.125	羽毛球(shuttlecock)头(head)	0.105
...	...	...	...
陶菲克(Taufik)	0.005	网球拍(racket)	0.002

Table 2: Translation tables of "badminton" before and after incorporation of LCS data.

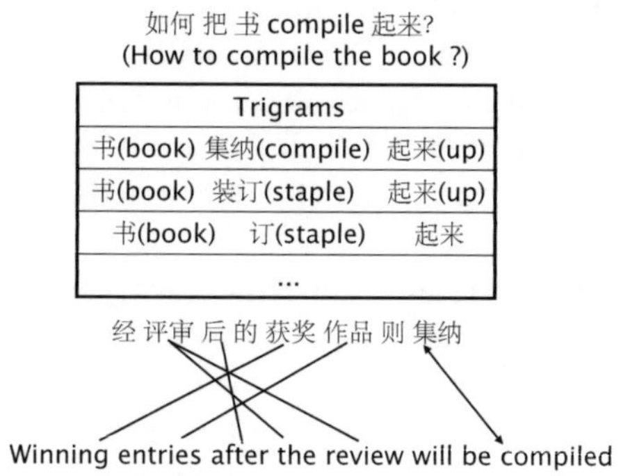

Figure 6: After incorporating the EA constraint from the LCS data, the word "compiled(集纳)" is aligned correctly.

use different word alignment models' outputs as the first step for Moses and keep the rest of Moses system the same. We incorporate Moses's eight standard features as well as the lexicalized reordering model. We also use the grow-diag-final and alignment symmetrization heuristic.

Table 3 shows the machine translation results. We can see that 3 techniques we proposed for word alignment all improve the machine translation result over the baseline system as well as the IBM 3 model. However, although co-training has a bigger improvement on the word alignment compared with PR^+, it actually has a lower BLEU score. This phenomenon shows that the improvement in the word alignment does not necessarily lead to the improvement on machine translation. After combining the co-training and the PR^+ together, co-training+PR^+ improved slightly over PR^+ for MT.

System	BLEU score
Baseline	29.15
IBM 3	30.24
PR^+	31.59*
co-training	31.04*
co-training+PR^+	31.79*

Table 3: Machine translation results. All entries marked with an asterisk are better than the baseline with 95% statistical significance computed using paired bootstrap resampling (Koehn, 2004).

7 Conclusion and Future Work

In this paper, we explored two different ways to use LCS data in a MT system: 1) PR framework to incorporate with Blocked Alignment and Encouraged Alignment constraints. 2) A semi-supervised co-training procedure. Both techniques improve the performance of word alignment and MT over the baseline. Our techniques are currently limited to sentences where the LCS data contains very short (usually one word) phrases from a minority language. An important line of investigation for generalizing these approaches is to consider techniques that cover longer phrases in the minority language; this can help add more of the LCS data into training.

Acknowledgements

This work was supported in part by NSF awards 1065397 and 1218692.

References

S.and Carbonell J. Ambati, V.and Vogel. 2010. Active semi-supervised learning for improving word alignment. In *In Proceedings of the Active Learning for NLP Workshop, NAACL.*

Avrim Blum and Tom Mitchell. 1998. Combining labeled and unlabeled data with co-training. In *Annual Conference on Computational Learning Theaory.*

P. F. Brown, S. Della Pietra, V. J. Della Pietra, and R. L. Mercer. 1994. The mathematics of statistical machine translation: Parameter estimation. *Computational Linguistics*, 19(2):263–311.

Chris Callison-Burch and Miles Osborne. 2003. Co-training for statistical machine translation. In *In Proceedings of the 6th Annual CLUK Research Colloquium.*

Chris Callison-Burch, David Talbot, and Miles Osborne. 2004. Statistical machine translation with word- and sentence-aligned parallel corpora. In *In Proceedings of ACL.*

J. Y. C. Chan, P. C. Ching, and H. M. LEE, T.and Meng. 2004. Detection of language boundary in code-switching utterances by bi-phone probabilities. In *In Proceedings of the International Symposium on Chinese Spoken Language Processing.*

A De Fina. 2007. Code-switching and the construction of ethnic identity in a community of practice. In *Language in Society*, volume 36.

A. P. Dempster, N. M. Laird, and D. B. Rubin. 1977. Maximum likelihood from incomplete data via the em algorithm. In *Royal Statistical Society, Ser*, volume 39.

Andreas Eisele. 2006. Parallel corpora and phrase-based statistical machine translation for new language pairs via multiple intermediaries. In *International Conference on Language Resources and Evaluation.*

Alex Fraser and Daniel Marcu. 2006. Semi-supervised training for statistical word alignment. In *In Proceedings of ACL.*

Kuzman Ganchev, J. Graca, Jennifer Gillenwater, and Ben Taskar. 2010. Posterior regularization for structured latent variable models. In *Journal of Machine Learning Research*, volume 11.

J. Graca, K. Ganchev, and B. Taskar. 2008. Expectation maximization and posterior constraints. In *NIPS.*

Philipp Koehn, Franz Josef Och, and Daniel Marcu. 2003. Statistical phrase-based translation. In *NAACL-HLT.*

Philipp Koehn. 2004. Statistical significance tests for machine translation evaluation. In *In Proceedings of EMNLP.*

Shankar Kumar, Franz Josef Och, and Wolfgang Macherey. 2007. Improving word alignment with bridge languages. In *EMNLP.*

Esme Manandise and Claudia Gdaniec. 2011. Morphology to the rescue redux: Resolving borrowings and code-mixing in machine translation. In *SFCM.*

C. Nilep. 2006. Code switching in sociocultural linguistics. In *Colorado Research in Linguistics*, volume 19.

Franz Josef Och. 2003. Minimum error rate training for statistical machine translation. In *ACL.*

R.M.K. Sinha and A. Thakur. 2005. Machine translation of bi-lingual hindi-english (hinglish) text. In *In Proceedings of the 10th Conference on Machine Translation.*

T. Solorio and Y. Liu. 2008. Learning to predict code-switching points. In *In Proceedings of the Conference on Empirical Methods in Natural Language Processing (EMNLP).*

A. Stolcke. 2002. An extensible language modeling toolkit. In *Proc. Intl. Conf. on Spoken Language Processing*, volume 2, pages 901–904.

S. Vogel, H. Ney, and C. Tillmann. 1996. Hmm-based word alignment in statistical translation. In *In Proc.COLING.*

Ian H. Witten and Timothy C. Bell. 1991. The zero-frequency problem: Estimating the probabil- ities of novel events in adaptive text compression. In *IEEE Transactions on Information Theory*, volume 4, pages 1085–1094.

Undirected Machine Translation with Discriminative Reinforcement Learning

Andrea Gesmundo
Google Inc.
andrea.gesmundo@gmail.com

James Henderson
Xerox Research Centre Europe
james.henderson@xrce.xerox.com

Abstract

We present a novel Undirected Machine Translation model of Hierarchical MT that is not constrained to the standard bottom-up inference order. Removing the ordering constraint makes it possible to condition on top-down structure and surrounding context. This allows the introduction of a new class of contextual features that are not constrained to condition only on the bottom-up context. The model builds translation-derivations efficiently in a greedy fashion. It is trained to learn to choose jointly the best action and the best inference order. Experiments show that the decoding time is halved and forest-rescoring is 6 times faster, while reaching accuracy not significantly different from state of the art.

1 Introduction

Machine Translation (MT) can be addressed as a structured prediction task (Brown et al., 1993; Yamada and Knight, 2001; Koehn et al., 2003). MT's goal is to learn a mapping function, f, from an input sentence, x, into $y = (t, h)$, where t is the sentence translated into the target language, and h is the hidden correspondence structure (Liang et al., 2006). In Hierarchical MT (HMT) (Chiang, 2005) the hidden correspondence structure is the synchronous-tree composed by instantiations of synchronous rules from the input grammar, G.

Statistical models usually define f as: $f(x) = \arg\max_{y \in \mathcal{Y}} \mathsf{Score}(x, y)$, where $\mathsf{Score}(x, y)$ is a function whose parameters can be learned with a specialized learning algorithm. In MT applications, it is not possible to enumerate all $y \in \mathcal{Y}$. HMT decoding applies pruning (e.g. Cube Pruning (Huang and Chiang, 2005)), but even then HMT has higher complexity than Phrase Based MT (PbMT) (Koehn et al., 2003). On the other hand, HMT improves over PbMT by introducing the possibility of exploiting a more sophisticated reordering model not bounded by a window size, and producing translations with higher syntactic-semantic quality. In this paper, we present the Undirected Machine Translation (UMT) framework, which retains the advantages of HMT and allows the use of a greedy decoder whose complexity is lower than standard quadratic beam-search PbMT.

UMT's fast decoding is made possible through even stronger pruning: the decoder chooses a single action at each step, never retracts that action, and prunes all incompatible alternatives to that action. If this extreme level of pruning was applied to the CKY-like beam-decoding used in standard HMT, translation quality would be severely degraded. This is because the bottom-up inference order imposed by CKY-like beam-decoding means that all pruning decisions must be based on a bottom-up approximation of contextual features, which leads to search errors that affect the quality of reordering and lexical-choice (Gesmundo and Henderson, 2011). UMT solves this problem by removing the bottom-up inference order constraint, allowing many different inference orders for the same tree structure, and learning the inference order where the decoder can be the most confident in its pruning decisions.

Removing the bottom-up inference order constraint makes it possible to condition on top-down structure and surrounding context. This undirected approach allows us to integrate contextual features such as the Language Model (LM) in a more flexible way. It also allows us to introduce a new class of undirected features. In particular, we introduce the Context-Free Factor (CFF) features. CFF features compute exactly and efficiently a bound on the context-free cost of a partial derivation's missing branches, thereby estimating the future cost of partial derivations. The new class of undirected features is fundamental for the success of a greedy approach to HMT, because the additional non-bottom-up context is sometimes crucial to have the necessary information to make greedy decisions.

Because UMT prunes all but the single chosen action at each step, both choosing a good inference order and choosing a correct action reduce to a single choice of what action to take next. To learn this decoding policy, we propose a novel Discriminative Reinforcement Learning (DRL) framework. DRL is used to train models that construct incrementally structured output using a local discriminative function, with the goal of optimizing a global loss function. We apply DRL to learn the UMT scoring function's parameters, using the BLEU score as the global loss function. DRL learns a weight vector for a linear classifier that discriminates between decisions based on which one leads to a complete translation-derivation with a better BLEU score. Promotions/demotions of translations are performed by applying a Perceptron-style update on the sequence of decisions that produced the translation, thereby training local decisions to optimize the global BLEU score of the final translation, while keeping the efficiency and simplicity of the Perceptron Algorithm (Rosenblatt, 1958; Collins, 2002).

Our experiments show that UMT with DRL reduces decoding time by over half, and the time to rescore translations with the Language Model by 6 times, while reaching accuracy non-significantly different from the state of the art.

2 Undirected Machine Translation

In this section, we present the UMT framework. For ease of presentation, and following synchronous-grammar based MT practice, we will henceforth restrict our focus to binary grammars (Zhang et al., 2006; Wang et al., 2007).

A UMT decoder can be formulated as a function, f, that maps a source sentence, $x \in \mathcal{X}$, into a structure defined by $y = (t, h) \in \mathcal{Y}$, where t is the translation in the target language, and h is the synchronous tree structure generating the input sentence on the source side and its translation on the target side. Synchronous-trees are composed of instantiations of synchronous-rules, r, from a grammar, G. A UMT decoder builds synchronous-trees, h, by recursively expanding partial synchronous-trees, τ. τ includes a partial translation. Each τ is required to be a connected sub-graph of some synchronous-tree h. Thus, τ is composed of a subset of the rules from any h that generates x on the source side, such that there is a connected path between any two rules in τ. Differently from the partial structures built by a bottom-up decoder, τ does not have to cover a contiguous span on x. Formally, τ is defined by:
1) The set of synchronous-rule instantiations in τ: $I \equiv \{r_1, r_2, \cdots, r_k | r_i \in G, 1 \leq i \leq k\}$;
2) The set of connections among the synchronous-rule instantiations, C.
Let $c_i = (r_i, r_{j_i})$ be the notation to represent the connection between the i-th rule and the rule r_{j_i}. The set of connections can be expressed as:
$C \equiv \{(r_1, r_{j_1}), (r_2, r_{j_2}), \cdots, (r_{k-1}, r_{j_{k-1}})\}$
3) The postcondition set, P, which specifies the non-terminals in τ that are available for creating new connections. Each postcondition, $p_i = (r_x, X_{\boxed{y}})_i$, indicates that the rule r_x has the non-terminal $X_{\boxed{y}}$ available for connections. The index $\boxed{y}$ identifies the non-terminal in the rule. In a binary grammar $\boxed{y}$ can take only 3 values: $\boxed{1}$ for the first non-terminal (the left child of the source side), $\boxed{2}$ for the second non-terminal, and $\boxed{h}$ for the head. The postcondition set can be expressed as:
$P \equiv \{(r_{x_1}, X_{y_1})_1, \cdots, (r_{x_m}, X_{y_m})_m\}$
4) The set of carries, K. We define a different carry, κ_i, for each non-terminal available for connections. Each carry stores the extra information required to correctly score the non-local interactions between τ and the rule that will be connected at that non-terminal. Thus $|K| = |P|$. Let κ_i be the carry associated with the postcondition p_i. The set of carries can be expressed as:
$K \equiv \{\kappa_1, \kappa_2, \cdots, \kappa_m\}$

Partial synchronous-trees, τ, are expanded by performing connection-actions. Given a τ we can connect to it a new rule, $\hat{r}$, using one available non-terminal represented by postcondition, $p_i \in P$, and obtain a new partial synchronous-tree $\hat{\tau}$. Formally: $\hat{\tau} \equiv \langle \tau \lessdot \hat{a} \rangle$, where, $\hat{a} = [\hat{r}, p_i]$, represents the connection-action.

Algorithm 1 UMT Decoding

1: **function** Decoder (x; $\mathbf{w}$, G) : (t,h)
2: $\tau.\{I, C, P, K\} \leftarrow \{\emptyset, \emptyset, \emptyset, \emptyset\}$;
3: $\mathbf{Q} \leftarrow$ LeafRules(G);
4: **while** $|\mathbf{Q}| > 0$ **do**
5: $[\hat{r}, p_i] \leftarrow$ PopBestAction ($\mathbf{Q}$,$\mathbf{w}$);
6: $\tau \leftarrow$ CreateConnection($\tau, \hat{r}, p_i$);
7: UpdateQueue($\mathbf{Q}$, $\hat{r}$, p_i);
8: **end while**
9: Return(τ);

10: **procedure** CreateConnection(τ, $\hat{r}, p_i$) : $\hat{\tau}$
11: $\hat{\tau}.I \leftarrow \tau.I + \hat{r}$;
12: $\hat{\tau}.C \leftarrow \tau.C + (\hat{r}, r_{p_i})$;
13: $\hat{\tau}.P \leftarrow \tau.P - p_i$;
14: $\hat{\tau}.K \leftarrow \tau.K - \kappa_i$;
15: $\hat{\tau}.K$.UpdateCarries($\hat{r}, p_i$);
16: $\hat{\tau}.P$.AddAvailableConnectionsFrom($\hat{r}, p_i$);
17: $\hat{\tau}.K$.AddCarriesForNewConnections($\hat{r}, p_i$);
18: Return($\hat{\tau}$);

19: **procedure** UpdateQueue($\mathbf{Q}$, $\hat{r}$, p_i) :
20: $\mathbf{Q}$.RemoveActionsWith(p_i);
21: $\mathbf{Q}$.AddNewActions($\hat{r}$, p_i);

2.1 Decoding Algorithm

Algorithm 1 gives details of the UMT decoding algorithm. The decoder takes as input the source sentence, x, the parameters of the scoring function, $\mathbf{w}$, and the synchronous-grammar, G. At *line* 2 the partial synchronous-tree τ is initialized by setting I, C, P and K to empty sets $\emptyset$. At *line* 3 the queue of candidate connection-actions is initialized as $\mathbf{Q} \equiv \{\ [r_{leaf},\ \mathbf{null}] \mid r_{leaf}$ is a leaf rule$\}$, where **null** means that there is no post-condition specified, since the first rule does not need to connect to anything. A leaf rule r_{leaf} is any synchronous rule with only terminals on the right-hand sides. At *line* 4 the main loop starts. Each iteration of the main loop will expand τ using one connection-action. The loop ends when $\mathbf{Q}$ is empty, implying that τ covers the full sentence and has no more missing branches or parents. The best scoring action according to the parameter vector $\mathbf{w}$ is popped from the queue at *line* 5. The scoring of connection-actions is discussed in details in Section 3.2. At *line* 6 the selected connection-action is used to expand τ. At *line* 7 the queue of candidates is updated accordingly (see *lines* 19-21). At *line* 8 the decoder iterates the main loop, until τ is complete and is returned at *line* 9.

Lines 10-18 describe the CreateConnection($\cdot$) procedure, that connects the partial synchronous-tree τ to the selected rule $\hat{r}$ via the postcondition p_i specified by the candidate-action selected in *line* 5. This procedure returns the resulting partial synchronous-tree: $\hat{\tau} \equiv \langle\ \tau \lessdot [\hat{r}, p_i]\ \rangle$. At *line* 11, $\hat{r}$ is added to the rule set I. At *line* 12 the connection between $\hat{r}$ and r_{p_i} (the rule specified in the postcondition) is added to the set of connections C. At *line* 13, p_i is removed from P. At *line* 14 the carry k_i matching with p_i is removed from K. At *line* 15 the set of carries K is updated, in order to update those carries that need to provide information about the new action. At *line* 16 new postconditions representing the non-terminals in $\hat{r}$ that are available for subsequent connections are added in P. At *line* 17 the carries associated with these new postconditions are computed and added to K. Finally at *line* 18 the updated partial synchronous-tree is returned.

In the very first iteration, the CreateConnection($\cdot$) procedure has nothing to compute for some lines. *Line* 11 is not executed since the first leaf rule needs no connection and has nothing to connect to. *lines* 12-13 are not executed since P and K are $\emptyset$ and p_i is not specified for the first action. *Line* 15 is not executed since there are no carries to be updated. *Lines* 16-17 only add the postcondition and carry relative to the leaf rule head link.

The procedure used to update $\mathbf{Q}$ is reported in *lines* 19-21. At *line* 20 all the connection-actions involving the expansion of p_i are removed from $\mathbf{Q}$. These actions are the incompatible alternatives to the selected action. In the very first iteration, all actions in $\mathbf{Q}$ are removed because they are all incompatible with the connected-graph constraint. At *line* 21 new connection-actions are added to $\mathbf{Q}$. These are the candidate actions proposing a connection to the available non-terminals of the selected action's new rule $\hat{r}$. The rules used for these new candidate-actions must not be in conflict with the current structure of τ (e.g. the rule cannot generate a source side terminal that is already covered by τ).

3 Discriminative Reinforcement Learning

Training a UMT model simply means training the parameter vector $\mathbf{w}$ that is used to choose the best scoring action during decoding. We propose a novel method to apply a kind of minimum error rate training (MERT) to $\mathbf{w}$. Because each action choice must be evaluated in the context of the complete translation-derivation, we formalize this method in terms of Reinforcement Learning. We propose Discriminative Reinforcement Learning as an appropriate way to train a UMT model to maximize the BLEU score of the complete derivation. First we define DRL as a novel generic training framework.

3.1 Generic Framework of DRL

RL can be applied to any task, $\mathcal{T}$, that can be formalized in terms of:

1) The set of states S[1];

2) A set of actions A_s for each state $s \in S$;

3) The transition function $T : S \times A_s \rightarrow S$, that specifies the next state given a source state and performed action[2];

4) The reward function, $R : S \times A_s \rightarrow \mathbb{R}$;

5) The discount factor, $\gamma \in [0, 1]$.

A policy is defined as any map $\pi : S \rightarrow A$. Its value function is given by:

$$V^{\pi}(s_0) = \sum_{i=0}^{\sigma} \gamma^i R(s_i, \pi(s_i)) \qquad (1)$$

where $\mathsf{path}(s_0|\pi) \equiv \langle s_0, s_1, \cdots, s_\sigma|\pi\rangle$ is the sequence of states determined by following policy π starting at state s_0. The Q-function is the total future reward of performing action a_0 in state s_0 and then following policy π:

$$Q^{\pi}(s_0, a_0) = R(s_0, a_0) + \gamma V^{\pi}(s_1) \qquad (2)$$

Standard RL algorithms search for a policy that maximizes the given reward.

Because we are taking a discriminative approach to learn $\mathbf{w}$, we formalize our optimization task similarly to an inverse reinforcement learning problem (Ng and Russell, 2000): we are given information about the optimal action sequence and we want to learn a discriminative reward function. As in other discriminative approaches, this approach simplifies the task of learning the reward function in two respects: the learned reward function only needs to be monotonically related to the true reward function, and this property only needs to hold for the best competing alternatives. This is all we need in order to use the discriminative reward function in an optimal classifier, and this simplification makes learning easier in cases where the true reward function is too complicated to model directly.

In RL, an optimal policy π^* is one which, at each state s, chooses the action which maximizes the future reward $Q^{\pi^*}(s, a)$. We assume that the future discriminative reward can be approximated with a linear function $\tilde{Q}^{\pi}(s, a)$ in some feature-vector representation $\phi : S \times A_s \rightarrow \mathbb{R}^d$ that maps a state-action pair to a d-dimensional features vector:

$$\tilde{Q}^{\pi}(s, a) = \mathbf{w}\,\phi(s, a) \qquad (3)$$

where $\mathbf{w} \in \mathbb{R}^d$. This gives us the following policy:

$$\pi_{\mathbf{w}}(s) = \arg\max_{a \in A_s} \mathbf{w}\,\phi(s, a) \qquad (4)$$

The set of parameters of this policy is the vector $\mathbf{w}$. With this formalization, all we need to learn is a vector $\mathbf{w}$ such that the resulting decisions are compatible with the given information about the optimal action sequence. We propose a Perceptron-like algorithm to learn these parameters.

Algorithm 2 Discriminative RL

1: **function** Trainer $(\phi, \mathcal{T}, D)$: $\mathbf{w}$
2: **repeat**
3: $\quad s \leftarrow$SampleState(S);
4: $\quad \hat{a} \leftarrow \pi_{\mathbf{w}}(s)$;
5: $\quad a' \leftarrow$SampleAction(A_s);
6: $\quad$**if** $Q^{\pi_{\mathbf{w}}}(s, \hat{a}) < Q^{\pi_{\mathbf{w}}}(s, a')$ in D **then**
7: $\quad\quad \mathbf{w} \leftarrow \mathbf{w} + \Phi^{\mathbf{w}}(s, a') - \Phi^{\mathbf{w}}(s, \hat{a})$;
8: $\quad$**end if**
9: **until** convergence
10: Return($\mathbf{w}$);

Algorithm 2 describes the DRL meta-algorithm. The Trainer takes as input ϕ, the task $\mathcal{T}$, and a generic set of data D describing the behaviors we want to learn. The output is the weight vector $\mathbf{w}$ of the learned policy that fits the data D. The algorithm consists in a single training loop that is repeated until convergence (*lines* 2-9). At *line* 3 a state, s, is sampled from S. At *line* 4, $\hat{a}$ is set to

[1] S can be either finite or infinite.

[2] For simplicity we describe a deterministic process. To generalize to the stochastic process, replace the transition function with the transition probability: $P_{sa}(s')$, $s' \in S$.

be the action that would be preferred by the current $\mathbf{w}$-policy. At *line* 5 an action, a', is sampled from A_s such that $a' \neq \hat{a}$. At *line* 6 the algorithm checks if preferring $\mathsf{path}(T(s,\hat{a}),\pi_{\mathbf{w}})$ over $\mathsf{path}(T(s,a'),\pi_{\mathbf{w}})$ is a correct choice according to the behaviors data D that the algorithm aims to learn. If the current $\mathbf{w}$-policy contradicts D, *line* 7 is executed to update the weight vector to promote $\Phi^{\mathbf{w}}(s,a')$ and penalize $\Phi^{\mathbf{w}}(s,\hat{a})$, where $\Phi^{\mathbf{w}}(s,a)$ is the summation of the features vectors of the entire derivation path starting at (s,a) and following policy $\pi_{\mathbf{w}}$. This way of updating $\mathbf{w}$ has the effect of increasing the $\tilde{Q}(\cdot)$ value associated with all the actions in the sequence that generated the promoted structure, and reducing the $\tilde{Q}(\cdot)$ value of the actions in the sequence that generated the penalized structure[3].

We have described the DRL meta-algorithm to be as general as possible. When applied to a specific problem, more details can be specified: **1)** it is possible to choose specific sampling techniques to implement *lines* 3 and 5; **2)** the test at *line* 6 needs to be detailed according to the nature of $\mathcal{T}$ and D; **3)** the update statement at *line* 7 can be replaced with a more sophisticated update approach. We address these issues and describe a range of alternatives as we apply DRL to UMT in Section 3.2.

3.2 Application of DRL to UMT

To apply DRL we formalize the task of translating x with UMT as $\mathcal{T} \equiv \{S,\{A_s\},T,R,\gamma\}$:

1) The set of states S is the space of all possible UMT partial synchronous-trees, τ;

2) The set $A_{\tau,x}$ is the set of connection-actions that can expand τ connecting new synchronous-rule instantiations matching the input sentence x on the source side;

3) The transition function T is the connection function $\hat{\tau} \equiv \langle\, \tau \lessdot a \,\rangle$ formalized in Section 2 and detailed by the procedure CreateConnection($\cdot$) in Algorithm 1;

4) The true reward function R is the BLEU score. BLEU is a loss function that quantifies the difference between the reference translation and the output translation t. The BLEU score can be computed only when a terminal state is reached and a full translation is available. Thus, the rewards are all zero except at terminal states, called a Pure Delayed Reward function;

5) Considering the nature of the problem and reward function, we choose an undiscounted setting: $\gamma = 1$.

Next we specify the details of the DRL algorithm. The data D consists of a set of pairs of sentences, $D \equiv \{(x,t^*)\}$, where x is the source sentence and t^* is the reference translation. The feature-vector representation function ϕ maps a pair (τ,a) to a real valued vector having any number of dimensions. Each dimension corresponds to a distinct feature function that maps: $\{\tau\} \times A_{\tau,x} \rightarrow \mathbb{R}$. Details of the features functions implemented for our model are given in Section 4. Each loop of the DRL algorithm analyzes a single sample $(x,t^*) \in D$. The state s is sampled from a uniform distribution over $\langle s_0, s_1, \cdots, s_\sigma | \pi \rangle$. The action a' is sampled from a Zipfian distribution over $\{A_{\tau,x} - \hat{a}\}$ sorted with the $\tilde{Q}^{\pi_{\mathbf{w}}}(s,a)$ function. In this way actions with higher score have higher probability to be drawn, while actions at the bottom of the rank still have a small probability to be selected. The **if** at *line* 6 tests if the translation produced by $\mathsf{path}(T(s,a'),\pi_{\mathbf{w}})$ has higher BLEU score than the one produced by $\mathsf{path}(T(s,\hat{a}),\pi_{\mathbf{w}})$.

For the update statement at *line* 7 we use the Averaged Perceptron technique (Freund and Schapire, 1999). Algorithm 2 can be easily adapted to implement the efficient Averaged Perceptron updates (e.g. see Section 2.1.1 of (Daumé III, 2006)). In preliminary experiments, we found that other more aggressive update technique, such as Passive-Aggressive (Crammer et al., 2006), Aggressive (Shen et al., 2007), or MIRA (Crammer and Singer, 2003), lead to worst accuracy. To see why this might be, consider that a MT decoder needs to learn to construct structures (t,h), while the training data specifies the gold translation t^* but gives no information on the hidden-correspondence structure h. As discussed in (Liang et al., 2006), there are output structures that match the reference translation using a wrong internal structure (e.g. assuming wrong internal alignment). While in other cases the output translation can be a valid alternative translation but gets a low BLEU score because it differs from t^*. Aggressively promoting/penalizing structures whose correctness can be only partially verified can be expected to harm generalization ability.

[3]Preliminary experiments with updating only the features for $\hat{a}$ and a' produced substantially worse results.

4 Undirected Features

In this section we show how the features designed for bottom-up HMT can be adapted to the undirected approach, and we introduce a new feature from the class of undirected features that are made possible by the undirected approach.

Local features depend only on the action rule r. These features can be used in the undirected approach without adaptation, since they are independent of the surrounding structure. For our experiments we use a standard set of local features: the probability of the source phrase given the target phrase; the lexical translation probabilities of the source words given the target words; the lexical translation probabilities of the target words given the source words; and the Word Penalty feature.

Contextual features are dependent on the interaction between the action rule r and the available context. In UMT all the needed information about the available context is stored in the carry κ_i. Therefore, the computation of contextual features whose carry's size is bounded (like the LM) requires constant time.

The undirected adaptation of the LM feature computes the scores of the new n-grams formed by adding the terminals of the action rule r to the current partial translation τ. In the case that the action rule r is connected to τ via a child non-terminal, the carry is expressed as $\kappa_i \equiv ([W_L \star W_R])$. Where W_L and W_R are respectively the left and right boundary target words of the span covered by τ. This notation is analogous to the standard star notation used for the bottom-up decoder (e.g. (Chiang, 2007) Section 5.3.2). In the case that r is connected to τ via the head non-terminal, the carry is expressed as $\kappa_i \equiv (W_R]\text{-}[W_L)$. Where W_L and W_R are respectively the left and right boundary target words of the surrounding context provided by τ. The boundary words stored in the carry and the terminals of the action rule are all the information needed to compute and score the new n-grams generated by the connection-action.

In addition, we introduce the Context-Free Factor (CFF) features. An action rule r is connected to τ via one of r's non-terminals, $X_{r,\tau}$. Thus, the score of the interaction between r and the context structure attached to $X_{r,\tau}$ can be computed exactly, while the score of the structures attached to other r nonterminals (i.e. those in postconditions) cannot be computed since these branches are missing. Each of these postcondition nonterminals has an associated CFF feature, which is an upper bound on the score of its missing branch. More precisely, it is an upper bound on the context-free component of this score. This upper bound can be exactly and efficiently computed using the Forest Rescoring Framework (Huang and Chiang, 2007; Huang, 2008). This framework separates the MT decoding in two steps. In the first step only the context-free factors are considered. The output of the first step is a hypergraph called the context-free-forest, which compactly represents an exponential number of synchronous-trees. The second step introduces contextual features by applying a process of state-splitting to the context-free-forest, rescoring with non-context-free factors, and efficiently pruning the search space.

To efficiently compute CFF features we run the Inside-Outside algorithm with the $(max, +)$ semiring (Goodman, 1999) over the context-free-forest. The result is a map that gives the maximum Inside and Outside scores for each node in the context-free forest. This map is used to get the value of the CFF features in constant time while running the forest rescoring step.

5 Experiments

We implement our model on top of Cdec (Dyer et al., 2010). Cdec provides a standard implementation of the HMT decoder (Chiang, 2007) and MERT training (Och, 2003) that we use as baseline.

We experiment on the NIST Chinese-English parallel corpus. The training corpus contains $239k$ sentence pairs with $6.9M$ Chinese words and $8.9M$ English words. The test set contains 919 sentence pairs. The hierarchical translation grammar was extracted using the Joshua toolkit (Li et al., 2009) implementation of the suffix array rule extractor algorithm (Callison-Burch et al., 2005; Lopez, 2007).

Table 1 reports the decoding time measures. HMT with $beam1$ is the fastest possible configuration for HMT, but it is 71.59% slower than UMT. This is because HMT $b1$ constructs $O(n^2)$ subtrees, many of which end up not being used in the final result, whereas UMT only constructs the rule instantiations that are required. HMT with $beam30$ is the fastest configuration that reaches state of the art accuracy, but increases the average time per sentence by an additional 131.36% when compared with UMT. The rescoring time is

Model	sent. t.	sent. t. var.	resc. t.	resc. t. var.
UMT	135.2ms	-	38.9 ms	-
HMT $b1$	232.0ms	+71.59%	141.3 ms	+263.23%
HMT $b30$	312.8ms	+131.36%	226.9 ms	+483.29%

Table 1: Decoding speed comparison.

Model	sent. t.	sent. t. var.
UMT with DRL	267.4 ms	-
HMT $b1$	765.2 ms	+186.16%
HMT $b30$	1153.5 ms	+331.37%

Table 2: Training speed comparison.

Model	BLEU	relative loss	p-value
UMT with DRL	30.14	6.33%	0.18
HMT $b1$	30.87	4.07%	0.21
HMT $b30$	32.18	-	-

Table 3: Accuracy comparison.

the average time spent on the forest rescoring step, which is the only step where the decoders actually differ. This is the step that involves the integration of the Language Model and other contextual features. For HMT $b30$, rescoring takes two thirds of the total decoding time. Thus rescoring is the most time consuming step in the pipeline. The rescoring time comparison shows even bigger gains for UMT. HMT $b30$ is almost 6 times slower than UMT.

Table 2 reports the training time measures. These results show HMT $b30$ training is more than 4 times slower than UMT training with DRL. Comparing with Table 1, we notice that the relative gain on average training time is higher than the gain measured at decoding time. This is because MERT has an higher complexity than DRL. Both of the training algorithms requires 10 training epochs to reach convergence.

Table 3 reports the accuracy measures. As expected, accuracy degrades the more aggressively the search space is pruned. UMT trained with DRL loses 2.0 BLEU points compared to HMT $b30$. This corresponds to a relative-loss of 6.33%. Although not inconsequential, this variation is not considered big (e.g. at the WMT-11 Machine Translation shared task (Callison-Burch et al., 2011)). To measure the significance of the variation, we compute the sign test and measure the one-tail p-value for the presented models in comparison to HMT $b30$. From the values reported in the fourth column, we can observe that the BLEU score variations would not normally be considered significant. For example, at WMT-11 two systems were considered equivalent if $p > 0.1$, as in these cases. The accuracy cannot be compared in terms of search score since the models we are comparing are trained with distinct algorithms and thus the search scores are not comparable.

To test the impact of the CFF features, we trained and tested UMT with DRL with and without these features. This resulted in an accuracy decrease of 2.3 BLEU points. Thus these features are important for the success of the greedy approach. They provide an estimate of the score of the missing branches, thus helping to avoid some actions that have a good local score but lead to final translations with low global score.

To validate the results, additional experiments were executed on the French to Italian portion of the Europarl corpus v6. This portion contains $190k$ pairs of sentences. The first $186k$ sentences were used to extract the grammar and train the two models. The final tests were performed on the remaining $4k$ sentence pairs. With this corpus we measured a similar speed gain. HMT $b30$ is 2.3 times slower at decoding compared to UMT, and 6.1 times slower at rescoring, while UMT loses 1.1 BLEU points in accuracy. But again the accuracy differences are not considered significant. We measured a p-value of 0.25, which is not significant at the 0.1 level.

6 Related Work

Models sharing similar intuitions have been previously applied to other structure prediction tasks. For example, Nivre et al. (2006) presents a linear time syntactic dependency parser, which is constrained in a left-to-right decoding order. This model offers a different accuracy/complexity balance than the quadratic time graph-based parser of Mcdonald et al. (2005).

Other approaches learning a model specifically for greedy decoding have been applied with success to other less complex tasks. Shen et al. (2007) present the Guided Learning (GL) framework for bidirectional sequence classification. GL successfully combines the tasks of learning the order of inference and training the local classifier in a single Perceptron-like algorithm, reaching state of the art accuracy with complexity lower than the exhaustive counterpart (Collins, 2002).

Goldberg and Elhadad (2010) present a similar training approach for a Dependency Parser that builds the tree-structure by recursively creating the easiest arc in a non-directional manner. This model also integrates the tasks of learning the order of inference and training the parser in a single Perceptron. By "non-directional" they mean the removal of the constraint of scanning the sentence from left to right, which is typical of shift-reduce models. However this algorithm still builds the tree structures in a bottom-up fashion. This model has a $O(n \log n)$ decoding complexity and accuracy performance close to the $O(n^2)$ graph-based parsers (Mcdonald et al., 2005).

Similarities can be found between DRL and previous work that applies discriminative training to structured prediction: Collins and Roark (2004) present an Incremental Parser trained with the Perceptron algorithm. Their approach is specific to dependency parsing and requires a function to test exact match of tree structures to trigger parameter updates. On the other hand, DRL can be applied to any structured prediction task and can handle any kind of reward function. LASO (Daumé III and Marcu, 2005; Daumé III et al., 2005) and SEARN (Daumé III et al., 2009; Daumé III et al., 2006) are generic frameworks for discriminative training for structured prediction: LASO requires a function that tests correctness of partial structures to trigger early updates, while SEARN requires an optimal policy to initialize the learning algorithm. Such a test function or optimal policy cannot be computed for tasks such as MT where the hidden correspondence structure h is not provided in the training data.

7 Discussion and Future Work

In general, we believe that greedy-discriminative solutions are promising for tasks like MT, where there is not a single correct solution: normally there are many correct ways to translate the same sentence, and for each correct translation there are many different derivation-trees generating that translation, and each correct derivation tree can be built greedily following different inference orders. Therefore, the set of correct decoding paths is a reasonable portion of UMT's search space, giving a well-designed greedy algorithm a chance to find a good translation even without beam search.

In order to directly evaluate the impact of our proposed decoding strategy, in this paper the only novel features that we consider are the CFF features. But to take full advantage of the power of discriminative training and the lower decoding complexity, it would be possible to vastly increase the number of features. The UMT's undirected nature allows the integration of non-bottom-up contextual features, which cannot be used by standard HMT and PbMT. And the use of a history-based model allows features from an arbitrarily wide context, since the model does not need to be factorized. Exploring the impact of this advantage is left for future work.

8 Conclusion

The main contribution of this work is the proposal of a new MT model that offers an accuracy/complexity balance that was previously unavailable among the choices of hierarchical models.

We have presented the first Undirected framework for MT. This model combines advantages given by the use of hierarchical synchronous-grammars with a more efficient decoding algorithm. UMT's nature allows us to design novel undirected features that better approximate contextual features (such as the LM), and to introduce a new class of undirected features that cannot be used by standard bottom-up decoders. Furthermore, we generalize the training algorithm into a generic Discriminative Reinforcement Learning meta-algorithm that can be applied to any structured prediction task.

References

Peter F. Brown, Vincent J. Della Pietra, Stephen A. Della Pietra, and Robert L. Mercer. 1993. The mathematics of statistical machine translation: parameter estimation. *Computational Linguistics*, 19:263–311.

Chris Callison-Burch, Colin Bannard, and Josh Schroeder. 2005. Scaling phrase-based statistical machine translation to larger corpora and longer phrases. In *ACL '05: Proceedings of the 43rd Conference of the Association for Computational Linguistics*, Ann Arbor, MI, USA.

Chris Callison-Burch, Philipp Koehn, Christof Monz, and Omar Zaidan. 2011. Findings of the 2011 workshop on statistical machine translation. In *WMT '11: Proceedings of the 6th Workshop on Statistical Machine Translation*, Edinburgh, Scotland.

David Chiang. 2005. A hierarchical phrase-based model for statistical machine translation. In *ACL '05: Proceedings of the 43rd Conference of the Association for Computational Linguistics*, Ann Arbor, MI, USA.

David Chiang. 2007. Hierarchical phrase-based translation. *Computational Linguistics*, 33(2):201–228.

Michael Collins and Brian Roark. 2004. Incremental parsing with the perceptron algorithm. In *ACL '04: Proceedings of the 42rd Conference of the Association for Computational Linguistics*.

Michael Collins. 2002. Discriminative training methods for hidden markov models: Theory and experiments with perceptron algorithms. In *EMNLP '02: Proceedings of the 2002 Conference on Empirical Methods in Natural Language Processing*, Philadelphia, PA, USA.

Koby Crammer and Yoram Singer. 2003. Ultraconservative online algorithms for multiclass problems. *Journal of Machine Learning Research*, 3:951–991.

Koby Crammer, Ofer Dekel, Shai Shalev-Shwartz, and Yoram Singer. 2006. Online passive-aggressive algorithms. *Journal of Machine Learning Research*, 7:551–585.

Hal Daumé III and Daniel Marcu. 2005. Learning as search optimization: approximate large margin methods for structured prediction. In *ICML '05: Proceedings of the 22nd International Conference on Machine Learning*, Bonn, Germany.

Hal Daumé III, John Langford, and Daniel Marcu. 2005. Search-based structured prediction as classification. In *ASLTSP '05: Proceedings of the NIPS Workshop on Advances in Structured Learning for Text and Speech Processing*, Whistler, British Columbia, Canada.

Hal Daumé III, John Langford, and Daniel Marcu. 2006. Searn in practice. Technical report.

Hal Daumé III, John Langford, and Daniel Marcu. 2009. Search-based structured prediction. *Submitted to Machine Learning Journal*.

Hal Daumé III. 2006. Practical structured learning techniques for natural language processing. Ph.D. thesis, University of Southern California.

Chris Dyer, Adam Lopez, Juri Ganitkevitch, Jonathan Weese, Hendra Setiawan, Ferhan Ture, Vladimir Eidelman, Phil Blunsom, and Philip Resnik. 2010. cdec: A decoder, alignment, and learning framework for finite-state and context-free translation models. In *ACL '10: Proceedings of the ACL 2010 System Demonstrations*, Uppsala, Sweden.

Yoav Freund and Robert E. Schapire. 1999. Large margin classification using the perceptron algorithm. *Machine Learning*, 37(3):277–296.

Andrea Gesmundo and James Henderson. 2011. Heuristic Search for Non-Bottom-Up Tree Structure Prediction. In *EMNLP '11: Proceedings of the 2011 Conference on Empirical Methods in Natural Language Processing*, Edinburgh, Scotland, UK.

Yoav Goldberg and Michael Elhadad. 2010. An efficient algorithm for easy-first non-directional dependency parsing. In *NAACL '10: Proceedings of the 11th Conference of the North American Chapter of the Association for Computational Linguistics*, Los Angeles, CA, USA.

Joshua Goodman. 1999. Semiring parsing. *Computational Linguistics*, 25:573–605.

Liang Huang and David Chiang. 2005. Better k-best parsing. In *IWPT '05: Proceedings of the 9th International Workshop on Parsing Technology*, Vancouver, British Columbia, Canada.

Liang Huang and David Chiang. 2007. Forest rescoring: Faster decoding with integrated language models. In *ACL '07: Proceedings of the 45th Conference of the Association for Computational Linguistics*, Prague, Czech Republic.

Liang Huang. 2008. Forest-based algorithms in natural language processing. Ph.D. thesis, University of Pennsylvania.

Philipp Koehn, Franz Josef Och, and Daniel Marcu. 2003. Statistical phrase-based translation. In *NAACL '03: Proceedings of the 4th Conference of the North American Chapter of the Association for Computational Linguistics*, Edmonton, Canada.

Zhifei Li, Chris Callison-Burch, Chris Dyer, Sanjeev Khudanpur, Lane Schwartz, Wren Thornton, Jonathan Weese, and Omar Zaidan. 2009. Joshua: An open source toolkit for parsing-based machine translation. In *WMT '09: Proceedings of the 4th Workshop on Statistical Machine Translation*, Athens, Greece.

Percy Liang, Alexandre Bouchard-Côté, Dan Klein, and Ben Taskar. 2006. An end-to-end discriminative approach to machine translation. In *COLING-ACL '06: Proceedings of the 21st International Conference on Computational Linguistics and the 44th Conference of the Association for Computational Linguistics*, Sydney, Australia.

Adam Lopez. 2007. Hierarchical phrase-based translation with suffix arrays. In *EMNLP-CoNLL '07: Proceedings of the 2007 Joint Conference on Empirical Methods in Natural Language Processing and Computational Natural Language Learning*, Prague, Czech Republic.

Ryan Mcdonald, Koby Crammer, and Fernando Pereira. 2005. Online large-margin training of dependency parsers. In *ACL '05: Proceedings of the 43rd Conference of the Association for Computational Linguistics*, Ann Arbor, MI, USA.

Andrew Y. Ng and Stuart Russell. 2000. Algorithms for inverse reinforcement learning. In *ICML '00: Proceedings of the 17th International Conference on Machine Learning*, Stanford University, CA, USA.

Joakim Nivre, Johan Hall, and Jens Nilsson. 2006. Maltparser: A data-driven parser-generator for dependency parsing. In *LREC '06: Proceedings of the 5th International Conference on Language Resources and Evaluation*, Genoa, Italy.

Franz Josef Och. 2003. Minimum error rate training in statistical machine translation. In *ACL '03: Proceedings of the 41st Conference of the Association for Computational Linguistics*, Sapporo, Japan.

Frank Rosenblatt. 1958. The Perceptron: A probabilistic model for information storage and organization in the brain. *Psychological Review*, 65(6):386–408.

Libin Shen, Giorgio Satta, and Aravind Joshi. 2007. Guided learning for bidirectional sequence classification. In *ACL '07: Proceedings of the 45th Conference of the Association for Computational Linguistics*, Prague, Czech Republic.

Wei Wang, Kevin Knight, and Daniel Marcu. 2007. Binarizing syntax trees to improve syntax-based machine translation accuracy. In *EMNLP-CoNLL '07: Proceedings of the 2007 Joint Conference on Empirical Methods in Natural Language Processing and Computational Natural Language Learning*, Prague, Czech Republic.

Kenji Yamada and Kevin Knight. 2001. A syntax-based statistical translation model. In *ACL '01: Proceedings of the 39th Conference of the Association for Computational Linguistics*, Toulouse, France.

Hao Zhang, Liang Huang, Daniel Gildea, and Kevin Knight. 2006. Synchronous binarization for machine translation. In *NAACL '06: Proceedings of the 7th Conference of the North American Chapter of the Association for Computational Linguistics*, New York, New York.

Minimum Translation Modeling with Recurrent Neural Networks

Yuening Hu
Department of Computer Science
University of Maryland, College Park
ynhu@cs.umd.edu

Michael Auli, Qin Gao, Jianfeng Gao
Microsoft Research
Redmond, WA, USA
{michael.auli,qigao,jfgao}@microsoft.com

Abstract

We introduce recurrent neural network-based Minimum Translation Unit (MTU) models which make predictions based on an unbounded history of previous bilingual contexts. Traditional back-off n-gram models suffer under the sparse nature of MTUs which makes estimation of high-order sequence models challenging. We tackle the sparsity problem by modeling MTUs both as bags-of-words and as a sequence of individual source and target words. Our best results improve the output of a phrase-based statistical machine translation system trained on WMT 2012 French-English data by up to 1.5 BLEU, and we outperform the traditional n-gram based MTU approach by up to 0.8 BLEU.

1 Introduction

Classical phrase-based translation models rely heavily on the language model and the reordering model to capture dependencies between phrases. Sequence models over Minimum Translation Units (MTUs) have been shown to complement both syntax-based (Quirk and Menezes, 2006) as well as phrase-based (Zhang et al., 2013) models by explicitly modeling relationships between phrases. MTU models have been traditionally estimated using standard back-off n-gram techniques (Quirk and Menezes, 2006; Crego and Yvon, 2010; Zhang et al., 2013), similar to word-based language models (§2).

However, the estimation of higher-order n-gram models becomes increasingly difficult due to *data sparsity* issues associated with large n-grams, even when training on over one hundred billion words (Heafield et al., 2013); bilingual units are much sparser than words and are therefore even harder to estimate. Another drawback of n-gram models is that future predictions are based on a limited amount of previous context that is often not sufficient to capture important aspects of human language (Rastrow et al., 2012).

Recently, several feed-forward neural network-based models have achieved impressive improvements over traditional back-off n-gram models in language modeling (Bengio et al., 2003; Schwenk et al., 2007; Schwenk et al., 2012; Vaswani et al., 2013), as well as translation modeling (Allauzen et al., 2011; Le et al., 2012; Gao et al., 2013). These models tackle the data sparsity problem by representing words in continuous space rather than as discrete units. Similar words are grouped in the same sub-space rather than being treated as separate entities. Neural network models can be seen as functions over continuous representations exploiting the similarity between words, thereby making the estimation of probabilities over higher-order n-grams easier.

However, feed-forward networks do not directly address the limited context issue either, since predictions are based on a fixed-size context, similar to back-off n-gram models. We therefore focus in this paper on recurrent neural network architectures, which address the limited context issue by basing predictions on an *unbounded history* of previous events which allows to capture long-span dependencies. Recurrent architectures have recently advanced the state of the art in language modeling (Mikolov et al., 2010; Mikolov et al., 2011a; Mikolov, 2012) outperforming multi-layer feed-forward based networks in perplexity and word error rate for speech recognition (Arisoy et al., 2012; Sundermeyer et al., 2013). Recent work has also shown successful applications to machine translation (Mikolov, 2012; Auli et al., 2013; Kalchbrenner and Blunsom, 2013). We extend this work by modeling Minimum Translation Units with recurrent neural networks.

Specifically, we introduce two recurrent neural network-based MTU models to address the is-

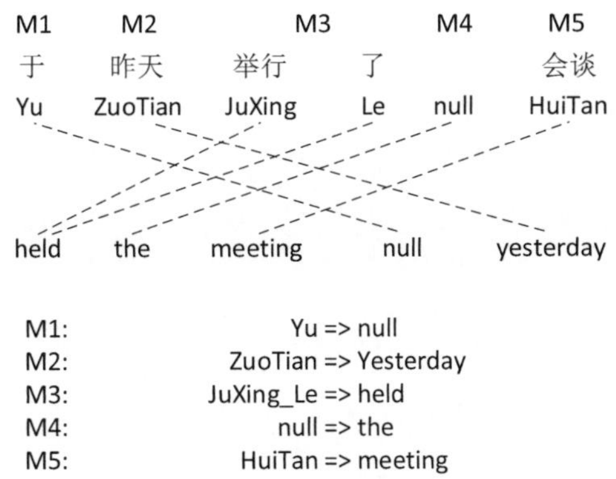

Figure 1: Example Minimum Translation Unit partitioning based on Zhang et al. (2013).

sues regarding data sparsity and limited context sizes by leveraging continuous representations and the unbounded history of the recurrent architecture. Our first approach frames the problem as a sequence modeling task over minimal units (§3). The second model improves over the first by modeling an MTU as a bag-of-words, thereby allowing us to learn representations over sub-structures of minimal units that are shared across MTUs (§4). Our models significantly outperform the traditional back-off n-gram based approach and we show that they act complementary to a very strong recurrent neural network-based language model based solely on target words (§5).

2 Minimum Translation Units

Banchs et al. (2005) introduced the idea of framing translation as a sequence modeling problem where a sentence pair is generated in left-to-right order as a sequence of bilingual n-grams. Minimum Translation Units (Quirk and Menezes, 2006; Zhang et al., 2013) are an extension which additionally permit tuples with empty source or target sides, thereby allowing insertion or deletion phrase pairs. The two basic requirements for MTUs are that there are no overlapping word alignment links between phrase pairs and it should not be possible to extract smaller phrase pairs without violating the word alignment constraints. Informally, we can think of MTUs as small phrase pairs that cannot be broken down any further without violating the two requirements.

Minimum Translation Units partition a sentence pair into a set of minimal bilingual units or tu-

	Words	MTUs
Tokens	34,769,416	14,853,062
Types	143,524	1,315,512
Singleton types	34.9%	80.1%

Table 1: Token and type counts for both source and target words as well as MTUs based on the WMT 2006 German to English data set (cf. §5).

ples obtained by an algorithm similar to phrase-extraction (Koehn et al., 2003). Figure 1 illustrates such a partitioning. Modeling minimal units has two advantages over considering larger phrase pairs that are effectively composed of MTUs: First, minimal units result in a *unique partitioning* of a sentence pair. This has the advantage that we avoid modeling spurious derivations, that is, multiple derivations generating the same sentence pair. Second, minimal units result in smaller models with a smoother distribution than models based on composed units (Zhang et al., 2013).

Sentence pairs can be generated in multiple orders, such as left-to-right or right-to-left, either in source or target order. For example, the source left-to-right order of the sentence pair in Figure 1 is simply M1, M2, M3, M4, M5, while the target left-to-right order is M3, M4, M5, M1, M2. We deal with inserted or deleted words similar to Zhang et al. (2013): The source side null token of an inserted target phrase is placed next to the last source word aligned to the closest preceding non-null aligned target phrase; a similar rule is applied to null tokens on the target side. For example, in Figure 1 we place M4 straight after M3 because "the", the aligned target phrase, is after "held", the previous non-null aligned target phrase.

We can straightforwardly estimate an n-gram model over MTUs to estimate the probability of a sentence pair using standard back-off techniques commonly employed in language modeling. For example, a trigram model in target left-to-right order factors the sentence pair in Figure 1 as $p(M3)\, p(M4|M3)\, p(M5|M3, M4)\, p(M1|M4, M5) p(M2|M5, M1)$.

If we would like to model larger contexts, then we quickly run into data sparsity issues. To illustrate this point, consider the parameter growth of an n-gram model which is driven by the vocabulary size $|V|$ and the n-gram order n: $\mathcal{O}(|V|^n)$. Clearly, the exact estimation of higher-order n-gram probabilities becomes more difficult with large n, leading to the estimation of events with increasingly sparse statistics, or having to rely on statistics from lower-order events with back-off models, which is less desirable. Even word-based language models rarely ventured so far much beyond 5-gram statistics as demonstrated by Heafield et al. (2013) who trained a, by today's standards, very large 5-gram model on 130B words. Data sparsity is therefore an even more significant issue for MTU models relying on much larger vocabularies. In our setting, the MTU vocabulary is an order of magnitude larger than a word vocabulary obtained from the same data (Table 1). Furthermore, most MTUs are observed only once making the reliable estimation of probabilities very challenging.

Neural network-based sequence models tackle the data sparsity problem by learning continuous word representations, that group similar words together in continuous space. For example, the distributional representations induced by recurrent neural networks have been found to have interesting syntactic and semantic regularities (Mikolov et al., 2013). Furthermore, these representations can be exploited to estimate more reliable statistics over higher-order n-grams than with discrete word units. Recurrent neural networks go beyond fixed-size contexts and allow the model to keep track of long-span dependencies that are important for future predictions. In the next sections we will present Minimum Translation Unit models based on recurrent architectures.

3 Atomic MTU RNN Model

The first model we introduce is based on the recurrent neural network language model of Mikolov et al. (2010). We frame the problem as a traditional sequence modeling task which treats MTUs as atomic units, similar to the approach taken by the traditional back-off n-gram models.

The model is factored into an input layer, a hidden layer with recurrent connections, and an output layer (Figure 2). The input layer encodes the MTU at time t as a 1-of-N vector $\mathbf{m}_t$ with all values being zero except for the entry representing the MTU. The output layer $\mathbf{y}_t$ represents a probability distribution over possible next MTUs; both the input and output layers are of size $|V|$, the size of the MTU vocabulary. The hidden layer state $\mathbf{h}_t$ encodes the history of all MTUs observed in the sequence up to time step t.

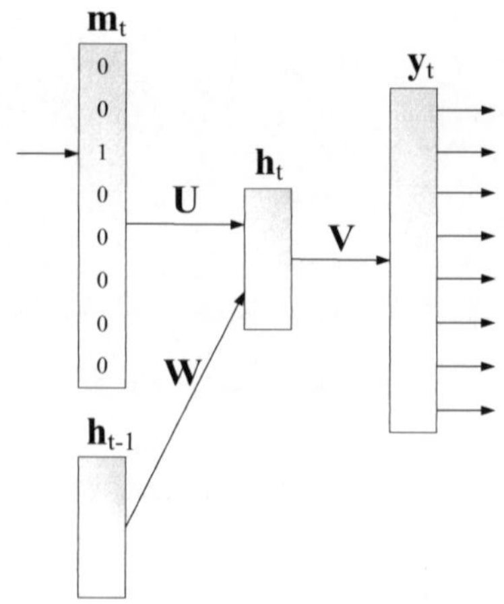

Figure 2: Structure of the atomic recurrent neural network MTU model following the word-based RNN model of Mikolov (2012).

The state of the hidden layer is determined by the input layer and the hidden layer configuration of the previous time step $\mathbf{h}_{t-1}$. The weights of the connections between the layers are summarized in a number of matrices: $\mathbf{U}$ represents weights from the input layer to the hidden layer, and $\mathbf{W}$ represents connections from the previous hidden layer to the current hidden layer. Matrix $\mathbf{V}$ contains weights between the current hidden layer and the output layer.

The hidden and output layers are computed via a series of matrix-vector products and non-linearities:

$$\mathbf{h}_t = s(\mathbf{U}\mathbf{m}_t + \mathbf{W}\mathbf{h}_{t-1})$$
$$\mathbf{y}_t = g(\mathbf{V}\mathbf{h}_t)$$

where

$$s(z) = \frac{1}{1+\exp\{-z\}}, \quad g(z_m) = \frac{\exp\{z_m\}}{\sum_k \exp\{z_k\}}$$

are sigmoid and softmax functions, respectively. Additionally, the network is interpolated with a maximum entropy model of sparse n-gram features over input MTUs (Mikolov et al., 2011a). The maximum entropy weights $\mathbf{D}$ are added to the output activations before applying the softmax function and are estimated jointly with all other parameters (Figure 3).[1]

[1]While these features depend on multiple input MTUs, we

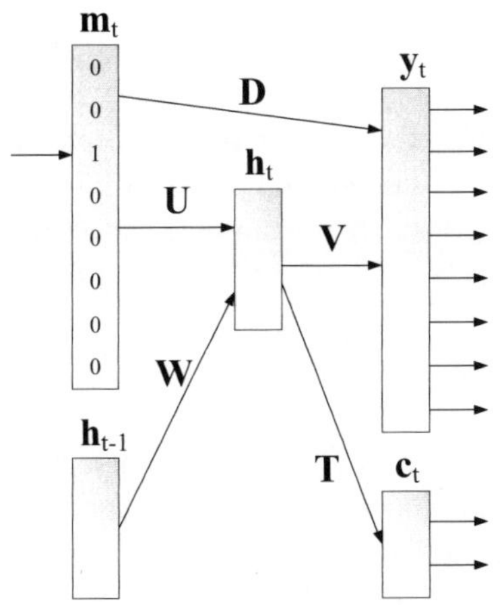

Figure 3: Structure of atomic recurrent neural network MTU model with classing layer $\mathbf{c}_t$ and direct connections $\mathbf{D}$ between the input and output layers (cf. Figure 2).

The model is optimized via a maximum likelihood objective function using stochastic gradient descent. Training is based on the truncated back propagation through time algorithm, which unrolls the network and then computes error gradients over multiple time steps (Rumelhart et al., 1986); we use a cross entropy criterion to obtain the error vector with respect to the output activations and the desired prediction. After training, the output layer represents posteriors $p(m_{t+1}|m_{t-n+1}^t, \mathbf{h}_t)$, the probability of the next MTU given the previous n input MTUs $m_{t-n+1}^t = m_t, \ldots, m_{t-n+1}$ and the current hidden layer configuration $\mathbf{h}_t$.

Naïve computation of the probability distribution over the next MTU is very expensive for large vocabularies, such as commonly encountered for MTU models (Table 1). A well established efficiency trick assigns each possible output to a unique class and then uses a two-step process to find the probability of an MTU, instead of computing the probability of all possible outputs (Goodman, 2001; Emami and Jelinek, 2005; Mikolov et al., 2011b). Under this scheme we compute the probability of an MTU by multiplying the probability of its class c_t^i with the probability of the minimal unit conditioned on the class:

$$p(m_{t+1}|m_{t-n+1}^t, \mathbf{h}_t) = \\ p(c_t^i|m_{t-n+1}^t, \mathbf{h}_t)\, p(m_{t+1}|c_t^i, m_{t-n+1}^t, \mathbf{h}_t)$$

This factorization reduces the complexity of computing the output probabilities from $\mathcal{O}(|V|)$ to $\mathcal{O}(|C| + \max_i |c^i|)$ where $|C|$ is the number of classes and $|c^i|$ is the number of minimal units in class c^i. The best case complexity $\mathcal{O}(\sqrt{|V|})$ requires the number of classes and MTUs to be evenly balanced, i.e., each class contains exactly as many minimal units as there are classes.

Figure 3 illustrates how classing changes the structure of the network by adding an additional output layer for the class probabilities.

4 Bag-of-words MTU RNN Model

The previous model treats MTUs as atomic symbols which leads to large vocabularies requiring large parameter sets and expensive inference. However, similar MTUs may share the same words, or words which are related in continuous space. The atomic MTU model does not exploit this since it cannot access the internal structure of a minimal unit.

The approach we pursue next is to break MTUs into individual source and target words (Le et al., 2012) in order to exploit structural similarities between infrequently observed minimal units. Singletons represent the vast majority of our MTU vocabulary (Table 1). This resembles the word-hashing trick of Huang et al. (2013) who represented individual words as a bag-of-character n-grams to reduce the vocabulary size of a neural network-based model in an information retrieval setting.[2]

We first describe a theoretically appealing but computationally expensive model and then discuss a more practical variation. The input layer of this model accepts the current minimal unit as a K-of-N vector representing K source and target words as opposed to the 1-of-N encoding of entire MTUs in the previous model (Figure 4). Larger MTUs may contain the same word more than once and we simply adjust their count to one.[3] Different to the

depicted them for simplicity as a connection between the current input vector $\mathbf{m}_t$ and the output layer.

[2]Applying the same technique would likely result in too many collisions since we are dealing with multi-word units instead of single words.

[3]We found no effect on accuracy when using the unmodified count in initial experiments.

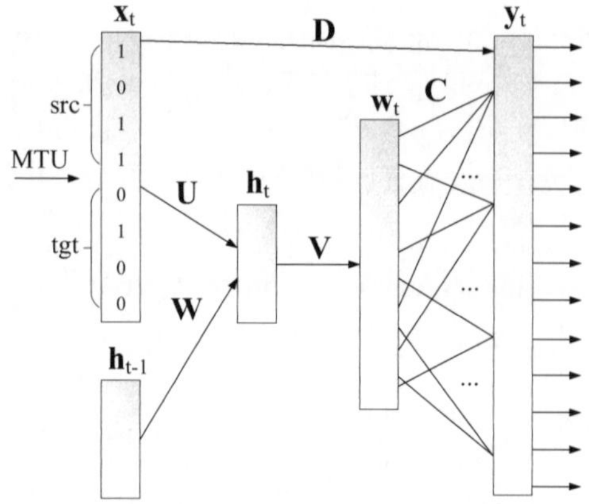

Figure 4: Structure of MTU bag-of-words recurrent neural network model. The input layer represents a minimal unit as a bag-of-words and the output layer $\mathbf{y}_t$ is a probability distribution over possible next MTUs depending on the activations of the word layer $\mathbf{w}_t$ representing source and target words of minimal units.

previous model, the input vector has now multiple active entries whose signals are absorbed into the new hidden layer configuration.

This bag-of-words encoding of minimal units dramatically reduces the vocabulary size but it inevitably maps different MTUs to the same encoding. On our data set, we observe less than 0.2% of minimal units that are involved in collisions, a rate that is similar to Huang et al. (2013). In practice collisions are unlikely to affect accuracy in our setting because MTUs that are mapped to the same encoding usually do not differ much in semantic meaning as illustrated by the following examples: *erfolg haben* $\rightarrow$ *succeed* collides with *haben erfolg* $\rightarrow$ *succeed*, or *damit* , $\rightarrow$ *to* and , *damit* $\rightarrow$ *to*; in both examples either the auxiliary verb *haben* or the comma changes position, neither of which significantly changes the meaning for this particular pair of MTUs.

The structure of the bag-of-words MTU RNN models is shown in Figure 4. Similar to the atomic MTU RNN model (§3), the hidden layer combines the signal from the input layer and the previous hidden layer configuration. The hidden layer activations feed into a word layer $\mathbf{w}_t$ representing the source and target words that part of all possible MTUs; it is of the same size as the input layer. The word layer is connected to a *convolutional* output layer $\mathbf{y}_t$ by weights summarized in the sparse matrix $\mathbf{C}$. The output layer represents all possible next minimal units, where each MTU entry is only connected to neurons in the word layer representing its source and target words. The word and MTU layers are then computed as follows:

$$\mathbf{w}_t = s(\mathbf{V}\mathbf{h}_t)$$
$$\mathbf{y}_t = g(\mathbf{C}\mathbf{w}_t)$$

However, there are a number of computational issues with this model: First, we cannot efficiently factor the word layer $\mathbf{w}_t$ into classes such as for the atomic MTU RNN model because we require all its activations to compute the MTU output layer $\mathbf{y}_t$. This reduces the best case complexity of computing the word layer from $\mathcal{O}(\sqrt{|V|})$ back to linear in the number of source and target words $|V|$. In practice this results in between 200-1000 more activations that need to be computed, depending on the word vocabulary size. Second, turning the MTU output layer into a convolutional layer is not enough to sufficiently reduce the computational effort to compute the output activations since the number of connections between the word and MTU layers is very imbalanced. This is because frequent words, such as function words, are part of many MTUs and therefore have a very high out-degree, e.g., the neuron representing "the" has over 82K outgoing edges. On the other hand, infrequent words, have a very low out-degree. This imbalance makes it hard to efficiently compute activations and error gradients, even on a GPU, since some neurons require substantially more work than others.[4]

For these reasons we decided to design a simpler, more tractable version of this model (Figure 5). The simplified model still represents an input MTU as a bag-of-words but minimal units are generated word-by-word, first emitting source words and then target words. This is in contrast to the original model which predicted an MTU as a single unit. Decomposing the next MTU into individual words dramatically reduces the size of the output layer, thereby resulting in faster computation of the outputs and making normalization

[4]In initial experiments we found this model to be over twenty times slower than the atomic MTU RNN model with estimated training times of over 6 weeks. This was despite using a vastly smaller vocabulary and by computing the word layer on a, by current standards, high-end GPU (NVIDIA Tesla K20c) using sparse matrix optimizations (cuSPARSE) for the convolutional layer.

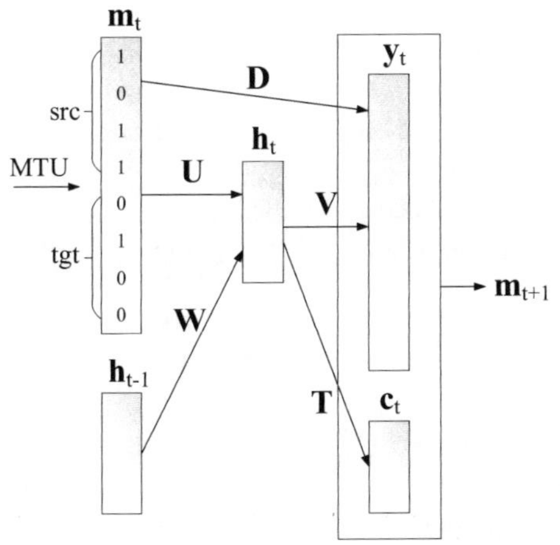

Figure 5: Simplified MTU bag-of-words recurrent neural network model (cf. Figure 4). An MTU is input as bag-of-words and the next MTU is predicted as a sequence of both source and target words.

into probabilities easier. Furthermore, the output layer can be factorized into classes requiring only a fraction of the neurons to be computed, a much more efficient solution compared to the original model which required calculation of the entire output layer.

The simplified model computes the probability of the next MTU m_{t+1} as a product of individual word probabilities:

$$p(m_{t+1}|m_{t-n+1}^{t}, \mathbf{h}_t) = \prod_{a^1,\dots,a^u \in m_{t+1}} p(c^k|m_{t-n+1}^{t}, \mathbf{h}_t) \, p(a^k|c^k, m_{t-n+1}^{t}, \mathbf{h}_t) \quad (1)$$

where we predict a sequence of source and target words $a^1, \dots, a^u \in m_{t+1}$ with a class-structured output layer, similar to the atomic model (§3).

Training still uses a cross entropy criterion and back propagation through time, however, error vectors are computed on a per-word basis, instead of a per-MTU basis. Direct connections between the input and output layers are based on source and target words which is less sparse than basing direct features on entire MTUs such as for the original bag-of-words model.

Overall, the simplified model retains the bag-of-words input representation of the original model, while permitting the efficient factorization of the word-output layer into classes.

5 Experiments

We evaluate the effectiveness of both the atomic MTU RNN model (§3) and the simplified bag-of-words MTU RNN model (§4) in an n-best rescoring setting, comparing against a trigram back-off MTU model as well as the phrasal decoder 1-best output which we denote as the baseline.

5.1 Experimental Setup

Baselines. We experiment with an in-house phrase-based system similar to Moses (Koehn et al., 2007), scoring translations by a set of common features including maximum likelihood estimates of source given target mappings $p_{MLE}(e|f)$ and vice versa $p_{MLE}(f|e)$, as well as lexical weighting estimates $p_{LW}(e|f)$ and $p_{LW}(f|e)$, word and phrase-penalties, a linear distortion feature and a lexicalized reordering feature. The baseline includes a standard modified Kneser-Ney word-based language model trained on the target-side of the parallel corpora described below. Log-linear weights are estimated with minimum error rate training (MERT; Och, 2003).

The 1-best output by the phrase-based decoder is the baseline accuracy. As a second baseline we experiment with a trigram back-off MTU model trained on all extracted MTUs, denoted as n-gram MTU. The trigram MTU model is estimated with the same modified Kneser-Ney framework as the target side language model. All MTU models are trained in target left-to-right MTU order which performed well in initial experiments.

Evaluation. We test our approach on two different data sets. First, we train a German to English system based on the data of the WMT 2006 shared task (Koehn and Monz, 2006). The parallel corpus includes about 35M words of parliamentary proceedings for training, a development set and two test sets with 2000 sentences each.

Second, we experiment with a French to English system based on 102M words of training data from the WMT 2012 campaign. The majority of the training data set is parliamentary proceedings except for about 5m words which are newswire; all MTU models are trained on the newswire subset since we found similar accuracy to using all data in initial experiments. We evaluate on four newswire domain test sets from 2008, 2010 and 2011 as well as the 2010 system combination test set containing between 2034 to 3003 sentences. Log-linear weights are estimated on the 2009 data set comprising 2525 sentences. We evaluate all systems in a single reference BLEU setting.

Rescoring Setup. We rescore the 1000-best output of the baseline phrase-based decoder by either the trigram back-off MTU model or the RNN models. The baseline accuracy is obtained by choosing the 1-best decoder output. We re-estimate the log-linear weights for rescoring by running a further iteration of MERT with the additional feature values; we initialize the rescoring feature weight to zero and try 20 random restarts. At test time we use the new set of log-linear weights to rescore the test set n-best list.

Neural Network Setup. We trained the recurrent neural network models on between 88% and 93% of each data set and used the remainder as validation data. The vocabulary of the atomic MTU RNN model is comprised of all MTU types which were observed more than once in the training data.[5] Similarly, we modeled all non-singleton words for the bag-of-words MTU RNN model. We obtain classes for words or MTUs using a version of Brown-Clustering with an additional regularization term to optimize the runtime of the language model (Brown et al., 1992; Zweig and Makarychev, 2013). Direct connections use features over unigrams, bigrams and trigrams of words or MTUs, depending on the model. Features are hashed to a table with at most 500 million values following Mikolov et al. (2011a). We use the standard settings for the model with the default learning rate $\alpha = 0.1$ that decays exponentially if the validation set entropy does not decrease. Back propagation through time computes error gradients over the past twenty time steps. Training is stopped after 20 epochs or when the validation entropy does not decrease over two epochs. Throughout, we use a hidden layer size of 100 which provided a good trade-off between time and accuracy in initial experiments.

5.2 Results

We first report the decoder 1-best output as the first baseline and then rescore our two data sets (Table 2 and Table 3) with the n-gram back-off MTU model to establish a second baseline (n-gram MTU). The n-gram model improves by 0.4 BLEU over the decoder 1-best on all test sets for German to English. On French-English accuracy improves on three out of five sets by up to 0.7 BLEU.

	dev	test1	test2
Baseline	25.8	26.0	26.0
n-gram MTU	26.3	26.6	26.4
atomic MTU RNN	26.5	26.8	26.5
BoW MTU RNN	26.5	27.0	26.9
word RNNLM	26.5	27.1	26.8
Combined	26.8	27.3	27.1

Table 2: German to English BLEU results for the decoder 1-best output (Baseline) compared to rescoring with a target left-to-right trigram MTU model (n-gram MTU), our two recurrent neural network-based MTU models, a word-based RNN-based language model (word RNNLM), as well as a combination of the three RNN-based models (Combined).

Next, we evaluate the accuracy of the MTU RNN models. The atomic MTU RNN model improves over the n-gram MTU model on all test sets for German to English, however, for French to English the back-off model performs better on two out of four test sets.

The next question we answer is if breaking MTUs into individual units to leverage similarities in the internal structure can help accuracy. The results (Table 2 and Table 3) for the bag-of-words model (BoW MTU RNN) clearly show that this is the case for both language pairs. We significantly improve over the n-gram MTU model as well as the atomic RNN model on all test sets. We observe gains of up to 0.5 BLEU over the n-gram MTU model for German to English as well as French to English; improvements over the decoder baseline are up to 1.2 BLEU for French to English.

How do our models compare to other neural network approaches that rely only on target side information? To answer this question we compare to the strong language model of Mikolov (2012; RNNLM) which has recently improved the state-of-the-art in language modeling perplexity. The results (Table 2 and Table 3) show that RNNLM performs competitively. However, our approaches model translation since we use both source and target information as opposed to scoring only the fluency of the target side, such as done by RNNLM.

Can our models act complementary to a strong RNN language model? Our final experiment combines the atomic MTU RNN model, the BoW

[5] We tried modeling all MTUs which did not contain a singleton *word* but observed no significant effect on accuracy.

	dev	news2008	news2010	news2011	newssyscomb2010
Baseline	24.3	20.5	24.4	25.1	24.3
n-gram MTU	24.6	20.8	24.4	25.8	24.3
atomic MTU RNN	24.6	20.7	24.4	25.5	24.3
BoW MTU RNN	25.2	21.2	24.8	26.3	24.6
word RNNLM	25.1	21.4	25.1	26.4	24.9
Combined	25.4	21.4	25.1	26.6	24.9

Table 3: French to English BLEU results for the decoder 1-best output (Baseline) compared to various MTU models (cf. Table 2).

MTU RNN model, and the RNNLM (Combined). The results (Table 2 and Table 3) confirm that this is the case. For German to English translation accuracy improves by 0.2 to 0.3 BLEU over the RNNLM alone, with gains of up to 1.3 BLEU over the baseline and up to 0.7 BLEU over the n-gram MTU model. Improvements for French to English are lower but we can see some gains on news2011 and on the dev set. Overall, we improve accuracy on the French to English task by up to 1.5 BLEU over the decoder 1-best, and by up to 0.8 BLEU over the n-gram MTU model.

6 Related Work

Our approach of modeling Minimum Translation Units is very much in line with recent work on n-gram-based translation models (Crego and Yvon, 2010), and more recently, continuous space-based translation models (Le et al., 2012). The models presented in this paper differ in a number of key aspects: We use a recurrent architecture representing an unbounded history of MTUs rather than a feed-forward style network. Feed-forward networks as well as back-off n-gram models rely on a finite history which results in predictions independent of anything but a short context of words. A recent side-by-side comparison between recurrent and feed-forward style neural networks (Sundermeyer et al., 2013) has shown that recurrent architectures outperform feed-forward networks in a language modeling task, a similar problem to modeling sequences over Minimum Translation Units.

Furthermore, the input of our best model is a bag-of-words representation of an MTU, unlike the ordered source and target word n-grams used by Crego and Yvon (2010) as well as Le et al. (2012). Finally, we model both source and target words in a single recurrent neural network. The approach of Le et al. (2012) factorizes the joint probability over an MTU sequence in a way that suggests the use of separate neural network models for the source and the target sides, where each model generates words on the respective side only.

Other work on applying recurrent neural networks to machine translation (Mikolov, 2012; Auli et al., 2013; Kalchbrenner and Blunsom, 2013) concentrated on word-based language and translation models, whereas we model Minimum Translation Units.

7 Conclusion and Future Work

Minimum Translation Unit models based on recurrent neural networks lead to substantial gains over their classical n-gram back-off models. We introduced two models of which the best improves accuracy by up to 1.5 BLEU over the 1-best decoder output, and by 0.8 BLEU over a trigram MTU model in an n-best rescoring setting.

Our experiments have shown that representing MTUs as bags-of-words leads to better accuracy since this exploits similarities in the internal structure of Minimum Translation Units, which is not possible when modeling them as atomic symbols. We have also shown that our models are complementary to a very strong RNN language model (Mikolov, 2012).

In future work, we would like to make the initial version of the bag-of-words model computationally more tractable using a better GPU implementation. This model combines the efficient bag-of-words input representation with the ability to predict MTUs as single units while explicitly modeling the constituent words in an intermediate layer.

8 Acknowledgements

We would like to thank Kristina Toutanova for providing a dataset and for helpful discussions related to this work. We also thank the four anonymous reviewers for their comments.

References

Alexandre Allauzen, Hélène Bonneau-Maynard, Hai-Son Le, Aurélien Max, Guillaume Wisniewski, François Yvon, Gilles Adda, Josep Maria Crego, Adrien Lardilleux, Thomas Lavergne, and Artem Sokolov. 2011. LIMSI @ WMT11. In *Proc. of WMT*, pages 309–315, Edinburgh, Scotland, July. Association for Computational Linguistics.

Ebru Arisoy, Tara N. Sainath, Brian Kingsbury, and Bhuvana Ramabhadran. 2012. Deep Neural Network Language Models. In *NAACL-HLT Workshop on the Future of Language Modeling for HLT*, pages 20–28, Stroudsburg, PA, USA. Association for Computational Linguistics.

Michael Auli, Michel Galley, Chris Quirk, and Geoffrey Zweig. 2013. Joint Language and Translation Modeling with Recurrent Neural Networks. In *Proc. of EMNLP*, October.

Rafael E. Banchs, Josep M. Crego, Adrià de Gispert, Patrik Lambert, and José B. Mariño. 2005. Statistical Machine Translation of Euparl Data by Using bilingual n-grams. In *Proc. of ACL Workshop on Building and Using Parallel Texts*, pages 133–136, Jun.

Yoshua Bengio, Réjean Ducharme, Pascal Vincent, and Christian Jauvin. 2003. A Neural Probabilistic Language Model. *Journal of Machine Learning Research*, 3:1137–1155.

Peter F. Brown, Peter V. deSouza, Robert L. Mercer, Vincent J. Della Pietra, and Jenifer C. Lai. 1992. Class-based n-gram models of natural language. *Computational Linguistics*, 18(4):467–479, Dec.

Josep Crego and François Yvon. 2010. Factored bilingual n-gram language models for statistical machine translation. *Machine Translation*, 24(2):159–175.

Ahmad Emami and Frederick Jelinek. 2005. A Neural Syntactic Language Model. *Machine Learning*, 60(1-3):195–227, September.

Jianfeng Gao, Xiaodong He, Wen-tau Yih, and Li Deng. 2013. Learning Semantic Representations for the Phrase Translation Model. Technical Report MSR-TR-2013-88, Microsoft Research, September.

Joshua Goodman. 2001. Classes for Fast Maximum Entropy Training. In *Proc. of ICASSP*.

Kenneth Heafield, Ivan Pouzyrevsky, Jonathan H. Clark, and Philipp Koehn. 2013. Scalable Modified Kneser-Ney Language Model Estimation. In *Proc. of ACL*, August.

Po-Sen Huang, Xiaodong He, Jianfeng Gao, Li Deng, Alex Acero, and Larry Heck. 2013. Learning Deep Structured Semantic Models for Web Search using Clickthrough Data. In *Proc. of CIKM*, October.

Nal Kalchbrenner and Phil Blunsom. 2013. Recurrent Continuous Translation Models. In *Proc. of EMNLP*, pages 1700–1709, Seattle, Washington, USA, October. Association for Computational Linguistics.

Philipp Koehn and Christof Monz. 2006. Manual and automatic evaluation of machine translation between european languages. In *Proc. of NAACL Workshop on Statistical Machine Translation*, pages 102–121.

Philipp Koehn, Franz Josef Och, and Daniel Marcu. 2003. Statistical Phrase-Based Translation. In *Proc. of HLT-NAACL*, pages 127–133, Edmonton, Canada, May.

Philipp Koehn, Hieu Hoang, Alexandra Birch, Chris Callison-Burch, Marcello Federico, Nicola Bertoldi, Brooke Cowan, Wade Shen, Christine Moran, Richard Zens, Chris Dyer, Ondrej Bojar, Alexandra Constantin, and Evan Herbst. 2007. Moses: Open Source Toolkit for Statistical Machine Translation. In *Proc. of ACL Demo and Poster Sessions*, pages 177–180, Prague, Czech Republic, Jun.

Hai-Son Le, Alexandre Allauzen, and François Yvon. 2012. Continuous Space Translation Models with Neural Networks. In *Proc. of HLT-NAACL*, pages 39–48, Montréal, Canada. Association for Computational Linguistics.

Tomáš Mikolov, Karafiát Martin, Lukáš Burget, Jan Cernocký, and Sanjeev Khudanpur. 2010. Recurrent Neural Network based Language Model. In *Proc. of INTERSPEECH*, pages 1045–1048.

Tomáš Mikolov, Anoop Deoras, Daniel Povey, Lukáš Burget, and Jan Černocký. 2011a. Strategies for Training Large Scale Neural Network Language Models. In *Proc. of ASRU*, pages 196–201.

Tomáš Mikolov, Stefan Kombrink, Lukáš Burget, Jan Cernocký, and Sanjeev Khudanpur. 2011b. Extensions of Recurrent Neural Network Language Model. In *Proc. of ICASSP*, pages 5528–5531.

Tomáš Mikolov, Wen-tau Yih, and Geoffrey Zweig. 2013. Linguistic Regularities in Continuous Space-Word Representations. In *Proc. of NAACL*, pages 746–751, Stroudsburg, PA, USA, June. Association for Computational Linguistics.

Tomáš Mikolov. 2012. *Statistical Language Models based on Neural Networks*. Ph.D. thesis, Brno University of Technology.

Franz Josef Och. 2003. Minimum Error Rate Training in Statistical Machine Translation. In *Proc. of ACL*, pages 160–167, Sapporo, Japan, July.

Chris Quirk and Arul Menezes. 2006. Do we need phrases? Challenging the conventional wisdom in Statistical Machine Translation. In *Proc. of NAACL*, pages 8–16, New York, Jun.

Ariya Rastrow, Sanjeev Khudanpur, and Mark Dredze. 2012. Revisiting the Case for Explicit Syntactic Information in Language Models. In *NAACL-HLT Workshop on the Future of Language Modeling for HLT*, pages 50–58. Association for Computational Linguistics.

David E. Rumelhart, Geoffrey E. Hinton, and Ronald J. Williams. 1986. Learning Internal Representations by Error Propagation. In *Symposium on Parallel and Distributed Processing*.

Holger Schwenk, Marta R. Costa-jussà, and José A. R. Fonollosa. 2007. Smooth Bilingual N-Gram Translation. In *Proc. of EMNLP*, pages 430–438, Prague, Czech Republic, June. Association for Computational Linguistics.

Holger Schwenk, Anthony Rousseau, and Mohammed Attik. 2012. Large, Pruned or Continuous Space Language Models on a GPU for Statistical Machine Translation. In *NAACL-HLT Workshop on the Future of Language Modeling for HLT*, pages 11–19. Association for Computational Linguistics.

Martin Sundermeyer, Ilya Oparin, Jean-Luc Gauvain, Ben Freiberg, Ralf Schlüter, and Hermann Ney. 2013. Comparison of Feedforward and Recurrent Neural Network Language Models. In *IEEE International Conference on Acoustics, Speech, and Signal Processing*, pages 8430–8434, Vancouver, Canada, May.

Ashish Vaswani, Yinggong Zhao, Victoria Fossum, and David Chiang. 2013. Decoding with Large-scale Neural Language Models improves Translation. In *Proc. of EMNLP*. Association for Computational Linguistics, October.

Hui Zhang, Kristina Toutanova, Chris Quirk, and Jianfeng Gao. 2013. Beyond left-to-right: Multiple decomposition structures for smt. In *Proc. of NAACL*, pages 12–21, Atlanta, Georgia, June. Association for Computational Linguistics.

Geoff Zweig and Konstantin Makarychev. 2013. Speed Regularization and Optimality in Word Classing. In *Proc. of ICASSP*.

Maximizing Component Quality in Bilingual Word-Aligned Segmentations

Spyros Martzoukos   Christophe Costa Florêncio   Christof Monz
Intelligent Systems Lab Amsterdam, University of Amsterdam
Science Park 904, 1098 XH Amsterdam, The Netherlands
{S.Martzoukos, C.CostaFlorencio, C.Monz}@uva.nl

Abstract

Given a pair of source and target language sentences which are translations of each other with known word alignments between them, we extract bilingual phrase-level segmentations of such a pair. This is done by identifying two appropriate measures that assess the quality of phrase segments, one on the monolingual level for both language sides, and one on the bilingual level. The monolingual measure is based on the notion of partition refinements and the bilingual measure is based on structural properties of the graph that represents phrase segments and word alignments. These two measures are incorporated in a basic adaptation of the Cross-Entropy method for the purpose of extracting an N-best list of bilingual phrase-level segmentations. A straight-forward application of such lists in Statistical Machine Translation (SMT) yields a conservative phrase pair extraction method that reduces phrase-table sizes by 90% with insignificant loss in translation quality.

1 Introduction

Given a pair of source and target language sentences which are translations of each other with known word alignments between them, the problem of extracting high quality bilingual phrase segmentations is defined as follows: Maximize the quality of phrase segments, i.e., groupings of consecutive words, in both language sides, subject to constraints imposed by the underlying word alignments. The purpose of this work is to provide a solution to this maximization problem and investigate the effect of the resulting high quality bilingual phrase segments on SMT. For brevity, 'phrase-level sentence segmentation' and 'phrase segment' will henceforth be simply referred to as 'segmentation' and 'segment' respectively.

The exact definition of segments' quality depends on the application. Our notion of a segmentation of maximum quality is defined as the set of consecutive words of the sentence that captures maximum collocational and/or grammatical characteristics. This implies that a sequence of tokens is identified as a segment if its fully compositional expressive power is higher than the expressive power of any combination of partial compositions. Since this definition is fairly general it is thus suitable for most NLP tasks. In particular, it is tailored to the type of segments that are suitable for the purposes of SMT and is in line with previous work (Blackwood et al., 2008; Paul et al., 2010).

With this definition in mind, we introduce a monolingual segment quality measure that is based on assessing the cost of converting one segmentation into another by means of an elementary operation. This operation, namely the 'splitting' of a segment into two segments, together with all possible segmentations of a sentence are known to form a partially ordered set (Guo, 1997). Such a construction is known as partition refinement and gives rise to the desired monolingual *surface* quality measure.

The presence of word alignments between the sentence pair provides additional structure which should not be ignored. In the language of graph theory, a segment can also be viewed as a chain, i.e., a graph in which vertices are the segment's words and an edge between two words exists if and only if these words are consecutive. Then, a bilingual segmentation is represented by the graph that is formed by all its source and target language chains together with edges induced by word alignments. Motivated by the phrase pair extraction methods of SMT (Och et al., 1999; Koehn et al., 2003), we focus on the connected components, or simply components of such a representation. We explain that the extent to which we can delete word alignments from a component without violating its component status, gives rise to a bilingual, purely *structural* quality measure.

The surface and structural measures are incorporated in one algorithm that extracts an N-best list of bilingual word-aligned segmentations. This algorithm, which is an adaptation of the Cross-Entropy method (Rubinstein, 1997), performs joint maximization of surface (in both languages) and structural quality measures. Components of graph representations of the resulting N-best lists give rise to high quality translation units. These units, which form a small subset of all possible (continuous) consistent phrase pairs, are used to construct SMT models. Results on Czech–English and German–English datasets show a 90% reduction in phrase-table sizes with insignificant loss in translation quality which are in line with other pruning techniques in SMT (Johnson et al., 2007; Zens et al., 2012).

2 Monolingual Surface Quality Measure

Given a sentence $s_1 s_2 ... s_k$ that consists of words s_i, $1 \leq i \leq k$, we introduce an empirical count-based measure that assesses the quality of its segmentations. By fixing a segmentation σ, we are interested in assessing the cost of perturbing σ and generating another segmentation σ'. A perturbation of σ is achieved by splitting a segment of σ into two new segments, while keeping all other segments fixed. For example, for a sentence with five words, if $\sigma : (s_1 s_2)(s_3 s_4 s_5)$, where brackets are used to distinguish the segments $s_1 s_2$ and $s_3 s_4 s_5$, then σ can be perturbed in three different ways:

- $\sigma' : (s_1)(s_2)(s_3 s_4 s_5)$, by splitting the first segment of σ.
- $\sigma'' : (s_1 s_2)(s_3)(s_4 s_5)$, by splitting at the first position of the second segment of σ.
- $\sigma''' : (s_1 s_2)(s_3 s_4)(s_5)$, by splitting at the second position of the second segment of σ,

so that σ', σ'' and σ''' are the perturbations of σ. Such perturbations are known as partition refinements in the literature (Stanley, 1997). The set of all segmentations of a sentence, equipped with the splitting operation forms a partially ordered set (Guo, 1997), and its visual representation is known as the *Hasse diagram*. Figure 1 shows such a partially ordered set for a sentence with four words.

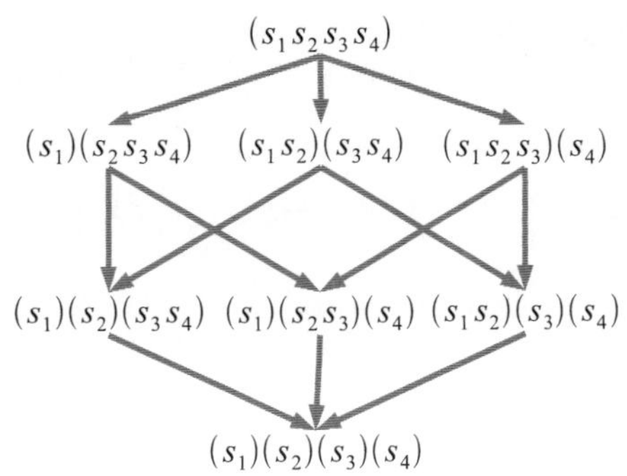

Figure 1: Hasse diagram of segmentation refinements for a sentence with four words.

The cost of perturbing a segmentation into another, i.e., the weight of a directed edge in the Hasse diagram, is calculated from n-gram counts that are extracted from a monolingual training corpus. Let $n(s)$ be the empirical count of phrase s in the corpus. Given a segmentation σ of a sentence, let $seg(\sigma)$ denote the set of σ's segments. In the above example we have for instance $seg(\sigma'') = \{s_1 s_2, s_3, s_4 s_5\}$. The probability of s in σ is given by relative frequencies

$$p_\sigma(s) = \frac{n(s)}{\sum_{s' \in seg(\sigma)} n(s')}. \tag{1}$$

The cost of perturbing σ into σ' by splitting a segment $s\bar{s}$ of σ into segments s and $\bar{s}$ is defined by

$$\text{cost}_{\sigma \to \sigma'}(s, \bar{s}) = \log \frac{p_\sigma(s\bar{s})}{p_{\sigma'}(s) p_{\sigma'}(\bar{s})}, \tag{2}$$

and we say that s and $\bar{s}$ are co-responsible for the perturbation $\sigma \to \sigma'$. Intuitively, this cost function yields the amount of energy (log of probability) that is lost when performing a perturbation. On a more technical level, it is closely related to metric spaces on partially ordered sets (Monjardet, 1981; Orum and Joslyn, 2009), but we do not go into further details here.

The cost function admits a measure for the segments that are co-responsible for perturbing σ into σ' and we define the gain of s from the perturbation $\sigma \to \sigma'$ as

$$gain_{\sigma \to \sigma'}(s) = -\text{cost}_{\sigma \to \sigma'}(s, \bar{s}). \quad (3)$$

A segment s may be co-responsible for different perturbations, and we have to consider all such perturbations. Let

$$R(s) = \{\sigma \to \sigma' : s \notin seg(\sigma), s \in seg(\sigma')\} \quad (4)$$

denote the set of perturbations for which s is co-responsible. Then, the average gain of s in the sentence is given by

$$gain(s) = \frac{1}{|R(s)|} \sum_{\{\sigma \to \sigma'\} \in R(s)} gain_{\sigma \to \sigma'}(s). \quad (5)$$

Intuitively, $gain(s)$ measures how difficult it is to break phrase s into sub-phrases. Finally, the surface quality measure of a segmentation σ of a sentence is given by

$$g(\sigma) = \sum_{s \in seg(\sigma)} gain(s). \quad (6)$$

Note that g is a real number. The relation $g(\sigma) > g(\sigma')$ implies that σ is a better segmentation than σ'.

We conclude this section with two remarks: (i) The exact computation of $gain(s)$ for each possible segment s is computationally expensive since all perturbations need to be considered. In practice we can simply generate a random sample of no more than 1500 segmentations and compute $gain(\cdot)$ based on that sample only. (ii) Each sentence of the monolingual training corpus (from which the n-gram counts are extracted) should have the beginning and end-of-sentence tokens. The count for each of them is equal to the number of sentences in the corpus, and they are treated as regular words. Without going into further details they provide the purpose of normalization.

3 Bilingual Structural Quality Measure

Given a word-aligned sentence pair, we introduce a purely structural measure that assesses the quality of its bilingual segmentations. By 'purely structural' we mean that the focus is entirely on combinatorial aspects of the bilingual segmentations and the word alignments. For that reason we turn to a graph theoretic framework.

A segment can also be viewed as a chain, i.e., a graph in which vertices are the segment's words and an edge between two words exists if and only if these words are consecutive. Then, a source segmentation σ and a target segmentation τ are graphs that consist of source chains and target chains respectively. The graph formed by σ, τ and the translation edges induced by word alignments is thus a graph representation of a bilingual word-aligned segmentation.

We focus on a particular type of subgraphs of this representation, namely its connected components, or simply components. A component is a graph such that (a) there exists a path between any two of its vertices, and (b) there does not exist a path between a vertex of the component and a vertex outside the component. Condition (a) means, both technically and intuitively, that a component is connected and Condition (b) requires connectivity to be maximal.

Components play a key role in SMT. The most widely used strategy for extracting high quality phrase-level translations without linguistic information, namely the consistency method (Och et al., 1999; Koehn et al., 2003) is entirely based on components of word aligned unsegmented sentence pairs (Martzoukos et al., 2013). In particular, each extracted translation is either a component or the union of components. Since an unsegmented sentence pair is just one possible configuration of all possible bilingual segmentations, we consequently have no direct reason to investigate further than components.

In order to get an intuition of the measure that will be introduced in this section, we begin with an example. Figure 2, shows two different configurations of the pair (σ, τ) for the same sentence pair with known and fixed word alignments. Both configurations have the same number of edges that connect source vertices (3) and the same number of edges that connect target vertices (2). However, one would

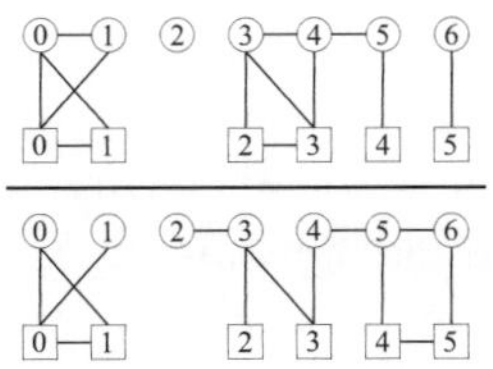

Figure 2: Graph representations of two bilingual segmentations with fixed word alignments. Source and target vertices are shown with circles and squares respectively.

expect the top configuration to represent a better bilingual segmentation. This is because it has more components (4 opposed to 2 for the bottom configuration) and because it consists of 'tighter' clusters, i.e., 'tighter' components.

A general measure that would capture this observation requires a balance between the number of edges of source and target chains, the number of components and the number of translation edges, all coupled with how these edges and vertices are connected. This might seem as a daunting task that can be tackled with a combination of heuristics, but there is actually a graph-theoretic measure that can fully describe the sought structure. We proceed with introducing this measure.

Let C denote the set of components of the graph representation of a bilingual word-aligned segmentation. We are interested in measuring the extent to which we can delete translation edges from $c \in C$, while retaining its component status. Let a_c denote the subset of translation edges that are restricted to the component c. We define the positive integer

$$gain(c) = \text{number of ways of deleting translation edges from } a_c, \text{ while keeping } c \text{ connected,} \quad (7)$$

where the option of deleting nothing is counted. Intuitively, by keeping the edges of the chains fixed the quantity $gain(c)$ measures how difficult it is to perturb a component from its connected state to a disconnected state.

Figure 3 shows two components c and c' that satisfy $gain(c) = gain(c') = 3$. Both components are equally difficult to be perturbed into a disconnected state, but only superficially. The actual structural quality of c is revealed when it is 'compared' to component $\tilde{c}$ that consists of the same source and target vertices, the same translation edges but its source vertices form exactly one chain and similarly for its target vertices; $\tilde{c}$ is essentially the 'upper bound' of c. In general, the maximum value of $gain(c)$, with

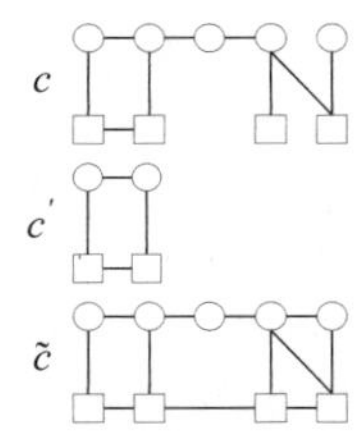

Figure 3: Superficially similar components c and c'. Comparing c with $\tilde{c}$ yields c's true structural quality.

respect to a fixed set of source and target vertices and translation edges, is attained when it consists of exactly one source chain and exactly one target chain. It is not difficult to see that the desired maximum value is always $2^{|a_c|} - 1$. In the example of Figure 3, the structural quality of c and c' is thus $3/(2^5 - 1) = 9.7\%$ and $3/(2^2 - 1) = 100\%$ respectively. Hence, the measure that evaluates the structural quality of a bilingual word-aligned segmentation (σ, τ) is given by

$$f(\sigma, \tau) = \left(\prod_{c \in C} \frac{gain(c)}{2^{|a_c|} - 1} \right)^{\frac{1}{|C|}}, \quad (8)$$

which takes values in $(0, 1]$. The relation $f(\sigma, \tau) > f(\sigma', \tau')$ implies that (σ, τ) is a better bilingual segmentation than (σ', τ').

We conclude this section with two remarks: (i) A component with no translation edges, i.e., a source or target segment whose words are all unaligned, has a contribution of $1/0$ in (8). In practice we exclude such components from C. (ii) In graph theory the quantity $gain(c)$ is known as the number of connected spanning subgraphs (CSSGs) of graph c and is the key quantity of network reliability (Valiant, 1979; Coulbourn, 1987). Finding the number of CSSGs of a general graph is a known #P-hard problem (Welsh, 1997). In our setting, graphs have specific formation (source and target chains connected via translation edges) and we are interested in the deletion of translation edges only; it is possible to compute $gain(\cdot)$ in polynomial time, but we do not go into further details here.

4 Extracting Bilingual Segmentations with the Cross-Entropy Method

Equipped with the measures of Sections 2 and 3 we turn to extracting an N-best list of bilingual segmentations for a given sentence pair. The search space is exponential in the total number of words of the sentence pair. We propose a new approach for this task, by noting a direct connection with the combinatorial problems that can be solved efficiently and effectively with the Cross-Entropy (CE) method (Rubinstein, 1997).

The CE method is an iterative self-tuning sampling method that has applications in various combinatorial and continuous global optimization problems as well as in rare event detection. A detailed account on the CE method is beyond the scope of this work, and we thus simply describe its application to our problem.

In particular, we first establish the connection between the most basic form of the CE method and the problem of finding the best *monolingual* segmentation of a sentence, with respect to some scoring function (not necessarily the one that was introduced in Section 2). This connection yields a simple, efficient and effective algorithm for the monolingual maximization problem. Then, the transition to the bilingual level is done by incorporating the measure of Section 3 in the algorithm, thus performing joint maximization of surface and structural quality. Finally, the generation of the N-best list will be trivial.

A segmentation of a given sentence has a bit-string representation in the following way: If two consecutive words in the sentence belong to the same segment in the segmentation, then this pair of words is encoded by '1', otherwise by '0'. Such a representation is bijective and, thus, for the rest of this section, we do not distinguish between a segmentation and its bit-string representation. In this setting, the CE method takes its most basic form (De Boer et al., 2005). In a nutshell, it is a repeated application of (a) sampling bit-strings from a parametrized probability mass function, (b) scoring them and keeping only a small high-performing subsample, and (c) updating the parameters of the probability mass function based on that subsample only.

We assume no prior knowledge on the quality of bit-strings, so that they are all equally likely. In other words, each position of a randomly chosen bit-string can be either a '0' or a '1' with probability $1/2$. The aim is to tune these position probabilities towards the best bit-string, with respect to some scoring function g. In particular, let the sentence have n words and let $\ell = n - 1$ be the length of bit-strings. A bit-string labeled by an integer i is denoted by b_i and its jth bit by b_{ij}. The algorithm is as follows:

0. Initialize the bit-string position probabilities $p^0 = (p^0_1, ..., p^0_\ell) = (1/2, ..., 1/2)$ and set $M = 20\ell$ (sample size), $\rho = \lceil 1\% M \rceil$ (keep top 1% of samples), $\alpha = 0.7$ (smoothing parameter) and $t = 1$ (iteration).

1. Generate a sample $b_1, ..., b_M$ of bit-strings, each of length ℓ, such that $b_{ij} \sim$Bernoulli(p^{t-1}_j), for all $i = 1, ..., M$ and $j = 1, ..., \ell$.

1.1 Compute scores $g(b_1), ..., g(b_M)$.

1.2 Order them descendingly as $g(b_{\pi(1)}) > ... > g(b_{\pi(M)})$.

2. Focus on the best performing ones: Compute $\gamma_t = g(b_{\pi(\rho)})$; samples performing less than this threshold will be ignored.

3. Use the best performing sub-sample of $b_1, ..., b_M$ to update position probabilities:

$$p^t_j = \frac{\sum_{i=1}^M I_i(\gamma_t) b_{ij}}{\sum_{i=1}^M I_i(\gamma_t)}, \quad j = 1, ..., \ell, \tag{9}$$

where the choice function I_i is given by

$$I_i(\gamma_t) = \begin{cases} 1, & \text{if } g(b_i) > \gamma_t \\ 0, & \text{otherwise.} \end{cases}$$

4. Smooth the updated position probabilities as

$$p^t_j := \alpha p^t_j + (1 - \alpha) p^{t-1}_j, \quad j = 1, ..., \ell. \tag{10}$$

E. If for some $t > 5$ we have $\gamma_t = \gamma_{t-1} = ... = \gamma_{t-5}$ then stop. Else, $t := t + 1$ and go to Step 1.

The values for the parameters M, ρ and α reported here are in line with the ones suggested in the literature (Rubinstein and Kroese, 2004) for combinatorial problems such as this one. After the execution of the algorithm, the updated vector of position probabilities converges to sequence of '0's and '1's, which corresponds to the best segmentation under g.

The extension to bilingual level is done by incorporating the structural quality measure of Section 3. The setting is similar, i.e., samples are again bit-strings, but of length $\ell = n + m - 2$, where n and m are the number of words in the source and target sentence respectively. The first $n - 1$ bits correspond to the source sentence and the rest to the target sentence. The surface quality score of such a bit-string is given by the harmonic mean of its source and target surface quality scores.[1] The bit-string scoring function throughout Steps 1 – 3 is given by the harmonic mean of surface and structural quality scores. Finally, N-best lists are trivially generated, simply by collecting the top-N performing accumulated samples of a maximization process.

5 Experiments

Given a sentence pair with known and fixed word alignments, the result of the method described in Section 4 is an N-best list of bilingual segmentations of such a pair. The objective function provides a balance between compositional expressive power of segments in both languages and synchronization via word alignments. Thus, each (continuous) component of such a bilingual segmentation leads to the extraction of a high quality phrase pair.

As was mentioned in Section 3, each extracted phrase pair of standard phrase-based SMT is constructed from a component or from the union of components of an unsegmented word-aligned sentence pair. For each sentence pair, all possible (continuous) components and (continuous) unions of components give rise to the extracted (continuous) phrase pairs. In this section we investigate the impact to SMT models and translation quality, when extracting phrase pairs (from the N-best lists) that correspond to components *only*. A reduction in phrase-table size is guaranteed because we are essentially extracting only a subset of all possible continuous phrase pairs. The challenge is to verify whether this subset can provide a sufficient translation model.

	Cz–En	De–En
Europarl (v7)	642,505	1,889,791
News Commentary (v8)	139,679	177,079
Total	782,184	2,066,870

Table 1: Number of filtered parallel sentences for Czech–English and German–English.

Both the baseline and our system are standard phrase-based MT systems. Bidirectional word alignments are generated with GIZA++ (Och and Ney, 2003) and 'grow-diag-final-and'. These are used to construct a phrase-table with bidirectional phrase probabilities, lexical weights and a reordering model with monotone, swap and discontinuous orientations, conditioned on both the previous and the next phrase. 4-gram interpolated language models with Kneser-Ney smoothing are built with SRILM (Stolcke, 2002). A distortion limit of 6 and a phrase-penalty are also used. All model parameters are tuned with MERT (Och, 2003). Decoding during tuning and testing is done with Moses (Koehn et. al, 2007). Since our system only affects which phrases are extracted, lexical weights and reordering orientations are the same for both systems.

Datasets are from the WMT'13 translation task (Bojar et al., 2013): Translation and reordering models are trained on Czech–English and German–English corpora (Table 1). Language models and segment measures *gain*, as defined in (5), are trained on 35.3M Czech, 50.0M German and 94.5M English sentences from the provided monolingual data. Tuning is done on newstest2010 and performance is evaluated on newstest2008, newstest2009, newstest2011 and newstest2012 with BLEU (Papineni et al., 2001).

In our experiments the size of an N-best list varies according to the total number of words in the sentence pair, say w. For the purposes of phrase extraction in SMT we would ideally require all local maxima to be part of an N-best list. This would

[1] As it was mentioned in Section 2 the surface quality score in (6) is a real number. At each iteration of the algorithm the surface score of a segmentation can be converted into a number in [0, 1] via Min-Max normalization. This holds for both source and target sides of a bit-string (independently).

Method	Czech→English				English→Czech				Czech–English
	'08	'09	'11	'12	'08	'09	'11	'12	PT size (retain%)
Baseline	19.6	20.6	22.6	20.6	14.8	15.6	16.6	14.9	44.6M (100%)
N-best	19.7	20.4	22.4	20.3	14.4	15.2	16.3	14.3	4.4M (9.8%)
N-best & unseg.	19.6	20.5	22.6	20.7	14.6	15.4	16.8	14.7	4.6M (10.4%)

Table 2: BLEU scores and phrase-table (PT) sizes for Czech–English. Phrase-table of 'Baseline' is constructed from all consistent phrase pairs. Phrase-table of 'N-best' is constructed from consistent phrase pairs that are components of the top-N bilingual word-aligned segmentations of each sentence pair. Similarly for 'N-best & unseg.', but consistent phrase pairs that are components of each (unsegmented) sentence pair are also included.

Method	German→English				English→German				German–English
	'08	'09	'11	'12	'08	'09	'11	'12	PT size (retain%)
Baseline	21.4	20.8	21.3	22.1	15.1	15.1	16.0	16.5	102.3M (100%)
N-best	21.3	20.6	21.3	21.8	15.0	15.0	15.6	16.0	9.4M (9.2%)
N-best & unseg.	21.5	20.8	21.5	22.0	15.4	15.2	15.7	16.2	9.9M (9.7%)

Table 3: Similar to Table 2, but for German–English.

guarantee the extraction of all high quality phrase pairs, with (empirically) desired variations, while keeping N small. Since the CE method performs global optimization, the resulting members of an N-best list are in the vicinity of the global maximum. Consequently, we cannot guarantee the inclusion of local maxima. We set $N = \lceil 30\%w \rceil$ so that at least some variation from the global maximum is included, but is not large enough to contaminate the lists with noisy bilingual segmentations. The resulting lists have 22 bilingual segmentations on average for both language pairs. Figure 4 shows typical German–English best performing bilingual segmentations.

BLEU scores are reported in Tables 2 and 3 for Czech–English and German–English respectively. Methods 'Baseline' and 'N-best' are the ones described above. Phrase-table sizes are reduced as expected and performance when translating to English is comparable. The significant drops in newstest2012 when translating from the morphologically poorer language (English) prompts us to include more 'basic' phrase pairs in the phrase-tables. This leads to augmenting each N-best list by its unsegmented sentence pair. Consequently, method 'N-best & unseg.' extracts the same phrase pairs as 'N-best', together with those from components of the unsegmented sentence pairs. As a result, translation quality is comparable to 'Baseline' across all language directions and small phrase-table sizes are retained.

6 Discussion and Future Work

This work can also be viewed as an attempt to understand bilinguality as a *generalization* of monolinguality. There is conceptual common ground on what $gain(x)$ for phrase x (Section 2) or component x (Section 3) computes. In both cases it measures how 'stable' a unit is. The stability of a phrase x is determined by how difficult it is to split x into multiple phrases. The partially ordered set framework of partition refinements is the natural setting for such computations. In order to determine the stability of a component we turn to empirical evidence from SMT: 'good' phrase pairs are extracted from components or unions of components of the graph that represents word-aligned sentence pairs. The stability of a component x is therefore determined by how difficult it is to break x into multiple components. It is thus interesting to investigate whether there exists a general approach that unifies partition refinements and network reliability for the purpose of identifying highly stable multilingual units.

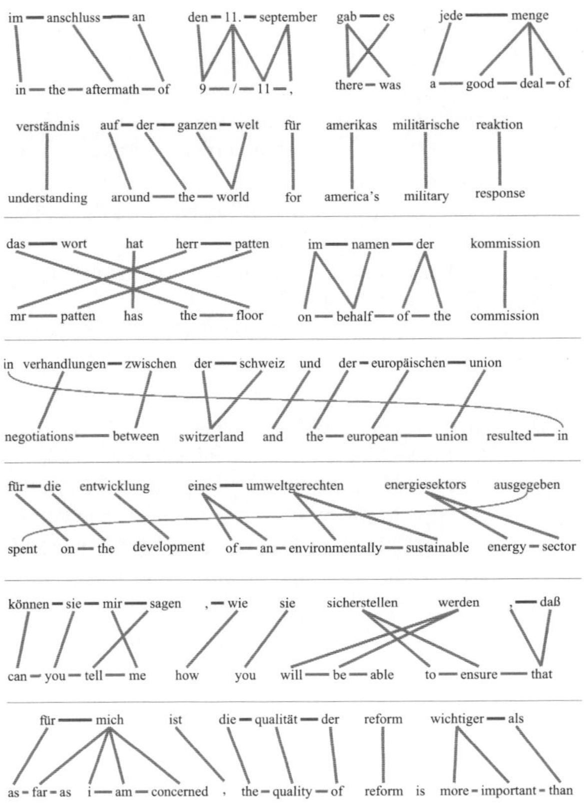

Figure 4: Typical fragments from best performing German–English segmentations.

The focus has been on bilingual segmentations, but as was mentioned in Section 2, it is possible to apply the CE method for generating monolingual segmentations. By using (6) as the objective function, we observed that the resulting segmentations yield promising applications in n-gram topic modeling, named entity recognition and Chinese segmentation. However, in the spirit of Ries et al. (1996), attempts to minimize perplexity instead of maximizing (6), resulted in larger segments and the segment quality definition of Section 1 was not met.

The sizes of the resulting phrase-tables together with the type of phrase pairs that are extracted lead to applications involving discontinuous phrase pairs. In (Galley and Manning, 2010) there was evidence that discontinuous phrase pairs that are extracted from discontinuous components of word-aligned sentence pairs can improve translation quality.[1] As the number of such components is much bigger than the continuous ones, (Gimpel and Smith, 2011) propose a Bayesian nonparametric model for finding the most probable discontinuous phrase pairs. This can also be done from the N-best lists that are generated in Section 4, and it would be interesting to see the effect of such phrase pairs in our existing models.

In a longer version of this work we intend to study the effect in translation quality when varying some of the parameters (size of N-best lists, sample sizes for training $gain$ in Section 2 and for the CE method), as well as when extracting source-driven bilingual segmentations as in (Sanchis-Trilles et al., 2011).

7 Conclusions

In this work, we have presented a solution to the problem of extracting bilingual segmentations in the presence of word alignments. Two measures that assess the quality of bilingual segmentations based on the expressive power of segments in both languages and their synchronization via word alignments have been introduced. We have established the link between the CE method and finding the best monolingual and bilingual segmentations. These measures formed the objective function of the CE method whose maximization resulted in an N-best list of bilingual segmentations for a given sentence pair. By extracting only phrase pairs that correspond to components from bilingual segmentations of those lists, we found that phrase table sizes can be reduced with insignificant loss in translation quality.

Acknowledgements

This research was funded in part by the European Commission through the CoSyne project FP7-ICT-4-248531 and the Netherlands Organisation for Scientific Research (NWO) under project nr. 639.022.213.

[1] By 'discontinuous component' we mean a component whose source or target words (vertices) form a discontinuous substring in the source or target sentence respectively.

References

Graeme Blackwood, Adria de Gispert, and William Byrne. 2008. Phrasal Segmentation Models for Statistical Machine Translation. In *COLING*.

Ondřej Bojar, Christian Buck, Chris Callison-Burch, Christian Federmann, Barry Haddow, Philipp Koehn, Christof Monz, Matt Post, Radu Soricut, and Lucia Specia. 2013. Findings of the 2013 Workshop on Statistical Machine Translation. In *WMT*.

Charlie J. Coulbourn. 1987. The Combinatorics of Network Reliability. Oxford University Press.

Pieter-Tjerk De Boer, Dirk P. Kroese, Shie Mannor, and Reuven Y. Rubinstein. 2005. A Tutorial on the Cross-Entropy Method. *Annals of Operations Research*, vol. 134, pages 19–67.

Michel Galley and Christopher D. Manning. 2010. Accurate Non-Hierarchical Phrase-Based Translation. In *NAACL*.

Kevin Gimpel and Noah A. Smith. 2011. Generative Models of Monolingual and Bilingual Gappy Patterns. In *WMT*.

Jin Guo. 1997. Critical Tokenization and its Properties. *Computational Linguistics*, vol. 23(4), pages 569–596.

Howard Johnson, Joel Martin, George Foster, and Roland Kuhn. 2007. Improving translation quality by discarding most of the phrase-table. In *EMNLP-CoNLL*.

Philipp Koehn, Hieu Hoang, Alexandra Birch, Chris Callison-Burch, Marcello Federico, Nicola Bertoldi, Brooke Cowan, Wade Shen, Christine Moran, Richard Zens, Chris Dyer, Ondřej Bojar, Alexandra Constantin, and Evan Herbst. 2007. Moses: Open Source Toolkit for Statistical Machine Translation. In *ACL, demonstration session*.

Philipp Koehn, Franz J. Och, and Daniel Marcu. 2003. Statistical Phrase-Based Translation. In *HLT-NAACL*.

Spyros Martzoukos, Christophe Costa Florêncio, and Christof Monz. 2013. Investigating Connectivity and Consistency Criteria for Phrase Pair Extraction in Statistical Machine Translation. In *Meeting on Mathematics of Language*.

Bernard Monjardet. 1981. Metrics on partially ordered sets – a survey. *Discrete Mathematics*, vol. 35, pages 173–184.

Franz J. Och. 2003. Minimum error rate training in statistical machine translation. In *ACL*.

Franz J. Och and Hermann Ney. 2003. A Systematic Comparison of Various Statistical Alignment Models. *Computational Linguistics*, vol. 29 (1), pages 19–51.

Franz J. Och, Christoph Tillmann, and Hermann Ney. 1999. Improved Alignment Models for Statistical Machine Translation. In *EMNLP-VLC*.

Chris Orum and Cliff A. Joslyn. 2009. Valuations and Metrics on Partially Ordered Sets. *Computing Research Repository - CORR*, vol. abs/0903.2.

Kishore Papineni, Salim Roukos, Todd Ward, and Wei-Jing Zhu. 2001. Bleu: a method for automatic evaluation of machine translation. In *ACL*.

Michael Paul, Andrew Finch, and Eiichiro Sumita. 2010. Integration of Multiple Bilingually-Learned Segmentation Schemes into Statistical Machine Translation. In *WMT and MetricsMATR*.

Klaus Ries, Finn Dag Bu, and Alex Waibel. 1996. Class phrase models for language modeling. In *ICSLP*.

Reuven Y. Rubinstein. 1997. Optimization of Computer Simulation Models with Rare Events. *European Journal of Operations Research*, vol. 99, pages 89–112.

Reuven Y. Rubinstein and Dirk P. Kroese. 2004. The Cross-Entropy Method: A Unified Approach to Combinatorial Optimization, Monte-Carlo Simulation and Machine Learning. Springer-Verlag, New York.

Germán Sanchis-Trilles, Daniel Ortiz-Martínez, Jesús González-Rubio, Jorge González, and Francisco Casacuberta. 2011. Bilingual segmentation for phrasetable pruning in Statistical Machine Translation. In *EAMT*.

Richard P. Stanley. 1997. Enumerative Combinatorics, Volume 1. Cambridge University Press.

Andreas Stolcke. 2002. SRILM – An Extensible Language Modeling Toolkit. In *ICSLP*.

Leslie G. Valiant. 1979. The complexity of enumeration and reliability problems. *SIAM Journal on Computing*, vol. 8, pages 410–421.

Dominic J. A. Welsh. 1997. Approximate counting. *Surveys in Combinatorics*, London Math. Soc. Lecture Notes Ser., 241, pages 287–324.

Richard Zens, Daisy Stanton, and Peng Xu. 2012. A Systematic Comparison of Phrase Table Pruning Techniques. In *EMNLP*.

A Joint Model for Quotation Attribution and Coreference Resolution

Mariana S. C. Almeida[*†] **Miguel B. Almeida**[*†] **André F. T. Martins**[*†]
[*]Priberam Labs, Alameda D. Afonso Henriques, 41, 2°, 1000-123 Lisboa, Portugal
[†]Instituto de Telecomunicações, Instituto Superior Técnico, 1049-001 Lisboa, Portugal
{mla,mba,atm}@priberam.pt

Abstract

We address the problem of automatically attributing quotations to speakers, which has great relevance in text mining and media monitoring applications. While current systems report high accuracies for this task, they either work at mention-level (getting credit for detecting uninformative mentions such as pronouns), or assume the coreferent mentions have been detected beforehand; the inaccuracies in this preprocessing step may lead to error propagation. In this paper, we introduce a joint model for entity-level quotation attribution and coreference resolution, exploiting correlations between the two tasks. We design an evaluation metric for attribution that captures all speakers' mentions. We present results showing that both tasks benefit from being treated jointly.

1 Introduction

Quotations are a crucial part of news stories, giving the perspectives of the participants in the narrated event, and making the news sound objective. The ability of extracting and organizing these quotations is highly relevant for text mining applications, as it may aid journalists in fact-checking, help users browse news threads, and reduce human intervention in media monitoring. This involves assigning the correct speaker to each quote—a problem called **quotation attribution** (§2).

There is significant literature devoted to this task, both for narrative genres (Mamede and Chaleira, 2004; Elson and McKeown, 2010) and newswire domains (Pouliquen et al., 2007; Sarmento et al., 2009; Schneider et al., 2010). While the earliest works focused on devising lexical and syntactic rules and hand-crafting grammars, there has been a recent shift toward machine learning approaches (Fernandes et al., 2011; O'Keefe et al., 2012; Pareti et al., 2013), with latest works reporting high accuracies for speaker identification in newswire (in the range 80–95% for direct and mixed quotes, according to O'Keefe et al. (2012)). Despite these encouraging results, quotation mining systems are not yet fully satisfactory, even when only direct quotes are considered. Part of the problem, as we next describe, has to do with inaccuracies in **coreference resolution** (§3).

The "easiest" instances of quotation attribution problems arise when the speaker and the quote are semantically connected, *e.g.*, through a reported speech verb like *said*. However, in newswire text, the subject of this verb is commonly a pronoun or another uninformative anaphoric mention. While the speaker thus determined may well be correct—being in most cases consistent with human annotation choices (Pareti, 2012)—from a practical perspective, it will be of little use without a coreference system that correctly resolves the anaphora. Since the current state of the art in coreference resolution is far from perfect, errors at this stage tend to propagate to the quote attribution system.

Consider the following examples for illustration (taken from the WSJ-1057 and WSJ-0089 documents in the Penn Treebank), where we have annotated with subscripts some of the mentions:

(a) Rivals carp at "the principle of [Pilson]$_{M_1}$," as [NBC's Arthur Watson]$_{M_2}$ once put it – *"[he]$_{M_3}$'s always expounding that rights are too high, then [he]$_{M_4}$'s going crazy."* But [the 49-year-old Mr. Pilson]$_{M_5}$ is hardly a man to ignore the numbers.

(b) [English novelist Dorothy L. Sayers]$_{M_1}$ described [ringing]$_{M_2}$ as a *"passion that finds its satisfaction in [mathematical completeness]$_{M_3}$ and [mechanical perfection]$_{M_4}$."* [Ringers]$_{M_5}$, [she]$_{M_6}$ added, are *"filled with the solemn intoxication that comes of intricate ritual faultlessly performed."*

In example (a), the pronoun coreference system used by O'Keefe et al. (2012) erroneously clusters together mentions M_2, M_3 and M_4 (instead of the correct clustering $\{M_1, M_3, M_4\}$). Since it is unlikely that the speaker is co-referent to a third-person pronoun *he* inside the quote, a pipeline system would likely attribute (incorrectly) this quote to *Pilson*. In example (b), there are two quotes with the same speaker entity (as indicated by the cue *she added*). This gives evidence that M_1 and M_6 should be coreferent. A pipeline approach would not be able to exploit these correlations.

We argue that this type of mistakes, among others, can be prevented by a system that performs quote attribution and coreference resolution **jointly** (§4). Our joint model is inspired by recent work in coreference resolution that independently ranks the possible mention's antecedents, forming a latent coreference tree structure (Denis and Baldridge, 2008; Fernandes et al., 2012; Durrett et al., 2013; Durrett and Klein, 2013). We consider a generalization of these structures which we call a **quotation-coreference tree**. To effectively couple the two tasks, we need to go beyond simple arc-factored models and consider paths in the tree. We formulate the resulting problem as a logic program, which we tackle using a dual decomposition strategy (§5). We provide an empirical comparison between our method and baselines for each of the tasks and a pipeline system, defining suitable metrics for entity-level quotation attribution (§6).

2 Quotation Attribution

The task of quotation attribution can be formally defined as follows. Given a document containing a sequence of quotations, $\langle q_1, \ldots, q_L \rangle$, and a set of candidate speakers, $\{s_1, \ldots, s_M\}$, the goal is to a assign a speaker to every quote.

Previous work has handled direct and mixed quotations (Sarmento et al., 2009; O'Keefe et al., 2012), easily extractable with regular expressions for detecting quotation marks, as well as indirect quotations (Pareti et al., 2013), which are more involved and require syntactic or semantic patterns. In this work, we resort to direct and mixed quotations. Pareti (2012) defines quotation attributions in terms of their *content span* (the quotation text itself), their *cue* (a lexical anchor of the attribution relation, such as a reported speech verb), and the *source span* (the author of the quote). The same reference introduced the PARC dataset, which we use in our experiments (§6) and which is based on the annotation of a database of attribution relations from the Penn Discourse Treebank (Prasad et al., 2008). Several machine learning algorithms have been applied to this task, either framing the problem as classification (an independent decision for each quote), or sequence labeling (using greedy methods or linear-chain conditional random fields); see O'Keefe et al. (2012) for a comparison among these different methods.

In this paper, we distinguish between **mention-level** quotation attribution, in which the candidate speakers are individual mentions, and **entity-level** quotation attribution, in which they are entity clusters comprised of one or more mentions. With this distinction, we attempt to clarify how prior work has addressed this task, and design suitable baselines and evaluation metrics. For example, O'Keefe et al. (2012) applies a coreference resolver *before* quotation attribution, whereas de La Clergerie et al. (2011) does it *afterwards*, as a post-processing stage. An important issue when evaluating quotation attribution systems is to prevent them from getting credit for detecting uninformative speakers such as pronouns; we will get back to this topic in §6.2.

3 Coreference Resolution

In coreference resolution, we are given a set of mentions $M := \{m_1, \ldots, m_K\}$, and the goal is to cluster them into discourse entities, $E := \{e_1, \ldots, e_J\}$, where each $e_j \subseteq M$ and $e_j \neq \varnothing$. We follow Haghighi and Klein (2007) and distinguish between proper, nominal, and pronominal mentions. Each requires different types of information to be resolved. Thus, the task involves determining anaphoricity, resolving pronouns, and identifying semantic compatibility among mentions. To resolve these references, one typically exploits contextual and grammatical clues, as well as semantic information and world knowledge, to understand whether mentions refer to people, places, organizations, and so on. The importance of coreference resolution has led to it being the subject of recent CoNLL shared tasks (Pradhan et al., 2011; Pradhan et al., 2012).

There has been a variety of approaches for this problem. Early work used local discriminative classifiers, making independent decisions for each mention or pair of mentions (Soon et al., 2001; Ng and Cardie, 2002). Lee et al. (2011) proposed a competitive non-learned sieve-based method, which constructs clusters by aglomerating mentions in a greedy manner. Entity-centric models define scores for the entire entity clusters (Culotta et al., 2007; Haghighi and Klein, 2010;

Rahman and Ng, 2011) and seek the set of entities that optimize the sum of scores; this can also be promoted in a decentralized manner (Durrett et al., 2013). Pairwise models (Bengtson and Roth, 2008; Finkel et al., 2008; Versley et al., 2008), on the other hand, define scores for each pair of mentions to be coreferent, and define the clusters as the transitive closure of these pairwise relations. A disadvantage of these two methods is that they lead to intractable decoding problems, so approximate methods must be used. For comprehensive overviews, see Stoyanov et al. (2009), Ng (2010), Pradhan et al. (2011) and Pradhan et al. (2012).

Our joint approach (to be fully described in §4) draws inspiration from recent work that shifts from entity clusters to **coreference trees** (Fernandes et al., 2012; Durrett and Klein, 2013). These models define scores for each mention to link to its antecedent or to an artifical root symbol $ (in which case it is not anaphoric). The computation of the best tree can be done exactly with spanning tree algorithms, or by independently choosing the best antecedent (or the root) for each mention, if only left-to-right arcs are allowed. The same idea underlies the antecedent ranking approach of Denis and Baldridge (2008). Once the coreference tree is computed, the set of entity clusters E is obtained by associating each entity set to a branch of the tree coming out from the root. This is illustrated in Figure 1 (left).

4 Joint Quotations and Coreferences

In this work, we propose that quotation attribution and coreference resolution are solved jointly by treating both mentions and quotations as nodes in a generalized structure called a **quotation-coreference tree** (Figure 1, right). The joint system's decoding process consists in creating such a tree, from which a clustering of the nodes can be immediatelly obtained. The clustering is interpreted as follows:

- All mention nodes in the cluster are coreferent, thus they describe one single entity (just like in a standard coreference tree).
- Quotation nodes that appear together with those mentions in a cluster will be assigned that entity as the speaker.

For example, in Figure 1 (right), the entity *Dorothy L. Sayers* (formed by mentions $\{M_1, M_6\}$) is assigned as the speaker of quotations Q_1 and Q_2. We forbid arcs between quotes and from a quote to a mention, effectively constraining the quotes to be *leaves* in the tree, with mentions as parents.[1] We force a tree with only left-to-right arcs, by choosing a total ordering of the nodes that places all the quotations in the rightmost positions (which implies that any arc connecting a mention to a quotation will point to the right). The quotation-coreference tree is obtained as the best spanning tree that maximizes a score function, to be described next.

4.1 Basic Model

Our basic model is a feature-based linear model which assigns a score to each candidate arc linking two mentions (*mention-mention arcs*), or linking a mention to a quote (*mention-quotation arcs*). Our basic system is called QUOTEBEFORECOREF for reasons we will detail in section 4.2.

4.1.1 Coreference features

For the mention-mention arcs, we use the same coreference features as the SURFACE model of the Berkeley Coreference Resolution System (Durrett and Klein, 2013), plus features for gender and number obtained through the dataset of Bergsma and Lin (2006). This is a very simple lexical-driven model which achieves state-of-the-art results. The features are shown in Table 1.

4.1.2 Quotation features

For the quote attribution features, we use features inspired by O'Keefe et al. (2012), shown in Table 2. The same set of features works for speakers that are individual mentions (in the model just described), and for speakers that are clusters of mentions (used in §6 for the baseline QUOTEAFTERCOREF). These features include various distances between the mention and the quote, the indication of the speaker being inside the quote span, and various contextual features.

4.2 Final Model

While the basic model just described puts quotations and mentions together, it is not more expressive than having separate models for the two tasks. In fact, if we just have scores for individual arcs, the two problems are *decoupled*: the optimal

[1] This is implemented by defining $-\infty$ scores for all the outgoing arcs in a quotation node, as well as incoming arcs originating from the root.

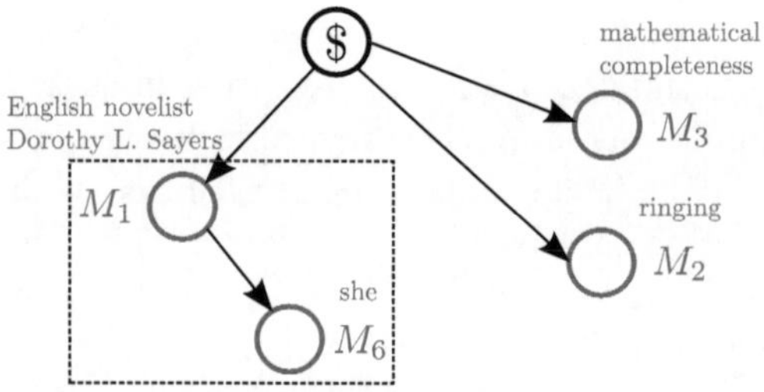

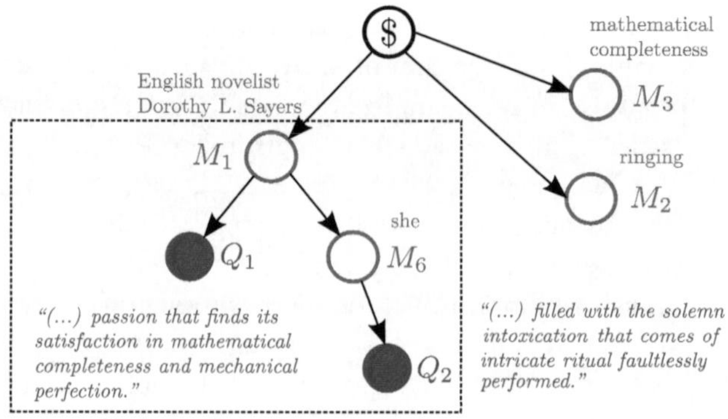

Figure 1: *Left:* A typical coreference tree for the text snippet in §1, example (b), with mentions M_1 and M_6 clustered together and M_2 and M_3 left as singletons. *Right:* A quotation-coreference tree for the same example. Mention nodes are depicted as green circles, and quotation nodes in shaded blue. The dashed rectangle represents a branch of the tree, containing the entity cluster associated with the speaker *Dorothy L. Sayers*, as well as the quotes she authored.

Features on the child mention
[ANAPHORIC (T/F)] + [CHILD HEAD WORD]
[ANAPHORIC (T/F)] + [CHILD FIRST WORD]
[ANAPHORIC (T/F)] + [CHILD LAST WORD]
[ANAPHORIC (T/F)] + [CHILD PRECEDING WORD]
[ANAPHORIC (T/F)] + [CHILD FOLLOWING WORD]
[ANAPHORIC (T/F)] + [CHILD LENGTH]
Features on the parent mention
[PARENT HEAD WORD]
[PARENT FIRST WORD]
[PARENT LAST WORD]
[PARENT PRECEDING WORD]
[PARENT FOLLOWING WORD]
[PARENT LENGTH]
[PARENT GENDER]
[PARENT NUMBER]
Features on the pair
[EXACT STRING MATCH (T/F)]
[HEAD MATCH (T/F)]
[SENTENCE DISTANCE, CAPPED AT 10]
[MENTION DISTANCE, CAPPED AT 10]

Table 1: Coreference features, associated to each candidate mention-mention arc in the tree. As in Durrett and Klein (2013), we also include conjunctions of each feature with the child and parent mention types (proper, nominal, or, if pronominal, the pronoun word).

Features on the quote-speaker pair
[WORD DISTANCE]
[SENTENCE DISTANCE]
[# IN-BETWEEN QUOTES]
[# IN-BETWEEN SPEAKERS]
[SPEAKER IN QUOTE, 1ST PERS. SG. PRONOUN (T/F)]
[SPEAKER IN QUOTE, 1ST PERS. PL. PRONOUN (T/F)]
[SPEAKER IN QUOTE, OTHER (T/F)]
Features on the speaker
[PREVIOUS WORD IS QUOTE (T/F)]
[PREVIOUS WORD IS SAME QUOTE (T/F)]
[PREVIOUS WORD IS ANOTHER QUOTE (T/F)]
[PREVIOUS WORD IS SPEAKER (T/F)]
[PREVIOUS WORD IS PUNCTUATION (T/F)]
[PREVIOUS WORD IS REPORTED SPEECH VERB (T/F)]
[PREVIOUS WORD IS VERB (T/F)]
[NEXT WORD IS QUOTE (T/F)]
[NEXT WORD IS SAME QUOTE (T/F)]
[NEXT WORD IS ANOTHER QUOTE (T/F)]
[NEXT WORD IS SPEAKER (T/F)]
[NEXT WORD IS PUNCTUATION (T/F)]
[NEXT WORD IS REPORTED SPEACH VERB (T/F)]
[NEXT WORD IS VERB (T/F)]

Table 2: Quotation attribution features, associated to each quote-speaker candidate. These features are used in the QUOTEONLY, QUOTEBEFORECOREF, and JOINT systems (where the speaker is a mention) and in the QUOTEAFTERCOREF system (where the speaker is an entity).

quotation-coreference tree can be obtained by first assigning the highest scored mention to each quotation, and then building a standard coreference tree involving only the mention nodes. This corresponds to the QUOTEBEFORECOREF baseline, to be used in §6.

To go beyond separate models, we introduce a final JOINT model, which includes additional scores that depend not just on arcs, but also on *paths* in the tree. Concretely, we select certain pairs of nodes and introduce scores for the event that both nodes are in the same branch of the tree. Rather than doing this for all pairs—which essentially would revert to the computationally demanding pairwise coreference models discussed in §3—we focus on a small set of pairs that are mostly related with the interaction between the two tasks we address jointly. Namely, we consider the mention-quotation pairs such that the mention

Mention-inside-quote features
[MENTION IS 1ST PERSON, SING. PRONOUN (T/F)]
[MENTION IS 1ST PERSON, PLUR. PRONOUN (T/F)]
[OTHER MENTION (T/F)]
Consecutive quote features
[DISTANCE IN NUMBER OF WORDS]
[DISTANCE IN NUMBER OF SENTENCES]

Table 3: Features used in the JOINT system for mention-quote pairs (only for mentions inside quotes) and for quote pairs (only for consecutive quotes). These features are associated to pairs in the same branch of the quotation-coreference tree.

span is within the quotation span (*mention-inside-quotation pairs*), and pairs of quotations that appear consecutively in the document (*consecutive-quotation pairs*). The idea is that, if consecutive quotations appear on the same branch of the tree, they will have the same speaker (the entity class associated with that branch), even though they are not necessarily siblings. These two pairs are aligned with the motivating examples (a) and (b) shown in §1.

4.2.1 Mention-inside-quotation features

The top rows of Table 3 show the features we defined for mentions inside quotes. The features indicate whether the mention is first-person singular pronominal (*I*, *me*, *my*, *myself*), which provides strong evidence that it co-refers with the quotation author, whether it is first-person plural pronominal (*we*, *us*, *our*, *ourselves*), which provides a weaker evidence (but sometimes works for colective entities that are organizations), and whether none of the above happens—in which case, the speaker is *unlikely* to be co-referent with the mention.

4.2.2 Consecutive quotation features

We show our consecutive quote features in the bottom rows of Table 3. We use only distance features, measuring both distance in sentences and in words, with binning. These simple features are enough to capture the trend of consecutive quotes that are close apart to have the same speaker.

5 Joint Decoding and Training

While decoding in the basic model is easy—as pointed out above, it can even be done by running a mention-level quotation attributor and the coreference resolver independently (QUOTEBEFORECOREF)—exact decoding with the JOINT model is in general intractable, since this model breaks the independence assumption between the arcs. However, given the relatively small amount of node pairs that have scores (only mentions inside quotations and consecutive quotations), we expect this "perturbation" to be small enough not to affect the quality of an approximate decoder. The situation resembles other problems in NLP, such as non-projective dependency parsing, which becomes intractable if higher order interactions between the arcs are considered, but can still be well approximated. Inspired by work in parsing (Martins et al., 2009) using linear relaxations with multi-commodity flow models, we propose a similar strategy by defining auxiliary variables and coupling them in a logic program.

5.1 Logic Formulation

We next derive the logic program for joint decoding of coreferences and quotations. The input is a set of nodes (including an artificial node), a set of candidate arcs with scores, and a set of node pairs with scores. To make the exposition lighter, we index nodes by integers (starting by the root node 0) and we do not distinguish between mention and quotation nodes. Only arcs from left to right are allowed. The variables in our logic program are:

- Arc variables $a_{i\to j}$, which take the value 1 if there is an arc from i to j, and 0 otherwise.
- Pair variables $p_{i,j}$, which indicate that nodes i and j are in the same branch of the tree.
- Path variables $\pi_{j\to^* k}$, indicating if there is a path from j to k.
- Common ancestor variables $\psi_{i\to^* j,k}$, indicating that node i is a common ancestor of nodes j and k in the tree.

Consistency among these variables is ensured by the following set of constraints:

- Each node except the root has exactly one parent:

$$\sum_{i=0}^{j-1} a_{i\to j} = 1, \ \forall j \neq 0 \quad (1)$$

- There is a path from each node to itself:

$$\pi_{i\to^* i} = 1, \ \forall i \quad (2)$$

- There is a path from i to k iff there is some j such that i is connected to j and there is path from j to k:

$$\pi_{i \to^* k} = \bigvee_{i<j \leq k} (a_{i \to j} \wedge \pi_{j \to^* k}), \ \forall i, k \quad (3)$$

- Node i is a common ancestor of k and ℓ iff there is a path from i to k and from i to ℓ:

$$\psi_{i \to^* k, \ell} = \pi_{i \to^* k} \wedge \pi_{i \to^* \ell}, \ \forall i, k, \ell \quad (4)$$

- Nodes k and ℓ are in the same branch if they have a common ancestor which is not the root:

$$p_{k,\ell} = \bigvee_{i \neq 0} \psi_{i \to^* k, \ell}, \ \forall k, l. \quad (5)$$

The objective to optimize is linear in the arc and pair variables (hence the problem can be represented as an integer linear program by turning the logical constraints into linear inequalities).

5.2 Dual Decomposition

To decode, we employ the alternating directions dual decomposition algorithm (AD^3), which solves a relaxation of the ILP above. AD^3 has been used successfully in various NLP tasks, such as dependency parsing (Martins et al., 2011; Martins et al., 2013), semantic role labeling (Das et al., 2012), and compressive summarization (Almeida and Martins, 2013). At test time, if the solution is not integer, we apply a simple rounding procedure to obtain an actual tree: for each node j, obtain the antecedent (or root) i with the highest $a_{i \to j}$, solving ties arbitrarily.

5.3 Learning the Model

We train the joint model with the max-loss variant of the MIRA algorithm (Crammer et al., 2006), adapted to latent variables (we simply obtain the best tree consistent with the gold clustering at each step of MIRA, before doing cost-augmented decoding). The resulting algorithm is very similar to the latent perceptron algorithm in Fernandes et al. (2011), but it uses the aggressive stepsize of MIRA. We set the same costs for coreference mistakes as Durrett and Klein (2013), and a unit cost for missing the correct speaker of a quotation. For speeding up decoding, we first train a basic pruner for the coreference system (using only the features described in §4.1.1), limiting the number of candidate antecedents to 10, and discarding scores whose difference with respect to the best antecedent is below a threshold. We also freeze the best coreference trees consistent with the gold clustering using the pruner model, to eliminate the need of latent variables in the second stage.

6 Experiments

6.1 Dataset

We used the 597 documents of the Wall Street Journal (WSJ) corpus that were disclosed for the CoNLL-2011 coreference shared task (Pradhan et al., 2011) as a dataset for coreference resolution. This dataset includes train, development and test partitions, annotated with coreference information, as well as gold and automatically generated syntactic and semantic information.

The CoNLL-2011 corpus does not contain annotations of quotation attribution. For that reason, we used the WSJ quotation annotations in the PARC dataset (Pareti, 2012). We used the same version of the corpus as O'Keefe et al. (2012), but with different splits, to match the dataset partitions in the coreference resolution data. This attribution corpus contains 279 documents of the 597 CoNLL-2011 files, having a total of 1199 annotated quotes. As in that work, we only considered directed speech quotes and the direct part of mixed quotes (quotes with both direct and undirected speech).

6.2 Metrics for quotation attribution

Previous evaluations of quotation attribution systems were designed at *mention level*, and are thus assessed by comparing the predicted speaker mention span with the gold one. This metric assesses the amount of speaker mentions that were correctly identified. For compatibility with previous assessments, we report this score, which we call *Exact Match (EM)*: this is the percentage of predicted speakers with the same span as the gold one.

However, for several quotations (about 30% in the PARC corpus) this information is of little value, since the gold mention is a pronoun, which *per se* does not give any useful information about the actual speaker entity. Considering this fact, we propose two other metrics that capture information at the *entity level*, reflecting the amount of information a system is able to extract about the speakers:

- *Representative Speaker Match (RSM):* for each annotated quote, we obtain the full gold coreference set of the gold annotated speaker, and choose a *representative speaker* from that cluster. We define this representative speaker as the proper mention which is the closest to the quote (if available); if the cluster does not contain proper mentions, we use the closest nominal mention; if only pronominal mentions are available, we use the original annotated speaker. The final measure is the percentage of predicted speakers that match the string of the corresponding representative speakers.

- *Entity Cluster F_1 (ECF$_1$).* Considering that a system outputs a set of mentions coreferent to the predicted speakers, we compute the F_1 score between the predicted set and the gold coreference cluster of the correct speaker.

The entity level metrics are not only useful for assessing the quality of an quotation attribution system—they also reflect the quality of the underlying coreference system used to cluster the related mentions.

6.3 Attribution baselines

To analyze the task of entity-level quotation attribution, we implemented three baseline systems.

- QUOTEONLY: A quotation attribution system trained on the representative speaker, instead of the gold speaker. For fairness, this baseline was trained with an extra feature indicating the type of the mention (nominal, pronominal or proper).
- QUOTEAFTERCOREF: An attribution system directly applied to the output of a predicted coreference chain. This baseline uses a coreference pre-processing, as applied in O'Keefe et al. (2012).
- QUOTEBEFORECOREF: An attribution system trained on the gold speaker, and post-combined with the output of a coreference system. This system should be able to provide a set of informative mentions about a quote, post-resolving the problem of the pronominal speakers. This kind of post-coreference approach was used by de La Clergerie et al. (2011).

6.4 Coreference Resolution

We use the coreference results of our basic QUOTEBEFORECOREF system as a baseline for coreference resolution. Since this system effectively solves the two problems separately, this can be considered our implementation of the SURFACE system of Durrett and Klein (2013) . As reported in Table 4, the perfromance of our baseline is comparable with the one of the SURFACE system of Durrett and Klein (2013), which is denoted as SURFACE-DK-2013.[2]

Table 4 also show the CoNLL metrics obtained for the proposed system of joint coreference resolution and quotation attribution. Our joint system outperformed the baseline with statistical significance (with $p < 0.05$ and according to a bootstrap resampling test (Koehn, 2004)) for all metrics expect for the CEAFE F_1 measure, whose value was only slighty improved. These results confirm that the coreference resolution task benefits for being tackled jointly with quotation attribution.

6.5 Quotation attribution

We implemented and trained the three attribution systems that were described in §6.3 and the system for joint coreference and author attribution that is detailed in §4. For each system, Table 5 shows the mention-based and entity-based metrics that were described in §6.2.

Training a quotation attribution system using representative speakers instead of the gold speakers (QUOTEONLY) leads to rather disappointing results. As expected, we conclude that assigning the semantically related speaker is considerably easier than selecting another mention that is coreferent with the correct speaker.

Using (predicted) coreference information, both QUOTEAFTERCOREF and QUOTEBEFORECOREF systems considerably increase our entity-based metrics. This was also expected, since the coreference chain allows these baselines to output a set of related mentions. We observed that, using the coreference resolution clusters as the attribution entity (QUOTEAFTERCOREF) influences the results negatively when compared to a more basic system that runs coreference on top of attribution result of the QUOTEONLY system (QUOTEBEFORECOREF). These results indicate that the quotation attribution task performs better by looking at the speaker mention that connects more strongly with the quotation, instead of trying to match the whole cluster.

Finally, the scores achieved by our JOINT

[2]To make the systems comparable, we re-trained Durrett et al.'s coreference system (version 0.9) on the WSJ portion of the Ontonotes datasets (the portion which has quote annotations from Pareti et al.'s PARC dataset). For this reason, the values in Table 4 differ from those reported in Durrett and Klein (2013), which where trained and tested in the entire Ontonotes.

	MUC F_1	BCUB F_1	CEAFE F_1	Avg.
SURFACE-DK-2013	**58.87**	62.74	45.46	55.7
SURFACE-OURS [QUOTEBEFORECOREF]	57.89	62.50	45.48	55.3
JOINT	58.78	**63.79**	**45.50**	**56.0**

Table 4: Coreference obtained with the CoNLL scorer (version 5) in the test partition of the WJS corpus, for the SURFACE system of Durrett and Klein (2013), our baseline implementation of the that system (SURFACE-OURS), and our JOINT approach. All systems were trained in the WSJ portion of the Ontonotes.

	EM	RSM	ECF_1
QUOTEONLY	49.1%	49.4%	41.2%
QUOTEAFTERCOREF	76.7%	64.6%	70.0%
QUOTEBEFORECOREF	**88.7%**	74.7%	73.7%
JOINT	88.1%	**76.6%**	**74.1%**

Table 5: Attribution results obtained, in the test set, for the three baseline systems and our joint system.

model are slightly above the best baseline system QUOTEBEFORECOREF, yielding the best performance on the entity-level quotation attribution task. The differences, however, were not found statistically significant, probably due to the small number of quotes (159) in the test set.

The average decoding runtime of the JOINT model is 1.6 sec. per document, against 0.2 sec. for the pipeline system. This slowdown is expectable given the fact that the pipeline system only needs to make independent decisions, while the joint version needs to solve a harder combinatorial problem. Yet, this runtime is within the order of magnitude of the time necessary to preprocess the documents (which includes tagging and parsing the sentences).

6.6 Error Analysis

To understand the type of errors that are prevented with the JOINT system, consider the following example (from document WSJ-2428):

- [Robert Dow, a partner and portfolio manager at Lord, Abbett & Co.]$_{M_1}$, which manages \$4 billion of high-yield bonds, says [he]$_{M_2}$ doesn't *"think there is any fundamental economic rationale (for the junk bond rout). It was [herd instinct]$_{M_3}$."* [He]$_{M_4}$ adds: *"The junk market has witnessed some trouble and now some people think that if the equity market gets creamed that means the economy will be terrible and that's bad for junk."*

The basic QUOTEBEFORECOREF system wrongly clusters together M_3 and M_4 as coreferent, and wrongly assigns M_3 as the representative speaker. On the other hand, the JOINT system correctly clusters M_1, M_2 and M_4 as coreferent. This is due to the presence of the consecutive quote features which aid in understanding that both quotes have the same speaker, and the mention-inside-quote features which prevent *herd instinct*, which is inside a quote, from being coreferent with *He*, which is very likely the author of the quotes due to the verb *adds*.

7 Conclusions

We presented a framework for joint coreference resolution and quotation attribution. We represented the problem as finding an optimal spanning tree in a graph including both quotation nodes and mention nodes. To couple the two tasks, we introduce variables that look at paths in the tree, indicating if pairs of nodes are in the same branch, and we formulate decoding as a logic program. Each branch from the root can then be interpreted as a cluster containing all coreferent mentions of an entity and all quotes from that entity.

In addition, we designed an evaluation metric suitable for entity-level quotation attribution that takes into account informative speakers. Experimental results show mutual improvements in the coreference resolution and quotation attribution tasks.

Future work will include extensions to tackle indirect quotations, possibly exploring connections to semantic role labeling.

Acknowledgements

We thank all reviewers for their valuable comments, and Silvia Pareti and Tim O'Keefe for providing us the PARC dataset and answering several questions. This work was partially supported by the EU/FEDER programme, QREN/POR Lisboa (Portugal), under the Intelligo project (contract 2012/24803) and by a FCT grant PTDC/EEI-SII/2312/2012.

References

M. B. Almeida and A. F. T. Martins. 2013. Fast and robust compressive summarization with dual decomposition and multi-task learning. In *Proc. of the Annual Meeting of the Association for Computational Linguistics*.

Eric Bengtson and Dan Roth. 2008. Understanding the value of features for coreference resolution. In *Proceedings of the Conference on Empirical Methods in Natural Language Processing*, pages 294–303. Association for Computational Linguistics.

Shane Bergsma and Dekang Lin. 2006. Bootstrapping path-based pronoun resolution. In *Proceedings of the 21st International Conference on Computational Linguistics and the 44th annual meeting of the Association for Computational Linguistics*, pages 33–40. Association for Computational Linguistics.

K. Crammer, O. Dekel, J. Keshet, S. Shalev-Shwartz, and Y. Singer. 2006. Online Passive-Aggressive Algorithms. *Journal of Machine Learning Research*, 7:551–585.

Aron Culotta, Michael Wick, Robert Hall, and Andrew McCallum. 2007. First-order probabilistic models for coreference resolution. In *Human Language Technology Conference of the North American Chapter of the Association for Computational Linguistics (HLT/NAACL)*, pages 81–88.

D. Das, A. F. T. Martins, and N. A. Smith. 2012. An Exact Dual Decomposition Algorithm for Shallow Semantic Parsing with Constraints. In *Proc. of First Joint Conference on Lexical and Computational Semantics (*SEM)*.

Éric de La Clergerie, Benoît Sagot, Rosa Stern, Pascal Denis, Gaëlle Recourcé, and Victor Mignot. 2011. Extracting and visualizing quotations from news wires. In *Human Language Technology. Challenges for Computer Science and Linguistics*, pages 522–532. Springer.

Pascal Denis and Jason Baldridge. 2008. Specialized models and ranking for coreference resolution. In *Proceedings of the Conference on Empirical Methods in Natural Language Processing*, pages 660–669. Association for Computational Linguistics.

Greg Durrett and Dan Klein. 2013. Easy victories and uphill battles in coreference resolution. In *Proceedings of the 2013 Conference on Empirical Methods in Natural Language Processing*.

Greg Durrett, David Hall, and Dan Klein. 2013. Decentralized entity-level modeling for coreference resolution. In *Proc. of Annual Meeting of the Association for Computational Linguistics*.

David K Elson and Kathleen McKeown. 2010. Automatic attribution of quoted speech in literary narrative. In *AAAI*.

William Paulo Ducca Fernandes, Eduardo Motta, and Ruy Luiz Milidiú. 2011. Quotation extraction for portuguese. In *Proceedings of the 8th Brazilian Symposium in Information and Human Language Technology (STIL 2011), Cuiabá*, pages 204–208.

Eraldo Rezende Fernandes, Cícero Nogueira dos Santos, and Ruy Luiz Milidiú. 2012. Latent structure perceptron with feature induction for unrestricted coreference resolution. In *Joint Conference on EMNLP and CoNLL-Shared Task*, pages 41–48. Association for Computational Linguistics.

J.R. Finkel, A. Kleeman, and C.D. Manning. 2008. Efficient, feature-based, conditional random field parsing. *Proc. of Annual Meeting on Association for Computational Linguistics*, pages 959–967.

Aria Haghighi and Dan Klein. 2007. Unsupervised coreference resolution in a nonparametric bayesian model. In *Annual meeting-Association for Computational Linguistics*, volume 45, page 848.

Aria Haghighi and Dan Klein. 2010. Coreference resolution in a modular, entity-centered model. In *Human Language Technologies: The 2010 Annual Conference of the North American Chapter of the Association for Computational Linguistics*, pages 385–393. Association for Computational Linguistics.

P. Koehn. 2004. Statistical signicance tests for machine translation evaluation. In *Proc. of the Annual Meeting of the Association for Computational Linguistics*.

Heeyoung Lee, Yves Peirsman, Angel Chang, Nathanael Chambers, Mihai Surdeanu, and Dan Jurafsky. 2011. Stanford's multi-pass sieve coreference resolution system at the conll-2011 shared task. In *Proceedings of the Fifteenth Conference on Computational Natural Language Learning: Shared Task*, pages 28–34. Association for Computational Linguistics.

Nuno Mamede and Pedro Chaleira. 2004. Character identification in children stories. In *Advances in Natural Language Processing*, pages 82–90. Springer.

A. F. T. Martins, N. A. Smith, and E. P. Xing. 2009. Concise Integer Linear Programming Formulations for Dependency Parsing. In *Proc. of Annual Meeting of the Association for Computational Linguistics*.

A. F. T. Martins, N. A. Smith, P. M. Q. Aguiar, and M. A. T. Figueiredo. 2011. Dual Decomposition with Many Overlapping Components. In *Proc. of Empirical Methods for Natural Language Processing*.

A. F. T. Martins, M. B. Almeida, and N. A. Smith. 2013. Turning on the turbo: Fast third-order non-projective turbo parsers. In *Proc. of the Annual Meeting of the Association for Computational Linguistics*.

Vincent Ng and Claire Cardie. 2002. Improving machine learning approaches to coreference resolution. In *Proceedings of the 40th Annual Meeting on Association for Computational Linguistics*, pages 104–111. Association for Computational Linguistics.

V. Ng. 2010. Supervised noun phrase coreference research: The first fifteen years. In *Proc. of the Annual Meeting of the Association for Computational Linguistics*.

Tim O'Keefe, Silvia Pareti, James R Curran, Irena Koprinska, and Matthew Honnibal. 2012. A sequence labelling approach to quote attribution. In *Proceedings of the 2012 Joint Conference on Empirical Methods in Natural Language Processing and Computational Natural Language Learning*, pages 790–799. Association for Computational Linguistics.

Silvia Pareti, Tim O'Keefe, Ioannis Konstas, James R. Curran, and Irena Koprinska. 2013. Automatically detecting and attributing indirect quotations. In *Proceedings of the 2013 Conference on Empirical Methods in Natural Language Processing*.

Silvia Pareti. 2012. A database of attribution relations. In *LREC*, pages 3213–3217.

Bruno Pouliquen, Ralf Steinberger, and Clive Best. 2007. Automatic detection of quotations in multilingual news. In *Proceedings of Recent Advances in Natural Language Processing*, pages 487–492.

Sameer Pradhan, Lance Ramshaw, Mitchell Marcus, Martha Palmer, Ralph Weischedel, and Nianwen Xue. 2011. Conll-2011 shared task: Modeling unrestricted coreference in ontonotes. In *Proceedings of the Fifteenth Conference on Computational Natural Language Learning: Shared Task*, pages 1–27. Association for Computational Linguistics.

Sameer Pradhan, Alessandro Moschitti, Nianwen Xue, Olga Uryupina, and Yuchen Zhang. 2012. Conll-2012 shared task: Modeling multilingual unrestricted coreference in ontonotes. In *Proceedings of the Joint Conference on EMNLP and CoNLL: Shared Task*, pages 1–40.

Rashmi Prasad, Nikhil Dinesh, Alan Lee, Eleni Miltsakaki, Livio Robaldo, Aravind K Joshi, and Bonnie L Webber. 2008. The penn discourse treebank 2.0. In *LREC*. Citeseer.

Altaf Rahman and Vincent Ng. 2011. Narrowing the modeling gap: A cluster-ranking approach to coreference resolution. *Journal of Artificial Intelligence Research*, 40(1):469–521.

Luis Sarmento, Sergio Nunes, and E Oliveira. 2009. Automatic extraction of quotes and topics from news feeds. In *4th Doctoral Symposium on Informatics Engineering*.

Nathan Schneider, Rebecca Hwa, Philip Gianfortoni, Dipanjan Das, Michael Heilman, Alan W Black, Frederick L Crabbe, and Noah A Smith. 2010. Visualizing topical quotations over time to understand news discourse. Technical report, Technical Report CMU-LTI-01-103, CMU.

Wee Meng Soon, Hwee Tou Ng, and Daniel Chung Yong Lim. 2001. A machine learning approach to coreference resolution of noun phrases. *Computational linguistics*, 27(4):521–544.

Veselin Stoyanov, Nathan Gilbert, Claire Cardie, and Ellen Riloff. 2009. Conundrums in noun phrase coreference resolution: Making sense of the state-of-the-art. In *Proceedings of the Joint Conference of the 47th Annual Meeting of the ACL and the 4th International Joint Conference on Natural Language Processing of the AFNLP: Volume 2-Volume 2*, pages 656–664. Association for Computational Linguistics.

Yannick Versley, Simone Paolo Ponzetto, Massimo Poesio, Vladimir Eidelman, Alan Jern, Jason Smith, Xiaofeng Yang, and Alessandro Moschitti. 2008. Bart: A modular toolkit for coreference resolution. In *Proceedings of the 46th Annual Meeting of the Association for Computational Linguistics on Human Language Technologies: Demo Session*, pages 9–12. Association for Computational Linguistics.

A Hierarchical Bayesian Model for Unsupervised Induction of Script Knowledge

Lea Frermann[1] l.frermann@ed.ac.uk
Ivan Titov[2] titov@uva.nl
Manfred Pinkal[3] pinkal@coli.uni-sb.de

[1] ILCC, School of Informatics, University of Edinburgh, United Kingdom
[2] ILLC, University of Amsterdam, Netherlands
[3] Department of Computational Linguistics, Saarland University, Germany

Abstract

Scripts representing common sense knowledge about stereotyped sequences of events have been shown to be a valuable resource for NLP applications. We present a hierarchical Bayesian model for unsupervised learning of script knowledge from crowdsourced descriptions of human activities. Events and constraints on event ordering are induced jointly in one unified framework. We use a statistical model over permutations which captures event ordering constraints in a more flexible way than previous approaches. In order to alleviate the sparsity problem caused by using relatively small datasets, we incorporate in our hierarchical model an informed prior on word distributions. The resulting model substantially outperforms a state-of-the-art method on the event ordering task.

1 Introduction

A *script* is a "predetermined, stereotyped sequence of actions that define a well-known situation" (Schank and Abelson, 1975). While humans acquire such common-sense knowledge over their lifetime, it constitutes a bottleneck for many NLP systems. Effective question answering and summarization are impossible without a form of story understanding, which in turn has been shown to benefit from access to databases of script knowledge (Mueller, 2004; Miikkulainen, 1995). Knowledge about the typical ordering of events can further help assessing document coherence and generating coherent text. Here, we present a general method for acquiring data bases of script knowledge.

Our work may be regarded as complementary to existing work on learning script knowledge from natural text (cf. (Chambers and Jurafsky, 2008)), as not all types of scripts are elaborated in natural text – being left implicit because of assumed readers' world knowledge. Our model, operating on data obtained in a cheap way by crowdsourcing, is applicable to any kind of script and can fill this gap. We follow work in inducing script knowledge from explicit instantiations of scripts, so-called *event sequence descriptions* (ESDs) (Regneri et al., 2010). Our data consists of sets of ESDs, each set describing a well-known situation we will call *scenario* (e.g., "washing laundry"). An ESD consists of a sequence of *events*, each describing an action defining part of the scenario (e.g., "place the laundry in the washing machine"). We refer to descriptions of the same event across ESDs as *event types*. We refer to entities involved in a scenario as *participants* (e.g., a "washing machine" or a "detergent"), and to sets of participant descriptions describing the same entity as *participant types*.

For each type of scenario, our model clusters descriptions which refer to the same type of event, and infers constraints on the temporal order in which the events types occur in a particular scenario. Common characteristics of ESDs such as event optionality and varying degrees of temporal flexibility of event types make this task nontrivial. We propose a model which, in contrast to previous approaches, explicitly targets these characteristics. We develop a Bayesian formulation of the script learning problem, and present a generative model for *joint* learning of event types and ordering constraints, arguing that the temporal position of an event in an ESD provides a strong cue for its type, and vice versa. Our model is unsupervised in that no event- or participant labels are required for training.

We model constraints on the order of event types using a statistical model over permutations, the Generalized Mallows Model (GMM; Fligner and Verducci (1986)). With the GMM we can flexibly model apparent characteristics of scripts, such as event type-specific temporal flexibility. Assuming that types of participants provide a strong cue for the type of event they are observed in, we use participant types as a latent variable in our model. Finally, by modeling event type occurrence using Binomial distributions, we can model event optionality, a characteristic of scripts that previous approaches did not capture.

We evaluate our model on a data set of ESDs collected via web experiments from non-expert annotators by Regneri et al. (2010) and compare our model against their approach. Our model achieves an absolute average improvement of 7% over the model of Regneri et al. on the task of event ordering.

For our unsupervised Bayesian model the limited size of this training set constitutes an additional challenge. In order to alleviate this problem, we use an informed prior on the word distributions. Instead of using Dirichlet priors which do not encode a-priori correlations between words, we incorporate a logistic normal distribution with the covariance matrix derived from WordNet. While we will show that prior knowledge as defined above enables the application of our model to small data sets, we emphasize that the model is generally widely applicable for two reasons. First, the data, collected using crowdsourcing, is comparatively easy and cheap to extend. Secondly, our model is domain independent and can be applied to scenario descriptions from any domain without any modification. Note that parameters were tuned on held-out scenarios, and no scenario-specific tuning was performed.

2 Related Work

In the 1970s, scripts were introduced as a way to equip AI systems with world knowledge (Schank and Abelson, 1975; Barr and Feigenbaum, 1986). Task-specific script databases were developed manually. FrameNet (Baker et al., 1998) follows a similar idea, in defining verb frames together with argument types that can fill the verbs' argument slots. Frames can then be combined into "scenario frames". Manual composition of such databases, is arguably expensive and does not scale well.

This paper follows a series of more recent work which aims to infer script knowledge automatically from data. Chambers and Jurafsky (2008) present a system which learns *narrative chains* from newswire texts. Relevant phrases are identified based on shared protagonists. The phrases are clustered into equivalence classes and temporally ordered using a pipeline of methods. We work with explicit event sequence descriptions of a specific scenario, arguing that large-scale common sense knowledge is hard to acquire from natural text, since it is often left implicit. Regneri et al. (2010) induce script knowledge from explicit ESDs using a graph-based method. Event types and ordering constraints are induced by aligning descriptions of equivalent events using WordNet-based semantic similarity. On this basis an abstract graph-representation (Temporal Script Graph; TSG) of the scenario is computed, using Multiple Sequence Alignment (MSA). Our work follows the work of Regneri et al. (2010), in that we use the same data and aim to focus on the same task. However, the two approaches described above employ a pipeline architecture and treat event learning and learning ordering constraints as separate problems. In contrast, we propose to learn both tasks *jointly*. We incorporate both tasks in a hierarchical Bayesian model, thus using one unified framework.

A related task, unsupervised frame induction, has also been considered in the past (Titov and Klementiev, 2011; Modi et al., 2012; O'Connor, 2012); the frame representations encode events and participants but ignore the temporal aspect of script knowledge.

We model temporal constraints on event type orderings with the Generalized Mallows Model (GMM; Mallows (1957); Fligner and Verducci (1986); Klementiev et al. (2008)), a statistical model over permutations. The GMM is a flexible model which can specify item-specific sensitivity to perturbation from the item's position in the canonical permutation. With the GMM we are thus able to model event type-specific temporal flexibility – a feature of scripts that MSA cannot capture.

The GMM has been successfully applied to modeling ordering constraints in NLP tasks. Chen et al. (2009) augment classical topic models with a GMM, under the assumption that topics in structured domains (e.g., biographies in Wikipedia) tend to follow an underlying canonical ordering, an assumption which matches well our data (the annotators were asked to follow the temporal order of events in their descriptions (Regneri et al., 2010)). Chen et al. show that for these domains their approach significantly outperforms Markovian modeling of topics. This is expected as Markov models (MMs) are not very appropriate for representing linear structure with potentially missing topics (e.g., they cannot encode that every topic is assigned to at most one continuous fragment of text). Also GMMs are preferable for smaller collections such as ours, as the parameter number is linear in the number of topics (i.e., for us, event types) rather than quadratic as in Markov models. We are not aware of previous work on modeling events with GMMs. Conversely, MMs were considered in the very recent work of Cheung et al. (2013) in the context of script induction from news corpora where the Markovian assumption is much more natural.

There exists a body of work for learning participant types involved in scripts. Regneri et al. (2011) extend their work by inducing participant types on the basis of the TSG, using structural information about participant mentions in the TSG as well as WordNet similarity, which they then combine into an Integer Linear Program. Similarly, Chambers and Jurafsky (2009) extend their work on narrative chains, presenting a system with which they jointly learn event types and semantic roles of the participants involved, but do not consider event orderings. We include participant types as a latent feature in our model, assuming that participant mentions in an event description are a predictive feature for the corresponding event type.

One way of alleviating the problem of small data sets is incorporating informed prior knowledge. Raina et al. (2006) encode word correlations in a variance-covariance matrix of a multivariate normal distribution (MVN), and sample prior parameter vectors from it, thus introducing dependencies among the parameters. They induce the covariances from supervised learning tasks in the transfer learning set-up. We use the same idea, but obtain word covariances from WordNet relations. In a slightly different setting, covariance matrices of MVNs have been used in topic models to induce correlation between topics in documents (Blei and Lafferty, 2006).

3 Problem Formulation

Our input consists of a corpus of scenario-specific ESDs, and our goal is to label each event description in an ESD with one event type e. We specify the number of possible event types E a priori as a number exceeding the number of event types in all the scripts considered. The model will select an effective subset of those types.

Assume a scenario-specific corpus c, consisting of D ESDs, $c = \{d_1, ..., d_D\}$. Each ESD d_i consists of N_d event descriptions $d_i = \{d_{i,1}, ..., d_{i,N_i}\}$. Boundaries between descriptions of single events are marked in the data. For each event description $d_{i,n}$ a bag of participant descriptions is extracted. Each participant description corresponds to one noun phrase as identified automatically by a dependency parser (cf. Regneri et al. (2011)). We also associate participant types with participant descriptions, these types are latent and induced at the inference stage.

Given such a corpus of ESDs, our model assigns each event description $d_{i,n}$ in an ESD d_i one event type $z_{d_{i,n}} = e$, where $e \in \{1, ..., E\}$. Assuming that all ESDs are generated from the same underlying set of event types, our objective is to assign the same event type to equivalent event descriptions across all ESDs in the corpus.

We furthermore assume that there exists a canonical temporal ordering of event types for each scenario type, and that events in observed scenarios tend to follow this ordering, but allowing for some flexibility. The event labeling sequence $\mathbf{z}_{d_i}$ of an entire ESD should reflect this canonical ordering. This allows us to use global structural patterns of ESDs in the event type assignments, and thus introducing dependence between event types through their position in the sequence.

4 The Model

Before we describe our model, we briefly explain the Generalized Mallows Model (GMM) which we use to encode a preference for linear ordering of events in a script.

4.1 The (Generalized) Mallows Model

The Mallows Model (MM) is a statistical model over orderings (Mallows, 1957). It takes two parameters $\boldsymbol{\sigma}$, the canonical ordering, and $\rho > 0$, a dispersion parameter. The dispersion parameter is a penalty for the divergence $d(\boldsymbol{\pi}, \boldsymbol{\sigma})$ of an observed ordering $\boldsymbol{\pi}$ from the canonical ordering $\boldsymbol{\sigma}$. The divergence can be any distance metric but Kendall's tau distance ("bubble-sort" distance), a number of swaps needed to bring $\boldsymbol{\pi}$ in the order $\boldsymbol{\sigma}$, is arguably the most common choice. The probability of an observed ordering $\boldsymbol{\pi}$ is defined as

$$P(\boldsymbol{\pi}|\rho, \boldsymbol{\sigma}) = \frac{e^{-\rho\, d(\boldsymbol{\pi},\boldsymbol{\sigma})}}{\psi(\rho)},$$

where $\psi(\rho)$ is a normalization factor. The distribution is centered around the canonical ordering (as $d(\boldsymbol{\sigma},\boldsymbol{\sigma}) = 0$), and the probability decreases exponentially with an increasing distance. For our purposes, without loss of generality, we can assume that $\boldsymbol{\sigma}$ is the identity permutation, that is $\boldsymbol{\sigma} = [1, \ldots, n]$, where n is the number of items.

The Mallows model has been generalized to take as a parameter a vector of *item-specific* dispersion parameters $\boldsymbol{\rho}$ (Fligner and Verducci, 1986). In order to introduce this extension, we first need to reformulate Kendall's tau in a way that captures item-specific distance. An ordering $\boldsymbol{\pi}$ of n items can be equivalently represented by a vector of inversion counts $\boldsymbol{v}$ of length $n - 1$, where each component v_i equals the number of items $j > i$ that occur before item i in $\boldsymbol{\pi}$. For example, for an observed ordering $\boldsymbol{\pi}$ = [2,1,0] the inversion vector $\boldsymbol{v} = (2, 1)$.[1] Then the generalized Mallows model (GMM) is defined as

$$GMM(\boldsymbol{\pi}|\boldsymbol{\rho}) \propto \prod_i e^{-\rho_i\, v_i}.$$

The GMM can be factorized into item-specific components, which allows for efficient inference:

$$GMM_i(v_i|\rho_i) \propto e^{-\rho_i\, v_i}. \quad (1)$$

Intuitively, we will be able to induce event type-specific penalty parameters, and will thus be able to model individual degrees of temporal flexibility among the event types.

Since the GMM is member of the exponential family, a conjugate prior can be defined, which allows for efficient learning of the parameters $\boldsymbol{\rho}$ (Fligner and Verducci, 1990). Like the GMM, its prior distribution GMM_0 can be factorized into independent components for each item i:

$$GMM_0(\rho_i|v_{i,0}, \nu_0) \propto e^{-\rho_i v_{i,0} - log(\psi_i(\rho_i))\nu_0}. \quad (2)$$

The parameters $v_{i,0}$ and ν_0 represent our prior beliefs about flexibility for each item i, and the strength of these beliefs, respectively.

[1]Trivially, the inversion count for the last element in the canonical ordering is always 0.

4.2 The Generative Story

Our model encodes two fundamental assumptions, based on characteristics observed in the data: (1) We assume that each event type can occur at most once per ESD; (2) Each participant type is assumed to occur at most once per event type.

The formalized generative story is given in Figure 1. For each document (ESD) d, we decide independently for each event type e whether to realize it or not by drawing from $Binomial(\theta_e)$.[2] We obtain a binary event vector $\boldsymbol{t}$ where $t_e = 1$ if event type e is realized and $t_e = 0$ otherwise. We draw an event ordering $\boldsymbol{\pi}$ from $GMM(\boldsymbol{\rho})$, represented as a vector of inversion counts.

Now, we pass event types in the order defined by $\boldsymbol{\pi}$. For each realized event type i (i.e., i : $t_i = 1$), we first generate a word (normally a predicate) from the corresponding language model $Mult(\vartheta_i)$. Then we independently decide for each participant type p whether to realize it or not with the probability $Binomial(\varphi_p^i)$. If realized, the participant word (its syntactic head) is generated from the participant language model $Mult(\varpi_p)$.

Note that though the distribution controlling frequency of participant generation (φ_j^i) is event type-specific, the language model associated with the participant ($Mult(\varpi_j)$) is shared across events, thus, ensuring that participant types are defined across events.

The learnt binary realization parameters $\boldsymbol{\theta}$ and $\boldsymbol{\varphi}^e$ should ensure that an appropriate number of events and participants is generated (e.g. the realization probability for obligatory events, observed in almost every ESD for a particular scenario, should be close to 1).

Priors We draw the parameters for the binomial distributions from the Beta distribution, which allows us to model a global preference for using only few event types and only few participant types for each event type. We draw the parameters of the multinomials from the Dirichlet distribution, and can thus model a preference towards sparsity. The GMM parameter vector $\boldsymbol{\rho}$ is drawn from GMM_0 (c.f. Equation (2)).

4.3 Adding Prior Knowledge

Since we are faced with a limited amount of training data, we augment the model described above

[2]We slightly abuse the notation by dropping the superscript d for ESD-specific variables.

Generation of parameters

for event type $e = 1, \ldots, E$ **do**
  $\theta_e \sim Beta(\alpha^+, \alpha^-)$ [freq of event]
  $\vartheta_e \sim Dirichlet(\boldsymbol{\gamma})$ [event lang mod]
  for participant type $p = 1, \ldots, P$ **do**
    $\varphi_p^e \sim Beta(\beta^+, \beta^-)$ [freq of ptcpt]
for participant type $p = 1, \ldots, P$ **do**
  $\varpi_p \sim Dirichlet(\boldsymbol{\delta})$ [ptcpt lang mod]
for event type $e = 1, \ldots, E - 1$ **do**
  $\rho_e \sim GMM_0(\boldsymbol{\rho}_0, \boldsymbol{\nu}_0)$ [ordering params]

Generation of ESD d

for event type $e = 1, \ldots, E$ **do**
  $t_e \sim Binomial(\theta^e)$ [realized events]
$\boldsymbol{\pi} \sim GMM(\boldsymbol{\rho}, \boldsymbol{\nu})$ [event ordering]
for event i from $\boldsymbol{\pi}$ s.th. t_i=1 **do**
  $w_i \sim Mult(\vartheta_i)$ [event lexical unit]
  for participant type $p = 1, \ldots, P$ **do**
    $u_p \sim Binomial(\varphi_p^e)$ [realized ptcpts]
    if $u_p = 1$ **then**
      $w_p \sim Mult(\varpi_p)$ [ptcpt lexical unit]

Figure 1: The generative story of the basic model.

to encode correlations between semantically similar words in the priors for language models. We describe our approach by first introducing the model extension allowing for injecting prior correlations between words, and then explaining how the word correlations are derived from WordNet (Fellbaum, 1998). Since the event vocabulary and the participant vocabulary are separate in our model, the following procedure is carried out separately, but equivalently, for the two vocabularies.

4.3.1 Modeling Word Correlation

Dirichlet distributions do not provide a way to encode correlations between words. To tackle this problem we add another level in the model hierarchy: instead of specifying priors $Dirichlet(\boldsymbol{\gamma})$ and $Dirichlet(\boldsymbol{\delta})$ directly, we generate them for each event type e and participant type p using multivariate normal distributions.

The modification for the generative story is shown in Figure 2. In this extension, each event type e and participant type p has a different associated (nonsymmetric) Dirichlet prior, $\boldsymbol{\gamma}^e$ and $\boldsymbol{\delta}^p$, respectively. The generative story for choosing $\boldsymbol{\gamma}^e$ is the following: A vector $\boldsymbol{\eta}_e$ is drawn from the zero-mean normal distribution $N(\Sigma_\eta, \mathbf{0})$, where Σ_η is the covariance matrix encoding the semantic relatedness of words (see Section 4.3.2). The vector's dimensionality corresponds to size of the vocabulary of event words. Then, the vector is exponentiated and normalized to yield $\boldsymbol{\gamma}^e$.[3] The same procedure is used to choose $\boldsymbol{\delta}^p$ as shown in Figure 2.

Generation of parameters ϑ_e **and** ϖ_p

for event type $e = 1, \ldots, E$ **do**
  $\boldsymbol{\eta}^e \sim N(\Sigma_\eta, 0)$
  for all words w **do**
    $\gamma_w^e = \exp(\eta_w^e) / \sum_{w'} \exp(\eta_{w'}^e)$ [Dir prior]
  $\vartheta_e \sim Dirichlet(\boldsymbol{\gamma}^e)$ [event lang mod]
for participant type $p = 1, \ldots, P$ **do**
  $\boldsymbol{\xi}^p \sim N(\Sigma_\xi, 0)$
  for all words w **do**
    $\delta_w^p = \exp(\xi_w^p) / \sum_{w'} \exp(\xi_{w'}^p)$ [Dir prior]
  $\varpi_p \sim Dirichlet(\boldsymbol{\delta}^p)$ [ptcpt lang mod]

Figure 2: The modified parameter generation procedure for ϑ_e and ϖ_p to encode word correlations.

4.3.2 Defining Semantic Similarity

We use WordNet to obtain semantic similarity scores for each pair of words in our vocabulary. Since we work on limited domains, we define a subset of WordNet as all synsets that any word in our vocabulary is a member of, plus the hypernym sets of all these synsets. We then create a feature vector for each word $f(w_i)$ as follows:

$$f(w_i)_n = \begin{cases} 1 & \text{any sense of } w_i \in \text{synset } n \\ 0 & \text{otherwise} \end{cases}$$

The similarity of two words w_i and w_j is defined as the dot product $f(w_i) \cdot f(w_j)$. We use this similarity to define the covariance matrices Σ_η and Σ_ξ. Each component (i, j) stores the similarity between words w_i and w_j as defined above. Note that the matrices are guaranteed to be valid covariance matrices, as they are positive semidefinite by construction.

5 Inference

Our goal is to infer the set of labelings $\boldsymbol{z}$ of our corpus of ESDs. A labeling $\boldsymbol{z}$ consists of event

[3] In fact, Dirichlet concentration parameters do not need to sum to one. We experimented with normalizing them to yield a different constant, thus regulating the influence of the prior, but have not observed much of improvement from this extension.

types $\boldsymbol{t}$, participant types $\boldsymbol{u}$ and event ordering $\boldsymbol{\pi}$. Additionally, we induce parameters of our model: ordering dispersion parameters ($\boldsymbol{\rho}$) and the language model parameters $\boldsymbol{\eta}$ and $\boldsymbol{\xi}$. We induce these variables conditioned on all the observable words in the data set $\boldsymbol{w}$. Since direct joint sampling from the posterior distributions is intractable, we use Gibbs sampling for approximate inference. Since we chose conjugate prior distributions over the parameter distributions, we can "collapse" the Gibbs sampler by integrating out all parameters (Griffiths and Steyvers, 2004), except for the ones listed above. The unnormalized posterior can be written as the following product of terms:

$$P(\boldsymbol{z}, \boldsymbol{\rho}, \boldsymbol{\eta}, \boldsymbol{\xi} | \boldsymbol{w}) \propto \prod_e DCM_e \prod_p DCM_p$$
$$\prod_e BBM_e \prod_p BBM_{ep}$$
$$\prod_e GMM_e \quad MN_e \prod_p MN_p.$$

The terms DCM_e and DCM_p are Dirichlet compound multinomials associated with event-specific and participant-specific language models:

$$DCM_e = \frac{\Gamma(\sum_v \gamma_v^e)}{\Gamma(\sum_v N_v^e + \gamma_v^e)} \prod_v \frac{\Gamma(N_v^e + \gamma_v^e)}{\Gamma(\gamma_v^e)}$$
$$DCM_p = \frac{\Gamma(\sum_v \delta_v^p)}{\Gamma(\sum_v N_v^p + \delta_v^p)} \prod_v \frac{\Gamma(N_v^p + \delta_v^p)}{\Gamma(\delta_v^p)},$$

where N_v^e and N_v^p is the number of times word type v is assigned to event e and participant p, respectively. The terms BBM_e and BBM_{ep} are the Beta-Binomial distributions associated with generating event types and generating participant types for each event type (i.e. encoding optionality of events and participants):

$$BBM_e \propto \frac{\Gamma(N_e^+ + \alpha^+)\Gamma(N_e^- + \alpha^-)}{\Gamma(N_e^+ + N_e^- + \alpha^+ + \alpha^-)}$$
$$BBM_{ep} \propto \prod_e \prod_p \frac{\Gamma(N_{ep}^+ + \beta^+)\Gamma(N_{ep}^- + \beta^-)}{\Gamma(N_{ep}^+ + N_{ep}^- + \beta^+ + \beta^-)},$$

where N_e^+ and N_e^- is the number of ESDs where event type is generated and the number of ESD where it is not generated, respectively. N_{ep}^+ and N_{ep}^- are analogously defined for participant types (for each event type e). The term GMM_e is associated with the inversion count distribution for event type e and has the form

$$GMM_e \propto GMM_0(\rho_e; \frac{\sum_d v_e^d + v_{e,0}\nu_0}{N + \nu_0}, N + \nu_0),$$

where GMM_0 is defined in expression (2) and v_e^d is the inversion count for event e in ESD d. N is the cumulative number of event occurrences in the data set.

Finally, MN_e and MN_p correspond to the probability of drawing $\boldsymbol{\eta}^e$ and $\boldsymbol{\xi}^p$ from the corresponding normal distributions, as discussed in Section 4.3.1.

Though, at each step of Gibbs sampling, components of $\boldsymbol{z}$ could potentially be sampled by considering the full unnormalized posterior, this clearly can be made much more efficient by observing that only a fraction of terms affect the corresponding conditional probability. For example, when sampling an event type for a given event in a ESD d, only the terms DCM_e, BBM_{ep} and BBM_e for all e and p are affected. For DCMs it can be simplified further as only a few word types are affected. Due to space constraints, we cannot describe the entire sampling algorithms but it naturally follows from the above equations and is similar to the one described in Chen et al. (2009).

For sampling the other parameters of our model, ranking dispersion parameters $\boldsymbol{\rho}$ and the language model parameters $\boldsymbol{\eta}$ and $\boldsymbol{\xi}$, we use slice sampling (MacKay, 2002). For each event type e we draw its dispersion parameter ρ_e independently from the slice sampler.

After every n^{th} iteration we resample $\boldsymbol{\eta}$ and $\boldsymbol{\xi}$ for all language models to capture the correlations. However, to improve mixing time, we also resample components η_i^k and η_i^l when word i has changed event membership from type k to type l. In addition we define classes of closely related words (heuristically based on the covariance matrix) by classifying words as related when their similarity exceeds an empirically determined threshold. We also resample all components η_j^k and η_j^l for each word j that related to word i. We re-normalize $\boldsymbol{\eta}^m$ and $\boldsymbol{\eta}^n$ after resampling to update the Dirichlet concentration parameters. The same procedure is used for participant language models (parameters $\boldsymbol{\xi}$).

6 Evaluation

In our evaluation, we evaluate the quality of the event clusters induced by the model and the extent to which the clusters capture the global event ordering underlying the script, as well as the benefit of the GMM and the informed prior knowledge. We start by describing data and evaluation metrics.

Scenario Name	♯ESDs	Avg len
OMICS corpus		
Cook in microwave	59	5.03
Answer the telephone	55	4.47
Buy from vending machine	32	4.53
Make coffee	38	5.00
R10 corpus		
Iron clothes	19	8.79
Make scrambled eggs	20	10.3
Eat in fast food restaurant	15	8.93
Return food (in a restaurant)	15	5.93
Take a shower	21	11.29
Take the bus	19	8.53

Table 1: Test scenarios used in experiments (left), the size of the corresponding corpus (middle), and the average length of an ESD in events (right).

	Event Paraphrase			Evt. Ordering		
	P	R	F	P	R	F
Ret. Food	0.92	0.52	**0.67**	0.87	0.72	**0.79**
-GMM	0.70	0.30	0.42	0.46	0.44	0.45
-COVAR	0.92	0.52	**0.67**	0.77	0.67	0.71
Vending	0.76	0.78	0.77	0.90	0.74	**0.81**
-GMM	0.74	0.39	0.51	0.64	0.47	0.54
-COVAR	0.74	0.87	**0.80**	0.85	0.73	0.78
Shower	0.68	0.67	**0.67**	0.85	0.84	**0.85**
-GMM	0.36	0.17	0.23	0.42	0.38	0.40
-COVAR	0.64	0.44	0.52	0.77	0.73	0.75
Microwave	0.85	0.80	0.82	0.91	0.74	0.82
-GMM	0.88	0.30	0.45	0.67	0.62	0.64
-COVAR	0.89	0.81	**0.85**	0.92	0.82	**0.87**

Table 2: Comparison of model variants: For each scenario: The full model (top), a version without the GMM (`-GMM`), and a version with a uniform Dirichlet prior over language models (`-COVAR`).

6.1 Data

We use the data sets presented in Regneri et al. (2010) (henceforth R10) for development and testing. The data is comprised of ESDs from two corpora. R10 collected a corpus, consisting of sets of ESDs for a variety of scenarios, via a web experiment from non-expert annotators. In addition we use ESDs from the OMICS corpus[4] (Kochenderfer and Gupta, 2003), which consists of instantiations of descriptions of several 'stories', but is restricted to indoor activities. The details of our data are displayed in Table 1. For each event description we extract all noun phrases, as automatically identified by Regneri et al. (2011), separating participant descriptions from action descriptions. We remove articles and pronouns, and reduce NPs to their head words.

6.2 Gold Standard and Evaluation Metrics

We follow R10 in evaluating induced event types and orderings in a binary classification setting. R10 collected a gold standard by classifying pairs of event descriptions w.r.t. whether or not they are paraphrases. Our model classifies two event descriptions as equivalent whenever $z_{e_1} = z_{e_2}$.

Equivalently, R10 classify ordered pairs of event descriptions as to whether they are presented in their natural order. Assuming the identity ordering as canonical ordering in the Generalized Mallows Model, event types tending to occur earlier in the script should be assigned lower cluster IDs than event types occurring later. Thus, whenever $z_{e_1} < z_{e_2}$, our the model predicts that two event descriptions occur in their natural order.

[4]http://csc.media.mit.edu/

We evaluate the output of our model against the described gold standard, using Precision, Recall and F1 as evaluation metrics, so that our results are directly comparable to R10. We tune our parameters on a development set of 5 scenarios which are not used in testing.

6.3 Results

Table 3 presents the results of our two evaluation tasks. While on the event paraphrase task the R10 system performs slightly better, our model outperforms the R10 system on the event ordering task by a substantial margin of 7 points average F-score. While both systems perform similarly on the task of event type induction, we induce a *joint* model for both objectives. The results show that, despite the limited amount of data, and the more complex learning objective, our model succeeds in inducing event types and ordering constraints.

In order to demonstrate the benefit of the GMM, we compare the performance of our model to a variant which excludes this component (`-GMM`), cf. Table 2. The results confirm our expectation that biasing the model towards encouraging a linear ordering on the event types provides a strong cue for event cluster inference.

As an example of a clustering learnt by our model, consider the following event chain:

$\{$get$\}$ → $\{$open,take$\}$ → $\{$put,place$\}$ → $\{$close$\}$ → $\{$set,select,enter,turn$\}$ → $\{$start$\}$ → $\{$wait$\}$ → $\{$remove,take,open$\}$ → $\{$push,press,turn$\}$

We display the most frequent words in the clusters

Scenario	Event Paraphrase Task						Event Ordering Task					
	Precision		Recall		F1		Precision		Recall		F1	
	R10	BS	R10	BS	R10	BS	R10	BS	R10	BS	R10	BS
Coffee	0.50	0.47	0.94	0.58	**0.65**	0.52	0.70	0.68	0.78	0.57	**0.74**	0.62
Telephone	0.93	0.92	0.85	0.72	**0.89**	0.81	0.83	0.92	0.86	0.87	0.84	**0.89**
Bus	0.65	0.52	0.87	0.43	**0.74**	0.47	0.80	0.76	0.80	0.76	**0.80**	0.76
Iron	0.52	0.65	0.94	0.56	**0.67**	0.60	0.78	0.87	0.72	0.69	0.75	**0.77**
Scr. Eggs	0.58	0.92	0.86	0.65	0.69	**0.76**	0.67	0.77	0.64	0.59	0.66	**0.67**
Vending	0.59	0.76	0.83	0.78	0.69	**0.77**	0.84	0.90	0.85	0.74	**0.84**	0.81
Microwave•	0.75	0.85	0.75	0.80	0.75	**0.82**	0.47	0.91	0.83	0.74	0.60	**0.82**
Shower•	0.70	0.68	0.88	0.67	**0.78**	0.67	0.48	0.85	0.82	0.84	0.61	**0.85**
Fastfood•	0.50	0.74	0.73	0.87	0.59	**0.80**	0.53	0.97	0.81	0.65	0.64	**0.78**
Ret. Food•	0.73	0.92	0.68	0.52	**0.71**	0.67	0.48	0.87	0.75	0.72	0.58	**0.79**
Average	0.645	**0.743**	**0.833**	0.658	**0.716**	0.689	0.658	**0.850**	**0.786**	0.717	0.706	**0.776**

Table 3: Results of our model for the event paraphrase task (left) and event type ordering task (right). Our system (BS) is compared to the system in Regneri et al. (2010) (R10). We were able to obtain the R10 system from the authors and evaluate on additional scenarios for which no results are reported in the paper. These additional scenarios are marked with a dot (•).

inferred for the "Microwave" scenario. Clusters are sorted by event type ID. Note that the word 'open' is assigned to two event types in the sequence, which is intuitively reasonable. This illustrates why assuming a deterministic mapping from predicates to events (as in Chambers and Jurafsky (2008)) is limiting for our dataset.

We finally examined the influence of the informed prior component, comparing to a model variant which uses uniform Dirichlet parameters (`-COVAR`; see Table 2). As expected, using an informed prior component leads to improved performance on scenario types with fewer training ESDs available ('Take a shower' and 'Return food'; cf. Table 1). For scenarios with a larger set of training documents no reliable benefit from the informed prior is observable. We did not optimize this component, e.g. by testing more sophisticated methods for construction of the covariance matrix, but expect to be able to improve its reliability.

7 Discussion

The evaluation shows that our model is able to create meaningful event type clusters, which resemble the underlying event ordering imposed by the scenario. We achieve an absolute average improvement of 7% over a state-of-the-art model. In contrast to previous approaches to script induction, our model does not include specifically customized components, and is thus flexibly applicable without additional engineering effort.

Our model provides a clean, statistical formulation of the problem of jointly inducing event types and their ordering. Using a Bayesian model allows for flexible enhancement of the model. One straightforward next step would be to explore the influence of participants, and try to jointly infer them with our current set of latent variables.

Statistical models highly rely on a sufficient amount of training data in order to be able to induce latent structures. The limited amount of training data in our case is a bottleneck for the performance. The model performs best on the two scenarios with the most training data ('Telephone' and 'Microwave'), which supports this assumption. We showed, however, that our model can be applied to small data sets through incorporation of informed prior knowledge without supervision.

8 Conclusion

We presented a hierarchical Bayesian model for joint induction of event clusters and constraints on their orderings from sets of ESDs. We incorporate the Generalized Mallows Model over orderings. The evaluation shows that our model successfully induces event clusters and ordering constraints.

We compare our joint, statistical model to a pipeline based model using MSA for event clustering. Our system outperforms the system on the task of event ordering induction by a substantial margin, while achieving comparable results in the event induction task. We could further explicitly show the benefit of modeling global ESD structure, using the GMM.

In future work we plan to apply our model to larger data sets, and to examine the role of participants in our model, exploring the potential of inferring them jointly with our current objectives.

Acknowledgments

We thank Michaela Regneri for substantial support with the script data, and Mirella Lapata for helpful comments.

References

Collin F. Baker, Charles J. Fillmore, and John B. Lowe. 1998. The berkeley framenet project. In *Proceedings of the 36th Annual Meeting of the Association for Computational Linguistics and 17th International Conference on Computational Linguistics*, pages 86–90.

A. Barr and E.A. Feigenbaum. 1986. *The handbook of artificial intelligence. 1 (1981).* The Handbook of Artificial Intelligence. Addison-Wesley.

David Blei and John Lafferty. 2006. Correlated topic models. In *Advances in Neural Information Processing Systems 18*, pages 147–154.

Nathanael Chambers and Dan Jurafsky. 2008. Unsupervised learning of narrative event chains. In *Proceedings of ACL-08: HLT*, pages 789–797.

Nathanael Chambers and Dan Jurafsky. 2009. Unsupervised learning of narrative schemas and their participants. In *Proceedings of the 47th Annual Meeting of the Association for Computational Linguistics*, pages 602–610.

H. Chen, S. R. K. Branavan, R. Barzilay, and D. R. Karger. 2009. Content modeling using latent permutations. *Journal of Artificial Intelligence Research*, 36(1):129–163.

Christiane Fellbaum, editor. 1998. *WordNet: an electronic lexical database*. MIT Press.

M. Fligner and J. Verducci. 1986. Distance based ranking models. *Journal of the Royal Statistical Society, Series B*, 48:359–369.

M. Fligner and J. Verducci. 1990. Posterior probabilities for a consensus ordering. *Psychometrika*, 55:53–63.

T. L. Griffiths and M. Steyvers. 2004. Finding scientific topics. *Proceedings of the National Academy of Sciences*, 101(Suppl. 1):5228–5235.

Alexandre Klementiev, Dan Roth, and Kevin Small. 2008. Unsupervised rank aggregation with distance-based models. In *Proceedings of the 25th International Conference on Machine Learning*, pages 472–479.

Mykel J. Kochenderfer and Rakesh Gupta. 2003. Common sense data acquisition for indoor mobile robots. In *Proceedings of the Nineteenth National Conference on Artificial Intelligence (AAAI-04)*, pages 605–610.

D. J. C. MacKay. 2002. *Information Theory, Inference & Learning Algorithms*. Cambridge University Press, New York, NY, USA.

C. L. Mallows. 1957. Non-null ranking models. *Biometrika*, 44:114–130.

Risto Miikkulainen. 1995. Script-based inference and memory retrieval in subsymbolic story processing. *Applied Intelligence*, pages 137–163.

Ashutosh Modi, Ivan Titov, and Alexandre Klementiev. 2012. Unsupervised induction of frame-semantic representations. In *Proceedings of the NAACL-HLT Workshop on the Induction of Linguistic Structure*, pages 1–7.

Erik T. Mueller. 2004. Understanding script-based stories using commonsense reasoning. *Cognitive Systems Research*, 5(4):307–340.

Brendan O'Connor. 2012. Bayesian unsupervised frame learning from text. Technical report, Carnegie Mellon University.

Rajat Raina, Andrew Y. Ng, and Daphne Koller. 2006. Constructing informative priors using transfer learning. In *Proceedings of the 23rd International Conference on Machine Learning*, pages 713–720.

Michaela Regneri, Alexander Koller, and Manfred Pinkal. 2010. Learning script knowledge with web experiments. In *Proceedings of the 48th Annual Meeting of the Association for Computational Linguistics*, pages 979–988.

Michaela Regneri, Alexander Koller, Josef Ruppenhofer, and Manfred Pinkal. 2011. Learning script participants from unlabeled data. In *Proceedings of RANLP 2011*, pages 463–470.

Roger C. Schank and Robert P. Abelson. 1975. Scripts, plans, and knowledge. In *Proceedings of the 4th International Joint Conference on Artificial Intelligence*, IJCAI'75, pages 151–157.

Ivan Titov and Alexandre Klementiev. 2011. A bayesian model for unsupervised semantic parsing. In *Proceedings of the 49th Annual Meeting of the Association for Computational Linguistics: Human Language Technologies*, pages 1445–1455.

Inducing Example-based Semantic Frames from a Massive Amount of Verb Uses

Daisuke Kawahara[†] **Daniel W. Peterson**[‡] **Octavian Popescu**[§] **Martha Palmer**[‡]
[†]Kyoto University, Kyoto, Japan
[‡]University of Colorado at Boulder, Boulder, CO, USA
[§]Fondazione Bruno Kessler, Trento, Italy
dk@i.kyoto-u.ac.jp, {Daniel.W.Peterson, Martha.Palmer}@colorado.edu, popescu@fbk.eu

Abstract

We present an unsupervised method for inducing semantic frames from verb uses in giga-word corpora. Our semantic frames are verb-specific example-based frames that are distinguished according to their senses. We use the Chinese Restaurant Process to automatically induce these frames from a massive amount of verb instances. In our experiments, we acquire broad-coverage semantic frames from two giga-word corpora, the larger comprising 20 billion words. Our experimental results indicate the effectiveness of our approach.

1 Introduction

Semantic frames are indispensable knowledge for semantic analysis or text understanding. In the last decade, semantic frames, such as FrameNet (Baker et al., 1998) and PropBank (Palmer et al., 2005), have been manually elaborated. These resources are effectively exploited in many natural language processing (NLP) tasks, including not only semantic parsing but also machine translation (Boas, 2002), information extraction (Surdeanu et al., 2003), question answering (Narayanan and Harabagiu, 2004), paraphrase acquisition (Ellsworth and Janin, 2007) and recognition of textual entailment (Burchardt and Frank, 2006).

There have been many attempts to automatically acquire frame knowledge from raw corpora with the goal of either adding frequency information to an existing resource or of inducing similar frames for other languages. Most of these approaches, however, focus on syntactic frames, i.e., subcategorization frames (e.g., (Manning, 1993; Briscoe and Carroll, 1997; Korhonen et al., 2006; Lippincott et al., 2012; Reichart and Korhonen, 2013)). Since subcategorization frames represent argument patterns of verbs and are purely syntactic, expressions that have the same subcategorization frame can have different meanings (e.g., metaphors). Semantics-oriented NLP applications based on frames, such as paraphrase acquisition and machine translation, require consistency in the meaning of each frame, and thus these subcategorization frames are not suitable for these semantic tasks.

Recently, there have been a few studies on automatically acquiring semantic frames (Materna, 2012; Materna, 2013). Materna induced semantic frames (called LDA-Frames) from triples of (subject, verb, object) in the British National Corpus (BNC) based on Latent Dirichlet Allocation (LDA) and the Dirichlet Process. LDA-Frames capture limited linguistic phenomena of these triples, and are defined across verbs based on probabilistic topic distributions.

This paper presents a method for automatically building verb-specific semantic frames from a large raw corpus. Our semantic frames are verb-specific like PropBank and semantically distinguished. A frame has several syntactic case slots, each of which consists of words that are eligible to fill the slot. For example, let us show three semantic frames of the verb "observe":[1]

observe:1
nsubj:{we, author, ...} dobj:{effect, result, ...}
prep_in:{study, case, ...} ...

observe:2
nsubj:{teacher, we, ...} dobj:{child, student, ...}
prep_in:{classroom, school, ...} ...

observe:3
nsubj:{child, people, ...} dobj:{bird, animal, ...}
prep_at:{range, time, ...} ...

[1]In this paper, we use the dependency relation names of the Stanford collapsed dependencies (de Marneffe et al., 2006) as the notations of case slots. For instance, "nsubj" means a nominal subject, "dobj" means a direct object, "iboj" means an indirect object, "ccomp" means a clausal complement and "prep_*" means a preposition.

Frequencies, which are not shown in the above examples, are attached to each semantic frame, case slot and word, and can be effectively exploited for the applications of these semantic frames. The frequencies of words in each case slot become good sources of selectional preferences.

Our novel contributions are summarized as follows:

- induction of semantic frames based on the Chinese Restaurant Process (Aldous, 1985) from only automatic parses of a web-scale corpus,
- exploitation of the assumption of one sense per collocation (Yarowsky, 1993) to make the computation feasible,
- providing broad-coverage knowledge for selectional preferences, and
- evaluating induced semantic frames by using an existing annotated corpus with verb classes.

2 Related Work

The most closely related work to our semantic frames are LDA-Frames, which are probabilistic semantic frames automatically induced from a raw corpus (Materna, 2012; Materna, 2013). He used a model based on LDA and the Dirichlet Process to cluster verb instances of a triple (subject, verb, object) to produce semantic frames and slots. Both of these are represented as a probabilistic distribution of words across verbs. He applied this method to the BNC and acquired 427 frames and 144 slots (Materna, 2013). These frames are overgeneralized across verbs and might be difficult to provide with fine-grained selectional preferences. In addition, Grenager and Manning (2006) proposed a method for inducing PropBank-style frames from Stanford typed dependencies extracted from raw corpora. Although these frames are based on typed dependencies and more semantic than subcategorization frames, they are not distinguished in terms of the senses of words filling a case slot.

There are hand-crafted semantic frames in the lexicons of FrameNet (Baker et al., 1998) and PropBank (Palmer et al., 2005). Corpus Pattern Analysis (CPA) frames (Hanks, 2012) are another manually created repository of patterns for verbs. Each pattern represents a prototypical word usage as extracted by lexicographers from the BNC. Creating CPA is time consuming, but our proposed method may be employed to assist in the creation of this type of resource, as shown in Section 4.4.

Our task can be regarded as clustering of verb instances. In this respect, the models of Parisien and Stevenson are related to our method (Parisien and Stevenson, 2009; Parisien and Stevenson, 2010). Parisien and Stevenson (2009) proposed a Dirichlet Process model for clustering usages of the verb "get." Later, Parisien and Stevenson (2010) proposed a Hierarchical Dirichlet Process model for jointly clustering argument structures (i.e., subcategorization frames) and verb classes. However, their argument structures are not semantic but syntactic, and also they did not evaluate the resulting frames. There have also been related approaches to clustering verb types (Vlachos et al., 2009; Sun and Korhonen, 2009; Falk et al., 2012; Reichart and Korhonen, 2013). These methods induce verb clusters in which multiple verbs participate, and do not consider the polysemy of verbs. Our objective is different from theirs.

Another line of related work is unsupervised semantic parsing or semantic role labeling (Poon and Domingos, 2009; Lang and Lapata, 2010; Lang and Lapata, 2011a; Lang and Lapata, 2011b; Titov and Klementiev, 2011; Titov and Klementiev, 2012). These approaches basically cluster predicates and their arguments to distinguish predicate senses and semantic roles of arguments. Modi et al. (2012) extended the model of Titov and Klementiev (2012) to jointly induce semantic roles and frames using the Chinese Restaurant Process, which is also used in our approach. However, they did not aim at building a lexicon of semantic frames, but at distinguishing verbs that have different senses in a relatively small annotated corpus. Applying this method to a large corpus could produce a frame lexicon, but its scalability would be a big problem.

For other languages than English, Kawahara and Kurohashi (2006a) proposed a method for automatically compiling Japanese semantic frames from a large web corpus. They applied conventional agglomerative clustering to predicate-argument structures using word/frame similarity based on a manually-crafted thesaurus. Since Japanese is head-final and has case-marking postpositions, it seems easier to build semantic frames with it than with other languages such as English. They also achieved an improvement in dependency parsing and predicate-argument structure analysis by using their resulting frames (Kawahara and Kurohashi, 2006b).

3 Method for Inducing Semantic Frames

Our objective is to automatically induce verb-specific example-based semantic frames. Each semantic frame consists of a partial set of syntactic slots: nsubj, dobj, iobj, ccomp and prep_*. Each slot consists of words with frequencies, which could provide broad-coverage selectional preferences.

Frames for a verb should be semantically distinguished. That is to say, each frame should consist of predicate-argument structures that have consistent usages or meanings.

Our procedure to automatically generate semantic frames from verb usages is as follows:

1. apply dependency parsing to a raw corpus and extract predicate-argument structures for each verb from the automatic parses,
2. merge the predicate-argument structures that have presumably the same meaning based on the assumption of one sense per collocation to get a set of initial frames, and
3. apply clustering to the initial frames based on the Chinese Restaurant Process to produce the final semantic frames.

Each of these steps is described in the following sections in detail.

3.1 Extracting Predicate-argument Structures from a Raw Corpus

We first apply dependency parsing to a large raw corpus. We use the Stanford parser with Stanford dependencies (de Marneffe et al., 2006).[2] Collapsed dependencies are adopted to directly extract prepositional phrases.

Then, we extract predicate-argument structures from the dependency parses. Dependents that have the following dependency relations to a verb are extracted as arguments:

nsubj, xsubj, dobj, iobj, ccomp, xcomp, prep_∗

Here, we do not distinguish adjuncts from arguments. All extracted dependents of a verb are handled as arguments. This distinction is left for future work, but this will be performed using slot

[2]http://nlp.stanford.edu/software/lex-parser.shtml

Sentences:
They observed the effects of ...
This statistical ability to observe an effect ...
We did not observe a residual effect of ...
He could observe the results at the same time ...
My first opportunity to observe the results of ...
You can observe beautiful birds ...
Children may then observe birds ...
⋮

Predicate-argument structures:
nsubj:they observe dobj:effect
observe dobj:effect
nsubj:we observe dobj:effect
nsubj:he observe dobj:result prep_at:time
observe dobj:result
nsubj:you observe dobj:bird
nsubj:child observe dobj:bird
⋮

Initial frames:
nsubj:{they, we, ...} observe dobj:{effect}
nsubj:{he, ...} observe dobj:{result} prep_at:{time}
nsubj:{you, child, ...} observe dobj:{bird}
⋮

Figure 1: Examples of predicate-argument structures and initial frames for the verb "observe."

frequencies in the applications of semantic frames or the method proposed by Abend and Rappoport (2010).

We apply the following processes to extracted predicate-argument structures:

- A verb and an argument are lemmatized, and only the head of an argument is preserved for compound nouns.
- Phrasal verbs are also distinguished from non-phrasal verbs. For example, "look up" has independent frames from "look."
- The passive voice of a verb is distinguished from the active voice, and thus these have independent frames. Passive voice is detected using the part-of-speech tag "VBN" (past participle). The alignment between frames of active and passive voices will be done after the induction of frames using the model of Sasano et al. (2013) in the future.
- "xcomp" (open clausal complement) is renamed to "ccomp" (clausal complement) and "xsubj" (controlling subject) is renamed to "nsubj" (nominal subject). This is because

these usages as predicate-argument structures are not different.

- A capitalized argument with the part-of speech "NNP" (singular proper noun) or "NNPS" (plural proper noun) is generalized to ⟨name⟩. Similarly, an argument of "ccomp" is generalized to ⟨comp⟩ since the content of a clausal complement is not important.

Extracted predicate-argument structures are collected for each verb and the subsequent processes are applied to the predicate-argument structures of each verb. Figure 1 shows examples of predicate-argument structures for "observe."

3.2 Constructing Initial Frames from Predicate-argument Structures

A straightforward way to produce semantic frames is to cluster the extracted predicate-argument structures directly. Since our objective is to compile broad-coverage semantic frames, a massive amount of predicate-argument structures should be fed into the clustering. It would take prohibitive computational costs to conduct the sampling procedure, which is described in the next section.

To make the computation feasible, we merge the predicate-argument structures that have the same or similar meaning to get initial frames. These initial frames are the input of the subsequent clustering process. For this merge, we assume one sense per collocation (Yarowsky, 1993) for predicate-argument structures.

For each predicate-argument structure of a verb, we couple the verb and an argument to make a unit for sense disambiguation. We select an argument in the following order by considering the degree of effect on the verb sense:[3]

dobj, ccomp, nsubj, prep_*, iobj.

This selection of a predominant argument order above is justified by relative comparisons of the discriminative power of the different slots for CPA frames (Popescu, 2013). If a predicate-argument structure does not have any of the above slots, it is discarded.

Then, the predicate-argument structures that have the same verb and argument pair (slot and word, e.g., "dobj:effect") are merged into an initial frame (Figure 1). After this process, we discard minor initial frames that occur fewer than 10 times.

For example, we have 732,292 instances (predicate-argument structures) for the verb "observe" in the web corpus that is used in our experiment (its details are described in Section 4.1). As the result of this merging process, we obtain 6,530 initial frames, which become an input for the clustering. This means that this process accelerates the speed of clustering more than 100 times.

The precision of this process will be evaluated in Section 4.3.

3.3 Clustering using Chinese Restaurant Process

We cluster initial frames for each verb to produce final semantic frames using the Chinese Restaurant Process (Aldous, 1985). We regard each initial frame as an instance in the usual clustering of the Chinese Restaurant Process.

We calculate the posterior probability of a semantic frame f_j given an initial frame v_i as follows:

$$P(f_j|v_i) \propto \begin{cases} \frac{n(f_j)}{N+\alpha} \cdot P(v_i|f_j) & f_j \neq new \\ \frac{\alpha}{N+\alpha} \cdot P(v_i|f_j) & f_j = new, \end{cases} \quad (1)$$

where N is the number of initial frames for the target verb and $n(f_j)$ is the current number of initial frames assigned to the semantic frame f_j. α is a hyper-parameter that determines how likely it is for a new semantic frame to be created. In this equation, the first term is the Dirichlet process prior and the second term is the likelihood of v_i.

$P(v_i|f_j)$ is defined based on the Dirichlet-Multinomial distribution as follows:

$$P(v_i|f_j) = \prod_{w \in V} P(w|f_j)^{count(v_i,w)}, \quad (2)$$

where V is the vocabulary in all case slots cooccurring with the verb. It is distinguished by the case slot, and thus consists of pairs of slots and words, e.g., "nsubj:child" and "dobj:bird." $count(v_i, w)$ is the number of w in the initial frame v_i.

$P(w|f_j)$ is defined as follows:

$$P(w|f_j) = \frac{count(f_j, w) + \beta}{\sum_{t \in V} count(f_j, t) + |V| \cdot \beta}, \quad (3)$$

[3] If a predicate-argument structure has multiple prepositional phrases, one of them is randomly selected.

where $count(f_j, w)$ is the current number of w in the frame f_j, and β is a hyper-parameter of Dirichlet distribution. For a new semantic frame, this probability is uniform $(1/|V|)$.

We use Gibbs sampling to realize this clustering.

4 Experiments and Evaluations

4.1 Experimental Settings

We use two kinds of large-scale corpora: a web corpus and the English Gigaword corpus.

To prepare a web corpus, we first crawled the web. We extracted sentences from each web page that seems to be written in English based on the encoding information. Then, we selected sentences that consist of at most 40 words, and removed duplicated sentences. From this process, we obtained a corpus of one billion sentences, totaling approximately 20 billion words. We focused on verbs whose frequency was more than 1,000. There were 19,649 verbs, including phrasal verbs, and separating passive and active constructions. We extracted 2,032,774,982 predicate-argument structures.

We also used the English Gigaword corpus (LDC2011T07; English Gigaword Fifth Edition) to induce semantic frames. This corpus consists of approximately 180 million sentences, which totaling four billion words. There were 7,356 verbs after applying the same frequency threshold as the web corpus. We extracted 423,778,278 predicate-argument structures from this corpus.

We set the hyper-parameters α in (1) and β in (3) to 1.0. The frame assignments for all the components were initialized randomly. We took 100 samples for each initial frame and selected the frame assignment that has the highest probability. These parameters were determined according to a preliminary experiment to manually examine the quality of resulting frames.

4.2 Experimental Results

We executed the per-verb clustering tasks on a PC cluster. It finished within a few hours for most verbs, but it took a couple of days for very frequent verbs, such as "get" and "say." The clustering produced an average number of semantic frames per verb of 15.2 for the web corpus and 18.5 for the Gigaword corpus. Examples of induced semantic frames from the web corpus are shown in Table 1.

	slot	instances
observe:1	nsubj	i:5850, we:5201, he:3796, you:3669, ...
	dobj	what:7091, people:2272, this:2262, ...
	prep_in	way:254, world:204, life:194, ...
	⋮	
observe:2	nsubj	we:11135, you:1321, i:1317, ...
	dobj	change:5091, difference:2719, ...
	prep_in	study:622, case:382, cell:362, ...
	⋮	
observe:3	nsubj	student:3921, i:2240, we:2174, ...
	dobj	child:2323, class:2184, student:2025, ...
	prep_in	classroom:555, action:509, ...
	⋮	
accept:1	nsubj	we:44833, i:6873, order:4051, ...
	dobj	card:28835, payment:22569, ...
	prep_for	payment:1166, convenience:1147, ...
	⋮	
accept:2	nsubj	i:10568, we:9300, you:5106, ...
	dobj	that:14180, this:12061, it:7756, ...
	prep_as	part:1879, fact:1085, truth:926, ...
	⋮	
accept:3	nsubj	people:7459, he:6696, we:5515, ...
	dobj	christ:13766, jesus:6528, it:5612, ...
	prep_as	savior:5591, lord:597, one:469, ...
	⋮	

Table 1: Examples of resulting frames for the verb "observe" and "accept" induced from the web corpus. The number following an instance word represents its frequency.

4.3 Evaluation of Induced Semantic Frames

We evaluate precision and coverage of induced semantic frames. To measure the precision of induced semantic frames, we adopt the purity metric, which is usually used to evaluate clustering results. However, the problem is that it is impossible to assign gold-standard classes to the huge number of instances. To automatically measure the purity of the induced semantic frames, we make use of the SemLink corpus (Loper et al., 2007), in which VerbNet classes (Kipper-Schuler, 2005) and PropBank/FrameNet frames are assigned to each instance. We make a test set that contains 157 polysemous verbs that occur 10 or more times in the SemLink corpus (sections 02-21 of the Wall Street Journal). We first add these instances to the instances from a raw corpus and apply clustering to these merged instances. Then, we compare the induced semantic frames of the SemLink instances with their gold-standard classes. We adopt VerbNet classes and PropBank frames as gold-standard classes.

For each group of verb-specific semantic frames, we measure the purity of the frames as the percentage of SemLink instances belonging to the majority gold class in their respective cluster. Let

		PU		CO		F_1	
		Mac	Mic	Mac	Mic	Mac	Mic
against VerbNet	One frame	0.799	0.802	**0.917**	**0.952**	0.854	0.870
	Initial frames	**0.985**	**0.982**	0.755	0.812	0.855	0.889
	Induced sem frames	0.900	0.901	0.886	0.928	**0.893**	**0.914**
against PropBank	One frame	0.901	0.872	↑	↑	0.909	0.910
	Initial frames	**0.994**	**0.993**	↑	↑	0.858	0.893
	Induced sem frames	0.965	0.949	↑	↑	**0.924**	**0.939**

Table 2: Evaluation results of semantic frames from the web corpus against VerbNet classes and PropBank frames. "Mac" means a macro average and "Mic" means a micro average.

		PU		CO		F_1	
		Mac	Mic	Mac	Mic	Mac	Mic
against VerbNet	One frame	0.799	0.804	**0.855**	**0.920**	0.826	0.858
	Initial frames	**0.985**	**0.981**	0.666	0.758	0.795	0.855
	Induced sem frames	0.916	0.909	0.796	0.880	**0.852**	**0.894**
against PropBank	One frame	0.901	0.874	↑	↑	**0.877**	0.896
	Initial frames	**0.994**	**0.993**	↑	↑	0.798	0.859
	Induced sem frames	0.968	0.953	↑	↑	0.874	**0.915**

Table 3: Evaluation results of semantic frames from the Gigaword corpus against VerbNet classes and PropBank frames. "Mac" means a macro average and "Mic" means a micro average.

N denote the total number of SemLink instances of the target verb, G_j the set of instances belonging to the j-th gold class and F_i the set of instances belonging to the i-th frame. The purity (PU) can then be written as follows:

$$\text{PU} = \frac{1}{N} \sum_i \max_j |G_j \cap F_i|. \quad (4)$$

For example, a frame of the verb "observe" contains 11 SemLink instances, and eight out of them belong to the class SAY-37.7, which is the majority class among these 11 instances. PU is calculated by summing up such counts over all the frames of this verb.

Usually, inverse purity or collocation is used to measure the recall of normal clustering tasks. However, these recall measures do not fit our task. This is because it is not a real error to have similar separate frames. Instead, we want to avoid having so many frames that we cannot provide broad-coverage selectional preferences due to sparsity. To judge this aspect, we measure coverage.

The coverage (CO) measures to what extent predicate-argument structures of the target verb in a test set are included in one of frames of the verb. We use the predicate-argument structures of the above 157 verbs from the SemLink corpus, which are the same ones used in the evaluation of PU. We judge a predicate-argument structure as correct if all of its argument words (of the target slot described in Section 3.1) are included in the corresponding slot of a frame. If the clustering gets better, the value of CO will get higher, because merging instances by clustering alleviates data sparsity.

These per-verb scores are aggregated into an overall score by averaging over all verbs. We use two ways of averaging: a macro average and a micro average. The macro average is a simple average of scores for individual verbs. The micro average is obtained by weighting the scores for individual verbs proportional to the number of instances for that verb. Finally, we use the harmonic mean (F_1) of purity and coverage as a single measure of clustering quality.

For comparison, we adopt the following two baseline methods:

One frame a frame into which all the instances for a verb are merged

Initial frames the initial frames without clustering (described in Section 3.2)

Table 2 and Table 3 list evaluation results for semantic frames induced from the web corpus and the Gigaword corpus, respectively.[4] Note that CO does not consider gold-standard classes, and thus the values of CO are the same for the VerbNet

[4]We did not adopt inverse purity, but its values for the induced semantic frames range from 0.42 to 0.49.

and PropBank evaluations. The induced frames outperformed the two baseline methods in terms of F_1 in most cases. While the coverage of the web frames was higher than that of the Gigaword frames, as expected, the purity of the web frames was slightly lower than that of the Gigaword frames. This degradation might be caused by the noise in the web corpus.

The purity of the initial frames was around 98%-99%, which means that there were few cases that the one-sense-per-collocation assumption was violated.

Modi et al. (2012) reported a purity of 77.9% for the assignment of FrameNet frames to the FrameNet corpus. We also conducted the above purity evaluation against FrameNet frames for 140 verbs.[5] We obtained a macro average of 92.9% and a micro average of 89.2% for the web frames, and a macro average of 93.2% and a micro average of 89.8% for the Gigaword frames. It is difficult to directly compare these results with Modi et al. (2012), but our frame assignments seem to have higher accuracy.

4.4 Evaluation against CPA Frames

Corpus Pattern Analysis (CPA) is a technique for linking word usage to prototypical syntagmatic patterns.[6] The resource was built manually by investigating examples in the BNC, and the set of corpus examples used to induce each pattern is given. For example, the following three patterns describe the usage of the verb "accommodate."

[Human 1] accommodate [Human 2]
[Building] accommodate [Eventuality]
[Human] accommodate [Self] to [Eventuality]

In this paper, we use CPA to evaluate the quality of the automatically induced frames. By comparing the induced frames to CPA patterns, we can evaluate the correctness and relevance of this approach from a human point of view. To do that, we associate semantic features to the set of words in each slot in the frames, using SUMO (Niles and Pease, 2001). For example, take the following frame for the verb "accomplish":

accomplish:1
nsubj:{you, leader, employee, ...}
dobj:{developing, progress, objective, ...}.

[5]Since FrameNet frames are not assigned to all the verbs of SemLink, the number of verbs is different from the evaluations against VerbNet and PropBank.

[6]http://deb.fi.muni.cz/pdev/

	all	K-means
Entropy (E)	0.790	0.516
Recovery Rate (RC)	0.347	0.630
Purity (P)	0.462	0.696

Table 4: CPA Evaluation.

Using SUMO, we map this frame to the following:
nsubj: [Human]
dobj: [SubjectiveAssessmentAttribute],
which corresponds to pattern 3 for "accomplish" in CPA.

We also associate SUMO attributes to the CPA patterns with more than 10 examples (716 verbs). There are many patterns of SUMO attributes for any CPA frame or induced frame, since each filler word in a particular slot can have more than one SUMO attribute. We filter out the non-discriminative SUMO attributes following the technique described in Popescu (2013). Using this, we obtain SUMO attributes for both CPA clusters and induced frames, and we can use the standard entropy-based measures to evaluate the match between the two types of patterns: E — entropy, RC — recovery rate, and P — purity (Li et al., 2004):

$$E = \sum_{j=1}^{K} \frac{m_j}{m} \cdot e_j, \quad RC = 1 - \sum_{j,i=1}^{K,L} \frac{p_{ij}}{m_i}, \tag{5}$$

$$P = \sum_{j=1}^{K} \frac{m_j}{m} \cdot p_j, \quad p_j = \max_i p_{ij}, \tag{6}$$

$$e_j = \sum_{i=1}^{L} p_{ij} \log_2 p_{ij}, \quad p_{ij} = \frac{m_{ij}}{m_i}, \tag{7}$$

where m_j is the number of induced frames corresponding to topic j, m_{ij} is the number of induced frames in cluster j and annotated with the CPA pattern i, m is the total number of induced frames, L is the number of CPA patterns, and K is the number of induced frames.

We also consider a K-means clustering process, with K set as 2 or 3 depending on the number of SUMO-attributed patterns. The K-means evaluation is carried out considering only the centroid of the cluster, which corresponds to the prototypical induced semantic frame with SUMO attributes. We compute E, RC and P using formulae (5) - (7) for each verb and then compute the macro average, considering all the frames and only the K-means centroids, respectively. The results for the induced web frames are displayed in Table 4.

The evaluation method presented here overcomes some of the drawbacks of the previous approaches (Materna, 2012; Materna, 2013). First, we did not limit the evaluation to the most frequent patterns. Second, the mapping was carried out automatically and not by hand. The results above compare favorably with the previous approaches, especially considering that no filtering procedures were applied to the induced frames. We anticipate that the results based on the prototypical induced frames with SUMO attributes would be competitive. Our post-analysis revealed that the entropy can be lowered further if an automatic filtering based on frequencies is applied.

4.5 Evaluation of the Quality of Selectional Preferences

We also investigated the quality of selectional preferences within the induced semantic frames. The only publicly available test data for selectional preferences, to our knowledge, is from Chambers and Jurafsky (2010). This data consists of quadruples (verb, relation, word, confounder) and does not contain their context.[7]

A typical way for using our semantic frames is to select an appropriate frame for an input sentence and judge the eligibility of the word uses against the selected frame. However, due to the lack of context for the above data, it is difficult to select a corresponding semantic frame for a test quadruple and thus the induced semantic frames cannot be naturally applied to this data. To investigate the potential for selectional preferences of the semantic frames, we approximately match a quadruple with each of the semantic frames of the verb and select the frame that has the highest probability as follows:

$$P(w) = \max_i P(w|v, rel, f_i), \tag{8}$$

where w is the word or confounder, v is the verb, rel is the relation and f_i is a semantic frame. By comparing the probabilities of the word and the confounder, we select either of them according to the higher probability. For tie breaking in the case that no frames are found for the verb or both the word and confounder are not found in the case slot, we randomly select either of them in the same way as Chambers and Jurafsky (2010).

We use the "neighbor frequency" set, which is the most difficult among the three sets included in the data. It contains 6,767 quadruples and the relations consist of three classes: subject, object and preposition, which has no distinction of actual prepositions. To link these relations with our case slots, we manually aligned the subject with the nsubj (nominal subject) slot, the object with the dobj (direct object) slot and the preposition with prep_* (all the prepositions) slots. For the preposition relation, we choose the highest probability among all the preposition slots in a frame. To match the generalized ⟨name⟩ with the word in a quadruple, we change the word to ⟨name⟩ if it is capitalized and not a capitalized personal pronoun.

Our semantic frames from the Gigaword corpus achieved an accuracy of 81.7%[8] and those from the web corpus achieved an accuracy of 80.2%. This slight deterioration seems to come from the noise in the web corpus. The best performance in Chambers and Jurafsky (2010) is 81.7% on this "neighbor frequency" set, which was achieved by conditional probabilities with the Erk (2007)'s smoothing method calculated from the English Gigaword corpus. Our approach for selectional preferences does not use smoothing like Erk (2007), but it achieved equivalent performance to the previous work. If we applied our semantic frames to a verb instance with its context, a more precise judgment of selectional preferences would be possible with appropriate frame selection.

5 Conclusion

This paper has described an unsupervised method for inducing semantic frames from instances of each verb in giga-word corpora. This method is clustering based on the Chinese Restaurant Process. The resulting frame data are open to the public and also can be searched by inputting a verb via our web interface.[9]

As applications of the resulting frames, we plan to integrate them into syntactic parsing, semantic role labeling and verb sense disambiguation. For instance, Kawahara and Kurohashi (2006b) improved accuracy of dependency parsing based on Japanese semantic frames automatically induced from a large raw corpus. It is valuable and promising to apply our semantic frames to these NLP tasks.

[7] A document ID of the English Gigaword corpus is available, but it is difficult to recover the context of each instance from this information.

[8] Since the dataset was created from the NYT 2001 portion of the English Gigaword Corpus, we built semantic frames again from the Gigaword corpus except this part.

[9] http://nlp.ist.i.kyoto-u.ac.jp/member/kawahara/cf/crp.en/

Acknowledgments

This work was supported by Kyoto University John Mung Program and JST CREST. We gratefully acknowledge the support of the National Science Foundation Grant NSF 1116782 - RI: Small: A Bayesian Approach to Dynamic Lexical Resources for Flexible Language Processing. Any opinions, findings, and conclusions or recommendations expressed in this material are those of the authors and do not necessarily reflect the views of the National Science Foundation.

References

Omri Abend and Ari Rappoport. 2010. Fully unsupervised core-adjunct argument classification. In *Proceedings of the 48th Annual Meeting of the Association for Computational Linguistics*, pages 226–236.

David Aldous. 1985. Exchangeability and related topics. *École d'Été de Probabilités de Saint-Flour XIII —1983*, pages 1–198.

Collin Baker, Charles J. Fillmore, and John Lowe. 1998. The Berkeley FrameNet Project. In *Proceedings of the 36th Annual Meeting of the Association for Computational Linguistics and 17th International Conference on Computational Linguistics*, pages 86–90.

Hans C. Boas. 2002. Bilingual framenet dictionaries for machine translation. In *Proceedings of the 3rd International Conference on Language Resources and Evaluation*, pages 1364–1371.

Ted Briscoe and John Carroll. 1997. Automatic extraction of subcategorization from corpora. In *Proceedings of the 5th Conference on Applied Natural Language Processing*, pages 356–363.

Aljoscha Burchardt and Anette Frank. 2006. Approximating textual entailment with LFG and FrameNet frames. In *Proceedings of the 2nd PASCAL Recognizing Textual Entailment Workshop*, pages 92–97.

Nathanael Chambers and Daniel Jurafsky. 2010. Improving the use of pseudo-words for evaluating selectional preferences. In *Proceedings of the 48th Annual Meeting of the Association for Computational Linguistics*, pages 445–453.

Marie-Catherine de Marneffe, Bill MacCartney, and Christopher D. Manning. 2006. Generating typed dependency parses from phrase structure parses. In *Proceedings of the 5th International Conference on Language Resources and Evaluation*, pages 449–454.

Michael Ellsworth and Adam Janin. 2007. Mutaphrase: Paraphrasing with framenet. In *Proceedings of the ACL-PASCAL Workshop on Textual Entailment and Paraphrasing*, pages 143–150.

Katrin Erk. 2007. A simple, similarity-based model for selectional preferences. In *Proceedings of the 45th Annual Meeting of the Association of Computational Linguistics*, pages 216–223.

Ingrid Falk, Claire Gardent, and Jean-Charles Lamirel. 2012. Classifying french verbs using french and english lexical resources. In *Proceedings of the 50th Annual Meeting of the Association for Computational Linguistics*, pages 854–863.

Trond Grenager and Christopher D. Manning. 2006. Unsupervised discovery of a statistical verb lexicon. In *Proceedings of the 2006 Conference on Empirical Methods in Natural Language Processing*, pages 1–8.

Patrick Hanks. 2012. How people use words to make meanings: Semantic types meet valencies. *Input, Process and Product: Developments in Teaching and Language Corpora*, pages 54–69.

Daisuke Kawahara and Sadao Kurohashi. 2006a. Case frame compilation from the web using high-performance computing. In *Proceedings of the 5th International Conference on Language Resources and Evaluation*, pages 1344–1347.

Daisuke Kawahara and Sadao Kurohashi. 2006b. A fully-lexicalized probabilistic model for Japanese syntactic and case structure analysis. In *Proceedings of the Human Language Technology Conference of the NAACL*, pages 176–183.

Karin Kipper-Schuler. 2005. *VerbNet: A Broad-Coverage, Comprehensive Verb Lexicon*. Ph.D. thesis, University of Pennsylvania.

Anna Korhonen, Yuval Krymolowski, and Ted Briscoe. 2006. A large subcategorization lexicon for natural language processing applications. In *Proceedings of the 5th International Conference on Language Resources and Evaluation*, pages 345–352.

Joel Lang and Mirella Lapata. 2010. Unsupervised induction of semantic roles. In *Human Language Technologies: The 2010 Annual Conference of the North American Chapter of the Association for Computational Linguistics*, pages 939–947.

Joel Lang and Mirella Lapata. 2011a. Unsupervised semantic role induction via split-merge clustering. In *Proceedings of the 49th Annual Meeting of the Association for Computational Linguistics: Human Language Technologies*, pages 1117–1126.

Joel Lang and Mirella Lapata. 2011b. Unsupervised semantic role induction with graph partitioning. In *Proceedings of the 2011 Conference on Empirical Methods in Natural Language Processing*, pages 1320–1331.

Tao Li, Sheng Ma, and Mitsunori Ogihara. 2004. Entropy-based criterion in categorical clustering. In *Proceedings of the 21st International Conference on Machine Learning*, volume 4, pages 536–543.

Thomas Lippincott, Anna Korhonen, and Diarmuid Ó Séaghdha. 2012. Learning syntactic verb frames using graphical models. In *Proceedings of the 50th Annual Meeting of the Association for Computational Linguistics*, pages 420–429.

Edward Loper, Szu-Ting Yi, and Martha Palmer. 2007. Combining lexical resources: mapping between PropBank and VerbNet. In *Proceedings of the 7th International Workshop on Computational Linguistics*.

Christopher Manning. 1993. Automatic acquisition of a large subcategorization dictionary from corpora. In *Proceedings of the 31st Annual Meeting of the Association for Computational Linguistics*, pages 235–242.

Jiří Materna. 2012. LDA-Frames: An unsupervised approach to generating semantic frames. In Alexander Gelbukh, editor, *Proceedings of the 13th International Conference CICLing 2012, Part I*, volume 7181 of *Lecture Notes in Computer Science*, pages 376–387. Springer Berlin / Heidelberg.

Jiří Materna. 2013. Parameter estimation for LDA-Frames. In *Proceedings of the 2013 Conference of the North American Chapter of the Association for Computational Linguistics: Human Language Technologies*, pages 482–486.

Ashutosh Modi, Ivan Titov, and Alexandre Klementiev. 2012. Unsupervised induction of frame-semantic representations. In *Proceedings of the NAACL-HLT Workshop on the Induction of Linguistic Structure*, pages 1–7.

Srini Narayanan and Sanda Harabagiu. 2004. Question answering based on semantic structures. In *Proceedings of the 20th International Conference on Computational Linguistics*, pages 693–701.

Ian Niles and Adam Pease. 2001. Towards a standard upper ontology. In *Proceedings of the International Conference on Formal Ontology in Information Systems*, pages 2–9.

Martha Palmer, Daniel Gildea, and Paul Kingsbury. 2005. The proposition bank: An annotated corpus of semantic roles. *Computational Linguistics*, 31(1):71–106.

Christopher Parisien and Suzanne Stevenson. 2009. Modelling the acquisition of verb polysemy in children. In *Proceedings of the CogSci2009 Workshop on Distributional Semantics beyond Concrete Concepts*, pages 17–22.

Christopher Parisien and Suzanne Stevenson. 2010. Learning verb alternations in a usage-based Bayesian model. In *Proceedings of the 32nd annual meeting of the Cognitive Science Society*.

Hoifung Poon and Pedro Domingos. 2009. Unsupervised semantic parsing. In *Proceedings of the 2009 Conference on Empirical Methods in Natural Language Processing*, pages 1–10.

Octavian Popescu. 2013. Learning corpus patterns using finite state automata. In *Proceedings of the 10th International Conference on Computational Semantics*, pages 191–203.

Roi Reichart and Anna Korhonen. 2013. Improved lexical acquisition through DPP-based verb clustering. In *Proceedings of the 51st Annual Meeting of the Association for Computational Linguistics*, pages 862–872.

Ryohei Sasano, Daisuke Kawahara, Sadao Kurohashi, and Manabu Okumura. 2013. Automatic knowledge acquisition for case alternation between the passive and active voices in Japanese. In *Proceedings of the 2013 Conference on Empirical Methods in Natural Language Processing*, pages 1213–1223.

Lin Sun and Anna Korhonen. 2009. Improving verb clustering with automatically acquired selectional preferences. In *Proceedings of the 2009 Conference on Empirical Methods in Natural Language Processing*, pages 638–647.

Mihai Surdeanu, Sanda Harabagiu, John Williams, and Paul Aarseth. 2003. Using predicate-argument structures for information extraction. In *Proceedings of the 41st Annual Meeting of the Association for Computational Linguistics*, pages 8–15.

Ivan Titov and Alexandre Klementiev. 2011. A Bayesian model for unsupervised semantic parsing. In *Proceedings of the 49th Annual Meeting of the Association for Computational Linguistics: Human Language Technologies*, pages 1445–1455.

Ivan Titov and Alexandre Klementiev. 2012. A Bayesian approach to unsupervised semantic role induction. In *Proceedings of the 13th Conference of the European Chapter of the Association for Computational Linguistics*, pages 12–22.

Andreas Vlachos, Anna Korhonen, and Zoubin Ghahramani. 2009. Unsupervised and constrained dirichlet process mixture models for verb clustering. In *Proceedings of the Workshop on Geometrical Models of Natural Language Semantics*, pages 74–82.

David Yarowsky. 1993. One sense per collocation. In *Proceedings of the Workshop on Human Language Technology*, pages 266–271.

Automated Verb Sense Labelling Based on Linked Lexical Resources

Kostadin Cholakov[1] **Judith Eckle-Kohler**[2,3] **Iryna Gurevych**[2,3]
[1] Humboldt-Universität zu Berlin, kostadin.cholakov@anglistik.hu-berlin.de
[2] Ubiquitous Knowledge Processing Lab (UKP-TUDA)
Dept. of Computer Science, Technische Universität Darmstadt
[3] Ubiquitous Knowledge Processing Lab (UKP-DIPF)
German Institute for Educational Research and Educational Information
http://www.ukp.tu-darmstadt.de

Abstract

We present a novel approach for creating sense annotated corpora automatically. Our approach employs shallow syntactico-semantic patterns derived from linked lexical resources to automatically identify instances of word senses in text corpora. We evaluate our labelling method intrinsically on SemCor and extrinsically by using automatically labelled corpus text to train a classifier for verb sense disambiguation. Testing this classifier on verbs from the English MASC corpus and on verbs from the Senseval-3 all-words disambiguation task shows that it matches the performance of a classifier which has been trained on manually annotated data.

1 Introduction

Sense annotated corpora are important resources in NLP as they can be used as training data (e.g., for word sense disambiguation (WSD) or semantic role labelling) or as sources for the acquisition of lexical information (e.g., selectional preference information). Typically, a particular sense inventory from a lexical resource is used to annotate some or all words with word senses from this sense inventory. For instance, various sense-annotated corpora based on WordNet (WN; (Fellbaum, 1998)) exist, such as the data from the Senseval competitions,[1] or the SemCor corpus.[2] Such corpora are usually created manually which is expensive and time consuming. Furthermore, the corpora are often domain specific (e.g. newspaper texts) which makes statistical systems trained on them strongly biased.

We present a novel approach for creating sense annotated corpora automatically. Our approach employs shallow syntactico-semantic patterns derived from linked lexical resources (LLRs) to automatically identify instances of word senses in text corpora. We significantly extend previous work on this task by making two important contributions: (i) we employ a large-scale LLR for automatically creating sense annotated data and (ii) we perform meaningful intrinsic and application-based evaluations of our method on large sense annotated datasets.

LLRs are the result of integrating several lexical-semantic resources by linking them at the word sense level. Examples of large LLRs are the multilingual BabelNet (Navigli and Ponzetto, 2012), an integration of wordnets and Wikipedia[3], or UBY, (Gurevych et al., 2012), the resource we employ in our work here. UBY is an integration of multiple resources, such as wordnets, Wikipedia, Wiktionary (WKT)[4], FrameNet (FN; (Baker et al., 1998)) and VerbNet (VN; (Kipper et al., 2008)) for English and German.

A distinguishing feature of LLRs is the enriched sense representation for word senses that are interlinked since different resources provide different, often complementary information. Annotating corpora with such enriched sense representations turns them into versatile training data for statistical systems.

Our first contribution (i) also addresses a considerable gap in recent research regarding automated sense labelling of verbs. Most previous work is done on nouns. However, verbs pose a bigger challenge due to their high polysemy and the fact that, unlike nouns, syntax is of crucial importance because it often reflects particular aspects of verb meaning. That is why, here we focus on verbs and present results and evaluations for this previously neglected part-of-speech (POS). Our method, however, can be applied to other parts-of

[1] http://www.senseval.org

[2] http://www.cse.unt.edu/~rada/downloads.html#semcor

[3] http://www.wikipedia.org

[4] http://www.wiktionary.org

speech as well.

Regarding (ii), we are the first to perform meaningful intrinsic and extrinsic evaluations of automatically labelled data on a larger scale. The intrinsic evaluation measures the performance of our method on the manually annotated SemCor corpus. The extrinsic evaluation compares the performance of a classifier for verb sense disambiguation (VSD) which has been trained (a) on automatically sense labelled data and (b) on manually annotated data. Both settings achieve very similar results which means that competitive VSD can be performed without the need of costly manually created training data. This could be beneficial in languages (e.g., German, Spanish) for which elaborate lexical-semantic resources exist but large, high-quality sense annotated corpora are unavailable. Moreover, we experiment with various linkings between lexical resources in order to investigate how different resource combinations affect the performance of automated sense labelling. We show that combining all available resources might not be the best option.

The remainder of the paper is organised as follows. Section 2 presents our method. Section 3 describes the data used in the experiments. Section 4 presents the results of the evaluations. Section 5 analyses in detail the differences between our method and previous work. Section 6 concludes the paper.

2 Automated Labelling of Verb Senses

This section describes our novel approach for automated sense labelling of verbs in a corpus, which exploits the added value of LLRs.

2.1 Approach

Our approach to automatically label corpus instances of verb senses with sense identifiers from an LLR is based on a *pattern-based representation of verb senses*. Such patterns constitute a *common format* for the representation of verb senses available in LLRs and verb instances found in corpora. The common format we developed resembles a syntactico-semantic clause pattern which we call a sense pattern (SP). Based on a comparison of the derived SPs by means of a similarity metric, verb instances in a corpus can automatically be labelled with sense identifiers from an LLR.

SPs can be derived from corpus instances and from information given in LLRs, in particular, sense examples and more abstract predicate argument structure information.

2.2 Step 1: Creation of SPs from LLRs

For the creation of SPs, we employ the large-scale LLR UBY which combines 10 lexical resources for English and German to make use of the enriched verb sense representations provided by the sense links between various resources available in UBY. Although our method can work with any LLR, we choose UBY because the various resources are represented in a standardised format (Eckle-Kohler et al., 2012) and sense links between them can uniformly and conveniently be accessed via the freely available UBY-API.[5]

Since we evaluate our method on data annotated with WN senses, we create SPs for *enriched* WN senses (see example given in Table 1). We enrich WN senses by aggregating lexical information that can be accessed through links given in UBY to corresponding verb senses in other resources.

In this setting, enrichment means that we make use of sense examples from WN, from FN via the WN–FN linking, and from WKT via the WN–WKT linking. In addition, we use abstract predicate-argument structure information from VN via the WN–VN linking (see Table 1).[6]

For phrasal verb senses (e.g., *write up*) and other verbal multiword expressions (e.g., *know what's going on*) listed in WN, UBY rarely provides links to other resources. Therefore, we induced sense links by following the one sense per collocation assumption.[7] Based on this assumption, we linked each sense of a verbal multiword verb lemma in WN with each sense of the same multiword lemma in FN and WKT.

From sense examples, we derive two different kinds of SPs. Based on a fragment of a sense example given by a window w around the target verb lemma we create: (i) lemma SPs (LSPs) consisting only of lemmas (including the target verb) and (ii) abstract SPs (ASPs) consisting of the target verb lemma and items from a fixed, linguistically motivated vocabulary. This is based on the intuition that LSPs are important to identify relatively fixed

[5] `http://code.google.com/p/uby/`

[6] Although VN is linked to sense examples given in the PropBank corpus, the rationale behind using just abstract predicate-argument structure information was to explore, which effect this type of information has on the performance of an automated labelling algorithm.

[7] It assumes that nearby words provide strong and consistent clues to the sense of a target word, see Yarowsky (1995).

	WN sense tell%2:32:00:: (*let something be known*)	Corresponding sense patterns (SPs)
WN	*Tell them that you will be late*	LSP – **tell** them that you will be ASP – **tell** PP that PP be JJ
WN–FN	*But an insider told TODAY : ' There was no animosity.'*	LSP – but an insider **tell** Today : ' there be ASP – person **tell** location be feeling
WN–WKT	*Please tell me the time.*	LSP – Please **tell** me the time ASP – **tell** PP event
WN–VN	Agent$[+animate \| + organization]$ V Recipient$[+animate \| + organization]$ about Topic$[+communication]$	ASP – PP **tell** group about communication

Table 1: Examples of SPs derived from an enriched WN sense in UBY. PP, JJ, and VV are POS tags from the Penn Treebank tagset, standing for personal pronoun, adjective and full verb.

verbal multiword expressions in a corpus, whereas ASPs are necessary to identify productively used verb senses that are constrained in their use only by their syntactic behaviour and particular semantic properties, such as selectional preferences on their arguments.

The fixed vocabulary used for the creation of ASPs consists of (i) the target verb lemma, (ii) selected POS tags from the Penn Treebank Tagset (Marcus et al., 1993), (iii) a list of particular function words that play an important role in fine-grained subcategorisation frames of verbs (Eckle-Kohler and Gurevych, 2012) and (iv) semantic categories of nouns given by WN semantic fields. We selected POS tags that play an important role in syntactic realisations of verbs, e.g. POS tags for personal pronouns which are potential verb arguments. In our experiments, we tried different sets of function words and POS tags. For instance, we found that some function words (e.g., reflexive pronouns) and some POS tags (e.g., those for past participles and comparative adjectives) introduced too much noise in the data and therefore we did not select them for the final vocabulary.[8]

In order to create SPs from sense examples, we apply POS tagging and lemmatisation using the TreeTagger (Schmid, 1994) and named entity tagging using the Stanford Named Entity Recogniser (Klein et al., 2003). The named entity tags attached by the Named Entity Recogniser are mapped to WN semantic fields.

For the generation of ASPs from sense examples, we used a window size of $w = 7$, while the generation of LSPs has been performed with $w = 5$ in order to put a focus on the closely neighbouring lexemes in multiword verb lemmas. The window size was set empirically using the English Lexical Sample task of the Senseval-2 dataset as a development set. The same set was also used for the development of the linguistically motivated vocabulary for ASPs.[9]

From the abstract predicate-argument structure information given in VN, we derived only ASPs. For this, we employed the subcategorisation frames, as well as the semantic role and selectional preference information from VN, and created ASPs based on manually created mappings between these information types and the controlled vocabulary used for ASPs.

2.3 Step 2: Automated Labelling

For the automated labelling of verbs in a corpus, we first derive SPs from each corpus sentence containing a target verb. SPs are derived from corpus sentences by applying the same procedure as described in Step 1 for the creation of SPs from sense examples, the window size used is $w = 7$.

To compare two SPs, we propose a similarity metric based on Dice's coefficient which calculates the sum of the weighted number of their common bi-grams, tri-grams, and four-grams. Formally, the similarity score $sim_w \in [0..1]$ of two SPs p_1, p_2 is defined as:

$$(1) \qquad sim_w(p_1, p_2) = \frac{\sum_{n=2}^{4} |G_n(p_1) \cap G_n(p_2)| \cdot n}{norm_w}$$

where $w >= 1$ is the size of the window around the target verb, $G_n(p_i), i \in \{1, 2\}$ is the set of n-

[8]The vocabulary used for the creation of ASPs is available at http://www.ukp.tu-darmstadt.de/data/.

[9]However, the Senseval-2 data are annotated with sense keys of the WN pre-release version 1.7 and therefore, we had to employ an automated mapping of WN 1.7 pre-release to WN 3.0 sense keys provided by Rada Mihalcea. Since this mapping turned out to be rather noisy, we did not use the Senseval-2 data in our evaluations.

Automated labelling of corpus instances

for each sentence s_i with verb v
derive LSP_i and ASP_i

forall $j = sizeOf$(UBY-LSP(v))
compare LSP_i with LSP_j in UBY-LSP(v):
$maxSim(LSP_i) = argmax_j score(LSP_i, LSP_j)$
add sense($argmax_j$) to MostSimilarSenses(LSP_i)

forall $k = sizeOf$(UBY-ASP(v))
compare ASP_i with ASP_k in UBY-ASP(v):
$maxSim(ASP_i) = argmax_k score(ASP_i, ASP_k)$
add sense($argmax_k$) to MostSimilarSenses(ASP_i)

if $maxSim_{i,j} >=$ threshold t and
$maxSim_{i,j} >= maxSim_{i,k}$
label(s_i) = random(MostSimilarSenses(LSP_i))
else if $maxSim_{i,k} >=$ threshold t
label(s_i) = random(MostSimilarSenses(ASP_i))
end if
end for

Table 2: Algorithm for labelling corpus instances with WordNet senses.

grams occurring in SP p_i, and $norm_w$ is the normalisation factor defined by the sum of the maximum number of common bigrams, trigrams and fourgrams in the window w. Similarity metrics based on Dice's coefficient have often been used in Lesk-based WSD (Lesk, 1986) to calculate the overlap of two sets (e.g., Baldwin et al. (2010)). In our case, however, the elements of the two sets are bigrams, trigrams and fourgrams, while in Lesk-based algorithms typically sets of unigrams are compared, thus not accounting for word order.

Table 2 shows the algorithm used for automated labelling of corpus instances in pseudo-code. The algorithm assumes that for each verb v, the corresponding set of SPs derived from UBY sense examples (UBY-LSP(v) and UBY-ASP(v) in Table 2) has already been computed.

For each corpus sentence containing a target verb v, the corresponding SPs for verb v derived from UBY are scored by the similarity metric in (1). The SPs with the maximum score that is above a threshold t form the set of most similar senses. From this set, the algorithm picks one sense randomly as a label. How often this happens, depends on the value of t: the percentage of randomly selected senses ranges from about 33% for $t = 0.14$ to about 50% for $t = 0.04$.

3 Data

Web corpora. For the automated labelling of corpus data with WN senses, we use two very large web corpora: the English ukWaC corpus (Baroni et al., 2009) and the article pages extracted from the English Wikipedia using the Java-based Wikipedia API JWPL (Zesch et al., 2008). Further, for the evaluation of our method, we use three manually sense annotated data sets.

SemCor. We use the SemCor 3.0 corpus which is annotated with WN 3.0 senses.

MASC. MASC is a balanced subset of 500K words of written texts and transcribed speech drawn primarily from the Open American National Corpus (OANC).[10] The texts come from 19 different genres which allows us to test our method on real-life data from multiple sources. The corpus is annotated with various types of linguistic information, including WN 3.0 sense annotations for instances of selected words. Therefore, MASC is a *lexical sample* corpus.

We extracted instances of 16 MASC verbs (11,997 instances) which have been sense annotated. Most instances are annotated by multiple annotators and, to create a gold standard, we took the sense preferred by the majority of annotators and ignored instances where there were ties.

Senseval-3. In the test corpus of the Senseval-3 all-words disambiguation task sense annotations are provided for each content word in a chunk of the WSJ corpus (5,000 words of running text). The third annotated data set for our experiment is formed by extracting all verb instances from this test corpus. Note that the gold standard annotations in Senseval-3 were made using WN 1.7.1. In our experiments, we use Rada Mihalcea's conversion of the corpus to WN 3.0.[11] However, we found out that some verb instances were converted to sense labels that do not exist in WN 3.0. After removing those instances, there were 305 verbs with 592 instances left.

4 Experiments and Evaluation

Next, we present the intrinsic and the application-based evaluations of our method.

4.1 Intrinsic Evaluation

We intrinsically evaluate the performance of the automated labelling algorithm for the Senseval-3 verbs which occur in the SemCor corpus. Occurrences of these 152 verbs in SemCor are processed

[10] http://www.americannationalcorpus.org/

[11] http://www.cse.unt.edu/~rada/downloads.html#sensevalsemcor

	WN–FN–WKT			WN–FN–WKT–VN		
t	Cov (Inst.)	Cov (Sense)	Acc	Cov (Inst.)	Cov (Sense)	Acc
0.04	0.55	0.27	0.32	0.48	0.25	0.35
0.07	0.15	0.17	0.36	0.13	0.15	0.42
0.1	0.11	0.14	0.35	0.10	0.13	0.42
0.14	0.02	0.07	0.41	0.02	0.05	0.47

Table 3: Performance of the automated labelling algorithm evaluated for occurrences of Senseval-3 verbs in SemCor.

by the labelling algorithm with a window size $w = 7$ and the automatically annotated WN 3.0 senses are compared with the gold senses available in SemCor 3.0.

Quantitative Evaluation. We calculated the accuracy as the percentage of correctly labelled instances and the instance coverage as the percentage of labelled instances. The sense coverage is calculated as the percentage of all predicted (not annotated) senses relative to all gold verb senses given in SemCor.

A random sense baseline yields 15% accuracy. Note that a MFS baseline based on WN would not be meaningful, because the WordNet MFS is based on the frequency distribution of annotated senses in SemCor.

Table 3 shows accuracy and coverage results of the automated labelling algorithm for different values of the threshold t and two combinations of sense links from UBY. Depending on the threshold t, 2% to 55% of the verb instances in SemCor can automatically be labelled, and the instance coverage goes largely in parallel to the coverage of predicted WN senses. Accuracy ranges between 32% and 47% and exceeds the random sense baseline by a large margin. Lowering the threshold increases the coverage of the labelling method, but it also leads to a decrease in accuracy of 9 percentage points (12 for the configuration with VN).

Adding more patterns from VN via the WN–VN alignment, leads to a decrease in both instance and sense coverage combined with an increase in accuracy. Since SemCor is a rather small corpus, the increase in instance coverage is not as clear as for large Web corpora such as the ukWaC corpus. Labelling a 1GB subset of the ukWaC corpus based on patterns derived from the WN–FN–WKT alignments resulted in 15MB of labelled data, whereas 25MB labelled data could be created from the same subset with the additional patterns from the WN–VN alignment.

Qualitative Analysis. In Table 4, we show examples of the highest ranking patterns and the corresponding labelled SemCor instances for senses that were correctly and falsely annotated. The examples in Table 4 show that the similarity metric assigns the highest values to instances where function words (e.g., *in, to, who*) or POS tags (e.g., PP, VV) from the ASP vocabulary occur in the immediate neighbourhood of the target verb. Since such functions words play an important role in the ASPs derived from VN, the VN ASPs possibly tend to dominate over the SPs derived from sense examples, which explains the observed decrease in coverage (see Table 3).

The falsely labelled instances turn out to be examples of WN senses where the gold sense is very similar to the automatically attached sense as evident from the synset definition given in the rightmost column.

4.2 Extrinsic Evaluation

We extrinsically evaluate our method for automated verb sense labelling by using it for learning a classifier for VSD in a train-test setting. We use features which have been widely used in supervised WSD systems, in particular features based on dependency parsing. While this might seem to be in contrast to our labelling algorithm which is based on shallow linguistic preprocessing, it is fully justified by the purpose of our extrinsic evaluation: The main purpose of the extrinsic evaluation is not to outperform state-of-the-art VSD systems, but to show that, when operating with reasonable features, a classifier trained on the data automatically labelled with our method performs equally well as when this classifier is trained on manually annotated data.

4.2.1 Features

The training and test data are parsed with the Stanford parser (Klein and Manning, 2003) which provides Stanford Dependencies output (De Marneffe et al., 2006) as well as phrase structure trees. We employ the Stanford Named Entity Recogniser to identify named entities. We then extract lexical, syntactic, and semantic features from the parse results for classification.

Lexical features include the lemmas and POS tags of the two words before and after the target verb. To extract **syntactic features** we select all dependency relations from the parser output in

SemCor instance	SP derived from SemCor	score	WN sense ID (gold sense in brackets)
Some of the New York Philharmonic musicians who **live** *in the suburbs spent yesterday morning digging themselves free from snow.*	of group person who **live** in location VVD time time VVG	0.29	live%2:42:08:: (live%2:42:08::)
These societies can **expect** *to face difficult times.*	group **expect** to VV JJ event	0.22	expect%2:31:01:: (expect%2:31:01::)
As autumn starts its annual sweep , few Americans and Canadians **realize** *how fortunate they are in having the world 's finest fall coloring.*	JJ attribute JJ person **realize** how JJ PP be in	0.22	realize%2:31:00:: – perceive (an idea or situation) mentally (realize%2:31:01:: – be fully aware or cognizant of)
Dan Morgan told himself he would **forget** *Ann Turner.*	person person VVD PP PP **forget** person location	0.16	forget%2:31:00:: – be unable to remember (forget%2:31:01:: – dismiss from the mind; stop remembering)

Table 4: Examples of SemCor instances with high similarity scores (upper half shows correctly labelled instances, lower half incorrectly labelled instances.

which the target verb is related to a noun, a pronoun, or a named entity. For each selected word, the lemma of the word (or the named entity tag in case of proper nouns) is combined with the type of the dependency relation which exists between it and the verb to form a separate feature. In a similar feature, the lemma of the selected word is replaced by its POS tag. The **semantic features** include all synsets found in WN for nominal arguments of the verb. Personal pronouns are mapped to 'person' and the three synsets found in WN 3.0 for this word are taken as features.

4.2.2 Train and Test Data

Using exactly the same method as intrinsically evaluated in section 4.1, we automatically labelled occurrences of the 16 MASC verbs and the 305 Senseval-3 verbs in both web corpora with WN senses. Only occurrences with similarity score above 0.1 are labelled – all other occurrences are discarded. We refer to the resulting data as *automatically labelled corpus* (ALC) and use it as training data for statistical VSD.

Instances of the test verbs found in SemCor are also used as training data in order to compare the performance of the classifier in a fully supervised setting.

MASC. There are 22 senses with instances in MASC which are not found in SemCor. For the ALC this number is 34. However, in the latter there are 27 senses, instances of which are unseen in MASC. 20 of those represent phrasal verbs which we attribute to the special treatment of such verbs in our method.

The classifier cannot correctly classify senses which are not seen in the training data. The coverage of the ALC is 88.05% and that of SemCor — 94.8%. The SemCor data can mainly cover more test instances of 3 verbs — *launch*, *rule*, and *transfer* — the WN senses of which lack sense examples or links to other senses in UBY. Unlike the hand-labelled SemCor data, our automated sense labelling method is limited to the information found in the LLR used. However, there are also 330 MASC instances covered by the ALC only. Those are mostly instances of phrasal verbs, such as *rip off* and *show up*. Note that the definition of coverage we use here makes its values the upper bounds for the performance of the classifier.

Senseval-3. We also generated training data automatically for the 305 Senseval verbs. However, only 152 of those verbs (442 instances) are found in SemCor. This means we cannot train the classifier for the remaining Senseval verbs. The coverage of the SemCor training data for the 152 verbs which can be classified is 96.15% and that of the ALC — 95.25%. For all 592 Senseval test instances, the coverage of the ALC is 90.38%.

4.2.3 Results and Analysis

We trained a separate logistic regression classifier for each test verb in the two datasets using the WEKA data mining software (Hall et al., 2009) with default parameters. The classifiers were trained with features extracted from (i) the SemCor hand-labelled data and (ii) the ALC.

MASC. The classifier achieves 50.23% accuracy when SemCor is used and 49% when the ALC is employed. The difference in the results is not statistically significant at $p < 0.05$. The MFS baseline scores at 41.72%.

Senseval-3. The classifier achieves 43.24% with the ALC. We assigned the MFS to each of the 143 test verbs not found in SemCor since we cannot train the classifier for those. The achieved accuracy is 45.2%. We also measured accuracy in a setup where no MFS back-off strategy was employed for SemCor (152 test verbs with 442 instances). When trained on SemCor data, the classifier achieves 48.64% accuracy compared to 47.51% for the ALC. All differences in the results are not statistically significant at $p < 0.05$. Finally, the MFS baseline accuracy is significantly lower at 25.34% for all 305 test verbs.

For both test datasets, the overall performance of the classifier when trained on automatically labelled data is very close to the setting in which manually created training data is employed. We thus conclude that the quality of the data produced by our sense labelling method is sufficient and these data can be directly used for training a statistical VSD classifier. As a reference, the state-of-the-art supervised VSD system described in Chen and Palmer (2009) achieves 64.8% accuracy on the Senseval-2 fine-grained data. However, we cannot compare to this result due to the different sense inventory which the Senseval-2 data were annotated with.

4.2.4 Sense Links

In order to investigate the effect of LLRs, we performed experiments in which sense examples found in WN only were used. We also experimented with various combinations of the resources available in UBY to determine the contribution of each of those to our method. Table 5 shows the results. The setting which includes only WN has the worst performance, thus clearly showing the benefits of using LLRs. Next, the inclusion of WKT improves both coverage and accuracy. We conclude that WKT plays an important role in discovering additional verb senses. Finally, similarly to the results of the intrinsic evaluation, adding VN to the mix increases slightly the coverage but decreases accuracy.

5 Related Work and Discussion

Our work is related to previous research on (i) using a combination of lexical resources for knowledge-based WSD, (ii) using lexical resources for distant supervision, and (iii) the automated acquisition of sense-annotated data.

	MASC		Senseval	
	Cov	Acc	Cov	Acc
WN	0.6573	0.3498	0.6372	0.3209
WN–FN	0.8562	0.4810	0.8812	0.4172
WN–FN–WKT	0.8805	0.4900	0.9038	0.4324
WN–FN–WKT–VN	0.8822	0.4688	0.9139	0.4054

Table 5: Performance of the various combinations of lexical resources.

Knowledge-based WSD. While the combination of sense-annotated data and wordnets has been described for knowledge-based WSD before (e.g., Navigli and Velardi (2005; Agirre and Soroa (2009) who use graph algorithms), only recently Ponzetto and Navigli (2010) have investigated the impact of the combination of different *lexical resources* on the performance of WSD. They aligned WN senses with Wikipedia articles and employed two simple knowledge-based algorithms, i.e., a Lesk-based algorithm and a graph-based algorithm, to evaluate the resulting LLR for WSD. While their evaluation demonstrates that the use of an LLR boosts the performance of knowledege-based WSD, it is restricted to nouns only since Wikipedia provides very few verb senses. Moreover, lexical resources that are rich in lexical-syntactic information such as VN have not been involved.

Miller et al. (2012) employ a Lesk-based algorithm which makes use of a combination of WN and an automatically acquired distributional thesaurus. Lesk-based algorithms play a central role in knowledge-based WSD. Based on the overlap of the context of the target word and sense definitions in a given sense inventory, they assign the sense with the highest overlap as disambiguation result. We were kindly provided with the system described in Miller et al. (2012) and we were able to test its performance on our test sets. The system achieved only 33.86% and 30.16% accuracy for the MASC and the Senseval-3 verbs, respectively, which is far below the results we presented. This low performance is due to the fact that Lesk-based algorithms do not account for word order. Such information is important especially for verb senses, as the syntactic behaviour of a verb reflects aspects of its meaning.

Distant supervision. Distant supervision is a learning paradigm similar to semi-supervised learning. Unlike semi-supervised methods which typically employ a supervised classifier and a small number of seed instances to do bootstrap learning (Yarowsky, 1995; Mihalcea, 2004; Fujita and Fujino, 2011), in distant supervision training data are created in a single run from scratch by aligning corpus instances with entries in a knowledge base. Distant supervision methods that have used LLRs as knowledge bases have been previously applied in relation extraction, e.g. Freebase (Mintz et al., 2009; Surdeanu et al., 2012) and BabelNet (Krause et al., 2012; Moro et al., 2013). However, as far as we are aware, we are the first to apply distant supervision to the task of verb sense disambiguation.

Acquisition of sense-annotated data. Most previous work on using lexical resources for automatically acquiring sense-annotated data either was mostly restricted to noun senses or, unlike us, did not present a meaningful evaluation. Leacock et al. (1998) describe the automated creation of training data for supervised WSD on the basis of WN as a lexical resource combined with corpus statistics, but they evaluate their approach just on one noun, verb, and adjective, and thus it is unclear whether their results can be generalized. Cuadros and Rigau (2008) used the approach of Leacock et al. (1998) to automatically build a large *KnowNet* from the Web, but they evaluated this resource only for WSD of nouns. However, the system based on KnowNet yields results below the SemCor-MFS baseline. Mihalcea and Moldovan (1999) use WordNet glosses to extract sense examples from the Web via a search engine and use this approach in a subsequent paper (Mihalcea, 2002) to generate a sense tagged corpus. For five randomly selected nouns, they performed a comparative evaluation of a WSD classifier trained on an automatically tagged corpus on the one hand, and on the manually annotated data from the Senseval-2 English lexical sample task on the other hand. The results obtained for these five nouns seem to be similar but the dataset used is too small to draw meaningful conclusions and moreover, it does not cover verbs. Mostow and Duan (2011) presented a system that extracts example contexts for nouns and apply these contexts in (Duan and Yates, 2010) for WSD by using them to label text and train a statistical classifier. An evaluation of this classifier yielded results similar to those obtained by a supervised WSD system.

Kübler and Zhekova (2009) extract example sentences from several English dictionaries and various types of corpora, including web corpora. They employ a Lesk-based algorithm to automatically annotate the target word instances in the extracted example sentences with WN senses and use them in one of their experiments as training data for a WSD classifier. However, the performance of the system decreased significantly achieving the lowest accuracy among all system configurations. The authors provide only the overall accuracy score, so we do not know how disambiguation of verbs was affected.

Summary. We consider the ability to establish a link between the rich knowledge available in LLRs and corpora of any kind to be the main advantage of our automated labelling method. However, to automatically label a suffcient amount of data for supervised learning, very large corpora are required. Our method can be extended to other POS (using sense examples and possibly other types of lexical information), as well as to other languages where (linked) lexical resources are available.

6 Conclusion

In this paper, we presented a novel method for creating sense labelled corpora automatically. We exploit LLRs and perform large-scale intrinsic and application-based evaluations. The results of those evaluations show that the quality of the sense labelled corpora created with our method matches that of manually annotated corpora.

In future research, we plan to use PropBank (Palmer et al., 2005) in order to extract sense examples for VN as well. This might improve the performance of lexical resource combinations which include VN. We will also apply our method to languages (e.g., German) for which lexical resources are available but no or little sense annotated corpora exist.

Acknowledgments

This work has been supported by the Volkswagen Foundation as part of the Lichtenberg- Professorship Program under grant No. I/82806 and by the German Research Foundation under grant No. GU 798/9-1. We would like to thank the anonymous reviewers for their valuable feedback.

References

Eneko Agirre and Aitor Soroa. 2009. Personalizing PageRank for Word Sense Disambiguation. In *Proceedings of the 12th Conference of the European Chapter of the Association for Computational Linguistics (EACL 2009)*, pages 33–41, Athens, Greece.

C.F. Baker, C.J. Fillmore, and J.B. Lowe. 1998. The Berkeley FrameNet project. In *Proceedings of the 36th Annual Meeting of the Association for Computational Linguistics and 17th International Conference on Computational Linguistics-Volume 1*, pages 86–90, Montreal, Canada.

Timothy Baldwin, Sunam Kim, Francis Bond, Sanae Fujita, David Martinez, and Takaaki Tanaka. 2010. A Reexamination of MRD-Based Word Sense Disambiguation. *ACM Transactions on Asian Language Information Processing (TALIP)*, 9(1):4:1–4:21.

Marco Baroni, Silvia Bernardini, Adriano Ferraresi, and Eros Zanchetta. 2009. The WaCky wide web: a collection of very large linguistically processed web-crawled corpora. *Language Resources and Evaluation*, 43(3):209–226.

Jinying Chen and Martha Palmer. 2009. Improving English verb sense disambiguation performance with linguistically motivated features and clear sense distinction boundaries. *Language Resources and Evaluation*, 43:181–208.

Montse Cuadros and German Rigau. 2008. Knownet: Building a large net of knowledge from the web. In *22nd International Conference on Computational Linguistics (COLING)*, pages 161–168, Manchester, UK.

M.C. De Marneffe, B. MacCartney, and C.D. Manning. 2006. Generating typed dependency parses from phrase structure parses. In *Proceedings of the 5th International Conference on Language Resources and Evaluation (LREC 2006)*, pages 449–454, Genoa, Italy.

Weisi Duan and Alexander Yates. 2010. Extracting glosses to disambiguate word senses. In *Human Language Technologies: The 2010 Annual Conference of the North American Chapter of the Association for Computational Linguistics*, HLT '10, pages 627–635, Los Angeles, USA.

Judith Eckle-Kohler and Iryna Gurevych. 2012. Subcat-LMF: Fleshing out a standardized format for subcategorization frame interoperability. In *Proceedings of the 13th Conference of the European Chapter of the Association for Computational Linguistics (EACL 2012)*, pages 550–560, Avignon, France.

Judith Eckle-Kohler, Iryna Gurevych, Silvana Hartmann, Michael Matuschek, and Christian M. Meyer. 2012. UBY-LMF – A uniform format for standardizing heterogeneous lexical-semantic resources in ISO-LMF. In *Proceedings of the 8th International Conference on Language Resources and Evaluation (LREC 2012)*, pages 275–282, Istanbul, Turkey.

Christiane Fellbaum. 1998. *WordNet: An Electronic Lexical Database*. MIT Press, Cambridge, MA, USA.

Sanae Fujita and Akinori Fujino. 2011. Word sense disambiguation by combining labeled data expansion and semi-supervised learning method. In *Proceedings of the 5th International Joint Conference on Natural Language Processing*, pages 676–685, Chiang Mai, Thailand.

Iryna Gurevych, Judith Eckle-Kohler, Silvana Hartmann, Michael Matuschek, Christian M. Meyer, and Christian Wirth. 2012. UBY - a large-scale unified lexical-semantic resource based on LMF. In *Proceedings of the 13th Conference of the European Chapter of the Association for Computational Linguistics (EACL 2012)*, pages 580–590.

Mark Hall, Eibe Frank, Geoffrey Holmes, Bernhard Pfahringer, Peter Reutemann, and Ian H. Witten. 2009. The WEKA data mining software: An update. *ACM SIGKDD Explorations Newsletter*, 11(1):10–18.

Karin Kipper, Anna Korhonen, Neville Ryant, and Martha Palmer. 2008. A large-scale classification of English verbs. *Language Resources and Evaluation*, 42:21–40.

D. Klein and C.D. Manning. 2003. Accurate unlexicalized parsing. In *Proceedings of the 41st Annual Meeting on Association for Computational Linguistics-Volume 1*, pages 423–430, Sapporo, Japan. Association for Computational Linguistics.

Dan Klein, Joseph Smarr, Huy Nguyen, and Christopher D. Manning. 2003. Named entity recognition with character-level models. In *Proceedings of the Seventh Conference on Natural Language Learning at HLT-NAACL 2003*, pages 180–183, Edmonton, Canada.

Sebastian Krause, Hong Li, Hans Uszkoreit, and Feiyu Xu. 2012. Large-scale learning of relation-extraction rules with distant supervision from the web. In *Proceedings of the 11th International Semantic Web Conference*, pages 263–278, Boston, Masachusetts, USA, 11. Springer.

Sandra Kübler and Desislava Zhekova. 2009. Semi-Supervised Learning for Word Sense Disambiguation: Quality vs. Quantity. In *Proceedings of the International Conference RANLP-2009*, pages 197–202, Borovets, Bulgaria.

Claudia Leacock, George A. Miller, and Martin Chodorow. 1998. Using corpus statistics and wordnet relations for sense identification. *Computational Linguistics*, 24(1):147–165.

Michael Lesk. 1986. Automatic sense disambiguation using machine readable dictionaries: how to tell a pine cone from an ice cream cone. In *Proceedings of the 5th Annual International Conference on Systems Documentation*, pages 24–26, Toronto, Ontario, Canada.

Mitchell P. Marcus, Mary Ann Marcinkiewicz, and Beatrice Santorini. 1993. Building a large annotated corpus of english: the penn treebank. *Computational Linguistics*, 19(2):313–330.

Rada Mihalcea and Dan Moldovan. 1999. An automatic method for generating sense tagged corpora. In *Proceedings of the American Association for Artificial Intelligence (AAAI 1999)*, Orlando, Florida, USA.

Rada Mihalcea. 2002. Bootstrapping large sense tagged corpora. In *Proceedings of the Third International Conference of Language Resources and Evaluation (LREC 2002)*, pages 1407–1411, Las Palmas, Canary Islands, Spain.

Rada Mihalcea. 2004. Co-training and self-training for word sense disambiguation. In *Proceedings of the Conference on Computational Natural Language Learning (CoNLL-2004)*, Boston, MA, USA.

Tristan Miller, Chris Biemann, Torsten Zesch, and Iryna Gurevych. 2012. Using distributional similarity for lexical expansion in knowledge-based word sense disambiguation. In *Proceedings of the 24th International Conference on Computational Linguistics (COLING 2012)*, pages 1781–1796, Mumbai, India.

Mike Mintz, Steven Bills, Rion Snow, and Daniel Jurafsky. 2009. Distant supervision for relation extraction without labeled data. In *Proceedings of the Joint Conference of the 47th Annual Meeting of the ACL and the 4th International Joint Conference on Natural Language Processing of the AFNLP*, pages 1003–1011, Suntec, Singapore.

Andrea Moro, Hong Li, Sebastian Krause, Feiyu Xu, Roberto Navigli, and Hans Uszkoreit. 2013. Semantic rule filtering for web-scale relation extraction. In *Proceedings of the 12th International Semantic Web Conference*, Sydney, Australia, 10. Springer.

Jack Mostow and Weisi Duan. 2011. Generating example contexts to illustrate a target word sense. In *Proceedings of the Sixth Workshop on Innovative Use of NLP for Building Educational Applications*, pages 105–110, Portland, Oregon, June. Association for Computational Linguistics.

Roberto Navigli and Simone Paolo Ponzetto. 2012. BabelNet: The automatic construction, evaluation and application of a wide-coverage multilingual semantic network. *Artificial Intelligence*, 193:217–250.

Roberto Navigli and Paola Velardi. 2005. Structural semantic interconnections: A knowledge-based approach to word sense disambiguation. *IEEE Transactions on Pattern Analysis and Machine Intelligence*, 27(7):1075–1086.

Martha Palmer, Dan Gildea, and Paul Kingsbury. 2005. The Proposition Bank: A corpus annotated with semantic roles. *Computational Linguistics*, 31(1):71–105.

Simone Paolo Ponzetto and Roberto Navigli. 2010. Knowledge-rich word sense disambiguation rivaling supervised systems. In *Proceedings of the 48th Annual Meeting of the Association for Computational Linguistics (ACL 2010)*, pages 1522–1531, Uppsala, Sweden.

Helmut Schmid. 1994. Probabilistic part-of-speech tagging using decision trees. In *Proceedings of the International Conference on New Methods in Language Processing*, pages 44–49, Manchester, UK.

Mihai Surdeanu, Julie Tibshirani, Ramesh Nallapati, and Christopher D. Manning. 2012. Multi-instance multi-label learning for relation extraction. In *Proceedings of the 2012 Joint Conference on Empirical Methods in Natural Language Processing and Computational Natural Language Learning*, pages 455–465, Jeju Island, Korea.

David Yarowsky. 1995. Unsupervised word sense disambiguation rivaling supervised methods. In *Proceedings of the 33rd annual meeting on Association for Computational Linguistics*, pages 189–196, Cambridge, Massachusetts, USA.

Torsten Zesch, Christof Müller, and Iryna Gurevych. 2008. Extracting lexical semantic knowledge from wikipedia and wiktionary. In *Proceedings of the 6th International Conference on Language Resources and Evaluation (LREC 2008)*, volume 8, pages 1646–1652, Marrakech, Morocco.

Multi-Granular Aspect Aggregation in Aspect-Based Sentiment Analysis

John Pavlopoulos and **Ion Androutsopoulos**
Department of Informatics
Athens University of Economics and Business
Patission 76, GR-104 34 Athens, Greece
http://nlp.cs.aueb.gr/

Abstract

Aspect-based sentiment analysis estimates the sentiment expressed for each particular aspect (e.g., battery, screen) of an entity (e.g., smartphone). Different words or phrases, however, may be used to refer to the same aspect, and similar aspects may need to be aggregated at coarser or finer granularities to fit the available space or satisfy user preferences. We introduce the problem of aspect aggregation at multiple granularities. We decompose it in two processing phases, to allow previous work on term similarity and hierarchical clustering to be reused. We show that the second phase, where aspects are clustered, is almost a solved problem, whereas further research is needed in the first phase, where semantic similarity measures are employed. We also introduce a novel sense pruning mechanism for WordNet-based similarity measures, which improves their performance in the first phase. Finally, we provide publicly available benchmark datasets.

1 Introduction

Given a set of texts discussing a particular entity (e.g., reviews of a laptop), *aspect-based sentiment analysis* (ABSA) attempts to identify the most prominent (e.g., frequently discussed) aspects of the entity (e.g., battery, screen) and the average sentiment (e.g., 1 to 5 stars) for each aspect or group of aspects, as in Fig. 1. Most ABSA systems perform all or some of the following (Liu, 2012): *subjectivity detection* to retain only sentences (or other spans) expressing subjective opinions; *aspect extraction* to extract (and possibly rank) terms corresponding to aspects (e.g., 'battery'); *aspect aggregation* to group aspect terms that are near-synonyms (e.g., 'price', 'cost') or to obtain aspects at a coarser granularity (e.g., 'chicken','steak', and 'fish' may be replaced by 'food' in restaurant reviews); and *aspect sentiment score estimation* to estimate the average sentiment for each aspect or group of aspects. In this paper, we focus on aspect aggregation, the least studied stage of the four.

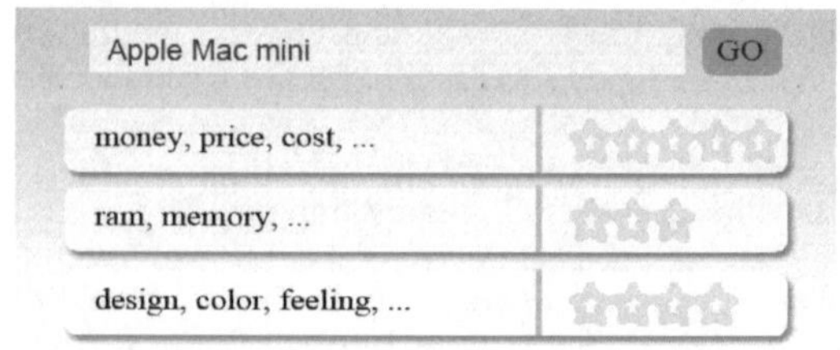

Figure 1: Aspect groups and scores of an entity.

Aspect aggregation is needed to avoid reporting separate sentiment scores for aspect terms that are very similar. In Fig. 1, for example, showing separate lines for 'money', 'price', and 'cost' would be confusing. The extent to which aspect terms should be aggregated, however, also depends on the available space and user preferences. On devices with smaller screens, it may be desirable to aggregate aspect terms that are similar, though not necessarily near-synonyms (e.g., 'design', 'color', 'feeling') to show fewer lines (Fig. 1), but finer aspects may be preferable on larger screens. Users may also wish to adjust the granularity of aspects, e.g., by stretching or narrowing the height of Fig. 1 on a smartphone to view more or fewer lines. Hence, aspect aggregation should be able to produce groups of aspect terms for *multiple granularities*. We assume that the aggregated aspects are displayed as lists of terms, as in Fig. 1. We make no effort to order (e.g., by frequency) the terms in each list, nor do we attempt to produce a single (more general) term to describe each aggregated aspect, leaving such tasks for future work.

ABSA systems usually group synonymous (or near-synonymous) aspect terms (Liu, 2012). Aggregating only synonyms (or near-synonyms), however, does not allow users to select the desirable aspect granularity, and ignores the hierarchical relations between aspect terms. For example, 'pizza' and 'steak' are kinds of 'food' and, hence, the three terms can be aggregated to show fewer, coarser aspects, even though they are not synonyms. Carenini et al. (2005) used a predefined domain-specific taxonomy to hierarchically aggregate aspect terms, but taxonomies of this kind are often not available. By contrast, we use only general-purpose taxonomies (e.g., WordNet), term similarity measures based on general-purpose taxonomies or corpora, and hierarchical clustering.

We define *multi-granular aspect aggregation* to be the task of partitioning a given set of aspect terms (generated by a previous aspect extraction stage) into k non-overlapping clusters, for multiple values of k. A further constraint is that the clusters have to be *consistent* for different k values, meaning that if two aspect terms t_1, t_2 are placed in the same cluster for $k = k_1$, then t_1 and t_2 must also be grouped together (in the same cluster) for every $k = k_2$ with $k_2 < k_1$, i.e., for every coarser grouping. For example, if 'waiter' and 'service' are grouped together for $k = 5$, they must also be grouped together for $k = 4, 3, 2$ and (trivially) $k = 1$, to allow the user to feel that selecting a smaller number of aspect groups (narrowing the height of Fig. 1) has the effect of zooming out (without aspect terms jumping unexpectedly to other aspect groups), and similarly for zooming in.[1] This requirement is satisfied by using agglomerative hierarchical clustering algorithms (Manning and Schütze, 1999; Hastie et al., 2001), which in our case produce term hierarchies like the ones of Fig. 2. By using slices (nodes at a particular depth) of the hierarchies that are closer to the root or the leaves, we obtain fewer or more clusters. The vertical dotted lines of Fig. 2 illustrate two slices for $k = 4$. By contrast, flat clustering algorithms (e.g., k-means) do not satisfy the consistency constraint for different k values.

Agglomerative clustering algorithms require a measure of the distance between individuals, in our case a measure of how similar two aspect terms are, and a linkage criterion to specify which clusters should be merged to form larger (coarser) clusters. To experiment with different term sim-

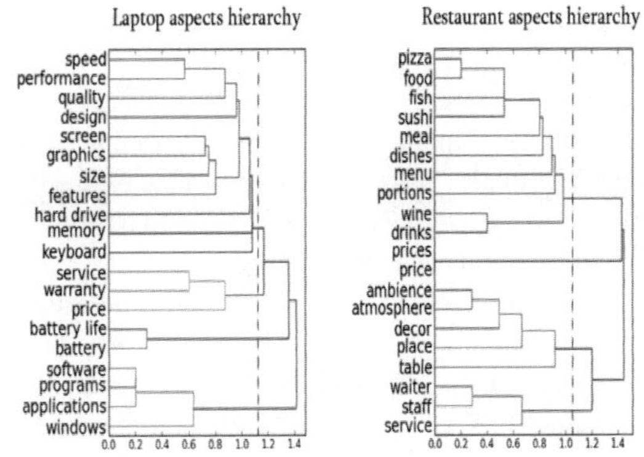

Figure 2: Example aspect hierarchies produced by agglomerative hierarchical clustering.

	food	*fish*	*sushi*	*dishes*	*wine*
food	5	4	4	4	2
fish	4	5	4	2	1
sushi	4	4	5	3	1
dishes	4	2	3	5	2
wine	2	1	1	2	5

Table 1: An aspect term similarity matrix.

ilarity measures and linkage criteria, we decompose multi-granular aspect aggregation in two processing phases. Phase A fills in a symmetric matrix, like the one of Table 1, with scores showing the similarity of each pair of input aspect terms; the matrix in effect defines the distance measure to be used by agglomerative clustering. In Phase B, the aspect terms are grouped into k non-overlapping clusters, for varying values of k, given the matrix of Phase A and a linkage criterion; a hierarchy like the ones of Fig. 2 is first formed via agglomerative clustering, and fewer or more clusters (for different values of k) are then obtained by using different slices of the hierarchy, as already discussed. Our two-phase decomposition can also accommodate non-hierarchical clustering algorithms, provided that the consistency constraint is satisfied, but we consider only agglomerative hierarchical clustering in this paper.

The decomposition in two phases has three main advantages. Firstly, it allows reusing previous work on term similarity measures (Zhang et al., 2013), which can be used to fill in the matrix of Phase A. Secondly, the decomposition allows different linkage criteria to be experimentally compared (in Phase B) using the same similarity matrix (of Phase A), i.e., the same distance

[1] We also require the clusters to be non-overlapping to make this zooming in and out metaphor clearer to the user.

measure. Thirdly, the decomposition leads to high inter-annotator agreement, as we show experimentally. By contrast, in preliminary experiments we found that asking humans to directly evaluate aspect hierarchies produced by hierarchical clustering, or to manually create gold aspect hierarchies led to poor inter-annotator agreement.

We show that existing term similarity measures perform reasonably well in Phase A, especially when combined, but there is a large scope for improvement. We also propose a novel *sense pruning* method for WordNet-based similarity measures, which leads to significant improvements in Phase A. In Phase B, we experiment with agglomerative clustering using four different linkage criteria, concluding that they all perform equally well and that Phase B is almost a solved problem when the gold similarity matrix of Phase A is used; however, further improvements are needed in the similarity measures of Phase A to produce a sufficiently good similarity matrix. We also make publicly available the datasets of our experiments.

Our main contributions are: (i) to the best of our knowledge, we are the first to consider multi-granular aspect aggregation (not just merging near-synonyms) in ABSA *without* manually crafted domain-specific ontologies; (ii) we propose a two-phase decomposition that allows previous work on term similarity and hierarchical clustering to be reused and evaluated with high inter-annotator agreement; (iii) we introduce a novel sense pruning mechanism that improves WordNet-based similarity measures; (iv) we provide the first public datasets for multi-granular aspect aggregation; (v) we show that the second phase of our decomposition is almost a solved problem, and that research should focus on the first phase. Although we experiment with customer reviews of products and services, ABSA and the work of this paper in particular are, at least in principle, also applicable to texts expressing opinions about other kinds of entities (e.g., politicians, organizations).

Section 2 below discusses related work. Sections 3 and 4 present our work for Phase A and B, respectively. Section 5 concludes.

2 Related work

Most existing approaches to aspect aggregation aim to produce a single, *flat* partitioning of aspect terms into aspect groups, rather than aspect groups at multiple granularities. The most common approaches (Liu, 2012) are to aggregate only synonyms or near-synonyms, using WordNet (Liu et al., 2005), statistics from corpora (Chen et al., 2006; Bollegala et al., 2007a; Lin and Wu, 2009), or semi-supervised learning (Zhai et al., 2010; Zhai et al., 2011), or to cluster the aspect terms using (latent) topic models (Titov and McDonald, 2008a; Guo et al., 2009; Brody and Elhadad, 2010; Jo and Oh, 2011). Topic models do not perform better than other methods (Zhai et al., 2010), and their clusters may overlap.[2] The topic model of Titov et al. (2008b) uses two granularity levels; we consider many more (3–10 levels).

Carenini et al. (2005) used a *predefined domain-specific* taxonomy and similarity measures to aggregate related terms. Yu et al. (2011) used a tailored version of an existing taxonomy. By contrast, we assume no domain-specific taxonomy. Kobayashi et al. (2007) proposed methods to extract aspect terms and relations between them, including hierarchical relations. They extract, however, relations by looking for clues in texts (e.g., particular phrases). By contrast, we employ similarity measures and hierarchical clustering, which allows us to group similar aspect terms even when they do not cooccur in texts. Also, in contrast to Kobayashi et al. (2007), we respect the consistency constraint discussed in Section 1.

A similar task is taxonomy induction. Cimiano and Staab (2005) automatically construct taxonomies from texts via agglomerative clustering, much as in our Phase B, but not in the context of ABSA, and without trying to learn a similarity matrix first. They also label the hierarchy's concepts, a task we do not consider. Klapaftis and Manandhar (2010) show how word sense induction can be combined with agglomerative clustering to obtain more accurate taxonomies, again not in the context of ABSA. Our sense pruning method was influenced by their work, but is much simpler than their word sense induction. Fountain and Lapata (2012) study unsupervised methods to induce concept taxonomies, without considering ABSA.

3 Phase A

We now discuss our work for Phase A. Recall that in this phase the input is a set of aspect terms and

[2]Topic models are typically also used to perform aspect extraction, apart from aspect aggregation, but simple heuristics (e.g., most frequent nouns) often outperform them in aspect extraction (Liu, 2012; Moghaddam and Ester, 2012).

the goal is to fill in a matrix (Table 1) with scores showing the similarity of each pair of aspect terms.

3.1 Datasets used in Phase A

We used two benchmark datasets that we had previously constructed to evaluate ABSA methods for subjectivity detection, aspect extraction, and aspect score estimation, but not aspect aggregation. We extended them to support aspect aggregation, and we make them publicly available.[3]

The two original datasets contain sentences from customer reviews of restaurants and laptops, respectively. The reviews are manually split into sentences, and each sentence is manually annotated as 'subjective' (expressing opinion) or 'objective' (not expressing opinion). The restaurants dataset contains 3,710 English sentences from the restaurant reviews of Ganu et al. (2009). The laptops dataset contains 3,085 English sentences from 394 customer reviews, collected from sites that host customer reviews. In the experiments of this paper, we use only the 3,057 (out of 3,710) subjective restaurant sentences and the 2,631 (out of 3,085) subjective laptop sentences.

For each subjective sentence, our datasets show the words that human annotators marked as aspect terms. For example, in "The *dessert* was divine!" the aspect term is 'dessert', and in "Really bad *waiter*." it is 'waiter'. Among the 3,057 subjective restaurant sentences, 1,129 contain exactly one aspect term, 829 more than one, and 1,099 no aspect term; a subjective sentence may express an opinion about the restaurant (or laptop) being reviewed without mentioning a specific aspect (e.g., "Really nice restaurant!"), which is why no aspect terms are present in some subjective sentences. There are 558 distinct multi-word aspect terms and 431 distinct single-word aspect terms in the subjective restaurant sentences. Among the 2,631 subjective sentences of the laptop reviews, 823 contain exactly one aspect term, 389 more than one, and 1,419 no aspect term. There are 273 distinct multi-word aspect terms and 330 distinct single-word aspect terms in the subjective laptop sentences.

From each dataset, we selected the 20 (distinct) aspect terms that the human annotators had annotated most frequently, taking annotation frequency to be an indicator of importance; there are only two multi-word aspect terms ('hard drive', 'battery life') among the 20 most frequent ones in the laptops dataset, and none among the 20 most frequent aspect terms of the restaurants dataset. We then formed all the 190 possible pairs of the 20 terms and constructed an empty similarity matrix (Fig. 1), one for each dataset, which was given to three human judges to fill in (1: strong dissimilarity, 5: strong similarity).[4] For each aspect term, all the subjective sentences mentioning the term were also provided, to help the judges understand how the terms are used in the particular domains (e.g., 'window' and 'Windows' have domain-specific meanings in laptop reviews).

The Pearson correlation coefficient indicated high inter-annotator agreement (0.81 for restaurants, 0.74 for laptops). We also measured the absolute inter-annotator agreement $a(l_1, l_2)$, defined below, where l_1, l_2 are lists containing the scores (similarity matrix values) of two judges, N is the length of each list, and v_{max}, v_{min} are the largest and smallest possible scores (5 and 1).

$$a(l_1, l_2) = \frac{1}{N} \sum_{i=1}^{N} \left[1 - \frac{|l_1(i) - l_2(i)|}{v_{max} - v_{min}} \right]$$

The absolute interannotator agreement was also high (0.90 for restaurants, 0.91 for laptops).[5] With both measures, we compute the agreement of each judge with the averaged (for each matrix cell) scores of the other two judges, and we report the mean of the three agreement estimates. Finally, we created the *gold* similarity matrix of each dataset by placing in each cell the average scores that the three judges had provided for that cell.

In preliminary experiments, we gave aspect terms to human judges, asking them to group any terms they considered near-synonyms. We then asked the judges to group the aspect terms into fewer, coarser groups by grouping terms that could be viewed as direct hyponyms of the same broader term (e.g., 'pizza' and 'steak' are both kinds of 'food'), or that stood in a hyponym-hypernym relation (e.g., 'pizza' and 'food'). We used the Dice coefficient to measure inter-annotator agreement, and we obtained reasonably good agreement for near-synonyms (0.77 for restaurants, 0.81 for laptops), but poor agreement for the coarser as-

[3]The datasets are available at `http://nlp.cs.aueb.gr/software.html`.

[4]The matrix is symmetric; hence, the judges had to fill in only half of it. The guidelines and an annotation tool that were given to the judges are available upon request.

[5]The Pearson correlation ranges from −1 to 1, whereas the absolute inter-annotator agreement ranges from 0 to 1.

pects (0.25 and 0.11).[6] In other preliminary experiments, we asked human judges to rank alternative aspect hierarchies that had been produced by applying agglomerative clustering with different linkage criteria to 20 aspect terms, but we obtained very poor inter-annotator agreement (Pearson score -0.83 for restaurants and 0 for laptops).

3.2 Phase A methods

We employed five term similarity measures. The first two are WordNet-based (Budanitsky and Hirst, 2006). The next two combine WordNet with statistics from corpora. The fifth one is a corpus-based distributional similarity measure.

The first measure is *Wu and Palmer's* (1994). It is actually a sense similarity measure (a term may have multiple senses). Given two senses $s_{ij}, s_{i'j'}$ of terms $t_i, t_{i'}$, the measure is defined as follows:

$$WP(s_{ij}, s_{i'j'}) = 2 \cdot \frac{depth(lcs(s_{ij}, s_{i'j'}))}{depth(s_{ij}) + depth(s_{ij})},$$

where $lcs(s_{ij}, s_{i'j'})$ is the *least common subsumer*, i.e., the most specific common ancestor of the two senses in WordNet, and $depth(s)$ is the depth of sense s in WordNet's hierarchy.

Most terms have multiple senses, however, and word sense disambiguation methods (Navigli, 2009) are not yet robust enough. Hence, when given two aspect terms $t_i, t_{i'}$, rather than particular senses of the terms, a simplistic *greedy* approach is to compute the similarities of all the possible pairs of senses $s_{ij}, s_{i'j'}$ of $t_i, t_{i'}$, and take the similarity of $t_i, t_{i'}$ to be the maximum similarity of the sense pairs (Bollegala et al., 2007b; Zesch and Gurevych, 2010). We use this greedy approach with all the WordNet-based measures, but we also propose a sense pruning mechanism below, which improves their performance. In all the WordNet-based measures, if a term is not in WordNet, we take its similarity to any other term to be zero.[7]

The second measure, $PATH(s_{ij}, s_{i'j'})$, is simply the inverse of the length (plus one) of the shortest path connecting the senses $s_{ij}, s_{i'j'}$ in WordNet (Zhang et al., 2013). Again, the greedy approach can be used with terms having multiple senses.

The third measure is *Lin's* (1998), defined as:

$$LIN(s_{ij}, s_{i'j'}) = \frac{2 \cdot ic(lcs(s_{ij}, s_{i'j'}))}{ic(s_{ij}) + ic(s_{i'j'})},$$

where $s_{ij}, s_{i'j'}$ are senses of terms $t_i, t_{i'}$, $lcs(s_{ij}, s_{i'j'})$ is the least common subsumer of $s_{ij}, s_{i'j'}$ in WordNet, and $ic(s) = -\log P(s)$ is the *information content* of sense s (Pedersen et al., 2004), estimated from a corpus. When the corpus is not sense-tagged, we follow the common approach of treating each occurrence of a word as an occurrence of all of its senses, when estimating $ic(s)$.[8] We experimented with two variants of Lin's measure, one where the $ic(s)$ scores were estimated from the Brown corpus (Marcus et al., 1993), and one where they were estimated from the (restaurant or laptop) reviews of our datasets.

The fourth measure is *Jiang and Conrath's* (1997), defined below. Again, we experimented with two variants of $ic(s)$, as above.

$$JCN(s_{ij}, s_{i'j'}) = \frac{1}{ic(s_{ij}) + ic(s_{i'j'}) - 2 \cdot lcs(s_{ij}, s_{i'j'})}$$

For all the above WordNet-based measures, we experimented with a *sense pruning* mechanism, which discards some of the senses of the aspect terms, before applying the greedy approach. For each aspect term t_i, we consider all of its WordNet senses s_{ij}. For each s_{ij} and each other aspect term $t_{i'}$, we compute (using $PATH$) the similarity between s_{ij} and each sense $s_{i'j'}$ of $t_{i'}$, and we consider the *relevance* of s_{ij} to $t_{i'}$ to be:[9]

$$rel(s_{ij}, t_{i'}) = \max_{s_{i'j'} \in senses(t_{i'})} PATH(s_{ij}, s_{i'j'})$$

The relevance of s_{ij} to *all* of the N other aspect terms $t_{i'}$ is taken to be:

$$rel(s_{ij}) = \frac{1}{N} \cdot \sum_{i' \neq i} rel(s_{ij}, t_{i'})$$

For each aspect term t_i, we retain only its senses s_{ij} with the top $rel(s_{ij})$ scores, which tends to

[6] The Dice coefficient ranges from 0 to 1. There was a very large number of possible responses the judges could provide and, hence, it would be inappropriate to use Cohen's K.

[7] This never happened in the restaurants dataset. In the laptops dataset, it only happened for 'hard drive' and 'battery life'. We use the NLTK implementation of the first four measures (see `http://nltk.org/`) and our own implementation of the distributional similarity measure.

[8] `http://www.d.umn.edu/~tpederse/Data/README-WN-IC-30.txt`. We use the default counting.

[9] We also experimented with other similarity measures when computing $rel(s_{ij}, t_{i'})$, instead of $PATH$, but there was no significant difference. We use NLTK to tokenize, remove punctuation, and stop-words.

	without SP		with SP	
Method	*Rest.*	*Lapt.*	*Rest.*	*Lapt.*
WP	0.475	0.216	0.502	0.265
PATH	**0.524**	0.301	0.529	0.332
LIN@domain	0.390	0.256	0.456	0.343
LIN@Brown	0.434	0.329	0.471	0.391
JCN@domain	0.467	0.348	0.509	0.448
JCN@Brown	0.403	0.469	0.419	0.539
DS	0.283	**0.517**	(0.283)	(0.517)
AVG	0.499	0.352	0.537	0.426
WN	0.490	0.328	0.530	0.395
WNDS	0.523	0.453	**0.545**	**0.546**

Table 2: Phase A results (Pearson correlation to gold similarities) *with* and *without* sense pruning.

prune senses that are very irrelevant to the particular domain (e.g., laptops). This sense pruning mechanism is novel, and we show experimentally that it improves the performance of all the WordNet-based similarity measures we examined.

We also implemented a *distributional similarity* measure (Harris, 1968; Padó and Lapata, 2007; Cimiano et al., 2009; Zhang et al., 2013). Following Lin and Wu (2009), for each aspect term t, we create a vector $\vec{v}(t) = \langle PMI(t, w_1), \ldots, PMI(t, w_n)\rangle$. The vector components are the Pointwise Mutual Information scores of t and each word w_i of a corpus:

$$PMI(t, w_i) = -\log \frac{P(t, w_i)}{P(t) \cdot P(w_i)}$$

We treat $P(t, w_i)$ as the probability of t, w_i cooccurring in the same sentence, and we use the (laptop or restaurant) reviews of our datasets as the corpus to estimate the probabilities. The distributional similarity $DS(t, t')$ of two aspect terms t, t' is the cosine similarity of $\vec{v}(t), \vec{v}(t')$.[10]

Finally, we tried combinations of the similarity measures: *AVG* is the average of all five; *WN* is the average of the first four, which employ WordNet; and *WNDS* is the average of *WN* and *DS*; all the scores range in $[0, 1]$. We also tried regression (e.g., SVR), but there was no improvement.

3.3 Phase A experimental results

Each similarity measure was evaluated by computing its Pearson correlation with the scores of the gold similarity matrix. Table 2 shows the results.

Our sense pruning consistently improves all four WordNet-based measures. It does not apply to *DS*, which is why the *DS* results are identical with and without pruning. A paired t test indicates that the other differences (with and without pruning) of Table 2 are statistically significant ($p < 0.05$). We used the senses with the top five $rel(s_{ij})$ scores for each aspect term t_i during sense pruning. We also experimented with keeping fewer senses, but the results were inferior or there was no improvement.

Lin's measure performed better when information content was estimated on the (much larger, but domain-independent) Brown corpus (*LIN@Brown*), as opposed to using the (domain-specific) reviews of our datasets (*LIN@domain*), but we observed no similar consistent pattern for *JCN*. Given its simplicity, *PATH* performed remarkably well in the restaurants dataset; it was the best measure (including combinations) without sense pruning, and the best uncombined measure with sense pruning. It performed worse, however, compared to several other measures in the laptops dataset. Similar comments apply to *WP*, which is among the top-performing uncombined measures in restaurants, both with and without sense pruning, but the worst overall measure in laptops. *DS* is the best overall measure in laptops when compared to measures without sense pruning, and the third best overall when compared to measures that use sense pruning, but the worst overall in restaurants both with and without pruning. *LIN* and *JCN*, which use both WordNet and corpus statistics, have a more balanced performance across the two datasets, but they are not top-performers in any of the two. *Combinations of similarity measures seem more stable across domains*, as the results of *AVG*, *WN*, and *WNDS* indicate, though experiments with more domains are needed to investigate this issue. *WNDS is the best overall method with sense pruning*, and among the best three methods without pruning in both datasets.

To get a better view of the performance of *WNDS* with sense pruning, i.e., the best overall measure of Table 2, we compared it to two state of the art semantic similarity systems. First, we applied the system of Han et al. (2013), one of the best systems of the recent *Sem 2013 semantic text similarity competition, to our Phase A data. The performance (Pearson correlation with gold similarities) of the same system on the widely used *WordSim353* word similarity dataset (Agirre et al., 2009) is 0.73, much higher than the same system's performance on our Phase A data (see Table 3),

[10] We also experimented with Euclidean distance, a normalized *PMI* (Bouma, 2009), and the Brown corpus, but there was no improvement.

Method	Restaurants	Laptops
Han et al. (2013)	0.450	0.471
Word2Vec	0.434	0.485
WNDS with SP	**0.545**	**0.546**
Judge 1	0.913	0.875
Judge 2	0.914	0.894
Judge 3	0.888	0.924

Table 3: Phase A results (Pearson correlation to gold similarities) of *WNDS* with SP against semantic similarity systems and human judges.

which suggests that our data are more difficult.[11]

We also employed the recent *Word2Vec* system, which computes continuous vector space representations of words from large corpora and has been reported to improve results in word similarity tasks (Mikolov et al., 2013). We used the English Wikipedia to compute word vectors with 200 features.[12] The similarity between two aspect terms was taken to be the cosine similarity of their vectors. This system performed better than Han et al.'s with laptops, but not with restaurants.

Table 3 shows that *WNDS (with sense pruning) performed clearly better than the system of Han et al. and Word2Vec*. Table 3 also shows the Pearson correlation of each judge's scores to the gold similarity scores, as an indication of the best achievable results. Although *WNDS* (with sense pruning) performs reasonably well in both domains,[13] *there is large scope for improvement.*

4 Phase B

In Phase B, the aspect terms are to be grouped into k non-overlapping clusters, for varying values of k, given a Phase A similarity matrix. We experimented with both the gold similarity matrix of Phase A and similarity matrices produced by *WNDS* (with SP), the best Phase A method.

4.1 Phase B methods

We experimented with agglomerative clustering and four linkage criteria: *single*, *complete*, *average*, and *Ward* (Manning and Schütze, 1999; Hastie et al., 2001). Let $d(t_1, t_2)$ be the distance of two individual instances t_1, t_2; in our case, the instances are aspect terms and $d(t_1, t_2)$ is the inverse of the similarity of t_1, t_2, defined by the Phase A similarity matrix (gold or produced by *WNDS*). Different linkage criteria define differently the distance of two clusters $D(C_1, C_2)$, which affects the choice of clusters that are merged to produce coarser (higher-level) clusters:

$$D_{single}(C_1, C_2) = \min_{t_1 \in C_1, t_2 \in C_2} d(t_1, t_2)$$

$$D_{compl}(C_1, C_2) = \max_{t_1 \in C_1, t_2 \in C_2} d(t_1, t_2)$$

$$D_{avg}(C_1, C_2) = \frac{1}{|C_1||C_2|} \sum_{t_1 \in C_1} \sum_{t_2 \in C_2} d(t_1, t_2)$$

Complete linkage tends to produce more compact clusters, compared to single linkage, with average linkage being in between. Ward minimizes the total in-cluster variance; consult Milligan (1980) for further details.[14]

4.2 Phase B experimental results

To evaluate the k clusters produced at each aspect granularity by the different linkage criteria, we used the *Silhouette Index* (*SI*) (Rousseeuw, 1987), a cluster evaluation measure that considers both inter- and intra-cluster coherence.[15] Given a set of clusters $\{C_1, \ldots, C_k\}$, each $SI(C_i)$ is defined as:

$$SI(C_i) = \frac{1}{|C_i|} \cdot \sum_{j=1}^{|C_i|} \frac{b_j - a_j}{\max(b_j, a_j)},$$

where a_j is the mean distance from the j-th instance of C_i to the other instances in C_i, and b_j is the mean distance from the j-th instance of C_i to the instances in the cluster nearest to C_i. Then:

$$SI(\{C_1, \ldots, C_k\}) = \frac{1}{k} \cdot \sum_{i=1}^{k} SI(C_i)$$

We always use the correct (gold) distances of the instances (terms) when computing the *SI* scores.

As shown in Fig. 3, *no linkage criterion clearly outperforms the others, when the gold matrix of Phase A is used*; all four criteria perform reasonably well. Note that the *SI* ranges from -1 to

[11]The system of Han et al. (2013) is available from http://semanticwebarchive.cs.umbc.edu/SimService/; we use the STS similarity.

[12]*Word2Vec* is available from https://code.google.com/p/word2vec/. We used the continuous bag of words model with default parameters, the first billion characters of the English Wikipedia, and the preprocessing of http://mattmahoney.net/dc/textdata.html.

[13]Recall that the Pearson correlation ranges from -1 to 1.

[14]We used the SciPy implementations of agglomerative clustering with the four criteria (see http://www.scipy.org), relying on *maxclust* to obtain the slice of the resulting hierarchy that leads to k (or approx. k) clusters.

[15]We used the *SI* implementation of Pedregosa et al. (2011); see http://scikit-learn.org/. We also experimented with the Dunn Index (Dunn, 1974) and the Davies-Bouldin Index (1979), but we obtained similar results.

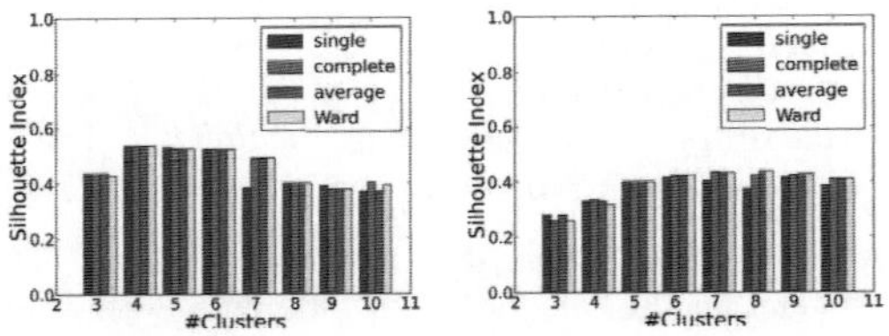

(a) restaurants (b) laptops

Figure 3: Silhouette Index (SI) results for Phase B, using the **gold** similarity matrix of Phase A.

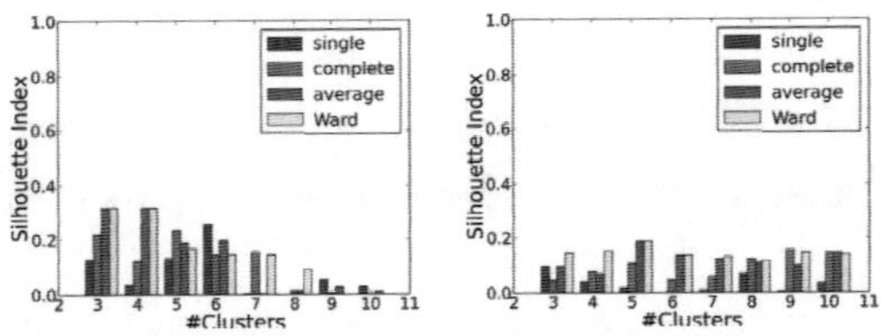

(a) restaurants (b) laptops

Figure 4: SI results for Phase B, using the **WNDS (with SP)** similarity matrix of Phase A.

1, with higher values indicating better clustering. Figure 4 shows that *when the similarity matrix of WNDS (with SP) is used, the SI scores deteriorate significantly*; again, there is no clear winner among the linkage criteria, but average and Ward seem to be overall better than the others.

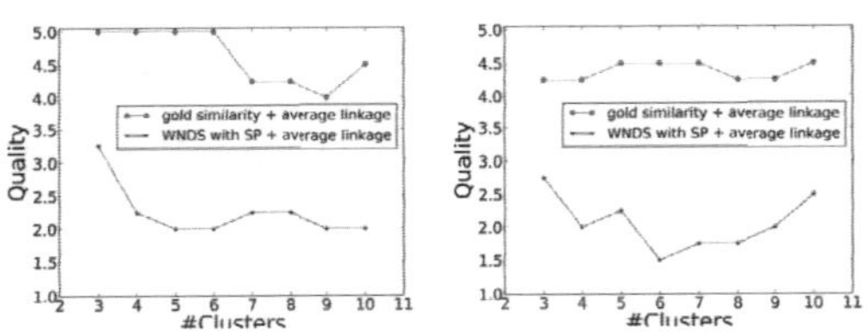

(a) Restaurants (b) Laptops

Figure 5: Human evaluation of aspect groups.

In a final experiment, we showed clusterings of varying granularities (k values) to four human judges (graduate CS students). The clusterings were produced by two systems: one that used the *gold similarity matrix* of Phase A and agglomerative clustering with average linkage in Phase B, and one that used the *similarity matrix of WNDS* (with SP) and again agglomerative clustering with average linkage. We showed all the clusterings to all the judges. Each judge was asked to evaluate each clustering on a 1–5 scale. We measured the absolute inter-annotator agreement, as in Section 3.1, and found high agreement in all cases (0.93 and 0.83 for the two systems, respectively, in restaurants; 0.85 for both in laptops).[16]

Figure 5 shows the average human scores of the two systems for different granularities. The judges considered the aspect groups always perfect or near-perfect when the gold similarity matrix of Phase A was used, but they found the aspect groups to be of rather poor quality when the similarity matrix of the best Phase A measure was used. These results, along with those of Fig. 3–4, show that *more effort needs to be devoted to improving the similarity measures of Phase A, whereas Phase B is in effect an almost solved problem*, if a good similarity matrix is available.

5 Conclusions

We considered a new, more demanding form of aspect aggregation in ABSA, which aims to aggregate aspects at multiple granularities, as opposed to simply merging near-synonyms, and without assuming that manually crafted domain-specific ontologies are available. We decomposed the problem in two processing phases, which allow previous work on term similarity and hierarchical clustering to be reused and evaluated appropriately with high inter-annotator agreement. We showed that the second phase, where we used agglomerative clustering, is an almost solved problem, whereas further research is needed in the first phrase, where term similarity measures are employed. We also introduced a sense pruning mechanism that significantly improves WordNet-based similarity measures, leading to a measure that outperforms state of the art similarity methods in the first phase of our decomposition. We also made publicly available the datasets of our experiments.

Acknowledgments

We thank G. Batistatos, A. Zosakis, and G. Lampouras for their annotations in Phase A. We thank A. Kosmopoulos, G. Lampouras, P. Malakasiotis, and I. Lourentzou for their annotations in Phase B.

[16]The Pearson correlation cannot be computed, as several judges gave the same rating to the first system, for all k.

References

E. Agirre, E. Alfonseca, K. Hall, J. Kravalova, M. Paşca, and A. Soroa. 2009. A study on similarity and relatedness using distributional and wordnet-based approaches. In *Proceedings of the Annual Conference of NAACL*, pages 19–27, Boulder, CO, USA.

D. Bollegala, Y. Matsuo, and M. Ishizuka. 2007a. An integrated approach to measuring semantic similarity between words using information available on the web. In *Proceedings of HLT-NAACL*, pages 340–347, Rochester, NY, USA.

D. Bollegala, Y. Matsuo, and M. Ishizuka. 2007b. Measuring semantic similarity between words using web search engines. In *Proceedings of the 16th International Conference of WWW*, volume 766, pages 757–766, Banff, Alberta, Canada.

G. Bouma. 2009. Normalized (pointwise) mutual information in collocation extraction. *Proceedings of the Biennial Conference of GSCL*, pages 31–40.

S. Brody and N. Elhadad. 2010. An unsupervised aspect-sentiment model for online reviews. In *Proceedings of the Annual Conference of NAACL*, pages 804–812, Los Angeles, CA, USA.

A. Budanitsky and G. Hirst. 2006. Evaluating WordNet-based measures of lexical semantic relatedness. *Computational Linguistics*, 32(1):13–47.

G. Carenini, R. T. Ng, and E. Zwart. 2005. Extracting knowledge from evaluative text. In *Proceedings of the 3rd International Conference on Knowledge Capture*, pages 11–18, Banff, Alberta, Canada.

H. Chen, M. Lin, and Y. Wei. 2006. Novel association measures using web search with double checking. In *Proceedings of the 21st International Conference of COLING and the 44th Annual Meeting of ACL*, pages 1009–1016, Sydney, Australia.

P. Cimiano and S. Staab. 2005. Learning concept hierarchies from text with a guided hierarchical clustering algorithm. In *Proceedings of ICML – Workshop on Learning and Extending Lexical Ontologies with Machine Learning Methods*, Bonn, Germany.

P. Cimiano, A. Mädche, S. Staab, and J. Völker. 2009. Ontology learning. In *Handbook on Ontologies*, pages 245–267. Springer.

D. L. Davies and D. W. Bouldin. 1979. A cluster separation measure. *IEEE Transactions on Pattern Analysis and Machine Intelligence*, 1(2):224–227.

J. C. Dunn. 1974. Well-separated clusters and optimal fuzzy partitions. *Journal of Cybernetics*, 4(1):95–104.

T. Fountain and M. Lapata. 2012. Taxonomy induction using hierarchical random graphs. In *Proceedings of NAACL:HLT*, pages 466–476, Montreal, Canada.

G. Ganu, N. Elhadad, and A. Marian. 2009. Beyond the stars: Improving rating predictions using review text content. In *Proceedings of the 12th International Workshop on the Web and Databases*, Providence, RI, USA.

H. Guo, H. Zhu, Z. Guo, X. Zhang, and Z. Su. 2009. Product feature categorization with multilevel latent semantic association. In *Proceedings of the 18th CIKM*, pages 1087–1096.

L. Han, A. Kashyap, T. Finin, J. Mayfield, and J. Weese. 2013. Umbc_ebiquity-core: Semantic textual similarity systems. In *Proceedings of the 2nd Joint Conference on Lexical and Computational Semantics*, pages 44–52, Atlanta, GA, USA.

Z. Harris. 1968. *Mathematical Structures of Language*. Wiley.

T. Hastie, R. Tibshirani, and J. Friedman. 2001. *The Elements of Statistical Learning*. Springer.

J. J. Jiang and D. W. Conrath. 1997. Semantic similarity based on corpus statistics and lexical taxonomy. In *Proceedings of ROCLING*, pages 19–33, Taiwan, China.

Y. Jo and A. H. Oh. 2011. Aspect and sentiment unification model for online review analysis. In *Proceedings of the 4th International Conference of WSDM*, pages 815–824, Hong Kong, China.

I. P. Klapaftis and S. Manandhar. 2010. Taxonomy learning using word sense induction. In *Proceedings of NAACL*, pages 82–90, Los Angeles, CA, USA.

N. Kobayashi, K. Inui, and Y. Matsumoto. 2007. Extracting aspect-evaluation and aspect-of relations in opinion mining. In *Proceedings of the Joint Conference on EMNLP-CoNLL*, pages 1065–1074, Prague, Czech Republic.

D. Lin and X. Wu. 2009. Phrase clustering for discriminative learning. In *Proceedings of ACL*, pages 1030–1038, Suntec, Singapore. ACL.

D. Lin. 1998. An information-theoretic definition of similarity. In *Proceedings of the 15th ICML*, pages 296–304, Madison, WI, USA.

B. Liu, M. Hu, and J. Cheng. 2005. Opinion observer: analyzing and comparing opinions on the web. In *Proceedings of the 14th International Conference of WWW*, pages 342–351, Chiba, Japan.

B. Liu. 2012. *Sentiment Analysis and Opinion Mining*. Synthesis Lectures on Human Language Technologies. Morgan & Claypool.

C. D. Manning and H. Schütze. 1999. *Foundations of Statistical Natural Language Processing*. MIT Press, Cambridge, MA, USA.

M. P. Marcus, M. A. Marcinkiewicz, and B. Santorini. 1993. Building a large annotated corpus of english: The penn treebank. *Computational Linguistics*, 19(2):313–330.

T. Mikolov, C. Kai, G. Corrado, and J. Dean. 2013. Efficient estimation of word representations in vector space. *CoRR*, abs/1301.3781.

G.W. Milligan. 1980. An examination of the effect of six types of error perturbation on fifteen clustering algorithms. *Psychometrika*, 45(3):325–342.

S. Moghaddam and M. Ester. 2012. On the design of lda models for aspect-based opinion mining. In *Proceedings of the 21st CIKM*, pages 803–812, Maui, HI, USA.

R. Navigli. 2009. Word sense disambiguation: A survey. *ACM Computing Surveys*, 41(2):10:1–10:69.

S. Padó and M. Lapata. 2007. Dependency-based construction of semantic space models. *Computational Linguistics*, 33(2):161–199.

T. Pedersen, S. Patwardhan, and J. Michelizzi. 2004. Wordnet::similarity: measuring the relatedness of concepts. In *Proceedings of NAACL:HTL – Demonstrations*, pages 38–41, Boston, MA, USA.

F. Pedregosa, G. Varoquaux, A. Gramfort, V. Michel, B. Thirion, O. Grisel, M. Blondel, P. Prettenhofer, R. Weiss, V. Dubourg, J. Vanderplas, A. Passos, D. Cournapeau, M. Brucher, M. Perrot, and E. Duchesnay. 2011. Scikit-learn: Machine learning in python. *Journal of Machine Learning Research*, 12:2825–2830.

P. Rousseeuw. 1987. Silhouettes: a graphical aid to the interpretation and validation of cluster analysis. *Journal of Computational and Applied Mathematics*, 20(1):53–65.

I. Titov and R. T. McDonald. 2008a. A joint model of text and aspect ratings for sentiment summarization. In *Proceedings of the 46th Annual Meeting of ACL-HLT*, pages 308–316, Columbus, OH, USA.

I. Titov and R. T. McDonald. 2008b. Modeling online reviews with multi-grain topic models. In *Proceedings of the 17th International Conference of WWW*, pages 111–120, Beijing, China.

Z. Wu and M. Palmer. 1994. Verbs semantics and lexical selection. In *Proceedings of the 32nd ACL*, pages 133–138, Las Cruces, NM, USA.

J. Yu, Z. Zha, M. Wang, K. Wang, and T. Chua. 2011. Domain-assisted product aspect hierarchy generation: towards hierarchical organization of unstructured consumer reviews. In *Proceedings of EMNLP*, pages 140–150, Edinburgh, UK.

T. Zesch and I. Gurevych. 2010. Wisdom of crowds versus wisdom of linguists - measuring the semantic relatedness of words. *Natural Language Engineering*, 16(1):25–59.

Z. Zhai, B. Liu, H. Xu, and P. Jia. 2010. Grouping product features using semi-supervised learning with soft-constraints. In *Proceedings of the 23rd International Conference of COLING*, pages 1272–1280, Beijing, China.

Z. Zhai, B. Liu, H. Xu, and P. Jia. 2011. Clustering product features for opinion mining. In *Proceedings of the 4th International Conference of WSDM*, pages 347–354, Hong Kong, China.

Z. Zhang, A. Gentile, and F. Ciravegna. 2013. Recent advances in methods of lexical semantic relatedness - a survey. *Natural Language Engineering*, FirstView(1):1–69.

Simple, Robust and (almost) Unsupervised Generation of Polarity Lexicons for Multiple Languages

Iñaki San Vicente, Rodrigo Agerri, German Rigau
IXA NLP Group
University of the Basque Country (UPV/EHU)
Donostia-San Sebastián
{inaki.sanvicente,rodrigo.agerri,german.rigau}@ehu.es

Abstract

This paper presents a simple, robust and (almost) unsupervised dictionary-based method, *qwn-ppv* (Q-WordNet as Personalized PageRanking Vector) to automatically generate polarity lexicons. We show that *qwn-ppv* outperforms other automatically generated lexicons for the four extrinsic evaluations presented here. It also shows very competitive and robust results with respect to manually annotated ones. Results suggest that no single lexicon is best for every task and dataset and that the intrinsic evaluation of polarity lexicons is not a good performance indicator on a Sentiment Analysis task. The *qwn-ppv* method allows to easily create quality polarity lexicons whenever no domain-based annotated corpora are available for a given language.

1 Introduction

Opinion Mining and Sentiment Analysis are important for determining opinions about commercial products, on companies reputation management, brand monitoring, or to track attitudes by mining social media, etc. Given the explosion of information produced and shared via the Internet, it is not possible to keep up with the constant flow of new information by manual methods.

Sentiment Analysis often relies on the availability of words and phrases annotated according to the positive or negative connotations they convey. 'Beautiful', 'wonderful', and 'amazing' are examples of positive words whereas 'bad', 'awful', and 'poor' are examples of negatives.

The creation of lists of sentiment words has generally been performed by means of manual-, dictionary- and corpus-based methods. Manually collecting such lists of polarity annotated words is labor intensive and time consuming, and is thus usually combined with automated approaches as the final check to correct mistakes. However, there are well known lexicons which have been fully (Stone et al., 1966; Taboada et al., 2010) or at least partially *manually created* (Hu and Liu, 2004; Riloff and Wiebe, 2003).

Dictionary-based methods rely on some dictionary or lexical knowledge base (LKB) such as WordNet (Fellbaum and Miller, 1998) that contain synonyms and antonyms for each word. A simple technique in this approach is to start with some sentiment words as seeds which are then used to perform some iterative propagation on the LKB (Hu and Liu, 2004; Strapparava and Valitutti, 2004; Kim and Hovy, 2004; Takamura et al., 2005; Turney and Littman, 2003; Mohammad et al., 2009; Agerri and García-Serrano, 2010; Baccianella et al., 2010).

Corpus-based methods have usually been applied to obtain domain-specific polarity lexicons: they have been created by either starting from a seed list of known words and trying to find other related words in a corpus or by attempting to directly adapt a given lexicon to a new one using a domain-specific corpus (Hatzivassiloglou and McKeown, 1997; Turney and Littman, 2003; Ding et al., 2008; Choi and Cardie, 2009; Mihalcea et al., 2007). One particular issue arising from corpus methods is that for a given domain the same word can be positive in one context but negative in another. This is also a problem shared by manual and dictionary-based methods, and that is why *qwn-ppv* also produces synset-based lexicons for approaches on Sentiment Analysis at sense level.

This paper presents a simple, robust and (almost) unsupervised dictionary-based method, *QWordNet-PPV* (QWordNet by Personalized PageRank Vector) to automatically generate polarity lexicons based on propagating some automatically created seeds using a Personalized

PageRank algorithm (Agirre et al., 2014; Agirre and Soroa, 2009) over a LKB projected into a graph. We see *qwn-ppv* as an effective methodology to easily create polarity lexicons for any language for which a WordNet is available.

This paper empirically shows that: (i) *qwn-ppv* outperforms other automatically generated lexicons (e.g. SentiWordNet 3.0, MSOL) on the 4 extrinsic evaluations presented here; it also displays competitive and robust results also with respect to manually annotated lexicons; (ii) no single polarity lexicon is fit for every Sentiment Analysis task; depending on the text data and the task itself, one lexicon will perform better than others; (iii) if required, *qwn-ppv* efficently generates many lexicons on demand, depending on the task on which they will be used; (iv) intrinsic evaluation is not appropriate to judge whether a polarity lexicon is fit for a given Sentiment Analysis (SA) task because good correlation with respect to a *gold-standard* does not correspond with *correlation* with respect to a SA task; (v) it is easily applicable to create *qwn-ppv(s)* for *other languages*, and we demonstrate it here by creating many polarity lexicons not only for English but also for Spanish; (vi) the method works at *both word and sense* levels and it only requires the availability of a LKB or dictionary; finally, (vii) a dictionary-based method like *qwn-ppv* allows to easily create quality polarity lexicons whenever no domain-based annotated reviews are available for a given language. After all, there usually is available a dictionary for a given language; for example, the Open Multilingual WordNet site lists WordNets for up to 57 languages (Bond and Foster, 2013).

Although there has been previous work using graph methods for obtaining lexicons via propagation, the *qwn-ppv* method to combine the seed generation and the Personalized PageRank propagation is novel. Furthermore, it is considerable simpler and obtains better and easier to reproduce results than previous automatic approaches (Esuli and Sebastiani, 2007; Mohammad et al., 2009; Rao and Ravichandran, 2009).

Next section reviews previous related work, taking special interest on those that are currently available for evaluation purposes. Section 3 describes the *qwn-ppv* method to automatically generate lexicons. The resulting lexical resources are evaluated in section 4. We finish with some concluding remarks and future work in section 5.

2 Related Work

There is a large amount of work on Sentiment Analysis and Opinion Mining, and good comprehensive overviews are already available (Pang and Lee, 2008; Liu, 2012), so we will review the most representative and closest to the present work. This means that we will not be reviewing corpus-based approaches but rather those constructed manually or upon a dictionary or LKB. We will in turn use the approaches here reviewed for comparison with *qwn-ppv* in section 4.

The most popular manually-built polarity lexicon is part of the General Inquirer (Stone et al., 1966), and consists of 1915 words labelled as "positive" and 2291 as "negative". Taboada *et al.* (2010) manually created their lexicons annotating the polarity of 6232 words on a scale of 5 to -5. Liu *et al.*, starting with Hu and Liu (2004), have along the years collected a manually corrected polarity lexicon which is formed by 4818 negative and 2041 positive words. Another manually corrected lexicon (Riloff and Wiebe, 2003) is the one used by the Opinion Finder system (Wilson et al., 2005) and contains 4903 negatively and 2718 positively annotated words respectively.

Among the automatically built lexicons, Turney and Littman (2003) proposed a minimally supervised algorithm to calculate the polarity of a word depending on whether it co-ocurred more with a previously collected small set of positive words rather than with a set of negative ones. Agerri and García Serrano presented a very simple method to extract the polarity information starting from the *quality* synset in WordNet (Agerri and García-Serrano, 2010). Mohammad *et al.* (2009) developed a method in which they first identify (by means of affixes rules) a set of positive/negative words which act as seeds, then used a Roget-like thesaurus to mark the synonymous words for each polarity type and to generalize from the seeds. They produce several lexicons the best of which, MSOL(ASL and GI) contains 51K and 76K entries respectively and uses the full General Inquirer as seeds. They performed both intrinsic and extrinsic evaluations using the MPQA 1.1 corpus.

Finally, there are two approaches that are somewhat closer to us, because they are based on WordNet and graph-based methods. SentiWordNet 3.0 (Baccianella et al., 2010) is built in 4 steps: (i) they select the synsets of 14 paradigmatic positive and negative words used as seeds (Turney and Littman, 2003). These seeds are then iteratively extended following the construction of WordNet-Affect (Strapparava and Valitutti, 2004). (ii) They train 7 supervised classifiers with the synsets' glosses which are used to assign *polarity* and *objectivity* scores to WordNet senses. (iii) In SentiWordNet 3.0 (Esuli and Sebastiani, 2007) they take the output of the supervised classifiers as input to applying PageRank to WordNet 3.0's graph. (iv) They intrinsically evaluate it with respect to MicroWnOp-3.0 using the *p-normalized Kendall* τ *distance* (Baccianella et al., 2010). Rao and Ravichandran (2009) apply different semi-supervised graph algorithms (Mincuts, Randomized Mincuts and Label Propagation) to a set of seeds constructed from the General Inquirer. They evaluate the generated lexicons intrinsically taking the General Inquirer as the gold standard for those words that had a match in the generated lexicons.

In this paper, we describe two methods to automatically generate seeds either by following Agerri and García-Serrano (2010) or using Turney and Littman's (2003) seeds. The automatically obtained seeds are then fed into a Personalized PageRank algorithm which is applied over a WordNet projected on a graph. This method is fully automatic, simple and unsupervised as it only relies on the availability of a LKB.

3 Generating qwn-ppv

The overall procedure of our approach consists of two steps: **(1)** automatically creates a set of seeds by iterating over a LKB (e.g. a WordNet) relations; and **(2)** uses the seeds to initialize contexts to propagate over the LKB graph using a Personalized Pagerank algorithm. The result is *qwn-ppv(s)*: Q-WordNets as Personalized PageRanking Vectors.

3.1 Seed Generation

We generate seeds by means of two different automatic procedures.

1. **AG**: We start at the *quality synset* of WordNet and iterate over WordNet relations following the original Q-WordNet method described in Agerri and García Serrano (2010).

2. **TL**: We take a short manually created list of 14 positive and negative words (Turney and Littman, 2003) and iterate over WordNet using five relations: *antonymy, similarity, derived-from, pertains-to and also-see*.

The **AG** method starts the propagation from the attributes of the *quality synset* in WordNet. There are five noun quality senses in WordNet, two of which contain attribute relations (to adjectives). From the $quality^1_n$ synset the attribute relation takes us to $positive^1_a$, $negative^1_a$, $good^1_a$ and bad^1_a; $quality^2_n$ leads to the attributes $superior^1_a$ and $inferior^2_a$. The following step is to iterate through every WordNet relation collecting (i.e., annotating) those synsets that are accessible from the seeds. Both *AG* and *TL* methods to generate seeds rely on a number of relations to obtain a more balanced POS distribution in the output synsets. The output of both methods is a list of (assumed to be) positive and negative synsets. Depending on the number of iterations performed a different number of seeds to feed UKB is obtained. Seed numbers vary from 100 hundred to 10K synsets. Both seed creation methods can be applied to any WordNet, not only Princeton WordNet, as we show in section 4.

3.2 PPV generation

The second and last step to generate *qwn-ppv*(s) consists of propagating over a WordNet graph to obtain a Personalized PageRanking Vector (PPV), one for each polarity. This step requires:

1. A LKB projected over a graph.

2. A Personalized PageRanking algorithm which is applied over the graph.

3. Seeds to create contexts to start the propagation, either words or synsets.

Several undirected graphs based on WordNet 3.0 as represented by the MCR 3.0 (Agirre et al., 2012) have been created for the experimentation, which correspond to 4 main sets: (G1) two graphs consisting of every synset linked by the *synonymy* and *antonymy* relations; (G2) a graph with the nodes linked by every relation, including glosses; (G3) a graph consisting of the synsets linked by every relation except those that are linked by *antonymy*; finally, (G4) a graph consisting of the nodes related by every relation except the *antonymy* and *gloss* relations.

Using the (G1) graphs, we propagate from the seeds over each type of graph (synonymy and antonymy) to obtain two rankings per polarity.

	Synset Level							Word level						
		Positives			Negatives				Positives			Negatives		
Lexicon	size	P	R	F	P	R	F	size	P	R	F	P	R	F
Automatically created														
MSOL(ASL-GI)*	32706	.65	.45	.53	.58	.76	.66	76400	.70	.49	.58	.61	.79	.69
QWN	15508	.69	.53	.60	.62	.76	.68	11693	.64	.53	.58	.60	.70	.65
SWN	27854	.73	.57	.64	.65	.79	.71	38346	.70	.55	.62	.63	.77	.69
QWN-PPV-AG(s03_G1/w01_G1)	2589	.77	.63	.69	.69	.81	.74	5119	.68	.77	**.72**	.73	.64	**.68**
QWN-PPV-TL(s04_G1/w01_G1)	5010	.76	.66	**.70**	.70	.79	**.74**	4644	.68	.71	.69	.70	.67	.68
(Semi-) Manually created														
GI*	2791	.74	.57	.64	.65	.80	.72	3376	.79	.64	.71	.70	.83	.76
OF*	4640	.77	.61	.68	.68	.81	.74	6860	.82	.71	.76	.74	.84	.79
Liu*	4127	.81	.63	**.71**	.70	.85	**.76**	6786	.85	.74	**.79**	.77	.87	**.82**
SO-CAL*	4212	.75	.57	.64	.65	.81	.72	6226	.82	.70	.76	.74	.85	.79

Table 1: Evaluation of lexicons at document level using Bespalov's Corpus.

The graphs created in (G2), (G3) and (G4) are used to obtain two ranks, one for each polarity by propagating from the seeds. In all four cases the different polarity rankings have to be combined in order to obtain a final polarity lexicon: the polarity score *pol(s)* of a given synset *s* is computed by adding its scores in the positive rankings and subtracting its scores in the negative rankings. If *pol(s)* > 0 then *s* is included in the final lexicon as positive. If *pol(s)* < 0 then *s* is included in the final lexicon as negative. We assume that synsets with *null* polarity scores have no polarity and consequently they are excluded from the final lexicon.

The Personalized PageRanking propagation is performed starting from both synsets and words and using both *AG* and *TL* styles of seed generation, as explained in section 3.1. Combining the various possibilities will produce at least 6 different lexicons for each iteration, depending on which decisions are taken about which graph, seeds and word/synset to create the *qwn-ppv*(s). In fact, the experiments produced hundreds of lexicons, according to the different iterations for seed generation[1], but we will only refer to those that obtain the best results in the extrinsic evaluations.

With respect to the algorithm to propagate over the WordNet graph from the automatically created seeds, we use a Personalized PageRank algorithm (Agirre et al., 2014; Agirre and Soroa, 2009). The famous PageRank (Brin and Page, 1998) algorithm is a method to produce a rank from the vertices in a graph according to their relative structural importance. PageRank has also been viewed as the result of a Random Walk process, where the final rank of a given node represents the probability of a random walk over the graph which ends on that same node. Thus, if we take the created WordNet graph G with N vertices $v_1, \ldots, v_n$ and d_i as being the outdegree of node i, plus a $N \times N$ transition probability matrix M where $M_{ji} = 1/d_i$ if a link from i to j exists and 0 otherwise, then calculating the PageRank vector over a graph G amounts to solve the following equation (1):

$$\mathbf{Pr} = cM\mathbf{Pr} + (1 - c)\mathbf{v} \qquad (1)$$

In the traditional PageRank, vector **v** is a uniform normalized vector whose elements values are all $1/N$, which means that all nodes in the graph are assigned the same probabilities in case of a random walk. Personalizing the PageRank algorithm in this case means that it is possible to make vector **v** non-uniform and assign stronger probabilities to certain nodes, which would make the algorithm to propagate the initial importance of those nodes to their vicinity. Following Agirre *et al.* (2014), in our approach this translates into initializing vector **v** with those senses obtained by the seed generation methods described above in section 3.1. Thus, the initialization of vector **v** using the seeds allows the Personalized propagation to assign greater importance to those synsets in the graph identified as being positive and negative, which resuls in a PPV with the weigths skewed towards those nodes initialized/personalized as positive and negative.

4 Evaluation

Previous approaches have provided intrinsic evaluation (Mohammad et al., 2009; Rao and Ravichandran, 2009; Baccianella et al., 2010) using manually annotated resources such as the General Inquirer (Stone et al., 1966) as gold standard. To facilitate comparison, we also provide such evaluation in section 4.3. Nevertheless, and as demonstrated by the results of the extrinsic evaluations, we believe that polarity lexicons should

[1]The total time to generate the final 352 QWN-PPV propagations amounted to around two hours of processing time in a standard PC.

	Synset Level							Word level						
		Positives			Negatives				Positives			Negatives		
Lexicon	size	P	R	F	P	R	F	size	P	R	F	P	R	F
Automatically created														
MSOL(ASL-GI)*	32706	.56	.37	.44	.76	.87	.81	76400	.67	.5	.57	.80	.89	.85
QWN	15508	.63	.22	.33	.73	.94	.83	11693	.58	.22	.31	.73	.93	.82
SWN	27854	.57	.33	.42	.75	.89	.81	38346	.55	.55	.55	.80	.8	.80
QWN-PPV-AG (w10_G3/s09_G4)	117485	.60	.63	**.62**	.83	.82	**.83**	144883	.65	.50	.57	.80	.88	.84
QWN-PPV-TL (s05_G4)	114698	.61	.58	.59	.82	.83	.83	144883	.66	.53	**.59**	.81	.88	**.84**
(Semi-) Manually created														
GI*	2791	.70	.32	.44	.76	.94	.84	3376	.71	.56	.62	.82	.90	.86
OF*	4640	.67	.37	**.48**	.77	.92	**.84**	6860	.75	.68	**.71**	.87	.90	**.88**
Liu*	4127	.67	.33	.44	.76	.93	.83	6786	.78	.45	.57	.79	.94	.86
SO-CAL*	4212	.69	.3	.42	.75	.94	.84	6226	.73	.53	.61	.81	.91	.86

Table 2: Evaluation of lexicons using *averaged ratio* on the MPQA 1.2_{test} Corpus.

in general be evaluated *extrinsically*. After all, any polarity lexicon is as good as the results obtained by using it for a particular Sentiment Analysis task.

Our goal is to evaluate the polarity lexicons simplifying the evaluation parameters to avoid as many external influences as possible on the results. We compare our work with most of the lexicons reviewed in section 2, both at synset and word level, both manually and automatically generated: General Inquirer (**GI**), Opinion Finder (**OF**), **Liu**, Taboada *et al.'s* (**SO-CAL**), Agerri and García-Serrano (2010) (**QWN**), Mohammad *et al's*, (**MSOL(ASL-GI)**) and SentiWordNet 3.0 (**SWN**). The results presented in section 4.2 show that *extrinsic* evaluation is more meaningful to determine the adequacy of a polarity lexicon for a specific Sentiment Analysis task.

4.1 Datasets and Evaluation System

Three different corpora were used: Bespalov *et al.'s* (2011) and MPQA (Riloff and Wiebe, 2003) for English, and HOpinion[2] in Spanish. In addition, we divided the corpus into two subsets (75% development and 25% test) for applying our ratio system for the phrase polarity task too. Note that the development set is only used to set up the polarity classification task, and that the generation of *qwn-ppv* lexicons is unsupervised.

For Spanish we tried to reproduce the English settings with Bespalov's corpus. Thus, both development and test sets were created from the HOpinion corpus. As it contains a much higher proportion of positive reviews, we created also subsets which contain a balanced number of positive and negative reviews to allow for a more meaningful comparison than that of table 6. Table 3 shows the number of documents per polarity for Bespalov's, MPQA 1.2 and HOpinion.

[2]http://clic.ub.edu/corpus/hopinion

Corpus	POS docs	NEG docs	Total
Bespalov_{dev}	23,112	23,112	46,227
Bespalov_{test}	10,557	10,557	21,115
MPQA 1.2_{dev}	2,315	5,260	7,575
MPQA 1.2_{test}	771	1,753	2,524
MPQA 1.2_{total}	3,086	7,013	10,099
$\text{HOpinion\_Balanced}_{dev}$	1,582	1,582	3,164
$\text{HOpinion\_Balanced}_{test}$	528	528	1,056
HOpinion_{dev}	9,236	1,582	10,818
HOpinion_{test}	3,120	528	3,648

Table 3: Number of positive and negative documents in train and test sets.

We report results of 4 extrinsic evaluations or tasks, three of them based on a simple *ratio average system*, inspired by Turney (2002), and another one based on Mohammad *et al.* (2009). We first implemented a simple *average ratio classifier* which computes the average ratio of the polarity words found in document d:

$$polarity(d) = \frac{\sum_{w \in d} pol(w)}{|d|} \qquad (2)$$

where, for each polarity, *pol(w)* is 1 if *w* is included in the polarity lexicon and 0 otherwise. Documents that reach a certain threshold are classified as positive, and otherwise as negative. To setup an evaluation enviroment as fair as possible for every lexicon, the threshold is optimised by maximising accuracy over the development data.

Second, we implemented a phrase polarity task identification as described by Mohammad *et al.* (2009). Their method consists of: (i) if any of the words in the target phrase is contained in the negative lexicon, then the polarity is negative; (ii) if none of the words are negative, and at least one word is in the positive lexicon, then is positive; (iii) the rest are not tagged.

We chose this very simple polarity estimators because our aim was to minimize the role other

	Synset Level							Word level						
		Positives			Negatives				Positives			Negatives		
Lexicon	size	P	R	F	P	R	F	size	P	R	F	P	R	F
Automatically created														
MSOL(ASL-GI)*	32706	.52	.48	.50	.85	.62	.71	76400	.68	.56	.62	.82	.86	.84
QWN	15508	.50	.36	.42	.84	.32	.46	11693	.45	.49	.47	.78	.51	.61
SWN	27854	.50	.45	.47	.85	.48	.61	38346	.49	.52	.50	.78	.68	.73
QWN-PPV-AG (s09_G3/w02_G3)	117485	.59	.67	**.63**	.85	.78	**.82**	147194	.64	.64	.64	.84	.83	.83
QWN-PPV-TL (w02_G3/s06_G3)	117485	.59	.57	.58	.82	.81	.81	147194	.63	.67	**.65**	.85	.81	**.83**
(Semi-) Manually created														
GI*	2791	.60	.40	.47	.91	.38	.54	3376	.70	.60	.65	.93	.52	.67
OF*	4640	.63	.42	**.50**	.93	.46	**.62**	6860	.75	.71	**.73**	.95	.66	**.78**
Liu*	4127	.65	.36	.47	.94	.45	.60	6786	.78	.49	.60	.97	.61	.75
SO-CAL*	4212	.65	.37	.47	.92	.45	.60	6226	.73	.57	.64	.96	.59	.73

Table 4: Evaluation of lexicons at phrase level using Mohammad *et al.'s* (2009) method on MPQA 1.2_{total} Corpus.

aspects play in the evaluation and focus on how, other things being equal, polarity lexicons perform in a Sentiment Analysis task. The *average ratio* is used to present results of tables 1 and 2 (with Bespalov corpus), and 5 and 6 (with HOpinion), whereas Mohammad *et al.'s* is used to report results in table 4. Mohammad *et al.'s* (2009) testset based on MPQA 1.1 is smaller, but both MPQA 1.1 and 1.2 are hugely skewed towards negative polarity (30% positive vs. 70% negative).

All datasets were POS tagged and Word Sense Disambiguated using FreeLing (Padró and Stanilovsky, 2012; Agirre and Soroa, 2009). Having word sense annotated datasets gives us the opportunity to evaluate the lexicons both at word and sense levels. For the evaluation of those lexicons that are synset-based, such as *qwn-ppv* and SentiWordNet 3.0, we convert them from senses to words by taking every word or variant contained in each of their senses. Moreover, if a lemma appears as a variant in several synsets the most frequent polarity is assigned to that lemma.

With respect to lexicons at word level, we take the most frequent sense according to WordNet 3.0 for each of their positive and negative words. Note that the latter conversion, for synset based evaluation, is mostly done to show that the evaluation at synset level is harder independently of the quality of the lexicon evaluated.

4.2 Results

Although tables 1, 2 and 4 also present results at synset level, it should be noted that the only polarity lexicons available to us for comparison at synset level were Q-WordNet (Agerri and García-Serrano, 2010) and SentiWordNet 3.0 (Baccianella et al., 2010). *QWN-PPV-AG* refers to the lexicon generated starting from **AG**'s seeds, and *QWN-PPV-TL* using **TL**'s seeds as described in section 3.1. Henceforth, we will use *qwn-ppv* to refer to the overall method presented in this paper, regardless of the seeds used.

For every *qwn-ppv* result reported in this section, we have used every graph described in section 3.2. The configuration of each *qwn-ppv* in the results specifies which seed iteration is used as the initialization of the Personalized PageRank algorithm, and on which graph. Thus, QWN-PPV-TL (s05_G4) in table 2 means that the 5th iteration of synset seeds was used to propagate over graph G4. If the configuration were (w05_G4) it would have meant 'the 5th iteration of word seeds were used to propagate over graph G4'. The simplicity of our approach allows us to generate many lexicons simply by projecting a LKB over different graphs.

The lexicons marked with an asterisk denote those that have been converted from word to senses using the most frequent sense of WordNet 3.0. We would like to stress again that the purpose of such word to synset conversion is to show that SA tasks at synset level are harder than at word level. In addition, it should also be noted that in the case of SO-CAL (Taboada et al., 2010), we have reduced what is a graded lexicon with scores ranging from 5 to -5 into a binary one.

Table 1 shows that (at least partially) manually built lexicons obtain the best results on this evaluation. It also shows that *qwn-ppv* clearly outperforms any other automatically built lexicons. Moreover, manually built lexicons suffer from the evaluation at synset level, obtaining most of them lower scores than *qwn-ppv*, although Liu's (Hu and Liu, 2004) still obtains the best results. In any case, for an unsupervised procedure, *qwn-ppv* lexicons obtain very competitive results with respect to manually created lexicons and is the best among the automatic methods. It should also be noted that the best results of *qwn-ppv* are obtained with graph

G1 and with very few seed iterations.

Table 2 again sees the manually built lexicons performing better although overall the differences are lower with respect to automatically built lexicons. Among these, *qwn-ppv* again obtains the best results, both at synset and word level, although in the latter the differences with MSOL(ASL-GI) are not large. Finally, table 4 shows that *qwn-ppv* again outperforms other automatic approaches and is closer to those have been (partially at least) manually built. In both MPQA evaluations the best graph overall to propagate the seeds is G3 because this type of task favours high recall.

		Positives			Negatives		
Lexicon	size	P	R	F	P	R	F
Automatically created							
SWN	27854	.87	.99	.93	.70	.16	.27
QWN-PPV-AG (wrd01_G1)	3306	.86	.00	.92	.67	.01	.02
QWN-PPV-TL (s04_G1)	5010	.89	.96	**.93**	.58	.30	**.39**

Table 5: Evaluation of Spanish lexicons using the full HOpinion corpus at synset level.

We report results on the Spanish HOpinion corpus in tables 5 and 6. Mihalcea(f) is a manually revised lexicon based on the automatically built Mihalcea(m) (Pérez-Rosas et al., 2012). ElhPolar (Saralegi and San Vicente, 2013) is semi-automatically built and manually corrected. SO-CAL is built manually. SWN and QWN-PPV have been built via the MCR 3.0's ILI by applying the synset to word conversion previously described on the Spanish dictionary of the MCR. The results for Spanish at word level in table 6 show the same trend as for English: *qwn-ppv* is the best of the automatic approaches and it obtains competitive although not as good as the best of the manually created lexicons (ElhPolar). Due to the disproportionate number of positive reviews, the results for the negative polarity are not useful to draw any meaningful conclusions. Thus, we also performed an evaluation with HOpinion Balanced set as listed in table 3.

The results with a balanced HOpinion, not shown due to lack of space, also confirm the previous trend: *qwn-ppv* outperforms other automatic approaches but is still worse than the best of the manually created ones (ElhPolar).

		Positives			Negatives		
Lexicon	size	P	R	F	P	R	F
Automatically created							
Mihalcea(m)	2496	.86	.00	.92	.00	.00	.00
SWN	9712	.88	.97	.92	.55	.19	.28
QWN-PPV-AG (s11_G1)	1926	.89	.97	.93	.59	.26	.36
QWN-PPV-TL (s03_G1)	939	.89	.98	**.93**	.71	.26	**.38**
(Semi-) Manually created							
ElhPolar	4673	.94	.94	**.94**	.64	.64	**.64**
Mihalcea(f)	1347	.91	.96	.93	.61	.41	.49
SO-CAL	4664	.92	.96	.94	.70	.51	.59

Table 6: Evaluation of Spanish lexicons using the full HOpinion corpus at word level.

4.3 Intrinsic evaluation

To facilitate intrinsic comparison with previous approaches, we evaluate our automatically generated lexicons against GI. For each *qwn-ppv* lexicon shown in previous extrinsic evaluations, we compute the intersection between the lexicon and GI, and evaluate the words in that intersection. Table 7 shows results for the best-performing QWN-PPV lexicons (both using AG and TL seeds) in the extrinsic evaluations at word level of tables 1 (first two rows), 2 (rows 3 and 4) and 4 (rows 5 and 6). We can see that QWN-PPV lexicons systematically outperform SWN in number of correct entries. *QWN-PPV-TL* lexicons obtain 75.04% of correctness on average. The best performing lexicon contains up to 81.07% of correct entries. Note that we did not compare the results with MSOL(ASL-GI) because it contains the GI.

Lexicon	**∩ wrt. GI**	**Acc.**	**Pos**	**Neg**
SWN	2,755	.74	.76	.73
QWN-PPV-AG (w01_G1)	849	.71	.68	.75
QWN-PPV-TL (w01_G1)	713	.78	.80	.76
QWN-PPV-AG (s09_G4)	3,328	.75	.75	.77
QWN-PPV-TL (s05_G4)	3,333	**.80**	**.84**	**.77**
QWN-PPV-AG (w02_G3)	3,340	.74	.71	.77
QWN-PPV-TL (s06_G3)	3,340	.77	.79	.77

Table 7: Accuracy QWN-PPV lexicons and SWN with respect to the GI lexicon.

4.4 Discussion

QWN-PPV lexicons obtain the best results among the evaluations for English and Spanish. Furthermore, across tasks and datasets *qwn-ppv* provides a more consistent and robust behaviour than most of the manually-built lexicons apart from OF. The results also show that for a task requiring high recall the larger graphs, e.g. G3, are preferable, whereas for a more balanced dataset and document level task smaller G1 graphs perform better.

These are good results considering that our method to generate *qwn-ppv* is simpler, more robust and adaptable than previous automatic approaches. Furthermore, although also based on a Personalized PageRank application, it is much simpler than SentiWordNet 3.0, consistently outperformed by *qwn-ppv* on every evaluation and dataset. The main differences with respect to SentiWordNet's approach are the following: (i) the seed generation and training of 7 supervised classifiers corresponds in *qwn-ppv* to only one simple step, namely, the automatic generation of seeds as explained in section 3.1; (ii) the generation of *qwn-ppv* only requires a LKB's graph for the Personalized PageRank propagation, no disambiguated glosses; (iii) the graph they use to do the propagation also depends on disambiguated glosses, not readily available for any language.

The fact that *qwn-ppv* is based on already available WordNets projected onto simple graphs is crucial for the robustness and adaptability of the *qwn-ppv* method across evaluation tasks and datasets: Our method can quickly create, over different graphs, many lexicons of diffent sizes which can then be evaluated on a particular polarity classification task and dataset. Hence the different configurations of the *qwn-ppv* lexicons, because for some tasks a G3 graph with more AG/TL seed iterations will obtain better recall and viceversa. This is confirmed by the results: the tasks using MPQA seem to clearly benefit from high recall whereas the Bespalov's corpus has overall, more balanced scores. This could also be due to the size of Bespalov's corpus, almost 10 times larger than MPQA 1.2.

The experiments to generate Spanish lexicons confirm the trend showed by the English evaluations: Lexicons generated by *qwn-ppv* consistenly outperform other automatic approaches, although some manual lexicon is better on a given task and dataset (usually a different one). Nonetheless the Spanish evaluation shows that our method is also robust across languages as it gets quite close to the manually corrected lexicon of Mihalcea(full) (Pérez-Rosas et al., 2012).

The results also confirm that no single lexicon is the most appropriate for any SA task or dataset and domain. In this sense, the adaptability of *qwn-ppv* is a desirable feature for lexicons to be employed in SA tasks: the unsupervised *qwn-ppv* method only relies on the availability of a LKB to build hundreds of polarity lexicons which can then be evaluated on a given task and dataset to choose the best fit. If not annotated evaluation set is available, G3-based propagations provide the best recall whereas the G1-based lexicons are less noisy. Finally, we believe that the results reported here point out to the fact that intrinsic evaluations are not meaningful to judge the adequacy a polarity lexicon for a specific SA task.

5 Concluding Remarks

This paper presents an unsupervised dictionary-based method *qwn-ppv* to automatically generate polarity lexicons. Although simpler than similar automatic approaches, it still obtains better results on the four extrinsic evaluations presented. Because it only depends on the availability of a LKB, we believe that this method can be valuable to generate on-demand polarity lexicons for a given language when not sufficient annotated data is available. We demonstrate the adaptability of our approach by producing good performance polarity lexicons for different evaluation scenarios and for more than one language.

Further work includes investigating different graph projections of WordNet relations to do the propagation as well as exploiting synset weights. We also plan to investigate the use of annotated corpora to generate lexicons at word level to try and close the gap with those that have been (at least partially) manually annotated.

The *qwn-ppv* lexicons and graphs used in this paper are publicly available (under CC-BY license): *http://adimen.si.ehu.es/web/qwn-ppv*. The *qwn-ppv tool* to automatically generate polarity lexicons given a WordNet in any language will soon be available in the aforementioned URL.

Acknowledgements

This work has been supported by the OpeNER FP7 project under Grant No. 296451, the FP7 NewsReader project, Grant No. 316404 and by the Spanish MICINN project SKATER under Grant No. TIN2012-38584-C06-01.

References

R. Agerri and A. García-Serrano. 2010. Q-WordNet: extracting polarity from WordNet senses. In *Seventh Conference on International Language Resources and Evaluation, Malta. Retrieved May*, volume 25, page 2010.

Eneko Agirre and Aitor Soroa. 2009. Personalizing pagerank for word sense disambiguation. In *Proceedings of the 12th Conference of the European Chapter of the Association for Computational Linguistics (EACL-2009)*, Athens, Greece.

Aitor González Agirre, Egoitz Laparra, German Rigau, and Basque Country Donostia. 2012. Multilingual central repository version 3.0: upgrading a very large lexical knowledge base. In *GWC 2012 6th International Global Wordnet Conference*, page 118.

Eneko Agirre, Oier Lopez de Lacalle, and Aitor Soroa. 2014. Random walks for knowledge-based word sense disambiguation. *Computational Linguistics*, (Early Access).

S. Baccianella, A. Esuli, and F. Sebastiani. 2010. SentiWordNet 3.0: An enhanced lexical resource for sentiment analysis and opinion mining. In *Seventh conference on International Language Resources and Evaluation (LREC-2010), Malta.*, volume 25.

Dmitriy Bespalov, Bing Bai, Yanjun Qi, and Ali Shokoufandeh. 2011. Sentiment classification based on supervised latent n-gram analysis. In *Proceedings of the 20th ACM international conference on Information and knowledge management*, pages 375–382.

Francis Bond and Ryan Foster. 2013. Linking and extending an open multilingual wordnet. In *51st Annual Meeting of the Association for Computational Linguistics: ACL-2013.*

Sergey Brin and Lawrence Page. 1998. The anatomy of a large-scale hypertextual web search engine. *Computer networks and ISDN systems*, 30(1):107117.

Y. Choi and C. Cardie. 2009. Adapting a polarity lexicon using integer linear programming for domain-specific sentiment classification. In *Proceedings of the 2009 Conference on Empirical Methods in Natural Language Processing: Volume 2-Volume 2*, pages 590–598.

X. Ding, B. Liu, and P. S. Yu. 2008. A holistic lexicon-based approach to opinion mining. In *Proceedings of the international conference on Web search and web data mining*, pages 231–240.

Andrea Esuli and Fabrizio Sebastiani. 2007. Pageranking wordnet synsets: An application to opinion mining. In *Proceedings of the 45th Annual Meeting of the Association of Computational Linguistics*, pages 424–431, Prague, Czech Republic, June. Association for Computational Linguistics.

C. Fellbaum and G. Miller, editors. 1998. *Wordnet: An Electronic Lexical Database*. MIT Press, Cambridge (MA).

V. Hatzivassiloglou and K. R McKeown. 1997. Predicting the semantic orientation of adjectives. In *Proceedings of the eighth conference on European chapter of the Association for Computational Linguistics*, pages 174–181.

M. Hu and B. Liu. 2004. Mining and summarizing customer reviews. In *Proceedings of the tenth ACM SIGKDD international conference on Knowledge discovery and data mining*, pages 168–177.

Soo-Min Kim and Eduard Hovy. 2004. Determining the sentiment of opinions. In *Proceedings of Coling 2004*, pages 1367–1373, Geneva, Switzerland, Aug 23–Aug 27. COLING.

Bing Liu. 2012. Sentiment analysis and opinion mining. *Synthesis Lectures on Human Language Technologies*, 5(1):1–167.

R. Mihalcea, C. Banea, and J. Wiebe. 2007. Learning multilingual subjective language via cross-lingual projections. In *Annual Meeting of the Association for Computational Linguistics*, volume 45, page 976.

S. Mohammad, C. Dunne, and B. Dorr. 2009. Generating high-coverage semantic orientation lexicons from overtly marked words and a thesaurus. In *Proceedings of the 2009 Conference on Empirical Methods in Natural Language Processing: Volume 2-Volume 2*, pages 599–608.

Lluís Padró and Evgeny Stanilovsky. 2012. Freeling 3.0: Towards wider multilinguality. In *Proceedings of the Language Resources and Evaluation Conference (LREC 2012)*, Istanbul, Turkey, May. ELRA.

B. Pang and L. Lee. 2008. Opinion mining and sentiment analysis. *Foundations and Trends in Information Retrieval*, 2(1-2):1–135.

Verónica Pérez-Rosas, Carmen Banea, and Rada Mihalcea. 2012. Learning sentiment lexicons in spanish. In *LREC*, pages 3077–3081.

D. Rao and D. Ravichandran. 2009. Semi-supervised polarity lexicon induction. In *Proceedings of the 12th Conference of the European Chapter of the Association for Computational Linguistics*, pages 675–682.

E. Riloff and J. Wiebe. 2003. Learning extraction patterns for subjective expressions. In *Proceedings of the International Conference on Empirical Methods in Natural Language Processing (EMNLP'03).*

Xabier Saralegi and Iñaki San Vicente. 2013. Elhuyar at TASS2013. In *XXIX Congreso de la Sociedad Espaola de Procesamiento de lenguaje natural, Workshop on Sentiment Analysis at SEPLN (TASS2013)*, pages 143–150, Madrid.

P. Stone, D. Dunphy, M. Smith, and D. Ogilvie. 1966. *The General Inquirer: A Computer Approach to Content Analysis*. Cambridge (MA): MIT Press.

Carlo Strapparava and Alessandro Valitutti. 2004. Wordnet-affect: an affective extension of wordnet. In *Proceedings of the 4th International Conference on Languages Resources and Evaluation (LREC 2004)*, pages 1083–1086, Lisbon, May.

M. Taboada, J. Brooke, M. Tofiloski, K. Voll, and M. Stede. 2010. Lexicon-based methods for sentiment analysis. *Computational Linguistics*, (Early Access):141.

Hiroya Takamura, Takashi Inui, and Manabu Okumura. 2005. Extracting semantic orientations of words using spin model. In *Proceedings of the 43rd Annual Meeting of the Association for Computational Linguistics (ACL'05)*, page 133140, Ann Arbor, Michigan, June. Association for Computational Linguistics.

P. Turney and M. Littman. 2003. Measuring praise and criticism: Inference of semantic oreintation from association. *ACM Transaction on Information Systems*, 21(4):315–346.

P.D. Turney. 2002. Thumbs up or thumbs down?: semantic orientation applied to unsupervised classification of reviews. In *Proceedings of the 40th Annual Meeting on Association for Computational Linguistics*, page 417424.

Theresa Wilson, Janyce Wiebe, and Paul Hoffmann. 2005. Recognizing contextual polarity in phrase-level sentiment analysis. In *Proceedings of the conference on Human Language Technology and Empirical Methods in Natural Language Processing*, page 347354.

Mapping dialectal variation by querying social media

Gabriel Doyle
Department of Linguistics
University of California, San Diego
La Jolla, CA, USA 92093-0108
gdoyle@ucsd.edu

Abstract

We propose a Bayesian method of estimating a conditional distribution of data given metadata (e.g., the usage of a dialectal variant given a location) based on queries from a big data/social media source, such as Twitter. This distribution is structurally equivalent to those built from traditional experimental methods, despite lacking negative examples. Tests using Twitter to investigate the geographic distribution of dialectal forms show that this method can provide distributions that are tightly correlated with existing gold-standard studies at a fraction of the time, cost, and effort.

1 Introduction

Social media provides a linguist with a new data source of unprecedented scale, opening novel avenues for research in empirically-driven areas, such as corpus and sociolinguistics. Extracting the right information from social media, though, is not as straightforward as in traditional data sources, as the size and format of big data makes it too unwieldy to observe as a whole. Researchers often must interact with big data through queries, which produce only positive results, those matching the search term. At best, this can be augmented with a set of "absences" covering results that do not match the search term, but explicit negative data (e.g., confirmation that a datapoint could never match the search term) does not exist. In addition to the lack of explicit negative data, query-derived data has a conditional distribution that reverses the dependent and independent variables compared to traditional data sources, such as sociolinguistic interviews.

This paper proposes a Bayesian method for overcoming these two difficulties, allowing query-derived data to be applied to traditional problems without requiring explicit negative data or the ability to view the entire dataset at once. The test case in this paper is dialect geography, where the positive data is the presence of a dialectal word or phrase in a tweet, and the metadata is the location of the person tweeting it. However, the method is general and applies to any queryable big data source that includes metadata about the user or setting that generated the data.

The key to this method lies in using an independent query to estimate the overall distribution of the metadata. This estimated distribution corrects for non-uniformity in the data source, enabling the reversal of the conditionality on the query-derived distribution to convert it to the distribution of interest.

Section 2 explains the mathematical core of the Bayesian analysis. Section 3 implements this analysis for Twitter and introduces an open-source program for determining the geographic distribution of tweets. Section 4 tests the method on problems in linguistic geography and shows that its results are well-correlated with those of traditional sociolinguistic research. Section 5 addresses potential concerns about noise or biases in the queries.

2 Reversing the conditionality of query data

2.1 Corpora and positive-only data

In traditional linguistic studies, the experimenter has control over the participants' metadata, but not over their data. For instance, a sociolinguist may select speakers with known ages or locations, but will not know their usages in advance. Corpus queries reverse the direction of investigation; the experimenter selects a linguistic form to search for, but then lacks control over the metadata of the participants who use the query. The direction of conditionality must be reversed to get comparable information from query-derived and traditional data.

Queries also complicate the problem by providing only positive examples. This lack of explicit negative data is common in language acquisition, as children encounter mostly grammatical statements during learning, and receive few explicitly ungrammatical examples, yet still develop a consistent grammaticality classification system as they mature. Similar positive-only problems abound in cognitive science and artificial intelligence, and a variety of proposals have been offered to overcome it in different tasks. These include biases like the Size Principle (Tenenbaum and Griffiths, 2001), heuristics like generating pseudo-negatives from unobserved data (Okanohara and Tsujii, 2007; Poon et al., 2009), or innate prespecifications like Universal Grammar in the Principles and Parameters framework.

For query-derived data, Bayesian reasoning can address both problems by inverting the conditionality of the distribution and implying negative data. The key insight is that a lack of positive examples where positive examples are otherwise expected is implicit negative evidence. This method allows a researcher to produce an estimated distribution that approximates the true conditional distribution up to a normalizing factor. This conditional distribution is that of data (e.g., a dialectal form) conditioned on metadata (e.g., a location).

This distribution can be written as $p(D|M)$, where D and M are random variables representing the data and metadata. A query for a data value d returns metadata values m distributed according to $p(M|D = d)$. All of the returned results will have the searched-for data value, but the metadata can take any value.

For most research, $p(M|D = d)$ is not the distribution of interest, as it is conflated with the overall distribution of the metadata. For instance, if the query results indicate that 60% of users of the linguistic form d live in urban areas, this seems to suggest that the linguistic form is more likely in urban areas. But if 80% of people live in urban areas, the linguistic form is actually underrepresented in these areas, and positively associated with rural areas. An example of the effect of such misanalysis is shown in Sect. 4.2.

2.2 Reversing the conditionality

Bayesian reasoning allows a researcher to move from the sampled $p(M|D)$ distribution to the desired $p(D|M)$. We invoke Bayes' Rule:

$$p(D|M) = \frac{p(M|D)p(D)}{p(M)}$$

In some situations, these underlying distributions will be easily obtainable. For small corpora, $p(D)$ and $p(M)$ can be calculated by enumeration. For data with explicit negative examples available, $p(D)$ can be estimated as the ratio of positive examples to the sum of positive and negative examples.[1] But for queries in general, neither of these approximations is possible. Instead, we estimate $p(M)$ through the querying mechanism itself.

This is done by choosing a "baseline" query term q whose distribution is approximately independent of the metadata – that is, a query q such that $p(q|m)$ is approximately constant for all metadata values $m \in M$. If $p(q|m)$ is constant, then by Bayes' Rule:

$$p(m|q) = \frac{p(q|m)p(m)}{p(q)} \approx p(m), \quad \forall m \in M$$

Thus we can treat results from a baseline query as though they are draws directly from $p(M)$, and estimate the denominator from this distribution. The remaining unknown distribution $p(d)$ is constant for a given data value d, so combining the above equations yields the unnormalized probability $\tilde{p}(d|M)$:

$$p(d|M) \propto \tilde{p}(d|M) = \frac{p(M|d)}{p(M|q)}. \qquad (1)$$

This switch to the unnormalized distribution can improve interpretability as well. If $\tilde{p}(d|m) = 1$, then $p(m|d) = p(m|q)$, which means that the metadata m is observed for the linguistic form d just as often as it is for the baseline query. When $\tilde{p}(d|m) > 1$, the linguistic form is more common for metadata m than average, and when $\tilde{p}(d|m) < 1$, the form is less common for that metadata.[2]

[1] This can be extended to multi-class outcomes; if D has more than two outcomes, each possible outcome is an implicit negative example for the other possible outcomes.

[2] If a normalized distribution is needed, $p(d)$ may be estimable, depending on the data source. In the Twitter data presented here, tweets are sequentially numbered, so $p(d)$ could be estimated using these index numbers. This paper only uses unnormalized distributions.

2.3 Coverage and confidence

Due to the potentially non-uniform distribution of metadata, the amount of error in the estimate in Eq. 1 can vary with m. Intuitively, the confidence in the conditional probability estimates depends on the amount of data observed for each metadata value. Because queries estimate $p(M|d)$ by repeated draws from that distribution, the error in the estimate decreases as the number of draws increases. The overall error in the estimate of $\tilde{p}(d|m)$ decreases as the number of datapoints observed at m increases. This suggests estimating confidence as the square root of the count of observations of the metadata m, as the standard error of the mean decreases in proportion to the square root of the number of observations. More complex Bayesian inference can be used improve error estimates in the future.

3 Sample Implementation: SeeTweet

This section implements the method described in the previous section on a case study of the geographic distributions of linguistic forms, calculated from recent tweets. It is implemented as a suite of novel open-source Python/R programs called SeeTweet, which queries Twitter, obtains tweet locations, performs the mathematical analysis, and maps the results. The suite is available at `http://github.com/gabedoyle/seetweet`.

3.1 SeeTweet goals

Traditionally, sociolinguistic studies are highly time-intensive, and broad coverage is difficult to obtain at reasonable costs. Two data sources that we compare SeeTweet to are the *Atlas of North American English* (Labov et al., 2008, ANAE) and the *Harvard Dialect Survey* (Vaux and Golder, 2003, HDS), both of which obtained high-quality data, but over the course of years. Such studies remain the gold-standard for most purposes, but SeeTweet presents a rapid, cheap, and surprisingly effective alternative for broad coverage on some problems in dialect geography.

3.2 Querying Twitter

SeeTweet queries Twitter through its API, using Mike Verdone's Python Twitter Tools[3]. The API returns the 1000 most recent query-matching tweets or all query-matching tweets within the last week, whichever is smaller, and can be geographically limited to tweets within a certain radius of a center point. In theory, the contiguous United States are covered by a 2500km radius (Twitter's maximum) around the geographic center, approximately 39.8°N, 98.6°W, near the Kansas-Nebraska border. In practice, though, such a query only returns tweets from a non-circular region within the Great Plains.

Through trial-and-error, four search centers were found that span the contiguous U.S. with minimal overlap and nearly complete coverage,[4] located near Austin, Kansas City, San Diego, and San Francisco. All results presented here are based on these four search centers. Tweets located outside the U.S. or with unmappable locations are discarded.

The need for multiple queries and the API's tweet limit complicate the analysis. The four searches must be balanced against each other to avoid overrepresenting certain areas, especially in constructing the baseline $p(M)$. If any searches reach the 1000-tweet limit, only the search with the most recent 1000th tweet has all of its tweets used. All tweets before that tweet are removed, balancing the searches by having them all span the same timeframe. Due to the seven-day limit for recent tweets, many searches do not return 1000 hits; if none of the searches max out, all returned tweets are accepted.

3.3 Establishing the baseline

For the baseline query (used to estimate $p(M)$), SeeTweet needs a query with approximately uniform usage across the country. Function or stop words are reasonable candidates for this task. We use the word *I* here, which was chosen as it is common in all American English dialects but not other major languages of the U.S., and it has few obvious alternative forms. Other stop words were tested, but the specific baseline query had little impact on the learned distribution; correlations between maps with *I, of, the* or *a* baselines were all above .97 on both baseline distributions and estimated conditional distributions.

Each tweet from the target query requires its own baseline estimate, as the true distribution of metadata varies over time. For instance, there will be relatively more tweets on the East Coast in

[3] `http://mike.verdone.ca/twitter/`

[4] Northern New England has limited coverage, and the Mountain West returns little data outside the major cities.

the early morning (when much of the West Coast is still asleep). Thus, SeeTweet builds the baseline distribution by querying the baseline term *I*, and using the first 50 tweets preceding each target tweet. This query is performed for each search center for each tweet, with the centers balanced as discussed in the previous section.[5]

3.4 Determining coordinates and mapping

A tweet's geographic information can be specified in many ways. These include coordinates specified by a GPS system ("geotags"), user-specified coordinates, or user specification of a home location whose coordinates can be geocoded. Some tweets may include more that one of these, and SeeTweet uses this hierarchy: geotags are accepted first, followed by user-specified coordinates, followed by user-specified cities. This hierarchy moves from sources with the least noise to the most.

Obtaining coordinates from user-specified locations is done in two steps. First, if the user's location follows a "city, state" format, it is searched for in the US Board on Geographic Names's Geographic Names Information System[6], which matches city names to coordinates. Locations that do not fit the "city, state" format are checked against a manually compiled list of coordinates for 100 major American cities. This second step catches many cities that are sufficiently well-known that a nickname is used for the city (e.g., Philly) and/or the state is omitted.

Tweets whose coordinates cannot be determined by these methods are discarded; this is approximately half of the returned tweets in the experiments discussed here.

This process yields a database of tweet coordinates for each query. To build the probability distributions, SeeTweet uses a two-dimensional Gaussian kernel density estimator. Gaussian distributions account for local geographic dependency and uncertainty in the exact location of a tweeter as well as smoothing the distributions. The standard deviation ("bandwidth") of the kernels is a free parameter, and can be scaled to supply appropriate coverage/granularity of the map. We use 3 degrees (approximately 200 miles) of bandwidth for all maps in this paper, but found consistently high correlation (at least .79 by Hosmer-Lemeshow) to the ANAE data in Sect. 4.1 with bandwidths between 0.5 and 10 degrees.

The KDE estimates probabilities on a grid overlaid on the map; we make each grid box a square one-tenth of a degree on each side and calculate $\tilde{p}(d|m)$ for each box m. SeeTweet maps plot the value of $\tilde{p}(d|M)$ on a color gradient with approximately constant luminosity. Orange indicates high probability of the search term, and blue low probability. Constant luminosity is used so that confidence in the estimate can be represented by opacity; regions with higher confidence in the estimated probability appear more opaque.[7] Unfortunately, this means that the maps will not be informative if printed in black and white.

4 Experiments in dialect geography

Our first goal is to test the SeeTweet results against an existing gold standard in dialect geography; for this, we compare SeeTweet distributions of the *needs done* construction to those found by long-term sociolinguistic studies and show that the quick-and-dirty unsupervised SeeTweet distributions are accurate reflections of the slow-and-clean results. Our second goal is show the importance of using the correct conditional distribution, by comparing it to the unadjusted distribution. With these points established, we then use SeeTweet to create maps of previously uninvestigated problems.

4.1 Method verification on *need* + past participle

The *Atlas of North American English* (Labov et al., 2008) is the most complete linguistic atlas of American English dialect geography. It focuses on phonological variation, but also includes a small set of lexical/syntactic alternations. One is the *needs* + past participle construction, as in *The car needs (to be) washed.* This construction has a limited geographic distribution, and ANAE provides the first nationwide survey of its usage.

We compare SeeTweet's conditional probabilities for this construction to the ANAE responses to see how the relatively uncontrolled Twitter source compares to the tightly controlled telephone survey data that ANAE reports. We create a SeeTweet

[5]An alternative baseline, perhaps even more intuitive, would be to use some number of sequential tweets preceding the target tweet. However, the Twitter API query mechanism subsamples from the overall set of tweets, so sequential tweets may not follow the same distribution as the queries and would provide an inappropriate baseline.

[6]`http://geonames.usgs.gov/domestic/download_data.htm`

[7]Confidence is given by the square root of the smoothed number of tweets in a grid box m, $p(m|d) * C(d)$.

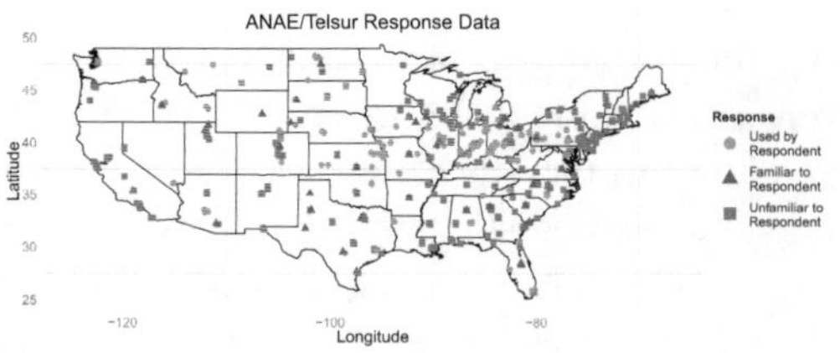

(a) ANAE/Telsur survey responses for *need*+past participle.

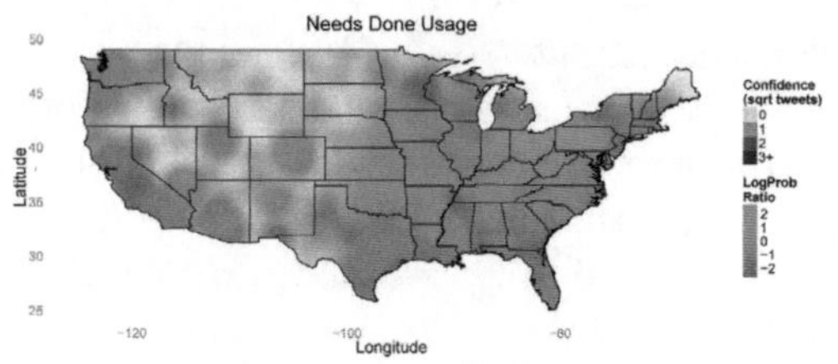

(b) SeeTweet search for "needs done".

Figure 1: Comparing the SeeTweet distribution and ANAE responses for *needs done* usage. Orange indicates higher local usage, purple moderate, and blue lower. Increased opacity indicates more confidence (i.e., more tweets) in a region.

map and visually compare this to the ANAE map, along with a Hosmer-Lemeshow-style analysis. The SeeTweet map is not calibrated to the ANAE map; they are each built independently.

The ANAE map (Fig. 1a) shows the responses of 577 survey participants who were asked about *needs done*. Three possible responses were considered: they used the construction themselves, they did not use it but thought it was used in their area, or they neither used it nor believed it to be used in their area.

The SeeTweet map (Fig. 1b) is built from five searches for the phrase "needs done", yielding 480 positive tweets and 32275 baseline tweets.[8] The component distributions $p(M|d)$ and $p(M)$ are estimated by Gaussian kernels with bandwidth 3. The log of $\tilde{p}(f|M)$, calculated as in Eq. 1, determines the color of a region; orange indicates a higher value, purple a middle (approx. 1) value, and blue a low value. Confidence in the estimate is reflected by opacity; higher opacity indicates higher confidence in the estimate. Confidence values above 3 (corresponding to 9 tweets per bin) are fully opaque. This description holds for all other maps in this paper.

We start with a qualitative comparison of the maps. Both maps show the construction to be most prominent in the area between the Plains states and central Pennsylvania (the North Midland dialect region), with minimal use in New England and Northern California and limited use elsewhere. SeeTweet lacks data in the Mountain West and Great Plains, and ANAE lacks data for Minnesota and surrounding states.[9] The most notable deviation between the maps is that SeeTweet finds the construction more common in the Southeast than ANAE does.

Quantitative comparison is possible by comparing SeeTweet's estimates of the unnormalized conditional probability of *needs done* in a location with the ANAE informants' judgments there. Two such comparisons are shown in Fig. 2.

The first comparison (Fig. 2a) is a violin plot with the ANAE divided into the three response categories. The vertical axis represents the SeeTweet estimates, and the width of a violin is proportional to the likelihood of that ANAE response coming from a region of the given SeeTweet estimate. The violins' mass shifts toward regions with lower SeeTweet estimates (down in the graph) as the respondents report decreasing use/familiarity with the construction (moving left to right).

Users of the construction are most likely to come from regions with above-average conditional probability of *needs done*, as seen in the left-most violin. Non-users, whether familiar with the construction or not, are more likely to come from regions with below-average conditional probability. Non-users who are unfamiliar with it tend to live in regions with the lowest conditional probabilities of the three groups. This shows the expected correspondence trend between the ANAE responses and the estimated prevalence of the construction in an area; the mean SeeTweet estimates for the three groups are 0.45, -0.34, and -0.61, respectively.

The second comparison (Fig. 2b) is a Hosmer-Lemeshow plot. The respondents are first divided into deciles based on the SeeTweet estimate at their location. Two mean values are calculated for each decile: the mean SeeTweet log-probability

[8]The verb *do* was used as it was found to be the most common verb in corpus work on *needs to be [verbed]* constructions (Doyle and Levy, 2008), appearing almost three times as often as the second-most common verb (*replace*).

[9]Murray et al. (1996)'s data suggest that these untested areas would not use the construction; the SeeTweet data suggests this as well.

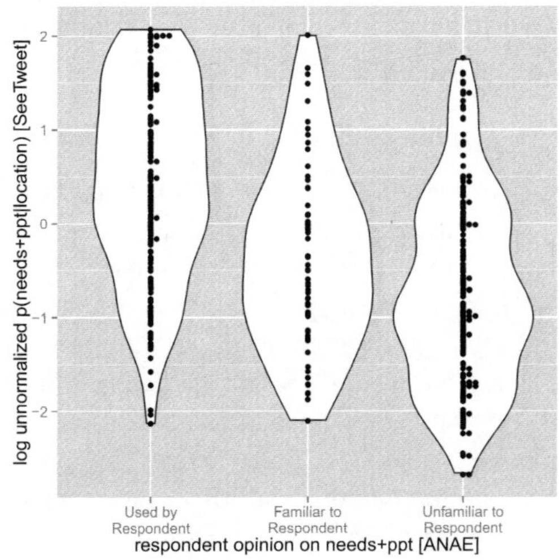

(a) Violin plot of SeeTweet estimated conditional probability against ANAE response type.

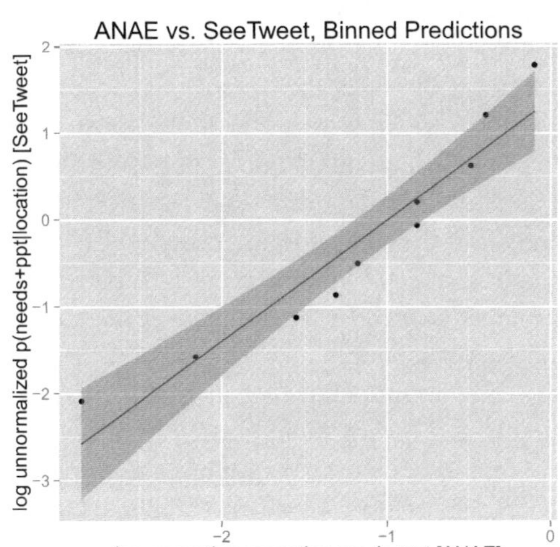

(b) Hosmer-Lemeshow plot of SeeTweet distribution deciles against average probability of ANAE respondent usage.

Figure 2: Quantifying the relationship between the SeeTweet distribution and ANAE reports for *needs done*.

estimate (increasing with each decile) and the log-proportion of respondents in that decile who use the construction.[10] If SeeTweet estimates of the conditional distribution are an adequate reflection of the ANAE survey data, we should see a tight correlation between the SeeTweet and ANAE values in each decile. The correlation between the two is $R^2 = 0.90$. This is an improvement over the inappropriate conditional distribution $p(M|d)$ that is obtained by smoothing the tweet map without dividing by the overall tweet distribution $p(M)$. Its Hosmer-Lemeshow correlation is $R^2 = 0.79$

These experiments verify two important points: the SeeTweet method can generate data that is tightly correlated with gold-standard data from controlled surveys, and conditionality inversion establishes a more appropriate distribution to correct for different baseline frequencies in tweeting. This second point will be examined further with double modals in the next section.

4.2 Double modals and the importance of the baseline

The double modal construction provides a second test case. While ungrammatical in Standard American English, forms like *I might could use your help* are grammatical and common in Southern American dialects. This construction is interesting both for its theoretical syntax implications on the nature of modals as well as the relationship between its sociolinguistic distribution and its pragmatics (Hasty, 2011).

The ANAE does not have data on double modals' distribution, but another large-scale sociolinguistic experiment does: the Harvard Dialect Survey (Vaux and Golder, 2003). This online survey obtained 30788 responses to 122 dialect questions, including the use of double modals. Katz (2013) used a nearest-neighbor model to create a $p(d|M)$ distribution over the contiguous U.S. for double modal usage, mapped in Fig. 3a.[11] Lighter colors indicate higher rates of double modal acceptance.

SeeTweet generates a similar map (Fig. 3b), based on three searches with 928 positive and 66272 baseline tweets. As with the ANAE test, the

[10] We remove all respondents who do not use the construction but report it in their area. Such respondents are fairly rare (slightly over 10% of the population), and removing this response converts the data to a binary classification problem appropriate to Hosmer-Lemeshow analysis.

[11] `http://spark.rstudio.com/jkatz/Data/comp-53.png`

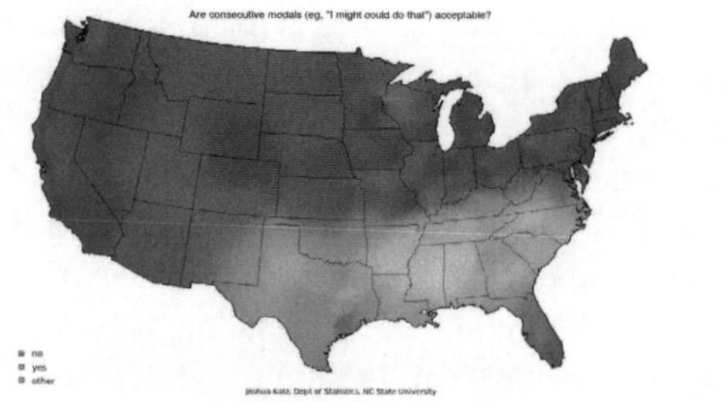

(a) Katz's nearest-neighbor estimates of the double modal's distribution in the Harvard Dialect Survey.

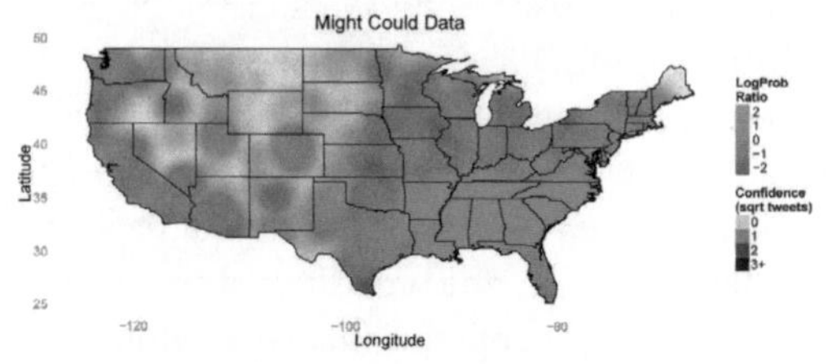

(b) SeeTweet distribution for *might could.*

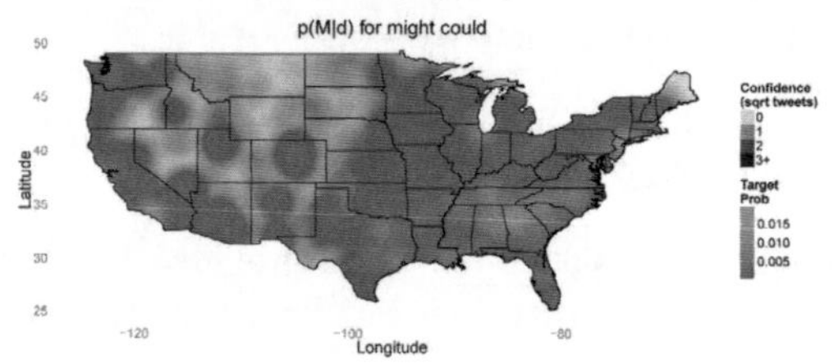

(c) Inappropriate $p(M|d)$ distribution directly estimated from Twitter hits.

Figure 3: Maps of the double modal's distribution.

SeeTweet map is built independently of the HDS data and is not calibrated to it.

The notable difference between the maps is that SeeTweet does not localize double modals as sharply to the Southeast, with pockets in cities throughout the country. This may reflect the difference in the meaning of locations on Twitter and in the HDS; Twitter locations will be a user's current home, whereas the HDS explicitly asks for a respondent's location during their formative years. SeeTweet may partly capture the spread of dialectal features due to migration.

Double modals also provide an illustration of the importance of the Bayesian inversion in Eqn. 1, as shown in Fig. 3c. This map, based on the inappropriate distribution $p(M|d)$, which does not account for the overall distribution $p(M)$, disagrees with general knowledge of the double modal's geography and the HDS map. Although both maps find double modals to be prominent around Atlanta, the inappropriate distribution find New York City, Chicago, and Los Angeles to be the next most prominent double modal regions, with only moderate probability in the rest of the Southeast. This is not incorrect, per se, as these are the sources of many double modal tweets; but these peaks are incidental, as major cities produce more tweets than the rest of the country. This is confirmed by their absence in the HDS map as well as the appropriate SeeTweet map.

4.3 Extending SeeTweet to new problems

Given SeeTweet's success in mapping *needs done* and double modals, it can also be used to test new questions. An understudied issue in past work on the *need* + past participle construction is its relationship with alternative forms *need to be* + past participle and *need* + present participle. Murray et al. (1996) suggest that their *need* + past participle users reject both alternatives, although it is worth noting that their informants are more accepting of the *to be* alternative, calling it merely "too formal", as opposed to an "odd" or "ungrammatical" opinion about the present participle form. Their analysis of the opinions on alternative forms does not go beyond this anecdotal evidence.

SeeTweet provides the opportunity to examine this issue, and finds that the *to be* form is persistent across the country (Fig. 4c), both in areas with and without the *need* + past participle form, whereas the present participle alternant (Fig. 4b) is strongest in areas where *need* + past participle is not used. Although further analysis is necessary to see if the same people use both the past participle forms, the current data suggests that the bare past participle and bare present participle forms are in complementary distribution, while the *to be* form is acceptable in most locations.

We also compare the alternative constructions to the ANAE data. Using Hosmer-Lemeshow analysis, we find negative correlations: $R^2 = -.65$ for *needs doing* and $R^2 = -.25$ for *needs to be done*. In addition, mean SeeTweet estimates of *needs doing* usage were lower for regions where respondents use *needs done* than for regions where they do not: $-.93$ versus $-.49$.[12] Thus, SeeTweet provides evidence that *needs done* and *needs doing* are in a geographically distinct distribution, while *needs done* and *needs to be done* are at most weakly distinct.

[12] SeeTweet estimates of *needs to be done* usage were comparable in both regions, $-.018$ against $.019$.

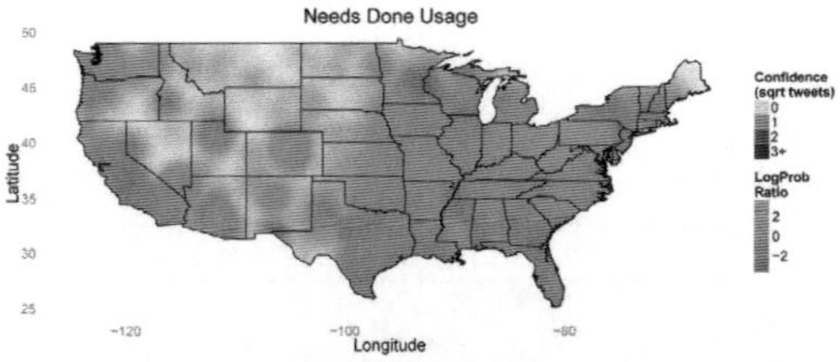

(a) "Needs done" distribution

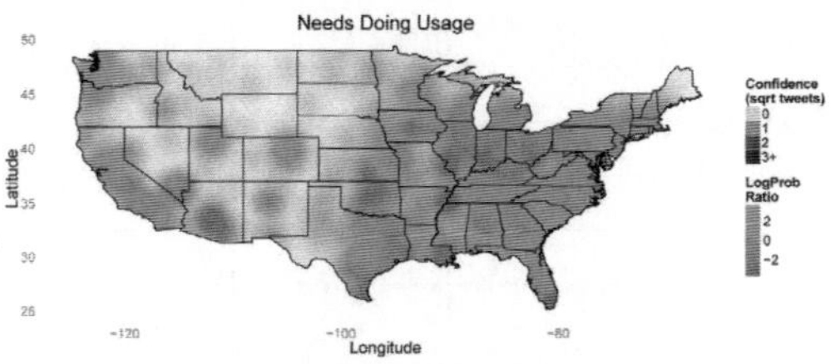

(b) "Needs doing" distribution

(c) "Needs to be done" distribution

Figure 4: SeeTweet distributions for *needs done*, *needs to be done*, and *needs doing*.

5 The appropriateness of Twitter as a data source

A possible concern with this analysis is that Twitter could be a biased and noisy dataset, inappropriate for sociolinguistic investigation. Twitter skews toward the young and slightly toward urbanites (Duggan and Brenner, 2013). However, as young urbanites tend to drive language change (Labov et al., 2008), any such bias would make the results more useful for examining sociolinguistic changes and emergent forms. The informality of the medium also provides unedited writing data that is more reflective of non-standard usage than most corpora, and its large amounts of data in short timescales offers new abilities to track emerging linguistic change.

As for noise in the tweet data and locations, the strong correlations between the gold-standard and SeeTweet results show that, at least for these features, the noise is mitigated by the size of dataset. We examined the impact of noise on the *needs done* dataset by manually inspecting the data for false positives and re-mapping the clean data. Although the false positive rate was 12%, the conditional distribution learned with and without the false positives removed remained tightly correlated, at $R^2 = .94$. The SeeTweet method appears to be robust to false positives, although noisier queries may require manual inspection.

A final point to note is that while the datasets used in constructing these maps are relatively small, they are crucially derived from big data. Because the *needs done* and double modal constructions are quite rare, there would be very few examples in a standard-sized corpus. Only because there are so many tweets are we able to get the hundreds of examples we used in this study.

6 Conclusion

We have shown that Bayesian inversion can be used to build conditional probability distributions over data given metadata from the results of queries on social media, connecting query-derived data to traditional data sources. Tests on Twitter show that such calculations can provide dialect geographies that are well correlated with existing gold-standard sources at a fraction of the time, cost, and effort.

Acknowledgments

We wish to thank Roger Levy, Dan Michel, Emily Morgan, Mark Myslín, Bill Presant, Agatha Ventura, and the reviewers for their advice, suggestions, and testing. This work was supported in part by NSF award 0830535.

References

Gabriel Doyle and Roger Levy. 2008. Environment prototypicality in syntactic alternation. In *Proceedings of the 34th Annual Meeting of the Berkeley Linguistics Society*.

Maeve Duggan and Joanna Brenner. 2013. The demographics of social media users – 2012. Pew Internet and American Life Project.

J. Daniel Hasty. 2011. I might would not say that: A sociolinguistic study of double modal acceptance. In *University of Pennsylvania Working Papers in Linguistics*, volume 17.

Joshua Katz. 2013. Beyond "soda, pop, or coke": Regional dialect variation in the continental US. Retrieved from `http://www4.ncsu.edu/~jakatz2/project-dialect.html`.

William Labov, Sharon Ash, and Charles Boberg. 2008. *The Atlas of North American English. Phonetics, Phonology, and Sound Change*. de Gruyter Mouton.

Thomas Murray, Timothy Frazer, and Beth Lee Simon. 1996. Need + past participle in American English. *American Speech*, 71:255–271.

Daisuke Okanohara and Jun'ichi Tsujii. 2007. A discriminative language model with pseudo-negative samples. In *Proceedings of the 45th Annual Meeting of the Association of Computational Linguistics*.

Hoifung Poon, Colin Cherry, and Kristina Toutanova. 2009. Unsupervised morphological segmentation with log-linear models. In *Proceedings of the North American Chapter of the Association for Computational Linguistics*.

Joshua Tenenbaum and Thomas Griffiths. 2001. Generalization, similiarity, and Bayesian inference. *Behavioral and Brain Sciences*, 24:629–640.

Bert Vaux and Scott Golder. 2003. Harvard dialect survey. Available at `http://www4.uwm.edu/FLL/linguistics/dialect/index.html`.

Modeling the Use of Graffiti Style Features to Signal Social Relations within a Multi-Domain Learning Paradigm

Mario Piergallini[1], A. Seza Doğruöz[2], Phani Gadde[1], David Adamson[1], Carolyn P. Rosé[1,3]

[1]Language Technologies Institute
Carnegie Mellon University
5000 Forbes Avenue,
Pittsburgh PA, 15213
{mpiergal,pgadde,
dadamson}@cs.cmu.edu

[2]Tilburg University, TSH,
5000 LE Tilburg, The Netherlands/
Language Technologies Institute, Carnegie Mellon University, 5000 Forbes Ave.,Pittsburgh PA 15213
a.s.dogruoz@gmail.com

[3]Human-Computer Interaction Institute
Carnegie Mellon University
5000 Forbes Avenue,
Pittsburgh PA, 15213
cprose@cs.cmu.edu

Abstract

In this paper, we present a series of experiments in which we analyze the usage of graffiti style features for signaling personal gang identification in a large, online street gangs forum, with an accuracy as high as 83% at the gang alliance level and 72% for the specific gang. We then build on that result in predicting how members of different gangs signal the relationship between their gangs within threads where they are interacting with one another, with a predictive accuracy as high as 66% at this thread composition prediction task. Our work demonstrates how graffiti style features signal social identity both in terms of personal group affiliation and between group alliances and oppositions. When we predict thread composition by modeling identity and relationship simultaneously using a multi-domain learning framework paired with a rich feature representation, we achieve significantly higher predictive accuracy than state-of-the-art baselines using one or the other in isolation.

1 Introduction

Analysis of linguistic style in social media has grown in popularity over the past decade. Popular prediction problems within this space include gender classification (Argamon et al., 2003), age classification (Argamon et al., 2007), political affiliation classification (Jiang & Argamon, 2008), and sentiment analysis (Wiebe et al., 2004). From a sociolinguistic perspective, this work can be thought of as fitting within the area of machine learning approaches to the analysis of style (Biber & Conrad, 2009), perhaps as a counterpart to work by variationist sociolinguists in their effort to map out the space of language variation and its accompanying social interpretation (Labov, 2010; Eckert & Rickford, 2001). One aspiration of work in social media analysis is to contribute to this literature, but that requires that our models are interpretable. The contribution of this paper is an investigation into the ways in which stylistic features behave in the language of participants of a large online community for street gang members. We present a series of experiments that reveal new challenges in modeling stylistic variation with machine learning approaches. As we will argue, the challenge is achieving high predictive accuracy without sacrificing interpretability.

Gang language is a type of sociolect that has so far not been the focus of modeling in the area of social media analysis. Nevertheless, we argue that the gangs forum we have selected as our data source provides a strategic source of data for exploring how social context influences stylistic language choices, in part because it is an area where the dual goals of predictive accuracy and interpretability are equally important. In particular, evidence that gang related crime may account for up to 80% of crime in the United States attests to the importance of understanding the social practices of this important segment of society (Johnsons, 2009). Expert testimony attributing meaning to observed, allegedly gang-related social practices is frequently used as evidence of malice in criminal investigations (Greenlee, 2010). Frequently, it is police officers who are given the authority to serve as expert witnesses on this interpretation because of their routine interaction with gang members.

Nevertheless, one must consider their lack of formal training in forensic linguistics (Coulthard & Johnson, 2007) and the extent to which the nature of their interaction with gang members may subject them to a variety of cognitive biases that may threaten the validity of their interpretation (Kahneman, 2011).

Gang-related social identities are known to be displayed through clothing, tattoos, and language practices including speech, writing, and gesture (Valentine, 1995), and even dance (Philips, 2009). Forensic linguists have claimed that these observed social practices have been over-interpreted and inaccurately interpreted where they have been used as evidence in criminal trials and that they may have even resulted in sentences that are not justified by sufficient evidence (Greenlee, 2010). Sociolinguistic analysis of language varieties associated with gangs and other counter-cultural groups attests to the challenges in reliable interpretation of such practices (Bullock, 1996; Lefkowitz, 1989). If we as a community can understand better how stylistic features behave due to the choices speakers make in social contexts, we will be in a better position to achieve high predictive accuracy with models that are nevertheless interpretable. And ultimately, our models may offer insights into usage patterns of these social practices that may then offer a more solid empirical foundation for interpretation and use of language as evidence in criminal trials.

In the remainder of the paper we describe our annotated corpus. We then motivate the technical approach we have taken to modeling linguistic practices within the gangs forum. Next, we present a series of experiments evaluating our approach and conclude with a discussion of remaining challenges.

2 The Gangs Forum Corpus

The forum that provides data for our experiments is an online forum for members of street gangs. The site was founded in November, 2006. It was originally intended to be an educational resource compiling knowledge about the various gang organizations and the street gang lifestyle. Over time, it became a social outlet for gang members. There are still traces of this earlier focus in that there are links at the top of each page to websites dedicated to information about particular gangs. At the time of scraping its contents, it had over a million posts and over twelve thousand active users. Our work focuses on analysis of stylistic choices that are influenced by social context, so it is important to consider some details about the social context of this forum. Specifically, we discuss which gangs are present in the data and how the gangs are organized into alliances and rivalries. Users are annotated with their gang identity at two levels of granularity, and threads are annotated with labels that indicate which gang dominates and how the participating gangs relate to one another.

2.1 User-Level Annotations

At the fine-grained level, we annotated users with the gang that they indicated being affiliated with, including Bloods, Crips, Hoovers, Gangster Disciples, other Folk Nation, Latin Kings, Vice Lords, Black P. Stones, other People Nation, Trinitarios, Norteños, and Sureños. There was also an Other category for the smaller gangs. For a coarser grained annotation of gang affiliation, we also noted the nation, otherwise known as gang alliance, each gang was associated with.

For our experiments, a sociolinguist with significant domain expertise annotated the gang identity of 3384 users. Information used in our annotation included the user's screen name, their profile, which included a slot for gang affiliation, and the content of their posts. We used regular expressions to find gang names or other identifiers occurring within the gang affiliation field and the screen names and annotated the users that matched. If the value extracted for the two fields conflicted, we marked them as claiming multiple gangs. For users whose affiliation could not be identified automatically, we manually checked their profile to see if their avatar (an image that accompanies their posts) or other fields there contained any explicit information. Otherwise, we skimmed their posts for explicit statements of gang affiliation.

Affiliation was unambiguously identified automatically for 56% of the 3384 users from their affiliation field. Another 36% were identified automatically based on their screen name. Manual inspection was only necessary in 9% of the cases. Users that remained ambiguous, were clearly fake or joke accounts, or who claimed multiple gangs were grouped together in an "Other" category, which accounts for 6.2% of the total. Thus, 94% of the users were classified into the 12 specific gangs mentioned above.

At a coarse-grained level, users were also associated with a nation. The nation category was inspired by the well-known gang alliances known as the People Nation and Folks Nation, which are city-wide alliances of gangs in Chicago. We labeled the Crips and Hoovers as a nation since they are closely allied gangs. Historically, the Hoovers began breaking away from the Crips and are rivals with certain subsets of Crips, but allies with the majority of other Crips gangs. The complex inner structure of the Crips alliance will be discussed in Section 5 where we interpret our quantitative results.

There are a large number of gangs that comprise the People and Folks Nations. The major gangs within the People Nation are the Latin Kings, Vice Lords and Black P. Stones. The Folks Nation is dominated by the Gangster Disciples with other Folks Nation gangs being significantly smaller. The People Nation, Blood and Norteños gangs are in a loose, national alliance against the opposing national alliance of the Folks Nation, Crips and Sureños. Remaining gangs were annotated as other, such as the Trinitarios, that don't fit into this national alliance system nor even smaller alliances.

2.2 Thread-Level Annotations

In addition to person-level annotations of gang and nation, we also annotated 949 threads with dominant gang as well as thread composition, by which we mean whether the users who participated on the thread were only from allied gangs, included opposing gangs, or contained a mix of gangs that were neither opposing nor allied. These 949 threads were ones where a majority of the users who posted were in the set of 3384 users annotated with a gang identity.

For the dominant gang annotation at the gang level, we consider only participants on the thread for whom there was an annotated gang affiliation. If members of a single gang produced the majority of the posts in the thread, then that was annotated as the dominant gang of the thread. If no gang had a majority in the thread, it was instead labeled as Mixed. For dominant gang at the nation level, the same procedure was used, but instead of looking for which gang accounted for more of the members, we looked for which gang alliance accounted for the majority of users.

For the thread composition annotation, we treated the Bloods, People Nation, and Norteños as allied with each other as the "Red set". We treated Crips, Hoovers, Folks Nation, and Sureños as allies with each other as the "Blue set". The Red and Blue sets oppose one another. The Latin Kings and Trinitarios also oppose one another. Thread composition was labeled as Allied, Mixed or Opposing depending on the gangs that appeared in the thread. As with the dominant gang annotation, only annotated users were considered. If all of the posts were by users of the same gang or allied gangs, the thread was labeled as Allied. If there were any posts from rival gangs, it was labeled as Opposing. Otherwise, it was labeled as Mixed. If the users were all labeled with Other as their gang it was also labeled as Mixed.

3 Modeling Language Practices at the Feature Level

In this section, we first describe the rich feature representation we developed for this work. Finally, we discuss the motivation for employing a multi-domain learning framework in our machine-learning experiments.

3.1 Feature Space Design: Graffiti Style Features

While computational work modeling gang-related language practices is scant, we can learn lessons from computational work on other types of sociolects that may motivate a reasonable approach. Gender prediction, for example, is a problem where there have been numerous publications in the past decade (Corney et al., 2002; Argamon et al., 2003; Schler et al., 2005; Schler, 2006; Yan & Yan, 2006; Zhang et al., 2009). Because of the complex and subtle way gender influences language choices, it is a strategic example to motivate our work.

Gender-based language variation arises from multiple sources. Among these, it has been noted that within a single corpus comprised of samples of male and female language that the two genders do not speak or write about the same topics. This is problematic because word-based features such as unigrams and bigrams, which are very frequently used, are highly likely to pick up on differences in topic (Schler, 2006) and possibly perspective. Thus, in cases where linguistic style variation is specifically of interest, these features do not offer good generalizability (Gianfortoni et al., 2011). Similarly, in our work, members of different gangs are located in different areas associated with different concerns and levels of socioeconomic status. Thus, in working to model the stylistic choices of gang forum members, it is important to consider how to avoid overfitting to content-level distinctions.

Typical kinds of features that have been used in gender prediction apart from unigram features include part-of-speech (POS) ngrams (Argamon et al., 2003), word-structure features that cluster words according to endings that indicate part of speech (Zhang et al., 2009), features that indicate the distribution of word lengths within a corpus (Corney et al., 2002), usage of punctuation, and features related to usage of jargon (Schler et al., 2005). In Internet-based communication, additional features have been investigated such as usage of internet specific features including "internet speak" (e.g., lol, wtf, etc.), emoticons, and URLs (Yan & Yan, 2006).

Transformation	Origin or meaning
b^, c^, h^, p^	"Bloods up" Positive towards Bloods, Crips, Hoovers, Pirus, respectively
b → bk, c → ck	Blood killer, Crip killer
h → hk, p → pk	Hoover killer, Piru killer
ck → cc, kc	Avoid use of 'ck' since it represents Crip killer
o → x, o → ø	Represents crosshairs, crossing out the '0's in a name like Rollin' **60s** Crips
b → 6	Represents the six-pointed star. Symbol of Folk Nation and the affiliated Crips.
e → 3	Various. One is the trinity in Trinitario.
s → 5	Represents the five-pointed star. Symbol of People Nation and the affiliated Bloods.

Table 1: Orthographical substitutions from gang graffiti symbolism

In order to place ourselves in the best position to build an interpretable model, our space of graffiti style features was designed based on a combination of qualitative observations of the gangs forum data and reading about gang communication using web accessible resources such as informational web pages linked to the forum and other resources related to gang communication (Adams & Winter, 1997; Garot, 2007). Specifically, in our corpus we observed gang members using what we refer to as graffiti style features to mark their identity. Gang graffiti employs shorthand references to convey affiliation or threats (Adams & Winter, 1997). For example, the addition of a <k> after a letter representing a rival gang stands for "killer." So, writing <ck> would represent "crip killer." A summary of these substitutions can be seen in Table 1. Unfortunately, only about 25% of the users among the 12,000 active users employ these features in their posts, which limits their ability to achieve a high accuracy, but nevertheless offers the opportunity to model a frequent social practice observed in the corpus.

The graffiti style features were extracted using a rule-based algorithm that compares words against a standard dictionary as well as using some phonotactic constraints on the position of certain letters. The dictionary was constructed using all of the unique words found in the AQUAINT corpus (Graff, 2002). If a word in a post did not match any word from the AQUAINT corpus, we tested it against each of the possible transformations in Table 1. Transformations were applied to words using finite state transducers. If some combination transformations from that table applied to the observed word could produce some term from the AQUAINT corpus, then we counted that observed word as containing the features associated with the applied transformations.

The transformations were applied in the order of least likely to occur in normal text to the most likely. Since 'bk' only occurs in a handful of obscure words, for example, almost any occurrence of it can be assumed to be a substitution and the 'k' can safely be removed before the next step. By contrast, 'cc' and 'ck' occur in many common words so they must be saved for last to ensure that the final dictionary checks have any simultaneous substitutions already removed.

When computing values for the graffiti style features for a text, the value for each feature was computed as the number of words (tokens) that contained the feature divided by the total number of words (tokens) in the document. We used a set of 13 of these features, chosen on the basis of how frequently they occurred and how strongly they distinguished gangs from one another (for example, substituting '$' for 's' was a transformation that was common across gangs in our qualitative analysis, and thus did not seem beneficial to include).

Transformation	Freq.	False Positive rate	False Negative rate
b^, c^, h^, p^	15103	0%	0%
b → bk	26923	1%	0%
c → ck	16144	25%	8%
h → hk	10053	1%	0%
p → pk	5669	3%	0%
ck → cc, kc	72086	2%	0%
o → x, o → ø	13646	15%	5%
b → 6	2470	16%	0%
e → 3	8628	28%	1%
s → 5	13754	6%	0%

Table 2: Evaluation of extraction of graffiti style features over the million post corpus

The feature-extraction approach was developed iteratively. After extracting the features over the corpus of 12,000 active users, we created lists of words where the features were detected, sorted by frequency. We then manually examined the words to determine where we observed errors occurring and then made some minor adjustments to the extractors. Table 2 displays a quantitative evaluation of the accuracy of the graffiti style feature extraction.

Performance of the style features was estimated for each style-feature rule. For each rule, we compute a false positive and false negative rate. For false positive rate, we begin by retrieving the list of words marked by the feature extraction rule containing the associated style marking. From the full set of words that matched a style feature rule, we selected the 200 most frequently occurring word types. We manually checked that complete set of word tokens and counted the number of misfires. The false positive rate was then calculated for each feature by dividing the number of tokens that were misfires over the total number of tokens in the set. In all cases, we ensured that at least 55% of the total word tokens were covered, so additional words may have been examined.

In the case of false negatives, we started with the set of word types that did not match any word in the dictionary and also did not trigger the style feature rule. Again we sorted word types in this list by frequency and selected the top 200 most frequent. We then manually checked for missed instances where the associated style feature was used but not detected. The false negative rate was then the total number of word tokens within this word type set divided by the total number of word tokens in the complete set of word types.

Another type of feature we used referenced the nicknames gangs used for themselves and other gangs, which we refer to as Names features. The intuition behind this is simple: someone who is a member of the Crips gang will talk about the Crips more often. The measure is simply how often a reference to a gang occurs per document. Some of these nicknames we included were gang-specific insults, with the idea that if someone uses insults for Crips often, they are likely not a Crip. The last type of reference is words that refer to gang alliances like the People Nation and Folks Nation. Members of those Chicago-based gangs frequently refer to their gang as the "Almighty [gang name] Nation".

Gang	Positive/Neutral Mentions	Insults
Crips	crip, loc	crab, ckrip, ck
Bloods	blood, damu, piru, ubn	slob, bklood, pkiru, bk, pk
Hoovers	hoover, groover, crim, hgc, hcg	snoover, hkoover, hk
Gangster Disciples	GD, GDN, Gangster Disciple	gk, dk, nigka
Folks Nations	folk, folknation, almighty, nation	
People Nation	people, peoplenation, almighty, nation	
Latin Kings	alkqn, king, queen	
Black P. Stones	stone, abpsn, moe, black p.	
Vice Lords	vice, lord, vl, avln, foe, 4ch	

Table 3: Patterns used for gang name features. For all gangs listed in the table, there are slang terms used as positive mentions of the gang. For some gangs there are also typical insult names.

We used regular expressions to capture occurrences of these words and variations on them such as the use of the orthographic substitutions mentioned previously, plurals, feminine forms, etc. Additionally, in the Blood and Hoover features, they sometimes use numbers to replace the 'o's representing the street that their gang is located on. So the Bloods from 34th Street, say, might write "Bl34d".

3.2 Computational Paradigm: Multi-domain learning

The key to training an interpretable model in our work is to pair a rich feature representation with a model that enables accounting for the structure of the social context explicitly. Recent work in the area of multi-domain learning offers such an opportunity (Arnold, 2009; Daumé III, 2007; Finkel & Manning, 2009). In our work, we treat the dominant gang of a thread as a domain for the purpose of detecting thread composition. This decision is based on the observation that while it is a common practice across gangs to express their attitudes towards allied and opposing gangs using stylistic features like the Graffiti style features, the particular features that serve the purpose of showing affiliation or opposition differ by gang. Thus, it is not the features themselves that carry significance, but rather a combination of who is saying it and how it is being said.

As a paradigm for multi-domain learning, we use Daume's Frustratingly Easy Domain Adaptation approach (Daumé III, 2007) as implemented in LightSIDE (Mayfield & Rosé, 2013). In this work, Daumé III proposes a very simple "easy adapt" approach, which was originally proposed in the context of adapting to a specific target domain, but easily generalizes to multi-domain learning. The key idea is to create domain-specific versions of the original input features depending on which domain a data point belongs to. The original features represent a domain-general feature space. This allows any standard learner to appropriately optimize the weights of domain-specific and domain-general features simultaneously. In our work, this allows us to model how different gangs signal within-group identification and across-group animosity or alliance using different features. The resulting model will enable us to identify how gangs differ in their usage of style features to display social identity and social relations.

It has been noted in prior work that style is often expressed in a topic-specific or even domain-specific way (Gianfortoni et al., 2011). What exacerbates these problems in text processing approaches is that texts are typically represented with features that are at the wrong level of granularity for what is being modeled. Specifically, for practical reasons, the most common types of features used in text classification tasks are still unigrams, bigrams, and part-of-speech bigrams, which are highly prone to over-fitting. When text is represented with features that operate at too fine-grained of a level, features that truly model the target style are not present within the model. Thus, the trained models are not able to capture the style itself and instead capture features that correlate with that style within the data (Gianfortoni et al., 2011).

This is particularly problematic in cases where the data is not independent and identically distributed (IID), and especially where instances that belong to different subpopulations within the non-IID data have different class value distributions. In those cases, the model will tend to give weight to features that indicate the subpopulation rather than features that model the style. Because of this insight from prior work, we contrast our stylistic features with unigram features and our multi-domain approach with a single-domain approach wherever appropriate in our experiments presented in Section 4.

4 Prediction Experiments

In this section we present a series of prediction experiments using the annotations described in Section 2. We begin by evaluating our ability to identify gang affiliation for individual users. Because we will use dominant gang as a domain feature in our multi-domain learning approach to detect thread composition, we also present an evaluation of our ability to automatically predict dominant gang for a thread. Finally, we evaluate our ability to predict thread composition. All of our experiments use L1 regularized Logistic regression.

4.1 Predicting Gang Affiliation per User

The first set of prediction experiments we ran was to identify gang affiliation. For this experiment, the full set of posts contributed by a user was concatenated together and used as a document from which to extract text features. We conducted this experiment using a 10-fold cross-validation over the full set of users annotated for gang affiliation. Results contrasting alternative feature spaces at the gang level and nation level are displayed in Table 4. We begin with a unigram feature space as the baseline. We contrast this with the Graffiti style features described above in Section 3.1. Because all of the Graffiti features are encoded in words as pairs of characters, we contrast the carefully extracted Graffiti style features with character bigrams. Next we test the nickname features also described in Section 3.1. Finally, we test combinations of these features.

	Gang	Nation
Unigrams	70%	81%
Character Bigrams	64%	76%
Graffiti Features	44%	68%
Name Features	63%	78%
Name + Graffiti	67%	81%
Unigrams + Name	70%	82%
Unigrams + Character Bigrams	71%	82%
Unigrams + Graffiti	71%	82%
Unigrams + Name + Graffiti	<u>72%</u>	<u>83%</u>
Unigrams + Name + Character Bigrams	<u>72%</u>	79%

Table 4: Results (percent accuracy) for gang affiliation prediction at the gang and nation level.

We note that the unigram space is a challenging feature space to beat, possibly because only about 25% of the users employ the style features we identified with any regularity. The character bigram space actually significantly outperforms the Graffiti features, in part because it captures aspects of both the Graffiti features, the name features, and also some other gang specific jargon. When we combine the stylistic features with unigrams, we start to see an advantage over unigrams alone. The best combination is Unigrams, Graffiti style features, and Name features, at 72% accuracy (.65 Kappa) at the gang level and 83% accuracy (.69 Kappa) at the nation level. Overall the accuracy is reasonable and offers us the opportunity to expand our analysis of social practices on the gangs forum to a much larger sample in our future work than we present in this first foray.

4.2 Predicting Dominant Gang per Thread

In Section 4.3 we present our multi-domain learning approach to predicting thread composition. In that work, we use dominant gang on a thread as a domain. In those experiments, we contrast results with hand-annotated dominant gang and automatically-predicted dominant gang. In order to compute an automatically-identified dominant gang for the 949 threads used in that experiment, we build a model for gang affiliation prediction using data from the 2689 users who did not participate on any of those threads as training data so there is no overlap in users between train and test.

The feature space for that classifier included unigrams, character bigrams, and the gang name features since this feature space tied for best performing at the gang level in Section 4.1 and presents a slightly lighter weight solution than Unigrams, graffiti style features, and gang name features. We applied that trained classifier to the users who participated on the 949 threads. From the automatically-predicted gang affiliations, we computed a dominant gang using the gang and nation level for each thread using the same rules that we applied to the annotated user identities for the annotated dominant gang labels described in Section 2.2. We then evaluated our performance by comparing the automatically-identified dominant gang with the more carefully annotated one. Our automatically identified dominant gang labels were 73.3% accurate (.63 Kappa) at the gang level and 76.6% accurate (.72 Kappa) at the nation level. This experiment is mainly important as preparation for the experiment presented in Section 4.3.

4.3 Predicting Thread Composition

Our final and arguably most important prediction experiments were for prediction of thread composition. This is where we begin to investigate how stylistic choices reflect the relationships between participants in a discussion. We conducted this experiment twice, specifically, once with the annotated dominant gang labels (Table 5) and once with the automatically predicted ones (Table 6). In both cases, we evaluate gang and nation as alternative domain variables. In both sets of experiments, the multi-domain versions significantly outperform the baseline across a variety of feature spaces, and the stylistic features provide benefit above the unigram baseline. In both tables the domain and nation variables are hand-annotated. * indicates the results are significantly better than the no domain unigram baseline. <u>Underline</u> indicates best result per column. And **bold** indicates overall best result.

The best performing models in both cases used a multi-domain model paired with a stylistic feature space rather than a unigram space. Both models performed significantly better than any of the unigram models, even the multi-domain versions with annotated domains. Where gang was used as the domain variable and Graffiti style features were the features used for prediction, we found that the high weight features associated with Allied threads were either positive about gang identity for a variety of gangs other than their own (like B^ in a Crips dominated thread) or protective (like CC in a Bloods dominated thread).

	No Domain	Dominant Gang	Dominant Nation
Unigrams	53%	58%*	60%*
Character Bigrams	49%	55%	56%
Graffiti Features	53%	54%	61%*
Name Features	54%	63%*	**66%***
Name + Graffiti	54%	61%*	65%*
Unigrams + Name	52%	58%*	61%*
Unigrams + Graffiti	53%	57%	57%
Unigrams + Name + Graffiti	54%	61%*	65%*

Table 5: Results (percent accuracy) for thread composition prediction, contrasting a single domain approach with two multi-domain approaches, one with dominant gang as the domain variables, and the other with dominant nation as the domain variable. In this case, the domain variables are annotated.

	No Domain	Dominant Gang	Dominant Nation
Unigrams	53%	57%	57%
Character Bigrams	49%	53%	55%
Graffiti Features	53%	**65%***	58%*
Name Features	54%	61%*	59%*
Name + Graffiti	54%	60%*	59%*
Unigrams + Name	52%	56%	56%
Unigrams + Graffiti	53%	58%*	57%
Unigrams + Name + Graffiti	54%	60%*	59%*

Table 6: Results (percent accuracy) for thread composition prediction, contrasting a single domain approach with two multi-domain approaches with predicted domain variables, one with dominant gang as the domain variables, and the other with dominant nation as the domain variable.

Crips-related features were the most frequent within this set, perhaps because of the complex social structure within the Crips alliance, as discussed above. We saw neither features associated with negative attitudes of the gang towards others nor other gangs towards them in these Allied threads, but in opposing threads, we see both, for example, PK in Crips threads or BK in Bloods threads. Where unigrams are used as the feature space, the high weight features are almost exclusively in the general space rather than the domain space, and are generally associated with attitude directly rather than gang identity. For example, "lol," and "wtf."

5 Conclusions

We have presented a series of experiments in which we have analyzed the usage of stylistic features for signaling personal gang identification and between gang relations in a large, online street gangs forum. This first foray into modeling the language practices of gang members is one step towards providing an empirical foundation for interpretation of these practices. In embarking upon such an endeavor, however, we must use caution. In machine-learning approaches to modeling stylistic variation, a preference is often given to accounting for variance over interpretability, with the result that interpretability of models is sacrificed in order to achieve a higher prediction accuracy. Simple feature encodings such as unigrams are frequently chosen in a (possibly misguided) attempt to avoid bias. As we have discussed above, however, rather than cognizant introduction of bias informed by prior linguistic work, unknown bias is frequently introduced because of variables we have not accounted for and confounding factors we are not aware of, especially in social data that is rarely IID. Our results suggest that a strategic combination of rich feature encodings and structured modeling approach leads to high accuracy and interpretability. In our future work, we will use our models to investigate language practices in the forum at large rather than the subset of users and threads used in this paper[1].

[1] An appendix with additional analysis and the specifics of the feature extraction rules can be found at http://www.cs.cmu.edu/~cprose/Graffiti.html. This work was funded in part by ARL 000665610000034354.

References

Adams, K. & Winter, A. (1997). Gang graffiti as a discourse genre, *Journal of Sociolinguistics* 1/3. Pp 337-360.

Argamon, S., Koppel, M., Fine, J., & Shimoni, A. (2003). Gender, genre, and writing style in formal written texts, *Text*, 23(3), pp 321-346.

Argamon, S., Koppel, M., Pennebaker, J., & Schler, J. (2007). Mining the blogosphere: age, gender, and the varieties of self-expression. *First Monday* 12(9).

Arnold, A. (2009). Exploiting Domain And Task Regularities For Robust Named Entity Recognition. PhD thesis, Carnegie Mellon University, 2009.

Biber, D. & Conrad, S. (2009). *Register, Genre, and Style*, Cambridge University Press

Bullock, B. (1996). Derivation and Linguistic Inquiry: Les Javnais, *The French Review* 70(2), pp 180-191.

Corney, M., de Vel, O., Anderson, A., Mohay, G. (2002). Gender-preferential text mining of e-mail discourse, in the Proceedings of the 18th Annual Computer Security Applications Conference.

Coulthard, M. & Johnson, A. (2007). *An Introduction to Forensic Linguistics: Language as Evidence*, Routledge

Daumé III, H. (2007). Frustratingly Easy Domain Adaptation. In Proceedings of the 45th Annual Meeting of the Association of Computational Linguistics, pages 256-263.

Eckert, P. & Rickford, J. (2001). *Style and Sociolinguistic Variation*, Cambridge: University of Cambridge Press.

Finkel, J. & Manning, C. (2009). Hierarchical Bayesian Domain Adaptation. In *Proceedings of Human Language Technologies: The 2009 Annual Conference of the North American Chapter of the Association for Computational Linguistics.*

Garot, R. (2007). "Where You From!": Gang Identity as Performance, Journal of Contemporary Ethnography, 36, pp 50-84.

Gianfortoni, P., Adamson, D. & Rosé, C. P. (2011). Modeling Stylistic Variation in Social Media with Stretchy Patterns, in *Proceedings of First Workshop on Algorithms and Resources for Modeling of Dialects and Language Varieties,* Edinburgh, Scottland, UK, pp 49-59.

Graff, D. (2002). The AQUAINT Corpus of English News Text, Linguistic Data Consortium, Philadelphia

Greenlee, M. (2010). Youth and Gangs, in M. Coulthard and A. Johnson (Eds.). *The Routledge Handbook of Forensic Linguistics*, Routledge.

Jiang, M. & Argamon, S. (2008). Political leaning categorization by exploring subjectivities in political blogs. In *Proceedings of the 4th International Conference on Data Mining*, pages 647-653.

Johnsons, K. (2009). FBI: Burgeoning gangs behind up to 80% of U.S. Crime, in USA Today, January 29, 2009.

Kahneman, D. (2011). *Thinking Fast and Slow*, Farrar, Straus, and Giroux

Krippendorff, K. (2013). *Content Analysis: An Introduction to Its Methodology* (Chapter 13), SAGE Publications

Labov, W. (2010). *Principles of Linguistic Change: Internal Factors (Volume 1)*, Wiley-Blackwell.

Lefkowitz, N. (1989). Talking Backwards in French, *The French Review* 63(2), pp 312-322.

Mayfield, E. & Rosé, C. P. (2013). LightSIDE: Open Source Machine Learning for Text Accessible to Non-Experts, in *The Handbook of Automated Essay Grading*, Routledge Academic Press. http://lightsidelabs.com/research/

Philips, S. (2009). Crip Walk, Villian Dance, Pueblo Stroll: The Embodiment of Writing in African American Gang Dance, Anthropological Quarterly 82(1), pp69-97.

Schler, J., Koppel, M., Argamon, S., Pennebaker, J. (2005). Effects of Age and Gender on Blogging, Proceedings of AAAI Spring Symposium on Computational Approaches for Analyzing Weblogs.

Schler, J. (2006). Effects of Age and Gender on Blogging. *Artificial Intelligence*, *86*, 82-84.

Wiebe, J., Bruce, R., Martin, M., Wilson, T., & Ball, M. (2004). Learning Subjective Language, *Computational Linguistics*, 30(3).

Yan, X., & Yan, L. (2006). Gender classification of weblog authors. *AAAI Spring Symposium Series Computational Approaches to Analyzing Weblogs* (p. 228–230).

Zhang, Y., Dang, Y., Chen, H. (2009). Gender Difference Analysis of Political Web Forums : An Experiment on International Islamic Women's Forum, Proceedings of the 2009 IEEE international conference on Intelligence and security informatics, pp 61-64.

Modelling the Lexicon in Unsupervised Part of Speech Induction

Greg Dubbin
Department of Computer Science
University of Oxford
United Kingdom
Gregory.Dubbin@wolfson.ox.ac.uk

Phil Blunsom
Department of Computer Science
University of Oxford
United Kingdom
Phil.Blunsom@cs.ox.ac.uk

Abstract

Automatically inducing the syntactic part-of-speech categories for words in text is a fundamental task in Computational Linguistics. While the performance of unsupervised tagging models has been slowly improving, current state-of-the-art systems make the obviously incorrect assumption that all tokens of a given word type must share a single part-of-speech tag. This one-tag-per-type heuristic counters the tendency of Hidden Markov Model based taggers to over generate tags for a given word type. However, it is clearly incompatible with basic syntactic theory. In this paper we extend a state-of-the-art Pitman-Yor Hidden Markov Model tagger with an explicit model of the lexicon. In doing so we are able to incorporate a soft bias towards inducing few tags per type. We develop a particle filter for drawing samples from the posterior of our model and present empirical results that show that our model is competitive with and faster than the state-of-the-art without making any unrealistic restrictions.

1 Introduction

Research on the unsupervised induction of part-of-speech (PoS) tags has the potential to improve both our understanding of the plausibility of theories of first language acquisition, and Natural Language Processing applications such as Speech Recognition and Machine Translation. While there has been much prior work on this task (Brown et al., 1992; Clark, 2003; Christodoulopoulos et al., 2010; Toutanova and Johnson, 2008; Goldwater and Griffiths, 2007; Blunsom and Cohn, 2011), a common thread in many of these works is that models based on a Hidden Markov Model (HMM) graphical structure suffer from a tendency to assign too many different tags to the tokens of a given word type. Models which restrict word types to only occur with a single tag show a significant increase in performance, even though this restriction is clearly at odds with the gold standard labeling (Brown et al., 1992; Clark, 2003; Blunsom and Cohn, 2011). While the empirically observed expectation for the number of tags per word type is close to one, there are many exceptions, e.g. words that occur as both nouns and verbs (*opening*, *increase*, *related* etc.).

In this paper we extend the Pitman-Yor HMM tagger (Blunsom and Cohn, 2011) to explicitly include a model of the lexicon that encodes from which tags a word type may be generated. For each word type we draw an ambiguity class which is the set of tags that it may occur with, capturing the fact that words are often ambiguous between certain tags (e.g. *Noun* and *Verb*), while rarely between others (e.g. *Determiner* and *Verb*). We extend the type based Sequential Monte Carlo (SMC) inference algorithm of Dubbin and Blunsom (2012) to incorporate our model of the lexicon, removing the need for the heuristic inference technique of Blunsom and Cohn (2011).

We start in Section 3 by introducing the original PYP-HMM model and our extended model of the lexicon. Section 4 introduces a Particle Gibbs sampler for this model, a basic SMC method that generates samples from the model's posterior. We evaluate these algorithms in Section 5, analyzing their behavior in comparisons to previously proposed state-of-the-art approaches.

2 Background

From the early work in the 1990's, much of the focus on unsupervised PoS induction has been on hidden Markov Models (HMM) (Brown et al., 1992; Kupiec, 1992; Merialdo, 1993). The HMM has proven to be a powerful model of PoS tag assignment. Successful approaches generally build upon the HMM model by expanding its context and smoothing the sparse data. Constraints such as tag dictionaries simplify inference by restricting the number of tags to explore for each word (Goldwater and Griffiths, 2007). Ganchev et al. (2010) used posterior regularization to ensure that word types have a sparse posterior distribution over tags. A similar approach constrains inference to only explore tag assignments such that all tokens of the same word type are assigned the same tag. These constraints reduce tag assignment ambiguity while also providing a bias towards the natural sparsity of tag distributions in language (Clark, 2003). However they do not provide a model based solution to tag ambiguity.

Recent work encodes similar sparsity information with non-parametric priors, relying on Bayesian inference to achieve strong results without any tag dictionaries or constraints (Goldwater and Griffiths, 2007; Johnson, 2007; Gao and Johnson, 2008). Liang et al. (2010) propose a type-based approach to this Bayesian inference similar to Brown et al. (1992), suggesting that there are strong dependencies between tokens of the same word-type. Lee et al. (2010) demonstrate strong results with a similar model and the introduction of a one-tag-per-type constraint on inference.

Blunsom and Cohn (2011) extend the Bayesian inference approach with a hierarchical non-parametric prior that expands the HMM context to trigrams. However, the hierarchical non-parametric model adds too many long-range dependencies for the type-based inference proposed earlier. The model produces state-of-the art results with a one-tag-per-type constraint, but even with this constraint the tag assignments must be roughly inferred from an approximation of the expectations.

Ambiguity classes representing the set of tags each word-type can take aid inference by making the sparsity between tags and words explicit. Toutanova and Johnson (2008) showed that modelling ambiguity classes can lead to positive results with a small tag-dictionary extracted from the data. By including ambiguity classes in the model, this approach is able to infer ambiguity classes of unknown words.

Many improvements in part-of-speech induction over the last few years have come from the use of semi-supervised approaches in the form of projecting PoS constraints across languages with parallel corpora (Das and Petrov, 2011) or extracting them from the wiktionary (Li et al., 2012). These semi-supervised methods ultimately rely on a strong unsupervised model of PoS as their base. Thus, further improvements in unsupervised models, especially in modelling tag constrains, should lead to improvements in semi-supervised part-of-speech induction.

We find that modelling the lexicon in part-of-speech inference can lead to more efficient algorithms that match the state-of-the-art unsupervised performance. We also note that the lexicon model relies heavily on morphological information, and suffers without it on languages with flexible word ordering. These results promise further improvements with more advanced lexicon models.

3 The Pitman-Yor Lexicon Hidden Markov Model

This article proposes enhancing the standard Hidden Markov Model (HMM) by explicitly incorporating a model of the lexicon that consists of word types and their associated tag ambiguity classes. The ambiguity class of a word type is the set of possible lexical categories to which tokens of that type can be assigned. In this work we aim to learn the ambiguity classes unsupervised rather than have them specified in a tag dictionary.

The Lexicon HMM (Lex-HMM) extends the Pitman-Yor HMM (PYP-HMM) described by Blunsom and Cohn (2011). When the ambiguity class of all of the word types in the lexicon is the complete tagset, the two models are the same.

3.1 PYP-HMM

The base of the model applies a hierarchical Pitman-Yor process (PYP) prior to a trigram hidden Markov model to jointly model the distribution of a sequence of latent word tags, $\mathbf{t}$, and word tokens, $\mathbf{w}$. The joint probability defined by the transition, $P_\theta(t_l|t_{n-1}, t_{n-2})$, and emission, $P_\theta(w_n|t_n)$, distributions of a trigram HMM is

$$P_\theta(\mathbf{t}, \mathbf{w}) = \prod_{n=1}^{N+1} P_\theta(t_l|t_{n-1}, t_{n-2}) P_\theta(w_n|t_n)$$

where $N = |\mathbf{t}| = |\mathbf{w}|$ and the special tag \$ is added to denote the sentence boundaries. The model defines a generative process in which the tags are selected from a transition distribution, $t_l|t_{l-1}, t_{l-2}, T$, determined by the two previous tags in their history, and the word tokens are selected from the emission distribution, $w_l|t_l, E$, of the latest tag.

$$\begin{aligned} t_n|t_{n-1}, t_{n-2}, T &\sim T_{t_{n-1}, t_{n-2}} \\ w_n|t_n, E &\sim E_{t_n} \end{aligned}$$

The PYP-HMM draws the above multinomial distributions from a hierarchical Pitman-Yor Process prior. The Pitman-Yor prior defines a smooth back off probability from more complex to less complex transition and emission distributions. In the PYP-HMM trigram model, the transition distributions form a hierarchy with trigram transition distributions drawn from a PYP with the bigram transitions as their base distribution, and the bigram transitions similarly backing off to the unigram transitions. The hierarchical prior can be intuitively understood to smooth the trigram transition distributions with bigram and unigram distributions in a similar manner to an ngram language model (Teh, 2006). This back-off structure greatly reduces sparsity in the trigram distributions and is achieved by chaining together the PYPs through their base distributions:

$$\begin{aligned} T_{ij}|a^T, b^T, B_i &\sim \mathrm{PYP}(a^T, b^T, B_i) \\ B_i|a^B, b^B, U &\sim \mathrm{PYP}(a^B, b^B, U) \\ U|a^U, b^U &\sim \mathrm{PYP}(a^U, b^U, \mathrm{Uniform}). \\ E_i|a^E, b^E, C &\sim \mathrm{PYP}(a^E, b^E, C_i), \end{aligned}$$

where T_{ij}, B_i, and U are trigram, bigram, and unigram transition distributions respectively, and C_i is either a uniform distribution (PYP-HMM) or a bigram character language model distribution to model word morphology (PYP-HMM+LM).

Sampling from the posterior of the hierarchical PYP is calculated with a variant of the Chinese Restaurant Process (CRP) called the Chinese Restaurant Franchise (CRF) (Teh, 2006; Goldwater et al., 2006). In the CRP analogy, each latent variable (tag) in a sequence is represented by a customer entering a restaurant and sitting at one of an infinite number of tables. A customer chooses to sit at a table in a restaurant according to the probability

$$P(z_n = k|\mathbf{z}_{1:n-1}) = \begin{cases} \frac{c_k^- - a}{n-1+b} & 1 \leq k \leq K^- \\ \frac{K^- a + b}{n-1+b} & k = K^- + 1 \end{cases} \quad (1)$$

where z_n is the index of the table chosen by the nth customer to the restaurant, $\mathbf{z}_{1:n-1}$ is the seating arrangement of the previous $n-1$ customers to enter, c_k^- is the count of the customers at table k, and K^- is the total number of tables chosen by the previous $n-1$ customers. All customers at a table share the same dish, representing the value assigned to the latent variables. When customers sit at an empty table, a new dish is assigned to that table according to the base distribution of the PYP. To expand the CRP analogy to the CRF for hierarchical PYPs, when a customer sits at a new table, a new customer enters the restaurant of the PYP of the base distribution.

Blunsom and Cohn (2011) explored two Gibbs sampling methods for inference with the PYP-HMM model. The first individually samples tag assignments for each token. The second employs a tactic shown to be effective by earlier works by constraining inference to only one tag per word type (PYP-1HMM). However marginalizing over all possible table assignments for more than a single tag is intractable. Blunsom and Cohn (2011) approximates the PYP-1HMM tag posteriors for a particular sample according to heuristic fractional table counts. This approximation is shown to be particularly inaccurate for values of a close to one.

3.2 The Lexicon HMM

We define the lexicon to be the set of all word types (W) and a function ($\mathcal{L}$) which maps each word type ($W_i \in W$) to an element in the power set of possible tags T,

$$\mathcal{L} : W \rightarrow \mathcal{P}(T).$$

The Lexicon HMM (Lex-HMM) generates the lexicon with all of the word types and their ambiguity classes before generating the standard HMM parameters. The set of tags associated with each word type is referred to as its ambiguity class $s_i \subseteq T$. The ambiguity classes are generated from a multinomial distribution with a sparse, Pitman-Yor Process prior,

$$\begin{aligned} s_i|S &\sim S \\ S|a^S, b^S &\sim PYP(a^S, b^S, G) \end{aligned}$$

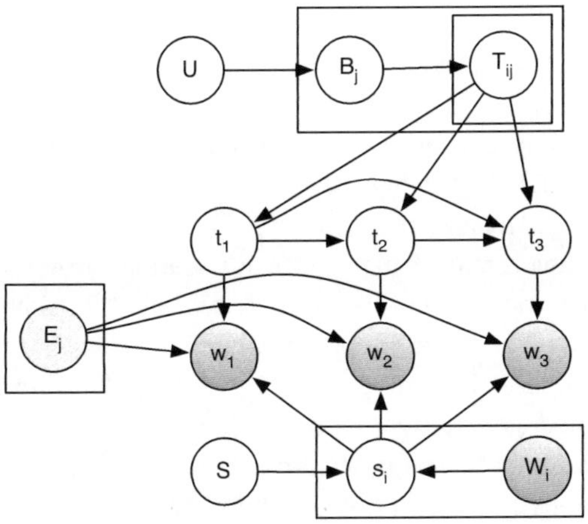

Figure 1: **Lex-HMM Structure:** The graphical structure of the Lex-HMM model. In addition to the trigram transition (T_{ij}) and emission (E_j), the model includes an ambiguity class (s_i) for each word type (W_i) drawn from a distribution S with a PYP prior.

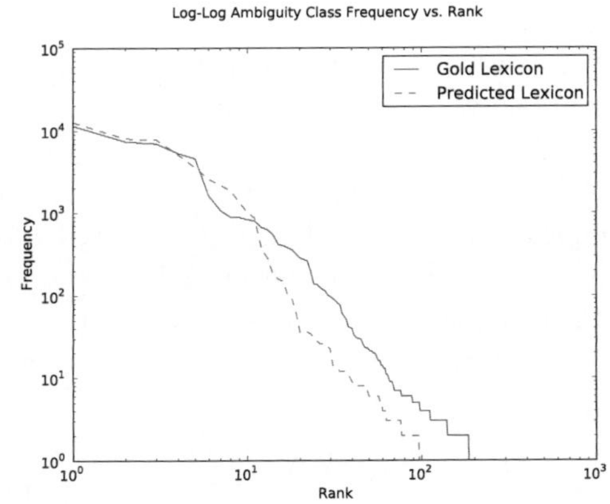

Figure 2: **Ambiguity Class Distribution:** Log-log plot of ambiguity class frequency over rank for the Penn-Treebank WSJ Gold Standard lexicon highlighting a Zipfian distribution and the ambiguity of classes extracted from the predicted tags.

where S is the multinomial distribution over all possible ambiguity classes. The base distribution of the PYP, G, chooses the size of the ambiguity class according to a geometric distribution (normalized so that the size of the class is at most the number of tags $|T|$). G assigns uniform probability to all classes of the same size. A plate diagram for this model is shown in Figure 1.

This model represents the observation that there are relatively few distinct ambiguity classes over all of the word types in a corpus. For example, the full Penn-Treebank Wall Street Journal (WSJ) corpus with 45 possible tags and 49,206 word types has only 343 ambiguity classes. Figure 2 shows that ambiguity classes in the WSJ have a power-law distribution. Furthermore, these classes are generally small; the average ambiguity class in the WSJ corpus has 2.94 tags. The PYP prior favors power-law distributions and the modified geometric base distribution favors smaller class sizes.

Once the lexicon is generated, the standard HMM parameters can be generated as described in section 3.1. The base emission probabilities C are constrained to fit the generated lexicon. The standard Lex-HMM model emission probabilities for tag t_i are uniform over all word types with t_i in their ambiguity class. The character language model presents a challenge because it is non-trivial to renormalise over words with t_i in their ambiguity class. In this case word types without t_i in their ambiguity class are assigned an emission probability of 0 and the model is left deficient.

Neither of the samplers proposed by Blunsom and Cohn (2011) and briefly described in section 3.1 are well suited to inference with the lexicon. Local Gibbs sampling of individual token-tag assignments would be very unlikely to explore a range of confusion classes, while the type based approximate sample relies on a one-tag-per-type restriction. Thus in the next section we extend the Particle Filtering solution presented in Dubbin and Blunsom (2012) to the problem of simultaneous resampling the ambiguity class as well as the tags for all tokens of a given type. This sampler provides both a more attractive inference algorithm for the original PYP-HMM and one adaptable to our Lex-HMM.

4 Inference

To perform inference with both the lexicon and the tag assignments, we block sample the ambiguity class assignment as well as all tag assignments for tokens of the same word type. It would be intractable to exactly calculate the probabilities to sample these blocks. Particle filters are an example of a Sequential Monte Carlo technique which generates unbiased samples from a distribution without summing over the intractable number of possibilities.

The particle filter samples multiple independent sequences of ambiguity classes and tag assignments. Each sequence of samples, called a particle, is generated incrementally. For each particle, the particle filter first samples an ambiguity class, and then samples each tag assignment in sequence based only on the previous samples in the particle. The value of the next variable in a sequence is sampled from a proposal distribution based only on the earlier values in the sequence. Each particle is assigned an importance weight such that a particle sampled proportional to its weight represents an unbiased sample of the true distribution.

Each particle represents a specific sampling of an ambiguity class, tag sequence, $\mathbf{t}_{1:n}^{W,p}$, and the count deltas, $\mathbf{z}_{1:n}^{W,p}$. The term $\mathbf{t}_{1:n}^{W,p}$ denotes the sequence of n tags generated for word-type W and stored as part of particle $p \in [1, P]$. The count deltas store the differences in the seating arrangement neccessary to calculate the posterior probabilities according to the Chinese restaurant franchise described in section 3.1. The table counts from each particle are the only data necessary to calculate the probabilities described in equation (1).

The ambiguity class for a particle is proposed by uniformly sampling one tag from the tagset to add to or remove from the previous iteration's ambiguity class with the additional possibility of using the same ambiguity class. The particle weights are then set to

$$\frac{P(s_{W,p}|S^{-W})}{\prod_{t \in s_{W,p}} (e_t + 1)^{\#(E_t)} \prod_{t \in T - s_{W,p}} (e_t)^{\#(E_t)}}$$

where $P(s_{W,p}|S^{-W})$ is the probability of the ambiguity class proposed for particle p for word type W given the ambiguity classes for the rest of the vocabulary, e_t is the number of word types with t in their ambiguity class, and $\#(E_t)$ is the number of tables in the CRP for the emission distribution of tag t. The last two terms of the equation correct for the difference in the base probabilities of the words that have already been sampled with a different lexicon.

At each token occurrence n, the next tag assignment, $t_n^{W,p}$ for each particle $p \in [1, P]$ is determined by the seating decisions $z_n^{W,p}$, which are made according the proposal distribution:

$$\begin{aligned} q_n^{W,p}(z_n^{W,p}|\mathbf{z}_{1:n-1}^{W,p}, \mathbf{z}^{-W}) \propto \\ P(z_n^{W,p}|c^{-2}, c^{-1}, \mathbf{z}_{1:n-1}^{W,p}, \mathbf{z}^{-W}) \\ \times P(c_n^{+1}|c_n^{-1}, z_n^{W,p}, \mathbf{z}_{1:n-1}^{W,p}, \mathbf{z}^{-W}) \\ \times P(c_n^{+2}|z_n^{W,p}, c_n^{+1}, \mathbf{z}_{1:n-1}^{W,p}, \mathbf{z}^{-W}) \\ \times P(w_n^{W}|z_n^{W,p}, z_{1:n-1}^{W,p}, z^{-W}). \end{aligned}$$

In this case, $c_n^{\pm k}$ represents a tag in the context of site t_n^W offset by k, while $\mathbf{z}_{1:n-1}^{W,p}$ and $\mathbf{z}^{-W}$ represent the table counts from the seating decisions previously chosen by particle p and the values at all of the sites where a word token of type W does not appear, respectively. This proposal distribution ignores changes to the seating arrangement between the three transitions involving the site n. The specific tag assignement, t^W, p_n, is completely determined by the seating decisions sampled according to this proposal distribution. Once all of the particles have been sampled, one of them is sampled with probability proportional to its weight. This final sample is a sample from the target distribution.

As the Particle Filter is embedded in a Gibbs sampler which cycles over all word types this algorithm is an instance of Particle Gibbs. Andrieu et al. (2010) shows that to ensure the samples generated by SMC for a Gibbs sampler have the target distribution as the invariant density, the particle filter must be modified to perform a *conditional SMC update*. This means that the particle filter guarantees that one of the final particles is assigned the same values as the previous Gibbs iteration. Therefore, a special 0th particle is automatically assigned the value from the prior iteration of the Gibbs sampler at each site n, though the proposal probability $q_n^W(t_n^{W,0}|\mathbf{t}_{1:n-1}^{W,p}, \mathbf{z}_{1:n-1}^{W,p})$ still has to be calculated to update the weight $\omega_n^{W,p}$ properly. This ensures that the sampler has a chance of reverting to the prior iteration's sequence.

5 Experiments and Results

We provide an empirical evaluation of our proposed Lex-HMM in terms of the accuracy of the taggings learned according to the most popular metric, and the distributions over ambiguity classes. Our experimental evaluation considers the impact of our improved Particle Gibbs inference algorithm both for the original PYP-HMM and when used for inference in our extended model.

We intend to learn whether the lexicon model can match or exceed the performance of the other models despite focusing on only a subset of the possible tags each iteration. We hypothesize that an accurate lexicon model and the sparsity it induces over the number of tags per word-type will improve the performance over the standard PYP-HMM model while also decreasing training time. Furthermore, our lexicon model is novel, and its

Sampler	M-1 Accuracy	Time (h)
Meta-Model (CGS10)	76.1	—
MEMM (BBDK10)	75.5	~40*
Lex-HMM	71.1	7.9
Type PYP-HMM	70.1	401.2
Local PYP-HMM	70.2	8.6
PYP-1HMM	75.6	20.6
Lex-HMM+LM	77.5	16.9
Type PYP-HMM+LM	73.5	446.0
PYP-1HMM+LM	77.5	34.9

Table 1: **M-1 Accuracy on the WSJ Corpus:** Comparison of the accuracy of each of the samplers with and without the language model emission prior on the English WSJ Corpus. The second column reports run time in hours where available*. Note the Lex-HMM+LM model matches the PYP-1HMM+LM approximation despite finishing in half the time. The abbreviations in parentheses indicate that the results were reported in CGS10 (Christodoulopoulos et al., 2010) and BBDK10 (Berg-Kirkpatrick et al., 2010) *CGS10 reports that the MEMM model takes approximately 40 hours on 16 cores.

accuracy in representing ambiguity classes is an important aspect of its performance. The model focuses inference on the most likely tag choices, represented by ambiguity classes.

5.1 Unsupervised Part-of-Speech Tagging

The most popular evaluation for unsupervised part-of-speech taggers is to induce a tagging for a corpus and compare the induced tags to those annotated by a linguist. As the induced tags are simply integer labels, we must employ a mapping between these and the more meaningful syntactic categories of the gold standard. We report results using the many-to-one (M-1) metric considered most intuitive by the evaluation of Christodoulopoulos et al. (2010). M-1 measures the accuracy of the model after mapping each predicted class to its most frequent corresponding tag. While Christodoulopoulos et al. (2010) found V-measure to be more stable over the number of parts-of-speech, this effect doesn't appear when the number of tags is constant, as in our case. For experiments on English, we report results on the entire Penn. Treebank (Marcus et al., 1993). For other languages we use the corpora made available for the CoNLL-X Shared Task (Buchholz and Marsi, 2006). All Lex-HMM results are reported with 10 particles as no significant improvement was found with 50 particles.

Table 1 compares the M-1 accuracies of both the PYP-HMM and the Lex-HMM models on the Penn. Treebank Wall Street Journal corpus. Blunsom and Cohn (2011) found that the Local PYP-HMM+LM sampler is unable to mix, achieving accuracy below 50%, therefore it has been left out of this analysis. The Lex-HMM+LM model achieves the same accuracy as the state-of-the-art PYP-1HMM+LM approximation. The Lex-HMM+LM's focus on only the most likely tags for each word type allows it to finish training in half the time as the PYP-1HMM+LM approximation without any artificial restrictions on the number of tags per type. This contrasts with other approaches that eliminate the constraint at a much greater cost, e.g. the Type PYP-HMM, the MEMM, and the Meta-Model [1]

The left side of table 2 compares the M-1 accuracies of the Lex-HMM model to the PYP-HMM model. These models both ignore word morphology and rely on word order. The 1HMM approximation achieves the highest average accuracy. The Lex-HMM model matches or surpasses the type-based PYP-HMM approach in six languages while running much faster due to the particle filter considering a smaller set of parts-of-speech for each particle. However, in the absence of morphological information, the Lex-HMM model has a similar average accuracy to the local and type-based PYP-HMM samplers. The especially low performance on Hungarian, a language with free word ordering and strong morphology, suggests that the Lex-HMM model struggles to find ambiguity classes without morphology. The Lex-HMM model has a higher average accuracy than the type-based or local PYP-HMM samplers when Hungarian is ignored.

The right side of table 2 compares the M-1 accuracies of the Lex-HMM+LM model to the PYP-HMM+LM. The language model leads to consistently improved performance for each of the samplers excepting the token sampler, which is unable to mix properly with the additional complexity. The accuracies achieved by the 1HMM+LM

[1] While were unable to get an estimate on the runtime of the Meta-Model, it uses a system similar to the feature-based system of the MEMM with an additional feature derived from the proposed class from the brown model. Therefore, it is likely that this model has a similar runtime.

Language	Lex-HMM	PYP-HMM	Local	1HMM	Lex-HMM+LM	PYP-HMM+LM	1HMM+LM
WSJ	71.1	70.1	70.2	75.6	**77.5**	73.5	**77.5**
Arabic	57.2	57.6	56.2	61.9	62.1	**62.7**	62.0
Bulgarian	67.2	67.8	67.6	71.4	72.7	72.1	**76.2**
Czech	61.3	61.6	64.5	65.4	**68.2**	67.4	67.9
Danish	68.6	70.3	69.1	70.6	**74.7**	73.1	74.6
Dutch	70.3	71.6	64.1	73.2	71.7	71.8	**72.9**
Hungarian	57.9	61.8	64.8	69.6	64.4	69.9	**73.2**
Portuguese	69.5	71.1	68.1	72.0	76.3	73.9	**77.1**
Spanish	73.2	69.1	68.5	74.7	**80.0**	75.2	78.8
Swedish	66.3	63.5	67.6	67.2	**70.4**	67.6	68.6
Average	66.3 (67.2)	66.5 (67.0)	66.1 (66.2)	70.2 (70.3)	71.8 (72.6)	70.7 (70.8)	72.9 (72.9)

Table 2: **M-1 Accuracy of Lex-HMM and PYP-HMM models:** Comparison of M-1 accuracy for the lexicon based model (Lex-HMM) and the PYP-HMM model on several languages. The Lex-HMM and PYP-HMM columns indicate the results of word type based particle filtering with 10 and 100 particles, respectively, while the Local and 1HMM columns use the token based sampler and the 1HMM approximation described by Blunsom and Cohn (2011). The token based sampler was run for 500 iterations and the other samplers for 200. The percentages in brakets represent the average accuracy over all languages except for Hungarian.

sampler represent the previous state-of-the-art. These results show that the Lex-HMM+LM model achieves state-of-the-art M-1 accuracies on several datasets, including the English WSJ. The Lex-HMM+LM model performs nearly as well as, and often better than, the 1HMM+LM sampler without any restrictions on tag assignments.

The drastic improvement in the performance of the Lex-HMM model reinforces our hypothesis that morphology is critical to the inference of ambiguity classes. Without the language model representing word morphology, the distinction between ambiguity classes is too ambiguous. This leads the sampler to infer an excess of poor ambiguity classes. For example, the tag assignments from the Lex-PYP model on the WSJ dataset consist of 660 distinct ambiguity classes, while the Lex-PYP+LM tag assignments only have 182 distinct ambiguity classes.

Note that while the Lex-HMM and Lex-HMM+LM samplers do not have any restrictions on inference, they do not sacrifice time. The additional samples generated by the particle filter are mitigated by limiting the number of tags each particle must consider. In practice, this results in the Lex-HMM samplers with 10 particles running in half time as the 1HMM samplers. The Lex-HMM+LM sampler with 10 particles took 16.9 hours, while the 1HMM+LM sampler required 34.9 hours. Furthermore, the run time evaluation does not take advantage of the inherent distributed nature of particle filters. Each of the particles can be sampled completely independentally from the others, making it trivial to run each on a seperate core.

5.2 Lexicon Analysis

While section 5.1 demonstrates that the Lex-HMM+LM sampler performs similarly to the more restricted 1HMM+LM, we also seek to evaluate the accuracy of the lexicon model itself. We compare the ambiguity classes extracted from the gold standard and predicted tag assignments of the WSJ corpus. We also explore the relationship between the actual and sampled ambiguity classes.

The solid curve in figure 2 shows the distribution of the number of word types assigned to each ambiguity set extracted from the gold standard tag assignments from the Penn Treebank Wall Street Journal corpus. The straight line strongly indicates that ambiguity classes follow a Zipfian distribution. Figure 2 also graphs the distribution of the ambiguity classes extracted from the best tag-assignment prediction from the model. The predicted graph has a similar shape to the gold standard but represents half as many distinct ambiguity classes - 182 versus 343.

For a qualitative analysis of the generated lexicon, table 3 lists frequent ambiguity classes and the most common words assigned to them. The 14 most frequent ambiguity classes contain only one tag each, the top half of table 3 shows the 5 most frequent. One third of the word-types in the first five rows of the table are exactly matched with the ambiguity classes from the gold standard. Most of the remaining words in those rows are assigned to

Rank	Gold Rank	Tags	Top Word Types
1	1	NNP	**Mr.**, Corp. (1), Inc. (.99), Co. (1), Exchange (.99)
2	2	NN	% (1), **company**, stock (.99), -RRB- (0), years (0)
3	3	JJ	**new**, **other**, first (.9), most (0), major (1)
4	5	NNS	**companies**, prices (1), quarter (0), week (0), **investors**
5	4	CD	$ (0), million (1), **billion**, **31**, # (0)
15	303	NN, CD	yen (.47, 0), dollar (1, 0), 150 (0, 1), 29 (0, 1), 33 (0, 1)
16	17	VB, NN	plan (.03, .9), offer (.2, .74), issues (0, 0), increase (.34, .66), end (.18, .81)
17	115	DT, NNP	As (0, 0), One (0, .01), First (0, .82), Big (0, .91), On (0, .01)
18	11	NN, JJ	market (.99, 0), U.S. (0, 0), bank (1, 0), cash (.98, 0), high (.06, .9)
20	22	VBN, JJ	estimated (.58, .15), lost (.43, .03), failed (.35, .04), related (.74, .23), reduced (.57, .12)

Table 3: **Selection of Predicted Ambiguity Classes:** Common ambiguity classes from the predicted part-of-speech assignments from the WSJ data set, and the five most common word types associated with each ambiguity class. The sets are ranked according to the number of word types associated to them. Words in bold are matched to exactly the same ambiguity set in the gold standard. The lower five ambiguity classes are the most common with more than one part-of-speech. Numbers in parentheses represent the proportion of tokens of that type assigned to each tag in the gold standard for that ambiguity class.

a class representing almost all of the words' occurrences in the gold standard, e.g., 'Corp.' is an NNP in 1514 out of 1521 occurrences. Some words are assigned to classes with similar parts of speech, e.g. {NNS} rather than {NN} for week.

The lower half of table 3 shows the most frequent ambiguity classes with more than a single tag. The words assigned to the {NN,CD}, {DT,NNP}, and {NN,JJ} classes are not themselves ambiguous. Rather words that are unambiguously one of the two tags are often assigned to an ambiguity class with both. The most common types in the {NN, CD} set are unambiguously either NN or CD. In many cases the words are merged into broader ambiguity classes because the Lex-HMM+LM uses the language model to model the morphology of words over individual parts-of-speech, rather than entire ambiguity classes. Therefore, a word-type is likely to be assigned a given ambiguity class as long as at least one part-of-speech in that ambiguity class is associated with morphologically similar words. These results suggest modifying the Lex-HMM+LM to model word morphology over ambiguity classes rather than parts-of-speech.

The {VB,NN} and {VBN,JJ} are representative of true ambiguity classes. Occurrences of words in these classes are likely to be either of the possible parts-of-speech. These results show that the Lex-HMM is modelling ambiguity classes as intended.

6 Conclusion

This paper described an extension to the PYP-HMM part-of-speech model that incorporates a sparse prior on the lexicon and an SMC based inference algorithm. These contributions provide a more plausible model of part-of-speech induction which models the true ambiguity of tag to type assignments without the loss of performance of earlier HMM models. Our empirical evaluation indicates that this model is able to meet or exceed the performance of the previous state-of-the-art across a range of language families.

In addition to the promising empirical results, our analysis indicates that the model learns ambiguity classes that are often quite similar to those in the gold standard. We believe that further improvements in both the structure of the lexicon prior and the inference algorithm will lead to additional performance gains. For example, the model could be improved by better modelling the relationship between a word's morphology and its ambiguity class. We intend to apply our model to recent semi-supervised approaches which induce partial tag dictionaries from parallel language data (Das and Petrov, 2011) or the Wiktionary (Li et al., 2012). We hypothesize that the additional data should improve the modelled lexicon and consequently improve tag assignments.

The Lex-HMM models ambiguity classes to focus the sampler on the most likely parts-of-speech for a given word-type. In doing so, it matches or improves on the accuracy of other models while running much faster.

References

Christophe Andrieu, Arnaud Doucet, and Roman Holenstein. 2010. Particle markov chain monte carlo methods. *Journal Of The Royal Statistical Society Series B*, 72(3):269–342.

Taylor Berg-Kirkpatrick, Alexandre Bouchard-Côté, John DeNero, and Dan Klein. 2010. Painless unsupervised learning with features. In *Human Language Technologies: The 2010 Annual Conference of the North American Chapter of the Association for Computational Linguistics*, pages 582–590, Los Angeles, California, June. Association for Computational Linguistics.

Phil Blunsom and Trevor Cohn. 2011. A hierarchical Pitman-Yor process hmm for unsupervised part of speech induction. In *Proceedings of the 49th Annual Meeting of the Association for Computational Linguistics: Human Language Technologies*, pages 865–874, Portland, Oregon, USA, June. Association for Computational Linguistics.

Peter F. Brown, Peter V. deSouza, Robert L. Mercer, Vincent J. Della Pietra, and Jenifer C. Lai. 1992. Class-based n-gram models of natural language. *Comput. Linguist.*, 18:467–479, December.

Sabine Buchholz and Erwin Marsi. 2006. Conll-x shared task on multilingual dependency parsing. In *Proceedings of the Tenth Conference on Computational Natural Language Learning*, CoNLL-X '06, pages 149–164, Morristown, NJ, USA. Association for Computational Linguistics.

Christos Christodoulopoulos, Sharon Goldwater, and Mark Steedman. 2010. Two decades of unsupervised POS induction: How far have we come? In *Proceedings of the 2010 Conference on Empirical Methods in Natural Language Processing*, pages 575–584, Cambridge, MA, October. Association for Computational Linguistics.

Alexander Clark. 2003. Combining distributional and morphological information for part of speech induction. In *Proceedings of the tenth Annual Meeting of the European Association for Computational Linguistics (EACL)*, pages 59–66.

Dipanjan Das and Slav Petrov. 2011. Unsupervised part-of-speech tagging with bilingual graph-based projections. In *Proceedings of the 49th Annual Meeting of the Association for Computational Linguistics: Human Language Technologies - Volume 1*, HLT '11, pages 600–609, Stroudsburg, PA, USA. Association for Computational Linguistics.

Gregory Dubbin and Phil Blunsom. 2012. Unsupervised bayesian part of speech inference with particle gibbs. In Peter A. Flach, Tijl De Bie, and Nello Cristianini, editors, *ECML/PKDD (1)*, volume 7523 of *Lecture Notes in Computer Science*, pages 760–773. Springer.

Kuzman Ganchev, João Graça, Jennifer Gillenwater, and Ben Taskar. 2010. Posterior regularization for structured latent variable models. *Journal of Machine Learning Research*, 99:2001–2049, August.

Jianfeng Gao and Mark Johnson. 2008. A comparison of bayesian estimators for unsupervised hidden markov model pos taggers. In *Proceedings of the Conference on Empirical Methods in Natural Language Processing*, EMNLP '08, pages 344–352, Morristown, NJ, USA. Association for Computational Linguistics.

Sharon Goldwater and Tom Griffiths. 2007. A fully bayesian approach to unsupervised part-of-speech tagging. In *Proc. of the 45th Annual Meeting of the ACL (ACL-2007)*, pages 744–751, Prague, Czech Republic, June.

Sharon Goldwater, Tom Griffiths, and Mark Johnson. 2006. Interpolating between types and tokens by estimating power-law generators. In Y. Weiss, B. Schölkopf, and J. Platt, editors, *Advances in Neural Information Processing Systems 18*, pages 459–466. MIT Press, Cambridge, MA.

Mark Johnson. 2007. Why doesnt EM find good HMM POS-taggers? In *Proc. of the 2007 Conference on Empirical Methods in Natural Language Processing (EMNLP-2007)*, pages 296–305, Prague, Czech Republic.

Julian Kupiec. 1992. Robust part-of-speech tagging using a hidden Markov model. *Computer Speech and Language*, 6:225–242.

Yoong Keok Lee, Aria Haghighi, and Regina Barzilay. 2010. Simple type-level unsupervised pos tagging. In *Proceedings of the 2010 Conference on Empirical Methods in Natural Language Processing*, EMNLP '10, pages 853–861, Morristown, NJ, USA. Association for Computational Linguistics.

Shen Li, João V. Graça, and Ben Taskar. 2012. Wiki-ly supervised part-of-speech tagging. In *Proceedings of the 2012 Joint Conference on Empirical Methods in Natural Language Processing and Computational Natural Language Learning*, EMNLP-CoNLL '12, pages 1389–1398, Stroudsburg, PA, USA. Association for Computational Linguistics.

P. Liang, M. I. Jordan, and D. Klein. 2010. Type-based MCMC. In *North American Association for Computational Linguistics (NAACL)*.

Mitchell P. Marcus, Mary Ann Marcinkiewicz, and Beatrice Santorini. 1993. Building a large annotated corpus of English: the Penn treebank. *Computational Linguistics*, 19(2):313–330.

Bernard Merialdo. 1993. Tagging english text with a probabilistic model. *Computational Linguistics*, 20:155–171.

Yee Whye Teh. 2006. A hierarchical bayesian language model based on Pitman-Yor processes. In *Proceedings of the 21st International Conference on Computational Linguistics and the 44th annual meeting of the Association for Computational Linguistics*, ACL-44, pages 985–992, Morristown, NJ, USA. Association for Computational Linguistics.

Kristina Toutanova and Mark Johnson. 2008. A Bayesian LDA-based model for semi-supervised part-of-speech tagging. In J.C. Platt, D. Koller, Y. Singer, and S. Roweis, editors, *Advances in Neural Information Processing Systems 20*, pages 1521–1528. MIT Press, Cambridge, MA.

Generalizing a Strongly Lexicalized Parser using Unlabeled Data

Tejaswini Deoskar[1], **Christos Christodoulopoulos**[2], **Alexandra Birch**[1], **Mark Steedman**[1]
[1]School of Informatics, University of Edinburgh, Edinburgh, EH8 9AB
[2]University of Illinois, Urbana-Champaign, Urbana, IL 61801
{tdeoskar,abmayne,steedman}@inf.ed.ac.uk, christod@illinois.edu

Abstract

Statistical parsers trained on labeled data suffer from sparsity, both grammatical and lexical. For parsers based on strongly lexicalized grammar formalisms (such as CCG, which has complex lexical categories but simple combinatory rules), the problem of sparsity can be isolated to the lexicon. In this paper, we show that semi-supervised Viterbi-EM can be used to extend the lexicon of a generative CCG parser. By learning complex lexical entries for low-frequency and unseen words from unlabeled data, we obtain improvements over our supervised model for both in-domain (WSJ) and out-of-domain (questions and Wikipedia) data. Our learnt lexicons when used with a discriminative parser such as C&C also significantly improve its performance on unseen words.

1 Introduction

An important open problem in natural language parsing is to generalize supervised parsers, which are trained on hand-labeled data, using unlabeled data. The problem arises because further hand-labeled data in the amounts necessary to significantly improve supervised parsers are very unlikely to be made available. Generalization is also necessary in order to achieve good performance on parsing in textual domains other than the domain of the available labeled data. For example, parsers trained on Wall Street Journal (WSJ) data suffer a fall in accuracy on other domains (Gildea, 2001).

In this paper, we use self-training to generalize the lexicon of a Combinatory Categorial Grammar (CCG) (Steedman, 2000) parser. CCG is a strongly lexicalized formalism, in which every word is associated with a syntactic category (similar to an elementary syntactic structure) indicating its subcategorization potential. Lexical entries are fine-grained and expressive, and contain a large amount of language-specific grammatical information. For parsers based on strongly lexicalized formalisms, the problem of grammar generalization can be cast largely as a problem of lexical extension.

The present paper focuses on learning lexical categories for words that are *unseen* or *low-frequency* in labeled data, from unlabeled data. Since lexical categories in a strongly lexicalized formalism are complex, fine-grained (and far more numerous than simple part-of-speech tags), they are relatively sparse in labeled data. Despite performing at state-of-the-art levels, a major source of error made by CCG parsers is related to unseen and low-frequency words (Hockenmaier, 2003; Clark and Curran, 2007; Thomforde and Steedman, 2011). The unseen words for which we learn categories are surprisingly commonplace words of English; examples are *conquered, apprehended, subdivided, scoring, denotes, hunted, obsessed, residing, migrated* (Wikipedia). Correctly learning to parse the predicate-argument structures associated with such words (expressed as lexical categories in the case of CCG), is important for open-domain parsing, not only for CCG but indeed for any parser.

We show that a simple self-training method, Viterbi-EM (Neal and Hinton, 1998) when used to enhance the lexicon of a strongly-lexicalized parser can be an effective strategy for self-training and domain-adaptation. Our learnt lexicons improve on the lexical category accuracy of two supervised CCG parsers (Hockenmaier (2003) and the Clark and Curran (2007) parser, C&C) on within-domain (WSJ) and out-of-domain test sets (a question corpus and a Wikipedia corpus).

In most prior work, when EM was initialized based on labeled data, its performance did not improve over the supervised model (Merialdo, 1994;

Charniak, 1993). We found that in order for performance to improve, unlabeled data should be used only for parameters which are not well covered by the labeled data, while those that are well covered should remain fixed.

In an additional contribution, we compare two strategies for treating unseen words (a smoothing-based, and a part-of-speech back-off method) and find that a smoothing-based strategy for treating unseen words is more effective for semi-supervised learning than part-of-speech back-off.

2 Combinatory Categorial Grammar

Combinatory Categorial Grammar (CCG) (Steedman, 2000) is a strongly lexicalized grammar formalism, in which the lexicon contains all language-specific grammatical information. The lexical entry of a word consists of a syntactic category which expresses the subcategorization potential of the word, and a semantic interpretation which defines the compositional semantics (Lewis and Steedman, 2013). A small number of combinatory rules are used to combine constituents, and it is straightforward to map syntactic categories to a logical form for semantic interpretation.

For statistical CCG parsers, the lexicon is learnt from labeled data, and is subject to sparsity due to the fine-grained nature of the categories. Figure 1 illustrates this with a simple CCG derivation. In this sentence, *bake* is used as a ditransitive verb and is assigned the ditransitive category **S\NP/NP/NP**. This category defines the verb syntactically as mapping three **NP** arguments to a sentence **S**, and semantically as a ternary relation between its three arguments, thus providing a complete analysis of the sentence.

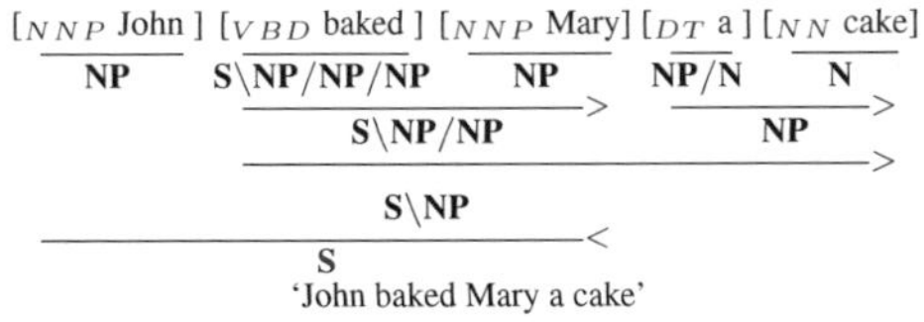

Figure 1: Example CCG derivation

For a CCG parser to obtain the correct derivation above, its lexicon must include the ditransitive category **S\NP/NP/NP** for the verb *bake*. It is not sufficient to have simply seen the verb in another context (say a transitive context like "John baked a cake", which is a more common context). This is in contrast to standard treebank parsers where the verbal category is simply VBD (past tense verb) and a ditransitive analysis of the sentence is not ruled out as a result of the lexical category.

In addition to sparsity related to open-class words like verbs as in the above example, there are also missing categories in labeled data for closed-class words like question words, due to the small number of questions in the Penn Treebank. In general, lexical sparsity for a statistical CCG parser can be broken down into three types: *(i)* where a word is unseen in training data but is present in test data, *(ii)* where a word is seen in the training data but not with the category type required in the test data (but the category type is seen with other words) and *(iii)* where a word bears a category type required in the test data but the category type is completely unseen in the training data.

In this paper, we deal with the first two kinds. The third kind is more prevalent when the size of labeled data is comparatively small (although, even in the case of the English WSJ CCG treebank, there are several attested category types that are entirely missing from the lexicon, Clark et al., 2004). We make the assumption here that all category types in the language have been seen in the labeled data. In principle new category types may be introduced independently without affecting our semi-supervised process (for instance, manually, or via a method that predicts new category types from those seen in labeled data).

3 Related Work

Previous attempts at harnessing unlabeled data to improve supervised CCG models using methods like self-training or co-training have been unsatisfactory (Steedman et al., 2003, 43-44). Steedman et al. (2003) experimented with self-training a generative CCG parser, and co-training a generative parser with an HMM-based supertagger. Co-training (but not self-training) improved the results of the parser when the seed labeled data was small. When the seed data was large (the full treebank), i.e., the supervised baseline was high, co-training and self-training both failed to improve the parser.

More recently, Honnibal et al. (2009) improved the performance of the C&C parser on a domain-adaptation task (adaptation to Wikipedia text) using self-training. Instead of self-training the parsing model, they re-train the supertagging model, which in turn affects parsing accuracy. They obtained an improvement of 1.09% (dependency score) on supertagger accuracy on Wikipedia (although performance on WSJ text dropped) but did not attempt to re-train the parsing model.

An orthogonal approach for extending a CCG lexicon using unlabeled data is that of Thomforde and Steedman (2011), in which a CCG category for an unknown word is derived from partial parses of sentences with just that one word unknown. The method is capable of inducing unseen categories *types* (the third kind of sparsity mentioned in §2.1), but due to algorithmic and efficiency issues, it did not achieve the broad-coverage needed for grammar generalisation of a high-end parser. It is more relevant for low-resource languages which do not have substantial labeled data and category type discovery is important.

Some notable positive results for non-CCG parsers are McClosky et al. (2006) who use a parser-reranker combination. Koo et al. (2008) and Suzuki et al. (2009) use unsupervised word-clusters as features in a dependency parser to get lexical dependencies. This has some notional similarity to categories, since, like categories, clusters are less fine-grained than words but more fine-grained than POS-tags.

4 Supervised Parser

The CCG parser used in this paper is a re-implementation of the generative parser of Hockenmaier and Steedman (2002) and Hockenmaier (2003)[1], except for the treatment of unseen and low-frequency words.

We use a model (the *LexCat* model in Hockenmaier (2003)) that conditions the generation of constituents in the parse tree on the *lexical category* of the head word of the constituent, but not on the head word itself. While fully-lexicalized models that condition on words (and thus model word-to-word dependencies) are more accurate than unlexicalized ones like the *LexCat* model, we use an unlexicalized model[2] for two reasons: first, our lexicon smoothing procedure (described in the next section) introduces new words and new categories for words into the lexicon. Lexical categories are added to the lexicon for seen and unseen words, but no new category types are introduced. Since the *LexCat* model conditions rule expansions on lexical categories, but not on words, it is still able to produce parses for sentences with new words. In contrast, a fully lexicalized model would need all components of the grammar to be smoothed, a task that is far from trivial due to the resulting explosion in grammar size (and one that we leave for future work).

Second, although lexicalized models perform better on in-domain WSJ data (the *LexCat* model has an accuracy of 87.9% on Section 23, as opposed to 91.03% for the head-lexicalized model in Hockenmaier (2003) and 91.9% for the C&C parser), our parser is more accurate on a question corpus, with a lexical category accuracy of 82.3%, as opposed to 71.6% and 78.6% for the C&C and Hockenmaier (2003) respectively.

4.1 Handling rare and unseen words

Existing CCG parsers (Hockenmaier (2003) and Clark and Curran (2007)) back-off rare and unseen words to their POS tag. The POS-backoff strategy is essentially a pipeline approach, where words are first tagged with coarse tags (POS tags) and finer tags (CCG categories) are later assigned, by the parser (Hockenmaier, 2003) or the supertagger (Clark and Curran, 2007). As POS-taggers are much more accurate than parsers, this strategy has given good performance in general for CCG parsers, but it has the disadvantage that POS-tagging errors are propagated. The parser can never recover from a tagging error, a problem that is serious for words in the Zipfian tail, where these words might also be unseen for the POS tagger and hence more likely to be tagged incorrectly. This issue is in fact more generally relevant than for CCG parsers alone—the dependence of parsers on POS-taggers was cited as one of the problems in domain-adaptation of parsers in the NAACL-2012 shared task on parsing the web (Petrov and McDonald, 2012). Lease and Charniak (2005) obtained an improvement in the accuracy of the Charniak (2000) parser on a biomedical domain simply by training a new POS tagger model.

In the following section, we describe an alternative smoothing-based approach to handling un-

[1]These generative models are similar to the Collins' head-based models (Collins, 1997), where for every node, a head is generated first, and then a sister conditioned on the head. Details of the models are in Hockenmaier and Steedman (2002) and Hockenmaier 2003:pg 166.

[2]A terminological clarification: *unlexicalized* here refers to the model, in the sense that head-word information is not used for rule-expansion. The formalism itself (CCG) is referred to as *strongly-lexicalized*, as used in the title of the paper. Formalisms like CCG and LTAG are considered strongly-lexicalized since linguistic knowledge (functions mapping words to syntactic structures/semantic interpretations) is included in the lexicon.

seen and rare words. This method is less sensitive to POS tagging errors, as described below. In this approach, in a pre-processing step prior to parsing, categories are introduced into the lexicon for unseen and rare words from the data to be parsed. Some probability mass is taken from seen words/categories and given to unseen word and category pairs. Thus, at parse time, no word is unseen for the parser.

4.1.1 Smoothing

In our approach, we introduce lexical entries for words from the unlabeled corpus that are unseen in the labeled data, and also add categories to existing entries for rarely seen words. The most general case of this would be to assign all known categories to a word. However, doing this reduces the lexical category accuracy.[3] A second option, chosen here, is to limit the number of categories assigned to the word by using some information about the word (for instance, its part-of-speech). Based on the part-of-speech of an unseen word in the unlabeled or test corpus, we add an entry to the lexicon of the word with the top n categories that have been seen with that part-of-speech in the labeled data. Each new entry of (w, cat), where w is a word and cat is a CCG category, is associated with a count $c(w, cat)$, obtained as described below. Once all (w, cat) entries are added to the lexicon along with their counts, a probability model $P(w|cat)$ is calculated over the entire lexicon.

Our smoothing method is based on a method used in Deoskar (2008) for smoothing a PCFG lexicon. Eq. 1 and 2 apply it to CCG entries for unseen and rare words. In the first step, an out-of-the-box POS tagger is used to tag the unlabeled or test corpus (we use the C&C tagger). Counts of words and POS-tags $c_{corpus}(w, T)$ are obtained from the tagged corpus. For the CCG lexicon, we ultimately need a count for a word w and a CCG category cat. To get this count, we split the count of a word and POS-tag amongst all categories seen with that tag in the supervised data in the same ratio as the ratio of the categories in the supervised data. In Eq. 1, this ratio is $c_{tb}(cat_T)/c_{tb}(T)$ where $c_{tb}(cat_T)$ is the treebank count of a category cat_T seen with a POS-tag T, and $c_{tb}(T)$ is the marginal count of the tag T in the treebank. This ratio makes a more frequent category type more likely than a rarer one for an unseen word. For example, for unseen verbs, it would make the transitive category more likely than a ditransitive one (since transitives are more frequent than ditransitives). There is an underlying assumption here that relative frequencies of categories and POS-tags in the labeled data are maintained in the unlabeled data, which in fact can be thought of as a prior while estimating from unlabeled data (Deoskar et al., 2012).

$$c_{corpus}(w, cat) = \frac{c_{tb}(cat_T)}{c_{tb}(T)} \cdot c_{corpus}(w, T) \quad (1)$$

Additionally, for seen but low-frequency words, we make use of the existing entry in the lexicon. Thus in a second step, we interpolate the count $c_{corpus}(w, cat)$ of a word and category with the supervised count of the same $c_{tb}(w, cat)$ (if it exists) to give the final smoothed count of a word and category $c_{smooth}(w, cat)$ (Eq. 2).

$$c_{smooth}(w, cat) = \lambda \cdot c_{tb}(w, cat) + (1 - \lambda) \cdot c_{corpus}(w, cat) \quad (2)$$

When this smoothed lexicon is used with a parser, POS-backoff is not necessary since all needed words are now in the lexicon. Lexical entries for words in the parse are determined not by the POS-tag from a tagger, but directly by the parsing model, thus making the parse less susceptible to tagging errors.

5 Semi-supervised Learning

We use Viterbi-EM (Neal and Hinton, 1998) as the self-training method. Viterbi-EM is an alternative to EM where instead of using the model parameters to find a true posterior from unlabeled data, a posterior based on the single maximum-probability (Viterbi) parse is used. Viterbi-EM has been used in various NLP tasks before and often performs better than classic EM (Cohen and Smith, 2010; Goldwater and Johnson, 2005; Spitkovsky et al., 2010). In practice, a given parsing model is used to obtain Viterbi parses of unlabeled sentences. The Viterbi parses are then treated as training data for a new model. This process is iterated until convergence.

Since we are interested in learning the lexicon, we only consider lexical counts from Viterbi parses of the unlabeled sentences. Other parameters of the model are held at their supervised values. We conducted some experiments where we

[3] For instance, we find that assigning all categories to unseen verbs gives a lexical category accuracy of 52.25 %, as opposed to an accuracy of 65.4% by using top 15 categories, which gave us the best results, as reported later in Table 3.

self-trained all components of the parsing model, which is the usual case of self-training. We obtained negative results similar to Steedman et al. (2003), where self-training reduced the performance of the parsing model. We do not report them here. Thus, using unlabeled data only to estimate parameters that are badly estimated from labeled data (lexical entries in CCG, due to lexical sparsity) results in improvements, in contrast to prior work with semi-supervised EM.

As is common in semi-supervised settings, we treated the count of each lexical event as the weighted count of that event in the labeled data (treebank)[4] and the count from the Viterbi-parses of unlabeled data. Here we follow Bacchiani et al. (2006) and McClosky et al. (2006) who show that count merging is more effective than model interpolation.

We placed an additional constraint on the contribution that the unlabeled data makes to the semi-supervised model—we only use counts (from unlabeled data) of lexical events that are rarely seen/unseen in the labeled data. Our reasoning was that many lexical entries are estimated accurately from the treebank (for example, those related to function words and other high-frequency words) and estimation from unlabeled data might hurt them. We thus had a cut-off frequency (of words in labeled data) above which we did not allow the unlabeled counts to affect the semi-supervised model. In practise, our experiments turned out to be fairly insensitive to the value of this parameter, on evaluations over rare or unseen verbs. However, overall accuracy would drop slightly if this cut-off was increased. We experimented with cut-offs of 5, 10 and 15, and found that the most conservative value (of 5) gave the best results on in-domain WSJ experiments, and a higher value of 10 gave the best results for out-of-domain experiments.

We also conducted some limited experiments with classical semi-supervised EM, with similar settings of weighting labeled counts, and using unlabeled counts only for rare/unseen events. Since it is a much more computationally expensive procedure, and most of the results did not come close to the results of Viterbi-EM, we did not pursue it.

[4]The labeled count is weighted in order to scale up the labeled data which is usually smaller in size than the unlabeled data, to avoid swamping the labeled counts with much larger unlabeled counts.

5.1 Data

Labeled: Sec. 02-21 of CCGbank (Hockenmaier and Steedman, 2007). In one experiment, we used Sec. 02-21 minus 1575 sentences that were held out to simulate test data containing unseen verbs—see §6.2 for details.

Unlabeled: For in-domain experiments, we used sentences from the unlabeled WSJ portion of the ACL/DCI corpus (LDC93T1, 1993), and the WSJ portion of the ANC corpus (Reppen et al., 2005), limited to sentences containing 20 words or less, creating datasets of approximately 10, 20 and 40 million words each. Additionally, we have a dataset of 140 million words – 40M WSJ words plus an additional 100M from the New York Times.

For domain-adaptation experiments, we use two different datasets. The first one consists of question-sentences – 1328 unlabeled questions, obtained by removing the manual annotation of the question corpus from Rimell and Clark (2008). The second out-of-domain dataset consists of Wikipedia data, approximately 40 million words in size, with sentence length < 20 words.

5.2 Experimental setup

We ran our semi-supervised method using our parser with a smoothed lexicon (from §4.1.1) as the initial model, on unlabeled data of different sizes/domains. For comparison, we also ran experiments using a POS-backed off parser (the original Hockenmaier and Steedman (2002) *LexCat* model) as the initial model. Viterbi-EM converged at 4-5 iterations. We then parsed various test sets using the semi-supervised lexicons thus obtained. In all experiments, the labeled data was scaled to match the size of the unlabeled data. Thus, the scaling factor of labeled data was 10 for unlabeled data of 10M words, 20 for 20M words, etc.

5.3 Evaluation

We focused our evaluations on unseen and low-frequency verbs, since verbs are the most important open-class lexical entries and the most ambiguous to learn from unlabeled data (approx. 600 categories, versus 150 for nouns). We report lexical category accuracy in parses produced using our semi-supervised lexicon, since it is a direct measure of the effect of the lexicon.[5] We discuss four

[5]Dependency recovery accuracy is also used to evaluate performance of CCG parsers and is correlated with lexical

	All words	All Verbs	Unseen Verbs
SUP	87.76	78.10	52.54
SEMISUP	**88.14**	**78.46**	**57.28
SUP_{bkoff}	87.91	76.08	54.14
SEMISUP_{bkoff}	87.79	75.68	54.60

Table 1: Lexical category accuracy on TEST-4SEC
**: $p < 0.004$, McNemar test

experiments below. The first two are on in-domain (WSJ) data. The last two are on out-of-domain data – a question corpus and a Wikipedia corpus.

6 Results

6.1 In-domain: WSJ unseen verbs

Our first testset consists of a concatenation of 4 sections of CCGbank (01, 22, 24, 23), a total of 7417 sentences, to form a testset called TEST-4SEC. We use all these sections in order to get a reasonable token count of unseen verbs, which was not possible with Sec. 23 alone.

Table 1 shows the performance of the smoothed supervised model (SUP) and the semi-supervised model (SEMISUP) on this testset. There is a significant improvement in performance on unseen verbs, showing that the semi-supervised model learns good entries for unseen verbs over and above the smoothed entry in the supervised lexicon. This results in an improvement in the overall lexical category accuracy of the parser on all words, and all verbs.

We also performed semi-supervised training using a supervised model that treated unseen words with a POS-backoff strategy SUP_{bkoff}. We used the same settings of cut-off and the same scaling of labeled counts as before. The supervised backed-off model performs somewhat better than the supervised smoothed model. However, it did not improve as much as the smoothed one from unlabeled data. Additionally, the overall accuracy of SEMISUP_{bkoff} fell below the supervised level, in contrast to the smoothed model, where overall numbers improved. This could indicate that the accuracy of a POS tagger on unseen words, especially verbs, may be an important bottleneck in semi-supervised learning.

Low-frequency verbs We also obtain improvements on verbs that are seen but with a low frequency in the labeled data (Table 2). We divided

category accuracy, but a dependency evaluation is more relevant when comparing performance with parsers in other formalisms and does not have much utility here.

Freq. Bin	1-5	6-10	11-20
SUP	64.13	75.19	77.6
SEMISUP	**66.72**	**76.21**	**79.8**

Table 2: Seen but rare verbs, TEST-4SEC

verbs occurring in TEST-4SEC into different bins according to their occurrence frequency in the labeled data (bins of frequency 1-5, 6-10 and 11-20). Semi-supervised training improves over the supervised baseline for all bins of low-frequency verbs. Note that our cut-off frequency for using unlabeled data is 5, but there are improvements in the 6-10 and 11-20 bins as well, suggesting that learning better categories for rare words (below the cut-off) impacts the accuracy of words above the cut-off as well, by affecting the rest of the parse positively.

6.2 In-domain : heldout unseen verbs

The previous section showed significant improvement in learning categories for verbs that are unseen in the training sections of CCGbank. However, these verbs are in the Zipfian tail, and for this reason have fairly low occurrence frequencies in the unlabeled corpus. In order to estimate whether our method will give further improvements in the lexical categories for these verbs, we would need unlabeled data of a much larger size. We therefore designed an experimental scenario in which we would be able to get high counts of unseen verbs from a similar size of unlabeled data. We first made a list of N verbs from the treebank and then extracted all sentences containing them (either as verbs or otherwise) from CCGbank training sections. These sentences form a testset of 1575 sentences, called TEST-HOV (for *held out verbs*). The verbs in the list were chosen based on occurrence frequency f in the treebank, choosing all verbs that occurred with a frequency of $f = 11$. This number gave us a large enough set and a good type/token ratio to reliably evaluate and analyze our semi-supervised models—112 verb types, with 1115 token occurrences [6]. Since these verbs are actually mid-frequency verbs in the supervised data, they have a correspondingly large occurrence frequency in the unlabeled data, occurring much more often than true unseen verbs. Thus, the unlabeled data size is effectively magnified—as far as these verbs are concerned, the unlabeled data is approximately 11 times larger than it actually is.

Table 3 shows lexical category accuracy on

[6] Selecting a different but close value of f such as $f = 10$ or $f = 12$ would have also served this purpose.

	All Words	All Verbs	Unseen Verbs
SUP	87.26	74.55	65.49
SEMISUP	**87.78**	**75.30**	*** **70.43**
SUP_{bkoff}	87.58	73.06	67.25
SEMISUP_{bkoff}	87.52	72.89	68.05

Table 3: Lexical category accuracy in TEST-HOV. ***p<0.0001, McNemar test

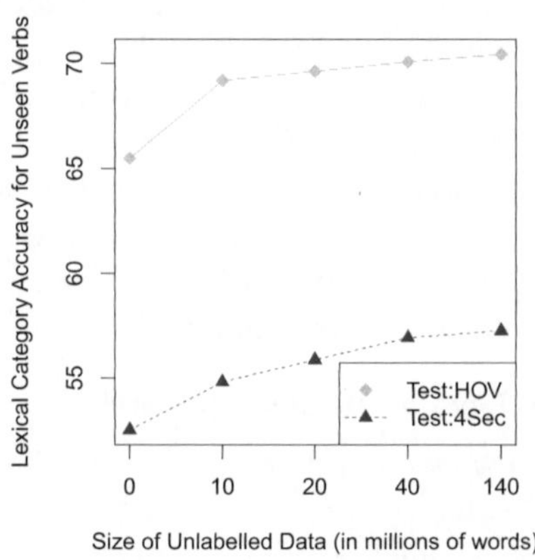

Figure 2: Increasing accuracy on unseen verbs with increasing amounts of unlabeled data.

this testset. The baseline accuracy of the parser on these verbs is much higher than that on the truly unseen verbs.[7] The semi-supervised model (SEMISUP) improves over the supervised model SUP very significantly on these unseen verbs. We also see an overall improvement on all verbs (seen and unseen) in the test data, and in the overall lexical category accuracy as well. Again, the backed-off model does not improve as much as the smoothed model, and moreover, overall performance falls below the supervised level.

Figure 2 shows the effect of different sizes of unlabeled data on accuracy of unseen verbs for the two testsets TEST-HOV and TEST-4SEC . Improvements are monotonic with increasing unlabeled data sizes, up to 40M words. The additional 100M words of NYT also improve the models but to a lesser degree, possibly due to the difference in domain. The graphs indicate that the method will lead to more improvements as more unlabeled data (especially WSJ data) is added.

[7]This could be because verbs in the Zipfian tail have more idiosyncratic subcategorization patterns than mid-frequency verbs, and thus are harder for a parser. Another reason is that they may have been seen as nouns or other parts of speech, leading to greater ambiguity in their case.

	QUESTIONS		WIKIPEDIA	
	All words	wh words	All words	Unseen words
SUP	82.36	61.77	84.31	79.5
SEMISUP	***83.21**	**63.22**	***85.6**	**80.25**

Table 4: Out-of-domain: Questions and Wikipedia, *p<0.05, McNemar test

6.2.1 Out-of-Domain

Questions The question corpus is not strictly a different domain (since questions form a different kind of construction rather than a different domain), but it is an interesting case of adaptation for several reasons: WSJ parsers perform poorly on questions due to the small number of questions in the Penn Treebank/CCGbank. Secondly, unsupervised adaptation to questions has not been attempted before for CCG (Rimell and Clark (2008) did supervised adaptation of their supertagger).

The supervised model SUP already performs at state-of-the-art on this corpus, on both overall scores and on wh(question)-words alone. C&C and Hockenmaier (2003) get 71.6 and 78.6% overall accuracies respectively, and only 33.6 and 50.7 on wh-words alone. To our original unlabeled WSJ data (40M words), we add 1328 unlabeled question-sentences from Rimell and Clark, 2008, scaled by ten, so that each is counted ten times. We then evaluated on a testset containing questions (500 question sentences, from Rimell and Clark (2008)). The overall lexical category accuracy on this testset improves significantly as a result of the semi-supervised learning (Table 4). The accuracy on the question words alone *(who, what, where, when, which, how, whose, whom)* also improves numerically, but by a small amount (the number of tokens that improve are only 7). This could be an effect of the small size of the testset (500 sentences, i.e. 500 wh-words).

Wikipedia We obtain statistically significant improvements in overall scores over a testset consisting of Wikipedia sentences hand-annotated with CCG categories (from Honnibal et al. (2009)) (Table 4). We also obtained improvements in lexical category accuracy on unseen words, and on unseen verbs alone (not shown), but could not prove significance. This testset contains only 200 sentences, and counts for unseen words are too small for significance tests, although there are numeric improvements. However, the overall improvement is statistically significantly, showing that adapting the lexicon alone is effective for a new domain.

6.3 Using semi-supervised lexicons with the C&C parser

To show that the learnt lexical entries may be useful to parsers other than our own, we incorporate our semi-supervised lexical entries into the C&C parser to see if it benefits performance. We do this in a naive manner, as a proof of concept, making no attempt to optimize the performance of the C&C parser (since we do not have access to its internal workings). We take all entries of unseen words from our best semi-supervised lexicon (word, category and count) and add them to the dictionary of the C&C supertagger (tagdict). The C&C is a discriminative, lexicalized model that is more accurate than an unlexicalized model. Even so, the lexical entries that we learn improve the C&C parsers performance over and above its back-off strategy for unseen words. Table 5 shows the results on WSJ data TEST-4SEC and TEST-HOV. There were numeric improvements on the TEST-4SEC test set as shown in Table 5[8]. We obtain significance on the TEST-HOV testset which has a larger number of tokens of unseen verbs and entries that were learnt from effectively larger unlabeled data. We tested two cases: when these verbs were seen for the POS tagger used to tag the test data, and when they were unseen for the POS tagger, and found statistically significant improvement for the case when the verbs were unseen for the POS tagger[9], indicating sensitivity to POS-tagger errors.

6.4 Entropy and KL-divergence

We also evaluated the quality of the semi-supervised lexical entries by measuring the overall entropy and the average Kullback-Leibler (KL) divergence of the learnt entries of unseen verbs from entries in the gold testset. The gold entry for each verb from the TEST-HOV testset was obtained from the heldout gold treebank trees. Supervised (smoothed) and semi-supervised entries were obtained from the respective lexicons. These metrics use the conditional probability of a category given a word, which is not a factor in the generative model (which considers probabilities of words given categories), but provide a good measure of how close the learnt lexicons are to the gold lexicon. We find that the average KL divergence reduces from **2.17** for the baseline supervised entries to **1.40** for the semi-supervised entries. The overall entropy for unseen verb distributions also goes down from **2.23** (supervised) to **1.37** (semi-supervised), showing that semi-supervised distributions are more peaked, and bringing them closer to the true entropy of the gold distribution (**0.93**).

	TEST-4SEC	TEST-HOV	
	(590)	POS-seen (1134)	POS-unseen (1134)
C&C	62.03 (366)	76.71 (870)	72.39 (821)
C&C (enhanced)	**63.89** (377)	**77.34** (877)	***73.98** (839)

Table 5: TEST-4SEC: Lexical category accuracy of C&C parser on unseen verbs. Numbers in brackets are the number of tokens.*$p<0.05$, McNemar test

7 Conclusions

We have shown that it is possible to learn CCG lexical entries for unseen and low-frequency words from unlabeled data. When restricted to learning only lexical entries, Viterbi-EM improved the performance of the supervised parser (both in-domain and out-of-domain). Updating all parameters of the parsing model resulted in a decrease in the accuracy of the parser. We showed that the entries we learnt with an unlexicalized model were accurate enough to also be useful to a highly-accurate lexicalized parser. It is likely that a lexicalized parser will provide even better lexical entries. The lexical entries continued to improve with increasing size of unlabeled data. For the out-of-domain testsets, we obtained statistically significant overall improvements, but we were hampered by the small sizes of the testsets in evaluating unseen/wh words.

In future work, we would like to add unseen but predicted category *types* to the initial lexicon using an independent method, and then apply the same semi-supervised learning to words of these types.

Acknowledgements

We thank Mike Lewis, Shay Cohen and the three anonymous EACL reviewers for helpful comments. This work was supported by the ERC Advanced Fellowship 249520 GRAMPLUS.

[8]There were also improvements on the question and Wikipedia testsets (not shown) (8 and 6 tokens each) but the size of these testsets is too small for significance.

[9]Note that for this testset TEST-HOV, the numbers are the supertagger's accuracy, and not the parser's. We were only able to retrain the supertagger on training data with TEST-HOV sentences heldout, but could not retrain the parser, despite consultation with the authors.

References

Michiel Bacchiani, Michael Riley, Brian Roark, and Richard Sproat. 2006. MAP adaptation of stochastic grammars. *Computer Speech and Language*, 20(1):41–68.

Eugene Charniak. 1993. *Statistical Language Learning*. MIT Press.

Stephen Clark and James R. Curran. 2007. Wide-Coverage Efficient Statistical Parsing with CCG and Log-Linear Models. *Computational Linguistics*, 33(4):493–552.

Stephen Clark, Mark Steedman, and James Curran. 2004. Object-extraction and question-parsing using CCG. In *Proceedings of EMNLP 2004*.

Shay Cohen and Noah Smith. 2010. Viterbi Training for PCFGs: Hardness Results and Competitiveness of Uniform Initialization. In *Proceedings of ACL 2010*.

Michael Collins. 1997. Three generative, lexicalised models for statistical parsing. In *Proceedings of the 35th ACL*.

Tejaswini Deoskar. 2008. Re-estimation of Lexical Parameters for Treebank PCFGs. In *Proceedings of COLING 2008*.

Tejaswini Deoskar, Markos Mylonakis, and Khalil Sima'an. 2012. Learning Structural Dependencies of Words in the Zipfian Tail. *Journal of Logic and Computation*.

Daniel Gildea. 2001. Corpus Variation and Parser Performance. In *Proceedings of EMNLP 2001*.

Sharon Goldwater and Mark Johnson. 2005. Bias in learning syllable structure. In *Proceedings of CoNLL05*.

Julia Hockenmaier. 2003. *Data and Models for Statistical Parsing with Combinatory Categorial Grammar*. Ph.D. thesis, School of Informatics, University of Edinburgh.

Julia Hockenmaier and Mark Steedman. 2002. Generative Models for Statistical Parsing with Combinatory Categorial Grammar. In *ACL40*.

Julia Hockenmaier and Mark Steedman. 2007. CCGbank: A Corpus of CCG Derivations and Dependency Structures Extracted from the Penn Treebank. *Computational Linguistics*, 33:355–396.

Matthew Honnibal, Joel Nothman, and James R. Curran. 2009. Evaluating a Statistial CCG Parser on Wikipedia. In *Proceedings of the 2009 Workshop on the People's Web Meets NLP, ACL-IJCNLP*.

Terry Koo, Xavier Carreras, and Michael Collins. 2008. Simple Semi-supervised Dependency Parsing. In *Proceedings of ACL-08: HLT*, pages 595–603. Association for Computational Linguistics, Columbus, Ohio.

LDC93T1. 1993. LDC93T1. *Linguistic Data Consortium, Philadelphia*.

Matthew Lease and Eugene Charniak. 2005. Parsing Biomedical Literature. In R. Dale, K.-F. Wong, J. Su, and O. Kwong, eds., *Proceedings of the 2nd International Joint Conference on Natural Language Processing (IJCNLP'05)*, vol. 3651 of *Lecture Notes in Computer Science*, pages 58 – 69. Springer-Verlag, Jeju Island, Korea.

Mike Lewis and Mark Steedman. 2013. Combined Distributional and Logical Semantics. *Transactions of the Association for Computational Linguistics*.

David McClosky, Eugene Charniak, and Mark Johnson. 2006. Effective Self-Training for Parsing. In *Proceedings of HLT-NAACL 2006*.

Bernard Merialdo. 1994. Tagging English Text with a Probabilistic Model. *Computational Linguistics*, 20(2):155–171.

Radford M. Neal and Geoffrey E. Hinton. 1998. A view of the EM algorithm that justifies incremental, sparse, and other variants. In *Learning and Graphical Models*, pages 355 – 368. Kluwer Academic Publishers.

Slav Petrov and Ryan McDonald. 2012. Overview of the 2012 Shared Task on Parsing the Web. In *First Workshop on Syntactic Analysis of Non-Canonical Language (SANCL) Workshop at NAACL 2012*.

Randi Reppen, Nancy Ide, and Keith Suderman. 2005. LDC2005T35, American National Corpus (ANC) Second Release. *Linguistic Data Consortium, Philadelphia*.

Laura Rimell and Stephen Clark. 2008. Adapting a Lexicalized-Grammar Parser to Contrasting Domains. In *Proceedings of the Conference on Empirical Methods in Natural Language Processing (EMNLP-08)*.

Valentin I. Spitkovsky, Hiyan Alshawi, Daniel Jurafsky, and Christopher D. Manning. 2010. Viterbi Training Improves Unsupervised Dependency Parsing. In *Proceedings of CoNLL-2010*.

Mark Steedman. 2000. *The Syntactic Process*. MIT Press/Bradford Books.

Mark Steedman, Steven Baker, Jeremiah Crim, Stephen Clark, Julia Hockenmaier, Rebecca Hwa, Miles Osbornn, Paul Ruhlen, and Anoop Sarkar. 2003. Semi-Supervised Training for Statistical Parsing. Tech. rep., CLSP WS-02.

Jun Suzuki, Hideki Isozaki, Xavier Carreras, and Michael Collins. 2009. An Empirical Study of Semi-supervised Structured Conditional Models for Dependency Parsing. In *Proceedings of the 2009 Conference on Empirical Methods in Natural Language Processing*, pages 551–560. Association for Computational Linguistics, Singapore.

Emily Thomforde and Mark Steedman. 2011. Semi-supervised CCG Lexicon Extension. In *Proceedings of the Conference on Empirical Methods in Natural Language Processing, Edinburgh UK*.

Special Techniques for Constituent Parsing of Morphologically Rich Languages

Zsolt Szántó, Richárd Farkas
University of Szeged
Department of Informatics
{szanto,rfarkas}@inf.u-szeged.hu

Abstract

We introduce three techniques for improving constituent parsing for morphologically rich languages. We propose a novel approach to automatically find an optimal preterminal set by clustering morphological feature values and we conduct experiments with enhanced lexical models and feature engineering for rerankers. These techniques are specially designed for morphologically rich languages (but they are language-agnostic). We report empirical results on the treebanks of five morphologically rich languages and show a considerable improvement in accuracy and in parsing speed as well.

1 Introduction

From the viewpoint of syntactic parsing, the languages of the world are usually categorized according to their level of morphological richness (which is negatively correlated with configurationality). At one end, there is English, a strongly configurational language while there is Hungarian at the other end of the spectrum with rich morphology and free word order (Fraser et al., 2013). A large part of the methodology for syntactic parsing has been developed for English but many other languages of the world are fundamentally different from English. In particular, morphologically rich languages – the other end of the configurational spectrum – convey most sentence-level syntactic information by morphology (i.e. at the word level), not by configuration. Because of these differences the parsing of morphologically rich languages requires techniques that differ from or extend the methodology developed for English (Tsarfaty et al., 2013). In this study, we present three techniques to improve constituent parsing and these special techniques are dedicated to handle the challenges of morphologically rich languages.

Constituency parsers have advanced considerably in the last two decades (Charniak, 2000; Charniak and Johnson, 2005; Petrov et al., 2006; Huang, 2008) boosted by the availability of the Penn Treebank (Marcus et al., 1993). While there is a progress on parsing English (especially the Penn Treebank), the treebanks of morphologically rich languages have been attracted much less attention. For example, a big constituent treebank has been available for Hungarian for almost 10 years (Csendes et al., 2005) and to the best of our knowledge our work is the first one reporting results on this treebank. One reason for the moderate level of interest in constituent parsing of morphologically rich languages is the widely held belief that dependency structures are better suited for representing syntactic analyses for morphologically rich languages than constituent representations because they allow non-projective structures (i.e. discontinuous constituents). From a theoretical point of view, Tsarfaty et al. (2010) point out, however, this is not the same as proving that dependency parsers function better than constituency parsers for parsing morphologically rich languages. For a detailed discussion, please see Fraser et al. (2013).

From an empirical point of view, the organizers of the recent shared task on 'Statistical Parsing of Morphologically Rich Languages' (Seddah et al., 2013) provided datasets only for languages having treebanks in both dependency and constituency format and their cross-framework evaluation – employing the unlabeled TedEval (Tsarfaty et al., 2012) as evaluation procedure – revealed that at 4 out of 9 morphologically rich languages, the results of constituent parsers were higher than the scores achieved by the best dependency parsing system. Based on these theoretical issues and empirical results, we support the conclusion of

Fraser et al. (2013) that "... *there is no clear evidence for preferring dependency parsing over constituency parsing in analyzing languages with rich morphology and instead argue that research in both frameworks is important.*"

In this study, we propose answers to the two main challenges of constituent parsing of morphologically rich languages, which are finding the optimal preterminal set and handling the huge number of wordforms. The size of the preterminal set in the standard context free grammar environment is crucial. If we use only the main POS tags as preterminals, we lose a lot of information encoded in the morphological description of the tokens. On the other hand, using the full morphological description as preterminal yields a set of over a thousand preterminals, which results in data sparsity and performance problems as well. The chief contribution of this work is to propose a novel automatic procedure to find the optimal set of preterminals by **merging morphological feature values**. The main novelties of our approach over previous work are that it is very fast – it operates inside a probabilistic context free grammar (PCFG) instead of using a parser as a black box with re-training for every evaluation of a feature combination – and it can investigate particular morphological feature values instead of removing a feature with all of its values.

Another challenge is that because of the inflectional nature of morphologically rich languages the number of wordforms is much higher compared with English. Hence the number of unknown and very rare tokens – i.e. the tokens that do not appear in the training dataset – is higher here, which hurts the performance of PCFG parsers. Following Goldberg and Elhadad (2013), we **enhance the lexical model** by exploiting an external lexicon. We investigate the applicabilities of fully supervised taggers instead of unsupervised ones for gathering external lexicons.

Lastly, we introduce novel feature templates for an n-best reranker operating on the top of a PCFG parser. These feature templates are **exploiting atomic morphological features** and achieve improvements over the standard feature set engineered for English.

We conducted experiments by the above mentioned three techniques on Basque, French, German, Hebrew and Hungarian, five morphologically rich languages. The BerkeleyParser (Petrov et al., 2006) enriched with these three techniques achieved state-of-the-art results on each language.

2 Related Work

Constituent parsing of English is a well researched area. The field has been dominated by data-driven, i.e. treebank-based statistical approaches in the last two decades (Charniak, 2000; Charniak and Johnson, 2005; Petrov et al., 2006). We extend here BerkeleyParser (Petrov et al., 2006), which is a PCFG parser using latent annotations at non-terminals. Its basic idea is to iteratively split each non-terminal into subsymbols thus capturing the different subusage of them instead of manually designed annotations.

The constituent parsing of morphologically rich languages is a much less investigated field. There exist constituent treebanks for several languages along with a very limited number of parsing reports on them. For instance, Petrov (2009) trained BerkeleyParser on Arabic, Bulgarian, French, German and Italian and he reported good accuracies, but there has been previous work on Hebrew (Goldberg and Elhadad, 2013), Korean (Choi et al., 1994) and Spanish (Le Roux et al., 2012) etc. The recently organized 'Statistical Parsing of Morphologically Rich Languages' (Seddah et al., 2013) addressed the dependency and constituency parsing of nine morphologically rich languages and provides useful benchmark datasets for these languages.

Our chief contribution in this paper is a procedure to merge preterminal labels. The related work for this line of research includes the studies on manual refinement of preterminal sets such as Marton et al. (2010) and Le Roux et al. (2012). The most closely related approach to our proposal is Dehdari et al. (2011), who defines metaheuristics to incrementally insert or remove morphological features. Their approach uses parser – training and parsing – as a black box evaluation of a preterminal set. In contrast, our proposal operates as a submodule of the BerkeleyParser, hence does not require the re-training of the parser for every possible preterminal set candidate, thus it is way more faster.

The most successful supervised constituent parsers contain a second feature-rich discriminative parsing step (Charniak and Johnson, 2005; Huang, 2008; Chen and Kit, 2012) as well. At the first stage they apply a PCFG to extract pos-

	Basque	French	German	Hebrew	Hungarian
#sent. in training	7577	14759	40472	5000	8146
#sent. in dev	948	1235	5000	500	1051
#sent. in test	946	2541	5000	716	1009
avg. token/sent.	12.92	30.13	17.51	25.33	21.76
#non-terminal labels	3000	770	994	1196	890
#main POS labels	16	33	54	46	16
unknown token ratio (dev)	18.35%	3.22%	6.34%	19.94%	19.94%

Table 1: Basic statistics of the treebanks used.

sible parses. The *n-best list parsers* keep just the 50-100 best parses according to the PCFG (Charniak and Johnson, 2005). These methods employ a large feature set (usually a few million features) (Collins, 2000; Charniak and Johnson, 2005). These feature sets are engineered for English. In this study, we introduce feature templates for exploiting morphological information and investigate their added value over the standard feature sets.

3 Experimental Setup

We conducted experiments on the treebanks of the 2013 shared task on 'Statistical Parsing of Morphologically Rich Languages' (Seddah et al., 2013). We used the train/dev/test splits of the shared task's Basque (Aduriz et al., 2003), French (Abeillé et al., 2003), Hebrew (Sima'an et al., 2001), German (Brants et al., 2002) and Hungarian (Csendes et al., 2005) treebanks. Table 1 shows the basic statistics of these treebanks, for a more detailed description about their annotation schemata, domain, preprocessing etc. please see Seddah et al. (2013).

As evaluation metrics we employ the PARSEVAL score (Abney et al., 1991) along with the exact match accuracy (i.e. the ratio of perfect parse trees). We use the evalb implementation of the shared task[1].

4 Enhanced Lexical Models

Before introducing our proposal and experiments with preterminal set optimisation, we have to offer a solution for the out-of-vocabulary (OOV) problem, which – because of the inflectional nature – is a crucial problem in morphologically rich languages. We follow here Goldberg and Elhadad (2013) and enhance a lexicon model trained on the training set of the treebank with frequency information about the possible morphological analyses of tokens. We estimate the tagging probability $P(t|w)$ of the tag t given the word w by

$$P(t|w) = \begin{cases} P_{tb}(t|w), & \text{if } c(w) \geq K \\ \frac{c(w)P_{tb}(t|w)+P_{ex}(t|w)}{1+c(w)}, & \text{otherwise} \end{cases}$$

where $c(w)$ is the count of w in the training set, K is predefined constant, $P_{tb}(t|w)$ is the probability estimate from the treebank (the relative frequency with smoothing) and $P_{ex}(t|w)$ is the probability estimate from an external lexicon. We calculate the emission probabilities $P(w|t)$ from the tagging probabilities $P(t|w)$ by applying the Bayesian rule.

The key question here is how to construct the external lexicon. For a baseline, Goldberg and Elhadad (2013) suggest using the uniform distribution over all possible morphological analyses coming from a morphological analyser ('uniform').

Goldberg and Elhadad (2013) also report considerable improvements over the 'uniform' baseline by relative frequencies counted on a large corpus which was automatically annotated in the unsupervised POS tagging paradigm (Goldberg et al., 2008). Here we show that even a supervised morphological tagger without a morphological analyzer can achieve the same level of improvement. We employ MarMot[2] (Mueller et al., 2013) for predicting full morphological analysis (i.e. POS tags and morphological features jointly). MarMot is a Conditional Random Field tagger which incrementally creates forward-backward lattices of increasing order to prune the

[1]Available at `http://pauillac.inria.fr/~seddah/evalb_spmrl2013.tar.gz`. An important change in this version compared to the original evalb is the penalization of unparsed sentences.

[2]`https://code.google.com/p/cistern/`

sizable space of possible morphological analyses. We used MarMoT with the default parameters. This purely data-driven tagger achieves a tagging accuracy of 97.6 evaluated at full morphological analyses on the development set of the Hungarian treebank, which is competitive with the state-of-the-art Hungarian taggers which employ language-specific rules (e.g. magyarlanc (Zsibrita et al., 2013)). The chief advantage of using MarMot instead of an unsupervised tagger is that the former does not require any morphological lexicon/analyser (which can lists the possible tags for a given word). This morphological lexicon/analyser is language-dependent, usually handcrafted and it has to be compatible with the treebank in question. In contrast, a supervised morphological tagger can build a reasonable tagging model on the training part of the treebanks – especially for morphologically rich languages, where the tag ambiguity is generally low – thus each of these problems is avoided.

Table 2 shows the results of various $P_{ex}(t|w)$ estimates on the Hungarian development set. The first row 'BerkeleyParser' is our absolute baseline, i.e. the original implementation of BerkeleyParser[3] defining signatures for OOVs. For the 'uniform' results, we used the morphological analyser module of magyarlanc (Zsibrita et al., 2013). The last two rows show the results achieved by training MarMot on the treebank's training dataset, having tagged the development set plus a huge unlabeled corpus (10M sentences from the Hungarian National Corpus (Váradi, 2002)) with it then having counted relative tag frequencies. We report scores on only using the frequencies from the development set ('dev') and from the concatenation of the development set and the huge corpus ('huge').

After a few preliminary experiments, we set $K = 7$ and use this value thereafter.

Table 2 shows that even 'dev' yields a considerable improvement over the baseline parser and 'uniform'. These results are also in line with the findings of Goldberg and Elhadad (2013), i.e. 'uniform' has some added value and using relative frequencies gathered from automatically tagged corpora contributes more. Although we can see another nice improvement by exploiting unlabeled corpora ('huge'), we will use the 'dev' setting in

	PARSEVAL	EX
BerkeleyParser	87.22	12.75
uniform	87.31	14.78
dev	88.29	15.22
huge	89.27	16.97

Table 2: The results achieved by using various external lexical models on the Hungarian development set.

the experiments of the next sections as we did not have access to huge, in-domain unlabeled corpora for each language used in this study.

5 Morphological Feature Values as Preterminals

Finding the optimal set of morphological features incorporating into the perterminal labels is crucial for any PCFG parsers. Removing morphological features might reduce data sparsity problems while it might lead to loss of information for the syntactic parser. In this section, we propose a novel method for automatically finding the optimal set of preterminals then we present empirical results with this method and compare it to various baselines.

Merge Procedure for Morphological Feature Values: There have been studies published on the automatic reduction of the set of preterminals for constituent parsing. For instance, Dehdari et al. (2011) proposed a system which iteratively removes morphological features as a unit then evaluates the preterminal sets by running the training and parsing steps of a black-box constituent parser. Our motivation here is two-fold. First, morphological features should not be handled as a unit because different values of a feature might behave differently. Take for instance the degree feature in Hungarian adjectives. Here the values positive and superlative behave similarly (can be merged) while distinguishing comparative and positive+superlative is useful for syntactic parsing because comparative adjectives often have an argument (e.g. x is more beautiful than y) while positive and superlative adjectives are not syntactic governors thus have no arguments. Second, keeping a morphological feature can be useful for particular POS tags and useless at other particular POS tags (e.g. the number of possessed in Hungarian for nouns and pronouns).

[3] `http://code.google.com/p/berkeleyparser/`

Algorithm 1 The preterminal set merger algorithm.

1. training the standard BerkeleyParser using only main POS tags as preterminals
2. merging each subsymbols at the preterminal level
3. for each POS tag - morphological feature pair
   (a) split the POS tag for the values of the morphological feature[4]
   (b) recalculating the rule probabilities where there are preterminals in the right-hand side by uniformly distribute the probability mass among subsymbols
   (c) set the lexical probabilities according to the relative frequencies of morphological values counted on gold standard morphological tags of the treebank
   (d) running 10 iterations of the Expectation-Maximization procedure on the whole treebank initialized with (b)-(c)
   (e) constructing a fully connected graph whose nodes are the morphological values of the feature in question
   (f) for every edge of the graph, calculate the loss in likehood for the merging the two subsymbols (the same way as for BerkeleyParser's merge procedure)
4. removing edges from the entire set of graphs (controlled by the parameter th)
5. merge the morphological values of the graphs' connected components

Based on these observations we propose a procedure which starts from the full morphological description of a treebank then iteratively merges particular morphological feature values and it handles the same feature at the different POS tags separately. The result of this procedure is a clustering of the possible values of each morphological feature. The removal of a morphological feature is a special case of our approach because if the values of the feature in question form one single cluster it does not have any discriminative function anymore. Hence our proposal can be regarded as a generalisation of the previous approaches.

This general approach requires much more evaluation of intermediate candidate preterminal sets, which is not feasible within the external black-box parser evaluation scenario (training and parsing an average sized treebank by the BerkeleyParser takes more than 1 hour). Our idea here is that re-training a parser for the evaluation of each preterminal set candidates is not necessary. They key objective here is to select among preterminal sets based on their usefulness for the syntactic parser. This is the motivation of the merge procedure of the BerkeleyParser. After randomly splitting non-terminals, BerkeleyParser calculates for each split the loss in likelihood incurred when merging the subsymbols back. If this loss is small, the new annotation does not carry enough useful information and can be removed (Petrov et al., 2006). Our task is the same at the preterminal level. Hence at the preterminal level, – instead of using the automatic subsymbol splits of the BerkeleyParser – we call this merging procedure over the morphological feature values. Algorithm 1 shows our proposal for the preterminal merging procedure.

Baseline Preterminal Set Constructions: The two basic approaches for preterminal set construction are the use of only the main POS tag set ('mainPOS') and the use of the full morphological description as preterminals ('full'). For Hungarian, we also had access to a linguistically motivated, hand-crafted preterminal set ('manual') which was designed for a morphological tagger (Zsibrita et al., 2013). This manual code set keeps different morphological features at different POS tags and merges morphological values instead of fully removing features hence it inspired our automatic merge procedure introduced in the previous section.

Our last baseline is the repetition of the experiments of Dehdari et al. (2011). For this, we started from the full morphological feature set and completely removed features (from all POS) one-by-one then re-trained our parser. We observed the greatest drop in PARSEVAL score at removing the

	Basque	French	German	Hebrew	Hungarian
mainPOS	68.8/3.9 16	78.4/13.9 33	82.3/38.7 54	88.3/12.0 46	82.6/7.3 16
full	**81.8/18.4** 2976	78.9/15.0 676	**82.3/40.3** 686	88.9/**15.2** 257	88.3/15.2 680
preterminal merger	81.6/16.9 2791	**79.7/15.6** 480	82.3/39.3 111	**89.0**/14.6 181	**88.5/15.4** 642

Table 3: PARSEVAL / exact match scores on the development sets. The third small numbers in cells show the size of the preterminal sets.

'Num' feature and the least severe one at removing 'Form'. 'Num' denotes number for verbs and nominal elements (nouns, adjectives and numerals), and since subject-verb agreement is determined by the number and person features of the predicate (the verb) and the subject (the noun), deleting the feature 'Num' results in a serious decline in performance. On the other hand, 'Form' denotes whether a conjunction is single or compound (which is a lexical feature) or whether a number is spelt with letters, Arabic or Roman numbers (which is an orthographic feature). It is interesting to see that their deletion hardly harms the PARSEVAL scores, moreover, it can even improve the exact match scores, which is probably due to the fact that the distinction between different orthographic versions of the same number (e.g. *6* and *VI*) just confused the parser. On the other hand, members of a compound conjunction are not attached to each other in any way in the parse tree, and behave similar to single compounds, so this distinction might also be problematic for parsing.

Results with Various Preterminal Sets: Table 4 summarizes the results achieved by our four baseline methods along with the scores of two preterminal sets output by our merger approach at two different merging threshold th value.

	#pt	PARSEVAL	EX
mainPOS	16	82.36	5.52
manual	72	85.38	9.23
full	680	88.29	15.22
full - Num	479	87.43	14.49
full - Form	635	88.24	15.73
merged ($th = 0.5$)	378	88.36	**15.92**
merged ($th = 0.1$)	642	**88.52**	15.44

Table 4: The results achieved by using various preterminal sets on the Hungarian development set.

The difference between mainPOS and full is surprisingly high, which indicates that the morphological information carried in preterminals is extremely important for the constituent parser and the BerkeleyParser can handle preterminal sets of the size of several hundreds. For Hungarian, we found that the full removal of any feature cannot increase the results. This finding is contradictory with Dehdari et al. (2011) in Arabic, where removing 'Case' yielded a gain of 1.0 in PARSEVAL. We note that baselines for Arabic and Hungarian are also totally different, Dehdari et al. (2011) reports basically no difference between mainPOS and full in Arabic.

We report results of our proposed procedure with two different merging thresholds. The $th = 0.1$ case merges only a few morphological feature values and it can slightly outperform the 'full' setting (statistically significant[5] in exact match.). On the other hand, the $th = 0.5$ setting is competitive with the 'full' setting in terms of parsing accuracy but it uses only the third of the preterminals used by 'full'. Although it is not statistically better than 'full' in accuracy, it almost halves the running time of parsing[6].

Table 3 summarizes the results achieved by the most important baselines and our approach along with the size of the particular preterminal sets applied. The 'full' results outperform 'mainPOS' at each language with a striking difference at Basque and Hungarian. These results show that – contradictory to the general belief – the detailed morphological description is definitely useful in constituent parsing as well. The last row of the table contains the result achieved by our merger approach. Here we run experiments with several merging threshold th values and show the highest scores for each language.

Our merging proposal could find a better preterminal set than full on French and Hungarian, it found a competitive tag set in terms of accuracies

[5]According to two sample t-test with $p<0.001$.

[6]Parsing the 1051 sentences of the Hungarian development set takes 15 and 9 minutes with full and $th = 0.5$ respectively (on an Intel Xeon E7 2GHz).

which are much smaller than full on German and Hebrew and it could not find any useful merge at Basque. The output of the merger procedure consists of one sixth of preterminals compared with full. Manually investigating the clusters, we can see that it basically merged every morphological feature except case at nouns and adjectives (but merged case at personal pronouns). This finding is in line with the experimental results of Fraser et al. (2013).

6 Morphology-based Features in n-best Reranking

n-best rerankers (Collins, 2000; Charniak and Johnson, 2005) are used as second stage after a PCFG parser and they usually achieve considerable improvement over the first stage parser. They extract a large feature set to describe the n best output of a PCFG parser and they select the best parse from this set (i.e. rerank the parses). Here, we define feature templates exploiting morphological information and investigate their added value for the standard feature sets (engineered for English). We reimplemented the feature templates from Charniak and Johnson (2005) and Versley and Rehbein (2009) excluding the features based on external corpora and use them as our baseline feature set.

We used $n = 50$ in our experiment and followed a 5-fold-cross-parsing (a.k.a. jackknifing) approach for generating unseen parse candidates for the training sentences (Charniak and Johnson, 2005). The reranker is trained for the maximum entropy objective function of Charniak and Johnson (2005), i.e. the sum of posterior probabilities of the oracles. We used a slightly modified version of the Mallet toolkit for reranking (McCallum, 2002) and L2 regularizer with its default value for coefficient.

The feature templates of the baseline feature set frequently incorporate preterminals as atomic feature. As a first step, we investigated which preterminal set is the most useful for the baseline feature set. We took the 50 best output from the parser using the merged preterminal set and used its preterminals ('merged') or only the main POS tag ('mainPOS') as atomic building blocks for the reranker's feature extractor. Table 5 shows that mainPOS outperformed full. This is probably due to data sparsity problems.

Based on this observation, we decided to use mainPOS as preterminal in the atomic building block of the baseline features and designed new feature templates capturing the information in the morphological analysis. We experimented with the following templates:

For each preterminal of the candidate parse and for each morphological feature value inside the preterminal we add the pair of wordform and morphological feature value as a new feature. In a similar way, we define a reranker feature from every morphological feature value of the head word of the constituent. For each head-daughter attachment in the candidate parse we add each pair of the morphological feature values from the head words of the attachment's participants. Similarly we take each combination of head word's morphological features values from sister constituents.

The first two templates enable the reranker to incorporate information into its learnt model from the rich morphology of the language at the lexical and constituent levels, while the last two templates might capture (dis)agreement at the morphological level. The motivation for using these features is that because of the free(er) word order of morphologically rich languages, morphological (dis)agreement can be a good indicator of attachment.

Table 5 shows the added value of these feature templates over mainPOS ('extended'), which is again statistically significant in exact match. Exploiting the morphological agreement in syntactic parsing has been investigated in previous studies, e.g. the Bohnet parser (Bohnet, 2010) employs morphological feature value pairs similar to our feature templates and Seeker and Kuhn (2013) introduces an integer linear programming framework including constraints for morphological agreement. However, these works focus on dependency parsing and to the best of our knowledge, this is the first study on experimenting with atomic morphological features and their agreement in a constituency parsing.

	PARSEVAL	EX
reranker (merged morph)	89.05	18.45
reranker (mainPOS)	89.33	18.64
reranker (extended)	**89.47**	**20.35**

Table 5: The results achieved by using various feature template sets for 50-best reranking on the Hungarian development set.

	Basque	French	German	Hebrew	Hungarian
BerkeleyParser	79.21 / 19.03	79.53 / 18.46	74.77 / 26.56	87.87 / 14.53	88.22 / 26.96
+ Lexical model	82.02 / 25.69	78.91 / 17.87	75.64 / 28.36	88.53 / 13.69	89.09 / 26.76
+ Preterminal merger	83.19 / 24.74	79.53 / 18.58	77.12 / **30.02**	88.07 / 13.83	89.15 / 28.05
+ reranker	83.81 / 25.66	80.31 / 18.91	**77.78** / 29.80	88.38 / 15.12	89.57 / 30.23
+ reranker + morph feat	**84.03 / 26.28**	**80.41 / 20.07**	77.74 / 29.23	**88.55 / 15.24**	**89.91 / 30.55**

Table 6: PARSEVAL / exact match scores on the test sets.

7 Results of the Full System

After our investigations focusing on building blocks of our system independently from each other on the development set, we parsed the test sets of the treebanks adding steps one-by-one. Table 6 summarizes our final results. We start from the BerkeleyParser using the full morphological descriptions as preterminal set, then we enrich the lexical model with tagging frequencies gathered from the automatic parsing of the test sets ('+ lexical model'). In the third step we replace the full preterminal set by the output of our preterminal merger procedure ('+ preterminal merger'). We tuned the merging threshold of our method on the development set for each language. The last two rows contain the results achieved by the 50-best reranker with the standard feature set ('+ reranker') and with the feature set extended by morphological features ('+ morph features').

The enhanced lexical model contributes a lot at Basque and considerable improvements are present at German and Hungarian as well while it harmed the results in French. The advance of the preterminal merger approach over the full setting is clear at French and Hungarian, similarly to the development set. It is interesting that an rationalized preterminal set could compensate the loss suffered by a inadequate lexical model at French.

Although the reranking step could further improve the results at each languages we have to note that the gain (0.5 in average) is much smaller here than the gains reported on English (over 1.5). This might be because of the high number of wordforms at morphologically rich languages i.e. most of feature templates are incorporate the words itself and the huge dictionary can indicate data sparsity problems again. Our morphology-based reranking features yielded a moderate improvement at four languages, but we believe there a lots of space for improvement here.

8 Conclusions

In this study we introduced three techniques for better constituent parsing of morphologically rich languages. We believe that research in constituency parsing is important next to dependency parsing. In general, we report state-of-the-art results with constituent parsers with our entirely language-agnostic techniques.

Our chief contribution here is the preterminal merger procedure. This is a more general approach than previous proposals and still much faster thank to operating on probabilities from a PCFG instead of employing a full train+parse step for evaluating every preterminal set candidate. We found that the inclusion of the rich morphological description into the preterminal level is crucial for parsing morphologically rich languages. Our proposed preterminal merger approach could outperform the full setting at 2 out of 5 languages, i.e. we have reported gains in parsing accuracies by merging morphological feature values. At the other languages, the results with the full preterminal set and our approach are competitive in terms of parsing accuracies while our approach could achieve these scores with a smaller preterminal set, which leads to considerable parsing time advantages.

We also experimented with exploiting external corpora in the lexical model. Here we showed that automatic tagging of an off-the-shelf supervised morphological tagger (MarMot) can contribute to the results. Our last experiment was carried out with the feature set of an n-best reranker. We showed that incorporating feature templates built on morphological information improves the results.

Acknowledgments

This work was supported in part by the European Union and the European Social Fund through project FuturICT.hu (grant no.: TÁMOP-4.2.2.C-11/1/KONV-2012-0013).

References

Anne Abeillé, Lionel Clément, and François Toussenel. 2003. Building a treebank for french. In Anne Abeillé, editor, *Treebanks*. Kluwer, Dordrecht.

S. Abney, S. Flickenger, C. Gdaniec, C. Grishman, P. Harrison, D. Hindle, R. Ingria, F. Jelinek, J. Klavans, M. Liberman, M. Marcus, S. Roukos, B. Santorini, and T. Strzalkowski. 1991. Procedure for quantitatively comparing the syntactic coverage of english grammars. In E. Black, editor, *Proceedings of the workshop on Speech and Natural Language*, pages 306–311.

I. Aduriz, M. J. Aranzabe, J. M. Arriola, A. Atutxa, A. Díaz de Ilarraza, A. Garmendia, and M. Oronoz. 2003. Construction of a Basque dependency treebank. In *TLT-03*, pages 201–204.

Bernd Bohnet. 2010. Top accuracy and fast dependency parsing is not a contradiction. In *Proceedings of the 23rd International Conference on Computational Linguistics (Coling 2010)*, pages 89–97.

Sabine Brants, Stefanie Dipper, Silvia Hansen, Wolfgang Lezius, and George Smith. 2002. The TIGER treebank. In Erhard Hinrichs and Kiril Simov, editors, *Proceedings of the First Workshop on Treebanks and Linguistic Theories (TLT 2002)*, pages 24–41.

Eugene Charniak and Mark Johnson. 2005. Coarse-to-fine n-best parsing and maxent discriminative reranking. In *Proceedings of the 43rd Annual Meeting on Association for Computational Linguistics*, ACL '05, pages 173–180.

Eugene Charniak. 2000. A maximum-entropy-inspired parser. In *Proceedings of the 1st North American chapter of the Association for Computational Linguistics conference*, pages 132–139.

Xiao Chen and Chunyu Kit. 2012. Higher-order constituent parsing and parser combination. In *Proceedings of the 50th Annual Meeting of the Association for Computational Linguistics (Volume 2: Short Papers)*, pages 1–5.

Key-Sun Choi, Young S Han, Young G Han, and Oh W Kwon. 1994. Kaist tree bank project for korean: Present and future development. In *Proceedings of the International Workshop on Sharable Natural Language Resources*, pages 7–14. Citeseer.

Michael Collins. 2000. Discriminative reranking for natural language parsing. In *Proceedings of the Seventeenth International Conference on Machine Learning*, ICML '00, pages 175–182.

Dóra Csendes, János Csirik, Tibor Gyimóthy, and András Kocsor. 2005. The Szeged Treebank. In *TSD*, pages 123–131.

Jon Dehdari, Lamia Tounsi, and Josef van Genabith. 2011. Morphological features for parsing morphologically-rich languages: A case of arabic. In *Proceedings of the Second Workshop on Statistical Parsing of Morphologically Rich Languages*, pages 12–21, Dublin, Ireland, October. Association for Computational Linguistics.

Alexander Fraser, Helmut Schmid, Richárd Farkas, Renjing Wang, and Hinrich Schütze. 2013. Knowledge sources for constituent parsing of german, a morphologically rich and less-configurational language. *Computational Linguistics*, 39(1):57–85.

Yoav Goldberg and Michael Elhadad. 2013. Word segmentation, unknown-word resolution, and morphological agreement in a hebrew parsing system. *Computational Linguistics*, 39(1):121–160.

Yoav Goldberg, Meni Adler, and Michael Elhadad. 2008. EM can find pretty good HMM POS-taggers (when given a good start). In *Proceedings of ACL-08: HLT*, pages 746–754.

Liang Huang. 2008. Forest reranking: Discriminative parsing with non-local features. In *Proceedings of ACL-08: HLT*, pages 586–594.

Joseph Le Roux, Benoit Sagot, and Djamé Seddah. 2012. Statistical parsing of spanish and data driven lemmatization. In *Proceedings of the ACL 2012 Joint Workshop on Statistical Parsing and Semantic Processing of Morphologically Rich Languages*, pages 55–61.

Mitchell P. Marcus, Mary Ann Marcinkiewicz, and Beatrice Santorini. 1993. Building a large annotated corpus of english: the penn treebank. *Computational Linguistics*, 19(2):313–330.

Yuval Marton, Nizar Habash, and Owen Rambow. 2010. Improving arabic dependency parsing with lexical and inflectional morphological features. In *Proceedings of the NAACL HLT 2010 First Workshop on Statistical Parsing of Morphologically-Rich Languages*, pages 13–21.

Andrew Kachites McCallum. 2002. Mallet: A machine learning for language toolkit. http://mallet.cs.umass.edu.

Thomas Mueller, Helmut Schmid, and Hinrich Schütze. 2013. Efficient higher-order CRFs for morphological tagging. In *Proceedings of the 2013 Conference on Empirical Methods in Natural Language Processing*, pages 322–332.

Slav Petrov, Leon Barrett, Romain Thibaux, and Dan Klein. 2006. Learning accurate, compact, and interpretable tree annotation. In *Proceedings of the 21st International Conference on Computational Linguistics and 44th Annual Meeting of the Association for Computational Linguistics*, pages 433–440.

Slav Petrov. 2009. *Coarse-to-Fine Natural Language Processing*. Ph.D. thesis, University of California at Bekeley, Berkeley, CA, USA.

Djamé Seddah, Reut Tsarfaty, Sandra Kübler, Marie Candito, Jinho D. Choi, Richárd Farkas, Jennifer Foster, Iakes Goenaga, Koldo Gojenola Galletebeitia, Yoav Goldberg, Spence Green, Nizar Habash, Marco Kuhlmann, Wolfgang Maier, Yuval Marton, Joakim Nivre, Adam Przepiórkowski, Ryan Roth, Wolfgang Seeker, Yannick Versley, Veronika Vincze, Marcin Woliński, and Alina Wróblewska. 2013. Overview of the SPMRL 2013 shared task: A cross-framework evaluation of parsing morphologically rich languages. In *Proceedings of the Fourth Workshop on Statistical Parsing of Morphologically-Rich Languages*, pages 146–182.

Wolfgang Seeker and Jonas Kuhn. 2013. Morphological and syntactic case in statistical dependency parsing. *Computational Linguistics*, 39(1):23–55.

Khalil Sima'an, Alon Itai, Yoad Winter, Alon Altman, and Noa Nativ. 2001. Building a Tree-Bank for Modern Hebrew Text. In *Traitement Automatique des Langues*.

Reut Tsarfaty, Djamé Seddah, Yoav Goldberg, Sandra Kuebler, Yannick Versley, Marie Candito, Jennifer Foster, Ines Rehbein, and Lamia Tounsi. 2010. Statistical parsing of morphologically rich languages (spmrl) what, how and whither. In *Proceedings of the NAACL HLT 2010 First Workshop on Statistical Parsing of Morphologically-Rich Languages*, pages 1–12.

Reut Tsarfaty, Joakim Nivre, and Evelina Andersson. 2012. Cross-framework evaluation for statistical parsing. In *Proceedings of the 13th Conference of the European Chapter of the Association for Computational Linguistics*, pages 44–54.

Reut Tsarfaty, Djamé Seddah, Sandra Kübler, and Joakim Nivre. 2013. Parsing morphologically rich languages: Introduction to the special issue. *Computational Linguistics*, 39(1):15–22.

Tamás Váradi. 2002. The hungarian national corpus. In *In Proceedings of the Second International Conference on Language Resources and Evaluation*, pages 385–389.

Yannick Versley and Ines Rehbein. 2009. Scalable discriminative parsing for german. In *Proceedings of the 11th International Conference on Parsing Technologies (IWPT'09)*, pages 134–137.

János Zsibrita, Veronika Vincze, and Richárd Farkas. 2013. magyarlanc: A toolkit for morphological and dependency parsing of hungarian. In *Proceedings of RANLP*.

Leveraging Verb-Argument Structures to Infer Semantic Relations

Eduardo Blanco and **Dan Moldovan**
Lymba Corporation
Richardson, TX 75080 USA
{eduardo,moldovan}@lymba.com

Abstract

This paper presents a methodology to infer implicit semantic relations from verb-argument structures. An annotation effort shows implicit relations boost the amount of meaning explicitly encoded for verbs. Experimental results with automatically obtained parse trees and verb-argument structures demonstrate that inferring implicit relations is a doable task.

1 Introduction

Automatic extraction of semantic relations is an important step towards capturing the meaning of text. Semantic relations explicitly encode links between concepts. For example, in *The accident left him a changed man*, the '*accident*' is the CAUSE of the man undergoing some '*change*'. A question answering system would benefit from detecting this relation when answering *Why did he change?*

Extracting *all* semantic relations from text is a monumental task and is at the core of language understanding. In recent years, approaches that aim at extracting a subset of all relations have achieved great success. In particular, previous research (Carreras and Màrquez, 2005; Punyakanok et al., 2008; Che et al., 2010; Zapirain et al., 2010) focused on verb-argument structures, i.e., relations between a verb and its syntactic arguments. PropBank (Palmer et al., 2005) is the corpus of reference for verb-argument relations. However, relations between a verb and its syntactic arguments are only a fraction of the relations present in texts.

Consider the statement *[Mr. Brown]*$_{NP_1}$ *succeeds [Joseph W. Hibben, who retired last August]*$_{NP_2}$ and its parse tree (Figure 1). Verb-argument relations encode that NP_1 is the AGENT and NP_2 is the THEME of verb '*succeeds*' (PropBank uses labels ARG_0 and ARG_1). Any semantic relation between '*succeeds*' and concepts dominated in the parse tree by one of its syntactic arguments NP_1 or NP_2, e.g., '*succeeds*' occurred after '*last August*', are missing. Note that in this example, verb-argument structures encode that '*retired*' has TIME '*last August*', and this knowledge could be exploited to infer the missing relation. The work presented here stems from two observations: (1) verbs are semantically connected with concepts that are not direct syntactic arguments (henceforth, *implicit relations*); and (2) verb-argument structures can be leveraged to infer implicit relations.

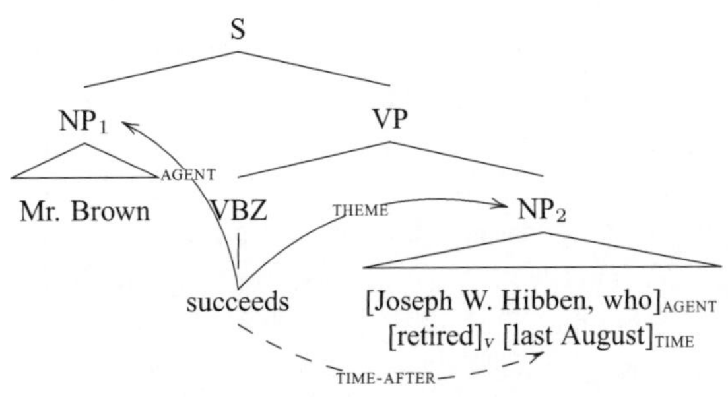

Figure 1: Example of parse tree and verb-argument structures (solid arrows). The relation between '*succeeds*' and '*last August*' is missing, but a TIME-AFTER holds (dashed arrow).

This paper goes beyond verb-argument structures and targets implicit relations like the one depicted above. TIME, LOCATION, MANNER, PURPOSE and CAUSE are inferred without imposing syntactic restrictions between their arguments: systems trained over PropBank do not attempt to extract these relations. An annotation effort demonstrates implicit relations reveal as much as 30% of meaning on top of verb-argument structures. The main contributions are: (1) empirical study of verb-argument structures and implicit relations in PropBank; (2) annotations of implicit relations on top of PropBank; (3) novel features extracted from verb-argument structures; and (4) experimental results with features derived from gold and automatically obtained linguistic information, showing implicit relations can be extracted in a realistic environment.

2 Related Work

Several systems to extract verb-argument structures from plain text have been proposed (Johansson and Nugues, 2008; Che et al., 2010). The work presented here complements them with additional semantic relations. The TimeBank corpus (Pustejovsky et al., 2003) and TempEval competitions (UzZaman et al., 2013) target events and detailed temporal information; this work also targets LOCATION, MANNER, PURPOSE and CAUSE. Extracting missing relations is not a new problem. Early work focused on a very limited domain (Palmer et al., 1986; Tetreault, 2002) or did not attempt to automate the task (Whittemore et al., 1991). This section focuses on more recent work.

Gerber and Chai (2010) augment NomBank annotations (Meyers et al., 2004) of 10 predicates with additional core arguments. Their supervised systems obtain F-measures of 42.3 and 50.3 (Gerber and Chai, 2012). Laparra and Rigau (2013a) present a deterministic algorithm and obtain an F-measure of 45.3. In contrast, our approach does not focus on a few selected predicates or core arguments. It targets *all predicates* and argument modifiers (AM-TMP, AM-MNR, AM-LOC, etc.), whose meaning is shared across verbs.

The SemEval-2010 Task 10: Linking Events and their Participants in Discourse (Ruppenhofer et al., 2009) targeted cross-sentence missing core arguments in both PropBank and FrameNet (Baker et al., 1998). Ruppenhofer et al. (2013) detail the annotations and results. The task proved extremely difficult, participants (Chen et al., 2010; Tonelli and Delmonte, 2010) reported overall F-measures around 2 (out of 100). Posterior work (Silberer and Frank, 2012; Laparra and Rigau, 2013b) reported F-measures below 20 for the same task. The work presented here does not target missing core arguments but modifiers within the same sentence. Furthermore, results show our proposal is useful in a real environment.

Finally, our previous work (Blanco and Moldovan, 2011; Blanco and Moldovan, 2014) proposed composing new relations out of chains of previously extracted relations. This approach is unsupervised and accurate (88% with gold annotations), but inferences are made only between the ends of chains of existing relations. Our current proposal also leverages relations previously extracted, but productivity is higher and results with automatic annotations are presented.

[But]$_{\text{MDIS}}$ [the surprisingly durable seven-year economic expansion]$_{\text{ARG}_0}$ has [made]$_v$ [mincemeat]$_{\text{ARG}_1}$ [of more than one forecast]$_{\text{ARG}_2}$.
Also, financial planners advising on insurance say that to their knowledge there has not yet been [a tax ruling]$_{\text{ARG}_0}$ [exempting]$_v$ [these advance payments]$_{\text{ARG}_1}$ [from taxes]$_{\text{ARG}_2}$.

Table 1: Examples of verb-argument structures from PropBank.

3 Verb-Argument Structures and Implicit Relations

Throughout this paper, R(x, y) denotes a semantic relation R holding between x and y. R(x, y) is interpreted "*x has* R *y*", e.g., AGENT(*took*, *Bill*) could be read "*took* has AGENT *Bill*". Verb-argument structures, or semantic roles, account for semantic relations between a verb and its syntactic arguments. In other words, R(x, y) is a semantic role if 'x' is a verb and 'y' a syntactic argument of 'x', and all semantic roles with 'x' as first argument form the verb-argument structure of verb 'x'. Implicit relations are relations R(x, y) where x is a verb and y is not a syntactic argument of x.

The work presented in this paper aims at complementing verb-argument structures with implicit semantic relations. We follow a practical approach by inferring implicit relations from PropBank's verb-argument structures. We believe this is an advantage since PropBank is well-known in the field and several tools to predict PropBank annotations are documented and publicly available.[1] The work presented here could be incorporated in any NLP pipeline after role labeling without modifications to other components. Furthermore, working on top of PropBank allows us to quantify the impact of features derived from gold and automatically extracted linguistic information when inferring implicit relations (Section 6).

3.1 Verb-Argument structures in PropBank

PropBank (Palmer et al., 2005) annotates verb-argument structures on top of the syntactic trees of the Penn TreeBank (Marcus et al., 1994). It uses a set of numbered arguments[2] (ARG$_0$, ARG$_1$, ARG$_2$, etc.) and modifiers (AM-TMP, AM-MNR, etc.). Numbered arguments do not share a common meaning across verbs, they are defined on a

[1]E.g., Illinois SRL, http://cogcomp.cs.illinois.edu/page/software; SENNA, http://ml.nec-labs.com/senna/; SwiRL, http://www.surdeanu.info/mihai/swirl/

[2]Numbered arguments are also referred to as *core*.

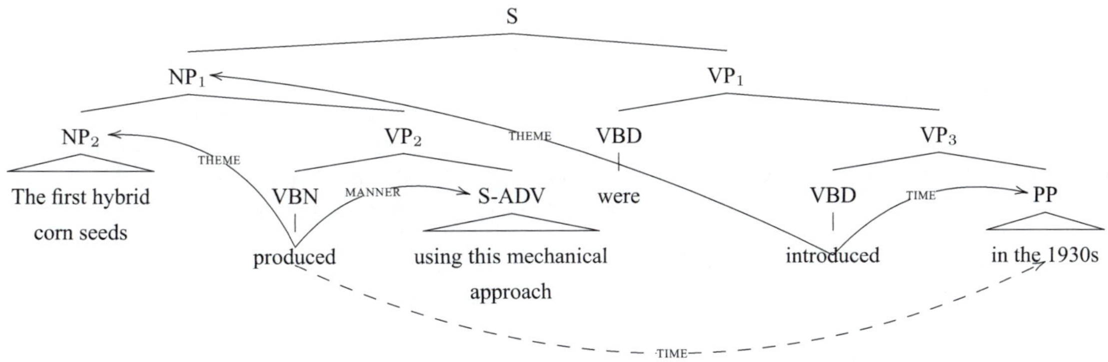

Figure 2: Verb-argument structures (solid arrows) and inferred implicit semantic relation (dashed arrow).

AM-LOC: location	AM-CAU: cause
AM-EXT: extent	AM-TMP: time
AM-DIS: discourse connective	AM-PNC: purpose
AM-ADV: general-purpose	AM-MNR: manner
AM-NEG: negation marker	AM-DIR: direction
AM-MOD: modal verb	

Table 2: Argument modifiers in PropBank.

Label	# predicates	% predicates
ARG_0	79,334	70.26%
ARG_1	106,331	94.17%
ARG_2	24,560	21.75%
AM-TMP	19,756	17.50%
AM-MNR	7,833	6.94%
AM-LOC	7,198	6.37%
AM-PNC	2,784	2.47%
AM-CAU	1,563	1.38%

Table 3: Counts of selected PropBank semantic roles. Total number of predicates is 112,917.

verb by verb basis in each frameset. For example, ARG_2 is used to indicate "*created-from, thing changed*" with verb *make* and "*entity exempted from*" with verb *exempt* (Table 1).

Unlike numbered arguments, modifiers share a common meaning across verbs (Table 2). Some modifiers are arguably not a semantic relation and are not present in most relation inventories (Tratz and Hovy, 2010; Hendrickx et al., 2009). For example, AM-NEG and AM-MOD signal the presence of negation and modals, e.g., $[wo]_{\text{AM-MOD}}[n't]_{\text{AM-NEG}}\ [go]_{\text{V}}$. For more information about PropBank annotations and examples, refer to the annotation guidelines.[3]

Inspecting PropBank annotations one can easily conclude that numbered arguments dominate the annotations and only a few modifiers are annotated (Table 3). ARG_0 and ARG_1 are present in most verb-argument structures, other numbered arguments are often not defined in the corresponding frameset and are thus not annotated.

Examining PropBank one can also conclude that information regarding TIME, LOCATION, MANNER, CAUSE and PURPOSE for a given verb is often present, yet not annotated because the text encoding this knowledge is not a direct syntactic argument of the verb (Section 4.3). Because of this fact, we decided to focus on these five relations.

3.2 Implicit relations in PropBank

Two scenarios are possible when inferring an implicit relation $R(x, y)$: (1) a semantic role $R'(x', y)$ exists; or (2) such a semantic role does not exists. In (1), y is a syntactic argument of some verb x', where $x \neq x'$ and in (2) that is not the case. Inferences under scenario (1) can be further classified into (1a) when a semantic role $R''(x, y')$ such that y' contains y exists; or (1b) when such a semantic roles does not exist. The remainder of this section exemplifies the three scenarios.

The example in Figure 1 falls under scenario (1a). Semantic roles encode, among others, '*retired*' has TIME '*last August*', and '*succeeds*' has AGENT '*Mr. Brown*' and THEME '*Joseph W. Hibben, who retired last August*'. The second argument of implicit relation TIME-AFTER(*succeeds, last August*) is a semantic role of '*retired*' and is contained in the THEME of '*succeeds*'.

Figure 2 shows a statement in which implicit relation TIME(*produced, in the 1930s*) could be inferred under scenario (1b). Semantic roles of '*produced*' only indicate that NP_2 is the THEME and S-ADV the MANNER; roles of '*introduced*' indicate that NP_1 is the THEME and '*[in the 1930s]$_{PP}$*' the TIME. In this case, there is no connection be-

[3] http://verbs.colorado.edu/~mpalmer/projects/ace/PBguidelines.pdf

```
rs = {TIME, LOCATION, MANNER, CAUSE, PURPOSE};
foreach semantic role R'(x', y) such that R' ∈ rs do
    foreach verb x in the same sentence do
        generate potential implicit relation R(x, y);
```

Algorithm 1. Procedure to generate all potential implicit relations in scenario (1) (Section 3.2).

tween '*produced*' and '*[in the 1930s]$_{PP}$*' or any other node subsuming this PP in the parse tree.

Scenario (2) occurs whenever the second argument of implicit relation R(x, y) is not a syntactic argument of a verb. If it were, a semantic role R$'(x', y)$ would exist and it would fall under scenario (1). For example, in *[I]*$_{\text{AGENT}}$ *[gave]*$_v$ *[her]*$_{\text{RECIPIENT}}$ *[a book from 1945]*$_{\text{THEME}}$, we could infer the implicit semantic relation "*gave* occurred after *1945*".

4 Annotating Implicit Relations

Inferring all implicit semantic relations is a challenging task. This paper targets implicit relations that can be inferred under scenarios (1a, 1b); scenario (2) is reserved for future work. All potential implicit relations under scenario (1) are generated using Algorithm 1. A manual annotation effort discards potential implicit relations that do not hold in order to create a gold standard.

4.1 Annotation Guidelines

Annotators are faced with the task of deciding whether a potential implicit relation R(x, y) holds. If it does, they mark it with YES, otherwise with NO. Annotators were initially trained with the original PropBank annotation guidelines[4] as this task is very similar to annotating PropBank semantic roles. Indeed, the only difference is that 'y' is not a syntactic argument of 'x'.

After some preliminary annotations, we found it useful to account for three subtypes of TIME. This way, richer semantic connections are inferred. When the task is to decide whether implicit relation TIME(x, y) holds, annotators have four labels to choose from: (1) TIME-BEFORE: x occurred before y; (2) TIME-AFTER: x occurred after y; (3) TIME-SAME x occurred at/during y; and (4) NO: y does not describe temporal information of x. If more than one label is valid, annotators choose the one encoding the temporal context y of x starting the earliest. Namely, TIME-BEFORE has the highest priority, followed by TIME-SAME, TIME-AFTER and finally NO.

Annotation examples are detailed in Section 4.2, the more complex annotations involving TIME are illustrated below. Consider the following statement and PropBank annotations:

> [The government's decision]$_{\text{ARG}_2,\, v_1}$ [reflects]$_{v_1}$ [their true desires before [the next election]$_{\text{ARG}_1,\, v_2}$, [expected]$_{v_2}$ [in late 1991]$_{\text{TIME},\, v_2}$]$_{\text{ARG}_1,\, v_1}$.

When annotating potential implicit semantic relation R(*reflects*, *in late 1991*), annotators may select TIME-BEFORE, TIME-SAME and TIME-AFTER. However, they select TIME-BEFORE because it indicates the temporal context of '*reflects*' that starts the earliest.

4.2 Annotation Examples

Several annotations examples are shown in Table 4. Semantic roles for statement (1) include TIME(*remain*, *in 1990*), MANNER(*remain*, *at about 1,200 cars*) and no other TIME or MANNER. Implicit relations reveal two extra semantic connections: TIME-BEFORE(*said*, *in 1990*) and TIME-BEFORE(*expects*, *in 1990*), i.e., '*said*' and '*expects*' occurred before '*1990*'. The potential implicit relations MANNER(*said*, *at about 1,200 cars*) and MANNER(*expects*, *at about 1,200 cars*) do not hold and are annotated N.

Interpreting statement (2) one can see that '*this past summer*' is not only indicating the TIME of '*proposed*'; events encoded by verbs '*make*' and '*exempt*' occurred after '*this past summer*'. In this example, two implicit semantic relations are inferred from a single semantic role.

Statement (3) shows that two potential implicit relations R(x, y) and R(x', y) sharing the second argument 'y' may be assigned different labels. Regarding time, semantic roles only include TIME(*report*, *in December*). Implicit relations add TIME-BEFORE(*proposed*, *in December*) and TIME-SAME(*allow*, *in December*).

Two implicit LOCATION relations are inferred in statement (4): '*discovered*' and '*preserving*' occurred '*in the test-tube experiments*'. The potential implicit relation LOCATION(*said*, *in the test-tube experiments*) is discarded (annotated N). Statement (5) shows two potential implicit MANNER that can be inferred. The '*program*' was '*aired*' and '*seen by 12 million viewers*' in the following manner: '*With Mr. Vila as host*'.

[4] http://verbs.colorado.edu/~mpalmer/projects/ace/PBguidelines.pdf

Statement	TMP				LOC		MNR		PRP		CAU	
	B	A	S	N	Y	N	Y	N	Y	N	Y	N
1: Rolls-Royce said it expects [its U.S. sales]$_{\text{ARG}_1}$ to [remain]$_{\text{V}}$ [steady]$_{\text{ARG}_3}$ [at about 1,200 cars]$_{\text{MANNER}}$ [in 1990]$_{\text{TIME}}$.												
– *said*, [in 1990]$_{\text{TIME}}$	✓	-	-	-								
– *expects*, [in 1990]$_{\text{TIME}}$	✓	-	-	-								
– *said*, [at about 1,200 cars]$_{\text{MANNER}}$							-	✓				
– *expects*, [at about 1,200 cars]$_{\text{MANNER}}$							-	✓				
2: They make the argument in letters to the agency about [rule changes]$_{\text{ARG}_1}$ [proposed]$_{\text{V}}$ [this past summer]$_{\text{TIME}}$ that, among other things, exempt many middle-management executives from government supervision.												
– *make*, [this past summer]$_{\text{TIME}}$	-	✓	-	-								
– *exempt*, [this past summer]$_{\text{TIME}}$	-	✓	-	-								
3: The proposed changes also allow [executives]$_{\text{ARG}_0}$ to [report]$_{\text{V}}$ [exercises of options]$_{\text{ARG}_1}$ [in December]$_{\text{TIME}}$.												
– *proposed*, [in December]$_{\text{TIME}}$	✓	-	-	-								
– *allow*, [in December]$_{\text{TIME}}$	-	-	✓	-								
4: Two Japanese scientists said they discovered [an antibody that]$_{\text{ARG}_0}$, [in laboratory test-tube experiments]$_{\text{LOCATION}}$, [kills]$_{\text{V}}$ [AIDS-infected cells]$_{\text{ARG}_1}$ [while preserving healthy cells]$_{\text{TIME}}$.												
– *said*, [in laboratory test-tube experiments]$_{\text{LOCATION}}$					-	✓						
– *discovered*, [in laboratory test-tube experiments]$_{\text{LOCATION}}$					✓	-						
– *preserving*, [in laboratory test-tube experiments]$_{\text{LOCATION}}$					✓	-						
5: [With Mr. Vila as host]$_{\text{MANNER}}$, "[This Old House]$_{\text{ARG}_1}$" [became]$_{\text{V}}$ [one of the Public Broadcasting Service's top 10 programs]$_{\text{ARG}_2}$, [airing weekly on about 300 of the network 's stations and seen by an average of 12 million viewers]$_{\text{AM-ADV}}$.												
– *airing*, [With Mr. Vila as host]$_{\text{MANNER}}$							✓	-				
– *seen*, [With Mr. Vila as host]$_{\text{MANNER}}$							✓	-				
[6: It]$_{\text{ARG}_0}$ [raised]$_{\text{V}}$ [financing of 300 billion lire]$_{\text{ARG}_1}$ [for the purchase this summer by another Agnelli-related group of the food concern Galbani S.p.A.]$_{\text{PURPOSE}}$, [by selling a chunk of its IFI shares to Mediobanca S.p.A.]$_{\text{MANNER}}$												
– *selling*, [for the purchase this summer by another ...]$_{\text{PURPOSE}}$									✓	-		
7: [Greece and Turkey]$_{\text{ARG}_0}$, for example, are suspected of [overstating]$_{\text{V}}$ [their arsenals]$_{\text{ARG}_1}$ [in hopes that they can emerge from the arms-reduction treaty with large remaining forces to deter each other]$_{\text{PURPOSE}}$.												
– *suspected*, [in hopes that they can emerge from the ...]$_{\text{PURPOSE}}$									-	✓		
8: ...the rationalization that [given the country's lack of natural resources]$_{\text{CAUSE}}$, [they]$_{\text{ARG}_0}$ [must]$_{\text{AM-MOD}}$ [work]$_{\text{V}}$ [hard]$_{\text{MANNER}}$ [to create value through exports]$_{\text{ARG}_1}$ and buy food with the surplus.												
– *create*, [given the country's lack of natural resources]$_{\text{CAUSE}}$											✓	-
– *buy*, [given the country's lack of natural resources]$_{\text{CAUSE}}$											✓	-
9: Its third-quarter earnings were lower than analysts had forecast, and the company said [it]$_{\text{ARG}_0}$ had [lowered]$_{\text{V}}$ [its projections for earnings growth through the end of 1990]$_{\text{ARG}_1}$ [because of planned price cuts]$_{\text{CAUSE}}$.												
– *forecast*, [because of planned price cuts]$_{\text{CAUSE}}$											-	✓
– *said*, [because of planned price cuts]$_{\text{CAUSE}}$											-	✓

Table 4: Examples of potential implicit relations and their annotations. All of them but the ones annotated with N can be inferred. B stands for BEFORE, A for AFTER, S for SAME, N for NO and Y for YES. PropBank semantic roles from which implicit relations are generated are indicated between brackets.

Statement (6, 7) exemplify potential implicit PURPOSE relations. While the '*selling*' event in statement (6) has as its purpose '*the purchase [...]*' (label Y), the '*suspected*' event in statement (7) is clearly not done so that '*they (Greece and Turkey) can emerge from the [...]*' (label N).

Finally, statements (8, 9) exemplify potential implicit CAUSE relations. In (8), both '*create*' and '*buy*' are done due to the '*country's lack of natural resources*'. However, in (9), the analysts '*forecasting*' and the company '*saying*' do not have as their cause '*planned price cuts*'.

4.3 Annotation Analysis

Table 5 shows counts for all potential implicit relations annotated. All labels except N indicate a valid implicit relation. 94.1% of potential implicit relations generated from a TIME semantic role can be inferred. Other roles yield less inferences in relative terms, but substantial additional meaning: LOCATION 39.4%, MANNER 16.7%, PURPOSE 29.4%, and CAUSE 30.2%.

Two annotators performed the annotations. A simple script generated all potential implicit relations and prompted for a label: BEFORE, AFTER, SAME or NO if the potential implicit relation was generated from a TIME semantic role; YES or NO otherwise. Annotators are not concerned with argument identification, as arguments of implicit relations are retrieved from the verb-argument structures in PropBank (Algorithm 1). This makes the annotation process easier and faster.

Annotation quality was calculated with two agreement coefficients: observed agreement (raw percentage of equal annotations) and Cohen's κ (Artstein and Poesio, 2008). The actual num-

	Source	No.	Name	Description
basic	x	1,2	word, POS tag	x's surface form and part-of-speech tag
		3	voice	whether x is in active or passive voice
	y	4,5	first word, POS tag	first word and part of speech tag in y
		6,7	last word, POS tag	last word and part-of-speech tag in y
		8,9	head, POS tag	head of y and its part-of-speech tag
		10–12	node, left and right sibling	syntactic nodes of y, and its left and right siblings
		13	subcategory	concatenation of y's children nodes
	x, y	14	direction	whether x occurs before or after y
		15	subsumer	common syntactic node between x and y
		16	path	syntactic path between x and y
pred structures	x_ps	17–31	**verb semantic roles**	flags indicating presence of semantic roles in *x_ps*
	y_ps	32,33	**verb, POS tag**	verb in *y_ps* and its part-of-speech tag
		34	**arg label**	semantic role between verb in *y_ps* and y
		35–49	**arg semantic roles**	flags indicating presence of semantic roles in *y_ps*
	x_ps, y_ps	50	**overlapping semantic role**	role R$''$ linking x and y', where y' contains y
		51	**overlapping head**	head of y' in semantic role detected in feature 50
		52	**overlapping direct**	whether feature 51 is the verb in *y_ps*

Table 6: Complete feature set to determine whether a potential implicit semantic relation R(x, y) should be inferred. Second column indicates the source: first or second argument (x, y), or their respective predicate structures (*x_ps*, *y_ps*). Features in bold are novel and specially designed for our task.

Label		# instances	% instances
TIME	B	3,033	38.4%
	A	2,886	36.5%
	S	1,514	19.2%
	N	463	5.9%
	All	7,896	100.0%
LOCATION	Y	3,345	39.4%
	N	5,151	60.6%
	All	8,496	100.0%
MANNER	Y	1,600	16.7%
	N	7,987	83.3%
	All	9,587	100.0%
PURPOSE	Y	821	29.4%
	N	1,971	70.6%
	All	2,792	100.0%
CAUSE	Y	404	30.2%
	N	909	69.2%
	All	1,313	100.0%

Table 5: Number of potential implicit relations (instances) annotated and counts for each label. Total number of instances is 30,084.

bers are: 78.16% (observed) / 0.687 (κ) for TIME, 86.63% / 0.733 for LOCATION, 93.02% / 0.782 for MANNER, 88.60% / 0.734 for PURPOSE, and 90.91% / 0.810 for CAUSE. These agreements are either comparable or superior to similar previous annotation efforts. Girju et al. (2007) reported observed agreements between 47.8% and 86.1% when annotating 7 semantic relations between nominals, and Bethard et al. (2008) observed agreements of 81.2% and 77.8% (Kappa: 0.715 and 0.556) when annotating temporal and causal relations between event pairs.

5 Inferring Implicit Relations

Inferring implicit relations is reduced to (1) generating potential implicit relations (Algorithm 1) and (2) labeling them. The second task determines if potential implicit relations should be discarded or inferred, all labels but N indicate potential implicit relations that should be inferred. We follow a standard supervised machine learning approach where each potential implicit relation is an instance.

Instances were divided into training (70%) and test (30%). The feature set (Section 5.1) and model parameters were tuned using 10-fold stratified cross-validation over the training split, and results (Section 6) are reported using the test split. More features than the ones presented were tried and discarded because they did not improve performance, e.g., syntactic path between verbs in the verb-argument structures of x and y, depth of both structures, number of tokens in y.

5.1 Feature Selection

The full set of features to determine whether a potential implicit relation R(x, y) can be inferred is summarized in Table 6. Features are classified into *basic* and *predicate structures*. The former are commonly used by semantic role labelers. The latter exploit the output of role labelers, i.e., verb-argument structures, and, to our knowledge, are novel. Results show *predicate structures* features improve performance (Section 6.2).

Basic features are derived from lexical and syntactic information. We do not elaborate more on

Feat No.	Value
1,2	succeeds, VBZ
3	active
4,5	last, JJ
6,7	August, NNP
8,9	August, NNP
10–12	NP, VBD, nil
13	JJ-NNP
14	after
15	VP
16	VBZ+VP-NP-SBAR-S-VP-NP
17–31	ARG_0 and ARG_1 true, rest false
32,33	retired, VBD
34	AM-TMP
35-49	ARG_0 and AM-TMP true, rest false
50	ARG_1
51	Hibben
52	false

Table 7: Feature values when deciding if R(*succeeds, last summer*) can be inferred from the verb-argument structures in Figure 1.

these features, detailed descriptions and examples are provided by Gildea and Jurafsky (2002).

Features (17–52) are derived from the *predicate structures* of x and y and specially defined to infer implicit semantic relations. Features (17–31, 35–49) are flags indicating the presence of semantic roles in the predicate structures of x and y.

Features (32–34) characterize the semantic role $\text{R}'(x', y)$ from which the potential implicit relation was generated. They specify verb x', its part-of-speech, and label R'. Note that x' is not present in the potential implicit relation $\text{R}(x, y)$, but incorporating this information helps determining whether a relation actually holds as well as label R (TIME-BEFORE, TIME-AFTER, TIME-SAME, etc.).

Finally, features 50–52 apply to inferences under scenario (1a) (Section 3.2). Feature (50) indicates the semantic role $\text{R}''(x, y')$, if any, such that y' contains y. Feature (51) indicates the head of argument y' found in feature (50). Feature (52) captures whether the head calculated in feature (51) is the verb in the predicate structure of y.

Table 7 exemplifies all features when deciding whether TIME-AFTER(*succeeds, last August*) can be inferred from the verb-argument structures in *Mr. Brown succeeds Joseph W. Hibben, who retired last August* (Figure 1). Table 8 provides an additional example for features 50–52.

6 Experiments and Results

Experiments were carried out using Support Vector Machines with RBF kernel as implemented in LIBSVM (Chang and Lin, 2011). Parameters α and γ were tuned by grid search using 10-fold cross validation over training instances.

Mr. Corr resigned to pursue other interests, the airline said.	
ARG_0(*resigned, Mr. Corr*) AM-PNC(*resigned, to pursue other interests*)	
ARG_0(*pursue, Mr. Corr*) ARG_1(*pursue, other interests*)	
ARG_0(*said, the airline*) ARG_1(*said, Mr. Corr resigned to pursue other interests*)	
feature 50, overlapping sem rel	ARG_1
feature 51, overlapping head	resigned
feature 52, overlapping direct	true

Table 8: PropBank roles and values for features (50–52) when predicting potential implicit relation R(*said, to pursue other interests*), labeled N.

Results are reported using features extracted from gold and automatic annotations. Gold annotations are taken directly from the Penn TreeBank and PropBank. Automatic annotations are obtained with Polaris (Moldovan and Blanco, 2012), a semantic parser that among others is trained with PropBank. Results using gold (automatic) annotations are obtained with a model trained with gold (automatic) annotations.

6.1 Detailed Results

Table 9 presents per-relation and overall results. In general terms, there is a decrease in performance when using automatic annotations. The difference is most noticeable in recall and it is due to missing semantic roles, which in turn are often due to syntactic parsing errors. This is not surprising as in order for an implicit relation $\text{R}(x, y)$ to be generated as potential and fed to the learning algorithm for classification, a semantic role $\text{R}'(x', y)$ must be extracted first (Algorithm 1). However, using automatic annotations brings very little decrease in precision. This leads to the conclusion that as long as 'y' is identified as a semantic role of some verb, even if it is mislabeled, one can still infer the right implicit relations. Since results obtained with automatic parse trees and semantic roles are a realistic estimation of performance, the remainder of the discussion focuses on those. Results with gold annotations are provided for informational purposes.

Overall results for inferring implicit semantic relations are encouraging: precision 0.66, recall 0.58 and F-measure 0.616. Direct comparison with previous work is not possible because the implicit relations we aim at inferring have not been considered before. However, we note the top

		gold						automatic					
		basic			basic + ps			basic			basic + ps		
		P	R	F	P	R	F	P	R	F	P	R	F
TIME	B	.66	.72	.689	.72	.74	*.730	.64	.65	.643	.68	.67	**.677**
	A	.63	.74	.681	.67	.75	**.708**	.61	.68	.642	.66	.72	**.687**
	S	.57	.41	.477	.54	.45	**.491**	.55	.36	.437	.55	.38	**.450**
LOCATION	Y	.71	.61	.656	.70	.64	**.669**	.71	.56	.624	.71	.58	**.635**
MANNER	Y	.65	.38	.480	.60	.45	**.514**	.54	.45	.489	.64	.41	**.500**
PURPOSE	Y	.65	.58	.613	.69	.60	**.642**	.56	.49	.525	.68	.49	**.572**
CAUSE	Y	.71	.60	.650	.74	.62	**.675**	.69	.65	.670	.71	.63	**.669**
All		.66	.61	.625	.67	.64	*.651	.63	.57	.591	.66	.58	*.616

Table 9: Results obtained with the test split using features extracted from gold and automatic annotations, and using basic and *predicate structures* (ps) features. Statistical significance between F-measures using *basic* and *basic + predicate structures* features is indicated with * (confidence 95%).

performer (Koomen et al., 2005) at CoNLL-2005 Shared Task on role labeling obtained the following F-measures when extracting the same relations between a verb and its syntactic arguments: 0.774 (TIME), 0.6033 (LOCATION), 0.5922 (MANNER), 0.4541 (PURPOSE) and 0.5397 (CAUSE).

The most difficult relations are TIME-SAME and MANNER, F-measures are 0.450 and 0.500 respectively. Even when using gold annotations these two relations are challenging: F-measures are 0.491 for TIME-SAME, an increase of 9.1%, and 0.514 for MANNER, an increase of 2.8%. Results show that other relations can be inferred with F-measures between 0.635 and 0.687, the only exception is PURPOSE with an F-measure of 0.572.

6.2 Feature Ablation

Results in Table 9 suggest that while implicit relations can be inferred using *basic* features, it is beneficial to complement them with the novel features derived from *predicate structures*. This is true for all relations except CAUSE when using automatic annotations with a negligible difference of 0.001. When considering all implicit relations, the difference in performance is $0.616 - 0.591 = 0.025$, an increase of 4.2% that is statistically significant (Z-test, confidence 95%).

The positive impact of features derived from *predicate structures* is most noticeable when inferring PURPOSE, with an increase of 8.9% ($0.572 - 0.525 = 0.047$). TIME-BEFORE and TIME-AFTER also benefit, with increases of 5.3% ($0.677 - 0.643 = 0.034$) and 7.0% ($0.687 - 0.642 = 0.045$) respectively. The improvement *predicate structures* features bring is statistically significant when taking into account all relations (confidence 95%). However, due to the lower number of instances, differences in performance when considering individual relations is not statistically significant.

7 Conclusions

Verb-argument structures, or semantic roles, comprise semantic relations between a verb and its syntactic arguments. The work presented in this paper leverages verb-argument structures to infer implicit semantic relations. A relation R(x, y) is implicit if x is a verb and y is not a syntactic argument of x. The method could be incorporated into any NLP pipeline after role labeling without modifications to other components.

An analysis of verb-argument structures and implicit relations in PropBank has been presented. Out of all potential implicit relations R(x, y), this paper targets those that can be generated from a semantic role R′(x', y), where $x \neq x'$. A manual annotation effort demonstrates implicit relations yield substantial additional meaning. Most of the time (94.1%) a semantic role TIME(x', y) is present, we can infer temporal information for other verbs within the same sentence. Productivity is lower but substantial with other roles: 39.4% (LOCATION), 30.2% (CAUSE), 29.4% (PURPOSE) and 16.7% (MANNER).

Experimental results show that implicit relations can be inferred using automatically obtained parse trees and verb-argument structures. Standard machine learning is used to decide whether a potential implicit relation should be inferred, and novel features characterizing the verb-argument structures we infer from have been proposed.

References

Ron Artstein and Massimo Poesio. 2008. Inter-coder agreement for computational linguistics. *Computational Linguistics*, 34(4):555–596, December.

Collin F. Baker, Charles J. Fillmore, and John B. Lowe. 1998. The berkeley framenet project. In *Proceedings of the 36th Annual Meeting of the Association for Computational Linguistics and 17th International Conference on Computational Linguistics - Volume 1*, ACL '98, pages 86–90, Stroudsburg, PA, USA. Association for Computational Linguistics.

Steven Bethard, William Corvey, Sara Klingenstein, and James H. Martin. 2008. Building a Corpus of Temporal-Causal Structure. In *Proceedings of the Sixth International Language Resources and Evaluation (LREC'08)*, pages 908–915, Marrakech, Morocco. European Language Resources Association (ELRA).

Eduardo Blanco and Dan Moldovan. 2011. Unsupervised learning of semantic relation composition. In *Proceedings of the 49th Annual Meeting of the Association for Computational Linguistics: Human Language Technologies*, pages 1456–1465, Portland, Oregon, USA, June. Association for Computational Linguistics.

Eduardo Blanco and Dan Moldovan. 2014. Composition of semantic relations: Theoretical framework and case study. *ACM Trans. Speech Lang. Process.*, 10(4):17:1–17:36, January.

Xavier Carreras and Lluís Màrquez. 2005. Introduction to the CoNLL-2005 shared task: semantic role labeling. In *CONLL '05: Proceedings of the Ninth Conference on Computational Natural Language Learning*, pages 152–164, Morristown, NJ, USA. Association for Computational Linguistics.

Chih-Chung Chang and Chih-Jen Lin. 2011. LIBSVM: A library for support vector machines. *ACM Transactions on Intelligent Systems and Technology*, 2:27:1–27:27. Software available at `http://www.csie.ntu.edu.tw/~cjlin/libsvm`.

Wanxiang Che, Ting Liu, and Yongqiang Li. 2010. Improving Semantic Role Labeling with Word Sense. In *The 2010 Annual Conference of the North American Chapter of the Association for Computational Linguistics*, pages 246–249, Los Angeles, California, June. Association for Computational Linguistics.

Desai Chen, Nathan Schneider, Dipanjan Das, and Noah A. Smith. 2010. Semafor: Frame argument resolution with log-linear models. In *Proceedings of the 5th International Workshop on Semantic Evaluation*, pages 264–267, Uppsala, Sweden, July. Association for Computational Linguistics.

Matthew Gerber and Joyce Chai. 2010. Beyond NomBank: A Study of Implicit Arguments for Nominal Predicates. In *Proceedings of the 48th Annual Meeting of the Association for Computational Linguistics*, pages 1583–1592, Uppsala, Sweden, July. Association for Computational Linguistics.

Matthew Gerber and Joyce Chai. 2012. Semantic role labeling of implicit arguments for nominal predicates. *Computational Linguistics*, 38:755–798, 2012.

Daniel Gildea and Daniel Jurafsky. 2002. Automatic Labeling Of Semantic Roles. *Computational Linguistics*, 28:245–288.

Roxana Girju, Preslav Nakov, Vivi Nastase, Stan Szpakowicz, Peter Turney, and Deniz Yuret. 2007. SemEval-2007 Task 04: Classification of Semantic Relations between Nominals. In *Proceedings of the Fourth International Workshop on Semantic Evaluations (SemEval-2007)*, pages 13–18, Prague, Czech Republic, June. Association for Computational Linguistics.

Iris Hendrickx, Su N. Kim, Zornitsa Kozareva, Preslav Nakov, Diarmuid, Sebastian Padó, Marco Pennacchiotti, Lorenza Romano, and Stan Szpakowicz. 2009. SemEval-2010 Task 8: Multi-Way Classification of Semantic Relations Between Pairs of Nominals. In *Proceedings of the Workshop on Semantic Evaluations: Recent Achievements and Future Directions (SEW-2009)*, pages 94–99, Boulder, Colorado, June. Association for Computational Linguistics.

Richard Johansson and Pierre Nugues. 2008. Dependency-based semantic role labeling of propbank. In *Proceedings of the Conference on Empirical Methods in Natural Language Processing*, EMNLP '08, pages 69–78, Stroudsburg, PA, USA. Association for Computational Linguistics.

Peter Koomen, Vasin Punyakanok, Dan Roth, and Wen T. Yih. 2005. Generalized Inference with Multiple Semantic Role Labeling Systems. In *Proceedings of the Ninth Conference on Computational Natural Language Learning (CoNLL-2005)*, pages 181–184, Ann Arbor, Michigan, June. Association for Computational Linguistics.

Egoitz Laparra and German Rigau. 2013a. Impar: A deterministic algorithm for implicit semantic role labelling. In *Proceedings of the 51st Annual Meeting of the Association for Computational Linguistics (Volume 1: Long Papers)*, pages 1180–1189, Sofia, Bulgaria, August. Association for Computational Linguistics.

Egoitz Laparra and German Rigau. 2013b. Sources of evidence for implicit argument resolution. In *Proceedings of the 10th International Conference on Computational Semantics (IWCS 2013) – Long Papers*, pages 155–166, Potsdam, Germany, March. Association for Computational Linguistics.

Mitchel Marcus, Beatrice Santorini, and Mary A. Marcinkiewicz. 1994. Building a large annotated corpus of English: The Penn Treebank. *Computational linguistics*, 19(2):313–330.

A. Meyers, R. Reeves, C. Macleod, R. Szekely, V. Zielinska, B. Young, and R. Grishman. 2004. Annotating Noun Argument Structure for NomBank. In *Proceedings of LREC-2004*, pages 803–806, Lisbon, Portugal.

Dan Moldovan and Eduardo Blanco. 2012. Polaris: Lymba's semantic parser. In *Proceedings of the Eighth International Conference on Language Resources and Evaluation (LREC-2012)*, pages 66–72, Istanbul, Turkey, May. European Language Resources Association (ELRA).

Martha S. Palmer, Deborah A. Dahl, Rebecca J. Schiffman, Lynette Hirschman, Marcia Linebarger, and John Dowding. 1986. Recovering implicit information. In *Proceedings of the 24th Annual Meeting of the Association for Computational Linguistics*, pages 10–19, New York, New York, USA, July. Association for Computational Linguistics.

Martha Palmer, Daniel Gildea, and Paul Kingsbury. 2005. The Proposition Bank: An Annotated Corpus of Semantic Roles. *Computational Linguistics*, 31(1):71–106.

Vasin Punyakanok, Dan Roth, and Wen T. Yih. 2008. The importance of syntactic parsing and inference in semantic role labeling. *Computational Linguistics*, 34(2):257–287, June.

James Pustejovsky, Patrick Hanks, Roser Sauri, Andrew See, Robert Gaizauskas, Andrea Setzer, Dragomir Radev, Beth Sundheim, David Day, Lisa Ferro, et al. 2003. The timebank corpus. *Corpus linguistics*, 2003:40.

Josef Ruppenhofer, Caroline Sporleder, Roser Morante, Collin Baker, and Martha Palmer. 2009. SemEval-2010 Task 10: Linking Events and Their Participants in Discourse. In *Proceedings of the Workshop on Semantic Evaluations: Recent Achievements and Future Directions (SEW-2009)*, pages 106–111, Boulder, Colorado, June. Association for Computational Linguistics.

Josef Ruppenhofer, Russell Lee-Goldman, Caroline Sporleder, and Roser Morante. 2013. Beyond sentence-level semantic role labeling: linking argument structures in discourse. *Language Resources and Evaluation*, 47(3):695–721.

Carina Silberer and Anette Frank. 2012. Casting implicit role linking as an anaphora resolution task. In **SEM 2012: The First Joint Conference on Lexical and Computational Semantics*, pages 1–10, Montréal, Canada, 7-8 June. Association for Computational Linguistics.

Joel R Tetreault. 2002. Implicit role reference. In *International Symposium on Reference Resolution for Natural Language Processing*, pages 109–115.

Sara Tonelli and Rodolfo Delmonte. 2010. Venses++: Adapting a deep semantic processing system to the identification of null instantiations. In *Proceedings of the 5th International Workshop on Semantic Evaluation*, pages 296–299, Uppsala, Sweden, July. Association for Computational Linguistics.

Stephen Tratz and Eduard Hovy. 2010. A Taxonomy, Dataset, and Classifier for Automatic Noun Compound Interpretation. In *Proceedings of the 48th Annual Meeting of the Association for Computational Linguistics*, pages 678–687, Uppsala, Sweden, July. Association for Computational Linguistics.

Naushad UzZaman, Hector Llorens, Leon Derczynski, James Allen, Marc Verhagen, and James Pustejovsky. 2013. Semeval-2013 task 1: Tempeval-3: Evaluating time expressions, events, and temporal relations. In *Second Joint Conference on Lexical and Computational Semantics (*SEM), Volume 2: Proceedings of the Seventh International Workshop on Semantic Evaluation (SemEval 2013)*, pages 1–9, Atlanta, Georgia, USA, June. Association for Computational Linguistics.

Greg Whittemore, Melissa Macpherson, and Greg Carlson. 1991. Event-building through role-filling and anaphora resolution. In *Proceedings of the 29th Annual Meeting of the Association for Computational Linguistics*, pages 17–24, Berkeley, California, USA, June. Association for Computational Linguistics.

Be N. Zapirain, Eneko Agirre, Lluís Màrquez, and Mihai Surdeanu. 2010. Improving Semantic Role Classification with Selectional Preferences. In *The 2010 Annual Conference of the North American Chapter of the Association for Computational Linguistics*, pages 373–376, Los Angeles, California, June. Association for Computational Linguistics.

Structured and Unstructured Cache Models for SMT Domain Adaptation

Annie Louis
School of Informatics
University of Edinburgh
10 Crichton Street
Edinburgh EH8 9AB
alouis@inf.ed.ac.uk

Bonnie Webber
School of Informatics
University of Edinburgh
10 Crichton Street
Edinburgh EH8 9AB
bonnie@inf.ed.ac.uk

Abstract

We present a French to English translation system for Wikipedia biography articles. We use training data from out-of-domain corpora and adapt the system for biographies. We propose two forms of domain adaptation. The first biases the system towards words likely in biographies and encourages repetition of words across the document. Since biographies in Wikipedia follow a regular structure, our second model exploits this structure as a sequence of topic segments, where each segment discusses a narrower subtopic of the biography domain. In this structured model, the system is encouraged to use words likely in the current segment's topic rather than in biographies as a whole. We implement both systems using cache-based translation techniques. We show that a system trained on Europarl and news can be adapted for biographies with 0.5 BLEU score improvement using our models. Further the structure-aware model outperforms the system which treats the entire document as a single segment.

1 Introduction

This paper explores domain adaptation of statistical machine translation (SMT) systems to contexts where the target documents have predictable regularity in topic and document structure. Regularities can take the form of high rates of word repetition across documents, similarities in sentence syntax, similar subtopics and discourse organization. Domain adaptation for such documents can exploit these similarities. In this paper we focus on topic (lexical) regularities in a domain. We present a system that translates Wikipedia biographies from French to English by adapting a system trained on Europarl and news commentaries. This task is interesting for the following two reasons.

Many techniques for SMT domain adaption have focused on rather diverse domains such as using systems trained on Europarl or news to translate medical articles (Tiedemann, 2010a), blogs (Su et al., 2012) and transcribed lectures (Federico et al., 2012). The main challenge for such systems is translating out-of-vocabulary words (Carpuat et al., 2012). In contrast, words in biographies are closer to a training corpus of news commentaries and parlimentary proceedings and allow us to examine how well domain adaptation techniques can disambiguate lexical choices. Such an analysis is harder to do on very divergent domains.

In addition, biographies have a fairly regular discourse structure: a central entity (person who is the topic of the biography), recurring subtopics such as 'childhood', 'schooling', 'career' and 'later life', and a likely chronological order to these topics. These regularities become more predictable in documents from sources such as Wikipedia. This setting allows us to explore the utility of models which make translation decisions depending on the discourse structure. Translation methods for structured documents have only recently been explored in Foster et al. (2010). However, their system was developed for parlimentary proceedings and translations were adapted using separate language models based upon the identity of the speaker, text type (questions, debate, etc.) and the year when the proceedings took place. Biographies constitute a more realistic discourse context to develop structured models.

This paper introduces a new corpus consisting of paired French-English translations of biography articles from Wikipedia.[1] We translate this corpus by developing cache-based domain adaptation methods, a technique recently proposed by Tiede-

[1] Corpus available at http://homepages.inf.ed.ac.uk/alouis/wikiBio.html.

mann (2010a). In such methods, cache(s) can be filled with relevant items for translation and translation hypotheses that match a greater number of cache items are scored higher. These cache scores are used as additional features during decoding. We use two types of cache—one which encourages the use of words more indicative of the biography domain and another which encourages word repetition in the same document.

We also show how cache models allow for straightforward implementation of structured translation by refreshing the cache in response to topic segment boundaries. We fill caches with words relevant to the topic of the current segment which is being translated. The cache contents are obtained from an unsupervised topic model which induces clusters of words that are likely to appear in the same topic segment. Evaluation results show that cache-based models give upto 0.5 BLEU score improvements over an out-of-domain system. In addition, models that take topical structure into account score 0.3 BLEU points higher than those which ignore discourse structure.

2 Related work

The study that is closest to our work is that of Tiedemann (2010a), which proposed cache models to adapt a Europarl-trained system to medical documents. The system used caching in two ways: a cache-based language model (stores target language words from translations of preceding sentences in the same document) and a cache-based translation model (stores phrase pairs from preceding sentence translations). These caches encouraged the system to imitate the 'consistency' aspect of domain-specific texts i.e., the property that words or phrases are likely to be repeated in a domain and within the same document.

Cache models developed in later work, Tiedemann (2010b) and Gong et al. (2011), were applied for translating in-domain documents. Gong et al. (2011) introduced additional caches to store *(i)* words and phrase pairs from training documents most similar to a current source article, and *(ii)* words from topical clusters created on the training set. However, a central issue in these systems is that caches become noisy over time, since they ignore topic shifts in the documents. This paper presents cache models which not only take advantage of likely words in the domain and consistency, but which also adapt to topic shifts.

A different line of work very relevant to our study is the creation of topic-specific translations by either inferring a topic for the source document as a whole, or at the other extreme, finer topics for individual sentences (Su et al., 2012; Eidelman et al., 2012). Neither of these granularities seem intuitive in natural discourse. In this work, we propose that tailoring translations to topics associated with discourse segments in the article is likely to be beneficial for two reasons: a) subtopics of such granularity can be assumed with reasonable confidence to re-occur in documents from the same domain and b) we can hypothesize that a domain will have a small number of segment-level topics.

3 System adaptation for biographies

We introduce two types of translation systems adapted for biographies:

General domain models (domain-) that use information about biographies but treat the document as a whole.

Structured models (struct-) that are sensitive to topic segment boundaries and the specific topic of the segment currently being translated.

We implement both models using caches. Since we do not have parallel corpora for the biography domain, our caches contain items in the target language only. We use two types of caches:

Topic cache stores target language words (unigrams) likely in a particular topic. Each unigram has an associated score.

Consistency cache favours repetition of words in the sentences from the same document. It stores target language words (unigrams) from the 1-best translations of previous sentences in the same document. Each word is associated with an age value and a score. Age indicates when a word entered the cache and introduces a 'decay effect'. Words used in immediately previous sentences have a low age value while higher age values indicate words from sentences much prior in the document. Scores are inversely proportional to age.

Both the types of caches are present in both the general domain and structured models, but the cache words and scores are computed differently.

3.1 A general domain model

This system seeks to bias translations towards words which occur often in biography articles.

The topic cache is filled with word unigrams that are more likely to occur in biographies compared to general news documents. We compare the words from 1,475 English Wikipedia biographies articles to those in a large collection (64,875 articles) of New York Times (NYT) news articles (taken from the NYT Annotated Corpus (Sandhaus, 2008)). We use a log-likelihood ratio test (Lin and Hovy, 2000) to identify words which occur with significantly higher probability in biographies compared to NYT. We collect only words indicated with 0.0001 significance by the test to be more likely in biographies. We rank this set of 18,597 words in decreasing order of frequency in the biography article set and assign to each word a score equal to $1/\text{rank}$ of the word. These words with their associated scores form the contents of the topic cache. In the general domain model, these same words are assumed to be useful for the full document and so the cache contents remain constant during translation of the full document.

The consistency cache stores words from the translations of preceding sentences of the same document. After each sentence is translated, we collect the words from the 1-best translation and filter out punctuation marks and out of vocabulary words. The remaining words are assigned an age of 1. Words already present in the cache have their age incremented by one. The new words with age 1 are added to the cache[2] and the scores for all cache words are recomputed as $e^{1/age}$. The age therefore gets incremented as each sentence's words are inserted into the cache creating a decay. The cache is cleared at the end of each document.

During decoding, a candidate phrase is split into unigrams and checked against each cache. Scores for matching unigrams are summed up to obtain a score for the phrase. Separate scores are computed for matches with the topic and consistency caches.

3.2 A structured model

Here we consider topic and consistency at a narrower level—within topic segments of the article.

The topic cache is filled with words likely in individual topic segments of an article. To do this, we need to identify the topic of smaller segments of the article and also store a set of most probable words for each topic. The topics should also have bilingual mappings which will allow us to infer for every French document segment, words that are likely in such a segment in the English language.

We designed and implemented an unsupervised topic model based on Latent Dirichlet Allocation (LDA) (Blei et al., 2003) to induce such word clusters. In a first step, we induce subtopics from monolingual articles in English and French separately. The topics are subsequently aligned between the languages as explained below.

In the *first step*, we learn a topic model which incorporates two main ideas a) adds sensitivity to topic boundaries by assigning a single topic per topic segment b) allows for additional flexibility by not only drawing the words of a segment from the segment-level topic, but also allows some words to be either specific to the document (such as named entities) or stop words. To address idea b), we have a "switching variable" to switch between document-specific word, stopword or domain-words.

The generative story to create a monolingual dataset of biographies is as follows:

- Draw a distribution η for the proportion of the three word types in the full corpus (domain subtopic, document-specific, stopwords) $\sim$ Dirichlet(γ)
- For each domain subtopic ϕ_l, $1 \leq l \leq T$, draw a distribution over word vocabulary $\sim$ Dirichlet(β)
- Draw a distribution ψ over word vocabulary for stopwords $\sim$ Dirichlet(ϵ)
- For each document D_i:
  - Draw a distribution π_i over vocabulary for document-specific words $\sim$ Dirichlet(μ)
  - Draw a distribution θ_i giving the mixture of domain subtopics for this document $\sim$ Dirichlet(α)
  - For each topic segment M_{ij} in D_i:
    - Draw a domain subtopic z_{ij} $\sim$ Multinomial(θ_i)
    - For each word w_{ijk} in segment M_{ij}:
      - Draw a word type s_{ijk} $\sim$ Multinomial(η)
      - Depending on the chosen switch value s_{ijk}, draw the word from the subtopic of the segment $\phi_{z_{ij}}$ or document-specific vocabulary π_i, or stopwords ψ

We use the section markings in the Wikipedia articles as topic segment boundaries while learning the model. We use symmetric Dirichlet priors

[2] If the word already exists in the cache, it is first removed.

for the vocabulary distributions associated with domain subtopics, document-specific words and stopwords. The concentration parameters are set to 0.001 to encourage sparsity. The distribution θ_i for per-document subtopics is also drawn from a symmetric Dirichlet distribution with concentration parameter 0.01. We use asymmetric Dirichlet priors for η set to (5, 3, 2) for (domain topic, document-specific, stopwords). The hyperparameter values were minimally tuned so that the different vocabulary distributions behaved as intended.

We perform inference using collapsed Gibbs sampling where we integrate out many multinomials. The sampler chooses a topic z_{ij} for every segment and then samples a word type s_{ijk} for each word in the segment. We initialize these variables randomly and the assignment after 1000 Gibbs iterations are taken as the final ones. We create these models separately for English and French, in each case obtaining T domain subtopics.

The *second step* creates an alignment between the source and target topics using a bilingual dictionary[3]. For each French topic, we find the top matching English topic by scoring the number of dictionary matches. It is unlikely for every French topic to have a closely corresponding English topic. Based on observations about the quality of topic alignment, we select the top 60% (out of T) pairs of French-English aligned topics only.

Note that our method uses two steps to learn bilingual topics in contrast to some multilingual topic models which learn aligned topics directly from parallel or comparable corpora (Zhao and Xing, 2006; Boyd-Graber and Blei, 2009; Jagarlamudi and Daumé III, 2010). These methods induce topic-specific translations of words. Rather we choose a less restrictive pairing of word clusters by topic since (i) we have monolingual biographies in the two languages which could be quite heterogenous in the types of personalities discussed, (ii) we seek to identify words likely in a topic segment for example 'career-related' words rather than specific translations for source words.

During translation, for each topic segment in the source document, we infer the French topic most likely to have produced the segment and find the corresponding English-side topic. The most probable words for that English topic are then loaded into the topic cache. The score for a word is its probability in that topic. When a topic segment boundary is reached, the topic cache is cleared and the topic words for the new segment are filled.

The consistency cache's contents are computed similarly to the general domain case. However, the cache gets cleared at segment boundaries.

4 Training and test data

We distinguish two resources for data. The out-of-domain system is trained using the WMT'12 datasets comprising Europarl and news commentary texts. It has 2,144,820 parallel French-English sentence pairs. The language model is trained using the English side of the training corpus. The tuning set has 2,489 sentence pairs.

Our test set is a corpus of French to English translations of biographies compiled from Wikipedia. To create the biography corpus, we collect articles which are marked with a "Translation template" in Wikipedia metadata. These markings indicate a page which is translated from a corresponding page in a different language and also contains a link to the source article. (Note that these article pairs are **not** those written on the same topic separately in the two languages.) We collect pairs of French-English pages with this template and filter those which do not belong to the Biography topic (using Wikipedia metadata).

Note, however, that these article pairs are not very close translations. During translation an editor may omit or add information and also reorganize parts of the article. So we filter out the paired documents which differ significantly in length. We use LFAligner[4] to create sentence alignments for the remaining document pairs. We constrain the alignments to be within documents but since section headings were not maintained in translations, we did not further constrain alignments within sections. We manually corrected the resulting alignments and keep only documents which have good alignments and have manually marked topic segments (Wikipedia section headings). Unaligned sentences were filtered out. Table 1 shows a summary of this data and the split for tuning and test. The articles are 12 to 87 sentences long and contain 5 topic segments on average.

We also collect a larger set of monolingual French and English Wikipedia biographies to create the domain subtopics. We select only articles that have at least 10 segments (sections) to ensure

[3] A filtered set of 13,400 entries from www.dict.cc

[4] http://sourceforge.net/projects/aligner/

	Tuning	Test
No. of article pairs	15	30
Total sentences pairs	430	1008
Min. article size (in sentences)	13	12
Max. article size (in sentences)	59	85
Average no. of segments per article	4.7	5.3

Table 1: Summary of Wikipedia biographies data

that they are comprehensive ones. This collection contains 1000 French and 1000 English articles.

5 Experimental settings

We use the Moses phrase-based translation system (Koehn et al., 2007) to implement our models.

5.1 Out-of-domain model

This baseline model is trained on the WMT 2012 training sets described in the previous section and uses the six standard features from Koehn et al. (2003). We build a 5-gram language model using SRILM. The features were tuned using MERT (Och, 2003) on the WMT 2012 tuning sets. This system does not use any data about biographies.

5.2 Biography-adapted models

First we perform experiments using the manually marked sections in Wikipedia as topic segments. We also report results with automatic segmentation in Section 7.

The domain and structured models have two extra features 'topic cache' and 'consistency cache'. For the structured model, topic segment boundaries and inferred topic is passed as XML markup on the source documents. For the consistency cache, we use a wrapper which passes the 1-best translation (also using XML markup) of the preceding sentence and updates the cache before translating every next sentence.

We tune the weights for these new cache features as follows. The weights for the baseline features from the out-of-domain model are kept constant. The weights for the new cache features are set using a grid search. This tuning uses the biographies documents listed in Table 1 as tuning data. We run the decoding using the baseline feature weights and a weight for a cache feature and compute the (case-insensitive) BLEU (Papineni et al., 2002) scores of each tuning document. The weight for the cache feature which maximizes the average BLEU value over the tuning documents is chosen. We have not tuned the features using MERT in this study since a grid search allowed us to quantify the influence of increasing

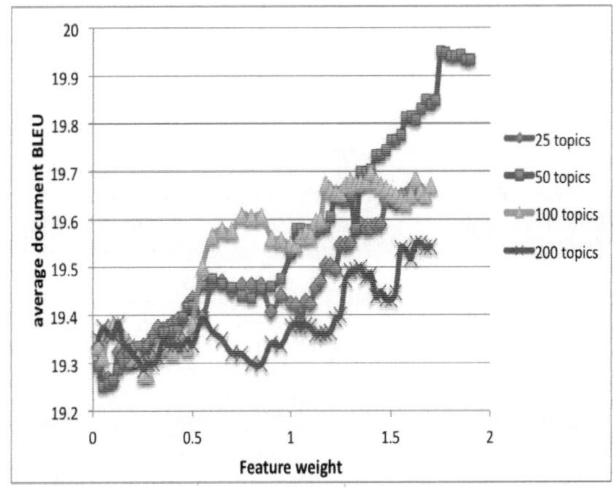

Figure 1: Effect of feature weights and number of topics on accuracy for structured topic cache

weights on the new features directly. Previous work has noted that MERT fails to find good settings for cache models (Tiedemann, 2010b). In future work, we will explore how successful optimization of baseline and cache feature weights could be done jointly. We present the findings from our grid search below.

The struct-topic cache has two parameters, the number of topics T and the number of most probable words from each topic which get loaded into the cache. We ran the tuning for $T = 25$, 50, 100 and 200 topics (note that 60% of the topics will be kept after bilingual alignment, see Section 3.2). We also varied the number of topic words chosen—50, 100, 250 and 500.

The performance did not vary with the number of topic words used and 50 words gave the same performance as 500 words for topic models with any number of topics. This interesting result suggests that only the most likely and basic words from each topic are useful. The top 50 words from two topics (one capturing early life and the other an academic career) taken from the 50-topic model on English biographies are shown in Table 2.

In Figure 1, we show the performance of systems using different number of topics. In each case, the same number of topic words (50) was added to the cache. We find that 50 topics model performs best confirming our hypothesis that only a small number of domain subtopics is plausible. We choose the 50 topic model with top 50 words for each topic for the structured topic cache.

The best weights and average document level BLEU scores on the tuning set are given in Table 3. The scores were computed using the *mteval-v13a.pl* script in Moses. BLEU scores for the

his	a	s	family	on	life	She	child	St	mother
of	in	married	children	They	death	became	whom	friends	attended
and	had	He	that	daughter	son	marriage	lived	later	work
to	was	born	died	wife	years	met	couple	I	age
he	her	at	she	father	home	moved	about	husband	house
of	is	He	received	has	included	National	original	Academy	French
and	The	by	its	used	works	study	list	book	College
his	work	Award	Medal	award	His	Institute	life	contributed	Year
in	he	are	awarded	also	title	Arts	Royal	edition	awards
s	University	Prize	Society	A	honorary	Library	include	Sciences	recognition

Table 2: Top 50 words from 2 topics of the $T = 50$ topic model

Cache type	**weight**	**BLEU-doc**
Domain-topic	0.075	19.79
Domain-consistency	0.05	19.70
Domain-topic + consis.	0.05, 0.05	19.80
Struct-topic (50 topics)	1.75	**19.94**
Struct-consistency	0.125	19.70
Struct-topic + consis.	0.4, 0.1	19.84
Domain-consis. + struct-topic	0.1, 0.25	19.86
Out-of-domain		19.33

Table 3: Best weights for cache features and BLEU scores (averaged for tuning documents).

Model	**BLEU-doc**	**BLEU-sent**
Domain-topic	17.63	17.61
Domain-consistency	17.70	17.75
Domain-topic + consis.	17.63	17.63
Struct-topic (50 topics)	**17.76**	**17.84**
Struct-consistency	17.33	17.34
Struct-topic + consis.	17.47	17.51
Struct-topic + dom-consis.	17.29	17.25
Out-of-domain	17.37	17.43

Table 4: BLEU scores on the test set. 'doc' indicates BLEU scores averaged over documents, 'sent' indicates sentence-level BLEU

out-of-domain model are shown on the last line. Note that these scores are overall on a lower scale for a French-English system due to out-of-domain differences and because the reference translations from Wikipedia are not very close ones.

These numbers show that cache models have the potential to provide better translations compared to an out-of-domain baseline. The structured topic model system is the best system outperforming the out-of-domain system and also the domain-topic system. Hence, treating documents as composed of topical segments is a useful setting for automatic translation.

The domain and structured versions of the consistency cache however, show no difference. This result could arise due to the decay factor incorporated in the consistency cache. Higher scores are given to words from immediately previous sentences compared to those far off. This decay implicitly gives lower scores to words from earlier topic segments than those from recent ones. Explicitly refreshing the cache in the structured model does not give additional benefits.

When consistency and topic caches are used together in both general domain and structured settings, the combination is not better than individual caches. We also tried a setting where the consistency cache is document-range and the topic cache works at segment level (domain-consis. + struct-topic). This combination also does not outperform using the structured topic cache alone.

6 Results on the test corpus

The best weights chosen on the tuning corpus are used to decode the biographies test corpus (summarized in Table 1). Table 4 reports the average BLEU of documents as well as sentence level BLEU scores of the corpus. We used the paired bootstrap resampling method (Koehn 2004) to compute significance.

The struct-topic model gives the highest improvement of 0.4 sentence level BLEU over the out-of-domain model. Struct-topic is also 0.23 BLEU points better compared to the domain-topic model confirming the usefulness of modeling structure regularities. These improvements at significant at 95% confidence level.

The second best model is the domain-consistency model (significantly better than out-of-domain model at 90% confidence level). But the performance of this cache decreases in the structured setting. Moreover, combinations of caches fail to improve over individual caches. One hypothesis for this result is that biography subtopic words which give good performance in the topic cache differ from the words which provide benefits in the consistency cache. For example, words related to named entities and other document-specific content words could be ones that are more consistent within the document. Then clearing the consistency cache at topic boundaries would remove such words from the cache leading to low performance of the 'structured' version. In our current model, we do not distinguish between words making up the consistency cache. In future, we plan to experiment with consistency caches of different ranges and which hold different types of words. This approach would require identifying named entities and parts of speech on the automatic translations of previous sentences, which is likely to be error-prone and so require methods for associating a confidence measure with the cache words.

7 Understanding factors that influence structured cache models

The documents in our test corpus have varying lengths, number of segments and segment sizes. This section explores the behavior of structured models on these different document types. For this analysis, we compare the BLEU scores from the *domain* and the *structured* versions of the two caches. We do not consider the out-of-domain system here since we are interested in quantifying gains from using document structure.

For each document in our test corpus, we compute *(i)* the difference between the BLEU scores of struct-topic and domain-topic systems (*BLEU-gain-topic*), and *(ii)* the difference in BLEU scores between the struct-consistency and domain-consistency systems (*BLEU-gain-consis*). Table 5 reports the average BLEU gains binned by a) the document length (in sentences) b) number of topic segments in the document and c) the average size of topic segments in a document (in sentences).

The numbers clearly indicate that performance is not uniform across different types of documents. The struct-topic cache performs much better on longer documents of over 30 sentences giving 0.3 to 0.4 BLEU points increase compared to the general domain model. On the other hand, the performance worsens when the structured cache is applied on documents with less than 20 sentences. Similarly, the struct-topic cache is beneficial for documents where the average segment size is larger than 5 sentences and when the number of topic segments is around 5 to 7.

The struct-consistency cache generally performs worse than the unstructured version and there does not appear to be a niche set according to any of the properties—document length, number of segments and segment size.

Given these findings, it is possible that the struct-topic cache can benefit by modifying the document structure to match that handled better by the structured model. We test this hypothesis by segmenting all test documents with an ideal segment size. The model seems to perform better when each segment has around 5 to 10 sentences (longer segments are also preferred but we have few very long documents in our corpus), so we try to re-segment the articles to contain approximately 7 sentences in each segment. We use an automatic topic segmentation method (Eisenstein and Barzilay, 2008) to segment the source articles in our test corpus. For each article we request (document length)/7 segments to be created.[5]

We then run the structured topic and consistency models on the automatically segmented corpus using the same feature weights as before. The results are shown in Table 6.

(a) Average BLEU gains and document length

doc. length	**no. docs**	**gain-topic**	**gain-consis**
12 to 19	7	-0.41	-0.20
20 to 29	10	0.17	-0.63
30 to 49	8	0.44	-0.16
50 to 85	5	0.34	-0.45

(b) Average BLEU gains and no. of topic segments

no. segments	**no. docs**	**gain-topic**	**gain-consis**
3 to 4	9	-0.09	-0.21
5	13	0.24	-0.37
6 to 7	5	0.34	-0.74
9	3	-0.03	-0.26

(c) Average BLEU gains and topic segment size

avg. segment size	**no. docs**	**gain-topic**	**gain-consis**
< 5	10	-0.23	-0.41
5 to 10	18	0.33	-0.37
11 to 17	2	0.39	-0.24

Table 5: Average BLEU score gains from a structured cache (compared to domain caches) split by different properties of documents in the test set

Model	**BLEU (doc)**	**BLEU (sent)**
Struct-topic	**17.94**	**17.94**
Struct-consistency	17.51	17.46

Table 6: Translation performance on automatically segmented test corpus

The struct-topic cache now reaches our best result of 0.5 BLEU improvement over the out-of-domain model and 0.3 improvement over the unstructured domain model. The consistency cache is also slightly better using the automatic segmentation than the manual sections. Choosing the right granularity appears to be important for structured caches and coarse section headers may not be ideal. This result also shows automatic segmen-

[5]Note that we only specify the number of segments, but the system could create long or short segments.

of (42)	he (36)	his (36)	the (22)	to (11)	in (9)	was (7)	one (6)	a (3)	at (3)
head (3)	that (3)	construction (3)	empire	office	french	bases	reconstruction	only	such
all	ban	marseille	main	charged	have	well	researchers	openness	retreat
an	two	mechanical	events	army	iron	class	surrender	order	thirty
and	black	objectives	factory	disciple	largest	close	budget	part	time
as	who	ceremony	figure	majority	level	even	sentence	project	trained
on	seat	diplomatic	wheat	working	winner	life	archaeological	9	during

Table 7: Impact words computed on the test corpus. The number of times each word was found in the impact list is indicated within parentheses. Words listed without parentheses appeared once in the list.

(1) **(S)** Pendant la Première Guerre mondiale, mobilisé dans les troupes de marine, il combat dans les Balkans et les Dardanelles.
(R) During the First World War, conscripted into the navy, **he** fought in the Balkans and the Dardanelles.
(B) During World War I, mobilized in troops navy, it fight in the Balkans and Dardanelles.
(C) During World War I, mobilized troops in the navy, **he** fight in the Balkans and the Dardanelles.

(2) **(S)** À l'âge de 15 ans, elle a été choisie par la troupe d'opéra de l'armée chinoise pour être formée au chant.
(R) At the age of 15, she was selected by the Chinese Armys Operatic troupe to be **trained** as a singer.
(B) In the age of 15 years, she was chosen by the pool of opera of the Chinese military to be formed the call.
(C) In the age of 15 years, she was chosen by the pool of opera of the Chinese military to be **trained** to call.

(3) **(S)** La figure de la Corriveau n'a cessé, depuis, d'inspirer romans, chansons et pièces de théâtre et d'alimenter les controverses.
(R) The **figure** of Corriveau still inspires novels, songs and plays and is the subject of argument.
(B) The perceived the Corriveau has stopped, since, inspire novels, songs and parts of theater and fuel controversies.
(C) The **figure** of the Corriveau has stopped, since, inspire novels, songs and parts of theater and fuel controversies.

Table 8: Three examples of impact words in test translations. Abbreviations: S - source sentence, R - reference translation, B - baseline translation, C - structured topic cache translation

tation can be successfully used in these models.

8 Changes made by the cache models

Here we examine the kinds of changes made by the cache models which have lead to the improved BLEU scores. We focus on the the topic cache since its changes are straightforward to compute compared to consistency. We analyze the struct-topic cache translations on automatically segmented documents as that provided the best performance overall.

To do this analysis, we define the notion of an *impact word*. An *impact word* is one which satisfies three conditions: (i) the word **is not present** in the out-of-domain translation of a sentence, (ii) it **is present** in the translation produced by the topic cache model (iii) the word **matches the reference** translation for the sentence.

These impact words provide a simple (albeit approximate) way to analyze useful changes made by the topic cache over the out-of-domain system.

On the test corpus (30 documents), 231 impact word tokens were found and they come from 70 unique word types. So topic cache model significantly affects translation decisions and over 200 useful word changes were made in the 30 documents. The impact word types and counts are shown in Table 7. Several of these changes relate to function words and pronouns. For example, the pronoun 'he' and the past tense verb 'was' were correctly introduced in several sentences such as Example (1) in Table 8. A content word change is indicated in examples (2) and (3). These changes appear to be appropriate for biographies.

9 Conclusions

We have introduced a new corpus of biography translations which we propose as suitable for examining discourse-motivated SMT methods. We showed that cache-based techniques which also take the topic organization into account, make more appropriate lexical choices for the domain. In future work, we plan to explore how other domain similarities such as sentence syntax and entity reference, for example biographies have a central entity (person), can be used to improve translation performance. We also plan to take advantage of recent methods to do document level decoding (Hardmeier et al., 2012).

Acknowledgements

The first author was supported by a Newton International Fellowship (NF120479) from the Royal Society and The British Academy. We also thank the NLP group at Edinburgh for their comments and feedback on this work.

References

David M. Blei, Andrew Y. Ng, and Michael I. Jordan. 2003. Latent dirichlet allocation. *the Journal of machine Learning research*, 3:993–1022.

Jordan Boyd-Graber and David M. Blei. 2009. Multilingual topic models for unaligned text. In *Proceedings of UAI*, pages 75–82.

Marine Carpuat, Hal Daumé III, Alexander Fraser, Chris Quirk, Fabienne Braune, Ann Clifton, Ann Irvine, Jagadeesh Jagarlamudi, John Morgan, Majid Razmara, Aleš Tamchyna, Katharine Henry, and Rachel Rudinger. 2012. Domain adaptation in machine translation: Final report. In *2012 Johns Hopkins Summer Workshop Final Report*.

Vladimir Eidelman, Jordan Boyd-Graber, and Philip Resnik. 2012. Topic models for dynamic translation model adaptation. In *Proceedings of ACL*, pages 115–119.

Jacob Eisenstein and Regina Barzilay. 2008. Bayesian unsupervised topic segmentation. In *Proceedings of EMNLP*, pages 334–343.

Marcello Federico, Mauro Cettolo, Luisa Bentivogli, Michael Paul, and Sebastian Stueker. 2012. Overview of the IWSLT 2012 evaluation campaign. *Proceedings of IWSLT*.

George Foster, Pierre Isabelle, and Roland Kuhn. 2010. Translating structured documents. In *Proceedings of AMTA*.

Zhengxian Gong, Min Zhang, and Guodong Zhou. 2011. Cache-based document-level statistical machine translation. In *Proceedings of EMNLP*, pages 909–919.

Christian Hardmeier, Joakim Nivre, and Jörg Tiedemann. 2012. Document-wide decoding for phrase-based statistical machine translation. In *Proceedings of the EMNLP-CoNLL*, pages 1179–1190.

Jagadeesh Jagarlamudi and Hal Daumé III. 2010. Extracting multilingual topics from unaligned comparable corpora. In *Advances in Information Retrieval*, Lecture Notes in Computer Science, pages 444–456. Springer Berlin Heidelberg.

Philipp Koehn, Franz Josef Och, and Daniel Marcu. 2003. Statistical phrase-based translation. In *Proceedings of NAACL-HLT*, pages 48–54.

Philipp Koehn, Hieu Hoang, Alexandra Birch, Chris Callison-Burch, Marcello Federico, Nicola Bertoldi, Brooke Cowan, Wade Shen, Christine Moran, Richard Zens, Chris Dyer, Ondřej Bojar, Alexandra Constantin, and Evan Herbst. 2007. Moses: open source toolkit for statistical machine translation. In *Proceedings of the ACL meeting on Interactive Poster and Demonstration Sessions*, pages 177–180.

Chin-Yew Lin and Eduard Hovy. 2000. The automated acquisition of topic signatures for text summarization. In *Proceedings of COLING*, pages 495–501.

Franz Josef Och. 2003. Minimum error rate training in statistical machine translation. In *Proceedings of ACL*, pages 160–167.

Kishore Papineni, Salim Roukos, Todd Ward, and Wei-Jing Zhu. 2002. Bleu: A method for automatic evaluation of machine translation. In *Proceedings of ACL*, pages 311–318.

Evan Sandhaus. 2008. The New York Times Annotated Corpus. *Corpus number LDC2008T19, Linguistic Data Consortium, Philadelphia*.

Jinsong Su, Hua Wu, Haifeng Wang, Yidong Chen, Xiaodong Shi, Huailin Dong, and Qun Liu. 2012. Translation model adaptation for statistical machine translation with monolingual topic information. In *Proceedings of ACL*, pages 459–468.

Jörg Tiedemann. 2010a. Context adaptation in statistical machine translation using models with exponentially decaying cache. In *Proceedings of the 2010 Workshop on Domain Adaptation for Natural Language Processing*.

Jörg Tiedemann. 2010b. To cache or not to cache?: experiments with adaptive models in statistical machine translation. In *Proceedings of the Joint Fifth Workshop on Statistical Machine Translation and MetricsMATR*, pages 189–194.

Bing Zhao and Eric P. Xing. 2006. Bitam: bilingual topic admixture models for word alignment. In *Proceedings of the COLING-ACL*, pages 969–976.

Regularized Structured Perceptron: A Case Study on Chinese Word Segmentation, POS Tagging and Parsing

Kaixu Zhang
Xiamen University
Fujian, P.R. China
kareyzhang@gmail.com

Jinsong Su
Xiamen University
Fujian, P.R. China
jssu@xmu.edu.cn

Changle Zhou
Xiamen University
Fujian, P.R. China
dozero@xmu.edu.cn

Abstract

Structured perceptron becomes popular for various NLP tasks such as tagging and parsing. Practical studies on NLP did not pay much attention to its regularization. In this paper, we study three simple but effective task-independent regularization methods: (1) one is to average weights of different trained models to reduce the bias caused by the specific order of the training examples; (2) one is to add penalty term to the loss function; (3) and one is to randomly corrupt the data flow during training which is called dropout in the neural network. Experiments are conducted on three NLP tasks, namely Chinese word segmentation, part-of-speech tagging and dependency parsing. Applying proper regularization methods or their combinations, the error reductions with respect to the averaged perceptron for some of these tasks can be up to 10%.

1 Introduction

Structured perceptron is a linear classification algorithm. It is used for word segmentation (Zhang and Clark, 2011), POS (part-of-speech) tagging (Collins, 2002), syntactical parsing (Collins and Roark, 2004), semantical parsing (Zettlemoyer and Collins, 2009) and other NLP tasks.

The averaged perceptron or the voted perceptron (Collins, 2002) is proposed for better generalization. Early update (Collins and Roark, 2004; Huang et al., 2012) is used for inexact decoding algorithms such as the beam search. Distributed training (McDonald et al., 2010) and the minibatch and parallelization method (Zhao and Huang, 2013) are recently proposed. Some other related work focuses on the task-specified feature engineering.

Regularization is to improve the ability of generalization and avoid over-fitting for machine learning algorithms including online learning algorithms (Do et al., 2009; Xiao, 2010). But practical studies on NLP did not pay much attention to the regularization of the structured perceptron. As a result, for some tasks the model learned using perceptron algorithm is not as good as the model learned using regularized condition random field.

In this paper, we treat the perceptron algorithm as a special case of the stochastic gradient descent (SGD) algorithm and study three kinds of simple but effective task-independent regularization methods that can be applied. The *averaging* method is to average the weight vectors of different models. We propose a "shuffle-and-average" method to reduce the bias caused by the specific order of the training examples. The traditional *penalty* method is to add penalty term to the loss function. The *dropout* method is to randomly corrupt the data flow during training. We show that this dropout method originally used in neural network also helps the structured perceptron.

In Section 2, we describe the perceptron algorithm as a special case of the stochastic gradient descent algorithm. Then we discuss three kinds of regularization methods for structured perceptron in Section 3, 4 and 5, respectively. Experiments conducted in Section 6 shows that these regularization methods and their combinations improve performances of NLP tasks such as Chinese word segmentation, POS tagging and dependency parsing. Applying proper regularization methods, the error reductions of these NLP tasks can be up to 10%. We finally conclude this work in Section 7.

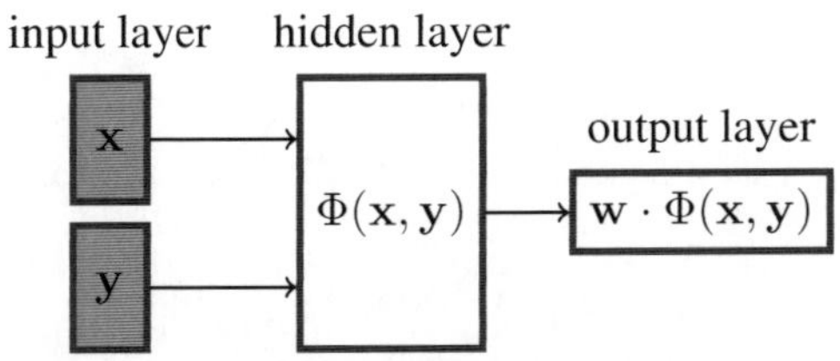

Figure 1: A structured perceptron can be seen as a multi-layer feed-forward neural network.

2 Structured Perceptron

We treat the structured perceptron architecture as a multi-layer feed-forward neural network as in Figure 1 and treat the perceptron algorithm as a special case of the stochastic gradient descent algorithm in order to describe all the regularization methods.

The network of the structured perceptron has three layers. The input vector $\mathbf{x}$ and output vector $\mathbf{y}$ of the structured classification task are concatenated as the input layer. The hidden layer is the feature vector $\Phi(\mathbf{x}, \mathbf{y})$. The connections between the input layer and the hidden layer are usually hand-crafted and fixed during training and predicting. And the output layer of the network is a scalar $\mathbf{w} \cdot \Phi(\mathbf{x}, \mathbf{y})$ which is used to evaluate the matching of the vector $\mathbf{x}$ and $\mathbf{y}$.

Besides the common process to calculate the output layer given the input layer, there is a process called decoding, which is to find a vector $\mathbf{z}$ to maximum the activation of the output layer:

$$\mathbf{z}_i = \arg\max_{\mathbf{z}} \mathbf{w} \cdot \Phi(\mathbf{x}_i, \mathbf{z}) \tag{1}$$

By carefully designing the feature vector, the decoding can be efficiently performed using dynamic programming. Beam search is also commonly used for the decoding of syntactical parsing tasks.

In the predicting precess, the vector $\mathbf{z}$ is the structured output corresponding to $\mathbf{x}$. In the training precess, what we expect is that for every input $\mathbf{x}_i$, the vector $\mathbf{z}_i$ that maximums the activation of the output layer is exactly the gold standard output $\mathbf{y}_i$.

We define the loss function as the sum of the margins of the whole training data:

$$\begin{aligned}\mathcal{L}(\mathbf{w}) &= \sum_i \{\mathbf{w} \cdot \Phi(\mathbf{x}_i, \mathbf{z}_i) - \mathbf{w} \cdot \Phi(\mathbf{x}_i, \mathbf{y}_i)\} \\ &= \mathbf{w} \sum_i \cdot \Delta\Phi_i\end{aligned} \tag{2}$$

where

$$\Delta\Phi_i = \Phi(\mathbf{x}_i, \mathbf{z}_i) - \Phi(\mathbf{x}_i, \mathbf{y}_i) \tag{3}$$

The unconstrained optimization problem of the training process is

$$\arg\min_{\mathbf{w}} \mathcal{L}(\mathbf{w}) \tag{4}$$

The loss function is not convex but calculating the derivative is easy. One of the algorithms to solve this optimization problem is SGD. Here we use the minibatch with size of 1, which means in every iteration we use only one training example to approximate the loss function and the gradient to update the weight vector:

$$\mathbf{w}^{(t+1)} \leftarrow \mathbf{w}^{(t)} - \eta \left.\frac{\partial \mathcal{L}}{\partial \mathbf{w}}\right|_{\mathbf{w}^{(t)}} \approx \mathbf{w}^{(t)} - \eta \Delta\Phi^{(t)} \tag{5}$$

where $\mathbf{w}^{(t)}$ is the weight vector after t updates. Note that in this case, the learning rate η can be set to an arbitrary positive real number. In the perceptron algorithm commonly used in NLP (Collins, 2002) , η is not changed respect to t. We fix η to be 1 in this paper without loss of generality.

3 Averaging

3.1 Averaged Perceptron

Averaging the weight vectors in the learning process is one of the most popular regularization techniques of the structured perceptron (Collins, 2002). And it is also the only used regularization technique for many practical studies on NLP (Jiang et al., 2009; Huang and Sagae, 2010).

Suppose the learning algorithm stopped after T updates. The final weight vector is calculated as:

$$\mathbf{w} = \frac{1}{T} \sum_{t=1}^{T} \mathbf{w}^{(t)} \tag{6}$$

The intuition might be that the learned weight vector is dependent on the order of the training examples. The final vector $\mathbf{w}^{(T)}$ may be more appropriate for the last few training examples than the previous ones. The averaging method is used to avoid such tendency. Similar treatment is used in other sequential algorithm such as the Markov chain Monte Carlo sampling method.

Since this regularization technique is widely used and tested, it is used for all the models in the experiments of this paper. Any other regularization methods are applied to this basic averaged perceptron.

3.2 Shuffle and Average

As we has mentioned that the learned weight vector is strongly dependent on the order of the training examples, randomly shuffling the training examples results in different weight vectors. Based on such observation, we training different weight vectors using the same training examples with different orders, and average them to get the final weight vector. We use this method to further minimize the side effect caused by this online algorithm.

Suppose we shuffle and train n different weight vectors $\mathbf{w}^{[1]}, \ldots, \mathbf{w}^{[n]}$, the j-th component of the final vector can be simply calculated as

$$w_j = \frac{\sum_{i=1}^{n} w_j^{[i]}}{n} \tag{7}$$

Note that generally these models do not share the same feature set. Features may be used in one model but not in another one. When $w_j^{[i]} = 0$, it does not imply that this feature has no effect on this problem. It only implies that this feature does not have chances to be tested. We propose a modified equation to only average the non-zero components:

$$w_j = \frac{\sum_{i=1}^{n} w_j^{[i]}}{\left|\{i | w_j^{[i]} \neq 0, i = 1, \cdots, n\}\right|} \tag{8}$$

This equation makes the low-frequency features more important in the final model.

4 Penalty

Adding penalty term to the loss function is a common and traditional regularization method to avoid over-fitting. It is widely used for the optimization problems of logistic regression, support vector machine, conditional random field and other models. Penalty terms for probabilistic models can be interpreted as a prior over the weights (Chen and Rosenfeld, 1999). It is also called "weight decay" in artificial neural network (Moody et al., 1995). The use of the penalty term is to prevent the components of the weight vector to become too large.

In Section 2 we have modeled the perceptron algorithm as an SGD algorithm with an explicit loss function, the additional penalty term is therefore easy to be employed.

4.1 L2-norm penalty

We can add a square of the L2-norm of the weight vector as the penalty term to the loss function as

$$\mathcal{L} = \mathbf{w} \cdot \sum_i \Delta\Phi_i + \frac{\lambda_2}{2} \|\mathbf{w}\|_2^2 \tag{9}$$

where λ_2 is a hyper-parameter to determine the strength of the penalty.

In the SGD algorithm, the update method of the weight vector is thus

$$\mathbf{w}^{(t+1)} \leftarrow (1 - \eta\lambda_2)\mathbf{w}^{(t)} - \eta\Delta\Phi^{(t)} \tag{10}$$

The term $(1 - \eta\lambda_2)$ is used to decay the weight in every updates. This forces the weights to be close to zero.

4.2 L1-norm penalty

Another commonly used penalty term is the L1-norm of the weight vector. This kinds of terms usually results in sparse weight vector. Since the averaged perceptron is used, the final averaged weight vector will not be sparse.

The loss function using the L1-nrom penalty is

$$\mathcal{L} = \mathbf{w} \cdot \sum_i \Delta\Phi_i + \lambda_1 \|\mathbf{w}\|_1 \tag{11}$$

where λ_1 is the hyper-parameter to determine the strength of the penalty.

The derivative of the penalty term is discontinuous. We update the weights as

$$w_i^{(t+1)} \leftarrow \frac{\max\{0, |w_i^{(t)}| - \eta\lambda_1\}}{|w_i^{(t)}|} w_i^{(t)} - \eta\Delta\phi_i^{(t)} \tag{12}$$

This ensures that the weight decay will not change the sign of the weight.

An modified version of the L1 penalty for the online learning is the cumulative L1 penalty (Tsuruoka et al., 2009), which is used to make the stochastic gradient of the penalty term more close to the true gradient. The update is divided into two steps. In the first step, the weight vector is updated according to the loss function without the penalty term

$$w_i^{(t+\frac{1}{2})} \leftarrow w_i^{(t)} - \eta\Delta\phi_i^{(t)} \tag{13}$$

And the cumulative penalty is calculated separately

$$c_i^{(t+\frac{1}{2})} \leftarrow c_i^{(t)} + \eta\lambda_1 \tag{14}$$

In the second step, $|w_i|$ and c_i are compared and at most one of them is non-zero before the next update

$$m \leftarrow \min\{|w_i^{(t+\frac{1}{2})}|, c_i^{(t+\frac{1}{2})}\} \tag{15}$$

$$w_i^{(t+1)} \leftarrow \frac{\max\{0, |w_i^{(t+\frac{1}{2})}| - m\}}{|w_i^{(t+\frac{1}{2})}|} w_i^{(t+\frac{1}{2})} \tag{16}$$

$$c_i^{(t+1)} \leftarrow c_i^{(t+\frac{1}{2})} - m \tag{17}$$

5 Dropout

Dropout (Hinton et al., 2012) is originally a regularization method used for the artificial neural network. It corrupts one or more layers of a feed-forward network during training, by randomly omitting some of the neurons. If the input layer is corrupted during the training of an autoencoder, the model is called denoising autoencoder (Vincent et al., 2008).

The reason why such treatment can regularize the parameters are explained in different ways. Hinton et al. (2012) argued that the final model is an average of a large number of models and the dropout forces the model to learn good features which are less co-adapted. Vincent et al. (2008) argued that by using dropout of the input layer, the model can learn how to deal with examples outside the low-dimensional manifold that the training data concentrate.

Models not so deep such as the structured perceptron may also benefit from this idea. Following the dropout method used in neural network, we give the similar method for structured perceptron.

5.1 Input Layer

We can perform dropout for structured perceptron by corrupting the input layer in Figure 1. Since we concern that what $\mathbf{y}$ exactly is, we only corrupt $\mathbf{x}$. The components of the corrupted vector $\tilde{\mathbf{x}}$ is calculated as

$$\tilde{x}_i = x_i n_i \tag{18}$$

where $n_i \sim \text{Bern}(p)$ obey a Binomial distribution with the hyper-parameter p.

During training, the decoding processing with the corrupted input is

$$\mathbf{z} = \arg\max_{\mathbf{z}} \mathbf{w} \cdot \Phi(\tilde{\mathbf{x}}, \mathbf{z}) \tag{19}$$

The $\mathbf{x}$ in the loss function is also substituted with the corrupted version $\tilde{\mathbf{x}}$.

Note that the corruption decreases the number of non-zero components of the feature vector Φ, which makes the decoding algorithm harder to find the gold standard $\mathbf{y}$.

For NLP tasks, the input vector $\mathbf{x}$ could be a sequence of tokens (words, POS tags, etc.). The corruption substitutes some of the tokens with a special token null. Any features contain such token will be omitted (This is also the case for the out-of-vocabulary words during predicting). So the dropout of $\mathbf{x}$ in NLP during training can be explained as to randomly mask some of the input tokens. The decoder algorithm needs to find out the correct answer even if some parts of the input are unseen. This harder situation could force the learning algorithm to learn better models.

5.2 Hidden Layer

The dropout can also be performed at the hidden layer. Likewise, the components of the corrupted feature vector $\tilde{\Phi}$ is calculated as

$$\tilde{\phi}_i = \phi_i m_i \tag{20}$$

where $m_i \sim \text{Bern}(q)$ obey a Binomial distribution with the hyper-parameter q.

The Φ in the decoding processing during training and the loss function is substituted with $\tilde{\Phi}$.

6 Experiments

In this section, we first introduce three NLP tasks using structured perceptron namely Chinese word segmentation, POS tagging and dependency parsing. Then we investigate the effects of regularization methods for structured perceptron mainly on the development set of character-based Chinese word segmentation. Finally, we compare the final performances on the test sets of these three tasks using regularization methods with related work.

6.1 Tasks

6.1.1 Chinese Word Segmentation

A Chinese word consists of one or more Chinese characters. But there is no spaces in the sentences to indicating words. Chinese word segmentation is the task to segment words in the sentence.

We use a character-based Chinese word segmentation model as the baseline. Like part-of-speech tagging which is to assign POS tags to words sequence, character-based Chinese word segmentation is to assign tags to character sequence. The tag set of four tags is commonly used:

Type	Templates
Unigram	$\langle x_{i-1}, y_i\rangle$, $\langle x_i, y_i\rangle$, $\langle x_{i+1}, y_i\rangle$
Bigram	$\langle x_{i-2}, x_{i-1}, y_i\rangle$, $\langle x_{i-1}, x_i, y_i\rangle$
	$\langle x_i, x_{i+1}, y_i\rangle$, $\langle x_{i+1}, x_{i+2}, y_i\rangle$
transition	$\langle y_{i-1}, y_i\rangle$

Table 1: Feature templates for the character-based Chinese word segmentation model and the joint Chinese word segmentation and POS tagging model.

tag S indicates that the character forms a single-character words; tag B / E indicates that the character is at the beginning / end of a multi-character words; tag M indicates that the character is in the middle of a multi-character words.

For example, if the tag sequence for the input

$$\mathbf{x} = \text{菊次郎的夏天} \tag{21}$$

is

$$\mathbf{y} = \text{BMESBE}, \tag{22}$$

the corresponding segmentation result is

$$\text{菊次郎 的 夏天}. \tag{23}$$

Table 1 shows the set of the feature templates which is a subset of some related work (Ng and Low, 2004; Jiang et al., 2009) .

Following Sun (2011), we split the Chinese treebank 5 into training set, development set and test set. F-measure (Emerson, 2005) is used as the measurement of the performance.

6.1.2 Part-of-Speech Tagging

The second task is joint Chinese word segmentation and POS tagging. This can also be modeled as a character-based sequence labeling task.

The tag set is a Cartesian product of the tag set for Chinese word segmentation and the set of POS tags. For example, the tag B-NN indicates the character is the first character of a multi-character noun. The tag sequence

$$\mathbf{y} = \text{B-NR M-NR E-NR S-DEG B-NN E-NN}, \tag{24}$$

for the input sentence in Equation (21) results in

$$\text{菊次郎\_NR 的\_DEG 夏天\_NN}. \tag{25}$$

The same feature templates shown in Table 1 are used for joint Chinese word segmentation and POS tagging.

Also, we use the same training set, development set and test set based on CTB5 corpus as the Chinese word segmentation task. F-measure for joint Chinese word segmentation and POS tagging is used as the measurement of the performance.

6.1.3 Dependency Parsing

The syntactical parsing tasks are different with previously introduced tagging tasks. To investigate the effects of regularization methods on the parsing tasks, we fully re-implement the linear-time incremental shift-reduce dependency parser by Huang and Sagae (2010). The structure perceptron is used to train such model. The model totally employs 28 feature templates proposed by Huang and Sagae (2010).

Since the search space for parsing tasks is quite larger than the search space for tagging tasks, Exact search algorithms such as dynamic programming can not be used. Besides, beam search with state merging is used for decoding. The early update strategy (Collins and Roark, 2004) is also employed.

In order to compare to the related work, unlike the Chinese word segmentation and the POS tagging task, we split the CTB5 corpus following Zhang et al.(2008). Two types of accuracies are used to measure the performances, namely word and complete match (excluding punctuations) (Huang and Sagae, 2010).

6.2 Averaging

First, we investigate the effect of averaging techniques for regularization. Figure 2 shows the influence of the number of the averaged models by using the "shuffle-and-average" method described in section 3.2. The performances of the Chinese word segmentation, POS tagging and parsing tasks are all increased by averaging models trained with the same training data with different orders. The "shuffle-and-average" method is effective to reduce the bias caused by the specific order of the training examples.

For the Chinese word segmentation task which is a relatively simple task, averaging about five different models can achieve the best effect; whereas for POS tagging and parsing, averaging more models will continually increase the performance even when the number of models approaches 10.

The dotted lines in Figure 2 indicate the performances by using Equation (7) for model averaging. The solid lines indicate the performances by

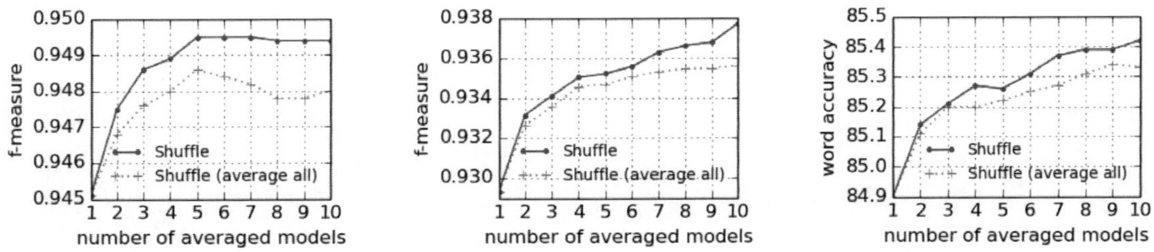

(a) Chinese word segmentation (b) POS tagging (c) Dependency parsing

Figure 2: The influence of the number of the averaged models using the "shuffle-and-average" method for (a) Chinese word segmentation, (b) POS tagging and (c) dependency parsing. "Shuffle" means to only average the non-zero weights (Equation (8)), while "Shuffle (average all)" means to average all weights (Equation (7)).

using Equation (8) for model averaging. According to these three different tasks, Equation (8) always performs better than Equation (7). We will use Equation (8) denoted as "Shuffle" for the rest of the experiments.

6.3 Penalty

Here we investigate the penalty techniques for regularization only using the character-based Chinese word segmentation task.

Figure 3 shows the effect of adding L1-norm and L2-norm penalty terms to the loss function.

With appropriate hyper-parameters, the performances are increased. According to the performances, adding L2 penalty is slightly better than adding L1 penalty or adding cumulative L1 penalty.

We then combine the "shuffle-and-average" method with the penalty methods. The performances (solid lines in Figure 3) are further improved and are better than those of models that only use one regularization method.

6.4 Dropout

We also investigate the dropout method for regularization using the character-based Chinese word segmentation task.

Figure 4 shows the effect of the dropout method ("dropout" for the input layer and "dropout (Φ)" for the hidden layer) and the combination of the dropout and "shuffle-and-average" method (solid line). We observed that the dropout for the hidden layer is not effective for structured perceptron. This may caused by that the connections between the input layer and the hidden layer are fixed during training. Neurons in the hidden layer can not changes the weights to learn different representations for the input layer. On the other hand, the dropout for the input layer improves the performance. Combining the dropout and the "shuffle-and-average" method, the performance is further improved.

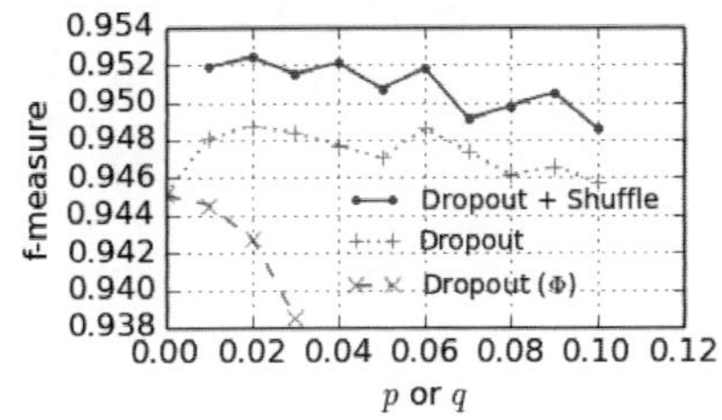

Figure 4: Influences of the hyper-parameter p (for the input layer, denoted as "dropout") or q (for the hidden layer, denoted as "dropout (Φ)") for the dropout method.

Figure 5 shows the effect of the combination of the three regularization methods. We see that no matter what other regularization methods are already used, adding "shuffle-and-average" method can always improve the performance. The effects of the penalty method and the dropout method have some overlap, since combining these two method does not result in a significant improvement of the performance.

6.5 Final Results

6.5.1 Chinese Word Segmentation

Table 2 shows the final results of the character-based Chinese word segmentation task on the test set of the CTB5 corpus.

Structure perceptron with feature templates in

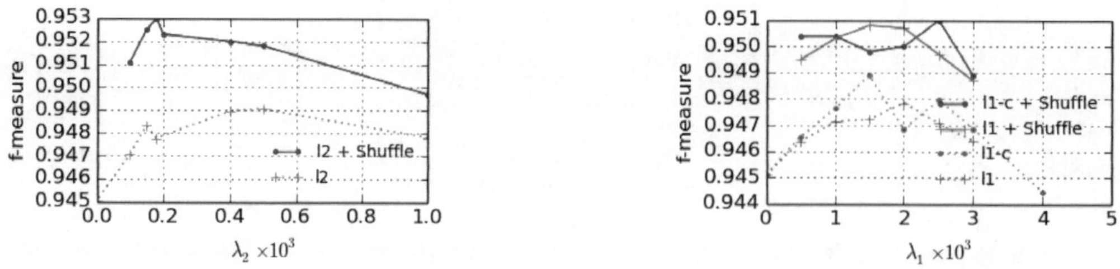

(a) L2-norm penalty (b) L1-norm penalty

Figure 3: influence of the hyper-parameter λ_2 in the L2-norm penalty term and λ_1 in the L1-norm penalty term ("l1-c" indicates the cumulative L1 penalty) for the character-based Chinese word segmentation task.

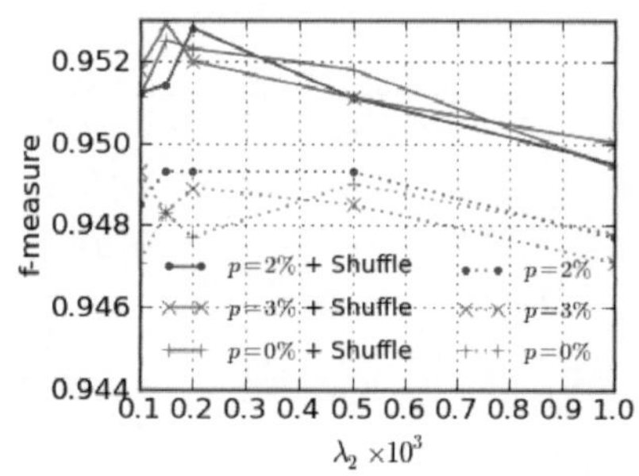

Figure 5: The combination of these three regularization methods.

Table 1 is used. We use the "shuffle-and-average" (5 models), the L2 penalty method ($\lambda_2 = 10^{-4}$), the dropout method ($p = 3\%$) and their combinations to regularize the structured perceptron.

To compare with the perceptron algorithm, we use the conditional random field model (CRF) with the same feature templates in Table 1 to train the model parameters. The toolkit CRF++[1] with the L2-norm penalty is used to train the weights. The hyper-parameter $C = 20$ is tuned using the development set.

Jiang et al. (2009) proposed a character-based model employing similar feature templates using averaged perceptron. The feature templates are following Ng and Low (2004). Zhang and Clark (2011) proposed a word-based model employing both character-based features and more sophisticated word-based features using also averaged perceptron. There are other related results (Jiang et al., 2012) of open test including the final result of Jiang et al. (2009). Since their models used extra resources, they are not comparable with the results in this paper.

	sf
(Jiang et al., 2009)	0.9735
(Zhang and Clark, 2011)	0.9750†
CRF++ ($C = 20$)	0.9742
Averaged Percetron	0.9734
+ Shuffle	0.9755
+ L2	0.9736
+ L2 + Shuffle	**0.9772**
+ Dropout	0.9741
+ Dropout+ Shuffle	0.9765
+ L2 + Dropout	0.9749
+ L2 + Dropout+ Shuffle	0.9771

Table 2: Final results of the character-based Chinese word segmentation task on CTB5. † This result is read from a figure in that paper.

	sf
Word-based model	0.9758
+ Shuffle	0.9787
+ L2 + Shuffle	**0.9791**
+ L2 + Dropout+ Shuffle	**0.9791**

Table 3: Final results of the word-based Chinese word segmentation task on CTB5.

The results in Table 2 shows that with proper regularization methods, the models trained using perceptron algorithm can outperform CRF models with the same feature templates and other models with more sophisticated features trained using the averaged perceptron without other regularization methods.

We further re-implemented a word-based Chinese word segmentation model with the feature templates following Zhang et al. (2012), which

[1] http://crfpp.googlecode.com/svn/trunk/doc/index.html

	sf	jf
(Jiang et al., 2008)	0.9785	0.9341
(Kruengkrai et al., 2009)	0.9787	0.9367
(Zhang and Clark, 2010)	0.9778	0.9367
(Sun, 2011)	0.9817	0.9402
Character-based model	0.9779	0.9336
+ Shuffle	0.9802	0.9375
+ Dropout	0.9789	0.9361
+ Dropout+ Shuffle	0.9809	0.9407
+ word-based re-ranking	0.9813	**0.9438**

Table 4: Final results of the POS tagging task on CTB5.

	word	compl.
(Huang and Sagae, 2010)	85.20	33.72
our re-implementation	85.22	34.15
+ Shuffle	85.65	34.52
+ Dropout	85.32	34.04
+ Dropout+ Shuffle	**85.71**	34.57

Table 5: Final results of the dependency parsing task on CTB5.

is similar with the model proposed by Zhang and Clark (2011). Beam search with early-update is used for decoding instead of dynamic programming. The results with different regularization methods are shown in Figure 3. These regularization methods show similar characteristics for the word-based model.

6.5.2 POS Tagging

The results of the POS tagging models on the CTB5 corpus are shown in Table 4. Structure perceptron with feature templates in Table 1 is used. The F-measures for word segmentation (sf) and for joint word segmentation and POS tagging (jf) are listed.

We use the "shuffle-and-average" (10 models), the dropout method ($p = 5\%$) and their combination to regularize the structured perceptron.

Jiang et al. (2008) used a character-based model using perceptron for POS tagging and a log-linear model for re-ranking. Kruengkrai et al. (2009) proposed a hybrid model including character-based and word-based features. Zhang and Clark (2010) proposed a word-based model using perceptron. Sun (2011) proposed a framework based on stacked learning consisting of four sub-models. For the closed test, this model has the best performance on the CTB5 corpus to our knowledge. Other results (Wang et al., 2011; Sun and Wan, 2012) for the open test are not listed since they are not comparable with the results in this paper.

If we define the error rate as $1 - \text{jf}$, the error reduction by applying regularization methods for the character-based model is more than 10%. Comparing to the related work, the character-based model that we used is quite simple. But using the regularization methods discussed in this paper, it provides a comparable performance to the best model in the literature.

6.5.3 Dependency Parsing

Table 5 shows the final results of the dependency parsing task on the CTB5 corpus. We use the "shuffle-and-average" (10 models), the dropout method ($p = 5\%$ only for the words in the input) and their combination to regularize the structured perceptron based on Huang and Sagae's (2010).

The performance of the parsing model is also improved by using more regularization methods, although the improvement is not as remarkable as those for tagging tasks. For the parsing tasks, there are many other factors that impact the performance.

7 Conclusion

The "shuffle-and-average" method can effectively reduce the bias caused by the specific order of the training examples. It can improve the performance even if some other regularization methods are applied.

When we treat the perceptron algorithm as a special case of the SGD algorithm, the traditional penalty methods can be applied. And our observation is that L2 penalty is better than L1 penalty.

The dropout method is derived from the neural network. Corrupting the input during training improves the ability of generalization. The effects of the penalty method and the dropout method have some overlap.

Experiments showed that these regularization methods help different NLP tasks such as Chinese word segmentation, POS tagging and dependency parsing. Applying proper regularization methods, the error reductions for some of these NLP tasks can be up to 10%. We believe that these methods can also help other models which are based on structured perceptron.

Acknowledgments

The authors want to thanks all the reviews for many pertinent comments which have improved the quality of this paper. The authors are supported by NSFC (No. 61273338 and No. 61303082), the Doctoral Program of Higher Education of China (No. 20120121120046) and China Postdoctoral Science Foundation (No. 2013M541861).

References

Stanley F Chen and Ronald Rosenfeld. 1999. A gaussian prior for smoothing maximum entropy models. Technical report, DTIC Document.

Michael Collins and Brian Roark. 2004. Incremental parsing with the perceptron algorithm. In *Proceedings of the 42nd Meeting of the Association for Computational Linguistics (ACL'04), Main Volume*, page 111118, Barcelona, Spain, July.

Michael Collins. 2002. Discriminative training methods for hidden markov models: theory and experiments with perceptron algorithms. pages 1–8.

Chuong B Do, Quoc V Le, and Chuan-Sheng Foo. 2009. Proximal regularization for online and batch learning. In *Proceedings of the 26th Annual International Conference on Machine Learning*, pages 257–264. ACM.

Thomas Emerson. 2005. The second international chinese word segmentation bakeoff. In *Proceedings of the Fourth SIGHAN Workshop on Chinese Language Processing*, pages 123–133. Jeju Island, Korea.

Geoffrey E. Hinton, Nitish Srivastava, Alex Krizhevsky, Ilya Sutskever, and Ruslan R. Salakhutdinov. 2012. Improving neural networks by preventing co-adaptation of feature detectors. *arXiv preprint arXiv:1207.0580*.

Liang Huang and Kenji Sagae. 2010. Dynamic programming for linear-time incremental parsing. In *Proceedings of the 48th Annual Meeting of the Association for Computational Linguistics*, pages 1077–1086, Uppsala, Sweden, July. Association for Computational Linguistics.

Liang Huang, Suphan Fayong, and Yang Guo. 2012. Structured perceptron with inexact search. In *Proceedings of the 2012 Conference of the North American Chapter of the Association for Computational Linguistics: Human Language Technologies*, pages 142–151. Association for Computational Linguistics.

Wenbin Jiang, Liang Huang, Qun Liu, and Yajuan L ü. 2008. A cascaded linear model for joint chinese word segmentation and part-of-speech tagging. In *Proceedings of ACL-08: HLT*, pages 897–904, Columbus, Ohio, June. Association for Computational Linguistics.

Wenbin Jiang, Liang Huang, and Qun Liu. 2009. Automatic adaptation of annotation standards: Chinese word segmentation and POS tagging - a case study. In *Proceedings of the 47th ACL*, pages 522–530, Suntec, Singapore, August. Association for Computational Linguistics.

Wenbin Jiang, Fandong Meng, Qun Liu, and Yajuan L ü. 2012. Iterative annotation transformation with predict-self reestimation for chinese word segmentation. In *Proceedings of the 2012 Joint Conference on Empirical Methods in Natural Language Processing and Computational Natural Language Learning*, pages 412–420, Jeju Island, Korea, July. Association for Computational Linguistics.

Canasai Kruengkrai, Kiyotaka Uchimoto, Jun'ichi Kazama, Yiou Wang, Kentaro Torisawa, and Hitoshi Isahara. 2009. An error-driven word-character hybrid model for joint chinese word segmentation and POS tagging. In *Proc. of ACL-IJCNLP 2009*, pages 513–521, Suntec, Singapore. Association for Computational Linguistics.

Ryan McDonald, Keith Hall, and Gideon Mann. 2010. Distributed training strategies for the structured perceptron. In *Human Language Technologies: The 2010 Annual Conference of the North American Chapter of the Association for Computational Linguistics*, pages 456–464. Association for Computational Linguistics.

JE Moody, SJ Hanson, Anders Krogh, and John A Hertz. 1995. A simple weight decay can improve generalization. *Advances in neural information processing systems*, 4:950–957.

Hwee Tou Ng and Jin Kiat Low. 2004. Chinese part-of-speech tagging: One-at-a-time or all-at-once? word-based or character-based? In Dekang Lin and Dekai Wu, editors, *Proceedings of EMNLP 2004*, pages 277–284, Barcelona, Spain, July. Association for Computational Linguistics.

Weiwei Sun and Xiaojun Wan. 2012. Reducing approximation and estimation errors for chinese lexical processing with heterogeneous annotations. In *Proceedings of the 50th Annual Meeting of the Association for Computational Linguistics (Volume 1: Long Papers)*, pages 232–241, Jeju Island, Korea, July. Association for Computational Linguistics.

Weiwei Sun. 2011. A stacked sub-word model for joint chinese word segmentation and part-of-speech tagging. In *Proceedings of the 49th Annual Meeting of the Association for Computational Linguistics: Human Language Technologies*, pages 1385–1394, Portland, Oregon, USA, June. Association for Computational Linguistics.

Yoshimasa Tsuruoka, Jun'ichi Tsujii, and Sophia Ananiadou. 2009. Stochastic gradient descent training for l1-regularized log-linear models with cumulative penalty. In *Proceedings of the Joint Conference of the 47th Annual Meeting of the ACL and the*

4th International Joint Conference on Natural Language Processing of the AFNLP: Volume 1-Volume 1, pages 477–485. Association for Computational Linguistics.

Pascal Vincent, Hugo Larochelle, Yoshua Bengio, and Pierre-Antoine Manzagol. 2008. Extracting and composing robust features with denoising autoencoders. In *Proceedings of the 25th international conference on Machine learning*, page 10961103.

Yiou Wang, Jun'ichi Kazama, Yoshimasa Tsuruoka, Wenliang Chen, Yujie Zhang, and Kentaro Torisawa. 2011. Improving chinese word segmentation and POS tagging with semi-supervised methods using large auto-analyzed data. In *Proceedings of 5th International Joint Conference on Natural Language Processing*, pages 309–317, Chiang Mai, Thailand, November. Asian Federation of Natural Language Processing.

Lin Xiao. 2010. Dual averaging methods for regularized stochastic learning and online optimization. *The Journal of Machine Learning Research*, 9999:2543–2596.

Luke S Zettlemoyer and Michael Collins. 2009. Learning context-dependent mappings from sentences to logical form. In *Proceedings of the Joint Conference of the 47th Annual Meeting of the ACL and the 4th International Joint Conference on Natural Language Processing of the AFNLP: Volume 2-Volume 2*, pages 976–984. Association for Computational Linguistics.

Yue Zhang and Stephen Clark. 2008. A tale of two parsers: Investigating and combining graph-based and transition-based dependency parsing. In *Proceedings of the 2008 Conference on Empirical Methods in Natural Language Processing*, page 562571, Honolulu, Hawaii, October. Association for Computational Linguistics.

Yue Zhang and Stephen Clark. 2010. A fast decoder for joint word segmentation and POS-Tagging using a single discriminative model. In *Proceedings of the 2010 Conference on Empirical Methods in Natural Language Processing*, pages 843–852, Cambridge, MA, October. Association for Computational Linguistics.

Y. Zhang and S. Clark. 2011. Syntactic processing using the generalized perceptron and beam search. *Computational Linguistics*, (Early Access):1–47.

Kaixu Zhang, Maosong Sun, and Changle Zhou. 2012. Word segmentation on chinese mirco-blog data with a linear-time incremental model. In *Proceedings of the Second CIPS-SIGHAN Joint Conference on Chinese Language Processing*, pages 41–46, Tianjin, China, December. Association for Computational Linguistics.

Kai Zhao and Liang Huang. 2013. Minibatch and parallelization for online large margin structured learning. In *Proceedings of NAACL-HLT*, pages 370–379.

About Inferences in a Crowdsourced Lexical-Semantic Network

Manel Zarrouk
UM2-LIRMM
161 rue Ada
34095 Montpellier, FRANCE
manel.zarrouk@lirmm.fr

Mathieu Lafourcade
UM2-LIRMM
161 rue Ada
34095 Montpellier, FRANCE
mathieu.lafourcade@lirmm.fr

Alain Joubert
UM2-LIRMM
161 rue Ada
34095 Montpellier, FRANCE
alain.joubert@lirmm.fr

Abstract

Automatically inferring new relations from already existing ones is a way to improve the quality of a lexical network by relation densification and error detection. In this paper, we devise such an approach for the JeuxDeMots lexical network, which is a freely avalaible lexical network for French. We first present deduction (generic to specific) and induction (specific to generic) which are two inference schemes ontologically founded. We then propose abduction as a third form of inference scheme, which exploits examples similar to a target term.

1 Introduction

Building resources for Computational Linguistics (CL) is of crucial interest. Most of existing lexical-semantic networks have been built by hand (like for instance WordNet (Miller et al., 1990)) and, despite that tools are generally designed for consistency checking, the task remains time consuming and costly. Fully automated approaches are generally limited to term co-occurrences as extracting precise semantic relations between terms from corpora remains really difficult. Meanwhile, crowdsourcing approaches are flowering in CL especially with the advent of Amazon Mechanical Turk or in a broader scope Wikipedia and Wiktionary, to cite the most well-known examples. WordNet is such a lexical network, constructed by hand at great cost, based on synsets which can be roughly considered as concepts (Fellbaum, 1988). EuroWordnet (Vossen., 1998) a multilingual version of WordNet and WOLF (Sagot., 2008) a French version of WordNet, were built by automated crossing of WordNet and other lexical resources along with some manual checking. Navigli (2010) constructed automatically BabelNet a large multilingual lexical network from term co-occurrences in Wikipedia.

A lexical-semantic network can contain lemmas, word forms and multi-word expressions as entry points (nodes) along with word meanings and concepts. The idea itself of *word senses* in the lexicographic tradition may be debatable in the context of resources for semantic analysis, and we generally prefer to consider *word usages*. A given polysemous word, as identified by locutors, has several usages that might differ substantially from word senses as classically defined. A given usage can also in turn have several deeper refinements and the whole set of usages can take the form of a decision tree. For example, *frigate* can be a bird or a ship. A *frigate>boat* can be distinguished as a modern ship with missiles and radar or an ancient vessel with sails. In the context of a collaborative construction, such a lexical resource should be considered as being constantly evolving and a general rule of thumb is to have no definite certitude about the state of an entry. For a polysemic term, some refinements might be just missing at a given time notwithstanding evolution of language which might be very fast, especially in technical domains. There is no way (unless by inspection) to know if a given entry refinements are fully completed, and even if this question is really relevant.

The building of a collaborative lexical network (or, in all generality, any similar resource) can be devised according to two broad strategies. First, it can be designed as a contributive system like Wikipedia where people willingly add and complete entries (like for Wiktionary). Second, contributions can be made indirectly thanks to games (better known as GWAP (vonAhn, 2008)) and in this case players do not need to be aware that while playing they are helping building a lexical resource. In any case, the built lexical network is not free of errors which are corrected along their discovery. Thus, a large number of obvious relations are not contained in the lexical network but are indeed necessary for a high quality resources usable in various NLP applications and notably semantic analysis. For example, contributors seldom indicate that a particular bird type can fly, as it is considered as an obvious generality. Only notable facts which are not easily deductible are naturally contributed. Well known exceptions are also generally contributed and take the form of a negative weight and annotated as such (for example, *fly* $\xrightarrow{agent:-100}$ *ostrich* [exception: bird]).

In order to consolidate the lexical network, we adopt a strategy based on a simple inference mechanism to propose new relations from those already existing. The approach is strictly endogenous (i.e. self-contained) as it doesn't rely on any other external resources. Inferred relations are submitted either to contributors for voting or to experts for direct validation/invalidation. A large percentage of the inferred relations has been found to be correct however, a non-negligible part of them are found to be wrong and understanding why is both interesting and useful. The explanation process can be viewed as a *reconciliation* between the inference engine and contributors who are guided through a dialog to explain why they found the considered relation incorrect. The possible causes for a wrong inferred relation may come from three possible origins: false premises that were used by the inference engine, exception or confusion due to some polysemy.

In (Sajous et al., 2013) an endogenous enrichment of Wiktionary is done thanks to a crowdsourcing tool. A quite similar approach of using crowdsourcing has been considered by (Zeichner, 2012) for evaluating inference rules that are discovered from texts. In (Krachina, 2006), some specific inference methods are conducted on text with the help of an ontology. Similarly, (Besnard, 2008) capture explanation with ontology-based inference. OntoLearn (Velardi, 2006) is a system that automatically build ontologies of specific domains from texts and also makes use of inferences. There have been also researchs on taxonomy induction based on WordNet (Snow, 2006). Although extensive work on inference from texts or handcrafted resources has been done, almost none endogenously on lexical network built by the crowds. Most probably the main reason of that situation is the lack of such specific resources.

In this article, we first present the principles behind the lexical network construction with crowdsourcing and *games with a purpose* (also know as human-based computation games) and illustrated them with the JeuxDeMots (JDM) project. Then, we present the outline of an *elicitation engine* based on an *inference engine* using deduction, induction and especially abduction schemes. An experimentation is then presented.

2 Crowdsourced Lexical Networks

For validating our approach, we used the JDM lexical network, which is constructed thanks to a set of associatory games (Lafourcade, 2007) and has been made freely available by its authors. There is an increasing trend of using online GWAPs (game with a purpose (Thaler et al., 2011)) method for feeding such resources. Beside manual or automated strategies, contributive approaches are flowering and becoming more and more popular as they are both cheap to set up and efficient in quality.

The network is composed of terms (as vertices) and typed relations (as links between vertices) with weight. It contains terms and possible refinements. There are more than 50 types of relations, that range from ontological (hypernym, hyponym), to lexical-semantic (synonym, antonym) and to semantic role (agent, patient, instrument). The weight of a relation is interpreted as a strength, but not directly as a probability of being valid. The JDM network is not an ontology with some clean hierarchy of concepts or terms. A given term can have a substantial set of hypernyms that covers a large part of the ontological chain to upper concepts. For example, hypernym(cat) = {feline, mammal, living being, pet, vertebrate, ...}. Heavier weights associated to relations are those felt by users as being the most relevant. The

1st January 2014, there are more than 6 700 000 relations and roughly 310 000 lexical items in the JDM lexical network (according to the figures given by the game site: http://jeuxdemots.org).

To our knowledge, there is no other existing freely available crowdsourced lexical-network, especially with weighted relations, thus enabling strongly heuristic methods.

3 Inferring with Deduction & Induction

Adding new relations to the JDM lexical network may rely on two components: (a) an inference engine and (b) a reconciliator. The inference engine proposes relations as a contributor to be validated by other human contributors or experts. In case of invalidation of an inferred relation, the reconciliator is invoked to try to assess why the inferred relation was found wrong. Elicitation here should be understood as the process to transform some implicit knowledge of the user into explicit relations in the lexical network. The core ideas about inferences in our engine are the following:

- inferring is to derive new premises (as relations between terms) from previously known premises, which are existing relations;
- candidate inferences may be logically blocked on the basis of the presence or the absence of some other relations;
- candidate inferences can be filtered out on the basis of a strength evaluation.

3.1 Deduction Scheme

Inferring by deduction is a top-down scheme based on the transitivity of the relation *is-a* (hypernym). If a term A is a kind of B and B holds some relation R with C, then we can expect that A holds the same relation type with C. The scheme can be formally written as follows: $\exists A \xrightarrow{is-a} B \wedge \exists B \xrightarrow{R} C \Rightarrow A \xrightarrow{R} C$.

For example, *shark* $\xrightarrow{is-a}$ *fish* and *fish* $\xrightarrow{has-part}$ *fin*, thus we can expect that *shark* $\xrightarrow{has-part}$ *fin*. The inference engine is applied on terms having at least one hypernym (the scheme could not be applied otherwise). Of course, this scheme is far too naive, especially considering the resource we are dealing with and may produce wrong relations (noise). In effect, the central term B is possibly polysemous and ways to avoid probably wrong inferences can be done through a *logical blocking*: if there are two distinct meanings for B that hold respectively the first and the second relation, then most probably the inferred relation R(3) is wrong (see figure 1) and hence should be blocked. Moreover, if one of the premises is tagged by contributors as *true but irrelevant*, then the inference is blocked.

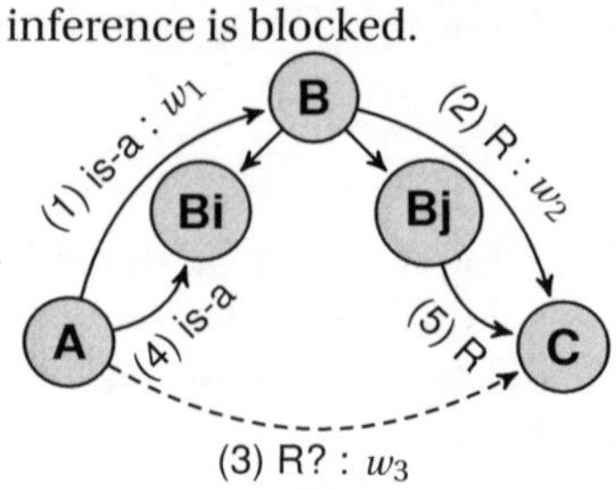

Figure 1: Triangular inference scheme where the logical blocking based on the polysemy of the central term B which has two distinct meanings B_i and B_j is applied. The two arrows without label are those of word meanings.

It is possible to evaluate a confidence level (on an open scale) for each produced inference, in a way that dubious inferences can be eliminated out through *statistical filtering*. The weight w of an inferred relation is the geometric mean of the weight of the premises (relations (1) and (2) in Figure 1). If the second premise has a negative value, the weight is not a number and the proposal is discarded. As the geometric mean is less tolerant to small values than the arithmetic mean, inferences which are not based on two rather strong relations (premises) are unlikely to pass.

$$w(A \xrightarrow{R} C) = (\, w(A \xrightarrow{is-a} B) \times w(B \xrightarrow{R} C)\,)^{1/2}$$
$$\Rightarrow \quad w3 = (w1 \times w2)^{1/2}$$

Inducing a transitive closure over a knowledge base is not new, but doing so considering word meanings over a crowdsourced lexical network is an original approach.

3.2 Induction Scheme

As for the deductive inference, induction exploits the transitivity of the relation *is-a*. If a term A is a kind of B and A holds a relation R with C, then we might expect that B could hold the same type of relation with C. More formally we can write: $\exists A \xrightarrow{is-a} B \wedge \exists A \xrightarrow{R} C \Rightarrow B \xrightarrow{R} C$. For example, *shark* $\xrightarrow{is-a}$ *fish* and *shark* $\xrightarrow{has-part}$ *jaw*, thus we might expect that *fish* $\xrightarrow{has-part}$ *jaw*.

This scheme is a generalization inference. The principle is similar to the one applied to the deduction scheme and similarly some logical and statistical filtering may be undertaken.

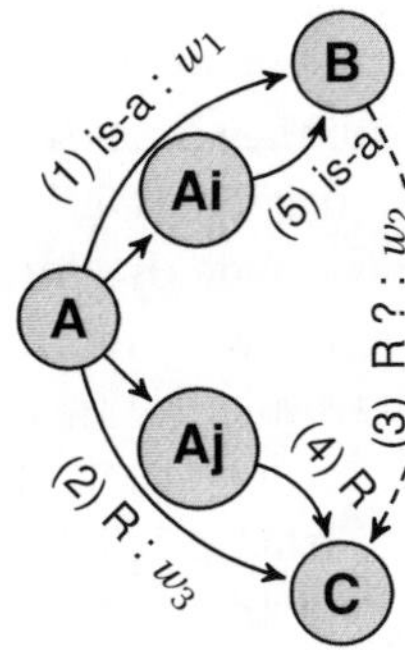

Figure 2: (1) and (2) are the premises, and (3) is the induction proposed for validation. Term A may be polysemous with meanings holding premises, thus inducing a probably wrong relation.

The central term here A, is possibly polysemous (as shown in Figure 2). In that case, we have the same polysemy issues than with the deduction, and the inference may be blocked. The estimated weight for the induced relation is:

$$w(B \xrightarrow{R} C) = (w(A \xrightarrow{R} C))^2 \,/\, w(A \xrightarrow{is-a} B)$$
$$\Rightarrow \quad w2 = (w_3)^2 / w_1$$

3.3 Performing Reconciliation

Inferred relations are presented to the validator to decide of their status. In case of invalidation, a reconciliation procedure is launched in order to diagnose the reasons: error in one of the premises (previously existing relations are false), exception or confusion due to polysemy (the inference has been made on a polysemous central term). A dialog is initiated with the user (Cohen's kappa of 0.79). To know in which order to proceed, the reconciliator checks if the weights of the premises are rather strong or weak.

Errors in the premises. We suppose that relation (1) (in Figure 1 and 2) has a relatively low weight. The reconciliation process asks the validator if the relation (1) is true. It sets a negative weight to this relation if not so that the engine blocks further inferences. Else, if relation (1) is true, we ask about relation (2) and proceed as above if the answer is negative. Otherwise, we check the other cases (exception, polysemy).

Errors due to Exceptions. For the *deduction*, in case we have two trusted relations, the reconciliation process asks the validators if the inferred relation is a kind of exception relatively to the term B. If it is the case, the relation is stored in the lexical network with a negative weight and annotated as *exception*. Relations that are exceptions do not participate further as premises for deducing. For the *induction*, in case we have two trusted relations, the reconciliator asks the validators if the relation ($A \xrightarrow{R} C$) (which served as premise) is an exception relatively to the term B. If it is the case, in addition to storing the false inferred relation ($B \xrightarrow{R} C$) in the lexical network with a negative weight, the relation ($A \xrightarrow{R} C$) is annotated as exception. In the induction case, the exception is a true premise which leads to a false induced relation. In both cases of induction and deduction, the *exception* tag concerns always the relation ($A \xrightarrow{R} C$). Once this relation is annotated as an exception, it will not participate as a premise in inferring generalized relations (bottom-up model) but can still be used in inducing specified relations (top-down model).

Errors due to Polysemy. If the central term (B for deduction and A for induction) presenting a polysemy is mentioned as polysemous in the network, the refinement terms $term_1$, $term_2$, ... $term_n$ are presented to the validator so she/he can choose the appropriate one. The validator can propose new terms as refinements if she/he is not satisfied with the listed ones (inducing the creation of new appropriate refinements). If there is no meta information indicating that the term is polysemous, we ask first the validator if it is indeed the case. After this procedure, new relations will be included in the network with positive values and the inference engine will use them later on as premises.

4 Abductive Inference

The last inferring scheme is built upon abduction and can be viewed as an example based strategy. Hence abduction relies on similarity between terms, which may be formalized in our context as sharing some outgoing relations between terms. The abductive inferring layout supposes that relations held by a term can be proposed to similar terms. Here, abduction first selects a set of similar terms to the target term A which are considered as proper examples. The outgoing relations from the examples which are not common with those of A are proposed as potential relations for A and then presented for validation/invalidation to users. Unlike induction and deduction, abduction can be applied on terms with missing or irrelevant ontological relations, and can generate ontological relations to be used afterward by the inference loop.

4.1 Abduction Scheme

We note an *outgoing relation* as a 3-uple of a type t, a weight w and a target node n:$R_i = \langle\, t_i\,,\, w_i\,,\, n_i\,\rangle$. For example, consider the term A having n outgoing relations. Amongst these relations, we have for example:

- *beak* $\xleftarrow{has-part}$ A & • *nest* $\xleftarrow{location}$ A.

We found 3 examples sharing those two relations with the term A:

- *beak* $\xleftarrow{has-part}$ $\{ex_1, ex_2, ex_3\}$
- *nest* $\xleftarrow{location}$ $\{ex_1, ex_2, ex_3\}$

We consider these terms as a set of examples to follow and similar to A. These examples have also other outgoing relations which are proposed as potential relations for A. For example :

- $\{ex_1, ex_2\}$ $\xrightarrow{agent-1}$ *fly* • $\{ex_2\}$ $\xrightarrow{carac}$ *colorful*
- $\{ex_1, ex_2, ex_3\}$ $\xrightarrow{has-part}$ *feather*
- $\{ex_3\}$ $\xrightarrow{agent-1}$ *sing*

We infer that A can hold these relations and we propose them for validation.

- A $\xrightarrow{agent-1}$ *fly* ? • A $\xrightarrow{has-part}$ *feather* ?
- A $\xrightarrow{carac}$ *colorful* ? • A $\xrightarrow{agent-1}$ *sing* ?

4.2 Abduction Filtering

Applying the abduction procedure crudely on the terms generates a lot of waste as a considerable amount of erroneous inferred relations. Hence, we elaborated a filtering strategy to avoid having a lot of dubious proposed candidates. For this purpose, we define two different threshold pairs. The first threshold pair (δ_1, ω_1) is used to select proper examples x_1,x_2...x_n and is defined as follows:

$$\delta_1 = \max(3, \text{nbogr}(A) \times 0.1) \qquad (1)$$

where *nbogr(A)* is the number of outgoing relations from the term A.

$$\omega_1 = \max(25, \text{mwogr}(A) \times 0.5) \qquad (2)$$

where *mwogr(A)* is the mean of weights of outgoing relations from A. The second threshold pair (δ_2, ω_2) is used to select proper candidate relations from outgoing relations of the examples R'_1,R'_2...R'_q.

$$\delta_2 = \max(3, \overline{\{x_i\}} \times 0.1) \qquad (3)$$

where $\overline{\{x_i\}}$ is the cardinal of the set $\{x_i\}$.

$$\omega_2 = \max(25, \text{mwogr}(\{x_i\}) \times 0.5) \qquad (4)$$

where *mwogr*$(\{x_i\})$ is the mean of weights of outgoing relations from the set of examples x_i.

If a term A is sharing at least δ_1 relations, having a weight over ω_1, of the total of the relations R_1, R_2, $\ldots R_p$ toward terms T_1, T_2, $\ldots T_p$ with a group of examples x_1, x_2, $\ldots x_n$, we admit that this term has a degree of similarity strong enough with these examples. After building up a set of examples on which we can apply our abduction engine we proceed with the second part of the strategy. If we have at least δ_2 examples x_i holding a specific relation R'_k weighting over ω_2 with a term B_k, more formally $R'_k = \langle\, t\,,\, w \geq \omega_2,\, B_k\,\rangle$, we can suppose that the term A may hold this same relation R'_k with the same target term B_k (figure 3).

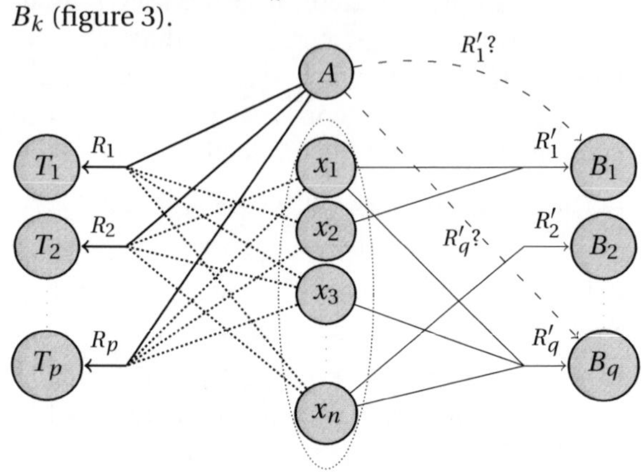

Figure 3: Abduction scheme with examples x_i sharing relations with A and proposing new abducted relations.

On figure 3, we simplified thresholds to 2 for illustrative purpose. So, to be selected, the examples x_1 ,x_2, x_3, $\ldots x_n$ must have at least 2 common relations with A. A relation $R'_{1 \to q}$ must be hold by at least 2 examples to be proposed as a potential relation for A. More clearly:

► $x_1 \xrightarrow{R'_1} B_1$ and $x_2 \xrightarrow{R'_1} B_1 \Rightarrow R'_1 : 2$
$\Longrightarrow$ propose $A \xrightarrow{R'_1?} B_1$

► $x_n \xrightarrow{R'_2} B_2$ $\Rightarrow R'_2 : 1$
$\Longrightarrow$ do not propose this relation.

► $x_1 \xrightarrow{R'_q} B_q$, $x_3 \xrightarrow{R'_q} B_q$ and $x_n \xrightarrow{R'_q} B_q$
$\Rightarrow R'_q : 3$
$\Longrightarrow$ propose $A \xrightarrow{R'_q?} B_q$

For statistical filtering, we can act on the

threshold (δ_2, ω_2) as the minimum number of examples x_i being R' related with a target term B_k. It is also possible to evaluate the weight of the abducted relation as following:

$$w(A \xrightarrow{R'_k} B_k) = \frac{1}{nb_{R'_{cd}}} \sum_{i=1,j=1,k=1}^{n,p,q} \sqrt[3]{w_1 w_2 w_3} \quad (5)$$

where $nb_{R'_{cd}}$ is the number of the relations R' candidate to be proposed and $w_1 = A \xrightarrow{R_j} T_j$ & $w_2 = x_i \xrightarrow{R_j} T_j$ & $w_3 = x_i \xrightarrow{R'_k} B_k$.

This filtering parameters are adjustable according to the user's requirements, so it can fulfil various expectations. Constant values in threshold formulas have been determined empirically.

5 Experimentation

We made an experiment with a unique run of the deduction, induction and abduction engines over the lexical network. Contributors have either accepted or rejected a subset of those candidates during the normal course of their activity. This experiment is for an evaluation purpose only, as actually the system is running iteratively along with contributors and games. The experiment has been done with the parameters given previously, which are determined emprically as those maximizing recall and precision (over a very small subset of the JDM lexical network, around 1‰).

5.1 Appliying Deductions and Inductions

We applied the inference engine on around 25 000 randomly selected terms having at least one hypernym or one hyponym and thus produced by deduction more than 1 500 000 inferences and produced by induction over 360 000 relation candidates. The threshold for filtering was set to a weight of 25. This value is relevant as when a human contributor proposed relation is validated by experts, it is introduced with a default weight of 25.

The transitive *is-a* (Table1) is not very productive which might seems surprising at first glance. In fact, the *is-a* relation is already quite populated in the network, and as such, fewer new relations can be inferred. The figures are inverted for some other relations that are not so well populated in the lexical network but still are potentially valid. The *has-parts* relation and the agent semantic role (the *agent-1* relation) are by far the most productive types.

Relation type	**Proposed %**
is-a (x is a type of y)	6.1
has-parts (x is composed of y)	25.1
holonym (y specific of x)	7.2
typical place (of x)	7.2
charac (x as characteristic y)	13.7
agent-1 (x can do y)	13.3
instr-1 (x instrument of y)	1.7
patient-1 (x can be y)	1
place-1 (x located in the place y)	9.8
place > action (y can be done in place x)	3.4
object > mater (x is made of y)	0.3

Table 1: Global percentages of relations proposed per type for deduction and induction.

Deduction	**% valid**		**% error**		
Relation type	**rlvt**	**¬ rlvnt**	**prem**	**excep**	**pol**
is-a	76%	13%	2%	0%	9%
has-parts	65%	8%	4%	13%	10%
holonym	57%	16%	2%	20%	5%
typical place	78%	12%	1%	4%	5%
charac	82%	4%	2%	8%	4%
agent-1	81%	11%	1%	4%	3%
instr-1	62%	21%	1%	10%	6%
patient-1	47%	32%	3%	7%	11%
place-1	72%	12%	2%	10%	6%
place > action	67%	25%	1%	4%	3%
object > mater	60%	3%	7%	18%	12%

Table 2: Number of propositions produced by deduction and ratio of relations found as true or false.

In tables 2 and 3 are presented some evaluations of the status of the inferences proposed by the inference engine through deduction and induction respectively. Inferences are valid for an overall of 80-90% with around 10% valid but not relevant (like for instance *dog* $\xrightarrow{has-parts}$ *proton*). We observe that error number in premises is quite low, and nevertheless errors can be easily corrected. Of course, not all possible errors are detected through this process. More interestingly, the reconciliation allows in 5% of the cases to identify polysemous terms and refinements. Globally false negatives (inferences voted false while being true) and false positives (inferences voted true while being false) are evaluated to less than 0.5%.

For the induction process, the relation *is-a* is not obvious (a lexical network is not reductible to an ontology and multiple inheritance is possible). Result seems about 5% better than for the deduction process: inferences are valid for an overall of 80-95%. The error number is very low. The main difference with the deduction process is on errors due to polysemy which is lower with the induction process.

To try to assess a baseline for those results, we compute the full closure of the lexical network, i.e. we produce iteratively all possible candidate relations until no more could be found, each candidate being considered as correct and participating to the process. We got more than 6 000 000 relations out of which 45% were wrong (evaluation on around 1 000 candidates randomly chosen).

5.2 Unleashing the Abductive Engine

We applied systematically the abduction engine on the lexical items contained in the network, and produce 629 987 abducted relations out of which 137 416 were not already existing in the network. Those 137 416 are candidate relations concerning 10 889 distinct lexical entries, hence producing a mean of around 12 new relations per entry. The distribution of the proposed relations follows a power law, which is not totally surprising as the relation distribution in the lexical network is by itself governed by such a distribution. Those figures indicate that abduction seems to be still quite productive in terms of raw candidates, even not relying on ontological existing relations.

The table 4 presents the number of relations proposed by the inference engine through abduction. The different relation types are variously productive, and this is mainly due to the number of existing relations and the distribution of their type. The most productive relation is *has-part* and the least one is *holo* (holonym/whole). Correct relations represent around 80% of the relations that have been evaluated (around 5.6% of the total number of produced relations).

One suprising fact, is that the 80% seem to be quite constant notwithstanding the relation type, the lowest value being 77% (for *instr-1* which is the relation specifying what can be done with x as an instrument) and the highest being 85% (for *action-place* which is the relation associating for an action the typical locations where it can occur). The abduction process is not ontologically based, and hence does not rely on the generic (is-a) or specific (hyponym) relations, but on the contrary on any set of examples that seems to be alike the target term. The apparent stability of 80% correct abducted relations may be a positive consequence of relying on a set of examples, with a potentially irreductible of 20% wrong abducted relations.

Figure 4 presents two types of data: (1) the percentage of correct abducted relations according to the number of examples required to produce the inference, and (2) the proportion between the produced relations and the total of 107 416 relations according to the minimal number of examples allowed. What can clearly be seen is that when the number of required examples is increased, the ratio of correct abductions increases accordingly, but the number of proposed relations dramaticaly falls. The number of abductions is an inverse power law of the number of examples required.

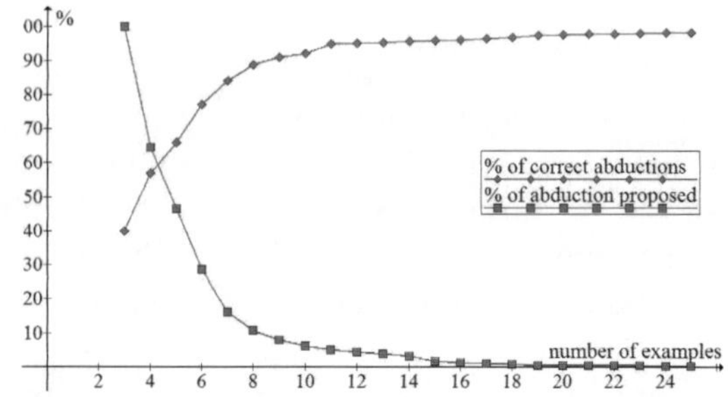

Figure 4: Production of abducted relations and percentage of correctness according to examples number.

At 3 examples, only 40% of the proposed relations are correct, and with a minimum of 6 examples, more than 3/4 of the proposals are deemed correct. The balanced F-score is optimal at the intersection of both curves, that is to say for at least 4 examples.

In figure 5, is showed the mean number of new relations during an iteration of the inference engine on abduction. Between two runs, users and validators are invited to accept or reject abducted relations. This process is done at their discretion and users may leave some propostions unvoted. Experiments showed that users are willing to validate strongly true relations and invalidate clearly false relations. Relations whose status may be difficult are more often left aside than other easiest proposals. The third run is the most productive with a mean of almost 20 new abducted relations. After 3 runs, the abductive process begins to be less productive by attrition of new possible candidates. Notice that the abduction process may, on subsequent runs, remove some previsouly done proposals and as such is not monotonous.

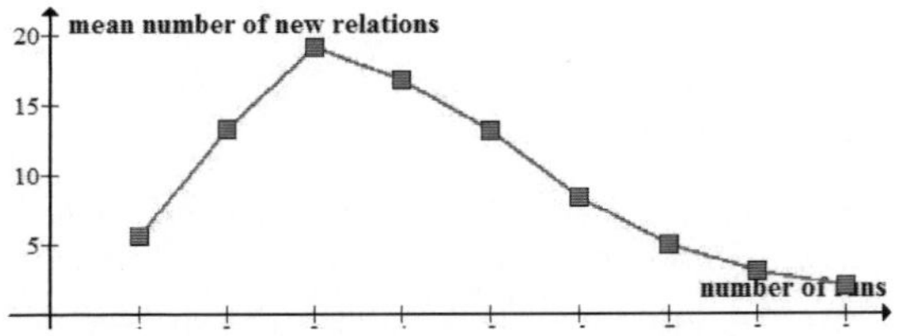

Figure 5: Mean number of new relations relatively to runs in iterated abduction.

5.3 Figures on Reconciliation

Reconciliation in abduction is simpler than in deduction or induction, as the potential adverse effect of polysemy is counterbalanced by the statistical approach implemented by the large number of examples (when available). The reconciliation in the case of abduction is to determine if the wrong proposal has been produced logically considering the support examples. In 97% of the cases, the wrong abducted relation has been qualified as *wrong but logical* by voters or validators. For examples: • *Boeing 747* $\xrightarrow{has-part}$ *propeller** • *whale* $\xrightarrow{place}$ *lake* * • *pelican* $\xrightarrow{agent-1}$ *sing* *. All those wrong abducted relations given as examples above might have been correct. Considering the examples exploited to produce the candidates, in those cases there is no possible way to guess those relations are wrong. This is even reinforced by the fact that abduction does not rely on ontological relations, which in some cases could have avoided wrong abduction. However, abduction compared to induction and deduction, can be used on terms that do not hold ontological relations, either they are missing or they are not relevant (for verbs, instances...).

6 Conclusion

We presented some issues in inferring new relations from existing ones to consolidate a lexical-semantic network built with games and user contributions. New inferred relations are stored to avoid having to infer them again and again dynamically. To be able to enhance the network quality and coverage, we proposed an elicitation engine based on inferences (induction, deduction and abduction) and reconciliation. If an inferred relation is proven wrong, a reconciliation process is conducted in order to identify the underlying cause and solve the problem. The abduction scheme does not rely on the ontological relation (is-a) but merely on examples that are similarly close to the target term. Experiments showed that abduction is quite productive (compared to deduction and induction), and is stable in correctness. User evaluation showed that wrong abducted relations (around 20% of all abducted relations) are still logically sound and could not have been dismissed *a priori*. Abduction can conclusively be considered as a usefull and efficient tool for relation inference. The main difficulty relies in setting the various parameter in order to achieve a fragile tradeoff between an overrestrictive filter (many false negatives, resulting in information losses) and the opposite (many false postive, more human effort).

The elicitation engine we presented through schemas based on deduction, induction and abduction is an efficient error detector, a polysemy identifier but also a classifier by abduction. The actions taken during the reconciliation forbid an inference proven wrong or exceptional to be inferred again. Each inference scheme is supported by the two others, and if a given inference has been produced by more than one of these three schemas, it is almost surely correct.

Induction	**% valid**		**% error**		
Relation types	**rlvt**	**¬rlvnt**	**prem**	**excep**	**pol**
is-a	-	-	-	-	-
has-parts	78%	10%	3%	2%	7%
holonyme	68%	17%	2%	8%	5%
typical place	81%	13%	1%	2%	3%
charac	87%	6%	2%	2%	3%
agent-1	84%	12%	1%	2%	1%
instr-1	68%	24%	1%	4%	3%
patient-1	57%	36%	3%	2%	2%
place-1	75%	16%	2%	5%	2%
place > action	67%	28%	1%	3%	1%
object > mater	75%	10%	7%	5%	3%

Table 3: Number of propositions produced by induction and ratio of relations found as true or false.

Abduction	**#prop**	**#eval (%)**	**True (%)**	**False (%)**
is-a	7141	421 (5.9)	343 (81.5)	78 (18.5)
has-parts	26517	720 (2.7)	578 (80.3)	142 (19.7)
holo	1592	153 (9.6)	124 (81)	29 (18.9)
agent	7739	298 (3.9)	236 (79.2)	62 (20.8)
place	17148	304 (1.8)	253 (83.2)	51 (16.8)
instr	10790	431 (4)	356 (82.6)	75 (17.4)
charac	7443	319 (4.3)	251 (78.7)	68 (21.3)
agent-1	18147	955 (5.3)	780 (81.7)	175 (18.3)
instr-1	11867	886 (7.5)	682 (77)	204 (23)
place-1	14787	1106 (7.5)	896 (81)	210 (19)
place>act	8268	270 (3.3)	214 (79.3)	56 (20.7)
act>place	5976	170 (2.8)	145 (85.3)	25 (14.7)
Total	137416	6033 (4.3)	4858 (81)	1175 (19)

Table 4: Number of propositions produced by abduction and ratio of relations found as true or false.

References

von Ahn, L. and Dabbish, L. 2008. *Designing games with a purpose.* in Communications of the ACM, number 8, volume 51. p 58-67.

Besnard, P. Cordier, M.-O., and Moinard, Y. 2008. *Ontology-based inference for causal explanation.* Integrated Computer-Aided Engineering , IOS Press, Amsterdam, Vol. 15 , No. 4, 351-367, 2008.

Fellbaum, C. and Miller, G. 1988. *(eds) WordNet.* The MIT Press.

Krachina, O., Raskin, V. 2006. *Ontology-Based Inference Methods.* CERIAS TR 2006-76, 6 p.

Lafourcade, M. 2007. *Making people play for Lexical Acquisition.* In Proc. SNLP 2007, 7th Symposium on Natural Language Processing. Pattaya, Thailande, 13-15 December. 8 p.

Lafourcade, M., Joubert, A. 2012. *Long Tail in Weighted Lexical Networks.* In proc of Cognitive Aspects of the Lexicon (CogAlex-III), COLING, Mumbai, India, December 2012.

Lieberman, H, Smith, D. A and Teeters, A 2007. *Common consensus: a web-based game for collecting commonsense goals.* In Proc. of IUI, Hawaii,2007.12 p .

Marchetti, A and Tesconi, M and Ronzano, F and Mosella, M and Minutoli, S. 2007. *SemKey: A Semantic Collaborative Tagging System.* in Procs of WWW2007, Banff, Canada. 9 p.

Mihalcea, R and Chklovski, T. 2003. *Open MindWord Expert: Creating large annotated data collections with web users help..* In Proceedings of the EACL 2003, Workshop on Linguistically Annotated Corpora (LINC). 10 p.

Miller, G.A. and Beckwith, R. and Fellbaum, C. and Gross, D. and Miller, K.J. 1990. *Introduction to WordNet: an on-line lexical database.* International Journal of Lexicography. Volume 3, p 235-244.

Navigli, R and Ponzetto, S. 2010. *BabelNet: Building a very large multilingual semantic network.* in Proceedings of the 48th Annual Meeting of the Association for Computational Linguistics, Uppsala, Sweden, 11-16 July 2010.p 216-225.

Sagot, B. and Fier, D. 2010. *Construction d'un wordnet libre du français à partir de ressources multilingues.* in Proceedings of TALN 2008, Avignon, France, 2008.12 p.

Sajous, F., Navarro, E., Gaume, B,. Prévot, L. and Chudy, Y. 2013. *Semi-Automatic Enrichment of Crowdsourced Synonymy Networks: The WISIGOTH system applied to Wiktionary.* Language Resources & Evaluation, 47(1), pp. 63-96.

Siorpaes, K. and Hepp, M. 2008. *Games with a Purpose for the Semantic Web.* in IEEE Intelligent Systems, number 3, volume 23.p 50-60.

Snow, R. Jurafsky, D., Y. Ng., A. 2006. *Semantic taxonomy induction from heterogenous evidence.* in Proceedings of COLING/ACL 2006, 8 p.

Thaler, S and Siorpaes, K and Simperl, E. and Hofer, C. 2011. *A Survey on Games for Knowledge Acquisition.* STI Technical Report, May 2011.19 p.

Velardi, P. Navigli, R. Cucchiarelli, A. Neri, F. 2006. *Evaluation of OntoLearn, a methodology for Automatic Learning of Ontologies.* in Ontology Learning and Population, Paul Buitelaar Philipp Cimmiano and Bernardo Magnini Editors, IOS press 2006).

Vossen, P. 2011. *EuroWordNet: a multilingual database with lexical semantic networks.* Kluwer Academic Publishers.Norwell, MA, USA.200 p.

Zeichner, N., Berant J., and Dagan I. 2012. *Crowdsourcing Inference-Rule Evaluation.* in proc of ACL 2012 (short papers).

Incremental Query Generation

Laura Perez-Beltrachini
Faculty of Computer Science
Free University of Bozen-Bolzano
Bozen-Bolzano, Italy
laura.perez@loria.fr

Claire Gardent
CNRS/LORIA
Nancy, France
claire.gardent@loria.fr

Enrico Franconi
Faculty of Computer Science
Free University of Bozen-Bolzano
Bozen-Bolzano, Italy
franconi@inf.unibz.it

Abstract

We present a natural language generation system which supports the incremental specification of ontology-based queries in natural language. Our contribution is two fold. First, we introduce a chart based surface realisation algorithm which supports the kind of incremental processing required by ontology-based querying. Crucially, this algorithm avoids confusing the end user by preserving a consistent ordering of the query elements throughout the incremental query formulation process. Second, we show that grammar based surface realisation better supports the generation of fluent, natural sounding queries than previous template-based approaches.

1 Introduction

Previous research has shown that formal ontologies could be used as a means not only to provide a uniform and flexible approach to integrating and describing heterogeneous data sources, but also to support the final user in querying them, thus improving the usability of the integrated system. To support the wide access to these data sources, it is crucial to develop efficient and user-friendly ways to query them (Wache et al., 2001).

In this paper, we present a Natural Language (NL) interface of an ontology-based query tool, called Quelo[1], which allows the end user to formulate a query without any knowledge either of the formal languages used to specify ontologies, or of the content of the ontology being used. Following the conceptual authoring approach described in (Tennant et al., 1983; Hallett et al., 2007), this interface masks the composition of a formal query as the composition of an English text describing the equivalent information needs using natural language generation techniques. The natural language generation system that we propose for Quelo's NL interface departs from similar work (Hallett et al., 2007; Franconi et al., 2010a; Franconi et al., 2011b; Franconi et al., 2010b; Franconi et al., 2011a) in that it makes use of standard grammar based surface realisation techniques. Our contribution is two fold. First, we introduce a chart based surface realisation algorithm which supports the kind of incremental processing required by ontology driven query formulation. Crucially, this algorithm avoids confusing the end user by preserving a consistent ordering of the query elements throughout the incremental query formulation process. Second, we show that grammar based surface realisation better supports the generation of fluent, natural sounding queries than previous template-based approaches.

The paper is structured as follows. Section 2 discusses related work and situates our approach. Section 3 describes the task being addressed namely, ontology driven query formulation. It introduces the input being handled, the constraints under which generation operates and the operations the user may perform to build her query. In Section 4, we present the generation algorithm used to support the verbalisation of possible queries. Section 5 reports on an evaluation of the system with respect to fluency, clarity, coverage and incrementality. Section 6 concludes with pointers for further research.

2 Related Work

Our approach is related to two main strands of work: incremental generation and conceptual authoring.

Incremental Generation (Oh and Rudnicky, 2000) used an n-gram language model to stochas-

[1] krdbapp.inf.unibz.it:8080/quelo

tically generate system turns. The language model is trained on a dialog corpus manually annotated with word and utterance classes. The generation engine uses the appropriate language model for the utterance class and generates word sequences randomly according to the language model distribution. The generated word sequences are then ranked using a scoring mechanism and only the best-scored utterance is kept. The system is incremental is that each word class to be verbalised can yield a new set of utterance candidates. However it supports only addition not revisions. Moreover it requires domain specific training data and manual annotation while the approach we propose is unsupervised and generic to any ontology.

(Dethlefs et al., 2013) use Conditional Random Fields to find the best surface realisation from a semantic tree. They show that the resulting system is able to modify generation results on the fly when new or updated input is provided by the dialog manager. While their approach is fast to execute, it is limited to a restricted set of domain specific attributes; requires a training corpus of example sentences to define the space of possible surface realisations; and is based on a large set (800 rules) of domain specific rules extracted semi-automatically from the training corpus. In contrast, we use a general, small size grammar (around 50 rules) and a lexicon which is automatically derived from the input ontologies. The resulting system requires no training and thus can be applied to any ontology with any given signature of concepts and relations. Another difference between the two approaches concerns revisions: while our approach supports revisions anywhere in the input, the CRF approach proposed by (Dethlefs et al., 2013) only supports revisions occurring at the end of the generated string.

There is also much work (Schlangen and Skantze, 2009; Schlangen et al., 2009) in the domain of spoken dialog systems geared at modelling the incremental nature of dialog and in particular, at developing dialog systems where processing starts before the input is complete. In these approaches, the focus is on developing efficient architectures which support the timely interleaving of parsing and generation. Instead, our aim is to develop a principled approach to the incremental generation of a user query which supports revision and additions at arbitrary points of the query being built; generates natural sounding text; and maximally preserves the linear order of the query.

Conceptual authoring Our proposal is closely related to the conceptual authoring approach described in (Hallett et al., 2007). In this approach, a text generated from a knowledge base, describes in natural language the knowledge encoded so far, and the options for extending it. Starting with an initial very general query (e.g., all things), the user can formulate a query by choosing between these options. Similarly, (Franconi et al., 2010a; Franconi et al., 2011b; Franconi et al., 2010b; Franconi et al., 2011a) describes a conceptual authoring approach to querying semantic data where in addition , logical inference is used to semantically constrain the possible completions/revisions displayed to the user.

Our approach departs from this work in that it makes use of standard grammars and algorithms. While previous work was based on procedures and templates, we rely on a Feature-Based Tree Adjoining Grammar to capture the link between text and semantics required by conceptual authoring; and we adapt a chart based algorithm to support the addition, the revision and the substitution of input material. To avoid confusing the user, we additionally introduce a scoring function which helps preserve the linear order of the NL query. The generation system we present is in fact integrated in the Quelo interface developed by (Franconi et al., 2011a) and compared with their previous template-based approach.

3 Incremental Generation of Candidate Query Extensions

The generation task we address is the following. Given a knowledge base K, some initial formal query q and a focus point p in that query, the reasoning services supported by Quelo's query logic framework (see (Guagliardo, 2009)) will compute a set of new queries $rev(q)$ formed by adding, deleting and revising the current query q at point p. The task of the generator is then to produce a natural language sentence for each new formal query $q' \in rev(q)$ which results from this revision process. In other words, each time the user refines a query q to produce a new query q', the system computes all revisions $rev(q)$ of q' that are compatible with the underlying knowledge base using a reasoner. Each of these possible revisions is then input to the generator and the resulting revised NL queries are displayed to the user. In what follows, we assume that formal queries are represented using Description Logics (Baader, 2003).

The following examples show a possible sequence of NL queries, their corresponding DL representation and the operations provided by Quelo that can be performed on a query (bold face is used to indicate the point in the query at which the next revision takes place). For instance, the query in (1c) results from adding the concept $Young$ to the query underlying (1b) at the point highlighted by **man**.

(1) a. I am looking for **something** (initial query)
$\top$

b. I am looking for **a man** (substitute concept)
Man

c. I am looking for a young **man** (add compatible concept)
$Man \sqcap Young$

d. I am looking for a young **man who is married to a person** (add relation)
$Man \sqcap Young \sqcap \exists isMarried.(Person)$

e. I am looking for a **young** married man (substitute selection)
$MarriedMan \sqcap Young$

f. I am looking for a married man (delete concept)
$MarriedMan$

4 Generating Queries

Generation of KB queries differs from standard natural language generation algorithms in two main ways. First it should support the revisions, deletions and additions required by incremental processing. Second, to avoid confusing the user, the revisions (modifications, extensions, deletions) performed by the user should have a minimal effect on the linear order of the NL query. That is the generator is not free to produce any NL variant verbalising the query but should produce a verbalisation that is linearly as close as possible, modulo the revision applied by the user, to the query before revisions. Thus for instance, given the DL query (2) and assuming a linearisation of that formula that matches the linear order it is presented in (see Section 4.2.1 below for a definition of the linearisation of DL formulae), sentence (2b) will be preferred over (2c).

(2) a. $Car \sqcap \exists runOn.(Diesel) \sqcap \exists equippedWith.(AirCond)$

b. A car which runs on Diesel and is equipped with air conditioning

c. A car which is equipped with air conditioning and runs on Diesel

In what follows, we describe the generation algorithm used to verbalise possible extensions of user queries as proposed by the Quelo tool. We start by introducing and motivating the underlying formal language supported by Quelo and the input to the generator. We then describe the overall architecture of our generator. Finally, we present the incremental surface realisation algorithm supporting the verbalisation of the possible query extensions.

4.1 The Input Language

Following (Franconi et al., 2010a; Franconi et al., 2011b; Franconi et al., 2010b; Franconi et al., 2011a) we assume a formal language for queries that targets the querying of various knowledge and data bases independent of their specification language. To this end, it uses a minimal query language $\mathcal{L}$ that is shared by most knowledge representation languages and is supported by Description Logic (DL) reasoners namely, the language of tree shaped conjunctive DL queries. Let $\mathcal{R}$ be a set of relations and $\mathcal{C}$ be a set of concepts, then the language of tree-shaped conjunctive DL queries is defined as follows: $S ::= C \mid \exists R.(S) \mid S \sqcap S$ where $R \in \mathcal{R}$, $C \in \mathcal{C}$, $\sqcap$ denotes conjunction and $\exists$ is the existential quantifier.

A tree shaped conjunctive DL query can be represented as a tree where nodes are associated with a set of concept names (*node labels*) and edges are labelled with a relation name (*edge labels*). Figure 1 shows some example query trees.

4.2 NLG architecture

Our generator takes as input two $\mathcal{L}$ formula: the formula representing the current query q and the formula representing a possible revision r (addition/deletion/modification) of q. Given this input, the system architecture follows a traditional pipeline sequencing a document planner which (i) linearises the input query and (ii) partition the input into sentence size chunks; a surface realiser mapping each sentence size $\mathcal{L}$ formula into a sentence; and a referring expression generator verbalising NPs.

4.2.1 Document Planning

The document planning module linearises the input query and segments the resulting linearised

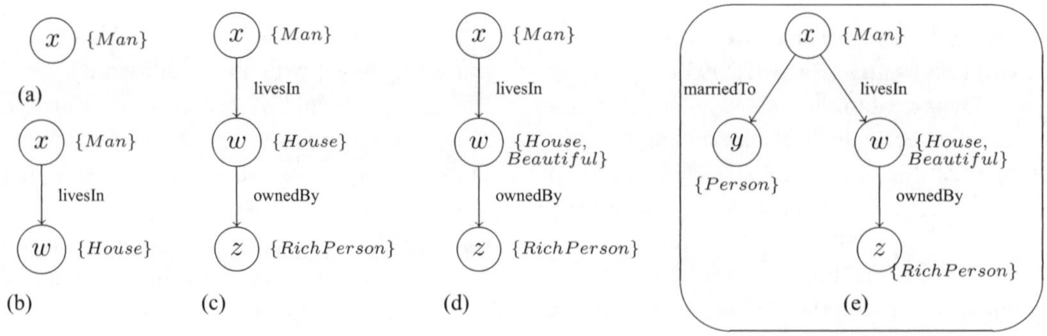

Figure 1: Example of query tree and incremental query construction.

query into sentence size chunks.

Query Linearisation Among the different strategies investigated in (Dongilli, 2008) to find a good order for the content contained in a query tree the *depth-first planning*, i.e. depth-first traversal of the query tree, was found to be the most appropriate one. Partly because it is obtained straightforward from the query tree but mostly due to the fact that it minimizes the changes in the text plan that are required by incremental query modifications. Thus, (Franconi et al., 2010a) defines a *query linearisation* as a strict total order[2] on the query tree that satisfies the following conditions:

- all labels associated with the edge's leaving node precede the edge label
- the edge label is followed by at least one label associated with the edge's arriving node
- between any two labels of a node there can only be (distinct) labels of the same node

The specific linearisation adopted in Quelo is defined by the depth-first traversal strategy of the query tree and a total order on the children which is based on the query operations. That is, the labels of a node are ordered according to the sequence applications of the `add compatible concept` operation. The children of a node are inversely ordered according to the sequence of applications of the `add relation` operation.

According to this linearisation definition, for the query tree (e) in Figure 1 the following linear order is produced:

(3) a. Man marriedTo $Person$ livesIn $House$ $Beautiful$ ownedBy $RichPeron$

[2]A strict total order can be obtained by fixing an order in the children nodes and traversing the tree according to some tree traversal strategy.

Query Segmentation Given a linearised query q, the document planner uses some heuristics based on the number and the types of relations/concepts present in q to output a sequence of sub-formulae each of which will be verbalised as a sentence.

4.2.2 Incremental Surface Realisation and Linearisation Constraints

We now describe the main module of the generator namely the surface realiser which supports both the incremental refinement of a query and a minimal modification of the linear order between increments. This surface realiser is caracterised by the following three main features.

Grammar-Based We use a symbolic, grammar-based approach rather than a statistical one for two reasons. First, there is no training corpus available that would consist of knowledge base queries and their increments. Second, the approach must be portable and should apply to any knowledge base independent of the domain it covers and independent of the presence of a training corpus. By combining a lexicon automatically extracted from the ontology with a small grammar tailored to produce natural sounding queries, we provide a generator which can effectively apply to any ontology without requiring the construction of a training corpus.

Chart-Based A chart-based architecture enhances efficiency by avoiding the recomputation of intermediate structures while allowing for a natural implementation of the revisions (addition, deletion, substitution) operations required by the incremental formulation of user queries. We show how the chart can be used to implement these operations.

Beam search. As already mentioned, for ergonomic reasons, the linear order of the generated NL query should be minimally disturbed during query formulation. The generation system should also be sufficiently fast to support a timely Man/Machine interaction. We use beam search and a customised scoring function both to preserve linear order and to support efficiency.

We now introduce each of these components in more details.

Feature-Based Tree Adjoining Grammar A tree adjoining grammar (TAG) is a tuple $\langle \Sigma, N, I, A, S \rangle$ with Σ a set of terminals, N a set of non-terminals, I a finite set of initial trees, A a finite set of auxiliary trees, and S a distinguished non-terminal ($S \in N$). Initial trees are trees whose leaves are labeled with substitution nodes (marked with a down-arrow) or with terminal categories[3]. Auxiliary trees are distinguished by a foot node (marked with a star) whose category must be the same as that of the root node.

Two tree-composition operations are used to combine trees: substitution and adjunction. Substitution inserts a tree onto a substitution node of some other tree while adjunction inserts an auxiliary tree into a tree. In a Feature-Based Lexicalised TAG (FB-LTAG), tree nodes are furthermore decorated with two feature structures which are unified during derivation; and each tree is anchored with a lexical item. Figure 2 shows an example toy FB-LTAG with unification semantics. The dotted arrows indicate possible tree combinations (substitution for *John*, adjunction for *often*). As the trees are combined, the semantics is the union of their semantics modulo unification. Thus given the grammar and the derivation shown, the semantics of *John often runs* is as shown namely, *named(j john), run(a,j), often(a)*.

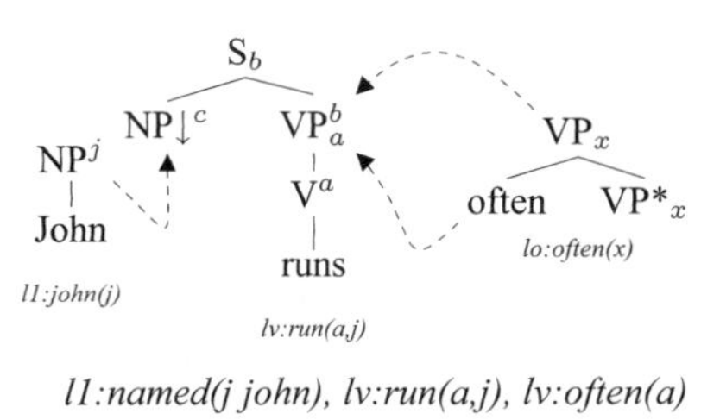

Figure 2: Derivation and Semantics for "John often runs"

Chart-Based Surface Realisation Given an FB-LTAG G of the type described above, sentences can be generated from semantic formulae by (i) selecting all trees in G whose semantics subsumes part of the input formula and (ii) combining these trees using the FB-LTAG combining operations namely substitution and adjunction. Thus for instance, in Figure 2, given the semantics *l1:named(j john), lv:run(a,j), lv:often(a)*, the three trees shown are selected. When combined they produce a complete phrase structure tree whose yield (*John runs often*) is the generated sentence.

Following (Gardent and Perez-Beltrachini, 2011), we implement an Earley style generation algorithm for FB-LTAG which makes use of the fact that the derivation trees of an FB-LTAG are context free and that an FB-LTAG can be converted to a a Feature-Based Regular Tree Grammar (FB-RTG) describing the derivation trees of this FB-LTAG[4].

On the one hand, this Earley algorithm enhances efficiency in that (i) it avoids recomputing intermediate structures by storing them and (ii) it packs locally equivalent structures into a single representative (the most general one). Locally equivalent structures are taken to be partial derivation trees with identical semantic coverage and similar combinatorics (same number and type of substitution and adjunction requirements).

On the other hand, it naturally supports the range of revisions required for the incremental formulation of ontology-based queries. Let C be the current chart i.e., the chart built when generating a NL query from the formal query. Then additions, revisions and deletion can be handled as follows.

- Add concept or property X: the grammar units selected by X are added to the agenda[5] and tried for combinations with the elements of C.
- Substitute selection X with Y: all chart items derived from a grammar unit selected by an element of X are removed from the chart. Conversely, all chart items derived from a grammar unit selected by an element of Y are added to the agenda. All items in the agenda are then processed until generation halts.
- Delete selection X: all chart items derived from a grammar unit selected by an element of X are removed from the chart. Intermediate structures that had previously used X are moved to the agenda and the agenda is processed until generation halts.

[3]For a more detailed introduction to TAG and FB-LTAG, see (Vijay-Shanker and Joshi, 1988).

[4]For more details on this algorithm, we refer the reader to (Gardent and Perez-Beltrachini, 2010).

[5]The agenda is a book keeping device which stores all items that needs to be processed i.e., which need to be tried for combination with elements in the chart.

Beam Search To enhance efficiency and favor those structures which best preserve the word order while covering maximal input, we base our beam search on a scoring function combining linear order and semantic coverage information. This works as follows. First, we associate each literal in the input query with its positional information e.g.,

(4) a. `man(x)[0] marriedTo(x y)[1] person(y)[2] livesIn(x w)[3] house(w)[4]`

This positional information is copied over to each FB-LTAG tree selected by a given literal and is then used to compute a *word order cost* (C_{wo}) for each derived tree as follows:

$$C_{wo}(t_{i+j}) = C_{wo}(t_i) + C_{wo}(t_j) + C_{wo}(t_i + t_j)$$

That is the cost of a tree t_{i+j} obtained by combining t_i and t_j is the sum of the cost of each of these trees plus the cost incurred by combining these two trees. We define this latter cost to be proportional to the distance separating the actual position (ap_i) of the tree (t_i) being substituted/adjoined in from its required position (rp_i). If t_i is substituted/adjoined at position n to the right (left) of the anchor of a tree t_j with position p_j, then the actual position of t_i is $pj + n$ ($pj - n$) and the cost of combining t_i with t_j is $\mid pj + n - rp_i \mid / \alpha$ ($\mid pj - n - rp_i \mid / \alpha$) where we empirically determined α to be 100[6].

Finally, the total score of a tree reflects the relation between the cost of the built tree, i.e. its word order cost, and its semantic coverage, i.e. nb. of literals from the input semantics:

$$S(t_i) = \begin{cases} -(|\text{literals}| - 1) & C_{wo}(t_i) = 0 \\ C_{wo}(t_i)/(|\text{literals}| - 1) & \text{otherwise} \end{cases}$$

The total score is defined by cases. Those trees with $C_{wo} = 0$ get a negative value according to their input coverage (i.e. those that cover a larger subset of the input semantics are favored as the trees in the agenda are ordered by increasing total score). Conversely, those trees with $C_{wo} > 0$ get a score that is the word order cost proportional to the covered input.

In effect, this scoring mechanism favors trees with low word order cost and large semantic coverage. The beam search will select those trees with lowest score.

[6]In the current implementation we assume that $n = 1$. Furthermore, as t_i might be a derived tree we also add to $C_{wo}(t_i + t_j)$ the cost computed on each tree t_k used in the derivation of t_i with respect to t_j.

4.2.3 Referring Expression Generation

The referring expression (RE) module takes as input the sequence of phrase structure trees output by the surface realiser and uses heuristics to decide for each NP whether it should be verbalised as a pronoun, a definite or an indefinite NP. These heuristics are based on the linear order and morpho-syntactic information contained in the phrase structure trees of the generated sentences.

5 Experiments and evaluation

We conducted evaluation experiments designed to address the following questions:

- Does the scoring mechanism appropriately capture the ordering constraints on the generated queries ? That is, does it ensure that the generated queries respect the strict total order of the query tree linearisation ?
- Does our grammar based approach produce more fluent and less ambiguous NL query than the initial template based approach currently used by Quelo ?
- Does the automatic extraction of lexicons from ontology support generic coverage of arbitrary ontologies ?

We start by describing the grammar used. We then report on the results obtained for each of these evaluation points.

5.1 Grammar and Lexicon

We specify an FB-LTAG with unification semantics which covers a set of basic constructions used to formulate queries namely, active and passive transitive verbs, adjectives, prepositional phrases, relative and elliptical clauses, gerund and participle modifiers. The resulting grammar consists of 53 FB-LTAG pairs of syntactic trees and semantic schema.

To ensure the appropriate syntax/semantic interface, we make explicit the arguments of a relation using the variables associated with the nodes of the query tree. Thus for instance, given the rightmost query tree shown in Figure 1, the flat semantics input to surface realisation is {*Man(x), Person(y), House(w), Beautiful(w), RichPerson(z), marriedTo(x,y), livesIn(x,w), ownedBy(w,z)*}.

For each ontology, a lexicon mapping concepts and relations to FB-LTAG trees is automatically derived from the ontology using (Trevisan, 2010)'s approach. We specify for each experiment below, the size of the extracted lexicon.

5.2 Linearisation

In this first experiment, we manually examined whether the incremental algorithm we propose supports the generation of NL queries whose word order matches the linearisation of the input query tree.

We created four series of queries such that each serie is a sequence $q_1 \dots q_n$ where q_{i+1} is an increment of q_i. That is, q_{i+1} is derived from q_i by adding, removing or substituting to q_i a concept or a relation. The series were devised so as to encompass the whole range of possible operations at different points of the preceding query (e.g., at the last node/edge or on some node/edge occurring further to the left of the previous query); and include 14 revisions on 4 initial queries.

For all queries, the word order of the best NL query produced by the generator was found to match the linearisation of the DL query.

5.3 Fluency and Clarity

Following the so-called *consensus model* (Power and Third, 2010), the current, template based version of Quelo generates one clause per relation[7]. Thus for instance, template-based Quelo will generate (5a) while our grammar based approach supports the generation of arguably more fluent sentences such as (5b).

(5) a. I am looking for a car. Its make should be a Land Rover. The body style of the car should be an off-road car. The exterior color of the car should be beige.

b. I am looking for car whose make is a Land Rover, whose body style is an off-road car and whose exterior color is beige.

We ran two experiments designed to assess how fluency impacts users. The first experiment aims to assess how Quelo template based queries are perceived by the users in terms of clarity and fluency, the second aims to compare these template based queries with the queries produced by our grammar-based approach.

Assessing Quelo template-based queries Using the Quelo interface, we generated a set of 41 queries chosen to capture different combinations of concepts and relations. Eight persons (four native speakers of English, four with C2 level of competence for foreign learners of English) were then asked to classify (a binary choice) each query in terms of clarity and fluency. Following (Kow and Belz, 2012), we take *Fluency* to be a single quality criterion intended to capture language quality as distinct from its meaning, i.e. how well a piece of text reads. In contrast, *Clarity/ambiguity* refers to ease of understanding (Is the sentence easy to understand?). Taking the average of the majority vote, we found that the judges evaluated the queries as non fluent in 50% of the cases and as unclear in 10% of the cases. In other words, template based queries were found to be disfluent about half of the time and unclear to a lesser extent. The major observation made by most of the participants was that the generated text is too repetitive and lacks aggregation.

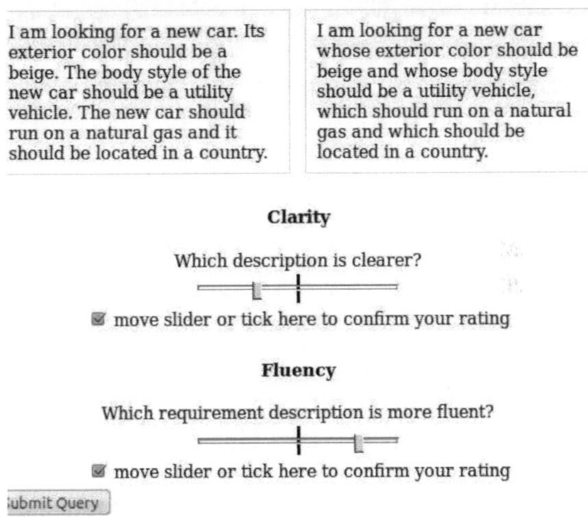

Figure 3: Online Evaluation.

Comparing template- and grammar-based queries In this second experiment, we asked 10 persons (all proficient in the English language) to compare pairs of NL queries where one query is produced using templates and the other using our grammar-based generation algorithm. The evaluation was done online using the LG-Eval toolkit (Kow and Belz, 2012) and geared to collect relative quality judgements using visual analogue scales. After logging in, judges were given a description of the task. The sentence pairs were displayed as shown in Figure 3 with one sentence to the left and the other to the right. The judges were instructed to move the slider to the left to favor the sentence shown on the left side of the screen; and to the right to favor the sentence appearing to the right. Not moving the slider means that both sentences rank equally. To avoid creating a bias,

[7]This is modulo aggregation of relations. Thus two subject sharing relations may be realised in the same clause.

the sentences from both systems were equally distributed to both sides of the screen.

For this experiment, we used 14 queries built from two ontologies, an ontology on cars and the other on universities. The extracted lexicons for each of these ontology contained 465 and 297 entries respectively.

The results indicate that the queries generated by the grammar based approach are perceived as more fluent than those produced by the template based approach (19.76 points in average for the grammar based approach against 7.20 for the template based approach). Furthermore, although the template based queries are perceived as clearer (8.57 for Quelo, 6.87 for our approach), the difference is not statistically significant ($p < 0.5$). Overall thus, the grammar based approach appears to produce verbalisations that are better accepted by the users. Concerning clarity, we observed that longer sentences let through by document planning were often deemed unclear. In future work, we plan to improve clarity by better integrating document planning and sentence realisation.

5.4 Coverage

One motivation for the symbolic based approach was the lack of training corpus and the need for portability: the query interface should be usable independently of the underlying ontology and of the existence of a training corpus. To support coverage, we combined the grammar based approach with a lexicon which is automatically extracted from the ontology using the methodology described in (Trevisan, 2010). When tested on a corpus of 200 ontologies, this approach was shown to be able to provide appropriate verbalisation templates for about 85% of the relation identifiers present in these ontologies. 12 000 relation identifiers were extracted from the 200 ontologies and 13 syntactic templates were found to be sufficient to verbalise these relation identifiers (see (Trevisan, 2010) for more details on this evaluation).

That is, in general, the extracted lexicons permit covering about 85% of the ontological data. In addition, we evaluated the coverage of our approach by running the generator on 40 queries generated from five distinct ontologies. The domains observed are cinema, wines, human abilities, disabilities, and assistive devices, e-commerce on the Web, and a fishery database for observations about an aquatic resource. The extracted lexicons contained in average 453 lexical entries and the coverage (proportion of DL queries for which the generator produced a NL query) was 87%.

Fuller coverage could be obtained by manually adding lexical entries, or by developing new ways of inducing lexical entries from ontologies (c.f. e.g. (Walter et al., 2013)).

6 Conclusion

Conceptual authoring (CA) allows the user to query a knowledge base without having any knowledge either of the formal representation language used to specify that knowledge base or of the content of the knowledge base. Although this approach builds on a tight integration between syntax and semantics and requires an efficient processing of revisions, existing CA tools predominantly make use of ad hoc generation algorithms and restricted computational grammars (e.g., Definite Clause Grammars or templates). In this paper, we have shown that FB-LTAG and chart based surface realisation provide a natural framework in which to implement conceptual authoring. In particular, we show that the chart based approach naturally supports the definition of an incremental algorithm for query verbalisation; and that the added fluency provided by the grammar based approach potentially provides for query interfaces that are better accepted by the human evaluators.

In the future, we would like to investigate the interaction between context, document structuring and surface realisation. In our experiments we found out that this interaction strongly impacts fluency whereby for instance, a complex sentence might be perceived as more fluent than several clauses but a too long sentence will be perceived as difficult to read (non fluent). Using data that can now be collected using our grammar based approach to query verbalisation and generalising over FB-LTAG tree names rather than lemmas or POS tags, we plan to explore how e.g., Conditional Random Fields can be used to model these interactions.

Acknowledgments

We would like to thank Marco Trevisan, Paolo Guagliardo and Alexandre Denis for facilitating the access to the libraries they developed and to Natalia Korchagina and the judges who participated in the evaluation experiments.

References

Franz Baader. 2003. *The description logic handbook: theory, implementation, and applications*. Cambridge university press.

Nina Dethlefs, Helen Hastie, Heriberto Cuayáhuitl, and Oliver Lemon. 2013. Conditional Random Fields for Responsive Surface Realisation using Global Features. *Proceedings of ACL, Sofia, Bulgaria.*

Paolo Dongilli. 2008. Natural language rendering of a conjunctive query. *KRDB Research Centre Technical Report No. KRDB08-3). Bozen, IT: Free University of Bozen-Bolzano*, 2:5.

E. Franconi, P. Guagliardo, and M. Trevisan. 2010a. An intelligent query interface based on ontology navigation. In *Workshop on Visual Interfaces to the Social and Semantic Web, VISSW*, volume 10. Citeseer.

E. Franconi, P. Guagliardo, and M. Trevisan. 2010b. Quelo: a NL-based intelligent query interface. In *Pre-Proceedings of the Second Workshop on Controlled Natural Languages*, volume 622.

E. Franconi, P. Guagliardo, S. Tessaris, and M. Trevisan. 2011a. A natural language ontology-driven query interface. In *9th International Conference on Terminology and Artificial Intelligence*, page 43.

E. Franconi, P. Guagliardo, M. Trevisan, and S. Tessaris. 2011b. Quelo: an Ontology-Driven Query Interface. In *Description Logics*.

C. Gardent and L. Perez-Beltrachini. 2010. RTG based Surface Realisation for TAG. In *COLING'10*, Beijing, China.

B. Gottesman Gardent, C. and L. Perez-Beltrachini. 2011. Using regular tree grammar to enhance surface realisation. *Natural Language Engineering*, 17:185–201. Special Issue on Finite State Methods and Models in Natural Language Processing.

Paolo Guagliardo. 2009. Theoretical foundations of an ontology-based visual tool for query formulation support. Technical report, KRDB Research Centre, Free University of Bozen-Bolzano, October.

C. Hallett, D. Scott, and R. Power. 2007. Composing questions through conceptual authoring. *Computational Linguistics*, 33(1):105–133.

Eric Kow and Anja Belz. 2012. LG-Eval: A Toolkit for Creating Online Language Evaluation Experiments. In *LREC*, pages 4033–4037.

Alice H Oh and Alexander I Rudnicky. 2000. Stochastic language generation for spoken dialogue systems. In *Proceedings of the 2000 ANLP/NAACL Workshop on Conversational systems-Volume 3*, pages 27–32. Association for Computational Linguistics.

R. Power and A. Third. 2010. Expressing owl axioms by english sentences: dubious in theory, feasible in practice. In *Proceedings of the 23rd International Conference on Computational Linguistics: Posters*, pages 1006–1013. Association for Computational Linguistics.

David Schlangen and Gabriel Skantze. 2009. A general, abstract model of incremental dialogue processing. In *Proceedings of the 12th Conference of the European Chapter of the Association for Computational Linguistics*, pages 710–718. Association for Computational Linguistics.

David Schlangen, Timo Baumann, and Michaela Atterer. 2009. Incremental reference resolution: The task, metrics for evaluation, and a bayesian filtering model that is sensitive to disfluencies. In *Proceedings of the SIGDIAL 2009 Conference: The 10th Annual Meeting of the Special Interest Group on Discourse and Dialogue*, pages 30–37. Association for Computational Linguistics.

H. R Tennant, K. M Ross, R. M Saenz, C. W Thompson, and J. R Miller. 1983. Menu-based natural language understanding. In *Proceedings of the 21st annual meeting on Association for Computational Linguistics*, pages 151–158. Association for Computational Linguistics.

Marco Trevisan. 2010. *A Portable Menuguided Natural Language Interface to Knowledge Bases for Querytool*. Ph.D. thesis, Masters thesis, Free University of Bozen-Bolzano (Italy) and University of Groningen (Netherlands).

K. Vijay-Shanker and A. Joshi. 1988. Feature based tags. In *Proceedings of the 12th International Conference of the Association for Computational Linguistics*, pages 573–577, Budapest.

Holger Wache, Thomas Voegele, Ubbo Visser, Heiner Stuckenschmidt, Gerhard Schuster, Holger Neumann, and Sebastian Hübner. 2001. Ontology-based integration of information-a survey of existing approaches. In *IJCAI-01 workshop: ontologies and information sharing*, volume 2001, pages 108–117. Citeseer.

Sebastian Walter, Christina Unger, and Philipp Cimiano. 2013. A corpus-based approach for the induction of ontology lexica. In *Natural Language Processing and Information Systems*, pages 102–113. Springer.

PARADIGM: Paraphrase Diagnostics through Grammar Matching

Jonathan Weese and **Juri Ganitkevitch**
Johns Hopkins University

Chris Callison-Burch
University of Pennsylvania

Abstract

Paraphrase evaluation is typically done either manually or through indirect, task-based evaluation. We introduce an intrinsic evaluation PARADIGM which measures the goodness of paraphrase collections that are represented using synchronous grammars. We formulate two measures that evaluate these paraphrase grammars using gold standard sentential paraphrases drawn from a monolingual parallel corpus. The first measure calculates how often a paraphrase grammar is able to synchronously parse the sentence pairs in the corpus. The second measure enumerates paraphrase rules from the monolingual parallel corpus and calculates the overlap between this reference paraphrase collection and the paraphrase resource being evaluated. We demonstrate the use of these evaluation metrics on paraphrase collections derived from three different data types: multiple translations of classic French novels, comparable sentence pairs drawn from different newspapers, and bilingual parallel corpora. We show that PARADIGM correlates with human judgments more strongly than BLEU on a task-based evaluation of paraphrase quality.

1 Introduction

Paraphrases are useful in a wide range of natural language processing applications. A variety of data-driven approaches have been proposed to generate paraphrase resources (see Madnani and Dorr (2010) for a survey of these methods). Few objective metrics have been established to evaluate these resources. Instead, paraphrases are typically evaluated using subjective manual evaluation or through task-based evaluations.

Different researchers have used different criteria for manual evaluations. For example, Barzilay and McKeown (2001) evaluated their paraphrases by asking judges whether paraphrases were "approximately conceptually equivalent." Ibrahim et al. (2003) asked judges whether their paraphrases were "roughly interchangeable given the genre." Bannard and Callison-Burch (2005) replaced phrases with paraphrases in a number of sentences and asked judges whether the substitutions "preserved meaning and remained grammatical." The results of these subjective evaluations are not easily reusable.

Other researchers have evaluated their paraphrases through task-based evaluations. Lin and Pantel (2001) measured their potential impact on question-answering. Cohn and Lapata (2007) evaluate their applicability in the text-to-text generation task of sentence compression. Zhao et al. (2009) use them to perform sentence compression and simplification and to compute sentence similarity. Several researchers have demonstrated that paraphrases can improve machine translation evaluation (c.f. Kauchak and Barzilay (2006), Zhou et al. (2006), Madnani (2010) and Snover et al. (2010)).

We introduce an automatic evaluation metric called PARADIGM, PARAphrase DIagnostics through Grammar Matching. This metric evaluates paraphrase collections that are represented using synchronous grammars. Synchronous tree-adjoining grammars (STAGs), synchronous tree substitution grammars (STSGs), and synchronous context free grammars (SCFGs) are popular formalisms for representing paraphrase rules (Dras, 1997; Cohn and Lapata, 2007; Madnani, 2010; Ganitkevitch et al., 2011). We present two measures that evaluate these paraphrase grammars using gold standard sentential paraphrases drawn from a monolingual parallel corpus, which have been previously proposed as a good resource for paraphrase evaluation (Callison-Burch et al., 2008; Cohn et al., 2008).

The first of our two proposed metrics calculates how often a paraphrase grammar is able to synchronously parse the sentence pairs in a test set. The second measure enumerates paraphrase rules from a monolingual parallel corpus and calculates the overlap between this reference paraphrase collection, and the paraphrase resource being evaluated.

2 Related work and background

The most closely related work is ParaMetric (Callison-Burch et al., 2008), which is a set of objective measures for evaluating the quality of *phrase-based* paraphrases. ParaMetric extracts a set of gold-standard phrasal paraphrases from sentential paraphrases that have been manually word-aligned. The sentential paraphrases used in ParaMetric were drawn from a data set originally created to evaluate machine translation output using the BLEU metric. Cohn et al. (2008) argue that these sorts of monolingual parallel corpora are appropriate for evaluating paraphrase systems, because they are naturally occurring sources of paraphrases.

Callison-Burch et al. (2008) calculated three types of metrics in ParaMetric. The manual word alignments were used to calculate how well an automatic paraphrasing technique is able *to align* the paraphrases in a sentence pair. This measure is limited to a class of paraphrasing techniques that perform alignment (like MacCartney et al. (2008)). Most methods produce a list of paraphrases for a given input phrase. So Callison-Burch et al. (2008) calculate two more generally applicable measures by comparing the paraphrases in an automatically extracted resource to gold standard paraphrases extracted via the alignments. These allow a *lower-bound on precision* and *relative recall* to be calculated.

Liu et al. (2010) introduce the PEM metric as an alternative to BLEU, since BLEU prefers identical paraphrases. PEM uses a second language as a pivot to judge semantic equivalence. This requires use of some bilingual data. Chen and Dolan (2011) suggest using BLEU together with their metric PINC, which uses n-grams to measure lexical difference between paraphrases.

PARADIGM extends the ideas in ParaMetric from *lexical* and *phrasal* paraphrasing techniques to paraphrasing techniques that also generate *syntactic templates*, such as Zhao et al. (2008), Cohn and Lapata (2009), Madnani (2010) and Ganitkevitch et al. (2011). Instead of extracting gold standard paraphrases using techniques from phrase-based machine translation, we use grammar extraction techniques (Weese et al., 2011) to extract gold standard paraphrase grammar rules from ParaMetric's word-aligned sentential paraphrases. Using these rules, we calculate the overlap between a gold standard paraphrase grammar and an automatically generated paraphrase grammar.

Moreover, like ParaMetric, PARADIGM is able to do further analysis on a restricted class of paraphrasing models. In this case, PARADIGM evaluates how well certain models are able to produce synchronous parses of sentence pairs drawn from monolingual parallel corpora. PARADIGM's different metrics are explained in Section 4, but first we give background on synchronous parsing and synchronous grammars.

2.1 Synchronous parsing with SCFGs

Synchronous context-free grammars

An SCFG (Lewis and Stearns, 1968; Aho and Ullman, 1972) is similar to a context-free grammar, except that it generates *pairs* of strings in correspondence. Each production rule in an SCFG rewrites a non-terminal symbol as a pair of phrases, which may have contain a mix of words and non-terminals symbols. The grammar is *synchronous* because both phrases in the pair must have an identical set of non-terminals (though they can come in different orders), and corresponding non-terminals must be rewritten using the same rule.

Much recent work in MT (and, by extension, paraphrasing approaches that use MT machinery) has been focused on choosing an appropriate set of non-terminal symbols. The Hiero model (Chiang, 2007) used a single non-terminal symbol X. Other approaches have read symbols from constituent parses of the training data (Galley et al., 2004; Galley et al., 2006; Zollmann and Venugopal, 2006). Labels based combinatory categorial grammar (Steedman and Baldridge, 2011) have also been used (Almaghout et al., 2010; Weese et al., 2012).

Synchronous parsing

Wu (1997) introduced a parsing algorithm using a variant of CKY. Dyer recently showed (2010)

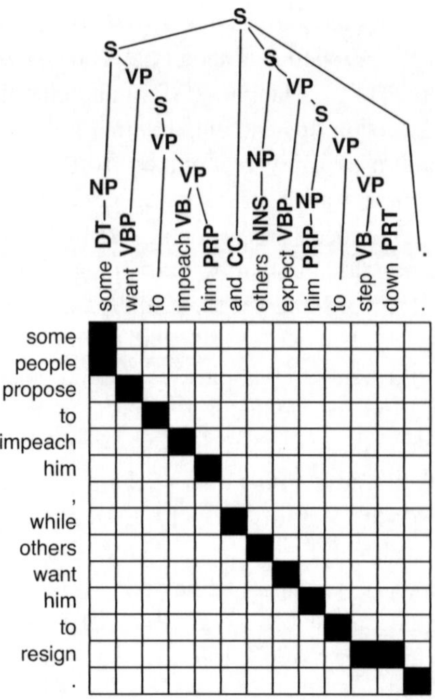

Figure 1: PARADIGM extracts lexical, phrasal and syntactic paraphrases from parsed, word-aligned sentence pairs.

that the average parse time can be significantly improved by using a two-pass algorithm.

The question of whether a source-reference pair is reachable under a model must be addressed in end-to-end discriminative training in MT (Liang et al., 2006a; Gimpel and Smith, 2012). Auli et al. (2009) showed that only approximately 30% of training pairs are reachable under a phrase-based model. This result is confirmed by our results in paraphrasing.

3 Paraphrase grammar extraction

Like ParaMetric, PARADIGM extracts gold standard paraphrases from word-aligned sentential paraphrases. PARADIGM goes further by parsing one of the two input sentences, and uses the parse tree to extract *syntactic* paraphrase rules, following recent advances in syntactic approaches to machine translation (like Galley et al. (2004), Zollmann and Venugopal (2006), and others). Figure 1 shows an example of a parsed sentence pair. From that pair it is possible to extract a wide variety of non-identical paraphrases, which include lexical paraphrases (single word synonyms), phrasal paraphrases, and syntactic paraphrases that include a mix of words and syntactic non-terminal symbols. Figure 2 shows a set of four examples for each type that can be extracted from Figure 1.

CC →	and	while
VBP →	want	propose
VBP →	expect	want
DT →	some	some people
S →	him to step down	him to resign
VP →	step down	resign
VP →	to step down	to resign
VP →	want to impeach him	propose to impeach him
VP →	want VP	propose VP
VP →	want to impeach PRP	propose to impeach PRP
VP →	VBP him to step down	VBP him to resign
S →	PRP to step down	PRP to resign

Figure 2: Four examples each of lexical, phrasal, and syntactic paraphrases that can be extracted from the sentence pair in Figure 1.

These rules are formulated as SCFG rules, with a syntactic left-hand nonterminal symbol and two English right-hand sides representing the paraphrase. The examples above include non-terminal symbols that represent whole syntactic constituents. It is also possible to create more complex non-terminal symbols that describe CCG-like non-constituent phrases. For example, we could extract a rule like

S/VP → <NNS want him to, NNS expect him to>

Using constituents only, we are able to extract 45 paraphrase rules from Figure 1. Adding CCG-style slashed constituents yields 66 additional rules.

4 PARADIGM: Evaluating paraphrase grammars

By considering a paraphrase model as a synchronous context-free grammar, we propose to measure the model's goodness using the following criteria:

1. What percentage of sentential paraphrases are reachable under the model? That is, given a collection of sentence pairs (a_i, b_i) and an SCFG G, where each pair of a and b are sentential paraphrases, how many of the pairs are in the language of G? We evaluate this by producing a synchronous parse for the pairs, as shown in Figure 3.

2. Given a collection of gold-standard paraphrase rules, how many of those paraphrases exist as rules in G? To calculate this, we look at the overlap of grammars (described in

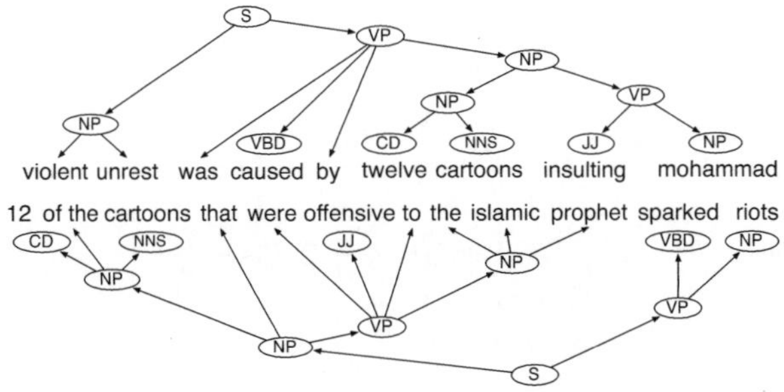

Figure 3: We measure the goodness of paraphrase grammars by determine how often they can be used to synchronously parse gold-standard sentential paraphrases. Note we do not require the synchronous derivation to match a gold-standard parse tree.

Section 4.2 below), examining different categories of rules and thresholding based on how frequently the rule was used in the gold standard data.

These criteria correspond to properties that we think are desirable in paraphrase models. They also have the advantage that they do not depend on human judgments and so can be calculated automatically.

4.1 Synchronous parse coverage

Paraphrase grammars should be able to explain sentential paraphrases. For example, Figure 3 shows a sentence pair that is synchronously parseable by one paraphrase grammar. In general, we say that the more such sentence pairs that a paraphrase grammar can synchronously parse, the better it is.

The synchronous derivation allows us to draw inferences about parts of the sentence pair that are in correspondence; for instance, in Figure 3, *violent unrest* corresponds to *riots* and *mohammad* corresponds to *the islamic prophet*.

4.2 Grammar overlap defined

We measure grammar overlap by comparing the sets of production rules for two different grammars. If the grammars contain rules that are equivalent, the equivalent rules are in the grammars' overlap.

We consider two types of overlapping, which we will call *strict* and *non-strict* overlap. For strict overlap, we say that two rules are equivalent if they are identical, that is, if they have the same left-hand side non-terminal symbol, their source sides are identical strings, and their target sides are identical strings. (This includes identical indexing on non-terminal symbols on the right hand sides of the rule.)

To calculate non-strict overlap, we ignore the identities of non-terminal symbols in the left-hand and right-hand sides of the rules. That is, two rules are considered equivalent if they are identical after all the non-terminal symbols have been replaced by one equivalent symbol.

For example, in non-strict overlap, the syntactic rule

$$NP \rightarrow \langle N_1 \text{ 's } N_2;\ \text{the } N_2 \text{ of } N_1 \rangle$$

would match the Hiero rule

$$X \rightarrow \langle X_1 \text{ 's } X_2;\ \text{the } X_2 \text{ of } X_1 \rangle$$

If we are considering two Hiero grammars, strict and non-strict intersection are the same operation since they only have on non-terminal X.

4.3 Precision lower bound and relative recall

Callison-Burch et al. (2008) use the notion of overlap between two paraphrase sets to define two metrics, *precision lower bound* and *relative recall*. These are calculated the same way as standard precision and recall. Relative recall is qualified as "relative" because it is calculated on a potentially incomplete set of gold standard paraphrases. There may exist valid paraphrases that do not occur in that set. Similarly, only a lower bound on precision can be calculated because the candidate set may contain valid paraphrases that do not occur in the gold standard set.

5 Experiments

5.1 Data

We extracted paraphrase grammars from a variety of different data sources, including four collections of sentential paraphrases. These included:

- **Multiple translation corpora** that were compiled by the Linguistics Data Consortium (LDC) for the purposes of evaluating machine translation quality with the BLEU metric. We collected eight LDC corpora that all have multiple English translations.[1]

[1]LDC Catalog numbers LDC2002T01, LDC2005T05, LDC2010T10, LDC2010T11, LDC2010T12, LDC2010T14, LDC2010T17, and LDC2010T23.

Corpus	sentence pairs	total words
LDC Multiple Translations	83,284	2,254,707
Classic French Literature	75,106	682,978
MSR Paraphrase Corpus	5,801	219,492
ParaMetric	970	21,944

Table 1: Amount of English–English parallel data. LDC data has 4 parallel translations per sentence. Literature data is from Barzilay and McKeown (2001). MSR data is from Quirk et al. (2004) and Dolan et al. (2004). ParaMertic data is from Callison-Burch et al. (2008).

- **Classic French Literature** that were translated by different translators, and which were compiled by Barzilay and McKeown (2001).
- **The MSR Paraphrase corpus** which consists of sentence pairs drawn from comparable news articles drawn from different web sites in the same date rate. The sentence pairs were aligned heuristically aligned and then manually judged to be paraphrases.
- **The ParaMetric data** which consists of 900 manually word-aligned sentence pairs collected by Cohn et al. (2008). 300 sentence pairs were drawn from each of the 3 above sources. We use this to extract the gold standard paraphrase grammar.

The size of the data from each source is summarized in Table 1.

For each dataset, after tokenizing and normalizing, we parsed one sentence in each English pair using the Berkeley constituency parser (Liang et al., 2006b). We then obtained word-level alignments, either using GIZA++ (Och and Ney, 2000) or, in the case of ParaMetric, using human annotations.

We used the Thrax grammar extractor (Weese et al., 2011) to extract Hiero-style and syntactic SCFGs from the paraphrase data. In the syntactic setting we allowed labeling of rules with either constituent labels or CCG-style slashed categories. The size of the extracted grammars is shown in Table 2.

We also used version 0.2 of the SCFG-based paraphrase collection known as the ParaPhrase DataBase or PPDB (Ganitkevitch et al., 2013). The PPDB paraphrases were extracted using the pivoting technique (Bannard and Callison-Burch, 2005) on bilingual parallel corpora containing over 42 million sentence pairs.

The PPDB release includes a tool for pruning the grammar to a smaller size by retaining only high-precision paraphrases. We include PPDB grammars for several different pruning settings in our analysis.

Grammar	Rules
LDC Hiero	52,784,462
Lit. Hiero	3,288,546
MSR Hiero	2,456,513
ParaMetric Hiero	584,944
LDC Syntax	23,978,477
Lit. Syntax	715,154
MSR Syntax	406,115
ParaMetric Syntax	317,772
PPDB-v0.2-small	1,292,224
PPDB-v0.2-large	9,456,356
PPDB-v0.2-xl	46,592,161

Table 2: Size of various paraphrase grammars.

Grammar	freq. ≥ 1	freq. ≥ 2
ParaMetric Syntax	317,772	21,709
LDC Hiero	5,840 (1.8%)	416 (1.9%)
Lit. Hiero	6,152 (1.9%)	359 (1.7%)
MSR Hiero	10,012 (3.2%)	315 (1.5%)
LDC Syntax	**48,833 (15.3%)**	7,748 (35.6%)
Lit. Syntax	14,431 (4.5%)	1,960 (9.0%)
MSR Syntax	21,197 (6.7%)	2,053 (9.5%)
PPDB-v0.2-small	15,831 (5.0%)	5,673 (26.1%)
PPDB-v0.2-large	31,277 (9.8%)	8,245 (37.9%)
PPDB-v0.2-xl	47,720 (15.0%)	**10,049 (46.2%)**

Table 3: Size of strict overlap (number of rules and % of the gold standard) of each grammar with a syntactic grammar derived from ParaMetric. freq. $\geq$ 2 means we first removed all rules that appeared only once from the ParaMetric grammar. The number in parentheses shows the percentage of ParaMetric rules that are present in the overlap.

5.2 Experimental setup

We calculated our two metrics for each of the grammars listed in Table 2.

To perform synchronous parsing, we used the Joshua decoder (Post et al., 2013), which includes an implementation of Dyer's two-pass parsing algorithm (2010). After splitting the LDC data into 10 equal pieces, we trained paraphrase models on nine-tenths of the data and parsed the other tenth.

Grammars trained from other sources (the MSR corpus, French literature domain, and PPDB) were also evaluated on the held-out tenth of LDC data.

Grammar	freq. ≥ 1	freq. ≥ 2
ParaMetric Syntax	200,385	20,699
LDC Hiero	41,346 (20.6%)	5,323 (25.8%)
Lit. Hiero	36,873 (18.4%)	4,606 (22.3%)
MSR Hiero	**58,970 (29.4%)**	**6,741 (32.6%)**
LDC Syntax	37,231 (11.7%)	5,055 (24.5%)
Lit. Syntax	19,530 (9.7%)	3,121 (15.1%)
MSR Syntax	28,016 (14.0%)	3,564 (17.2%)
PPDB-v0.2-small	13,003 (6.5%)	3,661 (17.7%)
PPDB-v0.2-large	22,431 (11.2%)	4,837 (23.4%)
PPDB-v0.2-xl	31,294 (15.6%)	5,590 (27.0%)

Table 4: Size of non-strict overlap of each grammar with the syntactic grammar derived from ParaMetric. The number in parentheses shows the percentage of ParaMetric rules that are present in the overlap.

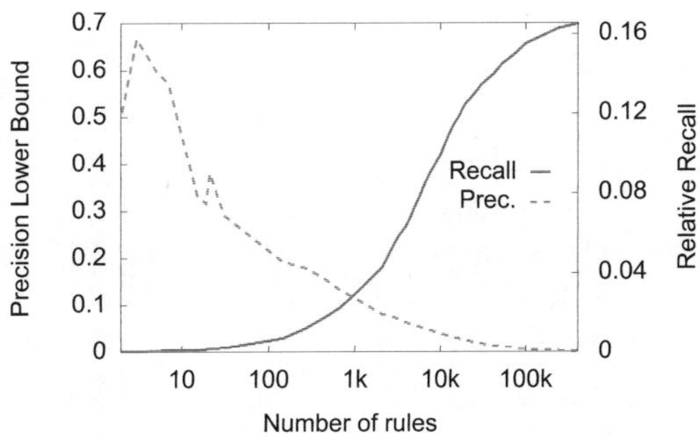

Figure 4: Precision lower bound and relative recall when overlapping different sizes of PPDB with the syntactic ParaMetric grammar.

Grammar	syntactic	phrasal	lexical
ParaMetric	238,646	73,320	5,806
LDC_{Syn}	36,375 (15%)	8,806 (12%)	3,652 (62%)
MSR_{Syn}	7,734 (3%)	11,254 (15%)	2,209 (38%)
PPDB-xl	40,822 (17%)	3,765 (5%)	3,142 (54%)

Table 5: Number of paraphrases of each type in each grammar's strict overlap with the syntactic ParaMetric grammar. Numbers in parentheses show the percentage of ParaMetric rules of each type.

Note that the LDC data contains 4 independent translations of each foreign sentence, giving 6 possible (unordered) paraphrase pairs. We evaluated coverage in two ways (corresponding to the two columns in Table 6): first, considering all possible sentence pairs from the test data, how many were able to be parsed?

Secondly, if we consider all the English sentences that correspond to one foreign sentence, how many foreign sentences had at least one pair of English translations that could be parsed synchronously?

For grammar overlap, we perform both strict and non-strict calculations (see Section 4.2) against a syntactic grammar derived from hand-aligned ParaMetric data.

5.3 Grammar overlap results

In Table 5 we see a breakdown of the types of paraphrases in the overlap for three of the models. Although the PPDB-xl overlap is much larger than the other two, about 80% of its rules are syntactic transformations. The LDC and MSR models have a much larger proportion of phrasal and lexical rules.

Next we will look at the grammar overlap numbers presented in Table 3 and Table 4.

Note the non-intuitive result that for some grammars (notably PPDB), the non-strict overlap is smaller than the strict overlap. This is because rules with different non-terminals only count once in the non-strict overlap; for example, in PPDB-small,

$$NN \rightarrow \langle \text{ answer ; reply } \rangle$$
$$VB \rightarrow \langle \text{ answer ; reply } \rangle$$

count as separate entries when calculating strictly, but when ignoring non-terminals, they count as only one type of rule.

The fact that the non-strict overlaps are smaller means that there must be many rules in PPDB that are identical except for non-terminal labels.

5.4 Precision and recall results

Figure 4 shows relative recall and precision lower bound calculated for various sizes of PPDB relative to the ParaMetric grammar. The x-axis represents the size of the grammar as we vary from keeping only the most probable rules to including less probable ones. Restricting to high probability rules makes the grammar much smaller, resulting in higher precision.

5.5 Synchronous parsing results

Table 6 shows the percentage of sentence pairs that were reachable in a held-out portion of the LDC multiple-translation data.

We find that a grammar trained on LDC data vastly outperforms data from any other domain. This is not surprising — we shouldn't expect a model trained on French literature to be able to

Grammar	% (all)	% (any)
LDC Hiero	9.5	33.0
Lit. Hiero	1.8	9.6
MSR Hiero	1.7	9.2
LDC Syntax	9.1	30.2
Lit. Syntax	2.0	10.7
MSR Syntax	1.9	10.4
PM Syntax	1.7	9.8
PPDB-v0.2-small	1.8	3.3
PPDB-v0.2-large	2.5	4.5
PPDB-v0.2-xl	3.5	6.2

Table 6: Parse coverage on held-out LDC data. The *all* column considers every possible sentential paraphrase in the test set. The *any* column considers a sentence parsed if any of its paraphrases was able to parsed.

handle some of the vocabulary found in news stories that were originally in Arabic or Chinese.

The PPDB data outperforms both French literature and MSR models if we look all possible sentence pairs from test data (the column labeled "all" in the table). However, when we consider whether *any* pair from a set of 4 translations can be translated, the PPDB models do not do as well. This implies that PPDB tends to be able to reach many pairs from the same set of translations, but there are many translations that it cannot handle at all. By contrast, the literature- and MSR-trained models can reach at least one pair from 10% of the test examples, even though the absolute number of pairs they can reach is lower.

5.6 Effects of grammar size and choice of syntactic labels

Table 2 shows that the PPDB-derived grammars are much larger than the syntactic models derived from other domains. It may seem surprising that they should perform worse, but adding more rules to the grammar just by varying non-terminal labels isn't likely to help overall parse coverage. This suggests a new pruning method: keep only the top k label variations for each rule type.

If we compare the syntactic models to the Hiero models trained from the same data, we see that their overall reachability performance is not very different. This implies that paraphrases can be annotated with linguistic information without necessarily hurting their ability to explain particular sentence pairs. Contrast this result, with, for example, those of Koehn et al. (2003), showing that restricting translation models to only syntactic phrases hurts overall translation performance. The comparable performance between Hiero and syntactic models seems to hold regardless of domain.

6 Correlation with human judgments

To validate PARADIGM, we calculated its correlation with human judgments of paraphrase quality on the sentence compression text-to-text generation task, which has been used to evaluate paraphrase grammars in previous research (Cohn and Lapata, 2007; Zhao et al., 2009; Ganitkevitch et al., 2011; Napoles et al., 2011). We created sentence compression systems for five of the paraphrase grammars described in Section 5.1. We followed the methodology outlined by Ganitkevitch et al. (2011) and did the following:

- Each paraphrase grammar was augmented with an appropriate set of rule-level features that capture information pertinent to the task. In this case, the paraphrase rules were given two additional features that shows how the number of words and characters changed after applying the rule.

- Similarly to how the weights of the models are set using minimum error rate training in statistical machine translation, the weights for each of the paraphrase grammars using the PRO tuning method (Hopkins and May, 2011).

- Instead of optimizing to the BLEU metric, as is done in machine translation, we optimized to PRÉCIS, a metric developed for sentence compression that adapts BLEU so that it includes a "verbosity penalty" (Ganitkevitch et al., 2011) to encourage the compression systems to produce shorter output.

- We created a development set with sentence compressions by selecting 1000 pairs of sentences from the multiple translation corpus where two English translations of the same foreign sentences differed in each other by a length ratio of 0.67–0.75.

- We decoded a test set of 1000 sentences using each of the grammars and its optimized weights with the Joshua decoder (Ganitkevitch et al., 2012). The selected in the same fashion as the dev sentences, so each one had a human-created reference compression.

We conducted a human evaluation to judge the meaning and grammaticality of the sentence compressions derived from each paraphrase grammar. We presented workers on Mechanical Turk with the input sentence to the compression sentence (the long sentence), along with 5 shortened outputs from our compression systems. To ensure that workers were producing reliable judgments we also presented them with a positive control (a reference compression written by a person) and a negative controls (a compressed output that was generated by randomly deleted words). We excluded judgments from workers who did not perform well on the positive and negative controls.

Meaning and grammaticality were scored on 5-point scales where 5 is best. These human scores were averaged over 2000 judgments (1000 sentences x 2 annotators) for each system. The systems' outputs were then scored with BLEU, PRÉCIS, and their paraphrase grammars were scored PARADIGM's relative recall and precision lower-bound estimates. For each grammar, we also calculated the average length of parseable sentences.

We calculated the correlation between the human judgements and the automatic scores, using Spearman's rank correlation coefficient ρ. This is methodology is the same that is used to quantify the goodness of automatic evaluation metrics in the machine translation literature (Przybocki et al., 2008; Callison-Burch et al., 2010). The possible values of ρ range between 1 (where all systems are ranked in the same order) and -1 (where the systems are ranked in the reverse order). Thus an automatic evaluation metric with a higher absolute value for ρ is making predictions that are more similar to the human judgments than an automatic evaluation metric with a lower absolute ρ.

Table 7 shows that our PARADIGM scores correlate more highly with human judgments than either BLEU or PRÉCIS for the 5 systems in our evaluation. This suggests that it may be a better predictor of the goodness of paraphrase grammars than MT metrics, when the paraphrase grammars are used for text-to-text generation tasks.

	MEANING	GRAMMAR
BLEU	-0.7	-0.1
PRÉCIS	-0.6	+0.2
PINC	+0.1	**+0.4**
PARADIGM$_{precision}$	**+0.6**	+0.1
PARADIGM$_{recall}$	+0.1	**+0.4**
PARADIGM$_{avg-len}$	-0.3	**+0.4**

Table 7: The correlation (Spearman's ρ) of different automatic evaluation metrics with human judgments of paraphrase quality for the text-to-text generation task of sentence compression.

7 Summary

We have introduced two new metrics for evaluating paraphrase grammars, and looked at several models from a variety of domains. Using these metrics we can perform a variety of analyses about SCFG-based paraphrase models:

- Automatically-extracted grammars can parse a small fraction of held-out data ($\leq$30%). This is comparable to results in MT (Auli et al., 2009).
- In-domain training data is necessary in order to parse held-out data. A model trained on newswire data parsed 30% of held-out newswire sentence pairs, versus to $<$10% for literature or parliamentary data.
- SCFGs with syntactic labels perform just as well as simpler models with a single nonterminal label.
- Automatically-extracted syntactic grammars tend to have a reasonable overlap with grammars derived from human-aligned data, including more 45% of the gold-standard grammar's paraphrase rules that occurred at least twice.
- We showed that PARADIGM more strongly correlates with human judgments of the meaning and grammaticality of paraphrases produced by sentence compression systems than standard automatic evaluation measures like BLEU.

PARADIGM will help researchers developing paraphrase resources to perform similar diagnostics on their models, and quickly evaluate their systems.

Acknowledgements

This material is based on research sponsored by the NSF under grant IIS-1249516 and DARPA under agreement number FA8750-13-2-0017 (the DEFT program). The U.S. Government is authorized to reproduce and distribute reprints for Governmental purposes. The views and conclusions contained in this publication are those of the authors and should not be interpreted as representing official policies or endorsements of DARPA or the U.S. Government.

References

Alfred V. Aho and Jeffrey D. Ullman. 1972. *The Theory of Parsing, Translation, and Compiling*. Prentice Hall.

Hala Almaghout, Jie Jiang, and Andy Way. 2010. CCG augmented hierarchical phrase-based machine translation. In *Proc. of IWSLT*.

Michael Auli, Adam Lopez, Hieu Hoang, and Philipp Koehn. 2009. A systematic analysis of translation model search spaces. In *Proc. WMT*.

Colin Bannard and Chris Callison-Burch. 2005. Paraphrasing with bilingual parallel corpora. In *Proceedings of ACL*.

Regina Barzilay and Kathleen R. McKeown. 2001. Extracting paraphrases from a parallel corpus. In *Proc. of ACL*.

Chris Callison-Burch, Trevor Cohn, and Mirella Lapata. 2008. ParaMetric: An automatic evaluation metric for paraphrasing. In *Proc. of COLING*.

Chris Callison-Burch, Philipp Koehn, Christof Monz, Kay Peterson, Mark Przybocki, and Omar F. Zaidan. 2010. Findings of the 2010 joint workshop on statistical machine translation and metrics for machine translation. In *Proceedings of the Fourth Workshop on Statistical Machine Translation (WMT10)*.

David L. Chen and William Dolan. 2011. Collecting highly parallel data for paraphrase evaluation. In *Proc. of ACL*.

David Chiang. 2007. Hierarchical phrase-based translation. *Computational Linguistics*, 33(2):201–228.

Trevor Cohn and Mirella Lapata. 2007. Large margin synchronous generation and its application to sentence compression. In *Proceedings of EMNLP-CoLing*.

Trevor Cohn and Mirella Lapata. 2009. Sentence compression as tree transduction. *Journal of Artificial Intelligence Research (JAIR)*, 34:637–674.

Trevor Cohn, Chris Callison-Burch, and Mirella Lapata. 2008. Constructing corpora for the development and evaluation of paraphrase systems. *Computational Linguistics*, 34(4).

William Dolan, Chris Quirk, and Chris Brockett. 2004. Unsupervised construction of large paraphrases corpora: Exploiting massively parallel news sources. In *Proc. of COLING*.

Mark Dras. 1997. Representing paraphrases using synchronous tree adjoining grammars. In *Proceedings of the 35th Annual Meeting of the Association for Computational Linguistics*, pages 516–518, Madrid, Spain, July. Association for Computational Linguistics.

Chris Dyer. 2010. Two monolingual parses are better than one (synchronous parse). In *Proceedings of HLT/NAACL*, pages 263–266. Association for Computational Linguistics.

Michel Galley, Mark Hopkins, Kevin Knight, and Daniel Marcu. 2004. What's in a translation rule? In *HLT-NAACL 2004: Main Proceedings*, pages 273–280.

Michel Galley, Jonathan Graehl, Kevin Knight, Daniel Marcu, Steve Deneefe, Wei Wang, and Ignacio Thayer. 2006. Scalable inference and training of context-rich syntactic translation models. In *Proc. of ACL*, pages 961–968.

Juri Ganitkevitch, Chris Callison-Burch, Courtney Napoles, and Benjamin Van Durme. 2011. Learning sentential paraphrases from bilingual parallel corpora for text-to-text generation. In *Proceedings of EMNLP*.

Juri Ganitkevitch, Yuan Cao, Jonathan Weese, Matt Post, and Chris Callison-Burch. 2012. Joshua 4.0: Packing, pro, and paraphrases. In *Proceedings of the Seventh Workshop on Statistical Machine Translation*, pages 283–291, Montréal, Canada, June. Association for Computational Linguistics.

Juri Ganitkevitch, Benjamin Van Durme, and Chris Callison-Burch. 2013. PPDB: The paraphrase database. In *Proc. NAACL*.

Kevin Gimpel and Noah A. Smith. 2012. Structured ramp loss minimization for machine translation. In *Proc. of NAACL*.

Mark Hopkins and Jonathan May. 2011. Tuning as ranking. In *Proceedings of the 2011 Conference on Empirical Methods in Natural Language Processing*, pages 1352–1362, Edinburgh, Scotland, UK., July. Association for Computational Linguistics.

Ali Ibrahim, Boris Katz, and Jimmy Lin. 2003. Extracting structural paraphrases from aligned monolingual corpora. In *Proc. of the Second International Workshop on Paraphrasing*.

David Kauchak and Regina Barzilay. 2006. Paraphrasing for automatic evaluation. In *Proceedings of EMNLP*.

Philipp Koehn, Franz Josef Och, and Daniel Marcu. 2003. Statistical phrase-based translation. In *NAACL '03: Proceedings of the 2003 Conference of the North American Chapter of the Association for Computational Linguistics on Human Language Technology*, pages 48–54, Morristown, NJ, USA. Association for Computational Linguistics.

Philip M. Lewis and Richard E. Stearns. 1968. Syntax-directed transduction. *Journal of the ACM*, 15(3):465–488.

Percy Liang, Alexandre Bouchard-Côté, Dan Klein, and Ben Taskar. 2006a. An end-to-end discriminative approach to machine translation. In *Proc. of ACL*.

Percy Liang, Ben Taskar, and Dan Klein. 2006b. Alignment by agreement. In *Proceedings of the Human Language Technology Conference of the NAACL, Main Conference*, pages 104–111, New York City, USA, June. Association for Computational Linguistics.

Dekang Lin and Patrick Pantel. 2001. Discovery of inference rules from text. *Natural Language Engineering*, 7(3):343–360.

Chang Liu, Daniel Dahlmeier, and Hwee Tou Ng. 2010. PEM: a paraphrase evaluation metric exploiting parallel texts. In *Proc. of EMNLP*.

Bill MacCartney, Michel Galley, and Christopher D. Manning. 2008. A phrase-based alignment model for natural language inference. In *Proceedings of the 2008 Conference on Empirical Methods in Natural Language Processing*, pages 802–811, Honolulu, Hawaii, October. Association for Computational Linguistics.

Nitin Madnani and Bonnie Dorr. 2010. Generating phrasal and sentential paraphrases: A survey of data-driven methods. *Computational Linguistics*, 36(3):341–388.

Nitin Madnani. 2010. *The Circle of Meaning: From Translation to Paraphrasing and Back*. Ph.D. thesis, Department of Computer Science, University of Maryland College Park.

Courtney Napoles, Benjamin Van Durme, and Chris Callison-Burch. 2011. Evaluating sentence compression: Pitfalls and suggested remedies. In *Proceedings of the Workshop on Monolingual Text-To-Text Generation*, pages 91–97, Portland, Oregon, June. Association for Computational Linguistics.

Franz Och and Hermann Ney. 2000. Improved statistical alignment models. In *Proceedings of the 38th Annual Meeting of the Association for Computational Linguistics*, pages 440–447, Hong Kong, China, October.

Matt Post, Juri Ganitkevitch, Luke Orland, Jonathan Weese, Yuan Cao, and Chris Callison-Burch. 2013. Joshua 5.0: Sparser, better, faster, server. In *Proc. of WMT*.

Mark Przybocki, Kay Peterson, and Sebastian Bronsart. 2008. Official results of the NIST 2008 "Metrics for MAchine TRanslation" challenge (MetricsMATR08). In *AMTA-2008 workshop on Metrics for Machine Translation*.

Chris Quirk, Chris Brockett, and William Dolan. 2004. Monlingual machine translation for paraphrase generation. In *Proc. of EMNLP*.

Matthew Snover, Nitin Madnani, Bonnie Dorr, and Richard Schwartz. 2010. Ter-plus: paraphrase, semantic, and alignment enhancements to translation edit rate. *Machine Translation*, 23(2-3):117–127.

Mark Steedman and Jason Baldridge. 2011. Combinatory categorial grammar. In Robert Borsley and Kersti Börjars, editors, *Non-Transformational Syntax*. Wiley-Blackwell.

Idan Szpektor, Eyal Shnarch, and Ido Dagan. 2007. Instance-based evaluation of entailment rule acquisition. In *Proc. of ACL*.

Jonathan Weese, Juri Ganitkevitch, Chris Callison-Burch, Matt Post, and Adam Lopez. 2011. Joshua 3.0: Syntax-based machine translation with the thrax grammar extractor. In *Proceedings of the Sixth Workshop on Statistical Machine Translation*, pages 478–484, Edinburgh, Scotland, July. Association for Computational Linguistics.

Jonathan Weese, Chris Callison-Burch, and Adam Lopez. 2012. Using categorial grammar to label translation rules. In *Proc. of WMT*.

Dekai Wu. 1997. Stochastic inversion transduction grammars and bilingual parsing of parallel corpora. *Computational Linguistics*, 23(3):377–404.

Shiqi Zhao, Haifeng Wang, Ting Liu, and Sheng Li. 2008. Pivot approach for extracting paraphrase patterns from bilingual corpora. In *Proceedings of ACL/HLT*.

Shiqi Zhao, Xiang Lan, Ting Liu, and Sheng Li. 2009. Application-driven statistical paraphrase generation. In *Proceedings of ACL*.

Liang Zhou, Chin-Yew Lin, Dragos Stefan Munteanu, and Eduard Hovy. 2006. Paraeval: Using paraphrases to evaluate summaries automatically. In *Proceedings of HLT/NAACL*.

Andreas Zollmann and Ashish Venugopal. 2006. Syntax augmented machine translation via chart parsing. In *Proceedings on the Workshop on Statistical Machine Translation*, pages 138–141, New York City, June. Association for Computational Linguistics.

Translation Memory Retrieval Methods

Michael Bloodgood
Center for Advanced Study of Language
University of Maryland
College Park, MD 20742 USA
meb@umd.edu

Benjamin Strauss
Center for Advanced Study of Language
University of Maryland
College Park, MD 20742 USA
bstrauss@umd.edu

Abstract

Translation Memory (TM) systems are one of the most widely used translation technologies. An important part of TM systems is the matching algorithm that determines what translations get retrieved from the bank of available translations to assist the human translator. Although detailed accounts of the matching algorithms used in commercial systems can't be found in the literature, it is widely believed that edit distance algorithms are used. This paper investigates and evaluates the use of several matching algorithms, including the edit distance algorithm that is believed to be at the heart of most modern commercial TM systems. This paper presents results showing how well various matching algorithms correlate with human judgments of helpfulness (collected via crowdsourcing with Amazon's Mechanical Turk). A new algorithm based on weighted n-gram precision that can be adjusted for translator length preferences consistently returns translations judged to be most helpful by translators for multiple domains and language pairs.

1 Introduction

The most widely used computer-assisted translation (CAT) tool for professional translation of specialized text is translation memory (TM) technology (Christensen and Schjoldager, 2010). TM consists of a database of previously translated material, referred to as the TM vault or the TM bank (TMB in the rest of this paper). When a translator is translating a new sentence, the TMB is consulted to see if a similar sentence has already been translated and if so, the most similar previous translation is retrieved from the bank to help the translator. The main conceptions of TM technology occurred in the late 1970s and early 1980s (Arthern, 1978; Kay, 1980; Melby and others, 1981). TM has been widely used since the late 1990s and continues to be widely used today (Bowker and Barlow, 2008; Christensen and Schjoldager, 2010; Garcia, 2007; Somers, 2003).

There are a lot of factors that determine how helpful TM technology will be in practice. Some of these include: quality of the interface, speed of the back-end database lookups, speed of network connectivity for distributed setups, and the comfort of the translator with using the technology. A fundamentally important factor that determines how helpful TM technology will be in practice is how well the TM bank of previously translated materials matches up with the workload materials to be translated. It is necessary that there be a high level of match for the TM technology to be most helpful. However, having a high level of match is not sufficient. One also needs a successful method for retrieving the useful translations from the (potentially large) TM bank.

TM similarity metrics are used for both evaluating the expected helpfulness of previous translations for new workload translations and the metrics also directly determine what translations get provided to the translator during translation of new materials. Thus, the algorithms that compute the TM similarity metrics are not only important, but they are doubly important.

The retrieval algorithm used by commercial TM systems is typically not disclosed (Koehn and Senellart, 2010; Simard and Fujita, 2012; Whyman and Somers, 1999). However, the best-performing method used in current systems is widely believed to be based on edit distance (Baldwin and Tanaka, 2000; Simard and Fujita, 2012; Whyman and Somers, 1999; Koehn and Senellart, 2010; Christensen and Schjoldager, 2010; Mandreoli et al., 2006; He et al., 2010). Recently

Simard and Fujita (2012) have experimented with using MT (machine translation) evaluation metrics as TM fuzzy match, or similarity, algorithms. A limitation of the work of (Simard and Fujita, 2012) was that the evaluation of the performance of the TM similarity algorithms was also conducted using the same MT evaluation metrics. Simard and Fujita (2012) concluded that their evaluation of TM similarity functions was biased since whichever MT evaluation metric was used as the TM similarity function was also likely to obtain the best score under that evaluation metric.

The current paper explores various TM fuzzy match algorithms ranging from simple baselines to the widely used edit distance to new methods. The evaluations of the TM fuzzy match algorithms use human judgments of helpfulness. An algorithm based on weighted n-gram precision consistently returns translations judged to be most helpful by translators for multiple domains and language pairs. In addition to being able to retrieve useful translations from the TM bank, the fuzzy match scores ought to be indicative of how helpful a translation can be expected to be. Many translators find it counter-productive to use TM when the best-matching translation from the TM is not similar to the workload material to be translated. Thus, many commercial TM products offer translators the opportunity to set a fuzzy match score threshold so that only translations with scores above the threshold will ever be returned. It seems to be a widely used practice to set the threshold at 70% but again it remains something of a black-box as to why 70% ought to be the setting. The current paper uncovers what expectations of helpfulness can be given for different threshold settings for various fuzzy match algorithms.

The rest of this paper is organized as follows. Section 2 presents the TM similarity metrics that will be explored; section 3 presents our experimental setup; section 4 presents and analyzes results; and section 5 concludes.

2 Translation Memory Similarity Metrics

In this section we define the methods for measuring TM similarity for which experimental results are reported in section 4. All of the metrics compute scores between 0 and 1, with higher scores indicating better matches. All of the metrics take two inputs: M and C, where M is a workload sentence from the MTBT (Material To Be Translated) and C is the source language side of a candidate pre-existing translation from the TM bank. The metrics range from simple baselines to the surmised current industrial standard to new methods.

2.1 Percent Match

Perhaps the simplest metric one could conceive of being useful for TM similarity matching is percent match (PM), the percent of tokens in the MTBT segment found in the source language side of the candidate translation pair from the TM bank.

Formally,

$$PM(M,C) = \frac{|M_{unigrams} \bigcap C_{unigrams}|}{|M_{unigrams}|}, \quad (1)$$

where M is the sentence from the MTBT that is to be translated, C is the source language side of the candidate translation from the TM bank, $M_{unigrams}$ is the set of unigrams in M, and $C_{unigrams}$ is the set of unigrams in C.

2.2 Weighted Percent Match

A drawback of PM is that it weights the matching of each unigram in an MTBT segment equally, however, it is not the case that the value of assistance to the translator is equal for each unigram of the MTBT segment. The parts that are most valuable to the translator are the parts that he/she does not already know how to translate. Weighted percent match (WPM) uses inverse document frequency (IDF) as a proxy for trying to weight words based on how much value their translations are expected to provide to translators. The use of IDF-based weighting is motivated by the assumption that common words that permeate throughout the language will be easy for translators to translate but words that occur in relatively rare situations will be harder to translate and thus more valuable to match in the TM bank. For our implementation of WPM, each source language sentence in the parallel corpus we are experimenting with is treated as a "document" when computing IDF.

Formally,

$$WPM(M,C) = \frac{\sum_{u \in \{M_{unigrams} \bigcap C_{unigrams}\}} idf(u,D)}{\sum_{u \in M_{unigrams}} idf(u,D)}, \quad (2)$$

where M, C, $M_{unigrams}$, and $C_{unigrams}$ are as defined in Eq. 1, D is the set of all source language sentences in the parallel corpus, and $idf(x, D) = log(\frac{|D|}{|\{d \in D: x \in d\}|})$.

2.3 Edit Distance

A drawback of both the PM and WPM metrics are that they are only considering coverage of the words from the workload sentence in the candidate sentence from the TM bank and not taking into account the context of the words. However, words can be translated very differently depending on their context. Thus, a TM metric that matches sentences on more than just (weighted) percentage coverage of lexical items can be expected to perform better for TM bank evaluation and retrieval. Indeed, as was discussed in section 1, it is widely believed that most TM similarity metrics used in existing systems are based on string edit distance.

Our implementation of edit distance (Levenshtein, 1966), computed on a word level, is similar to the version defined in (Koehn and Senellart, 2010).

Formally, our TM metric based on Edit Distance (ED) is defined as

$$ED = max\left(1 - \frac{edit\text{-}dist(M, C)}{|M_{unigrams}|}, 0\right), \quad (3)$$

where M, C, and $M_{unigrams}$ are as defined in Eq. 1, and $edit\text{-}dist(M, C)$ is the number of word deletions, insertions, and substitutions required to transform M into C.

2.4 N-Gram Precision

Although ED takes context into account, it does not emphasize local context in matching certain high-value words and phrases as much as metrics that capture n-gram precision between the MTBT workload sentence and candidate source-side sentences from the TMB. We note that n-gram precision forms a fundamental subcomputation in the computation of the corpus-level MT evaluation metric BLEU score (Papineni et al., 2002). However, although TM fuzzy matching metrics are related to automated MT evaluation metrics, there are some important differences. Perhaps the most important is that TM fuzzy matching has to be able to operate at a sentence-to-sentence level whereas automated MT evaluation metrics such as BLEU score are intended to operate over a whole corpus. Accordingly, we make modifications to how we use n-gram precision for the purpose of TM matching than how we use it when we compute BLEU scores. The rest of this subsection and the next two subsections describe the innovations we make in adapting the notion of n-gram precision to the TM matching task.

Our first metric along these lines, N-Gram Precision (NGP), is defined formally as follows:

$$NGP = \sum_{n=1}^{N} \frac{1}{N} p_n, \quad (4)$$

where the value of N sets the upper bound on the length of n-grams considered[1], and

$$p_n = \frac{|M_{n\text{-}grams} \cap C_{n\text{-}grams}|}{Z * |M_{n\text{-}grams}| + (1 - Z) * |C_{n\text{-}grams}|}, \quad (5)$$

where M and C are as defined in Eq. 1, $M_{n\text{-}grams}$ is the set of n-grams in M, $C_{n\text{-}grams}$ is the set of n-grams in C, and Z is a user-set parameter that controls how the metric is normalized.[2]

As seen by equation 4, we use an arithmetic mean of precisions instead of the geometric mean that BLEU score uses. An arithmetic mean is better than a geometric mean for use in translation memory metrics since translation memory metrics are operating at a segment level and not at the aggregate level of an entire test set. At the extreme, the geometric mean will be zero if any of the n-gram precisions p_n are zero. Since large n-gram matches are unlikely on a segment level, using a geometric mean can be a poor method to use for matching on a segment level, as has been described for the related task of MT evaluation (Doddington, 2002; Lavie et al., 2004). Additionally, for the related task of MT evaluation at a segment level, Lavie et al. (2004) have found that using an arithmetic mean correlates better with human judgments than using a geometric mean.

Now we turn to discussing the parameter Z for controlling how the metric is normalized. At one extreme, setting Z=1 will correspond to having no penalty on the length of the candidate retrieved from the TMB and leads to getting longer translation matches retrieved. At the other extreme,

[1] We used $N = 4$ in our experiments.

[2] Note that the n in n-grams is intended to be substituted with the corresponding integer. Accordingly, for p_1, $n = 1$ and therefore $M_{n\text{-}grams} = M_{1\text{-}grams}$ is the set of unigrams in M and $C_{n\text{-}grams} = C_{1\text{-}grams}$ is the set of unigrams in C; for p_2, $n = 2$ and therefore $M_{n\text{-}grams} = M_{2\text{-}grams}$ is the set of bigrams in M and $C_{n\text{-}grams} = C_{2\text{-}grams}$ is the set of bigrams in C; and so on.

setting Z=0 will correspond to a normalization that penalizes relatively more for length of the retrieved candidate and leads to shorter translation matches being retrieved. There is a precision/recall tradeoff in that one wants to retrieve candidates from the TMB that have high recall in the sense of matching what is in the MTBT sentence yet one also wants the retrieved candidates from the TMB to have high precision in the sense of not having extraneous material not relevant to helping with the translation of the MTBT sentence. The optimal setting of Z may differ for different scenarios based on factors like the languages, the corpora, and translator preference. We believe that for most TM applications there will usually be an asymmetric valuation of precision/recall in that recall will be more important since the value of getting a match will be more than the cost of extra material up to a point. Therefore, we believe a Z setting in between 0.5 and 1.0 will be an optimal default. We use Z=0.75 in all of our experiments described in section 3 and reported on in section 4 except for the experiments explicitly showing the impact of changing the Z parameter.

2.5 Weighted N-Gram Precision

Analogous to how we improved PM with WPM, we seek to improve NGP in a similar fashion. As can be seen from the numerator of Equation 5, NGP is weighting the match of all n-grams as uniformly important. However, it is not the case that each n-gram is of equal value to the translator. Similar to WPM, we use IDF as the basis of our proxy for weighting n-grams according to the value their translations are expected to provide to translators. Specifically, we define the weight of an n-gram to be the sum of the IDF values for each constituent unigram that comprises the n-gram.

Accordingly, we formally define method Weighted N-Gram Precision (WNGP) as follows:

$$WNGP = \sum_{n=1}^{N} \frac{1}{N} wp_n, \tag{6}$$

where N is as defined in Equation 4, and

$$wp_n = \frac{\sum_{i \in \{M_{n\text{-}grams} \cap C_{n\text{-}grams}\}} w(i)}{Z\left[\sum_{i \in M_{n\text{-}grams}} w(i)\right] + (1-Z)\left[\sum_{i \in C_{n\text{-}grams}} w(i)\right]}, \tag{7}$$

where Z, $M_{n\text{-}grams}$, and $C_{n\text{-}grams}$ are as defined in Equation 5, and

$$w(i) = \sum_{1\text{-}gram \in i} idf(1\text{-}gram, D), \tag{8}$$

where i is an n-gram and $idf(x, D)$ is as defined above for Equation 2.

2.6 Modified Weighted N-gram Precision

Note that in Equation 6 each wp_n contributes equally to the average. Modified Weighted N-Gram Precision (MWNGP) improves on WNGP by weighting the contribution of each wp_n so that shorter n-grams contribute more than longer n-grams. The intuition is that for TM settings, getting more high-value shorter n-gram matches at the expense of fewer longer n-gram matches will be more helpful since translators will get relatively more assistance from seeing new high-value vocabulary. Since the translators already presumably know the rules of the language in terms of how to order words correctly, the loss of the longer n-gram matches will be mitigated.

Formally we define MWNGP as follows:

$$MWNGP = \frac{2^N}{2^N - 1} \sum_{n=1}^{N} \frac{1}{2^n} wp_n, \tag{9}$$

where N and wp_n are as they were defined for Equation 6.

3 Experimental Setup

We performed experiments on two corpora from two different technical domains with two language pairs, French-English and Chinese-English. Subsection 3.1 discusses the specifics of the corpora and the processing we performed. Subsection 3.2 discusses the specifics of our human evaluations of how helpful retrieved segments are for translation.

3.1 Corpora

For Chinese-English experiments, we used the OpenOffice3 (OO3) parallel corpus (Tiedemann, 2009), which is OO3 computer office productivity software documentation. For French-English experiments, we used the EMEA parallel corpus (Tiedemann, 2009), which are medical documents from the European Medecines Agency. The corpora were produced by a suite of automated tools as described in (Tiedemann, 2009) and come sentence-aligned.

The first step in our experiments was to preprocess the corpora. For Chinese corpora we tokenize each sentence using the Stanford Chinese Word Segmenter (Tseng et al., 2005) with the Chinese Penn Treebank standard (Xia, 2000). For all corpora we remove all segments that have fewer than 5 tokens or more than 100 tokens. We call the resulting set the valid segments. For the purpose of computing match statistics, for French corpora we remove all punctuation, numbers, and scientific symbols; we case-normalize the text and stem the corpus using the NLTK French snowball stemmer. For the purpose of computing match statistics, for Chinese corpora we remove all but valid tokens. Valid tokens must include at least one Chinese character. A Chinese character is defined as a character in the Unicode range 0x4E00-0x9FFF or 0x4000-0x4DFF or 0xF900-0xFAFF. The rationale for removing these various tokens from consideration for the purpose of computing match statistics is that translation of numbers (when they're written as Arabic numerals), punctuation, etc. is the same across these languages and therefore we don't want them influencing the match computations. But once a translation is selected as being most helpful for translation, the original version (that still contains all the numbers, punctuation, case markings, etc.) is the version that is brought back and displayed to the translator.

For the TM simulation experiments, we randomly sampled 400 translations from the OO3 corpus and pretended that the Chinese sides of those 400 translations constitute the workload Chinese MTBT. From the rest of the corpus we randomly sampled 10,000 translations and pretended that that set of 10,000 translations constitutes the Chinese-English TMB. We also did similar sampling from the EMEA corpus of a workload French MTBT of size 300 and a French-English TMB of size 10,000.

After the preprocessing and selection of the TMB and MTBT, we found the best-matching segment from the TMB for each MTBT segment according to each TM retrieval metric defined in section 2.[3] The resulting sets of (MTBT segment,best-matching TMB segment) pairs formed the inputs on which we conducted our evaluations of the performance of the various TM retrieval metrics.

3.2 Human Evaluations

To conduct evaluations of how helpful the translations retrieved by the various TM retrieval metrics would be for translating the MTBT segments, we used Amazon Mechanical Turk, which has been used productively in the past for related work in the context of machine translation (Bloodgood and Callison-Burch, 2010b; Bloodgood and Callison-Burch, 2010a; Callison-Burch, 2009).

For each (MTBT segment,best-matching TMB segment) pair generated as discussed in subsection 3.1, we collected judgments from Turkers (i.e., the workers on MTurk) on how helpful the TMB translation would be for translating the MTBT segment on a 5-point scale. The 5-point scale was as follows:

- 5 = Extremely helpful. The sample is so similar that with trivial modifications I can do the translation.
- 4 = Very helpful. The sample included a large amount of useful words or phrases and/or some extremely useful words or phrases that overlapped with the MTBT.
- 3 = Helpful. The sample included some useful words or phrases that made translating the MTBT easier.
- 2 = Slightly helpful. The sample contained only a small number of useful words or phrases to help with translating the MTBT.
- 1 = Not helpful or detrimental. The sample would not be helpful at all or it might even be harmful for translating the MTBT.

After a worker rated a (MTBT segment,TMB segment) pair the worker was then required to give

[3] If more than one segment from the TMB was tied for being the highest-scoring segment, the segment located first in the TMB was considered to be the best-matching segment.

metric	PM	WPM	ED	NGP	WNGP	MWNGP
PM	100.0	69.5	23.0	32.0	31.5	35.5
WPM	69.5	100.0	25.8	37.0	39.0	44.2
ED	23.0	25.8	100.0	41.5	35.8	35.0
NGP	32.0	37.0	41.5	100.0	77.8	67.0
WNGP	31.5	39.0	35.8	77.8	100.0	81.2
MWNGP	35.5	44.2	35.0	67.0	81.2	100.0

Table 1: OO3 Chinese-English: The percent of the time that each pair of metrics agree on the most helpful TM segment

metric	PM	WPM	ED	NGP	WNGP	MWNGP
PM	100.0	64.7	30.3	40.3	38.3	41.3
WPM	64.7	100.0	32.0	46.3	47.0	54.3
ED	30.3	32.0	100.0	42.3	40.3	39.3
NGP	40.3	46.3	42.3	100.0	76.3	67.7
WNGP	38.3	47.0	40.3	76.3	100.0	81.3
MWNGP	41.3	54.3	39.3	67.7	81.3	100.0

Table 2: EMEA French-English: The percent of the time that each pair of metrics agree on the most helpful TM segment

Metric	Found Best	Total MTBT Segments
PM	178	400
WPM	200	400
ED	193	400
NGP	251	400
WNGP	271	400
MWNGP	282	400

Table 3: OO3 Chinese-English: The number of times that each metric found the most helpful TM segment (possibly tied).

Metric	Found Best	Total MTBT Segments
PM	166	300
WPM	184	300
ED	148	300
NGP	188	300
WNGP	198	300
MWNGP	201	300

Table 4: EMEA French-English: The number of times that each metric found the most helpful TM segment (possibly tied).

an explanation for their rating. These explanations proved quite helpful as discussed in section 4. For each (MTBT segment,TMB segment) pair, we collected judgments from five different Turkers. For each (MTBT segment,TMB segment) pair these five judgments were then averaged to form a mean opinion score (MOS) on the helpfulness of the retrieved TMB translation for translating the MTBT segment. These MOS scores form the basis of our evaluation of the performance of the different TM retrieval metrics.

4 Results and Analysis

4.1 Main Results

Tables 1 and 2 show the percent of the time that each pair of metrics agree on the choice of the most helpful TM segment for the Chinese-English OO3 data and the French-English EMEA data, respectively. A main observation to be made is that the choice of metric makes a big difference in the choice of the most helpful TM segment. For example, we can see that the surmised industrial standard ED metric agrees with the new MWNGP metric less than 40% of the time on both sets of data (35.0% on Chinese-English OO3 and 39.3% on French-English EMEA data).

Tables 3 and 4 show the number of times each metric found the TM segment that the Turkers judged to be the most helpful out of all the TM segments retrieved by all of the different metrics. From these tables one can see that the MWNGP method consistently retrieves the best TM segment more often than each of the other metrics. Scatterplots showing the exact performance on every MTBT segment of the OO3 dataset for various metrics are shown in Figures 1, 2, and 3. To conserve space, scatterplots are only shown for metrics PM (baseline metric), ED (strong surmised industrial standard metric), and MWNGP (new highest-performing metric). For each MTBT segment, there is a point in the scatterplot. The y-coordinate is the value assigned by the TM metric to the segment retrieved from the TM bank and the x-coordinate is the MOS of the five Turkers on how helpful the retrieved TM segment would be for translating the MTBT segment. A point is depicted as a dark blue diamond if none of the other metrics retrieved a segment with higher MOS judgment for that MTBT segment. A point is depicted as a yellow circle if another metric retrieved a different segment from the TM bank for that MTBT segment that had a higher MOS.

A main observation from Figure 1 is that PM is failing as evidenced by the large number of points in the upper left quadrant. For those points, the metric value is high, indicating that the retrieved segment ought to be helpful. However, the MOS is low, indicating that the humans are judging it to not be helpful. Figure 2 shows that the ED metric does not suffer from this problem. However, Figure 2 shows that ED has another problem, which is a lot of yellow circles in the lower left quadrant. Points in the lower left quadrant are not necessarily indicative of a poorly performing metric, depending on the degree of match of the TMB with the MTBT workload. If there is nothing available in the TMB that would help with the MTBT, it is appropriate for the metric to assign a low value and the humans to correspondingly agree that the retrieved sentence is not helpful. However, the fact that so many of ED's points are yellow circles indicates that there were better segments available in the TMB that ED was not able to retrieve yet another metric was able to retrieve them. Observing the scatterplots for ED and those for MWNGP one can see that both methods have the vast majority of points concentrated in the lower left and upper right quadrants, solving the upper left quadrant problem of PM. However, MWNGP has a relatively more densely populated upper right quadrant populated with dark blue diamonds than ED does whereas ED has a more densely populated lower left quadrant with yellow circles than MWNGP does. These results and trends are consistent across the EMEA French-English dataset so those scatterplots are omitted to conserve space.

Examining outliers where MWNGP assigns a high metric value yet the Turkers indicated that the translation has low helpfulness such as the point in Figure 3 at (1.6,0.70) is informative. Looking only at the source side, it looks like the translation retrieved from the TMB ought to be very helpful. The Turkers put in their explanation of their scores that the reason they gave low helpfulness is because the English translation was incorrect. This highlights that a limitation of MWNGP, and all other TM metrics we're aware of, is that they only consider the source side.

4.2 Adjusting for length preferences

As discussed in section 2, the Z parameter can be used to control for length preferences. Table 5 shows how the average length, measured by number of tokens of the source side of the translation pairs returned by MWNGP, changes as the Z parameter is changed.

Table 6 shows an example of how the optimal translation pair returned by MWNGP changes from Z=0.00 to Z=1.00. The example illustrates

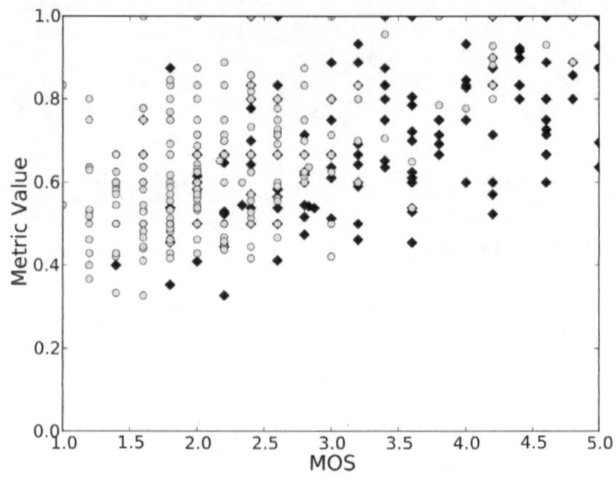

Figure 1: OO3 PM scatterplot

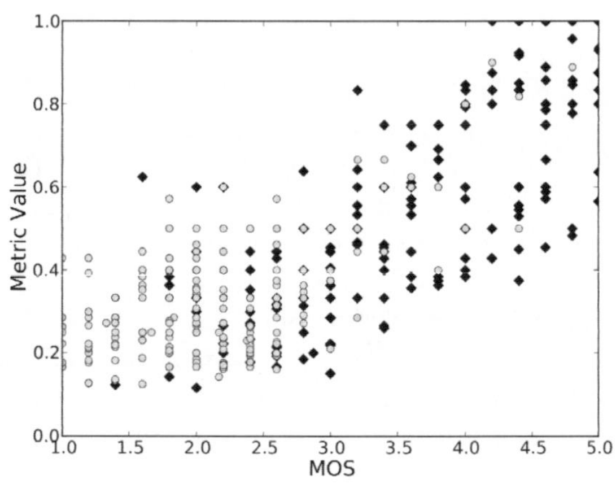

Figure 2: OO3 ED scatterplot

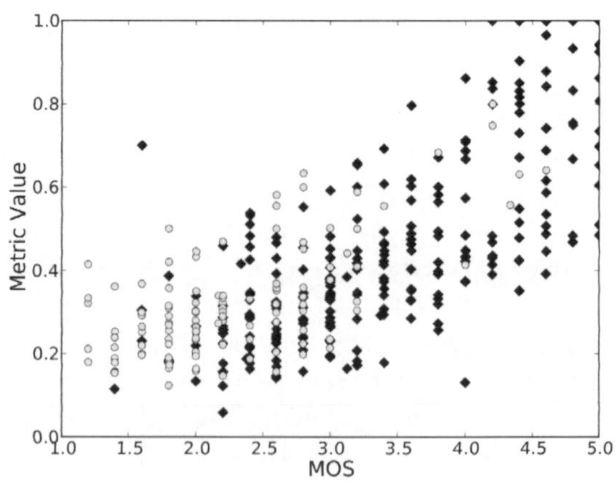

Figure 3: OO3 MWNGP scatterplot

MTBT	**French:** Ne pas utiliser durant la gestation et la lactation, car l' innocuité du médicament vétérinaire n' a pas été établie pendant la gestation ou la lactation. **English:** Do not use during pregnancy and lactation because the safety of the veterinary medicinal product has not been established during pregnancy and lactation.
MWNGP (Z=0.00)	**French:** Peut être utilisé pendant la gestation et la lactation. **English:** Can be used during pregnancy and lactation.
MWNGP (Z=1.00)	**French:** Ne pas utiliser chez l' animal en gestation ou en période de lactation, car la sécurité du robenacoxib n' a pas été établie chez les femelles gestantes ou allaitantes ni chez les chats et chiens utilisés pour la reproduction. **English:** Do not use in pregnant or lactating animals because the safety of robenacoxib has not been established during pregnancy and lactation or in cats and dogs used for breeding.

Table 6: This table shows for an example MTBT workload sentence from the EMEA French-English data how the optimal translation pair returned by MWNGP changes when going from Z = 0.00 to Z = 1.00. We provide the English translation of the MTBT workload sentence for the convenience of the reader since it was available from the EMEA parallel corpus. Note that in a real setting it would be the job of the translator to produce the English translation of the MTBT-French sentence using the translation pairs returned by MWNGP as help.

Z Value	Avg Length
0.00	9.9298
0.25	13.204
0.50	16.0134
0.75	19.6355
1.00	27.8829

(a) EMEA French-English

Z Value	Avg Length
0.00	7.2475
0.25	9.5600
0.50	11.1250
0.75	14.1825
1.00	25.0875

(b) OO3 Chinese-English

Table 5: Average TM segment length, measured by number of tokens of the source side of the translation pairs returned by MWNGP, for varying values of the Z parameter

the impact of changing the Z value on the nature of the translation matches that get returned by MWNGP. As discussed in section 2, smaller settings of Z are appropriate for preferences for shorter matches that are more precise in the sense that a larger percentage of their content will be relevant. Larger settings of Z are appropriate for preferences for longer matches that have higher recall in the sense that they will have more matches with the content in the MTBT segment overall, although at the possible expense of having more irrelevant content as well.

5 Conclusions

Translation memory is one of the most widely used translation technologies. One of the most important aspects of the technology is the system for assessing candidate translations from the TM bank for retrieval. Although detailed descriptions of the apparatus used in commercial systems are lacking, it is widely believed that they are based on an edit distance approach. We have defined and examined several TM retrieval approaches, including a new method using modified weighted n-gram precision that performs better than edit distance according to human translator judgments of helpfulness. The MWNGP method is based on the following premises: local context matching is desired; weighting words and phrases by expected helpfulness to translators is desired; and allowing shorter n-gram precisions to contribute more to the final score than longer n-gram precisions is desired. An advantage of the method is that it can be adjusted to suit translator length preferences of returned matches. A limitation of MWNGP, and all other TM metrics we are aware of, is that they only consider the source language side. Examples from our experiments reveal that this can lead to poor retrievals. Therefore, future work is called for to examine the extent to which the target language sides of the translations in the TM bank influence TM system performance and to investigate ways to incorporate target language side information to improve TM system performance.

References

Peter J Arthern. 1978. Machine translation and computerized terminology systems: a translator's viewpoint. In *Translating and the Computer: Proceedings of a Seminar*, pages 77–108.

Timothy Baldwin and Hozumi Tanaka. 2000. The effects of word order and segmentation on translation retrieval performance. In *Proceedings of the 18th conference on Computational linguistics-Volume 1*, pages 35–41. Association for Computational Linguistics.

Michael Bloodgood and Chris Callison-Burch. 2010a. Bucking the trend: Large-scale cost-focused active learning for statistical machine translation. In *Proceedings of the 48th Annual Meeting of the Association for Computational Linguistics*, pages 854–864. Association for Computational Linguistics.

Michael Bloodgood and Chris Callison-Burch. 2010b. Using mechanical turk to build machine translation evaluation sets. In *Proceedings of the NAACL HLT 2010 Workshop on Creating Speech and Language Data with Amazon's Mechanical Turk*, pages 208–211. Association for Computational Linguistics.

Lynne Bowker and Michael Barlow. 2008. A comparative evaluation of bilingual concordancers and translation memory systems. *Topics in Language Resources for Translation and Localization, Ámsterdam-Filadelfia: John Benjamins*, pages 1–22.

Chris Callison-Burch. 2009. Fast, cheap, and creative: Evaluating translation quality using Amazon's Mechanical Turk. In *Proceedings of the 2009 Conference on Empirical Methods in Natural Language Processing*, pages 286–295, Singapore, August. Association for Computational Linguistics.

Tina Paulsen Christensen and Anne Gram Schjoldager. 2010. Translation-memory (tm) research: what do we know and how do we know it? *Hermes*, 44:89–101.

George Doddington. 2002. Automatic evaluation of machine translation quality using n-gram cooccurrence statistics. In *Proceedings of the second international conference on Human Language Technology Research*, HLT '02, pages 138–145, San Francisco, CA, USA. Morgan Kaufmann Publishers Inc.

Ignacio Garcia. 2007. Power shifts in web-based translation memory. *Machine Translation*, 21(1):55–68.

Yifan He, Yanjun Ma, Andy Way, and Josef Van Genabith. 2010. Integrating n-best smt outputs into a tm system. In *Proceedings of the 23rd International Conference on Computational Linguistics: Posters*, pages 374–382. Association for Computational Linguistics.

Martin Kay. 1980. The proper place of men and machines in language translation. In *Research Report CSL-80-11*, Xerox PARC, Palo Alto, CA. Reprinted in *Machine Translation* 12, 3-23, 1997.

Philipp Koehn and Jean Senellart. 2010. Convergence of translation memory and statistical machine translation. In *Proceedings of AMTA Workshop on MT Research and the Translation Industry*, pages 21–31.

Alon Lavie, Kenji Sagae, and Shyamsundar Jayaraman. 2004. The significance of recall in automatic metrics for mt evaluation. In *In Proceedings of the 6th Conference of the Association for Machine Translation in the Americas (AMTA-2004*.

Vladimir I Levenshtein. 1966. Binary codes capable of correcting deletions, insertions and reversals. In *Soviet physics doklady*, volume 10, page 707.

Federica Mandreoli, Riccardo Martoglia, and Paolo Tiberio. 2006. Extra: a system for example-based translation assistance. *Machine Translation*, 20(3):167–197.

Alan K Melby et al. 1981. A bilingual concordance system and its use in linguistic studies. In *The Eighth Lacus Forum*, pages 541–549, Columbia, SC.

Kishore Papineni, Salim Roukos, Todd Ward, and Wei-Jing Zhu. 2002. Bleu: a method for automatic evaluation of machine translation. In *Proceedings of the 40th annual meeting on association for computational linguistics*, pages 311–318. Association for Computational Linguistics.

Michel Simard and Atsushi Fujita. 2012. A poor man's translation memory using machine translation evaluation metrics. In *Conference of the Association for Machine Translation in the Americas 2012*, San Diego, California, USA, October.

Harold L Somers. 2003. *Computers and translation: a translator's guide*, volume 35. John Benjamins Publishing Company.

Jörg Tiedemann. 2009. News from OPUS - A collection of multilingual parallel corpora with tools and interfaces. In N. Nicolov, K. Bontcheva, G. Angelova, and R. Mitkov, editors, *Recent Advances in Natural Language Processing*, volume V, pages 237–248. John Benjamins, Amsterdam/Philadelphia, Borovets, Bulgaria.

Huihsin Tseng, Pichuan Chang, Galen Andrew, Daniel Jurafsky, and Christopher Manning. 2005. A conditional random field word segmenter for sighan bakeoff 2005. In *Proceedings of the Fourth SIGHAN Workshop on Chinese Language Processing*, volume 171. Jeju Island, Korea.

Edward K. Whyman and Harold L. Somers. 1999. Evaluation metrics for a translation memory system. *Software-Practice and Experience*, 29:1265–1284.

Fei Xia. 2000. The segmentation guidelines for the penn chinese treebank (3.0). Technical Report IRCS-00-06, University of Pennsylvania.

Frame Semantic Tree Kernels for Social Network Extraction from Text

Apoorv Agarwal
Dept. of Computer Science
Columbia University
New York, NY, USA

Sriramkumar Balasubramanian
Dept. of Computer Science
Columbia University
New York, NY, USA

Anup Kotalwar
Microsoft, Inc.
Redmonad, WA, USA

Jiehan Zheng
The Peddie School
Hightstown, NJ, USA

Owen Rambow
CCLS
Columbia University
New York, NY, USA

apoorv@cs.columbia.edu

Abstract

In this paper, we present work on extracting social networks from unstructured text. We introduce novel features derived from semantic annotations based on FrameNet. We also introduce novel semantic tree kernels that help us improve the performance of the best reported system on *social event detection* and *classification* by a statistically significant margin. We show results for combining the models for the two aforementioned subtasks into the overall task of *social network extraction*. We show that a combination of features from all three levels of abstractions (lexical, syntactic and semantic) are required to achieve the best performing system.

1 Introduction

Social network extraction from text has recently been gaining a considerable amount of attention (Agarwal and Rambow, 2010; Elson et al., 2010; Agarwal et al., 2013a; Agarwal et al., 2013b; He et al., 2013). One of the reason for this attention, we believe, is that being able to extract social networks from unstructured text may provide a powerful new tool for historians, political scientists, scholars of literature, and journalists to analyze large collections of texts around *entities* and their *interactions*. The tool would allow researchers to quickly extract networks and assess their size, nature, and cohesiveness, a task that would otherwise be impossible with corpora numbering millions of documents. It would also make it possible to make falsifiable claims about these networks, bringing the experimental method to disciplines like history, where it is still relatively rare.

In our previous work (Agarwal et al., 2010), we proposed a definition of a network based on *interactions*: *nodes* are entities and *links* are *social events*. We defined two broad types of *links*: one-directional links (one person thinking about or talking about another person) and bi-directional links (two people having a conversation, a meeting, etc.). For example, in the following sentence, we would add two links to the network: a one-directional link between **Toujan Faisal** and the **committee**, triggered by the word *said* (because **Toujan** is talking *about* the committee) and a bi-directional link between the same entities triggered by the word *informed* (a mutual interaction).

(1) [Toujan Faisal], 54, said [she] was informed of the refusal by an [Interior Ministry committee] overseeing election preparations.

In this paper, we extract networks using the aforementioned definition of social networks. We introduce and add tree kernel representations and features derived from frame-semantic parses to our previously proposed system. Our results show that hand-crafted frame semantic features, which are linguistically motivated, add less value to the overall performance in comparison with the frame-semantic tree kernels. We believe this is due to the fact that hand-crafted features require frame parses to be highly accurate and complete. In contrast, tree kernels are able to find and leverage less strict patterns without requiring the semantic parse to be entirely accurate or complete.

Apart from introducing semantic features and tree structures, we evaluate on the task of social network extraction, which is a combination of two sub-tasks: social event *detection* and social event *classification*. In our previous work (Agarwal and Rambow, 2010), we presented results for the two sub-tasks, but no evaluation was presented for the task of social network extraction. We experiment with two different designs of combining models for the two sub-tasks: 1) One-versus-All and 2) Hierarchical. We find that the hierarchical design outperforms the more commonly used One-versus-All by a statistically significant margin.

Following are the contributions of this paper:

1. We design and propose novel frame semantic features and tree-based representations and show that tree kernels are well suited to work with noisy semantic parses.
2. We show that in order to achieve the best performing system, we need to include features and tree structures from all levels of abstractions, lexical, syntactic, and semantic, and that the convolution kernel framework is well-suited for creating such a combination.
3. We combine the previously proposed sub-tasks (social event detection and classification) into a single task, social network extraction, and show that combining the models using a hierarchical design is significantly better than the one-versus-all design.

The rest of the paper is structured as follows: In Section 2, we give a precise definition of the task and describe the data. In Section 3, we give a brief overview of frame semantics and motivate the need to use frame semantics for the tasks addressed in this paper. In Section 4, we present semantic features and tree kernel representations designed for the tasks. In Section 5, we briefly review tree kernels and support vector machines (SVM). In Section 6 we present experiments and discuss the results. In Section 7 we discuss related work. We conclude and give future directions of work in Section 8.

2 Data and Task Definition

In Agarwal et al. (2010), we presented the annotation details of *social events* on a well-known corpus – Automated Content Extraction[1] (ACE2005). We defined a social event to be a *happening* between two entities (of type person) $E1$ and $E2$ ($E1 \neq E2$), in which at least one entity is cognitively aware of the other and of the happening taking place. We defined two broad categories of social events: Interaction (INR) and Observation (OBS). In a social event of type INR, the two participating entities are mutually aware of each other, i.e., INR is a bi-directional social event. For example, meetings and dinners are social events of type interaction. In a social event of type OBS, only one of the two participating entities is aware of the other and therefore, OBS is a one-directional social event, directed from the entity that is aware of the other to the other entity. For example, thinking about someone, or missing someone are social events of type OBS. Table 1 shows the distribution of the data. There are 199 INR type of social events, 199 OBS events, and 1,609 pairs of entity mentions have no event between them.

	No-Event	INR	OBS
# of Examples	1,609	199	199

Table 1: Data distribution; INR are interaction social events. OBS are observation social events.

Task definition : The task is, given a pair of entity mentions in a sentence, to predict if the entities are participating in a social event or not (social event detection, SED), and if they are, to further predict the type of social event (INR or OBS, social event classification, SEC). In this paper, we evaluate our system on the above tasks as well as a combined task: social network extraction (SNE): given a sentence and a pair of entity mentions, predict the class of the example from one of the following three categories: {No-Event, INR, OBS}.

For the purposes of this paper, we use gold named entity mentions to avoid errors caused due to named entity recognition systems. This is a common practice used in the literature for reporting relation extraction systems (Zelenko et al., 2003; Kambhatla, 2004; Zhao and Grishman, 2005; GuoDong et al., 2005; Harabagiu et al., 2005; Nguyen et al., 2009). We use standard terminology from the literature to refer to the pair of entities mentions as *target* entities T_1 and T_2.

3 Frame Semantics and FrameNet

FrameNet (Baker et al., 1998) is a resource which associates words of English with their meaning. Word meanings are based on the notion of "semantic frame". A frame is a conceptual description of a type of event, relation, or entity, and it

[1]Version: 6.0, Catalog number: LDC2005E18

includes a list of possible participants in terms of the roles they play; these participants are called "frame elements". Through the following example, we present the terminology and acronyms that will be used throughout the paper.

Example (2) shows the frame annotations for the sentence *Toujan Faisal said she was informed of the refusal by an Interior Ministry committee.* One of the semantic frames in the sentence is **Statement**. The *frame evoking element (FEE)* for this frame is *said*. It has two *frame elements (FE)*: one of type **Speaker** (*Toujan Faisal*) and the other of type **Message** (*she was informed ... by an Interior Ministry committee*).

(2) [$_{\mathbf{FE-Speaker}}$ Toujan Faisal] [$_{\mathbf{FEE-Statement}}$ said] [$_{\mathbf{FE-Message}}$ she was informed of the refusal by an Interior Ministry committee]

In example (2), the speaker of the message (*Toujan Faisal*) is *mentioning* another group of people (the *Interior Ministry committee*) in her message. By definition, this is a social event of type OBS. In general, there is an OBS social event between any **Speaker** and any person mentioned in the frame element **Message** of the frame **Statement**. This close relation between frames and social events is the reason for our investigation and use of frame semantics for the tasks addressed in this paper.

4 Feature space and data representation

We convert examples[2] into two kinds of structured representations: feature vectors and tree structures. Each of these structural representations may broadly be categorized into one or more of the following levels of abstraction: {Lexical, Syntactic, Semantic}. Table 2 presents this distribution. Our final results show that all of our top performing models use a data representation that is a combination of features and structures from all levels of abstraction. We review previously proposed features and tree structures in subsections 4.1, 4.2, and 4.3. To the best of our knowledge, the remaining features and structures presented in this section are novel.

4.1 Bag of words (BOW)

We create a vocabulary from our training data by using the Stanford tokenizer (Klein and Manning, 2003) followed by removal of stop words and Porter Stemming. We convert each example ($\vec{x}$) to a set of three boolean vectors: $\{\vec{b_1}, \vec{b_2}, \vec{b_3}\}$. $\vec{b_1}$ is the occurrence of words before the first target, $\vec{b_2}$ between the two targets and $\vec{b_3}$ after the second target. Here the *first target* and *second target* are defined in terms of the surface order of words. Though these features have been previously proposed for relation extraction on ACE (GuoDong et al., 2005), they have not been utilized for the task we address in this paper.

4.2 Syntactic structures (AR2010)

In Agarwal and Rambow (2010), we explored a wide range of syntactic structures for the two tasks of social event detection (SED) and classification (SEC). All our previous structures were derived from a variation of two underlying tree structures: phrase structure trees and dependency trees. The best structure we proposed was PET_GR_SqGRW, which was a linear combination of two tree kernels and one word kernel: 1) a structure derived from a phrase structure tree (PET); 2) a grammatical role tree (GR), which is a dependency tree in which words are replaced with their grammatical roles; and 3) a path from one entity to the other in a dependency tree, in which grammatical roles of words are inserted as additional nodes between the dependent and parent (SqGRW). We refer the reader to Agarwal and Rambow (2010) for details of these structures. For the rest of the paper, we refer to this structure, PET_GR_SqGRW, as "AR2010". We use AR2010 as one of our baselines.

4.3 Bag of frames (BOF)

We use Semafor (Chen et al., 2010) for obtaining the semantic parse of a sentence. Semafor found instances of 1,174 different FrameNet frames in our corpus. Each example ($\vec{x}$) is converted to a vector of dimension 1,174, in which x_i (the ith component of vector $\vec{x}$) is 1 if the frame number i appears in the example, and 0 otherwise.

4.4 Hand-crafted semantic features (RULES)

We use the manual of the FrameNet resource to hand-craft 199 rules that are intended to detect the presence and determine the type of social events between two entities mentioned in a sentence. An example of one such rule is given in section 3, which we reformulate here. We also present another example:

[2]An input example is a sentence with a pair of entity mentions between whom we predict and classify social events.

	Feature Vectors			Tree Structures			
	BOW	BOF	RULES	AR2010	FrameForest	FrameTree	FrameTreeProp
Lexical	✓			✓	✓		
Syntactic				✓	✓		
Semantic (novel)		✓	✓		✓	✓	✓

Table 2: Features and tree structures and the level of abstraction they fall into.

(3) If the frame is **Statement**, and the first target entity mention is contained in the FE **Speaker**, and the second is contained in the FE **Message**, then there is an OBS social event from the first entity to the second.

(4) If the frame is **Commerce_buy**, and one target entity mention is contained in the FE **Buyer**, and the other is contained in the FE **Seller**, then there is an INR social event between the two entities.

Each rule corresponds to a binary feature: it takes a value 1 if the rule fires for an input example, and 0 otherwise. Consider the following sentence:

(5) [Coleman]$_{T1-Ind}$ {claimed} [he]$_{T1'-Ind}$ {bought} drugs from the [defendants]$_{T2-Grp}$.

In this sentence, there are two social events: 1) an OBS event triggered by the word *claimed* between *Coleman* and *defendants* and 2) an INR event triggered by the word *bought* between *he* (co-referential with *Coleman*) and the *defendants*.

Semafor correctly detects two frames in this sentence: 1) the frame **Statement**, with *Coleman* as **Speaker**, and *he bought ... defendants* as **Message**, and 2) the frame **Commerce_buy**, with *he* as the **Buyer**, *drugs* as the **Goods** and *the defendants* as the **Seller**. Both hand-crafted rules (3 and 4) fire and the corresponding feature values for these rules is set to 1. Firing of these rules (and thus the effectiveness these features) is of course highly dependent on the fact that Semafor provides an accurate frame parse for the sentence.

4.5 Semantic trees (FrameForest, FrameTree, FrameTreeProp)

Semafor labels *text spans* in sentences as frame evoking elements (FEE) or frame elements (FE). A sentence usually has multiple frames and the frame annotations may overlap. There may be two ways in which spans overlap (Figure 1): (a) one frame annotation is completely embedded in the other frame annotation and (b) some of the frame elements overlap (in terms of text spans). We now present the three frame semantic tree kernel representations that handle these overlapping issues, along with providing a meaningful semantic kernel representation for the tasks addressed in this paper.

Figure 1: Two overlapping scenarios for frame annotations of a sentence, where $F1, F2$ are frames.

For each of the following representations, we assume that for each sentence s, we have the set of semantic frames, $\mathbb{F}_s = \{F = \langle FEE, [FE_1, FE_2, \ldots, FE_n]\rangle\}$ with each frame F having an FEE and a list of FEs. . We illustrate the structures using sentence (5).

4.5.1 FrameForest Tree Representation

We first create a tree for each frame annotation F in the sentence. Consider a frame, $F = \langle FEE, [FE_1, FE_2, \ldots, FE_n]\rangle$. For the purposes of tree construction, we treat FEE as another FE (call it FE_0) of type *Target*. For each FE_i, we choose the subtree from the dependency parse tree that is the smallest subtree containing all words annotated as FE_i by Semafor. Call this subtree extracted from the dependency parse $DepTree\_FE_i$. We then create a larger tree by adding $DepTree\_FE_i$ as a child of a new node labeled with frame element FE_i: $(FE_i\ DepTree\_FE_i)$. Call this resulting tree $SubTree\_FE_i$. We then connect all the $SubTree\_FE_i$ ($i \in \{0, 1, 2, \ldots, n\}$) to a new root node labeled with the frame F: $(F\ SubTree\_FE_0\ \ldots\ SubTree\_FE_n)$. This is the tree for a frame F. Since the sentence could have multiple frames, we connect the *forest* of frame trees to a new node called $ROOT$.

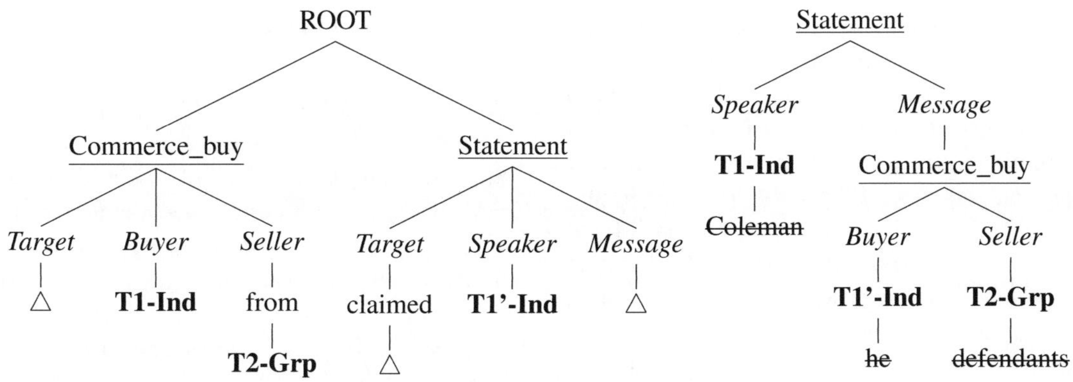

Figure 2: Semantic trees for the sentence "Coleman claimed [he]$_{T1-Ind}$ bought drugs from the [defendants]$_{T2-Grp}$.". The tree on the left is FrameForest and the tree on the right is FrameTree. △ in FrameForest refers to the subtree (bought (T1-Ind) (from T2-Grp)). **Ind** refers to individual and **Grp** refers to group.

We prune away all subtrees that do not contain the target entities. We refer to the resulting tree as FrameForest.

For example, in Figure 2, the left tree is the FrameForest tree for sentence (5). There are two frames in this sentence that appear in the final tree because both these frames contain the target entities and thus are not pruned away. The two frames are **Commerce_buy** and **Statement**. We first create trees for each of the frames. For the **Commerce_buy** frame, there are three frame elements: *Target* (the frame evoking element), *Buyer* and *Seller*. For each frame element, we get the subtree from the dependency tree that contains all the words belonging to that frame element. The subtree for FEE *Target* is (*bought* T1-Ind (*from* T2-Grp)). The subtree for FE *Buyer* is (T1-Ind) and the subtree for FE *Seller* is (*from* T2-Grp). We connect these subtrees to their respective frame elements and connect the resulting subtrees to the frame (**Commerce_buy**). Similarly, we create a tree for the frame **Statement**. Finally, we connect all frame trees to the $ROOT$.

In this representation, we have avoided the frame overlapping issues by repeating the common subtrees: the subtree (*bought* T1-Ind (*from* T2-Grp)) is repeated under the FEE **Target** of the **Statement** frame as well as under the FE **Message** of the **Statement** frame.

4.5.2 FrameTree Tree Representation

For the design of this tree, we deal with the two overlapping conditions shown in Figure 1 differently. If one frame is fully embedded in another frame, we add the former as a child of the latter frame. In Figure 2, the frame **Commerce_buy** is fully embedded in the frame element **Message** of the frame **Statement**. Therefore, the frame subtree for **Commerce_buy** appears as a subtree of **Message**.

If the frames overlap partially, we copy over the overlapping portions of the structures to each of the frame sub-trees.

For the design of this representation, we remove all lexical nodes (struck out nodes in Figure 2) and trees that do not span any of the target entities (not shown in the figure). As a result, this structure is the smallest semantic structure that contains the two target entities. The right tree in Figure 2 is the FrameTree tree for sentence (5).

4.5.3 FrameTreeProp Tree Representation

We are using a partial tree kernel (PTK) for calculating the similarity of two trees (as detailed in section 5). The PTK does not *skip* over nodes of the tree that lie on the same path. For establishing an OBS social event between *Coleman* and the *defendants*, all the structure needs to encode is the fact that one target appears as a *Speaker* and the other appears in the *Message* (of the speaker). In FrameTree, this information is encoded but in an unclear manner – there are two nodes (Commerce_buy and *Seller*) that come in between the node *Message* and **T2-Grp**.

For this reason, we copy the nodes labeled with the target annotations ($T1-*$, $T2-*$) to all nodes (that are frame elements of a frame) on the path from them to the root in FrameTree. We call this variation of FrameTree, in which we *propagate* $T1 - *, T2 - *$ nodes to the root, FrameTreeProp. For the running example, FrameTreeProp will be: (Statement (*Speaker* **T1-Ind**) (*Message* (Commerce_buy ...) (**T2-Grp**))). Using this tree representation, one of the sub-trees in the implicit feature space will be (Statement (*Speaker* **T1-Ind**) (*Message* (**T2-Grp**)), which encodes the relation between the two targets in a more direct manner as compared to FrameTree.

5 Machine Learning

We represent our data in form of feature vectors and tree structures. We use convolution kernels (Haussler, 1999) that make use of the dual form of Support Vector Machines (SVMs). In the dual form, the optimization problem that SVM solves is the following (Burges, 1998):

$$max \ \Sigma_i \mu_i - \Sigma_{i,j} \mu_i \mu_j y_i y_j K(x_i, x_j)$$

$$\text{s.t.} \quad \Sigma_i \mu_i y_i = 0$$

$$\mu_i \geq 0 \quad \forall i = 1, 2, \ldots, l$$

Here, x_i is the input example, y_i is the class of the example x_i, μ_i is the Lagrange multiplier associated with example x_i, l is the number of training examples, and K is the kernel function that returns a similarity between two examples. More formally, K is the function, $K : X \times X \rightarrow \mathbb{R}$, that maps a pair of objects belonging to the set X to a real number. For example, if we represent our input examples as feature vectors, the set X would be the set of feature vectors. For feature vectors, we use a linear kernel, i.e. $K(x_i, x_j) = x_i \cdot x_j$ (dot product of the two vectors). For our tree representations, we use a Partial Tree Kernel (PTK), first proposed by Moschitti (2006). PTK is a relaxed version of the Subset Tree (SST) kernel proposed by Collins and Duffy (2002). A subset tree kernel measures the similarity between two trees by counting all subtrees common to the two trees. However, there is one constraint: all daughter nodes of a parent node must be included (in the sub-trees). In PTK, this constraint is removed. Therefore, in contrast to SST, PT kernels compare many more substructures. For a combination of feature vectors and tree representations, we simply use the linear combination of their respective kernels.

6 Experiments and Results

We present 5-fold cross-validation results on the ACE2005 corpus annotated for social events. Since the number of types of features and structures is not large (Table 2), we run an exhaustive set of $2^7 - 1 = 127$ experiments for each of three tasks: Social Event Detection (SED), Social Event Classification (SEC) and Social Network Extraction (SNE). To avoid over-fitting to a particular partition into folds, we run each 5-fold experiment 50 times, for 50 randomly generated partitions. The results reported in the following tables are all averaged over these 50 partitions. The absolute standard deviation on an average is less than 0.004. This means that the performance of our models across 50 random folds does not fluctuate and hence the system is robust. We use McNemar's significance test and refer to statistical significance as $p < 0.05$.

6.1 Social event detection (SED) and classification (SEC)

We report precision (P), recall (R) and F1 measure for the detection task, and % accuracy for the classification task. For both these tasks, our previous best performing system was PET_GR_SqGRW (which we refer to as AR2010). We use this as a baseline, and introduce two new baselines: the bag-of-words (BOW) baseline and a linear combination of BOW and AR2010, referred to as BOW_AR2010.

Table 3 presents the results for these two tasks for various features and structures. The results show that our purely semantic models (RULES, BOF, FrameTree, FrameTreeProp) do not perform well alone. FrameForest, which encodes some lexical and syntactic level features (but is primarily semantic), also performs worse than the baselines when used alone. However, a combination of lexical, syntactic and semantic structures improves the performance by an absolute of 1.1% in F1-measure for SED (from 0.574 to 0.585). This gain is statistically significant. For SEC, the absolute gain from our best baseline (BOW_AR2010) is 0.8% in F1-measure (from 82.3 to 83.1), which is not statistically significant. However, the gain of 2% from our previously proposed best system (AR2010) is statistically significant.

	SED			SEC	SNE Hierarchical		
Model	P	R	F1	%Acc	P	R	F1
BOW	0.343	0.391	0.365	70.9	0.247	0.277	0.261
AR2010	0.464	0.751	0.574	81.1	0.375	0.611	0.465
BOW_AR2010	0.488	0.645	0.555	82.3	0.399	0.532	0.456
RULES	0.508	0.097	0.164	60.2	0.301	0.059	0.099
BOF	0.296	0.416	0.346	64.4	0.183	0.266	0.217
FrameForest	0.331	0.594	0.425	74.5	0.247	0.442	0.317
FrameTree	0.295	0.594	0.395	68.3	0.206	0.405	0.273
FrameTreeProp	0.308	0.554	0.396	70.7	0.217	0.390	0.279
All	0.494	0.641	0.558	82.5	0.405	0.531	0.460
BOW_AR2010_FrameForest_FrameTreeProp	0.490	0.633	0.552	**83.1**	0.405	0.528	0.459
AR2010_FrameTreeProp	0.484	0.740	**0.585**	82.0	0.397	0.608	**0.480**

Table 3: Results for three tasks: "SED" is Social Event Detection, "SEC" is Social Event Classification, "SNE" is Social Network Extraction. The first three models are the baseline models. The next five models are the novel semantic features and structures we propose in this paper. "All" refers to the model that uses all the listed structures together. "BOW_AR2010_FrameForest_FrameTreeProp" refers to the model that uses a linear combination of mentioned structures. AR2010_FrameTreeProp is a linear combination of AR2010 and FrameTreeProp.

6.2 Social network extraction (SNE)

Social network extraction is a multi-way classification task, in which, given an example, we classify it into one of three categories: {No-Event, INR, OBS}. A popular technique of performing multi-way classification using a binary classifier like SVM, is one-versus-all (OVA). We try this along with a less commonly used technique, in which we stack two binary classifiers in a hierarchy. For the hierarchical design, we train two models: (1) the SED model ({INR + OBS} versus No-Event) and (2) the SEC model (INR versus OBS). Given a test example, it is first classified using the SED model. If the prediction is less than zero, we label it as No-Event. Otherwise, the test example is passed onto SEC and finally classified into either INR or OBS.

We see that none of the semantic features and structures alone outperform the baseline. However, a combination of structures from different levels of abstraction achieve the best performance: an absolute gain of 1.5% in F1 (statistically significant) when we use a hierarchical design (from 0.465 to 0.480).

Comparing hierarchical verus OVA approaches, we observe that the hierarchical approach outperforms the OVA approach for all our models by a statistically significant margin. The performance for our best reported model (AR2010_FrameTreeProp) for OVA in terms precision, recall, and F1-measure is 0.375, 0.592, 0.459 respectively. This is statistically significantly worse than hierarchical approach (0.397, 0.608, 0.480).

6.3 Discussion of results

Performing well on SED is more important than SEC, because if a social event is not detected in the first place, the goodness of the SEC model is irrelevant. Therefore, the best feature and structure combination we report in this paper is a combination of AR2010 and FrameTreeProp.

To gain insight into the how each type of semantic feature and structure contribute to our previously proposed lexical and syntactic model (AR2010), we perform experiments in which we add one semantic feature/structure at a time to AR2010. Table 4 presents the results for this study. We see that the hand-crafted RULES do not help in the overall task. We investigated the reason for RULES not being as helpful as we had expected. We found that when there is no social event, the rules fire in 7% of the cases. When there *is* a social event, they fire in 17% of cases. So while they fire more often when there is a social event, the percentage of cases in which they fire is small. We hypothesize that this is due the dependence of RULES on the correctness of semantic parses. For example, Rule (4) correctly detects the social event in sentence (5), since Semafor correctly parses the input. In contrast, Semafor does not correctly parse the input sentence (1): it correctly identifies the **Statement** frame and its **Message** frame element, but it fails to find the **Speaker**. As a result, Rule (3) does not fire, even though the semantic structure is partially identified. This, we believe, highlights the main strength of tree kernels – they are able to learn semantic patterns, without requiring correctness or completeness of the semantic parse.

Out of the semantic structures we propose, FrameTreeProp adds the most value to the baseline system as compared to other semantic features and structures. This supports our intuition that we need to reduce unbounded semantic dependencies between the target entities by propagating the target entity tags to the top of the semantic tree.

Model	SED (F1)	SEC (%A)	SNE Hier. (F1)
AR2010	0.574	81.1	0.465
+ RULES	0.576	80.8	0.465
+ BOF	0.569	80.7	0.459
+ FrameForest	0.571	**82.6**	0.472
+ FrameTree	0.579	81.5	0.473
+ FrameTreeProp	**0.585**	82.0	**0.480**

Table 4: A study to show which semantic features and structures add the most value to the baseline. The top row gives the performance of the baseline. Each consecutive row shows the result of the baseline plus the feature/structure mentioned in that row.

7 Related Work

There have been recent efforts to extract networks from text (Elson et al., 2010; He et al., 2013). However, these efforts extract a different type of network: a network of only bi-directional links, where the links are triggered by quotation marks. For example, Elson et al. (2010) and He et al. (2013) will extract an interaction link between *Emma* and *Harriet* in the following sentence. However, their system will not detect any interaction links in the other examples mentioned in this paper.

(6) "Take it," said Emma, smiling, and pushing the paper towards Harriet "it is for you. Take your own."

Our approach to extract and classify social events builds on our previous work (Agarwal and Rambow, 2010), which in turn builds on work from the relation extraction community (Nguyen et al., 2009). Therefore, the task of relation extraction is most closely related to the tasks addressed in this paper. Researchers have used other notions of semantics in the literature such as latent semantic analysis (Plank and Moschitti, 2013) and relation-specific semantics (Zelenko et al., 2003; Culotta and Sorensen, 2004). To the best of our knowledge, there is only one work that uses frame semantics for relation extraction (Harabagiu et al., 2005). Harabagiu et al. (2005) propose a novel semantic kernel that incorporates frame parse information in the kernel computation that calculates similarity between two dependency trees. They, however, do not propose data representations that are based on frame parses and the resulting arborescent structures, instead adding features to syntactic trees. We believe the implicit feature space of kernels based on our data representation encode a richer and larger feature space than the one proposed by Harabagiu et al. (2005).

8 Conclusion and Future Work

This work has only scratched the surface of possibilities for using frame semantic features and tree structures for the task of social event extraction. We have shown that tree kernels are well suited to work with possibly inaccurate semantic parses in contrast to hand-crafted features that require the semantic parses to be completely accurate. We have also extended our previous work by designing and evaluating a full system for social network extraction.

A more natural data representation for semantic parses is a graph structure. We are actively exploring the design of semantic graph structures that may be brought to bear with the use of graph kernels (Vishwanathan et al., 2010).

Acknowledgments

We would like to thank CCLS's IT heads, Hatim Diab and Manoj Pooleery, for providing the infrastructure support. This paper is based upon work supported in part by the DARPA DEFT Program. The views expressed are those of the authors and do not reflect the official policy or position of the Department of Defense or the U.S. Government.

References

Apoorv Agarwal and Owen Rambow. 2010. Automatic detection and classification of social events. In *Proceedings of the 2010 Conference on Empirical Methods in Natural Language Processing*, pages 1024–1034, Cambridge, MA, October. Association for Computational Linguistics.

Apoorv Agarwal, Owen C. Rambow, and Rebecca J. Passonneau. 2010. Annotation scheme for social network extraction from text. In *Proceedings of the Fourth Linguistic Annotation Workshop*.

Apoorv Agarwal, Anup Kotalwar, and Owen Rambow. 2013a. Automatic extraction of social networks from literary text: A case study on alice in wonderland. *In the Proceedings of the 6th International Joint Conference on Natural Language Processing (IJCNLP 2013)*.

Apoorv Agarwal, Anup Kotalwar, Jiehan Zheng, and Owen Rambow. 2013b. Sinnet: Social interaction network extractor from text. In *Sixth International Joint Conference on Natural Language Processing*, page 33.

Collin F. Baker, J. Fillmore, and John B. Lowe. 1998. The Berkeley FrameNet project. In *36th Meeting of the Association for Computational Linguistics and 17th International Conference on Computational Linguistics (COLING-ACL'98)*, pages 86–90, Montréal.

Chris Burges. 1998. A tutorial on support vector machines for pattern recognition. *Data mining and knowledge discovery*.

Desai Chen, Nathan Schneider, Dipanjan Das, and Noah A. Smith. 2010. Semafor: Frame argument resolution with log-linear models. In *Proceedings of the 5th International Workshop on Semantic Evaluation*, pages 264–267, Uppsala, Sweden, July. Association for Computational Linguistics.

Michael Collins and Nigel Duffy. 2002. New ranking algorithms for parsing and tagging: Kernels over discrete structures, and the voted perceptron. In *Proceedings of the 40th annual meeting on association for computational linguistics*, pages 263–270. Association for Computational Linguistics.

Aron Culotta and Jeffrey Sorensen. 2004. Dependency tree kernels for relation extraction. In *Proceedings of the 42nd Meeting of the Association for Computational Linguistics (ACL'04), Main Volume*, pages 423–429, Barcelona, Spain, July.

David K. Elson, Nicholas Dames, and Kathleen R. McKeown. 2010. Extracting social networks from literary fiction. *Proceedings of the 48th Annual Meeting of the Association for Computational Linguistics*, pages 138–147.

Zhou GuoDong, Su Jian, Zhang Jie, and Zhang Min. 2005. Exploring various knowledge in relation extraction. In *Proceedings of 43th Annual Meeting of the Association for Computational Linguistics*.

Sanda Harabagiu, Cosmin Adrian Bejan, and Paul Morarescu. 2005. Shallow semantics for relation extraction. In *International Joint Conference On Artificial Intelligence*.

David Haussler. 1999. Convolution kernels on discrete structures. Technical report, University of California at Santa Cruz.

Hua He, Denilson Barbosa, and Grzegorz Kondrak. 2013. Identification of speakers in novels. *The 51st Annual Meeting of the Association for Computational Linguistics (ACL 2013)*.

Nanda Kambhatla. 2004. Combining lexical, syntactic, and semantic features with maximum entropy models for extracting relations. In *Proceedings of the ACL 2004 on Interactive poster and demonstration sessions*, page 22. Association for Computational Linguistics.

Dan Klein and Christopher D. Manning. 2003. Accurate unlexicalized parsing. *Proceedings of the 41st Meeting of the Association for Computational Linguistics*, pages 423–430.

Alessandro Moschitti. 2006. Efficient convolution kernels for dependency and constituent syntactic trees. In *Proceedings of the 17th European Conference on Machine Learning*.

Truc-Vien T. Nguyen, Alessandro Moschitti, and Giuseppe Riccardi. 2009. Convolution kernels on constituent, dependency and sequential structures for relation extraction. *Conference on Empirical Methods in Natural Language Processing*.

Barbara Plank and Alessandro Moschitti. 2013. Embedding semantic similarity in tree kernels for domain adaptation of relation extraction. In *Proceedings of the 51st Annual Meeting of the Association for Computational Linguistics (Volume 1: Long Papers)*, pages 1498–1507, Sofia, Bulgaria, August. Association for Computational Linguistics.

SVN Vishwanathan, Nicol N Schraudolph, Risi Kondor, and Karsten M Borgwardt. 2010. Graph kernels. *The Journal of Machine Learning Research*, 11:1201–1242.

Dmitry Zelenko, Chinatsu Aone, and Anthony Richardella. 2003. Kernel methods for relation extraction. *The Journal of Machine Learning Research*, 3:1083–1106.

Shubin Zhao and Ralph Grishman. 2005. Extracting relations with integrated information using kernel methods. In *Proceedings of the 43rd Meeting of the ACL*.

Statistical Script Learning with Multi-Argument Events

Karl Pichotta
Department of Computer Science
The University of Texas at Austin
pichotta@cs.utexas.edu

Raymond J. Mooney
Department of Computer Science
The University of Texas at Austin
mooney@cs.utexas.edu

Abstract

Scripts represent knowledge of stereotypical event sequences that can aid text understanding. Initial statistical methods have been developed to learn probabilistic scripts from raw text corpora; however, they utilize a very impoverished representation of events, consisting of a verb and one dependent argument. We present a script learning approach that employs events with multiple arguments. Unlike previous work, we model the interactions between multiple entities in a script. Experiments on a large corpus using the task of inferring held-out events (the "narrative cloze evaluation") demonstrate that modeling multi-argument events improves predictive accuracy.

1 Introduction

Scripts encode knowledge of stereotypical events, including information about their typical ordered sequences of sub-events and corresponding arguments (Schank and Abelson, 1977). The classic example is the "restaurant script," which encodes knowledge about what normally happens when dining out. Such knowledge can be used to improve text understanding by supporting inference of missing actions and events, as well as resolution of lexical and syntactic ambiguities and anaphora (Rahman and Ng, 2012). For example, given the text "John went to Olive Garden and ordered lasagna. He left a big tip and left," an inference that scripts would ideally allow us to make is "John ate lasagna."

There is a small body of recent research on automatically learning probabilistic models of scripts from large corpora of raw text (Manshadi et al., 2008; Chambers and Jurafsky, 2008; Chambers and Jurafsky, 2009; Jans et al., 2012). However, this work uses a very impoverished representation of events that only includes a verb and a single dependent entity. We propose a more complex multi-argument event representation for use in statistical script models, capable of directly capturing interactions between multiple entities. We present a method for learning such a model, and provide experimental evidence that modeling entity interactions allows for better prediction of events in documents, compared to previous single-entity "chain" models. We also compare to a competitive baseline not used in previous work, and introduce a novel evaluation metric.

2 Background

The idea of representing stereotypical event sequences for textual inference originates in the seminal work of Schank and Abelson (1977). Early scripts were manually engineered for specific domains; however, Mooney and DeJong (1985) present an early knowledge-based method for learning scripts from a single document. These early scripts (and methods for learning them) were non-statistical and fairly brittle.

Chambers and Jurafsky (2008) introduced a method for learning statistical scripts that, using a much simpler event representation that allows for efficient learning and inference. Jans et al. (2012) use the same simple event representation, but introduce a new model that more accurately predicts test data. These methods only model the actions of a single participant, called the *protagonist*. Chambers and Jurafsky (2009) extended their approach to the multi-participant case, modeling the events in which all of the entities in a document are involved; however, their method cannot represent interactions between multiple entities.

Balasubramanian et al. (2012; 2013) describe the Rel-gram system, a Markov model similar to that of Jans et al. (2012), but with tuples instead of (verb, dependency) pairs. Our approach is similar, but instead of modeling a distribution over co-occurring verbs and nominal arguments, we model interactions between entities directly by incorporating coreference information into the model.

Previous statistical script learning systems proceed broadly as follows. For a document D:

1. Run a dependency parser on D, to match up verbs with their argument NPs.

2. Run a coreference resolver on D to determine which NPs likely refer to the same entity.

3. Construct a sequence of event objects, using syntactic and coreference information.

One can then build a statistical model of the event sequences produced by Step 3. Such a model may be evaluated using the narrative cloze evaluation, described in Section 4.1, in which we hold out an event from a sequence and attempt to infer it.

The major difference between the current work and previous work is that the event sequences produced in Step 3 are of a different sort from those in other models. Our events are more structured, as described in Section 3.1, and we produce one event sequence per document, instead of one event sequence per entity. This requires a different statistical model, as described in Section 3.2.

3 Script Models

In Section 3.1, we describe the multi-argument events we use as the basis of our script models. Section 3.2 describes a script model using these events, and Section 3.3 describes the baseline systems to which we compare.

3.1 Multi-Argument Events

Statistical scripts are models of stereotypical sequences of *events*. In Chambers and Jurafsky (2008; 2009) and Jans et al. (2012), events are (verb, dependency) pairs, forming "chains," grouped according to the entity involved. For example, the text

(1) Mary emailed Jim and he responded to her immediately.

yields two chains. First, there is a chain for Mary:

(*email*, subject)
(*respond*, object)

indicating that Mary was the subject of an *emailing* event and the object of a *responding* event. Second, there is a chain for Jim:

(*email*, object)
(*respond*, subject)

indicating that Jim was the object of an *emailing* event and the subject of a *responding* event. Thus, one document produces many chains, each corresponding to an entity. Note that a single verb may produce multiple pair events, each present in a chain corresponding to one of the verb's arguments. Note also that there is no connection between the different events produced by a verb: there is nothing connecting (*email*, subject) in Mary's chain with (*email*, object) in Jim's chain.

We propose a richer event representation, in which a document is represented as a single sequence of event tuples, the arguments of which are entities. Each entity may be mentioned in many events, and, unlike previous work, each event may involve multiple entities. For example, sentence (1) will produce a single two-event sequence, the first event representing Mary emailing Jim, and the second representing Jim responding to Mary.

Formally, an **entity** is represented by a constant, and noun phrases are mapped to entities, where two noun phrases are mapped to the same constant if and only if they corefer. A **multi-argument event** is a relational atom $v(e_s, e_o, e_p)$, where v is a verb lemma, and e_s, e_o, and e_p are possibly-null entities. The first entity, e_s, stands in a subject relation to the verb v; the second, e_o, is the direct object of v; the third e_p stands in a prepositional relation to v. One of these entities is **null** (written as "·") if and only if no noun phrase stands in the appropriate relation to v. For example, *Mary hopped* would be represented as $hop(mary, \cdot, \cdot)$, while *Mary gave the book to John* would be $give(mary, book, john)$. In this formulation, Example (1) produces the sequence

$email(m, j, \cdot)$
$respond(j, m, \cdot)$

where m and j are entity constants representing all mentions of Mary and Jim, respectively. Note that this formulation is capable of capturing interactions between entities: we directly encode the fact that after one person emails another, the latter responds to the former. In contrast, pair events can capture only that after an entity emails, they are responded to (or after they are emailed, they respond). Multi-argument events capture more of the basic event structure of text, and are therefore well-suited as a representation for scripts.

3.2 Multi-argument Statistical Scripts

We now describe our script model. Section 3.2.1 describes our method of estimating a joint probability distribution over pairs of events, modeling event co-occurrence, and Section 3.2.2 shows how this co-occurrence probability can be used to infer new events from a set of known events.

3.2.1 Estimating Joint Probabilities

Suppose we have a sequence of multi-argument events, each of which is a verb with entities as arguments. We are interested in predicting which event is most likely to have happened at some point in the sequence. Our model will require a conditional probability $P(a|a')$, the probability of seeing event a after event a', given we have observed a'. However, as described below, directly estimating this probability is more complicated than in previous work because events now have additional structure.

By definition, we have

$$P(a_2|a_1) = \frac{P(a_1, a_2)}{P(a_1)}$$

where $P(a_1, a_2)$ is the probability of seeing a_1 and a_2, in order. The most straightforward way to estimate $P(a_1, a_2)$ is, if possible, by counting the number of times we observe a_1 and a_2 co-occurring and normalizing the function to sum to 1 over all pairs (a_1, a_2). For Chambers and Jurafsky (2008; 2009) and Jans et al. (2012), such a Maximum Likelihood Estimate is straightforward to arrive at: events are (verb, dependency) pairs, and two events co-occur when they are in the same event chain, relating to the same entity (Jans et al. (2012) further require a_1 and a_2 to be near each other). One need simply traverse a training corpus and count the number of times each pair (a_1, a_2) co-occurs. The Rel-grams of Balasubramanian et al. (2012; 2013) admit a similar strategy: to arrive at a joint distribution of pairwise co-occurrence, one can simply count co-occurrence of ground relations in a corpus and normalize.

However, given two multi-argument events of the form $v(e_s, e_o, e_p)$, this strategy will not suffice. For example, if during training we observe the two co-occurring events

(2) *ask*$(mary, bob, question)$
answer$(bob, \cdot, \cdot)$

we would like this to lend evidence to the co-occurrence of events *ask*(x, y, z) and

Algorithm 1 Learning with entity substitution

```
for a1, a2 ∈ evs do
    N(a1, a2) ← 0
end for
for D ∈ documents do
    for a1, a2 ∈ coocurEvs(D) do
        for σ ∈ subs(a1, a2) do
            N(σ(a1), σ(a2)) += 1
        end for
    end for
end for
```

answer$(y, \cdot, \cdot)$ for all distinct entities x, y, and z. If we were to simply keep the entities as they are and calculate raw co-occurrence counts, we would get evidence only for $x = mary$, $y = bob$, and $z = question$.

One approach to this problem would be to deploy one of many previously described Statistical Relational Learning methods, for example Logical Hidden Markov Models (Kersting et al., 2006) or Relational Markov Models (Anderson et al., 2002). These methods can learn various statistical relationships between relational logical atoms with variables, of the sort considered here. However, we investigate a simpler option.

The most important relationship between the entities in two multi-argument events concerns their overlapping entities. For example, to describe the relationship between the three entities in (2), it is most important to note that the object of the first event is identical with the subject of the second (namely, both are *bob*). The identity of the non-overlapping entities *mary* and *question* is not important for capturing the relationship between the two events.

We note that two multi-argument events $v(e_s, e_o, e_p)$ and $v'(e'_s, e'_o, e'_p)$, share at most three entities. We thus introduce four variables x, y, z, and O. The three variables x, y, and z represent arbitrary distinct entities, and the fourth, O, stands for "Other," for entities not shared between the two events. We can rewrite the entities in our two multi-argument events using these variables, with the constraint that two identical (i.e. coreferent) entities must be mapped to the same variable in $\{x, y, z\}$, and no two distinct entities may map to the same variable in $\{x, y, z\}$. This formulation simplifies calculations while still capturing pairwise entity relationships between events.

Algorithm 1 gives the pseudocode for the learning method. This populates a co-occurrence matrix N, where entry $N(a_1, a_2)$ gives the co-occurrence count of events a_1 and a_2. The variable `evs` in line 1 is the set of all events in our model, which are of the form $v(e_s, e_o, e_p)$, with v a verb lemma and $e_s, e_o, e_p \in \{x, y, z, O\}$. The variable `documents` in line 4 is the collection of documents in our training corpus. The function `cooccurEvs` in line 5 takes a document D and returns all ordered pairs of co-occurring events in D, where, following the 2-skip bigram model of Jans et al. (2012), and similar to Balasubramanian et al. (2012; 2013), two events a_1 and a_2 are said to co-occur if they occur in order, in the same document, with at most two intervening events between them.[1] The function `subs` in line 6 takes two events and returns all variable substitutions σ mapping from entities mentioned in the events a_1 and a_2 to the set $\{x, y, z, O\}$, such that two coreferent entities map to the same element of $\{x, y, z\}$. A substitution σ applied to an event $v(e_s, e_o, e_p)$, as in line 7, is defined as $v(\sigma(e_s), \sigma(e_o), \sigma(e_p))$, with the null entity mapped to itself.

Once we have calculated $N(a_1, a_2)$ using Algorithm 1, we may define $P(a_1, a_2)$ for two events a_1 and a_2, giving an estimate for the probability of observing a_2 occurring after a_1, as

$$P(a_1, a_2) = \frac{N(a_1, a_2)}{\sum_{a_1', a_2'} N(a_1', a_2')}. \tag{3}$$

We may then define the conditional probability of seeing a_2 after a_1, given an observation of a_1:

$$\begin{aligned} P(a_2|a_1) &= \frac{P(a_1, a_2)}{\sum_{a'} P(a_1, a')} \\ &= \frac{N(a_1, a_2)}{\sum_{a'} N(a_1, a')}. \end{aligned} \tag{4}$$

3.2.2 Inferring Events

Suppose we have a sequence of multi-argument events extracted from a document. A natural task for a statistical script model is to infer what other events likely occurred, given the events explicitly stated in a document. Chambers and Jurafsky (2008; 2009) treat the events involving an entity as an unordered set, inferring the most likely additional event, with no relative ordering between the inferred event and known events. We adopt the model of Jans et al. (2012), which was demonstrated to give better empirical performance. This model takes an ordered sequence of events and a position in that sequence, and guesses events that likely occurred at that position. In that work, events are (verb, dependency) pairs, and an event sequence consists of all such pairs involving a particular entity. We use this model in the multi-argument event setting, in which a document produces a single sequence of multi-argument events.

Let A be an ordered list of events, and let p be an integer between 1 and $|A|$, the length of A. For $i = 1, \ldots, |A|$, define a_i to be the ith element of A. We follow Jans et al. (2012) by scoring a candidate event a according to its probability of following all of the events before position p, and preceding all events after position p. That is, we rank candidate events a by maximizing $S(a)$, defined as

$$S(a) = \sum_{i=1}^{p-1} \log P(a|a_i) + \sum_{i=p}^{|A|} \log P(a_i|a) \tag{5}$$

with conditional probabilities $P(a|a')$ calculated using (4). Each event in $a_i \in A$ independently contributes to a candidate a's score; the ordering between a and a_i is taken into account, but the ordering between the different events $a_i \in A$ does not directly affect a's score.

3.3 Baseline Systems

We describe the baseline systems against which we compare the performance of the multi-argument script system described in section 3.2. These systems infer new events (either multi-argument or pair events) given the events contained in a document.

Performance of these systems is measured using the narrative cloze task, in which we hold out a single event (either a multi-argument or pair event), and rate a system by its ability to infer this event, given the other events in a document. The narrative cloze task is described in detail in Section 4.1.

3.3.1 Random Model

The simplest baseline we compare to is the **random baseline**, which outputs randomly selected events observed during training. This model can guess either multi-argument or pair events.

3.3.2 Unigram Model

The **unigram** system guesses events ordered by prior probability, as calculated from the training set. If scripts are viewed as n-gram models

[1]Other notions of co-occurrence could easily be substituted here.

over events, this baseline corresponds to a bag-of-words unigram model. In this model, events are assumed to occur independently, drawn from a single distribution. This model can be used to guess either multi-argument or pair events.

3.3.3 Single Protagonist Model

We refer to the system of Jans et al. (2012) as the **single protagonist** system. This model takes a single sequence of (verb, dependency) pair events, all relating to a single entity. It then produces a list of pair events, giving the model's top predictions for additional events involving the entity. This model maximizes the objective given in (5), with the sequence A (and the candidate guesses a) comprised of pair events.

3.3.4 Multiple Protagonist Model

The **multiple protagonist** system infers multi-argument events. While this method is not described in previous work, it is the most direct way of guessing a full multi-argument event using a single protagonist script model.

The multiple protagonist system uses a single-protagonist model, which models pair events, to predict multi-argument events, given a sequence of known multi-argument events. Suppose we have a non-empty set E of entities mentioned in the known events. We describe the most direct method of using a single-protagonist system to infer additional multi-argument events involving E.

A multi-argument event $a = v(e_s, e_o, e_p)$ represents three pairs: (v, e_s), (v, e_o), and (v, e_p). The multiple protagonist model scores an event a according to the score the single protagonist model assigns to these three pairs individually.

For entity $e \in E$ in some multi-argument event in a document, we first extract the sequence of (verb, dependency) pairs corresponding to e from all known multi-argument events. For a pair d, we calculate the score $S_e(d)$, the score the single protagonist system assigns the pair d, given the known pairs corresponding to e. If e has no known pairs corresponding to it (in the cloze evaluation described below, this will happen if e occurs only in the held-out event), we fall back to calculating $S_e(d)$ with a unigram model, as described in Section 3.3.2, over (verb, dependency) pair events.

We then rank a multi-argument event $a = v(e_s, e_o, e_p)$, with $e_s, e_o, e_p \in E$, with the following objective function:

$$M(a) = S_{e_s}((v, \text{subj})) + S_{e_o}((v, \text{obj})) + S_{e_p}((v, \text{prep})) \quad (6)$$

where, for null entity e, we define $S_e(d) = 0$ for all d. In the cloze evaluation, E will be the entities in the held-out event. Each entity in a contributes independently to the score $M(a)$, based on the known (verb, dependency) pairs involving that entity. This model scores a multi-argument event a by combining one independent single-protagonist model for every entity in a.

This model is similar to the multi-participant narrative schemas described in Chambers and Jurafsky (2009), but whereas they infer bare verbs, we infer an entire multi-argument event.

4 Evaluation

4.1 Evaluation Task

We follow previous work in using the narrative cloze task to evaluate statistical scripts (Chambers and Jurafsky, 2008; Chambers and Jurafsky, 2009; Jans et al., 2012). The task is as follows: given a sequence of events $a_1, \ldots, a_n$ from a document, hold out some event a_p and attempt to predict that event, given the other events in the sequence. As we cannot automatically evaluate the prediction of truly unmentioned events in a document, this evaluation acts as a straightforward proxy.

In the aforementioned work, the cloze task is to guess a pair event, given the other events in which the held-out pair's entity occurs. In Section 4.2.2, we evaluate directly on this task of guessing pair events. However, in Section 4.2.1, we evaluate on the task of guessing a multi-argument event, given all other events in a document and the entities mentioned in the held-out event. This is, we argue, the most natural way to adapt the cloze evaluation to the multi-argument event setting: instead of guessing a held-out pair event based on the other events involving its lone entity, we will guess a held-out multi-argument event based on the other events involving any of its entities.

A document may contain arbitrarily many entities. The script model described in Section 3.2.1, however, only models events involving entities from a closed class of four variables $\{x, y, z, O\}$. We therefore rewrite entities in a document's sequences of events to the variables $\{x, y, z, O\}$ in a way that maintains all pairwise relationships between the held-out event and others. That is, if the held-out event shares an entity with another event, this remains true after rewriting.

We perform entity rewriting relative to a single held-out event, proceeding as follows:

- Any entity in the held-out event that is mentioned at least once in another event gets rewritten consistently to one of x, y, or z, such that distinct entities never get rewritten to the same variable.
- Any entity mentioned only in the held-out event is rewritten as O.
- All entities not present in the held-out event are rewritten as O.

This simplification removes structure from the original sequence, but retains the important pairwise entity relationships between the held-out event and the other events.

4.2 Experimental Evaluation

For each document, we use the Stanford dependency parser (De Marneffe et al., 2006) to get syntactic information about the document; we then use the Stanford coreference resolution engine (Raghunathan et al., 2010) to get (noisy) equivalence classes of coreferent noun phrases in a document.[2] We train on approximately 1.1M articles from years 1994-2006 of the NYT portion of the Gigaword Corpus, Third Edition (Graff et al., 2007), holding out a random subset of the articles from 1999 for development and test sets. Our test set consists of 10,000 randomly selected held-out events, and our development set is 500 disjoint randomly selected held-out events. To remove duplicate documents, we hash the first 500 characters of each article and remove any articles with hash collisions. We use add-one smoothing on all joint probabilities. To reduce the size of our model, we remove all events that occur fewer than 50 times.[3]

We evaluate performance using the following two metrics:

1. **Recall at 10**: Following Jans et al. (2012), we measure performance by outputting the top 10 guesses for each held-out event and calculating the percentage of such lists containing the correct answer.[4] This value will be between 0 and 1, with 1 indicating perfect system performance.
2. **Accuracy**: A multi-argument event $v(e_s, e_o, e_p)$ has four components; a pair event has two components. For a held-out event, we may judge the accuracy of a system's top guess by giving one point for getting each of its components correct and dividing by the number of possible points. We average this value over the test set, yielding a value between 0 and 1, with 1 indicating perfect system performance. This is a novel evaluation metric for the script learning task.

These metrics target a system's most confident predicted events: we argue that a script system is best evaluated by its top inferences.

In Section 4.2.1, we evaluate on the task of inferring multi-argument events. In Section 4.2.2, we evaluate on the task of guessing pair events.

4.2.1 System Comparison on Multi-argument Events

We first compare system performance on inferring multi-argument events, evaluated on the narrative cloze task as described in Section 4.1, using the corpora and metrics described in Section 4.2. We compare against three baselines: the uninformed **random** baseline from Section 3.3.1, the **unigram** system from 3.3.2, and the **multiple protagonist** system from Section 3.3.4.

The **joint** system guesses the held-out event, given the other events in the document that involve the entities in that held-out tuple. The system orders candidate events a by their scores $S(a)$, as given in Equation (5). This is the primary system described in this paper, modeling full multi-argument events directly.

Table 1 gives the recall at 10 ("R@10") and accuracy scores for the different systems. The unigram system is quite competitive, achieving performance comparable to the multiple protagonist system on accuracy, and superior performance on recall at 10.

Evaluating by the recall at 10 metric, the joint system provides a 2.9% absolute (**13.2%** relative) improvement over the unigram system, and a 3.6%

[2]We use version 1.3.4 of the Stanford CoreNLP system.

[3]A manual inspection reveals that the majority of these removed events come from noisy text or parse errors.

[4]Jans et al. (2012) instead use recall at 50, but we observe, as they also report, that the comparative differences between systems using recall at k for various values of k is similar.

Method	R@10	Accuracy
Random	0.001	0.334
Unigram	0.216	0.507
Multiple Protagonist	0.209	0.504
Joint	**0.245**	**0.549**

Table 1: Results for multi-argument events.

Method	R@10	Accuracy
Random	0.001	0.495
Unigram	0.297	0.552
Single Protagonist	0.282	0.553
Joint Pair	**0.336**	**0.561**

Table 2: Results for pair events.

absolute (**17.2**% relative) improvement over the multiple protagonist system. These differences are statistically significant ($p < 0.01$) by McNemar's test. By accuracy, the joint system provides a 4.2% absolute (**8.3**% relative) improvement over the unigram model, and a 4.5% absolute (**8.9**% relative) improvement over the multiple protagonist model. Accuracy differences are significant ($p < 0.01$) by a Wilcoxon signed-rank test.

These results provide evidence that directly modeling full multi-argument events, as opposed to modeling chains of (verb, dependency) pairs for single entities, allows us to better infer held-out verbs with all participating entities.

4.2.2 System Comparison on Pair Events

In Section 4.2.1, we adapted a baseline pair-event system to the task of guessing multi-argument events. We may also do the converse, adapting our multi-argument event system to the task of guessing the simpler pair events. That is, we infer a full multi-argument event and extract from it a (subject,verb) pair relating to a particular entity. This allows us to compare directly to previously published methods.

The **random**, **unigram**, and **single protagonist** systems are pair-event systems described in Sections 3.3.1, 3.3.2, and 3.3.3, respectively. The **joint pair** system takes the multi-argument events guessed by the joint system of Section 4.2.1 and converts them to pair events by discarding any information not related to the target entity; that is, if the held-out pair event relates to an entity e, then every occurrence of e as an argument of a guessed multi-argument event will be converted into a single pair event, scored identically to its original multi-argument event. Ties are broken arbitrarily.

Table 2 gives the comparative results for these four systems. The test set is constructed by extracting one pair event from each of the 10,000 multi-argument events in the test set used in Section 4.2.1, such that the extracted pair event relates to an entity with at least one additional known pair event. Evaluating by recall at 10, the joint system provides a 3.9% absolute (**13.1**% relative) improvement over the unigram baseline, and a 5.4% absolute (**19.1**% relative) improvement over the single protagonist system. These differences are significant ($p < 0.01$) by McNemar's test. By accuracy, the joint system provides a 0.9% absolute (**1.6**% relative) improvement over the unigram model, and a 0.8% absolute (**1.4**% relative) improvement over the single protagonist model. Accuracy differences are significant ($p < 0.01$) by a Wilcoxon signed-rank test.

These results indicate that modeling multi-argument event sequences allows better inference of simpler pair events. These performance improvements may be due to the fact that the joint model conditions on information not representable in the single protagonist model (namely, all of the events in which a multi-argument event's entities are involved).

5 Related Work

The procedural encoding of common situations for automated reasoning dates back decades. The frames of Minsky (1974), schemas of Rumelhart (1975), and scripts of Schank and Abelson (1977) are early examples. These models use quite complex representations for events, with many different relations between events. They are not statistical, and use separate models for different scenarios (e.g. the "restaurant script" is different from the "bank script"). Generally, they require humans to encode procedural information by hand; see, however, Mooney and DeJong (1985) for an early method for learning scripts automatically from a document. Miikkulainen (1990; 1993) gives a hierarchical Neural Network system which stores sequences of events from text in episodic memory, capable of simple question answering.

Regneri et al. (2010) and Li et al. (2012) give methods for using crowdsourcing to create situation-specific scripts. These methods help alleviate the bottleneck of the knowledge-engineering required for traditionally conceived script systems. These systems are precision-oriented: they create small, highly accurate scripts for very limited scenarios. The current work, in contrast, focuses on building high-recall models of general event sequences. There are also a number of systems addressing the related problem of modeling domain-specific human-human dialog for building dialog systems (Bangalore et al., 2006; Chotimongkol, 2008; Boyer et al., 2009).

There have been a number of recent approaches to learning statistical scripts. Chambers and Jurafsky (2008) and Jans et al. (2012) give methods for learning models of (verb, dependency) pairs, as described above. Manshadi et al. (2008) give an n-gram model for sequences of verbs and their patients. McIntyre and Lapata (2009; 2010) use script objects learned from corpora of fairy tales to automatically generate stories. Chambers and Jurafsky (2009) extend their previous model to incorporate multiple entities, but do not directly model the different arguments of an event. Bamman et al. (2013) learn latent character personas from film summaries, associating character types with stereotypical actions; they focus on identifying persona types, rather than event inference.

Manshadi et al. (2008) and Balasubramanian et al. (2012; 2013) give approaches similar to the current work for modeling sequences of events as n-grams. These methods differ from the current work in that they do not model entities directly, instead modeling co-occurrence of particular nouns standing as arguments to particular verbs. Lewis and Steedman (2013) build clusters of relations similar to these events, finding such clusters helpful to question answering and textual inference.

There has also been recent interest in the related problem of automatically learning event frames (Bejan, 2008; Chambers and Jurafsky, 2011; Cheung et al., 2013; Chambers, 2013). These approaches focus on identifying frames for information extraction tasks, as opposed to inferring events directly. Balasubramanian et al. (2013) give an event frame identification method, developed in parallel with the current work, using sequences of tuples similar to our multi-argument events, noting coherence issues with pair events. Their formulation differs from ours primarily in that they do not incorporate coreference information into their event co-occurrence distribution, and evaluate using human judgments of frame coherence rather than a narrative cloze test.

6 Future Work

We have evaluated only one type of multi-argument event inference, in which a script infers an event given a set of entities and the events involving those entities. We claim that this is the most natural adaptation of the cloze evaluation to the multi-argument event setting. However, other types of inferences would be useful as well for question-answering. Additional script inferences, and their applications to question answering, are worth investigating more fully.

The evaluation methodology used here has two serious benefits: it is totally automatic, and it does not require labeled data. The cloze evaluation is intuitively reasonable: a good script system should be able to predict stated events as having taken place. Basic pragmatic reasoning, however, tells us that the most obvious inferable events are not typically stated in text. This evaluation thus fails to capture some of the most important commonsense inferences. Further investigation into evaluation methodologies for script systems is needed.

7 Conclusion

We described multi-argument events for statistical scripts, which can directly encode the pairwise entity relationships between events in a document. We described a script model that can handle the important aspects of the additional complexity introduced by these events, and a baseline model that can infer multi-argument events using single-protagonist chains instead of directly modeling full relations. We introduced the novel unigram baseline model for comparison, as well as the novel accuracy metric, and provided empirical evidence that modeling full multi-argument events provides more predictive power than modeling event chains individually.

Acknowledgments

Thanks to Katrin Erk, Amelia Harrison, and the DEFT group at UT Austin for helpful discussions. Thanks also to the anonymous reviewers for their helpful comments. This research was supported in part by the DARPA DEFT program under AFRL grant FA8750-13-2-0026. Some of our experiments were run on the Mastodon Cluster, supported by NSF Grant EIA-0303609.

References

Corin R Anderson, Pedro Domingos, and Daniel S Weld. 2002. Relational Markov models and their application to adaptive web navigation. In *Proceedings of the Eighth ACM SIGKDD International Conference on Knowledge Discovery and Data Mining (KDD-2002)*, pages 143–152.

Niranjan Balasubramanian, Stephen Soderland, Mausam, and Oren Etzioni. 2012. Rel-grams: a probabilistic model of relations in text. In *Proceedings of the Joint Workshop on Automatic Knowledge Base Construction and Web-scale Knowledge Extraction at NAACL-HLT 2012 (AKBC-WEKEX 2012)*, pages 101–105.

Niranjan Balasubramanian, Stephen Soderland, Mausam, and Oren Etzioni. 2013. Generating coherent event schemas at scale. In *Proceedings of the 2013 Conference on Empirical Methods in Natural Language Processing (EMNLP-2013)*.

David Bamman, Brendan O'Connor, and Noah A. Smith. 2013. Learning latent personas of film characters. In *Proceedings of the 51st Annual Meeting of the Association for Computational Linguistics (ACL-13)*, pages 352–361.

Srinivas Bangalore, Giuseppe Di Fabbrizio, and Amanda Stent. 2006. Learning the structure of task-driven human–human dialogs. In *Proceedings of the 21st International Conference on Computational Linguistics and 44th Annual Meeting of the Association for Computational Linguistics (COLING/ACL-06)*, pages 201–208.

Cosmin Adrian Bejan. 2008. Unsupervised discovery of event scenarios from texts. In *Prodeedings of the 21st International Florida Artificial Intelligence Research Society Conference (FLAIRS-2008)*, pages 124–129.

Kristy Elizabeth Boyer, Robert Phillips, Eun Young Ha, Michael D. Wallis, Mladen A. Vouk, and James C. Lester. 2009. Modeling dialogue structure with adjacency pair analysis and Hidden Markov Models. In *Proceedings of Human Language Technologies: The Conference of the North American Chapter of the Association for Computational Linguistics, Companion Volume: Short Paper (NAACL-HLT-09 Short)*, pages 49–52.

Nathanael Chambers and Daniel Jurafsky. 2008. Unsupervised learning of narrative event chains. In *Proceedings of the 46th Annual Meeting of the Association for Computational Linguistics (ACL-08)*, pages 789–797.

Nathanael Chambers and Dan Jurafsky. 2009. Unsupervised learning of narrative schemas and their participants. In *Joint Conference of the 47th Annual Meeting of the Association for Computational Linguistics and the 4th International Joint Conference on Natural Language Processing of the Asian Federation of Natural Language Processing (ACL-IJCNLP)*, pages 602–610.

Nathanael Chambers and Dan Jurafsky. 2011. Template-based information extraction without the templates. In *Proceedings of the 49th Annual Meeting of the Association for Computational Linguistics: Human Language Technologies (ACL-HLT-11)*, pages 976–986.

Nathanael Chambers. 2013. Event schema induction with a probabilistic entity-driven model. In *Proceedings of the 2013 Conference on Empirical Methods in Natural Language Processing (EMNLP-2013)*.

Jackie Chi Kit Cheung, Hoifung Poon, and Lucy Vanderwende. 2013. Probabilistic frame induction. In *Proceedings of the 2013 Conference of the North American Chapter of the Association for Computational Linguistics: Human Language Technologies (NAACL-13)*.

Ananlada Chotimongkol. 2008. *Learning the structure of task-oriented conversations from the corpus of in-domain dialogs*. Ph.D. thesis, Carnegie Mellon University.

Marie-Catherine De Marneffe, Bill MacCartney, Christopher D Manning, et al. 2006. Generating typed dependency parses from phrase structure parses. In *Proceedings of the 5th International Conference on Language Resources & Evaluation (LREC-2006)*, volume 6, pages 449–454.

David Graff, Junbo Kong, Ke Chen, and Kazuaki Maeda. 2007. *English Gigaword Third Edition*. Linguistic Data Consortium.

Bram Jans, Steven Bethard, Ivan Vulić, and Marie Francine Moens. 2012. Skip n-grams and ranking functions for predicting script events. In *Proceedings of the 13th Conference of the European Chapter of the Association for Computational Linguistics (EACL-12)*, pages 336–344.

Kristian Kersting, Luc De Raedt, and Tapani Raiko. 2006. Logical Hidden Markov Models. *Journal of Artificial Intelligence Research*, 25:425–456.

Mike Lewis and Mark Steedman. 2013. Combined distributional and logical semantics. *Transactions of the Association for Computational Linguistics*, 1:179–192.

Boyang Li, Stephen Lee-Urban, Darren Scott Appling, and Mark O Riedl. 2012. Crowdsourcing narrative intelligence. *Advances in Cognitive Systems*, 2:25–42.

Mehdi Manshadi, Reid Swanson, and Andrew S Gordon. 2008. Learning a probabilistic model of event sequences from internet weblog stories. In *Prodeedings of the 21st International Florida Artificial Intelligence Research Society Conference (FLAIRS-2008)*, pages 159–164.

Neil McIntyre and Mirella Lapata. 2009. Learning to tell tales: A data-driven approach to story generation. In *Joint Conference of the 47th Annual Meeting of the Association for Computational Linguistics and the 4th International Joint Conference on Natural Language Processing of the Asian Federation of Natural Language Processing (ACL-IJCNLP)*, pages 217–225.

Neil McIntyre and Mirella Lapata. 2010. Plot induction and evolutionary search for story generation. In *Proceedings of the 48th Annual Meeting of the Association for Computational Linguistics (ACL-10)*, pages 1562–1572.

Risto Miikkulainen. 1990. *DISCERN: A Distributed Artificial Neural Network Model of Script Processing and Memory*. Ph.D. thesis, University of California.

Risto Miikkulainen. 1993. *Subsymbolic Natural Language Processing: An Integrated Model of Scripts, Lexicon, and Memory*. MIT Press, Cambridge, MA.

Marvin Minsky. 1974. A framework for representing knowledge. Technical report, MIT-AI Laboratory.

Raymond J. Mooney and Gerald F. DeJong. 1985. Learning schemata for natural language processing. In *Proceedings of the Ninth International Joint Conference on Artificial Intelligence (IJCAI-85)*, pages 681–687, Los Angeles, CA, August.

Karthik Raghunathan, Heeyoung Lee, Sudarshan Rangarajan, Nathanael Chambers, Mihai Surdeanu, Dan Jurafsky, and Christopher Manning. 2010. A multi-pass sieve for coreference resolution. In *Proceedings of the Conference on Empirical Methods in Natural Language Processing (EMNLP-2010)*, pages 492–501.

Altaf Rahman and Vincent Ng. 2012. Resolving complex cases of definite pronouns: the Winograd schema challenge. In *Proceedings of the 2012 Conference on Empirical Methods in Natural Language Processing and Computational Natural Language Learning (EMNLP-CoNLL-12)*, pages 777–789.

Michaela Regneri, Alexander Koller, and Manfred Pinkal. 2010. Learning script knowledge with web experiments. In *Proceedings of the 48th Annual Meeting of the Association for Computational Linguistics (ACL-10)*, Uppsala, Sweden, July.

David Rumelhart. 1975. Notes on a schema for stories. *Representation and Understanding: Studies in Cognitive Science.*

Roger C. Schank and Robert P. Abelson. 1977. *Scripts, Plans, Goals and Understanding: An Inquiry into Human Knowledge Structures*. Lawrence Erlbaum and Associates, Hillsdale, NJ.

Improving Distributional Semantic Vectors through Context Selection and Normalisation

Tamara Polajnar
University of Cambridge
Computer Laboratory
tp366@cam.ac.uk

Stephen Clark
University of Cambridge
Computer Laboratory
sc609@cam.ac.uk

Abstract

Distributional semantic models (DSMs) have been effective at representing semantics at the word level, and research has recently moved on to building distributional representations for larger segments of text. In this paper, we introduce novel ways of applying context selection and normalisation to vary model sparsity and the range of values of the DSM vectors. We show how these methods enhance the quality of the vectors and thus result in improved low dimensional and composed representations. We demonstrate these effects on standard word and phrase datasets, and on a new definition retrieval task and dataset.

1 Introduction

Distributional semantic models (DSMs) (Turney and Pantel, 2010; Clarke, 2012) encode word meaning by counting co-occurrences with other words within a context window and recording these counts in a vector. Various IR and NLP tasks, such as word sense disambiguation, query expansion, and paraphrasing, take advantage of DSMs at a word level. More recently, researchers have been exploring methods that combine word vectors to represent phrases (Mitchell and Lapata, 2010; Baroni and Zamparelli, 2010) and sentences (Coecke et al., 2010; Socher et al., 2012). In this paper, we introduce two techniques that improve the quality of word vectors and can be easily tuned to adapt the vectors to particular lexical and compositional tasks.

The quality of the word vectors is generally assessed on standard datasets that consist of a list of word pairs and a corresponding list of gold standard scores. These scores are gathered through an annotation task and reflect the similarity between the words as perceived by human judges (Bruni et al., 2012). Evaluation is conducted by comparing the word similarity predicted by the model with the gold standard using a correlation test such as Spearman's ρ.

While words, and perhaps some frequent shorter phrases, can be represented by distributional vectors learned through co-occurrence statistics, infrequent phrases and novel constructions are impossible to represent in that way. The goal of compositional DSMs is to find methods of combining word vectors, or perhaps higher-order tensors, into a single vector that represents the meaning of the whole segment of text. Elementary approaches to composition employ simple operations, such as addition and elementwise product, directly on the word vectors. These have been shown to be effective for phrase similarity evaluation (Mitchell and Lapata, 2010) and detection of anomalous phrases (Kochmar and Briscoe, 2013).

The methods that will be introduced in this paper can be applied to co-occurrence vectors to produce improvements on word similarity and compositional tasks with simple operators. We chose to examine the use of sum, elementwise product, and circular convolution (Jones and Mewhort, 2007), because they are often used due to their simplicity, or as components of more complex models (Zanzotto and Dell'Arciprete, 2011).

The first method is context selection (CS), in which the top N highest weighted context words per vector are selected, and the rest of the values are discarded (by setting to zero). This technique is similar to the way that Explicit Semantic Analysis (ESA) (Gabrilovich and Markovitch, 2007) selects the number of topics that represent a word, and the word filtering approach in Gamallo and Bordag (2011). It has the advantage of improving word representations and vector sum representations (for compositional tasks) while using vectors with fewer non-zero elements. Programming languages often have efficient strategies for storing these *sparse* vectors, leading to lower memory usage. As an example of the resulting accuracy improvements, when vectors with up to 10,000 non-zero elements are reduced to a maximum of $N = 240$ non-zero elements, the Spearman ρ improves from 0.61 to 0.76 on a standard word similarity task. We also see an improvement when used in conjunction with further, standard dimensionality reduction techniques: the CS sparse vectors lead to reduced-dimensional representations that produce higher correlations with human similarity judgements than the original full vectors.

The second method is a weighted l^2-normalisation of the vectors prior to application of singular value decomposition (SVD) (Deerwester et al., 1990) or compositional vector operators. It has the effect of drastically improving SVD with 100 or fewer dimensions. For example, we find that applying normalisation before SVD improves correlation from $\rho = 0.48$ to $\rho = 0.70$ for 20 dimensions, on the word similarity task. This is an essential finding as many more complex models of compositional semantics (Coecke et al., 2010; Baroni and Zamparelli, 2010; Andreas and Ghahramani, 2013) work with tensor objects and require good quality low-dimensional representations of words in order to lower computational costs. This technique also improves the performance of vector addition on texts of any length and vector elementwise product on shorter texts, on both the similarity and definitions tasks.

The definition task and dataset are an additional contribution. We produced a new dataset of words and their definitions, which is separated into nine parts, each consisting of definitions of a particular length. This allows us to examine how compositional operators interact with CS and normalisation as the number of vector operations increases.

This paper is divided into three main sections. Section 2 describes the construction of the word vectors that underlie all of our experiments and the two methods for adaptation of the vectors to specific tasks. In Section 3 we assess the effects of CS and normalisation on standard word similarity datasets. In Section 4 we present the compositional experiments on phrase data and our new definitions dataset.

2 Word Vector Construction

The distributional hypothesis assumes that words that occur within similar contexts share similar meanings; hence semantic vector construction first requires a defintition of context. Here we use a window method, where the context is defined as a particular sequence of words either side of the target word. The vectors are then populated through traversal of a large corpus, by recording the number of times each of the target words co-occurs with a context word within the window, which gives the raw target-context co-occurrence frequency vectors (Freq).

The rest of this section contains a description of the particular settings used to construct the raw word vectors and the weighting schemes (tTest, PPMI) that we considered in our experiments. This is followed by a detailed description of the context selection (CS) and normalisation techniques. Finally, dimensionality reduction (SVD) is proposed as a way of combating sparsity and random indexing (RI) as an essential step of encoding vectors for use with the convolution operator.

Raw Vectors We used a cleaned-up corpus of 1.7 billion lemmatised tokens (Minnen et al., 2001) from the October, 2013 snapshot of Wikipedia, and constructed context vectors by using sentence boundaries to provide the window. The set of context words C consisted of the 10,000 most frequent words occurring in this dataset, with the exception of stopwords from a standard stopword list. Therefore, a frequency vector for a target word $w_i \in W$ is represented as $\vec{w_i} = \{f_{w_i c_j}\}_j$, where $c_j \in C$ ($|C| = 10,000$), W is a set of target words in a particular evaluation dataset, and $f_{w_i c_j}$ is the co-occurrence frequency between the target word, w_i and context word, c_j.

Vector Weighting We used the tTest and PPMI weighting schemes, since they both performed well on the development data. The vectors resulting from the application of the weighting schemes are as follows, where the tTest and PPMI functions give weighted values for the basis vector corresponding to context word c_j for target word w_i:

$$\text{tTest}(\vec{w_i}, c_j) = \frac{p(w_i, c_j) - p(w_i)p(c_j)}{\sqrt{p(w_i)p(c_j)}} \quad (1)$$

$$\text{PPMI}(\vec{w_i}, c_j) = p(w_i, c_j) \log \left(\frac{p(w_i, c_j)}{p(w_i)p(c_j)} \right) \quad (2)$$

where $p(w_i) = \frac{\sum_j f_{w_i c_j}}{\sum_k \sum_l f_{w_k c_l}}$, $p(c_j) = \frac{\sum_i f_{w_i c_j}}{\sum_k \sum_l f_{w_k c_l}}$, and $p(w_i, c_j) = \frac{f_{w_i c_j}}{\sum_k \sum_l f_{w_k c_l}}$.

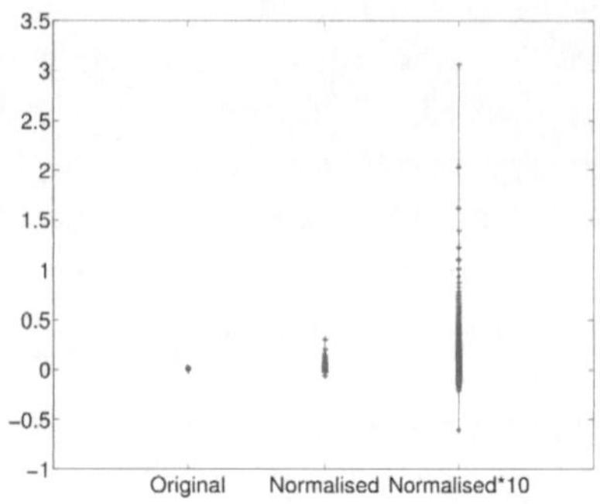

Figure 1: The range of context weights on tTest weighted vectors before and after normalisation.

Context Ranking and Selection The weighting schemes change the importance of individual target-context raw co-occurrence counts by considering the frequency with which each context word occurs with other target words. This is similar to term-weighting in IR and many retrieval functions are also used as weighting functions in DSMs. In the retrieval-based model ESA (Gabrilovich and Markovitch, 2007), only the N highest-weighted contexts are kept as a representative set of "topics" for a particular target word, and the rest are set to zero. Here we use a similar technique and, for each target word, retain only the N-highest weighted context words, using a word-similarity development set to choose the N that maximises correlation across all words in that dataset. Throughout the paper, we will refer to this technique as context selection (**CS**) and use N to indicate the maximum number of contexts per word. Hence all word vectors have at most N non-zero elements, effectively adjusting the sparsity of the vectors, which may have an effect on the sum and elementwise product operations when composing vectors.

Normalisation PPMI has only positive values that span the range $[0, \infty]$, while tTest spans $[-1, 1]$, but generally produces values tightly concentrated around zero. We found that these ranges can produce poor performance due to numerical problems, so we corrected this through weighted row normalisation: $\vec{w} := \lambda \frac{\vec{w}}{||\vec{w}||_2}$. With $\lambda = 10$ this has the effect of restricting the values to $[-10, 10]$ for tTest and $[0, 10]$ for PPMI. Figure 1 shows the range of values for tTest. In general we use $\lambda = 1$, but for some experiments we use $\lambda = 10$ to push the highest weights above 1, as a way of combating the numerical errors that are likely to arise due to repeated multiplications of small numbers. This normalisation has no effect on the ordering of context weights or cosine similarity calculations between single-word vectors. We apply normalisation prior to dimensionality reduction and RI.

SVD SVD transforms vectors from their target-context representation into a target-topic space. The resulting space is *dense*, in that the vectors no longer contain any zero elements. If $\mathbf{M}$ is a $|w| \times |C|$ matrix whose rows are made of word vectors $\vec{w_i}$, then the lower dimensional representation of those vectors is encoded in the $|W| \times K$ matrix $\hat{\mathbf{M}}_K = \mathbf{U}_K\mathbf{S}_K$ where $\text{SVD}(\mathbf{M}, K) = \mathbf{U}_K\mathbf{S}_K\mathbf{V}_K$ (Deerwester et al., 1990). We also tried non-negative matrix factorisation (NNMF) (Seung and Lee, 2001), but found that it did not perform as well as SVD. We used the standard Matlab implementation of SVD.

Random Indexing There are two ways of creating RI-based DSMs, the most popular being to initialise all target word vectors to zero and to generate a random vector for each context word. Then, while traversing through the corpus, each time a target word and a context word co-occur, the context word vector is added to the vector representing the target word. This method allows the RI vectors to be created in one step through a single traversal of the corpus. The other method, following Jones and Mewhort (2007), is to create the RI vectors through matrix multiplication rather than sequentially. We employ this method and assign each context word a random vector $\vec{e_{c_j}} = \{r_k\}_k$ where r_k are drawn from the normal distribution $\mathcal{N}(0, \frac{1}{D})$ and $|\vec{e_{c_j}}| = D = 4096$. The RI representation of a target word $RI(\vec{w_i}) = \vec{w_i}\mathbf{R}$ is constructed by multiplying the word vector $\vec{w_i}$, obtained as before, by the $|C| \times D$ matrix $\mathbf{R}$ where each column represents the vectors $\vec{e_{c_j}}$. Weighting is performed prior to random indexing.

3 Word Similarity Experiments

In this section we investigate the effects of context selection and normalisation on the quality of word vectors using standard word similarity datasets. The datasets consist of word pairs and a gold standard score that indicates the human judgement of the similarity between the words within each pair. We calculated the similarity between word vectors for each pair and compared our results with the gold standard using Spearman correlation.

	tTest		PPMI		Freq	
Data	Max ρ	Full ρ	Max ρ	Full ρ	Max ρ	Full ρ
MENdev†	**0.75**	0.73	**0.76**	0.61	**0.66**	0.57
MENtest	**0.76**	0.73	**0.76**	0.61	**0.66**	0.56
WS353	**0.70**	0.63	**0.70**	0.41	**0.57**	0.41

Table 1: Values N learned on dev (†) also improve performance on the test data. Max ρ indicates correlation at the values of N that lead to the highest Spearman correlation on the development data. For each weighting scheme these are: 140 (tTest), 240 (PPMI), and 20 (Freq). Full ρ indicates the correlation when using full vectors without CS.

The cosine, Jaccard, and Lin similarity measures (Curran, 2004) were all used to ensure the results reflect genuine effects of context selection, and not an artefact of any particular similarity measure. The similarity measure and value of N were chosen, given a particular weighting scheme, to maximise correlation on the development part of the MEN data (Bruni et al., 2012) (**MENdev**). Testing was performed on the remaining section of MEN and the entire WS353 dataset (Finkelstein et al., 2002). The MEN dataset consists of 3,000 word pairs rated for similarity, which is divided into a 2,000-pair development set and a 1,000-pair test set. WS353 consists only of 353 pairs, but has been consistently used as a benchmark word similarity dataset throughout the past decade.

Results Figure 2 shows how correlation varies with N for the MEN development data. The peak performance for tTest is achieved when using around 140 top-ranked contexts per word, while for PPMI it is at $N = 240$, and for Freq $N = 20$. The dramatic drop in performance is demonstrated when using all three similarity measures, although Jaccard seems particularly sensitive to the negative tTest weights that are introduced when lower-ranked contexts are added to the vectors. The remaining experiments only consider cosine similarity. We also find that context selection improves correlation for tTest, PPMI, and the unweighted Freq vectors on the test data (Table 1). Moreover, the lower the correlation from the full vectors, the larger the improvement when using CS.

3.1 Dimensionality Reduction

Figure 3 shows the effects of dimensionality reduction described in the following experiments.

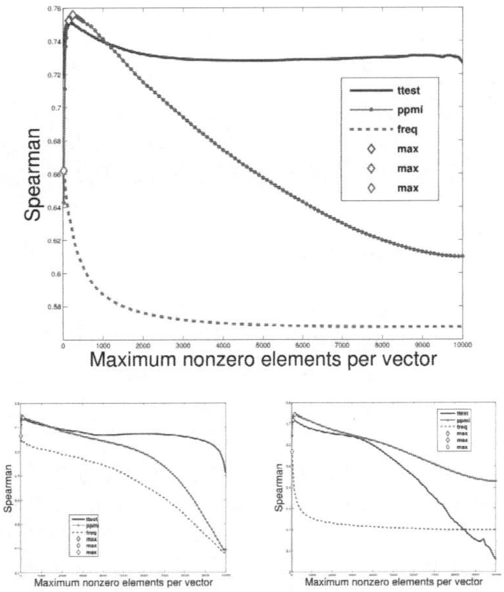

Figure 2: Correlation decreases as more lower-ranked context words are introduced (MENdev), with cosine (top), Lin (bottom left), and Jaccard (bottom right) simialrity measures.

3.1.1 SVD and CS

To check whether CS improves the correlation through increased sparsity or whether it improves the contextual representation of the words, we investigated the behaviour of SVD on three different levels of vector sparsity. To construct the most sparse vectors, we chose the best performing N for each weighting scheme (from Table 1). Thus sparse tTest vectors had $\frac{140}{10000} = 0.0140$, or 1.4%, non-zero elements. We also chose a mid-range of $N = 3300$ for up to 33% of non-zero elements per vector, and finally the full vectors with $N = 10000$.

Results In general the CS-tuned vectors lead to better lower-dimensional representations. The mid-range contexts in the tTest weighting scheme seem to hold information that hinders SVD, while the lowest-ranked negative weights appear to help (when the mid-range contexts are present as well). For the PPMI weighting, fewer contexts consistently lead to better representations, while the unweighted vectors seem to mainly hold information in the top 20 most frequent contexts for each word.

3.1.2 SVD, CS, and Normalisation

We also consider the combination of normalisation and context selection followed by SVD.

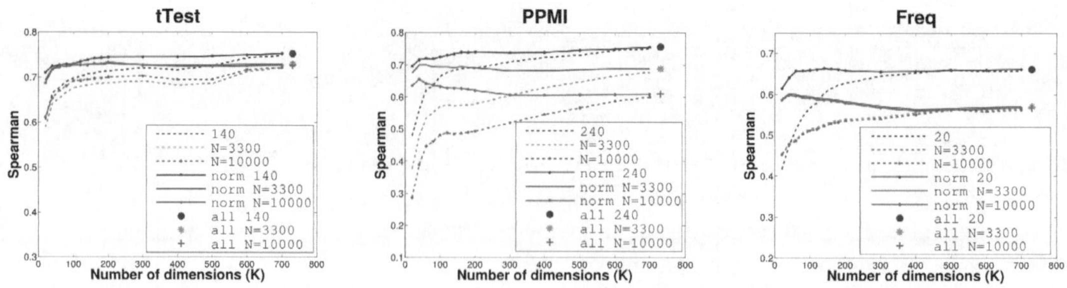

Figure 3: Vectors tuned for sparseness (blue) consistently produce equal or better dimensionality reductions (results on MENdev). The solid lines show improvement in lower dimensional representations of SVD when dimensionality reduction is applied after normalisation.

Results Normalisation leads to more stable SVD representations, with a large improvement for small numbers of dimensions (K) as demonstrated by the solid lines in Figure 3. At $K = 20$ the Spearman correlation increases from 0.61 to 0.71. In addition, for tTest there is an improvement in the mid-range vectors, and a knock-on effect for the full vectors. As the tTest values effectively range from -0.1 to 0.1, the mid-range values are very small numbers closely grouped around zero. Normalisation spreads and increases these numbers, perhaps making them more relevant to the SVD algorithm. The effect is also visible for PPMI weighting where at $K = 20$ the correlation increases from 0.48 to 0.70. For PPMI and Freq we also see that, for the full and mid-range vectors, the SVD representations have slightly higher correlations than the unreduced vectors.

3.2 Random Indexing

We use random indexing primarily to produce a vector representation for convolution (Section 4). While this produces a lower-dimensional representation, it may not use less memory since the resulting vectors, although smaller, are fully dense.

In summary, the RI encoded vectors with dimensions of $D = 4096$ lead to only slightly reduced correlation values compared to their unencoded counterparts. We find that for tTest we get similar performance with or without CS at any level, while for PPMI CS helps especially for $D \geqslant 512$. On Freq we find that CS with $N = 60$ leads to higher correlation, but mid-range and full vectors have equivalent performance. For Freq, the correlation is equivalent to full vectors from $D = 128$, while for the weighted vectors 512 dimensions appear to be sufficient. Unlike for SVD, normalisation slightly reduces the performance for mid-range dimensions.

4 Compositional Experiments

We examine the performance of vectors augmented by CS and normalisation in two compositional tasks. The first is an extension of the word similarity task to phrase pairs, using the dataset of Mitchell and Lapata (2010). Each entry in the dataset consists of two phrases, each consisting of two words (in various syntactic relations, such as verb-object and adjective noun), and a gold standard score. We combine the two word vectors into a single phrase vector using various operators described below. We then calculate the similarity between the phrase vectors using cosine and compare the resulting scores against the gold standard using Spearman correlation. The second task is our new definitions task where, again, word vectors from each definition are composed to form a single vector, which can then be compared for similarity with the target term.

We use PPMI- and tTest-weighted vectors at three CS cutoff points: the best chosen N from Section 3, the top third of the ranked contexts at $N = 3300$, and the full vectors without CS at $N = 10000$. This gives us a range of values to examine, without directly tuning on this dataset. For dimensionality reduction we consider vectors reduced with SVD to 100 and 700 dimensions. In some cases we exclude the results for SVD_{700} because they are very close to the scores for unreduced vectors. We experiment with 3 values of D from $\{512, 1024, 4096\}$ for the RI vectors.

Operators To combine distributional vectors into a single-vector sentence representation, we use a representative set of methods from Mitchell and Lapata (2010). In particular, we use vector addition, elementwise (Hadamard) product, Kronecker product, and circular convolution (Plate, 1991; Jones and Mewhort, 2007), which are defined as follows for two word vectors $\vec{x}, \vec{y}$:

$$\begin{array}{ll} \textbf{Sum} & \vec{x} + \vec{y} = \{\vec{x}_i + \vec{y}_i\}_i \\ \textbf{Prod} & \vec{x} \odot \vec{y} = \{\vec{x}_i \cdot \vec{y}_i\}_i \\ \textbf{Kron} & \vec{x} \otimes \vec{y} = \{\vec{x}_i \cdot \vec{y}_j\}_{ij} \\ \textbf{Conv} & \vec{x} \circledast \vec{y} = \left\{\sum_{j=0}^{n} (\vec{x})_{j\%n} \cdot (\vec{y})_{(i-j)\%n}\right\}_i \end{array}$$

Repeated application of the **Sum** operation adds contexts for each of the words that occur in a phrase, which maintains (and mixes) any noisy parts of the component word vectors. Our intention was that use of the CS vectors would lead to less noisy word vectors and hence less noisy phrase and sentence vectors. The **Prod** operator, on the other hand, provides a phrase or sentence representation consisting only of the contexts that are common to all of the words in the sentence (since zeros in any of the word vectors lead to zeros in the same position in the sentence vector). This effect is particularly problematic for rare words which may have sparse vectors, leading to a sparse vector for the sentence.[1] We address the sparsity problem through the use of dimensionality reduction, which produces more dense vectors.

Kron, the Kronecker (or tensor) product of two vectors, produces a matrix (second order tensor) whose diagonal matches the result of the **Prod** operation, but whose off-diagonal entries are all the other products of elements of the two vectors. We only apply **Kron** to SVD-reduced vectors, and to compare two matrices we turn them into vectors by concatenating matrix rows, and use cosine similarity on the resulting vectors. While in the more complex, type-driven methods (Baroni and Zamparelli, 2010; Coecke et al., 2010) tensors represent functions, and off-diagonal entries have a particular transformational interpretation as part of a linear map, the significance of the off-diagonal elements is difficult to interpret in our setting, apart from their role as encoders of the order of operands. We only examine **Kron** as the unencoded version of the **Conv** operator to see how the performance is affected by the random indexing and the modular summation by which **Conv** differs from **Kron**.[2] We cannot use **Kron** for combining more than two words as the size of the resulting tensor grows exponentially with the number of vector operations, but we can use **Conv** as an encoded alternative as it results in a vector of the same dimension as the two operands.

[1]Sparsity is a problem that may be addressable through smoothing (Zhai and Lafferty, 2001), although we do not investigate that avenue in this paper.

[2]**Conv** also differs from **Kron** in that it is commutative, unless one of the operands is permuted. In this paper we do not permute the operands.

Oper		N=140	N=3300	N=10000
sum	ttest	0.40 (**0.41**)	0.40 (0.40)	0.40 (0.40)
	SVD_{100}	0.37 (**0.42**)	0.35 (**0.41**)	0.37 (0.40)
prod	ttest	0.32 (0.32)	**0.40 (0.40)**	0.32 (0.32)
	SVD_{100}	0.25 (0.23)	0.23 (0.23)	0.21 (0.23)
kron	SVD_{100}	0.31 (0.34)	0.34 (**0.38**)	0.29 (0.32)
	SVD_{700}	**0.39 (0.39)**	**0.37 (0.37)**	0.30 (0.30)
conv	RI_{512}	0.10 (0.12)	**0.26** (0.21)	0.25 (0.25)
	RI_{1024}	0.22 (0.15)	0.29 (0.27)	0.25 (0.26)
	RI_{4096}	0.16 (0.19)	**0.33 (0.34)**	0.28 (0.30)

Table 2: Behaviour of vector operators with tTest vectors on ML2010 (Spearman correlation). Values for normalised vectors in parentheses.

Oper		N=240	N=3300	N=10000
sum	ppmi	**0.40** (0.39)	**0.40 (0.39)**	0.29 (0.29)
	SVD_{100}	**0.40** (0.40)	0.38 (**0.40**)	0.29 (0.30)
prod	ppmi	0.28 (0.28)	**0.40 (0.40)**	0.30 (0.30)
	SVD_{100}	0.23 (0.17)	0.18 (0.22)	0.14 (0.12)
kron	SVD_{100}	0.37 (0.30)	0.36 (**0.38**)	0.27 (0.27)
	SVD_{700}	**0.38 (0.37)**	**0.37 (0.37)**	0.26 (0.26)
conv	RI_{512}	0.09 (0.09)	0.27 (**0.30**)	0.25 (0.24)
	RI_{1024}	0.08 (0.14)	0.33 (**0.37**)	0.25 (0.27)
	RI_{4096}	0.18 (0.19)	**0.37 (0.38)**	0.27 (0.27)

Table 3: Behaviour of vector operators with PPMI vectors on ML2010 (Spearman correlation). Values for normalised vectors in parentheses.

4.1 Phrase Similarity

To test how CS, normalisation, and dimensionality reduction affect simple compositional vector operations we use the test portion of the phrasal similarity dataset from Mitchell and Lapata (2010) (ML2010). This dataset consists of pairs of two-word phrases and a human similarity judgement on the scale of 1-7. There are three types of phrases: noun-noun, adjective-noun, and verb-object. In the original paper, and some subsequent works, these were treated as three different datasets; however, here we combine the datasets into one single phrase pair dataset. This allows us to summarise the effects of different types of vectors on phrasal composition in general.

Results Our results (Tables 2 and 3) are comparable to those in Mitchell and Lapata (2010) averaged across the phrase-types ($\rho = 0.44$), but are achieved with much smaller vectors. We find that with normalisation, and the optimal choice of N, there is little difference between **Prod** and **Sum**. **Sum** and **Kron** benefit from normalisation, especially in combination with SVD, but for **Prod** it either makes no difference or reduces performance. Product-based methods (**Prod, Kron,**

Conv) have a preference for context selection that includes the mid-rank contexts ($N = 3300$), but not the full vector ($N = 10000$). On tTest vectors **Sum** is relatively stable across different CS and SVD settings, but with PPMI weighting, there is a preference for lower N. SVD reduces performance for **Prod**, but not for **Kron**. Finally, **Conv** gets higher correlation with higher-dimensional RI vectors and with PPMI weights.

4.2 Definition Retrieval

In this task, which is formulated as a retrieval task, we investigate the behaviour of different vector operators as multiple operations are chained together. We first encode each definition into a single vector through repeated application of one of the operators on the distributional vectors of the content words in the definition. Then, for each head (defined) word, we rank all the different definition vectors in decreasing order according to inner product (unnormalised cosine) similarity with the head word's distributional vector.

Performance is measured using precision and Mean Reciprocal Rank (MRR). If the correct definition is ranked first, the precision (P@1) is 1, otherwise 0. Since there is only one definition per head word, the reciprocal rank (RR) is the inverse of the rank of the correct definition. So if the correct definition is ranked fourth, for example, then RR is $\frac{1}{4}$. MRR is the average of the RR across all head words.

The difficulty of the task depends on how many words there are in the dataset and how similar their definitions are. In addition, if a head word occurs in the definition of another word in the same dataset, it may cause the incorrect definition to be ranked higher than the correct one. These problems are more likely to occur with higher frequency words and in a larger dataset. In order to counter these effects, we average our results over ten repeated random samplings of 100 word-definition pairs. The sampling also gives us a random **baseline** for P@1 of 0.0130 ± 0.0106 and for MRR 0.0576 ± 0.0170, which can be interpreted as there is a chance of slightly more than 1 in 100 of ranking the correct definition first, and on average the correct definition is ranked around the 20 mark.

For this task all experiments were performed using the tTest-weighted vectors. When applying normalisation we use $\lambda = 1$ (**Norm**) and $\lambda = 10$ (**Norm10**). In addition, we examine the effect of continually applying **Norm** after every operation (**CNorm**).

DD2	DD3	DD4	DD5	DD6	DD7	DD8	DD9	DD10
346	547	594	537	409	300	216	150	287

Table 4: Number of definitions per dataset.

Dataset We developed a new dataset (**DD**) consisting of 3,386 definitions from the Wiktionary BNC spoken-word frequency list.[3] Most of the words have several definitions, but we considered only the first definition with at least two non-stopwords. The word-definition pairs were divided into nine separate datasets according to the number of non-stopwords in the definition. For example, all of the definitions that have five content words are in **DD5**. The exception is **DD10**, which contains all the definitions of ten or more words. Table 4 shows the number of definitions in each dataset.

Results Figure 4 shows how the MRR varies with different **DD** datasets for **Sum**, **Prod**, and **Conv**. The CS, SVD, and RI settings for each operator correspond to the best average settings from Table 5. In some cases other settings had similar performance, but we chose these for illustrative purposes. We can see that all operators have relatively higher MRR on smaller datasets (**DD6-9**). Compensating for that effect, we can hypothesise that **Sum** has a steady performance across different definition sizes, while the performance of both **Prod** and **Conv** declines as the number of operations increases. Normalisation helps with **Sum** throughout, with little difference in performance between **Norm** and **Norm10**, but with a slight decrease when **CNorm** is used. On the other hand, only **CNorm** improves the ranking of **Prod**-based vectors. Normalisation makes no difference for RI vectors combined with convolution and the results in Table 5 show that, on average, **Conv** performs worse than the random baseline.

In Figure 5 we can see that, although dimensionality reduction leads to lower MRR, for **Sum**, normalisation prior to SVD counteracts this effect, while, for **Prod**, dimensionality reduction, in general, reduces the performance.

[3] http://simple.wiktionary.org/wiki/Wiktionary:BNC_spoken_freq

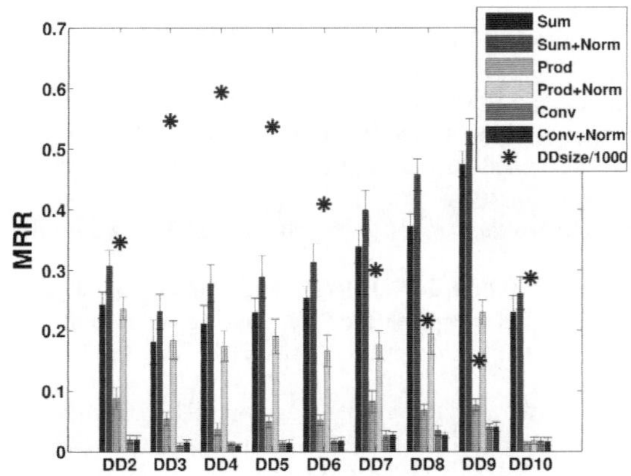

Figure 4: Per-dataset breakdown of best normalised and unnormalised vectors for each vector operator. Stars indicate the dataset size from Table 4 divided by 1000.

	Sum		Prod		Conv	
Norm	**No**	**Yes**	**No**	**CN**	**No**	**Yes**
CS (N)	140	140	3300	10000	140	3300
SVD(K)**/RI**(D)	700	700	None	None	2048	512
mean P@1	0.18	**0.23**	0.01	0.11	0.00	0.00
mean MRR	0.28	**0.35**	0.06	0.17	0.02	0.02

Table 5: Best settings for operators calculated from the highest average MRR across all the datasets, with and without normalisation. The results for vectors with no normalisation or CS are: **Sum** - P@1=0.1567, MRR=0.2624; **Prod** - P@1=0.0147, MRR=0.0542; **Conv** P@1=0.0027, MRR=0.0192.

5 Discussion

In this paper we introduced context selection and normalisation as techniques for improving the semantic vector space representations of words. We found that, although our untuned vectors perform better on WS353 data ($\rho = 0.63$) than vectors used by Mitchell and Lapata (2010) ($\rho = 0.42$), our best phrase composition model (**Sum**, $\rho = 0.40$) produces a lower performance than an estimate of their best model (**Prod**, $\rho = 0.44$).[4] This indicates that better performance on word-similarity data does not directly translate into better performance on compositional tasks; however, CS and normalisation are both effective in increasing the quality of the composed representation ($\rho = 0.42$). Since CS and normalisation are computationally inexpensive, they are an excellent way to improve model quality compared to the alternative, which is building several models with various context types, in order to find which one suits the data best.

[4]The estimate is computed as an average across the three phrase-type results.

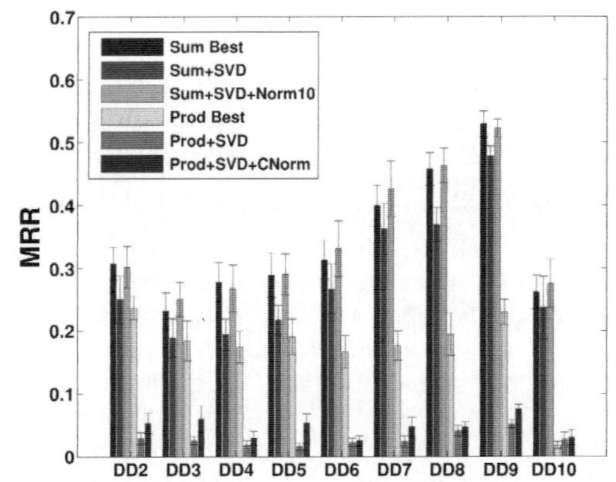

Figure 5: Per-dataset breakdown of best normalised and unnormalised SVD vectors for **Sum** and **Prod**. For both operators the best CS and SVD settings for normalised vectors were $N = 140$, $K = 700$, and for unnormalised were $N = 10000$, $K = 700$.

Furthermore, we show that, as the number of vector operations increases, **Sum** is the most stable operator and that it benefits from sparser representations (low N) and normalisation. Employing both of these methods, we are able to build an SVD-based representation that performs as well as full-dimensional vectors which, together with **Sum**, give the best results on both phrase and definition tasks. In fact, normalisation and CS both improve the SVD representations of the vectors across different weighting schemes. This is a key result, as many of the more complex compositional methods require low dimensional representations for computational reasons.

Future work will include application of CS and normalised lower-dimensional vectors to more complex compositional methods, and investigations into whether these strategies apply to other context types and other dimensionality reduction methods such as LDA (Blei et al., 2003).

Acknowledgements

Tamara Polajnar is supported by ERC Starting Grant DisCoTex (306920). Stephen Clark is supported by ERC Starting Grant DisCoTex (306920) and EPSRC grant EP/I037512/1. We would like to thank Laura Rimell for helpful discussion, and Laura and the anonymous reviewers for helpful comments on the paper.

References

Jacob Andreas and Zoubin Ghahramani. 2013. A generative model of vector space semantics. In *Proceedings of the ACL 2013 Workshop on Continuous Vector Space Models and their Compositionality*, Sofia, Bulgaria.

M. Baroni and R. Zamparelli. 2010. Nouns are vectors, adjectives are matrices: Representing adjective-noun constructions in semantic space. In *Conference on Empirical Methods in Natural Language Processing (EMNLP-10)*, Cambridge, MA.

David M. Blei, Andrew Y. Ng, and Michael I. Jordan. 2003. Latent dirichlet allocation. *J. Mach. Learn. Res.*, 3:993–1022.

Elia Bruni, Gemma Boleda, Marco Baroni, and Nam Khanh Tran. 2012. Distributional semantics in technicolor. In *Proceedings of the 50th Annual Meeting of the Association for Computational Linguistics (Volume 1: Long Papers)*, pages 136–145, Jeju Island, Korea, July. Association for Computational Linguistics.

Daoud Clarke. 2012. A context-theoretic framework for compositionality in distributional semantics. *Comput. Linguist.*, 38(1):41–71, March.

B. Coecke, M. Sadrzadeh, and S. Clark. 2010. Mathematical foundations for a compositional distributional model of meaning. In J. van Bentham, M. Moortgat, and W. Buszkowski, editors, *Linguistic Analysis (Lambek Festschrift)*, volume 36, pages 345–384.

James R. Curran. 2004. *From Distributional to Semantic Similarity*. Ph.D. thesis, University of Edinburgh.

Scott Deerwester, Susan T. Dumais, Thomas K. Landauer, George W. Furnas, and Richard Harshman. 1990. Indexing by latent semantic analysis. *Journal of the Society for Information Science*, 41(6):391–407.

Lev Finkelstein, Evgeniy Gabrilovich, Yossi Matias, Ehud Rivlin, Zach Solan, Gadi Wolfman, and Eytan Ruppin. 2002. Placing search in context: The concept revisited. *ACM Transactions on Information Systems*, 20:116–131.

Evgeniy Gabrilovich and Shaul Markovitch. 2007. Computing semantic relatedness using Wikipedia-based explicit semantic analysis. In *Proceedings of the 20th international joint conference on Artifical intelligence*, IJCAI'07, pages 1606–1611, San Francisco, CA, USA. Morgan Kaufmann Publishers Inc.

Pablo Gamallo and Stefan Bordag. 2011. Is singular value decomposition useful for word similarity extraction? *Language Resources and Evaluation*, 45(2):95–119.

Michael N. Jones and Douglas J. K. Mewhort. 2007. Representing word meaning and order information in a composite holographic lexicon. *Psychological Review*, 114:1–37.

Ekaterina Kochmar and Ted Briscoe. 2013. Capturing anomalies in the choice of content words in compositional distributional semantic space. In *Proceedings of the Recent Advances in Natural Language Processing (RANLP-2013)*, Hissar, Bulgaria.

Guido Minnen, John Carroll, and Darren Pearce. 2001. Applied morphological processing of English. *Natural Language Engineering*, 7(3):207–223.

Jeff Mitchell and Mirella Lapata. 2010. Composition in distributional models of semantics. *Cognitive Science*, 34(8):1388–1429.

T. A. Plate. 1991. Holographic reduced Representations: Convolution algebra for compositional distributed representations. In J. Mylopoulos and R. Reiter, editors, *Proceedings of the 12th International Joint Conference on Artificial Intelligence, Sydney, Australia, August 1991*, pages 30–35, San Mateo, CA. Morgan Kauffman.

D Seung and L Lee. 2001. Algorithms for non-negative matrix factorization. *Advances in neural information processing systems*, 13:556–562.

Richard Socher, Brody Huval, Christopher D. Manning, and Andrew Y. Ng. 2012. Semantic Compositionality Through Recursive Matrix-Vector Spaces. In *Proceedings of the 2012 Conference on Empirical Methods in Natural Language Processing (EMNLP)*, Jeju Island, Korea.

Peter Turney and Patrick Pantel. 2010. From frequency to meaning: Vector space models of semantics. *Journal of Artificial Intelligence Research*, 37:141–188.

Fabio Massimo Zanzotto and Lorenzo Dell'Arciprete. 2011. Distributed structures and distributional meaning. In *Proceedings of the Workshop on Distributional Semantics and Compositionality*, DiSCo-11, pages 10–15, Portland, Oregon. Association for Computational Linguistics.

Chengxiang Zhai and John Lafferty. 2001. A study of smoothing methods for language models applied to ad hoc information retrieval. In *Proceedings of the 24th annual international ACM SIGIR conference on Research and development in information retrieval*, SIGIR '01, pages 334–342, New York, NY, USA. ACM.

Source-side Preordering for Translation using Logistic Regression and Depth-first Branch-and-Bound Search*

Laura Jehl* Adrià de Gispert‡ Mark Hopkins‡ William Byrne‡

*Dept. of Computational Linguistics, Heidelberg University. 69120 Heidelberg, Germany
jehl@cl.uni-heidelberg.de
‡ SDL Research. East Road, Cambridge CB1 1BH, U.K.
{agispert,mhopkins,bbyrne}@sdl.com

Abstract

We present a simple preordering approach for machine translation based on a feature-rich logistic regression model to predict whether two children of the same node in the source-side parse tree should be swapped or not. Given the pair-wise children regression scores we conduct an efficient depth-first branch-and-bound search through the space of possible children permutations, avoiding using a cascade of classifiers or limiting the list of possible ordering outcomes. We report experiments in translating English to Japanese and Korean, demonstrating superior performance as (a) the number of crossing links drops by more than 10% absolute with respect to other state-of-the-art preordering approaches, (b) BLEU scores improve on 2.2 points over the baseline with lexicalised reordering model, and (c) decoding can be carried out 80 times faster.

1 Introduction

Source-side preordering for translation is the task of rearranging the order of a given source sentence so that it best resembles the order of the target sentence. It is a divide-and-conquer strategy aiming to decouple long-range word movement from the core translation task. The main advantage is that translation becomes computationally cheaper as less word movement needs to be considered, which results in faster and better translations, if preordering is done well and efficiently. Preordering also can facilitate better estimation of alignment and translation models as the parallel data becomes more monotonically-aligned, and translation gains can be obtained for various system architectures, e.g. phrase-based, hierarchical phrase-based, etc.

For these reasons, preordering has a clear research and commercial interest, as reflected by the extensive previous work on the subject (see Section 2). From these approaches, we are particularly interested in those that (i) involve little or no human intervention, (ii) require limited computational resources at runtime, and (iii) make use of available linguistic analysis tools.

In this paper we propose a novel preordering approach based on a logistic regression model trained to predict whether to swap nodes in the source-side dependency tree. For each pair of sibling nodes in the tree, the model uses a feature-rich representation that includes lexical cues to make relative reordering predictions between them. Given these predictions, we conduct a depth-first branch-and-bound search through the space of possible permutations of all sibling nodes, using the regression scores to guide the search. This approach has multiple advantages. First, the search for permutations is efficient and does not require specific heuristics or hard limits for nodes with many children. Second, the inclusion of the regression prediction directly into the search allows for finer-grained global decisions as the predictions that the model is more confident about are preferred. Finally, the use of a single regression model to handle any number of child nodes avoids incurring sparsity issues, while allowing the integration of a vast number of features into the preordering model.

We empirically contrast our proposed method against another preordering approach based on automatically-extracted rules when translating English into Japanese and Korean. We demonstrate a significant reduction in number of crossing links of more than 10% absolute, as well as translation gains of over 2.2 BLEU points over the baseline.

*This work was done during an internship of the first author at SDL Research, Cambridge.

We also show it outperforms a multi-class classification approach and analyse why this is the case.

2 Related work

One useful way to organize previous preordering techniques is by how they incorporate linguistic knowledge.

On one end of the spectrum we find those approaches that rely on syntactic parsers and human knowledge, typically encoded via a set of hand-crafted rules for parse tree rewriting or transformation. Examples of these can be found for French-English (Xia and McCord, 2004), German-English (Collins et al., 2005), Chinese-English (Wang et al., 2007), English-Arabic (Badr et al., 2009), English-Hindi (Ramanathan et al., 2009), English-Korean (Hong et al., 2009), and English-Japanese (Lee et al., 2010; Isozaki et al., 2010). A generic set of rules for transforming SVO to SOV languages has also been described (Xu et al., 2009). The main advantage of these approaches is that a relatively small set of good rules can yield significant improvements in translation. The common criticism they receive is that they are language-specific.

On the other end of the spectrum, there are preordering models that rely neither on human knowledge nor on syntactic analysis, but only on word alignments. One such approach is to form a cascade of two translation systems, where the first one translates the source to its preordered version (Costa-jussà and Fonollosa, 2006). Alternatively, one can define models that assign a cost to the relative position of each pair of words in the sentence, and search for the sequence that optimizes the global score as a linear ordering problem (Tromble and Eisner, 2009) or as a traveling salesman problem (Visweswariah et al., 2011). Yet another line of work attempts to automatically induce a parse tree and a preordering model from word alignments (DeNero and Uszkoreit, 2011; Neubig et al., 2012). These approaches are attractive due to their minimal reliance on linguistic knowledge. However, their findings reveal that the best performance is obtained when using human-aligned data which is expensive to create.

Somewhere in the middle of the spectrum are works that rely on automatic source-language syntactic parses, but no direct human intervention. Preordering rules can be automatically extracted from word alignments and constituent trees (Li et al., 2007; Habash, 2007; Visweswariah et al., 2010), dependency trees (Genzel, 2010) or predicate-argument structures (Wu et al., 2011), or simply part-of-speech sequences (Crego and Mariño, 2006; Rottmann and Vogel, 2007). Rules are assigned a cost based on Maximum Entropy (Li et al., 2007) or Maximum Likelihood estimation (Visweswariah et al., 2010), or directly on their ability to make the training corpus more monotonic (Genzel, 2010). The latter performs very well in practice but comes at the cost of a brute-force extraction heuristic that cannot incorporate lexical information. Recently, other approaches treat ordering the children of a node as a learning to rank (Yang et al., 2012) or discriminative multi-classification task (Lerner and Petrov, 2013). These are appealing for their use of finer-grained lexical information, but they struggle to adequately handle nodes with multiple children.

Our approach is closely related to this latter work, as we are interested in feature-rich discriminative approaches that automatically learn preordering rules from source-side dependency trees. Similarly to Yang et al. (2012) we train a large discriminative linear model, but rather than model each child's position in an ordered list of children, we model a more natural pair-wise swap / no-swap preference (like Tromble and Eisner (2009) did at the word level). We then incorporate this model into a global, efficient branch-and-bound search through the space of permutations. In this way, we avoid an error-prone cascade of classifiers or any limit on the possible ordering outcomes (Lerner and Petrov, 2013).

3 Preordering using logistic regression and branch-and-bound search

Like Genzel (2010), our method starts with dependency parses of source sentences (which we convert to shallow constituent trees; see Figure 1 for an example), and reorders the source text by permuting sibling nodes in the parse tree. For each non-terminal node, we first apply a logistic regression model which predicts, for each pair of child nodes, the probability that they should be swapped or kept in their original order. We then apply a depth-first branch-and-bound search to find the global optimal reordering of children.

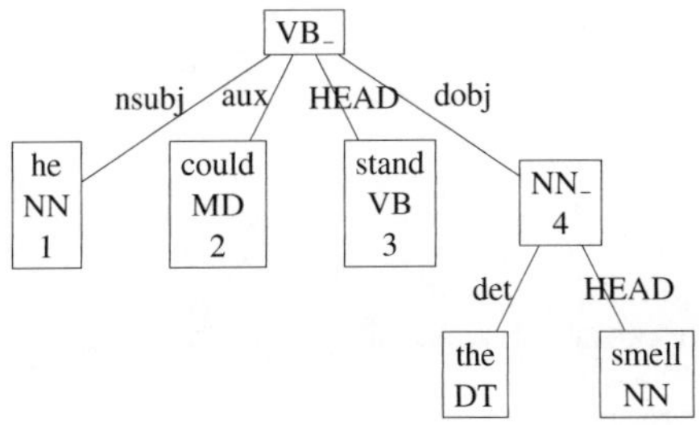

Figure 1: Shallow constituent tree generated from the dependency tree. Non-terminal nodes inherit the tag from the head.

3.1 Logistic regression

We build a regression model that assigns a probability of swapping any two sibling nodes, a and b, in the source-side dependency tree. The probability of swapping them is denoted $p(a, b)$ and the probability of keeping them in their original order is $1 - p(a, b)$. We use LIBLINEAR (Fan et al., 2008) for training an L1-regularised logistic regression model based on positively and negatively labelled samples.

3.1.1 Training data

We generate training examples for the logistic regression from word-aligned parallel data which is annotated with source-side dependency trees. For each non-terminal node, we extract all possible pairs of child nodes. For each pair, we obtain a binary label $y \in \{-1, 1\}$ by calculating whether swapping the two nodes would reduce the number of crossing alignment links. The crossing score of having two nodes a and b in the given order is

$$\mathrm{cs}(a, b) := |\{(i, j) \in A_a \times A_b : i > j\}|$$

where A_a and A_b are the target-side positions to which the words spanned by a and b are aligned. The label is then given as

$$y(a, b) = \begin{cases} 1 & , \quad \mathrm{cs}(a, b) > \mathrm{cs}(b, a) \\ -1 & , \quad \mathrm{cs}(b, a) > \mathrm{cs}(a, b) \end{cases}$$

Instances for which $\mathrm{cs}(a, b) = \mathrm{cs}(b, a)$ are not included in the training data. This usually happens if either A_a or A_b is empty, and in this case the alignments provide no indication of which order is better. We also discard any samples from nodes that have more than 16 children, as these are rare cases that often result from parsing errors.

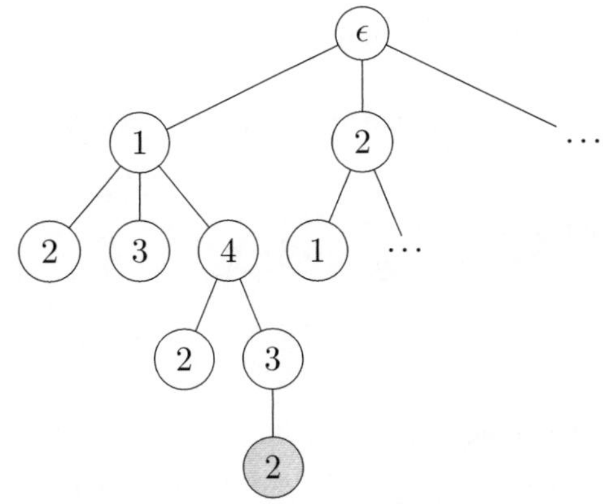

Figure 2: Branch-and-bound search: Partial search space of permutations for a dependency tree node with four children. The gray node marks a goal node. For the root node of the tree in Figure 1, the permutation corresponding to this path (1,4,3,2) would produce "he the smell stand could".

3.1.2 Features

Using a machine learning setup allows us to incorporate fine-grained information in the form of features. We use the following features to characterise pairs of nodes:

l	The dependency labels of each node
t	The part-of-speech tags of each node.
hw	The head words and classes of each node.
lm, rm	The left-most and right-most words and classes of a node.
dst	The distances between each node and the head.
gap	If there is a gap between nodes, the left-most and right-most words and classes in the gap.

In order to keep the size of our feature space manageable, we only consider features which occur at least 5 times[1]. For the lexical features, we use the top 100 vocabulary items from our training data, and 51 clusters generated by `mkcls` (Och, 1999). Similarly to previous work (Genzel, 2010; Yang et al., 2012), we also explore feature conjunctions. For the tag and label classes, we generate all possible combinations up to a given size. For the lexical and distance features, we explicitly specify conjunctions with the tag and label features. Results for various feature configurations are discussed in Section 4.3.1.

3.2 Search

For each non-terminal node in the source-side dependency tree, we search for the best possible

[1]Additional feature selection is achieved through L1-regularisation.

permutation of its children. We define the score of a permutation π as the product of the probabilities of its node pair orientations (swapped or unswapped):

$$\text{score}(\pi) = \prod_{1 \le i < j \le k | \pi[i] > \pi[j]} p(i,j) \cdot \prod_{1 \le i < j \le k | \pi[i] < \pi[j]} 1 - p(i,j)$$

Here, we represent a permutation π of k nodes as a k-length sequence containing each integer in $\{1, ..., k\}$ exactly once. Define a *partial permutation* of k nodes as a $k' < k$ length sequence containing each integer in $\{1, ..., k\}$ at most once. We can construct a search space over partial permutations in the natural way (see Figure 2). The root node represents the empty sequence ϵ and has score 1. Then, given a search node representing a k'-length partial permutation π', its successor nodes are obtained by extending it by one element:

$$\text{score}(\pi' \cdot \langle i \rangle) = \text{score}(\pi') \cdot \prod_{j \in V | i > j} p(i,j) \cdot \prod_{j \in V | i < j} 1 - p(i,j)$$

where $V = \{1, ..., k\} \backslash (\pi' \cdot \langle i \rangle)$ is the set of source child positions that have not yet been visited. Observe that the nodes at search depth k correspond exactly to the set of complete permutations. To search this space, we employ depth-first branch-and-bound (Balas and Toth, 1983) as our search algorithm. The idea of branch-and-bound is to remember the best scoring goal node found thus far, abandoning any partial paths that cannot lead to a better scoring goal node. Algorithm 1 gives pseudocode for the algorithm[2]. If the initial bound ($bound_0$) is set to 0, the search is guaranteed to find the optimal solution. By raising the bound, which acts as an under-estimate of the best scoring permutation, search can be faster but possibly fail to find any solution. All our experiments were done with $bound_0 = 0$, i.e. exact search, but we discuss search time in detail and pruning alternatives in Section 4.3.2.

Since we use a logistic regression model and incorporate its predictions directly as swap probabilities, our search prefers those permutations with swaps which the model is more confident about.

[2]See (Poole and Mackworth, 2010) for more details and a worked example.

Algorithm 1 Depth-first branch-and-bound

Require: k: maximum sequence length, ϵ: empty sequence, $bound_0$: initial bound

```
procedure BNBSEARCH(ε, bound_0, k)
    best_path ← ⊥
    bound ← bound_0
    SEARCH(⟨ε⟩)
    return best_path
end procedure

procedure SEARCH(π')
    if score(π') > bound then
        if |π'| = k then
            best_path ← ⟨π'⟩
            bound ← score(π')
            return
        else
            for each i ∈ {1, ..., k}\π' do
                SEARCH(π' · ⟨i⟩)
            end for
        end if
    end if
end procedure
```

4 Experiments

4.1 Setup

We report translation results in English-to-Japanese/Korean. Our corpora are comprised of generic parallel data extracted from the web, with some documents extracted manually and some automatically crawled. Both have about 6M sentence pairs and roughly 100M words per language.

The dev and test sets are also generic. Source sentences were extracted from the web and one target reference was produced by a bilingual speaker. These sentences were chosen to evenly represent 10 domains, including world news, chat/SMS, health, sport, science, business, and others. The dev/test sets contain 602/903 sentences and 14K/20K words each. We do English part-of-speech tagging using SVMTool (Giménez and Màrquez, 2004) and dependency parsing using MaltParser (Nivre et al., 2007).

For translation experiments, we use a phrase-based decoder that incorporates a set of standard features and a hierarchical reordering model (Galley and Manning, 2008) with weights tuned using MERT to optimize the character-based BLEU score on the dev set. The Japanese and Korean language models are 5-grams estimated on > 350M words of generic web text.

For training the logistic regression model, we automatically align the parallel training data and intersect the source-to-target and target-to-source alignments. We reserve a random 5K-sentence

approach	EJ cs (%)	EK cs (%)
rule-based (Genzel, 2010)	61.9	64.2
multi-class	65.2	-
df-bnb	51.4	51.8

Table 1: Percentage of the original crossing score on the heldout set, obtained after applying each preordering approach in English-Japanese (EJ, left) and Korean (EK, right). Lower is better.

subset for intrinsic evaluation of preordering, and use the remainder for model parameter estimation.

We evaluate our preordering approach with logistic regression and depth-first branch-and-bound search (in short, 'df-bnb') both in terms of reordering via crossing score reduction on the heldout set, and in terms of translation quality as measured by character-based BLEU on the test set.

4.2 Preordering baselines

We contrast our work against two data-driven preordering approaches. First, we implemented the rule-based approach of Genzel (2010) and optimised its multiple parameters for our task. We report only the best results achieved, which correspond to using ~100K training sentences for rule extraction, applying a sliding window width of 3 children, and creating rule sequences of ~60 rules. This approach cannot incorporate lexical features as that would make the brute-force rule extraction algorithm unmanageable.

We also implemented a multi-class classification setup where we directly predict complete permutations of children nodes using multi-class classification (Lerner and Petrov, 2013). While this is straightforward for small numbers of children, it leads to a very large number of possible permutations for larger sets of children nodes, making classification too difficult. While Lerner and Petrov (2013) use a cascade of classifiers and impose a hard limit on the possible reordering outcomes to solve this, we follow Genzel's heuristic: rather than looking at the complete set of children, we apply a sliding window of size 3 starting from the left, and make classification/reordering decisions for each window separately. Since the windows overlap, decisions made for the first window affect the order of nodes in the second window, etc. We address this by soliciting decisions from the classifier on the fly as we preorder. One limitation of this approach is that it is able to move children only within the window. We try to remedy this by applying the method iteratively, each time re-training the classifier on the preordered data from the previous run.

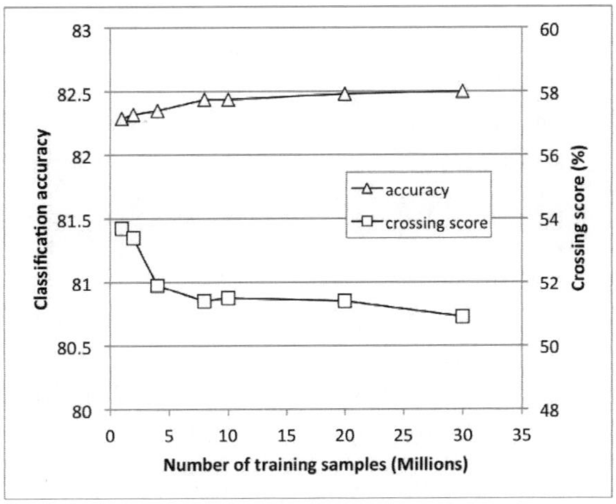

Figure 3: Crossing scores and classification accuracy improve with training data size.

4.3 Crossing score

We now report contrastive results in the intrinsic preordering task, as measured by the number of crossing links (Genzel, 2010; Yang et al., 2012) on the 5K held-out set. Without preordering, there is an average of 22.2 crossing links in English-Japanese and 20.2 in English-Korean. Table 1 shows what percentage of these links remain after applying each preordering approach to the data. We find that the 'df-bnb' method outperforms the other approaches in both language pairs, achieving more than 10 additional percentage points reduction over the rule-based approach. Interestingly, the multi-class approach is not able to match the rule-based approach despite using additional lexical cues. We hypothesise that this is due to the sliding window heuristic, which causes a mismatch in train-test conditions: while samples are not independent of each other at test time due to window overlaps, they are considered to be so when training the classifier.

4.3.1 Impact of training size and feature configuration

We now report the effects of feature configuration and training data size for the English-Japanese case. We assess our 'df-bnb' approach in terms of the classification accuracy of the trained logistic

features used	acc (%)	cs (%)
l,t,hw,lm,rm,dst,gap	82.43	51.3
l,t,hw,lm,rm,dst	82.44	51.4
l,t,hw,lm,rm	82.32	53.1
l,t,hw	82.02	55
l,t	81.07	58.4

Table 2: Ablation tests showing crossing scores and classification accuracy as features are removed. All models were trained on 8M samples.

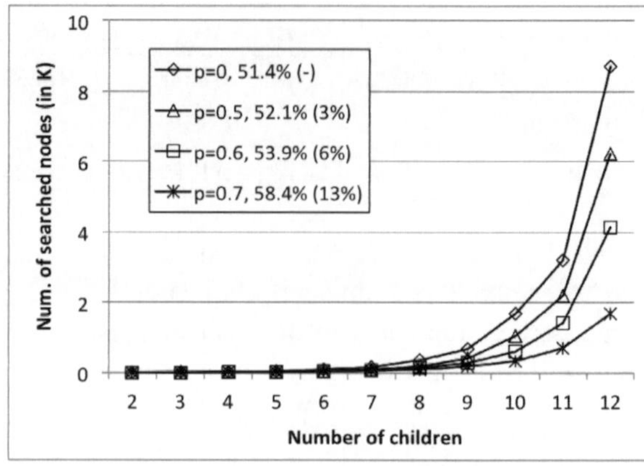

Figure 4: Average number of nodes explored in branch-and-bound search by number of children.

regression model (using it to predict ± 1 labels in the held-out set) and by the percentage of crossing alignment links reduced by preordering.

Figure 3 shows the performance of the logistic regression model over different training set sizes, extracted from the training corpus as described in Section 3. We observe a constant increase in prediction accuracy, mirrored by a steady decrease in crossing score. However, gains are less for more than 8M training examples. Note that a small variation in accuracy can produce a large variation in crossing score if two nodes are swapped which have a large number of crossing alignments.

Table 2 shows an ablation test for various feature configurations. We start with all features, including head word and class (*hw*), left-most and right-most word in each node's span (*lm*, *rm*), each node's distance to the head (*dst*), and left-most and right-most word of the gap between nodes (*gap*). We then proceed by removing features to end with only label and tag features (*l,t*), as in Genzel (2010). For each configuration, we generated all tag- and label- combinations of size 2. We then specified combinations between tag and label and all other features. For the lexical features we always used conjunctions of the word itself, and its class. Class information is included for all words, not just those in the top 100 vocabulary. Table 2 shows that lexical and distance feature groups contribute to prediction accuracy and crossing score, except for the *gap* features, which we omit from further experiments.

4.3.2 Run time

We now demonstrate the efficiency of branch-and-bound search for the problem of finding the optimum permutation of n children at runtime. Even though in the worst case the search could explore all $n!$ permutations, making it prohibitive for nodes with many children, in practice this does not happen. Many low-scoring paths are discarded early by branch-and-bound search so that the optimal solution can be found quickly. The top curve in Figure 4 shows the average number of nodes explored in searches run on our validation set (5K sentences) as a function of the number of children. All instances are far from the worst case[3].

In our experiments, the time needed to conduct exact search ($bound_0 = 0$) was not a problem except for a few bad cases (nodes with more than 16 children), which we simply chose not to preorder; in our data, 90% of the nodes have less than 6 children, while only 0.9% have 10 children or more, so this omission does not affect performance noticeably. We verified this on our held-out set, by carrying out exhaustive searches. We found that not preordering nodes with 16 children did not worsen the crossing score. In fact, setting a harsher limit of 10 nodes would still produce a crossing score of 51.9%, compared to the best score of 51.4%.

There are various ways to speed up the search, if needed. First, one could impose a hard limit on the number of explored nodes[4]. As shown in Figure 4, a limit of 4K would still allow exact search on average for permutations of up to 11 children, while stopping search early for more children. We tested this for limits of 1K/4K nodes and obtained crossing scores of 51.9/51.5%. Alternatively, one could define a higher initial bound; since the score of a path is a product of probabilities, one would select a threshold probability

[3]Note that $12! \approx 479$M nodes, whereas our search finds the optimal permutation path after exploring <10K nodes.

[4]As long as the limit exceeds the permutation length, a solution will always be found as search is depth-first.

d	approach	−LRM	Δ	+LRM	Δ
10	baseline	25.39	-	26.62	-
	rule-based	25.93	**+0.54**	27.65	**+1.03**
	multi-class	25.60	**+0.21**	26.10	**−0.52**
	df-bnb	26.73	**+1.34**	28.09	**+1.47**
4	baseline	25.07	-	25.92	-
	rule-based	26.35	**+1.28**	27.54	**+1.62**
	multi-class	25.37	**+0.30**	26.31	**+0.39**
	df-bnb	26.98	**+1.91**	28.13	**+2.21**

Table 3: English-Japanese BLEU scores with various preordering approaches (and improvement over baseline) under two distortion limits d. Results reported both excluding and including lexicalised reordering model features (LRM).

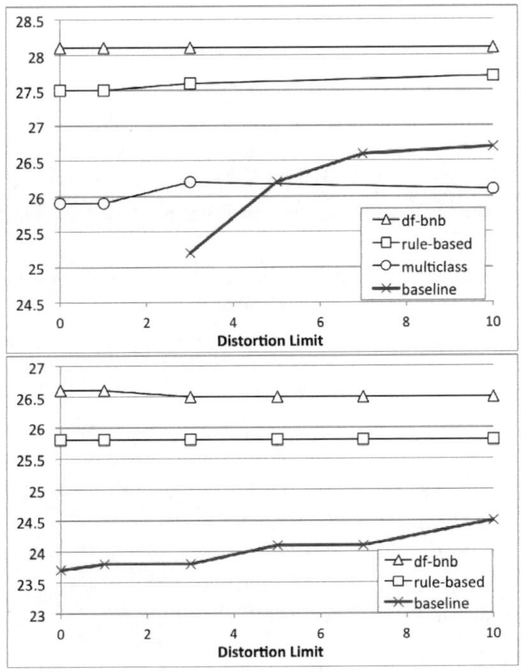

Figure 5: BLEU scores as a function of distortion limit in decoder (+LRM case). Top: English-Japanese. Bottom: English-Korean.

p and calculate a bound depending on the size n of the permutation as $bound_0 = p^{\frac{n \cdot (n-1)}{2}}$. Examples of this would be the lower curves of Figure 4. The curve labels show the crossing score produced with each threshold, and in parenthesis the percentage of searches that fail to find a solution with a better score than $bound_0$, in which case children are left in their original order. As shown, this strategy proves less effective than simply limiting the number of explored nodes, because the more frequent cases with less children remain unaffected.

4.4 Translation performance

Table 3 reports English-Japanese translation results for two different values of the distortion limit d, i.e. the maximum number of source words that the decoder is allowed to jump during search. We draw the following conclusions. Firstly, all the preordering approaches outperform the baseline and the BLEU score gain they provide increases as the distortion limit decreases. This is further analysed in Figure 5, where we report BLEU as a function of the distortion limit in decoding for both English-Japanese and English-Korean. This reveals the power of preordering as a targeted strategy to obtain high performance at fast decoding times, since d can be drastically reduced without performance degradation which leads to huge decoding speed-ups; this is consistent with the observations in (Xu et al., 2009; Genzel, 2010; Visweswariah et al., 2011). We also find that with preordering it is possible to apply harsher pruning conditions in decoding while still maintaining the exact same performance, achieving further speedups. With preordering, our system is able to decode 80 times faster while producing translation output of the same quality.

Secondly, we observe that the preordering gains, which are correlated with the crossing score reductions of Table 1, are largely orthogonal to the gains obtained when incorporating a lexicalised reordering model (LRM). In fact, preordering gains are slightly larger with LRM, suggesting that this reordering model can be better estimated with preordered text. This echoes the notion that reordering models are particularly sensitive to alignment noise (DeNero and Uszkoreit, 2011; Neubig et al., 2012; Visweswariah et al., 2013), and that a 'more monotonic' training corpus leads to better translation models.

Finally, 'df-bnb' outperforms all other preordering approaches, and achieves an extra 0.5–0.8 BLEU over the rule-based one even at zero distortion limit. This is consistent with the substantial crossing score reductions reported in Section 4.3.

We argue that these improvements are due to the usage of lexical features to facilitate finer-grained ordering decisions, and to our better search through the children permutation space which is not restricted by sliding windows, does

Example 1	reference	[$_{1}$バーローは]$_{\text{Barlow}}$ [$_{2}$悪臭に]$_{\text{the smell}}$ [$_{3}$我慢]$_{\text{endure}}$ [$_{4}$できることを]$_{\text{could}}$ [$_{5}$願った]$_{\text{hoped}}$ [$_{6}$。]
	source	[$_{1}$Barlow] [$_{5}$hoped] he [$_{4}$could] [$_{3}$stand] [$_{2}$the smell] [$_{6}$.]
	preordered	[$_{1}$Barlow] he [$_{2}$the smell] [$_{3}$stand] [$_{4}$could] [$_{5}$hoped] [$_{6}$.]
Example 2	reference	[$_{1}$私自身の]$_{\text{my own}}$ [$_{2}$経験]$_{\text{experience}}$ [$_{3}$において]$_{\text{in}}$, [$_{4}$ローザパルクス]$_{\text{Rosa Parks}}$ [$_{5}$という]$_{\text{called}}$ [$_{6}$黒人の]$_{\text{black}}$ [$_{7}$女性は]$_{\text{woman}}$, [$_{8}$ある日]$_{\text{one day}}$ [$_{9}$とにかくとにかく]$_{\text{somehow}}$ [$_{10}$バスの]$_{\text{bus of}}$ [$_{11}$後部座席に]$_{\text{back seat in}}$ [$_{12}$坐る]$_{\text{sit}}$ ように [$_{13}$言われる]$_{\text{told being}}$ [$_{14}$ことに]$_{\text{of}}$ [$_{15}$うんざりす]$_{\text{was fed up with}}$ 。
	source	[$_{3}$In] [$_{1}$my own] [$_{2}$experience] , a [$_{6}$black] [$_{7}$woman] [$_{5}$named] [$_{4}$Rosa Parks] [$_{14}$was just tired] [$_{8}$one day] [$_{14}$of] [$_{13}$being told] [$_{12}$to sit] [$_{11}$in the back] [$_{10}$of the bus] .
	rule-based	[$_{1}$my own] [$_{2}$experience] [$_{3}$In] [$_{14}$was just tired] [$_{13}$being told] [$_{10}$the bus of] [$_{11}$the back in] [$_{12}$sit to] [$_{14}$of] [$_{8}$one day] , [$_{6}$a black] [$_{7}$woman] [$_{4}$Rosa Parks] [$_{5}$named] .
	df-bnb	[$_{1}$my own] [$_{2}$experience] [$_{3}$In] , [$_{5}$named] [$_{6}$a black] [$_{7}$woman] [$_{4}$Rosa Parks] [$_{10}$the bus of] [$_{11}$the back in] [$_{12}$sit to] [$_{13}$told being] [$_{14}$of] [$_{8}$one day] [$_{14}$was just tired] .
Example 3	reference	[$_{1}$私たちは]$_{\text{we}}$、[$_{2}$すっかり]$_{\text{quite}}$ [$_{3}$西安が]$_{\text{Xi'an}}$ [$_{4}$好き]$_{\text{like}}$ [$_{5}$に]$_{\text{to}}$ [$_{6}$なりました]$_{\text{come have}}$ 。
	source	[$_{1}$we] [$_{6}$have come] [$_{5}$to] [$_{2}$quite] [$_{4}$like] [$_{1}$xi'an] .
	rule-based	[$_{1}$we] [$_{2}$quite] [$_{4}$like] [$_{3}$xi'an] [$_{5}$to] [$_{6}$come have] .
	df-bnb	[$_{1}$we] have [$_{2}$quite] [$_{3}$xi'an] [$_{4}$like] [$_{5}$to] [$_{6}$come] .
	baseline	私たちはをかなり西安と同様です 。
	rule-based	私たちはかなりのように西安に来ます。
	df-bnb	私たちはかなり西安が好きになる。

Table 4: Examples from our test data illustrating the differences between the preordering approaches.

not depend heavily on getting the right decision in a multi-class scenario, and which incorporates regression to carry out a score-driven search.

4.5 Analysis

Table 4 gives three English-Japanese examples to illustrate the different preordering approaches. The first, very short, example is preordered correctly by the rule-based and the df-bnb approach, as the order of the brackets matches the order of the Japanese reference.

For longer sentences we see more differences between approaches, as illustrated by Example 2. In this case, both approaches succeed at moving prepositions to the back of the phrase ("my experience in", "the bus of"). However, while the df-bnb approach correctly moves the predicate of the second clause ("was just tired") to the back, the rule-based approach incorrectly moves the subject ("a black woman named Rosa Parks") to this position - possibly because of the verb "named" which occurs in the phrase. This could be an indication that the df-bnb is better suited for more complicated constructions. With the exception of phrases 4 and 8, all other phrases are in the correct order in the df-bnb reordering. None of the approaches manage to reorder "a black woman named Rosa Parks" to the correct order.

Example 3 shows that the translations into Japanese also reflect preordering quality. The original source results in "like" being translated as the main verb (which is incorrectly interpreted as "to be like, to be equal to"). The rule-based version correctly moves "have come" to the end, but fails to swap "xi'an" and "like", resulting in "come" being interpreted as a full verb, rather than an auxiliary. Only the df-bnb version achieves almost perfect reordering, resulting in the correct word choice of なる (to get to, to become) for "have come to".[5]

5 Conclusion

We have presented a novel preordering approach that estimates a preference for swapping or not swapping pairs of children nodes in the source-side dependency tree by training a feature-rich logistic regression model. Given the pair-wise scores, we efficiently search through the space of possible children permutations using depth-first branch-and-bound search. The approach is able to incorporate large numbers of features including lexical cues, is efficient at runtime even with a large number of children, and proves superior to other state-of-the-art preordering approaches both in terms of crossing score and translation performance.

[5]This translation is still not perfect, since it uses the wrong level of politeness, an important distinction in Japanese.

References

Ibrahim Badr, Rabih Zbib, and James Glass. 2009. Syntactic Phrase Reordering for English-to-Arabic Statistical Machine Translation. In *Proceedings of EACL*, pages 86–93, Athens, Greece.

Egon Balas and Paolo Toth. 1983. *Branch and Bound Methods for the Traveling Salesman Problem*. Carnegie-Mellon Univ. Pittsburgh PA Management Sciences Research Group.

Michael Collins, Philipp Koehn, and Ivona Kucerova. 2005. Clause Restructuring for Statistical Machine Translation. In *Proceedings of ACL*, pages 531–540, Ann Arbor, Michigan.

Marta R. Costa-jussà and José A. R. Fonollosa. 2006. Statistical Machine Reordering. In *Proceedings of EMNLP*, pages 70–76, Sydney, Australia.

Josep M. Crego and José B. Mariño. 2006. Integration of POStag-based Source Reordering into SMT Decoding by an Extended Search Graph. In *Proceedings of AMTA*, pages 29–36, Cambridge, Massachusetts.

John DeNero and Jakob Uszkoreit. 2011. Inducing Sentence Structure from Parallel Corpora for Reordering. In *Proceedings of EMNLP*, pages 193–203, Edinburgh, Scotland, UK.

Rong-En Fan, Kai-Wei Chang, Cho-Jui Hsieh, Xiang-Rui Wang, and Chih-Jen Lin. 2008. LIBLINEAR: A Library for Large Linear Classification. *Journal of Machine Learning Research*, 9:1871–1874.

Michel Galley and Christopher D. Manning. 2008. A Simple and Effective Hierarchical Phrase Reordering Model. In *Proceedings of EMNLP*, pages 847–855, Honolulu, Hawaii.

Dmitriy Genzel. 2010. Automatically learning source-side reordering rules for large scale machine translation. In *Proceedings of COLING*, pages 376–384, Beijing, China.

Jesús Giménez and Lluís Màrquez. 2004. SVMTool: A general POS tagger generator based on Support Vector Machines. In *Proceedings of LREC*, Lisbon, Portugal.

Nizar Habash. 2007. Syntactic Preprocessing for Statistical Machine Translation. In *Proceedings of MT-Summit*, pages 215–222, Copenhagen, Denmark.

Gumwon Hong, Seung-Wook Lee, and Hae-Chang Rim. 2009. Bridging Morpho-Syntactic Gap between Source and Target Sentences for English-Korean Statistical Machine Translation. In *Proceedings of ACL-IJCNLP*, pages 233–236, Suntec, Singapore.

Hideki Isozaki, Katsuhito Sudoh, Hajime Tsukada, and Kevin Duh. 2010. Head Finalization: A Simple Reordering Rule for SOV Languages. In *Proceedings of the Joint Fifth Workshop on Statistical Machine Translation and MetricsMATR*, pages 244–251, Uppsala, Sweden.

Young-Suk Lee, Bing Zhao, and Xiaoqian Luo. 2010. Constituent Reordering and Syntax Models for English-to-Japanese Statistical Machine Translation. In *Proceedings of COLING*, pages 626–634, Beijing, China.

Uri Lerner and Slav Petrov. 2013. Source-Side Classifier Preordering for Machine Translation. In *Proceedings of EMNLP*, Seattle, USA.

Chi-Ho Li, Minghui Li, Dongdong Zhang, Mu Li, Ming Zhou, and Yi Guan. 2007. A Probabilistic Approach to Syntax-based Reordering for Statistical Machine Translation. In *Proceedings of ACL*, pages 720–727, Prague, Czech Republic.

Graham Neubig, Taro Watanabe, and Shinsuke Mori. 2012. Inducing a Discriminative Parser to Optimize Machine Translation Reordering. In *Proceedings of EMNLP-CoNLL*, pages 843–853, Jeju Island, Korea.

Joakim Nivre, Johan Hall, Jens Nilsson, Atanas Chanev, Gülsen Eryigit, Sandra Kübler, Svetoslav Marinov, and Erwin Marsi. 2007. Maltparser: A language-independent system for data-driven dependency parsing. *Natural Language Engineering*, 13(2):95–135.

Franz Josef Och. 1999. An efficient method for determining bilingual word classes. In *Proceedings of EACL*, pages 71–76, Bergen, Norway.

David L. Poole and Alan K. Mackworth. 2010. *Artificial Intelligence: Foundations of Computational Agents*. Cambridge University Press. Full text online at http://artint.info.

Ananthakrishnan Ramanathan, Hansraj Choudhary, Avishek Ghosh, and Pushpak Bhattacharyya. 2009. Case markers and Morphology: Addressing the crux of the fluency problem in English-Hindi SMT. In *Proceedings of ACL-IJCNLP*, pages 800–808, Suntec, Singapore.

Kay Rottmann and Stephan Vogel. 2007. Word Reordering in Statistical Machine Translation with a POS-Based Distortion Model. In *Proceedings of TMI*, pages 171–180, Skövde, Sweden.

Roy Tromble and Jason Eisner. 2009. Learning linear ordering problems for better translation. In *Proceedings of EMNLP*, pages 1007–1016, Singapore.

Karthik Visweswariah, Jiri Navratil, Jeffrey Sorensen, Vijil Chenthamarakshan, and Nandakishore Kambhatla. 2010. Syntax based reordering with automatically derived rules for improved statistical machine translation. In *Proceedings of COLING*, pages 1119–1127, Beijing, China.

Karthik Visweswariah, Rajakrishnan Rajkumar, Ankur Gandhe, Ananthakrishnan Ramanathan, and Jiri Navratil. 2011. A word reordering model for improved machine translation. In *Proceedings of EMNLP*, pages 486–496, Edinburgh, United Kingdom.

Karthik Visweswariah, Mitesh M. Khapra, and Ananthakrishnan Ramanathan. 2013. Cut the noise: Mutually reinforcing reordering and alignments for improved machine translation. In *Proceedings of ACL*, pages 1275–1284, Sofia, Bulgaria.

Chao Wang, Michael Collins, and Philipp Koehn. 2007. Chinese Syntactic Reordering for Statistical Machine Translation. In *Proceedings of EMNLP-CoNLL*, pages 737–745, Prague, Czech Republic.

Xianchao Wu, Katsuhito Sudoh, Kevin Duh, Hajime Tsukada, and Masaaki Nagata. 2011. Extracting Pre-ordering Rules from Predicate-Argument Structures. In *Proceedings of IJCNLP*, pages 29–37, Chiang Mai, Thailand.

Fei Xia and Michael McCord. 2004. Improving a statistical MT system with automatically learned rewrite patterns. In *Proceedings of COLING*, Geneva, Switzerland.

Peng Xu, Jaeho Kang, Michael Ringgaard, and Franz Och. 2009. Using a Dependency Parser to Improve SMT for Subject-Object-Verb Languages. In *Proceedings of HTL-NAACL*, pages 245–253, Boulder, Colorado.

Nan Yang, Mu Li, Dongdong Zhang, and Nenghai Yu. 2012. A ranking-based approach to word reordering for statistical machine translation. In *Proceedings of ACL*, pages 912–920, Jeju Island, Korea.

Incremental Bayesian Learning of Semantic Categories

Lea Frermann and **Mirella Lapata**
Institute for Language, Cognition and Computation
School of Informatics, University of Edinburgh
10 Crichton Street, Edinburgh EH8 9AB
l.frermann@ed.ac.uk, mlap@inf.ed.ac.uk

Abstract

Models of category learning have been extensively studied in cognitive science and primarily tested on perceptual abstractions or artificial stimuli. In this paper we focus on categories acquired from *natural language* stimuli, that is words (e.g., *chair* is a member of the FURNITURE category). We present a Bayesian model which, unlike previous work, learns both categories and their features in a single process. Our model employs particle filters, a sequential Monte Carlo method commonly used for approximate probabilistic inference in an incremental setting. Comparison against a state-of-the-art graph-based approach reveals that our model learns qualitatively better categories and demonstrates cognitive plausibility during learning.

1 Introduction

Considerable psychological research has shown that people reason about novel objects they encounter by identifying the category to which these objects belong and extrapolating from their past experiences with other members of that category (Smith and Medin, 1981). *Categorization* is a classic problem in cognitive science, underlying a variety of common mental tasks including perception, learning, and the use of language.

Given its fundamental nature, categorization has been extensively studied both experimentally and in simulations. Indeed, numerous models exist as to how humans categorize objects ranging from strict *prototypes* (categories are represented by a single idealized member which embodies their core properties; e.g., Reed 1972) to full exemplar models (categories are represented by a list of previously encountered members; e.g., Nosofsky 1988) and combinations of the two (e.g., Griffiths et al. 2007). A common feature across different studies is the use of stimuli involving real-world objects (e.g., children's toys; Starkey 1981), perceptual abstractions (e.g., photographs of animals; Quinn and Eimas 1996), or artificial ones (e.g., binary strings, dot patterns or geometric shapes; Medin and Schaffer 1978; Posner and Keele 1968; Bomba and Siqueland 1983). Most existing models focus on adult categorization, in which it is assumed that a large number of categories have already been learnt (but see Anderson 1991 and Griffiths et al. 2007 for exceptions).

In this work we focus on categories acquired from *natural language* stimuli (i.e., words) and investigate how the statistics of the linguistic environment (as approximated by large corpora) influence category formation (e.g., *chair* and *table* are FURNITURE whereas *peach* and *apple* are FRUIT[1]). The idea of modeling categories using words as a stand-in for their referents has been previously used to explore categorization-related phenomena such as semantic priming (Cree et al., 1999) and typicality rating (Voorspoels et al., 2008), to evaluate prototype and exemplar models (Storms et al., 2000), and to simulate early language category acquisition (Fountain and Lapata, 2011). The idea of using naturalistic corpora has received little attention. Most existing studies use feature norms as a proxy for people's representation of semantic concepts. In a typical procedure, participants are presented with a word and asked to generate the most relevant features or attributes for its referent concept. The most notable collection of feature norms is probably the multi-year project of McRae et al. (2005), which obtained features for a set of 541 common English nouns.

Our approach replaces feature norms with representations derived from words' contexts in corpora. While this is an impoverished view of how categories are acquired — it is clear that they are learnt through exposure to the linguistic environment *and* the physical world — perceptual infor-

[1]Throughout this paper we will use small caps to denote CATEGORIES and italics for their *members*.

mation relevant for extracting semantic categories is to a large extent redundantly encoded in linguistic experience (Riordan and Jones, 2011). Besides, there are known difficulties with feature norms such as the small number of words for which these can be obtained, the quality of the attributes, and variability in the way people generate them (see Zeigenfuse and Lee 2010 for details). Focusing on natural language categories allows us to build categorization models with theoretically unlimited scope.

To this end, we present a probabilistic Bayesian model of category acquisition based on the key idea that learners can adaptively form category representations that capture the structure expressed in the observed data. We model category induction as two interrelated sub-problems: (a) the acquisition of features that discriminate among categories, and (b) the grouping of concepts into categories based on those features. An important modeling question concerns the exact mechanism with which categories are learned. To maintain cognitive plausibility, we develop an *incremental* learning algorithm. Incrementality is a central aspect of human learning which takes place sequentially and over time. Humans are capable of dealing with a situation even if only partial information is available. They adaptively learn as new information is presented and locally update their internal knowledge state without systematically revising everything known about the situation at hand. Memory and processing limitations also explain why humans must learn incrementally. It is not possible to store and have easy access to all the information one has been exposed to. It seems likely that people store the most prominent facts and generalizations, which they modify on they fly when new facts become available.

Our model learns categories using a particle filter, a Markov Chain Monte Carlo (MCMC) inference mechanism which sequentially integrates newly observed data and can be thus viewed as a plausible proxy for human learning. Experimental results show that the incremental learner obtains meaningful categories which outperform the state of the art whilst at the same time acquiring semantic representations of words and their features.

2 Related Work

The problem of category induction has achieved much attention in the cognitive science literature. Incremental category learning was pioneered by Anderson (1991) who develops a non-parametric model able to induce categories from abstract stimuli represented by binary features. Sanborn et al. (2006) present a fully Bayesian adaptation of Anderson's original model, which yields a better fit with behavioral data. A separate line of work examines the cognitive characteristics of category acquisition as well as the processes of generalizing and generating new categories and exemplars (Jern and Kemp, 2013; Kemp et al., 2012). The above models are conceptually similar to ours. However, they were developed with adult categorization in mind, and use rather simplistic categories representing toy-domains. It is therefore not clear whether they generalize to arbitrary stimuli and data sizes. We aim to show that it is possible to acquire natural language categories on a larger scale purely from linguistic context.

Our model is loosely related to Bayesian models of word sense induction (Brody and Lapata, 2009; Yao and Durme, 2011). We also assume that local linguistic context can provide important cues for word meaning and by extension category membership. However, the above models focus on performance optimization and learn in an ideal batch mode, while incorporating various kinds of additional features such as part of speech tags or dependencies. In contrast, we develop a cognitively plausible (early) language learning model and show that categories can be acquired purely from context, as well as in an incremental fashion.

From a modeling perspective, we learn categories incrementally using a particle filtering algorithm (Doucet et al., 2001). Particle filters are a family of sequential Monte Carlo algorithms which update the state space of a probabilistic model with newly encountered information. They have been successfully applied to natural language acquisition tasks such as word segmentation (Borschinger and Johnson, 2011), or sentence processing (Levy et al., 2009). Sanborn et al. (2006) also use particle filters for small-scale categorization experiments with artificial stimuli. To the best of our knowledge, we present the first particle filtering algorithm for large-scale category acquisition from natural text.

Our work is closest to Fountain and Lapata (2011) who also develop a model for inducing natural language categories. Specifically, they propose an incremental version of Chinese Whispers (Biemann, 2006), a randomized graph-clustering algorithm. The latter takes as input a graph which is constructed from corpus-based co-occurrence statistics and produces a hard clustering over the nodes in the graph. Contrary to our model, they treat the tasks of inferring a semantic representa-

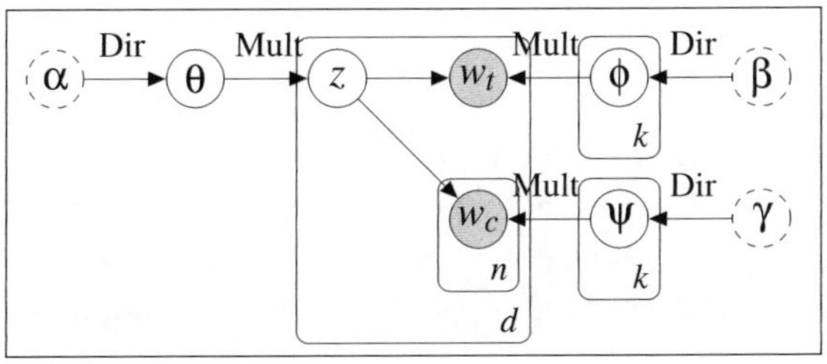

Figure 1: Plate diagram representation of the BayesCat model.

Draw distribution over categories $\theta \sim Dir(\alpha)$
for category k **do**
  Draw target word distribution $\phi_k \sim Dir(\beta)$
  Draw context word distribution $\psi_k \sim Dir(\gamma)$
for Document d **do**
  Draw category $z^d \sim Mult(\theta)$
  Draw target word $w_t^d \sim Mult(\phi_{z^d})$
  for context position $n = \{1..N\}$ **do**
    Draw context word $w_c^{d,n} \sim Mult(\psi_{z^d})$

Figure 2: The generative process of the BayesCat model.

tion for concepts and their class membership as two separate processes. This allows to experiment with different ways of initializing the co-occurrence matrix (e.g., from bags of words or a dependency parsed corpus), however at the expense of cognitive plausibility. It is unlikely that humans have two entirely separate mechanisms for learning the meaning of words and their categories. We formulate a more expressive model within a probabilistic framework which captures the meaning of words, their similarity, and the predictive power of their linguistic contexts.

3 The BayesCat Model

In this section we present our Bayesian model of category induction (BayesCat for short). The input to the model is natural language text, and its final output is a set of clusters representing categories of semantic concepts found in the input data. Like many other semantic models, BayesCat is inspired by the distributional hypothesis which states that a word's meaning is predictable from its context (Harris, 1954). By extension, we also assume that contextual information can be used to characterize *general semantic categories*. Accordingly, the input to our model is a corpus of documents, each defined as a target word t centered in a fixed-length context window:

$$[c_{-n} \dots c_{-1} \ t \ c_1 \dots c_n] \tag{1}$$

We assume that there exists one global distribution over categories from which all documents are generated. Each document is assigned a category label, based on two types of features: the document's target word and its context words, which are modeled through *separate* category-specific distributions. We argue that it is important to distinguish between these features, since words belonging to the same category do not necessarily co-occur, but tend to occur in the same contexts. For example, the words *polar bear* and *anteater* are both members of the category ANIMAL. However, they rarely co-occur (in fact, a cursory search using Google yields only three matches for the query "*polar bear * anteater*"). Nevertheless, we would expect to observe both words in similar contexts since both animals *eat, sleep, hunt, have fur, four legs*, and so on. This distinction contrasts our category acquisition task from the classical task of topic inference.

Figure 1 presents a plate diagram of the BayesCat model; an overview of the generative process is given in Figure 2. We first draw a global category distribution θ from the Dirichlet distribution with parameter α. Next, for each category k, we draw a distribution over target words ϕ_k from a Dirichlet with parameter β *and* a distribution over context words ψ_k from a Dirichlet with parameter γ. For each document d, we draw a category z^d, then a target word, and N context words from the category-specific distributions ϕ_{z^d} and ψ_{z^d}, respectively.

4 Learning

Our goal is to infer the joint distribution of all hidden model parameters, and observable data W. Since we use conjugate prior distributions throughout the model, this joint distribution can be simplified to:

$$P(W,Z,\theta,\phi,\psi;\alpha,\beta,\gamma) \propto \frac{\prod_k \Gamma(\mathcal{N}_k + \alpha_k)}{\Gamma(\sum_k \mathcal{N}_k + \alpha_k)} \times \prod_{k=1}^{K} \frac{\prod_r \Gamma(\mathcal{N}_r^k + \beta_r)}{\Gamma(\sum_r \mathcal{N}_r^k + \beta_r)} \times \prod_{k=1}^{K} \frac{\prod_s \Gamma(\mathcal{N}_s^k + \gamma_s)}{\Gamma(\sum_s \mathcal{N}_s^k + \gamma_s)}, \tag{2}$$

where r and s iterate over the target and context word vocabulary, respectively, and the distributions θ, ϕ, and ψ are integrated out and implicitly captured by the corresponding co-occurrence counts $\mathcal{N}_*^*$. $\Gamma()$ denotes the Gamma function, a generalization of the factorial to real numbers.

Since exact inference of the parameters of the BayesCat model is intractable, we use sampling-based approximate inference. Specifically, we present two learning algorithms, namely a Gibbs sampler and a particle filter.

The Gibbs Sampler Gibbs sampling is a well-established approximate learning algorithm, based on Markov Chain Monte Carlo methods (Geman and Geman, 1984). It operates in batch-mode by repeatedly iterating through all data points (documents in our case) and assigning the currently sampled document d a category z^d conditioned on the current labelings of all other documents z^{-d}:

$$z^d \sim P(z^d | z^{-d}, W^{-d}; \alpha, \beta, \gamma), \quad (3)$$

using equation (2) but ignoring information from the currently sampled document in all co-occurrence counts.

The Gibbs sampler can be seen as an ideal learner, which can view and revise any relevant information at any time during learning. From a cognitive perspective, this setting is implausible, since a human language learner encounters training data incrementally and does not systematically revisit previous learning decisions. Particle filters are a class of incremental, or sequential, Monte Carlo methods which can be used to model aspects of the language learning process more naturally.

The Particle Filter Intuitively, a particle filter (henceforth PF) entertains a fixed set of N weighted hypotheses (particles) based on previous training examples. Figure 3 shows an overview of the particle filtering learning procedure. At first, every particle of the PF is initialized from a base distribution P_0 (Initialization). Then a single iteration over the input data $\mathbf{y}$ is performed, during which the posterior distribution of each data point y^t under all current particles is computed given information from all previously encountered data points $\mathbf{y^{t-1}}$ (Sampling/Prediction). Crucially, each update is conditioned only on the previous model state z^{t-1}, which results in a constant state space despite an increasing amount of available data. A common problem with PF algorithms is weight degeneration, i.e., one particle tends to accumulate most of the weight. To avoid this problem, at regular intervals the set of particles is resampled in order to discard particles with

```
for particle p do                                   ▷ Initialization
    Initialize randomly or from z_p^0 ~ p_0(z)
for observation t do
    for particle n do                         ▷ Sampling/Prediction
        P_n(z_n^t|y^t) ~ p(z_n^t|z_n^{t-1}, α) P(y^t|z_n^t, y^{t-1})
    z^t ∝ Mult({P_n(z_n^t)}_{i=1}^N)                ▷ Resampling
```

Figure 3: The particle filtering procedure.

low probability and to ensure that the sample is representative of the state space at any time (Resampling).

This general algorithm can be straightforwardly adapted to our learning problem (Griffiths et al., 2011; Fearnhead, 2004). Each observation corresponds to a document, which needs to be assigned a category. To begin with, we assign the first observed document to category 0 in all particles (Initialization). Then, we iterate once over the remaining documents. For each particle n, we compute a probability distribution over K categories based on the simplified posterior distribution as defined in equation (2) (Sampling/Prediction), with co-occurrence counts based on the information from all previously encountered documents. Thus, we obtain a distribution over $N \cdot K$ possible assignments. From this distribution we sample with replacement N new particles, assign the current document to the corresponding category (Resampling), and proceed to the next input document.

5 Experimental Setup

The goal of our experimental evaluation is to assess the quality of the inferred clusters by comparison to a gold standard and an existing graph-based model of category acquisition. In addition, we are interested in the incremental version of the model, whether it is able to learn meaningful categories and how these change over time. In the following, we give details on the corpora we used, describe how model parameters were selected, and explain our evaluation procedure.

5.1 Data

All our experiments were conducted on a lemmatized version of the British National Corpus (BNC). The corpus was further preprocessed by removing stopwords and infrequent words (occurring less than 800 times in the BNC).

The model output was evaluated against a gold standard set of categories which was created by collating the resources developed by Fountain and

Lapata (2010) and Vinson and Vigliocco (2008). Both datasets contain a classification of nouns into (possibly multiple) semantic categories produced by human participants. We therefore assume that they represent psychologically salient categories which the cognitive system is in principle capable of acquiring. After merging the two resources, and removing duplicates we obtained 42 semantic categories for 555 nouns. We split this gold standard into a development (41 categories, 492 nouns) and a test set (16 categories, 196 nouns).[2]

The input to our model consists of short chunks of text, namely a target word centered in a symmetric context window of five words (see (1)). In our experiments, the set of target words corresponds to the set of nouns in the evaluation dataset. Target word mentions and their context are extracted from the BNC.

5.2 Parameters for the BayesCat Model

We optimized the hyperparameters of the BayesCat model on the development set. For the particle filter, the optimal values are $\alpha = 0.7, \beta = 0.1, \gamma = 0.1$. We used the same values for the Gibbs Sampler since it proved insensitive to hyperparameter variations. We run the Gibbs sampler for 200 iterations[3] and report results averaged over 10 runs. For the PF, we set the number of particles to 500, and report final scores averaged over 10 runs. For evaluation, we take the clustering from the particle with the highest weight [4].

5.3 Model Comparison

Chinese Whispers We compared our approach with Fountain and Lapata (2011) who present a non-parametric graph-based model for category acquisition. Their algorithm incrementally constructs a graph from co-occurrence counts of target words and their contexts (they use a symmetric context window of five words). Target words constitute the nodes of the graph, their co-occurrences are transformed into a vector of positive PMI values, and graph edges correspond to the cosine similarity between the PMI-vectors representing any two nodes. They use Chinese Whispers (Biemann, 2006) to partition a graph into categories.

[2]The dataset is available from `www.frermann.de/data`.

[3]We checked for convergence on the development set.

[4]While in theory particles should be averaged, we found that eventually they became highly similar — a common problem known as *sample impoverishment*, which we plan to tackle in the future. Nevertheless, diversity among particles is present in the initial learning phase, when uncertainty is greatest, so the model still benefits from multiple hypotheses.

We replicated the bag-of-words model presented in Fountain and Lapata (2011) and assessed its performance on our training corpora and test sets. The scores we report are averaged over 10 runs.

Chinese Whispers can only make hard clustering decisions, whereas the BayesCat model returns a soft clustering of target nouns. In order to be able to compare the two models, we convert the soft clusters to hard clusters by assigning each target word w to category c such that $cat(w) = \max_c P(w|c) \cdot P(c|w)$.

LDA We also compared our model to a standard topic model, namely Latent Dirichlet Allocation (LDA; Blei et al. 2003). LDA assumes that a document is generated from an individual mixture over topics, and each topic is associated with one word distribution. We trained a batch version of LDA using input identical to our model and the Mallet toolkit (McCallum, 2002).

Chinese Whispers is a parameter-free algorithm and thus determines the number of clusters automatically. While the Bayesian models presented here are parametric in that an upper bound for the potential number of categories needs to be specified, the models themselves decide on the specific value of this number. We set the upper bound of categories to 100 for LDA as well as the batch and incremental version of the BayesCat model.

5.4 Evaluation Metrics

Our aim is to learn a set of clusters each of which corresponds to one gold category, i.e., it contains *all* and *only* members of that gold category. We report evaluation scores based on three metrics which measure this tradeoff. Since in unsupervised clustering the cluster IDs are meaningless, all evaluation metrics involve a mapping from induced clusters to gold categories. The first two metrics described below perform a cluster-based mapping and are thus not ideal for assessing the output of soft clustering algorithms. The third metric performs an item-based mapping and can be directly used to evaluate soft clusters.

Purity/Collocation are based on member overlap between induced clusters and gold classes (Lang and Lapata, 2011). Purity measures the degree to which each cluster contains instances that share the same gold class, while collocation measures the degree to which instances with the same gold class are assigned to a single cluster. We report the harmonic mean of purity and collocation as a single measure of clustering quality.

V-Measure is the harmonic mean between homogeneity and collocation (Rosenberg and Hirschberg, 2007). Like purity, V-Measure performs cluster-based comparisons but is an entropy-based method. It measures the conditional entropy of a cluster given a class, and vice versa.

Cluster-F1 is an item-based evaluation metric which we propose drawing inspiration from the supervised metric presented in Agirre and Soroa (2007). Cluster-F1 maps each target word type to a gold cluster based on its soft class membership, and is thus appropriate for evaluation of soft clustering output. We first create a $K \times G$ soft mapping matrix $\mathcal{M}$ from each induced category k_i to gold classes g_j from $P(g_j|k_i)$. We then map each target word type to a gold class by multiplying its probability distribution over soft clusters with the mapping matrix $\mathcal{M}$, and taking the maximum value. Finally, we compute standard precision, recall and F1 between the mapped system categories and the gold classes.

6 Results

Our experiments are designed to answer three questions: (1) How do the induced categories fare against gold standard categories? (2) Are there performance differences between BayesCat and Chinese Whispers, given that the two models adopt distinct mechanisms for representing lexical meaning and learning semantic categories? (3) Is our incremental learning mechanism cognitively plausible? In other words, does the quality of the induced clusters improve over time and how do the learnt categories differ from the output of an ideal batch learner?

Clustering performance for the batch BayesCat model (BC-Batch), its incremental version (BC-Inc), Chinese Whispers (CW), and LDA is shown in Table 1. Comparison of the two incremental models, namely BC-Inc and CW, shows that our model outperforms CW under all evaluation metrics both on the test and the development set. Our BC models perform at least as well as LDA, despite the more complex learning objective. Recall that LDA does not learn category specific features. BC-Batch performs best overall, however this is not surprising. The BayesCat model learnt in batch mode uses a Gibbs sampler which can be viewed as an ideal learner with access to the entire training data at any time, and the ability to systematically revise previous decisions. This puts the incremental variant at a disadvantage since the particle filter encounters the data incrementally and never resamples previously seen documents. Nevertheless, as shown in Table 1 BC-Inc's performance is very close to BC-Batch. BC-Inc outperforms the Gibbs sampler in the PC-F1 metric, because it achieves higher collocation scores. Inspection of the output reveals that the Gibbs sampler induces larger clusters compared to the particle filter (as well as less distinct clusters). Although the general pattern of results is the same on the development and test sets, absolute scores for all systems are higher on the test set. This is expected, since the test set contains less categories with a smaller number of exemplars and more accurate clusterings can be thus achieved (on average) more easily.

Figure 4 displays the learning curves produced by CW and BC-Inc under the PC-F1 (left) and Cluster-F1 (right) evaluation metrics. Under PC-F1, CW produces a very steep initial learning curve which quickly flattens off, whereas no learning curve emerges for CW under Cluster-F1. The BayesCat model exhibits more discernible learning curves under both metrics. We also observe that learning curves for CW indicate much more variance during learning compared to BC-Inc, irrespectively of the evaluation metric being used. Figure 4b shows learning curves for BC-Inc when its output classes are interpreted in two ways, i.e., as soft or hard clusters. Interestingly, the two curves have a similar shape which points to the usefulness of Cluster-F1 as an evaluation metric for both types of clusters.

In order to better understand the differences in the learning process between CW and BC-Inc we tracked the evolution of clusterings over time, as well as the variance across cluster sizes at each point in time. The results are plotted in Figure 5. The top part of the figure compares the number of clusters learnt by the two models. We see that the number of clusters inferred by CW drops over time, but is closer to the number of clusters present in the gold standard. The final number of clusters inferred by CW is 26, whereas PF-Inc infers 90 clusters (there are 41 gold classes). The middle plot shows the variance in cluster size induced at any time by CW which is by orders of magnitude higher than the variance observed in the output of BayesCat (bottom plot). More importantly, the variance in BayesCat resembles the variance present in the gold standard much more closely. The clusterings learnt by CW tend to consist of

Metric		Development Set				Test Set			
		LDA	CW	BC-Inc	BC-Batch	LDA	CW	BC-Inc	BC-Batch
PC-F1	(Hard)	0.283	0.211	0.283	0.261	0.446	0.380	0.503	0.413
V-Measure	(Hard)	0.399	0.143	0.383	0.428	0.572	0.220	0.567	0.606
Cluster-F1	(Hard)	0.416	0.301	0.386	0.447	0.521	0.443	0.671	0.693
Cluster-F1	(Soft)	0.387	—	0.484	0.523	0.665	—	0.644	0.689

Table 1: Evaluation of model output against a gold standard. Results are reported for the BayesCat model trained incrementally (BC-Inc) and in batch mode (BC-Batch), and Chinese Whispers (CW). The type of clusters being evaluated is shown within parentheses.

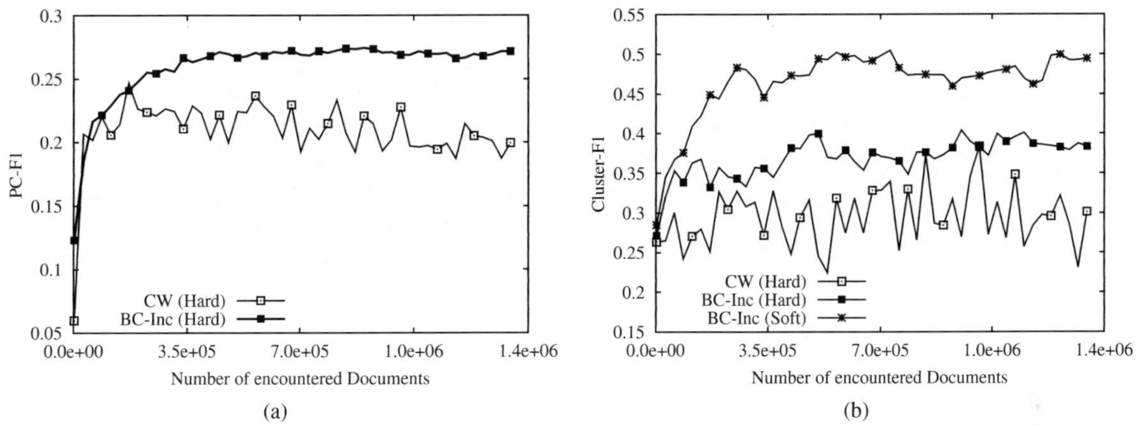

Figure 4: Learning curves for BC-Inc and CW based on PC-F1 (left), and Cluster-F1 (right). The type of clusters being evaluated is shown within parentheses. Results are reported on the development set.

few very large clusters and a large number of very small (mostly singleton) clusters. Although some of the bigger clusters are meaningful, the overall structure of clusterings does not faithfully represent the gold standard.

Finally, note that in contrast to CW and LDA, the BayesCat model learns not only how to induce clusters of target words, but also information about their category-specific contexts. Table 2 presents examples of the learnt categories together with their most likely contexts. For example, one of the categories our model discovers corresponds to BUILDINGS. Some of the context words or features relating to buildings refer to their location (e.g., *city, road, hill, north, park*), architectural style (e.g., *modern, period, estate*), and material (e.g., *stone*).

7 Discussion

In this paper we have presented a Bayesian model of category acquisition. Our model learns to group concepts into categories as well as their features (i.e., context words associated with them). Category learning is performed incrementally, using a particle filtering algorithm which is a natural choice for modeling sequential aspects of language learning.

We now return to our initial questions and summarize our findings. Firstly, we observe that our incremental model learns plausible linguistic categories when compared against the gold standard. Secondly, these categories are qualitatively better when evaluated against Chinese Whispers, a closely related graph-based incremental algorithm. Thirdly, analysis of the model's output shows that it simulates category learning in two important ways, it consistently improves over time and can additionally acquire category features.

Overall, our model has a more cognitively plausible learning mechanism compared to CW, and is more expressive, as it can simulate both category and feature learning. Although CW ultimately yields some meaningful categories, it does not acquire any knowledge pertaining to their features. This is somewhat unrealistic given that humans are good at inferring missing features for

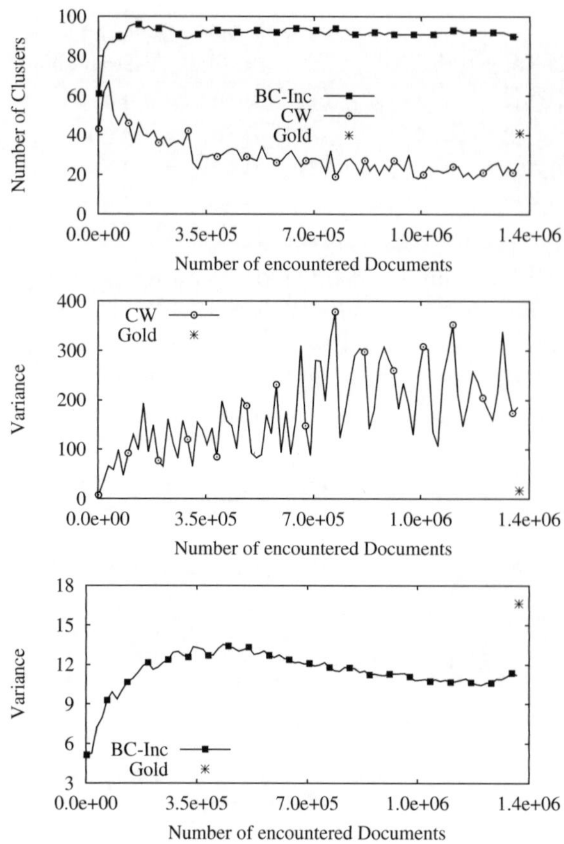

Figure 5: Number of clusters over time (top). Cluster size variance for CW (middle) and BC-Inc (bottom). Results shown on the development set.

BUILDINGS
wall, bridge, building, cottage, gate, house, train, bus, stone, chapel, brick, cathedral
plan, include, park, city, stone, building, hotel, lead, road, hill, north, modern, visit, main, period, cathedral, estate, complete, site, owner, parish

WEAPONS
shotgun, pistol, knife, crowbar, gun, sledgehammer, baton, bullet, motorcycle, van, ambulance
injure, ira, jail, yesterday, arrest, stolen, fire, officer, gun, police victim, hospital, steal, crash, murder, incident, driver, accident, hit

INSTRUMENTS
tuba, drum, harmonica, bagpipe, harp, violin, saxophone, rock, piano, banjo, guitar, flute, harpsichord, trumpet, rocker, clarinet, stereo, cello, accordion
amp, orchestra, sound, electric, string, sing, song, drum, piano, condition, album, instrument, guitar, band, bass, music

Table 2: Examples of categories induced by the incremental BayesCat model (upper row), together with their most likely context words (lower row).

unknown categories (Anderson, 1991). It is also symptomatic of the nature of the algorithm which does not have an explicit learning mechanism. Each node in the graph iteratively adopts (in random order) the strongest class in its neighborhood (i.e., the set of nodes with which it shares an edge). We also showed that LDA is less appropriate for the category learning task on account of its formulation which does not allow to simultaneously acquire clusters and their features.

There are several options for improving our model. The learning mechanism presented here is the most basic of particle methods. A common problem in particle filtering is sample impoverishment, i.e., particles become highly similar after a few iterations, and do not optimally represent the sample space. More involved resampling methods such as stratified sampling or residual resampling, have been shown to alleviate this problem (Douc, 2005).

From a cognitive perspective, the most obvious weakness of our algorithm is its strict incrementality. While our model simulates human memory restrictions and uncertainty by learning based on a limited number of current knowledge states (i.e., particles), it *never* reconsiders past categorization decisions. In many linguistic tasks, however, learners revisit past decisions (Frazier and Rayner, 1982) and intuitively we would expect categories to change based on novel evidence, especially in the early learning phase. In fixed-lag smoothing, a particle smoothing variant, model updates include systematic revision of a fixed set of previous observations in the light of newly encountered evidence (Briers et al., 2010). Based on this framework, we will investigate different schemes for informed sequential learning.

Finally, we would like to compare the model's predictions against behavioral data, and examine more thoroughly how categories and features evolve over time.

Acknowledgments We would like to thank Charles Sutton and members of the ILCC at the School of Informatics for their valuable feedback. We acknowledge the support of EPSRC through project grant EP/I037415/1.

References

Agirre, Eneko and Aitor Soroa. 2007. Semeval-2007 task 02: Evaluating word sense induction and discrimination systems. In *Proceedings of the 4th International Workshop on Semantic Evaluations*. Prague, Czech Republic, pages 7–12.

Anderson, John R. 1991. The adaptive nature of human categorization. *Psychological Review* 98:409–429.

Biemann, Chris. 2006. Chinese Whispers - an efficient graph clustering algorithm and its application to natural language processing problems. In *Proceedings of TextGraphs: the 1st Workshop on Graph Based Methods for Natural Language Processing*. New York City, pages 73–80.

Blei, David M., Andrew Y. Ng, and Michael I. Jordan. 2003. Latent Dirichlet allocation. *Journal of Machine Learning Research* 3:993–1022.

Bomba, Paul C. and Eimas R. Siqueland. 1983. The nature and structure of infant form categories. *Journal of Experimental Child Psychology* 35:294–328.

Borschinger, Benjamin and Mark Johnson. 2011. A particle filter algorithm for Bayesian word segmentation. In *Proceedings of the Australasian Language Technology Association Workshop*. Canberra, Australia, pages 10–18.

Briers, Mark, Arnaud Doucet, and Simon Maskell. 2010. Smoothing algorithms for state-space models. *Annals of the Institute of Statistical Mathematics* 62(1):61–89.

Brody, Samuel and Mirella Lapata. 2009. Bayesian word sense induction. In *Proceedings of the 12th Conference of the European Chapter of the ACL*. Athens, Greece, pages 103–111.

Cree, George S., Ken McRae, and Chris McNorgan. 1999. An attractor model of lexical conceptual processing: Simulating semantic priming. *Cognitive Science* 23(3):371–414.

Douc, Randal. 2005. Comparison of resampling schemes for particle filtering. In *4th International Symposium on Image and Signal Processing and Analysis*. Zagreb, Croatia, pages 64–69.

Doucet, Arnaud, Nando de Freitas, and Neil Gordon. 2001. *Sequential Monte Carlo Methods in Practice*. Springer, New York.

Fearnhead, Paul. 2004. Particle filters for mixture models with an unknown number of components. *Statistics and Computing* 14(1):11–21.

Fountain, Trevor and Mirella Lapata. 2010. Meaning representation in natural language categorization. In *Proceedings of the 32nd Annual Conference of the Cognitive Science Society*. Portland, Oregon, pages 1916–1921.

Fountain, Trevor and Mirella Lapata. 2011. Incremental models of natural language category acquisition. In *Proceedings of the 33nd Annual Conference of the Cognitive Science Society*. Boston, Massachusetts, pages 255–260.

Frazier, Lyn and Keith Rayner. 1982. Making and correcting errors during sentence comprehension: Eye movements in the analysis of structurally ambiguous sentences. *Cognitive Psychology* 14(2):178–210.

Geman, Stuart and Donald Geman. 1984. Stochastic relaxation, Gibbs distributions and the Bayesian restoration of images. *IEEE Transactions on Pattern Analysis and Machine Intelligence* 6(6):721–741.

Griffiths, Thomas L., Kevin R. Canini, Adam N. Sanborn, and Daniel J. Navarro. 2007. Unifying rational models of categorization via the hierarchical Dirichlet process. In *Proceedings of the 29th Annual Conference of the Cognitive Science Society*. Nashville, Tennessee, pages 323–328.

Griffiths, Thomas L., Adam N. Sanborn, Kevin R. Canini, John D. Navarro, and Joshua B. Tenenbaum. 2011. Nonparametric Bayesian models of categorization. In Emmanuel M. Pothos and Andy J. Wills, editors, *Formal Approaches in Categorization*, Cambridge University Press, pages 173–198.

Harris, Zellig. 1954. Distributional structure. *Word* 10(23):146–162.

Jern, Alan and Charles Kemp. 2013. A probabilistic account of exemplar and category generation. *Cognitive Psychology* 66:85–125.

Kemp, Charles, Patrick Shafto, and Joshua B. Tenenbaum. 2012. An integrated account of generalization across objects and features. *Cognitive Psychology* 64:35–75.

Lang, Joel and Mirella Lapata. 2011. Unsupervised semantic role induction with graph partitioning. In *Proceedings of the 2011 Conference on Empirical Methods in Natural Language Processing*. Edinburgh, Scotland, UK., pages 1320–1331.

Levy, Roger P., Florencia Reali, and Thomas L. Griffiths. 2009. Modeling the effects of memory on human online sentence processing with particle filters. In D. Koller, D. Schuurmans, Y. Bengio, and L. Bottou, editors, *Advances in Neural Information Processing Systems 21*, pages 937–944.

McCallum, Andrew Kachites. 2002. Mallet: A machine learning for language toolkit. http://mallet.cs.umass.edu.

McRae, Ken, George S. Cree, Mark S. Seidenberg, and Chris McNorgan. 2005. Semantic feature production norms for a large set of living and nonliving things. *Behavioral Research Methods* 37(4):547–59.

Medin, Douglas L. and Marguerite M. Schaffer. 1978. Context theory of classification learning. *Psychological Review* 85(3):207–238.

Nosofsky, Robert M. 1988. Exemplar-based accounts of relations between classification, recognition, and typicality. *Journal of Experimental Psychology: Learning, Memory, and Cognition* 14:700–708.

Posner, Michael I. and Steven W. Keele. 1968. On the genesis of abstract ideas. *Journal of Experimental Psychology* 21:367–379.

Quinn, Paul C. and Peter D. Eimas. 1996. Perceptual cues that permit categorical differentiation of animal species by infants. *Journal of Experimental Child Psychology* 63:189–211.

Reed, Stephen K. 1972. Pattern recognition and categorization. *Cognitive psychology* 3(3):382–407.

Riordan, Brian and Michael N. Jones. 2011. Redundancy in perceptual and linguistic experience: Comparing feature-based and distributional models of semantic representation. *Topics in Cognitive Science* 3(2):303–345.

Rosenberg, Andrew and Julia Hirschberg. 2007. V-measure: A conditional entropy-based external cluster evaluation measure. In *Proceedings of the 2007 Joint Conference on Empirical Methods in Natural Language Processing and Computational Natural Language Learning*. Prague, Czech Republic, pages 410–420.

Sanborn, Adam N., Thomas L. Griffiths, and Daniel J. Navarro. 2006. A more rational model of categorization. In *Proceedings of the 28th Annual Conference of the Cognitive Science Society*. Vancouver, Canada, pages 726–731.

Smith, Edward E. and Douglas L. Medin. 1981. *Categories and Concepts*. Harvard University Press, Cambridge, MA, USA.

Starkey, David. 1981. The origins of concept formation: Object sorting and object preference in early infancy. *Child Development* pages 489–497.

Storms, Gert, Paul De Boeck, and Wim Ruts. 2000. Prototype and exemplar-based information in natural language categories. *Journal of Memory and Language* 42:51–73.

Vinson, David and Gabriella Vigliocco. 2008. Semantic feature production norms for a large set of objects and events. *Behavior Research Methods* 40(1):183–190.

Voorspoels, Wouter, Wolf Vanpaemel, and Gert Storms. 2008. Exemplars and prototypes in natural language concepts: A typicality-based evaluation. *Psychonomic Bulletin & Review* 15(3):630–637.

Yao, Xuchen and Benjamin Van Durme. 2011. Nonparametric Bayesian word sense induction. In *Proceedings of TextGraphs-6: Graph-based Methods for Natural Language Processing*. Portland, Oregon, pages 10–14.

Zeigenfuse, Matthew D. and Michael D. Lee. 2010. Finding the features that represent stimuli. *Acta Psychologica* 133(3):283–295.

Word Ordering with Phrase-Based Grammars

Adrià de Gispert, Marcus Tomalin, William Byrne
Department of Engineering, University of Cambridge, UK
ad465@cam.ac.uk, mt126@cam.ac.uk, wjb31@cam.ac.uk

Abstract

We describe an approach to word ordering using modelling techniques from statistical machine translation. The system incorporates a phrase-based model of string generation that aims to take unordered bags of words and produce fluent, grammatical sentences. We describe the generation grammars and introduce parsing procedures that address the computational complexity of generation under permutation of phrases. Against the best previous results reported on this task, obtained using syntax driven models, we report huge quality improvements, with BLEU score gains of 20+ which we confirm with human fluency judgements. Our system incorporates dependency language models, large n-gram language models, and minimum Bayes risk decoding.

1 Introduction

Word ordering is a fundamental problem in NLP and has been shown to be NP-complete in discourse ordering (Althaus et al., 2004) and in SMT with arbitrary word reordering (Knight, 1999). Typical solutions involve constraints on the space of permutations, as in multi-document summarisation (Barzilay and Elhadad, 2011) and preordering in SMT (Tromble and Eisner, 2009; Genzel, 2010).

Some recent work attempts to address the fundamental word ordering task directly, using syntactic models and heuristic search. Wan et al. (2009) use a dependency grammar to address word ordering, while Zhang and Clark (2011; 2012) use CCG and large-scale n-gram language models. These techniques are applied to the unconstrained problem of generating a sentence from a multi-set of input words.

We describe GYRO (**G**et **Y**our **O**rder **R**ight), a phrase-based approach to word ordering. Given a bag of words, the system first scans a large, trusted text collection and extracts phrases consisting of words from the bag. Strings are then generated by concatenating these phrases in any order, subject to the constraint that every string is a valid reordering of the words in the bag, and the results are scored under an n-gram language model (LM). The motivation is that it is easier to make fluent sentences from phrases (snippets of fluent text) than from words in isolation.

GYRO builds on approaches developed for syntactic SMT (Chiang, 2007; de Gispert et al., 2010; Iglesias et al., 2011). The system generates strings in the form of weighted automata which can be rescored using higher-order n-gram LMs, dependency LMs (Shen et al., 2010), and Minimum Bayes Risk decoding, either using posterior probabilities obtained from GYRO or SMT systems.

We report extensive experiments using BLEU and conclude with human assessments. We show that despite its relatively simple formulation, GYRO gives BLEU scores over 20 points higher than the best previously reported results, generated by a syntax-based ordering system. Human fluency assessments confirm these substantial improvements.

2 Phrase-based Word Ordering

We take as input a bag of N words $\Omega = \{w_1, \ldots, w_N\}$. The words are sorted, e.g. alphabetically, so that it is possible to refer to the ith word in the bag, and repeated words are distinct tokens. We also take a set of phrases, $\mathcal{L}(\Omega)$ that are extracted from large text collections, and contain only words from Ω. We refer to phrases as u, i.e. $u \in \mathcal{L}(\Omega)$. The goal is to generate all permutations of Ω that can be formed by concatenation of phrases from $\mathcal{L}(\Omega)$.

2.1 Word Order Generation Grammar

Consider a subset $A \subset \Omega$. We can represent A by an N-bit binary string $I(A) = I_1(A) \ldots I_N(A)$, where $I_i(A) = 1$ if $w_i \in A$, and $I_i(A) = 0$ otherwise. A Context-Free Grammar (CFG) for generation can then be defined by the following rules:
Phrase-based Rules: $\forall A \subset \Omega$ and $\forall u \in \mathcal{L}(A)$

$$I(A) \rightarrow u$$

Concatenation Rules: $\forall A \subset \Omega, B \subset A, C \subset A$ such that $I(A) = I(B) + I(C)$ and $I(B) \bullet I(C) = 0$

$$I(A) \rightarrow I(B)\, I(C)$$

where $\bullet$ is the bit-wise logical AND
Root: $S \rightarrow I(\Omega)$
We use this grammar to 'parse' the list of the words in the bag Ω. The grammar has one nonterminal per possible binary string, so potentially 2^N distinct nonterminals might be needed to generate the language. Each nonterminal can produce either a phrase $u \in \mathcal{L}(A)$, or the concatenation of two binary strings that share no bits in common. A derivation is sequence of rules that starts from the bit string $I(\Omega)$. Rules are unweighted in this basic formulation.

For example, assume the following bag $\Omega = \{a, b, c, d, e\}$, which we sort alphabetically. Assume the phrases are $\mathcal{L}(\Omega) = \{$"$a\,b$", "$b\,a$", "$d\,e\,c$"$\}$. The generation grammar contains the following 6 rules:

R^1: 11000$\rightarrow$ ab
R^2: 11000$\rightarrow$ ba
R^3: 00111$\rightarrow$ dec
R^4: 11111$\rightarrow$ 11000 00111
R^5: 11111$\rightarrow$ 00111 11000
R^6: $S\rightarrow$ 11111

Figure 1 represents all the possible derivations in a hypergraph, which generate four alternative strings. For example, string "$d\,e\,c\,b\,a$" is obtained with derivation R^{6}R^{5}R^{3}R^2, whereas string "$a\,b\,d\,e\,c$" is obtained via R^{6}R^{4}R^{1}R^3.

2.2 Parsing a Bag of Words

We now describe a general algorithm for parsing a bag of words with phrase constraints. The search

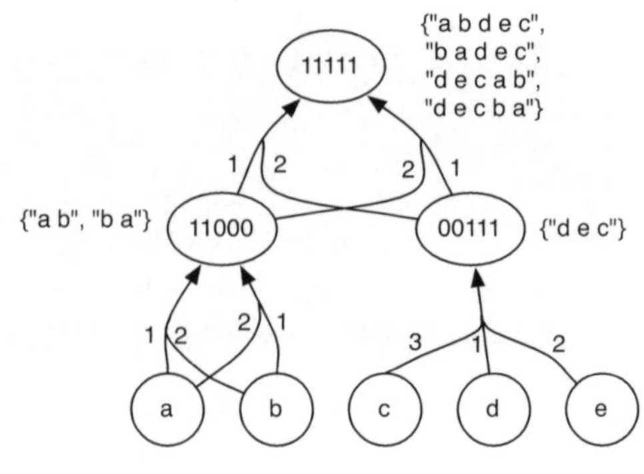

Figure 1: Hypergraph representing generation from $\{a, b, c, d, e\}$ with phrases $\{$"$a\,b$", "$b\,a$", "$d\,e\,c$"$\}$.

is organized along a two-dimensional grid $M[x, y]$ of 2^N–1 cells, where each cell is associated with a unique nonterminal in the grammar (a bit string I with at least one bit set to 1). Each row x in the grid has $\binom{N}{x}$ cells, representing all the possible ways of covering exactly x words from the bag. There are N rows in total.

For a bit string I, $X(I)$ is the length of I, i.e. the number of 1's in I. In this way $X(I(A))$ points to the row associated with set A. There is no natural ordering of cells within a row, so we introduce a second function $Y(I)$ which indicates which cell in row $X(I)$ is associated with I. Hence $M[X(I), Y(I)]$ is the cell associated with bit string I. In the inverse direction, we using the notation $I_{x,y}$ to indicate a bit string associated with the cell $M[x, y]$.

The basic parsing algorithm is given in Figure 2. We first initialize the grid by filling the cells linked to phrase-based rules (lines 1-4 of Figure 2). Then parsing proceeds as follows. For each row in increasing order (line 5), and for each of the nonempty cells in the row (line 6), try to combine its bit string with any other bit strings (lines 7-8). If combination is admitted, then form the resultant bit string and add the concatenation rule to the associated cell in the grid (lines 9-10). The combination will always yield a bit string that resides in a higher row of the grid, so search is exhaustive. If a rule is found in cell $M[N, 1]$, there is a parse (line 11); otherwise none exists. The complexity of the algorithm is $O(2^N \cdot K)$. If back-pointers are kept, traversing these from cell $M[N, 1]$ yields all the generated word sequences.

The number of cells will grow exponentially as the bag grows in size. In practice, the number of

PARSE-BAG-OF-WORDS

Input: bag of words Ω of size N
Input: list of phrases $\mathcal{L}(\Omega)$
Initialize - Add phrase-based rules:
1 $M[x, y] \leftarrow \emptyset$
2 **for each** subset $A \in \Omega$
3   **for each** phrase $u \in \mathcal{L}(A)$
4   **add** rule $I(A) \rightarrow u$ to cell $M[X(I(A)), Y(I(A))]$
Parse:
5 **for each** row $x = 1, \ldots, N$
6   **for each** $y = 1, \ldots, \binom{N}{x}$
7   **for each** valid $A \in \Omega$
8   **if** $I_{x,y} \bullet I(A) = 0$, **then**
9         $I' \leftarrow I_{x,y} + I(A)$
10   **add** rule $I' \rightarrow I_{x,y}\, I(A)$ to cell $M[X(I'), Y(I')]$
11 **if** $|M[N, 1]| > 0$, **success**.

Figure 2: Parsing algorithm for a bag of words.

cells actually used in parsing can be smaller than $2^N - 1$. This depends strongly on the number of distinct phrase-based rules and the distinct subsets of Ω they cover. For example, if we consider 1-word subsets of Ω, then all cells are needed and GYRO attempts all word permutation. However, if only 10 distinct 5-word phrases and 20 distinct 4-word phrases are considered for a bag of N=9 words, then fewer than 431 cells will be used (20 + 10 for the initial cells at rows 4 and 5; plus all combinations of 4-word subsets into row 8, which is less than 400; plus 1 for the last cell at row 9).

2.3 Generation from Exact Parsing

We are interested in producing the space of word sequences generated by the grammar, and in scoring each of the sequences according to a word-based n-gram LM. Assuming that parsing the bag of words suceeded, this is a very similar scenario to that of syntax-based approaches to SMT: the output is a large collection of word sequences, which are built by putting together smaller units and which can be found by a process of *expansion*, i.e. by traversing the back-pointers from an initial cell in a grid structure. A significant difference is that in syntax-based approaches the parsing stage tends to be computationally easier than the parsing stage has only a quadratic dependency on the length of the input sentence.

We borrow techniques from SMT to represent and manipulate the space of generation hypotheses. Here we follow the approach of expanding this space onto a Finite-State Automata (FSA) described in (de Gispert et al., 2010; Iglesias et al., 2011). This means that in parsing, each cell $M[x, y]$ is associated with an FSA $F_{x,y}$, which encodes all the sequences generated by the grammar

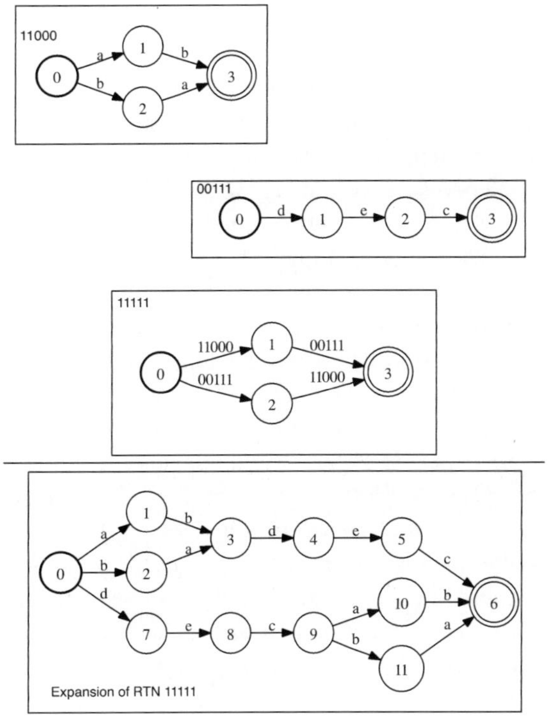

Figure 3: RTN representing generation from $\{a, b, c, d, e\}$ with phrases $\{\text{“}a\,b\text{”}, \text{“}b\,a\text{”}, \text{“}d\,e\,c\text{”}\}$ (top) and its expansion as an FSA (bottom).

when covering the words marked by the bit string of that cell. When a rule is added to a cell, a new path from the initial to the final state of $F_{x,y}$ is created so that each FSA is the union of all paths arising from the rules added to the cell. Importantly, when an instance of the concatenation rule is added to a cell, the new path is built with only two arcs. These point to other FSAs at lower rows in the grid so that the result has the form of a Recursive Transition Network with a finite depth of recursion. Following the example from Section 2.1, the top three FSAs in Figure 3 represent the RTN for example from Figure 1.

The parsing algorithm is modified as follows:

4 **add** rule $I(A) \rightarrow u$
  as path to FSA $F_{X(I(A)),Y(I(A))}$
...
10 **add** rule $I' \rightarrow I_{x,y}\, I(A)$
  as path to FSA $F_{X(I'),Y(I')}$
11 **if** NumStates$(F_{N,1}) > 1$, **success**.

At this point we specify two strategies:

Algorithm 1: Full expansion is described by the pseudocode in Figure 4, excluding lines 2-3. A recursive FSA replacement operation (Allauzen et al., 2007) can be used to expand the FSA in the top-most cell. In our running example, the result is the FSA at the bottom of Figure 3. We then apply a word-based LM to the resulting FSA via standard FSA composition. This outputs the complete (unpruned) language of interest, where each word sequence generated from the bag according to the phrasal constraints is scored by the LM.

Algorithm 2: Pruned expansion is described by the pseudocode in Figure 4, now including lines 2-3. We introduce pruning because full, unpruned expansion may not be feasible for large bags with many phrasal rules. Once parsing is done, we introduce the following bottom-up pruning strategy. For each row starting at row r, we union all FSAs of the row and expand the unioned FSA through the recursive replacement operation. This yields the space of all generation hypotheses of length r. We then apply the language model to this lattice and reduce it under likelihood-based pruning at weight β. We then update each cell in the row with a new FSA obtained as the intersection of its original FSA and the pruned FSA.[1] This intersection may yield an empty FSA for a particular cell (meaning that all its hypotheses were pruned out of the row), but it will always leave at least one surviving FSA per row, guaranteeing that if parsing succeeds, the top-most cell will expand into a non-empty FSA. As we process higher rows, the replacement operation will yield smaller FSAs because some back-pointers will point to empty FSAs. In this way memory usage can be controlled through parameters r and β. Of course, when pruning in this way, the final output lattice L will not contain the complete space of hypotheses that could be generated by the grammar.

2.4 Algorithm 3: Pruned Parsing and Generation

The two generation algorithms presented above rely on a completed initial parsing step. However, given that the complexity of the parsing stage is $O(2^N \cdot K)$, this may not be achievable in practice. Leaving aside time considerations, the memory required to store 2^N FSAs will grow exponentially in N, even if the FSAs contain only pointers to other FSAs. Therefore we also describe an algorithm to perform bottom-up pruning guided by the LM during parsing. The pseudocode is identical to that of Algorithm 1 except for the following changes: in parsing (Figure 2) we pass G as input and we call the row pruning function of Figure 4 after line 5 if $x \geq r$.

[1]This step can be performed much more efficiently with a single forward pass of the resultant lattice. This is possible because the replace operation can yield a transducer where the input symbols encode a pointer to the original FSA, so in traversing the arcs of the pruned lattice, we know which arcs will belong to which cell FSAs. However, for ease of explanation we avoid this detail.

```
FULL-PARSE-EXPANSION
    Input: bag of words Ω of size N
    Input: list phrases L(Ω)
    Input: word-based LM G
    Output: word lattice L of generated sequences
    Generate:
1   PARSE-BAG-OF-WORDS(Ω)
2   for each row x = r, ..., N − 1
3     PRUNE-ROW(x)
4   F ← FSA-REPLACE(F_{N,1})
5   return L ← F ∘ G

6   function PRUNE-ROW(x) :
7           F ← ∪_y F_{x,y}
8           F ← FSA-REPLACE(F)
9           F ← F ∘ G
10          F ← FSA-PRUNE(F, β)
11          for each cell y = 1, ..., (N choose x)
12            F_{x,y} ← F_{x,y} · F
13  return
```

Figure 4: Pseudocode for Algorithm 1 (excluding lines 2-3) and Algorithm 2 (including all lines).

We note that there is a strong connection between GYRO and the IDL approach of Soricut and Marcu (2005; 2006). Our bag of words parser could be cast in the IDL-formalism, and the FSA 'Replace' operation would be expressed by an IDL 'Unfold' operation. However, whereas their work applies pruning in the creation of the IDL-expression prior to LM application, GYRO uses unweighted phrase constraints so the LM must be considered for pruning while parsing.

3 Experimental Results

We now report various experiments evaluating the performance of the generation approach described above. The system is evaluated using the MT08-nw, and MT09-nw testsets. These correspond to the first English reference of the newswire portion of the Arabic-to-English NIST MT evaluation sets[2]. They contain 813 and 586 sentences respectively (53,325 tokens in total; average sentence length = 38.1 tokens after tokenization). In order to reduce the computational complexity, all sentences with more than 20 tokens were divided into sub-sentences, with 20 tokens being the upper limit. Between 70-80% of the sentences in the

[2]http://www.itl.nist.gov/iad/mig/tests/mt

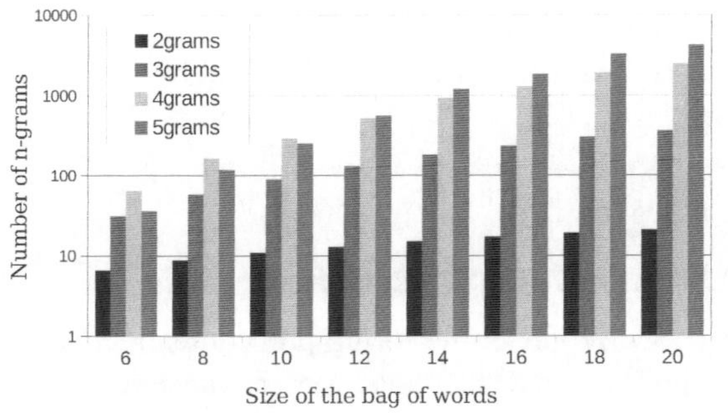

Figure 5: Average number of extracted phrases as a function of the bag of word size.

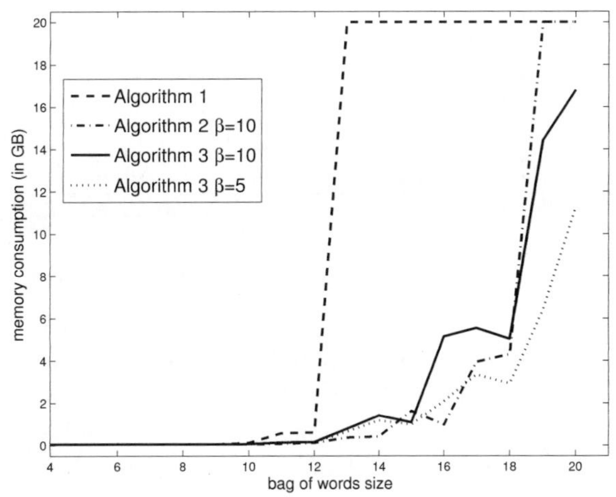

Figure 6: Worst-case memory required (GB) by each GYRO algorithm relative to the size of the bags.

testsets were divided in this way. For each of these sentences we create a bag.

The GYRO system uses a n-gram LM estimated over 1.3 billion words of English text, including the AFP and Xinhua portions of the GigaWord corpus version 4 (1.1 billion words) and the English side of various Arabic-English parallel corpora typically used in MT evaluations (0.2 billion words).

Phrases of up to length 5 are extracted for each bag from a text collection containing 10.6 billion words of English news text. We use efficient Hadoop-based look-up techniques to carry out this extraction step and to retrieve rules for generation (Pino et al., 2012). The average number of phrases extracted as a function of the size of the bag is shown in Figure 5. These are the phrase-based rules of our generation grammar.

3.1 Computational Analysis

We analyze here the computational requirements of the three alternative GYRO algorithms presented in Sections 2.3 and 2.4. We carry out this analysis on a subset of 200 random subsentences from MT08-nw and MT09-nw chosen to have the same sentence length distribution as the whole data set. For a fixed generation grammar comprised of 3-gram, 4-gram and 5-gram rules only, we run each algorithm with a memory limitation of 20GB. If the process reaches this limit, then it is killed. Figure 6 reports the worst-case memory memory required by each algorithm as a function of the size of the bag.

As shown, Full Expansion (Algorithm 1) is only feasible for bags that contain at most 12 words. By contrast, Pruned Expansion (Algorithm 2) with $\beta = 10$ is feasible for bags of up to 18 words. For bigger bags, the requirements of unpruned parsing make generation intractable under the memory limit. Finally, Pruned Parsing and Generation (Algorithm 3) is feasible at all bag sizes (up to 20 words), and its memory requirements can be controlled via the beam-width pruning parameter β. Harsher pruning (i.e. lower β) will incur more coverage problems, so it is desirable to use the highest feasible value of β.

We emphasise that Algorithm 3, with suitable pruning strategies, can scale up to larger problems quite readily and generate output from much larger input sets than reported here. We focus here on generation quality for moderate sized problems.

3.2 Generation Performance

We now compare the GYRO system with the Combinatory Categorial Grammar (CCG)-based system described in (Zhang et al., 2012). By means of extracted CCG rules, the CCG system searches for an optimal parse guided by large-margin training. Each partial hypothesis (or 'edge') is scored using the syntax model and a 4-gram LM trained similarly on one billion words of English Gigaword data. Both systems are evaluated using BLEU (Papineni et al., 2002; Espinosa et al., 2010).

For GYRO, we use the pruned parsing algorithm of Section 2.4 with $r = 6$ and $\beta = 10$ and a memory usage limit of 20G. The phrase-based rules of the grammar contain only 3-grams,

LM	System	MT08-nw	MT09-nw
4g	CCG	48.0	48.8
3g	GYRO	59.0	58.4
	GYRO +3g	63.0	64.1
4g	GYRO +4g	65.5	65.9
	100-best oracle	76.1	76.1
	lattice oracle	80.4	80.2

Table 1: CCG and GYRO BLEU scores.

4-grams and 5-grams.[3] Under these conditions, GYRO finds an output for 91.4% of the bags. For the remainder, we obtain an output either by pruning less or by adding bigram rules (in 7.2% of the bags), or simply by adding all words as unigram rules (1.4% of the bags).

Table 1 gives the results obtained by CCG and GYRO under a 3-gram or a 4-gram LM. Because GYRO outputs word lattices as opposed to a 1-best hypothesis, we can reapply the same LM to the concatenated lattices of any sentences longer than 20 to take into account context in subsentence boundaries. This is the result in the third row in the Table, labeled 'GYRO +3g'. We can see that GYRO benefits significantly from this rescoring, beating the CCG system across both sets. This is possibly explained by the CCG system's dependence upon in-domain data that have been explicitly marked-up using the CCG formalism. The final row reports the positive impact of increasing the LM order to 4.

Impact of generation grammar. To measure the benefits of using high-order n-grams as constraints for generation, we also ran GYRO with unigram rules only. This effectively does permutation under the LM with the pruning mechanisms described. The BLEU scores are 54.0 and 54.5 for MT08-nw and MT09 respectively. This indicates that a strong GYRO grammar is very much needed for this type of parsing and generation.

Quality of generated lattices. We assess the quality of the lattices output by GYRO under the 4-gram LM by computing the oracle BLEU score of either the 100-best lists or the whole lattices[4] in the last two rows of Table 1. In order to compute the latter, we use the linear approximation to BLEU that allows an efficient FST-based implementation of an Oracle search (Sokolov et al., 2012). We draw two conclusions from these results: (a) that there is a significant potential for improvement from rescoring, in that even for small 100-best lists the improvement found by the Oracle can exceed 10 BLEU points; and (b) that the output lattices are not perfect in that the Oracle score is not 100.

[3]Any word in the bag that does not occur in the large collection of English material is added as a 1-gram rule.

[4]Obtained by pruning at $\beta = 10$ in generation.

3.2.1 Rescoring GYRO output

We now report on rescoring procedures intended to improve the first-pass lattices generated by GYRO.

Higher-order language models. The first row in Table 2 reports the result obtained when applying a 5-gram LM to the GYRO lattices generated under a 4-gram. The 5-gram is estimated over the complete 10.6 billion word collection using the uniform backoff strategy of (Brants et al., 2007). We find improvements of 3.0 and 1.9 BLEU with respect to the 4-gram baseline.

Dependency language models. We now investigate the benefits of applying a dependency LM (Shen et al., 2010) in a rescoring mode. We run the MALT dependency parser[5] on the generation hypotheses and rescore them according to $log(p_{LM}) + \lambda_d log(p_{depLM})$, i.e. a weighted combination of the word-based LM and the dependency LM scores. Since it is not possible to run the parser on the entire lattice, we carry out this experiment using the 100-best lists generated from the previous experiment ('+5g'). The dependency LM is a 3-gram estimated on the entire GigaWord version 5 collection ($\sim$5 billion words). Results are shown in rows 2 and 3 in Table 2, where in each row the performance over the set used to tune the parameter λ_d is marked with $\star$. In either case, we observe modest but consistent gains across both sets. We find this very promising considering that the parser has been applied to noisy input sentences.

Minimum Bayes Risk Decoding. We also use Lattice-based Minimum Bayes Risk (LMBR) decoding (Tromble et al., 2008; Blackwood et al., 2010a). Here, the posteriors over n-grams are computed over the output lattices generated by the GYRO system. The result is shown in row labeled '+5g +LMBR', where again we find modest but consistent gains across the two sets with respect to the 5-gram rescored lattices.

LMBR with MT posteriors. We investigate LMBR decoding when applying to the generation lattice a linear combination of the n-gram pos-

[5]Available at www.maltparser.org

4g GYRO rescoring:	MT08-nw	MT09-nw
+5g	68.5	67.8
+5g +depLM $\lambda_d = 0.4$	68.7 *	68.1
+5g +depLM $\lambda_d = 0.33$	68.7	68.2 *
+5g +LMBR	68.6	68.3
+5g +LMBR-mt $\alpha = 0.25$	70.8 *	72.2
+5g +LMBR-mt $\alpha = 0.25$	70.8	72.2 *

Table 2: Results in BLEU when rescoring the lattices generated by GYRO using various strategies. Tuning conditions are marked by *.

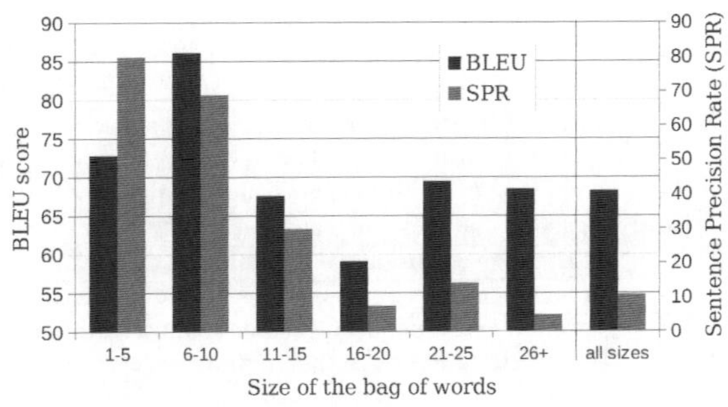

Figure 8: GYRO BLEU score and Sentence Precision Rate as a function of the bag of words size. Computed on the concatenation of MT08-nw and MT09-nw.

terior probabilities extracted from (a) the same generation lattice, and (b) from lattices produced by an Arabic-to-English hierarchical-phrase based MT system developed for the NIST 2012 OpenMT Evaluation. As noted, LMBR relies on a posterior distribution over n-grams as part of its computation or risk. Here, we use LMBR with a posterior of the form $\alpha\, p_{\text{GYRO}} + (1{-}\alpha)\, p_{\text{MT}}$. This is effectively performing a system combination between the GYRO generation system and the MT system (de Gispert et al., 2009; DeNero et al., 2010) but restricting the hypothesis space to be that of the GYRO lattice (Blackwood et al., 2010b). Results are reported in the last two rows of Table 2. Relative to 5-gram LM rescoring alone, we see gains in BLEU of 2.3 and 4.4 in MT08-nw and MT09-nw, suggesting that posterior distributions over n-grams provided by SMT systems can give good guidance in generation. These results also suggest that if we knew what words to use, we could generate very good quality translation output.

3.3 Analysis and examples

Figure 7 gives GYRO generation examples. These are often fairly fluent, and it is striking how the output can be improved with guidance from the SMT system. The examples also show the harshness of BLEU, e.g. 'german and turkish officials' is penalised with respect to ' turkish and german officials.' Metrics based on richer meaning representations, such as HyTER, could be valuable here (Dreyer and Marcu, 2012).

Figure 8 shows BLEU and Sentence Precision Rate (SPR), the percentage of exactly reconstructed sentences. As expected, performance is sensitive to length. For bags of up to 10, GYRO reconstructs the reference perfectly in over 65% of the cases. This is a harsh performance metric, and performance falls to less than 10% for bags of size 16-20. For bags of 6-10 words, we find BLEU scores of greater than 85. Performance is not as good for shorter segments, since these are often headlines and bylines that can be ambiguous in their ordering. The BLEU scores for bags of size 21 and higher are an artefact of our sentence splitting procedure. However, even for bag sizes of 16-to-20 GYRO has BLEU scores above 55.

3.4 Human Assessments

Finally, the CCG and 4g-GYRO+5g systems were compared using crowd-sourced fluency judgements gathered on CrowdFlower. Judges were asked 'Please read the reference sentence and compare the fluency of items 1 & 2.' The test was a selection of 75 fluent sentences of 20 words or less taken from the MT dev sets. Each comparison was made by at least 3 judges. With an average selection confidence of 0.754, GYRO was preferred in 45 cases, CCG was preferred in 14 cases, and systems were tied 16 times. This is consistent with the significant difference in BLEU between these systems.

4 Related Work and Conclusion

Our work is related to surface realisation within natural language generation (NLG). NLG typically assumes a relatively rich input representation intended to provide syntactic, semantic, and other relationships to guide generation. Example input representations are Abstract Meaning Representations (Langkilde and Knight, 1998), attribute-value pairs (Ratnaparkhi, 2000), lexical predicate-argument structures (Bangalore and Rambow, 2000), Interleave-Disjunction-Lock (IDL) expressions (Nederhof and Satta, 2004; Soricut and Marcu, 2005; Soricut and Marcu, 2006), CCG-bank derived grammars (White et al., 2007),

	Hypothesis	SBLEU
REF	a third republican senator joins the list of critics of bush 's policy in iraq .	
(a)	critics of bush 's iraq policy in a third of republican senator joins the list .	47.2
(b)	critics of bush 's policy in iraq joins the list of a third republican senator .	69.8
(c)	critics of bush 's iraq policy in a list of republican senator joins the third .	39.1
(d)	the list of critics of bush 's policy in iraq a third republican senator joins .	82.9
REF	it added that these messages were sent to president bashar al-asad through turkish and german officials .	
(a-c)	it added that president bashar al-asad through these messages were sent to german and turkish officials .	61.5
(d)	it added that these messages were sent to president bashar al-asad through german and turkish officials .	80.8
REF	a prominent republican senator has joined the ranks of critics of george bush 's policy in iraq , calling for a new strategy just days before a new confrontation in congress	
(a)	a prominent republican senator george has joined the ranks of critics of bush 's policy in iraq , just days before a new strategy in congress calling for a new confrontation	66.7
(b)	a prominent republican senator has joined the ranks of critics of george bush 's policy in iraq , just days before congress calling for a new strategy in a new confrontation	77.8
(c)	a prominent republican senator has joined the ranks of critics of george bush 's policy in iraq , just days before a new strategy in congress calling for a new confrontation	82.3
(d)	a prominent republican senator has joined the ranks of critics of george bush 's policy in iraq , calling for a new strategy just days before a new confrontation in congress	100

Figure 7: 4g GYRO (Table 2) output examples, with sentence level BLEU: (a) GYRO+4g; (b) GYRO+5g; (c) GYRO+5g+LMBR; (d) GYRO+5g+LMBR-mt. (a-c) indicates systems with identical hypotheses.

meaning representation languages (Wong and Mooney, 2007) and unordered syntactic dependency trees (Guo et al., 2011; Bohnet et al., 2011; Belz et al., 2011; Belz et al., 2012)[6].

These input representations are suitable for applications such as dialog systems, where the system maintains the information needed to generate the input representation for NLG (Lemon, 2011), or summarisation, where representations can be automatically extracted from coherent, well-formed text (Barzilay and Elhadad, 2011; Althaus et al., 2004). However, there are other applications, such as automatic speech recognition and SMT that could possibly benefit from NLG, but which do not generate reliable linguistic annotation in their output. For these problems it would be useful to have systems, as described in this paper, which do not require rich input representations. We plan to investigate these applications in future work.

There is much opportunity for future development. To improve coverage, the grammars of Section 2.1 could perform generation with overlapping, rather than concatenated, n-grams; and features could be included to define tuneable log-linear rule probabilities (Och and Ney, 2002; Chiang, 2007). The GYRO grammar could be extended using techniques from string-to-tree SMT, in particular by modifying the grammar so that output derivations respect dependencies (Shen et al., 2010); this will make it easier to integrate dependency LMs into GYRO. Finally, it would be interesting to couple the GYRO architecture with automata-based models of poetry and rhythmic text (Greene et al., 2010).

[6]Surface Realisation Task, Generation Challenges 2011, www.nltg.brighton.ac.uk/research/genchal11

Acknowledgement

The research leading to these results has received funding from the European Union Seventh Framework Programme (FP7-ICT-2009-4) under grant agreement number 247762, the FAUST project faust-fp7.eu/faust/, and the EPSRC (UK) Programme Grant EP/I031022/1 (Natural Speech Technology) natural-speech-technology.org.

References

Cyril Allauzen, Michael Riley, Johan Schalkwyk, Wojciech Skut, and Mehryar Mohri. 2007. OpenFst: A general and efficient weighted finite-state transducer library. In *Proceedings of CIAA*, pages 11–23, Prague, Czech Republic.

Ernst Althaus, Nikiforos Karamanis, and Alexander Koller. 2004. Computing locally coherent discourses. In *Proceedings of the 42nd Annual Meeting on Association for Computational Linguistics*, page 399. Association for Computational Linguistics.

Srinivas Bangalore and Owen Rambow. 2000. Exploiting a probabilistic hierarchical model for generation. In *Proceedings of the 18th conference on Computational linguistics - Volume 1*, COLING '00, pages 42–48, Stroudsburg, PA, USA. Association for Computational Linguistics.

Regina Barzilay and Noemie Elhadad. 2011. Inferring strategies for sentence ordering in multi-document news summarization. *arXiv preprint arXiv:1106.1820*.

Anja Belz, Mike White, Dominic Espinosa, Eric Kow, Deirdre Hogan, and Amanda Stent. 2011. The first surface realisation shared task: Overview and evaluation results. In *Proceedings of the Generation Challenges Session at the 13th European Workshop on Natural Language Generation*, pages 217–226, Nancy, France.

Anja Belz, Bernd Bohnet, Simon Mille, Leo Wanner, and Michael White. 2012. The surface realisation task: Recent developments and future plans. In *Proceedings of the 7th International Natural Language Generation Conference*, pages 136–140, Utica, IL, USA.

Graeme Blackwood, Adrià de Gispert, and William Byrne. 2010a. Efficient path counting transducers for minimum Bayes-risk decoding of statistical machine translation lattices. In *Proceedings of ACL: Short Papers*, pages 27–32, Uppsala, Sweden.

Graeme Blackwood, Adrià de Gispert, and William Byrne. 2010b. Fluency constraints for minimum Bayes-risk decoding of statistical machine translation lattices. In *Proceedings of COLING*, pages 71–79, Beijing, China.

Bernd Bohnet, Simon Mille, Benoît Favre, and Leo Wanner. 2011. <StuMaBa>: From deep representation to surface. In *Proceedings of the Generation Challenges Session at the 13th European Workshop on Natural Language Generation*, pages 232–235, Nancy, France.

Thorsten Brants, Ashok C. Popat, Peng Xu, Franz J. Och, and Jeffrey Dean. 2007. Large language models in machine translation. In *Proceedings of EMNLP-CoNLL*, pages 858–867, Prague, Czech Republic.

David Chiang. 2007. Hierarchical phrase-based translation. *Computational Linguistics*, 33(2):201–228.

Adrià de Gispert, Sami Virpioja, Mikko Kurimo, and William Byrne. 2009. Minimum Bayes risk combination of translation hypotheses from alternative morphological decompositions. In *Proceedings of HLT-NAACL: Short Papers*, pages 73–76, Boulder, CO, USA.

Adrià de Gispert, Gonzalo Iglesias, Graeme Blackwood, Eduardo R. Banga, and William Byrne. 2010. Hierarchical phrase-based translation with weighted finite-state transducers and shallow-n grammars. *Computational Linguistics*, 36(3):505–533.

John DeNero, Shankar Kumar, Ciprian Chelba, and Franz Och. 2010. Model combination for machine translation. In *Proceedings of HTL-NAACL*, pages 975–983, Los Angeles, CA, USA.

Markus Dreyer and Daniel Marcu. 2012. Hyter: Meaning-equivalent semantics for translation evaluation. In *Proceedings of NAACL-HLT*, pages 162–171, Montréal, Canada.

Dominic Espinosa, Rajakrishnan Rajkumar, Michael White, and Shoshana Berleant. 2010. Further meta-evaluation of broad-coverage surface realization. In *Proceedings of EMNLP*, pages 564–574, Cambridge, MA, USA.

Dmitriy Genzel. 2010. Automatically learning source-side reordering rules for large scale machine translation. In *Proceedings of COLING*, pages 376–384, Beijing, China.

Erica Greene, Tugba Bodrumlu, and Kevin Knight. 2010. Automatic analysis of rhythmic poetry with applications to generation and translation. In *Proceedings of EMNLP*, pages 524–533, Cambridge, MA, USA.

Yuqing Guo, Josef Van Genabith, and Haifeng Wang. 2011. Dependency-based n-gram models for general purpose sentence realisation. *Natural Language Engineering*, 17(04):455–483.

Gonzalo Iglesias, Cyril Allauzen, William Byrne, Adrià de Gispert, and Michael Riley. 2011. Hierarchical phrase-based translation representations. In *Proceedings of EMNLP*, pages 1373–1383, Edinburgh, Scotland, UK.

Kevin Knight. 1999. Decoding complexity in word-replacement translation models. *Computational Linguistics*, 25(4):607–615.

Irene Langkilde and Kevin Knight. 1998. Generation that exploits corpus-based statistical knowledge. In *Proceedings of ACL/COLING*, pages 704–710, Montreal, Quebec, Canada.

Oliver Lemon. 2011. Learning what to say and how to say it: Joint optimisation of spoken dialogue management and natural language generation. *Computer Speech & Language*, 25(2):210–221.

Mark-Jan Nederhof and Giorgio Satta. 2004. IDL-expressions: A formalism for representing and parsing finite languages in natural language processing. *Journal of Artificial Intelligence Research*, 21:287–317.

Franz Josef Och and Hermann Ney. 2002. Discriminative training and maximum entropy models for statistical machine translation. In *Proceedings of ACL*, pages 295–302, Philadelphia, PA, USA.

Kishore Papineni, Salim Roukos, Todd Ward, and Wei-Jing Zhu. 2002. BLEU: a method for automatic evaluation of machine translation. In *Proceedings of ACL*, pages 311–318, Philadelphia, PA, USA.

Juan Pino, Aurelien Waite, and William Byrne. 2012. Simple and efficient model filtering in statistical machine translation. *The Prague Bulletin of Mathematical Linguistics*, 98:5–24.

Adwait Ratnaparkhi. 2000. Trainable methods for surface natural language generation. In *Proceedings of NAACL*, pages 194–201, Seattle, WA, USA.

Libin Shen, Jinxi Xu, and Ralph Weischedel. 2010. String-to-dependency statistical machine translation. *Computational Linguistics*, 36(4):649–671.

Artem Sokolov, Guillaume Wisniewski, and Francois Yvon. 2012. Computing lattice bleu oracle scores for machine translation. In *Proceedings of EACL*, pages 120–129, Avignon, France.

Radu Soricut and Daniel Marcu. 2005. Towards developing generation algorithms for text-to-text applications. In *Proceedings of ACL*, pages 66–74, Ann Arbor, MI, USA.

Radu Soricut and Daniel Marcu. 2006. Stochastic Language Generation Using WIDL-Expressions and its Application in Machine Translation and Summarization. In *Proceedings of ACL*, pages 1105–1112, Sydney, Australia.

Roy Tromble and Jason Eisner. 2009. Learning linear ordering problems for better translation. In *Proceedings of EMNLP*, pages 1007–1016, Singapore.

Roy Tromble, Shankar Kumar, Franz Och, and Wolfgang Macherey. 2008. Lattice Minimum Bayes-Risk decoding for statistical machine translation. In *Proceedings of EMNLP*, pages 620–629, Honolulu, Hawaii, USA.

Stephen Wan, Mark Dras, Robert Dale, and Cécile Paris. 2009. Improving grammaticality in statistical sentence generation: Introducing a dependency spanning tree algorithm with an argument satisfaction model. In *Proceedings of EACL*, pages 852–860, Athens, Greece.

Michael White, Rajakrishnan Rajkumar, and Scott Martin. 2007. Towards broad coverage surface realization with ccg. In *Proc. of the Workshop on Using Corpora for NLG: Language Generation and Machine Translation (UCNLG+ MT)*.

Yuk Wah Wong and Raymond J Mooney. 2007. Generation by inverting a semantic parser that uses statistical machine translation. *Proceedings of Human Language Technologies: The Conference of the North American Chapter of the Association for Computational Linguistics (NAACL-HLT-07)*, pages 172–179.

Yue Zhang and Stephen Clark. 2011. Syntax-based Grammaticality Improvement using CCG and Guided Search. In *Proceedings of EMNLP*, pages 1147–1157, Edinburgh, Scotland, U.K.

Yue Zhang, Graeme Blackwood, and Stephen Clark. 2012. Syntax-based word ordering incorporating a large-scale language model. In *Proceedings of EACL*, pages 736–746, Avignon, France.

Iterative Constrained Clustering for Subjectivity Word Sense Disambiguation

Cem Akkaya, Janyce Wiebe
University of Pittsburgh
Pittsburgh PA, 15260, USA
{cem,wiebe}@cs.pitt.edu

Rada Mihalcea
University of North Texas
Denton TX, 76207, USA
rada@cs.unt.edu

Abstract

Subjectivity word sense disambiguation (SWSD) is a supervised and application-specific word sense disambiguation task disambiguating between subjective and objective senses of a word. Not surprisingly, SWSD suffers from the knowledge acquisition bottleneck. In this work, we use a "cluster and label" strategy to generate labeled data for SWSD semi-automatically. We define a new algorithm called *Iterative Constrained Clustering (ICC)* to improve the clustering purity and, as a result, the quality of the generated data. Our experiments show that the SWSD classifiers trained on the ICC generated data by requiring only 59% of the labels can achieve the same performance as the classifiers trained on the full dataset.

1 Introduction

Subjectivity lexicons (e.g., (Turney, 2002; Whitelaw et al., 2005; Riloff and Wiebe, 2003; Yu and Hatzivassiloglou, 2003; Kim and Hovy, 2004; Bloom et al., 2007; Andreevskaia and Bergler, 2008; Agarwal et al., 2009)) play an important role in opinion, sentiment, and subjectivity analysis. These systems typically look for the presence of clues in text. Recently, in (Akkaya et al., 2009), we showed that subjectivity clues are fairly ambiguous as to whether they express subjectivity or not – words in such lexicons may have both subjective and objective usages. We call this problem subjectivity sense ambiguity. Consider the following sentence containing the clue "attack":

(1) He was **attacked** by Milosevic for attempting to carve out a new party from the Socialists.

Knowing that "attack" is a subjectivity clue with negative polarity will help a system recognize the negative sentiment in the sentence. But for (2), the same information is simply misleading, because the clue is used with an objective meaning.

(2) A new treatment based on training T-cells to **attack** cancerous cells ...

Any opinion analysis system which relies on a subjectivity lexicon will be misled by subjectivity clues used with objective senses (false hits). In (Akkaya et al., 2009), we introduced the task, *Subjectivity Word Sense Disambiguation*, which is to automatically determine which word instances in a corpus are being used with subjective senses, and which are being used with objective senses. SWSD can be considered as a coarse-grained and application-specific word sense disambiguation task. We showed that sense subjectivity information about clues can be fed to subjectivity and sentiment analysis resulting in substantial improvement for both subjectivity and sentiment analysis by avoiding false hits.

Although SWSD is a promising tool, it suffers from the knowledge acquisition bottleneck. SWSD is defined as a supervised task, and follows a targeted approach common in the WSD literature for performance reasons. This means, for each target clue, a different classifier is trained requiring separate training data for each target clue. It is expensive and time-consuming to obtain annotated datasets to train SWSD classifiers limiting scalability. As a countermeasure, in (Akkaya et al., 2011), we showed that non-expert annotations collected through Amazon Mechanical Turk (MTurk) can replace expert annotations successfully and might be used to apply SWSD on a large scale.

Although non-expert annotations are cheap and fast, they still incur some cost. In this work, we aim to reduce the human annotation effort needed to generate the same amount of subjectivity sense tagged data by using a "cluster and label" strategy. We hypothesize that we can obtain large sets of labeled data by labelling clusters of instances of a target word instead of single instances.

The main contribution of this work is a novel constrained clustering algorithm called *Iterative Constrained Clustering (ICC)* utilizing an active constraint selection strategy. A secondary contribution is a mixed word representation that is a combination of previously proposed context representations. We show that a "cluster and label" strategy relying on these two proposed components generates training data of good purity. The resulting data has sufficient purity to train reliable SWSD classifiers. SWSD classifiers trained on only 59% of the data achieve the same performance as classifiers trained on 100% of the data, resulting in a significant reduction in the annotation effort. Our results take SWSD another step closer to large scale application.

2 Cluster and Label

Our approach is inspired by a method lexicographers commonly employ to create sense inventories, where they create inventories based on evidence found in corpora. They use concordance information to mine frequent usage patterns. (Kilgarriff, 1997) describes this process in detail. A lexicographer collects usages of a word in corpora and groups them into coherent sets. The instances in a set should have more in common with each other than with the instances in other sets, according to the criteria the lexicographer considers. After generating the sets, the lexicographer codes each set as a dictionary definition based on the common attributes of the instances. Our goal is similar. Instead of generating dictionary definitions, we are only interested in generating coherent sets of usages of a word, so that we can label each induced set – with its instances – to obtain labeled data for SWSD. Our high-level grouping criterion is that the instances in a cluster should be similar subjective (objective) usages of the word.

Training data for an SWSD classifier consists of instances of the target word tagged as having a subjective sense (*S*) or an objective sense (*O*) (*subjectivity sense tagged data*). We train a different SWSD classifier for each target word as in (Akkaya et al., 2009). Thus, we need a different training dataset for each target word. Our ultimate goal is to reduce the human annotation effort required to create training data for SWSD classifiers. For this purpose, we utilize a *"cluster and label"* strategy relying on context clustering. Each instance of a word is represented as a feature vector (i.e., a context vector). The annotation process has the following steps: (1) cluster the context vectors of word instances, (2) label the induced clusters as *S* or *O*, (3) propagate the given label to all instances in a cluster.

The induced clusters represent different usage patterns of a word. Thus, we build more than two clusters, even though SWSD is a binary task. This implies that two different instances of a word can both be subjective, but end up in different clusters, if they are different usages of the word.

Since we are labelling clusters as a whole, we will introduce noise in the labeled data. Thus, in developing the clustering process, we need to minimize that noise and find as pure clusters as possible.

The first step is to define the context representation of the instances. This is addressed in Section 3. Then, we turn in Section 4.2 to the clustering process itself.

To evaluate our "cluster and label" strategy, we use two gold standard subjectivity sense tagged datasets. [1]. The first one is called senSWSD generated in (Akkaya et al., 2009) and the second one is called mturkSWSD generated in (Akkaya et al., 2011). They consist of subjectivity sense tagged data for disjoint sets of 39 and 90 words, respectively. In this paper, we opt to use the smaller dataset senSWSD as our development set, on which we evaluate various context representations (in Section 3) and our proposed constrained clustering algorithm (in Section 4.2). Then, on mturkSWSD, we evaluate the quality of semi-automatically generated data for SWSD classification (in Section 4.3.2).

3 Context Representations

There has been much work on context representations of words for various NLP tasks. Clustering word instances in order to discriminate senses of a word is called *Word Sense Discrimination*. Context representations for this task rely on two main types of models: distributional semantic models (DSM) and feature-based models.

[1]Available at `http://mpqa.cs.pitt.edu/corpora`

(Schutze, 1998), which is still a competitive model for word-sense discrimination by context clustering, relies on a distributional semantic model (DSM) (Turney and Pantel, 2010; Sahlgren, 2006; Bullinaria and Levy, 2007). A DSM is usually a word-to-word co-occurrence matrix – also called *semantic space* – such that each row represents the distribution of a target word in a large text corpus. Each row gives the semantic signature of a word, which is basically a high dimensional numeric vector. Note that this high dimensional vector represents word types, not word tokens. Thus, it cannot model a word instance in context. For token-based treatment, (Schutze, 1998) utilizes a second-order representation by averaging co-occurrence vectors of the words (corresponding to rows of the co-occurrence matrix) that occur in that particular context. It is important to note that (Schutze, 1998) uses an additive model for compositional representation. Recently, in (Akkaya et al., 2012), we found that a DSM built using multiplicative composition – proposed by (Mitchell and Lapata, 2010) for a different task – gives better performance than the model described by (Schutze, 1998).

We test both methods in this paper, using the same semantic space. The space is built from a corpus consisting of 120 million tokens. The rows of the space correspond to word forms and the columns correspond to word lemmas present in the corpus. We adopt the parameters for our semantic space from (Mitchell and Lapata, 2010): window size of 10 and dimension size of 2000 (i.e., the 2000 most frequent lemmas). We do not filter out stop words, since they have been shown to be useful for various semantic similarity tasks in (Bullinaria and Levy, 2007). We use positive point-wise mutual information to compute values of the vector components, which has also been shown to be favourable in (Bullinaria and Levy, 2007).

Purandere and Pedersen is the prominent representative of feature-based models. (Purandare and Pedersen, 2004) creates context vectors from local feature representations similar to the feature vectors found in supervised WSD. In this work, we use the following features from (Mihalcea, 2002) to build the local feature representation: (1) the target word itself and its part of speech, (2) surrounding context of 3 words and their part of speech, (3) the head of the noun phrase, (4) the first noun and verb before the target word, (5) the first noun and verb after the target word.

	skew	local	dsm_add	dsm_mul	mix_rep
average	79.90	80.50	80.50	83.53	**85.23**
appear-v	53.83	54.85	54.85	57.40	69.39
fine-a	70.07	72.26	70.07	74.45	75.18
interest-n	54.41	54.78	55.88	81.62	81.62
restraint-n	70.45	71.97	75.00	71.21	81.82

Table 1: Evaluation of Various Context Representations

3.1 Evaluation of Context Representations

In this section, we evaluate context representations for the context clustering task on the subjectivity sense tagged data, senSWSD. The evaluation is done separately for each word.

We use the same clustering algorithm for all context representations: agglomerative hierarchical clustering with average linkage criteria. In all our experiments throughout the paper, we fix the cluster size to 7 as it is done in (Purandare and Pedersen, 2004). We think that is reasonable number since SENSEVAL III reports that the average number of senses per word is 6.47. We choose *cluster purity* as our evaluation metric. To compute cluster purity, we assign each cluster to a sense label, which is the most frequent one in the cluster. The number of the correctly assigned instances divided by the number of all the clustered instances gives us cluster purity.

Row 1 of Table 1 holds the cumulative results over all the words in senSWSD (micro averages). The table also reports detailed results for 4 sample selected words from senSWSD. *skew* stands for the percentage of the most frequent label. *dsm_add* is the representation based on (Schutze, 1998), *dsm_mul* stands for the representation as described in (Akkaya et al., 2012) and *local_features* is the local feature representation based on (Purandare and Pedersen, 2004). The results show that among *dsm_mul*, *dsm_add*, and *local_features*; *dsm_mul* performs the best.

When we look at the context clustering results for single words separately, we observe that the performance of different representations vary. There is not a single winner among all words. Thus, perhaps choosing one single representation for all the words is not optimal. Having that in mind, we try merging the *dsm_mul* and *local_features* representations. We leave out *dsm_add* representation, since both *dsm_mul* and *dsm_add* rely on the same type of semantic information (i.e., a DSM). We hypothesize that the two representations, one relying on a semantic space and the other relying on local WSD features, may complement each other.

To merge the representations, we concatenate the two feature vectors into one. First, however, we normalize each vector to unit length, since the individual vectors have different scales and would have unequal contribution, otherwise. We call this mixed representation *mix_rep*.

In Table 1, we see that, overall, *mix_rep* performs better than all the other representations. The improvement is statistically significant at the $p < .05$ level on a paired t-test. We observe that, even when *mix_rep* does not perform the best, it is never bad. *mix_rep* is the winner or ties for the winner for 25 out of 39 words. This number is 13, 13, and 15 for *dsm_add*, *dsm_mul* and *local_features*, respectively. For the words for which *mix_rep* is not the winner, it is, on average, 1.47 points lower than the winner. This number is 4.22, 6.83, and 7.07 for the others. The results provide evidence that *mix_rep* is consistently good and reliable. Thus, in our experiments, *mix_rep* will be our choice as the context representation.

4 Clustering Process

We now turn to the clustering process. In a "cluster and label" strategy, in order to be able to label clusters, we need to annotate some of the instances in each cluster. Then, we can accept the majority label found in a cluster as its label. Thus, some manual labelling is required, preferably a small amount.

We propose to provide this small amount of annotated data prior to clustering, and then perform semi-supervised clustering. This way the provided labels will guide the clustering algorithm to generate the clusters that are more suitable for our end task, namely clusters where subjective and objective instances are grouped together.

4.1 Constrained Clustering

Constrained clustering (Grira et al., 2004) also known as *semi-supervised clustering* is a recent development in the clustering literature. In addition to the similarity information required by unsupervised clustering, constrained clustering requires pairwise constraints. There are two types of constraints: (1) must-link and (2) cannot-link constraints. A must-link constraint dictates that two instances should be in the same cluster and a cannot-link dictates that two instances should not be in the same cluster. In this work, we only consider cannot-links, because of the definition of our SWSD task. Two instances sharing the same label do not need to be in the same cluster, since the induced clusters represent different usage patterns of a word. For example, two instances labeled S need not be similar to each other. They can be different usages, both having a subjective meaning. On the other hand, if two instances are labeled having opposing labels, we do not want them to be in the same cluster. Thus, we utilize cannot-links but not must-links.

Constraints can be obtained from domain knowledge or from available instance labels. In our work, constraints are generated from instance labels. Each instance pair with opposing labels is considered to be cannot-linked.

There are two general strategies to incorporate constraints into clustering. The first is to adapt the similarity between instances (Xing et al., 2002; Klein et al., 2002) by adjusting the underlying distance metric. The main idea is to make the distance between must-linked instances – their neighbourhoods – smaller and the distance between cannot-linked instances – their neighbourhoods – larger. The second strategy is modifying the clustering algorithm itself so that search is biased towards a partitioning for which the constraints hold (Wagstaff and Cardie, 2000; Basu et al., 2002; Demiriz et al., 1999).

Our proposed constrained clustering method relies on some ideas from (Klein et al., 2002). Thus, we explain it in more detail. (Klein et al., 2002) utilizes agglomerative hierarchical clustering with complete-linkage. The algorithm imposes constraints by changing the distance matrix according to the given constraints. The distances between must-linked instances are set to 0. That is not enough by itself, since if two instances are must-linked, other instances close to them should also get closer to each other. This means there is a need to propagate the constraints. This is done by calculating the shortest path between all the instances and updating the distance matrix accordingly. To impose cannot-links, the distance between two cannot-linked instances is set to some large number. The complete-linkage property indirectly propagates the cannot-link constraints, since it will not allow two clusters to be merged if they contain instances that are cannot-linked.

Although previous work report on average substantial improvement in the clustering purity, (Davidson et al., 2006) shows that even if the constraints are generated from gold-standard data, some constraint sets can decrease clustering purity. The results vary significantly depending on the specific set of constraints used. To our knowledge, there have been two approaches for selecting informative constraint sets (Basu et al., 2004; Klein et al., 2002). The method described in (Basu et al., 2004) uses the farthest-first traversal scheme. That strategy is not suitable in our setting, since we have only two labels. After selecting just one instance from both labels, this method becomes the same as random selection. The strategy described in (Klein et al., 2002) is more general. At first, the hierarchical clustering algorithm follows in a unconstrained fashion until some moderate number of clusters are remaining. Then, the algorithm starts to request constraints between roots whenever two clusters are merged.

4.2 Iterative Constrained Clustering

Our proposed algorithm is closely related to (Klein et al., 2002). We share the same backbone: (1) the agglomerative hierarchical clustering with complete-linkage and (2) the mechanism to impose cannot-link constraints described in Section 4.1. For our algorithm, we implement a second mechanism for imposing constraints proposed by (Xing et al., 2002) (Section 4.2.1) and use both mechanisms in combination. We also propose a novel constraint selection method (Section 4.2.2).

4.2.1 Imposing Constraints

(Klein et al., 2002) imposes cannot-link constraints by adjusting the distance between cannot-linked pairs heuristically and by relying on complete linkage for propagation. Although this approach was shown to be effective, we believe it does not make full use of the provided constraints. We believe that learning a new distance metric will result in more reliable distance estimates between all instances. For this purpose, we learn a Mahalanobis distance function following the method described in (Davis et al., 2007). (Davis et al., 2007) formulate the problem of distance metric learning as minimizing the differential relative entropy between two multivariate Gaussians under constraints. Note that using distance metric learning for imposing constraints was previously proposed by (Xing et al., 2002). (Xing et al., 2002) pose metric learning as a convex optimization problem. The reason we choose the metric learning method (Davis et al., 2007) over (Xing et al., 2002) is that it is computationally more efficient.

(Klein et al., 2002) has a favourable property we want to keep. The constraints are imposed strictly, meaning that no cannot-linked instances can appear in the same cluster. I.e., they are hard constraints. In the case of metric learning, the constraints are not imposed strictly. In a new learned distance metric, two cannot-linked instances will be relatively distant, but there is no guarantee they will not end up in the same cluster. Although we think that metric learning makes a better use of provided constraints, we do not want to lose the benefit of hard constraints. Thus, we use both mechanisms in combination to impose constraints. We first learn a Mahalanobis distance based on the provided constraints. Then, we compute distance matrix and employ the mechanism proposed by (Klein et al., 2002) on the learned distance matrix.

4.2.2 Active Constraint Generation

As mentioned before, the choice of the set of constraints affects the quality of the end clustering. In this work, we define a novel method to choose informative instances, which we believe will have maximum impact on the end cluster quality, when they are labeled and used to generate constraints for our task. We use an iterative approach. Each iteration consists of three steps: (1) generating clusters by the process described in Section 4.2.1 imposing available constraints, (2) choosing the most informative instance, considering the cluster boundaries, and acquiring its label, (3) extending the available constraints with the ones we generate from the newly labeled instance.

We consider an instance to be informative if there is a high probability that the knowledge of its label may change the cluster boundaries. The more probable that change is, the more informative is the instance. The basic idea is that if an instance is in a cluster holding instances of type a and it is close to another cluster holding instances of type b, that instance is most likely misclustered. Thus, it should be queried. Our hypothesis is that, in each iteration, the algorithm will choose the most problematic – informative – instance that will end up changing cluster boundaries. This will result in each iteration in a more reliable distance metric, which in return will provide more reliable estimates of problematic instances in future iterations. The imposed con-

Algorithm 1 Iterative Constrained Clustering

```
1: C = cluster(I)
2: I_{L} = labelprototypes(C)
3: while |I_{L}| < stop do
4:     Con = createconstraints(I_{L})
5:     Matrix_dist = learnmetric(I, Con)
6:     C = constraintedcluster(Matrix_dist, Con)
7:     L = labelmostinformative(C)
8:     I_{L} = I_{L} ∪ L
9: end while
10: propagatelabels(I_{L}, C)      {C...Clusters; Con...Constraints;
    I...Instances; I_{L}...Labeled Instances; Matrix_dist...Distance Matrix}
```

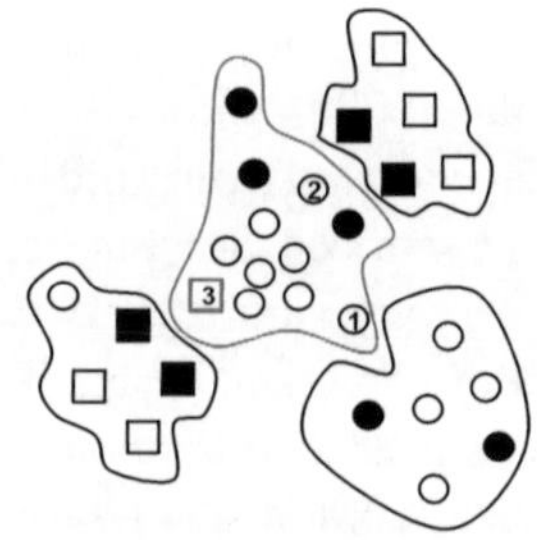

Figure 1: Behaviour of selection function

straints will move the clustering in each iteration towards better separation of S and O instances.

To define informativeness, we define a scoring function, which is used to score each data point on its goodness. The lower the score, the more likely it is that the instance is mis-clustered. Choosing the data point with the lowest score will likely change clustering borders in the next iteration. Our scoring function is based on the *silhouette coefficient*, a popular unsupervised cluster validation metric to measure goodness (Tan et al., 2005) of a cluster member. Basically, the silhouette score assigns a cluster member that is close to another cluster a lower score, and a cluster member that is closer to the cluster center a higher score. That is partly what we want. In addition, we do not want to penalize a cluster member that is close to another cluster having members with the same label. For this purpose, we calculate the silhouette score only over clusters with an opposing label (i.e., holding members with an opposing label). In addition, we consider only instances labeled so far when computing the score. We call this new coefficient silh_{const}. It is computed as follows: (1) for an instance i, compute its average distance from the other instances in its cluster x_i which are already labeled, (2) for an instance i, compute its average distance from the labeled instances of the clusters from an opposing label and take the minimum of these averages y_i, (3) compute the silhouette coefficient as $(y_i - x_i) / \max(y_i, x_i)$.

The silh_{const} coefficient has favourable properties. First, it scores members that are close to a cluster with an opposing label lower than the members that are close to a cluster with the same label. According to our definition, these members are more informative. Figure 1 holds a sample cluster setting. The shape of a member denotes its label and its fill denotes whether or not it has been queried. In this example, silh_{const} scores members 2 and 3 lower than 1. Thus, member 1 will not be selected, which is the right decision in this example. Both members 2 and 3 are close to clusters with an opposing label. In this example silh_{const} scores member 3 lower, which is farther away from already labeled members in the cluster. Thus, member 3 will be selected to be labeled. This type of behaviour results in an explorative strategy.

The active selection strategy proposed by (Klein et al., 2002) is single pass. Thus, it does not have the opportunity to observe the complete cluster structure before choosing constraints. We hypothesize that our strategy will provide more informative constraints, since it has the advantage of being able to base the decision of which constraints to generate on fully observed cluster structure in each iteration.

We call our proposed algorithm *Iterative Constrained Clustering (ICC)*. In our final implementation, ICC starts by simply clustering the instances without any constraints. The algorithm queries the label of the prototypical member – the member closest to the cluster center – of each cluster. Then, the described iterations begin. Algorithm 1 contains the complete ICC algorithm. Note that line 6 is equivalent to the algorithm of (Klein et al., 2002).

4.3 Experiments

This section gives details on experiments to evaluate the purity of the semi-automatically generated subjectivity sense tagged data by our "cluster and label" strategy. We carry out detailed analysis to quantify the effect of the proposed active selection strategy and of metric learning on the purity of the generated data. We compare our active selection strategy to random selection and also to (Klein et al., 2002). The comparison is done on the senSWSD dataset. SenSWSD consists of three subsets, SENSEVAL I,II and III. Since we devel-

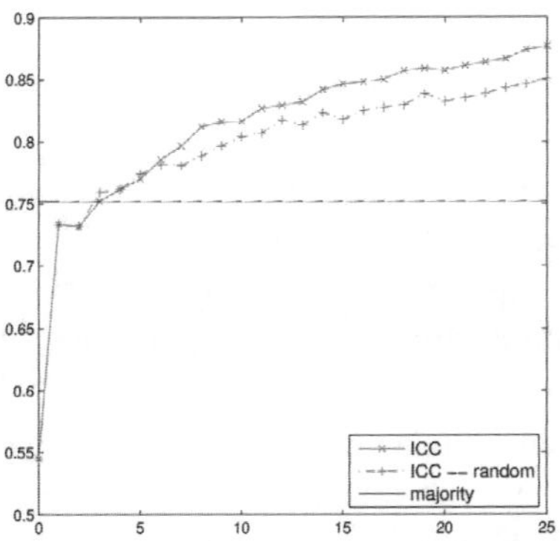

Figure 2: Label Purity – ICC vs. random selection

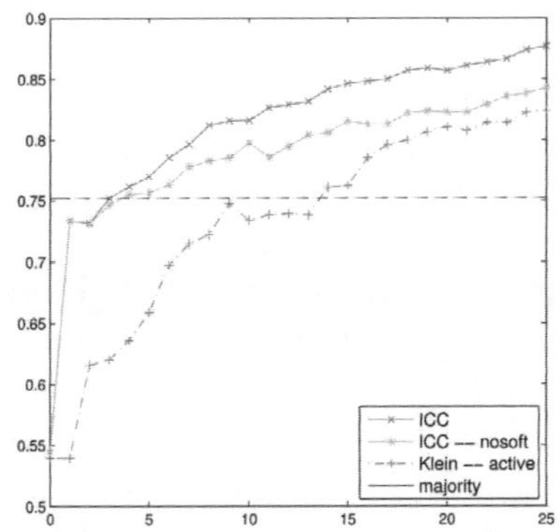

Figure 3: Label Purity – ICC vs. Klein

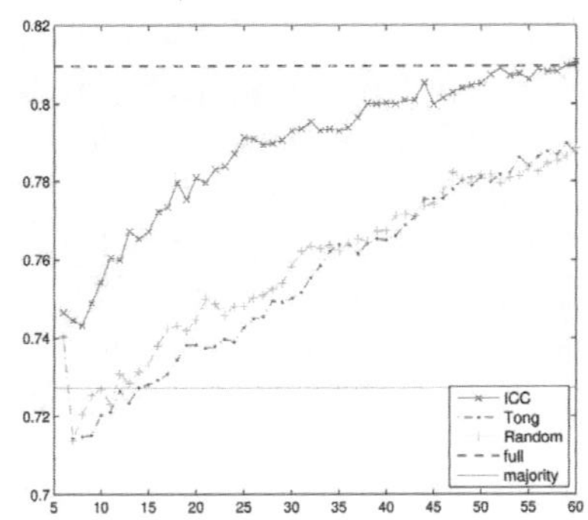

Figure 4: SWSD accuracy on ICC generated data

oped our active selection algorithm on the SENSEVAL I subset, we use only SENSEVAL II and III subsets for comparison. We apply ICC to each word in the comparison set separately, and report cumulative results for the purity of the generated data. We report results for different percentages of the queried data amount (e.g. 10% means that the algorithm queried 10% of the data to create constraints). This way, we obtain a learning curve. We fix the cluster number to 7 as in the context representation experiments.

4.3.1 Effect of Active Selection Strategy

Figure 2 holds the comparison of ICC with silh$_{const}$ selection to a random selection baseline. "majority" stands for majority label frequency in the dateset. We see that silh$_{const}$ performs better than the random selection. By providing labels to only 25% of the data, we can achieve 87.67% pure fully labeled data.

For comparison, we also evaluate the performance of (Klein et al., 2002) with their active constraint selection strategy as described in Section 4.1. Note that originally (Klein et al., 2002) requests the constraint between two roots. In our setting, it requests labels of the roots and then generates constraints from the obtained labels. Since we have a binary task, querying labels makes more sense. This has the advantage that more constraints from each request are obtained. Moreover, it allows a direct comparison to our algorithm. (Klein et al., 2002) does not use any metric learning. Thus, we run our algorithm also without metric learning, in order to compare the effectiveness of both active selection strategies fairly. In Figure 3, we see that silh$_{const}$ performs better than the active selection strategy described in (Klein et al., 2002). We also see that metric learning results in a big improvement. In addition, metric learning results in a smoother learning curve, which is a favourable property for a real-world application.

4.3.2 SWSD on semi-automatically generated annotations

Now that we have a tool to generate training data for SWSD, we want to evaluate it on the actual SWSD task. We want to see if the obtained purity is enough to create reliable SWSD classifiers. For this purpose, we test ICC on mturkSWSD dataset.

For each word in our dataset, we conduct 10-fold cross-validation experiments. ICC is applied to training folds to label instances semi-automatically. We train SWSD classifiers on the generated training fold labels and test the classifiers on the corresponding test fold. We distinguish between queried instances and propagated labels. The queried instances are weighted as 1 and the instances with propagated labels are weighted by their silh$_{const}$ score, since that measure gives the goodness of an instance. The score is defined between -1 and 1. This score is normalized between 0 and 1, before it is used as a weight. SVM classifiers from the Weka package (Witten and Frank., 2005) with its default settings are used as in (Akkaya et al., 2011).

We implement two baselines. The first is simple *random sampling* and the second is *uncertainty sampling*, which is an *active learning* (AL) method. We use "simple margin" selection as described in (Tong and Koller, 2001). It selects, in each iteration, the instance closest to the decision boundary of the trained SVM. Each method is run until it reaches the accuracy of training fully on the gold-standard data. ICC reaches that boundary when provided only 59% of the labels in the dataset. For uncertainty sampling and random sampling, these values are 92% and 100%, respectively. In Figure 4, we see the SWSD accuracy for different queried data percentages. "full" stands for training fully on gold-standard data. We see that training SWSD on semi-automatically labeled data by ICC does consistently better than uncertainty sampling and random sampling.

It is surprising to see that uncertainty sampling overall does not do better than random sampling. We believe that it might be because of sampling bias. During AL, as more and more labels are obtained, the training set quickly diverges from the underlying data distribution. (Schütze et al., 2006) states that AL can explore the feature space in such a biased way that it can end up ignoring entire clusters of unlabeled instances. We think that SWSD is highly prone for the mentioned missed cluster problem because of its unique nature. As mentioned, SWSD is a binary task where we distinguish between subjective and objective usages of a subjectivity word. Although the classification is binary, the underlying usages are grouped into multiple clusters corresponding to senses of the word. It is possible that two groups of usages which are represented quite differently in the feature space are both subjective or objective. Moreover, one usage group might be closer to a usage group from the opposing label than to a group with the same label.

We see that our method reduces the annotation amount by 36% in comparison to uncertainty sampling and by 41% in comparison to random sampling to reach the performance of the SWSD system trained on fully annotated data.

5 Related Work

One related line of research is constrained clustering also known as semi-supervised clustering (Xing et al., 2002; Wagstaff and Cardie, 2000; Grira et al., 2004; Demiriz et al., 1999). It has been applied to various datasets and tasks such as image and document categorization. To our knowledge, we are the first to utilize constrained clustering for a difficult NLP task.

There have been only two previous works selecting constraints for constrained clustering actively (Basu et al., 2004; Klein et al., 2002). The biggest difference of our approach is that it is iterative as opposed to single pass.

Active Learning (AL) (Settles, 2009; Settles and Craven, 2008; Hwa, 2004; Tong and Koller, 2001) builds another important set of related work. Our method is inspired by uncertainty sampling. We accomplish active selection in the clustering setting.

6 Conclusions

In this paper, we explore a "cluster and label" strategy to reduce the human annotation effort needed to generate subjectivity sense-tagged data. In order to keep the noise in the semi-automatically labeled data minimal, we investigate different feature space types and evaluate their expressiveness. More importantly, we define a new algorithm called iterative constrained clustering (ICC) with an active constraint selection strategy. We show that we can obtain a fairly reliable labeled data when we utilize ICC.

We show that the active selection strategy we propose outperforms a previous approach by (Klein et al., 2002) for generating subjectivity sense-tagged data. Training SWSD classifiers on ICC generated data improves over random sampling and uncertainty sampling (Tong and Koller, 2001). We can achieve on mturkSWSD 36% annotation reduction over uncertainty sampling and 41% annotation reduction over random sampling in order to reach the performance of SWSD classifiers trained on fully annotated data.

To our knowledge, this work is the first application of constrained clustering to a hard NLP problem. We showcase the power of constrained clustering. We hope that the same "cluster and label" strategy will be applicable to Word Sense Disambiguation. This will be part of our future work.

7 Acknowledgments

This material is based in part upon work supported by National Science Foundation awards #0917170 and #0916046.

References

Apoorv Agarwal, Fadi Biadsy, and Kathleen Mckeown. 2009. Contextual phrase-level polarity analysis using lexical affect scoring and syntactic N-grams. In *Proceedings of the 12th Conference of the European Chapter of the ACL (EACL 2009)*, pages 24–32, Athens, Greece, March. Association for Computational Linguistics.

Cem Akkaya, Janyce Wiebe, and Rada Mihalcea. 2009. Subjectivity word sense disambiguation. In *Proceedings of the 2009 Conference on Empirical Methods in Natural Language Processing*, pages 190–199, Singapore, August. Association for Computational Linguistics.

Cem Akkaya, Janyce Wiebe, Alexander Conrad, and Rada Mihalcea. 2011. Improving the impact of subjectivity word sense disambiguation on contextual opinion analysis. In *Proceedings of the Fifteenth Conference on Computational Natural Language Learning*, pages 87–96, Portland, Oregon, USA, June. Association for Computational Linguistics.

Cem Akkaya, Janyce Wiebe, and Rada Mihalcea. 2012. Utilizing semantic composition in distributional semantic models for word sense discrimination and word sense disambiguation. In *ICSC*, pages 45–51.

Alina Andreevskaia and Sabine Bergler. 2008. When specialists and generalists work together: Overcoming domain dependence in sentiment tagging. In *Proceedings of ACL-08: HLT*, pages 290–298, Columbus, Ohio, June. Association for Computational Linguistics.

Sugato Basu, Arindam Banerjee, and R. Mooney. 2002. Semi-supervised clustering by seeding. In *In Proceedings of 19th International Conference on Machine Learning (ICML-2002)*.

Sugato Basu, Arindam Banerjee, and Raymond J. Mooney. 2004. Active semi-supervision for pairwise constrained clustering. In *SDM*.

Kenneth Bloom, Navendu Garg, and Shlomo Argamon. 2007. Extracting appraisal expressions. In *HLT-NAACL 2007*, pages 308–315, Rochester, NY.

John Bullinaria and Joseph Levy. 2007. Extracting semantic representations from word co-occurrence statistics: A computational study. *Behavior Research Methods*, 39:510–526. 10.3758/BF03193020.

Ian Davidson, Kiri Wagstaff, and Sugato Basu. 2006. Measuring constraint-set utility for partitional clustering algorithms. In *PKDD*, pages 115–126.

Jason V. Davis, Brian Kulis, Prateek Jain, Suvrit Sra, and Inderjit S. Dhillon. 2007. Information-theoretic metric learning. In *Proceedings of the 24th international conference on Machine learning*, ICML '07, pages 209–216, New York, NY, USA. ACM.

Ayhan Demiriz, Kristin Bennett, and Mark J. Embrechts. 1999. Semi-supervised clustering using genetic algorithms. In *In Artificial Neural Networks in Engineering (ANNIE-99*, pages 809–814. ASME Press.

Nizar Grira, Michel Crucianu, and Nozha Boujemaa. 2004. Unsupervised and semi-supervised clustering: a brief survey. In *in A Review of Machine Learning Techniques for Processing Multimedia Content, Report of the MUSCLE European Network of Excellence*.

Rebecca Hwa. 2004. Sample selection for statistical parsing. *Comput. Linguist.*, 30(3):253–276, September.

Adam Kilgarriff. 1997. I dont believe in word senses. *Computers and the Humanities*, 31(2):91–113.

Soo-Min Kim and Eduard Hovy. 2004. Determining the sentiment of opinions. In *Proceedings of the Twentieth International Conference on Computational Linguistics (COLING 2004)*, pages 1267–1373, Geneva, Switzerland.

D. Klein, K. Toutanova, I.T. Ilhan, S.D. Kamvar, and C. Manning. 2002. Combining heterogeneous classifiers for word-sense disambiguation. In *Proceedings of the ACL Workshop on "Word Sense Disambiguatuion: Recent Successes and Future Directions*, pages 74–80, July.

R. Mihalcea. 2002. Instance based learning with automatic feature selection applied to Word Sense Disambiguation. In *Proceedings of the 19th International Conference on Computational Linguistics (COLING 2002)*, Taipei, Taiwan, August.

Jeff Mitchell and Mirella Lapata. 2010. Composition in distributional models of semantics. *Cognitive Science*, 34(8):1388–1429.

A. Purandare and T. Pedersen. 2004. Word sense discrimination by clustering contexts in vector and similarity spaces. In *Proceedings of the Conference on Computational Natural Language Learning (CoNLL 2004)*, Boston.

Ellen Riloff and Janyce Wiebe. 2003. Learning extraction patterns for subjective expressions. In *Proceedings of the Conference on Empirical Methods in Natural Language Processing (EMNLP-2003)*, pages 105–112, Sapporo, Japan.

Magnus Sahlgren. 2006. *The Word-Space Model: using distributional analysis to represent syntagmatic and paradigmatic relations between words in high-dimensional vector spaces.* Ph.D. thesis, Stockholm University.

Hinrich Schütze, Emre Velipasaoglu, and Jan O. Pedersen. 2006. Performance thresholding in practical text classification. In *Proceedings of the 15th ACM international conference on Information and knowledge management*, CIKM '06, pages 662–671, New York, NY, USA. ACM.

H. Schutze. 1998. Automatic word sense discrimination. *Computational Linguistics*, 24(1):97–124.

Burr Settles and Mark Craven. 2008. An analysis of active learning strategies for sequence labeling tasks. In *Proceedings of the Conference on Empirical Methods in Natural Language Processing*, EMNLP '08, pages 1070–1079, Stroudsburg, PA, USA. Association for Computational Linguistics.

Burr Settles. 2009. Active Learning Literature Survey. Technical Report 1648, University of Wisconsin–Madison.

Pang-Ning Tan, Michael Steinbach, and Vipin Kumar. 2005. *Introduction to Data Mining, (First Edition)*. Addison-Wesley Longman Publishing Co., Inc., Boston, MA, USA.

Simon Tong and Daphne Koller. 2001. Support vector machine active learning with applications to text classification. *Journal of Machine Learning Research*, 2:45–66.

Peter D. Turney and Patrick Pantel. 2010. From frequency to meaning: Vector space models of semantics. March.

Peter Turney. 2002. Thumbs up or thumbs down? Semantic orientation applied to unsupervised classification of reviews. In *Proceedings of the 40th Annual Meeting of the Association for Computational Linguistics (ACL-02)*, pages 417–424, Philadelphia, Pennsylvania.

Kiri Wagstaff and Claire Cardie. 2000. Clustering with instance-level constraints. In *Proceedings of the Seventeenth International Conference on Machine Learning (ICML-2000)*, pages 1103–1110.

Casey Whitelaw, Navendu Garg, and Shlomo Argamon. 2005. Using appraisal taxonomies for sentiment analysis. In *Proceedings of CIKM-05, the ACM SIGIR Conference on Information and Knowledge Management*, Bremen, DE.

I. Witten and E. Frank. 2005. *Data Mining: Practical Machine Learning Tools and Techniques, Second Edition*. Morgan Kaufmann, June.

Eric P. Xing, Andrew Y. Ng, Michael I. Jordan, and Stuart J. Russell. 2002. Distance metric learning with application to clustering with side-information. In *NIPS*, pages 505–512.

Hong Yu and Vasileios Hatzivassiloglou. 2003. Towards answering opinion questions: Separating facts from opinions and identifying the polarity of opinion sentences. In *Proceedings of the Conference on Empirical Methods in Natural Language Processing (EMNLP-2003)*, pages 129–136, Sapporo, Japan.

Identifying fake Amazon reviews as learning from crowds

Tommaso Fornaciari
Ministero dell'Interno
Dipartimento della Pubblica Sicurezza
Segreteria del Dipartimento
ComISSIT
tommaso.fornaciari@interno.it

Massimo Poesio
University of Essex
CSEE
University of Trento
CIMeC
poesio@essex.ac.uk

Abstract

Customers who buy products such as books online often rely on other customers reviews more than on reviews found on specialist magazines. Unfortunately the confidence in such reviews is often misplaced due to the explosion of so-called **sock puppetry**–authors writing glowing reviews of their own books. Identifying such deceptive reviews is not easy. The first contribution of our work is the creation of a collection including a number of genuinely deceptive Amazon book reviews in collaboration with crime writer Jeremy Duns, who has devoted a great deal of effort in unmasking sock puppeting among his colleagues. But there can be no certainty concerning the other reviews in the collection: all we have is a number of cues, also developed in collaboration with Duns, suggesting that a review may be genuine or deceptive. Thus this corpus is an example of a collection where it is not possible to acquire the actual label for all instances, and where clues of deception were treated as annotators who assign them heuristic labels. A number of approaches have been proposed for such cases; we adopt here the 'learning from crowds' approach proposed by Raykar et al. (2010). Thanks to Duns' certainly fake reviews, the second contribution of this work consists in the evaluation of the effectiveness of different methods of annotation, according to the performance of models trained to detect deceptive reviews.

1 Introduction

Customer reviews of books, hotels and other products are widely perceived as an important reason for the success of e-commerce sites such as amazon.com or tripadvisor.com. However, customer confidence in such reviews is often misplaced, due to the growth of the so-called **sock puppetry** phenomenon: authors / hoteliers writing glowing reviews of their own works / hotels (and occasionally also negative reviews of the competitors).[1] The prevalence of this phenomenon has been revealed by campaigners such as crime writer Jeremy Duns, who exposed a number of fellow authors involved in such practices.[2] A number of sites have also emerged offering Amazon reviews to authors for a fee.[3]

Several automatic techniques for exposing such deceptive reviews have been proposed in recent years (Feng et al., 2012; Ott et al., 2001). But like all work on deceptive language (computational or otherwise) (Newman et al., 2003; Strapparava and Mihalcea, 2009), such works suffer from a serious problem: the lack of a gold standard containing 'real life' examples of deceptive uses of language. This is because it is very difficult to find definite proof that an Amazon review is either deceptive or genuine. Thus most researchers recreate deceptive behavior in the lab, as done by Newman et al. (2003). For instance, Ott et al. (2001), Feng et al. (2012) and Strapparava and Mihalcea (2009) used crowdsourcing, asking turkers to produce instances of deceptive behavior. Finally, Li et al. (2011) classify reviews as deceptive or truthful by hand on the basis of a series of heuristics: they start by excluding anonymous reviews, then use their helpfulness and other criteria to decide

[1] The phenomenon predates Internet - see e.g., Amy Harmon, 'Amazon Glitch Unmasks War Of Reviewers', New York Times, February 14, 2004.

[2] See Andrew Hough, 'RJ Ellory: fake book reviews are rife on internet, authors warn', telegraph.co.uk, September 3, 2012

[3] See Alison Flood, 'Sock puppetry and fake reviews: publish and be damned', guardian.co.uk, September 4, 2012 and David Streitfeld, 'Buy Reviews on Yelp, Get Black Mark', nytimes.com, October 18, 2012.

whether they are deceptive or not. Clearly a more rigorous approach to establishing the truth or otherwise of reviews on the basis of such heuristic criteria would be useful.

In this work we develop a system for identifying deceptive reviews in Amazon. Our proposal makes two main contributions:

1. we identified in collaboration with Jeremy Duns a series of criteria used by Duns and other 'sock puppet hunters' to find suspicious reviews / reviewers, and collected a dataset of reviews some of which are certainly false as the authors admitted so, whereas others may be genuine or deceptive.

2. we developed an approach to the truthfulness of reviews based on the notion that the truthfulness of a review is a latent variable whose value cannot be known, but can be estimated using some criteria as potential indicators of such value–as *annotators*–and then we used the **learning from crowds** algorithm proposed by Raykar et al. (2010) to assign a class to each review in the dataset.

The structure of the paper is as follows. In Section 2 we describe how we collected our dataset; in Section 3 we show the experiments we carried out and in Section 4 we discuss the results.

2 Deception clues and dataset

2.1 Examples of Unmasked Sock Puppetry

After reading an article by Alison Flood on *The Guardian* of September 4th, 2012 [4], discussing how crime writer Jeremy Duns had unmasked a number of 'sock puppeteers,' we contacted him. Duns was extremely helpful; he pointed us to the other articles on the topic, mostly on *The New York Times*, and helped us create a set of **deception clues** and the dataset used in this work.

On July 25th, 2011, an article appeared on `www.moneytalksnews.com`, entitled '3 Tips for Spotting Fake Product Reviews - From Someone Who Wrote Them'.[5] Sandra Parker, author of the text, in that page described her experience as 'professional review writer'. According to her statements, advertising agencies were used to pay her $10-20 for writing reviews on sites like Amazon.com. She was not asked to lie, but 'if the review wasn't five star, they didn't pay'. In an article of August 19th, written by David Streitfeld on `www.nytimes.com`,[6] she actually denied that point: 'We were not asked to provide a five-star review, but would be asked to turn down an assignment if we could not give one'.

In any case, in her article Sandra Parker gave the readers some common sense-based advices, in order to help them to recognize possible fake reviews. One of these suggestions were also useful for this study, as discussed in Section 2.3. From our point of view, however, the most interesting aspect of the article relied in the fact that, letting know the name of an author of fake reviews, it made possible to identify them in Amazon.com, with an high degree of confidence.

A further article written on August 25th by David Streitfeld gave us another similar opportunity.[7] In fact, thanks to his survey, it was possible to come to know the titles of four books, whose the authors paid an agency in order to receive reviews.

2.2 The corpus

Using the suggestions of Jeremy Duns and the information in these articles we built a corpus we called DEREV (DEception in REViews), consisting of clearly fake, possibly fake, and possibly genuine book reviews posted on `www.amazon.com`. The corpus, which will be freely available on demand, consists of 6819 reviews downloaded from `www.amazon.com`, concerning 68 books and written by 4811 different reviewers. The 68 books were chosen trying to balance the number of reviews (our units of analysis) related to suspect books which probably or surely received fake reviews, with the number of reviews hypothesized to be genuine in that we expected the authors of the books not to have bought reviews. In particular, we put into the group of the suspect books - henceforth SB - the reviews of the four books indicated by David Streitfeld. To this first nucleus, we also added other four books, written by three of the authors of the previous group. We also in-

[4] *Sock puppetry and fake reviews: publish and be damned*, `http://www.guardian.co.uk/books/2012/sep/04/sock-puppetry-publish-be-damned`

[5] `http://www.moneytalksnews.com/2011/07/25/3-tips-for-spotting-fake-product-reviews---from-someone-who-wrote-them/`

[6] `http://www.nytimes.com/2011/08/20/technology/finding-fake-reviews-online.html?_r=1&`

[7] `http://www.nytimes.com/2012/08/26/business/book-reviewers-for-hire-meet-a-demand-for-online-raves.html?pagewanted=all`

cluded in the SB group the 22 books for which Sandra Parker wrote a review. Lastly, we noticed that some reviewers of the books pointed out by David Streitfeld tended to write reviews of the same books: we identified 16 of them, and considered suspect as well. In total, on November 17th, 2011 we downloaded the reviews of 46 books considered as suspect, which received 2707 reviews.[8] We also collected the reviews of 22 so called 'innocent books', for a total of 4112 reviews. These books were mainly chosen among classic authors, such as Conan Doyle or Kipling, or among living writers who are so renowned that any reviews' purchase would be pointless: this is the case, for example, of Ken Follett and Stephen King. As shown by the number of the reviews, the books of these authors are so famous that they receive a great amount of readers' opinions.

The size of DEREV is 1175410 tokens, considering punctuation blocks as single token. The mean size of the reviews is 172.37 tokens. The titles of the reviews were neither included in these statistics nor in the following analyses.

2.3 Deception clues

Once created the corpus, we identified a set of clues, whose presence suggested the deceptiveness of the reviews. These clues are:

Suspect Book - SB The first clue of deceptiveness was the reference of the reviews to a suspect book, identified as described above. This is the only clue which is constant for all the reviews of the same book.

Cluster - Cl The second clue comes from the suggestions given by Sandra Parker in her mentioned article. As she pointed out, the agencies she worked for were used to give her 48 hours to write a review. Being likely that the same deadline was given to other reviewers, Sandra Parker warns to pay attention if the books receive many reviews in a short period of time. Following her advice, we considered as positive this clue of deceptiveness if the review belonged to a group of at least two reviews posted within 3 days.

Nickname - NN A service provided by Amazon is the possibility for the reviewers to register in the website and to post comments using their real name. Since the real identity of the reviewers involves issues related to their reputation, we supposed it is less probable that the writers of fake reviews post their texts using their true name. Moreover, a similar assumption was probably accepted by Li et al. (2011), who considered the profile features of the reviewers, and among them the use or not of their real name.

Unknown Purchase - UP Lastly, the probably most interesting information provided by Amazon is whether the reviewer bought the reviewed book through Amazon itself. It is reasonable to think that, if the reviewer bought the book, he also read it. Therefore, the absence of information about the certified purchase was considered a clue of deceptiveness.

2.4 Gold and silver standard

The clues of deception discussed above give us a heuristic estimate of the truthfulness of the reviews. Such estimation represents a silver standard of our classes, as these are not determined through certain knowledge of the ground truth, but simply thanks to hints of deceptiveness. The methods we used in order to assign the heuristic classes to the reviews are described in the next Section; however for our purposes we needed a gold standard, that is at least a subset of reviews whose ground truth was known with a high degree of confidence. This subset was identified as follows.

First, we considered as false the 22 reviews published by Sandra Parker, even though not all her reviews are characterized by the presence of all the deception clues. Even though we cannot really say whether her reviews reflect her opinion of the books in question or not, she explicitly claimed to have been paid for writing them; and she only bought on Amazon three of these 22 books. This is the most accurate knowledge about fake reviews not artificially produced we have found in literature. Then we focused on the four books whose authors admitted to have bought the reviews.[9] Three of them received many reviews, which made it difficult to understand if they were truthful or not. However, one of these

[8] We specify the date of the download because, obviously, if the data collection would be repeated today, the overall number of reviews would be greater.

[9] `http://www.nytimes.com/2012/08/26/business/book-reviewers-for-hire-meet-a-demand-for-online-raves.html?pagewanted=all`

Table 1: The distribution of deception clues in the reviews

	Nr. clues	Reviews	Tot.	%
False	4	903		
rev.	3	1913	2816	41.30%
True	2	2528		
rev.	1	1210		
	0	265	4003	58.70%

books ('Write your first book', by Peter Biadasz) received only 20 reviews, which therefore could be considered as fake with high degree of probability. Even though we have no clear evidence that a small number of reviews correlates with a greater likelihood of deception, since we know this book received fake reviews, and there are only few reviews for it, we felt it is pretty likely that those are fake. Therefore we examined the reviews written by these twenty authors, and considered as false only those showing the presence of all the deception clues described above. In this way, we found 96 reviews published by 14 reviewers, and we added them to the 22 of Sandra Parker, for a total of 118 reviews written by 15 authors.

Once identified this subset of fake reviews, we selected other 118 reviews which did not show the presence of any deception clue, that is chosen from books above any suspicion, written by authors who published the review having made use of their real name and having bought the book through Amazon and so on.

In the end, we identified a subset of DEREV constituted by 236 reviews, whose class was known with high degree of confidence and considered them as our gold standard.

3 Experiments

We carried out two experiments, in which the classes assigned to the reviews of DEREV were found adopting two different strategies. In the first experiment the classes of the reviews were determined using majority voting of our deception clues. This experiment is thus conceptually similar to those of Li et al. (2011), who trained models using supervised methods with the aim of identifying fake reviews. We discuss this experiment in the next Section. In the second experiment, learning from crowds was used (Raykar et al., 2010). This approach is discussed in Section 3.2.1.

In both experiments we carried out a 10-fold cross-validation where in each iteration feature selection and training were carried out using 90% of the part of the corpus with only silver standard annotation and 90% of the subset with gold. The test set used in each iteration consisted of the remaining tenth of reviews with gold standard classes, which were employed in order to evaluate the predictions of the models. This allowed to estimate the efficiency of the strategies we used to determine our silver standard classes.

3.1 Majority Voting

3.1.1 Determining the class of reviews by majority voting

The deception clues discussed in Section 2.3 were used in our first experiment to identify the class of each review using majority voting. In other words, those clues were considered as independent predictors of the class; the class predicted by the majority of the annotators/clues was assigned to the review. Specifically, if 0, 1 or 2 deception clues were found, the review was classified as true; if there were 3 or 4, the review was considered false. Table 1 shows the distribution of the number of deception clues in the reviews in DEREV.

3.1.2 Feature selection

In both experiments each review was represented as feature vector. The features were just of unigrams, bigrams and trigrams of lemmas and part-of-speech (POS), as collected from the reviews through TreeTagger[10] (Schmid, 1994).

Since in each experiment we applied a 10-fold cross-validation, in every fold the features were extracted from the nine-tenths of DEREV employed as training set. Once identified the training set, we computed the frequency lists of the n-grams of lemmas and POS. The lists were collected separately from the reviews belonging to the class 'true' and to the class 'false'. Such separation was aimed to take into consideration the most highly frequent n-grams of both genuine and fake reviews. However, for the following steps of the feature selection, only the n-grams which appeared more than 300 times in every frequency list were considered: a threshold empirically chosen for ease of calculations. In fact, among the most

[10] http://www.ims.uni-stuttgart.de/projekte/corplex/TreeTagger/DecisionTreeTagger.html

Table 2: The most frequent n-grams collected

N-grams	Lemmas	POS	Total
Unigrams	34	21	
Bigrams	21	13	
Trigrams	13	8	
Total	68	42	110

frequents, in order to identify the features most effective in discriminating the two classes of reviews, the Information Gain (IG) of the selected n-grams was computed (Kullback and Leibler, 1951; Yang and Pedersen, 1997).

Then, after having found the Information Gain of the n-grams of lemmas and part-of-speech, a further reduction of the features was realized. In fact, we selected a relatively small amount of features, in order to facilitate the computation of the Raykar et al.'s algorithm (discussed in Sub-section 3.2.1), and only the n-grams with the highest IG values were selected to be taken as features of the vectors which represented the reviews. In particular, the n-grams were collected according to the scheme shown in Table 2. By the way, 8, 13, 21 and 34 are numbers belonging to the Fibonacci series (Sigler, 2003). They were chosen because they grow exponentially and are used, in our case, to give wider representation to the shortest n-grams.

Lastly, two more features were added to the feature set, that is the length of the review, considered with and without punctuation. Therefore, in each fold of the experiment, the vectors of the reviews were constituted by 112 values: 2 corresponding to the length of the review, and 110 representing the (not normalized) frequency, into the review itself, of the selected n-grams of lemmas and POS.

3.1.3 Baselines

The best way to assess the improvement coming from the algorithm would have been with respect to a supervised baseline. However this was not possible as we could only be certain regarding the classification of a fraction of the reviews (our gold standard: 236 reviews, for a total of about 23,000 tokens). We felt such a small dataset could not be used for training, but only for evaluation; therefore we used instead two simple heuristic baselines.

Majority baseline. The simplest metric for performance evaluation is the majority baseline: always assign to a review the class most represented in the dataset. Since in the subset of DEREV with gold standard we had 50% of true and false reviews, simply 50% is our majority baseline.

Random baseline. Furthermore, we estimated a random baseline through a Monte Carlo simulation. This kind of simulation allows to estimate the performance of a classifier which performs several times a task over random outputs whose distribution reflects that of real data.

In particular, for this experiment, since we had 236 reviews whose 50% were labeled as false, 100000 times we produced 236 random binomial predictions, having $p = .5$. In each simulation, the random prediction was compared with our real data. It turned out that in less than .01% of trials the level of 62.29% of correct predictions was exceeded. The thresholds for precision and recall in detecting deceptive reviews were 62.26% and 66.95% respectively.

3.1.4 Models

We tested a number of supervised learning methods to learn a classifier using the classes determined by majority voting, but the best results were obtained using Support Vector Machines (SVMs) (Cortes and Vapnik, 1995), already employed in many applications involving text classification (Yang and Liu, 1999).

3.1.5 Results

The results obtained by training a supervised classifier over the dataset with classes identified with majority voting are shown in the Table 3. The highest results are in bold. The methodological approach and performance achieved in this experiment seems to be comparable to that of Strapparava and Mihalcea (2009) and, more recently, of Li et al. (2011). However Li et al. (2011) evaluate the effectiveness of different kind of features with the aim of annotating unlabeled data, while we try to evaluate the reliability of heuristic classes in training.

3.2 Learning from Crowds

3.2.1 The Learning from Crowds algorithm

As pointed out by Raykar et al. (2010), majority voting is not necessarily the most effective way to determine the real classes in problems like

Table 3: The experiment with the majority voting classes

	Correctly classified reviews	Incorrectly classified reviews	Precision	Recall	F-measure
False reviews	75	43	**83.33%**	63.56%	72.12%
True reviews	103	15			
Total	178	58			
Total accuracy	**75.42%**				
Random baseline	62.29%		62.26%	**66.95%**	

those of reviews where there is no gold standard. This is because annotators are not equally reliable, and the reviews are not equally challenging. Hence the output of the majority voting may be affected by unevaluated biases. To address this problem, Raykar et al. (2010) presented a maximum-likelihood estimator that *jointly* learns the classifier/regressor, the annotator accuracy, and the actual true label.

For ease of exposition, Raykar et al. (2010) use as classifier the logistic regression, even though they specify their algorithm would work with any classifier. In case of logistic regression, the probability for an entity $x \in X$ of belonging to a class $y \in Y$ with $Y = \{1, 0\}$ is a sigmoid function of the weight vector w of the features of each instance x_i, that is $p[y = 1|x, w] = \sigma(w^\top x)$, where, given a threshold γ, the class $y = 1$ if $w^\top x \geq \gamma$.

Annotators' performance, then, is evaluated 'in terms of the sensitivity and specificity with respect to the unknown gold standard': in particular, in a binary classification problem, for the annotator j the sensitivity α^j is the rate of positive cases identified by the annotator –i.e., the recall of positive cases– while the specificity β^j is the annotator's recall of negative cases.

Given a dataset D constituted of independently sampled entities, a number of annotators R, and the relative parameters $\theta = \{w, \alpha, \beta\}$, the likelihood function which needs to be maximized, according to Raykar et al. (2010), would be $p[D|\theta] = \prod_{i=1}^{N} p[y_i^1, ...y_i^R|x_i, \theta]$, and the maximum-likelihood estimator is obtained by maximizing the log-likelihood, that is

$$\widehat{\theta}_{ML} = \{\widehat{\alpha}, \widehat{\beta}, \widehat{w}\} = \underset{\theta}{arg\,max}\{ln\,p[D|\theta]\}. \quad (1)$$

Raykar et al. (2010) propose to solve this maximization problem (Bickel and Doksum, 2000) through the technique of Expectation Maximization (EM) (Dempster et al., 1977). The EM algorithm can be used to recover the parameters of the hidden distributions accounting for the distribution of data. It consists of two steps, an Expectation step (E-step) followed by a Maximization step (M-step), which are iterated until convergence. During the E-step the expectation of the term y_i is computed starting from the current estimate of the parameters. In the M-step the parameters θ are updated by maximizing the conditional expectation. Regarding the third parameter, w, Raykar et al. (2010) admit there is not a closed form solution and suggest to use the Newton-Raphson method.

3.2.2 Determining the class of reviews using Learning from Crowds

In order to apply Raykar's algorithm, we proceeded as follows. First, we applied the procedure for feature selection described in Subsection 3.1.2 to create a single dataset: that is, the corpus was not divided in folds, but the feature selection involved all of DEREV. This dataset was built using the classes resulting from the majority voting approach and included these columns:

- The class assignments of the four clues discussed in Sub-section 2.3 – SB, Cl, NN, UP;
- The majority voting class;
- The 112 features identified according to the procedure presented in Sub-section 3.1.2.

Then, we implemented the algorithm proposed by Raykar et al. (2010) in R.[11] We computed a Logistic Regression (Gelman and Hill, 2007) on the dataset to compute the weight vector w, used to estimate for each instance the probability p_i for the review of belonging to the class 'true'. For the logistic regression we used the 112 surface features

[11] `http://www.r-project.org/`

Table 4: The experiment with Raykar et al.'s algorithm classes

	Correctly classified reviews	Incorrectly classified reviews	Precision	Recall	F-measure
False reviews	85	33	**78.70%**	**72.03%**	75.22%
True reviews	95	23			
Total	180	56			
Total accuracy	**76.27%**				
Random baseline	62.29%		62.26%	66.95%	

mentioned above, adopting as class the majority voting, as suggested by Raykar et al. (2010).

The parameters α and β were estimated regarding the three clues Cl - Cluster, NN - Nickname and UP - Unknown Purchase. The attribute SB - Suspect Book was not used, in order to carry out the EM algorithm exclusively on heuristic data, removing the information obtained through sources external to the dataset. The parameters α and β of the three clues were obtained not from random classes, as the EM algorithm would allow, but again comparing the clues' labels with the majority voting class. In fact, aware of the local maximum problem of EM, in this way we tried to enhance the reliability of the results posing a configuration which could be, at least theoretically, better than a completely random one.

Knowing these values for each instance of the dataset, we computed the E-step and we updated our parameters in M-step.

The E-step and the M-step were iterated 100 times, in which the log-likelihood increases monotonically, indicating a convergence to a local maximum.

The final value of p_i determined the new class of each instance: if $p_i > .5$ the review was labeled as true, otherwise as false. In the end, the EM clusterization allowed to label 3267 reviews as false and 3552 as true, that is 47.91% and 52.09% of DEREV respectively.

3.2.3 Feature selection

The feature selection for this experiment was exactly the same presented for the previous one in Sub-section 3.1.2; the only, fundamental difference was that in the first experiment the classes derived from the majority voting rule, while in the second experiment the classes were identified through the Raykar et al.'s strategy.

3.2.4 Baselines

As in the first experiment, we compared the performance of the models with the same majority and random baselines discussed in Sub-section 3.1.3.

3.2.5 Models

We used the classes determined through the Learning by Crowds algorithm to train SVMs models, with the same settings employed in the first experiments.

3.2.6 Results

Table 4 shows the results of the classifier trained over the dataset whose the classes were identified through the Raykar et al.'s algorithm.

4 Discussion

4.1 Deceptive language in reviews

Of the 4811 reviewers who wrote reviews included in our corpus, about 900 were anonymous, and only 16 wrote 10 or more reviews. If, in one hand, this prevented us from verifying the performance of the models with respect to particular reviewers, on the other hand we had the opportunity of evaluating the style in writing reviews across many subjects.

In our experiments, we extracted simple surface features constituted by short n-grams of lemmas and part-of-speech. In literature there is evidence that also other kinds of features are effective in detecting deception in reviews: for example, information about the syntactic structures of the texts (Feng et al., 2012). In our pilot studies we did not obtain improvements using syntactic features. But even the frequency of n-grams can provide some insight regarding deceptive language in reviews; and with this aim we focused on the unigrams appearing more than 50 times in the 236 reviews constituting the gold standard of DeRev, whose un/truthfulness is known. The use of self-referred pronouns and adjectives is remarkably different in true and fake reviews: in the genuine ones, the pronouns 'I', 'my' and 'me' are found 371, 74 and 51 times respectively, while in the fake ones the pronoun 'I' is present only 149 and 'me' and 'my' less than 50 times. This reduced number of self-references is coherent with the findings of other well-known studies regarding deception detection (Newman et al., 2003); however, while in truthful reviews the pronoun 'you' appears only 84 times, in the fake ones the frequency of 'you' and 'your' is 151 and 75. It seems that while the truth-tellers simple state their opinions, the deceivers address directly the reader. Probably they tend to give advice: after all, this is what they are paid for. The frequency of the word 'read' - that is the activity simulated in fake reviews - is also quite imbalanced: 137 in true reviews and 97 in the fake ones. Lastly, it is maybe surprising that in the false reviews terms related to positive feelings/judgments do not have the highest frequency; instead in truthful reviews we found 52 times the term 'good' (and 56 times the ambiguous term 'like'): also this outcome is similar to that of the mentioned study of Newman et al. (2003).

4.2 Estimating the gold standard

The estimation of the gold standard is a recurrent problem in many tasks of text classification and in particular with deceptive review identification, that is an application where the deceptiveness of the reviews cannot be properly determined but only heuristically assessed.

In this paper we introduced a new dataset for studying deceptive reviews, constituted by 6819 instances whose 236 (that is about 3.5% of the corpus) were labeled with the highest degree of confidence ever seen before. We used this subset to test the models that we trained on the other reviews of DeRev, whose the class was heuristically determined.

With this purpose, we adopted two techniques. First, we simply considered the value of our clues of deception as outputs of just as many annotators, and we assigned the classes to each review according to majority voting. Then we clustered our instances using the Learning from Crowd algorithm proposed by Raykar et al. (2010). Lastly we carried out the two experiments of text classification described above.

The results suggest that both methods achieve accuracy well above the baseline. However, the models trained using Learning from Crowd classes not only achieved the highest accuracy, but also outperformed the thresholds for precision and recall in detecting deceptive reviews (Table 4), while the models trained with the majority voting classes showed a very high precision, but at the expense of the recall, which was lower than the baseline (Table 3).

Since the results even with simple majority voting classes were positive, we carried out two more experiments, identical to those described above except that we included in the feature set the three deception clues Cluster - Cl, Nickname - NN and Unknown Purchase - UP. Both with majority voting and with learning from Crowds classes, the accuracy of the models exceeded 97%. This might seem to suggest that those clues are very effective; but given that the deception clues were used to derive the silver standard, their use as features could be considered to some extent circular (Subsection 2.4). Moreover, not all of our non-linguistic cues may be found in all review scenarios, and therefore the applicability of our methods to all review scenarios will have to be investigated. Specifically, Cluster is likely to be applicable to most review domains, Nickname and Unknown Purchase are Amazon features that may or may not be adopted by other services allowing users to provide reviews. However, our main concern was not to evaluate the effectiveness of these specific clues of deception, but to investigate whether better strategies for labeling instances than simple majority voting could be found.

In this perspective, the performance of our second experiment, in which the Learning from Crowds algorithm was employed, stands out. In fact in that case we tried to identify the classes of the instances abstaining from making use of any external information regarding the reviews: in particular, we ignored the Suspect Book - SB clue of deception which, by contrast, took part in the creation of the majority voting classes.

This outcome suggests that, even in scenarios where the gold standard is unknown, the Learning from Crowds algorithm is a reliable tool for labeling the reviews, so that effective models can be trained in order to classify them as truthful or not.

References

Bickel, P. and Doksum, K. (2000). *Mathematical statistics: basic ideas and selected topics*. Number v. 1 in Mathematical Statistics: Basic Ideas and Selected Topics. Prentice Hall.

Cortes, C. and Vapnik, V. (1995). Support-vector networks. *Machine Learning*, 20.

Dempster, A. P., Laird, N. M., and Rubin, D. B. (1977). Maximum Likelihood from Incomplete Data via the EM Algorithm. *Journal of the Royal Statistical Society. Series B (Methodological)*, 39(1):1–38.

Feng, S., Banerjee, R., and Choi, Y. (2012). Syntactic stylometry for deception detection. In *Proceedings of the 50th Annual Meeting of the Association for Computational Linguistics (Volume 2: Short Papers)*, pages 171–175, Jeju Island, Korea. Association for Computational Linguistics.

Gelman, A. and Hill, J. (2007). *Data Analysis Using Regression and Multilevel/Hierarchical Models*. Analytical Methods for Social Research. Cambridge University Press.

Kullback, S. and Leibler, R. A. (1951). On information and sufficiency. *Ann. Math. Statist.*, 22(1):79–86.

Li, F., Huang, M., Yang, Y., and Zhu, X. (2011). Learning to identify review spam. In *Proceedings of the Twenty-Second international joint conference on Artificial Intelligence-Volume Volume Three*, pages 2488–2493. AAAI Press.

Newman, M. L., Pennebaker, J. W., Berry, D. S., and Richards, J. M. (2003). Lying Words: Predicting Deception From Linguistic Styles. *Personality and Social Psychology Bulletin*, 29(5):665–675.

Ott, M., Choi, Y., Cardie, C., and Hancock, J. (2001). Finding deceptive opinion spam by any stretch of the imagination. In *Proceedings of the 49th Annual Meeting of the Association for Computational Linguistics: Human Language Technologies*, pages 309–319, Portland, Oregon, USA. Association for Computational Linguistics.

Raykar, V. C., Yu, S., Zhao, L. H., Valadez, G. H., Florin, C., Bogoni, L., and Moy, L. (2010). Learning from crowds. *Journal of Machine Learning Research*, 11:1297–1322.

Schmid, H. (1994). Probabilistic part-of-speech tagging using decision trees. In *Proceedings of International Conference on New Methods in Language Processing*.

Sigler, L., editor (2003). *Fibonacci's Liber Abaci: A Translation Into Modern English of Leonardo Pisano's Book of Calculation*. Sources and Studies in the History of Mathematics and Physical Sciences. Springer Verlag.

Strapparava, C. and Mihalcea, R. (2009). The Lie Detector: Explorations in the Automatic Recognition of Deceptive Language. In *Proceeding ACLShort '09 - Proceedings of the ACL-IJCNLP 2009 Conference Short Papers*.

Yang, Y. and Liu, X. (1999). A re-examination of text categorization methods. In *Proceedings of the 22nd annual international ACM SIGIR conference on Research and development in information retrieval*, SIGIR '99, pages 42–49, New York, NY, USA. ACM.

Yang, Y. and Pedersen, J. O. (1997). A comparative study on feature selection in text categorization. *CiteSeerX - Scientific Literature Digital Library and Search Engine [http://citeseerx.ist.psu.edu/oai2] (United States)*.

Assessing the relative reading level of sentence pairs for text simplification

Sowmya Vajjala and Detmar Meurers
LEAD Graduate School, Seminar für Sprachwissenschaft
Universität Tübingen
{sowmya,dm}@sfs.uni-tuebingen.de

Abstract

While the automatic analysis of the readability of texts has a long history, the use of readability assessment for text simplification has received only little attention so far. In this paper, we explore readability models for identifying differences in the reading levels of simplified and unsimplified versions of sentences.

Our experiments show that a relative ranking is preferable to an absolute binary one and that the accuracy of identifying relative simplification depends on the initial reading level of the unsimplified version. The approach is particularly successful in classifying the relative reading level of harder sentences.

In terms of practical relevance, the approach promises to be useful for identifying particularly relevant targets for simplification and to evaluate simplifications given specific readability constraints.

1 Introduction

Text simplification essentially is the process of rewriting a given text to make it easier to process for a given audience. The target audience can either be human users trying to understand a text or machine applications, such as a parser analyzing text. Text simplification has been used in a variety of application scenarios, from providing simplified newspaper texts for aphasic readers (Canning and Tait, 1999) to supporting the extraction of protein-protein interactions in the biomedical domain (Jonnalagadda and Gonzalez, 2009).

A related field of research is automatic readability assessment, which can be useful for evaluating text simplification. It can also be relevant for intermediate simplification steps, such as the identification of target sentences for simplification. Yet, so far there has only been little research connecting the two subfields, possibly because readability research typically analyzes documents, whereas simplification approaches generally targeted lexical and syntactic aspects at the sentence level. In this paper, we attempt to bridge this gap between readability and simplification by studying readability at a sentence level and exploring how well can a readability model identify the differences between unsimplified and simplified sentences.

Our main research questions in this paper are: 1. Can the readability features that worked at the document level successfully be used at the sentence level? 2. How accurately can we identify the differences in the sentential reading level before and after simplification? To pursue these questions, we started with constructing a document-level readability model. We then applied it to normal and simplified versions of sentences drawn from Wikipedia and Simple Wikipedia.

As context of our work, we first discuss relevant related research. Section 2 then describes the corpora and the features we used to construct our readability model. Section 3 discusses the performance of our readability model in comparison with other existing systems. Sections 4 and 5 present our experiments with sentence level readability analysis and the results. In Section 6 we present our conclusions and plans for future work.

1.1 Related Work

Research into automatic text simplification essentially started with the idea of splitting long sentences into multiple shorter sentences to improve parsing efficiency (Chandrasekar et al., 1996; Chandrasekar and Srinivas, 1996). This was followed by rule-based approaches targeting human and machine uses (Carroll et al., 1999; Siddharthan, 2002, 2004).

With the availability of a sentence-aligned corpus based on Wikipedia and SimpleWikipedia texts, data-driven approaches, partly inspired by statistical machine translation, appeared (Specia, 2010; Zhu et al., 2010; Bach et al., 2011; Coster and Kauchak, 2011; Woodsend and Lapata, 2011).

While simplification methods have evolved, understanding which parts of a text need to be simplified and methods for evaluating the simplified text so far received only little attention. The use of readability assessment for simplification has mostly been restricted to using traditional readability formulae for evaluating or generating simplified text (Zhu et al., 2010; Wubben et al., 2012; Klerke and Søgaard, 2013; Stymne et al., 2013). Some recent work briefly addresses issues such as classifying sentences by their reading level (Napoles and Dredze, 2010) and identifying sentential transformations needed for text simplification using text complexity features (Medero and Ostendorf, 2011). Some simplification approaches for non-English languages (Aluisio et al., 2010; Gasperin et al., 2009; Štajner et al., 2013) also touch on the use of readability assessment.

In the present paper, we focus on the neglected connection between readability analysis and simplification. We show through a cross-corpus evaluation that a document level, regression-based readability model successfully identifies the differences between simplified vs. unsimplified sentences. This approach can be useful in various stages of simplification ranging from identifying simplification targets to the evaluation of simplification outcomes.

2 Corpora and Features

2.1 Corpora

We built and tested our document and sentence level readability models using three publicly available text corpora with reading level annotations.

WeeBit Corpus: The WeeBit corpus (Vajjala and Meurers, 2012) consists of 3,125 articles belonging to five reading levels, with 625 articles per reading level. The texts compiled from the WeeklyReader and BBC Bitesize target English language learners from 7 to 16 years of age. We used this corpus to build our primary readability model by mapping the five reading levels in the corpus to a scale of 1–5 and considered readability assessment as a regression problem.

Common Core Standards Corpus: This corpus consists of 168 English texts available from the Appendix B of the Common Core Standards reading initiative of the U.S. education system (CCSSO, 2010). They are annotated by experts with grade bands that cover the grades 1 to 12. These texts serve as exemplars for the level of reading ability at a given grade level. This corpus was introduced as an evaluation corpus for readability models in the recent past (Sheehan et al., 2010; Nelson et al., 2012; Flor et al., 2013), so we used it to compare our model with other systems.

Wiki-SimpleWiki Sentence Aligned Corpus: This corpus was created by Zhu et al. (2010) and consists of ~100k aligned sentence pairs drawn from Wikipedia and Simple English Wikipedia. We removed all pairs of identical sentences, i.e., where the Wiki and the SimpleWiki versions are the same. We used this corpus to study reading level assessment at the sentence level.

2.2 Features

We started with the feature set described in Vajjala and Meurers (2012) and added new features focusing on the morphological and psycholinguistic properties of words. The features can be broadly classified into four groups.

Lexical richness and POS features: We adapted the lexical features from Vajjala and Meurers (2012). This includes measures of lexical richness from Second Language Acquisition (SLA) research and measures of lexical variation (noun, verb, adjective, adverb and modifier variation). In addition, this feature set also includes part-of-speech densities (e.g., the average # of nouns per sentence). The information needed to calculate these features was extracted using the Stanford Tagger (Toutanova et al., 2003). None of the lexical richness and POS features we used refer to specific words or lemmas.

Syntactic Complexity features: Parse tree based features and some syntactic complexity measures derived from SLA research proved useful for readability classification in the past, so we made use of all the syntactic features from Vajjala and Meurers (2012): mean lengths of various production units (sentence, clause, t-unit), measures of coordination and subordination (e.g., # of coordinate clauses per clause), the presence of particular syntactic structures (e.g., VPs per t-unit), the number of phrases of various categories (e.g., NP, VP, PP), the average lengths of phrases, the parse tree height, and the number of constituents per subtree. None of the syntactic features refer to specific words or lemmas. We used the BerkeleyParser (Petrov and Klein, 2007) for generating the parse trees and the Tregex tool (Levy and Andrew, 2006) to count the occurrences of the syntactic patterns.

While the first two feature sets are based on our previous work, as far as we know the next two are used in readability assessment for the first time.

Features from the Celex Lexical Database: The Celex Lexical Database (Baayen et al., 1995) is a database consisting of information about morphological, syntactic, orthographic and phonological properties of words along with word frequencies in various corpora. Celex for English contains this information for more than 50,000 lemmas. An overview of the fields in the Celex database is provided online[1] and the Celex user manual[2].

We used the morphological and syntactic properties of lemmas as features. We excluded word frequency statistics and properties which consisted of word strings. In all, we used 35 morphological and 49 syntactic properties that were expressed using either character or numeric codes in this database as features for our task.

The morphological properties in Celex include information about the derivational, inflectional and compositional features of the words, their morphological origins and complexity. The syntactic properties of the words in Celex describe the attributes of a word depending on its parts of speech. For the morphological and syntactic properties from this database, we used the proportion of occurrences per text as features. For example, the ratio of transitive verbs, complex morphological words, and vocative nouns to number of words. Lemmas from the text that do not have entries in the Celex database were ignored.

Word frequency statistics from Celex have been used before to analyze text difficulty in the past (Crossley et al., 2007). However, to our knowledge, this is the first time morphological and syntactic information from the Celex database is used for readability assessment.

Psycholinguistic features: The MRC Psycholinguistic Database (Wilson, 1988) is a freely available, machine readable dictionary annotated with 26 linguistic and psychological attributes of about 1.5 million words.[3] We used the measures of word familiarity, concreteness, imageability, meaningfulness, and age of acquisition from this database as our features, by encoding their average values per text.

Kuperman et al. (2012) compiled a freely available database that includes Age of Acquisition (AoA) ratings for over 50,000 English words.[4] This database was created through crowd sourcing and was compared with several other AoA norms, which are also included in the database. For each of the five AoA norms, we computed the average AoA of words per text.

Turning to the final resource used, we included the average number of senses per word as calculated using the MIT Java WordNet Interface as a feature.[5] We excluded auxiliary verbs for this calculation as they tend to have multiple senses that do not necessarily contribute to reading difficulty.

Combining the four feature groups, we encode 151 features for each text.

3 Document-Level Readability Model

In our first experiment, we tested the document-level readability model based on the 151 features using the WeeBit corpus. Under a regression perspective on readability, we evaluated the approach using Pearson Correlation and Root Mean Square Error (RMSE) in a 10-fold cross-validation setting. We used the SMO Regression implementation from WEKA (Hall et al., 2009) and achieved a Pearson correlation of 0.92 and an RMSE of 0.53.

The document-level performance of our 151 feature model is virtually identical to that of the regression model we presented in Vajjala and Meurers (2013). But compared to our previous work, the Celex and psycholinguistic features we included here provide more lexical information that is meaningful to compute even for the sentence-level analysis we turn to in the next section.

To be able to compare our document-level results with other contemporary readability approaches, we need a common test corpus. Nelson et al. (2012) compared several state of the art readability assessment systems using five test sets and showed that the systems that went beyond traditional formulae and wordlists performed better

[1]http://celex.mpi.nl/help/elemmas.html

[2]http://catalog.ldc.upenn.edu/docs/LDC96L14

[3]http://www.psych.rl.ac.uk

[4]http://crr.ugent.be/archives/806

[5]http://projects.csail.mit.edu/jwi

on these real-life test sets. We tested our model on one of the publicly accessible test corpora from this study, the Common Core Standards Corpus. Flor et al. (2013) used the same test set to study a measure of lexical tightness, providing a further performance reference.

Table 1 compares the performance of our model to that reported for several commercial (indicated in italics) and research systems on this test set. Nelson et al. (2012) used Spearman's Rank Correlation and Flor et al. (2013) used Pearson Correlation as evaluation metrics. To facilitate comparison, for our approach we provide both measures.

System	Spearman	Pearson
Our System	**0.69**	**0.61**
Nelson et al. (2012):		
REAP[6]	0.54	–
ATOS[7]	0.59	–
DRP[8]	0.53	–
Lexile[9]	0.50	–
Reading Maturity[10]	**0.69**	–
SourceRater[11]	**0.75**	–
Flor et al. (2013):		
Lexical Tightness	–	-0.44
Flesch-Kincaid	–	0.49
Text length	–	0.36

Table 1: Performance on CommonCore data

As the table shows, our model is the best non-commercial system and overall second (tied with the Reading Maturity system) to SourceRater as the best performing commercial system on this test set. These results on an independent test set confirm the validity of our document-level readability model. With this baseline, we turned to a sentence-level readability analysis.

4 Sentence-Level Binary Classification

For each of the pairs in the Wiki-SimpleWiki Sentence Aligned Corpus introduced above, we labeled the sentence from Wikipedia as *hard* and that from Simple English Wikipedia as *simple*. The corpus thus consisted of single sentences, each labeled either *simple* or *hard*. On this basis, we constructed a binary classification model.

[6]http://reap.cs.cmu.edu

[7]http://renlearn.com/atos

[8]http://questarai.com/Products/DRPProgram

[9]http://lexile.com

[10]http://readingmaturity.com

[11]http://naeptba.ets.org/SourceRater3

Our document-level readability model does not include discourse features, so all 151 features can also be computed for individual sentences. We built a binary sentence-level classification model using WEKA's Sequential Minimal Optimization (SMO) for training an SVM in WEKA on the Wiki-SimpleWiki sentence aligned corpus. The choice of algorithm was primarily motivated by the fact that it was shown to be efficient in previous work on readability classification (Feng, 2010; Hancke et al., 2012; Falkenjack et al., 2013).

The accuracy of the resulting classifier determining whether a given sentence is *simple* or *hard* was disappointing, reaching only 66% accuracy in a 10-fold cross-validation setting. Experiments with different classification algorithms did not yield any more promising results. To study how the classification performance is impacted by the size of the training data, we experimented with different sizes, using SMO as the classification algorithm. Figure 1 shows the classification accuracy with different training set sizes.

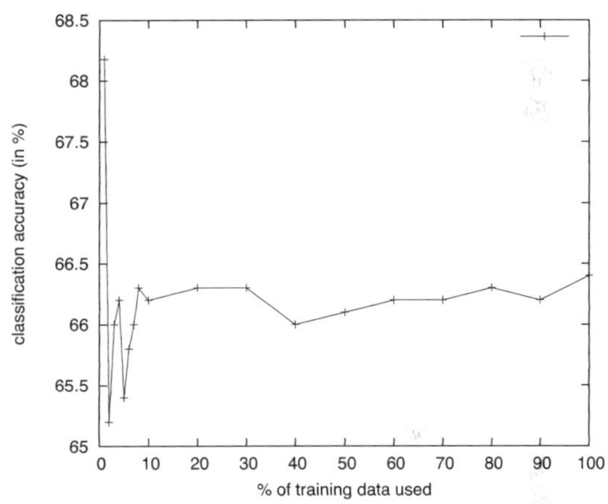

Figure 1: Training size vs. classification accuracy

The graph shows that beyond 10% of the training data, more training data did not result in significant differences in classification accuracy. Even at 10%, the training set contains around 10k instances per category, so the variability of any of the patterns distinguished by our features is sufficiently represented.

We also explored whether feature selection could be useful. A subset of features chosen by removing correlated features using the CfsSubsetEval method in WEKA did not improve the results, yielding an accuracy of 65.8%. A simple baseline based on the sentence length as single feature results in an accuracy of 60.5%, underscoring the limited value of the rich feature set in this binary classification setup.

For the sake of a direct comparison with the document-level model, we also explored modeling the task as a regression on a 1–2 scale. In comparison to the document-level model, which as discussed in section 3 had a correlation of 0.92, the sentence-level model achieves only a correlation of 0.4. A direct comparison is also possible when we train the document-level model as a five-class classifier with SMO. This model achieved a classification accuracy of ~90% on the documents, compared to the 66% accuracy of the sentence-level model classifying sentences. So under each of these perspectives, the sentence-level models on the sentence task are much less successful than the document-level models on the document task.

But does this indicate that it is not possible to accurately identify the reading level distinctions between simplified and unsimplified versions at the sentence level? Is there not enough information available when considering a single sentence?

We hypothesized that the drop in the classification accuracy instead results from the relative nature of simplification. For each pair of the Wiki-SimpleWiki sentence aligned corpus we used, the Wiki sentence was harder than the SimpleWikipedia sentence. But this does not necessarily mean that each of the Wikipedia sentences is harder than each of the SimpleWikipedia sentences. The low accuracy of the binary classifier may thus simply result from the inappropriate assumption of an absolute, binary classification viewing each of the sentences originating from SimpleWikipedia as simple and each from the regular Wiki as hard.

The confusion matrices of the binary classification suggests some support for this hypothesis, as more *simple* sentences were classified as *hard* compared to the other way around. This can result when a *simple* sentence is simpler than its *hard* version, but could actually be simplified further – and as such may still be harder than another unsimplified sentence. The hypothesis thus amounts to saying that the two-class classification model mistakenly turned the relative difference between the sentence pairs into a global classification of individual sentences, independent of the pairs they occur in.

How can we verify this hypothesis? The sentence corpus only provides the relative ranking of the pairs, but we can try to identify more fine-grained readability levels for sentences by applying the five class readability model for documents that was introduced in section 3.

5 Relative Reading Levels of Sentences

We applied the document-level readability model to the individual sentences from the Wiki-SimpleWiki corpus to study which reading levels are identified by our model. As we are using a regression model, the values sometimes go beyond the training corpus' scale of 1–5. For ease of comparison, we rounded off the reading levels to the five level scale, i.e., 1 means 1 or below, and 5 means 5 or above. Figure 2 shows the distribution of Wikipedia and SimpleWikipedia sentences according to the predictions of our document-level readability model trained on the WeeBit corpus.

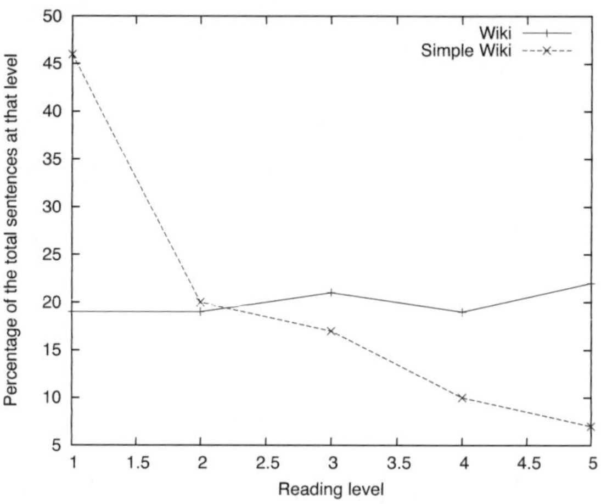

Figure 2: Reading level distribution of the Wikipedia and SimpleWikipedia sentences

The model determines that a high percentage of the SimpleWiki sentences belong to lower reading levels, with over 45% at the lowest reading level; yet there also are some SimpleWikipedia sentences which are aligned even to the highest readability level. In contrast, the regular Wikipedia sentences are evenly distributed across all reading levels.

The distributions identified by the model support our hypothesis that some Wiki sentences are simpler than some SimpleWikipedia sentences. Note that this is fully compatible with the fact that for each pair of (SimpleWiki,Wiki) sentences included in the corpus, the former is higher in reading level than the latter; e.g., just consider two sentence pairs with the levels $(1, 2)$ and $(3, 5)$.

5.1 On the discriminating power of the model

Zooming in on the relative reading levels of the paired unsimplified and simplified sentences, we wanted to determine for how many sentence pairs the sentence reading levels determined by our model are compatible with the pair's ranking. In other words, we calculated the percentage of pairs (S, N) in which the reading level of a simplified sentence (S) is identified as less than, equal to, or greater than the unsimplified (normal) version of the sentence (N), i.e., $S < N$, $S = N$, and $S > N$. Where simplification split a sentence into multiple sentences, we computed S as the average reading level of the split sentences.

Given the regression model setup, we can consider how big the difference between two reading levels determined by the model should be in order for us to interpret it as a categorical difference in reading level. Let us call this discriminating reading-level difference the *d-level*. For example, with $d = 0.3$, a sentence pair determined to be at levels $(3.4, 3.2)$ would be considered a case of $S = N$, whereas $(3.4, 3.7)$ would be an instance of $S < N$. The d-value can be understood as a measure of how fine-grained the model is in identifying reading-level differences between sentences.

If we consider the percentage of samples identified as $S <= N$ as an accuracy measure, Figure 3 shows the accuracy for different d-values.

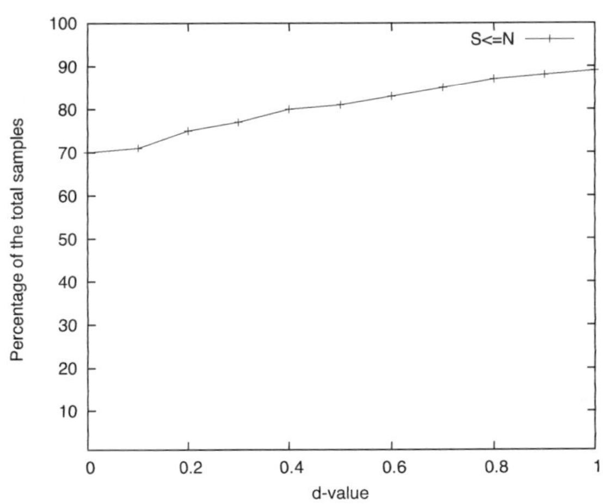

Figure 3: Accurately identified $S <= N$

We can observe that the percentage of instances that the model correctly identifies as $S <= N$ steadily increases from 70% to 90% as *d* increases. While the value of d in theory can be anything, values beyond 1 are uninteresting in the context of this study. At $d = 1$, most of the sentence pairs already belong to $S = N$, so increasing this further would defeat the purpose of identifying reading-level differences. The higher the d-value, the more of the simplified and unsimplified pairs are lumped together as indistinguishable.

Spelling out the different cases from Figure 3, the number of pairs identified correctly, equated, and misclassified as a function of the d-value is shown in Figure 4.

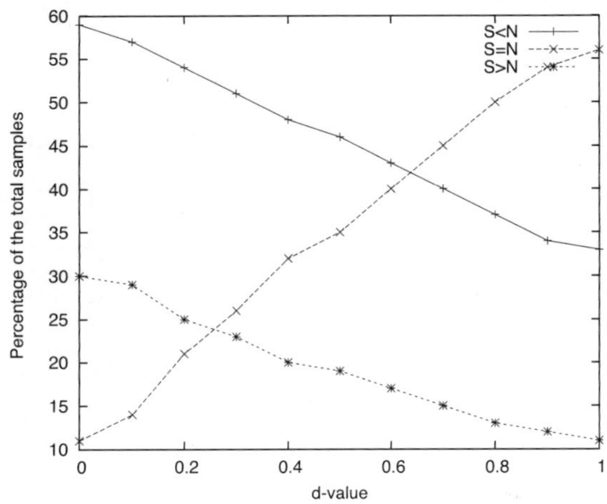

Figure 4: Correctly $(S < N)$, equated $(S = N)$, and incorrectly $(S > N)$ identified sentence pairs

At $d = 0.4$, around 50% of the pairs are correctly classified, 20% are misclassified, and 30% equated. At $d = 0.7$, the rate of pairs for which no distinction can be determined already rises above 50%. For d-values between 0.3 and 0.6, the percentage of correctly identified pairs exceeds the percentage of equated pairs, which in turn exceeds the percentage of misclassified pairs.

5.2 Influence of reading-level on accuracy

We saw in Figure 2 that the Wikipedia sentences are uniformly distributed across the reading levels, and for each of these sentences, a human simplified version is included in the corpus. Even sentences identified by our readability model as belonging to the lower reading levels thus were further simplified. This leads us to investigate whether the reading level of the unsimplified sentence influences the ability of our model to correctly identify the simplification relationship.

To investigate this, we separately analyzed pairs where the unsimplified sentences had a higher reading level and those where it had a lower reading level, taking the middle of the scale (2.5) as the cut-off point. Figure 5 shows the accuracies obtained when distinguishing unsimplified sentences of two readability levels.

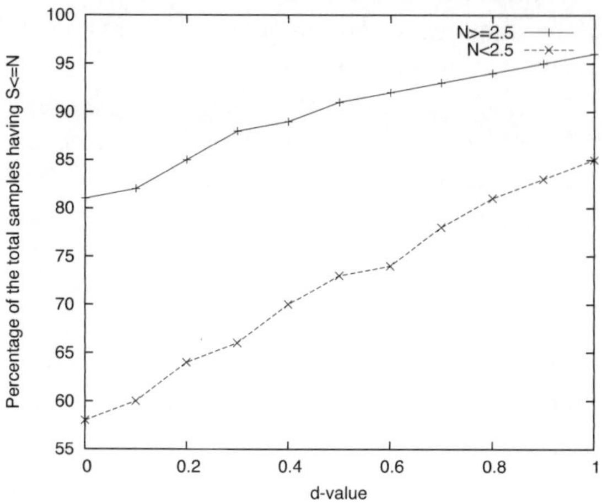

Figure 5: Accuracy ($S\!<=\!N$) for different N types

For the pairs where the reading level of the unsimplified version is high, the accuracy of the readability model is high (80–95%). In the other case, the accuracy drops to 65–75% (for $0.3 <= d <= 0.6$). Presumably the complex sentences for which the model performs best offer more syntactic and lexical material informing the features used.

When we split the graph into the three cases again ($S < N$, $S = N$, $S > N$), the pairs with a high-level unsimplified sentence in Figure 6 follow the overall picture of Figure 4.

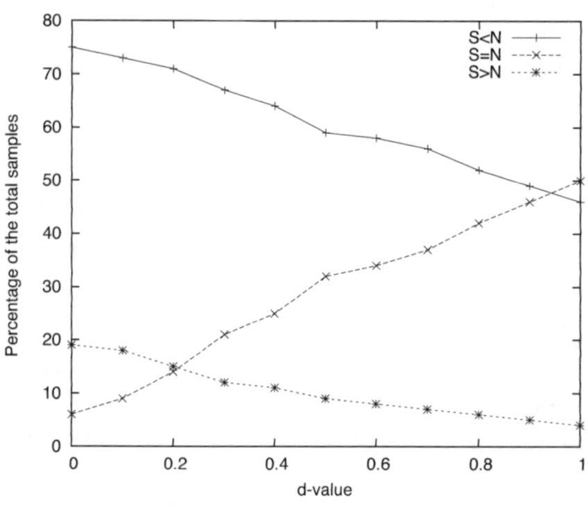

Figure 6: Results for $N\!>=\!2.5$

On the other hand, the results in Figure 7 for the pairs with an unsimplified sentence at a low readability level establish that the model essentially is incapable to identify readability differences.

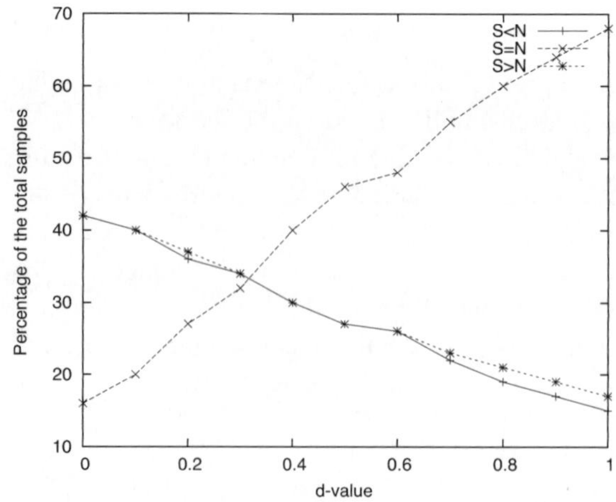

Figure 7: Results for $N\!<\!2.5$

The correctly identified $S < N$ and the incorrectly identified $S > N$ cases mostly overlap, indicating chance-level performance. Increasing the d-level only increases the number of equated pairs, without much impact on the number of correctly distinguished pairs.

In real-world terms, this means that it is difficult to identify simplifications of an already simple sentence. While some of this difficulty may stem from the fact that simple sentences are likely to be shorter and thus offer less linguistic material on which an analysis can be based, it also points to a need for more research on features that can reliably distinguish lower levels of readability.

Summing up, the experiments discussed in this section show that a document-level readability model trained on the WeeBit corpus can provide insightful perspectives on the nature of simplification at the sentence level. The results emphasize the relative nature of readability and the need for more features capable of identifying characteristics distinguishing sentences at lower levels.

6 Conclusions

We started with constructing a document-level readability model and compared its performance with other readability systems on a standard test set. Having established the state-of-the-art performance of our document-level model, we moved on to investigate the use of the features and the model at the sentence level.

In the sentence-level research, we first used the same feature set to construct a two-class readability model on the sentences from the Wikipedia-SimpleWikipedia sentence aligned corpus. The model only achieved a classification accuracy of 66%. Exploring the causes for this low performance, we studied the sentences in the aligned pairs through the lens of our document-level readability model, the regression model based on the five level data of the WeeBit corpus. Our experiment identifies most of the Simple Wikipedia sentences as belonging to the lower levels, with some sentences also showing up at higher levels. The sentences from the normal Wikipedia, on the other hand, display a uniform distribution across all reading levels. A simplified sentence (S) can thus be at a lower reading level than its paired unsimplified sentence (N) while also being at a higher reading level than another unsimplified sentence. Given this distribution of reading levels, the low performance of the binary classifier is expected. Instead of an absolute, binary difference in reading levels that counts each Wikipedia sentence from the corpus as hard and each Simple Wikipedia sentence as simple, a relative ranking of reading levels seems to better suit the data.

Inspecting the relative difference in the reading levels of the aligned unsimplified-simplified sentence pairs, we characterized the accuracy of predicting the relative reading level ranking in a pair correctly depending on the reading-level difference d required to required to identify a categorical difference. While the experiments were performed to verify the hypothesis that simplification is relative, they also confirm that the document-level readability model trained on the WeeBit corpus generalized well to Wikipedia-SimpleWikipedia as a different, sentence-level corpus.

The analysis revealed that the accuracy depends on the initial reading level of the unsimplified sentence. The model performs very well when the reading level of the unsimplified sentence is higher, but the features seem limited in their ability to pick up on the differences between sentences at the lowest levels. In future work, we thus intend to add more features identifying differences between lower levels of readability.

Taking the focus on the relative ranking of the readability of sentences one step further, we are currently studying if modeling the readability problem as preference learning or ordinal regression will improve the accuracy in predicting the relation between simplified and unsimplified sentence versions.

Overall, the paper contributes to the state of the art by providing a methodology to quantitatively evaluate the degree of simplification performed by an automatic system. The results can also be potentially useful in providing assistive feedback for human writers preparing simplified texts given specific target user constraints. We plan to explore the idea of generating simplified text with readability constraints as suggested in Stymne et al. (2013) for Machine Translation.

Acknowledgements

We thank the anonymous reviewers for their detailed comments. Our research was funded by the LEAD Graduate School (GSC 1028, `http://purl.org/lead`), a project of the Excellence Initiative of the German federal and state governments, and the European Commission's 7th Framework Program under grant agreement number 238405 (CLARA).

References

Sandra Aluisio, Lucia Specia, Caroline Gasperin, and Carolina Scarton. 2010. Readability assessment for text simplification. In *Proceedings of the NAACL HLT 2010 Fifth Workshop on Innovative Use of NLP for Building Educational Applications*, pages 1–9.

R. H. Baayen, R. Piepenbrock, and L. Gulikers. 1995. The CELEX lexical databases. CDROM, `http://www.ldc.upenn.edu/Catalog/readme_files/celex.readme.html`.

Nguyen Bach, Qin Gao, Stephan Vogel, and Alex Waibel. 2011. Tris: A statistical sentence simplifier with log-linear models and margin-based discriminative training. In *Proceedings of 5th International Joint Conference on Natural Language Processing*, pages 474–482. Asian Federation of Natural Language Processing.

Yvonne Canning and John Tait. 1999. Syntactic simplification of newspaper text for aphasic readers. In *Proceedings of SIGIR-99 Workshop on Customised Information Delivery*, pages 6–11.

John Carroll, Guido Minnen, Darren Pearce, Yvonne Canning, Siobhan Devlin, and John Tait. 1999. Simplifying text for language-impaired readers. In *Proceedings of the 9th Conference of the European Chapter of the Association for Computational Linguistics (EACL)*, pages 269–270.

CCSSO. 2010. Common core state standards for english language arts & literacy in history/social studies, science, and technical subjects. appendix B: Text exemplars and sample performance tasks. Technical report, National Governors Association Center for

Best Practices, Council of Chief State School Officers. http://www.corestandards.org/assets/Appendix_B.pdf.

R. Chandrasekar and B. Srinivas. 1996. Automatic induction of rules for text simplification. Technical Report IRCS Report 96–30, Upenn, NSF Science and Technology Center for Research in Cognitive Science.

R. Chandrasekar, Christine Doran, and B. Srinivas. 1996. Motivations and methods for text simplification. In *Proceedings of the 16th International Conference on Computational Linguistics (COLING)*, pages 1041–1044.

William Coster and David Kauchak. 2011. Simple english wikipedia: A new text simplification task. In *Proceedings of the 49th Annual Meeting of the Association for Computational Linguistics: Human Language Technologies*, pages 665–669, Portland, Oregon, USA, June. Association for Computational Linguistics.

Scott A. Crossley, David F. Dufty, Philip M. McCarthy, and Danielle S. McNamara. 2007. Toward a new readability: A mixed model approach. In Danielle S. McNamara and Greg Trafton, editors, *Proceedings of the 29th annual conference of the Cognitive Science Society*. Cognitive Science Society.

Johan Falkenjack, Katarina Heimann Mühlenbock, and Arne Jönsson. 2013. Features indicating readability in swedish text. In *Proceedings of the 19th Nordic Conference of Computational Linguistics (NODALIDA)*.

Lijun Feng. 2010. *Automatic Readability Assessment*. Ph.D. thesis, City University of New York (CUNY).

Michael Flor, Beata Beigman Klebanov, and Kathleen M. Sheehan. 2013. Lexical tightness and text complexity. In *Proceedings of the Second Workshop on Natural Language Processing for Improving Textual Accessibility*.

Caroline Gasperin, Lucia Specia, Tiago F. Pereira, and Sandra M. Aluisio. 2009. Learning when to simplify sentences for natural text simplification. In *Encontro Nacional de Inteligência Artificial (ENIA-2009)*.

Mark Hall, Eibe Frank, Geoffrey Holmes, Bernhard Pfahringer, Peter Reutemann, and Ian H. Witten. 2009. The weka data mining software: An update. In *The SIGKDD Explorations*, volume 11, pages 10–18.

Julia Hancke, Detmar Meurers, and Sowmya Vajjala. 2012. Readability classification for german using lexical, syntactic, and morphological features. In *Proceedings of the 24th International Conference on Computational Linguistics (COLING)*, pages 1063–1080, Mumbay, India.

Siddhartha Jonnalagadda and Graciela Gonzalez. 2009. Sentence simplification aids protein-protein interaction extraction. In *Proceedings of The 3rd International Symposium on Languages in Biology and Medicine, Jeju Island, South Korea, November 8-10, 2009*.

Sigrid Klerke and Anders Søgaard. 2013. Simple, readable sub-sentences. In *Proceedings of the ACL Student Research Workshop*.

Victor Kuperman, Hans Stadthagen-Gonzalez, and Marc Brysbaert. 2012. Age-of-acquisition ratings for 30,000 english words. *Behavior Research Methods*, 44(4):978–990.

Roger Levy and Galen Andrew. 2006. Tregex and tsurgeon: tools for querying and manipulating tree data structures. In *5th International Conference on Language Resources and Evaluation*, Genoa, Italy.

Julie Medero and Marie Ostendorf. 2011. Identifying targets for syntactic simplification. In *ISCA International Workshop on Speech and Language Technology in Education (SLaTE 2011)*.

Courtney Napoles and Mark Dredze. 2010. Learning simple wikipedia: a cogitation in ascertaining abecedarian language. In *Proceedings of the NAACL HLT 2010 Workshop on Computational Linguistics and Writing: Writing Processes and Authoring Aids*, CL&W '10, pages 42–50, Stroudsburg, PA, USA. Association for Computational Linguistics.

J. Nelson, C. Perfetti, D. Liben, and M. Liben. 2012. Measures of text difficulty: Testing their predictive value for grade levels and student performance. Technical report, The Council of Chief State School Officers.

Slav Petrov and Dan Klein. 2007. Improved inference for unlexicalized parsing. In *Human Language Technologies 2007: The Conference of the North American Chapter of the Association for Computational Linguistics; Proceedings of the Main Conference*, pages 404–411, Rochester, New York, April.

Kathleen M. Sheehan, Irene Kostin, Yoko Futagi, and Michael Flor. 2010. Generating automated text complexity classifications that are aligned with targeted text complexity standards. Technical Report RR-10-28, ETS, December.

Advaith Siddharthan. 2002. An architecture for a text simplification system. In *In Proceedings of the Language Engineering Conference 2002 (LEC 2002)*.

Advaith Siddharthan. 2004. Syntactic simplification and text cohesion. Technical Report UCAM-CL-TR-597, University of Cambridge Computer Laboratory.

Lucia Specia. 2010. Translating from complex to simplified sentences. In *Proceedings of the 9th international conference on Computational Processing of the Portuguese Language (PROPOR'10)*.

Sara Stymne, Jörg Tiedemann, Christian Hardmeier, and Joakim Nivre. 2013. Statistical machine translation with readability constraints. In *Proceedings of the 19th Nordic Conference of Computational Linguistics (NODALIDA 2013)*.

K. Toutanova, D. Klein, C. Manning, and Y. Singer. 2003. Feature-rich part-of-speech tagging with a cyclic dependency network. In *HLT-NAACL*, pages 252–259, Edmonton, Canada.

Sowmya Vajjala and Detmar Meurers. 2012. On improving the accuracy of readability classification using insights from second language acquisition. In *In Proceedings of the 7th Workshop on Innovative Use of NLP for Building Educational Applications*, pages 163—-173.

Sowmya Vajjala and Detmar Meurers. 2013. On the applicability of readability models to web texts. In *Proceedings of the Second Workshop on Predicting and Improving Text Readability for Target Reader Populations*.

M.D. Wilson. 1988. The MRC psycholinguistic database: Machine readable dictionary, version 2. *Behavioural Research Methods, Instruments and Computers*, 20(1):6–11.

Kristian Woodsend and Mirella Lapata. 2011. Learning to simplify sentences with quasi-synchronous grammar and integer programming. In *Proceedings of the Conference on Empirical Methods in Natural Language Processing (EMNLP)*.

Sander Wubben, Antal van den Bosch, and Emiel Krahmer. 2012. Sentence simplification by monolingual machine translation. In *Proceedings of ACL 2012*.

Zhemin Zhu, Delphine Bernhard, and Iryna Gurevych. 2010. A monolingual tree-based translation model for sentence simplification. In *Proceedings of The 23rd International Conference on Computational Linguistics (COLING), August 2010. Beijing, China*.

Sanja Štajner, Biljana Drndarevic, and Horaccio Saggion. 2013. Corpus-based sentence deletion and split decisions for spanish text simplification. In *CICLing 2013: The 14th International Conference on Intelligent Text Processing and Computational Linguistics*.

Subcategorisation Acquisition from Raw Text for a Free Word-Order Language

Will Roberts and **Markus Egg** and **Valia Kordoni**
Institute für Anglistik und Amerikanistik, Humboldt University
10099 Berlin, Germany
{will.roberts,markus.egg,evangelia.kordoni}@anglistik.hu-berlin.de

Abstract

We describe a state-of-the-art automatic system that can acquire subcategorisation frames from raw text for a free word-order language. We use it to construct a subcategorisation lexicon of German verbs from a large Web page corpus. With an automatic verb classification paradigm we evaluate our subcategorisation lexicon against a previous classification of German verbs; the lexicon produced by our system performs better than the best previous results.

1 Introduction

We introduce a state-of-the-art system for the acquisition of subcategorisation frames (SCFs) from large corpora, which can deal with languages with very free word order. The concrete language we treat is German; its word order variability is illustrated in (1)–(4), all of which express the sentence *The man gave the old dog a chop*:

(1) Dem alten Hund gab der Mann ein Schnitzel.

(2) Ein Schnitzel gab dem alten Hund der Mann.

(3) Ein Schnitzel gab der Mann dem alten Hund.

(4) Der Mann gab dem alten Hund ein Schnitzel.

On the basis of raw text, the system can be used to build extensive SCF lexicons for German verbs. Subcategorisation means that lexical items require specific obligatory concomitants or arguments; we focus on verb subcategorisation. E.g., the verb *geben* 'give' requires three arguments, the nominative subject *der Mann* 'the man', the dative indirect object *dem alten Hund* 'the old dog', and the accusative direct object *ein Schnitzel* 'a chop'. Other syntactic items may be subcategorised for, too, e.g. both *stellen* and its English translation *put* subcategorise for subject, direct object, and a prepositional phrase (PP) like *on the shelf*:

(5) *[$_{NP}$ Al] put [$_{NP}$ the book] [$_{PP}$ on the shelf].*

Subcategorisation frames describe a combination of arguments required by a specific verb. The set of SCFs for a verb is called its *subcategorisation preference*. Our system follows much previous work by counting PPs that accompany the verb among its complements, even though they are not obligatory (so-called 'adjuncts'), because PP adjuncts are excellent clues to a verb's semantics (Sun et al., 2008). However, nominal and clausal adjuncts do not count as verbal complements.

SCF information can benefit all applications that need information on predicate-argument structure, e.g., parsing, verb clustering, semantic role labelling, or machine translation. Automatic acquisition of SCF information with minimal supervision is also crucial to construct useful resources quickly.

The main innovation of the presented new system is to address two challenges simultaneously, viz., SCF acquisition from *raw text* and the focus on languages with a *very free word order*. With this system, we create an SCF lexicon for German verbs and evaluate this lexicon against a previously published manual verb classification, showing better performance than has been reported until now.

After an overview of previous work on SCF acquisition in Section 2, Section 3 describes our subcategorisation acquisition system, and Section 4 the SCF lexicon that we build using it. In Sections 5 and 6 we evaluate the SCF lexicon on a verb classification task and discuss our results; Section 7 then concludes with directions for future work.

2 Previous work

To date, research on SCF acquisition from corpora has mostly targeted English. Brent and Berwick (1991) detect five SCFs by looking for attested contexts where argument slots are filled by closed-class lexical items (pronouns or proper names). Briscoe and Carroll (1997) detect 163 SCFs with a system that builds an SCF lexicon whose entries include the relative frequency of SCF classes. Potential SCF patterns are extracted from a corpus parsed with a dependency-based parser, and then filtered by hypothesis testing on binomial frequency data. Korhonen (2002) refines Briscoe and Carroll (1997)'s system using back-off estimates on the WordNet semantic class of the verb's predominant sense, assuming that semantically similar verbs have similar SCFs, following Levin (1993). Some current statistical methods for Semantic Role Labelling build models that also capture subcategorisation information, e.g., Grenager and Manning (2006). Schulte im Walde (2009) offers a recent survey of the SCF acquisition literature.

SCF acquisition is also an important step in the automatic semantic role labelling (Grenager and Manning, 2006; Lang and Lapata, 2010; Titov and Klementiev, 2012). Semantic roles of a verb describe the kind of involvement of entities in the event introduced by the verb, e.g., as agent (active, often not affected by the event) or patient (passive, often affected). On the basis of these SCFs, semantic roles can be assigned due to the interdependence between semantic roles and their syntactic realisations, called *Argument Linking* (Levin, 1993; Levin and Rappaport Hovav, 2005).

Acquiring SCFs for languages with a very fixed word order like English needs only a simple syntactic analysis, which mainly relies on the predetermined sequencing of arguments in the sentence, e.g., Grenager and Manning (2006). When word order is freer, the analysis gets more complicated, and must include a full syntactic parse.

What is more, German is a counterexample to Manning's (1993) expectation that freedom of word order should be matched by an increase in case and/or agreement marking. This is due to a very high degree of syncretism (identity of word forms) in German paradigms for nouns, adjectives, and determiners. E.g., the noun *Auto* 'car' has only two forms, *Auto* for nominative, dative, and accusative singular, and *Autos* for genitive singular and all four plural forms. This is in contrast to some other free word order languages for which SCF acquisition has been studied, like Modern Greek (Maragoudakis et al., 2000) and Czech (Sarkar and Zeman, 2000). A one-many relation between word forms and case is also one of the problems for SCF acquisition in Urdu (Ghulam, 2011).

For German, initial studies used semi-automatic techniques and manual evaluation (Eckle-Kohler, 1999; Wauschkuhn, 1999). The first automatic subcategorisation acquisition system for German is described by Schulte im Walde (2002a), who defined an SCF inventory and manually wrote a grammar to analyse verb constructions according to these frames. A lexicalised PCFG parser using this grammar was trained on 18.7 million words of German newspaper text; the trained parser model contained explicit subcategorisation frequencies, which could then be extracted to construct a subcategorisation lexicon for 14,229 German verbs. This work was evaluated against a German dictionary, the *Duden Stilwörterbuch* (Schulte im Walde, 2002b).

Schulte im Walde and Brew (2002) used the subcategorisation lexicon created by the system to automatically induce a set of semantic verb classes with an unsupervised clustering algorithm. This clustering was evaluated against a small manually created semantic verb classification. Schulte im Walde (2006) continues this work using a larger manual verb classification. The SCFs used in this study are defined at three levels of granularity. The first level (38 different SCFs) lists only the complements in the frame; the second one adds head and case information for PP complements (183 SCFs). The third level examined the effect of adding selectional preferences, but results were inconclusive.

A recent paper (Scheible et al., 2013) describes a system similar to ours, built on a statistical dependency parser, and using some of the same kinds of rules as we describe in Section 3.1; this system is evaluated in a task-based way (e.g., to improve the performance of a SMT system) and cannot be directly compared to our system in this paper.

3 The SCF acquisition system

This section describes the first contribution of this paper, a state-of-the-art subcategorisation acquisition system for German. Its core component is a rule-based SCF tagger which operates on phrase structure analyses, as delivered by a statistical parser. Given a parse of a sentence, the tagger assigns each finite verb in the sentence an SCF type.

We use the SCF inventory of Schulte im Walde (2002a), which includes complements like `n` for nominative subject, `a` for accusative direct object, `d` for dative indirect object, `r` for reflexive pronoun, and `x` for expletive *es* ('it') subject. Clausal complements can be infinite (`i`); finite ones can have the verb in second position (`S-2`) or include the complementiser *dass* 'that' (`S-dass`). Complements can be combined as in `na` (transitive verb); for PPs in SCFs, the head is specified, e.g., `p:für` for PP complements headed by *für* 'for'[1].

Due to the free word order, simple phrase structure like that used for analysis of English is not enough to specify the syntax of German sentences. Therefore we use the annotation scheme in the manually constructed German treebanks NEGRA and TIGER (Skut et al., 1997; Brants et al., 2002), which decorate parse trees with edge labels specifying the syntactic roles of constituents. We automatically annotate the parse trees from our statistical parser using a simple machine learning model.

In the next section, we illustrate the operation of the SCF tagger with reference to examples; then in Section 3.2 we describe our edge labeller.

3.1 The SCF tagger

The SCF tagger begins by collecting complements co-occurring with a verb instance using the phrase structure of the sentence. In our system, we obtain phrase structure information for unannotated text using the Berkeley Parser (Petrov et al., 2006), a statistical unlexicalised parser trained on TIGER. Fig. 1 illustrates the phrase structure analysis and edge labels in the TIGER corpus for (6):

(6) *Das hielte ich für moralisch außerordentlich fragwürdig.*
'I'd consider that morally extremely questionable'.

Its finite verb *hielte* (from *halten* 'hold') has three complements, the subject *ich* 'I', edge-labelled with `SB`, the direct object *das* 'that', labelled with `OA`, and a PP headed by *für* 'for' (`MO` stands for 'modifier'). After collecting complements, the SCF tagger uses this edge label information to determine the complements' syntactic roles, and assigns the verb the corresponding SCF; in the case of *halten* above, the SCF is `nap:für`.

[1]We digress from Schulte im Walde's original SCF inventory in that we do not indicate case information in PPs.

The rule-based SCF tagger handles auxiliary and modal verb constructions, passive alternations, separable verb prefixes, and raising and control constructions. E.g., the subject *sie* 'they' of *anfangen* 'begin' in (7) doubles as the subject of its infinite clausal complement; hence, it shows up in the SCF of the complement's head *geben* 'give', too:

(7) *Sie fingen an, mir Stromschläge zu geben.*
'They started to give me electric shocks.'

The tagger also handles involved cases with many complements, including PPs and clauses as in (8). As the SCF inventory allows at most three complements in an SCF, such cases call for prioritising of verbal complements (e.g., subjects, objects, and clausal complements are preferred over PP complements). Consequently, the main verb *empfehlen* 'recommend' in (8), which has a subject, a dative object, a PP, and an infinitival clausal complement, is assigned the SCF `ndi`. Another challenging task which relies on edge label information is filtering out clausal adjuncts (relative clauses and parentheticals) so as not to include them in SCFs.

(8) *[$_{PP}$ Am Freitag] empfahl [$_{NP:Nom}$ der Aufsichtsrat] [$_{NP:Dat}$ den Aktionären], [$_{S}$ das Angebot abzulehnen].*
'On Friday the board of directors advised shareholders to turn down the offer.'

The 17 rules of the SCF tagger are simple; most of them categorise the complements of a specific verb instance; e.g., if a nominal complement to the verb is edge-labelled as a nominative subject, add `n` to the verb's SCF, unless the verb is in the passive, in which case add `a` to the SCF.

Our system was optimised by progressively refining the SCF tagger's rules through manual error analysis on sentences from TIGER. The result is an automatic SCF tagger that is resilient to variations in sentence structure and is firmly based on linguistically motivated knowledge. As a test case for its linguistic soundness, we chose the perfect parses in the TIGER treebank and found that the tagger is very accurate in capturing subcategorisation information inherent in these data.

3.2 The edge labeller

To obtain edge label information for the parses delivered by the Berkeley Parser, we built a novel machine learning classifier to annotate parse trees

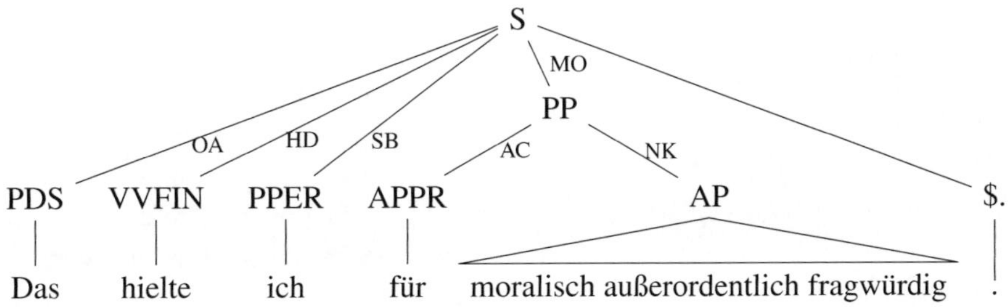

Figure 1: Edge labels in the TIGER corpus.

with TIGER edge label information. This edge labeller is a maximum entropy (multiclass logistic regression) model built using the Stanford Classifier package[2]. We include features such as:

- The part of speech of the complement;
- The first word of the complement;
- The lexical head of the complement;
- N-grams on the end of the lexical head of the complement;
- The kind of article of a complement;
- The presence or absence of specific article forms in other complements to the same verb;
- Position of the complement with respect to a reflexive pronoun in the sentence;
- The lemmatised form of the verb governing the complement (i.e., the verb on which the complement depends syntactically);
- The clause type of the governing verb; and,
- Active or passive voice of the governing verb.

We do no tuning and use the software's default hyperparameters (L2 regularisation with $\sigma = 3$).

This classifier was trained from edge label data extracted from the NEGRA and TIGER corpora; our training set contained 300,000 samples (approximately 25% from NEGRA and 75% from TIGER). On a held-out test set of 10% (containing 34,000 samples), the classifier achieves a final F-score of 95.5% on the edge labelling task.

The edge labeller makes the simplifying assumption that verbal complements can be labelled independently. Consequently, it tends to annotate multiple complements as subject for each verb. This has to do with the numerical dominance of subjects, which make up about 40% of all verb complements, more than three times the number of the next most common complement type (direct object).

Therefore we first collect all possible labels with associated probabilities that the edge labeller assigns to each complement of a verb. We then choose the set of labels with the highest probability that includes at most one subject and at most one accusative direct object for the verb, assuming that the joint probability of a set of labels is the product of the individual label probabilities.

We use our edge labeller in this work for morphological disambiguation of nominals and for identifying clausal adjuncts, but the edge labeller is a standalone reusable component, which might be equally well be used to mark up parse trees for, e.g., a semantic role labelling system.

4 The subcategorisation lexicon

With the system described in Sec. 3, we build a German subcategorisation lexicon that collects counts of ⟨lemma, SCF⟩ on deWaC (Baroni et al., 2009), a corpus of text extracted from Web search results, with 10^9 words automatically POS-tagged and lemmatised by the TreeTagger (Schmid, 1994). A subset of this corpus, SdeWaC (Faaß and Eckart, 2013), has been preprocessed to include only sentences which are maximally parsable; this smaller corpus includes 880 million words in 45 million sentences. We parsed 3 million sentences (80 million words) of SdeWaC; after filtering out those verb lemmas seen only five times or fewer in the corpus, we are left with statistics on 8 million verb instances, representing 9,825 verb lemmas.

As a concrete example for the resulting SCF lexicon, consider the entry for *sprechen* 'talk' in Fig. 2, which occurs 16,254 times in our SCF lexicon.

Sprechen refers to a conversation with speaker, hearer, topic, message, and code: Speakers are expressed by nominative NPs, hearers, by *mit-*, *bei-* or *zu*-PPs, topics, by *von-* and *über*-PPs. The code is expressed in *in*-PPs, and the message, by accusative NPs (*einige Worte sprechen* 'to say a few words'), main-clause complements or subordinate *dass* ('that') sentences. Other uses of the verb are

[2] `http://nlp.stanford.edu/software/classifier.shtml`

`np:von` (2715), `n` (2696), `na` (1380), `np:mit` (1247), `np:in` (1132), `nS-2` (1064), `np:über` (853), `np:für` (695), `nS-dass` (491), `np:zu` (307), `nap:in` (280), `nap:von` (275), `ni` (261), `np:bei` (212), `np:gegen` (192), `np:an` (186), `naS-2` (172), `np:aus` (168), `np:auf` (112), `nap:über` (112)

Figure 2: SCF lexicon for *sprechen*

figurative , e.g., *sprechen gegen* 'be a counterargument to'. As the distinction between arguments and adjuncts is gradual in our system, some adjunct patterns appear in the lexicon, too, but only with low frequency, e.g., `np:auf`, in which the *auf*-PP expresses the setting of the conversation, as in *auf der Tagung sprechen* 'speak at the convention'.

For reference, we also constructed an SCF lexicon from the NEGRA and TIGER corpora, which together comprise about 1.2 million words. This SCF lexicon contains statistics on 133,897 verb instances (5,316 verb lemmas). While the manual annotations in NEGRA and TIGER mean that this SCF lexicon has virtually no noise, the small size of the corpora results in problems with data sparsity and negatively impacts the utility of this resource (see discussion in Section 6.2).

5 Automatic verb classification

The remainder of the paper sets out to establish the relevance of our SCF acquisition system by comparison to previous work. As stated in Sec. 2, the only prior automatic German SCF acquisition system is that of Schulte im Walde (2002a), which was evaluated directly against an electronic version of a large dictionary; as this is not an open access resource, we cannot perform a similar evaluation.

We opt therefore to use a task-based evaluation to compare our system directly with Schulte im Walde's, and leave manual evaluation for future work. We refer back to the experiment set up by Schulte im Walde (2006) to automatically induce classifications of German verbs by clustering them on the basis of their SCF preferences as listed in her SCF lexicon. By casting this experiment as a fixed task, we can compare our system directly to hers. The link between subcategorisation and verb semantics is linguistically sound, due to the interdependence between verb meanings and the number and kinds of their syntactic arguments (Levin, 1993; Levin and Rappaport Hovav, 2005). E.g., only transitive verbs that denote a change of state like *cut* and *break* enter in the middle construction (*The bread cuts easily.*), with the patient or theme argument appearing as the syntactic subject. Thus, verbs whose SCF preferences show such an alternation can be predicted to denote a change of state.

We adopt the automatic verb classification paradigm to evaluate our system, replicating Schulte im Walde's (2006) experiment to the best of our ability. We argue that by evaluating our SdeWaC SCF lexicon described in the previous section, we simultaneously evaluate our subcategorisation acquisition system; this technique also allows us to demonstrate the semantic relevance of our SCF lexicon. Section 5.1 introduces the manual verb classification we use as a gold standard and Section 5.2 describes our unsupervised clustering technique. Our evaluation of the clustering against the gold standard then follows in Section 6.

5.1 Manual verb classifications

The semantic verb classification proposed by Schulte im Walde (2006, page 162ff.), hereafter SiW2006, comprises 168 high- and low-frequency verbs grouped into 43 semantic classes, with between 2 and 7 verbs per class. Examples of these classes are Aspect (e.g., *anfangen* 'begin'), Propositional Attitude (e.g., *denken* 'think'), Transfer of Possession (Obtaining) (e.g., *bekommen* 'get'), and Weather (e.g., *regnen* 'rain'). Some of the classes are subclassified[3], e.g., Manner of Motion, with the subclasses Locomotion (*klettern* 'climb'), Rotation (*rotieren* 'rotate'), Rush (*eilen* 'hurry'), Vehicle (*fliegen* 'fly'), and Flotation (*gleiten* 'glide').

These classes are related to Levin classes in that some are roughly equivalent to a Levin class (e.g., Aspect and Levin's Begin class), others are subgroups of Levin classes, e.g., Position is a subgroup of Levin's Dangle class; finally, some classes lump together Levin classes, e.g., Transfer of Possession (Obtaining) combines Levin's Get and Obtain classes. This shows that these classes could be integrated into a large-scale classification of German verbs in the style of Levin (1993).

5.2 Clustering

From the counts of ⟨lemma, SCF⟩ in the SCF lexicon, we can estimate the conditional probability that a particular verb v appears with an SCF f:

[3]For the purpose of our evaluation, we disregard class-subclass relations and consider subclasses as separate entities.

$P(\text{scf} = f|\text{lemma} = v)$. We smooth these conditional probability distributions by backing off to the prior probability $P(\text{scf})$ (Katz, 1987).

With these smoothed conditional probabilities, we cluster verbs with k-means clustering (Forgy, 1965), a hard clustering technique, which partitions a set of objects into k clusters. The algorithm is initialised with a starting set of k cluster centroids; it then proceeds iteratively, first assigning each object to the cluster whose centroid is closest under some distance measure, and then calculating new centroids to represent the centres of the updated clusters. The algorithm terminates when the assignment of objects to clusters no longer changes.

$$D(p\|q) = \sum_i p_i \log \frac{p_i}{q_i} \quad (9)$$

$$\text{irad}(p, q) = D(p\|\frac{p+q}{2}) + D(q\|\frac{p+q}{2}) \quad (10)$$

$$\text{skew}(p, q) = D(p\|\alpha q + (1-\alpha)p) \quad (11)$$

In our experiments, verbs are represented by their conditional probability distributions over SCFs. As distance measures, we use two variants of the Kullback-Leibler divergence (9), a measure of the dissimilarity of two probability distributions. The KL divergence from p to q is undefined if at some point q but not p is zero, so we use measures based on KL without this problem, viz., the *information radius* (aka Jensen-Shannon divergence, a symmetric metric, (10)), as well as *skew divergence* (an asymmetric dissimilarity measure which smoothes q by interpolating it to a small degree with p, (11)), where we set the interpolation parameter to be $\alpha = 0.9$, to make our results comparable to Schulte im Walde's (2006)[4].

As mentioned, the k-means algorithm is initialised with a set of cluster centroids; in this study, we initialise the centroids by random partitions (each of the n objects is randomly assigned to one of k clusters, and the centroids are then computed as the means of these random partitions). Because the random initial centroids influence the final clustering, we repeat the clustering a number of times.

We also initialise the k-means cluster centroids using agglomerative hierarchical clustering, a deterministic iterative bottom-up process. Hierarchical clustering initially assigns verbs to singleton clusters; the two clusters which are "nearest" to each other are then joined together, and this process is repeated until the desired number of clusters is obtained. Hierarchical clustering is performed to group the verbs into k clusters; the centroids of these clusters are then used to initialise the k-means algorithm. While there exist several variants of hierarchical clustering, we use Ward's method (Ward, Jr, 1963) for merging clusters, which attempts to minimise the variance inside clusters; Ward's criterion was previously found to be the most effective hierarchical clustering technique for verb classification (Schulte im Walde, 2006).

[4] Schulte im Walde (2006) takes $\alpha = 0.9$ although Lee (1999) recommends $\alpha = 0.99$ or higher values in her original description of skew divergence.

6 Evaluation

This section presents the results of evaluating the unsupervised verb clustering based on our SCF lexica against the gold standard described in Sec. 5.1.

6.1 Results

We use two cluster purity measures, defined in Fig. 3; we intentionally target our numerical evaluations to be directly comparable with previous results in the literature. As k-means is a hard clustering algorithm, we consider a clustering $\mathcal{C}$ to be an equivalence relation that partitions n verbs into k disjoint subsets $\mathcal{C} = \{C_1, \ldots, C_k\}$.

The first of these purity measures, *adjusted Rand index* (Rand_a in Eq. (12)) judges clustering similarity using the notion of the overlap between a cluster C_i in a given clustering $\mathcal{C}$ and a cluster G_j in a gold standard clustering $\mathcal{G}$, this value being denoted by $\mathcal{CG}_{ij} = |C_i \cap G_j|$; values of Rand_a range between 0 for chance and 1 for perfect correlation. The other metric, the *pairwise F-score* (PairF, Eq. (13)), operates by constructing a contingency table on the $\binom{n}{2}$ pairs of verbs, the idea being that the gold standard provides binary judgements about whether two verbs should be clustered together or not. If a clustering agrees with the gold standard in clustering a pair of verbs together or separately, this is a "correct" answer; by extension, information retrieval measures such as precision (P) and recall (R) can be computed.

Table 1 shows the performance of our SCF lexica, evaluated against the SiW2006 gold standard. The random baseline is given by PairF $= 2.08$ and $\text{Rand}_a = -0.004$ (calculated as the average of 50 random partitions). The optimal baseline is PairF $= 95.81$ and $\text{Rand}_a = 0.909$, calculated by evaluating the gold standard against itself. As the gold standard includes polysemous verbs, which belong

$$\text{Rand}_a(\mathcal{C},\mathcal{G}) = \frac{\sum_{i,j}\binom{\mathcal{CG}_{ij}}{2} - \left[\sum_i \binom{|C_i|}{2}\sum_j \binom{|G_j|}{2}\right]/\binom{n}{2}}{\frac{1}{2}\left[\sum_i \binom{|C_i|}{2} + \sum_j \binom{|G_j|}{2}\right] - \left[\sum_i \binom{|C_i|}{2}\sum_j \binom{|G_j|}{2}\right]/\binom{n}{2}} \quad (12)$$

$$\text{PairF}(\mathcal{C},\mathcal{G}) = \frac{2P(\mathcal{C},\mathcal{G})R(\mathcal{C},\mathcal{G})}{P(\mathcal{C},\mathcal{G}) + R(\mathcal{C},\mathcal{G})} \quad (13)$$

Figure 3: Evaluation metrics used to compare clusterings to gold standards.

Data Set	Eval	Distance	Manual	Random Best	Random Mean	Ward
Schulte im Walde	PairF	IRad	40.23	$1.34 \rightarrow 16.15$	13.37	$17.86 \rightarrow 17.49$
		Skew	47.28	$2.41 \rightarrow 18.01$	14.07	$15.86 \rightarrow 15.23$
	Rand_a	IRad	0.358	$0.001 \rightarrow 0.118$	0.093	$0.145 \rightarrow 0.142$
		Skew	0.429	$-0.002 \rightarrow 0.142$	0.102	$0.158 \rightarrow 0.158$
NEGRA/TIGER	PairF	IRad	30.77	$2.06 \rightarrow 14.67$	12.39	$16.13 \rightarrow 15.52$
		Skew	40.19	$3.47 \rightarrow 12.95$	11.48	$14.05 \rightarrow 14.31$
	Rand_a	IRad	0.281	$0.000 \rightarrow 0.122$	0.094	$0.134 \rightarrow 0.129$
		Skew	0.382	$-0.015 \rightarrow 0.102$	0.089	$0.112 \rightarrow 0.114$
SdeWaC	PairF	IRad	42.66	$1.62 \rightarrow 20.36$	18.26	$26.94 \rightarrow 27.50$
		Skew	50.38	$2.99 \rightarrow 20.75$	17.80	$24.60 \rightarrow 24.94$
	Rand_a	IRad	0.387	$-0.006 \rightarrow 0.167$	0.146	$0.232 \rightarrow 0.238$
		Skew	0.465	$0.008 \rightarrow 0.170$	0.143	$0.208 \rightarrow 0.211$

Table 1: Evaluation of the NEGRA/TIGER and SdeWaC SCF lexica using the SiW2006 gold standard.

to more than one cluster, the optimal baseline is calculated by randomly picking one of their senses; the average is then taken over 50 such trials.

We cluster using $k = 43$, matching the number of clusters in the gold standard. Of the 168 verbs in SiW2006, 159 are attested in NEGRA and TIGER (17,285 instances), and 167 are found in SdeWaC (1,047,042 instances)[5].

We report the results using k-means clustering initialised under a variety of conditions. "Manual" shows the quality of the clustering achieved when initialising k-means with the gold standard classes. We also initialise clustering 10 times using random partitions. For the best clustering[6] in these 10, "Random Best" shows the evaluation of both the starting random partition and the final clustering found by k-means; "Random Mean" shows the average cluster purity of the 10 final clusterings. "Ward" shows the evaluation of the clustering initialised with centroids found by hierarchical clustering of the verbs using Ward's method. Again, both the initial partition found by Ward's method and the k-means solution based on it are shown.

For comparison, we list the results of Schulte im Walde (2006, p. 174, Table 7) for the second level of SCF granularity, with PP head and case information (see Sec. 2 for Schulte im Walde's analysis). While this seems the most appropriate comparison to draw, since we also collect statistics about PPs, it is ambitious because, as noted in Section 3, our SCF lexica lack case information about PPs.[7] Compared to Schulte im Walde's numbers, the NEGRA/TIGER SCF lexicon scores significantly worse on the PairF evaluation metric under all conditions, and also on the Rand_a metric using the skew divergence measure (Rand_a/IRad is not significantly different). The SdeWaC SCF lexicon scores better on all metrics and conditions; these results are significant at the $p < 0.001$ level[8].

[5] Verbs missing from the clustering reduce the maximum achievable cluster purity score.

[6] Specifically, we take the clustering result with the minimum intra-cluster distance (not the clustering result with the best performance on the gold standard).

[7] PP case information is relevant for prepositions that can take both locative and directional readings, as in *in der Stadt* (dative) 'in town' und *in die Stadt* (accusative) 'to town'.

[8] Statistical significance is calculated by running repeated k-means clusterings with random partition initialisation and evaluating the results using the relevant purity metrics. These repeated clustering scores represent a random variable (a func-

6.2 Discussion

Sec. 6.1 compared the SCF lexicon created using SdeWaC with the lexicon built by Schulte im Walde (2002a), showing that our lexicon achieves significantly better results on the verb clustering task. We interpret this to be indicative of a more accurate subcategorisation lexicon, and, by extension, of a more accurate SCF acquisition system.

We attribute this superior performance primarily to our use of a statistical parser as opposed to a hand-written grammar. This design choice has several advantages. First, the parser delivers robust syntactic analyses, which we can expect to be relatively domain-independent. Second, we make no prior assumptions about the variety of subcategorisation phenomena that might appear in text, decoupling the identification of SCFs from the ability to parse natural language. Third, the fact that our parser and edge labeller are trained on the 800,000 word NEGRA/TIGER corpus means that we benefit from the linguistic expertise that went into building that treebank. Our use of off-the-shelf tools (the parser and our simple yet effective machine learning model describing edge label information) makes our system considerably simpler and easier to implement than Schulte im Walde's. We see our system as more easily extensible to other languages for which there is a parser and an initial syntactically annotated corpus to train the edge labeller on.

The NEGRA/TIGER SCF lexicon performs not as well on the verb clustering evaluations, as fewer verbs are attested in NEGRA/TIGER compared to the SdeWaC SCF lexicon and gold standard clusterings. Data sparsity can be a problem in SCF acquisition; all other factors being equal, using more data to construct an SCF lexicon should make patterns in the language more readily visible and reduce the chance of missing a particular lemma-SCF combination accidentally. A secondary effect is that models of verb subcategorisation preferences like the ones used here can be more precisely estimated as the counts of observed verb instances increase, particularly for low-frequency verbs.

Error analysis of our SCF lexicon reveals low counts of expletive subjects. The edge labeller is supposed to annotate semantically empty subjects (*es*, 'it') as expletive; for clusterings examined in Sec. 5.1, this would affect weather verbs (e.g., *es regnet*, 'it's raining'). However, in our SdeWaC SCF lexicon, expletive subjects are clearly underrepresented. Our SCF lexicon built on TIGER, where expletive subjects are systematically labelled, has the SCF `xa` as the most common SCF for the verb *geben* (in *es gibt* 'there is'). In contrast, in our SdeWaC SCF lexicon, the most common SCF is the transitive `na`, with `xa` in seventh place. I.e., the edge labeller does not identify all expletive subjects, which is due to the fact that expletive subjects are syntactically indistinguishable from neuter pronominal subjects, so the edge labeller does not have a rich feature set to inform it about this category. But since, statistically, expletive pronouns make up less than 1% of subjects in TIGER, the prior probability of labelling a constituent as expletive is very low. Due to these figures, we do not expect this issue to seriously impact the quality of our verb classification evaluations.

7 Future work

In this paper we have presented a state-of-the-art subcategorisation acquisition system for free-word order languages, and used it to create a large subcategorisation frame lexicon for German verbs. Our SCF lexicon resource is available at `http://amor.cms.hu-berlin.de/~robertsw/scflex.html`. We are performing a manual evaluation of the output of our system, which we will report soon.

We plan to continue this work first by expanding our SCF lexicon with case information and selectional preferences, second by using our SCF classifier and lexicon for verbal Multiword Expression identification in German, and last by comparing it to existing verb classifications, either by using available resources for German like the SALSA corpus (Burchardt et al., 2006), or by translating parts of VerbNet into German to create a more extensive gold standard for verb clustering in the spirit of Sun et al. (2010) who found that Levin's verb classification can be translated to French and still usefully allow generalisation over verb classes.

Finally, we plan to perform in vivo evaluation of our SCF lexicon, to determine what benefit it can deliver for NLP applications such as Semantic Role Labelling and Word Sense Disambiguation. Recent research has found that even automatically-acquired verb classifications can be useful for NLP applications (Shutova et al., 2010; Guo et al., 2011).

tion of the random cluster centroids used to initialise the k-means clustering). These samples are normally distributed, so we determine statistical significance using a t-test against the "Random Mean" results reported by Schulte im Walde (2006).

References

Marco Baroni, Silvia Bernardini, Adriano Ferraresi, and Eros Zanchetta. 2009. The WaCky wide web: A collection of very large linguistically processed web-crawled corpora. *Language Resources and Evaluation*, 43(3):209–226.

Sabine Brants, Stefanie Dipper, Silvia Hansen, Wolfgang Lezius, and George Smith. 2002. The TIGER treebank. In *TLT*, pages 24–41.

Michael R. Brent and Robert C. Berwick. 1991. Automatic acquisition of subcategorization frames from tagged text. In *HLT*, pages 342–345. Morgan Kaufmann.

Ted Briscoe and John Carroll. 1997. Automatic extraction of subcategorization from corpora. *CoRR*, cmp-lg/9702002.

Aljoscha Burchardt, Katrin Erk, Anette Frank, Andrea Kowalski, Sebastian Pado, and Manfred Pinkal. 2006. The SALSA corpus: A German corpus resource for lexical semantics. In *LREC*.

Judith Eckle-Kohler. 1999. *Linguistic knowledge for automatic lexicon acquisition from German text corpora*. Ph.D. thesis, Universität Stuttgart.

Gertrud Faaß and Kerstin Eckart. 2013. SdeWaC - A corpus of parsable sentences from the Web. In *Language processing and knowledge in the Web*, pages 61–68. Springer, Berlin, Heidelberg.

Edward W. Forgy. 1965. Cluster analysis of multivariate data: Efficiency versus interpretability of classifications. *Biometrics*, 21:768–769.

Raza Ghulam. 2011. *Subcategorization acquisition and classes of predication in Urdu*. Ph.D. thesis, Universität Konstanz.

Trond Grenager and Christopher D. Manning. 2006. Unsupervised discovery of a statistical verb lexicon. In *EMNLP*, pages 1–8.

Yufan Guo, Anna Korhonen, and Thierry Poibeau. 2011. A weakly-supervised approach to argumentative zoning of scientific documents. In *EMNLP*, pages 273–283.

Slava Katz. 1987. Estimation of probabilities from sparse data for the language model component of a speech recognizer. *IEEE Transactions on Acoustics, Speech and Signal Processing*, 35(3):400–401.

Anna Korhonen. 2002. Subcategorization acquisition. Technical report, University of Cambridge, Computer Laboratory.

Joel Lang and Mirella Lapata. 2010. Unsupervised induction of semantic roles. In *HLT*, pages 939–947.

Lillian Lee. 1999. Measures of distributional similarity. In *ACL*, pages 25–32.

Beth Levin and Malka Rappaport Hovav. 2005. *Argument realization*. Cambridge University Press, Cambridge.

Beth Levin. 1993. *English verb classes and alternations: A preliminary investigation*. University of Chicago Press, Chicago.

Christopher D. Manning. 1993. Automatic acquisition of a large subcategorization dictionary from corpora. In *ACL*, pages 235–242.

Manolis Maragoudakis, Katia Lida Kermanidis, and George Kokkinakis. 2000. Learning subcategorization frames from corpora: A case study for modern Greek. In *Proceedings of COMLEX 2000, Workshop on Computational Lexicography and Multimedia Dictionaries*, pages 19–22.

Slav Petrov, Leon Barrett, Romain Thibaux, and Dan Klein. 2006. Learning accurate, compact, and interpretable tree annotation. In *ACL*, pages 433–440.

Anoop Sarkar and Daniel Zeman. 2000. Automatic extraction of subcategorization frames for Czech. In *COLING*, pages 691–697.

Silke Scheible, Sabine Schulte im Walde, Marion Weller, and Max Kisselew. 2013. A compact but linguistically detailed database for German verb subcategorisation relying on dependency parses from Web corpora: Tool, guidelines and resource. In *Web as Corpus Workshop*.

Helmut Schmid. 1994. Probabilistic part-of-speech tagging using decision trees. In *NeMLaP*, volume 12, pages 44–49.

Sabine Schulte im Walde and Chris Brew. 2002. Inducing German semantic verb classes from purely syntactic subcategorisation information. In *ACL*, pages 223–230.

Sabine Schulte im Walde. 2002a. A subcategorisation lexicon for German verbs induced from a lexicalised PCFG. In *LREC*, pages 1351–1357.

Sabine Schulte im Walde. 2002b. Evaluating verb subcategorisation frames learned by a German statistical grammar against manual definitions in the Duden Dictionary. In *EURALEX*, pages 187–197.

Sabine Schulte im Walde. 2006. Experiments on the automatic induction of German semantic verb classes. *Computational Linguistics*, 32(2):159–194.

Sabine Schulte im Walde. 2009. The induction of verb frames and verb classes from corpora. In Anke Lüdeling and Merja Kytö, editors, *Corpus linguistics: An international handbook*, volume 2, chapter 44, pages 952–971. Mouton de Gruyter, Berlin.

Ekaterina Shutova, Lin Sun, and Anna Korhonen. 2010. Metaphor identification using verb and noun clustering. In *COLING*, pages 1002–1010.

Wojciech Skut, Brigitte Krenn, Thorsten Brants, and Hans Uszkoreit. 1997. An annotation scheme for free word order languages. In *ANLP*, pages 88–95.

Lin Sun, Anna Korhonen, and Yuval Krymolowski. 2008. Verb class discovery from rich syntactic data. In *CICLing*, pages 16–27, Haifa, Israel.

Lin Sun, Anna Korhonen, Thierry Poibeau, and Cédric Messiant. 2010. Investigating the cross-linguistic potential of VerbNet-style classification. In *COLING*, pages 1056–1064, Beijing, China.

Ivan Titov and Alexandre Klementiev. 2012. A Bayesian approach to unsupervised semantic role induction. In *EACL*, pages 12–22.

Joe H. Ward, Jr. 1963. Hierarchical grouping to optimize an objective function. *Journal of the American Statistical Association*, 58(301):236–244.

Oliver Wauschkuhn. 1999. *Automatische Extraktion von Verbvalenzen aus deutschen Textkorpora*. Shaker Verlag.

Classifying Temporal Relations with Simple Features

Paramita Mirza
Fondazione Bruno Kessler
and University of Trento
Trento, Italy
paramita@fbk.eu

Sara Tonelli
Fondazione Bruno Kessler
Trento, Italy
satonelli@fbk.eu

Abstract

Approaching temporal link labelling as a classification task has already been explored in several works. However, choosing the right feature vectors to build the classification model is still an open issue, especially for event-event classification, whose accuracy is still under 50%. We find that using a simple feature set results in a better performance than using more sophisticated features based on semantic role labelling and deep semantic parsing. We also investigate the impact of extracting new training instances using inverse relations and transitive closure, and gain insight into the impact of this bootstrapping methodology on classifying the full set of TempEval-3 relations.

1 Introduction

In recent years, temporal processing has gained increasing attention within the NLP community, in particular since TempEval evaluation campaigns have been organized on this topic (Verhagen et al., 2007; Verhagen et al., 2010; UzZaman et al., 2013). In particular, the classification of temporal relations holding between entities such as events and temporal expressions (timex) is crucial to build event timelines and to reconstruct the plot of a story. This could be exploited in decision support systems and document archiving applications, among others.

In this work we focus on the problem of classifying temporal relation types, assuming that the links between events and time expressions are already established. This task is part of Tempeval-3 evaluation campaign, hence we follow the guidelines and the dataset provided by the organizers, so that we can compare our system with other systems participating in the challenge. Recent works have tried to address this complex classification task by using sophisticated features, based on deep parsing, semantic role labelling and discourse parsing (D'Souza and Ng, 2013; Laokulrat et al., 2013). We argue that a simpler approach, based on lexico-syntactic features, achieves comparable results, while reducing the processing time needed to extract the features. Besides, the performance of complex NLP tools may strongly vary when moving to new domains, affecting in turn the classification performance, while our approach is likely to be more stable across different domains.

Our features include some basic information on the position, the attributes and the PoS tags of events and timexes, as well as other information obtained from external lexical resources such as a list of typical event durations and a list of temporal signals. The few processing steps required include PoS-tagging, dependency parsing and the semantic tagging of connectives (based on the parser output).

We also investigate the impact of extending the number of training instances through inverse relations and transitive closure, which is a 'simplified' version of temporal closure covering only entities connected via the same relation type.

2 Related Work

The task we deal with in this paper was proposed as part of the TempEval-3 shared task (UzZaman et al., 2012). Compared to previous TempEval campaigns, the TempEval-3 task involved recognizing the full set of temporal relations in TimeML (14 types) instead of a reduced set, increasing the task complexity. This specific temporal relation classification task becomes the main focus of this paper.

Supervised classification of temporal relation types has already been explored in some earlier works. Mani et al. (2006) built a MaxEnt classifier to label the temporal links using training data which were bootstrapped by applying temporal closure. Chambers et al. (2007) focused on classifying the temporal relation type of event-event pairs using previously learned event attributes as features. However, both works use a reduced set of temporal relations, obtained by collapsing the relation types that inverse each other into a single type.

Our work is most similar to the recent work by D'Souza and Ng (2013). The authors perform the same task on the full set of temporal relations, but adopt a much more complex approach. They utilize lexical relations extracted from the Merriam-Webster dictionary and WordNet (Fellbaum, 1998), as well as semantic and discourse features. They also introduce 437 hand-coded rules to build a hybrid classification model.

Since we conduct our experiments based on TempEval-3 task setup, this work is also comparable with the systems participating in the task. UzZaman et al. (2013) report that three groups submitted at least one system run to the task. The best performing one (Laokulrat et al., 2013) uses, among others, sentence-level semantic information from a deep syntactic parser, namely predicate-argument structure features. Another system (Chambers, 2013) is composed of four MaxEnt classifiers, two of which have been trained for event-event links (inter- and intra-sentence) and two for event-time links. The third-ranked system (Kolya et al., 2013), instead, implements a much simpler set of features accounting for event tense, modality and aspect, event and timex context, etc.

3 Temporal Link Labelling

In this section we detail the task of temporal relation labelling, the features implemented in our classification system and the strategy adopted to bootstrap new training data.

3.1 Task description

The full set of temporal relations specified in TimeML version 1.2.1 (Saurí et al., 2006) contains 14 types of relations, as illustrated in Table 1. Among them there are six pairs of relations that inverse each other.

Note that according to TimeML 1.2.1 annotation guidelines, the difference between *DURING* and *IS_INCLUDED* (also their inverses) is that *DURING* relation is specified when an event persists throughout a temporal duration (e.g. John *drove* for *5 hours*), while *IS_INCLUDED* relation is specified when an event happens within a temporal expression (e.g. John *arrived* on *Tuesday*).

a |——| b |——| (after a)	a is *BEFORE* b b is *AFTER* a
a |——| b |——| (starting where a ends)	a is *IBEFORE* b b is *IAFTER* a
a |——| b |————| (same start)	a *BEGINS* b b is *BEGUN_BY* a
a |——| b |————| (same end)	a *ENDS* b b is *ENDED_BY* a
a |——| b |——————|	a is *DURING* b b is *DURING_INV* a
a |——————| b |——|	a *INCLUDES* b b *IS_INCLUDED* in a
a |——| b |——|	a is *SIMULTANEOUS* with b
a |——| b	a is *IDENTITY* with b

Table 1: Temporal relations in TimeML annotation

In TimeML annotation, temporal links are used to (i) establish the temporal order of two events (*event-event* pair), (ii) anchor an event to a time expression (*event-timex* pair) and (iii) establish the temporal order of two time expressions (*timex-timex* pair).

The problem of determining the label of a given temporal link can be regarded as a classification problem. Given an ordered pair of entities (e_1, e_2) that could be either *event-event*, *event-timex* or *timex-timex* pair, the classifier has to assign a certain label, namely one of the 14 temporal relation types. We train a classification model for each category of entity pair, as suggested in several previous works (Mani et al., 2006; Chambers, 2013).

However, because there are very few examples of timex-timex pairs in the training corpus, it is not possible to train the classification model for these particular pairs. Moreover, they only add up to 3.2% of the total number of extracted entity pairs; therefore, we decided to disregard these pairs.

3.2 Feature set

We implement a number of features for temporal relation classification. Some of them are basic ones which take into account morpho-syntactic information on events and time expressions, their textual context and their attributes. Others rely on semantic information such as typical event durations and connective type. However, we avoid complex processing of data. Such semantic information is based on external lists of lexical items and on the output of the *addDiscourse* tagger (Pitler and Nenkova, 2009).

Some features are computed independently based on either e_1 or e_2, while some others are *pairwise features*, which are computed based on both elements. Some pairwise features are only relevant for event-event pairs, for example, the information on discourse connectives and the binary features representing whether two events have the same event attributes or not. Similarly, the features related to time expression attributes are only relevant for event-timex pairs, since this information can only be obtained if e_2 is a time expression. The selection of features that contribute to the improvement of event-event and event-timex classification will be detailed in Section 4.3.

String features. The tokens and lemmas of e_1 and e_2.

Grammatical features. The part of speech (PoS) tags of e_1 and e_2, and a binary feature indicating whether e_1 and e_2 have the same PoS tag. The binary feature only applies to event-event pairs since we do not include the PoS tag of a time expression in the feature set of event-timex pairs. The grammatical information is obtained using the Stanford CoreNLP tool.[1]

Textual context. The textual order, sentence distance and entity distance of e_1 and e_2. Textual order is the appearance order of e_1 and e_2 in the text, while sentence distance measures how far e_1 and e_2 are from each other in terms of sentences, i.e. 0 if they are in the same sentence. The entity distance is only measured if e_1 and e_2 are in the same sentence, and corresponds to the number of entities occurring between e_1 and e_2 (i.e. if they are adjacent, the distance is 0).

Entity attributes. Event attributes and time expression attributes of e_1 and e_2 as specified in TimeML annotation. Event attributes consist of *class*, *tense*, *aspect* and *polarity*, while the attributes of a time expression are its *type*, *value* and *dct* (indicating whether a time expression is the document creation time or not). Events falling under the category of noun, adjective and preposition do not have tense and aspect attributes in TimeML. We retrieve this information by extracting the tense and aspect of the verbs that govern them, based on their dependency relation. For event-event pairs we also include four binary features representing whether e_1 and e_2 have the same event attributes or not.

Dependency relations. Similar to D'Souza and Ng (2013), we use the information related to the dependency relation between e_1 and e_2. We include as features (i) the type of the dependency relation that exists between them, (ii) the dependency order which is either *governor-dependent* or *dependent-governor* and (iii) binary features indicating whether e_1/e_2 is the *root* of the sentence. This information is based on the collapsed representation of dependency relations provided by the parsing module of Stanford CoreNLP. Consider the sentence *"John **left** the office and **drove** back home for **20 minutes**"*. Using the collapsed typed dependencies we could get the direct relations between the existing entities, which are *conj_and(left, drove)* and *prep_for(drove, minutes)*.

Event durations. To our knowledge, we are the first to exploit event duration information as features for temporal relation classification. In fact, duration can be expressed not only by a predicate's tense and aspect but also by its *aktionsart*, i.e. the inherent temporal information connected to the meaning of a predicate. The typical event duration allows us to infer, for instance, that a punctual event is more likely to be contained in a durative one. If we consider the sentence *"State-run television **broadcast** footage of Cuban exiles **protesting** in Miami"*, this feature would tell us that *broadcast* lasts for *hours* while *protesting* lasts for *days*, thus contributing in determining the direction of *DURING* relation between the events.

The approximate duration for an event is obtained from the list of 1000 most frequent verbs and their duration distributions compiled by Gusev et al. (2011).[2] The types of duration include *seconds*, *minutes*, *hours*, *days*, *weeks*, *months*, *years* and *decades*. We also add the duration difference between e_1 and e_2 as a feature

[1] http://nlp.stanford.edu/software/corenlp.shtml

[2] The list is available at http://cs.stanford.edu/people/agusev/durations/

with the value varied between *same*, *less* or *more*. Similar to tense and aspect attributes for events, the duration of events under the category of noun, adjective and preposition are estimated by the governing verb. As for time expressions, their durations are estimated from their type and value attributes using a set of simple rules, e.g. the duration of *Thursday morning* (with the type of *TIME* and the value of *xxxx-xx-xxTMO*) is *hours*.

Temporal signals. Derczynski and Gaizauskas (2012) show the importance of temporal signals in temporal link labelling. We take this into account by integrating in our features the list of signals extracted from TimeBank 1.2 corpus[3]. We believe that the system performance will benefit from distinguishing between event-related signals and timex-related signals, therefore we manually split the signals into two separate lists. Signals such as *when*, *as* and *then* are commonly used to temporally connect events, while signals such as *at*, *for* and *within* more likely occur with time expressions. There are also signals that are used in both cases such as *before*, *after* and *until*, and those kind of signals are added to both lists.

Besides the signal token, the position of the signal with respect to the events or time expressions is also an important feature. Consider the position of a signal in the sentences (i) *"John taught high school* ***before*** *he worked at a bank"* and (ii) *"**Before** John taught high school, he worked at a bank"*, which is crucial to determine the order of John's occupations. We also include in the feature set whether a signal occurs at the beginning of a sentence, as it is usually used to temporally relate events in different sentences, e.g. *"John taught high school.* ***Previously****, he worked at a bank."*

Temporal discourse connectives. Consider the following sentences:

(i) *"John has been taking that driving course* ***since*** *the accident that took place last week."*
(ii) *"John has been taking that driving course* ***since*** *he wants to drive better."*

In order to label the temporal link holding between two events, it is important to know whether there are temporal connectives in the surrounding context, because they may contribute in identifying the relation type. For instance, it may be relevant to distinguish whether *since* is used as a temporal or a causal cue (example (i) and (ii) resp.). This information about discourse connectives is acquired using the *addDiscourse* tool (Pitler and Nenkova, 2009), which identifies connectives and assigns them to one of four semantic classes: *Temporal*, *Expansion*, *Contingency* and *Comparison*. Note that this is a much shallower approach than the one proposed by D'Souza and Ng (2013), who perform full discourse parsing.

We include as feature whether a discourse connective belonging to the *Temporal* class occurs in the textual context of e_1 and e_2. Similar to temporal signals, we also include in the feature set the position of the discourse connective with respect to the events.

3.3 Inverse Relations and Transitive Closure

Since Mani et al. (2006) demonstrate that bootstrapping training data through temporal closure results in quite significant improvements, we try to provide the classifier with more data to learn from using the inverse relations and closure-based inferred relations.

There are six pairs of relation types in TimeML that inverse each other (see Table 1). By switching the order of the entities in a given pair and labelling the pair with the inverse relation type, we basically multiply the number of training data.

As for temporal closure, there have been attempts to apply it to improve temporal relation classification. Mani et al. (2006) use SputLink (Verhagen, 2005), which was developed based on Allen's closure inference (Allen, 1983), to infer the relations based on temporal closure. UzZaman and Allen (2011b) employ Timegraph (Gerevini et al., 1995) to implement the scorer for TempEval-3 evaluation, since precision and recall for temporal relation classification are computed based on the closure graph.

We use a simpler approach to obtain the closure graph of temporal relations, by applying the *transitive closure* only within the same relation type, e.g. e_1 *BEFORE* $e_2 \wedge e_2$ *BEFORE e3* $\rightarrow e_1$ *BEFORE e3*. It can be seen as *partial temporal closure* since it produces only a subset of the relations produced by temporal closure, which covers more complex cases, e.g. e_1 *BEFORE* $e_2 \wedge e_2$ *INCLUDES e3* $\rightarrow e_1$ *BEFORE e3*.

[3]The list is available at `http://www.timeml.org/site/timebank/browser_1.2/displayTags.php?treshold=1&tagtype=signal&sort=alpha`

As shown in Fischer and Meyer (1971), the problem of finding the transitive closure of a directed acyclic graph can be reduced to a boolean matrix multiplication. For each temporal relation type, we build its boolean matrix with the size of $n \times n$, n being the number of entities in a text. Given a temporal relation type R and its boolean matrix M, the transitive closure-based relations of R can be inferred from the matrix M^2 by extracting its non-zero elements.

4 Experiment Description

4.1 Dataset

Since we want to compare our work with existing approaches to temporal relation classification, we use the same training and test data as in Tempeval-3 challenge[4]. Two types of training data were made available in the challenge: **TBAQ-cleaned** and **TE3-Silver-data**. The former includes a cleaned and improved version of the **AQUAINT** TimeML corpus, containing 73 news report documents, and the **TimeBank** corpus, with 183 news articles. TE3-Silver-data, instead, is a 600K word corpus annotated by the best performing systems at Tempeval-2, which we do not use in our experiments.

Our test data is the newly created **TempEval-3-platinum** evaluation corpus that was annotated/reviewed by the Tempeval-3 task organizers. The distribution of the relation types in all previously mentioned datasets is shown in Table 2. We report also the statistics obtained after applying inverse relations and transitive closure, that increase the number of training instances.

It is worth noticing that *DURING_INV* relation does not exist in the training data but appears in the test data. In this case, inverse relations help in automatically acquiring training instances. The *BEFORE* relation corresponds to the majority class and makes the instance distribution quite unbalanced, especially in the TBAQ corpus. Finally, five event-timex instances in the TBAQ training data are labeled with *IDENTITY* relation and can be assumed to be falsely annotated.

4.2 Experimental Setup

We build our classification models using the Support Vector Machine (SVM) implementation provided by YamCha[5]. The experiment involves conducting 5-fold cross validation on the TimeBank corpus to find the best combination of features for the event-event and event-timex classifiers. We first run our experiments using YamCha default parameters (pairwise method for multi-class classification and polynomial kernel of degree 2). After identifying the best feature sets for the two classifiers, we evaluate them using different kernel degrees (from 1 to 4).

4.3 Feature Engineering

In order to select from our initial set of features only those that improve the accuracy of the event-event and event-timex classifiers, we incrementally add them to the baseline (the model with string feature only), and compute their contribution. Table 3 shows the results of this selection process, by including the average accuracy from the 5-fold cross validation.

In Table 3, we report the feature contributions of the *entity attributes* and *dependency relations* sets in more details, because within those categories only some of the features have a positive impact on accuracy. Instead, for features within *textual context*, *signal* and *discourse* categories, incrementally adding each feature results in increasing accuracy, therefore we report only the overall accuracy of the feature group. Similarly, for *duration* features, adding each feature incrementally results in decreasing accuracy.

Regarding entity attributes, it can be seen that *aspect* and *class* features have no positive impact on the accuracy of event-event classification, along with pairwise features *same_class* and *same_polarity*. As for event-timex classification, all event attributes except for *polarity* contribute to accuracy improvements. Among time expression attributes, only the information about whether a time expression is a document creation time or not (*dct* feature) helps improving the classifier.

The *dependency_order* feature does not give positive contribution to the accuracy in both cases. Besides, information on whether an event is the root of the sentence (*dependency_is_root* feature) is not relevant for event-timex classification.

Adding the *temporal signal* feature very slightly improves the accuracy of event-event classification, not as much as its contribution to event-timex

[4]http://www.cs.york.ac.uk/semeval-2013/task1/index.php?id=data

[5]http://chasen.org/~taku/software/yamcha/

Relation	event-event					event-timex				
	train				test	train				test
	TB	TBAQ	TBAQ-I	TBAQ-IC	TE3-P	TB	TBAQ	TBAQ-I	TBAQ-IC	TE3-P
BEFORE	490	2,115	2,938	5,685	226	661	1,417	1,925	2,474	96
AFTER	458	823	2,938	5,685	167	205	509	1,925	2,474	29
IBEFORE	22	60	103	105	1	2	3	8	8	5
IAFTER	27	43	103	105	2	4	5	8	8	6
BEGINS	24	44	86	85	0	20	65	89	89	1
BEGUN_BY	24	42	86	85	1	22	24	89	89	1
ENDS	12	17	79	79	1	47	59	120	120	2
ENDED_BY	44	62	79	79	0	57	61	120	120	2
DURING	46	80	80	84	1	197	200	200	201	1
DURING_INV	0	0	80	84	0	0	0	200	201	1
INCLUDES	170	308	724	7,246	40	288	1,104	2,945	3,404	42
IS_INCLUDED	212	416	724	7,246	47	897	1,841	2,945	3,404	125
SIMULTANEOUS	456	519	519	518	81	58	58	58	58	6
IDENTITY	534	742	742	742	15	4	5	5	5	0
Total	**2,519**	**5,271**	**9,281**	**27,828**	**582**	**2,462**	**5,351**	**10,637**	**12,655**	**317**

Table 2: The distribution of each relation type in the datasets for both event-event and event-timex pairs. **TB** stands for TimeBank corpus, **TBAQ** denotes the combination of TimeBank and AQUAINT corpora, **TBAQ-I** denotes the TBAQ corpus augmented with inverse relations, **TBAQ-IC** is the TBAQ corpus with both inverse relations and transitive closure, and **TE3-P** is the TempEval-3-platinum evaluation corpus.

classification. However, together with the *temporal discourse* feature, they positively affect accuracy, confirming previous findings (Derczynski and Gaizauskas, 2012).

Surprisingly, adding event duration feature decreases the accuracy in both cases. This might be caused by the insufficient coverage of the event duration resource, since around 20% of the training pairs contain at least an event whose duration is unknown. Moreover, we employ the approximate duration of a verb event as a feature without considering the context and discourse. For example, according to the distributions in the duration resource, the event *attack* has two likely durations, *minutes* and *decades*, with *decades* being slightly more probable than *minutes*. In the sentence *"Israel has publicly declared that it will **respond** to an Iraqi **attack** on Jordan."*, the classifier fails to recognize the IBEFORE relation between *attack* and *respond* (*attack* happens immediately before *respond*), because the duration feature of *attack* is recognized as *decades*, while in this context the *attack* most probably occurs within *seconds*.

According to the analysis of the different feature contributions, we define the best classification models for both event-event pairs and event-timex pairs as the models using combinations of features that have positive impacts on the accuracy, based on Table 3. Given the best performing sets of features, we further experiment with different kernel degrees in the same 5-fold cross validation scenario.

The best classifier performances are achieved with the polynomial kernel of degree 4, both for event-event and event-timex classification. The accuracy for event-event classification is **43.69%**, while for event-timex classification it is **66.62%**. However, using a high polynomial kernel degree introduces more complexity in training the classification model, thus more time is required to train such models.

D'Souza and Ng (2013) evaluate their system on the same corpus, but with a slightly different setting. They also split TimeBank into 5 folds, but they only use two of them to perform 2-fold cross validation, while they use another part of the corpus to develop rules for their hybrid system. Their best configuration gives 46.8% accuracy for event-event classification and 65.4% accuracy for event-timex classification. Although the two approaches are not directly comparable, we can assume that the systems' performance are likely to be very similar, with a better accuracy on event-event classification by D'Souza and Ng (2013) and a better performance on event-timex pairs by our system. Probably, the hybrid system by D'Souza and Ng, which integrates supervised classification and manual rules, performs better on event-event classification because it is a more complex task than event-timex classification, where simple lexical and syntactic features are still very effective.

event-event			event-timex		
Feature	**Accuracy**		**Feature**	**Accuracy**	
majority class	22.17%	-	majority class	36.42%	-
string	31.07%	-	string	58.27%	-
+grammatical	36.15%	5.08%	+grammatical	61.30%	3.03%
+textual_context	39.44%	3.29%	+textual_context	61.71%	0.41%
+tense	41.10%	1.66%	+tense	63.10%	1.39%
+aspect	*41.10%*	*0.00%*	+aspect	64.51%	1.41%
+class	*39.96%*	*-1.14%*	+class	65.30%	0.79%
+polarity	40.44%	0.48%	*+polarity*	*64.88%*	*-0.42%*
+same_tense	40.55%	0.11%	+dct	65.21%	0.33%
+same_aspect	40.63%	0.08%	*+type*	*64.99%*	*-0.22%*
+same_class	*40.63%*	*0.00%*	*+value*	*64.60%*	*-0.39%*
+same_polarity	*40.47%*	*-0.16%*			
+ dependency	42.15%	1.68%	+dependecy	65.60%	1.00%
+dependency_order	*41.99%*	*-0.16%*	*+dependency_order*	*65.47%*	*-0.13%*
+dependency_is_root	42.63%	0.64%	*+dependency_is_root*	*65.22%*	*-0.25%*
+temporal_signal	42.66%	0.03%	+temporal_signal	65.43%	0.21%
+temporal_discourse	42.82%	0.16%			
+duration	*41.47%*	*-1.35%*	*+duration*	*64.19%*	*-1.24%*

Table 3: Feature contributions for event-event and event-timex classification. Features in *italics* have a negative impact on accuracy and are not included in the final feature set.

5 Evaluation

We perform two types of evaluation. In the first one, we evaluate the system performance with the best feature sets and the best parameter configuration using the four training sets presented in Table 2. Our test set is the TempEval-3-platinum corpus. The goal of this first evaluation is to specifically investigate the effect of enriching the training data with inverse relations and transitive closure. We compute the system accuracy as the percentage of the correct labels out of all annotated links.

In the second evaluation, we compare our system to the systems participating in the task on temporal relation classification at TempEval-3. The test set is again TempEval-3-platinum, i.e. the same one used in the competition. The task organizers introduced an evaluation metric (UzZaman and Allen, 2011a) capturing temporal awareness in terms of precision, recall and F1-score. To compute precision and recall, they verify the correctness of annotated temporal links using temporal closure, by checking the existence of the identified relations in the closure graph. In order to replicate this type of evaluation, we use the scorer made available to the task participants.

5.1 Evaluation of the Effects of Inverse Relations and Transitive Closure

Table 4 shows the classifiers' accuracies achieved using different training sets. After performing a randomization test between the best performing classifier and the others, we notice that on event-event classification the improvement is significant ($p < 0.005$) only between TBAQ and TimeBank. This shows that only extending the TimeBank corpus by adding AQUAINT is beneficial. In all other cases, the differences are not significant. Applying inverse relations and transitive closure extends the number of training instances but makes the dataset more unbalanced, thus it does not result in a significant improvement.

Training data	event-event	event-timex
TimeBank	42.61%	71.92%
TBAQ	**48.28%**	73.82%
TBAQ-I	47.77%	74.45%
TBAQ-IC	46.39%	**74.45%**

Table 4: Classifier accuracies with different training data

This result is in contrast with the improvement brought about by temporal closure reported in Mani et al. (2006). The difference between our approach and Mani et al.'s is that (i) we apply only the transitive closure instead of the full temporal one, and (ii) our classification task includes 14 relations, while the other authors classify 6 relations. In our future work, we will investigate whether the benefits of closure are affected by the number of relations, or whether our simplified version is actually outperformed by the full one.

Furthermore, we plan to investigate the effect of *over-sampling* to handle highly skewed datasets, for instance by applying inverse relations and transitive closure only to minority classes.

5.2 Evaluation of the System Performance in TempEval-3 task

We train our classifiers for event-event pairs and event-timex pairs by exploiting the best feature combination and best configuration acquired from the experiment, and using the best reported dataset for each classifier as the training data. Even though it has been shown that inverse relations and transitive closure do not bring significantly positive impact to the accuracy, using the TBAQ-IC corpus as the training set for event-timex classification is still the best option. The two classifiers are part of a temporal classification system called *TRelPro*.

We compare in Table 5 the performance of *TRelPro* to the other systems participating in Tempeval-3 task, according to the figures reported in (UzZaman et al., 2013). *TRelPro* is the best performing system both in terms of precision and of recall.

System	F1	Precision	Recall
TRelPro	**58.48%**	**58.80%**	**58.17%**
UTTime-1, 4	56.45%	55.58%	57.35%
UTTime-3, 5	54.70%	53.85%	55.58%
UTTime-2	54.26%	53.20%	55.36%
NavyTime-1	46.83%	46.59%	47.07%
NavyTime-2	43.92%	43.65%	44.20%
JU-CSE	34.77%	35.07%	34.48%

Table 5: Tempeval-3 evaluation on temporal relation classification

In order to analyze which are the most common errors made by *TRelPro*, we report in Table 6 the number of true positives (tp), false positives (fp) and false negatives (fn) scored by the system on each temporal relation. The system generally fails to recognize *IBEFORE*, *BEGINS*, *ENDS* and *DURING* relations, along with their inverse relations, primarily because of the skewed distribution of instances in the training data, especially in comparison with the majority classes. This explains also the large number of false positives labelled for the *BEFORE* class (event-event pairs) and for the *IS_INCLUDED* class (event-timex pairs), which are the majority classes for the two pairs respectively.

Relation	event-event			event-timex		
	tp	fp	fn	tp	fp	fn
BEFORE	186	186	40	82	17	14
AFTER	63	40	104	14	7	15
IBEFORE	0	0	1	0	0	5
IAFTER	0	0	2	0	0	6
BEGINS	0	0	0	0	0	1
BEGUN_BY	0	0	0	0	0	1
ENDS	0	0	1	0	0	2
ENDED_BY	1	1	0	0	0	2
DURING	0	0	1	0	2	1
DURING_INV	0	0	0	0	0	1
INCLUDES	1	2	39	27	13	15
IS_INCLUDED	2	4	45	114	40	11
SIMULTANEOUS	20	33	61	0	0	6
IDENTITY	9	35	6	0	1	0

Table 6: Relation type distribution for TempEval-3-platinum test data, annotated with TRelPro. The *tp* fields indicate the numbers of correctly annotated instances, while the *fp*/*fn* fields correspond to false positives/negatives.

6 Conclusion

We have described an approach to temporal link labelling using simple features based on lexico-syntactic information, as well as external lexical resources listing temporal signals and event durations. We find that by using a simple feature set we can build a system that outperforms the systems built using more sophisticated features, based on semantic role labelling and deep semantic parsing. This may depend on the fact that more complex features are usually extracted from the output of NLP systems, whose performance impacts on the quality of such features.

We find that bootstrapping the training data with inverse relations and transitive closure does not help improving the classifiers' performances significantly as it was reported in previous works, especially in event-event classification where the accuracy decreases instead. In the future, we will further investigate the reason of this difference. We will also explore other variants of closure, as well as over-sampling techniques to handle the highly skewed dataset introduced by closure.

Finally, the overall performance of our system, using the best models for both event-event and event-timex classification, outperforms the other systems participating in the TempEval-3 task. This confirms our intuition that using simple features and reducing the amount of complex semantic and discourse information is a valuable alternative to more sophisticated approaches.

Acknowledgments

The research leading to this paper was partially supported by the European Union's 7th Framework Programme via the NewsReader Project (ICT-316404).

References

James F. Allen. 1983. Maintaining knowledge about temporal intervals. *Commun. ACM*, 26(11):832–843, November.

Nathanael Chambers, Shan Wang, and Dan Jurafsky. 2007. Classifying temporal relations between events. In *Proceedings of the 45th Annual Meeting of the ACL on Interactive Poster and Demonstration Sessions*, ACL '07, pages 173–176, Stroudsburg, PA, USA. Association for Computational Linguistics.

Nate Chambers. 2013. Navytime: Event and time ordering from raw text. In *Second Joint Conference on Lexical and Computational Semantics (*SEM), Volume 2: Proceedings of the Seventh International Workshop on Semantic Evaluation (SemEval 2013)*, pages 73–77, Atlanta, Georgia, USA, June. Association for Computational Linguistics.

Leon Derczynski and Robert J. Gaizauskas. 2012. Using Signals to Improve Automatic Classification of Temporal Relations. *CoRR*, abs/1203.5055.

Jennifer D'Souza and Vincent Ng. 2013. Classifying Temporal Relations with Rich Linguistic Knowledge. In *Proceedings of the 2013 Conference of the North American Chapter of the Association for Computational Linguistics: Human Language Technologies*, pages 918–927.

Christiane Fellbaum, editor. 1998. *WordNet: An Electronic Lexical Database*. MIT Press.

Michael J. Fischer and Albert R. Meyer. 1971. Boolean matrix multiplication and transitive closure. In *SWAT (FOCS)*, pages 129–131. IEEE Computer Society.

Alfonso Gerevini, Lenhart Schubert, and Stephanie Schaeffer. 1995. The temporal reasoning tools Timegraph I-II. *International Journal of Artificial Intelligence Tools*, 4(1-2):281–299.

Andrey Gusev, Nathanael Chambers, Pranav Khaitan, Divye Khilnani, Steven Bethard, and Dan Jurafsky. 2011. Using query patterns to learn the duration of events. In *Proceedings of the Ninth International Conference on Computational Semantics*, IWCS '11, pages 145–154, Stroudsburg, PA, USA. Association for Computational Linguistics.

Anup Kumar Kolya, Amitava Kundu, Rajdeep Gupta, Asif Ekbal, and Sivaji Bandyopadhyay. 2013. Ju_cse: A crf based approach to annotation of temporal expression, event and temporal relations. In *Second Joint Conference on Lexical and Computational Semantics (*SEM), Volume 2: Proceedings of the Seventh International Workshop on Semantic Evaluation (SemEval 2013)*, pages 64–72, Atlanta, Georgia, USA, June. Association for Computational Linguistics.

Natsuda Laokulrat, Makoto Miwa, Yoshimasa Tsuruoka, and Takashi Chikayama. 2013. Uttime: Temporal relation classification using deep syntactic features. In *Second Joint Conference on Lexical and Computational Semantics (*SEM), Volume 2: Proceedings of the Seventh International Workshop on Semantic Evaluation (SemEval 2013)*, pages 88–92, Atlanta, Georgia, USA, June. Association for Computational Linguistics.

Inderjeet Mani, Marc Verhagen, Ben Wellner, Chong Min Lee, and James Pustejovsky. 2006. Machine learning of temporal relations. In *Proceedings of the 21st International Conference on Computational Linguistics and the 44th annual meeting of the Association for Computational Linguistics*, ACL-44, pages 753–760, Stroudsburg, PA, USA. Association for Computational Linguistics.

Emily Pitler and Ani Nenkova. 2009. Using syntax to disambiguate explicit discourse connectives in text. In *Proceedings of the ACL-IJCNLP 2009 Conference Short Papers*, ACLShort '09, pages 13–16, Stroudsburg, PA, USA. Association for Computational Linguistics.

Roser Saurí, Jessica Littman, Robert Gaizauskas, Andrea Setzer, and James Pustejovsky, 2006. *TimeML Annotation Guidelines, Version 1.2.1.*

Naushad UzZaman and James Allen. 2011a. Temporal Evaluation. In *Proceedings of the 49th Annual Meeting of the Association for Computational Linguistics: Human Language Technologies*, pages 351–356, Portland, Oregon, USA, June. Association for Computational Linguistics.

Naushad UzZaman and James F. Allen. 2011b. Temporal evaluation. In *ACL (Short Papers)*, pages 351–356. The Association for Computer Linguistics.

Naushad UzZaman, Hector Llorens, James F. Allen, Leon Derczynski, Marc Verhagen, and James Pustejovsky. 2012. TempEval-3: Evaluating Events, Time Expressions, and Temporal Relations. *CoRR*, abs/1206.5333.

Naushad UzZaman, Hector Llorens, Leon Derczynski, James Allen, Marc Verhagen, and James Pustejovsky. 2013. Semeval-2013 task 1: Tempeval-3: Evaluating time expressions, events, and temporal relations. In *Second Joint Conference on Lexical and Computational Semantics (*SEM), Volume 2: Proceedings of the Seventh International Workshop on Semantic Evaluation (SemEval 2013)*, pages 1–9, Atlanta, Georgia, USA, June. Association for Computational Linguistics.

Marc Verhagen, Robert Gaizauskas, Frank Schilder, Mark Hepple, Graham Katz, and James Pustejovsky. 2007. Semeval-2007 task 15: Tempeval temporal relation identification. In *Proceedings of the 4th International Workshop on Semantic Evaluations*, SemEval '07, pages 75–80, Stroudsburg, PA, USA. Association for Computational Linguistics.

Marc Verhagen, Roser Saurí, Tommaso Caselli, and James Pustejovsky. 2010. SemEval-2010 task 13: TempEval-2. In *Proceedings of the 5th International Workshop on Semantic Evaluation*, SemEval '10, pages 57–62, Stroudsburg, PA, USA. Association for Computational Linguistics.

Marc Verhagen. 2005. Temporal closure in an annotation environment. *Language Resources and Evaluation*, 39(2-3):211–241.

Using idiolects and sociolects to improve word prediction

Wessel Stoop
Centre for Language and Speech Technology
Radboud University Nijmegen
w.stoop@let.ru.nl

Antal van den Bosch
Centre for Language Studies
Radboud University Nijmegen
a.vandenbosch@let.ru.nl

Abstract

In this paper the word prediction system *Soothsayer*[1] is described. This system predicts what a user is going to write as he is keying it in. The main innovation of Soothsayer is that it not only uses *idiolects*, the language of one individual person, as its source of knowledge, but also *sociolects*, the language of the social circle around that person. We use Twitter for data collection and experimentation. The *idiolect* models are based on individual Twitter feeds, the *sociolect* models are based on the tweets of a particular person and the tweets of the people he often communicates with. The idea behind this is that people who often communicate start to talk alike; therefore the language of the friends of person x can be helpful in trying to predict what person x is going to say. This approach achieved the best results. For a number of users, more than 50% of the keystrokes could have been saved if they had used Soothsayer.

1 Introduction

The main aim of the study presented here is to show that the concepts of *idiolect* and *sociolect*, the language of one person and his or her social circle, can be used to improve *word prediction*, the task of predicting what a user is going to type, as he is typing. Word prediction technology reduces the number of keystrokes we have to make, thus saving time and preventing mistakes. With the rise of smartphones word prediction has become widely known and used. Preceding this popularization, word prediction systems were already developed up to three decades ago to assist people with speech and motor disabilities, like cerebral palsy or hemiplexia. By using a device equipped with word prediction technology, they can increase their communication rate considerably (Garay-Vitoria and Abascal, 2006). Indeed, most studies before the year 2000, when mobile phones were not widely used yet, targeted the disabled user group - Copestake (1997) even reports building a system for one individual user. More recent work targets a wider audience, but in this paper we return to the idea of using an individual's own language to train individualized models.

The concept of an idiolect, the language of a single person, is well-known, but rarely ever modelled or in some other way operationalized (Mollin, 2009; Barlow, 2010; Louwerse, 2004). Almost every claim in the field of linguistics concerns language as a whole; whether the subject of investigation is a particular syntactic construction, phonological variable, or some other linguistic phenomenon, the results are always supposed to hold for an entire language variety. According to Mollin (2009) idiolects are a 'neglected area in corpus linguistics', and Barlow (2010) states that the term 'is distinguished by the fact that there is probably no other linguistic term in which there is such a large gap between the familiarity of the concept and lack of empirical data on the phenomenon.' This is remarkable, since 'idiolects are the only kind of language we can collect data on', as Haugen (1972) points out; a language variety essentially is a collection of idiolects.

Word prediction systems typically operate with an algorithm and a language model, as the overview of related work in Section 2 will show. Language models are created from training material, typically a large collection of text. Section 3 introduces our algorithm step by step. The resulting best-performing algorithm is used in Section

[1]The system is available as an interactive demo at http://soothsayer.cls.ru.nl/ and its source code is publicly available at https://github.com/woseseltops/soothsayer

4, in which we investigate which language model should be used together with this algorithm. We start with the notion of an individual's idiolect in Section 4.1, and expand this by using the language of the people this individual communicates with, in Section 4.2. In Section 5 we offer our conclusions and formulate points for further research.

2 Related work

An early solution for word prediction was to use word frequency lists (Swiffin et al., 1985). Although it is possible to wait until a word unicity point has been reached (the point in a word where there there is no other word with the same prefix), more keystrokes may be saved if the prediction can be done before the unicity point. After this first data-driven improvement, numerous authors have shown that taking the contextof previously entered words into account improves prediction accuracy further. A simple approach to implementing context-sensitivity is applying the frequency list technique to word n-grams (Hunnicutt, 1987); in a string of work other statistical language modeling approaches have been proposed (Lesher et al., 1999; Langlais et al., 2000; Garay-Vitoria and Abascal, 2006; Tanaka-Ishii, 2007; Van den Bosch and Bogers, 2008).

The accuracy of a context-sensitive system largely depends on how often a similar context is available in the training material; the amount of training data will be an important factor for the system's success. A key publication by Lesher *et al.* (1999) indeed shows that the accuracy of a context-sensitive word prediction system is related to how much training material is provided. On the other hand, once most of the frequent combinations are covered, it takes more and more training material to improve the results a little bit. Van den Bosch (2011) demonstrates that the relation between the amount of training data and word completion performance is roughly log-linear. For instance, when going from 100 to 1,000 words in the training material, roughly 6% more keystrokes could be saved (from 15% to 21% keystrokes saved), while the same is true for the step from 1,000,000 to 10,000,000 words (from 40% to 46%).

A large portion of the work on word prediction includes linguistic knowledge in some way, for example by also training the system which PoS-tags are likely to follow each other, and using that to limit the pool of suggestions (Carlberger et al., 1997; Fazly and Hirst, 2003; Copestake, 1997; Matiasek et al., 2002; Garay-Vitoria and Gonzalez-Abascal, 1997). Interestingly, most authors conclude that including linguistic knowledge improves the results, but only slightly (Garay-Vitoria and Gonzalez-Abascal, 1997; Fazly and Hirst, 2003). Fazly and Hirst (2003) note that adding explicit linguistic knowledge 'might not be considered worth the considerable extra cost that it requires'. In the current study we have not used any explicit linguistic knowledge, thus making our system language-independent.

There have also been more successful optimizations of word completion systems. One is to use training material from the same domain. Verberne *et al.* (2012) show that trying to predict Wikipedia text, tweets, transcriptions of conversational speech and Frequently Asked Questions all worked best when using texts from the same type. As a second optimization, building on the idea of cache language models (Goodman, 2001), Van den Bosch (2011) proposes to make a word completion system learn about register and topic on the fly with a *recency buffer*. This buffer stores the n latest words; if a word the user is keying in matches one of the words in the recency buffer, this word is suggested instead of what the system would actually have suggested. The idea behind this is that if the user is writing about, for example, traveling, words like 'go', 'hotel', and 'see' are likely to be in the buffer and thus could be suggested quickly. In other words, the systems learns about the user and the topic on the fly.

Although both approaches help to increase the number of keystrokes saved, they also have downsides: for the system by Verberne *et al.* (2012) training texts in the same genre are needed, which might not be available, whereas the system by Van den Bosch (2011) ignores context information that it should weigh more intelligently. For example, while a context-sensitive text-prediction system will probably be able to predict *to* for the sentence *they were going t...*, the one with the recency buffer will predict *they*.

3 System description

Soothsayer predicts the next word the user is going to type, or the rest of the word in case the user already starting typing something. To do this, it works with a set of independent word prediction modules. Modules can be either context-insensitive or context-sensitive, and use one language model. We will work with two language models, one based on a large collection of texts sampling from many different authors, the 'general language model', and one based on a set of texts written by an individual, the 'idiolect'. We thus have four possible modules:

Module	Type	Model
1	Context-sensitive	idiolect
2	Context-sensitive	general language model
3	Context-insensitive	idiolect
4	Context-insensitive	general language model

Table 1: Four possible modules: combinations of type and language model

Modules can be concatenated in such a way that a second module takes over once the first modules no longer has predictions, a third module takes over once the second one no longer has predictions, etc. In future work, interpolation of the predictions of these modules should be investigated.

3.1 Context-insensitive modules

Context-insensitive modules only use information of the word the user is currently keying in. In sentence 1, for example, only the c will be used for prediction.

(1) I ate too much c

This means that a prediction like *communication* is fully possible, despite the context. This also means that at the beginning of each new word no prediction will be available, because the module has no material to work with. Despite these limitations, context-insensitive modules can already save a lot of keystrokes, because the first few letters of a word impose strong limitations on what letters can possibly follow, and some words have early unicity points. Predictions are done by going through a frequency list, so the most frequent (and thus more likely to occur again) words are considered first. Once a word is encountered that matches what has been keyed in so far, it is suggested.

3.2 Context-sensitive modules

Context-sensitive modules make use of the words that came before the current word to limit what words are predicted. Soothsayer approaches word prediction as a classification task, where the three words in the left context of the word to be predicted are the features, and the word following this context is the class label to be predicted. This means that we have a separate class for every word that could possibly be predicted. Soothsayer uses the k-nearest neighbour classification method, which is insensitive to the number of classes to be predicted. k-nearest neighbour classification (henceforth *KNN*) means that the class is determined on the basis of similar cases in a training corpus. How many cases are taken into consideration, k, can be determined beforehand. The similarity between a new instance and memorized instances is determined using a simularity function. A classic implementation of *KNN* suited for the type of symbolic features we have, the IB1-algorithm (Aha et al., 1991), simply counts how many features overlap. However, the IB1 algorithm generally is too slow to be used in practical applications, ours included. We adopt IGTree[2] (Daelemans et al., 1997), an approximation of IB1 that does not require a comparison of the complete context.

IGTree calculates which features contain most information about the class labels using the Information Gain or Gain Ratio metrics, orders the features from most informative to least informative, and compresses the training set in a decision tree. Classification of a new context reduces to making a small number of decisions (a maximum of three, because we have three features), instead of comparing a new context to thousands to millions of contexts. If we ask IGTree to classify unseen input, the algorithm may not come to a unique decision. Soothsayer asks the algorithm to return everything it considers a possibility at the deepest node it reached while traversing the decision tree. Analogous to the manner in which the context-insensitive module generates frequency-ranked lists of possible completions, IGTree will produce a frequency-ranked list of possible completions it found at this deepest node in the tree. Soothsayer then accepts the single (or three) top-ranking suggestion(s).

3.3 Evaluating the system

There is an ongoing discussion in the literature on what is the best way to evaluate word pre-

[2] IGTree is implemented in the TiMBL software package, `http://ilk.uvt.nl/timbl`

diction systems. A straightforward evaluation might be to calculate the percentage of correctly predicted words (the so-called *hit-ratio*), but as Garay-Vitoria and Abascal (2006) note, this is not enough: a system that has 100% of the words correct, but only gives this prediction at the last letter of every word saves very few keystrokes. A more natural way might be to test with real humans, and measure how much time they save when using the system (Carlberger et al., 1997; Koester and Levine, 1998; Garay-Vitoria and Abascal, 2006). However, this is a costly and time-consuming task, as the participants will need a considerable amount of time to get used to the system. Therefore, we will evaluate Soothsayer by simulating somebody keying in a text, and counting how many keystrokes this virtual user does not have to do when using the system.

However, even when using simulations, there are multiple ways to evaluate the system. One possibility is to provide the user with a list of the n most likely predictions (Lesher et al., 1999; Fazly and Hirst, 2003). This approach has the advantage that it results in high percentages of keystrokes saved - in particular when n is set to a high value, because this means the system can do multiple guesses at once, while only one has to be correct. As Van den Bosch (2011) notes, however, this also has important downsides:

> [I]n many devices and circumstances it is inefficient or impossible to present [...] suggestion lists. Inspecting a list of suggestions also poses a larger cognitive load than checking a single suggestion, and furthermore it is unclear how scrolling, browsing and selecting items from this list should be counted in terms of keystrokes.

For this reason, we calculate the number of keystrokes that could have been saved when the user was presented only one prediction at a time. Predictions can be accepted with the space key. Because this is sometimes problematic (for instance, if the user wanted to type *sun*, but Soothsayer predicts *sunday*, hitting space would lead to the wrong word), a rejection is also calculated as a keystroke. The number of keystrokes that can be saved if the word prediction system works this way will be called **Classical Keystrokes Saved** (CKS) in the remainder of this paper. Please note that CKS assumes that the user always accepts a prediction immediately when it is available, which might not always be the case in reality.

On the other hand, current popular smartphone applications suggest this approach might be too strict. The popular smartphone application SwiftKey[3] always shows the user three predictions, which seem to be (1) what the user has keyed in so far, (2) the most likely prediction and (3) the second most likely prediction. In case the user has not yet started typing the next word, option (1) is replaced by the third most likely prediction. The percentage of keystrokes that can be saved when two (and sometimes three) predictions were shown will be referred to as **SwiftKey Keystrokes Saved** (SKKS). This percentage will mostly be higher than CKS.

3.4 Other considerations

Context-sensitive before context-insensitive The context-sensitive module learns about which words in the training texts typically follow each other, and thus is potentially powerful when it comes to the more frequent, fixed combinations of words and words that often occur in each other's context, but is not useful with words that are also frequent, but were not used earlier in this context. The context-insensitive module, on the other hand, can predict any word, as long as it has been used before, but knows nothing about fixed combinations. In other words, the modules complement each other. Based on the fact that context-sensitive modules have been reported as scoring better than context-insensitive modules in direct comparisons in controlled experiments (Lesher et al., 1999), we rank context-sensitive modules before context-insensitive ones in all studies reported here. The context-insensitive module trained on idiolects precedes the final context-insensitive module trained on a general language corpus; this order reflects the order also found in the context-sensitive modules described in more detail in the next section.

Attenuation IGTree is fast in classification, but with tens of millions of training instances it becomes too slow for real-time use, where fast typists may reach as many as twenty keystrokes per second. To alleviate this issue we use a (simplified version of a) solution from the field of syntactic parsing called *attenuation* (Eisner, 1996). All

[3] `http://www.swiftkey.net/`

words in the training material that occur less often than a particular threshold are replaced by a dummy value. Replacing all low-frequent words by one dummy value makes the IGTree considerably smaller and thus faster to traverse during classification. In a pilot experiment an attenuation threshold of 3 turned out to be the most desirable: it leads to the largest increase in speed (from 28 classifications per second to 89) without any measurable decrease in prediction accuracy. For this reason, an attenuation threshold of 3 was used throughout the study.

Handling morphology Some aspects of morphology are inherently problematic for word completion, in particular compounding, inflections, and suffixes. For example, imagine a user has already written sentence 2, and wants to write the word *cookies*:

(2) I would really like the c

If in the training material the word *cookie* was more frequent, Soothsayer will suggest that instead of *cookies*. Normally, when a prediction is wrong, the algorithm will find out because the user keys in another letter (so the predicted word no longer matches what the user is typing), but that technique will not work here. For words that only differ in their suffix, the point of difference is at the end of the word, when there is nothing left to predict. Even if the correct word is the second most likely prediction, this will not be suggested, because Soothsayer has no reason to switch prediction.

However, there is a clue Soothsayer could use: normally, when a prediction is right, the user will accept it, instead of going on writing. He might not accept it immediately (typing often goes faster than mentally processing predictions), but once the user has not accepted a prediction for more than two or three keystrokes in a row, it gets more and more likely the user keeps on typing because the prediction is wrong. In that case, the second most likely prediction could be displayed, which in many cases will be the word with the second most likely suffix. We use this *early prediction switching* method throughout our experiments.

Recency As Church (2000) showed, the probability that a word recurs twice in a short stretch of text is far higher than its frequency in language would suggests, which is mainly related to the word's topicality. Whereas knowledge about topics could be covered by training and testing within the same coherent set of texts (e.g. all written by a single person), the aforementioned recency buffer by definition uses more recent text (that is, material from the same text), and might this way be able to do more accurate predictions. We implemented a buffer that remembers the n most recent words, and suggests the most recent one that matches with the word that is currently being keyed in. Following Van den Bosch (2011) we set n to 300. If no word matches, the next module will take over. In our experiments we have tested the insertion of the recency buffer module after the context-sensitive modules and before the context-insensitive modules.

4 The model: idiolects and sociolects

4.1 Idiolects

In this experiment the power of idiolects will be investigated by training and testing an array of systems on one hundred different idiolects of individuals. For this, the micro-blogging service Twitter[4] is used. Twitter is a micro-blogging service where each user can submit status updates known as tweets, which consist of 140 characters or less. Using the Twitter API, all tweets of a manually created seed set of 40 Dutch Twitter users were retrieved from January until June 2013. Retweets, messages these authors did not produce themselves, were excluded. These seed users were the starting point of an iterative expansion of the set of crawled Twitter uses by following mentions of other users (indicated with the syntax *'@username'*). The goal of this expansion was to find as much active Twitter users as possible for the system to follow, and to capture the network of these users. The set was extended with two users every 30 minutes with the following procedure:

- From the set of users mentioned in tweets already harvested and not yet tracked, the most frequently mentioned user is selected. This ensures that the new person communicates with at least one of the persons the system is already following.
- From the set of users mentioned by more than a single person already being tracked, the most frequently mentioned user is selected. This ensures the new person is well

[4] `http://www.twitter.com`

connected to the people the system is already following.

The system limits itself to Dutch tweets using a conservative Dutch word frequency list containing highly frequent Dutch words that have no counterpart in other languages.

Concerning the relation between number of tweets and Twitter users, many scholars have noticed that it follows a Pareto-distribution (Heil and Piskorski, 2009; Asur and Huberman, 2010; Rui and Whinston, 2012). That is, a small part of the Twitter users produce a large part of the tweets. This distribution means that using all or a random selection of Twitter users is not likely to lead to good results, because for most users not much material is available. Therefore, only data from the 100 Twitter users for which the most material was harvested are used to build the idiolect models. Twitter accounts run by something other than an individual person (such as a company) were excluded manually. The number of words ranged from 61,098 words for the least active user of the 100 users to 167,685 words for the most active user. As a general language model, a random selection of blogs, emails and Wikipedia articles from the SoNaR corpus for written Dutch (Oostdijk et al., 2013) was made. These texts were chosen because they were believed to be neither very formal nor very informal, and fall in the same new-media category as Twitter messages. The general language corpus consisted of 55,212,868 words.

First, we compared the general language model against each user's idiolect, and tested on all 100 Twitter feeds of individual users. We then combined the two models (the general model acting as back-off for the idiolect model). These three setups were tested with and without a recency buffer module, resulting in six runs. For each of these runs, we tried to predict the 10% most recent material, and trained on the remaining 90% (for idiolects). Tables 2 and 3 list the results on these six runs measured in CKS and SKKS, respectively. We observe that using the idiolect model leads to more keystrokes saved than using the general model. We also see that using the general language model as a background model leads to more keystrokes saved than using the idiolect model alone. Using the recency buffer leads to more keystrokes saved, especially when it is used in addition to the general mode,

An ANOVA for repeated measures showed that there is a significant effect of the training material $F(2, 198) = 109.495, p < .001$ and whether the recency buffer was used $F(1, 99) = 469.648, p < .001$. Contrast analyses revealed that both the differences between the results of the general model and the idiolect model $F(1, 99) = 41.902, p < .001$ and the idiolect model and the idiolect model with the background model $F(1, 99) = 232.140, p < .001$ were significant.

The high standard deviations indicate a lot of variation. The substantial individual differences are illustrated in Figure 1, where the users are ordered from least to most material. Contrary to expectations, no correlation between amount of training material and the results could be detected (Pearson's correlation, $p = .763$); apparently, the individual factor is that much stronger, and Soothsayer performs much better for one than for the other. Using the overall best-performing module set-up, the set-up with the idiolect model, backed up by the general language model, *and* the recency buffer, the worst result is 21.8% CKS and 24.1% SKKS for user 90, and the best result is 51.3% CKS and 52.4% SKKS for user 97.

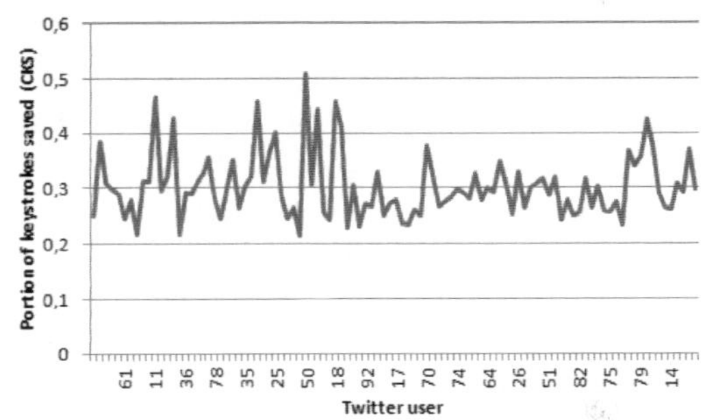

Figure 1: The proportion of keystrokes saved for individual Twitter users, ordered from by amount of tweets (from left to right: from least to most), when using the best-performing module set-up

The large amount of variation between individual Twitter users cannot easily be explained, with a few exceptions (for example, people with powerful idiolect models sometimes often repeated long words like *goedemorgen* 'good morning', *dankjewel* 'thank you', and *welterusten* 'sleep well'), but no clear patterns emerged. Trying to predict for which persons word prediction will go well and for which persons it will not might be an interesting topic for future research. It is a question that is related to the field of computational

Training material	Test material	Without recency buffer		With recency buffer	
		Mean	St. dev.	Mean	St. dev.
General	Twitter	14.4	5.1	23.2	5.2
Idiolect	Twitter	23.2	7.9	26.7	7.9
Idiolect + general	Twitter	26.4	6.2	29.7	6.4

Table 2: Mean percentage of keystrokes saved (**CKS**) and standard deviations for all module set-ups.

Training material	Test material	Without recency buffer		With recency buffer	
		Mean	St. dev.	Mean	St. dev.
General	Twitter	16.2	6.1	26	5.4
Idiolect	Twitter	24.8	8.3	27.9	7.2
Idiolect + general	Twitter	28.2	6.3	32.1	6.3

Table 3: Mean percentage of keystrokes saved (**SKKS**) and standard deviations for all module set-ups.

stylometry and in particular automatic authorship attribution, although authorship attribution is the exact opposite of the task described here (guessing the author on the basis of text instead of guessing the text on the basis of the author) (Bagavandas and Manimannan, 2008).

4.2 Social networks and language input

The findings by Lesher *et al.* (1999) suggest that more material leads to more keystrokes saved; this may also hold for idiolects. This material, however, might not be available, simply because not all people write or tweet that much. For a particular user x, what other sources of language do we have that might be similar to the idiolect of x? One of the more obvious answers might be the language of the people x often communicates with. The fact that people that are in some way related to each other speak alike using a 'group language' or a sociolect, is well established in sociolinguistics.

This approach of including the language of the people from a particular person's environment can also be viewed from a different perspective: so far, we have followed Mollin (2009) and Barlow(2010) in using only the *output* of speakers. This makes sense (since what comes out must have been inside), but can never be the full story. The sociolect model that will be constructed here can be seen as a feasible and rough approximation of recording everything a person reads or hears: by including the language of the socially related persons of person x, the system can have a rough idea of the kind of *input* person x gets.

On the basis of the data already collected for the idiolect experiments, sociolects were created by collecting all addressees mentioned with the *@addressee* syntax for each of the 100 Twitter users used in the previous experiment. For all addressees that were mentioned three times or more, it was checked if this addressee was in the dataset (which was almost always the case). If so, it was checked whether this addressee also mentioned the original Twitter user at least three times. If this was also the case, the system assumed the users speak to each other often enough to have their language adjusted to each other, and the tweets of this addressee were added to the sociolect of the original Twitter user. We thus end up with 100 sociolects built around the 100 most active Twitter users, all based on the tweets of a Twitter user and the tweets of the persons that this person communicated with at least six times (three times as writer, three times as reader).

The results of Verberne *et al.* (2012) would predict that adding tweets in general would lead to increases in the number of keystrokes saved, as this is using more texts from the same genre. To be sure that any improvements can be attributed to the fact that this is the language from friends, a control model will be built. While the sociolect model consists of the tweets of Twitter user x and the tweets of the friends of twitter user x, the control model consists of the tweets of Twitter user x and the tweets of random other Twitter users, and has approximately the same number of words.

For each of the 100 Twitter users, comparative runs are performed with the model created on the basis of the idiolect and the random Twitter users versus the sociolect model. The best performing module set-up from the previous experiments is used. The results are compared to the simulations with the idiolect model from the previous experi-

Training material	Test material	CKS		SKKS	
		Mean	St. dev.	Mean	St. dev.
Idiolect	Twitter feed	29.6	6.4	32.1	6.3
Control model	Twitter feed	31.2	6.3	33.9	6
Sociolect	Twitter feed	33.9	7.1	36.2	7.1

Table 4: Mean percentage of keystrokes saved when using an idiolect, a control model (consisting of an idiolect and random other Twitter feeds) and a sociolect.

Twitter user	Idiolect		Idiolect+random feeds		Sociolect	
	CKS	SKKS	CKS	SKKS	CKS	SKKS
24	31.2	36.3	34	36.4	31.6	34.3
49	27.2	29.1	26.2	29.7	24.6	27.2
71	27.5	30.2	34.2	35.8	30.8	32.9

Table 5: Percentage of keystrokes saved for 3 atypical Twitter users, using the the idiolect, control and sociolect models

ment. The results of the simulations are summarized in Table 4. We observe that adding more tweets to the idiolects leads to more keystrokes saved, and that the most keystrokes can be saved when using the tweets of the people the owner of the idiolect communicates with often.

An ANOVA for repeated measures showed that there is a significant effect for the training material $F(2, 198) = 69.466, p < .001$. Contrast analyses revealed that both the differences between the results of the idiolect model and the idiolect model and random feeds $F(1, 99) = 93.471, p < .001$ and the idiolect model and random feeds and the sociolect model $F(1, 99) = 61.871, p < .001$ are significant.

Again, the high standard deviations indicate notable variation among the individual results. Table 5 lists the deviating individual scores for three individual Twitter users. In these results we see an increase when random tweets are added, but a decrease when the tweets from their conversation partners are used. For user 24 and 49, the percentage of keystrokes saved when using the sociolect model is even lower than the idiolect model alone.

Using the best-performing module set-up in general, the set-up with the sociolect model, backed up by the general language model, *and* the recency buffer, the worst result is 21.3% CKS and 22% SKKS for user 90, and the best result is 56.2% CKS and 58.1% SKKS for user 38.

5 Conclusion

In this paper we presented the word prediction system *Soothsayer*. Testing the system we found that word prediction and idiolects are an effective combination; our results show that word prediction is best done with a combination of an idiolect-based context-sensitive system, backed up by a context-sensitive module equipped with a general language model. A recency buffer is a useful third module in the sequence. Our average best scores with these three modules are 29.7% keystrokes saved according to the strict (one-best) CKS metric, and 32.1% keystrokes saved according to the Swiftkey-inspired SKKS metric.

The fact that people speak like the people around them can also be useful to word prediction. When we approximate a sociolect by expanding a user's Twitter corpus by tweets from people this person communicates with, and retrain our first context-sensitive module with this data, average scores improve to 33.9% CKS and 36.2% SKKS.

What works well for one speaker, might not necessarily work for another, however. While we find significant advantages of idiolect-based and sociolect-based training, the variance among our 100 test users is substantial, and in individual cases idiolect-based training is not the best option. For other users the positive gains are substantially higher than the mean; the best result for a single user is 56.2% CKS and 58.1% SKKS.

In future research we aim to investigate methods that could predetermine which model and module order will work best for a user. Another set of open research questions concern the fact that we have not tested many of the system's settings. What would be the effects of predicting more words at the same time?

References

D. W. Aha, D. Kibler, and M. K. Albert. 1991. Instance-based learning algorithms. *Machine Learning*, 6:37–66.

S. Asur and B. A. Huberman. 2010. Predicting the future with social media. In *Proceedings of the 2010 IEEE/WIC/ACM International Conference on Web Intelligence and Intelligent Agent Technology - Volume 01*, WI-IAT '10, pages 492–499, Washington, DC, USA. IEEE Computer Society.

M. Bagavandas and G. Manimannan. 2008. Style consistency and authorship attribution: A statistical investigation. *Journal of Quantitative Linguistics*, 15(1):100–110.

M. Barlow. 2010. Individual usage: a corpus-based study of idiolects. In *LAUD Conference, Landau*. http://auckland.academia.edu/MichaelBarlow.

A. Carlberger, J. Carlberger, T. Magnuson, S. Hunnicutt, S. E. Palazuelos Cagigas, and S. Aguilera Navarro. 1997. Profet, a new generation of word prediction: An evaluation study. In *ACL Workshop on Natural Language Processing for Communication Aids*, pages 23 –28.

K. W. Church. 2000. Empirical estimates of adaptation: The chance of two noriegas is closer to p=2 than p2. In *Proceedings of the 18th Conference on Computational Linguistics*, volume 1, pages 180–186.

A. Copestake. 1997. Augmented and alternative nlp techniques for augmented and alternative nlp techniques for augmentative and alternative communication. In *Proceedings of the ACL workshop on Natural Language Processing for Communication Aids*, pages 37–42.

W. Daelemans, A. van den Bosch, and A. Weijters. 1997. Igtree: using trees for compression and classiffication in lazy learning algorithms. *Artificial Intelligence Review*, 11:407–423.

J. Eisner. 1996. An empirical comparison of probability models for dependency grammar. In *Technical Report IRCS-96-11, Institute for Research in Cognitive Science*. University of Pennsylvania.

A. Fazly and G. Hirst. 2003. Testing the efficacy of part-of-speech information in word completion. In *Proceedings of the 2003 EACL Workshop on Language Modeling for Text Entry Methods*, pages 9–16.

N. Garay-Vitoria and J. Abascal. 2006. Text prediction systems: a survey. *Univers. Access Inf. Soc.*, 4(3):188–203.

N. Garay-Vitoria and J. Gonzalez-Abascal. 1997. Intelligent word-prediction to enhance text input rate. In *Proceedings of the 2nd International Conference on Intelligent User Interfaces*, pages 241–244.

J. Goodman. 2001. A bit of progress in language modeling. *Computer Speech & Language*, 15(4):403–434.

E. Haugen. 1972. From idiolect to language. In E. Scherabon Firchow, K. Grimstad, N. Hasselmo, and W. A. ONeil, editors, *Studies by Einar Haugen. Presented on the Occasion of his 65th Birthday*, pages 415–421. Mouton, The Hague/Paris.

B. Heil and M. Piskorski. 2009. New twitter research: Men follow men and nobody tweets. `http://blogs.hbr.org/cs/2009/06/new\_twitter\_research\_men\_follo.html`.

S. Hunnicutt. 1987. Input and output alternatives in word prediction. *STL-QPSR*, 28(2-3):015–029.

H. H. Koester and S. P. Levine. 1998. Model simulations of user performance with word prediction. *Augmentative Alternative Commun*, pages 25–35.

P. Langlais, G. Foster, and G. Lapalme. 2000. Transtype: a computer-aided translation typing system. In *Proceedings of the 2000 NAACL-ANLP Workshop on Embedded machine translation systems-Volume 5*, pages 46–51. Association for Computational Linguistics.

G. W. Lesher, B. J. Moulton, and D. J. Higginbotham. 1999. Effects of ngram order and training text size on word prediction. In *Proceedings of the Annual Conference of the RESNA*.

M. M. Louwerse. 2004. Semantic variation in idiolect and sociolect: Corpus linguistic evidence from literary texts. *Computers and the Humanities*, 38(2):207–221.

J. Matiasek, M. Baroni, and H. Trost. 2002. FASTY: A multi-lingual approach to text prediction. In *Computers Helping People With Special Needs*, pages 165–176. Springer Verlag, Berlin, Germany.

S. Mollin. 2009. I entirely understand is a blairism: The methodology of identifying idiolectal collocations. *Journal of Corpus Linguistics*, 14 (3):367–392.

N. Oostdijk, M. Reynaert, V. Hoste, and I. Schuurman. 2013. The construction of a 500-million-word reference corpus of contemporary written Dutch. In *Essential Speech and Language Technology for Dutch*, pages 219–247. Springer.

H. Rui and A. Whinston. 2012. Information or attention? an empirical study of user contribution on twitter. *Information Systems and e-Business Management*, 10(3):309–324.

A. L. Swiffin, J. A. Pickering, J. L. Arnott, and A. F. Newell. 1985. PAL: An effort efficient portable communication aid and keyboard emulator. In *Proceedings of the 8th annual coonference on Rehabilitation Technology, RESNA*, pages 197–199.

K. Tanaka-Ishii. 2007. Word-based Predictive Text Entry using Adaptive Language Models. *Natural Language Engineering*, 13(1):51–74.

A. Van den Bosch and T. Bogers. 2008. Efficient context-sensitive word completion for mobile devices. In *MobileHCI 2008: Proceedings of the 10th International Conference on Human-Computer Interaction with Mobile Devices and Services, IOP-MMI special track*, pages 465–470.

A. Van den Bosch. 2011. Effects of context and recency in scaled word completion. *Computational Linguistics in the Netherlands Journal*, 1:79–94.

S. Verberne, A. Van den Bosch, H. Strik, and L. Boves. 2012. The effect of domain and text type on text prediction quality. In *Proceedings of the 13th Conference of the European Chapter of the Association for Computational Linguistics, Avignon, France*, pages 561–569, New Brunswick, NJ. ACL.

Dynamic Topic Adaptation for Phrase-based MT

Eva Hasler[1], **Phil Blunsom**[2], **Philipp Koehn**[1], **Barry Haddow**[1]
[1]School of Informatics, University of Edinburgh
[2]Dept. of Computer Science, University of Oxford

Abstract

Translating text from diverse sources poses a challenge to current machine translation systems which are rarely adapted to structure beyond corpus level. We explore topic adaptation on a diverse data set and present a new bilingual variant of Latent Dirichlet Allocation to compute topic-adapted, probabilistic phrase translation features. We dynamically infer document-specific translation probabilities for test sets of unknown origin, thereby capturing the effects of document context on phrase translations. We show gains of up to 1.26 BLEU over the baseline and 1.04 over a domain adaptation benchmark. We further provide an analysis of the domain-specific data and show additive gains of our model in combination with other types of topic-adapted features.

1 Introduction

In statistical machine translation (SMT), there has been a lot of interest in trying to incorporate information about the provenance of training examples in order to improve translations for specific target domains. A popular approach are mixture models (Foster and Kuhn, 2007) where each component contains data from a specific genre or domain. Mixture models can be trained for *cross-domain* adaption when the target domain is known or for *dynamic* adaptation when the target domain is inferred from the source text under translation. More recent domain adaptation methods employ corpus or instance weights to promote relevant training examples (Matsoukas et al., 2009; Foster et al., 2010) or do more radical data selection based on language model perplexity (Axelrod et al., 2011). In this work, we are interested in the dynamic adaptation case, which is challenging because we cannot tune our model towards any specific domain.

In previous literature, domains have often been loosely defined in terms of corpora, for example, news texts would be defined as belonging to the news domain, ignoring the specific content of news documents. It is often assumed that the data within a domain is homogeneous in terms of style and vocabulary, though that is not always true in practice. The term *topic* on the other hand can describe the thematic content of a document (e.g. politics, economy, medicine) or a latent cluster in a topic model. Topic modelling for machine translation aims to find a match between thematic context and topic clusters. We view topic adaptation as fine-grained domain adaptation with the implicit assumption that there can be multiple distributions over translations within the same data set. If these distributions overlap, then we expect topic adaptation to help separate them and yield better translations than an unadapted system. Topics can be of varying granularity and are therefore a flexible means to structure data that is not uniform enough to be modelled in its entirety. In recent years there have been several attempts to integrating topical information into SMT either by learning better word alignments (Zhao and Xing, 2006), by adapting translation features cross-domain (Su et al., 2012), or by dynamically adapting lexical weights (Eidelman et al., 2012) or adding sparse topic features (Hasler et al., 2012).

We take a new approach to topic adaptation by estimating probabilistic phrase translation features in a completely Bayesian fashion. The motivation is that automatically identifying topics in the training data can help to select the appropriate translation of a source phrase in the context of a document. By adapting a system to automatically induced topics we do not have to trust data from a given domain to be uniform. We also overcome the problem of defining the level of granularity for domain adaptation. With more and more training data automatically extracted from the web and little knowledge about its content, we believe this is an important area to focus on. Translation of web sites is already a popular application for MT systems and could be helped by dynamic model adaptation. We present results on a mixed data set of the TED corpus, parts of the Commoncrawl corpus which contains crawled web data and parts of the News Commentary corpus which contains

Figure 1: Phrasal LDA model for inference on training data.

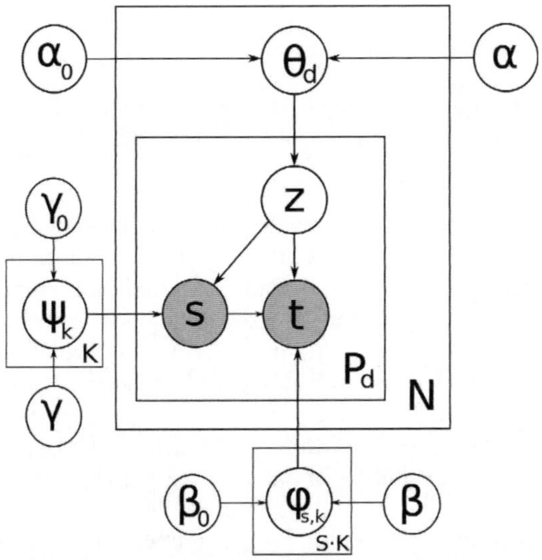

documents about politics and economics. We believe that the broad range of this data set makes it a suitable testbed for topic adaptation. We focus on translation model adaptation to learn how words and phrases translate in a given document-context without knowing the origin of the document. By learning translations over latent topics and combining several topic-adapted features we achieve improvements of more than 1 BLEU point.

2 Bilingual topic models over phrase pairs

Our model is based on LDA and infers topics as distributions over phrase pairs instead of over words. It is specific to machine translation in that the conditional dependencies between source and target phrases are modelled explicitly, and therefore we refer to it as phrasal LDA. Topic distributions learned on a training corpus are carried over to tuning and test sets by running a modified inference algorithm on the source side text of those sets. Translation probabilities are adapted separately to each source text under translation which makes this a dynamic topic adaptation approach. In the following we explain our approach to topic modelling with the objective of estimating better phrase translation probabilities for data sets that exhibit a heterogeneous structure in terms of vocabulary and style. The advantage from a modelling point of view is that unlike with mixture models, we avoid sparsity problems that would arise if we treated documents or sets of documents as domains and learned separate models for them.

2.1 Latent Dirichlet Allocation (LDA)

LDA is a generative model that learns latent topics in a document collection. In the original formulation, topics are multinomial distributions over words of the vocabulary and each document is assigned a multinomial distribution over topics (Blei et al., 2003). Our goal is to learn topic-dependent phrase translation probabilities and hence we modify this formulation by replacing words with phrase pairs. This is straightforward when both source and target phrases are observed but requires a modified inference approach when only source phrases are observed in an unknown test set. Different from standard LDA and previous uses of LDA for MT, we define a bilingual topic model that learns topic distributions over phrase pairs. This allows us to model the units of interest in a more principled way, without the need to map per-word or per-sentence topics to phrase pairs. Figure 1 shows a graphical representation of the following generative process.

For each of N documents in the collection

1. Choose topic distribution $\theta_d \sim \text{Dirichlet}(\alpha)$.
2. Choose the number of phrases pairs P_d in the document, $P_d \sim Poisson(\zeta)$.
3. For every position d_i in the document corresponding to a phrase pair $p_{d,i}$ of source and target phrase s_i and t_i[1]:
   (a) Choose a topic $z_{d,i} \sim \text{Multinomial}(\theta_d)$.
   (b) Conditioned on topic $z_{d,i}$, choose a source phrase $s_{d,i} \sim \text{Multinomial}(\psi_{z_{d,i}})$.
   (c) Conditioned on $z_{d,i}$ and $s_{d,i}$, choose target phrase $t_{d,i} \sim \text{Multinomial}(\phi_{s_{d,i},z_{d,i}})$.

α, β and γ are parameters of the Dirichlet distributions, which are asymmetric for $k = 0$. Our inference algorithm is an implementation of collapsed variational Bayes (CVB), with a first-order Gaussian approximation (Teh et al., 2006). It has been shown to be more accurate than standard VB and to converge faster than collapsed Gibbs sampling (Teh et al., 2006; Wang and Blunsom, 2013), with little loss in accuracy. Because we have to do inference over a large number of phrase pairs, CVB is more practical than Gibbs sampling.

2.2 Overview of training strategy

Ultimately, we want to learn translation probabilities for all possible phrase pairs that apply to a given test document during decoding. Therefore, topic modelling operates on phrase pairs as they will be seen during decoding. Given word-aligned parallel corpora from several domains, we extract lists of per-document phrase pairs produced by the extraction algorithm in the Moses toolkit (Koehn et al., 2007) which contain all phrase pairs consistent with the word alignment. We run CVB on the set of all training documents to learn latent topics without providing information about the domains.

[1] Parallel documents are modelled as bags of phrase pairs.

Using the trained model, CVB with modified inference is run on all test documents with the set of possible phrase translations that a decoder would load from a phrase table before decoding. When test inference has finished, we compute adapted translation probabilities at the document-level by marginalising over topics for each phrase pair.

3 Bilingual topic inference

3.1 Inference on training documents

The aim of inference on the training data is to find latent topics in the distributions over phrase pairs in each document.This is done by repeatedly visiting all phrase pair positions in all documents, computing conditional topic probabilities and updating counts. To bias the model to cluster stop word phrases in one topic, we place an asymmetric prior over the hyperparameters[2] as described in (Wallach et al., 2009) to make one of the topics a priori more probable in every document. We use a fixed-point update (Minka, 2012) to update the hyperparameters after every iteration. For CVB the conditional probability of topic $z_{d,i}$ given the current state of all variables except $z_{d,i}$ is

$$P(z_{d,i}=k|\mathbf{z}^{-(d,i)},\mathbf{s},\mathbf{t},d,\alpha,\beta,\gamma) \propto \frac{(\mathbb{E}_{\hat{q}}[n^{-(d,i)}_{.,k,s,t}]+\beta)}{(\mathbb{E}_{\hat{q}}[n^{-(d,i)}_{.,k,s,.}]+T_s\cdot\beta)} \frac{(\mathbb{E}_{\hat{q}}[n^{-(d,i)}_{.,k,s,.}]+\gamma)}{(\mathbb{E}_{\hat{q}}[n^{-(d,i)}_{.,k,.}]+S\cdot\gamma)} \cdot(\mathbb{E}_{\hat{q}}[n^{-(d,i)}_{d,k,.}]+\alpha) \quad (1)$$

where $\mathbf{s}$ and $\mathbf{t}$ are all source and target phrases in the collection. $n^{-(d,i)}_{.,k,s,t}$, $n^{-(d,i)}_{.,k,s,.}$ and $n^{-(d,i)}_{d,k,.}$ are cooccurrence counts of topics with phrase pairs, source phrases and documents respectively. $\mathbb{E}_{\hat{q}}$ is the expectation under the variational posterior and in comparison to Gibbs sampling where the posterior would otherwise look very similar, counts are replaced by their means. $n^{-(d,i)}_{.,k,.}$ is a topic occurrence count, T_s is the number of possible target phrases for a given source phrase and S is the total number of source phrases. By modelling phrase translation probabilities separately as $P(t_i|s_i,z_i=k,..)$ and $P(s_i|z_i=k,..)$, we can put different priors on these distributions. For example, we want a sparse distribution over target phrases for a given source phrase and topic to express our translation preference under each topic. The algorithm stops when the variational posterior has converged for all documents or after a maximum of 100 iterations.

3.2 Inference on tuning and test documents

To compute translation probabilities for tuning and test documents where target phrases are not observed, the variational posterior is adapted as shown in Equation 2

$$P(z_{d,i}=k,t_{i,j}|\mathbf{z}^{-(d,i)},\mathbf{s},\mathbf{t}^{-(d,i)},d,\alpha,\beta,\gamma) \propto \frac{(\mathbb{E}_{\hat{q}}[n^{-(d,i)}_{.,k,s,t_j}]+\beta)}{(\mathbb{E}_{\hat{q}}[n^{-(d,i)}_{.,k,s,.}]+T_s\cdot\beta)} \frac{(\mathbb{E}_{\hat{q}}[n^{-(d,i)}_{.,k,s,.}]+\gamma)}{(\mathbb{E}_{\hat{q}}[n^{-(d,i)}_{.,k,.}]+S\cdot\gamma)} \cdot(\mathbb{E}_{\hat{q}}[n^{-(d,i)}_{d,k,.}]+\alpha) \quad (2)$$

which now computes the joint conditional probability of a topic k and a target phrase $t_{i,j}$, given the source phrase s_i and the test document d. Therefore, the size of the support changes from K to $K\cdot T_s$. While during training inference we compute a distribution over topics for each source-target pair, in test inference we can use the posterior to marginalise out the topics and get a distribution over target phrases for each source phrase.

We use the Moses decoder to produce lists of translation options for each document in the tuning and test sets. These lists comprise all phrase pairs that will enter the search space at decoding time. By default, only 20 target phrases per source phrase are loaded from the phrase table, so in order to allow for new phrase pairs to enter the search space and for translation probabilities to be computed more accurately, we allow for up to 200 target phrases per source. For each source sentence, we consider all possible phrase segmentations and applicable target phrases. Unlike in training, we do not iterate over all phrase pairs in the list but over blocks of up to 200 target phrases for a given source phrase. The algorithm stops when all marginal translation probabilities have converged though in practice we stopped earlier to avoid overfitting.

3.3 Phrase translation probabilities

After topic inference on the tuning and test data, the forward translation probabilities $P(t|s,d)$ are computed. This is done separately for every document d because we are interested in the translation probabilities that depend on the inferred topic proportions for a given document. For every document, we iterate over source positions $p_{d,i}$ and use the current variational posterior to compute $P(t_{i,j}|s_i,d)$ for all possible target phrases by marginalizing over topics:

$$P(t_{i,j}|s_i,d)=\textstyle\sum_k P(z_i=k,t_{i,j}|\mathbf{z}^{-(d,i)},\mathbf{s},\mathbf{t}^{-(d,i)},d)$$

This is straightforward because during test inference the variational posterior is normalised to a distribution over topics and target phrases for a given source phrase. If a source phrase occurs multiple times in the same document, the probabilities are averaged over all occurrences. The inverse translation probabilities can be computed analogously except that in cases where we

[2]Omitted from the following equations for simplicity.

do not have variational posteriors for a given pair of source and target phrases, an approximation is needed. We omit the results here since our experiments so far did not indicate improvements with the inverse features included.

4 More topic-adapted features

Inspired by previous work on topic adaptation for SMT, we add three additional topic-adapted features to our model. All of these features make use of the topic mixtures learned by our bilingual topic model. The first feature is an adapted lexical weight, similar to the features in the work of Eidelman et al. (2012). Our feature is different in that we marginalise over topics to produce a single adapted feature where $v[k]$ is the kth element of a document topic vector for document d and w(t|s,k) is a topic-dependent word translation probability:

$$lex(\bar{t}|\bar{s},d) = \prod_{i}^{|t|} \frac{1}{\{j|(i,j) \in \mathbf{a}\}} \sum_{\forall(i,j)\in\mathbf{a}} \underbrace{\sum_{k} w(t|s,k) \cdot v[k]}_{w(t|s)} \quad (3)$$

The second feature is a target unigram feature similar to the lazy MDI adaptation of Ruiz and Federico (2012). It includes an additional term that measures the relevance of a target word w_i by comparing its document-specific probability P_{doc} to its probability under the asymmetric topic 0:

$$trgUnigrams_t = \prod_{i=1}^{|t|} \underbrace{f(\frac{P_{doc}(w_i)}{P_{baseline}(w_i)})}_{lazy\ MDI} \cdot \underbrace{f(\frac{P_{doc}(w_i)}{P_{topic0}(w_i)})}_{relevance} \quad (4)$$

$$f(x) = \frac{2}{1+\frac{1}{x}}, \quad x > 0 \quad (5)$$

The third feature is a document similarity feature, similar to the semantic feature described by Banchs and Costa-jussà (2011):

$$docSim_t = \max_i(1 - JSD(v_{train\ doc_i}, v_{test\ doc})) \quad (6)$$

where $v_{train\_doc_i}$ and v_{test_doc} are document topic vector of training and test documents. Because topic 0 captures phrase pairs that are common to many documents, we exclude it from the topic vectors before computing similarities.

4.1 Feature combination

We tried integrating the four topic-adapted features separately and in all possible combinations. As we will see in the results section, while all features improve over the baseline in isolation, the adapted translation feature P(t|s,d) is the strongest feature. For the features that have a counterpart in the baseline model (p(t|s,d) and lex(t|s,d)), we experimented with either adding or replacing them in the log-linear model. We found that while adding the features worked well and yielded close to zero weights for their baseline counterparts after tuning, replacing them yielded better results in combination with the other adapted features. We believe the reason could be that fewer phrase table features in total are easier to optimise.

Data	Mixed	CC	NC	TED
Train	354K (6450)	110K	103K	140K
Dev	2453 (39)	818	817	818
Test	5664 (112)	1892	1878	1894

Table 1: Number of sentence pairs and documents (in brackets) in the French-English data sets. The training data has 2.7M English words per domain.

5 Experimental setup

5.1 Data and baselines

Our experiments were carried out on a mixed data set, containing the TED corpus (Cettolo et al., 2012), parts of the News Commentary corpus (NC) and parts of the Commoncrawl corpus (CC) from the WMT13 shared task (Bojar et al., 2013) as described in Table 1. We were guided by two constraints in chosing our data set. 1) the data has document boundaries and the content of each document is assumed to be topically related, 2) there is some degree of topical variation within each data set. In order to compare to domain adaptation approaches, we chose a setup with data from different corpora. We want to abstract away from adaptation effects that concern tuning of length penalties and language models, so we use a mixed tuning set containing data from all three domains and train one language model on the concatenation of (equally sized) target sides of the training data. Word alignments are trained on the concatenation of all training data and fixed for all models.

Our baseline (ALL) is a phrase-based French-English system trained on the concatenation of all parallel data. It was built with the Moses toolkit (Koehn et al., 2007) using the 14 standard core features including a 5gram language model. Translation quality is evaluated on a large test set, using the average feature weights of three optimisation runs with PRO (Hopkins and May, 2011). We use the mteval-v13a.pl script to compute case-insensitive BLEU. As domain-aware benchmark systems, we use the phrase table fill-up method (FILLUP) of Bisazza et al. (2011) which preserves the translation scores of phrases from the IN model and the linear mixture models (LIN-TM) of Sennrich (2012b) (both available in the Moses toolkit). For both systems, we build separate phrase tables for each domain and use a wrapper to decode tuning and test sets with domain-specific tables. Both benchmarks have an advan-

Model	Mixed	CC	NC	TED
IN	26.77	18.76	**29.56**	**32.47**
ALL	26.86	**19.61**	29.42	31.88

Table 2: BLEU of in-domain and baseline models.

Model	Avg JSD	Rank1-diff
Ted-IN vs ALL	0.15	10.8%
CC-IN vs ALL	0.17	18.4%
NC-IN vs ALL	0.13	13.3%

Table 3: Average JSD of IN vs. ALL models. Rank1-diff: % PT entries where preferred translation changes.

tage over our model because they are aware of domain boundaries in the test set. Further, LIN-TM adapts phrase table features in both translation directions while we only adapt the forward features.

Table 2 shows BLEU scores of the baseline system as well as the performance of three in-domain models (IN) tuned under the same conditions. For the IN models, every portion of the test set is decoded with a domain-specific model. Results on the test set are broken down by domain but also reported for the entire test set (mixed). For Ted and NC, the in-domain models perform better than ALL, while for CC the all-domain model improves quite significantly over IN.

5.2 General properties of the data sets

In this section we analyse some internal properties of our three data sets that are relevant for adaptation. All of the scores were computed on the sets of source side tokens of the test set which were limited to contain content words (nouns, verbs, adjectives and adverbs). The test set was tagged with the French TreeTagger (Schmid, 1994). The top of Table 3 shows the average Jensen-Shannon divergence (using $\log_2$, JSD $\in [0,1]$) of each in-domain model in comparison to the all-domain model, which is an indicator of how much the distributions in the IN model change when adding out-of-domain data. Likewise, Rank1-diff gives the percentage of word tokens in the test set where the preferred translation according to $p(e|f)$ changes between IN and ALL. These are the words that are most affected by adding data to the IN model. Both numbers show that for Commoncrawl the IN and ALL models differ more than in the other two data sets. According to the JS divergence between NC-IN and ALL, translation distibutions in the NC phrase table are most similar to the ALL phrase table. Table 4 shows the average JSD for each IN model compared to a model trained on half of its in-domain data. This score gives an idea of how diverse a data set is, measured by comparing distributions over translations for source words in the test set. According to this score, Commoncrawl is the most diverse data set and Ted the most uniform. Note however, that these divergence scores do not provide information about the relative quality of the systems under comparison. For CC, the ALL model yields a much higher BLEU score than the IN model and it is likely that this is due to noisy data in the CC corpus. In this case, the high divergence is likely to mean that distributions are corrected by out-of-domain data rather than being shifted away from in-domain distributions.

Model	Avg JSD
Ted-half vs Ted-full	0.07
CC-half vs CC-full	0.17
NC-half vs NC-full	0.09

Table 4: Average JSD of in-domain models trained on half vs. all of the data.

5.3 Topic-dependent decoding

The phrase translation probabilities and additional features described in the last two sections are used as features in the log-linear translation model in addition to the baseline translation features. When combining all four adapted features, we replace $P(t|s)$ and $lex(t|s)$ by their adapted counterparts. We construct separate phrase tables for each document in the development and test sets and use a wrapper around the decoder to ensure that each input document is paired with a configuration file pointing to its document-specific translation table. Documents are decoded in sequence so that only one phrase table needs to be loaded at a time. Using the wrapped decoder we can run parameter optimisation (PRO) in the usual way to get one set of tuned weights for all test documents.

6 Results

In this section we present experimental results with phrasal LDA. We show BLEU scores in comparison to a baseline system and two domain-aware benchmark systems. We also evaluate the adapted translation distributions by looking at translation probabilities under specific topics and inspect translations of ambiguous source words.

6.1 Analyis of bilingual topic models

We experimented with different numbers of topics for phrasal LDA. The diagrams in Figure 2 shows blocks of training and test documents in each of the three domains for a model with 20 topics. Darker shading means that documents have a higher proportion of a particular topic in their document-topic distribution. The first topic is the one that was affected by the asymmetric prior and inspecting its most probable phrase pairs showed that it had 'collected' a large number of stop word phrases. This explains why it is the topic that is most shared across documents and domains.

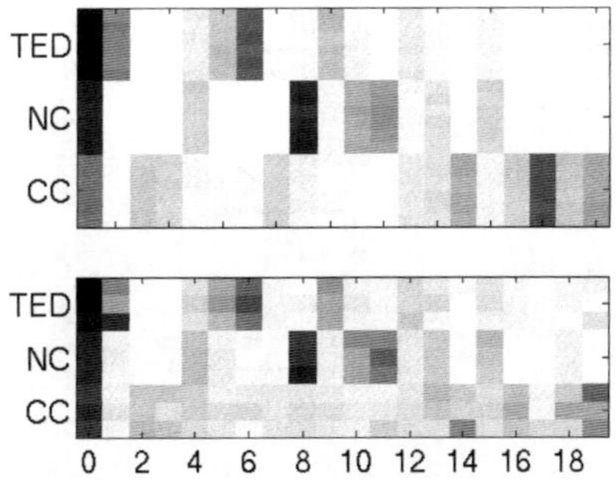

Figure 2: Document-topic distributions for training (top) and test (bottom) documents, grouped by domain and averaged into blocks for visualisation.

Topic 8	Topic 11
européenne → european	crise → crisis
politiques → political	taux → rate
politique → policy	financière → financial
intérêts → interests	monétaire → monetary
Topic 14	**Topic 19**
hôtel → hotel	web → web
plage → beach	utiliser → use
situé → located	logiciel → software
chambres → bedrooms	données → data

Figure 3: Frequent phrase pairs in learned topics.

There is quite a clear horizontal separation between documents of different domains, for example, topics 6, 8, 19 occur mostly in Ted, NC and CC documents respectively. The overall structure is very similar between training (top) and test (bottom) documents, which shows that test inference was successful in carrying over the information learned on training documents. There is also some degree of topic sharing across domains, for example topics 4 and 15 occur in documents of all three domains. Figure 3 shows examples of latent topics found during inference on the training data. Topic 8 and 11 seem to be about politics and economy and occur frequently in documents from the NC corpus. Topic 14 contains phrases related to hotels and topic 19 is about web and software, both frequent themes in the CC corpus.

6.2 Comparison according to BLEU

In Table 5 we compare our topic-adapted features when added separately to the baseline phrase table. The inclusion of each feature improves over the concatenation baseline but the combination of all four features gives the best overall results. Though the relative performance differs slightly for each domain portion in the test set, overall the adapted lexical weight is the weakest feature and the adapted translation probability is the strongest feature. We also performed feature ablation tests and found that no combination of features was superior to combining all four features. This confirms that the gains of each feature lead to additive improvements in the combined model.

In Table 6 we compare topic-adapted models with varying numbers of topics to the concatenation baseline. We see a consistent gain on all domains when increasing the number of topics from three to five and ten topics. This is evidence that the number of domain labels is in fact smaller than the number of underlying topics. The optimal number of latent topics varies for each domain and reflects our insights from section 5.2. The CC domain was shown to be the most diverse and the best performance on the CC portion of the test set is achieved with 100 topics. Likewise, the TED domain was shown to be least diverse and here the best performance is achieved with only 10 topics. The best performance on the entire test set is achieved with 50 topics, which is also the optimal number of topics for the NC domain. The botton row of the table indicates the relative improvement of the best topic-adapted model per domain over the ALL model. Using all four topic-adapted features yields an improvement of 0.81 BLEU on the mixed test set. The highest improvement on a given domain is achieved for TED with an increase of 1.26 BLEU. The smallest improvement is measured on the NC domain. This is in line with the observation that distributions in the NC in-domain table are most similar to the ALL table, therefore we would expect the smallest improvement for domain or topic adaptation. We used bootstrap resampling (Koehn, 2004) to measure significance on the mixed test set and marked all statistically significant results compared to the respective baselines with asterisk (*: $p \leq 0.01$).

To demonstrate the benefit of topic adaptation over more standard domain adaptation approaches for a diverse data set, we show the performance

Model	Mixed	CC	NC	TED
lex(e|f,d)	26.99	19.93	29.34	32.19
trgUnigrams	27.15	19.90	29.54	32.50
docSim	27.22	20.11	29.63	32.40
p(e|f,d)	27.31	20.23	29.52	32.58
All features	**27.67**	**20.40**	**30.04**	**33.08**

Table 5: BLEU scores of pLDA features (50 topics), separately and combined.

Model	Mixed	CC	NC	TED
ALL	26.86	19.61	29.42	31.88
3 topics	26.95	19.83	29.46	32.02
5 topics	*27.48	19.98	29.94	33.04
10 topics	*27.65	20.34	29.99	**33.14**
20 topics	*27.63	20.39	29.93	33.09
50 topics	***27.67**	20.40	**30.04**	33.08
100 topics	*27.65	**20.54**	30.00	32.90
>ALL	+0.81	+0.93	+0.62	+1.26

Table 6: BLEU scores of baseline and topic-adapted systems (pLDA) with all 4 features and largest improvements over baseline.

Model	Mixed	CC	NC	TED
FILLUP	27.12	19.36	29.78	32.71
LIN-TM	27.24	19.61	29.87	32.73
pLDA	***27.67**	**20.40**	**30.04**	**33.08**
>FILLUP	+0.55	+1.04	+0.26	+0.37
>LIN-TM	+0.43	+0.79	+0.17	+0.35

Table 7: Comparison of best pLDA system with two domain-aware benchmark systems.

Model	Mixed	CC	NC	TED
LIN-LM				
+ ALL	27.16	19.71	29.77	32.46
+ FILLUP	27.20	19.37	29.84	32.90
+ LIN-TM	27.34	19.59	29.92	33.02
+ pLDA	***27.84**	**20.48**	**30.03**	**33.57**
>ALL	+0.68	+0.77	+0.26	+1.11

Table 8: Combination of all models with additional LM adaptation (pLDA: 50 topics).

of two state-of-the-art domain-adapted systems in Table 7. Both FILLUP and LIN-TM improve over the ALL model on the mixed test set, by 0.26 and 0.38 BLEU respectively. The largest improvement is on TED while on the CC domain, FILLUP decreases in performance and LIN-TM yields no improvement either. This shows that relying on in-domain distributions for adaptation to a noisy and diverse domain like CC is problematic. The pLDA model yields the largest improvement over the domain-adapted systems on the CC test set, with in increase of 1.04 BLEU over FILLUP and 0.79 over LIN-TM. The improvements on the other two domains are smaller but consistent.

We also compare the best model from Table 6 to all other models in combination with linearly interpolated language models (LIN-LM), interpolated separately for each domain. Though the improvements are slightly smaller than without adapted language models, there is still a gain over the concatenation baseline of 0.68 BLEU on the mixed test set and similar improvements to before over the benchmarks (on TED the improvements are actually even larger). Thus, we have shown that topic-adaptation is effective for test sets of diverse documents and that we can achieve substantial improvements even in comparison with domain-adapted translation and language models.

6.3 Properties of adapted distributions and topic-specific translations

The first column of Table 9 shows the average entropy of phrase table entries in the adapted models according to $p(t|s,d)$ versus the all-domain model, computed over source tokens in the test set that are content words. The entropy decreases in the adapted tables in all cases which is an indicator that the distributions over translations of content

Set	Model	Avg entropy	Avg perplexity
CC	pLDA	**3.74**	**9.21**
	ALL	3.99	10.13
NC	pLDA	**3.42**	**6.96**
	ALL	3.82	7.51
TED	pLDA	**3.33**	**9.17**
	ALL	4.00	9.71

Table 9: Average entropy of translation distributions and test set perplexity of the adapted model.

régime		
topic 6	diet = 0.79	diet aids = 0.04
topic 8	regime* = 0.82	rule = 0.05
topic 19	restrictions = 0.53	diplomats = 0.10
noyau		
topic 9	nucleus* = 0.89	core = 0.01
topic 11	core* = 0.93	inner = 0.03
topic 19	kernel = 0.58	core = 0.11
démon		
topic 6	devil = 0.89	demon = 0.07
topic 8	demon* = 0.98	devil = 0.01
topic 19	daemon = 0.95	demon = 0.04

Table 10: The two most probable translations of *régime*, *noyau* and *démon* and probabilities under different latent topics (*: preferred by ALL).

words have become more peaked. The second column shows the average perplexity of target tokens in the test set which is a measure of how likely a model is to produce words in the reference translation. We use the alignment information between source and reference and therefore limit our analysis to pairs of aligned words, but nevertheless this shows that the adapted translation distributions model the test set distributions better than the baseline model. Therefore, the adapted distributions are not just more peaked but also more often peaked towards the correct translation.

Table 10 shows examples of ambiguous French words that have different preferred translations depending on the latent topic. The word *régime* can be translated as *diet*, *regime* and *restrictions* and the model has learned that the probability over translations changes when moving from one topic to another (preferred translations under the ALL model are marked with *). For example, the translation to *diet* is most probable under topic 6 and the translation to *regime* which would occur in a political context is most probable under topic 8. Topic 6 is most prominent among Ted documents while topic 8 is found most frequently in News Commentary documents which have a high percentage of politically related text. The French word *noyau* can be translated to *nucleus* (physics), *core* (generic) and *kernel* (IT) among other translations and the topics that exhibit these preferred translations can be attributed to Ted (which contains many talks about physics), NC and CC (with

Src:	"il suffit d'éjecter le *noyau* et d'en insérer un autre, comme ce qu'on fait pour le clônage."
BL:	"it is the **nucleus** eject and insert another, like what we do to the clônage."
pLDA:	"he just eject the **nucleus** and insert another, like what we do to the clônage." (nucleus = **0.77**)
Ref:	"you can just pop out the **nucleus** and pop in another one, and that's what you've all heard about with cloning."
Src:	"pourtant ceci obligerait les contribuables des pays de ce *noyau* à fournir du capital au sud"
BL:	"but this would force western taxpayers to provide the nucleus of capital in the south"
pLDA:	"but this would force western taxpayers to provide the **core** of capital in the south" (core = **0.78**)
Ref:	"but this would unfairly force taxpayers in the **core** countries to provide capital to the south"
Src:	"le *noyau* contient de nombreux pilotes, afin de fonctionner chez la plupart des utilisateurs."
BL:	"the nucleus contains many drivers, in order to work for most users."
pLDA:	"the **kernel** contains many drivers, to work for most users." (kernel = **0.53**)
Ref:	"the precompiled **kernel** includes a lot of drivers, in order to work for most users."

Figure 4: pLDA correctly translates *noyau* in test docs from Ted, NC and CC (adapted probabilities in brackets). The baseline (nucleus = 0.27, core = 0.27, kernel = 0.23) translates all instances to *nucleus*.

many IT-related documents). The last example, *démon*, has three frequent translations in English: *devil*, *demon* and *daemon*. The last translation refers to a computer process and would occur in an IT context. The topic-phrase probabilities reveal that its mostly likely translation as *daemon* occurs under topic 19 which clusters IT-related phrase pairs and is frequent in the CC corpus. These examples show that our model can disambiguate phrase translations using latent topics.

As another motivating example, in Figure 4 we compare the output of our adapted models to the output produced by the all-domain baseline for the word *noyau* from Table 10. While the ALL baseline translates each instance of *noyau* to *nucleus*, the adapted model translates each instance differently depending on the inferred topic mixtures for each document and always matches the reference translation. The probabilities in brackets show that the chosen translations were indeed the most likely under the respective adapted model. While the ALL model has a flat distribution over possible translations, the adapted models are peaked towards the correct translation. This shows that topic-specific translation probabilities are necessary when the translation of a word shifts between topics or domains and that peaked, adapted distributions can lead to more correct translations.

7 Related work

There has been a lot of previous work using topic information for SMT, most of it using monolingual topic models. For example, Gong and Zhou (2011) use the topical relevance of a target phrase, computed using a mapping between source and target side topics, as an additional feature in decoding. Axelrod et al. (2012) build topic-specific translation models from the TED corpus and select topic-relevant data from the UN corpus to improve coverage. Su et al. (2012) perform phrase table adaptation in a setting where only monolingual in-domain data and parallel out-of-domain data are available. Eidelman et al. (2012) use topic-dependent lexical weights as features in the translation model, which is similar to our work in that topic features are tuned towards usefulness of topic information and not towards a target domain. Hewavitharana et al. (2013) perform dynamic adaptation with monolingual topics, encoding topic similarity between a conversation and training documents in an additional feature. This is similar to the work of Banchs and Costa-jussà (2011), both of which inspired our document similarity feature. Also related is the work of Sennrich (2012a) who explore mixture-modelling on unsupervised clusters for domain adaptation and Chen et al. (2013) who compute phrase pair features from vector space representations that capture domain similarity to a development set. Both are cross-domain adaptation approaches, though. Instances of multilingual topic models outside the field of MT include Boyd-Graber and Blei (2009; Boyd-Graber and Resnik (2010) who learn cross-lingual topic correspondences (but do not learn conditional distributions like our model does). In terms of model structure, our model is similar to BiTAM (Zhao and Xing, 2006) which is an LDA-style model to learn topic-based word alignments. The work of Carpuat and Wu (2007) is similar to ours in spirit, but they predict the most probable translation in a context at the token level while our adaptation operates at the type level of a document.

8 Conclusion

We have presented a novel bilingual topic model based on LDA and applied it to the task of translation model adaptation on a diverse French-English data set. Our model infers topic distributions over phrase pairs to compute document-specific translation probabilities and performs dynamic adaptation on test documents of unknown origin. We have shown that our model outperforms a concatenation baseline and two domain-adapted benchmark systems with BLEU gains of up to 1.26 on domain-specific test set portions and 0.81 overall. We have also shown that a combination of topic-adapted features performs better than each feature in isolation and that these gains are additive. An analysis of the data revealed that topic adaptation compares most favourably to domain adaptation when the domain in question is rather diverse.

Acknowledgements

This work was supported by funding from the Scottish Informatics and Computer Science Alliance (Eva Hasler) and funding from the European Union Seventh Framework Programme (FP7/2007-2013) under grant agreement 287658 (EU BRIDGE) and grant agreement 288769 (ACCEPT). Thanks to Chris Dyer for an initial discussion about the phrasal LDA model.

References

Amittai Axelrod, Xiaodong He, and Jianfeng Gao. 2011. Domain adaptation via pseudo in-domain data selection. In *Proceedings of EMNLP*. Association for Computational Linguistics.

Amittai Axelrod, Xiaodong He, Li Deng, Alex Acero, and Mei-Yuh Hwang. 2012. New methods and evaluation experiments on translating TED talks in the IWSLT benchmark. In *Proceedings of ICASSP*. IEEE.

Rafael E. Banchs and Marta R. Costa-jussà. 2011. A semantic feature for statistical machine translation. In *Proceedings of the Fifth Workshop on Syntax, Semantics and Structure in Statistical Translation*, SSST-5. Association for Computational Linguistics.

Arianna Bisazza, Nick Ruiz, and Marcello Federico. 2011. Fill-up versus Interpolation Methods for Phrase-based SMT Adaptation. In *Proceedings of IWSLT*.

David M. Blei, Andrew Y. Ng, Michael I. Jordan, and John Lafferty. 2003. Latent dirichlet allocation. *JMLR*.

Ondřej Bojar, Christian Buck, Chris Callison-Burch, Christian Federmann, Barry Haddow, Philipp Koehn, Christof Monz, Matt Post, Radu Soricut, and Lucia Specia. 2013. Findings of WMT 2013. Association for Computational Linguistics.

Jordan Boyd-Graber and David Blei. 2009. Multilingual Topic Models for Unaligned Text. In *Proceedings of the Twenty-Fifth Conference on Uncertainty in Artificial Intelligence*. AUAI Press.

Jordan Boyd-Graber and Philip Resnik. 2010. Holistic Sentiment Analysis Across Languages: Multilingual Supervised Latent Dirichlet Allocation. In *Proceedings of EMNLP*. Association for Computational Linguistics.

Marine Carpuat and Dekai Wu. 2007. How phrase sense disambiguation outperforms word sense disambiguation for SMT. In *International Conference on Theoretical and Methodological Issues in MT*.

Mauro Cettolo, Christian Girardi, and Marcello Federico. 2012. Wit3: Web inventory of transcribed and translated talks. In *Proceedings of EAMT*.

Boxing Chen, Roland Kuhn, and George Foster. 2013. Vector space model for adaptation in SMT. In *Proceedings of ACL*. Association for Computational Linguistics.

Vladimir Eidelman, Jordan Boyd-Graber, and Philip Resnik. 2012. Topic models for dynamic translation model adaptation. In *Proceedings of ACL*. Association for Computational Linguistics.

G. Foster and R. Kuhn. 2007. Mixture-model adaptation for SMT. In *Proceedings of WMT*. Association for Computational Linguistics.

G. Foster, C. Goutte, and R. Kuhn. 2010. Discriminative instance weighting for domain adaptation in SMT. In *Proceedings of EMNLP*. Association for Computational Linguistics.

Zhengxian Gong and Guodong Zhou. 2011. Employing topic modeling for SMT. In *Proceedings of IEEE (CSAE)*, volume 4.

Eva Hasler, Barry Haddow, and Philipp Koehn. 2012. Sparse lexicalised features and topic adaptation for SMT. In *Proceedings of IWSLT*.

S. Hewavitharana, D. Mehay, S. Ananthakrishnan, and P. Natarajan. 2013. Incremental topic-based TM adaptation for conversational SLT. In *Proceedings of ACL*. Association for Computational Linguistics.

Mark Hopkins and Jonathan May. 2011. Tuning as ranking. In *Proceedings of EMNLP*. Association for Computational Linguistics.

Philipp Koehn, Hieu Hoang, Alexandra Birch, Chris Callison-Burch, Marcello Federico, Nicola Bertoldi, Brooke Cowan, Wade Shen, Christine Moran, Richard Zens, Chris Dyer, Ondrej Bojar, Alexandra Constantin, and Evan Herbst. 2007. Moses: Open source toolkit for SMT. In *ACL 2007: Demo and poster sessions*. Association for Computational Linguistics.

Philipp Koehn. 2004. Statistical significance tests for machine translation evaluation. In *Proceedings of EMNLP*. Association for Computational Linguistics.

S. Matsoukas, A. Rosti, and B. Zhang. 2009. Discriminative corpus weight estimation for MT. In *Proceedings of EMNLP*. Association for Computational Linguistics.

Thomas P Minka. 2012. Estimating a Dirichlet distribution. Technical report.

Nick Ruiz and Marcello Federico. 2012. MDI Adaptation for the Lazy: Avoiding Normalization in LM Adaptation for Lecture Translation. In *Proceedings of IWSLT*.

Helmut Schmid. 1994. Probabilistic part-of-speech tagging using decision trees. In *Proceedings of the International Conference on New Methods in Language Processing*.

Rico Sennrich. 2012a. Mixture-modeling with unsupervised clusters for domain adaptation in SMT. In *Proceedings of EAMT*.

Rico Sennrich. 2012b. Perplexity Minimization for Translation Model Domain Adaptation in SMT. In *Proceedings of EACL*. Association for Computational Linguistics.

J. Su, H. Wu, H. Wang, Y. Chen, X. Shi, H. Dong, and Q. Liu. 2012. Translation model adaptation for SMT with monolingual topic information. In *Proceedings of ACL*. Association for Computational Linguistics.

Yee Whye Teh, David Newman, and Max Welling. 2006. A collapsed variational Bayesian inference algorithm for LDA. In *Proceedings of NIPS*.

Hanna M. Wallach, David M. Mimno, and Andrew McCallum. 2009. Rethinking LDA: Why priors matter. In *Proceedings of NIPS*.

Pengyu Wang and Phil Blunsom. 2013. Collapsed variational Bayesian inference for Hidden Markov Models. In *AISTATS*, volume 31 of *JMLR Proceedings*, pages 599–607.

Bing Zhao and Eric P. Xing. 2006. Bilingual topic admixture models for word alignment. In *Proceedings of ACL*. Association for Computational Linguistics.

Deterministic Parsing using PCFGs

Mark-Jan Nederhof and **Martin McCaffery**
School of Computer Science
University of St Andrews, UK

Abstract

We propose the design of deterministic constituent parsers that choose parser actions according to the probabilities of parses of a given probabilistic context-free grammar. Several variants are presented. One of these deterministically constructs a parse structure while postponing commitment to labels. We investigate theoretical time complexities and report experiments.

1 Introduction

Transition-based dependency parsing (Yamada and Matsumoto, 2003; Nivre, 2008) has attracted considerable attention, not only due to its high accuracy but also due to its small running time. The latter is often realized through determinism, i.e. for each configuration a unique next action is chosen. The action may be a shift of the next word onto the stack, or it may be the addition of a dependency link between words.

Because of the determinism, the running time is often linear or close to linear; most of the time and space resources are spent on deciding the next parser action. Generalizations that allow nondeterminism, while maintaining polynomial running time, were proposed by (Huang and Sagae, 2010; Kuhlmann et al., 2011).

This work has influenced, and has been influenced by, similar developments in constituent parsing. The challenge here is to deterministically choose a shift or reduce action. As in the case of dependency parsing, solutions to this problem are often expressed in terms of classifiers of some kind. Common approaches involve maximum entropy (Ratnaparkhi, 1997; Tsuruoka and Tsujii, 2005), decision trees (Wong and Wu, 1999; Kalt, 2004), and support vector machines (Sagae and Lavie, 2005).

The programming-languages community recognized early on that large classes of grammars allow deterministic, i.e. linear-time, parsing, provided parsing decisions are postponed as long as possible. This has led to (deterministic) LR(k) parsing (Knuth, 1965; Sippu and Soisalon-Soininen, 1990), which is a form of shift-reduce parsing. Here the parser needs to commit to a grammar rule only after all input covered by the right-hand side of that rule has been processed, while it may consult the next k symbols (the lookahead). LR is the optimal, i.e. most deterministic, parsing strategy that has this property. Deterministic LR parsing has also been considered relevant to psycholinguistics (Shieber, 1983).

Nondeterministic variants of LR(k) parsing, for use in natural language processing, have been proposed as well, some using tabulation to ensure polynomial running time in the length of the input string (Tomita, 1988; Billot and Lang, 1989). However, nondeterministic LR(k) parsing is potentially as expensive as, and possibly more expensive than, traditional tabular parsing algorithms such as CKY parsing (Younger, 1967; Aho and Ullman, 1972), as shown by for example (Shann, 1991); greater values of k make matters worse (Lankhorst, 1991). For this reason, LR parsing is sometimes enhanced by attaching probabilities to transitions (Briscoe and Carroll, 1993), which allows pruning of the search space (Lavie and Tomita, 1993). This by itself is not uncontroversial, for several reasons. First, the space of probability distributions expressible by a LR automaton is incomparable to that expressible by a CFG (Nederhof and Satta, 2004). Second, because an LR automaton may have many more transitions than rules, more training data may be needed to accurately estimate all parameters.

The approach we propose here retains some important properties of the above work on LR parsing. First, parser actions are delayed as long as possible, under the constraint that a rule is committed to no later than when the input covered by its right-hand side has been processed. Second, the parser action that is performed at each step is the most likely one, given the left context, the lookahead, and a probability distribution over parses given by a PCFG.

There are two differences with traditional LR parsing however. First, there is no explicit representation of LR states, and second, probabilities of actions are computed dynamically from a PCFG rather than retrieved as part of static transitions. In particular, this is unlike some other early approaches to probabilistic LR parsing such as (Ng and Tomita, 1991).

The mathematical framework is reminiscent of that used to compute prefix probabilities (Jelinek and Lafferty, 1991; Stolcke, 1995). One major difference is that instead of a prefix string, we now have a stack, which does not need to be parsed. In the first instance, this seems to make our problem easier. For our purposes however, we need to add new mechanisms in order to take lookahead into consideration.

It is known, e.g. from (Cer et al., 2010; Candito et al., 2010), that constituent parsing can be used effectively to achieve dependency parsing. It is therefore to be expected that our algorithms can be used for dependency parsing as well. The parsing steps of shift-reduce parsing with a binary grammar are in fact very close to those of many dependency parsing models. The major difference is, again, that instead of general-purpose classifiers to determine the next step, we would rely directly on a PCFG.

The emphasis of this paper is on deriving the necessary equations to build several variants of deterministic shift-reduce parsers, all guided by a PCFG. We also offer experimental results.

2 Shift-reduce parsing

In this section, we summarize the theory of LR parsing. As usual, a *context-free grammar* (CFG) is represented by a 4-tuple (Σ, N, S, P), where Σ and N are two disjoint finite sets of *terminals* and *nonterminals*, respectively, $S \in N$ is the *start symbol*, and P is a finite set of *rules*, each of the form $A \rightarrow \alpha$, where $A \in N$ and $\alpha \in (\Sigma \cup N)^*$. By *grammar symbol* we mean a terminal or nonterminal. We use symbols $A, B, C, \ldots$ for nonterminals, $a, b, c, \ldots$ for terminals, $v, w, x, \ldots$ for strings of terminals, X for grammar symbols, and $\alpha, \beta, \gamma, \ldots$ for strings of grammar symbols. For technical reasons, a CFG is often *augmented* by an additional rule $S^\dagger \rightarrow S\$$, where $S^\dagger \notin N$ and $\$ \notin \Sigma$. The symbol $\$$ acts as an end-of-sentence marker.

As usual, we have a (right-most) 'derives' relation $\Rightarrow_{rm}$, $\Rightarrow_{rm}^*$ denotes derivation in zero or more steps, and $\Rightarrow_{rm}^+$ denotes derivation in one or more steps. If d is a string of rules $\pi_1 \cdots \pi_k$, then $\alpha \stackrel{d}{\Rightarrow}_{rm} \beta$ means that β can be derived from α by applying this list of rules in right-most order. A string α such that $S \Rightarrow_{rm}^* \alpha$ is called a *right-sentential form*.

The last rule $A \rightarrow \beta$ used in a derivation $S \Rightarrow_{rm}^+ \alpha$ together with the position of (the relevant occurrence of) β in α we call the *handle* of the derivation. In more detail, such a derivation can be written as $S = \underline{A_0} \Rightarrow_{rm} \alpha_1 A_1 \underline{\beta_1} \Rightarrow_{rm}^* \alpha_1 \underline{A_1} v_1 \Rightarrow_{rm} \alpha_1 \alpha_2 A_2 \underline{\beta_2} v_2 \Rightarrow_{rm}^* \ldots \Rightarrow_{rm}^* \alpha_1 \cdots \alpha_{k-1} \underline{A_{k-1}} v_{k-1} \cdots v_1 \Rightarrow_{rm} \alpha_1 \cdots \alpha_{k-1} \beta v_{k-1} \cdots v_1$, where $k \geq 1$, and $A_{i-1} \rightarrow \alpha_i A_i \beta_i$ $(1 \leq i < k)$ and $A_{k-1} \rightarrow \beta$ are in P. The underlined symbols are those that are (recursively) rewritten to terminal strings within the following relation $\Rightarrow_{rm}$ or $\Rightarrow_{rm}^*$. The handle here is $A_{k-1} \rightarrow \beta$, together with the position of β in the right-sentential form, just after $\alpha_1 \cdots \alpha_{k-1}$. A prefix of $\alpha_1 \cdots \alpha_{k-1} \beta$ is called a *viable prefix* in the derivation.

Given an input string w, a *shift-reduce parser* finds a right-most derivation of w, but in reverse order, identifying the last rules first. It manipulates configurations of the form $(\alpha, v\$)$, where α is a viable prefix (in at least one derivation) and v is a suffix of w. The initial configuration is $(\varepsilon, w\$)$, where ε is the empty string. The two allowable steps are $(\alpha, av\$) \vdash (\alpha a, v\$)$, which is called a *shift*, and $(\alpha\beta, v\$) \vdash (\alpha A, v\$)$ where $A \rightarrow \beta$ is in P, which is called a *reduce*. Acceptance happens upon reaching a configuration $(S, \$)$.

A *1-item* has the form $[A \rightarrow \alpha \bullet \beta, a]$, where $A \rightarrow \alpha\beta$ is a rule. The bullet separates the right-hand side into two parts, the first of which has been matched to processed input. The symbol $a \in \Sigma \cup \{\$\}$ is called the *follower*.

In order to decide whether to apply a shift or reduce after reaching a configuration $(X_1 \cdots X_k, w)$, one may construct the sets $I_0, \ldots, I_k$, inductively defined as follows, with $0 \leq i \leq k$:

- if $S \rightarrow \sigma$ in P, then $[S \rightarrow \bullet\, \sigma, \$] \in I_0$,

- if $[A \rightarrow \alpha \bullet B\beta, a] \in I_i$, $B \rightarrow \gamma$ in P, and $\beta \Rightarrow^*_{rm} x$, then $[B \rightarrow \bullet\ \gamma, b] \in I_i$, where $b = 1 : xa$,
- if $[A \rightarrow \alpha \bullet X_i\beta, a] \in I_{i-1}$ then $[A \rightarrow \alpha X_i \bullet \beta, a] \in I_i$.

(The expression $1 : y$ denotes a if $y = az$, for some a and z; we leave it undefined for $y = \varepsilon$.) Exhaustive application of the second clause above will be referred to as the *closure* of a set of items.

It is not difficult to show that if $[A \rightarrow \alpha\ \bullet, a] \in I_k$, then α is of the form $X_{j+1} \cdots X_k$, some j, and $A \rightarrow \alpha$ at position $j + 1$ is the handle of at least one derivation $S \Rightarrow^*_{rm} X_1 \cdots X_k ax$, some x. If furthermore $a = 1 : w$, where $1 : w$ is called the *lookahead* of the current configuration $(X_1 \cdots X_k, w)$, then this justifies a reduce with $A \rightarrow \alpha$, as a step that potentially leads to a complete derivation; this is only 'potentially' because the actual remaining input w may be unlike ax, apart from the matching one-symbol lookahead.

Similarly, if $[A \rightarrow \alpha \bullet a\beta, b] \in I_k$, then $\alpha = X_{j+1} \cdots X_k$, some j, and if furthermore $a = 1 : w$, then a shift of symbol a is a justifiable step. Potentially, if a is followed by some x such that $\beta \Rightarrow^*_{rm} x$, then we may eventually obtain a stack $X_1 \cdots X_j \alpha a\beta$, which is a prefix of a right-sentential form, with the handle being $A \rightarrow \alpha a\beta$ at position $j + 1$.

For a fixed grammar, the collection of all possible sets of 1-items that may arise in processing any viable prefix is a finite set. The technique of *LR(1) parsing* relies on a precomputation of all such sets of items, each of which is turned into a state of the *LR(1) automaton*. The initial state consists of $closure(\{[S \rightarrow \bullet\ \sigma, \$] \mid S \rightarrow \sigma \in P\})$. The automaton has a transition labeled X from I to J if $goto(I, X) = J$, where $goto(I, X) = closure(\{[A \rightarrow \alpha X \bullet \beta, a] \mid [A \rightarrow \alpha \bullet X\beta, a] \in I\})$. In the present study, we do not precompute all possible states of the LR(1) automaton, as this would require prohibitive amounts of time and memory. Instead, our parsers are best understood as computing LR states *dynamically*, while furthermore attaching probabilities to individual items.

In the sequel we will assume that all rules either have the (lexical) form $A \rightarrow a$, the (binary) form $A \rightarrow BC$, or the (unary) form $A \rightarrow B$. This means that $A \Rightarrow^*_{rm} \varepsilon$ is not possible for any A. The end-of-sentence marker is now introduced by two augmented rules $S^\dagger \rightarrow SS^\$$ and $S^\$ \rightarrow \$$.

3 Probabilistic shift-reduce parsing

A *probabilistic* CFG (PCFG) is a 5-tuple (Σ, N, S, P, p), where the extra element p maps rules to probabilities. The probability of a derivation $\alpha \overset{d}{\Rightarrow}_{rm} \beta$, with $d = \pi_1 \cdots \pi_k$, is defined to be $p(d) = \prod_i p(\pi_i)$. The probability $p(w)$ of a string w is defined to be the sum of $p(d)$ for all d with $S \overset{d}{\Rightarrow}_{rm} w$.

We assume *properness*, i.e. $\sum_{\pi = A \rightarrow \alpha} p(\pi) = 1$ for all A, and *consistency*, i.e. $\sum_w p(w) = 1$. Properness and consistency together imply that for each nonterminal A, the sum of $p(d)$ for all d with $\exists_w A \overset{d}{\Rightarrow}_{rm} w$ equals 1. We will further assume an augmented PCFG with extra rules $S^\dagger \rightarrow SS^\$$ and $S^\$ \rightarrow \$$ both having probability 1.

Consider a viable prefix $A_1 \cdots A_k$ on the stack of a shift-reduce parser, and lookahead a. Each right-most derivation in which the handle is $A \rightarrow A_{k-1}A_k$ at position $k - 1$ must be of the form sketched in Figure 1.

Because of properness and consistency, we may assume that all possible subderivations generating strings entirely to the right of the lookahead have probabilities summing to 1. To compactly express the remaining probabilities, we need additional notation. First we define:

$$\mathcal{V}(C, D) \;=\; \sum_{d : \exists_w C \overset{d}{\Rightarrow}_{rm} Dw} p(d)$$

for any pair of nonterminals C and D. This will be used later to 'factor out' a common term in a (potentially infinite) sum of probabilities of subderivations; the w in the expression above corresponds to a substring of the unknown input beyond the lookahead. In order to compute such values, we fix an ordering of the nonterminals by $N = \{C_1, \ldots, C_r\}$, with $r = |N|$. We then construct a matrix M, such that $M_{i,j} = \sum_{\pi = C_i \rightarrow C_j\alpha} p(\pi)$. In words, we sum the probabilities of all rules that have left-hand side C_i and a right-hand side beginning with C_j.

A downward path in a parse tree from an occurrence of C to an occurrence of D, restricted to following always the first child, can be of any length n, including $n = 0$ if $C = D$. This means we need to obtain the matrix $M^* = \sum_{0 \leq n} M^n$, and $\mathcal{V}(C_i, C_j) = M^*_{i,j}$ for all i and j. Fortunately, $M^*_{i,j}$ can be effectively computed as $(I - M)^{-1}$, where I is the identity matrix of size r and the superscript denotes matrix inversion.

We further define:

$$\mathcal{U}(C, D) = \sum_{d : C \stackrel{d}{\Rightarrow}_{rm} D} p(d)$$

much as above, but restricting attention to unit rules.

The expected number of times a handle $A \rightarrow A_{k-1}A_k$ at position $k-1$ occurs in a right-most derivation with viable prefix $A_1 \cdots A_k$ and lookahead a is now given by:

$$\begin{aligned}
&\mathcal{E}(A_1 \cdots A_k, a, A \rightarrow A_{k-1}A_k) = \\
&\quad \sum_{\substack{S^\dagger = E_0, \ldots, E_{k-2}, F_1, \ldots, F_{k-1} = A, \\ F, E, B, B', m \,:\, 0 \leq m < k-1}} \\
&\quad \prod_{i:\, 1 \leq i \leq m} \mathcal{V}(E_{i-1}, F_i) \cdot p(F_i \rightarrow A_i E_i) \cdot \\
&\quad \mathcal{V}(E_m, F) \cdot p(F \rightarrow EB) \cdot \mathcal{U}(E, F_{m+1}) \cdot \\
&\quad \prod_{i:\, m < i < k-1} p(F_i \rightarrow A_i E_i) \cdot \mathcal{U}(E_i, F_{i+1}) \cdot \\
&\quad p(F_{k-1} \rightarrow A_{k-1}A_k) \cdot \mathcal{V}(B, B') \cdot p(B' \rightarrow a)
\end{aligned}$$

Note that the value above is not a probability and may exceed 1. This is because the same viable prefix may occur several times in a single right-most derivation.

At first sight, the computation of $\mathcal{E}$ seems to require an exponential number of steps in k. However, we can use an idea similar to that commonly used for computation of forward probabilities for HMMs (Rabiner, 1989). We first define $\mathcal{F}$:

$$\mathcal{F}(\varepsilon, E) = \begin{cases} 1 \text{ if } E = S^\dagger \\ 0 \text{ otherwise} \end{cases}$$

$$\mathcal{F}(\alpha A, E) = \sum_{E', \pi = F \rightarrow AE} \mathcal{F}(\alpha, E') \cdot \mathcal{V}(E', F) \cdot p(\pi)$$

This corresponds to the part of the definition of $\mathcal{E}$ involving $A_1, \ldots, A_m$, $E_0, \ldots, E_m$ and $F_1, \ldots, F_m$. We build on this by defining:

$$\mathcal{G}(\alpha, E, B) = \sum_{E', \pi = F \rightarrow EB} \mathcal{F}(\alpha, E') \cdot \mathcal{V}(E', F) \cdot p(\pi)$$

One more recursive function is needed for what was $A_{m+1}, \ldots, A_{k-2}$, $E_{m+1}, \ldots, E_{k-2}$ and $F_{m+1}, \ldots, F_{k-2}$ in the earlier definition of $\mathcal{E}$:

$$\mathcal{H}(\varepsilon, E, B) = \mathcal{G}(\varepsilon, E, B)$$

$$\mathcal{H}(\alpha A, E, B) = \sum_{E', \pi = F \rightarrow AE} \mathcal{H}(\alpha, E', B) \cdot \mathcal{U}(E', F) \cdot p(\pi) + \mathcal{G}(\alpha A, E, B)$$

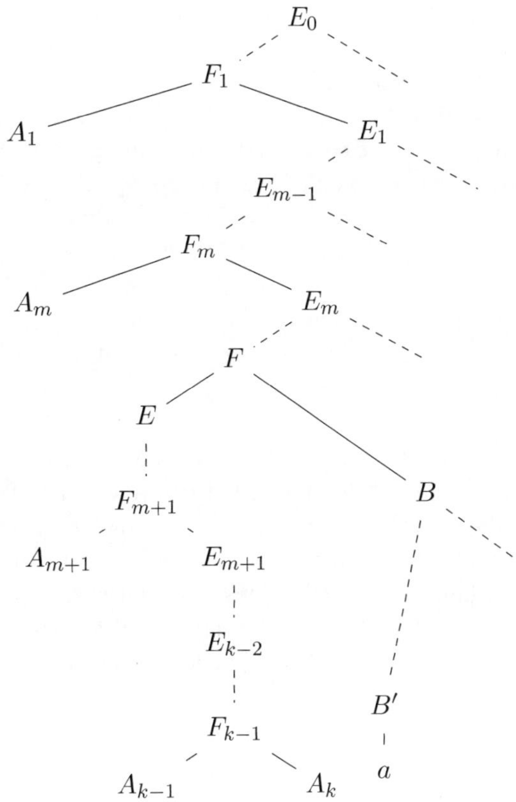

Figure 1: Right-most derivation leading to $F_{k-1} \rightarrow A_{k-1}A_k$ in viable prefix $A_1 \cdots A_k$ with lookahead a.

Finally, we can express $\mathcal{E}$ in terms of these recursive functions, considering the more general case of any rule $\pi = F \rightarrow \beta$:

$$\mathcal{E}(\alpha\beta, a, F \rightarrow \beta) = \sum_{E,B} \mathcal{H}(\alpha, E, B) \cdot \mathcal{U}(E, F) \cdot p(\pi) \cdot \mathcal{L}(B, a)$$

$$\mathcal{E}(\alpha, a, F \rightarrow \beta) = 0 \quad \text{if } \neg\exists_\gamma\ \alpha = \gamma\beta$$

where:

$$\mathcal{L}(B, a) = \sum_{\pi = B' \rightarrow a} \mathcal{V}(B, B') \cdot p(\pi)$$

The expected number of times the handle is to be found to the right of α, with the stack being α and the lookahead symbol being a, is:

$$\mathcal{E}(\alpha, a, \mathit{shift}) = \sum_B \mathcal{F}(\alpha, B) \cdot \mathcal{L}(B, a)$$

The expected number of times we see a stack α with lookahead a is:

$$\mathcal{E}(\alpha, a) = \mathcal{E}(\alpha, a, \mathit{shift}) + \sum_\pi \mathcal{E}(\alpha, a, \pi)$$

The probability that a reduce with rule π is the correct action when the stack is α and the lookahead is a is naturally $\mathcal{E}(\alpha, a, \pi)/\mathcal{E}(\alpha, a)$ and the probability that a shift is the correct action is $\mathcal{E}(\alpha, a, \textit{shift})/\mathcal{E}(\alpha, a)$. For determining the most likely action we do not need to compute $\mathcal{E}(\alpha, a)$; it suffices to identify the maximum value among $\mathcal{E}(\alpha, a, \textit{shift})$ and $\mathcal{E}(\alpha, a, \pi)$ for each rule π.

A deterministic shift-reduce parser can now be constructed that always chooses the most likely next action. For a given input string, the number of actions performed by this parser is linear in the input length.

A call of $\mathcal{E}$ may lead to a number of recursive calls of $\mathcal{F}$ and $\mathcal{H}$ that is linear in the stack size and thereby in the input length. Note however that by remembering the values returned by these function between parser actions, one can ensure that each additional element pushed on the stack requires a bounded number of additional calls of the auxiliary functions. Because only linearly many elements are pushed on the stack, the time complexity becomes linear in the input length.

Complexity analysis seems less favorable if we consider the number of nonterminals. The definitions of $\mathcal{G}$ and $\mathcal{H}$ each involve four nonterminals excluding the stack symbol A, so that the time complexity is $\mathcal{O}(|w| \cdot |N|^4)$, where $|w|$ is the length of the input w. A finer analysis gives $\mathcal{O}(|w| \cdot (|N| \cdot |P| + |N|^2 \cdot \|P\|))$, where $\|P\|$ is the maximum for all A of the number of rules of the form $F \rightarrow AE$. By splitting up $\mathcal{G}$ and $\mathcal{H}$ into smaller functions, we obtain complexity $\mathcal{O}(|w| \cdot |N|^3)$, which can still be prohibitive.

Therefore we have implemented an alternative that has a time complexity that is only quadratic in the size of the grammar, at the expense of a quadratic complexity in the length of the input string, as detailed in Appendix A. This is still better in practice if the number of nonterminals is much greater than the length of the input string, as in the case of the grammars we investigated.

4 Structural determinism

We have assumed so far that a deterministic shift-reduce parser chooses a unique next action in each configuration, an action being a shift or reduce. Implicit in this was that if the next action is a reduce, then also a unique rule is chosen. However, if we assume for now that all non-lexical rules are binary, then we can easily generalize the parsing algorithm to consider *all* possible rules whose right-hand sides match the top-most two stack elements, and postpone commitment to any of the nonterminals in the left-hand sides. This requires that stack elements now contain *sets* of grammar symbols. Each of these is associated with the probability of the most likely subderivation consistent with the relevant substring of the input.

Each reduce with a binary rule is implicitly followed by zero or more reduces with unary rules. Similarly, each shift is implicitly followed by a reduce with a lexical rule and zero or more reduces with unary rules; see also (Graham et al., 1980). This uses a precompiled table similar to $\mathcal{U}$, but using maximization in place of summation, defined by:

$$\mathcal{U}_{\max}(C, D) \quad = \quad \max_{d \,:\, C \overset{d}{\Rightarrow}_{rm} D} \quad p(d)$$

More concretely, configurations have the form $(Z_1 \ldots Z_k, v\$)$, $k \geq 0$, where each Z_i $(1 \leq i \leq k)$ is a set of pairs (A, p), where A is a nonterminal and p is a (non-zero) probability; each A occurs at most once in Z_i. A shift turns $(\alpha, av\$)$ into $(\alpha Z, v\$)$, where Z consists of all pairs (E, p) such that $p = \max_F \mathcal{U}_{\max}(E, F) \cdot p(F \rightarrow a)$. A generalized binary reduce now turns $(\alpha Z_1 Z_2, v\$)$ into $(\alpha Z, v\$)$, where Z consists of all pairs (E, p) such that:

$$p \quad = \quad \max_{\substack{\pi = F \rightarrow A_1 A_2, \\ (A_1, p_1) \in Z_1, (A_2, p_2) \in Z_2}} \quad \mathcal{U}_{\max}(E, F) \cdot p(\pi) \cdot p_1 \cdot p_2$$

We characterize this parsing procedure as *structurally deterministic*, as an unlabeled structure is built deterministically in the first instance. The exact choices of rules can be postponed until after reaching the end of the sentence. Then follows a straightforward process of 'backtracing', which builds the derivation that led to the computed probability associated with the start symbol.

The time complexity is now $\mathcal{O}(|w| \cdot |N|^5)$ in the most straightforward implementation, but we can reduce this to quadratic in the size of the grammar provided we allow an additional factor $|w|$ as before. For more details see Appendix B.

5 Other variants

One way to improve accuracy is to increase the size of the lookahead, beyond the current 1, comparable to the generalization from LR(1) to LR(k) parsing. The formulas are given in Appendix C.

Yet another variant investigates only the topmost n stack symbols when choosing the next parser action. In combination with Appendix A, this brings the time complexity down again to linear time in the length of the input string. The required changes to the formulas are given in Appendix D. There is a slight similarity to (Schuler, 2009), in that no stack elements beyond a bounded depth are considered at each parsing step, but in our case the stack can still have arbitrary height.

Whereas we have concentrated on determinism in this paper, one can also introduce a limited degree of nondeterminism and allow some of the most promising configurations at each input position to compete, applying techniques such as beam search (Roark, 2001; Zhang and Clark, 2009; Zhu et al., 2013), best-first search (Sagae and Lavie, 2006), or A* search (Klein and Manning, 2003) in order to keep the running time low. For comparing different configurations, one would need to multiply the values $\mathcal{E}(\alpha, a)$ as in Section 3 by the probabilities of the subderivations associated with occurrences of grammar symbols in stack α.

Further variants are obtained by replacing the parsing strategy. One obvious candidate is left-corner parsing (Rosenkrantz and Lewis II, 1970), which is considerably simpler than LR parsing. The resulting algorithm would be very different from the left-corner models of e.g. (Henderson, 2003), which rely on neural networks instead of PCFGs.

6 Experiments

We used the WSJ treebank from OntoNotes 4.0 (Hovy et al., 2006), with Sections 2-21 for training and the 2228 sentences of up to 40 words from Section 23 for testing. Grammars with different sizes, and in the required binary form, were extracted by using the tools from the Berkeley parser (Petrov et al., 2006), with between 1 and 6 split-merge cycles. These tools offer a framework for handling unknown words, which we have adopted.

The implementation of the parsing algorithms is in C++, running on a desktop with four 3.1GHz Intel Core i5 CPUs. The main algorithm is that of Appendix C, with lookahead k between 1 and 3, also in combination with structural determinism (Appendix B), which is indicated here by *sd*. The variant that consults the stack down to bounded depth n (Appendix D) will only be reported for $k = 1$ and $n = 5$.

Bracketing recall, precision and F-measure, are computed using evalb, with settings as in (Collins, 1997), except that punctuation was deleted.[1] Table 1 reports results.

A nonterminal B in the stack may occur in a small number of rules of the form $A \to BC$. The C of one such rule is needed next in order to allow a reduction. If future input does not deliver this C, then parsing may fail. This problem becomes more severe as nonterminals become more specific, which is what happens with an increase of the number of split-merge cycles. Even more failures are introduced by removing the ability to consult the complete stack, which explains the poor results in the case of $k = 1, n = 5$; lower values of n lead to even more failures, and higher values further increase the running time. That the running time exceeds that of $k = 1$ is explained by the fact that with the variant from Appendix D, every pop or push requires a complete recomputation of all function values.

Parse failures can be almost completely eliminated however by choosing higher values of k and by using structural determinism. A combination thereof leads to high accuracy, not far below that of the Viterbi parses. Note that one cannot expect the accuracy of our deterministic parsers to *exceed* that of Viterbi parses. Both rely on the same model (a PCFG), but the first is forced to make local decisions without access to the input string that follows the bounded lookahead.

7 Conclusions

We have shown that deterministic parsers can be constructed from a given PCFG. Much of the accuracy of the grammar can be retained by choosing a large lookahead in combination with 'structural determinism', which postpones commitment to nonterminals until the end of the input is reached.

Parsers of this nature potentially run in linear time in the length of the input, but our parsers are better implemented to run in quadratic time. In terms of the grammar size, the experiments suggest that the number of rules is the dominating factor. The size of the lookahead strongly affects running time. The extra time costs of structural determinism are compensated by an increase in accuracy and a sharp decrease of the parse failures.

[1] Evalb otherwise stumbles over e.g. a part of speech consisting of two single quotes in the parsed file, against a part of speech 'POS' in the gold file, for an input token consisting of a single quote.

Table 1: Total time required (seconds), number of parse failures, recall, precision, F-measure, for deterministic parsing, compared to the Viterbi parses as computed with the Berkeley parser.

	time	fail	R	P	F1		time	fail	R	P	F1
1-split-merge (12,059 rules)						4-split-merge (269,162 rules)					
$k = 1$	43	11	67.20	66.67	66.94	$k = 1$	870	115	75.69	73.30	74.48
$k = 2$	99	0	70.74	71.01	70.88	$k = 2$	2,257	1	83.48	82.35	82.91
$k = 3$	199	0	71.41	71.85	71.63	$k = 3$	4,380	1	84.95	84.06	84.51
$k = 1, sd$	62	0	68.12	68.52	68.32	$k = 1, sd$	2,336	1	80.82	80.65	80.74
$k = 2, sd$	135	0	70.98	71.72	71.35	$k = 2, sd$	4,747	0	85.52	85.64	85.58
$k = 3, sd$	253	0	71.31	72.50	71.90	$k = 3, sd$	7,728	0	86.62	86.82	86.72
$k = 1, n = 5$	56	170	66.19	65.67	65.93	$k = 1, n = 5$	1,152	508	76.21	73.92	75.05
Viterbi		0	72.45	74.55	73.49	Viterbi		0	87.95	88.10	88.02
2-split-merge (32,994 rules)						5-split-merge (716,575 rules)					
$k = 1$	120	33	72.65	70.50	71.56	$k = 1$	3,166	172	76.17	73.44	74.78
$k = 2$	275	1	78.44	77.26	77.84	$k = 2$	7,476	2	84.14	82.80	83.46
$k = 3$	568	0	79.81	79.27	79.54	$k = 3$	14,231	1	86.05	85.24	85.64
$k = 1, sd$	196	0	74.78	74.96	74.87	$k = 1, sd$	7,427	1	81.99	81.44	81.72
$k = 2, sd$	439	0	79.96	80.40	80.18	$k = 2, sd$	14,587	0	86.89	87.00	86.95
$k = 3, sd$	770	0	80.49	81.20	80.85	$k = 3, sd$	24,553	0	87.67	87.82	87.74
$k = 1, n = 5$	146	247	72.27	70.34	71.29	$k = 1, n = 5$	4,572	559	77.65	75.13	76.37
Viterbi		0	82.16	82.69	82.43	Viterbi		0	88.65	89.00	88.83
3-split-merge (95,647 rules)						6-split-merge (1,947,915 rules)					
$k = 1$	305	75	74.39	72.33	73.35	$k = 1$	7,741	274	76.60	74.08	75.32
$k = 2$	770	3	81.32	80.35	80.83	$k = 2$	19,440	5	84.60	83.17	83.88
$k = 3$	1,596	0	82.78	82.35	82.56	$k = 3$	35,712	0	86.02	85.07	85.54
$k = 1, sd$	757	0	78.11	78.37	78.24	$k = 1, sd$	19,530	1	82.64	81.95	82.29
$k = 2, sd$	1,531	0	82.85	83.39	83.12	$k = 2, sd$	39,615	0	87.36	87.20	87.28
$k = 3, sd$	2,595	0	83.66	84.25	83.96	$k = 3, sd$	64,906	0	88.16	88.26	88.21
$k = 1, n = 5$	404	401	74.52	72.39	73.44	$k = 1, n = 5$	10,897	652	77.89	75.57	76.71
Viterbi		0	85.38	86.03	85.71	Viterbi		0	88.69	88.99	88.84

There are many advantages over other approaches to deterministic parsing that rely on general-purpose classifiers. First, some state-of-the-art language models are readily available as PCFGs. Second, most classifiers require treebanks, whereas our algorithms are also applicable to PCFGs that were obtained in any other way, for example through intersection of language models. Lastly, our algorithms fit within well understood automata theory.

Acknowledgments We thank the reviewers.

A Formulas for quadratic time complexity

The following are the formulas that correspond to the first implemented variant. Relative to Section 3, some auxiliary functions are broken up, and associating the lookahead a with an appropriate nonterminal B is now done in $\mathcal{G}$:

$$
\begin{aligned}
\mathcal{F}(\varepsilon, E) &= \begin{cases} 1 \text{ if } E = S^{\dagger} \\ 0 \text{ otherwise} \end{cases} \\
\mathcal{F}(\alpha A, E) &= \sum_{\pi = F \to AE} \mathcal{F}'(\alpha, F) \cdot p(\pi) \\
\mathcal{F}'(\alpha, F) &= \sum_{E} \mathcal{F}(\alpha, E) \cdot \mathcal{V}(E, F) \\
\mathcal{G}(\alpha, E, a) &= \sum_{F} \mathcal{F}'(\alpha, F) \cdot \mathcal{G}'(F, E, a) \\
\mathcal{G}'(F, E, a) &= \sum_{\pi = F \to EB} p(\pi) \cdot \mathcal{L}(B, a) \\
\mathcal{H}(\varepsilon, E, a) &= \mathcal{G}(\varepsilon, E, a) \\
\mathcal{H}(\alpha A, E, a) &= \sum_{\pi = F \to AE} \mathcal{H}'(\alpha, F, a) \cdot p(\pi) \\
&\quad + \mathcal{G}(\alpha A, E, a) \\
\mathcal{H}'(\alpha, F, a) &= \sum_{E} \mathcal{H}(\alpha, E, a) \cdot \mathcal{U}(E, F)
\end{aligned}
$$

$$\begin{aligned}\mathcal{E}(\alpha\beta, a, F \to \beta) &= \mathcal{H}'(\alpha, F, a) \cdot p(F \to \beta)\\ \mathcal{E}(\alpha, a, F \to \beta) &= 0 \text{ if } \neg\exists_\gamma\ \alpha = \gamma\beta\\ \mathcal{E}(\alpha A, a, \mathit{shift}) &= \mathcal{G}(\alpha, A, a)\\ \mathcal{E}(\varepsilon, a, \mathit{shift}) &= \mathcal{L}(S^\dagger, a)\end{aligned}$$

These equations correspond to a time complexity of $\mathcal{O}(|w|^2 \cdot |N|^2 + |w| \cdot |P|)$. Each definition except that of $\mathcal{G}'$ involves one stack (of linear size) and, at most, one terminal plus two arbitrary nonterminals. The full grammar is only considered once for every input position, in the definition of $\mathcal{G}'$.

The values are stored as vectors and matrices. For example, for each distinct lookahead symbol a, there is a (sparse) matrix containing the value of $\mathcal{G}'(F, E, a)$ at a row and a column uniquely identified by F and E, respectively.

B Formulas for structural determinism

For the variant from Section 4, we need to change only two definitions of auxiliary functions:

$$\mathcal{F}(\alpha Z, E) = \sum_{(A,p)\in Z, \pi=F\to AE} \mathcal{F}'(\alpha, F) \cdot p(\pi) \cdot p$$

$$\mathcal{H}(\alpha Z, E, a) = \sum_{(A,p)\in Z, \pi=F\to AE} \mathcal{H}'(\alpha, F, a) \cdot p(\pi) \cdot p + \mathcal{G}(\alpha Z, E, a)$$

The only actions are shift and generalized binary reduce *red*. The definition of $\mathcal{E}$ becomes:

$$\mathcal{E}(\alpha Z_1 Z_2, a, \mathit{red}) = \sum_{\substack{(A_1,p_1)\in Z_1, (A_2,p_2)\in Z_2\\ \pi=F\to A_1A_2}} \mathcal{H}'(\alpha, F, a) \cdot p(\pi) \cdot p_1 \cdot p_2$$

$$\mathcal{E}(\alpha Z, a, \mathit{shift}) = \sum_{(A,p)\in Z} \mathcal{G}(\alpha, A, a) \cdot p$$

The time complexity now increases to $\mathcal{O}(|w|^2 \cdot (|N|^2 + |P|))$ due to the new $\mathcal{H}$.

C Formulas for larger lookahead

In order to handle k symbols of lookahead (Section 5) some technical problems are best avoided by having k copies of the end-of-sentence marker appended behind the input string, with a corresponding augmentation of the grammar. We generalize $\mathcal{L}(B, v)$ to be the sum of $p(d)$ for all d such that $B \overset{d}{\Rightarrow}_{rm} vx$, some x. We let $\mathcal{I}(B, v)$ be the sum of $p(d)$ for all d such that $B \overset{d}{\Rightarrow}_{rm} v$. If $\mathcal{I}$ is given for all prefixes of a fixed lookahead string of length k (this requires cubic time in k), we can compute $\mathcal{L}$ in linear time for all suffixes of the same string:

$$\mathcal{L}(B, v) = \sum_{B'} \mathcal{V}(B, B') \cdot \mathcal{L}'(B', v)$$

$$\mathcal{L}'(B, v) = \sum_{\substack{\pi=B\to B_1B_2, v_1, v_2:\\ v=v_1v_2, 1\le|v_1|, 1\le|v_2|}} p(\pi) \cdot \mathcal{I}(B_1, v_1) \cdot \mathcal{L}(B_2, v_2) \quad \text{if } |v| > 1$$

$$\mathcal{L}'(B, a) = \sum_{\pi=B\to a} p(\pi)$$

The function $\mathcal{H}$ is generalized straightforwardly by letting it pass on a string v ($1 \le |v| \le k$) instead of a single terminal a. The same holds for $\mathcal{E}$. The function $\mathcal{G}$ requires a slightly bigger modification, leading back to $\mathcal{H}$ if not all of the lookahead has been matched yet:

$$\mathcal{G}(\alpha, E, v) = \sum_F \mathcal{F}'(\alpha, F) \cdot \mathcal{G}'(F, E, v) + \sum_{F, v_1, v_2: v=v_1v_2, |v_2|>0} \mathcal{H}'(\alpha, F, v_2) \cdot \mathcal{G}''(F, E, v_1)$$

$$\mathcal{G}'(F, E, v) = \sum_{\pi=F\to EB} p(\pi) \cdot \mathcal{L}(B, v)$$

$$\mathcal{G}''(F, E, v) = \sum_{\pi=F\to EB} p(\pi) \cdot \mathcal{I}(B, v)$$

The time complexity is now $\mathcal{O}(k \cdot |w|^2 \cdot |N|^2 + k^3 \cdot |w| \cdot |P|)$.

D Investigation of top-most n stack symbols only

As discussed in Section 5, we want to predict the next parser action without consulting any symbols in α, when the current stack is $\alpha\beta$, with $|\beta| = n$. This is achieved by approximating $\mathcal{F}(\alpha, E)$ by the outside value of E, that is, the sum of $p(d)$ for all d such that $\exists_{\alpha,w} S \overset{d}{\Rightarrow}_{rm} \alpha E w$. Similarly, $\mathcal{H}'(\alpha, F, v)$ is approximated by $\sum_E \mathcal{G}(\alpha, E, v) \cdot \mathcal{W}(E, F)$ where:

$$\mathcal{W}(C, D) = \sum_{d\,:\, \exists_\delta C \overset{d}{\Rightarrow}_{rm} \delta D} p(d)$$

The time complexity (with lookahead k) is now $\mathcal{O}(k \cdot n \cdot |w| \cdot |N|^2 + k^3 \cdot |w| \cdot |P|)$.

References

A.V. Aho and J.D. Ullman. 1972. *Parsing*, volume 1 of *The Theory of Parsing, Translation and Compiling*. Prentice-Hall, Englewood Cliffs, N.J.

S. Billot and B. Lang. 1989. The structure of shared forests in ambiguous parsing. In *27th Annual Meeting of the ACL, Proceedings of the Conference*, pages 143–151, Vancouver, British Columbia, Canada, June.

T. Briscoe and J. Carroll. 1993. Generalized probabilistic LR parsing of natural language (corpora) with unification-based grammars. *Computational Linguistics*, 19(1):25–59.

M. Candito, J. Nivre, P. Denis, and E. Henestroza Anguiano. 2010. Benchmarking of statistical dependency parsers for French. In *The 23rd International Conference on Computational Linguistics*, pages 108–116, Beijing, China, August.

D. Cer, M.-C. de Marneffe, D. Jurafsky, and C. Manning. 2010. Parsing to Stanford dependencies: Trade-offs between speed and accuracy. In *LREC 2010: Seventh International Conference on Language Resources and Evaluation, Proceedings*, pages 1628–1632, Valletta , Malta, May.

M. Collins. 1997. Three generative, lexicalised models for statistical parsing. In *35th Annual Meeting of the ACL, Proceedings of the Conference*, pages 16–23, Madrid, Spain, July.

S.L. Graham, M.A. Harrison, and W.L. Ruzzo. 1980. An improved context-free recognizer. *ACM Transactions on Programming Languages and Systems*, 2:415–462.

J. Henderson. 2003. Generative versus discriminative models for statistical left-corner parsing. In *8th International Workshop on Parsing Technologies*, pages 115–126, LORIA, Nancy, France, April.

E. Hovy, M. Marcus, M. Palmer, L. Ramshaw, and R. Weischedel. 2006. OntoNotes: The 90% solution. In *Proceedings of the Human Language Technology Conference of the NAACL, Main Conference*, pages 57–60, New York, USA, June.

L. Huang and K. Sagae. 2010. Dynamic programming for linear-time incremental parsing. In *Proceedings of the 48th Annual Meeting of the ACL*, pages 1077–1086, Uppsala, Sweden, July.

F. Jelinek and J.D. Lafferty. 1991. Computation of the probability of initial substring generation by stochastic context-free grammars. *Computational Linguistics*, 17(3):315–323.

T. Kalt. 2004. Induction of greedy controllers for deterministic treebank parsers. In *Conference on Empirical Methods in Natural Language Processing*, pages 17–24, Barcelona, Spain, July.

D. Klein and C.D. Manning. 2003. A* parsing: Fast exact Viterbi parse selection. In *Proceedings of the 2003 Human Language Technology Conference of the North American Chapter of the ACL*, pages 40–47, Edmonton, Canada, May–June.

D.E. Knuth. 1965. On the translation of languages from left to right. *Information and Control*, 8:607–639.

M. Kuhlmann, C. Gómez-Rodríguez, and G. Satta. 2011. Dynamic programming algorithms for transition-based dependency parsers. In *49th Annual Meeting of the ACL, Proceedings of the Conference*, pages 673–682, Portland, Oregon, June.

M. Lankhorst. 1991. An empirical comparison of generalized LR tables. In R. Heemels, A. Nijholt, and K. Sikkel, editors, *Tomita's Algorithm: Extensions and Applications*, Proc. of the first Twente Workshop on Language Technology, pages 87–93. University of Twente, September.

A. Lavie and M. Tomita. 1993. GLR* – an efficient noise-skipping parsing algorithm for context free grammars. In *Third International Workshop on Parsing Technologies*, pages 123–134, Tilburg (The Netherlands) and Durbuy (Belgium), August.

M.-J. Nederhof and G. Satta. 2004. An alternative method of training probabilistic LR parsers. In *42nd Annual Meeting of the ACL, Proceedings of the Conference*, pages 551–558, Barcelona, Spain, July.

S.-K. Ng and M. Tomita. 1991. Probabilistic LR parsing for general context-free grammars. In *Proc. of the Second International Workshop on Parsing Technologies*, pages 154–163, Cancun, Mexico, February.

J. Nivre. 2008. Algorithms for deterministic incremental dependency parsing. *Computational Linguistics*, 34(4):513–553.

S. Petrov, L. Barrett, R. Thibaux, and D. Klein. 2006. Learning accurate, compact, and interpretable tree annotation. In *Proceedings of the 21st International Conference on Computational Linguistics and 44th Annual Meeting of the ACL*, pages 433–440, Sydney, Australia, July.

L.R. Rabiner. 1989. A tutorial on hidden Markov models and selected applications in speech recognition. *Proceedings of the IEEE*, 77(2):257–286, February.

A. Ratnaparkhi. 1997. A linear observed time statistical parser based on maximum entropy models. In *Proceedings of the Second Conference on Empirical Methods in Natural Language Processing*, pages 1–10, Providence, Rhode Island, USA, August.

B. Roark. 2001. Probabilistic top-down parsing and language modeling. *Computational Linguistics*, 27(2):249–276.

D.J. Rosenkrantz and P.M. Lewis II. 1970. Deterministic left corner parsing. In *IEEE Conference Record of the 11th Annual Symposium on Switching and Automata Theory*, pages 139–152.

K. Sagae and A. Lavie. 2005. A classifier-based parser with linear run-time complexity. In *Proceedings of the Ninth International Workshop on Parsing Technologies*, pages 125–132, Vancouver, British Columbia, Canada, October.

K. Sagae and A. Lavie. 2006. A best-first probabilistic shift-reduce parser. In *Proceedings of the 21st International Conference on Computational Linguistics and 44th Annual Meeting of the ACL*, pages 691–698, Sydney, Australia, July.

W. Schuler. 2009. Positive results for parsing with a bounded stack using a model-based right-corner transform. In *Proceedings of Human Language Technologies: The 2009 Annual Conference of the North American Chapter of the ACL*, pages 344–352, Boulder, Colorado, May–June.

P. Shann. 1991. Experiments with GLR and chart parsing. In M. Tomita, editor, *Generalized LR Parsing*, chapter 2, pages 17–34. Kluwer Academic Publishers.

S.M. Shieber. 1983. Sentence disambiguation by a shift-reduce parsing technique. In *21st Annual Meeting of the ACL, Proceedings of the Conference*, pages 113–118, Cambridge, Massachusetts, July.

S. Sippu and E. Soisalon-Soininen. 1990. *Parsing Theory, Vol. II: LR(k) and LL(k) Parsing*, volume 20 of *EATCS Monographs on Theoretical Computer Science*. Springer-Verlag.

A. Stolcke. 1995. An efficient probabilistic context-free parsing algorithm that computes prefix probabilities. *Computational Linguistics*, 21(2):167–201.

M. Tomita. 1988. Graph-structured stack and natural language parsing. In *26th Annual Meeting of the ACL, Proceedings of the Conference*, pages 249–257, Buffalo, New York, June.

Y. Tsuruoka and J. Tsujii. 2005. Chunk parsing revisited. In *Proceedings of the Ninth International Workshop on Parsing Technologies*, pages 133–140, Vancouver, British Columbia, Canada, October.

A. Wong and D. Wu. 1999. Learning a lightweight robust deterministic parser. In *Sixth European Conference on Speech Communication and Technology*, pages 2047–2050.

H. Yamada and Y. Matsumoto. 2003. Statistical dependency analysis with support vector machines. In *8th International Workshop on Parsing Technologies*, pages 195–206, LORIA, Nancy, France, April.

D.H. Younger. 1967. Recognition and parsing of context-free languages in time n^3. *Information and Control*, 10:189–208.

Y. Zhang and S. Clark. 2009. Transition-based parsing of the Chinese treebank using a global discriminative model. In *Proceedings of the 11th International Conference on Parsing Technologies*, pages 162–171, Paris, France, October.

M. Zhu, Y. Zhang, W. Chen, M. Zhang, and J. Zhu. 2013. Fast and accurate shift-reduce constituent parsing. In *51st Annual Meeting of the ACL, Proceedings of the Conference*, volume 1, pages 434–443, Sofia, Bulgaria, August.

Empirically-motivated Generalizations of CCG Semantic Parsing Learning Algorithms

Jesse Glass
Temple University
1801 N Broad Street
Philadelphia, PA 19122, USA
jglassemc2@gmail.com

Alexander Yates
Temple University
1801 N Broad Street
Philadelphia, PA 19122, USA
ayates@gmail.com

Abstract

Learning algorithms for semantic parsing have improved drastically over the past decade, as steady improvements on benchmark datasets have shown. In this paper we investigate whether they can generalize to a novel biomedical dataset that differs in important respects from the traditional geography and air travel benchmark datasets. Empirical results for two state-of-the-art PCCG semantic parsers indicates that learning algorithms are sensitive to the kinds of semantic and syntactic constructions used in a domain. In response, we develop a novel learning algorithm that can produce an effective semantic parser for geography, as well as a much better semantic parser for the biomedical dataset.

1 Introduction

Semantic parsing is the task of converting natural language utterances into formal representations of their meaning. In this paper, we consider in particular a grounded form of semantic parsing, in which the meaning representation language takes its logical constants from a given, fixed ontology. Several recent systems have demonstrated the ability to learn semantic parsers for domains like the GeoQuery database containing geography relations, or the ATIS database of air travel information. In these settings, existing systems can produce correct meaning representations with F1 scores approaching 0.9 (Wong and Mooney, 2007; Kwiatkowski et al., 2011).

These benchmark datasets have supported a diverse and influential line of research into semantic parsing learning algorithms for sophisticated semantic constructions, with continuing advances in accuracy. However, the focus on these datasets leads to a natural question — do other natural datasets have similar syntax and semantics, and if not, can existing algorithms handle the variability in syntax and semantics?

In an effort to investigate and improve the generalization capacity of existing learning algorithms for semantic parsing, we develop a novel, natural experimental setting, and we test whether current semantic parsers generalize to the new setting. For our datset, we use descriptions of clinical trials of experimental drugs in the United States, available from the U.S. National Institutes of Health[1]. Much of the text in the description of these clinical trials can be mapped neatly onto biomedical ontologies, thus permitting grounded semantic analysis. Crucially, the dataset was not designed specifically with semantic parsing or question-answering in mind, and as a result, it provides a natural source for the variety and complexity of utterances that humans use in this domain. As an added benefit, a successful semantic parser in this domain could yield a variety of useful bioinformatics applications by permitting comparisons between and across clinical trials using structured representations of the data, rather than unstructured text.

In this initial investigation of semantic parsing in this context, we ask:

- *Can existing semantic parsing learning algorithms handle the variety and complexity of the clinical trials dataset?* We show that two representative learning algorithms fare poorly on the clinical trials data: the best one achieves a 0.41 F1 in our tests.

- *What types of constructions are the major cause of errors on the clinical trials dataset,*

[1] clinicaltrials.gov

and can semantic parsers be extended to handle them? While this initial investigation does not cover all types of constructions, we identify three important types of constructions that existing learning algorithms do not handle. We propose a new learning algorithm that can handle these types of constructions, and we demonstrate empirically that the new algorithm produces a semantic parser that improves by over 23 points in F1 on the clinical trials dataset compared with existing parsers.

The rest of this paper is organized as follows. The next section provides background information on CCG and semantic parsing. Section 3 describes the text and ontology that form the new clinical trials dataset for semantic parsing, as well as some of the problems that exising approaches have on this dataset. Sections 4 describes our semantic parsing model, and learning and inference algorithms. Section 5 presents our experiments and results, and Section 6 concludes.

2 Background on Semantic Parsing with CCG

Our approach to learning a semantic parser falls into the general framework of context-free Probabilistic Combinatory Categorial Grammars (PCCG) (Zettlemoyer and Collins, 2005) with typed lambda calculus expressions for the semantics. PCCG grammars involve lexical entries, which are weighted unary rewrite rules of the form Syntax : Semantics → Phrase. For example:

Example Lexical Entries

NP : `melanoma` → skin cancer
$S\backslash NP$: $\lambda p \lambda d.$`has condition`(p, d) → patients with

In addition to lexical rules, PCCG grammars involve weighted binary rewrite rules like the following:

Example CCG Grammar Rules

$X : f(g) \rightarrow X/Y : f \quad Y : g$ (function application)
$X : f(g) \rightarrow Y : g \quad X\backslash Y : f$ (backward application)

These rules apply for any syntactic categories X and Y, and any logical forms f and g. The rules specify mechanisms for deducing syntactic categories for whole phrases based on their constituent parts. They also specify mechanisms for identifying semantics (logical forms) for phrases and sentences based on combinations of the semantics for the constituent parts. Besides function application, other ways to combine the semantics of children typically include conjunction, disjunction, function composition, and substitution, among others. Inference algorithms for PCCG can identify the best parse and logical form for a given sentence using standard dynamic programming algorithms for context-free grammars (Clark and Curran, 2007).

As a baseline in our experiments, we use a learning algorithm for semantic parsing known as Unification Based Learning (UBL) (Kwiatkowski et al., 2010). Source code for UBL is freely available. Its authors found that the semantic parsers it learns achieve results competitive with the state-of-the-art on a variety of standard semantic parsing data sets, including GeoQuery (0.882 F1). UBL uses a log-linear probabilistic model $P(L, T|S)$ over logical forms L and parse tree derivations T, given sentences S. During training, only S and L are observed, and UBL's gradient-based parameter estimation algorithm tries to maximize $\sum_T P(L, T|S)$ over the training dataset. To learn lexicon entries, it adopts a search procedure that involves unification in higher-order logic. The objective of the search procedure is to identify lexical entries for the words in a sentence that, when combined with the lexical entries for other words in the sentence, will produce the observed logical form in the training data. For each training sentence, UBL heuristically explores the space of all possible lexical entries to produce a set of promising candidates, and adds them to the lexicon.

Our second baseline is an extension of this work, called Factored Unification Based Learning (FUBL) (Kwiatkowski et al., 2011). Again, source code is freely available. FUBL factors the lexicon into a set of base lexical entries, and a set of templates that can construct more complex lexical entries from the base entries. This allows for a significantly more compact lexicon, as well as the ability to handle certain linguistic constructions, like ellipsis, that appear frequently in the ATIS dataset and which UBL struggles with. FUBL achieves an F1 of 0.82 on ATIS (compared with 66.3 for UBL), and an F1 of 0.886 on GeoQuery; both results are at or very near the best-reported results for those datasets.

2.1 Previous Work

Many supervised learning frameworks have been applied to the task of learning a semantic parser, including inductive logic programming (Zelle and Mooney, 1996; Thompson and Mooney, 1999; Thompson and Mooney, 2003), support vector machine-based kernel approaches (Kate et al., 2005; Kate and Mooney, 2006; Kate and Mooney, 2007), machine translation-style synchronous grammars (Wong and Mooney, 2007), and context-free grammar-based approaches like probabilistic Combinatory Categorial Grammar (Zettlemoyer and Collins, 2005; Zettlemoyer and Collins, 2007; Zettlemoyer and Collins, 2009; Kwiatkowski et al., 2010; Kwiatkowski et al., 2011; Lu et al., 2008) and discriminative reranking (Ge and Mooney, 2006; Ge and Mooney, 2009). These approaches have yielded steady improvements on standard test sets like GeoQuery. As far as we are aware, such systems have not been tested on domains besides ATIS and GeoQuery.

Because of the complexity involved in building a training dataset for a supervised semantic parser, there has been a recent push towards developing techniques which reduce the annotation cost or the data complexity of the models. Models have been developed which can handle some ambiguity in terms of which logical form is the correct label for each training sentence (Chen et al., 2010; Liang et al., 2009). Another set of approaches have investigated the case where no logical forms are provided, but instead some form of feedback or response from the world is used as evidence for what the correct logical form must have been (Clarke et al., 2010; Liang et al., 2011; Artzi and Zettlemoyer, 2011). Several projects have investigated unsupervised (Goldwasser et al., 2011; Poon, 2013; Krishnamurthy and Mitchell, 2012) and semi-supervised (Yahya et al., 2012; Cai and Yates, 2013) approaches. These techniques tend to handle either the same benchmark domains, or simpler questions over larger ontologies. While such techniques are important, their (unlabeled and labeled) sample complexity is higher than it could be, because the underlying grammars involved are not as general as they could be. Our work investigates techniques that will reduce this sample complexity.

3 The Clinical Trials Dataset

Clinical trials are scientific experiments that measure the effects of a medical procedure, instrument, or product on humans. Since September 2009 in the United States, any clinical trial that is funded by the federal government must make its results publicly available online at clinicaltrials.gov. This site provides a wealth of biomedical text and structured data, which we use to produce a novel test set for semantic parsing.

3.1 The text and ontology

We collected our utterances from a set of 47 random documents from clinicaltrials.gov. Many aspects of each study are reported in structured format; for example, the number of participants who were given a placebo and the number of participants who were given the intervention under consideration are both reported in a table in a standard format. However, certain crucial aspects of each study are reported only in text. Perhaps the most critical aspect of each study that is described only in text is the set of criteria for deciding who will be admitted to the study and who cannot be; these criteria are called inclusion criteria and exclusion criteria. We focus our semantic parsing tests on these criteria because they often form the longest portion of unstructured text for a given clinical trial report; because their meaning can be represented using a concise set of logical constants from a biomedical ontology; and because the criteria have a great deal of significance in the clinical trials domain. For example, these criteria are crucial for understanding why the results of two related studies about the same intervention might differ.

The criteria for a study can be logically represented as a function of candidate test subjects that returns true if they match the study criteria, and false otherwise. We use a variant of lambda calculus over a typed ontology to represent each inclusion and exclusion criterion in our dataset. We randomly collected 803 utterances and manually labeled each using our representation language. 401 were used for training, 109 for development, and 293 for our final tests.

To keep our semantic parsing study simple, we eschewed existing ontologies like UMLS (Bodenreider, 2004) that are large and overly-complex for this problem. We instead developed an ontology of 10 types, 38 relations and functions, and a dictionary of 591 named-entities to build the logical forms. The five most common types and relations in our dataset are listed in Table 1. On average, the logical forms in our dataset involved 3.7 relations per logical form, typically joined with conjunction, implication, or disjunction. If accepted, both the full ontology and dataset will be made publicly available.

3.2 Problems with semantic parsing the clinical trials data

We applied two state-of-the-art learning algorithms for learning PCCG semantic parsers — UBL and its extension, FUBL— to our training

Example Types	Example Functions
`(p)erson`	`t has condition(p, d)`
`(d)isease`	`t complication(d, d)`
`(t)est`	`i result(p, t)`
`(tr)eatment`	`t treated with(p, tr, date)`
`(bo)dy-part`	`t located(d, bo)`

Table 1: Common types and functions in our ontology. In the example functions, `t` indicates boolean type, `i` indicates real values, `p` indicates person, `d` disease, and so on.

patients with acute lymphoma λp . $\texttt{has condition}(p, \texttt{acute}(\texttt{lymphoma}))$
hypertension (*i.e.*, include patients with hypertension) λp . $\texttt{has condition}(p, \texttt{hypertension})$
AST $>$ 3 mg (*i.e.*, include patients with a level of the AST enzyme in the blood of greater than 3 mg) λp . $> (\texttt{result}(p, \texttt{AST}), \texttt{unit}(3, \texttt{mg}))$

Table 2: Example utterances from the clinical trials dataset, and their logical forms. Paraphrases in parentheses do not appear in the actual data.

data and tested the resulting parsers on development data. Results indicate that both systems have difficulty with the clinical trials datasets: FUBL achieves an F1 of 0.413, and UBL of just 0.281.

To help understand why state-of-the-art systems' performance differs so much from performance on benchmark datasets like GeoQuery, we performed an error analysis. Table 3 describes the most common errors we observed. The most common errors occurred on sentences containing coordination constructions, nested function applications, and for UBL, ellipsis, although a long tail of less common errors exists. FUBL manages to handle the elliptical constructions in Clinical Trials well, but not coordination or nested functions. Both systems tend to learn many, overly-specific lexical entries that include too much of the logical form in one lexical entry. For instance, from the coordination example in Table 3, UBL learns a lexical entry for the word "or" that includes the logical form $\lambda p \lambda d1 \lambda d2$. $\texttt{or}(\texttt{has condition}(p, d1), \texttt{has condition}(p, d2))$. While this entry works well when coordinating two diseases or conditions that patients must have, it will not work for coordinations between treatments or dates, or coordinations between diseases that patients should not have. UBL learns over 250 lexical entries for the word "or" from our training dataset of 401 sentences, each one with limited applicability to development sentences.

Based on these observed error types, we next develop novel learning procedures that properly handle coordination, nested function constructions, and ellipsis.

4 Learning to Handle Complex Constructions in Clinical Trials Data

4.1 Model and Inference

We introduce the GLL system for learning a semantic parser that generalizes to both GeoQuery and Clinical Trials data. The semantic parsing model involves a grammar that consists of a fixed set of binary CCG rewrite rules, a learned lexicon Λ, and a new set $\mathbf{T}$ of learned templates for constructing unary type-raising rules. We call these templates for type-raising rules *T-rules*; these are described below in Section 4.4.

Following Kwiatkowsi *et al.*(2010), we assign a probability $P(L, T|S, \vec{\theta}, G)$ to a logical form and parse tree for a sentence licensed by grammar G using a log-linear model with parameters $\vec{\theta}$. We use a set of feature functions $\vec{F}(L,T,S) = (f_1(L,T,S), \ldots, f_K(L,T,S))$, where each f_i counts the number of times that the ith grammar rule is used in the derivation of T and S. The probability of a particular logical form given a sentence and $\vec{\theta}$ is given by:

$$P(L|S, \vec{\theta}, G) = \frac{\sum_T \exp(\vec{\theta} \cdot \vec{F}(L,T,S))}{\sum_{T',L'} \exp(\vec{\theta} \cdot \vec{F}(L',T',S))} \quad (1)$$

where the trees T (and T') are restricted to those that are licensed by G and which produce L (L') as the logical form for the parent node of the tree. Inference is performed using standard dynamic programming algorithms for context-free parsing.

4.2 Learning

The input for the task of learning a semantic parser is a set of sentences $\vec{S}$, where each $S_i \in \vec{S}$ has been labeled with a logical form $L(S_i)$. We assume a fixed set of binary grammar productions, and use the training data to learn lexical entries, T-rules, and parameters. The training objective is to maximize the likelihood of the observed logical

Error Type	Freq.	Example	Description
Nested Funcs.	27%	patients > 18 years of age $\lambda p\ .\ >(\texttt{result}(\texttt{age}, p), \texttt{unit}(18, \texttt{year}))$	Many logical forms involve functions as arguments to other functions or relations.
Ellipsis	26%	diabetes $\lambda p\ .\ \texttt{has condition}(p, \texttt{diabetes})$	Many examples in the inclusion (exclusion) criteria simply list a disease or treatment, with the understanding that a patient p should be included (excluded) if p has the disease or is undergoing the treatment.
Coordination	16%	patient is pregnant or lactating $\lambda p\ .\ \texttt{or}(\texttt{has condition}(p, \texttt{pregnant}),$ $\texttt{has condition}(p, \texttt{lactating}))$	Clinical trials data has more coordination, especially noun phrase and adjective phrase coordination, than GeoQuery.

Table 3: Three common kinds of utterances in the clinical trials development set that caused UBL and FUBL to make errors. Frequency indicates the percentage of all development examples that exhibited that type of construction.

Input: set of labeled sentences $\{(S_i, L(S_i))\}$, initial grammar G_0, number of iterations MAX, learning rate α

$\Lambda \leftarrow \emptyset$
$\forall i : \Lambda \leftarrow \Lambda \cup \{S : L(S_i) \rightarrow S_i\}$
$G \leftarrow G_0 \cup \Lambda$
$\vec{\theta} \leftarrow \vec{0}$
For $iteration := 1$ to MAX:
  $TR \leftarrow$ TRLEARN(G)
  Add dimension θ_t to $\vec{\theta}$ for $t \in TR - G$
  $G \leftarrow G \cup TR$
  For each sentence S_i :
    $\Lambda \leftarrow$ LEXENTLEARN($S_i, L(S_i), G$)
    Add dimension θ_λ to $\vec{\theta}$ for all $\lambda \in \Lambda - G$
    $G \leftarrow G \cup \Lambda$
    $\vec{\theta} \leftarrow \vec{\theta} + \alpha \nabla_i CLL$
Return $G, \vec{\theta}$

Figure 1: The GLL Learning Algorithm. $\nabla_i CLL$ indicates the local gradient of the conditional log likelihood at sentence S_i.

forms, or to find G^* and $\vec{\theta^*}$ such that:

$$G^*, \vec{\theta^*} = \arg\max_{G,\vec{\theta}} \prod_i P(L(S_i)|S_i, \vec{\theta}, G)$$

This is a non-convex optimization problem. We use a greedy optimization procedure that iteratively updates G and $\vec{\theta}$. Figure 1 shows an overview of the full algorithm.

We use stochastic gradient updates to estimate parameters (LeCun et al., 1998). For each example sentence S_i in training, we compute the local gradient of the conditional log likelihood function $CLL = \log P(L(S_i)|S_i, \vec{\theta}, G)$, and update $\vec{\theta}$ by a step in the direction of this local gradient. The partial derivatives for this local gradient are:

$$\frac{\partial CLL}{\partial \theta_j} = \mathrm{E}_{P(T|L(S_i),S_i,\vec{\theta},G)} f_j(L(S_i), T, S_i) - \mathrm{E}_{P(T|S_i,\vec{\theta},G)} f_j(L(S_i), T, S_i)$$

4.3 Learning Lexical Entries with Inverse Function Composition

We adopt a greedy approach to learning new lexical entries. We first identify in our current parse any high-scoring lexical entries that cover multiple words, and then look for new lexical rules for the sub-phrases covered by these lexical entries that could combine to create the current parse chart entry using the existing grammar rules. This requires searching through the grammar rules to find children nodes that the nonterminal could be the parent of. In general, this produces an intractably large set, because it requires taking the inverse of function application and function composition for forming the semantics of the nonterminal, and those inverses are intractably large.

Figure 2 shows our algorithm for learning lexical entries, and Figure 3 shows the details of the critical component that generates the semantics of new potential lexical entries. For brevity, we omit the details of how we learn the syntax and mappings from semantics to words or phrases for new lexical entries, but these are borrowed from the existing techniques in UBL. The crucial difference from existing techniques is that the SPLITLEARN algorithm focuses on inverse function composition, while existing techniques focus on inverse

Input: training sentence $Sent$, its logical form L, current grammar G

Initialize:
  $PC \leftarrow$ parse chart from parsing $Sent$ with G
  $splits \leftarrow \emptyset$

For $len := length(Sent)$ to 1:
  For $pos := 0$ to $length(Sent) - len$:
    $e = \arg\max_{entry \in PC[len][pos]} entry.score$
    if e's only derivation is a lexical rule in G:
      $(score, \Lambda) \leftarrow$ SPLITLEARN(e, PC)
      $splits \leftarrow splits \cup \{(score, \Lambda)\}$

$split^* \leftarrow \arg\max_{split \in splits} split.score$
Return $split^*.\Lambda$

Figure 2: LEXENTLEARN Algorithm for learning lexical entries

function application. While *a priori* both techniques are reasonable choices (and both work well on GeoQuery), our empirical results show that inverse function composition can learn the same semantic forms as inverse function application, but in addition can handle nested functions (which are function compositions) and coordination — a form of function composition if one views logical connectives like `or` as boolean functions.

The SPLITLEARN algorithm uses a GETSUBEXPR subroutine to heuristically select only certain subexpressions of the input logical form for computing inverse composition. This is to avoid a combinatorial explosion in the number of learned splits of the input semantics. Mostly we consider any subexpression that forms an argument to some function in $le.sem$, but we take care to also include abstracted versions of these subexpressions, in which some of their arguments are in turn replaced by variables. The subroutine FREEVARS identifies all variables in a logical form that have no quantifier; REPEATVARS identifies all variables that appear at least twice. PCSCORE looks for any entry in the parse chart that has a matching semantics and returns the score of that entry, or 0 if no matches are found. We use PCSCORE to measure the improvement (delta) in the score of the parse if it uses the two new lexical entries, rather than the previous single lexical entry. SPLITLEARN returns the set of lexical entries that tie for the largest improvement in the score of the parse.

Figures 4 and 5 illustrate the difference between SPLITLEARN and lexical entry learning for UBL and FUBL. For both example sentences, there is a point in the learning process where a logical form must be split using inverse function composition in order for useful lexical entries to be learned. At those points, UBL and FUBL split the logical forms using inverse function application, resulting in splits where the semantics of different lexemes are mixed together in the two resulting subexpressions. In Figure 4, all three systems take the logical form $\lambda u.\lambda p. > (\texttt{result}(p, \texttt{bilirubin}), \texttt{unit}(1.5, u))$ and split it by removing some aspect of the final argument, $\texttt{unit}(1.5, u)$, from the full expression. In UBL and FUBL, the term that is left behind in the full expression is something that unifies with $\lambda u.\texttt{unit}(1.5, u)$. In GLL, however, only a variable is left behind, since that variable can be replaced by $\lambda u.\ \texttt{unit}(1.5, u)$ through function composition to obtain the original expression. Thus GLL's split yields one significantly simpler subexpression, which in the end yields simpler lexical entries. In both figures, and in general for most parses we have observed, inverse function composition yields simpler and cleaner subexpressions.

Input: lexical entry le, parse chart PC

Entries $\leftarrow \emptyset$
For $s \in$ GETSUBEXPR$(le.sem)$:
  $t \leftarrow$ copy of s
  $sem' \leftarrow$ copy of $le.sem$
  Apply$[t] \leftarrow \emptyset$
  For $v \in$ FREEVARS$(s) \cap$ REPEATVARS(sem'):
    Create variable v', $t \leftarrow t_{v' \text{ sub for } v}$
    Concatenate "$\lambda v'$" onto front of t
    Apply$[t] \leftarrow$ Apply$[t] \cup \{v\}$
  For $v \in$ FREEVARS(t):
    Remove "λv" from front of sem'
    Concatenate "λv" onto front of t
  Create new variable w
  $sub \leftarrow$ "(w" + each $a \in$ Apply$[t]$ + ")"
  $sem' \leftarrow sem'_{sub \text{ sub for } s}$
  Concatenate "λw" onto front of sem'
  Entries $\leftarrow$ Entries $\cup \{t, sem'\}$
  delta$[t]$, delta$[sem'] \leftarrow$ PCSCORE(t) + PCSCORE(sem') - PCSCORE(le)

$max \leftarrow \max_x$ delta$[x]$
Return $max, \{s \in$ Entries $|$ delta$[s] = max\}$

Figure 3: SPLITLEARN Algorithm for generating (the semantics of) new lexical entries.

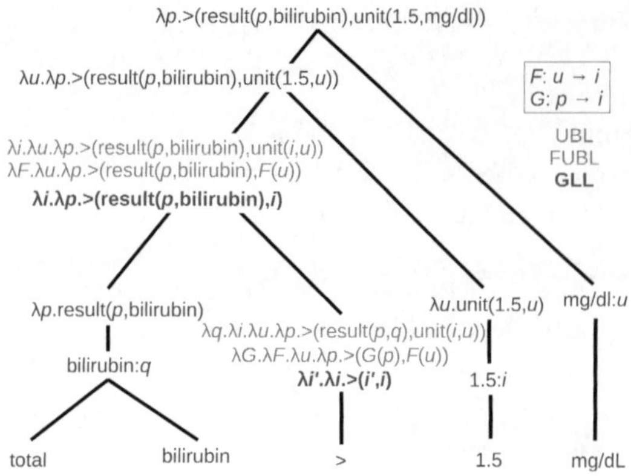

Figure 4: An example of a sentence with nested-function semantics. GLL's lexical entry learning procedure correctly identifies the most general semantics for the lexeme >, while UBL and FUBL learn more specific and complex semantics.

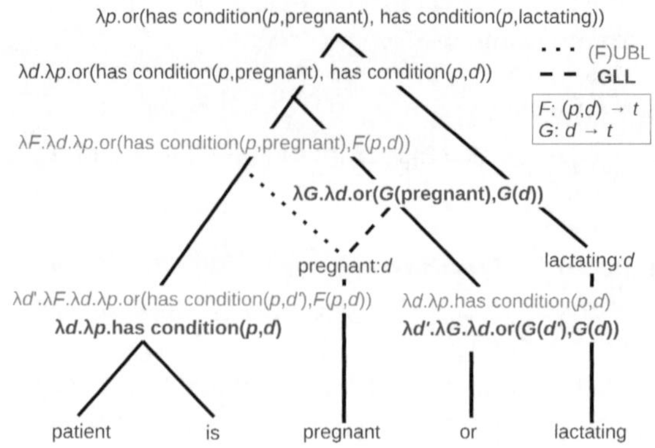

Figure 5: An example of a sentence with coordination semantics. GLL's lexical entry learning procedure correctly identifies the semantics for the lexeme or, while UBL and FUBL learn incorrect semantics.

4.4 Learning T-rules

We use T-rules to handle elliptical constructions. They are essentially a simplification of the factored lexicon used in FUBL that yields very similar results. Each T-rule $\tau \in \mathbf{T}$ is a function of the form λe . **if** $type(e)$ **then return** $Syn : f(e) \rightarrow Syn' : e$, where $type$ is a type from our ontology, Syn and Syn' are two syntactic CCG categories or variables, and f is an arbitrary lambda calculus expression. For example, consider the T-rule $\tau = (\lambda e$. **if** disease(e) **then return** $S\backslash N : \lambda p$. has condition(p, e) $\rightarrow N : e$). When applied to the entity diabetes, this T-rule results in an ordinary CCG rule: $S\backslash N : \lambda p$. has condition(p, diabetes) $\rightarrow N$: diabetes. Thus each T-rule is a template for constructing unary (type-raising) CCG grammar rules from an entity of the appropriate type.

TRLEARN works by first identifying a set of entity symbols E that appear in multiple lexical entries in the input grammar G. Let the lexical entries for entity $e \in E$ be denoted by $\Lambda(e)$; thus, E consists of all entities where $|\Lambda(e)| \geq 2$. TRLEARN then looks for patterns in each of these sets of lexical entries. If one of the lexical entries in $\Lambda(e)$ has a semantics that consists of just e (for example, the lexical entry N : diabetes $\rightarrow$ diabetes), we create candidate T-rules from every other lexical entry $l' \in \Lambda(e)$ that has the same child, such as $S\backslash N : \lambda p$. has condition(p, diabetes) $\rightarrow$ diabetes. From this lexical entry, we create the candidate T-rule τ = (λx . **if** disease(x) **then return** $S\backslash N : \lambda p$. has condition(p, x) $\rightarrow N : x$). In general, the test in the if statement in the T-rule contains a check for the type of entity e. The right-hand side of the implication contains a unary grammar rule whose parent matches the parent of the rule in l', except that entity e has been replaced by a variable x. The child of the grammar rule matches the parent of the basic lexical entry $N : e$, except again that the entity e has been replaced by the variable x.

Having constructed a set of candidate T-rules from this process, TRLEARN must select the ones that will actually be added to the grammar. We use a test of selecting T-rules that cover at least MIN existing grammar rules in the input grammar G. In our implementation, we set $MIN = 2$. When parsing a sentence, the parser checks any parse chart entry for semantics that consist solely of an entity; for any such entry, it looks in a hash-based index for applicable T-rules, applies them to the entity to construct new unary grammar rules, and then applies the unary grammar rules to the parse chart entry to create new nonterminal nodes.

5 Experiments

In our experiments, we test the generality of our learning algorithm by testing its ability to handle both GeoQuery and the Clinical Trials datasets.

5.1 Experimental setup

The clinical trials dataset is described above in Section 3. GeoQuery consists of a database of

System	Precision	Recall	F1
UBL	87.9	88.5	88.2
FUBL	**88.6**	**88.6**	**88.6**
GLL	84.6	86.1	85.5

Table 4: GLL performs comparably to two state-of-the-art learning algorithms for PCCG semantic parsing on the benchmark GeoQuery dataset.

System	Precision	Recall	F1
UBL	20.3	19.9	20.1
FUBL	42.3	39.7	40.8
GLL	**65.3**	**63.2**	**64.1**

Table 5: On the clinical trials dataset, GLL outperforms UBL and FUBL by more than 23 points in F1, for a reduction in error (*i.e.*, 1-F1) of nearly 40% over FUBL.

2400 geographical entities, such as nations, rivers, and mountains, as well as 8 geography relations, such as the location of a mountain, and whether one state borders another. The text for semantic parsing consists of a set of 880 geography questions, labeled with a lambda-calculus representation of the sentence's meaning. We follow the procedure described by Kwiatkowski *et al.*. (2010) in splitting these sentences into training, development, and test sentences. This dataset allows us to provide a comparison with other semantic parsers on a well-known dataset. We measured performance based on exact-match of the full logical form, modulo re-ordering of arguments to symmetric relations (like conjunction and disjunction).

5.2 Results and Discussion

Tables 4 and 5 show the results of semantic parsers learned by the UBL, FUBL, and GLL learning algorithms on the GeoQuery and clinical trials datasets, respectively. On the GeoQuery dataset, all three parsers perform very similarly, although GLL's performance is slightly worse. However, on the clinical trials dataset, GLL significantly outperforms both UBL and FUBL in terms of precision, recall, and F1. Of course, there clearly remain many syntactic and semantic constructions that none of these algorithms can currently handle, as all systems perform significantly worse on clinical trials than on GeoQuery.

Tables 6 shows the overall size of UBL's and GLL's learned lexicons, and Table 7 shows the number of learned entries for selected lexical items that appear frequently in the clinical trials corpus. FUBL uses a factored lexicon in which the semantics of a logical form is split across two data structures. As a result, FUBL's lexicon is not directly comparable to the other systems, so for these comparisons we restrict our attention to UBL and GLL. UBL tends to learn far more lexical entries than GLL, particularly for words that appear in multiple sentences. Yet the poorer performance of UBL on clinical trials is an indication that these lexical entries are overly specific.

	Lexicon Size	
System	GeoQuery	Clinical Trials
UBL	5,149	49,635
GLL	4,528	36,112

Table 6: GLL learns a lexicon that is 27% smaller than UBL's lexicon on clinical trials data.

Lexeme	UBL meanings	GLL meanings
$>$	36	2
$<$	28	2
$=$	35	2
and	6	4
or	254	9

Table 7: For certain common and critical lexical items in the clinical trials dataset, GLL learns far fewer (but more general) lexical entries; for the word "or", GLL learns only 3.5% of the entries that UBL learns.

6 Conclusion

We have introduced the clinical trials dataset, a naturally-occurring set of text where existing learning algorithms for semantic parsing struggle. Our new GLL algorithm uses a novel inverse function composition algorithm to handle coordination and nested function constructions, and pattern learning to handle elliptical constructions. These innovations allow GLL to handle GeoQuery and improve on clinical trials. Many sources of error on clinical trials remain for future research, including long-distance dependencies, attachment ambiguities, and coreference. In addition, further investigation is necessary to test how these algorithms handle additional domains and other types of natural linguistic constructions.

Acknowledgments

This work was supported by National Science Foundation grant 1218692. The authors appreciate the help that Anjan Nepal, Qingqing Cai, Avirup Sil, and Fei Huang provided.

References

Yoav Artzi and Luke Zettlemoyer. 2011. Bootstrapping Semantic Parsers from Conversations. In *Proceedings of the Conference on Empirical Methods in Natural Language Processing (EMNLP)*.

Olivier Bodenreider. 2004. The Unified Medical Language System (UMLS): integrating biomedical terminology. *Nucleic Acids Research*, 32:D267–D270.

Qingqing Cai and Alexander Yates. 2013. Large-scale Semantic Parsing via Schema Matching and Lexicon Extension. In *Proceedings of the Annual Meeting of the Association for Computational Linguistics (ACL)*.

David L. Chen, Joohyun Kim, and Raymond J. Mooney. 2010. Training a Multilingual Sportscaster: Using Perceptual Context to Learn Language. *Journal of Artificial Intelligence Research*, 37:397–435.

Stephen Clark and James R. Curran. 2007. Wide-coverage efficient statistical parsing with ccg and log-linear models. *Computational Linguistics*, 33(4):493–552.

J. Clarke, D. Goldwasser, M. Chang, and D. Roth. 2010. Driving semantic parsing from the world's response. In *Computational Natural Language Learning (CoNLL)*.

Ruifang Ge and Raymond J. Mooney. 2006. Discriminative Reranking for Semantic Parsing. In *Proceedings of the 21st International Conference on Computational Linguistics and 44th Annual Meeting of the Association for Computational Linguistics (COLING/ACL-06)*.

Ruifang Ge and Raymond J. Mooney. 2009. Learning a Compositional Semantic Parser using an Existing Syntactic Parser. In *Joint Conference of the 47th Annual Meeting of the Association for Computational Linguistics and the 4th International Joint Conference on Natural Language Processing of the Asian Federation of Natural Language Processing (ACL-IJCNLP 2009)*.

D. Goldwasser, R. Reichart, J. Clarke, and D. Roth. 2011. Confidence driven unsupervised semantic parsing. In *Association for Computational Linguistics (ACL)*.

Rohit J. Kate and Raymond J. Mooney. 2006. Using String-Kernels for Learning Semantic Parsers. In *Proceedings of the 21st International Conference on Computational Linguistics and the 44th annual meeting of the ACL*.

Rohit J. Kate and Raymond J. Mooney. 2007. Semi-Supervised Learning for Semantic Parsing using Support Vector Machines. In *Proceedings of the Human Language Technology Conference of the North American Chapter of the Association for Computational Linguistics, Short Papers (NAACL/HLT-2007)*.

Rohit J. Kate, Yuk Wah Wong, and Raymond J. Mooney. 2005. Learning to Transform Natural to Formal Languages. In *Proceedings of the Twentieth National Conference on Artificial Intelligence (AAAI-05)*.

Jayant Krishnamurthy and Tom Mitchell. 2012. Weakly Supervised Training of Semantic Parsers. In *Proceedings of the Conference on Empirical Methods in Natural Language Processing (EMNLP)*.

Tom Kwiatkowski, Luke Zettlemoyer, Sharon Goldwater, and Mark Steedman. 2010. Inducing Probabilistic CCG Grammars from Logical Form with Higher-order Unification. In *Proceedings of the Conference on Empirical Methods in Natural Language Processing (EMNLP)*.

Tom Kwiatkowski, Luke Zettlemoyer, Sharon Goldwater, and Mark Steedman. 2011. Lexical Generalization in CCG Grammar Induction for Semantic Parsing. In *Proceedings of the Conference on Empirical Methods in Natural Language Processing (EMNLP)*.

Y. LeCun, L. Bottou, Y. Bengio, and P. Haffner. 1998. Gradient-based learning applied to document recognition. In *Proceedings of the IEEE*.

P. Liang, M. I. Jordan, and D. Klein. 2009. Learning semantic correspondences with less supervision. In *Association for Computational Linguistics and International Joint Conference on Natural Language Processing (ACL-IJCNLP)*.

P. Liang, M. I. Jordan, and D. Klein. 2011. Learning dependency-based compositional semantics. In *Association for Computational Linguistics (ACL)*.

Wei Lu, Hwee Tou Ng, Wee Sun Lee, and Luke S. Zettlemoyer. 2008. A Generative Model for Parsing Natural Language to Meaning Representations. In *Proceedings of The Conference on Empirical Methods in Natural Language Processing (EMNLP)*.

Hoifung Poon. 2013. Grounded Unsupervised Semantic Parsing. In *Proceedings of the Annual Meeting of the Association for Computational Linguistics (ACL)*.

C.A. Thompson and R.J. Mooney. 1999. Automatic construction of semantic lexicons for learning natural language interfaces. In *Proc. 16th National Conference on Artificial Intelligence (AAAI-99)*, pages 487–493.

Cynthia A. Thompson and Raymond J. Mooney. 2003. Acquiring Word-Meaning Mappings for Natural Language Interfaces. *Journal of Artificial Intelligence Research (JAIR)*, 18:1–44.

Yuk Wah Wong and Raymond J. Mooney. 2007. Learning Synchronous Grammars for Semantic Parsing with Lambda Calculus. In *Proceedings of the 45th Annual Meeting of the Association for Computational Linguistics (ACL-2007)*.

Mohamed Yahya, Klaus Berberich, Shady Elbassuoni, Maya Ramanath, Volker Tresp, and Gerhard Weikum. 2012. Natural Language Questions for the Web of Data. In *Proceedings of the Conference on Empirical Methods in Natural Language Processing (EMNLP)*.

John M. Zelle and Raymond J. Mooney. 1996. Learning to Parse Database Queries using Inductive Logic Programming. In *AAAI/IAAI*, pages 1050–1055.

Luke S. Zettlemoyer and Michael Collins. 2005. Learning to Map Sentences to Logical Form: Structured Classification with Probabilistic Categorial Grammars. In *Proceedings of the Twenty First Conference on Uncertainty in Artificial Intelligence (UAI)*.

Luke S. Zettlemoyer and Michael Collins. 2007. Online Learning of Relaxed CCG Grammars for Parsing to Logical Form. In *Proceedings of the Joint Conference on Empirical Methods in Natural Language Processing and Computational Natural Language Learning (EMNLP-CoNLL)*.

Luke S. Zettlemoyer and Michael Collins. 2009. Learning Context-dependent Mappings from Sentences to Logical Form. In *Proceedings of the Joint Conference of the Association for Computational Linguistics and International Joint Conference on Natural Language Processing (ACL-IJCNLP)*.

Correcting Grammatical Verb Errors

Alla Rozovskaya
Columbia University
New York, NY 10115
ar3366@columbia.edu

Dan Roth
University of Illinois
Urbana, IL 61801
danr@illinois.edu

Vivek Srikumar
Stanford University
Stanford, CA 94305
svivek@cs.stanford.edu

Abstract

Verb errors are some of the most common mistakes made by non-native writers of English but some of the least studied. The reason is that dealing with verb errors requires a new paradigm; essentially all research done on correcting grammatical errors assumes a closed set of triggers – e.g., correcting the use of prepositions or articles – but identifying mistakes in verbs necessitates identifying potentially ambiguous triggers first, and then determining the type of mistake made and correcting it. Moreover, once the verb is identified, modeling verb errors is challenging because verbs fulfill many grammatical functions, resulting in a variety of mistakes. Consequently, the little earlier work done on verb errors assumed that the error type is known in advance.

We propose a linguistically-motivated approach to verb error correction that makes use of the notion of *verb finiteness* to identify triggers and types of mistakes, before using a statistical machine learning approach to correct these mistakes. We show that the linguistically-informed model significantly improves the accuracy of the verb correction approach.

1 Introduction

We address the problem of correcting grammatical verb mistakes made by English as a Second Language (ESL) learners. Recent work in ESL error correction has focused on errors in article and preposition usage (Han et al., 2006; Felice and Pulman, 2008; Gamon et al., 2008; Tetreault et al., 2010; Gamon, 2010; Rozovskaya and Roth, 2010b; Dahlmeier and Ng, 2011).

While verb errors occur as often as article and preposition mistakes, with a few exceptions (Lee and Seneff, 2008; Gamon et al., 2009; Tajiri et al., 2012), there has been little work on verbs. There are two reasons for why it is difficult to deal with verb mistakes. First, in contrast to articles and prepositions, verbs are more difficult to identify in text, as they can often be confused with other parts of speech, and processing tools are known to make more errors on noisy ESL data (Nagata et al., 2011). Second, verbs are more complex linguistically: they fulfill several grammatical functions, and these different roles imply different types of errors.

These difficulties have led all previous work on verb mistakes to assume prior knowledge of the mistake type; however, identifying the specific category of a verb error is nontrivial, since the surface form of the verb may be ambiguous, especially when that verb is used incorrectly. Consider the following examples of verb mistakes:

1. "We *discusses**/*discuss* this every time."
2. "I will be lucky if I {*will find*}*/*find* something that fits."
3. "They wanted to visit many places without *spend**/*spending* a lot of money."
4. "They arrived early to organized*/organize everything".

These examples illustrate three grammatical verb properties: *Agreement*, *Tense*, and non-finite *Form* choice that encompass the most common grammatical verb problems for ESL learners. The first two examples show mistakes on verbs that function as main verbs in a clause: sentence (1) shows an example of subject-verb *Agreement* error; (2) is an example of a *Tense* mistake where the ambiguity is between {*will find*} (Future tense) and *find* (Present tense). Examples (3) and (4) display *Form* mistakes: confusing the infinitive and gerund forms in (3) and including an inflection on an infinitive verb in (4).

This paper addresses the specific challenges of verb error correction that have not been addressed previously – identifying candidates for mistakes and determining which class of errors is present, before proceeding to correct the error. The experimental results show that our linguistically-motivated approach benefits verb error correction. In particular, in order to determine the error type, we build on the notion of *verb finiteness* to distinguish between *finite* and *non-finite* verbs (Quirk et al., 1985), that correspond to *Agreement* and *Tense* mistakes (examples (1) and (2) above) and *Form* mistakes (examples (3) and (4) above), respectively (see Sec. 3). The approach presented in this work was evaluated empirically and competitively in the context of the CoNLL shared task on error correction (Ng et al., 2013) where it was implemented as part of the highest-scoring University of Illinois system (Rozovskaya et al., 2013) and demonstrated superior performance on the verb error correction sub-task.

This paper makes the following contributions:

- We present a holistic, linguistically-motivated framework for correcting grammatical verb mistakes; our approach "starts from scratch" without any knowledge of which mistakes should be corrected or of the mistake type; in doing that we show that the specific challenges of verb error correction are better addressed by first identifying the *finiteness* of the verb in the error identification stage.
- Within the proposed model, we describe and evaluate several methods of *selecting verb candidates*, an algorithm for *determining the verb type*, and a type-driven *verb error correction system*.
- We annotate a subset of the FCE data set with gold verb candidates and gold verb type.[1]

2 Related Work

Earlier work in ESL error correction follows the methodology of the *context-sensitive spelling correction* task (Golding and Roth, 1996; Golding and Roth, 1999; Banko and Brill, 2001; Carlson et al., 2001; Carlson and Fette, 2007). Most of the effort in ESL error correction so far has been on article and preposition usage errors, as these are some of the most common mistakes among non-native English speakers (Dalgish, 1985; Leacock et al., 2010). These phenomena are generally modeled as multiclass classification problems: a single classifier is trained for a given error type where the set of classes includes all articles or the top *n* most frequent English prepositions (Izumi et al., 2003; Han et al., 2006; Felice and Pulman, 2008; Gamon et al., 2008; Tetreault et al., 2010; Rozovskaya and Roth, 2010b; Rozovskaya and Roth, 2011; Dahlmeier and Ng, 2011).

Mistakes on verbs have attracted significantly less attention in the error correction literature. Moreover, the little earlier work done on verb errors only considered subsets of these errors and assumed the error sub-type is known in advance. Gamon et al. (2009) mentioned a model for learning gerund/infinitive confusions and auxiliary verb presence/choice. Lee and Seneff (2008) proposed an approach based on pattern matching on trees combined with word n-gram counts for correcting agreement misuse and some types of verb form errors. However, they excluded tense mistakes, which is the most common error category for ESL learners (40% of all verb errors, Sec. 3). Tajiri et al. (2012) considered only tense mistakes. In the above studies, it was assumed that the type of mistake that needs to be corrected is known, and irrelevant verb errors were excluded (e.g., Tajiri et al. (2012) addressed only tense mistakes and excluded from the evaluation other kinds of verb errors). In other words, it was assumed that part of the task was solved. But, unlike in article and preposition error correction where the type of mistake is known based on the surface form of the word, in verb error correction, it is not obvious.

The key distinction of our work is that we propose a holistic approach that starts from "scratch" and, given an instance, first detects a mistake and identifies its type, and then proceeds to correct it. We also evaluate several methods for selecting verb candidates and show the significance of this step for improving verb error correction performance, while earlier studies do not discuss this aspect of the problem. In the CoNLL shared task (Ng et al., 2013) that included verb errors in agreement and form, the participating teams did not provide details on how specific challenges were handled, but the University of Illinois system obtained the highest score on the verb sub-task, even though

[1]The annotation is available at http://cogcomp.cs.illinois.edu/page/publication_view/743

Tag	Error type	Rel. freq. (%)
TV	Tense	40.0
FV	Form	22.3
AGV	Verb-subject agreement	11.5
MV	Missing verb	11.7
UV	Unneccesary verb	7.3
IV	Inflection	5.4
DV	Derivation	1.8
Total		6640

Table 1: **Grammatical verb errors in FCE.**

Category	Agreement	Kappa	Random
Correct verbs	0.97	0.95	0.51
Erroneous verbs	0.88	0.81	0.41

Table 3: **Inter-annotator agreement** based on 250 verb errors and 250 correct verbs, randomly selected.

all teams used similar resources (Ng et al., 2013).

3 Verb Errors in ESL Writing

Verb-related errors are very prominent among non-native English speakers: grammatical misuse of verbs constitutes one of the most common errors in several learner corpora, including those previously used (Izumi et al., 2003; Lee and Seneff, 2008) and the one employed in this work. We study verb errors using the FCE corpus (Yannakoudakis et al., 2011). The corpus possesses several desirable characteristics: it is large (500,000 words), has been annotated by native English speakers, and contains data by learners of multiple first-language backgrounds. The FCE corpus contains 5056 determiner errors, 5347 preposition errors, and 6640 grammatical verb mistakes (Table 1).

3.1 Verb Finiteness

There are many grammatical categories for which English verbs can be marked. The linguistic notion of *verb finiteness* or *verb type* (Radford, 1988; Quirk et al., 1985) distinguishes between verbs that function on their own in a clause as main verbs (finite) and those that do not (non-finite). Grammatical properties associated with each group are mutually exclusive: tense and agreement markers, for example, do not apply to non-finite verbs; non-finite verbs are not marked for many grammatical functions but may appear in several forms.

The most common verb problems for ESL learners – *Tense*, *Agreement*, non-finite *Form* – involve verbs both in finite and non-finite roles. Table 2 illustrates contexts that license finite and non-finite verbs.

Our intuition is that, because properties associated with each verb type are mutually exclusive, verb finiteness should benefit verb error correction models: an observed verb error may be due to several grammatical phenomena, and knowing which phenomena are active depends on the function of the verb in the current context. Note that *Agreement*, *Tense*, and *Form* errors account for about 74% of all grammatical verb errors in Table 1 but the finiteness distinction applies to all English verbs – every verb is either finite or non-finite in a specific syntactic context – and is also relevant for the remaining mistakes not addressed here.[2]

4 Annotation for Verb Finiteness

In order to evaluate the quality of the *algorithm for verb finiteness* and of the *candidate selection* methods, we annotated all verbs – correct and erroneous – in a random set of 124 documents from our corpus with the information about verb finiteness. We refer to these 124 documents as *gold subset*. We also annotated erroneous verbs in the remaining 1120 documents of the corpus. The annotation was performed by two students with background in Linguistics. The inter-annotator agreement is shown in Table 3 and is high.

Annotating Verb Errors For each verb error that was tagged as *Tense* (TV), *Agreement* (AGV), and *Form* (FV), the annotators marked verb finiteness. Additionally, the annotators also specified the type of error (*Tense*, *Agreement*, or *Form*) (Table 4), since the FCE tags do not always correspond to the three error types we study here. For example, the FV tag may mark errors on finite verbs. Overall, about 7% of verb errors have to do with phenomena different from the three verb properties considered in this work and thus are excluded from the present study.

Annotating Correct Verbs Correct verbs were identified in text using an automated procedure that relies on part-of-speech information (Sec. 5.1). Valid candidates were specified for verb finiteness. The candidates that were identified incorrectly due to mistakes by the part-of-speech tagger were marked as invalid.

5 The Computational Model

The verb error correction problem is formulated as a classification task in the spirit of the learn-

[2]For instance, the missing verb errors (MV, 11.7%) require an additional step to identify contexts for missing verbs, and then appropriate verb properties need to be determined based on verb finiteness.

Verb type	Example	Verb properties		
		Agreement	Tense	Form
Finite	"He *discussed* this with me last week"	-	Past Simple	-
	"He *discusses* this with me every week."	3rd person,Sing.	Present Simple	-
Non-finite	"He left without *discussing* it with me."	-	-	Gerund
	"They let him *discuss* this with me."	-	-	Infinitive
	"*To discuss* this now would be ill-advised."	-	-	to-Infinitive

Table 2: **Contexts that license finite and non-finite verbs and the corresponding active properties.**

Error on Verb Type	Subcategory	Example
Finite (67.7%)	Agreement (20%)	"We *discusses*/discuss* this every time."
	Tense (80%)	"If you buy something, you {*would be*}*/{*will be*} happy."
Non-finite (25.3%)		"If one is famous he has to accept the disadvantages of *be*/being* famous." "I am very glad {*for receiving*}*/{*to receive*} it." "They arrived early to *organized*/organize* everything."
Other errors (7.0%)	Passive/Active(42.3%)	"Our end-of-conference party {*is included*}*/*includes* dinner and dancing."
	Compound (40.7%)	"You ask me for some *informations*/information*- here *they*/it are*/is*."
	Other (16.8%)	"Nobody {*has to be*}*/{*should be*} late."

Table 4: **Verb error classification** based on 4864 mistakes marked as TV, AGV, and FV errors in the FCE corpus.

ing paradigm commonly used for correcting other ESL errors (Sec. 2), with the exception that the verb model includes additional components. All of the components are listed below:

1. Candidate selection (5.1)
2. Verb finiteness prediction (5.2)
3. Feature generation (5.3)
4. Error identification (5.4)
5. Error correction (5.5)

After verb candidates are selected, verb finiteness is determined and features are generated for each candidate. The *finiteness* prediction is used in the *error identification* component. Given the output of the error identification stage, the corresponding classifiers for each error type are invoked to propose an appropriate correction.

We split the corpus documents into two equal parts – training and test. We chose a train-test split and not cross-validation, since the FCE data set is quite large to allow for such a split. The training data is also used to develop the components for candidate selection and verb finiteness prediction.

5.1 Candidate Selection

This stage selects the set of verb instances that are presented as input to the classifier. A *verb instance* refers to the verb, including its auxiliaries or the infinitive marker (e.g. "found", "will find", "to find"). Candidate selection is a crucial step for models that correct mistakes on open-class words because those errors that are missed at this stage have no chance of being detected. We implement four candidate selection methods. Method (1) extracts all verbs heading a verb phrase, as identified by a shallow parser (Punyakanok and Roth, 2001).[3] Method (2) also includes words tagged with one of the verb tags: {VB, VBN, VBG, VBD, VBP, VBZ} predicted by the POS tagger.[4] However, relying on the POS information is not good enough, since the POS tagger performance on ESL data is known to be suboptimal (Nagata et al., 2011). For example, verbs lacking agreement markers are likely to be mistagged as nouns (Lee and Seneff, 2008). Methods (3) and (4) address the problem of pre-processing errors. Method (3) adds words that are on the list of valid English verb lemmas; the lemma list is constructed using a POS-tagged version of the NYT section of the Gigaword corpus and contains about 2,600 of frequently-occurring words tagged as *VB*; for example, (3) will add *shop* but not *shopping*, but (4) will add both.

For methods (3) and (4), we developed *verbMorph*,[5] a tool that performs morphological analysis on verbs and is used to lemmatize verbs and to generate morphological variants. The module makes uses of (1) the verb lemma list and (2) a list of irregular English verbs.

The quality of the candidate selection methods is evaluated in Table 5 on the gold subset by computing the recall, i.e. the percentage of erroneous verbs that have been selected as candidates. Methods that address pre-processing mistakes are able to recover more erroneous verb candidates in text. It is also interesting to note that across all methods, the highest recall is obtained for tense errors. This suggests that the POS tagger is more prone to fail-

[3] http://cogcomp.cs.illinois.edu/demo/shallowparse

[4] http://cogcomp.cs.illinois.edu/page/software_view/POS

[5] The tool and more detail about it can be found at http://cogcomp.cs.illinois.edu/page/publication_view/743

Method	Recall (%)	Recall by error group (%)		
		Agr.	Tense	Form
(1) All verb phrases	83.00	86.62	93.55	59.08
(2) + tokens tagged as verbs	91.96	90.30	94.33	87.79
(3) + tokens that are valid verb lemmas	95.50	95.99	96.46	93.23
(4) + tokens with inflections that are valid verb lemmas	96.09	96.32	96.62	94.84

Table 5: **Candidate selection methods performance.**

ure due to errors in agreement and form. The evaluation in Table 5 uses recall, as the goal is to assess the ability of the methods to select erroneous verbs as candidates. In Sec. 6.1, the contribution of each method to error identification is evaluated.

5.2 Predicting Verb Finiteness

Predicting verb finiteness is not trivial, as almost all English verbs can occur in both finite and non-finite form and the surface forms of a verb in finite and non-finite form may be the same (see Table 2).

While we cannot learn verb type automatically due to lack of annotation, we show, however, that, for the majority of verbs, finiteness can be reliably predicted using linguistic knowledge. We implement a decision-list classifier that makes use of linguistically-motivated rules (Table 6). The algorithm covers about 92% of all verb candidates, abstaining on the remaining highly-ambiguous 8%.

The evaluation of the method on the gold subset (last column in Table 6) shows that despite its simplicity, this method is highly effective: 98% on correct verbs and over 89% on errors.

5.3 Features

The *baseline* features are word n-grams in the 4-word window around the verb instance. Additional features are intended to characterize a given error type and are selected based on previous studies: for *Agreement* and *Form* errors, we use a parser (Klein and Manning, 2003) and define features that reflect dependency relations between the verb and its neighbors. We denote these features by *syntax*. Syntactic knowledge via tree patterns has been shown useful for *Agreement* mistakes (Lee and Seneff, 2008). Features for *Tense* include temporal adverbs in the sentence and tenses of other verbs in the sentence and are similar to the features used in other verb classification tasks (Reichart and Rappoport, 2010; Lee, 2011; Tajiri et al., 2012). The features are shown in Table 7.

5.4 Error Identification

The goal of this stage is to identify errors and to predict their type. We define a linear model where, given a verb, a weight vector $\mathbf{w}$ assigns a score to each label in the label space $\{$Correct, Form, Agreement, Tense$\}$. The prediction of the classifier is the label with the highest score.

The baseline error identification model, called *combined*, is agnostic to the type of the verb. In the *combined* model, for each verb v and label l, we generate a feature vector, $\phi(v, l)$ and the best label is predicted as

$$\arg\max_{l} \mathbf{w}^T \phi(v, l).$$

The *combined* model makes use of *all* the features we have defined earlier for each verb.

The *type-based* model uses the verb finiteness prediction made by the verb finiteness classifier. A *soft* way to use the finiteness prediction is to add the predicted finiteness value as a feature. The other – *hard*-decision approach – is to use only a subset of the features depending on the predicted finiteness: *Agreement* and *Tense* for the finite verbs, and *Form* features for non-finite. The hard-decision *type-driven* approach defines a feature vector for a verb based on its type. Thus, given the verb v *and* its type t, we define features $\phi(v, t, l)$ for each label l. Thus, the label is predicted as

$$\arg\max_{l} \mathbf{w}^T \phi(v, t, l).$$

5.5 Error Correction

The correction module consists of three components, one for each type of mistake. Given the output of the error identification model, the appropriate correction component is run for each instance predicted to be a mistake.[6] The verb finiteness prediction is used to select finite instances for training the *Agreement* and *Tense* components and non-finite – for the *Form* component. The label space for *Tense* specifies tense and aspect properties of the English verbs (see Tajiri et al., 2012 for more detail), the *Agreement* component specifies the person and number properties, while the *Form* component includes the commonly confusable non-finite English forms (see Table 2). These components are trained as multiclass classifiers.

[6] We assume that each verb contains at most one mistake. Less than 1% of all erroneous verbs have more than one error present.

A verb is Non-Finite if any of the following hold:	A verb is Finite if any of the following hold	Accuracy on	
		Correct verbs	Erroneous verbs
(1) $[numTokens = 2] \wedge [firstToken = to]$ (2) $firstToken = be$ (3) $[numTokens = 1] \wedge [pos = VBG]$	(1) All verbs identified by shallow parser (2) *can*; *could* (3) $[numTokens = 1] \wedge [pos \in \{VBD, VBP, VBZ\}]$ (4) $[numTokens = 2] \wedge [firstToken! = to]$ (5) $numTokens > 2$	98.01	89.4

Table 6: **Algorithm for determining verb type.** *numTokens* denotes the number of tokens in the verb instance, e.g., for the verb instance "to go", $numTokens = 2$. Verbs not covered by the rules, e.g. those that are not tagged with a verb-related POS in methods (3) and (4), are not assigned any verb type. The last column shows algorithm accuracy on the gold subset separately for correct and incorrect verbs.

	Agreement	Description
(1)	subjHead, subjPOS	The surface form and the POS tag of the subject head
(2)	subjDet {those,this,..}	Determiner of the subject phrase
(3)	subjDistance	Distance between the verb and the subject head
(4)	subjNumber {*Sing, Pl*}	*Sing* – singular pronouns and nouns; *Pl* – plural pronouns and nouns
(5)	subjPerson {*3rdSing, Not3rdSing, 1stSing*}	*3rdSing* – she,he,it,singular nouns; *Not3rdSing* – we,you,they, plural nouns; *1stSing* – "I"
(6)	conjunctions	$(1)\&(3);(4)\&(5)$
	Tense	**Description**
(1)	verb phrase (VP)	verb lemma, negation, surface forms and POS tags of all words in the verb phrase
(2)	verbs in sentence(4 features)	tenses and lemmas of the finite verbs preceding and following the verb instance
(3)	time adverbs (2 features)	temporal adverb before and after the verb instance
(4)	bag-of-words (BOW) (8 features)	Includes the following words in the sentence: {if, when, since, then, wish, hope, when, since, after}
	Form	**Description**
(1)	closest word	surface form, lemma, POS tag, and distance of the closest open-class word to the left of the verb
(2)	governor	surface form, POS tag and dependency type of the target
(3)	preposition	if the verb is preceded by a preposition: preposition itself and the surface form, POS tag and dependency of the governor of the preposition
(4)	pos and lemma	POS tag and lemma of the verb and their conjunctions with features in (2) and (3) and word ngrams

Table 7: **Features used, grouped by error type.**

6 Experiments

The main goal of this work is to propose a unified framework for correcting verb mistakes and to address the specific challenges of the problem. We thus do not focus on features or on the specific learning algorithm. Our experimental study addresses the following research questions:

I. **Linguistic questions**: (i) candidate selection methods; (ii) verb finiteness contribution to error identification
II. **Computational Framework**: error identification vs. correction
III. **Gold annotation**: (i) using gold candidates and verb type vs. automatic; (ii) performance comparison by error type

Learning Framework There is a lot of understanding for which algorithmic methods work best for ESL correction tasks, how they compare among themselves, and how they compare to n-gram based methods. Specifically, despite their intuitive appeal, language models were shown to not work well on these tasks, while the discriminative learning framework has been shown to be superior to other approaches and thus is commonly used for error correction tasks (see Sec. 2). Since we do not address the algorithmic aspect of the problem, we refer the reader to Rozovskaya and Roth (2011) for a discussion of these issues. We train all our models with the SVM learning algorithm implemented in JLIS (Chang et al., 2010).

Evaluation We report both Precision/Recall curves and AAUC (as a summary). Error correction is generally evaluated using F1 (Dale et al., 2012); Precision and Recall (Gamon, 2010; Tajiri et al., 2012); or Average Area Under Curve (AAUC) (Rozovskaya and Roth, 2011). For a discussion on these metrics with respect to error correction tasks, we refer the reader to Rozovskaya (2013). AAUC (Hanley and McNeil, 1983)) is a measure commonly used to generate a summary statistic, computed as an average precision value over a range of recall points. In this paper, AAUC is computed over the first 15 recall points:

$$AAUC = \frac{1}{15} \cdot \sum_{i=1}^{15} Precision(i).$$

6.1 Linguistic Questions

Candidate Selection Methods The contribution of the candidate selection component with respect to error identification is evaluated in Table 8, using the methods presented in Sec. 5.1. Overall,

Recall of candidate selection method (%)	AAUC	
	Combined	Type-based
(1) (83.00)	73.38	79.49
(2) (91.96)	80.36	86.48
(3) (95.50)	**81.39**	**87.05**
(4) (96.09)	81.27	86.81

Table 8: **Impact of candidate selection methods on error identification performance.** The first column shows the percentage of erroneous verbs selected by each method. *Type-based* models are discussed in Sec. 6.1.

	Correct verbs	Erroneous verbs	Error rate
Training	41721	1981	4.75%
Test	41836	2014	4.81%

Table 9: **Training and test data statistics.** Candidates are selected using method (3).

better performance is achieved by methods with higher recall, with the exception of method (4); its performance on error identification is behind that of method (3), perhaps due to the amount of noise that is also added. While the difference is small, method (3) is also simpler than method (4). We thus use method (3) in the rest of the paper. Table 9 shows the number of verb instances in training and test selected with this method.

Verb Finiteness Sec. 5.4 presented two ways of adding verb finiteness: (1) adding the predicted verb type as a feature and (2) selecting only the relevant features depending on the finiteness of the verb. Table 10 shows the results of using verb type in the error identification stage. While the first approach does not provide improvement over the *combined* model, the second method is very effective. We conjecture that because verb type prediction is quite accurate, the second, hard-decision approach is preferred, as it provides knowledge in a direct way. Henceforth, we will use the second method in the *type-based* model.

Fig. 1 compares the performance of the *combined* and the hard-decision *type-based* models shown in Table 10. Precision/Recall curves are generated by varying the threshold on the confidence of the classifier. This graph reveals the behavior of the systems at multiple recall points: we observe that at every recall point the *type-based* classifier has higher precision.

So far, the models used all features defined in Sec. 5.3. Table 11 reveals that the type-driven

Model	AAUC
Combined	81.39
Type-based I (soft)	81.11
Type-based II (hard)	**87.05**

Table 10: **Verb finiteness contribution to error identification.**

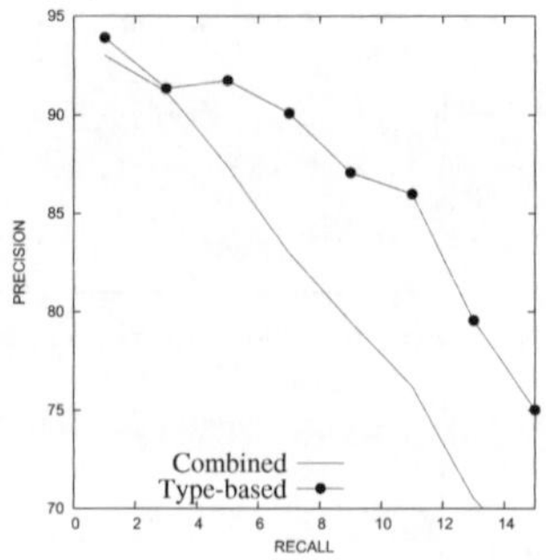

Figure 1: **Verb finiteness contribution to error identification: key result**. AAUC shown in Table 10. The *combined* model uses no verb type information. In the hard-decision *type-based* model, each verb uses the features according to its finiteness. The differences are statistically significant (McNemar's test, $p < 0.0001$).

Feature set	AAUC	
	Combined	Type-based
Baseline	46.62	49.72
All−Syntax	79.47	84.88
Full feature set	**81.39**	**87.05**

Table 11: **Verb finiteness contribution to error identification for different features.**

approach is superior to the combined approach across different feature sets, and the performance gap increases with more sophisticated feature sets, which is to be expected, since more complex features are tailored toward relevant verb errors. Furthermore, adding features specific to each error type significantly improves the performance over the word n-gram features. The rest of the experiments use all features (denoted *Full* feature set).

6.2 Identification vs. Correction

After running the error identification component, we apply the appropriate correction models to those instances identified as errors. The results for identification and correction are shown in Table 12. The correction models are also finiteness-aware models trained on the relevant verb instances (finite or non-finite), as predicted by the verb finiteness classifier.

We evaluate the correction components by fixing a recall point in the error identification stage.[7] We observe the relatively low recall obtained by the models. Error correction models tend to have low recall (see, for example, the recent shared tasks on ESL error correction (Dale and Kilgarriff, 2011; Dale et al., 2012; Ng et al., 2013)). The key reason for the low recall is the error sparsity: over 95% of verbs are correct, as shown in Table 9.

[7]We can increase recall using a different threshold but higher precision is preferred in error correction tasks.

Error type	Correction			Identification		
	P	R	F1	P	R	F1
Agreement	90.62	9.70	17.52	90.62	9.70	17.52
Tense	60.51	7.47	13.31	86.62	10.70	19.05
Form	81.82	16.34	27.24	83.47	16.67	27.79
Total	71.94	10.24	17.94	85.81	12.22	21.20

Table 12: **Performance of the complete model after the correction stage.** The results on *Agreement* mistakes are the same, since *Agreement* errors are always binary decisions, unlike *Tense* and *Form* mistakes.

The only way to improve over this 95% baseline is by forcing the system to have very good precision (at the expense of recall). The performance shown in Table 12 corresponds to an accuracy of 95.60% in identification (**error reduction of 8.7%**) and 95.40% in correction (**error reduction of 4.5%**) over the baseline of 95.19%.

6.3 Analysis on Gold Data

To further study the impact of each step of the system, we analyze our model on the gold subset of the data. The gold subset contains two additional pieces of information not available for the rest of the corpus: gold verb candidates and gold verb finiteness (Sec. 4). The set contains 7784 gold verbs, including 464 errors. Experiments are run in 10-fold cross-validation where on each run 90% of the documents are used for training and the remaining 10% are used for evaluation. The gold annotation can be used instead of automatic predictions in two system components: (1) candidate selection and (2) verb finiteness.

Table 13 shows the performance on error identification when gold vs. automatic settings are used. As expected, using the gold verb type is more effective than using the automatic one, both with automatic and gold candidates. The same is true for candidate selection. For instance, the *combined* model improves by 14 AAUC points (from 55.90 to 69.86) with gold candidates. These results indicate that candidate selection is an important component of the verb error correction system.

Note that compared to the performance on the entire data set (Table 10), the performance of the models shown here that use automatic components is lower, since the training size is smaller. On the other hand, because of the smaller training size, the gain due to the type-based approach is larger on the gold subset (19 vs. 6 AAUC points).

Finally, in Table 14, we evaluate the contribution of verb finiteness to error identification by error type. While performance varies by error, it is clear that all errors benefit from verb typing.

Candidate selection	Verb type prediction	AAUC
Automatic	None	55.90
	Automatic	74.72
	Gold	**89.45**
Gold	None	69.86
	Automatic	90.89
	Gold	**96.42**

Table 13: **Gold subset: error identification with gold vs. automatic candidates and finiteness information**. Value *None* for verb type prediction denotes the *combined* model.

Error type	AAUC		
	Combined	Type-based Automatic	Type-based Gold
Agreement	86.80	88.43	**89.21**
Tense	18.07	25.62	**26.87**
Form	97.08	98.23	**98.36**

Table 14: **Gold subset: gold vs. automatic finiteness contribution to error identification by error type.**

7 Conclusion

Verb errors are commonly made by ESL writers but difficult to address due to to their diversity and the fact that identifying verbs in (noisy) text may itself be difficult. We develop a linguistically-inspired approach that first identifies verb candidates in noisy learner text and then makes use of *verb finiteness* to identify errors and characterize the type of mistake. This is important, since most errors made by non-native speakers cannot be identified by considering only closed classes (e.g., prepositions and articles). Our model integrates a statistical machine learning approach with a rule-based system that encodes linguistic knowledge to yield the first general correction approach to verb errors (that is, one that does not assume prior knowledge of which mistake was made). This work thus provides a first step in considering more general algorithmic paradigms for correcting grammatical errors and paves the way for developing models to address other "open-class" mistakes.

Acknowledgments

The authors thank Graeme Hirst, Julia Hockenmaier, Mark Sammons, and the anonymous reviewers for their helpful feedback. This work was done while the first and the third authors were at the University of Illinois. This material is based on research sponsored by DARPA under agreement number FA8750-13-2-0008 and by the Army Research Laboratory (ARL) under agreement W911NF-09-2-0053. Any opinions, findings, conclusions or recommendations are those of the authors and do not necessarily reflect the view of the agencies.

References

M. Banko and E. Brill. 2001. Scaling to very very large corpora for natural language disambiguation. In *Proceedings of 39th Annual Meeting of the Association for Computational Linguistics*, pages 26–33, Toulouse, France, July.

A. Carlson and I. Fette. 2007. Memory-based context-sensitive spelling correction at web scale. In *Proceedings of the IEEE International Conference on Machine Learning and Applications (ICMLA)*.

A. Carlson, J. Rosen, and D. Roth. 2001. Scaling up context sensitive text correction. In *Proceedings of the National Conference on Innovative Applications of Artificial Intelligence (IAAI)*, pages 45–50.

M. Chang, V. Srikumar, D. Goldwasser, and D. Roth. 2010. Structured output learning with indirect supervision. In *Proc. of the International Conference on Machine Learning (ICML)*.

D. Dahlmeier and H. T. Ng. 2011. Grammatical error correction with alternating structure optimization. In *Proceedings of the 49th Annual Meeting of the Association for Computational Linguistics: Human Language Technologies*, pages 915–923, Portland, Oregon, USA, June. Association for Computational Linguistics.

R. Dale and A. Kilgarriff. 2011. Helping Our Own: The HOO 2011 pilot shared task. In *Proceedings of the 13th European Workshop on Natural Language Generation*.

R. Dale, I. Anisimoff, and G. Narroway. 2012. A report on the preposition and determiner error correction shared task. In *Proc. of the NAACL HLT 2012 Seventh Workshop on Innovative Use of NLP for Building Educational Applications*, Montreal, Canada, June. Association for Computational Linguistics.

G. Dalgish. 1985. Computer-assisted ESL research. *CALICO Journal*, 2(2).

R. De Felice and S. Pulman. 2008. A classifier-based approach to preposition and determiner error correction in L2 English. In *Proceedings of the 22nd International Conference on Computational Linguistics (Coling 2008)*, pages 169–176, Manchester, UK, August.

M. Gamon, J. Gao, C. Brockett, A. Klementiev, W. Dolan, D. Belenko, and L. Vanderwende. 2008. Using contextual speller techniques and language modeling for ESL error correction. In *Proceedings of IJCNLP*.

M. Gamon, C. Leacock, C. Brockett, W. B. Dolan, J. Gao, D. Belenko, and A. Klementiev. 2009. Using statistical techniques and web search to correct ESL errors. *CALICO Journal, Special Issue on Automatic Analysis of Learner Language*, 26(3):491–511.

M. Gamon. 2010. Using mostly native data to correct errors in learners' writing. In *NAACL*, pages 163–171, Los Angeles, California, June.

A. R. Golding and D. Roth. 1996. Applying Winnow to context-sensitive spelling correction. In *Proc. of the International Conference on Machine Learning (ICML)*, pages 182–190.

A. R. Golding and D. Roth. 1999. A Winnow based approach to context-sensitive spelling correction. *Machine Learning*, 34(1-3):107–130.

N. Han, M. Chodorow, and C. Leacock. 2006. Detecting errors in English article usage by non-native speakers. *Journal of Natural Language Engineering*, 12(2):115–129.

J. Hanley and B. McNeil. 1983. A method of comparing the areas under receiver operating characteristic curves derived from the same cases. *Radiology*, 148(3):839–843.

E. Izumi, K. Uchimoto, T. Saiga, T. Supnithi, and H. Isahara. 2003. Automatic error detection in the Japanese learners' English spoken data. In *The Companion Volume to the Proceedings of 41st Annual Meeting of the Association for Computational Linguistics*, pages 145–148, Sapporo, Japan, July.

T.-H. Kao, Y.-W. Chang, H. w. Chiu, T-.H. Yen, J. Boisson, J. c. Wu, and J.S. Chang. 2013. Conll-2013 shared task: Grammatical error correction nthu system description. In *Proceedings of the Seventeenth Conference on Computational Natural Language Learning: Shared Task*, pages 20–25, Sofia, Bulgaria, August. Association for Computational Linguistics.

D. Klein and C. D. Manning. 2003. Fast exact inference with a factored model for natural language parsing. In *Advances in Neural Information Processing Systems 15 NIPS*, pages 3–10. MIT Press.

C. Leacock, M. Chodorow, M. Gamon, and J. Tetreault. 2010. *Automated Grammatical Error Detection for Language Learners*. Morgan and Claypool Publishers.

J. Lee and S. Seneff. 2008. Correcting misuse of verb forms. In *ACL*, pages 174–182, Columbus, Ohio, June. Association for Computational Linguistics.

J. Lee. 2011. Verb tense generation. *Social and Behavioral Sciences*, 27:122–130.

R. Nagata, E. Whittaker, and V. Sheinman. 2011. Creating a manually error-tagged and shallow-parsed learner corpus. In *ACL*, pages 1210–1219, Portland, Oregon, USA, June. Association for Computational Linguistics.

H. T. Ng, S. M. Wu, Y. Wu, Ch. Hadiwinoto, and J. Tetreault. 2013. The CoNLL-2013 shared task on grammatical error correction. In *Proc. of the Seventeenth Conference on Computational Natural*

Language Learning. Association for Computational Linguistics.

V. Punyakanok and D. Roth. 2001. The use of classifiers in sequential inference. In *The Conference on Advances in Neural Information Processing Systems (NIPS)*, pages 995–1001. MIT Press.

R. Quirk, S. Greenbaum, G. Leech, and J. Svartvik. 1985. *A Comprehensive Grammar of the English Language*. Longman, New York.

A. Radford. 1988. *Transformational Grammar*. Cambridge University Press.

R. Reichart and A. Rappoport. 2010. Tense sense disambiguation: A new syntactic polysemy task. In *Proceedings of the 2010 Conference on Empirical Methods in Natural Language Processing*, pages 325–334, Cambridge, MA, October. Association for Computational Linguistics.

A. Rozovskaya and D. Roth. 2010a. Annotating ESL errors: Challenges and rewards. In *Proceedings of the NAACL Workshop on Innovative Use of NLP for Building Educational Applications*.

A. Rozovskaya and D. Roth. 2010b. Training paradigms for correcting errors in grammar and usage. In *Proceedings of the NAACL-HLT*.

A. Rozovskaya and D. Roth. 2011. Algorithm selection and model adaptation for esl correction tasks. In *ACL*, Portland, Oregon, 6. Association for Computational Linguistics.

A. Rozovskaya, K.-W. Chang, M. Sammons, and D. Roth. 2013. The University of Illinois system in the CoNLL-2013 shared task. In *CoNLL Shared Task*.

A. Rozovskaya. 2013. *Automated Methods for Text Correction*. Ph.D. thesis.

T. Tajiri, M. Komachi, and Y. Matsumoto. 2012. Tense and aspect error correction for esl learners using global context. In *Proceedings of the 50th Annual Meeting of the Association for Computational Linguistics (Volume 2: Short Papers)*, pages 198–202, Jeju Island, Korea, July. Association for Computational Linguistics.

J. Tetreault, J. Foster, and M. Chodorow. 2010. Using parse features for preposition selection and error detection. In *ACL*.

H. Yannakoudakis, T. Briscoe, and B. Medlock. 2011. A new dataset and method for automatically grading esol texts. In *Proceedings of the 49th Annual Meeting of the Association for Computational Linguistics*, pages 180–189, Portland, Oregon, USA, June. Association for Computational Linguistics.

Fast Statistical Parsing with Parallel Multiple Context-Free Grammars

Krasimir Angelov and **Peter Ljunglöf**
University of Gothenburg and Chalmers University of Technology
Göteborg, Sweden
krasimir@chalmers.se
peter.ljunglof@cse.gu.se

Abstract

We present an algorithm for incremental statistical parsing with Parallel Multiple Context-Free Grammars (PMCFG). This is an extension of the algorithm by Angelov (2009) to which we added statistical ranking. We show that the new algorithm is several times faster than other statistical PMCFG parsing algorithms on real-sized grammars. At the same time the algorithm is more general since it supports non-binarized and non-linear grammars.

We also show that if we make the search heuristics non-admissible, the parsing speed improves even further, at the risk of returning sub-optimal solutions.

1 Introduction

In this paper we present an algorithm for incremental parsing using Parallel Multiple Context-Free Grammars (PMCFG) (Seki et al., 1991). This is a non context-free formalism allowing discontinuity and crossing dependencies, while remaining with polynomial parsing complexity.

The algorithm is an extension of the algorithm by Angelov (2009; 2011) which adds statistical ranking. This is a top-down algorithm, shown by Ljunglöf (2012) to be similar to other top-down algorithms (Burden and Ljunglöf, 2005; Kanazawa, 2008; Kallmeyer and Maier, 2009). None of the other top-down algorithms are statistical.

The only statistical PMCFG parsing algorithms (Kato et al., 2006; Kallmeyer and Maier, 2013; Maier et al., 2012) all use bottom-up parsing strategies. Furthermore, they require the grammar to be binarized and linear, which means that they only support linear context-free rewriting systems (LCFRS). In contrast, our algorithm naturally supports the full power of PMCFG. By lifting these restrictions, we make it possible to experiment with novel grammar induction methods (Maier, 2013) and to use statistical disambiguation for hand-crafted grammars (Angelov, 2011).

By extending the algorithm with a statistical model, we allow the parser to explore only parts of the search space, when only the most probable parse tree is needed. Our cost estimation is similar to the estimation for the Viterbi probability as in Stolcke (1995), except that we have to take into account that our grammar is not context-free. The estimation is both admissible and monotonic (Klein and Manning, 2003) which guarantees that we always find a tree whose probability is the global maximum.

We also describe a variant with a non-admissible estimation, which further improves the efficiency of the parser at the risk of returning a suboptimal parse tree.

We start with a formal definition of a weighted PMCFG in Section 2, and we continue with a presentation of our algorithm by means of a weighted deduction system in Section 3. In Section 4, we prove that our estimations are admissible and monotonic. In Section 5 we calculate an estimate for the minimal inside probability for every category, and in Section 6 we discuss the non-admissible heuristics. Sections 7 and 8 describe the implementation and our evaluation, and the final Section 9 concludes the paper.

2 PMCFG definition

Our definition of weighted PMCFG (Definition 1) is the same as the one used by Angelov (2009; 2011), except that we extend it with weights for the productions. This definition is also similar to Kato et al (2006), with the small difference that we allow non-linear functions.

As an illustration for PMCFG parsing, we use a simple grammar (Figure 1) which can generate phrases like *"both black and white"* and *"either red or white"* but rejects the incorrect combina-

Definition 1
A parallel multiple context-free grammar is a tuple $G = (N, T, F, P, S, d, d_i, r, a)$ *where:*

- N *is a finite set of categories and a positive integer* $d(A)$ *called dimension is given for each* $A \in N$.
- T *is a finite set of terminal symbols which is disjoint with* N.
- F *is a finite set of functions where the arity* $a(f)$ *and the dimensions* $r(f)$ *and* $d_i(f)$ $(1 \leq i \leq a(f))$ *are given for every* $f \in F$. *For every positive integer d,* $(T^*)^d$ *denote the set of all d-tuples of strings over* T. *Each function* $f \in F$ *is a total mapping from* $(T^*)^{d_1(f)} \times (T^*)^{d_2(f)} \times \cdots \times (T^*)^{d_{a(f)}(f)}$ *to* $(T^*)^{r(f)}$, *defined as:*

  $$f := (\alpha_1, \alpha_2, \ldots, \alpha_{r(f)})$$

  Here α_i *is a sequence of terminals and* $\langle k; l \rangle$ *pairs, where* $1 \leq k \leq a(f)$ *is called argument index and* $1 \leq l \leq d_k(f)$ *is called constituent index.*
- P *is a finite set of productions of the form:*

  $$A \xrightarrow{w} f[A_1, A_2, \ldots, A_{a(f)}]$$

  where $A \in N$ *is called result category,* $A_1, A_2, \ldots, A_{a(f)} \in N$ *are called argument categories,* $f \in F$ *is the function symbol and* $w > 0$ *is a weight. For the production to be well formed the conditions* $d_i(f) = d(A_i)$ $(1 \leq i \leq a(f))$ *and* $r(f) = d(A)$ *must hold.*
- S *is the start category and* $d(S) = 1$.

tions *both-or* and *either-and*. We avoid these combinations by coupling the right pairs of words in a single function, i.e. we have the abstract conjunctions *both_and* and *either_or* which are linearized as discontinuous phrases. The phrase insertion itself is done in the definition of *conjA*. It takes the conjunction as its first argument, and it uses $\langle 1; 1 \rangle$ and $\langle 1; 2 \rangle$ to insert the first and the second constituent of the argument at the right places in the complete phrase.

A tree of function applications that yelds a complete phrase is the parse tree for the phrase. For instance, the phrase *"both red and either black or white"* is represented by the tree:

(*conjA both_and red*
(*conjA either_or black white*))

$$\begin{aligned}
A &\xrightarrow{w_1} \mathit{conjA}[\mathit{Conj}, A, A] \\
A &\xrightarrow{w_2} \mathit{black}[] \\
A &\xrightarrow{w_3} \mathit{white}[] \\
A &\xrightarrow{w_4} \mathit{red}[] \\
\mathit{Conj} &\xrightarrow{w_5} \mathit{both_and}[] \\
\mathit{Conj} &\xrightarrow{w_6} \mathit{either_or}[]
\end{aligned}$$

$$\begin{aligned}
\mathit{conjA} &:= (\langle 1;1\rangle\langle 2;1\rangle\langle 1;2\rangle\langle 3;1\rangle) \\
\mathit{black} &:= (\text{"black"}) \\
\mathit{white} &:= (\text{"white"}) \\
\mathit{red} &:= (\text{"red"}) \\
\mathit{both_and} &:= (\text{"both"}, \text{"and"}) \\
\mathit{either_or} &:= (\text{"either"}, \text{"or"})
\end{aligned}$$

Figure 1: Example Grammar

The weight of a tree is the sum of the weights for all functions that are used in it. In this case the weight for the example is $w_1 + w_5 + w_4 + w_1 + w_6 + w_2 + w_3$. If there are ambiguities in the sentence, the algorithm described in Section 3 always finds a tree which minimizes the weight.

Usually the weights for the productions are logarithmic probabilities, i.e. the weight of the production $A \rightarrow f[\vec{B}]$ is:

$$w = -\log P(A \rightarrow f[\vec{B}] \mid A)$$

where $P(A \rightarrow f[\vec{B}] \mid A)$ is the probability to choose this production when the result category is fixed. In this case the probabilities for all productions with the same result category sum to one:

$$\sum_{A \xrightarrow{w} f[\vec{B}] \in P} e^{-w} = 1$$

However, the parsing algorithm does not depend on the probabilistic interpretation of the weights, so the same algorithm can be used with any other kind of weights.

3 Deduction System

We define the algorithm as weighted deduction system (Nederhof, 2003) which generalizes Angelov's system.

A key feature in his algorithm is that the expressive PMCFG is reduced to a simple context-free grammar which is extended dynamically at parsing time in order to account for context dependent features in the original grammar. This can be exemplified with the grammar in Figure 1, where there are two productions for category *Conj*. Given the phrase *"both black and white"*, after accepting the token *both*, only the production *Conj* $\xrightarrow{w_5}$ *both_and*[] can be applied for parsing the second part of the conjunction. This is achieved by generating a new category $Conj_2$ which has just a single production:

$$Conj_2 \xrightarrow{w_5} both\_and[] \tag{1}$$

The parsing algorithm is basically an extension of Earley's (1970) algorithm, except that the parse items in the chart also keep track of the categories for the arguments. In the particular case, the corresponding chart item will be updated to point to $Conj_2$ instead of *Conj*. This guarantees that only *and* will be accepted as a second constituent after seeing that the first constituent is *both*.

Now since the set of productions is dynamic, the parser must keep three kinds of items in the chart, instead of two as in the Earley algorithm:

Productions The parser maintains a dynamic set with all productions that are derived during the parsing. The initial state is populated with the productions from the set P in the grammar.

Active Items The active items play the same role as the active items in the Earley algorithm. They have the form:

$$[^k_j A \xrightarrow{w} f[\vec{B}]; l : \alpha \bullet \beta; w_i; w_o]$$

and represent the fact that a constituent l of a category A has been partially recognized from position j to k in the sentence. Here $A \xrightarrow{w} f[\vec{B}]$ is the production and the concatenation $\alpha\beta$ is the sequence of terminals and $\langle k; r\rangle$ pairs which defines the l-th constituent of function f. The dot $\bullet$ between α and β separates the part of the constituent that is already recognized from the part which is still pending. Finally w_i and w_o are the inside and outside weights for the item.

Passive Items The passive items are of the form:

$$[^k_j A; l; \hat{A}]$$

and state that a constituent with index l from category A was recognized from position j to position k in the sentence. As a consequence the parser has created a new category $\hat{A}$. The set of productions derived for $\hat{A}$ compactly records all possible ways to parse the $j - k$ fragment.

3.1 Inside and outside weights

The inside weight w_i and the outside weight w_o in the active items deserve more attention since this is the only difference compared to Angelov (2009; 2011). When the item is complete, it will yield the forest of all trees that derive the sub-string covered by the item. For example, when the first constituent for category *Conj* is completely parsed, the forest will contain the single production in (1). The inside weight for the active item is the currently best known estimation for the lowest weight of a tree in the forest. The trees yielded by the item do not cover the whole sentence however. Instead, they will become part of larger trees that cover the whole sentence. The outside weight is the estimation for the lowest weight for an extension of a tree to a full tree. The sum $w_i + w_o$ estimates the weight of the full tree.

Before turning to the deduction rules we also need a notation for the lowest possible weight for a tree of a given category. If $A \in N$ is a category then w_A will denote the lowest weight that a tree of category A can have. For convenience, we also use $w_{\vec{B}}$ as a notation for the sum $\sum_i w_{B_i}$ of the weight of all categories in the vector $\vec{B}$. If the category A is defined in the grammar then we assume that the weight is precomputed as described in Section 5. When the parser creates the category, it will compute the weight dynamically.

3.2 Deduction rules

The deduction rules are shown in Figure 2. Here the assumption is that the active items are processed in the order of increasing $w_i + w_o$ weight. In the actual implementation we put all active items in a priority queue and we always take first the item with the lowest weight. We never throw away items but the processing of items with very high weight might be delayed indefinitely or they may never be processed if the best tree is found before that. Furthermore, we think of the deduction system as a way do derive a set of items, but in our case we ignore the weights when we consider whether two active items are the same. In this way, every item is derived only once and the weights for the active items are computed from the weights of the first antecedents that led to its derivation.

Finally, we use two more notations in the rules: rhs(g, r) denotes constituent with index r in function g; and ω_k denotes the k-th token in the sentence.

INITIAL PREDICT

$$\frac{S \xrightarrow{w} f[\vec{B}]}{[^0_0 S \xrightarrow{w} f[\vec{B}]; 1 : \bullet\, \gamma; w + w_{\vec{B}}; 0]} \quad S = \text{start category},\ \gamma = \text{rhs}(f, 1)$$

PREDICT

$$\frac{B_d \xrightarrow{w_1} g[\vec{C}] \quad [^k_j A \xrightarrow{w_2} f[\vec{B}]; l : \alpha \bullet \langle d; r\rangle\, \beta; w_i; w_o]}{[^k_k B_d \xrightarrow{w_1} g[\vec{C}]; r : \bullet\, \gamma; w_1 + w_{\vec{C}}; w_i - w_{B_d} + w_o]} \quad \gamma = \text{rhs}(g, r)$$

SCAN

$$\frac{[^k_j A \xrightarrow{w} f[\vec{B}]; l : \alpha \bullet s\, \beta; w_i; w_o]}{[^{k+1}_j A \xrightarrow{w} f[\vec{B}]; l : \alpha\, s \bullet \beta; w_i; w_o]} \quad s = \omega_{k+1}$$

COMPLETE

$$\frac{[^k_j A \xrightarrow{w} f[\vec{B}]; l : \alpha \bullet; w_i; w_o]}{\hat{A} \xrightarrow{w} f[\vec{B}] \qquad [^k_j A; l; \hat{A}]} \quad \hat{A} = (A, l, j, k),\ w_{\hat{A}} = w_i$$

COMBINE

$$\frac{[^u_j A \xrightarrow{w} f[\vec{B}]; l : \alpha \bullet \langle d; r\rangle\, \beta; w_i; w_o] \quad [^k_u B_d; r; \hat{B}_d]}{[^k_j A \xrightarrow{w} f[\vec{B}\{d := \hat{B}_d\}]; l : \alpha\, \langle d; r\rangle \bullet \beta; w_i + w_{\hat{B}_d} - w_{B_d}; w_o]}$$

Figure 2: Deduction Rules

The first rule on Figure 2 is INITIAL PREDICT and here we predict the initial active items from the productions for the start category S. Since this is the start category, we set the outside weight to zero. The inside weight is equal to the sum of the weight w for the production and the lowest possible weight $w_{\vec{B}}$ for the vector of arguments $\vec{B}$. The reason is that despite that we do not know the weight for the final tree yet, it cannot be lower than $w + w_{\vec{B}}$ since $w_{\vec{B}}$ is the lowest possible weight for the arguments of function f.

The interaction between inside and outside weights is more interesting in the PREDICT rule. Here we have an item where the dot is before $\langle d; r\rangle$ and from this we must predict one item for each production $B_d \xrightarrow{w_1} g[\vec{C}]$ of category B_d. The inside weight for the new item is $w_1 + w_{\vec{C}}$ for the same reasons as for the INITIAL PREDICT rule. The outside weight however is not zero because the new item is predicted from another item. The inside weight for the active item in the antecedents is now part of the outside weight of the new item. We just have to subtract w_{B_d} from w_i because the new item is going to produce a new tree which will replace the d-th argument of f. For this reason the estimation for the outside weight is $w_i - w_{B_d} + w_o$, where we also added the outside weight for the antecedent item.

In the SCAN rule, we just move the dot past a token, if it matches the current token ω_{k+1}. Both the inside and the outside weights are passed untouched from the antecedent to the consequent.

In the COMPLETE rule, we have an item where the dot has reached the end of the constituent. Here we generate a new category $\hat{A}$ which is unique for the combination (A, l, j, k), and we derive the production $\hat{A} \xrightarrow{w} f[\vec{B}]$ for it. We set the weight $w_{\hat{A}}$ for $\hat{A}$ to be equal to w_i and in Section 4, we will prove that this is indeed the lowest weight for a tree of category $\hat{A}$.

In the last rule COMBINE, we combine an active item with a passive item. The outside weight w_o for the new active item remains the same. However, we must update the inside weight since we have replaced the d-th argument in $\vec{B}$ with the newly generated category $\hat{B}_d$. The new weight is $w_i + w_{\hat{B}_d} - w_{B_d}$, i.e. we add the weight for the new category and we subtract the weight for the previous category B_d.

Now for the correctness of the weights we must prove that the estimations are both admissible and monotonic.

4 Admissibility and Monotonicity

We will first prove that the weights grow monotonically, i.e. if we derive one active item from another then the sum $w_i + w_o$ for the new item is always greater or equal to the sum for the previous item. PREDICT and COMBINE are the only two rules with an active item both in the antecedents and in the consequents.

Note that in PREDICT we choose one particular production for category B_d. We know that the lowest possible weight of a tree of this category is w_{B_d}. If we restrict the set of trees to those that not only have the same category B_d but also use the same production $B_d \xrightarrow{w_1} g[\vec{C}]$ on the top level, then the best weight for such a tree will be $w_1 + w_{\vec{C}}$. According to the definition of w_{B_d}, it must follow that:

$$w_1 + w_{\vec{C}} \geq w_{B_d}$$

From this we can trivially derive that:

$$(w_1 + w_{\vec{C}}) + (w_i - w_{B_d} + w_o) \geq w_i + w_o$$

which is the monotonicity condition for rule PREDICT. Similarly in rule COMBINE, the condition:

$$w_{\hat{B}_d} \geq w_{B_d}$$

must hold because the forest of trees for $\hat{B}_d$ is included in the forest for B_d. From this we conclude the monotonicity condition:

$$(w_i + w_{\hat{B}_d} - w_{B_d}) + w_o \geq w_i + w_o$$

The last two inequalities are valid only if we can correctly compute $w_{\hat{B}_d}$ for a dynamically generated category $\hat{B}_d$. This happens in rule COMPLETE, where we have a complete active item with a correctly computed inside weight w_i. Since we process the active items in the order of increasing $w_i + w_o$ weight and since we create $\hat{A}$ when we find the first complete item for category A, it is guaranteed that at this point we have an item with minimal $w_i + w_o$ value. Furthermore, all items with the same result category A and the same start position j must have the same outside weight. It follows that when we create $\hat{A}$ we actually do it from an active item with minimal inside weight w_i. This means that it is safe to assign that $w_{\hat{A}} = w_i$.

It is also easy to see that the estimation is admissible. The only places where we use estimations for the unseen parts of the sentence is in the rules INITIAL PREDICT and PREDICT where we use the weights $w_{\vec{B}}$ and $w_{\vec{C}}$ which may include components corresponding to function argument that are not seen yet. However by definition it is not possible to build a tree with weight lower than the weight for the category. This means that the estimation is always admissible.

5 Initial Estimation

The minimal weight for a dynamically created category is computed by the parser, but we must initialize the weights for the categories that are defined in the grammar. The easiest way is to just set all weights to zero, and this is safe since the weights for the predefined categories are used only as estimations for the yet unseen parts of the sentence. Essentially this gives us a statistical parser which performs Dijkstra search in the space of all parse trees. Any other reasonable weight assignment will give us an A^* algorithm (Hart et al., 1968).

In general it is possible to devise different heuristics which will give us different improvements in the parsing time. In our current implementation of the parser we use a weight assignment which considers only the already known probabilities for the productions in the grammar.

The weight for a category A is computed as:

$$w_A = \min_{A \xrightarrow{w} f[\vec{B}] \,\in\, P} (w + w_{\vec{B}})$$

Here the sum $w + w_{\vec{B}}$ is the minimal weight for a tree constructed with the production $A \xrightarrow{w} f[\vec{B}]$ at the root. By taking the minimum over all productions for A, we get the corresponding weight w_A. This is a recursive equation since its right-hand side contains the value $w_{\vec{B}}$ which depends on the weights for the categories in $\vec{B}$. It might happen that there are mutually dependent categories which will lead to a recursion in the equation.

The solution is found with iterative assignments until a fixed point is reached. In the beginning we assign $w_A = 0$ for all categories. After that we recompute the new weights with the equation above until we reach a fixed point.

6 Non-admissible heuristics

The set of active items is kept in a priority queue and at each step we process the item with the lowest weight. However, when we experimented with the algorithm we noticed that most of the time the item that is selected would eventually contribute with an alternative reading of the sentence but not to the best parse. What happens is that despite that there are already items ending at position k in the sentence, the current best item might have a span $i - j$ where $j < k$. The parser then picks the best item only to discover later that the item became much heavier until it reached the span $i - k$.

This suggests that when we compare the weights of items with different end positions, then we must take into account the weight that will be accumulated by the item that ends earlier until the two items align at the same end position.

We use the following heuristic to estimate the difference. The first time when we extend an item from position i to position $i+1$, we record the weight increment $w_\Delta(i+1)$ for that position. The increment w_Δ is the difference between the weights for the best active item reaching position $i+1$ and the best active item reaching position i. From now on when we compare the weights for two items x_j and x_k, with end positions j and k respectively ($j < k$), then we always add to the score w_{x_j} of the first item a fraction of the sum of the increments for the positions between j and k. In other words, instead of using w_{x_j} when comparing with w_{x_k}, we use

$$w_{x_j} + h \cdot \sum_{j<i\leq k} w_\Delta(i)$$

We call the constant $h \in [0,1]$ the "heuristics factor". If $h = 0$, we obtain the basic algorithm that we described earlier which is admissible and always returns the best parse. However, the evaluation in Section 8.3 shows that a significant speed-up can be obtained by using larger values of h. Unfortunately, if $h > 0$, we loose some accuracy and cannot guarantee that the best parse is always returned first.

Note that the heuristics does not change the completeness of the algorithm – it will succeed for all grammatical sentences and fail for all non-grammatical. But it does not guarantee that the first parse tree will be the optimal.

7 Implementation

The parser is implemented in C and is distributed as a part of the runtime system for the open-source Grammatical Framework (GF) programming language (Ranta, 2011).[1] Although the primary application of the runtime system is to run GF applications, it is not specific to one formalism, and it can serve as an execution platform for other frameworks where natural language parsing and generation is needed.

The GF system is distributed with a library of manually authored resource grammars (Ranta, 2009) for over 25 languages, which are used as a resource for deriving domain specific grammars. Adding a big lexicon to the resource grammar results in a highly ambiguous grammar, which can give rise to millions of trees even for moderately complex sentences. Previously, the GF system has not been able to parse with such ambiguous grammars, but with our statistical algorithm it is now feasible.

8 Evaluation

We did an initial evaluation on the GF English resource grammar augmented with a large-coverage lexicon of 40 000 lemmas taken from the Oxford Advanced Learner's Dictionary (Mitton, 1986). In total the grammar has 44 000 productions. The rule weights were trained from a version of the Penn Treebank (Marcus et al., 1993) which was converted to trees compatible with the grammar.

The trained grammar was tested on Penn Treebank sentences of length up to 35 tokens, and the parsing times were at most 7 seconds per sentence. This initial test was run on a computer with a 2.4 GHz Intel Core i5 processor with 8 GB RAM. This result was very encouraging, given the complexity of the grammar, so we decided to do a larger test and compare with an existing state-of-the-art statistical PMCFG parser.

Rparse (Kallmeyer and Maier, 2013) is a another state-of-the-art training and parsing system for PMCFG.[2] It is written in Java and developed at the Universities of Tübingen and Düsseldorf, Germany. Rparse can be used for training probabilistic PMCFGs from discontinuous treebanks. It can also be used for parsing new sentences with the trained grammars.

In our evaluation we used Rparse to extract PMCFG grammars from the discontinuous German Tiger Treebank (Brants et al., 2002). The reason for using this treebank is that the extracted grammars are non-context-free, and our parser is specifically made for such grammars.

8.1 Evaluation data

In our evaluations we got the same general results regardless of the size of the grammar, so we only report the results from one of these runs.

In this particular example, we trained the grammar on 40 000 sentences from the Tiger Treebank with lengths up to 160 tokens. We evaluated on

[1] http://www.grammaticalframework.org/

[2] https://github.com/wmaier/rparse

	Count
Training sentences	40 000
Test sentences	4 607
Non-binarized grammar rules	30 863
Binarized grammar rules	26 111

Table 1: Training and testing data.

4 600 Tiger sentences, with a length of 5–60 tokens. The exact numbers are shown in Table 1. All tests were run on a computer with a 2.3 GHz Intel Core i7 processor with 16GB RAM.

As a comparison, Maier et al (2012) train on approximately 15 000 sentences from the Negra Treebank, and only evaluate on sentences of at most 40 tokens.

8.2 Comparison with Rparse

We evaluated our parser by comparing it with Rparse's built-in parser. Note that we are only interested in the efficiency of our implementation, not the coverage and accuracy of the trained grammar. In the comparison we used only the admissible heuristics, and we did confirm that the parsers produce optimal trees with exactly the same weight for the same input.

Rparse extracts grammars in two steps. First it converts the treebank into a PMCFG, and then it binarizes that grammar. The binarization process uses markovization to improve the precision and recall of the final grammar (Kallmeyer and Maier, 2013). We tested both Rparse's standard (Kallmeyer and Maier, 2013) and its new improved parsing alogorithm (Maier et al., 2012). The new algorithm unfortunately works only with LCFRS grammars with a fan-out ≤ 2 (Maier et al., 2012).

In this test we used the optimal binarization method described in Kallmeyer (2010, chapter 7.2). This was the only binarization algorithm in Rparse that produced a grammar with fan-out ≤ 2.

As can be seen in Figure 3, our parser outperforms Rparse for all sentence lengths. For sentences longer than 15 tokens, the standard Rparse parser needs on average 100 times longer time than our parser. This difference increases with sentence length, suggesting that our algorithm has a better parsing complexity than Rparse.

The PGF parser also outperforms the improved Rparse parser, but the relative difference seems to stabilize on a speedup of 10–15 times.

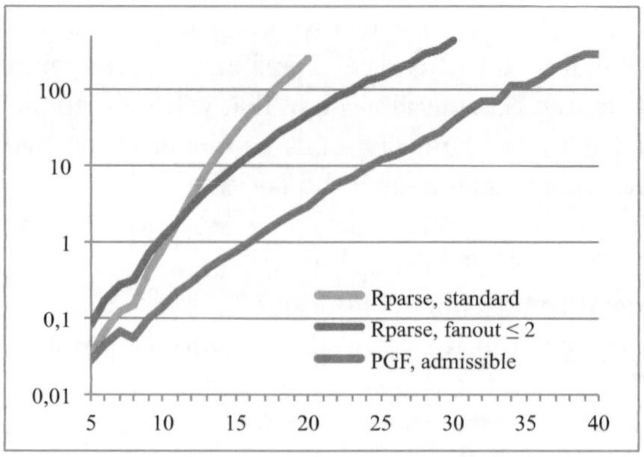

Figure 3: Parsing time (seconds) compared with Rparse.

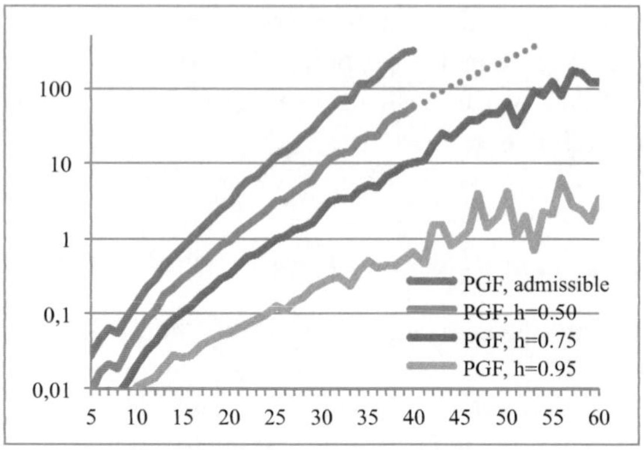

Figure 4: Parsing time (seconds) with different heuristics factors.

8.3 Comparing different heuristics

In another test we compared the effect of the heuristic factor h described in Section 6. We used the same training and testing data as before, and we tried four different heuristic factors: $h = 0$, 0.50, 0.75 and 0.95. As mentioned in Section 6, a factor of 0 gives an admissible heuristics, which means that the parser is guaranteed to return the tree with the best weight.

The parsing times are shown in Figure 4. As can be seen, a higher heuristics factor h gives a considerable speed-up. For 40 token sentences, $h = 0.50$ gives an average speedup of 5 times, while $h = 0.75$ is 30 times faster, and $h = 0.95$ is almost 500 times faster than using the admissible heuristics $h = 0$. This is more clearly seen in Figure 5, where the parsing times are shown relative to the admissible heuristics.

Note that all charts have a logarithmic y-axis, which means that a straight line is equivalent to exponential growth. If we examine the graph lines

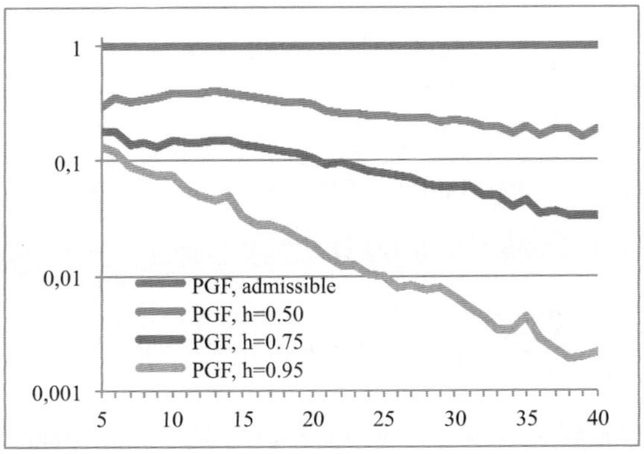

Figure 5: Relative parsing time for different values of h, compared to admissible heuristic.

more closely, we can see that they are not straight. The closest curves are in fact polynomial, with a degree of 4–6 depending on the parser and the value of h.[3]

8.4 Non-admissibility and parsing quality

What about the loss of parsing quality when we use a non-admissible heuristics? Firstly, as mentioned in Section 6, the parser still recognizes exactly the same language as defined by the grammar. The difference is that it is not guaranteed to return the tree with the best weight.

In our evaluation we saw that for a factor $h = 0.50$, 80% of the trees are optimal, and only 3% of the trees have a weight more than 5% from the optimal weight. The performance gradually gets worse for higher h, and with $h = 0.95$ almost 10% of the trees have a weight more than 20% from the optimum.

These numbers only show how the parsing quality degrades relative to the grammar. But since the grammar is trained from a treebank it is more interesting to evaluate how the parsing quality on the treebank sentences is affected when we use a non-admissible heuristics. Table 2 shows how the labelled precision and recall are changed with different values for h. The evaluation was done using the EVALB measure which is implemented in Rparse (Maier, 2010). As can be seen, a factor of $h = 0.50$ only results in a f-score loss of 3 points, which is arguably not very much. On the other extreme, for $h = 0.95$ the f-score drops 14 points.

[3]The exception is the standard Rparse parser, which has a polynomial degree of 8.

	Precision	Recall	F-score
admissible	71.1	67.7	69.3
$h = 0.50$	68.0	64.9	66.4
$h = 0.75$	63.0	60.8	61.9
$h = 0.95$	55.1	55.6	55.3

Table 2: Parsing quality for different values of h.

9 Discussion

The presented algorithm is an important generalization of the classical algorithms of Earley (1970) and Stolcke (1995) for parsing with probabilistic context-free grammars to the more general formalism of parallel multiple context-free grammars. The algorithm has been implemented as part of the runtime for the Grammatical Framework (Ranta, 2011), but it is not limited to GF alone.

9.1 Performance

To show the universality of the algorithm, we evaluated it on large LCFRS grammars trained from the Tiger Treebank.

Our parser is around 10–15 times faster than the latest, optimized version of the Rparse state-of-the-art parser. This improvement seems to be constant, which means that it can be a consequence of low-level optimizations. More important is that our algorithm does not impose any restrictions at all on the underlying PMCFG grammar. Rparse on the other hand requires that the grammar is both binarized and has a fan-out of at most 2.

By using a non-admissible heuristics, the speed improves by orders of magnitude, at the expense of parsing quality. This makes it possible to parse long sentences (more than 50 tokens) in just around a second on a standard desktop computer.

9.2 Future work

We would like to extend the algorithm to be able to use lexicalized statistical models (Collins, 2003). Furthermore, it would be interesting to develop better heuristics for A^* search, and to investigate how to incorporate beam search pruning into the algorithm.

References

Krasimir Angelov. 2009. Incremental parsing with parallel multiple context-free grammars. In *Proceedings of EACL 2009, the 12th Conference of the European Chapter of the Association for Computational Linguistics*, Athens, Greece.

Krasimir Angelov. 2011. *The Mechanics of the Grammatical Framework*. Ph.D. thesis, Chalmers University of Technology, Gothenburg, Sweden.

Sabine Brants, Stefanie Dipper, Silvia Hansen, Wolfgang Lezius, and George Smith. 2002. The TIGER treebank. In *Proceedings of TLT 2002, the 1st Workshop on Treebanks and Linguistic Theories*, Sozopol, Bulgaria.

Håkan Burden and Peter Ljunglöf. 2005. Parsing linear context-free rewriting systems. In *Proceedings of IWPT 2005, the 9th International Workshop on Parsing Technologies*, Vancouver, Canada.

Michael Collins. 2003. Head-driven statistical models for natural language parsing. *Computational Linguistics*, 29(4):589–637.

Jay Earley. 1970. An efficient context-free parsing algorithm. *Communications of the ACM*, 13(2):94–102.

Peter Hart, Nils Nilsson, and Bertram Raphael. 1968. A formal basis for the heuristic determination of minimum cost paths. *IEEE Transactions of Systems Science and Cybernetics*, 4(2):100–107.

Laura Kallmeyer and Wolfgang Maier. 2009. An incremental Earley parser for simple range concatenation grammar. In *Proceedings of IWPT 2009, the 11th International Conference on Parsing Technologies*, Paris, France.

Laura Kallmeyer and Wolfgang Maier. 2013. Data-driven parsing using probabilistic linear context-free rewriting systems. *Computational Linguistics*, 39(1):87–119.

Laura Kallmeyer. 2010. *Parsing Beyond Context-Free Grammars*. Springer.

Makoto Kanazawa. 2008. A prefix-correct Earley recognizer for multiple context-free grammars. In *Proceedings of TAG+9, the 9th International Workshop on Tree Adjoining Grammar and Related Formalisms*, Tübingen, Germany.

Yuki Kato, Hiroyuki Seki, and Tadao Kasami. 2006. Stochastic multiple context-free grammar for RNA pseudoknot modeling. In *Proceedings of TAGRF 2006, the 8th International Workshop on Tree Adjoining Grammar and Related Formalisms*, Sydney, Australia.

Dan Klein and Christopher D. Manning. 2003. A^* parsing: fast exact Viterbi parse selection. In *Proceedings of HLT-NAACL 2003, the Human Language Technology Conference of the North American Chapter of the Association for Computational Linguistics*, Edmonton, Canada.

Peter Ljunglöf. 2012. Practical parsing of parallel multiple context-free grammars. In *Proceedings of TAG+11, the 11th International Workshop on Tree Adjoining Grammar and Related Formalisms*, Paris, France.

Wolfgang Maier, Miriam Kaeshammer, and Laura Kallmeyer. 2012. PLCFRS parsing revisited: Restricting the fan-out to two. In *Proceedings of TAG+11, the 11th International Workshop on Tree Adjoining Grammar and Related Formalisms*, Paris, France.

Wolfgang Maier. 2010. Direct parsing of discontinuous constituents in German. In *Proceedings of SPRML 2010, the 1st Workshop on Statistical Parsing of Morphologically-Rich Languages*, Los Angeles, California.

Wolfgang Maier. 2013. LCFRS binarization and debinarization for directional parsing. In *Proceedings of IWPT 2013, the 13th International Conference on Parsing Technologies*, Nara, Japan.

Mitchell P. Marcus, Mary Ann Marcinkiewicz, and Beatrice Santorini. 1993. Building a large annotated corpus of English: the Penn Treebank. *Computational Linguistics*, 19:313–330.

Roger Mitton. 1986. A partial dictionary of English in computer-usable form. *Literary & Linguistic Computing*, 1(4):214–215.

Mark-Jan Nederhof. 2003. Weighted deductive parsing and Knuth's algorithm. *Computational Linguistics*, 29(1):135–143.

Aarne Ranta. 2009. The GF resource grammar library. *Linguistic Issues in Language Technology*, 2(2).

Aarne Ranta. 2011. *Grammatical Framework: Programming with Multilingual Grammars*. CSLI Publications, Stanford.

Hiroyuki Seki, Takashi Matsumura, Mamoru Fujii, and Tadao Kasami. 1991. On multiple context-free grammars. *Theoretical Computer Science*, 88(2):191–229.

Andreas Stolcke. 1995. An efficient probabilistic context-free parsing algorithm that computes prefix probabilities. *Computational Linguistics*, 21(2):165–201.

Sentiment Propagation via Implicature Constraints

Lingjia Deng
Intelligent Systems Program
University of Pittsburgh
lid29@pitt.edu

Janyce Wiebe
Department of Computer Science
University of Pittsburgh
wiebe@cs.pitt.edu

Abstract

Opinions may be expressed implicitly via inference over explicit sentiments and events that positively/negatively affect entities (*goodFor/badFor* events). We investigate how such inferences may be exploited to improve sentiment analysis, given goodFor/badFor event information. We apply Loopy Belief Propagation to propagate sentiments among entities. The graph-based model improves over explicit sentiment classification by 10 points in precision and, in an evaluation of the model itself, we find it has an 89% chance of propagating sentiments correctly.

1 Introduction

Previous research in sentiment analysis and opinion extraction has largely focused on the interpretation of explicitly stated opinions. However, many opinions are expressed implicitly via *opinion implicature* (i.e., opinion-oriented defeasible inference). Consider the following sentence:

Ex(**1**) The bill would lower health care costs, which would be a tremendous positive change across the entire health-care system.

The writer is clearly positive toward the idea of *lowering health care costs*. But how does s/he feel about the costs? If s/he is **positive** toward the idea of *lowering* them, then, presumably, she is **negative** toward the *costs* themselves (specifically, how high they are). The only explicit sentiment expression, *tremendous positive change*, is positive, yet we can infer a **negative** attitude toward the **object** of the event itself (i.e., *health care costs*).

Going further, since *the bill* is the **agent** of an event toward which the writer is positive, we may (defeasibly) infer that the writer is **positive** toward *the bill*, even though there are no explicit sentiment expressions describing it.

Now, consider *The bill would curb skyrocketing health care costs.* The writer expresses an explicit **negative** sentiment (*skyrocketing*) toward the **object** (*health care costs*) of the event. Note that *curbing* costs, like *lowering* them, is bad for them (the costs are reduced). We can reason that, because the event is bad for something toward which the writer is negative, the writer is **positive** toward the **event**. We can reason from there, as above, that the writer is **positive** toward *the bill*, since it is the **agent** of the positive event.

These examples illustrate how explicit sentiments toward one entity may be propagated to other entities via opinion implicature rules. The rules involve events that positively or negatively affect entities. We call such events *goodFor/badFor* (hereafter *gfbf*)events.

This work investigates how gfbf event interactions among entities, combined with opinion inferences, may be exploited to improve classification of the writer's sentiments toward entities mentioned in the text. We introduce four rule schemas which reveal sentiment constraints among gfbf events and their agents and objects. Those constraints are incorporated into a graph-based model, where a node represents an entity (agent/object), and an edge exists between two nodes if the two entities participate in one or more gfbf events with each other. Scores on the nodes represent the explicit sentiments, if any, expressed by the writer toward the entities. Scores on the edges are based on constraints derived from the rules. *Loopy Belief Propagation (LBP)* (Pearl, 1982) is applied to accomplish sentiment propagation in the graph.

Two evaluations are performed. The first shows that the graph-based model improves over an explicit sentiment classification system. The second evaluates the graph-based model itself (and hence the implicature rules), assessing its ability to correctly propagate sentiments to nodes whose polarities are unknown. We find it has an 89% chance of propagating sentiment values correctly.

This is the first paper to address this type of sentiment propagation to improve sentiment analysis. To eliminate interference introduced by other components, we use manually annotated gfbf information to build the graph. Thus, the evaluations in this paper are able to demonstrate the promise of the overall framework itself.

2 Related Work

Much work in sentiment analysis has been on document-level classification. Since different sentiments may be expressed toward different entities in a document, fine-grained analysis may be more informative for applications.

However, fine-grained sentiment analysis remains a challenging task for NLP systems. For fully-automatic systems evaluated on the MPQA corpus (Wiebe et al., 2005), for example, a recent paper (Johansson and Moschitti, 2013) reports results that improve over previous work, yet the F-measures are in the 40s and 50s.

Most work in NLP addresses explicit sentiment, but some address implicit sentiment. For example, (Zhang and Liu, 2011) identify noun product features that imply opinions, and (Feng et al., 2013) identify objective words that have positive or negative connotations. However, identifying terms that imply opinions is a different task than sentiment propagation between entities. (Dasigi et al., 2012) search for implicit attitudes shared between authors, while we address inferences within a single text.

Several papers apply compositional semantics to determine polarity (e.g., (Moilanen and Pulman, 2007; Choi and Cardie, 2008; Moilanen et al., 2010); see (Liu, 2012) for an overview). The goal of such work is to determine one overall polarity of an expression or sentence. In contrast, our framework commits to a holder having sentiments toward various events and entities in the sentence, possibly of different polarities.

The idea of gfbf events in sentiment analysis is not entirely new. For example, two papers mentioned above (Zhang and Liu, 2011; Choi and Cardie, 2008) include linguistic patterns for the tasks that they address that include gfbf events, but they don't define general implicature rules relating sentiments and gfbf events, agents, and objects as we do. Recently, in linguistics, Anand and Reschke (2010; 2011) identify classes of gfbf terms, and carry out studies involving artificially constructed gfbf triples and corpus examples matching fixed linguistic templates. Our work focuses on gfbf triples in naturally-occurring data and uses generalized implicature rules. Goyal et al. (2012) generate a lexicon of *patient polarity verbs*, which correspond to gfbf events whose spans are verbs. Riloff et al. (2013) investigate sarcasm where the writer holds a positive sentiment toward a negative situation. However, neither of these works performs sentiment inference.

Graph-based models have been used for various tasks in sentiment analysis. Some work (Wang et al., 2011; Tan et al., 2011) apply LBP on a graph capturing the relations between users and tweets in Twitter data . However, they assume the nodes and the neighbors of nodes share the same sentiments. In contrast, we don't assume that neighbors share the same sentiment, and the task we address is different.

3 Opinion Implicatures

This section describes the opinion-implicature framework motivating the design of the graph-based method for sentiment analysis proposed below. The components of the framework are gfbf events, explicit sentiments, and rules operating over gfbf events and sentiments.

The definition of a gfbf event is from (Deng et al., 2013). A GOODFOR event is an event that positively affects an entity (similarly, for BADFOR events). (Deng et al., 2013) point out that gfbf objects are not equivalent to benefactive/malefactive semantic roles. An example they give is *She baked a cake for me*: *a cake* is the object of GOODFOR event *baked* (creating something is good for it (Anand and Reschke, 2010)), while *me* is the filler of its benefactive semantic role (Zúñiga and Kittilä, 2010).

Four implicature rule schemas are relevant for this paper.[1] Four individual rules are covered by

[1] *Implicatures* "normally accompany the utterances of a given sentence unless special factors exclude that possibility

each schema. *sent*(α) = β means that the **writer's** sentiment toward α is β, where α is a GOODFOR event, a BADFOR event, or the agent or object of a gfbf event, and β is either *positive* or *negative* (*pos* or *neg*, for short). P $\rightarrow$ Q is to infer Q from P.

Rule1: sent(gfbf event) $\rightarrow$ sent(object)
1.1 sent(GOODFOR) = pos $\rightarrow$ sent(object) = pos
1.2 sent(GOODFOR) = neg $\rightarrow$ sent(object) = neg
1.3 sent(BADFOR) = pos $\rightarrow$ sent(object) = neg
1.4 sent(BADFOR) = neg $\rightarrow$ sent(object) = pos

Rule2: sent(object) $\rightarrow$ sent(gfbf event)
2.1 sent(object) = pos $\rightarrow$ sent(GOODFOR) = pos
2.2 sent(object) = neg $\rightarrow$ sent(GOODFOR) = neg
2.3 sent(object) = pos $\rightarrow$ sent(BADFOR) = neg
2.4 sent(object) = neg $\rightarrow$ sent(BADFOR) = pos

Rule3: sent(gfbf event) $\rightarrow$ sent(agent)
3.1 sent(GOODFOR) = pos $\rightarrow$ sent(agent) = pos
3.2 sent(GOODFOR) = neg $\rightarrow$ sent(agent) = neg
3.3 sent(BADFOR) = pos $\rightarrow$ sent(agent) = pos
3.4 sent(BADFOR) = neg $\rightarrow$ sent(agent) = neg

Rule4: sent(agent) $\rightarrow$ sent(gfbf event)
4.1 sent(agent) = pos $\rightarrow$ sent(GOODFOR) = pos
4.2 sent(agent) = neg $\rightarrow$ sent(GOODFOR) = neg
4.3 sent(agent) = pos $\rightarrow$ sent(BADFOR) = pos
4.4 sent(agent) = neg $\rightarrow$ sent(BADFOR) = neg

To explain the rules, we step through an example:

EX(**2**) Why would [President Obama] **support** [health care reform]? Because [reform] could **lower** [*skyrocketing* health care costs], and **prohibit** [private insurance companies] from **overcharging** [patients].

Suppose a sentiment analysis system recognizes only one explicit sentiment expression, *skyrocketing*. According to the annotations, there are several gfbf events. Each is listed below in the form $\langle$agent, gfbf, object$\rangle$.

E_1: $\langle$reform, lower, costs$\rangle$
E_2: $\langle$reform, prohibit, E_3 $\rangle$
E_3: $\langle$companies, overcharge, patients$\rangle$
E_4: $\langle$Obama, support, reform$\rangle$

In E_1, from the negative sentiment expressed by *skyrocketing* (the writer is negative toward the costs because they are too high), and the fact that *costs* is the object of a BADFOR event (*lower*), Rule2.4 infers **a positive attitude toward** E_1 .

Now, Rule3.3 applies. We infer the writer is **positive toward the *reform***, since it is the agent of E_1, toward which the writer is positive.

E_2 illustrates the case where the object is an event. Specifically, the object of E_2 is E_3, a BADFOR event (*overcharging*). As we can see, E_2 keeps E_3 from happening. Events such as E_2 are REVERSERS, because they reverse the polarity of a gfbf event (from BADFOR to GOODFOR, or vice versa). Note that REVERSERS may be seen as BADFOR events, because they make their objects irrealis (i.e., not happen). Similarly, a RETAINER such as *help* in *"help Mary save Bill"* can be viewed as a GOODFOR event. (We call a REVERSER or a RETAINER an INFLUENCER.) In this paper, RETAINERS are treated as GOODFOR events and REVERSERS are treated as BADFOR events.

Above, we inferred that the writer is positive toward *reform*, the agent of E_2. By Rule 4.3, the writer is **positive toward** E_2; then by Rule 1.3, the writer is **negative toward** E_3, the object of E_2.

For E_3, using Rule 1.4 we know the writer is **positive toward *patients*** and using Rule 3.4 we know the writer is **negative toward *companies***.

Turning to E_4, *support health care reform* is GOODFOR *reform*. We already inferred the writer is positive toward *reform*. Rule 2.1 infers that the writer is **positive toward** E_4. Rule 3.1 then infers that the writer is **positive toward the agent of** E_4, ***Obama***.

In summary, we infer that the writer is positive toward E_1, health care reform, E_2, patients, E_4, and Obama, and negative toward E_3 and private insurance companies.

4 Data

We use the data described in (Deng et al., 2013),[2] which consists of 134 documents about a controversial topic, "the Affordable Care Act." The documents are editorials and blogs, and are full of opinions.

In the data, gfbf triples are annotated specifying the spans of the gfbf event, its agent, and its object, as well as the polarity of the gfbf event (GOODFOR or BADFOR), and the writer's attitude toward the agent and object (positive, negative, or neutral). Influencers are also annotated. The agents of gfbf

(p. 39)." (Huddleston and Pullum, 2002)

[2]Available at http://mpqa.cs.pitt.edu

and influencer events are noun phrases. The object of a gfbf event is a noun phrase, but the object of an influencer is a gfbf event or another influencer. A *triple chain* is a chain of zero or more influencers ending in a gfbf event, where the object of each element of the chain is the following element in the chain. (e.g. in EX(2), the two event *prohibit* and *overcharging* is a triple chain.)

In total, there are 1,762 annotated gfbf triples, out of which 692 are GOODFOR or RETAINER and 1,070 are BADFOR or REVERSER. From the writer's perspective, 1,495 noun phrases are annotated positive, 1,114 are negative and the remaining 8 are neutral. This is not surprising, given that most of the sentences in the data are opinionated.

5 Graph-based Model

We propose a graph-based model of entities and the gfbf relations between them to enable sentiment propagation between entities. In this section, we introduce the definition of the graph (in 5.1), the LBP algorithm (in 5.2), and the definition of its functions for our task (in 5.3 and 5.4).

5.1 Definition of the Entity Graph

We define a gfbf entity graph $EG = \{N, E\}$, in which the node set N consists of nodes, each representing an annotated noun phrase agent or object span. The edge set E consists of edges, each linking two nodes if they co-occur in a triple chain with each other. Consider the triples of EX(2) in Section 3 below.

E_1: ⟨reform, lower, costs⟩
E_2: ⟨reform, prohibit, E_3 ⟩
E_3: ⟨companies, overcharge, patients⟩
E_4: ⟨Obama, support, reform⟩

The node of *reform* is linked to nodes of *costs* via E_1 and *Obama* via E_4.[3] Note that, for E_2 and E_3, the two are linked in a chain: ⟨*reform, prohibit,* ⟨*companies, overcharge, patients*⟩ ⟩. The three nodes *reform*, *companies* and *patients* participate in this triple chain; thus, pairwise edges exist among them. The edge linking *companies* and *patients* is BADFOR (because of *overcharging*). The edge linking *reform* and *companies* is also a BADFOR since we treat a REVERSER as BADFOR. The edge linking *reform* and *patients* encodes two BADFOR events (*prohibit-overcharge*); computationally we say two BADFORs result in a GOODFOR, so the edge linking the two is GOODFOR.[4]

Given a text, we get the spans of gfbf events and their agents and objects plus the polarities of the events (GOODFOR/BADFOR) from the manual annotations, and then build the graph upon them. However, the manual annotations of the writer's sentiments toward the agents and objects are used as the gold standard for evaluation.

5.2 Sentiment Inference via LBP

initialize all $m_{i\to j}(pos) = m_{i\to j}(neg) = 1$
repeat
foreach $n_i \in N$ **do**
foreach $n_j \in Neighbor(n_i)$ **do**
foreach $y \in pos, neg$ **do**
calculate $m_{i\to j}(y)$
normalize $m_{i\to j}(pos) + m_{i\to j}(neg) = 1$
until all $m_{i\to j}$ stop changing;
for each $n_i \in N$ **assign its polarity as**
$\underset{y\in pos,neg}{\text{argmax}}\ \Phi_i(y) * \prod_{n_k\in Neighbor(n_i)} m_{k\to i}(y)$
neutral, in case of a tie

Table 1: Loopy Belief Propagation

With graph EG containing cycles and no apparent structure, we utilize an approximate collective classification algorithm, *loopy belief propagation (LBP)* (Pearl, 1982; Yedidia et al., 2005), to classify nodes through belief message passing. The algorithm is shown in Table 1.

In LBP, each node has a score, $\Phi_i(y)$, and each edge has a score, $\Psi_{ij}(y_i, y_j)$. In our case, $\Phi_i(y)$ represents the writer's explicit sentiment toward n_i. $\Psi_{ij}(y_i, y_j)$ is the score on edge e_{ij}, representing the likelihood that node n_i has polarity y_i and n_j has polarity y_j. The specific definitions of the two functions are given in Sections 5.3 and 5.4.

LBP is an iterative message passing algorithm. A message from n_i to n_j over edge e_{ij} has two values: $m_{i\to j}(pos)$ is how much information from node n_i indicates node n_j is positive, and $m_{i\to j}(neg)$ is how much information from node n_i indicates node n_j is negative. In each iteration, the two are normalized such that $m_{i\to j}(pos) + m_{i\to j}(neg) = 1$. The message from n_i to its

[3]This assumes that the two instances of "reform" co-refer. However, the system does not resolve co-reference – the methods that we tried did not improve overall performance.

[4]Also, GOODFOR+BADFOR=BADFOR; GOODFOR+GOODFOR=GOODFOR

neighbor n_j is computed as:

$$m_{i\to j}(pos) = \Psi_{ij}(pos,pos) * \Phi_i(pos) * \prod_{n_k \in Neighbor(n_i)/n_j} m_{k\to i}(pos) + \Psi_{ij}(neg,pos) * \Phi_i(neg) * \prod_{n_k \in Neighbor(n_i)/n_j} m_{k\to i}(neg) \quad (1)$$

$$m_{i\to j}(neg) = \Psi_{ij}(neg,neg) * \Phi_i(neg) * \prod_{n_k \in Neighbor(n_i)/n_j} m_{k\to i}(neg) + \Psi_{ij}(pos,neg) * \Phi_i(pos) * \prod_{n_k \in Neighbor(n_i)/n_j} m_{k\to i}(pos) \quad (2)$$

For example, the first part of Equation (1) means that the positive message n_i conveys to n_j (i.e., $m_{i\to j}(pos)$) comes from n_i being positive itself ($\Phi_i(pos)$), the likelihood of edge e_{ij} with its nodes n_i being positive and n_j being positive ($\Psi_{ij}(pos,pos)$), and the positive message n_i's neighbors (besides n_j) convey to it ($\prod_{k \in Neighbor(n_i)/n_j} m_{k\to i}(pos)$).

After convergence, the polarity of each node is determined by its explicit sentiment and the messages its neighbors convey to it, as shown at the end of the algorithm in Table 1.

By this method, we take into account both sentiments and the interactions between entities via gfbf events in order to discover implicit attitudes.

Note that the node and edge scores are determined initially and do not change. Only $m_{i\to j}$ changes from iteration to iteration.

5.3 $\Psi_{ij}(y_i, y_j)$: GFBF Implicature Relations

The score $\Psi_{i,j}$ encodes constraints based on the gfbf relationships that nodes n_i and n_j participate in, together with the implicature rules given above.

Rule schemas 1 and 3 infer sentiments toward entities (agent/object) from sentiments toward gfbf events. All cases covered by them are shown in Table 2 (use s(α) to represent sent(α)).

			Rule 3	Rule1
s(gfbf)	gfbf type	→	s(agent)	s(object)
pos	GOODFOR	→	pos	pos
neg	GOODFOR	→	neg	neg
pos	BADFOR	→	pos	neg
neg	BADFOR	→	neg	pos

Table 2: Rule 1 & Rule 3

A table of Rule schemas 2 and 4 would be exactly the same, except that the inference (→) would be in the opposite direction (←).

From Table 2, we see that, regardless of the writer's sentiment toward the event, if the event is GOODFOR, then the writer's sentiment toward the agent and object are the same, while if the event is BADFOR, the writer's sentiment toward the agent and object are opposite. Thus, the event type and the writer's sentiments toward the agents and objects give us constraints. Therefore, we define $\Psi_{ij}(pos,pos)$ and $\Psi_{ij}(neg,neg)$ to be 1 if the two nodes are linked by a GOODFOR edge; otherwise, it is 0; and we define $\Psi_{ij}(neg,pos)$ and $\Psi_{ij}(pos,neg)$ to be 1 if the two nodes are linked by a BADFOR edge; otherwise, it is 0.

5.4 $\Phi_i(y)$: Explicit Sentiment Classifier

The score of a node, $\Phi_i(y)$, represents the sentiment explicitly expressed by the writer toward that entity in the document. Since y ranges over (pos, neg), each node has a positive and a negative score; the scores sum to 1. If it is a positive node, then its positive value ranges from 0.5 to 1, and its negative value ranges from 0 to 0.5 (similarly for negative nodes). For any node without explicit sentiment, both the positive and negative values are 0.5, indicating a neutral node.

Thus, we build a sentiment classifier that takes a node as input and outputs a positive and a negative score. It is built from widely-used, freely available resources: the OpinionFinder (Wilson et al., 2005) and General Inquirer (Stone et al., 1966) lexicons and the OpinionFinder system.[5] We also use a new Opinion Extraction system (Johansson and Moschitti, 2013) that shows better performance than previous work on fine-grained sentiment analysis,[6] and a new automatically developed connotation lexicon (Feng et al., 2013).[7]

We implement a weighted voting method among these various sentiment resources. After that, for nodes that have not yet been assigned polar values (positive or negative), we implement a simple local discourse heuristic to try to assign them polar values.

The particular strategies were chosen based only on a separate development set, which is not

[5] http://mpqa.cs.pitt.edu and http://www.wjh.harvard.edu/ inquirer/

[6] As evaluated on the MPQA corpus. Note that the authors ran their system for us on the data we use.

[7] http://www.cs.stonybrook.edu/~ychoi/connotation

included in the data used in the experiments.

5.4.1 Explicit Sentiment Tools

Opinion Extraction outputs a polarity expression with its source, and OpinionFinder outputs a polarity word. But neither of the tools extracts the target. To extract the target, for each word in the opinion expression, we select other words in the sentence which are in a *mod*, *obj* dependency parsing relation with it.

We match up the extracted expressions and the gfbf annotations according to their offsets in the text. For an opinion expression appearing in the sentence with no gfbf annotation, if the root word (in the dependency parse) of the expression span is the same as the root word of a gfbf span, or the root word of an agent span, or the root word of an object span, we assume they match up. Then we assign polarity as follows. If the expression refers only to the agent or object, then the agent or object is assigned the polarity of the expression. If the expression covers the gfbf event and its object, we assume the sentiment is toward the gfbf event and then assign sentiment according to Rule schema 1 (sent(gfbf event) $\rightarrow$ sent(object)).

5.4.2 Lexicons

To classify the sentiment expressed within the span of an agent or object, we check whether the words in the span appear in one or more of the lexicons.[8] If a lexicon finds both positive and negative words in the span, we resolve the conflict by choosing the polarity of the root word in the span. If the root word does not have a polar value, we choose the majority polarity of the sentiment words. If there are an equal number of positive and negative words, the polarity is neutral.

5.4.3 Voting Scheme among Resources

All together we have two sentiment systems and three lexicons. Before explicit sentiment classifying, each node has a positive value of 0.5 and a negative value of 0.5. We give the five votes equal weight (0.1), and add the number of positive votes multiplied by 0.1 to the positive value, and the number of negative votes multiplied by 0.1 to the negative value. After this addition, both values are in the range 0.5 to 1. If the positive value is larger, we maintain the positive value and assign the negative value to be 1-positive value (similarly if the negative value is larger).

5.4.4 Discourse

For a sentence s, we assume the writer's sentiments toward the gfbf events in the clauses of s, the previous sentence, and the next sentence, are the same. Consider EX(3):

EX(**3**) ... health-insurance regulations that will prohibit (a) denying coverage for pre-existing conditions, (b) dropping coverage if the client gets sick, and (c) capping insurance company reimbursement...

EX(3) has three clauses, (a)-(c). Suppose the explicit sentiment classifier recognizes that event (a), *denying coverage for pre-existing conditions*, is negative and it does not find any other explicit sentiments in the sentence. The system assumes the writer's sentiments toward (b) and (c) are negative as well.

After assigning all possible polarities to events within a sentence, polarities are propagated to the other still-neutral gfbf events in the previous and next sentences.

Finally, event-level polarities are propagated to still-neutral objects using Rule schema 1.[9] If there is a conflict, we take the majority sentiment; if there is a tie, the object remains neutral.

However, the confidence of the discourse voting is smaller than the explicit sentiment voting, since discourse structure is complex. If by discourse an object node is classified as positive, the positive value is $0.5 + random(0, 0.1)$ and the negative value is 1-positive value. Thus, the positive value of a positive node is larger than its negative value, but not exceeding too much (similarly for negative nodes).

6 Experiments and Results

6.1 Experiment Data

Of the 134 documents in the dataset, 6 were used as a development set, and 3 do not have any annotation. We use the remaining 125 for experiment.

6.2 Evaluation Metrics

To evaluate the performance of classifying the writer's sentiments toward agents and objects, we

[8]The comparison is done after lemmatization, using the wordNet lemmatization in NLTK, and with the same POS, according to the Stanford POStagger toolkit.

[9]Note that, in the gfbf entity graph, sentiments can be propagated from objects to agents, conceptually via Rule schemas 2 and 3. Thus, here we only classify objects.

define three metrics to evaluate performance. For the entire dataset, accuracy evaluates the percentage of nodes that are classified correctly. Precision and recall are defined to evaluate polar (non-neutral) classification.

$$Accuracy = \frac{\#\text{node auto=gold}}{\#\text{nodes}} \quad (3)$$

$$Precision = \frac{\#\text{node auto=gold \& gold != neutral}}{\#\text{node auto != neutral}} \quad (4)$$

$$Recall = \frac{\#\text{node auto=gold \& gold != neutral}}{\#\text{node gold != neutral}} \quad (5)$$

In the equations, *auto* is the system's output and *gold* is the gold-standard label from annotation.

6.3 Overall Performance

In this section, we evaluate the performance of the overall system. In 6.5, we evaluate the graph model itself.

Two baselines are defined. One is assigning the majority class label, which is positive, to all agents/objects ($Majority(+)$). The second is assuming that agents/objects in a GOODFOR relation are positive and agents/objects in a BADFOR relation are negative ($GFBF$). In addition, we evaluate the explicit sentiment classifier introduced in Section 5.4 ($Explicit$). The results are shown in Table 3.

	Accuracy	Precision	Recall
Majority(+)	0.5438	0.5621	0.5443
GFBF	0.5437	0.5523	0.5444
Explicit	0.3703	0.5698	0.3703
Graph-LBP	0.5412	**0.6660**	0.5419

Table 3: Performance of baselines and graph.

As can be seen, $Majority$ and $GFBF$ give approximately 56% precision. $Explicit$ sentiment classification alone performs hardly better in precision and much lower in recall. As mentioned in Section 2, fine-grained sentiment analysis is still very difficult for NLP systems. However, the graph model improves greatly over $Explicit$ in both precision and recall. While recall of the graph model is comparable to the $Majority$, precision is much higher.

During the experiment, if the LBP does not converge until 100 iterations, it is forced to stop. The average number of iteration is 34.192.

6.4 Error Analysis

Table 4 shows the results of an error analysis to determine what contributes to the graph model's errors.

1	wrong sentiment from voting	0.2132
2	wrong sentiment from discourse	0.0462
3	subgraph with wrong polarity	0.3189
4	subgraph with no polarity	0.4160
5	other	0.0056

Table 4: Errors for graph model.

Rows 1-2 are the error sources for nodes assigned a polar value before graph propagation. Row 1 errors are due to the sentiment-voting system, Row 2 are due to discourse processing.

Rows 3-4 are the error sources for nodes that have not been assigned a polar value by $Explicit$. Such a node receives a polar value only via propagation from other nodes in its subgraph (i.e., the connected component of the graph containing the node). Row 5 is the percentage of other errors.

As shown in Rows 1-2, 25.94% of the errors are due to $Explicit$. These may propagate incorrect labels to other nodes in the graph. As shown in Row 3, 31.89% of the errors are due to nodes not classified polar by $Explicit$, but given incorrect values because their subgraph has an incorrect polarity. Row 4 shows that 41.60% of the errors are due to nodes that are not assigned any polar value. Given non-ideal input from sentiment analysis, how does the graph model increase precision by 10 percentage points?

There are two main ways. For nodes which remain neutral after $Explicit$, they might be classified correctly via the graph. For nodes which are given incorrect polar labels by $Explicit$, they might be fixed by the graph. Table 5 shows the best the graph model could do, given the noisy input from $Explicit$. Over all of the nodes, more propagated labels are incorrect than correct. However, if there are no incorrect, or more correct than incorrect sentiments in the subgraph (connected component), then many more of the propagated labels are correct than incorrect. In all cases, more of the changed labels are correct than incorrect.

6.5 Consistency and Isolated Performance of Graph Model

The implicature rules are defeasible. In this section we introduce an experiment to valid the con-

propagated label correct	propagated label incorrect	changed correctly	changed incorrectly
all subgraphs			
399	536	424	274
subgraphs having no incorrect sentiment			
347	41	260	23
subgraphs having more correct than incorrect sentiment			
356	42	288	35

Table 5: Effects of graph model given $Explicit$ input

sistency of implicature rule. Recall that in Section 5.3, the definition of $\Psi_{i,j}$ is based on implicature rules and sentiment is propagated based on $\Psi_{i,j}$. Thus, this is also an evaluation of the performance of the graph model itself. We performed an experiment to assess the chance of a node being correctly classified only via the graph.

In each subgraph (connected component), we assign one of the nodes in the subgraph with its gold-standard polarity. Then we run LBP on the subgraph and record whether the other nodes in the subgraph are classified correctly or not. The experiment is run on the subgraph $|S|$ times, where $|S|$ is the number of nodes in the subgraph, so that each node is assigned its gold-standard polarity exactly once. Each node is given a propagated value $|S| - 1$ times, as each of the other nodes in its subgraph receives its gold-standard polarity.

To evaluate the chance of a node given a correct propagated label, we use Equations (6) and (7).

$$correct(a|b) = \begin{cases} 1 & \text{a is correct} \\ 0 & \text{otherwise} \end{cases} \quad (6)$$

$$correctness(a) = \frac{\sum_{b \in S_a, b \neq a} correct(a|b)}{|S_a| - 1} \quad (7)$$

where S_a is the set of nodes in a's subgraph. Given b being assigned its gold-standard polarity, if a is classified correctly, then $correct(a|b)$ is 1; otherwise 0. $|S_a|$ is the number of nodes in a's subgraph. $correctness(a)$ is the percentage of assignments to a that are correct. If it is 1, then a is correctly classified given the correct classification of any single node in its subgraph.

For example, suppose there are three nodes in a subgraph, A, B and C. For A we (1) assign B its gold label and carry out propagation on the subgraph, (2) assign C its gold label and carry out propagation again, then (3) calculate $correctness(A)$. Then the same process is repeated for B and C.

Some subgraphs contain only two nodes, the agent and the object. In this case, graph propagation corresponds to single applications of two implicature rules. Other subgraphs contain more nodes. Two results are shown in Table 6. One is the result on the whole experiment data, the other is the result for all nodes whose subgraphs have more than two nodes.

Dataset	# subgraph	correctness
all subgraphs	983	0.8874
multi-node subgraphs	169	0.9030

Table 6: Performance of graph model itself.

As we can see, a node has an 89% chance of being correct if there is one correct explicit subjectivity node in its subgraph. If we only consider subgraphs with more than two nodes, the correctness chance is higher. The results indicate that, if given correct sentiments, the graph model will assign the unknown nodes with correct labels 90% of the time. Further, the results indicate that the implicature rules are consistent for most of the times across the corpus.

7 Conclusions

We developed a graph-based model based on implicature rules to propagate sentiments among entities. The model improves over explicit sentiment classification by 10 points in precision and, in an evaluation of the model itself, we find it has an 89% chance of propagating sentiments correctly. An important question for future work is under what conditions do the implicatures not go through in context. Two cases we have discovered involve Rule schema 3: the inference toward the agent is defeated if the action was accidental or if the agent was forced to perform it. We are investigating lexical clues for recognizing such cases.

Acknowledgments. This work was supported in part by DARPA-BAA-12-47 DEFT grant #12475008 and National Science Foundation grant #IIS-0916046. We would like to thank Richard Johansson and Alessandro Moschitti for running their Opinion Extraction systems on our data.

References

Pranav Anand and Kevin Reschke. 2010. Verb classes as evaluativity functor classes. In *Interdisciplinary Workshop on Verbs. The Identification and Representation of Verb Features.*

Yejin Choi and Claire Cardie. 2008. Learning with compositional semantics as structural inference for subsentential sentiment analysis. In *Proceedings of the 2008 Conference on Empirical Methods in Natural Language Processing*, pages 793–801, Honolulu, Hawaii, October. Association for Computational Linguistics.

Pradeep Dasigi, Weiwei Guo, and Mona Diab. 2012. Genre independent subgroup detection in online discussion threads: A study of implicit attitude using textual latent semantics. In *Proceedings of the 50th Annual Meeting of the Association for Computational Linguistics (Volume 2: Short Papers)*, pages 65–69, Jeju Island, Korea, July. Association for Computational Linguistics.

Lingjia Deng, Yoonjung Choi, and Janyce Wiebe. 2013. Benefactive and malefactive event and writer attitude annotation. In *51st Annual Meeting of the Association for Computational Linguistics (ACL-2013, short paper).*

Song Feng, Jun Sak Kang, Polina Kuznetsova, and Yejin Choi. 2013. Connotation lexicon: A dash of sentiment beneath the surface meaning. In *Proceedings of the 51th Annual Meeting of the Association for Computational Linguistics (Volume 2: Short Papers)*, Sofia, Bulgaria, Angust. Association for Computational Linguistics.

Amit Goyal, Ellen Riloff, and Hal Daum III. 2012. A computational model for plot units. *Computational Intelligence*, pages 466–488.

Rodney D. Huddleston and Geoffrey K. Pullum. 2002. *The Cambridge Grammar of the English Language.* Cambridge University Press, April.

Richard Johansson and Alessandro Moschitti. 2013. Relational features in fine-grained opinion analysis. *Computational Linguistics*, 39(3).

Bing Liu. 2012. *Sentiment Analysis and Opinion Mining.* Morgan & Claypool.

Karo Moilanen and Stephen Pulman. 2007. Sentiment composition. In *Proceedings of RANLP 2007*, Borovets, Bulgaria.

Karo Moilanen, Stephen Pulman, and Yue Zhang. 2010. Packed feelings and ordered sentiments: Sentiment parsing with quasi-compositional polarity sequencing and compression. In *Proceedings of the 1st Workshop on Computational Approaches to Subjectivity and Sentiment Analysis (WASSA 2010)*, pages 36–43.

J. Pearl. 1982. Reverend bayes on inference engines: A distributed hierarchical approach. In *Proceedings of the American Association of Artificial Intelligence National Conference on AI*, pages 133–136, Pittsburgh, PA.

Kevin Reschke and Pranav Anand. 2011. Extracting contextual evaluativity. In *Proceedings of the Ninth International Conference on Computational Semantics*, IWCS '11, pages 370–374, Stroudsburg, PA, USA. Association for Computational Linguistics.

Ellen Riloff, Ashequl Qadir, Prafulla Surve, Lalindra De Silva, Nathan Gilbert, and Ruihong Huang. 2013. Sarcasm as contrast between a positive sentiment and negative situation. In *Proceedings of the 2013 Conference on Empirical Methods in Natural Language Processing*, pages 704–714, Seattle, Washington, USA, October. Association for Computational Linguistics.

P.J. Stone, D.C. Dunphy, M.S. Smith, and D.M. Ogilvie. 1966. *The General Inquirer: A Computer Approach to Content Analysis.* MIT Press, Cambridge.

Chenhao Tan, Lillian Lee, Jie Tang, Long Jiang, Ming Zhou, and Ping Li. 2011. User-level sentiment analysis incorporating social networks. In *Proceedings of the 17th ACM SIGKDD international conference on Knowledge discovery and data mining*, pages 1397–1405. ACM.

Xiaolong Wang, Furu Wei, Xiaohua Liu, Ming zhou, and Ming Zhang. 2011. Topic sentiment anaylsis in twitter: A graph-based hashtag sentiment classification appraoch. In *CIKM*, pages 1031–1040.

Janyce Wiebe, Theresa Wilson, and Claire Cardie. 2005. Annotating expressions of opinions and emotions in language ann. *Language Resources and Evaluation*, 39(2/3):164–210.

Theresa Wilson, Janyce Wiebe, and Paul Hoffmann. 2005. Recognizing contextual polarity in phrase-level sentiment analysis. In *HLT/EMNLP*, pages 347–354.

Jonathan S Yedidia, William T Freeman, and Yair Weiss. 2005. Constructing free-energy approximations and generalized belief propagation algorithms. *Information Theory, IEEE Transactions on*, 51(7):2282–2312.

Lei Zhang and Bing Liu. 2011. Identifying noun product features that imply opinions. In *Proceedings of the 49th Annual Meeting of the Association for Computational Linguistics: Human Language Technologies*, pages 575–580, Portland, Oregon, USA, June. Association for Computational Linguistics.

F. Zúñiga and S. Kittilä. 2010. Introduction. In F. Zúñiga and S. Kittilä, editors, *Benefactives and malefactives*, Typological studies in language. J. Benjamins Publishing Company.

Acquisition of Noncontiguous Class Attributes from Web Search Queries

Marius Paşca
Google Inc.
1600 Amphitheatre Parkway
Mountain View, California 94043
mars@google.com

Abstract

Previous methods for extracting attributes (e.g., *capital*, *population*) of classes (*Empires*) from Web documents or search queries assume that relevant attributes occur verbatim in the source text. The extracted attributes are short phrases that correspond to quantifiable properties of various instances (*ottoman empire*, *roman empire*, *mughal empire*) of the class. This paper explores the extraction of noncontiguous class attributes (*manner (it) claimed legitimacy of rule*), from fact-seeking and explanation-seeking queries. The attributes cover properties that are not always likely to be extracted as short phrases from inherently-noisy queries.

1 Introduction

Motivation: Resources such as Wikipedia (Remy, 2002) and Freebase (Bollacker et al., 2008) aim at organizing knowledge around classes (*Food ingredients*, *Astronomical objects*, *Religions*) and their instances (*wheat flower*, *uranus*, *hinduism*). Due to inherent limitations associated with maintaining and expanding human-curated resources, their content may be incomplete. For example, attributes representing the *energy* (or *energy per 100g*) or *solubility in water* are available in both Wikipedia and Freebase for many instances of *Food ingredients* (e.g., for *olive oil*, *honey*, *fennel*). But the attributes are missing for some instances (e.g., *cornmeal*). Moreover, structured information about *how long (it) lasts unopened* or *manner (it) helps in weight loss* is generally missing for *Food ingredients*, from both resources. Such information is also often absent from among the attributes acquired from either documents or queries by previous extraction methods (Paşca et al., 2007; Van Durme et al., 2008). Previously extracted attributes tend to be short, often nominal, phrases like *nutritional value* and *taste*. Even when extracted attributes are not nominal (Paşca, 2012), they remain relatively short phrases such as *good for skin*. As such, previous attributes have limited ability to capture the finer-grained properties being asked about in queries such as *"how long does olive oil last unopened"* and *"how does honey help in weight loss"*. The presence of such queries suggests that such information is relevant to Web users. Identifying noncontiguous properties, or attributes of interest to Web users, helps filling some of the gaps in existing knowledge resources, which otherwise could not be filled by attributes extracted with previous methods.

Contributions: The contributions of this paper are twofold. First, it introduces a method for the acquisition of noncontiguous class attributes, from fact or explanation-seeking Web search queries like *"how long does olive oil last unopened"* or *"how does honey help in weight loss"*. The resulting attributes are more diverse than, and therefore subsume, the scope of attributes extracted by previous methods. Indeed, previous methods are unlikely to extract attributes as specific as *length/duration (it) lasts unopened* and *manner (it) helps in weight loss*, for the instances *olive oil* and *honey* of the class *Food ingredients*. Conversely, previously extracted attributes like *nutritional value* and *solubility in water* are roughly equivalent to the finer-grained *nutritional value (it) has* and *reason (it) dissolves in water*, extracted from the queries *"what nutritional value does honey have"* and *"why does glucose dissolve in water"* respectively. Second, the noncontiguous attributes can be simultaneously interpreted as binary relations pertaining to instances and classes. The relations (*helps in weight loss*) connect an instance (*honey*) or, more generally, a class (*Food ingredients*), on one hand; and a loosely-typed unknown argument (*manner*) whose value is of interest to Web users, on the other hand. Because

Web users already inquire about the value of one of their arguments, the extracted relations are more likely to be relevant for the respective instances and classes, than relations extracted from arbitrary document sentences (Fader et al., 2011).

2 Noncontiguous Attributes

Intuitions: Users tend to formulate their Web search queries based on knowledge that they already possess at the time of the search (Paşca, 2007). Therefore, search queries play two roles simultaneously: in addition to requesting new information, they indirectly convey knowledge in the process. In particular, attributes correspond to quantifiable properties of instances and their classes. The extraction of attributes from queries starts from the intuition that, if an attribute A is relevant for a class C, then users are likely to ask for the value of the attribute A, for various instances I of the class C. If *nutritional value* and *diameter* are relevant attributes of the classes *Food ingredients* and *Astronomical objects* respectively, it is likely that users submit queries to inquire about the values of the attributes for instances of the two classes. Such queries could take the form *"what is the (nutritional value)$_A$ of (olive oil)$_I$"* and *"what is the (diameter)$_A$ of (jupiter)$_I$"*; or the more compact *"(nutritional value)$_A$ of (olive oil)$_I$"* and *"(diameter)$_A$ of (jupiter)$_I$"*. In this case, the attributes are relatively short phrases (*nutritional value*, *diameter*), and are expected to appear as contiguous phrases within queries. Previous methods on attribute extraction from queries specifically target this type of attributes. In fact, some methods apply dedicated extraction patterns (e.g., *A of I*) over either queries (Paşca et al., 2007) or documents (Tokunaga et al., 2005). Other methods expand manually-provided seed sets of attributes, with other phrases that co-occur with instances within queries, in similar contexts as the seed attributes do (Paşca, 2007).

While simpler properties are often mentioned in queries as short, contiguous phrases, finer-grained properties often are not. Queries seeking the *reason for solidification* for some *Food ingredients* could, but rarely do, contain the attribute verbatim (*"what is the reason for the solidification of honey"*). Instead, queries are more likely to inquire about the expected value, while specifying the instance and the properties encoded by the attribute (*"(why)$_A$ does (honey)$_I$ (solidify)$_A$"*). Readable descriptions (names) of the attributes can be recovered from the queries, by assembling the type of the expected value and the properties together (*reason (it) solidifies*). Thus, fact and explanation-seeking queries are an intriguing source of noncontiguous attributes that are not restricted to short phrases, and are not required to occur as contiguous phrases in queries.

Acquisition from Queries: The extraction method proposed in this paper takes as input a set of target classes, each of which is available as a set of instances that belong to the class; and a set of anonymized queries independent from one another. As illustrated in Figure 1, the method selects queries that contain an instance of a class together with what is deemed to be likely a noncontiguous attribute, and outputs ranked lists of attributes for each class. The extraction consists in several stages:

- selection of a subset of queries that contain an instance in a form that suggests the queries ask for the value of a noncontiguous attribute of the instance;
- extraction of noncontiguous attributes, from query fragments that describe the property of interest and the type of its expected value;
- aggregation and ranking of attributes of individual instances of a class, into attributes of a class.

Extraction Patterns: In order to determine whether a query contains an attribute of a class, the query is matched against the extraction patterns from Table 1. The use of patterns in attribute extraction has been previously suggested in (Paşca et al., 2007; Tokunaga et al., 2005), where the pattern *what is the A of I* extracts noun-phrase A attributes of instances I from queries and documents. In our case, the patterns are constructed such that they match fact-seeking and explanation-seeking questions that likely inquire about the value of a relevant property of an instance I of the class C. For example, the first pattern from Table 1 matches queries such as *"when did everquest become free to play"* and *"when was radon discovered as an element"*, which inquire about the date or time when certain events affected certain properties of the instances *everquest* and *radon* respectively. Instances I of the class C may be available as non-disambiguated items, that is, as strings (*java*) whose meaning is otherwise unknown; or as disambiguated items, that is, as strings associ-

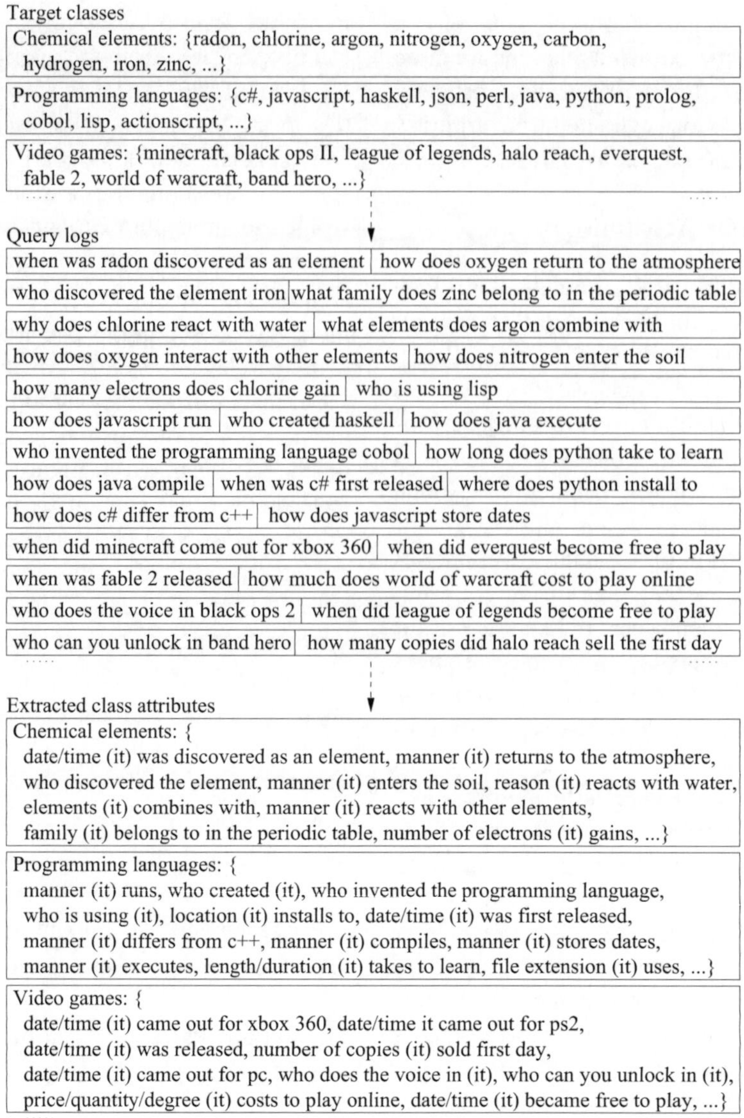

Figure 1: Overview of extraction of noncontiguous attributes from Web search queries

ated with pointers to knowledge base entries with a disambiguated meaning (*Java (programming language)*). In the first case, the matching of a query fragment, on one hand, to the portion of an extraction pattern corresponding to an instance I, on the other hand, consists in simple string matching. In the second case, the matching requires that the disambiguation of the query fragment, in the context of the query, matches the desired disambiguated meaning of I from the pattern. The subset of queries matching any of the extraction patterns, for any instances I of a class C, are the queries that contribute to extracting noncontiguous attributes of the class C.

Collecting Attributes of Individual Instances: A small set of rules optionally converts wh-prefixes into coarse-grained types of the expected values (e.g., *how long* into *length/duration*; or *when* into *date/time*). In the case of *what*-prefixed queries, the adjacent noun phrase, if any, is considered to be the expected type (*"what nutritional value .."* into *nutritional value*). Similar rules have been employed for shallow analysis of open-domain questions (Dumais et al., 2002). The predicate verbs in the remainder of the query are updated, to match the tense specified by the auxiliary verb (e.g., *"when did .."*), if any, following the wh-prefix. Thus, the verb *come* is converted to the past tense *came*, in the case of the query *"when did minecraft come out for xbox 360"*. An

<table>
<tr><td>Extraction Pattern
→ Examples of Matched Queries</td></tr>
<tr><td>when [does|did|do|was|were] [a|an|the|<nothing>] I A
→ when did everquest become free to play</td></tr>
<tr><td>why [does|did|do|was|were] [a|an|the|<nothing>] I A
→ why does chlorine interact with water</td></tr>
<tr><td>where [does|did|do|was|were] [a|an|the|<nothing>] I A
→ where does radon occur naturally</td></tr>
<tr><td>how [does|did|do|was|were] [a|an|the|<nothing>] I A
→ how does nitrogen enter the soil</td></tr>
<tr><td>who [does|did|do|was|were] [a|an|the|<nothing>] I A
→ who did claude monet study under</td></tr>
<tr><td>how A [does|did|do|was|were] [a|an|the|<nothing>] I A
→ how fast does oxygen dissolve in water</td></tr>
<tr><td>who A I
→ who invented the programming language cobol
(Note: A does not start with [is|are|was|were])</td></tr>
<tr><td>what A [does|did|do|was|were] [a|an|the|<nothing>] I A
→ what elements does argon combine with</td></tr>
<tr><td>which A [does|did|do|was|were] [a|an|the|<nothing>] I A
→ which ports does minecraft use</td></tr>
</table>

Table 1: The extraction patterns match queries that are likely to inquire about the value of a noncontiguous attribute of an instance (I=a required instance; A=a required non-empty sequence of arbitrary tokens)

attribute is constructed from the concatenation of the wh-prefix or expected type (*date/time*); the slot pronoun *it*, in lieu of the instance (*date/time (it)*); and the query remainder after tense conversion (*date/time (it) came out for xbox 360*). If the linking verb following the wh-prefix is a form of *be* (e.g., *was*), then the linking verb is also retained after the slot pronoun, to form a more coherent attribute (*date/time (it) was first released*). Since constructed attributes are noun phrases, they are more consistent with, and can be more easily inserted among, existing attributes in structured data repositories (infobox entries of articles in Wikipedia, or property names or topics in Freebase).

Aggregation into Class Attributes: Attributes of a class C are aggregated from attributes of individual instances I of the class. An attribute A is deemed more relevant for C if the attribute is extracted for more of the instances I of the class C, and for fewer instances I that do not belong to the class C. Concretely, the score of an attribute for a class is the lower bound of the Wilson score interval (Brown et al., 2001) where the number of positive observations is the number of queries for which the attribute A is extracted for some instance I in the class C, $|\{Query(I, A)\}_{I \in C}|$; and the number of negative observations is the number of queries for which the attribute A is extracted for some instances I outside of the class C, $|\{Query(I, A)\}_{I \notin C}|$. The scores are internally computed at 95% confidence. Attributes of each class are ranked in decreasing order of their scores.

Reduction of Near-Duplicate Attributes: Due to lexical variations across queries from which attributes are extracted, some of the attributes are equivalent or nearly equivalent to one another. For example, *gained independence*, *won its independence* and *gained its freedom* of the class *Countries* are roughly equivalent, although they employ distinct tokens. The diversity and potential usefulness of a ranked list of attributes can be increased, if groups of near-duplicate attributes are identified in the list, and merged together.

A lower-ranked attribute is marked as a near-duplicate of a higher-ranked (i.e., earlier) attribute from the list, if all tokens from the lower-ranked attribute match either tokens from the higher-ranked attribute (*gained independence* vs. *won its independence*), or tokens from synonyms of phrases from the earlier attribute (*gained independence* vs. *won its independence*; or *takes to show symptoms* vs. *takes to come out*). Stop words, which include linking verbs, pronouns, determiners, conjunctions, wh-prefixes and prepositions, are not required to match. Synonyms may be either derived from existing lexical resources (e.g., WordNet (Fellbaum, 1998)), or mined from large document collections (Madnani and Dorr, 2010). Lower-ranked near-duplicate attributes are merged with the higher-ranked ones from the ranked list, thus improving the diversity of the list.

3 Experimental Setting

Textual Data Sources: The experiments rely on a random sample of around 1 billion fully-anonymized queries in English, submitted to a general-purpose Web search engine. Each query is available independently from other queries, and is accompanied by its frequency of occurrence in the query logs.

Target Classes: Table 2 shows the set of 40 target classes for evaluating the attributes extracted from queries. In an effort to reuse experimental setup proposed in previous work, each of the 40 manually-compiled classes introduced in (Paşca, 2007) is mapped into the Wikipedia category that best matches it. For example, the evaluation classes *Aircraft Model*, *Movie*, *Religion* and *Ter-*

Class (Examples of Instances)
Actors (keanu reeves, milla jovovich, ben affleck), Aircraft (boeing 737, bombardier crj200, embraer 170), Animated characters (bugs bunny, pink panther (character), yosemite sam), Association football clubs (a.s. roma, fluminense football club, real madrid), Astronomical objects (alpha centauri, jupiter, delta corvi), Automobiles (nissan gt-r, tesla model s, toyota prius), Awards (grammy award, justin winsor prize (library), palme d'or), Battles and operations of world war ii (battle of midway, operation postmaster, battle of milne bay), Chemical elements (plutonium, radon, hydrogen), Cities (rio de janeiro, osaka, chiang mai), Companies (best buy, aveeno, pepsico), Countries (costa rica, rwanda, south korea), Currencies by country (japanese yen, swiss franc, korean won), Digital cameras (canon eos 400d, nikon d3000, pentax k10d), Diseases and disorders (anorexia nervosa, hyperlysinemia, repetitive strain injury), Drugs (fluticasone propionate, phentermine, tramadol), Empires (ottoman empire, roman empire, mughal empire), Films (the fifth element, mockingbird don't sing, ten thousand years older), Flowers (trachelospermum jasminoides, lavandula stoechas, evergreen rose), Food ingredients (carrot, olive oil, fennel), Holidays (good friday, easter, halloween), Hurricanes in North America (hurricane katrina, hurricane wilma, hurricane dennis), Internet search engines (google, baidu, lycos), Mobile phones (nokia n900, htc desire, samsung s5560), Mountains (mount rainier, cerro san luis obispo, steel peak), National Basketball Association teams (los angeles lakers, cleveland cavaliers, indiana pacers), National parks (yosemite national park, orang national park, tortuguero national park), Newspapers (the economist, corriere del trentino, seattle medium), Organizations designated as terrorist (taliban, shining path, eta), Painters (claude monet, domingo antonio velasco, tarcisio merati), Programming languages (javascript, prolog, obliq), Religious faiths traditions and movements (confucianism, fudoki, omnism), Rivers (danube, pingo river, viehmoorgraben), Skyscrapers (taipei 101, 15 penn plaza, eqt plaza), Sports events (tour de france, 1984 scottish cup final, rotlewi versus rubinstein), Stadiums (fenway park, chengdu longquanyi, stade geoffroy-guichard), Treaties (treaty of versailles, franco-indian alliance, treaty of cordoba), Universities and colleges (cornell university, nugaal university, gale college), Video games (minecraft, league of legends, everquest), Wine (madeira wine, yellow tail (wine), port wine)

Table 2: Set of 40 Wikipedia categories used as target classes in the evaluation of attributes

roristGroup from (Paşca, 2007) are mapped into the Wikipedia categories *Aircraft*, *Films*, *Religious faiths traditions and movements* and *Organizations designated as terrorist* respectively. The name of the Wikipedia category only serves as a convenience label for its target class, and is not otherwise exploited in any way during the evaluation. Instead, a target class consists in a set of titles of Wikipedia articles, of which sample titles (e.g., the Wikipedia article titled *nissan gt-r*) are shown in lowercase for each class (e.g., *Automobiles*) in Table 2. The set of instances of a class is selected from all articles listed under the respective category in Wikipedia, or listed under sub-categories of the respective category.

Label	Examples of Attributes
vital	Astronomical objects: manner (it) generates its energy
	Food ingredients: temperature (it) solidifies
	Religion: date/time (it) became a religion
okay	Astronomical objects: manner (it) became a constellation
	Food ingredients: reason (it) sparks in the microwave
	Religion: manner (it) feels about abortion
wrong	Astronomical objects: reason (it) has arms
	Food ingredients: manner (it) cleans pennies
	Religion: who owns (it)

Table 3: Correctness labels manually assigned to attributes extracted for various classes

The target classes contain between 41 (for *National Basketball Association teams*) and 66,934 (for *Films*) instances, with an average of 10,730 instances per class.

Synonym Repository: A synonym repository extracted separately from Web documents contains mappings from each of around 60,000 phrases in English, to lists of their synonym phrases. For example, the top synonyms available for the phrases *turn off* and *contagious* are [*switch off*, *extinguish*, *turn out*, ..] and [*infectious*, *catching*, *communicable*, ..] respectively.

Parameter Settings: Queries that match any of the extraction patterns from Table 1 are syntactically parsed (Petrov et al., 2010). As a prerequisite, the portion I of the patterns from the table must match a disambiguated instance from a query.

A variation of the tagger introduced in (Cucerzan, 2007) maps query fragments to their disambiguated, corresponding Wikipedia instances (i.e., to Wikipedia articles). The tagger is simplified to select the longest instance mentions, and does not use gazetteers or queries for training. Depending on the sources of textual data available for training, any taggers (Cucerzan, 2007; Ratinov et al., 2011; Pantel et al., 2012) that disambiguate text fragments relative to Wikipedia entries can be employed.

4 Evaluation Results

Attribute Accuracy: The top 50 attributes, from the ranked lists extracted for each target class, are manually assigned correctness labels. As shown in Table 3, an attribute is marked as *vital*, if it must be present among representative attributes of the

Class	Precision of Extracted Attributes			
	%vital	%okay	%wrong	Score
Awards	29	14	7	0.72
Chemical elements	46	2	2	0.94
Companies	42	1	7	0.85
Food ingredients	31	9	10	0.71
Programming languages	31	7	12	0.69
Stadiums	42	5	3	0.89
Video games	33	14	3	0.80
...				
Avg-All-Classes	33	10	7	0.76

Table 4: Accuracy of top 50 class attributes extracted from fact-seeking and explanation-seeking queries, over the evaluation set of 40 target classes

class; *okay*, if it provides useful but non-essential information; and *wrong*, if it is incorrect (Paşca, 2007). For example, the attributes *manner (it) generates its energy*, *manner (it) became a constellation* and *reason (it) has arms* are annotated as *vital*, *okay* and *wrong* respectively for the class *Astronomical objects*. To compute the precision score over a set of attributes, the correctness labels are converted to numeric values: *vital* to 1.0, *okay* to 0.5, and *wrong* to 0.0. Precision is the sum of the correctness values of the attributes, divided by the number of attributes.

Table 4 summarizes the precision scores over the evaluation set of target classes. The scores vary from one class to another, for example 0.71 for *Food ingredients* but 0.94 for *Chemical elements*. The average score is 0.76, indicating that attributes extracted from fact and explanation-seeking queries have encouraging levels of accuracy. The results already take into account the detection of near-duplicate attributes. More precisely, the highest-ranked attribute in each group of near-duplicate attributes, examples of which are shown in Table 5, is retained and evaluated; the lower-ranked attributes from each group are not considered in the evaluation. Attributes like *number of passengers (it) can hold*, *number of passengers it fits* and *number of passengers it seats* are nearly equivalent, but are still not marked as near-duplicates for the class *Aircraft*, when they should. Conversely, the attribute *location (it) lives* is marked as a near-duplicate of *location (it) lives in new york*, when it should not. Nevertheless, a significant number of near-duplicates, which would otherwise crowd the ranked lists of attributes with redundant information, are identified and discarded.

Target Class: Group of Near-Duplicate Attributes
Actors: movies (it) plays in, played in, acts in, acted in, played, played on
Automobiles: date (it) was first manufactured, first produced, first made
Battles and operations of World War II: reason (it) happened, took place, occurred
Chemical elements: manner (it) returns to the atmosphere, gets back into the atmosphere, got into the atmosphere, gets into the atmosphere, enters the environment, enters the atmosphere
Companies: location (it) makes its products, manufactures its products, produces its products, gets its products, makes its products, manufactures their products
Companies: date/time (it) began outsourcing, started outsourcing, outsourced
Countries: date (it) got its independence, gained independence, gained its independence, got independence, got their independence, won its independence, achieved independence, received its independence, gained its freedom
Diseases and disorders: length/duration (it) takes to show symptoms, takes to show up, takes to show, takes to appear, takes to manifest, takes to come out

Table 5: Groups of near-duplicate attributes identified for various classes. Attributes within a group are ranked according to their individual scores. Removing all but the first attribute of each group, from the ranked list of attributes of the respective class, improves the diversity of the list

Discussion: The set of patterns shown in Table 1 is extensible. Moreover, the patterns are subject to errors. They may cause false matches, resulting in erroneous extractions. The extent to which this occurs is indirectly measured in the overall precision results. The modification of some of the patterns, or the addition of new ones, would likely affect the expected coverage and precision of the extracted attributes. If a pattern is particularly noisy, it is likely to cause systematic errors, and therefore produce attributes of lower quality.

Since attributes in Wikipedia and Freebase are initially entered manually by human editors, their correctness is virtually guaranteed. As for attributes extracted automatically, previous comparisons indicate that attributes tend to have higher quality when extracted from queries instead of documents (Paşca, 2007). Indeed, a set of extraction patterns applied to text produces attributes whose average precision at rank 50 is 0.44 when extracted from documents, vs. 0.63 from queries (Paşca et al., 2007). More importantly, previously available or extracted attributes are virtually always simple, short noun phrases like *nutritional value*, *taste* or *solubility in water*. Even if not confined to noun phrases, they are still short,

Run: [Ranked Attributes for a Sample of Classes]
Class: Automobiles:
D: [(it) goes on sale, (it) will go on sale, (it) is an engineering playground, (it) will be available in japan, (it) shows up in japan, (it) is a technical tour de force, (it) unveiled at tas 2008, (it) runs a 7:38, (it) is a unique car, (it) uses a premium midship package, (it) features an all-new 3.8-litre, (it) is one of the fastest cars, (it) made a quick drive-by, ..]
Q: [price/quantity/degree (it) weights, year (it) was banned from bathurst, manner (it) launch control works, engine (it) has, kind of engine (it) has, price/quantity/degree (it) costs in japan, number of horsepower (it) has, price/quantity/degree horsepower (it) has, number of seats (it) has, speed (it) goes, who designed (it), ..]
Class: Mobile phones:
D: [(it) was announced on september 17 2008, (it) ceased with version, (it) was scheduled to be released in late 2010, (it) also supports qt (toolkit), (it) supports hardware capable, (it) can synchronize with microsoft outlook, (it) also supports python (programming language), ..]
Q: [date/time (it) came out in australia, who carries (it), reason (it) keeps rebooting, colours (it) comes in, video format (it) supports, date/time (it) was released, date/time (it) came out in the uk, length/duration (it)'s battery lasts, who sells (it), how much (it) costs, ..]
Class: Mountains:
D: [(it) is an active volcano, (it) is in the distance, (it) is the highest peak in cascade range, (it) is 14,410 feet, (it) was established in 1899, (it) comes into view, (it) was established as a national park, ..]
Q: [date/time (it) last erupted, manner (it) erupted in 1882, manner (it) formed, date/time (it) first became active, manner (it) got its name, number of eruptions (it) had, type of magma (it) has, reason (it) became a national park, kind of animals (it) has, ..]

Table 6: Top relations extracted for a sample of target classes via open-domain relations from documents (D) or via attributes from queries (Q)

like *vegan*, *healthy* or *gluten free* (Van Durme et al., 2008; Paşca, 2012). In comparison, attributes extracted in this paper accommodate properties that are sometimes awkward or even impossible to express through short phrases.

Noncontiguous Attributes as Relations: Noncontiguous attributes extracted from fact-seeking queries are embodiments of relations linking the instances mentioned in the queries, on one hand, and the values being requested by the queries, on the other hand. Therefore, the method proposed in this paper can also be regarded as a method for the acquisition of relevant relations of various classes. The extracted relations specify the left argument (i.e., the instance) and the linking relation name (i.e., the attribute). They only specify the type of the, but not the actual, right argument (i.e., the value being requested).

An additional experiment compares the accuracy of relations extracted as noncontiguous attributes from queries, vs. relations extracted by a previous open-domain method (Fader et al., 2011) from 500 million Web documents. The previous method, including its extraction patterns and its ranking scheme, is designed with instances rather than classes in mind. For fairness to the method in (Fader et al., 2011), the evaluation procedure is slightly adjusted. The set of instances associated with each target class, over which the two methods are evaluated, is reduced to a single representative instance selected a-priori. The instances are shown as the first instances in parentheses for each class in the earlier Table 2. Thus, the class attributes are extracted using only the instances *keanu reeves*, *boeing 737* and *bugs bunny* in the case of the classes *Actors*, *Aircraft* and *Animated characters* respectively.

Table 6 suggests that noncontiguous attributes extracted from queries tend to capture higher-quality relations than arbitrary relations extracted from documents. Because fact-seeking queries inquire about the value of some relations (attributes) of an instance, the relations themselves tends to be more relevant than relations extracted from arbitrary document sentences. Nevertheless, relations derived from queries likely serve as a useful complement, rather than replacement, of relations from documents. The former only discover what relations may be relevant; the latter also identify their occurrences within text.

5 Related Work

Sources of text from which relations (Zhu et al., 2009; Carlson et al., 2010; Lao et al., 2011) and, more specifically, attributes can be extracted include Web documents and data in human-compiled encyclopedia. In Web documents, attributes are available within unstructured (Tokunaga et al., 2005; Paşca et al., 2007), structured (Raju et al., 2008) and semi-structured text (Yoshinaga and Torisawa, 2007), layout formatting tags (Wong et al., 2008), itemized lists or tables (Cafarella et al., 2008). In human-compiled encyclopedia (Wu and Weld, 2010), data relevant to attribute extraction includes infoboxes and category labels (Nastase and Strube, 2008; Hoffart et al., 2013) associated with Wikipedia articles. In order to acquire class attributes, a common strategy is to first acquire attributes of instances, then aggregate or propagate (Talukdar and Pereira,

2010) attributes, from instances to the classes to which the instances belong. The role of Web search queries, as an alternative textual data source to Web documents in open-domain information extraction, has been investigated in the tasks of attribute extraction (Paşca, 2007; Paşca, 2012), as well as in collecting sets of related instances (Jain and Pennacchiotti, 2010).

To increase diversity within a ranked list of attributes, the extraction method in this paper employs a synonym vocabulary to approximately identify groups of near-duplicate attributes. As reported for previous methods, the resulting lists may still contain lexically different but semantically equivalent attributes. Scenarios where detecting all equivalent attributes is important may benefit from other techniques for paraphrase acquisition (Madnani and Dorr, 2010).

Sophisticated techniques are sometimes employed to identify the type of the expected answers of open-domain questions (Pinchak et al., 2009). In comparison, the loose typing of the values of our noncontiguous attributes is mostly coarse-grained. It relies on wh-prefixes (*when*, *how long*, *where*, *how*) and possibly subsequent words (*what nutritional value*) from the queries, to determine whether the values are expected to be a *date/time*, *length/duration*, *location*, *manner*, *nutritional value* etc.

Relations extracted from document sentences (e.g., *"Claude Monet was born in Paris"*) are tuples of an instance (*claude monet*), a text fragment acting as the lexicalized relation (*was born in*), and another instance (*paris*) (cf. (Fader et al., 2011; Mausam et al., 2012)). For convenience, the relation and second instance may be concatenated, as in *was born in paris* for *claude monet*. But document sentences mentioning an instance do not necessarily refer to properties of the instance that people other than the author of the document are likely to inquire about. Consequently, even top-ranked extracted relations occasionally include less informative ones, such as *comes into view* for *mount rainier*, *is on the table* for *madeira wine*, or *allows for features* for *javascript* (Fader et al., 2011). Comparatively, relations extracted via noncontiguous attributes from queries tend to refer to properties that have values that Web users inquire about in their search queries. Therefore, the relations extracted from queries are more likely to refer to salient properties, such as *date/time (it) had its last eruption* for *mount rainier*; *length/duration (it) lasts* for *madeira wine*; and *manner (it) stores date information* for *javascript*.

6 Conclusion

By requesting values for attributes of individual instances, fact-seeking and explanation-seeking queries implicitly assert the relevance of the properties encoded by the attributes, for the respective instances and their classes. The extracted attributes are not required to take the form of contiguous short phrases in the source queries, thus allowing for the acquisition of a broader range of attributes than those extracted by previous methods. Furthermore, since Web users are interested in their values, the relations to which the extracted attributes refer tend to be more relevant than relations extracted from arbitrary documents using previous methods. Current work explores the role of distributional similarities in expanding extracted attributes for narrow classes; and the extraction of noncontiguous attributes and relations from natural-language queries without a wh-prefix (e.g., *cars driven by james bond*).

Acknowledgments

The author would like to thank Efrat Farkash and Michael Kleyman for assistance with the synonym repository.

References

K. Bollacker, C. Evans, P. Paritosh, T. Sturge, and J. Taylor. 2008. Freebase: A collaboratively created graph database for structuring human knowledge. In *Proceedings of the 2008 International Conference on Management of Data (SIGMOD-08)*, pages 1247–1250, Vancouver, Canada.

L. Brown, T. Cai, and A. DasGupta. 2001. Interval estimation for a binomial proportion. *Statistical Science*, 16(2):101–117.

M. Cafarella, A. Halevy, D. Wang, E. Wu, and Y. Zhang. 2008. WebTables: Exploring the power of tables on the Web. In *Proceedings of the 34th Conference on Very Large Data Bases (VLDB-08)*, pages 538–549, Auckland, New Zealand.

A. Carlson, J. Betteridge, R. Wang, E. Hruschka, and T. Mitchell. 2010. Coupled semi-supervised learning for information extraction. In *Proceedings of the 3rd ACM Conference on Web Search and Data Mining (WSDM-10)*, pages 101–110, New York.

S. Cucerzan. 2007. Large-scale named entity disambiguation based on Wikipedia data. In *Proceedings of the 2007 Conference on Empirical Methods in Natural Language Processing (EMNLP-07)*, pages 708–716, Prague, Czech Republic.

S. Dumais, M. Banko, E. Brill, J. Lin, and A. Ng. 2002. Web question answering: Is more always better? In *Proceedings of the 24th ACM Conference on Research and Development in Information Retrieval (SIGIR-02)*, pages 207–214, Tampere, Finland.

A. Fader, S. Soderland, and O. Etzioni. 2011. Identifying relations for open information extraction. In *Proceedings of the 2011 Conference on Empirical Methods in Natural Language Processing (EMNLP-11)*, pages 1535–1545, Edinburgh, Scotland.

C. Fellbaum, editor. 1998. *WordNet: An Electronic Lexical Database and Some of its Applications*. MIT Press.

J. Hoffart, F. Suchanek, K. Berberich, and G. Weikum. 2013. YAGO2: a spatially and temporally enhanced knowledge base from Wikipedia. *Artificial Intelligence Journal. Special Issue on Artificial Intelligence, Wikipedia and Semi-Structured Resources*, 194:28–61.

A. Jain and M. Pennacchiotti. 2010. Open entity extraction from Web search query logs. In *Proceedings of the 23rd International Conference on Computational Linguistics (COLING-10)*, pages 510–518, Beijing, China.

N. Lao, T. Mitchell, and W. Cohen. 2011. Random walk inference and learning in a large scale knowledge base. In *Proceedings of the 2011 Conference on Empirical Methods in Natural Language Processing (EMNLP-11)*, pages 529–539, Edinburgh, Scotland.

N. Madnani and B. Dorr. 2010. Generating phrasal and sentential paraphrases: a survey of data-driven methods. *Computational Linguistics*, 36(3):341–387.

Mausam, M. Schmitz, S. Soderland, R. Bart, and O. Etzioni. 2012. Open language learning for information extraction. In *Proceedings of the 2012 Joint Conference on Empirical Methods in Natural Language Processing and Computational Natural Language Learning (EMNLP-CoNLL-12)*, pages 523–534, Jeju Island, Korea.

V. Nastase and M. Strube. 2008. Decoding Wikipedia categories for knowledge acquisition. In *Proceedings of the 23rd National Conference on Artificial Intelligence (AAAI-08)*, pages 1219–1224, Chicago, Illinois.

M. Paşca, B. Van Durme, and N. Garera. 2007. The role of documents vs. queries in extracting class attributes from text. In *Proceedings of the 16th International Conference on Information and Knowledge Management (CIKM-07)*, pages 485–494, Lisbon, Portugal.

M. Paşca. 2007. Organizing and searching the World Wide Web of facts - step two: Harnessing the wisdom of the crowds. In *Proceedings of the 16th World Wide Web Conference (WWW-07)*, pages 101–110, Banff, Canada.

M. Paşca. 2012. Attribute extraction from conjectural queries. In *Proceedings of the 24th International Conference on Computational Linguistics (COLING-12)*, Mumbai, India.

P. Pantel, T. Lin, and M. Gamon. 2012. Mining entity types from query logs via user intent modeling. In *Proceedings of the 50th Annual Meeting of the Association for Computational Linguistics (ACL-12)*, pages 563–571, Jeju Island, Korea.

S. Petrov, P. Chang, M. Ringgaard, and H. Alshawi. 2010. Uptraining for accurate deterministic question parsing. In *Proceedings of the 2010 Conference on Empirical Methods in Natural Language Processing (EMNLP-10)*, pages 705–713, Cambridge, Massachusetts.

C. Pinchak, D. Lin, and D. Rafiei. 2009. Flexible answer typing with discriminative preference ranking. In *Proceedings of the 12th Conference of the European Chapter of the Association for Computational Linguistics (EACL-09)*, pages 666–674, Athens, Greece.

S. Raju, P. Pingali, and V. Varma. 2008. An unsupervised approach to product attribute extraction. In *Proceedings of the 31st International Conference on Research and Development in Information Retrieval (SIGIR-08)*, pages 35–42, Singapore.

L. Ratinov, D. Roth, D. Downey, and M. Anderson. 2011. Local and global algorithms for disambiguation to Wikipedia. In *Proceedings of the 49th Annual Meeting of the Association for Computational Linguistics (ACL-11)*, pages 1375–1384, Portland, Oregon.

M. Remy. 2002. Wikipedia: The free encyclopedia. *Online Information Review*, 26(6):434.

P. Talukdar and F. Pereira. 2010. Experiments in graph-based semi-supervised learning methods for class-instance acquisition. In *Proceedings of the 48th Annual Meeting of the Association for Computational Linguistics (ACL-10)*, pages 1473–1481, Uppsala, Sweden.

K. Tokunaga, J. Kazama, and K. Torisawa. 2005. Automatic discovery of attribute words from Web documents. In *Proceedings of the 2nd International Joint Conference on Natural Language Processing (IJCNLP-05)*, pages 106–118, Jeju Island, Korea.

B. Van Durme, T. Qian, and L. Schubert. 2008. Class-driven attribute extraction. In *Proceedings of the 22nd International Conference on Computational Linguistics (COLING-08)*, pages 921–928, Manchester, United Kingdom.

T. Wong, W. Lam, and T. Wong. 2008. An unsupervised framework for extracting and normalizing product attributes from multiple Web sites. In *Proceedings of the 31st International Conference on Research and Development in Information Retrieval (SIGIR-08)*, pages 35–42, Singapore.

F. Wu and D. Weld. 2010. Open information extraction using Wikipedia. In *Proceedings of the 48th Annual Meeting of the Association for Computational Linguistics (ACL-10)*, pages 118–127, Uppsala, Sweden.

N. Yoshinaga and K. Torisawa. 2007. Open-domain attribute-value acquisition from semi-structured texts. In *Proceedings of the 6th International Semantic Web Conference (ISWC-07), Workshop on Text to Knowledge: The Lexicon/Ontology Interface (OntoLex-2007)*, pages 55–66, Busan, South Korea.

J. Zhu, Z. Nie, X. Liu, B. Zhang, and J. Wen. 2009. StatSnowball: a statistical approach to extracting entity relationships. In *Proceedings of the 18th World Wide Web Conference (WWW-09)*, pages 101–110, Madrid, Spain.

Learning from Post-Editing: Online Model Adaptation for Statistical Machine Translation

Michael Denkowski Chris Dyer Alon Lavie
Language Technologies Institute
Carnegie Mellon University
Pittsburgh, PA 15213 USA
{mdenkows,cdyer,alavie}@cs.cmu.edu

Abstract

Using machine translation output as a starting point for human translation has become an increasingly common application of MT. We propose and evaluate three computationally efficient online methods for updating statistical MT systems in a scenario where post-edited MT output is constantly being returned to the system: (1) adding new rules to the translation model from the post-edited content, (2) updating a Bayesian language model of the target language that is used by the MT system, and (3) updating the MT system's discriminative parameters with a MIRA step. Individually, these techniques can substantially improve MT quality, even over strong baselines. Moreover, we see super-additive improvements when all three techniques are used in tandem.

1 Introduction

Using machine translation outputs as a starting point for human translators is becoming increasingly common and is now arguably one of the most commercially important applications of MT. Considerable evidence has accumulated showing that human translators are more productive and accurate when *post-editing* MT output than when translating from scratch (Guerberof, 2009; Carl et al., 2011; Koehn, 2012; Zhechev, 2012, *inter alia*). An important (if unsurprising) insight from prior research in this area is that translators become more productive as MT quality improves (Tatsumi, 2009). While general improvements to MT continue to lead to further productivity gains, we explore how MT quality can be improved specifically in an online post-editing scenario in which sentence-level MT outputs are constantly being presented to human experts, edited, and then returned to the system for immediate learning. This task is challenging in two regards. First, from a technical perspective, post-edited outputs must be processed rapidly: a productive post-editor cannot wait for a standard batch MT training pipeline to be rerun after each sentence is corrected! Second, from a methodological perspective, it is expensive to run many human subject experiments, in particular when the human subjects must have translation expertise. We therefore use a **simulated post-editing paradigm** in which either non-post-edited reference translations or manually post-edited translations from a similar MT system are used in lieu of human post-editors (§2). This paradigm allows us to efficiently develop and evaluate systems that can go on to function in real-time post-editing scenarios without modification.

We present and evaluate three online methods for improving translation models using feedback from editors: adding new translations rules to the translation grammar (§3), updating a Bayesian language model with observations of the post-edited output (§4), and using an online discriminative parameter update to minimize model error (§5). These techniques are computationally efficient and make minimal use of approximation or heuristics, handling initial and incremental data in a uniform way. We evaluate these techniques in a variety of language and data scenarios that mimic the demands of real-world translation tasks. Compared to a competitive baseline, we show substantial improvement from updating the translation grammar or language model independently and super-additive gains from combining these techniques with a MIRA update (§6). We then discuss how our techniques relate to prior work (§7) and conclude (§8).

2 Simulated Post-Editing Paradigm

In post-editing scenarios, humans continuously edit machine translation outputs into production-quality translations, providing an additional, constant stream of data absent in batch translation. This data consists of highly domain-relevant reference translations that are minimally different from MT outputs, making them ideal for learning. However, true post-editing data is infeasible to collect during system development and internal testing as standard MT pipelines require tens of thousands of sentences to be translated with low latency. To address this problem, Hardt and Elming (2010) formulate the task of simulated post-editing, wherein pre-generated reference translations are used as a stand-in for actual post-editing. This approximation is equivalent to the case where humans edit each translation hypothesis to be identical to the reference rather than simply correcting the MT output to be grammatical and meaning-equivalent to the source. Our work uses this approximation for tuning and evaluation. We also introduce a more accurate approximation wherein MT output from the target system (or a similar system) is post-edited in advance, creating "offline" post-edited data that is similar to expected system outputs and should thus minimize unnecessary edits. An experiment in §6.4 compares the two approximations.

In our simulated post-editing tasks, decoding (for both the test corpus and each pass over the development corpus during optimization) begins with baseline models trained on standard bilingual and monolingual data. After each sentence is translated, the following take place in order: First, MIRA uses the new source–reference pair to update weights for the current models. Second, the source is aligned to the reference and used to update the translation grammar. Third, the reference is added to the Bayesian language model. As sentences are translated, the models gain valuable context information, allowing them to zero in on the target document and translator. Context is reset at the start of each development or test corpus.[1] This setup, which allows a uniform approach to tuning and decoding, is visualized in Figure 1.

3 Translation Grammar Adaptation

Translation models (either phrase tables or synchronous grammars) are typically generated offline from large bilingual text. This is reasonable in scenarios where available training data is fixed over long periods of time. However, this approach

[1]Initial experiments show this to outperform resetting models on more fine-grained document boundaries, although further investigation is warranted.

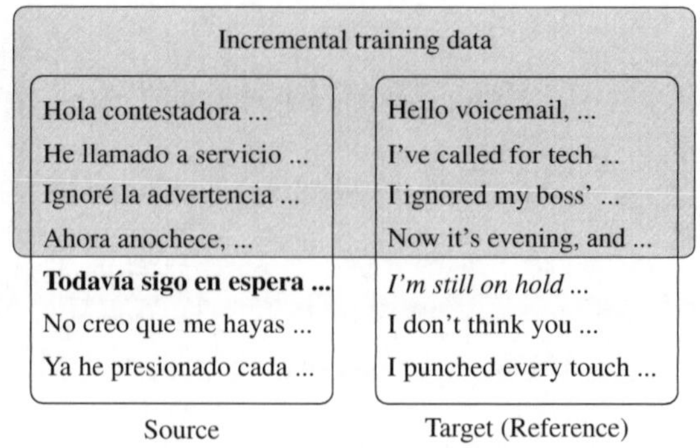

Figure 1: Context when translating an input sentence (bold) with simulated post-editing. Previous sentences and references (shaded) are added to the training data. *After* the current sentence is translated, it is aligned to the reference (italic) and added to the context for the next sentence.

does not allow adding new data without repeating model estimation in its entirety, which may take hours or days. In this section, we describe a simple technique for incorporating new bilingual training data as soon as it is available. Our approach is an extension of the on-demand grammar extractor described by Lopez (2008a). We extend the work initially designed for on-the-fly grammar extraction from static data (to mitigate the expense of storing large translation grammars), to specifically handle incremental data from post-editing.

3.1 Suffix Array Grammar Extraction

Lopez (2008a) introduces an alternative to traditional model estimation for hierarchical phrase-based statistical machine translation (Chiang, 2007). Rather than estimating a single grammar from all training data, the aligned bitext is indexed using a source-side suffix array (Manber and Myers, 1993). When an input sentence is to be translated, a grammar extraction program *samples* instances of aligned phrase pairs from the suffix array that match the source side of the sentence. Using statistics from these samples rather than the entire bitext, a sentence-specific grammar is rapidly generated. In addition to speed gains from sampling, indexing the source side of the bitext facilitates a more powerful feature set. Rules in on-demand grammars are generated using a sample $\mathcal{S}$ for each source phrase f in the input sentence. The sample, containing pairs $\langle f, e\rangle$, is used to calculate the following statistics:

Feature	Baseline	Adaptive
coherent $p(e\|f)$	$\frac{\mathcal{C}_{\mathcal{S}}(f,e)}{\|\mathcal{S}\|}$	$\frac{\mathcal{C}_{\mathcal{S}}(f,e)+\mathcal{C}_{\mathcal{L}}(f,e)}{\|\mathcal{S}\|+\|\mathcal{L}\|}$
sample size	$\|\mathcal{S}\|$	$\|\mathcal{S}\|+\|\mathcal{L}\|$
co-occurrence $\langle f,e\rangle$	$\mathcal{C}_{\mathcal{S}}(f,e)$	$\mathcal{C}_{\mathcal{S}}(f,e)+\mathcal{C}_{\mathcal{L}}(f,e)$
singleton f	$\mathcal{C}_{\mathcal{S}}(f) = 1$	$\mathcal{C}_{\mathcal{S}}(f)+\mathcal{C}_{\mathcal{L}}(f) = 1$
singleton $\langle f,e\rangle$	$\mathcal{C}_{\mathcal{S}}(f,e) = 1$	$\mathcal{C}_{\mathcal{S}}(f,e)+\mathcal{C}_{\mathcal{L}}(f,e) = 1$
post-edit support $\langle f,e\rangle$	0	$\mathcal{C}_{\mathcal{L}}(f,e) > 0$

Table 1: Phrase feature definitions for baseline and adaptive translation models.

- $\mathcal{C}_{\mathcal{S}}(f,e)$: count of instances in $\mathcal{S}$ where f aligns to e (phrase co-occurrence count).
- $\mathcal{C}_{\mathcal{S}}(f)$: count of instances in $\mathcal{S}$ where f aligns to any target phrase.
- $|\mathcal{S}|$: total number of instances in $\mathcal{S}$, equal to number of occurrences of f in training data, capped by the sample size limit.

These statistics are used to instantiate translation rules $X \rightarrow \langle f,e\rangle$ and calculate scores for the phrase feature set shown in the "Baseline" column of Table 1. Notably, the coherent phrase translation probability that conditions on f occurring in the data ($|\mathcal{S}|$) rather than f being extracted as part of a phrase pair ($\mathcal{C}_{\mathcal{S}}(f)$) is shown by Lopez (2008b) to yield significant improvement over the traditional translation probability.

3.2 Online Grammar Extraction

When a human translator post-edits MT output, a new bilingual sentence pair is created. However, in typical settings, it can be weeks or months before these training instances are incorporated into bilingual data and models retrained. Our extension to on-demand grammar extraction incorporates these new training instances into the model immediately. In addition to a static suffix array that indexes initial data, our system maintains a dynamic lookup table. Each new sentence pair is word-aligned with the model estimated from the initial data (a process often called forced alignment). This makes a generally insignificant approximation with respect to the original alignment model. Extractable phrase pairs are stored in the lookup table and phrase occurrences are counted on the source side. When subsequent grammars are extracted, the suffix array sample $\mathcal{S}$ for each f is accompanied by an exhaustive lookup $\mathcal{L}$ from the lookup table. Matching statistics are calculated from $\mathcal{L}$:

- $\mathcal{C}_{\mathcal{L}}(f,e)$: count of instances in $\mathcal{L}$ where f aligns to e.
- $\mathcal{C}_{\mathcal{L}}(f)$: count of instances in $\mathcal{L}$ where f aligns to any target phrase.
- $|\mathcal{L}|$: total number of instances of f in post-editing data (no size limit).

We use combined statistics from $\mathcal{S}$ and $\mathcal{L}$ to calculate scores for the "Adaptive" feature set defined in Table 1. In addition to updating existing features, we introduce a new indicator feature that identifies rules supported by post-editor feedback. Further, our approach allows us to extract rules that encode translations (phrase mappings and reorderings) *only* observed in the incremental post-editing data. This process, which can be seen as influencing the distribution from which grammars are sampled over time, produces comparable results to the infeasible process of rebuilding the translation model after every sentence is translated with the added benefit of allowing an optimizer to learn a weight for the post-edited data via the post-edit support feature. The simple aggregation of statistics allows our model to handle initial and incremental data in a formally consistent way. Further, any additional features that can be calculated on a suffix array sample can be matched by an incremental data lookup, making our translation model a viable platform for further exploration in online learning for MT.

4 Language Model Adaptation

Adapting language models in an online manner based on the content they are generating has long been seen as a promising technique for improving automatic speech recognition and machine translation (Kuhn and de Mori, 1990; Zhao et al., 2004; Sanchis-Trilles, 2012, *inter alia*). The post-editing scenario we are considering simplifies this process somewhat since rather than only having a posterior distribution over machine-generated outputs (any of which may be ungrammatical), the outputs, once edited by human translators, may be presumed to be grammatical.

We thus take a novel approach to language model adaptation, building on recent work showing that state-of-the-art language models can be inferred as the posterior predictive distribution of a Bayesian language model with hierarchical Pitman-Yor process priors, conditioned on the training corpus (Teh, 2006). The Bayesian formulation provides a natural way to incorporate progressively more data: by updating the posterior distribution given subsequent observations. Furthermore, the nonparametric nature of the model means that the model is well suited to potentially unbounded growth of vocabulary. Unfortunately, in general, Bayesian techniques are computationally difficult to work with. However, hierarchical Pitman-Yor process language models (HPYPLMs) are convenient in this regard since (1) inference can be carried out efficiently in a convenient collapsed representation (the "Chinese restaurant franchise") and (2) the posterior predictive distribution from a single sample provides a high quality language model.

We thus use the following procedure. Using the target side of the bitext as observations, we run the Gibbs sampling procedure described by Teh (2006) for 100 iterations in a 3-gram HPYPLM. The inferred "seating configuration" defines a posterior predictive distribution over words in 2-gram contexts (as with any 3-gram LM) as well as a posterior distribution over how the model will generate subsequent observations. We use the former as a language model component of a translation model. And, as post-edited sentences become available, we add their n-grams to the model using the later. We do not run any Gibbs sampling. Just updating the language model in this way, we obtain the results shown in Table 2 for the experimental conditions described in §6.

Spanish–English	*WMT10*	WMT11	TED1	TED2
HPYPLM	*25.5*	24.8	29.4	26.6
+data	***25.8***	**25.2**	**29.5**	**27.0**
English–Spanish	*WMT10*	WMT11	TED1	TED2
HPYPLM	*25.1*	26.8	26.0	24.3
+data	***25.4***	**27.2**	**26.2**	**25.0**
Arabic–English	*MT08*	MT09	TED1	TED2
HPYPLM	*19.3*	24.7	9.5	10.0
+data	***19.6***	**24.9**	**9.8**	**10.5**

Table 2: BLEU scores for systems with trigram HPYPLM (no large language model), with and without incremental updates from simulated post-editing data. Scores are averages over 3 optimizer runs. Bold scores indicate statistically significant improvement. Tuning set scores are italicized.

5 Learning Feature Weights

MT system parameter optimization (learning feature weights for the decoder) is also typically conducted as a batch process. Discriminative learning techniques such as minimum error rate training (Och, 2003) are used to find feature weights that maximize automatic metric score on a small development corpus. The resulting weight vector is then used to decode given input sentences. Using this approach with post-editing tasks presents two major issues. First, reference translation are only considered after all sentences are translated, a mismatch with post-editing where references are available incrementally. Second, despite the fact that adaptive feature sets become more powerful as post-editing data increases, an optimizer must learn a single corpus-level weight for each feature. This forces an averaging effect that can lead to decoding individual sentences with suboptimal weights. We address the first issue by using reference translations to simulate post-editing (Hardt and Elming, 2010) at tuning time and the second by using a version of the margin-infused relaxed algorithm (Crammer et al., 2006; Eidelman, 2012) to make online parameter updates during decoding. The result is a consistent approach to tuning and decoding that brings out the potential of adaptive models.

5.1 Parameter Optimization

In order to make our decoding process fully consistent with tuning, we introduce an online discriminative parameter update that allows our adaptive translation and language models be weighted appropriately as more data is available. This requires an optimization algorithm that can function as an online learner during decoding as well as a batch optimizer during tuning. Popular optimizers such as MERT (Och, 2003) and pairwise rank optimization (Hopkins and May, 2011) cannot be used due to their reliance on corpus-level optimization. We select the cutting-plane variant of the margin-infused relaxed algorithm (Chiang, 2012; Crammer et al., 2006) with additional extensions described by Eidelman (2012). MIRA is an online large-margin learner that makes a parameter update after each model prediction with the objective of choosing the correct output over the incorrect output by a margin at least as large as the cost of predicting the incorrect output. Applied to MT system optimization on a development corpus, MIRA proceeds as follows. The MT system generates a list of the k best translations for a single input sentence. From the list, a "hope" hypothesis is selected as a translation with both high model score and high automatic metric score. A "fear" hypothesis is selected as a translation with high model score but low metric score. Parameters are updated away from the fear hypothesis, toward the hope hypothesis, and the system processes the next input sentence. This process continues for a set number of passes over the development corpus. All adaptive systems used in our work are optimized with this variant of MIRA using the parameter settings described by Eidelman (2012). For each pass over the data, translation and language models have incremental access to reference translations (simulated post-editing data) as input sentences are translated. Translation and language models reset to using background data only at the beginning of each MIRA iteration.[2]

5.2 Online Parameter Updates

Our optimization strategy allows us to treat decoding as if it were simply the next iteration of MIRA (or alternatively that MIRA makes a single pass over an input corpus that consists of the development data concatenated n times followed by unseen input data). After each sentence is translated, a reference translation (resulting from actual human post-editing in production or simulated post-editing for our experiments) is provided to the models and MIRA makes a parameter update. In the only departure from our optimization setup, we decrease the maximum step size for MIRA (described in §6.2), effectively increasing regularization strength. This allows us to prefer small adjustments to already optimized decoding parameters over the large changes needed during tuning. It is also important to note that by using MIRA for updating weights during both tuning and decoding, we avoid scaling issues between multiple optimizers (such as when tuning with MERT and updating with a passive-aggressive algorithm).

6 Experiments

We evaluate our online extensions to standard machine translation systems in a series of simulated post-editing experiments that cover high-traffic languages and challenging domains. We show incremental improvement from our adaptive models and significantly larger gains when pairing our models with an online parameter update. We finally validate our adaptive system on actual post-edited data.

Spanish–English	*WMT10*	WMT11	TED1	TED2
Base MERT	*29.1*	27.9	32.8	29.6
Base MIRA	*29.2*	28.0	32.7	29.7
G	*29.8*	28.3	34.2	30.7
L	*29.2*	28.1	33.0	29.8
M	*29.2*	28.1	33.1	29.8
G+L+M	***30.0***	**28.8**	**35.2**	**31.3**
English–Spanish	*WMT10*	WMT11	TED1	TED2
Base MERT	*27.8*	29.4	26.5	25.7
Base MIRA	*27.7*	29.6	26.8	26.7
G	*28.1*	29.8	27.9	27.5
L	*27.9*	29.7	26.8	26.5
M	*27.9*	29.7	27.2	26.6
G+L+M	***28.4***	**30.4**	**28.6**	**27.9**
Arabic–English	*MT08*	MT09	TED1	TED2
Base MERT	*21.5*	25.0	10.4	10.5
Base MIRA	*21.2*	25.9	10.6	10.9
G	*21.8*	26.2	11.0	11.7
L	*20.6*	25.7	10.6	10.9
M	*21.3*	25.7	10.8	11.0
G+L+M	***21.8***	**26.5**	**11.4**	**11.8**

Table 3: BLEU scores for baseline and adaptive systems. Scores are averages over three optimizer runs. Highest scores are bold and tuning set scores are italicized. All fully adaptive systems (G+L+M) show statistically significant improvement over both MERT and MIRA baselines.

6.1 Data

We conduct a series of simulated post-editing experiments in three full scale language scenarios: Spanish–English, English–Spanish, and Arabic–English. Spanish–English and English–Spanish systems are trained on the 2012 NAACL WMT (Callison-Burch et al., 2012) constrained resources (2 million bilingual sentences, 300 million words of monolingual Spanish, and 1.1 billion words of monolingual English). Arabic–English systems are trained on the 2012 NIST OpenMT (Przybocki, 2012) constrained bilingual resources plus a selection from the English Gigaword corpus (Parker et al., 2011) (5 million bilingual sentences and 650 million words of monolingual En-

[2]Resetting translation and language models prevents contamination. If models retained state from previous passes over the development set, they would include data for input sentences before they were translated, rather than after as in post-editing.

glish). We tune and evaluate on standard news sets: WMT10 and WMT11 for Spanish–English and English–Spanish, and MT08 and MT09 for Arabic–English. To simulate real-world post editing where one translator works on a document at a time, we use only one of the four available reference translation sets for MT08 and MT09.

We also evaluate on a blind domain adaptation scenario that mimics the demands placed on MT systems in real-world translation tasks. The Web Inventory of Transcribed and Translated Talks (WIT^3) corpus (Cettolo et al., 2012) makes transcriptions of TED talks[3] available in several languages, including English, Spanish, and Arabic. For each language pair, we select two sets of 10 talk transcripts each (2000-3000 sentences) as blind evaluation sets. These sets consist of spoken language covering a broad range of topics. Systems have no access to any training or development data in this domain prior to translation.

6.2 Translation Systems

For each language scenario, we first construct a competitive baseline system. Bilingual data is word aligned using the model described by Dyer et al. (2013) and suffix array-backed translation grammars are extracted using the method described by Lopez (2008a). We add the standard lexical and derivation features[4] from Lopez (2008b) and Dyer et al. (2010). An unpruned, modified Kneser-Ney-smoothed 4-gram language model is estimated using the KenLM toolkit (Heafield et al., 2013). Feature weights are optimized using the lattice-based variant of MERT (Macherey et al., 2008; Och, 2003) on either WMT10 or MT08. Evaluation sets are translated using the `cdec` decoder (Dyer et al., 2010) and evaluated with the BLEU metric (Papineni et al., 2002). These results are listed as "Base MERT" in Table 3. To establish a baseline for our adaptive systems, we tune the same baseline system using cutting-plane MIRA with 500-best lists, the pseudo-document approximation described by Eidelman (2012), and a maximum update size of 0.01. We begin with uniform weights and make 20 passes over the development corpus. Results for this system are listed as "Base MIRA".

To evaluate the impact of each online model adaptation technique, we report the results for the following systems in Table 3:

- G: Baseline MIRA system with online grammar extraction, including incrementally updating existing phrase features plus an additional indicator feature for post-edit support.
- L: Baseline MIRA with a trigram hierarchical Pitman-Yor process language model that is incrementally updated, including a separate out-of-vocabulary feature.
- M: Baseline MIRA with online feature weight updates from cutting-plane MIRA.

Finally, we report results for a fully adaptive system that includes online grammar, language model, and feature weight updates. This system is reported as "G+L+M". To account for optimizer instability, all systems are tuned (consisting of running either MERT or MIRA) and evaluated 3 times. We report average scores over optimizer runs and conduct statistical significance tests using the methods described by Clark et al. (2011).

	News		TED Talks	
	New	Supp	New	Supp
Spanish–English	15%	19%	14%	18%
English–Spanish	12%	16%	9%	13%
Arabic–English	9%	12%	23%	28%

Table 5: Percentages of new rules (only seen in incremental data) and post-edit supported rules (Rules from all data for which the "post-edit support $\langle f, e\rangle$" feature fires) in grammars by domain.

6.3 Results

Our simulated translation post-editing experiments are summarized in Table 3. Simply moving from MERT to cutting-plane MIRA for parameter optimization yields improvement in most cases, corroborating existing work (Eidelman, 2012). Using incremental post-editing data to update translation grammars (G) yields further improvement in all cases evaluated. Gains are significantly larger for TED talks where translator feedback can bridge the gap between domains. Table 5 shows the aggregate percentages of rules in online grammars that are entirely new (extracted from post-editing instances only) or post-edit supported (superset of new rules). While percentages vary by data set, the overall trend is a combination of *learning* new vocabulary and reordering and *disambiguating* existing translation choices.

The introduction of a trigram Bayesian language model (L) yields mixed results: in some

[3] `http://www.ted.com/talks`

[4] Derivation features consist of word count, discretized rule-level non-terminal count (0, 1, or 2), glue rule count, and out-of-vocabulary pass-through count.

Base MERT	and changing the definition of what the **Zona Cero** is .
G+L+M	and the changing definition of what the **Ground Zero** is .
Reference	and the changing definition of what **Ground Zero** is .
Base MERT	was that when we **side by side** comparisons with **coal** , **timber**
G+L+M	was that when we did **side-by-side** comparisons with **wood charcoal** ,
Reference	was when we did **side-by-side** comparisons with **wood charcoal** ,
Base MERT	There was a way – **there was one** –
G+L+M	There was a way – **there had to be a way** –
Reference	There was a way – **there had to be a way** –

Table 4: Translation examples from baseline and fully adaptive systems of Spanish TED talks into English. Examples illustrate (from top to bottom) learning translations for new vocabulary items, selecting correct translation candidates for the domain, and learning domain-appropriate phrasing.

cases it leads to slight improvement and in others, degradation. It appears that a static but large 4-gram language model often outperforms an incrementally updated but smaller trigram model. Further, learning a single weight for the Bayesian model can lead to a harmful mismatch. As a tuning pass over the development corpus proceeds, the model incorporates additional data and MIRA learns a weight corresponding to its predictive ability at the end of the corpus. During decoding, *all* sentences are translated with this language model weight, even before the model can adequately adapt itself to the target domain. This problem is alleviated in our fully adaptive system.

Using cutting-plane MIRA to incrementally update weights during decoding (M) also leads to mixed results, frequently resulting in both small increases and decreases in score. This could be due to the noise incurred when making small adjustments to static features after each sentence: depending on the similarity between the previous and current sentence and the limit of the step size (regularization strength), a parameter update may slightly improve or degrade translation.

Finally, we see significantly larger gains for our fully adaptive system (G+L+M) that combines adaptive translation grammars and language models with online parameter updates. In many cases, the difference between the baseline systems and our adaptive system is *greater* than the sum of the differences from our individual techniques, demonstrating the effectiveness of combining online learning methods. Our final system has two key advantages over any individual extension. First, incremental updates from MIRA can *rescale* weights for features that *change* over time, keeping the model consistent. Second, the Bayesian language model's out-of-vocabulary feature can *discriminate* between true OOV items and vocabulary items in the post-editing data not present in the monolingual data. By contrast, the only OOVs in the baseline system are untranslated items, as the target side of the bitext is included in the language model training data. This interplay between the adaptive components in our translation system leads to significant gains over MERT and MIRA baselines. Table 4 contains examples from our system's output that exemplify key improvements in translation quality. With respect to performance, our fully adaptive system translates an average of 1.5 sentences per second per CPU core. The additional cost incurred updating translation grammars and language models is less than one second per sentence (though the baseline cost of on-demand grammar extraction can be up to a few seconds). In total, the system is well within the acceptable speed range needed to function in real-time human translation scenarios.

6.4 Evaluation Using Post-Edited References

The 2012 ACL Workshop on Machine Translation (Callison-Burch et al., 2012) makes available a set of 1832 English–Spanish parallel news source sentences, independent references, initial MT outputs, and post-edited MT outputs. The employed MT system is trained on largely the same resources as our own English–Spanish system, granting the opportunity for a much closer approximation to an actual post-editing task; our system configurations score between 54 and 56 BLEU against the sample MT, indicating that humans post-edited translations similar but not identical to our own. We split the data into development and test sets, each 916 sentences, and run 3 iterations of optimizing on the development set and evaluating on the test set with both the MERT baseline and our G+L+M system on both types of references. Using independent references for tuning and evaluation (as before), our system yields an improvement of 0.6 BLEU (23.3 to 23.9). With post-edited references, our system yields an improvement of 1.3 BLEU (43.0 to 44.3). This provides strong evidence that our adaptive systems would provide better translations (both in terms of absolute quality and improvement over a standard baseline) for real-world post-editing scenarios.

7 Related Work

Prior work has led to the extension of standard phrase-based translation systems to make use of incrementally available data.[5] Approaches generally fall into categories of adding new data to translation models and of using incremental data to adjust model parameters (feature weights). In the first case, Nepveu et al. (2004) use cache-based translation and language models to incorporate data from the current document into a computer-aided translation scenario. Ortiz-Martínez et al. (2010) augment a standard translation model by storing sufficient statistics in addition to feature scores for phrase pairs, allowing feature values to be incrementally updated as new sentence pairs are available for phrase extraction. Hardt and Elming (2010) demonstrate the benefit of maintaining a distinction between background and post-editing data in an adaptive model with simulated post-editing. Though not targeted at post-editing applications, the most similar work to our online grammar adaptation is the stream-based translation model described by Levenberg et al. (2010). The authors introduce a dynamic suffix array that can incorporate new training text as it becomes available. Sanchis-Trilles (2012) proposes a strategy for online language model adaptation wherein several smaller domain-specific models are built and their scores interpolated for each sentence translated based on the target domain.

Focusing on incrementally updating model parameters with post-editing data, Martínez-Gómez et al. (2012) and López-Salcedo et al. (2012) show improvement under some conditions when using techniques including passive-aggressive algorithms, perceptron, and discriminative ridge regression to adapt feature weights for systems initially tuned using MERT. This work also uses reference translations to simulate post-editing. Saluja et al. (2012) introduce a support vector machine-based algorithm capable of learning from binary-labeled examples. This learning algorithm is used to incrementally adjust feature weights given user feedback on whether a translation is "good" or "bad". As with our work, this strategy can be used during both optimization and decoding.

Finally, Simard and Foster (2013) apply a pipeline solution to the post-editing task wherein a second stage automatic post-editor (APE) system learns to replicate the corrections made to initial MT output by human translators. As incremental data accumulates, the APE (itself a statistical phrase-based system) attempts to "correct" the MT output before it is shown to humans.

8 Conclusion

Casting machine translation for post-editing as an online learning task, we have presented three methods for incremental model adaptation: adding data to the indexed bitext from which grammars are extracted, updating a Bayesian language model with incremental data, and using an online discriminative parameter update during decoding. These methods, which allow the system to handle all data in a uniform way, are applied to a strong baseline system optimized using MIRA in conjunction with simulated post-editing. In addition to showing gains for individual methods under various circumstances, we report super-additive improvement from combining our techniques to produce a fully adaptive system. Improvements generalize over language and data scenarios, with the greatest gains realized in blind out-of-domain tasks where the system must rely heavily on post-editor feedback to improve quality. Gains are also more significant when using offline post-edited references, showing promise for applying our techniques to real-world post-editing tasks. All software used for our online model adaptation experiments is freely available under an open source license as part of the `cdec` toolkit.[6]

Acknowledgements

This work is supported in part by the National Science Foundation under grant IIS-0915327, by the Qatar National Research Fund (a member of the Qatar Foundation) under grant NPRP 09-1140-1-177, and by the NSF-sponsored XSEDE program under grant TG-CCR110017.

[5] Prior to phrase-based systems, NISHIDA et al. (1988) use post-editing data to correct errors in transfer-based MT.

[6] `http://www.cs.cmu.edu/~mdenkows/cdec-realtime.html`

References

[Callison-Burch et al.2012] Chris Callison-Burch, Philipp Koehn, Christof Monz, Matt Post, Radu Soricut, and Lucia Specia. 2012. Findings of the 2012 workshop on statistical machine translation. In *Proceedings of the Seventh Workshop on Statistical Machine Translation*, pages 10–51, Montréal, Canada, June. Association for Computational Linguistics.

[Carl et al.2011] Michael Carl, Barbara Dragsted, Jakob Elming, Daniel Hardt, and Arnt Lykke Jakobsen. 2011. The process of post-editing: A pilot study. *Copenhagen Studies in Language*, 41:131–142.

[Cettolo et al.2012] Mauro Cettolo, Christian Girardi, and Marcello Federico. 2012. Wit^3: Web inventory of transcribed and translated talks. In *Proceedings of the Sixteenth Annual Conference of the European Association for Machine Translation*.

[Chiang2007] David Chiang. 2007. Hierarchical phrase-based translation. *Computational Linguistics*, 33.

[Chiang2012] David Chiang. 2012. Hope and fear for discriminative training of statistical translation models. *Journal of Machine Learning Research*, pages 1159–1187, April.

[Clark et al.2011] Jonathan H. Clark, Chris Dyer, Alon Lavie, and Noah A. Smith. 2011. Better hypothesis testing for statistical machine translation: Controlling for optimizer instability. In *Proceedings of the 49th Annual Meeting of the Association for Computational Linguistics: Human Language Technologies*, pages 176–181, Portland, Oregon, USA, June. Association for Computational Linguistics.

[Crammer et al.2006] Koby Crammer, Ofer Dekel, Joseph Keshet, Shai Shalev-Shwartz, and Yoram Singer. 2006. Online passive-aggressive algorithms. *Journal of Machine Learning Research*, pages 551–558, March.

[Dyer et al.2010] Chris Dyer, Adam Lopez, Juri Ganitkevitch, Jonathan Weese, Ferhan Ture, Phil Blunsom, Hendra Setiawan, Vladimir Eidelman, and Philip Resnik. 2010. cdec: A decoder, alignment, and learning framework for finite-state and context-free translation models. In *Proceedings of the ACL 2010 System Demonstrations*, pages 7–12, Uppsala, Sweden, July. Association for Computational Linguistics.

[Dyer et al.2013] Chris Dyer, Victor Chahuneau, and Noah A. Smith. 2013. A simple, fast, and effective reparameterization of IBM model 2. In *The 2013 Conference of the North American Chapter of the Association for Computational Linguistics: Human Language Technologies*.

[Eidelman2012] Vladimir Eidelman. 2012. Optimization strategies for online large-margin learning in machine translation. In *Proceedings of the Seventh Workshop on Statistical Machine Translation*, pages 480–489, Montréal, Canada, June. Association for Computational Linguistics.

[Guerberof2009] Ana Guerberof. 2009. Productivity and quality in mt post-editing. In *Proceedings of MT Summit XII - Workshop: Beyond Translation Memories: New Tools for Translators MT*.

[Hardt and Elming2010] Daniel Hardt and Jakob Elming. 2010. Incremental re-training for post-editing smt. In *Proceedings of the Ninth Conference of the Association for Machine Translation in the Americas*.

[Heafield et al.2013] Kenneth Heafield, Ivan Pouzyrevsky, Jonathan H. Clark, and Philipp Koehn. 2013. Scalable modified Kneser-Ney language model estimation. In *Proceedings of the 51st Annual Meeting of the Association for Computational Linguistics*, Sofia, Bulgaria, August.

[Hopkins and May2011] Mark Hopkins and Jonathan May. 2011. Tuning as ranking. In *Proceedings of the 2011 Conference on Empirical Methods in Natural Language Processing*, pages 1352–1362, Edinburgh, Scotland, UK., July. Association for Computational Linguistics.

[Koehn2012] Philipp Koehn. 2012. Computer-aided translation. Machine Translation Marathon.

[Kuhn and de Mori1990] Roland Kuhn and Renato de Mori. 1990. A cache-based natural language model for speech recognition. *IEEE Transactions on Pattern Analysis and Machine Intelligence*, 12(6).

[Levenberg et al.2010] Abby Levenberg, Chris Callison-Burch, and Miles Osborne. 2010. Stream-based translation models for statistical machine translation. In *Human Language Technologies: The 2010 Annual Conference of the North American Chapter of the Association for Computational Linguistics*, pages 394–402, Los Angeles, California, June. Association for Computational Linguistics.

[Lopez2008a] Adam Lopez. 2008a. Machine translation by pattern matching. In *Dissertation, University of Maryland*, March.

[Lopez2008b] Adam Lopez. 2008b. Tera-scale translation models via pattern matching. In *Proceedings of the 22nd International Conference on Computational Linguistics (Coling 2008)*, pages 505–512, Manchester, UK, August. Coling 2008 Organizing Committee.

[López-Salcedo et al.2012] Francisco-Javier López-Salcedo, Germán Sanchis-Trilles, and Francisco Casacuberta. 2012. Online learning of log-linear weights in interactive machine translation. *Advances in Speech and Language Technologies for Iberian Languages*, pages 277–286.

[Macherey et al.2008] Wolfgang Macherey, Franz Och, Ignacio Thayer, and Jakob Uszkoreit. 2008. Lattice-based minimum error rate training for statistical machine translation. In *Proceedings of the 2008 Conference on Empirical Methods in Natural Language Processing*, pages 725–734, Honolulu, Hawaii, October. Association for Computational Linguistics.

[Manber and Myers1993] Udi Manber and Gene Myers. 1993. Suffix arrays: A new method for on-line string searches. *SIAM Journal of Computing*, 22:935–948.

[Martínez-Gómez et al.2012] Pascual Martínez-Gómez, Germán Sanchis-Trilles, and Francisco Casacuberta. 2012. Online adaptation strategies for statistical machine translation in post-editing scenarios. *Pattern Recognition*, 45:3193–3203.

[Nepveu et al.2004] Laurent Nepveu, Guy Lapalme, Philippe Langlais, and George Foster. 2004. Adaptive language and translation models for interactive machine translation. In Dekang Lin and Dekai Wu, editors, *Proceedings of EMNLP 2004*, pages 190–197, Barcelona, Spain, July. Association for Computational Linguistics.

[NISHIDA et al.1988] Fujio NISHIDA, Shinobu TAKAMATSU, Tadaaki TANI, and Tsunehisa DOI. 1988. Feedback of correcting information in postediting to a machine translation system. In *Proc. of COLING*.

[Och2003] Franz Josef Och. 2003. Minimum error rate training in statistical machine translation. In *Proceedings of the 41st Annual Meeting of the Association for Computational Linguistics*, pages 160–167, Sapporo, Japan, July. Association for Computational Linguistics.

[Ortiz-Martínez et al.2010] Daniel Ortiz-Martínez, Ismael García-Varea, and Francisco Casacuberta. 2010. Online learning for interactive statistical machine translation. In *Human Language Technologies: The 2010 Annual Conference of the North American Chapter of the Association for Computational Linguistics*, pages 546–554, Los Angeles, California, June. Association for Computational Linguistics.

[Papineni et al.2002] Kishore Papineni, Salim Roukos, Todd Ward, and Wei-Jing Zhu. 2002. Bleu: a method for automatic evaluation of machine translation. In *Proceedings of 40th Annual Meeting of the Association for Computational Linguistics*, pages 311–318, Philadelphia, Pennsylvania, USA, July. Association for Computational Linguistics.

[Parker et al.2011] Robert Parker, David Graff, Junbo Kong, Ke Chen, and Kazuaki Maeda. 2011. English Gigaword Fifth Edition, June. Linguistic Data Consortium, LDC2011T07.

[Przybocki2012] Mark Przybocki. 2012. Nist open machine translation 2012 evaluation (openmt12). http://www.nist.gov/itl/iad/mig/openmt12.cfm.

[Saluja et al.2012] Avneesh Saluja, Ian Lane, and Ying Zhang. 2012. Machine translation with binary feedback: a large-margin approach. In *Proceedings of the Tenth Biennial Conference of the Association for Machine Translation in the Americas*.

[Sanchis-Trilles2012] Germán Sanchis-Trilles. 2012. Building task-oriented machine translation systems. In *Ph.D. Thesis, Universitat Politcnica de Valncia*.

[Simard and Foster2013] Michel Simard and George Foster. 2013. PEPr: Post-edit propagation using phrase-based statistical machine translation. In *Proceedings of the XIV Machine Translation Summit*, pages 191–198,, September.

[Tatsumi2009] Midori Tatsumi. 2009. Correlation between automatic evaluation metric scores, post-editing speed, and some other factors. In *Proceedings of the Twelfth Machine Translation Summit*.

[Teh2006] Yee Whye Teh. 2006. A hierarchical Bayesian language model based on Pitman-Yor processes. In *Proc. of ACL*.

[Zhao et al.2004] Bing Zhao, Matthias Eck, and Stephan Vogel. 2004. Language model adaptation for statistical machine translation with structured query models. In *Proc. of COLING*.

[Zhechev2012] Ventsislav Zhechev. 2012. Machine Translation Infrastructure and Post-editing Performance at Autodesk. In *AMTA 2012 Workshop on Post-Editing Technology and Practice (WPTP 2012)*, pages 87–96, San Diego, USA, October. Association for Machine Translation in the Americas (AMTA).

Predicting and Characterising User Impact on Twitter

Vasileios Lampos[1], **Nikolaos Aletras**[2], **Daniel Preoţiuc-Pietro**[2] and **Trevor Cohn**[3]

[1] Department of Computer Science, University College London
[2] Department of Computer Science, University of Sheffield
[3] Computing and Information Systems, The University of Melbourne
v.lampos@ucl.ac.uk, {n.aletras,d.preotiuc}@dcs.shef.ac.uk, trevor.cohn@gmail.com

Abstract

The open structure of online social networks and their uncurated nature give rise to problems of user credibility and influence. In this paper, we address the task of predicting the impact of Twitter users based only on features under their direct control, such as usage statistics and the text posted in their tweets. We approach the problem as regression and apply linear as well as nonlinear learning methods to predict a user impact score, estimated by combining the numbers of the user's followers, followees and listings. The experimental results point out that a strong prediction performance is achieved, especially for models based on the Gaussian Processes framework. Hence, we can interpret various modelling components, transforming them into indirect 'suggestions' for impact boosting.

1 Introduction

Online social networks have become a wide spread medium for information dissemination and interaction between millions of users (Huberman et al., 2009; Kwak et al., 2010), turning, at the same time, into a popular subject for interdisciplinary research, involving domains such as Computer Science (Sakaki et al., 2010), Health (Lampos and Cristianini, 2012) and Psychology (Boyd et al., 2010). Open access along with the property of structured content retrieval for publicly posted data have brought the microblogging platform of Twitter into the spotlight.

Vast quantities of human-generated text from a range of themes, including opinions, news and everyday activities, spread over a social network. Naturally, issues arise, like user credibility (Castillo et al., 2011) and content attractiveness (Suh et al., 2010), and quite often trustful or appealing information transmitters are identified by an impact assessment.[1] Intuitively, it is expected that user impact cannot be defined by a single attribute, but depends on multiple user actions, such as posting frequency and quality, interaction strategies, and the text or topics of the written communications.

In this paper, we start by predicting user impact as a statistical learning task (regression). For that purpose, we firstly define an impact score function for Twitter users driven by basic account properties. Afterwards, from a set of accounts, we measure several publicly available attributes, such as the quantity of posts or interaction figures. Textual attributes are also modelled either by word frequencies or, more generally, by clusters of related words which quantify a topic-oriented participation. The main hypothesis being tested is whether textual and non textual attributes encapsulate patterns that affect the impact of an account.

To model this data, we present a method based on nonlinear regression using Gaussian Processes, a Bayesian non-parametric class of methods (Rasmussen and Williams, 2006), proven more effective in capturing the multimodal user features. The modelling choice of excluding components that are not under an account's direct control (e.g. received retweets) combined with a significant user impact prediction performance ($r = .78$) enabled us to investigate further how specific aspects of a user's behaviour relate to impact, by examining the parameters of the inferred model.

Among our findings, we identify relevant features for this task and confirm that consistent activity and broad interaction are deciding impact factors. Informativeness, estimated by computing a joint user-topic entropy, contributes well to the separation between low and high impact accounts. Use case scenarios based on combinations of features are also explored, leading to findings such as that engaging about 'serious' or more 'light' topics may not register a differentiation in impact.

[1] For example, the influence assessment metric of Klout — http://www.klout.com.

2 Data

For the experimental process of this paper, we formed a Twitter data set ($\mathcal{D}1$) of more than 48 million tweets produced by $|U| = 38,020$ users geolocated in the UK in the period between 14/04/2011 and 12/04/2012 (both dates included, $\Delta t = 365$ days). $\mathcal{D}1$ is a temporal subset of the data set used for modelling UK voting intentions in (Lampos et al., 2013). Geolocation of users was carried out by matching the location field in their profile with UK city names on DBpedia as well as by checking that the user's timezone is set to G.M.T. (Rout et al., 2013). The use of a common greater geographical area (UK) was essential in order to derive a data set with language and topic homogeneity. A distinct Twitter data set ($\mathcal{D}2$) consisting of approx. 400 million tweets was formed for learning term clusters (Section 4.2). $\mathcal{D}2$ was retrieved from Twitter's Gardenhose stream (a 10% sample of the entire stream) from 02/01 to 28/02/2011. $\mathcal{D}1$ and $\mathcal{D}2$ were processed using TrendMiner's pipeline (Preoţiuc-Pietro et al., 2012).

3 User Impact Definition

On the microblogging platform of Twitter, user – or, in general, account – popularity is usually quantified by the raw number of followers ($\phi_{\text{in}} \geq 0$), i.e. other users interested in this account. Likewise, a user can follow others, which we denote as his set of followees ($\phi_{\text{out}} \geq 0$). It is expected that users with high numbers of followers are also popular in the real world, being well-known artists, politicians, brands and so on. However, non popular entities, the majority in the social network, can also gain a great number of followers, by exploiting, for example, a follow-back strategy.[2] Therefore, using solely the number of followers to quantify impact may lead to inaccurate outcomes (Cha et al., 2010). A natural alternative, the ratio of $\phi_{\text{in}}/\phi_{\text{out}}$ is not a reliable metric, as it is invariant to scaling, i.e. it cannot differentiate accounts of the type $\{\phi_{\text{in}}, \phi_{\text{out}}\} = \{m, n\}$ and $\{\gamma \times m, \gamma \times n\}$. We resolve this problem by squaring the number of followers $\left(\phi_{\text{in}}^2/\phi_{\text{out}}\right)$; note that the previous expression is equal to $(\phi_{\text{in}} - \phi_{\text{out}}) \times (\phi_{\text{in}}/\phi_{\text{out}}) + \phi_{\text{in}}$ and thus, it incorporates the ratio as well as the difference between followers and followees.

An additional impact indicator is the number of times an account has been listed by others ($\phi_{\lambda} \geq 0$). Lists provide a way to curate content on Twitter; thus, users included in many lists are attractors of

[2]An account follows other accounts randomly expecting that they will follow back.

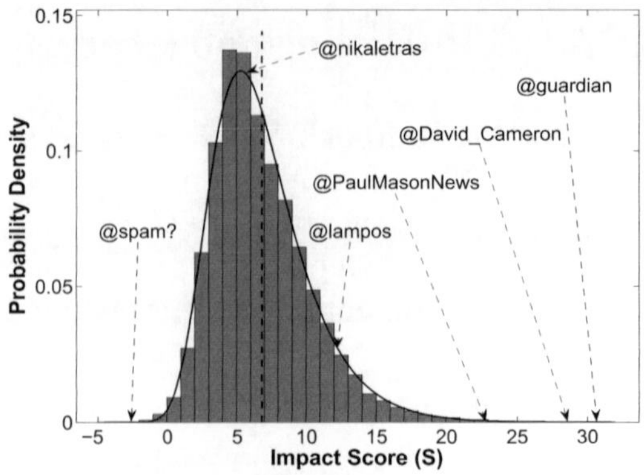

Figure 1: Histogram of the user impact scores in our data set. The solid black line represents a generalised extreme value probability distribution fitted in our data, and the dashed line denotes the mean impact score (= 6.776). User @spam? is a sample account with $\phi_{\text{in}} = 10$, $\phi_{\text{out}} = 1000$ and $\phi_{\lambda} = 0$; @lampos is a very active account, whereas @nikaletras is a regular user.

interest. Indeed, Pearson's correlation between ϕ_{in} and ϕ_{λ} for all the accounts in our data set is equal to .765 ($p < .001$); the two metrics are correlated, but not entirely and on those grounds, it would be reasonable to use both for quantifying impact.

Consequently, we have chosen to represent user impact (S) as a log function of the number of followers, followees and listings, given by

$$\text{S}(\phi_{\text{in}}, \phi_{\text{out}}, \phi_{\lambda}) = \ln\left(\frac{(\phi_{\lambda} + \theta)\,(\phi_{\text{in}} + \theta)^2}{\phi_{\text{out}} + \theta}\right), \tag{1}$$

where θ is a smoothing constant set equal to 1 so that the natural logarithm is always applied on a real positive number. Figure 1 shows the impact score distribution for all the users in our sample, including some pointers to less or more popular Twitter accounts. The depicted user impact scores form the response variable in the regression models presented in the following sections.

4 User Account Features

This section presents the features used in the user impact prediction task. They are divided into two categories: non-textual and text-based. All features have the joint characteristic of being under the user's direct control, something essential for characterising impact based on the actions of a user. Attributes such as the number of received retweets or @-mentions (of a user in the tweets of others) were not considered as they are not controlled by the account itself.

a_1	# of tweets
a_2	proportion of retweets
a_3	proportion of non-duplicate tweets
a_4	proportion of tweets with hashtags
a_5	hashtag-tokens ratio in tweets
a_6	proportion of tweets with @-mentions
a_7	# of unique @-mentions in tweets
a_8	proportion of tweets with @-replies
a_9	links ratio in tweets
a_{10}	# of favourites the account made
a_{11}	total # of tweets (entire history)
a_{12}	using default profile background (binary)
a_{13}	using default profile image (binary)
a_{14}	enabled geolocation (binary)
a_{15}	population of account's location
a_{16}	account's location latitude
a_{17}	account's location longitude
a_{18}	proportion of days with nonzero tweets

Table 1: Non textual attributes for a Twitter account used in the modelling process. All attributes refer to a set of 365 days (Δt) with the exception of a_{11}, the total number of tweets in the entire history of an account. Attributes a_i, $i \in \{2-6, 8, 9\}$ are ratios of a_1, whereas attribute a_{18} is a proportion of Δt.

4.1 Non textual attributes

The non-textual attributes (a) are derived either from general user behaviour statistics or directly from the account's profile. Table 1 presents the 18 attributes we extracted and used in our models.

4.2 Text features

We process the text in the tweets of $\mathcal{D}1$ and compute daily unigram frequencies. By discarding terms that appear less than 100 times, we form a vocabulary of size $|V| = 71,555$. We then form a user term-frequency matrix of size $|U| \times |V|$ with the mean term frequencies per user during the time interval Δt. All term frequencies are normalised with the total number of tweets posted by the user.

Apart from single word frequencies, we are also interested in deriving a more abstract representation for each user. To achieve this, we learn word clusters from a distinct reference corpus ($\mathcal{D}2$) that could potentially represent specific domains of discussion (or topics). From a multitude of proposed techniques, we have chosen to apply spectral clustering (Shi and Malik, 2000; Ng et al., 2002), a hard-clustering method appropriate for high-dimensional data and non-convex clusters (von Luxburg, 2007). Spectral clustering performs graph partitioning on the word-by-word similarity matrix. In our case, tweet-term similarity is reflected by the Normalised Pointwise Mutual Information (NPMI), an information theoretic measure indicating which words co-occur in the same context (Bouma, 2009). We use the random walk graph Laplacian and only keep the largest component of the resulting graph, eliminating most stop words in the process. The number of clusters needs to be specified in advance and each cluster's most representative words are identified by the following metric of centrality:

$$\mathrm{C}_w(c) = \frac{\sum_{v \in c} \mathrm{NPMI}(w, v)}{|c| - 1}, \tag{2}$$

where w is the target word and c the cluster it belongs ($|c|$ denotes the cluster's size). Examples of extracted word clusters are illustrated in Table 4. Other techniques were also applied, such as online LDA (Hoffman et al., 2010), but we found that the results were not satisfactory, perhaps due to the short message length and the foreign terms co-occuring within a tweet. After forming the clusters using $\mathcal{D}2$, we compute a topic score (τ) for each user-topic pair in $\mathcal{D}1$, representing a normalised user-word frequency sum per topic.

5 Methods

This section presents the various modelling approaches for the underlying inference task, the impact score (S) prediction of Twitter users based on a set of their actions.

5.1 Learning functions for regression

We formulate this problem as a regression task, i.e. we infer a real numbered value based on a set of observed features. As a simple baseline, we apply Ridge Regression (RR) (Hoerl and Kennard, 1970), a reguralised version of the ordinary least squares. Most importantly, we focus on nonlinear methods for the impact score prediction task given the multimodality of the feature space. Recently, it was shown by Cohn and Specia (2013) that Support Vector Machines for Regression (SVR) (Vapnik, 1998; Smola and Schölkopf, 2004), commonly considered the state-of-the-art for NLP regression tasks, can be outperformed by Gaussian Processes (GPs), a kernelised, probabilistic approach to learning (Rasmussen and Williams, 2006). Their setting is close to ours, in that they had few (17) features and were also aiming to predict a complex continuous phenomenon (human post-editing time). The initial stages of our experimental process confirmed that GPs performed better than SVR; thus, we based our modelling around them, including RR for comparison.

In GP regression, for the inputs $\boldsymbol{x} \in \mathbb{R}^d$ we want to learn a function $f \colon \mathbb{R}^d \rightarrow \mathbb{R}$ that is drawn from a GP prior

$$f(\boldsymbol{x}) \sim \mathcal{GP}\left(m(\boldsymbol{x}), k(\boldsymbol{x}, \boldsymbol{x}')\right), \qquad (3)$$

where $m(\boldsymbol{x})$ and $k(\boldsymbol{x}, \boldsymbol{x}')$ denote the mean (set to 0 in our experiments) and covariance (or kernel) functions respectively. The GP kernel function represents the covariance between pairs of input. We wish to limit f to smooth functions over the inputs, with different smoothness in each input dimension, assuming that some features are more useful than others. This can be accommodated by a squared exponential covariance function with Automatic Relevance Determination (ARD) (Neal, 1996; Williams and Rasmussen, 1996):

$$k_{\text{ard}}(\boldsymbol{x}, \boldsymbol{x}') = \sigma^2 \exp\left[\sum_i^d -\frac{(x_i - x_i')^2}{2\ell_i^2}\right], \qquad (4)$$

where σ^2 denotes the overall variance and ℓ_i is the length-scale parameter for feature x_i; all hyperparameters are learned from data during model inference. Parameter ℓ_i is inversely proportional to the feature's relevancy in the model, i.e. high values of ℓ_i indicate a low degree of relevance for the corresponding x_i. By setting $\ell_i = \ell$ in Eq. 4, we learn a common length-scale for all the dimensions – this is known as the isotropic squared exponential function (k_{iso}) since it is based purely on the difference $|\boldsymbol{x} - \boldsymbol{x}'|$. k_{iso} is a preferred choice when the dimensionality of the input space is high. Having set our covariance functions, predictions are conducted using Bayesian integration

$$\mathrm{P}(y_*|\boldsymbol{x}_*, \mathcal{O}) = \int_f \mathrm{P}(y_*|\boldsymbol{x}_*, f)\mathrm{P}(f|\mathcal{O}), \qquad (5)$$

where y_* is the response variable, $\mathcal{O}$ a labelled training set and $\boldsymbol{x}_*$ the current observation. We learn the hyperparameters of the model by maximising the log marginal likelihood $\mathrm{P}(y|\mathcal{O})$ using gradient ascent. However, inference becomes intractable when many training instances (n) are present as the number of computations needed is $\mathcal{O}(n^3)$ (Quiñonero-Candela and Rasmussen, 2005). Since our training samples are tens of thousands, we apply a sparse approximation method (FITC), which bases parameter learning on a few inducing points in the training set (Quiñonero-Candela and Rasmussen, 2005; Snelson and Ghahramani, 2006).

5.2 Models

For predicting user impact on Twitter, we develop three regression models that build on each other. The first and simplest one (A) uses only the non-textual attributes as features; the performance of A is tested using RR,[3] SVR as well as a GP model. For SVR we used an RBF kernel (equivalent to k_{iso}), whereas for the GP we applied the following covariance function

$$k(\boldsymbol{a}, \boldsymbol{a}') = k_{\text{ard}}(\boldsymbol{a}, \boldsymbol{a}') + k_{\text{noise}}(\boldsymbol{a}, \boldsymbol{a}') + \beta, \qquad (6)$$

where $k_{\text{noise}}(\boldsymbol{a}, \boldsymbol{a}') = \sigma^2 \times \delta(\boldsymbol{a}, \boldsymbol{a}')$, δ is a Kronecker delta function and β is the regression bias; this function consists of $(|a| + 3)$ hyperparameters. Note that the sum of covariance functions is also a valid covariance function (Rasmussen and Williams, 2006).

The second model (AW) extends model A by adding word-frequencies as features. The 500 most frequent terms in $\mathcal{D}1$ are discarded as stop words and we use the following $2,000$ ones (denoted by $\boldsymbol{w}$). Setting $\boldsymbol{x} = \{\boldsymbol{a}, \boldsymbol{w}\}$, the covariance function becomes

$$\begin{aligned} k(\boldsymbol{x}, \boldsymbol{x}') = k_{\text{ard}}(\boldsymbol{a}, \boldsymbol{a}') + k_{\text{iso}}(\boldsymbol{w}, \boldsymbol{w}') \\ + k_{\text{noise}}(\boldsymbol{x}, \boldsymbol{x}') + \beta, \end{aligned} \qquad (7)$$

where we apply k_{iso} on the term-frequencies due to their high dimensionality; the number of hyperparameters is $(|a| + 5)$. This is an intermediate model aiming to evaluate whether the incorporation of text improves prediction performance.

Finally, in the third model (AC) instead of relying on the high dimensional space of single words, we use topic-oriented collections of terms extracted by applying spectral clustering (see Section 4.2). By denoting the set of different clusters or topics as $\boldsymbol{\tau}$ and the entire feature space as $\boldsymbol{x} = \{\boldsymbol{a}, \boldsymbol{\tau}\}$, the covariance function now becomes

$$k(\boldsymbol{x}, \boldsymbol{x}') = k_{\text{ard}}(\boldsymbol{x}, \boldsymbol{x}') + k_{\text{noise}}(\boldsymbol{x}, \boldsymbol{x}') + \beta. \qquad (8)$$

The number of hyperparameters is equal to $(|a| + |\tau| + 3)$ and this model is applied for $|\tau| = 50$ and 100.

6 Experiments

Here we present the experimental results for the user impact prediction task and then investigate the factors that can affect it.

6.1 Predictive Accuracy

We evaluated the performance of the proposed models via 10-fold cross-validation. Results are presented in Table 2; Root Mean Squared Error

[3]Given that the representation of attributes a_{16} and a_{17} (latitude, longitude) is ambiguous in a linear model, they were not included in the RR-based models.

Model	Linear (RR)		Nonlinear (GP)	
	r	RMSE	r	RMSE
A	.667	2.642	.759	2.298
AW	.712	2.529	.768	2.263
AC, $\|\tau\| = 50$	.703	2.518	.774	2.234
AC, $\|\tau\| = 100$	.714	2.480	**.780**	**2.210**

Table 2: Average performance (RMSE and Pearson's r) derived from 10-fold cross-validation for the task of user impact score prediction.

Model	Top relevant features
A	$a_{13}^{\diamond}, a_{11}, a_7, a_1, a_9, a_8, a_{18}, a_4, a_6, a_3$
AW	$a_7, a_1, a_{11}, a_{13}^{\diamond}, a_9, a_8, a_{18}, a_4, a_6, a_{15}$
AC, $\tau = 50$	$a_{13}^{\diamond}, a_{11}, a_7, \tau_1', a_1, a_9, a_8, \tau_2', a_6, \tau_3'$
AC, $\tau = 100$	$a_{13}^{\diamond}, a_{11}, a_7, a_1, a_9, \tau_1, \tau_2, \tau_3, a_{18}, a_8$

Table 3: The 10 most relevant features in descending relevance order for all GP models. τ_i' and τ_i denote word clusters (may vary in each model).[6]

(RMSE) and Pearson's correlation (r) between predictions and responses were used as the performance metrics. Overall, the best performance in terms of both RMSE (2.21 impact points) and linear correlation ($r = .78$, $p < .001$) is achieved by the GP model (AC) that combines non-textual attributes with a 100 topic clusters; the difference in performance with all other models is statistically significant.[4] The linear baseline (RR) follows the same pattern of improvement through the different models, but never manages to reach the performance of the nonlinear alternative. As mentioned previously, we have also tried SVR with an RBF kernel for model A (parameters were optimised on a held-out development set) and the performance (RMSE: 2.33, $r = .75$, $p < .001$) was significantly worse than the one achieved by the GP model.[4]

Notice that when word-based features are introduced in model AW, performance improves. This was one of the motivations for including text in the modelling, apart from the notion that the posted content should also affect general impact. Lastly, turning this problem from regression to classification by creating 3 impact score pseudo-classes based on the .25 and the .9 quantiles of the response variable (4.3 and 11.4 impact score points respectively) and by using the outputs of model AC ($\tau = 100$) in each phase of the 10-fold cross-validation, we achieve a 75.86% classification accuracy.[5]

[4] Indicated by performing a t-test (5% significance level).

[5] Similar performance scores can be estimated for different class threshold settings.

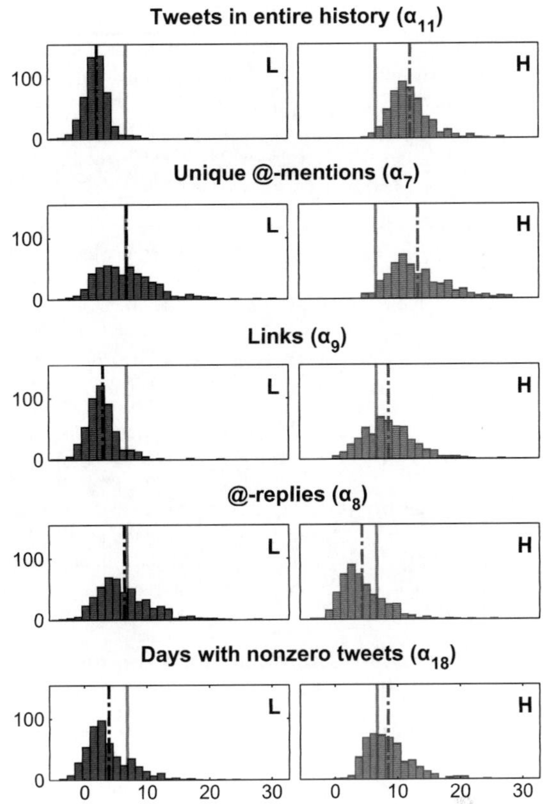

Figure 2: User impact distribution (x-axis: impact points, y-axis: # of user accounts) for users with a low (L) or a high (H) participation in a selection of relevant non-textual attributes. Dot-dashed lines denote the respective mean impact score; the red line is the mean of the entire sample (= 6.776).

6.2 Qualitative Analysis

Given the model's strong performance, we now conduct a more thorough analysis to identify and characterise the properties that affect aspects of the user impact. GP's length-scale parameters (ℓ_i) – which are inversely proportional to feature relevancy – are used for ranking feature importance. Note that since our data set consists of UK users, some results may be biased towards specific cultural properties.

Non-textual attributes. Table 3 lists the 10 most relevant attributes (or topics, where applicable) as extracted in each GP model. Ranking is determined by the mean value of the length-scale parameter for each feature in the 10-fold cross-validation process. We do not show feature ranking derived from the RR models as we focus on the models with the best performance. Despite this, it is worth mentioning

[6] Length-scales are comparable for features of the same variance (z-scored). Binary features (denoted by $\diamond$) are not z-scored, but for comparison purposes we have rescaled their length-scale using the feature's variance.

Label	$\mu(\ell) \pm \sigma(\ell)$	Cluster's words ranked by centrality	$\|c\|$
τ_1: Weather	3.73 ± 1.80	mph, humidity, barometer, gust, winds, hpa, temperature, kt, #weather [...]	309
τ_2: Healthcare Finance Housing	5.44 ± 1.55	nursing, nurse, rn, registered, bedroom, clinical, #news, estate, #hospital, rent, healthcare, therapist, condo, investment, furnished, medical, #nyc, occupational, investors, #ny, litigation, tutors, spacious, foreclosure [...]	1281
τ_3: Politics	6.07 ± 2.86	senate, republican, gop, police, arrested, voters, robbery, democrats, presidential, elections, charged, election, charges, #religion, arrest, repeal, dems, #christian, reform, democratic, pleads, #jesus, #atheism [...]	950
τ_4: Showbiz Movies TV	7.36 ± 2.25	damon, potter, #tvd, harry, elena, kate, portman, pattinson, hermione, jennifer, kristen, stefan, robert, catholic, stewart, katherine, lois, jackson, vampire, natalie, #vampirediaries, tempah, tinie, weasley, turner, rowland [...]	1943
τ_5: Commerce	7.83 ± 2.77	chevrolet, inventory, coupon, toyota, mileage, sedan, nissan, adde, jeep, 4x4, 2002, #coupon, enhanced, #deal, dodge, gmc, 20%, suv, 15%, 2005, 2003, 2006, coupons, discount, hatchback, purchase, #ebay, 10% [...]	608
τ_6: Twitter Hashtags	8.22 ± 2.98	#teamfollowback, #500aday, #tfb, #instantfollowback, #ifollowback, #instantfollow, #followback, #teamautofollow, #autofollow, #mustfollow [...]	194
τ_7: Social Unrest	8.37 ± 5.52	#egypt, #tunisia, #iran, #israel, #palestine, tunisia, arab, #jan25, iran, israel, protests, egypt, #yemen, #iranelection, israeli, #jordan, regime, yemen, #gaza, protesters, #lebanon, #syria, egyptian, #protest, #iraq [...]	321
τ_8: Non English	8.45 ± 3.80	yg, nak, gw, gue, kalo, itu, aku, aja, ini, gak, klo, sih, tak, mau, buat [...]	469
τ_9: Horoscope Gambling	9.11 ± 3.07	horoscope, astrology, zodiac, aries, libra, aquarius, pisces, taurus, virgo, capricorn, horoscopes, sagitarius, comprehensive, lottery, jackpot [...]	1354
τ_{10}: Religion Sports	10.29 ± 6.27	#jesustweeters, psalm, christ, #nhl, proverbs, unto, salvation, psalms, lord, kjv, righteousness, niv, bible, pastor, #mlb, romans, awards, nhl [...]	1610

Table 4: The 10 most relevant topics (for model AC, $|\tau| = 100$) in the prediction of a user's impact score together with their most central words. The topics are ranked by their mean length-scale, $\mu(\ell)$, in the 10-fold cross-validation process ($\sigma(\ell)$ is the respective standard deviation).

that RR's outputs also followed similar ranking patterns, e.g. the top 5 features in model A were a_{18}, a_7, a_3, a_{11} and a_9. Notice that across all models, among the strongest features are the total number of posts either in the entire account's history (a_{11}) or within the 365-day interval of our experiment (a_1) and the number of unique @-mentions (a_7), good indicators of user activity and user interaction respectively. Feature a_{13} is also a very good predictor, but is of limited utility for modelling our data set because very few accounts maintain the default profile photo (0.4%). Less relevant attributes (not shown) are the ones related to the location of a user (a_{16}, a_{17}) signalling that the whereabouts of a user may not necessarily relate to impact. Another low relevance attribute is the number of favourites that an account did (a_{10}), something reasonable, as those weak endorsements are not affecting the main stream of content updates in the social network.

In Figure 2, we present the distribution of user impact for accounts with low (left-side) and high (right-side) participation in a selection of non-textual attributes. Low (L) and high (H) participations are defined by selecting the 500 accounts with lowest and highest scores for this specific attribute. The means of (L) and (H) are compared with the mean impact score in our sample. As anticipated, accounts with low activity (a_{11}) are likely to be assigned impact scores far below the mean, while very active accounts may follow a quite opposite pattern. Avoiding mentioning (a_7) or replying (a_8) to others may not affect (on average) an impact score positively or negatively; however, accounts that do many unique @-mentions are distributed around a clearly higher impact score. On the other hand, users that overdo @-replies are distributed below the mean impact score. Furthermore, accounts that post irregularly with gaps longer than a day (a_{18}) or avoid using links in their tweets (a_9) will probably appear in the low impact score range.

Topics. Regarding prediction accuracy (Table 2), performance improves when topics are included. In turn, some of the topics replace non-textual attributes in the relevancy ranking (Table 3). Table 4 presents the 10 most relevant topic word-clusters based on their mean length-scale $\mu(\ell)$ in the 10-fold cross-validation process for the best performing GP model (AC, $|\tau| = 100$). We see that clusters with their most central words representing topics such as 'Weather', 'Healthcare/Finance', 'Politics' and 'Showbiz' come up on top.

Contrary to the non-textual attributes, accounts with low participation in a topic (for the vast majority of topics) were distributed along impact score values lower than the mean. Based on the fact that word clusters are not small in size, this is a rational outcome indicating that accounts with small word-frequency sums (i.e. the ones that do not tweet much) will more likely be users with small impact

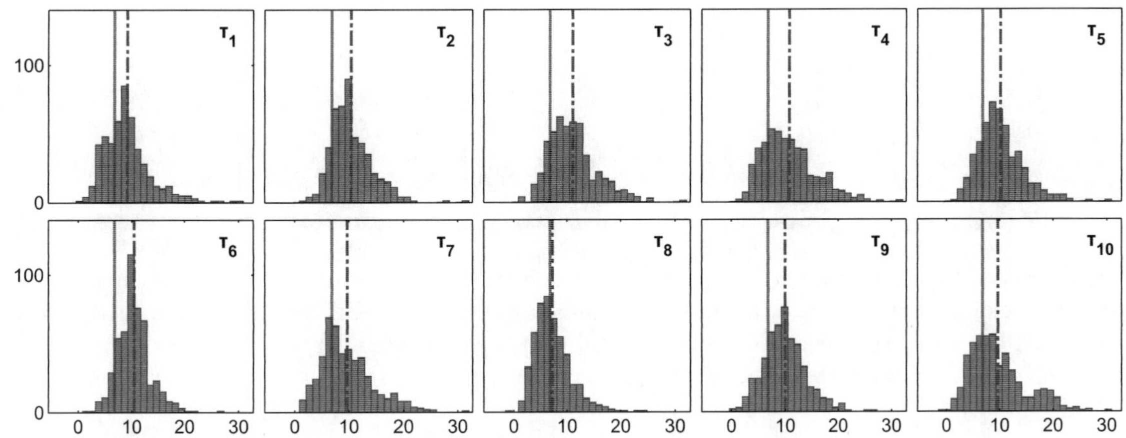

Figure 3: User impact distribution (x-axis: impact points, y-axis: # of user accounts) for accounts with a high participation in the 10 most relevant topics. Dot-dashed lines denote mean impact scores; the red line is the mean of the entire sample ($= 6.776$).

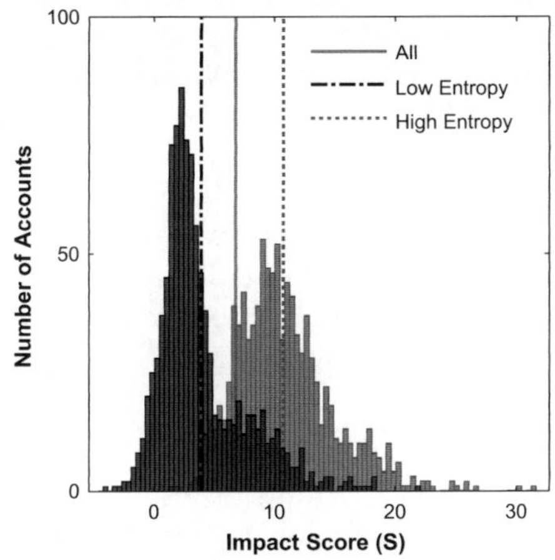

Figure 4: User impact distribution for accounts with high (blue) and low (dark grey) topic entropy. Lines denote the respective mean impact scores.

scores. Hence, in Figure 3 we only show the user impact distribution for the 500 accounts with the top participation in each topic. Informally, this is a way to quantify the contribution of each domain or topic of discussion in the impact score. Notice that the topics which 'push' users towards the highest impact scores fall into the domains of 'Politics' (τ_3) and 'Showbiz' (τ_4). An equally interesting observation is that engaging a lot about a specific topic will more likely result to a higher than average impact; the only exception is τ_8 which does not deviate from the mean, but τ_8 rather represents the use of a non-English language (Indonesian) and therefore, does not form an actual topic of discussion.

To further understand how participation in the 10 most relevant topics relates to impact, we also computed the joint user-topic entropy defined by

$$\mathrm{H}(u_i, \tau) = -\sum_{j=1}^{M} \mathrm{P}(u_i, \tau_j) \times \log_2 \mathrm{P}(u_i, \tau_j), \quad (9)$$

where u_i is a user and $M = 10$ (Shannon, 2001). This is a measure of user pseudo-informativeness, meaning that users with high entropy are considered as more informative (without assessing the quality of the information). Figure 4 shows the impact score distributions for the 500 accounts with the lowest and highest entropy. Low and high entropies are separated, with the former being placed clearly below the mean user impact score and the latter above. This pictorial assessment suggests that a connection between informativeness and impact may exist, at least in their extremes (their correlation in the entire sample is $r = .35$, $p < .001$).

Use case scenarios. Most of the previous analysis focused on the properties of single features. However, the user impact prediction models we learn depend on feature combinations. For that reason, it is of interest to investigate use case scenarios that bring various attributes together. To reduce notation in this paragraph, we use x_i^+ (x is either a non-textual attribute a or a topic τ) to express $x_i > \mu(x_i)$, the set of users for which the value of feature x_i is above the mean; equivalently $x_i^- : x_i < \mu(x_i)$. We also use τ_A^* to express the more complex set $\{\tau_A^+ \cap \tau_j^- \cap ... \cap \tau_z^-\}$, an intersection of users that are active in one topic (τ_A), but not very active in the rest. Figure 5 depicts the user impact distributions for five use case scenarios. Scenario A compares interactive to non interactive users, represented by $\mathrm{P}(a_1^+, a_6^+, a_7^+, a_8^+)$ and $\mathrm{P}(a_1^+, a_6^-, a_7^-, a_8^-)$ respectively; interactivity, defined by an intersection of accounts that tweet regularly, do many @-mentions and @-replies, but also

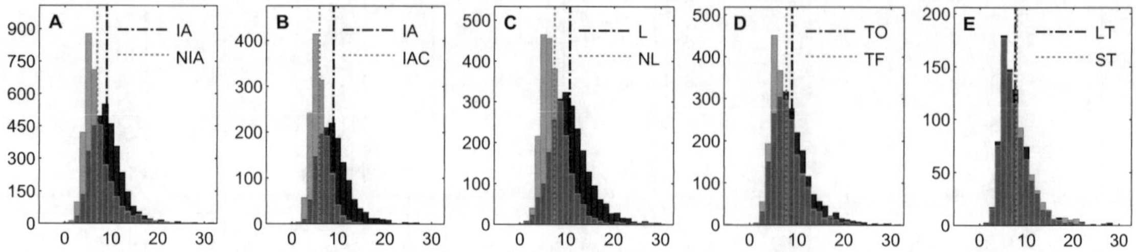

Figure 5: User impact distribution (x-axis: impact points, y-axis: # of user accounts) for five Twitter use scenarios based on subsets of the most relevant attributes and topics – IA: Interactive, IAC: Clique Interactive, L: Using many links, TO: Topic-Overall, TF: Topic-Focused, LT: 'Light' topics, ST: 'Serious' topics. (N) denotes negation and lines the respective mean impact scores.

mention many different users, seems to be rewarded on average with higher impact scores. Interactive users gain more impact than clique-interactive accounts represented by $\mathrm{P}(a_1^+, a_6^+, a_7^-, a_8^+)$, i.e. users who interact, but do not mention many different accounts, possibly because they are conducting discussions with a specific circle only (scenario B). The use of links when writing about the most prevalent topics ('Politics' and 'Showbiz') appears to be an important impact-wise factor (scenario C); the compared probability distributions in that case were $\mathrm{P}(a_1^+, (\tau_3^+ \cup \tau_4^+), a_9^+)$ against $\mathrm{P}(a_1^+, (\tau_3^+ \cup \tau_4^+), a_9^-)$. Surprisingly, when links were replaced by hashtags in the previous distributions, a clear class separation was not achieved. In scenario D, topic-focused accounts, i.e. users that write about one topic consistently, represented by $\mathrm{P}(a_1^+, (\tau_2^* \cup \tau_3^* \cup \tau_4^* \cup \tau_7^* \cup \tau_{10}^*))$, have on average slightly worse impact scores when compared to accounts tweeting about many topics, $\mathrm{P}(a_1^+, \tau_2^+, \tau_3^+, \tau_4^+, \tau_7^+, \tau_{10}^+)$. Finally, scenario E shows thats users engaging about more 'serious' topics, $\mathrm{P}(a_1^+, \tau_4^-, \tau_5^-, \tau_9^-, (\tau_3^+ \cup \tau_7^+))$, were not differentiated from the ones posting about more 'light' topics, $\mathrm{P}(a_1^+, (\tau_4^+ \cup \tau_5^+ \cup \tau_9^+), \tau_3^-, \tau_7^-)$.

7 Related Work

The task of user-impact prediction based on a machine learning approach that incorporates text features is novel, to the best of our knowledge. Despite this fact, our work is partly related to research approaches for quantifying and analysing user influence in online social networks. For example, Cha et al. (2010) compared followers, retweets and @-mentions received as measures of influence. Bakshy et al. (2011) aggregated all posts by each user, computed an individual-level influence and then tried to predict it by modelling user attributes (# of followers, followees, tweets and date of joining) together with past user influence. Their method, based on classification and regression trees (Breiman, 1984), achieved a modest performance ($r = .34$). Furthermore, Romero et al. (2011) proposed an algorithm for determining user influence and passivity based on information-forwarding activity, and Luo et al. (2013) exploited user attributes to predict retweet occurrences. The primary difference with all the works described above is that we aim to predict user impact by exploiting features under the user's direct control. Hence, our findings can be used as indirect insights for strategies that individual users may follow to increase their impact score. In addition, we incorporate the actual text posted by the users in the entire modelling process.

8 Conclusions and Future Work

We have introduced the task of user impact prediction on the microblogging platform of Twitter based on user-controlled textual and non-textual attributes. Nonlinear methods, in particular Gaussian Processes, were more suitable than linear approaches for this problem, providing a strong performance ($r = .78$). That result motivated the analysis of specific characteristics in the inferred model to further define and understand the elements that affect impact. In a nutshell, activity, non clique-oriented interactivity and engagement on a diverse set of topics are among the most decisive impact factors. In future work, we plan to improve various modelling components and gain a deeper understanding of the derived outcomes in collaboration with domain experts. For more general conclusions, the consideration of different cultures and media sources is essential.

Acknowledgments

This research was supported by EU-FP7-ICT project n.287863 ("TrendMiner"). Lampos also acknowledges the support from EPSRC IRC project EP/K031953/1.

References

Eytan Bakshy, Jake M. Hofman, Winter A. Mason, and Duncan J. Watts. 2011. Everyone's an influencer: quantifying influence on Twitter. In *4th International Conference on Web Search and Data Mining*, WSDM'11, pages 65–74.

Gerlof Bouma. 2009. Normalized (pointwise) mutual information in collocation extraction. In *Biennial GSCL Conference*, pages 31–40.

Danah Boyd, Scott Golder, and Gilad Lotan. 2010. Tweet, Tweet, Retweet: Conversational Aspects of Retweeting on Twitter. In *System Sciences*, HICSS'10, pages 1–10.

Leo Breiman. 1984. *Classification and regression trees*. Chapman & Hall.

Carlos Castillo, Marcelo Mendoza, and Barbara Poblete. 2011. Information credibility on Twitter. In *20th International Conference on World Wide Web*, WWW'11, pages 675–684.

Meeyoung Cha, Hamed Haddadi, Fabricio Benevenuto, and Krishna P. Gummadi. 2010. Measuring User Influence in Twitter: The Million Follower Fallacy. In *4th International Conference on Weblogs and Social Media*, ICWSM'10, pages 10–17.

Trevor Cohn and Lucia Specia. 2013. Modelling Annotator Bias with Multi-task Gaussian Processes: An Application to Machine Translation Quality Estimation. In *51st Annual Meeting of the Association for Computational Linguistics*, ACL'13, pages 32–42.

Arthur E. Hoerl and Robert W. Kennard. 1970. Ridge Regression: Biased Estimation for Nonorthogonal Problems. *Technometrics*, 12(1):55–67.

Matthew Hoffman, David Blei, and Francis Bach. 2010. Online Learning for Latent Dirichlet Allocation. In *Advances in Neural Information Processing Systems*, NIPS'10, pages 856–864.

Bernardo A. Huberman, Daniel M. Romero, and Fang Wu. 2009. Social Networks that Matter: Twitter Under the Microscope. *First Monday*, 14(1).

Haewoon Kwak, Changhyun Lee, Hosung Park, and Sue Moon. 2010. What is Twitter, a social network or a news media? In *19th International Conference on World Wide Web*, WWW'10, pages 591–600.

Vasileios Lampos and Nello Cristianini. 2012. Nowcasting Events from the Social Web with Statistical Learning. *ACM Transactions on Intelligent Systems and Technology*, 3(4):72:1–72:22.

Vasileios Lampos, Daniel Preoţiuc-Pietro, and Trevor Cohn. 2013. A user-centric model of voting intention from Social Media. In *51st Annual Meeting of the Association for Computational Linguistics*, ACL'13, pages 993–1003.

Zhunchen Luo, Miles Osborne, Jintao Tang, and Ting Wang. 2013. Who will retweet me?: finding retweeters in Twitter. In *36th International Conference on Research and Development in Information Retrieval*, SIGIR'13, pages 869–872.

Radford M. Neal. 1996. *Bayesian Learning for Neural Networks*. Springer.

Andrew Y. Ng, Michael I. Jordan, and Yair Weiss. 2002. On spectral clustering: Analysis and an algorithm. In *Advances in Neural Information Processing Systems*, NIPS'02, pages 849–856.

Daniel Preoţiuc-Pietro, Sina Samangooei, Trevor Cohn, Nicholas Gibbins, and Mahesan Niranjan. 2012. Trendminer: An Architecture for Real Time Analysis of Social Media Text. In *6th International Conference on Weblogs and Social Media*, ICWSM'12, pages 38–42.

Joaquin Quiñonero-Candela and Carl E. Rasmussen. 2005. A unifying view of sparse approximate Gaussian Process regression. *Journal of Machine Learning Research*, 6:1939–1959.

Carl E. Rasmussen and Christopher K. I. Williams. 2006. *Gaussian Processes for Machine Learning*. MIT Press.

Daniel M. Romero, Wojciech Galuba, Sitaram Asur, and Bernardo A. Huberman. 2011. Influence and Passivity in Social Media. In *Machine Learning and Knowledge Discovery in Databases*, volume 6913, pages 18–33.

Dominic Rout, Daniel Preoţiuc-Pietro, Bontcheva Kalina, and Trevor Cohn. 2013. Where's @wally: A classification approach to geolocating users based on their social ties. In *24th Conference on Hypertext and Social Media*, HT'13, pages 11–20.

Takeshi Sakaki, Makoto Okazaki, and Yutaka Matsuo. 2010. Earthquake shakes Twitter users: real-time event detection by social sensors. In *19th International Conference on World Wide Web*, WWW'10, pages 851–860.

Claude E. Shannon. 2001. A mathematical theory of communication. *SIGMOBILE Mob. Comput. Commun. Rev.*, 5(1):3–55 (reprint with corrections).

Jianbo Shi and Jitendra Malik. 2000. Normalized cuts and image segmentation. *Transactions on Pattern Analysis and Machine Intelligence*, 22(8):888–905.

Alex J. Smola and Bernhard Schölkopf. 2004. A tutorial on support vector regression. *Statistics and Computing*, 14(3):199–222.

Edward Snelson and Zoubin Ghahramani. 2006. Sparse Gaussian Processes using Pseudo-inputs. In *Advances in Neural Information Processing Systems*, NIPS'06, pages 1257–1264.

Bongwon Suh, Lichan Hong, Peter Pirolli, and Ed H. Chi. 2010. Want to be Retweeted? Large Scale Analytics on Factors Impacting Retweet in Twitter Network. In *Social Computing*, SocialCom'10, pages 177–184.

Vladimir N. Vapnik. 1998. *Statistical learning theory*. Wiley.

Ulrike von Luxburg. 2007. A tutorial on spectral clustering. *Statistics and computing*, 17(4):395–416.

Christopher K. I. Williams and Carl E. Rasmussen. 1996. Gaussian Processes for Regression. In *Advances in Neural Information Processing Systems*, NIPS'96, pages 514–520.

A Knowledge-based Representation for Cross-Language Document Retrieval and Categorization

Marc Franco-Salvador[1,2], **Paolo Rosso**[2] and **Roberto Navigli**[1]
[1] Department of Computer Science
Sapienza Università di Roma, Italy
{francosalvador,navigli}@di.uniroma1.it
[2] Natural Language Engineering Lab - PRHLT Research Center
Universitat Politècnica de València, Spain
{mfranco,prosso}@dsic.upv.es

Abstract

Current approaches to cross-language document retrieval and categorization are based on discriminative methods which represent documents in a low-dimensional vector space. In this paper we propose a shift from the supervised to the knowledge-based paradigm and provide a document similarity measure which draws on BabelNet, a large multilingual knowledge resource. Our experiments show state-of-the-art results in cross-lingual document retrieval and categorization.

1 Introduction

The huge amount of text that is available online is becoming ever increasingly multilingual, providing an additional wealth of useful information. Most of this information, however, is not easily accessible to the majority of users because of language barriers which hamper the cross-lingual search and retrieval of knowledge.

Today's search engines would benefit greatly from effective techniques for the cross-lingual retrieval of valuable information that can satisfy a user's needs by not only providing (Landauer and Littman, 1994) and translating (Munteanu and Marcu, 2005) relevant results into different languages, but also by reranking the results in a language of interest on the basis of the importance of search results in other languages.

Vector-based models are typically used in the literature for representing documents both in monolingual and cross-lingual settings (Manning et al., 2008). However, because of the large size of the vocabulary, having each term as a component of the vector makes the document representation very sparse. To address this issue several approaches to dimensionality reduction have been proposed, such as Principal Component Analysis (Jolliffe, 1986), Latent Semantic Indexing (Hull, 1994), Latent Dirichlet Allocation (LDA) (Blei et al., 2003) and variants thereof, which project these vectors into a lower-dimensional vector space. In order to enable multilinguality, the vectors of comparable documents written in different languages are concatenated, making up the document matrix which is then reduced using linear projection (Platt et al., 2010; Yih et al., 2011). However, to do so, comparable documents are needed as training. Additionally, the lower dimensional representations are not of easy interpretation.

The availability of wide-coverage lexical knowledge resources extracted automatically from Wikipedia, such as DBPedia (Bizer et al., 2009), YAGO (Hoffart et al., 2013) and BabelNet (Navigli and Ponzetto, 2012a), has considerably boosted research in several areas, especially where multilinguality is a concern (Hovy et al., 2013). Among these latter are cross-language plagiarism detection (Potthast et al., 2011; Franco-Salvador et al., 2013), multilingual semantic relatedness (Navigli and Ponzetto, 2012b; Nastase and Strube, 2013) and semantic alignment (Navigli and Ponzetto, 2012a; Matuschek and Gurevych, 2013). One main advantage of knowledge-based methods is that they provide a human-readable, semantically interconnected, representation of the textual item at hand (be it a sentence or a document).

Following this trend, in this paper we provide a knowledge-based representation of documents which goes beyond the lexical surface of text, while at the same time avoiding the need for training in a cross-language setting. To achieve this we leverage a multilingual semantic network, i.e., BabelNet, to obtain language-independent representations, which contain concepts together with semantic relations between them, and also include semantic knowledge which is just implied by the input text. The integration of our multilingual graph model with a vector representation enables us to obtain state-of-the-art results in comparable document retrieval and cross-language text categorization.

2 Related Work

The mainstream representation of documents for monolingual and cross-lingual document retrieval is vector-based. A document vector, whose components quantify the relevance of each term in the document, is usually highly dimensional, because of the variety of terms used in a document collection. As a consequence, the resulting document matrices are very sparse. To address the data sparsity issue, several approaches to the reduction of dimensionality of document vectors have been proposed in the literature. A popular class of methods is based on linear projection, which provides a low-dimensional mapping from a high dimensional vector space. A historical approach to linear projection is Principal Component Analysis (PCA) (Jolliffe, 1986), which performs a singular value decomposition (SVD) on a document matrix D of size $n \times m$, where each row in D is the term vector representation of a document. PCA uses an orthogonal transformation to convert a set of observations of possibly correlated variables into a set of values of linearly uncorrelated variables called principal components, which make up the low-dimensional vector. Latent Semantic Analysis (LSA) (Deerwester et al., 1990) is very similar to PCA but performs the SVD using the correlation matrix instead of the covariance matrix, which implies a lower computational cost. LSA preserves the amount of variance in an eigenvector $\vec{v}$ by maximizing its Rayleigh ratio: $\frac{\vec{v}^T C \vec{v}}{\vec{v}^T \vec{v}}$, where $C = D^T D$ is the correlation matrix of D.

A generalization of PCA, called Oriented Principal Component Analysis (OPCA) (Diamantaras and Kung, 1996), is based on a noise covariance matrix to project the similar components of D closely. Other projection models such as Latent Dirichlet Allocation (LDA) (Blei et al., 2003) are based on the extraction of generative models from documents. Another approach, named Explicit Semantic Analysis (ESA) (Gabrilovich and Markovitch, 2007), represents each document by its similarities to a document collection. Using a low domain specificity document collection such as Wikipedia, the model has proven to obtain competitive results.

Not only have these methods proven to be successful in a monolingual scenario (Deerwester et al., 1990; Hull, 1994), but they have also been adapted to perform well in tasks at a cross-language level (Potthast et al., 2008; Platt et al., 2010; Yih et al., 2011). Cross-language Latent Semantic Indexing (CL-LSI) (Dumais et al., 1997) was the first linear projection approach used in cross-lingual tasks. CL-LSI provides a cross-lingual representation for documents by reducing the dimensionality of a matrix D whose rows are obtained by concatenating comparable documents from different languages. Similarly, PCA and OPCA can be adapted to a multilingual setting. LDA was also adapted to perform in a multilingual scenario with models such as Polylingual Topic Models (Mimno et al., 2009), Joint Probabilistic LSA and Coupled Probabilistic LSA (Platt et al., 2010), which, however, are constrained to using word counts, instead of better weighting strategies, such as log(tf)-idf, known to perform better with large vocabularies (Salton and McGill, 1986). Another variant, named Canonical Correlation Analysis (CCA) (Thompson, 2005), uses a cross-covariance matrix of the low-dimensional vectors to find the projections. Cross-language Explicit Semantic Analysis (CL-ESA) (Potthast et al., 2008; Cimiano et al., 2009; Potthast et al., 2011), instead, adapts ESA to be used at cross-language level by exploiting the comparable documents across languages from Wikipedia. CL-ESA represents each document written in a language L by its similarities with a document collection in the same language L. Using a multilingual document collection with comparable documents across languages, the resulting vectors from different languages can be compared directly.

An alternative unsupervised approach, Cross-language Character n-Grams (CL-CNG) (Mcnamee and Mayfield, 2004), does not draw upon linear projections and represents documents as vectors of character n-grams. It has proven to obtain good results in cross-language document retrieval (Potthast et al., 2011) between languages with lexical and syntactic similarities.

Recently, a novel supervised linear projection model based on Siamese Neural Networks (S2Net) (Yih et al., 2011) achieved state-of-the-art performance in comparable document retrieval. S2Net performs a linear combination of the terms of a document vector $\vec{d}$ to obtain a reduced vector $\vec{r}$, which is the output layer of a neural network. Each element in $\vec{r}$ has a weight which is a linear combination of the original weights of $\vec{d}$, and captures relationships between the original terms.

However, linear projection approaches need a high number of training documents to achieve state-of-the-art performance (Platt et al., 2010; Yih et al., 2011). Moreover, although they are good at identifying a few principal components, the representations produced are opaque, in that they cannot explicitly model the semantic content of documents with a human-interpretable representation, thereby making the data analysis difficult. In this paper, instead, we propose a language-independent knowledge graph representation for documents which is obtained from a large multilingual semantic network, without using any training information. Our knowledge graph representation explicitly models the semantics of the document in terms of the concepts and relations evoked by its co-occurring terms.

3 A Knowledge-based Document Representation

We propose a knowledge-based document representation aimed at expanding the terms in a document's bag of words by means of a knowledge graph which provides concepts and semantic relations between them. Key to our approach is the use of a graph representation which does not depend on any given language, but, indeed, is multilingual. To build knowledge graphs of this kind we utilize BabelNet, a multilingual semantic network that we present in Section 3.1. Then, in Section 3.2, we describe the five steps needed to obtain our graph-based multilingual representation of documents. Finally, we introduce our knowledge graph similarity measure in Section 3.3.

3.1 BabelNet

BabelNet (Navigli and Ponzetto, 2012a) is a multilingual semantic network whose concepts and relations are obtained from the largest available semantic lexicon of English, WordNet (Fellbaum, 1998), and the largest wide-coverage collaboratively-edited encyclopedia, Wikipedia, by means of an automatic mapping algorithm. BabelNet is therefore a multilingual "encyclopedic dictionary" that combines lexicographic information with wide-coverage encyclopedic knowledge. Concepts in BabelNet are represented similarly to WordNet, i.e., by grouping sets of synonyms in the different languages into multilingual synsets. Multilingual synsets contain lexicalizations from WordNet synsets, the corresponding Wikipedia pages and additional translations output by a statistical machine translation system. The relations between synsets are collected from WordNet and from Wikipedia's hyperlinks between pages.

We note that, in principle, we could use any multilingual network providing a similar kind of information, e.g., EuroWordNet (Vossen, 2004). However, in our work we chose BabelNet because of its larger size, its coverage of both lexicographic and encyclopedic knowledge, and its free availability.[1] In our work we used BabelNet 1.0, which encodes knowledge for six languages, namely: Catalan, English, French, German, Italian and Spanish.

3.2 From Document to Knowledge Graph

We now introduce our five-step method for representing a given document d from a collection D of documents written in language L as a language-independent knowledge graph.

Building a Basic Vector Representation Initially we transform a document d into a traditional vector representation. To do this, we score each term $t_i \in d$ with a weight w_i. This weight is usually a function of term and document frequency. Following the literature, one method that works well is the log tf-idf weighting (Salton et al., 1983; Salton and McGill, 1986):

$$w_i = log_2(f_i + 1)log_2(n/n_i). \quad (1)$$

where f_i is the number of times term i occurs in document d, n is the total number of documents in the collection and n_i is the number of documents that contain t_i. We then create a weighted term vector $\vec{v} = (w_1, ..., w_n)$, where w_i is the weight corresponding to term t_i. We exclude stopwords from the vector.

Selecting the Relevant Document Terms We then create the set T of base forms, i.e., lemmas[2], of the terms in the document d. In order to keep only the most relevant terms, we sort the terms T according to their weight in vector $\vec{v}$ and retain a maximum number of K terms, obtaining a set of terms T_K.[3] The value of K is calculated as a function of the vector size, as follows:

$$K = (log_2(1 + |\vec{v}|))^2, \quad (2)$$

The rationale is that K must be high enough to ensure a good conceptual representation but not too high, so as to avoid as much noise as possible in the set T_K.

Populating the Graph with Initial Concepts Next, we create an initially-empty knowledge graph $G = (V, E)$, i.e., such that $V = E = \emptyset$.

We populate the vertex set V with the set S_K of all the synsets in BabelNet which contain any term in T_K in the document language L, that is:

[1] http://babelnet.org

[2] Following the setup of (Platt et al., 2010), our initial data is represented using term vectors. For this reason we lemmatize in this step.

[3] Since the vector $\vec{v}$ provides weights for all the word forms, and not only lemmas, occurring in d, we take the best weight among those word forms of the considered lemma.

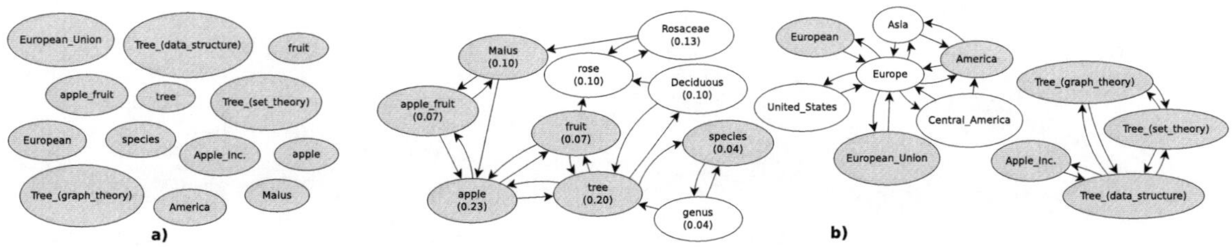

Figure 1: (a) initial graph from $T_K = \{$"European", "apple", "tree", "Malus", "species", "America"$\}$; (b) knowledge graph obtained by retrieving all paths from BabelNet. Gray nodes are the original concepts.

$$S_K = \bigcup_{t \in T_K} Synsets_L(t), \quad (3)$$

where $Synsets_L(t)$ is the set of synsets in BabelNet which contain a term t in the language of interest L. For example, in Figure 1(a) we show the initial graph obtained from the set $T_K = \{$"European", "apple", "tree", "Malus", "species", "America"$\}$. Note, however, that each retrieved synset is multilingual, i.e., it contains lexicalizations for the same concept in other languages too. Therefore, the nodes of our knowledge graph provide a language-independent representation of the document's content.

Creating the Knowledge Graph Similarly to Navigli and Lapata (2010), we create the knowledge graph by searching BabelNet for paths connecting pairs of synsets in V. Formally, for each pair $v, v' \in V$ such that v and v' do not share any lexicalization[4] in T_K, for each path in BabelNet $v \rightarrow v_1 \rightarrow \ldots \rightarrow v_n \rightarrow v'$, we set: $V := V \cup \{v_1, \ldots, v_n\}$ and $E := E \cup \{(v, v_1), \ldots, (v_n, v')\}$, that is, we add all the path vertices and edges to G. After prototyping, the path length is limited to maximum length 3, so as to avoid an excessive semantic drift.

As a result of populating the graph with intermediate edges and vertices, we obtain a knowledge graph which models the semantic context of document d. We point out that our knowledge graph might have different isolated components. We view each component as a different interpretation of document d. To select the main interpretation, we keep only the largest component, i.e., the one with the highest number of vertices, which we consider as the most likely semantic representation of the document content.

Figure 1(b) shows the knowledge graph obtained for our example term set. Note that our approach retains, and therefore weights, only the subgraph focused on the "apple fruit" meaning.

[4]This prevents different senses of the same term from being connected via a path in the resulting knowledge graph.

Knowledge Graph Weighting The final step consists of weighting all the concepts and semantic relations of the knowledge graph G. For weighting relations we use the original weights from BabelNet, which provide the degree of relatedness between the synset end points of each edge (Navigli and Ponzetto, 2012a). As for concepts, we weight them on the basis of the original weights of the terms in the vector $\vec{v}$. In order to score each concept in our knowledge graph G, we applied the topic-sensitive PageRank algorithm (Haveliwala et al., 2003) to G. While the well-known PageRank algorithm (Page et al., 1998) calculates the global importance of vertices in a graph, topic-sensitive PageRank is a variant in which the importance of vertices is biased using a set of representative "topics". Formally, the topic-sensitive PageRank vector $\vec{p}$ is calculated by means of an iterative process until convergence as follows: $\vec{p} = cM\vec{p} + (1-c)\vec{u}$, where c is the damping factor (conventionally set to 0.85), $1 - c$ represents the probability of a surfer randomly jumping to any node in the graph, M is the transition probability matrix of graph G, with $M_{ji} = degree(i)^{-1}$ if an edge from i to j exists, 0 otherwise, $\vec{u}$ is the random-jumping transition probability vector, where each u_i represents the probability of jumping randomly to the node i, and $\vec{p}$ is the resulting PageRank vector which scores the nodes of G. In contrast to vanilla PageRank, the "topic-sensitive" variant gives more probability mass to some nodes in G and less to others. In our case we perturbate $\vec{u}$ by concentrating the probability mass to the vertices in S_K, which are the synsets corresponding to the document terms T_K (cf. Formula 3).

3.3 Similarity between Knowledge Graphs

We can now determine the similarity between two documents $d, d' \in D$ in terms of the similarity of their knowledge graph representations G and G'.

Following the literature (Montes y Gómez et al., 2001) we calculate the similarity between the vertex sets in the two graphs using Dice's coefficient (Jackson et al., 1989):

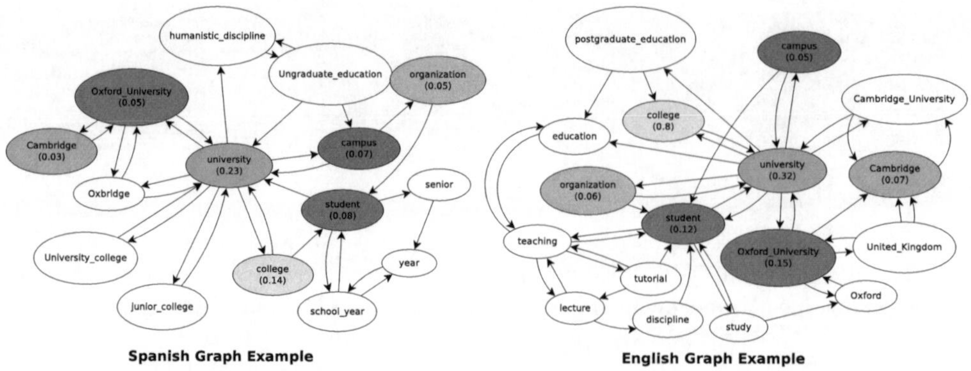

Figure 2: Knowledge graph examples from two comparable documents in different languages.

$$S_c(G,G') = \frac{2 \cdot \sum\limits_{c \in V(G) \cap V(G')} w(c)}{\sum\limits_{c \in V(G)} w(c) + \sum\limits_{c \in V(G')} w(c)}, \quad (4)$$

where $w(c)$ is the weight of a concept c (see Section 3.2). Likewise, we calculate the similarity between the two edge sets as:

$$S_r(G,G') = \frac{2 \cdot \sum\limits_{r \in E(G) \cap E(G')} w(r)}{\sum\limits_{r \in E(G)} w(r) + \sum\limits_{r \in E(G')} w(r)}, \quad (5)$$

where $w(r)$ is the weight of a semantic relation edge r.

We combine the two above measures of conceptual (S_c) and relational (S_r) similarity to obtain an integrated measure $S_g(G,G')$ between knowledge graphs:

$$S_g(G,G') = \frac{S_c(G,G') + S_r(G,G')}{2}. \quad (6)$$

Notably, since we are working with a language-independent representation of documents, this similarity measure can be applied to the knowledge graphs built from documents written in any language. In Figure 2 we show two knowledge graphs for comparable documents written in different languages (for clarity, labels are in English in both graphs). As expected, the graphs share several key concepts and relations.

4 A Multilingual Vector Representation

4.1 From Document to Multilingual Vector

Since our knowledge graphs will only cover the most central concepts of a document, we complement this core representation with a more traditional vector-based representation. However, as we are interested in the cross-language comparison of documents, we translate our monolingual vector $\vec{v}_L$ of a document d written in language L into its corresponding vector $\vec{v}_{L'}$ in language L' using BabelNet as our multilingual dictionary. We detail the document-vector translation process in Algorithm 1.

Algorithm 1 Dictionary-based term-vector translation.

Input: a weighted document vector $\vec{v}_L = (w_1, \ldots, w_n)$, a source language L and a target language L'
Output: a translated vector $\vec{v}_{L'}$

```
1: v_L' ← (0, ..., 0) of length n
2: for i = 1 to n
3:   if w_i = 0 continue
4:   // let t_i be the term corresponding to w_i in v_L
5:   S_L ← Synsets_L(t_i)
6:   for each synset s ∈ S_L
7:     T ← getTranslations(s, L')
8:     if T ≠ ∅ then
9:       for each tr ∈ T
10:        w_new = w_i · confidence(tr, t_i)
11:        // let index(tr) be the index of tr in v_L
12:        if ∃ index(tr) then
13:          v_L'(index(tr)) = w_new
14: return v_L'
```

The translated vector $\vec{v}_{L'}$ is obtained as follows: for each term t_i with non-zero weight in v_L we obtain all the possible meanings of t_i in BabelNet (see line 5) and, for each of these, we retrieve all the translations (line 7), i.e., lexicalizations of the concept, in language L' available in the synset. We set a non-zero value in the translation vector $\vec{v}_{L'}$,[5] in correspondence with each such translation tr, proportional to the weight of t_i in the original vector and the confidence of the translation (line 10), as provided by the BabelNet semantic network.[6]

In order to increase the amount of information available in the vector and counterbalance possible wrong translations, we avoid translating all vectors to one language. Instead, in the present work we create a multilingual vector representation of a

[5]To make the translation possible, while at the same time keeping the same number of dimensions in our vector representation, we use a shared vocabulary which covers both languages. See Section 6 for details on the experimental setup.

[6]Non-English lexicalizations in BabelNet have confidence 1 if originating from Wikipedia inter-language links and ≤ 1 if obtained by means of statistical machine translation (Navigli and Ponzetto, 2012a).

document d written in language L by concatenating the corresponding vector $\vec{v}_L$ with the translated vector $\vec{v}_{L'}$ of d for language L'. As a result, we obtain a multilingual vector $\vec{v}_{LL'}$, which contains lexicalizations in both languages.

4.2 Similarity between Multilingual Vectors

Following common practice for document similarity in the literature (Manning et al., 2008), we use the cosine similarity as the similarity measure between multilingual vectors:

$$S_v(\vec{v}_{LL'}, \vec{v}'_{LL'}) = \frac{\vec{v}_{LL'} \cdot \vec{v}'_{LL'}}{||\vec{v}_{LL'}|| \, ||\vec{v}'_{LL'}||}. \tag{7}$$

5 Knowledge-based Document Similarity

Given a source document d and a target document d', we calculate the similarities between the respective knowledge-graph and multilingual vector representations, and combine them to obtain a knowledge-based similarity as follows:

$$KBSim(d, d') = c(G)S_g(G, G') + (1 - c(G))S_v(\vec{v}_{LL'}, \vec{v}'_{LL'}), \tag{8}$$

where $c(G)$ is an interpolation factor calculated as the edge density of knowledge graph G:

$$c(G) = \frac{|E(G)|}{|V(G)|(|V(G)| - 1)}. \tag{9}$$

Note that, using the factor $c(G)$ to interpolate the two similarities in Eq. 8, we determine the relevance for the knowledge graphs and the multilingual vectors in a dynamic way. Indeed, $c(G)$ makes the contribution of graph similarity depend on the richness of the knowledge graph.

6 Evaluation

In this section we compare our knowledge-based document similarity measure, KBSim, against state-of-the-art models on two different tasks: comparable document retrieval and cross-lingual text categorization.

6.1 Comparable Document Retrieval

In our first experiment we determine the effectiveness of our knowledge-based approach in a comparable document retrieval task. Given a document d written in language L and a collection $D_{L'}$ of documents written in another language L', the task of comparable document retrieval consists of finding the document in $D_{L'}$ which is most similar to d, under the assumption that there exists one document $d' \in D_{L'}$ which is comparable with d.

6.1.1 Corpus and Task Setting

Dataset We followed the experimental setting described in (Platt et al., 2010; Yih et al., 2011) and evaluated KBSim on the Wikipedia dataset made available by the authors of those papers. The dataset is composed of Wikipedia comparable encyclopedic entries in English and Spanish. For each document in English there exists a "real" pair in Spanish which was defined as a comparable entry by the Wikipedia user community. The dataset of each language was split into three parts: 43,380 training, 8,675 development and 8,675 test documents. The documents were tokenized, without stemming, and represented as vectors using a log(tf)-idf weighting (Salton and Buckley, 1988). The vocabulary of the corpus was restricted to 20,000 terms, which were the most frequent terms in the two languages after removing the top 50 terms.

Methodology To evaluate the models we compared each English document against the Spanish dataset and vice versa. Following the original setting, the results are given as the average performance between these two experiments. For evaluation we employed the averaged top-1 accuracy and Mean Reciprocal Rank (MMR) at finding the real comparable document in the other language. We compared KBSim against the state-of-the-art supervised models S2Net, OPCA, CCA, and CL-LSI (cf. Section 2). In contrast to these models, KBSim does not need a training step, so we applied it directly to the testing partition.

In addition we also included the results of CL-ESA[7], CL-C3G[8] and two simple vector-based models which translate all documents into English on a word-by-word basis and compared them using cosine similarity: the first model (CosSim$_E$) uses a statistical dictionary trained with Europarl using Wavelet-Domain Hidden Markov Models (He, 2007), a model similar to IBM Model 4; the second model (CosSim$_{BN}$) instead uses Algorithm 1 to translate the vectors with BabelNet.

6.1.2 Results

As we can see from Table 1,[9] the CosSim$_{BN}$ model, which uses BabelNet to translate the document vectors, achieves better results than CCA and CL-LSI. We hypothesize that this is due to these linear projection models losing information during the projection. CosSim$_E$ yields results similar to CosSim$_{BN}$, showing that BabelNet is a good alternative statistical dictionary. In contrast to CCA

[7]Document collections with sizes higher than 10^5 provide high performance (Potthast et al., 2008). Here we used 15k documents from the training set to index the test documents.

[8]CL-C3G is CL-CNG using character 3-grams, which has proven to be the best length (Mcnamee and Mayfield, 2004).

[9]In this work, statistically significant results according to a χ^2 test are highlighted in bold.

Model	Dimension	Accuracy	MMR
S2Net	2000	**0.7447**	0.7973
KBSim	N/A	**0.7342**	0.7750
OPCA	2000	**0.7255**	0.7734
CosSim_E	N/A	0.7033	0.7467
CosSim_{BN}	N/A	0.7029	0.7550
CCA	1500	0.6894	0.7378
CL-LSI	5000	0.5302	0.6130
CL-ESA	15000	0.2660	0.3305
CL-C3G	N/A	0.2511	0.3025

Table 1: Test results for comparable document retrieval in Wikipedia. S2Net, OPCA, CosSim_E, CCA and CL-LSI are from (Yih et al., 2011).

Model	Dim.	EN News Accuracy	ES News Accuracy
KBSim	N/A	0.8189	**0.6997**
Full MT	50	**0.8483**	0.6484
CosSim_{BN}	N/A	0.8023	**0.6737**
OPCA	100	**0.8412**	0.5954
CCA	150	**0.8388**	0.5323
CL-LSI	5000	**0.8401**	0.5105
CosSim_E	N/A	0.8046	0.4481

Table 2: Test results for cross-language text categorization. Full MT, OPCA, CCA, CL-LSI and CosSim_E are from (Platt et al., 2010).

and CL-LSI, OPCA performs better thanks to its improved projection method using a noise covariance matrix, which enables it to obtain the main components in a low-dimensional space.

CL-C3G and CL-ESA obtain the lowest results. Considering that English and Spanish do not have many lexical similarities, the low performance of CL-C3G is justified because these languages do not share many character n-grams. The reason behind the low results of CL-ESA can be explained by the low number of intersecting concepts between Spanish and English in Wikipedia, as confirmed by Potthast et al. (2008). Despite both using Wikipedia in some way, KBSim obtains much higher performance than CL-ESA thanks to the use of our multilingual knowledge graph representation of documents, which makes it possible to expand and semantically relate its original concepts. As a result, in contrast to CL-ESA, KBSim can integrate conceptual and relational similarity functions which provide more accurate performance. Interestingly, KBSim also outperforms OPCA which, in contrast to our system, is supervised, and in terms of accuracy is only 1 point below S2Net, the supervised state-of-the-art model using neural networks.

6.2 Cross-language Text Categorization

The second task in which we tested the different models was cross-language text categorization. The task is defined as follows: given a document d_L in a language L and a corpus $D'_{L'}$ with documents in a different language L', and C possible categories, a system has to classify d_L into one of the categories C using the labeled collection $D'_{L'}$.

6.2.1 Corpus and Task Setting

Dataset To perform this task we used the Multilingual Reuters Collection (Amini et al., 2009), which is composed of five datasets of news from five different languages (English, French, German, Spanish and Italian) and classified into six possible categories. In addition, each dataset of news is translated into the other four languages using the Portage translation system (Sadat et al., 2005). As a result, we have five different multilingual datasets, each containing source news documents in one language and four sets of translated documents in the other languages. Each of the languages has an independent vocabulary. Document vectors in the collection are created using TFIDF-based weighting.

Methodology To evaluate our approach we used the English and Spanish news datasets. From the English news dataset we randomly selected 13,131 news as training and 1,875 as test documents. From the Spanish news dataset we selected all 12,342 news as test documents. To classify both test sets we used the English news training set. We performed the experiment at cross-lingual level using Spanish and English languages available for both Spanish and English news datasets, therefore we classified each test set selecting the documents in English and using the Spanish documents in the training dataset, and vice versa. We followed Platt et al. (2010) and averaged the values obtained from the two comparisons for each test set to obtain the final result. To categorize the documents we applied k-NN to the ranked list of documents according to the similarity measure employed for each model. We evaluated each model by estimating its accuracy in the classification of the English and Spanish test sets.

We compared our approach against the state-of-the-art supervised models in this task: OPCA, CCA and CL-LSI (Platt et al., 2010). In addition, we include the results of the CosSim_{BN} and CosSim_E models that we introduced in Section 6.1.1, as well as the results of a full statistical machine translation system trained with Europarl and post-processed by LSA (Full MT), as reported by Platt et al. (2010).

6.2.2 Results

Table 2 shows the cross-language text categorization accuracy. CosSim_E obtained the lowest results. This is because there is a significant number of untranslated terms in the translation process that the statistical dictionary cannot cover. This is not the case in the CosSim_{BN} model which achieves higher results using BabelNet as a statistical dictionary, especially on the Spanish news corpus.

On the other hand, however, the linear projection methods as well as Full MT obtained the highest results on the English corpus. The differences between the linear projection methods are evident when looking at the Spanish corpus results; OPCA performed best with a considerable improvement, which indicates again that it is one of the most effective linear projection methods. Finally, our approach, KBSim, obtained competitive results on the English corpus, performing best among the unsupervised systems, and the highest results on the Spanish news, surpassing all alternatives.

Since KBSim does not need any training for document comparison, and because it based, moreover, on a multilingual lexical resource, we performed an additional experiment to demonstrate its ability to carry out the same text categorization task in many languages. To do this, we used the Multilingual Reuters Collection to create a 3,000 document test dataset and 9,000 training dataset[10] for five languages: English, German, Spanish, French and Italian. Then we calculated the classification accuracy on each test set using each training set. Results are shown in Table 3.

The best results for each language were obtained when working at the monolingual level, which suggests that KBSim might be a good untrained alternative in monolingual tasks, too. In general, cross-language comparisons produced similar results, demonstrating the general applicability of KBSim to arbitrary language pairs in multilingual text categorization. However, we note that German, Italian and Spanish training partitions produced low results compared to the others. After analyzing the length of the documents in the different datasets we discovered that they have different average lengths in words: 79 (EN), 76 (FR), 75 (DE), 60 (ES) and 55 (IT). German, Spanish and especially Italian documents have the lowest average length, which makes it more difficult to build a representative knowledge graph of the content of each document when it is performing at cross-language level.

[10]Note that training is needed for the k-NN classifier, but not for document comparison.

Testing	Training datasets				
datasets	DE	EN	ES	FR	IT
DE	0.8053	0.6872	0.5373	0.6417	0.5920
EN	0.5827	0.8463	0.5540	0.6530	0.5820
ES	0.5883	0.6153	0.8707	0.6237	0.7010
FR	0.6867	0.7103	0.6667	0.8227	0.6887
IT	0.5973	0.5487	0.6263	0.5973	0.8317

Table 3: KBSim accuracy in a multilingual setup.

7 Conclusions

In this paper we introduced a knowledge-based approach to represent and compare documents written in different languages. The two main contributions of this work are: i) a new graph-based model for the language-independent representation of documents based on the BabelNet multilingual semantic network; ii) KBSim, a knowledge-based cross-language similarity measure between documents, which integrates our multilingual graph-based model with a traditional vector representation.

In two different cross-lingual tasks, i.e., comparable document retrieval and cross-language text categorization, KBSim has proven to perform on a par or better than the supervised state-of-the-art models which make use of linear projections to obtain the main components of the term vectors. We remark that, in contrast to the best systems in the literature, KBSim does not need any parameter tuning phase nor does it use any training information. Moreover, when scaling to many languages, supervised systems need to be trained on each pair, which can be very costly.

The gist of our approach is in the knowledge graph representation of documents, which relates the original terms using expanded concepts and relations from BabelNet. The knowledge graphs also have the nice feature of being human-interpretable, a feature that we want to exploit in future work. We will also explore the integration of linear projection models, such as OPCA and S2Net, into our multilingual vector-based similarity measure. Also, to ensure a level playing field, following the competing models, in this work we did not use multi-word expressions as vector components. We will study their impact on KBSim in future work.

Acknowledgments

The authors gratefully acknowledge the support of the ERC Starting Grant MultiJEDI No. 259234, EC WIQ-EI IRSES (Grant No. 269180) and MICINN DIANA-Applications (TIN2012-38603-C02-01). Thanks go to Yih et al. for their support and Jim McManus for his comments.

References

Massih-Reza Amini, Nicolas Usunier, and Cyril Goutte. 2009. Learning from multiple partially observed views - an application to multilingual text categorization. In *Advances in Neural Information Processing Systems 22 (NIPS 2009)*, pages 28–36.

Christian Bizer, Jens Lehmann, Georgi Kobilarov, Sören Auer, Christian Becker, Richard Cyganiak, and Sebastian Hellmann. 2009. Dbpedia - a crystallization point for the web of data. *J. Web Sem.*, 7(3):154–165.

David M. Blei, Andrew Y. Ng, and Michael I. Jordan. 2003. Latent dirichlet allocation. *the Journal of machine Learning research*, 3:993–1022.

Philipp Cimiano, Antje Schultz, Sergej Sizov, Philipp Sorg, and Steffen Staab. 2009. Explicit versus latent concept models for cross-language information retrieval. In *Proceedings of the International Joint Conference on Artificial Intelligence (IJCAI)*, volume 9, pages 1513–1518.

Scott Deerwester, Susan T. Dumais, George W. Furnas, Thomas K. Landauer, and Richard Harshman. 1990. Indexing by latent semantic analysis. *Journal of the American society for information science*, 41(6):391–407.

Konstantinos I. Diamantaras and Sun Y. Kung. 1996. *Principal component neural networks*. Wiley New York.

Susan T. Dumais, Todd A. Letsche, Michael L. Littman, and Thomas K. Landauer. 1997. Automatic cross-language retrieval using latent semantic indexing. In *Proc. of AAAI Spring Symposium on Cross-language Text and Speech Retrieval*, pages 18–24.

Christiane Fellbaum. 1998. *WordNet: An electronic lexical database*. Bradford Books.

Marc Franco-Salvador, Parth Gupta, and Paolo Rosso. 2013. Cross-language plagiarism detection using a multilingual semantic network. In *Proc. of the 35th European Conference on Information Retrieval (ECIR'13)*, volume LNCS(7814), pages 710–713. Springer-Verlag.

Evgeniy Gabrilovich and Shaul Markovitch. 2007. Computing semantic relatedness using wikipedia-based explicit semantic analysis. In *Proc. of the 20th International Joint Conference on Artifical Intelligence (IJCAI)*, pages 1606–1611.

Taher Haveliwala, Sepandar Kamvar, and Glen Jeh. 2003. An analytical comparison of approaches to personalizing pagerank. Technical Report 2003-35, Stanford InfoLab, June.

Xiaodong He. 2007. Using word dependent transition models in hmm based word alignment for statistical machine translation. In *Proceedings of the Second Workshop on Statistical Machine Translation*, pages 80–87. Association for Computational Linguistics.

Johannes Hoffart, Fabian M. Suchanek, Klaus Berberich, and Gerhard Weikum. 2013. Yago2: A spatially and temporally enhanced knowledge base from wikipedia. *Artificial Intelligence*, 194:28–61.

Eduard H. Hovy, Roberto Navigli, and Simone Paolo Ponzetto. 2013. Collaboratively built semi-structured content and Artificial Intelligence: The story so far. *Artificial Intelligence*, 194:2–27.

David Hull. 1994. Improving text retrieval for the routing problem using latent semantic indexing. In *Proceedings of the 17th Annual International ACM SIGIR Conference on Research and Development in Information Retrieval (SIGIR)*, pages 282–291. Springer.

Donald A. Jackson, Keith M. Somers, and Harold H. Harvey. 1989. Similarity coefficients: measures of co-occurrence and association or simply measures of occurrence? *American Naturalist*, pages 436–453.

Ian T. Jolliffe. 1986. *Principal component analysis*, volume 487. Springer-Verlag New York.

Thomas K. Landauer and Michael L. Littman. 1994. Computerized cross-language document retrieval using latent semantic indexing, April 5. US Patent 5,301,109.

Christopher D. Manning, Prabhakar Raghavan, and Hinrich Schütze. 2008. *Introduction to Information Retrieval*. Cambridge University Press, New York, NY, USA.

Michael Matuschek and Iryna Gurevych. 2013. Dijkstra-WSA: A graph-based approach to word sense alignment. *Transactions of the Association for Computational Linguistics (TACL)*, 1:151–164.

Paul Mcnamee and James Mayfield. 2004. Character n-gram tokenization for european language text retrieval. *Information Retrieval*, 7(1-2):73–97.

David Mimno, Hanna M. Wallach, Jason Naradowsky, David A. Smith, and Andrew McCallum. 2009. Polylingual topic models. In *Proceedings of the 2009 Conference on Empirical Methods in Natural Language Processing: Volume 2-Volume 2*, pages 880–889. Association for Computational Linguistics.

Manuel Montes y Gómez, Alexander F. Gelbukh, Aurelio López-López, and Ricardo A. Baeza-Yates. 2001. Flexible comparison of conceptual graphs. In *Proc. of the 12th International Conference on Database and Expert Systems Applications (DEXA)*, pages 102–111.

Dragos Stefan Munteanu and Daniel Marcu. 2005. Improving machine translation performance by exploiting non-parallel corpora. *Computational Linguistics*, 31(4):477–504.

Vivi Nastase and Michael Strube. 2013. Transforming wikipedia into a large scale multilingual concept network. *Artificial Intelligence*, 194:62–85.

Roberto Navigli and Mirella Lapata. 2010. An experimental study of graph connectivity for unsupervised word sense disambiguation. *IEEE Transactions on Pattern Analysis and Machine Intelligence*, 32(4):678–692.

Roberto Navigli and Simone Paolo Ponzetto. 2012a. BabelNet: The automatic construction, evaluation and application of a wide-coverage multilingual semantic network. *Artificial Intelligence*, 193:217–250.

Roberto Navigli and Simone Paolo Ponzetto. 2012b. BabelRelate! a joint multilingual approach to computing semantic relatedness. In *Proceedings of the Twenty-Sixth AAAI Conference on Artificial Intelligence (AAAI-12)*, pages 108–114, Toronto, Canada.

Lawrence Page, Sergey Brin, Rajeev Motwani, and Terry Winograd. 1998. The PageRank Citation Ranking: Bringing Order to the Web. Technical report, Stanford Digital Library Technologies Project.

John C. Platt, Kristina Toutanova, and Wen-tau Yih. 2010. Translingual document representations from discriminative projections. In *Proceedings of the 2010 Conference on Empirical Methods in Natural Language Processing*, pages 251–261.

Martin Potthast, Benno Stein, and Maik Anderka. 2008. A wikipedia-based multilingual retrieval model. In *Advances in Information Retrieval*, pages 522–530. Springer.

Martin Potthast, Alberto Barrón-Cedeño, Benno Stein, and Paolo Rosso. 2011. Cross-language plagiarism detection. *Language Resources and Evaluation*, 45(1):45–62.

Fatiha Sadat, Howard Johnson, Akakpo Agbago, George Foster, Joel Martin, and Aaron Tikuisis. 2005. Portage: A phrase-based machine translation system. In *Proceedings of the ACL Workshop on Building and Using Parallel Texts*, Ann Arbor, USA.

Gerard Salton and Christopher Buckley. 1988. Term-weighting approaches in automatic text retrieval. *Information processing & management*, 24(5):513–523.

Gerard Salton and Michael J. McGill. 1986. *Introduction to Modern Information Retrieval*. McGraw-Hill, Inc., New York, NY, USA.

Gerard Salton, Edward A. Fox, and Harry Wu. 1983. Extended boolean information retrieval. *Communications of the ACM*, 26(11):1022–1036.

Bruce Thompson. 2005. Canonical correlation analysis. *Encyclopedia of statistics in behavioral science*.

Piek Vossen. 2004. EuroWordNet: A multilingual database of autonomous and language-specific wordnets connected via an inter-lingual index. *International Journal of Lexicography*, 17(2):161–173.

Wen-tau Yih, Kristina Toutanova, John C. Platt, and Christopher Meek. 2011. Learning discriminative projections for text similarity measures. In *Proceedings of the Fifteenth Conference on Computational Natural Language Learning*, pages 247–256.

Dependency Tree Abstraction for Long-Distance Reordering in Statistical Machine Translation

Chenchen Ding
Department of Computer Science
University of Tsukuba
1-1-1 Tennodai, Tsukuba, Ibaraki , Japan
tei@mibel.cs.tsukuba.ac.jp

Yuki Arase
Microsoft Research
No. 5 Danling St., Haidian Dist.
Beijing, P.R. China
yukiar@microsoft.com

Abstract

Word reordering is a crucial technique in statistical machine translation in which syntactic information plays an important role. Synchronous context-free grammar has typically been used for this purpose with various modifications for adding flexibilities to its synchronized tree generation. We permit further flexibilities in the synchronous context-free grammar in order to translate between languages with drastically different word order. Our method pre-processes a parallel corpus by abstracting source-side dependency trees, and performs long-distance reordering on top of an off-the-shelf phrase-based system. Experimental results show that our method significantly outperforms previous phrase-based and syntax-based models for translation between English and Japanese.

1 Introduction

Since the inception of statistical machine translation (SMT), long-distance word reordering has been a notable challenge, particularly when translating between languages with drastically different word orders, such as subject-verb-object (SVO) and subject-object-verb (SOV) languages like English and Japanese, respectively. Phrase-based models (Koehn et al., 2003; Och and Ney, 2004; Xiong et al., 2006) have been strong in local translation and reordering. However, phrase-based models cannot effectively conduct long-distance reordering because they are based purely on statistics of syntax-independent phrases. As a complementary approach to phrase-based models, some researchers have incorporated syntactic information into an SMT framework (Wu, 1997; Yamada and Knight, 2001; Liu et al., 2006) using *synchronous context-free grammar* (SCFG) (Aho and Ullman, 1972). The original SCFG assumes that the syntactic trees of the source and target languages can be derived synchronously. However, this assumption is too strict for handling parallel sentences that are often comparable rather than parallel. For alleviating this assumption, some researchers have added flexibilities in synchronized tree generation (Wu, 1997; Burkett et al., 2010). In addition, in the SMT framework, there is an approach that alleviates the assumption by only generating the source-side syntactic tree and projecting it to the target-side sentence (Yamada and Knight, 2001; Liu et al., 2006).

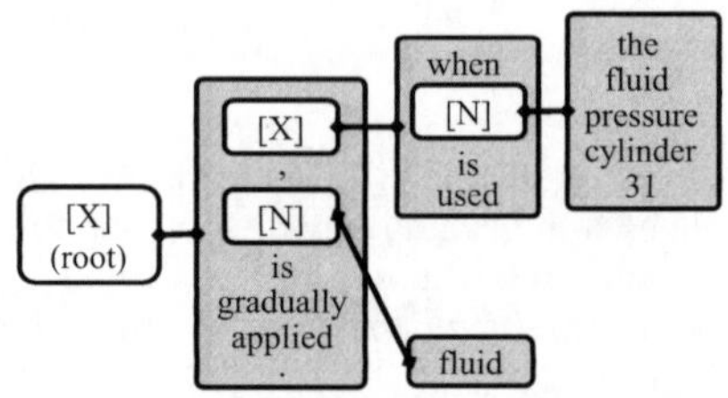

when the fluid pressure cylinder 31 is used, fluid is gradually applied.

Figure 1: English abstraction tree example

In practice, these existing methods are not flexible enough to handle parallel sentence pairs, especially those of SVO and SOV languages. Therefore, we permit further flexibility in SCFG aiming to effectively conduct long-distance reordering. We design our method as a pre-processing procedure so that we can use a well-developed phrase-based system without adding heavy computational complexity to the system. Specifically, we propose an *abstraction tree* that is a shallow and nested representation, *i.e.*, abstraction of the dependency tree as Fig. 1 depicts. Our method pre-processes a parallel corpus by generating source-side abstraction trees and projecting the trees onto the target-side sentences. It then decomposes the corpus by collecting corresponding node pairs as a new corpus, and finally trains the phrase-based model. In this manner, the source-side grammar is determined on the fly for each sentence based on a dependency parse of the source sentence. The target side of each production in the grammar is determined by running the phrase-based decoder.

We empirically show effectiveness of our method for English-to-Japanese and Japanese-to-English translations by comparing it to phrase-based and syntax-based models. Experimental results show that our method significantly outperforms the previous methods with respect to the BLEU (Papineni et al., 2002) metric.

2 Related Work

For adding flexibilities to SCFG under an SMT scenario, previous studies generate only a source-side syntactic tree and project it to the target-side sentence regardless of the true target-side syntactic structure. Liu et al. (2006) propose a tree-to-string model using a source-side constituency tree to extract correspondences between the source-side tree and the target-side sentence. Quirk et al. (2005) and Xie et al. (2011) use a dependency tree for the same purpose. Since these methods project a fine-grained source-side syntax tree, an accurate projection is possible only when the target-side sentence has a syntactic structure that is similar to the source-side. Zhu and Xiao (2011) and Huang and Pendus (2013) generalize rules obtained by the tree-to-string model to increase the chance of rule matching at decoding. Despite their merits, none of these methods resolves the problem of tree projection to the target-side.

The hierarchical phrase-based model (HIERO) proposed by Chiang (2007) is independent of any syntactic information and generates SCFG rules only from parallel sentence pairs. Li et al. (2012) and Feng et al. (2012) incorporate syntactic information into HIERO as soft constraints. Since these methods are bound by the original HIERO rules that are independent of syntactic information, their rules cannot represent the global syntactic structure of a sentence.

There are also pre-reordering methods for long-distance reordering in SVO-to-SOV translations using heuristics designed based on source-side syntactic structures (Xu et al., 2009; Isozaki et al., 2010; Isozaki et al., 2012). They are fine-tuned to handle only specific reordering problems in a predetermined language pair. Another approach is to statistically learn pre-reordering rules from a corpus; however, this requires a highly parallel training corpus consisting of literal translations to learn effective rules (Neubig et al., 2012; Navratil et al., 2012). Such a training dataset is not widely available in many languages.

Algorithm 1 CKY-style decoding

Input: Input sentence u and its dependency tree r_u, translation model TM, block-LM bLM, sentence-LM sLM, size of m-best m

$\tau_u \leftarrow$ generate abstraction tree of u using r_u
$NodeTrans[][] \leftarrow \emptyset$
for all $node$ in τ_u **do**
  $m\text{-}best \leftarrow Decode(node, TM, bLM, m)$
  $(start, end) \leftarrow$ start and end indices of $node$ in u
  $NodeTrans[start][end] \leftarrow m\text{-}best$
end for
for $start := 1$ **to** $|u|$ **do**
  for $span := 0$ **to** $|u| - 1$ **do**
    $end \leftarrow start + span$
    $ChildTrans[] \leftarrow \emptyset$
    for all (i, j) such that $start \leq i \leq j \leq end$ **do**
      if $NodeTrans[i][j] \neq \emptyset$ **then**
        add $NodeTrans[i][j]$ to $ChildTrans$
      end if
    end for
    $CubePruning(NodeTrans[start][end], ChildTrans, sLM, m)$
  end for
end for

3 Overview of the Proposed Method

Our method pre-processes sentences in a parallel corpus based on source-side abstraction trees. It first generates an abstraction tree τ_s of a source-side sentence s by abstracting its dependency tree r_s: $(s, r_s) \rightarrow \tau_s$. It then projects the tree to the target-side sentence t for generating a target-side abstraction tree τ_t that has exactly the same structure to τ_s, *i.e.*, $(\tau_s, t) \rightarrow \tau_t$. The abstraction-tree generation process can be adapted to translating languages by specifying source-side part-of-speeches (POSs) as input. Abstraction tree structures also depend on the dependency grammar that a parser uses. In this study, we assume commonly used Stanford typed dependency (de Marneffe et al., 2006) for English and the chunk-based dependency with ipadic (Asahara and Matsumoto, 2003) for Japanese. Investigation of effects of different dependency grammars is our future work.

We decompose the sentence pair into node pairs according to correspondences between the source and target abstraction trees, and generate a new corpus referred to as a *block-corpus* (Fig. 6). Using the block-corpus and the original corpus, we train a phrase-based model. Its translation model is trained with the block-corpus, and two target-side language models (LMs) are trained with the block-corpus (referred to as *block-LM*) and the

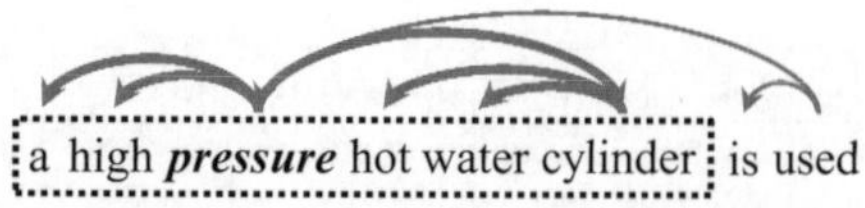

Figure 2: [N] node detection example

original corpus (referred to as *sentence-LM*), respectively. Thus the sentence-LM can be trained using a larger-scale monolingual corpus. Compared to previous methods that also decompose sentence pairs (Xu et al., 2005; Sudoh et al., 2010), our method is more syntax-oriented.

In decoding, we adopt the parsing algorithm with cube-pruning (Huang and Chiang, 2005) into a phrase-based decoder to translate the abstraction tree of an input sentence efficiently. As Algorithm 1 shows, our decoder first generates the abstraction tree of the input sentence (line 1), and independently translates each node using the block-LM that models ordering among non-terminals and lexical words (line 3–7). It then combines the m-best translation hypotheses of each node to construct a sentence-level translation (line 8–19). Specifically, we insert sets of the m-best translation hypotheses of child nodes into the m-best hypotheses of their parent node by replacing the corresponding non-terminals using the cube-pruning (line 17). The ordering of these child nodes has been determined in their parent node by the phrase-based model that regards non-terminals only as single words. By doing so, long-distance reordering is solved considering the global syntactic structure and contexts (lexical strings) preserved in the node. In cube-pruning, we use the sentence-LM to compose fluent sentence-level translation. The block-LM and sentence-LM scores are treated as independent features.

The computational complexity of our decoder (line 3–19) is $\mathcal{O}(|\mathcal{N}|C)$, where $|\mathcal{N}|$ is the number of nodes in the abstraction-tree and C is a constant representing the complexity of phrase-based decoder and cube-pruning. Since combinations of hypotheses in cube-pruning are determined by the abstraction-tree in our method, the computational cost is significantly smaller than HIERO's case.

4 Abstraction Tree Generation

In this section, we provide the formal definition of an abstraction tree and the generation method.

4.1 Definition of Abstraction Tree

We define an abstraction tree as $\tau = \{\mathcal{N}, \mathcal{E}\}$, where $\mathcal{N}$ is a set of nodes and $\mathcal{E}$ is a set of

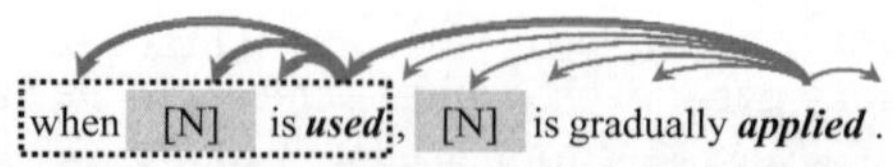

Figure 3: [X] and [P] node detection. Since the word "used" is a head, it and its governing span are detached from the root "applied" as a child node.

edges. For conducting abstraction based on syntactic structures, we merge a span governed by a dependency head as a node and represent it by a non-terminal in a parent node. As a result, the i-th node $\mathcal{N}_i$ consists of a sequence of lexical words w and non-terminals L that replace spans governed by heads in the corresponding child nodes:

$$\mathcal{N}_i = \{\Psi|\psi_1, \ldots, \psi_{|\mathcal{N}_i|}\}, \psi_k \in \{w, L\}.$$

The edge $\mathcal{E}_{ij}$ between a parent node $\mathcal{N}_i$ and its child node $\mathcal{N}_j$ corresponds to a governor-dependent relationship from the head in $\mathcal{N}_i$ to its dependent w_x in $\mathcal{N}_j$. w_x is another head and governs other words in $\mathcal{N}_j$. The span covered by $\mathcal{N}_j$ is replaced by a non-terminal in $\mathcal{N}_i$.

We use three kinds of labels to represent L for explicitly using syntactic information that is useful for long-distance reordering; [N], [P], and [X] according to the head in the corresponding node. We label a child node [N] when its head word is a noun and forms a base noun phrase, [P] when its head word is an adposition[1], and [X] for others like verb phrases, conjunctive phrases, and relative phrases. These nodes play different roles in a sentence. An [N] node, *i.e.*, a base noun phrase, adds context to a sentence. A [P] node depends on other phrases and generally appears relatively freely in a sentence. Thus, we assume that the [P] node requires special reordering.

The abstraction tree depicted in Fig. 1 has a parent [X] node "when [N] is used" and its child [N] node "the fluid pressure cylinder 31." The word "used" governs "cylinder" in the [N] node, and the [N] node folds the context in the [X] node.

4.2 Tree Construction

We begin with detecting [N] nodes, then proceed to [P] and [X] nodes. These processes require to specify source-side POSs as input for adapting to translating languages. We finally flatten fragmented nodes.

For detecting [N] nodes, we take a POS of noun as input and identify each noun and its governing span, *i.e.*, a string of all governed words, using the source-side dependency tree as Fig. 2 shows. We

[1]A preposition in English and a postposition in Japanese.

Algorithm 2 [P] and [X] node detection

```
Input: Source-side sentence s and its dependency tree r_s,
    POS list of adpositions PPos, [N] node list N-Nodes
Output: [P] and [X] nodes P-Nodes, X-Nodes
1: P-Nodes[] ← ∅, X-Nodes[] ← ∅
2: HeadList[] ← root of r_s
3: repeat
4:   head ← pop node from HeadList
5:   ChildList[] ← all dependents of head
6:   for all child in ChildList do
7:     if child ∉ N-Nodes and child has dependents
       then
8:       add child to HeadList
9:       remove child from ChildList
10:    end if
11:  end for
12:  start ← smallest start index of nodes in ChildList
13:  end ← largest end index of nodes in ChildList
14:  if POS of head ∈ PPos then
15:    add span [start, end] of s to P-Nodes
16:  else
17:    add span [start, end] of s to X-Nodes
18:  end if
19:  remove head from HeadList
20: until HeadList = ∅
```

regard descendant dependents as being governed by the noun for detecting a noun phrase of a complete form. We extract the span as a node and replace it by an [N] label in the sentence.

Next, we identify [P] and [X] nodes given a list of source-side POSs of adpositions as input. As Algorithm 2 shows, after [N] node detection, we trace the dependency tree from its root to leaves (line 3–20). We find all the dependents to the root, then check if each dependent is a head. If a dependent of the root is a head and governs other words, we detach the dependent to process later (line 6–11). We then find the smallest start index and largest end index of dependent words and set the corresponding span as a node (if a dependent is in an [N] node, we use the start and end indices of the [N] node). Each node is labeled according to the POS of its head as [P] or [X] (line 14–18). We then take the detached dependent as a new root and repeat the process until no more detachment is possible. The computational complexity is $\mathcal{O}(|s|^2)$. Through this process, a span with direct dependencies is extracted as a node, and other spans with descendant dependencies become descendant nodes, replaced by non-terminals in their parent node as shown in Fig. 3.

4.3 Handling Complex Noun Phrase

As described in Sec. 4.2, we detect a noun phrase as an [N] node. However, an [N] node becomes more complex than a base noun phrase when the head governs a clause, such as a relative

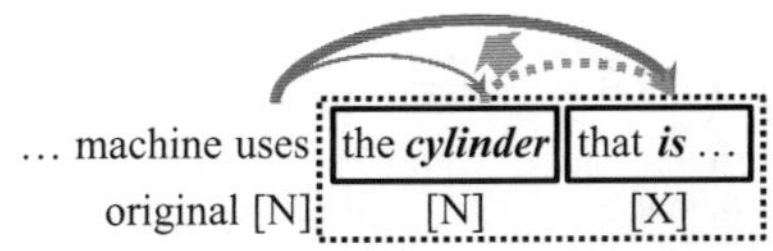

Figure 4: Handling a complex noun phrase

clause. Such a complex node may require long-distance reordering of an inside clause when translating. Therefore, we separate the noun phrase and clause. We take a POS list whose word can be a head of [P] and [X] nodes (preposition, verb, *to*, *Wh*-determiner/pronoun/adverb, and coordinating conjunction for English) as input. If the POS of a noun's dependent is in the list, we detach the dependency arc, and then re-attach the dependency arc to the head of the noun. As a result, the base noun phrase becomes an [N] node and its clause becomes a [P] or [X] node that is transformed to a sibling of the [N] node.

In Fig. 4, the word "cylinder" in the original [N] node has a relative clause and governs "is." We detach the dependency arc and re-attach it to "uses" (the head of "cylinder"), so that the noun phrase and the clause become sibling [N] and [X] nodes.

4.4 Flattening Fragmented Nodes

The above processes are independent of the size of each node, meaning they produce fragmented nodes of only a few words. Such fragmented nodes make the tree projection to the target-side difficult. To solve this problem, we flatten the abstraction tree as shown in Algorithm 3. We process an internal node in τ_s from bottom to top. If the covering span of an internal node is less than a threshold $\gamma \in \mathbb{N}$, its child nodes are merged (line 3 and 4, Algorithm 3). Specifically, we reinsert the child nodes by replacing the corresponding non-terminals with lexical strings that the child nodes have been covered by. The computational cost is $\mathcal{O}(|\mathcal{N}|)$. We investigate the effect of γ in the following evaluation section (Table 2).

5 Abstraction Tree Projection

In this section, we describe a method for projecting the obtained source-side abstraction tree onto the target-side sentence.

5.1 Tree Structure Projection

We use word alignment results for tree structure projection. However, accurate word alignment is challenging when handling language pairs in which long-distance reordering is needed, and the alignment noise propagates to the tree projection.

Algorithm 3 Tree flattening

Input: Abstraction tree τ_s, threshold γ

Output: Flattened tree τ'_s

for all internal $node$ in τ_s, from bottom to top **do**
  $(start, end) \leftarrow$ start and end indices of $node$
  if $end - start + 1 < \gamma$ **then**
    $\tau'_s \leftarrow MergeChildNodes(node, \tau_s)$
  end if
end for

To avoid this problem, we first omit alignment links of function words whose alignment quality tends to be lower than that of the content words. We then complement the quality of word alignment by adapting the *syntactic cohesion assumption* (Yamada and Knight, 2001) that assumes a word string covered by a sub-tree of the source-side syntactic tree corresponds to a string of *contiguous* words in the target-side sentence. Following the assumption, we project the k-th node of the source-side abstraction tree $\mathcal{N}_k^{(s)}$ to a string of contiguous words in the target-side:

$$\mathcal{N}_k^{(s)} \mapsto t_i, \ldots, t_j, \text{ s.t. } 1 \le i \le j \le |t|,$$

where t_i is the i-th word in the target-side sentence and $|t|$ is the number of words in the sentence.

For each node of the source-side abstraction tree, we first obtain its covering span. We then define a vector $\boldsymbol{c} \in \{0,1\}^n$ whose elements represent word alignment links in a binary manner. If and only if the i-th target word is aligned to a word in the span, the i-th element of $\mathbf{c}$ becomes 1, otherwise it is 0. Since the original word alignment represented by the vector $\mathbf{c}$ may be noisy, we find a vector $\boldsymbol{c}^* \in \{0,1\}^n$ that maximizes the syntactic cohesion assumption. In $\mathbf{c}^*$, *only* consecutive elements between two indices i and j are 1, and others are 0. We derive such $\mathbf{c}^*$ as follows:

$$C_{min}(\boldsymbol{c}) = \{\boldsymbol{c}' | \operatorname*{argmin}_{\boldsymbol{c}'} \|\boldsymbol{c}' - \mathbf{c}\|\}, \quad (1)$$
$$\text{s.t. } \exists\, i,\ j,\ 1 \le i \le j \le n \text{ and } c'_k = \begin{cases} 1 & i \le k \le j, \\ 0 & \text{otherwise}, \end{cases}$$
$$\boldsymbol{c}^* = \operatorname*{argmax}_{\boldsymbol{c}' \in C_{min}(\boldsymbol{c})} \|\boldsymbol{c}'\|. \quad (2)$$

The operator $\|\cdot\|$ computes the Euclidean norm of a vector and c'_k is the k-th element of a vector $\mathbf{c}'$. Finally, $\mathbf{c}^*$ represents the best possible word links that maximize the syntactic cohesion assumption, *i.e.*, the longest contiguous word string in the target-side, and that are closest to the original word alignment. Specifically, Eq. (1) determines vectors that have the smallest distance to

Algorithm 4 Tree projection

Input: Source-side abstraction tree τ_s, target-side sentence t, word alignment $\boldsymbol{A_w}$ between s and t

Output: Target-side abstraction tree τ_t

1: $\tau_t[] \leftarrow \emptyset$
2: remove links of function words in $\boldsymbol{A_w}$
3: **for** $span := |s| - 1$ **to** 0 **do**
4:   **for** $start := 1$ **to** $|s|$ **do**
5:     $end \leftarrow start + span$
6:     **if** span $[start, end] \in \tau_s$ **then**
7:       $\mathbf{c} \leftarrow GenerateVector([start, end], \boldsymbol{A_w})$
8:       $\mathbf{c}^* \leftarrow Solve(\mathbf{c})$ ◁ Eq. (1) and Eq. (2)
9:       $(i, j) \leftarrow$ start and end indices of $\mathbf{c}^*$
10:       add span $[i, j]$ of t as a node into τ_t
11:       $\boldsymbol{A_w} \leftarrow UpdateWordAlignment(\mathbf{c}, \mathbf{c}^*)$
12:     **end if**
13:   **end for**
14: **end for**

the original vector $\mathbf{c}$ while satisfying the hard constraint, and Eq. (2) selects the one whose norm is largest, *i.e.*, a vector that has longest contiguous word links to the target-side. For computational efficiency, we use the greedy-search so that the computational cost is $\mathcal{O}(|t|)$. When Eq. (2) has multiple solutions, word links in these solutions are equally likely, and thus we merge them into a unique solution. Specifically, we take the union of the solutions and find the smallest index i_l and largest index i_r whose elements are 1. We then set all elements between i_l and i_r to 1.

As Algorithm 4 shows, we conduct this process in a top-down manner throughout the abstraction tree (line 3–14). When processing each node, word alignment links are updated by overwriting links in $\mathbf{c}$ with the ones in $\mathbf{c}^*$ (line 11). The computational cost is $\mathcal{O}(|\mathcal{N}^{(s)}||t|)$, where $|\mathcal{N}^{(s)}|$ is the number of nodes in τ_s. Figure 5 shows a projection example of a node. A node of "when [N] is used" covers a span of "when the fluid pressure cylinder 31 is used." The words in the span are aligned to the 1st, 2nd, and 5th target words (chunks)[2]; however, the link to the 5th target word (chunk) is a mis-alignment. With the alignment vector $\boldsymbol{c}$ of $[1, 1, 0, 0, \mathbf{1}, 0, 0]$, we can remove this misalignment and derive $\boldsymbol{c}^*$ of $[1, 1, 0, 0, \mathbf{0}, 0, 0]$.

5.2 Fixed-Expression Recovery

The abstraction tree generation and projection are based on a dependency tree, and thus may over-segment a *fixed-expression*, such as idioms and multi-word expressions. Since a fixed-expression composes a complete meaning using a contiguous word string, splitting it into different nodes results

[2]In Japanese, a unit of dependency is a chunk in general, and thus we conduct chunking before projection.

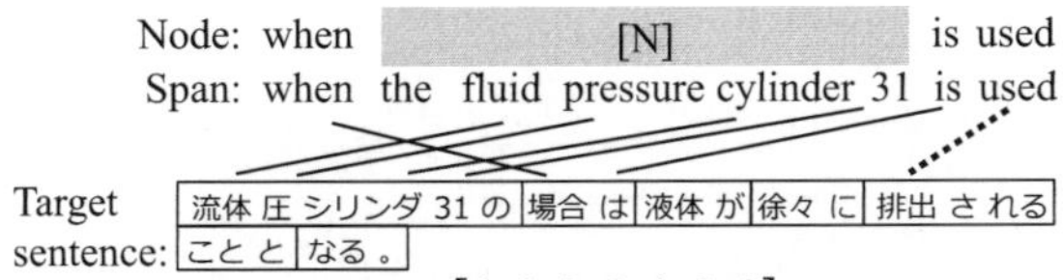

$$c = [1, 1, 0, 0, 1, 0, 0]$$

Figure 5: Abstraction tree projection

Input parallel corpus	
When the fluid pressure cylinder 31 is used , fluid is gradually applied .	流体 圧 シリンダ 31 の 場合 は 流体 が 徐々 に 排出 さ れる こと と なる 。
Block-Corpus	
$[X]_{\boxed{0}}$, $[N]_{\boxed{0}}$ is gradually applied .	$[X]_{\boxed{0}}$ $[N]_{\boxed{0}}$ が 徐々 に 排出 さ れる こと と なる 。
when $[N]_{\boxed{1}}$ is used	$[N]_{\boxed{1}}$ の 場合 は
the fluid pressure cylinder 31	流体 圧 シリンダ 31
fluid	流体

Figure 6: Block-corpus example. Boxed indices link non-terminals in the source and target exemplars.

in poor translation. To avoid this issue, we generate a list of fixed-expressions using conventional methods (Evert, 2008) and force them to remain in one node. On both the source and target abstraction trees, we recursively reinsert nodes to their parent node when such a fixed-expression is over-segmented and spread over multiple nodes.

5.3 Block-Corpus Construction

After tree structure projection, we extract corresponding node pairs as a block-corpus. Each node pair has a form $\langle \Psi_s, \Psi_t, \boldsymbol{A_L} \rangle$, where $\Psi_s \in \{\Omega_s, L\}^n$ represents the source-side node of length n. It consists of a sequence of lexical words in the source-side vocabulary Ω_s and non-terminals L. $\Psi_t \in \{\Omega_t, L\}^m$ similarly represents the target-side node of length m. $\boldsymbol{A_L}$ preserves correspondences between the non-terminals in the source and target nodes.

Specifically, we extract a pair of leaf nodes as a pair of lexical strings. As for internal nodes, we use the same non-terminal labels appearing in the source-side node at the target-side node. Namely, the span covered by child nodes are replaced by corresponding non-terminal labels in the source-side node. At the same time, we record the correspondence between the non-terminals. Figure 6 shows an example of the block-corpus, in which the boxed indices indicate correspondences of non-terminals in the source and target nodes.

6 Evaluation

We evaluate our method in English-to-Japanese (EJ) and Japanese-to-English (JE) translation tasks, since long-distance reordering is a serious problem in this language pair.

6.1 Experiment Corpus

We use NTCIR-7 PATMT (Fujii et al., 2008), a publicly available standard evaluation dataset, for EJ and JE machine translation. The dataset is constructed using English and Japanese patents and consists of 1.8 million parallel sentence pairs for training, 915 sentence pairs for development, and 1,381 sentence pairs for testing. The development and test sets have one reference per sentence. This dataset is bidirectional and can be used for both EJ and JE translation evaluation.

6.2 Implementation of Proposed Method

We implement our method for EJ and JE translation tasks. In both cases, we use an in-house implementation of English POS tagger (Collins, 2002) and a Japanese morphological analyzer (Kudo et al., 2004) for tokenization and POS tagging. As for EJ translation, we use the Stanford parser (de Marneffe et al., 2006) to obtain English abstraction trees. We also use an in-house implementation of a Japanese chunker (Kudo and Matsumoto, 2002) to obtain chunks in Japanese sentences. We apply the chunker just before tree projection for using a chunk as a projection unit, since a chunk is the basic unit in Japanese. As for JE translation, we use a popular Japanese dependency parser (Kudo and Matsumoto, 2002) to obtain Japanese abstraction trees. We convert Japanese chunk-level dependency tree to a word-level using a simple heuristic. We use GIZA++ (Och and Ney, 2003) with the grow-diag-final-and heuristic for word alignment.

We use an in-house implementation of the bracketing transduction grammar (BTG) model (Xiong et al., 2006) as the phrase-based model that our method relies on for translation. Non-terminals in our block-corpus are regarded as a single word, and their alignments $\boldsymbol{A_L}$ determined in the block-corpus are exclusively used to align them. We set the maximum phrase length to 5 when training the translation model, since we find that the performance is stable even setting larger values as in (Koehn et al., 2003). We then train the sentence-LM and block-LM using the original corpus and the obtained block-corpus, respectively. We ignore a sentence-end tag (</s>) in the block-LM. With each corpus, we train a 5-gram LM using the SRI toolkit (Stolcke, 2002).

6.3 Comparison Method

Since our method pre-processes the parallel corpus based on SCFG with increased flexibility and trains a BTG model using the processed corpus, we compare our method to another BTG model trained only with the original corpus (simply referred to as the BTG model). We also compare to the tree-to-string model and HIERO using state-of-the-art implementations available in the Moses system (Koehn et al., 2007), since they are based on SCFG. The tree-to-string model requires source-side constituency trees. For EJ translation, we use a state-of-the-art English constituency parser (Miyao and Tsujii, 2005; Miyao and Tsujii, 2008). For JE translation, we transform a Japanese dependency tree into a constituency tree using a simple heuristic because there is no publicly available constituency parser. During the translation model training, we use the same setting as our method. In addition, we set the maximum span of rule extraction to infinity for the tree-to-string model and 10 for HIERO following Moses' default. We use the sentence-LM in these models as they assume.

In addition, we compare our method to Head-Finalization (Isozaki et al., 2010; Isozaki et al., 2012) because it has achieved the best BLEU score in EJ translation by handling long-distance reordering. It is a specialized method to EJ translation, where a syntactic head in an English sentence is reordered behind its constituents for complying with the head-final nature of the Japanese language. We pre-process the parallel corpus using the Head-Finalization and train a BTG model using the same setting with our method to observe the effect of different pre-processing methods.

During decoding, we set the translation table size to 10 for each source string, and the stack and beam sizes in the cube pruning to 100 for our method (*i.e.*, m-best = 100) and all other models. The maximum reordering span in the tree-to-string model and HIERO is the same as the rule extraction setting (infinity and 10, respectively). We set the word reordering limit to infinity for our method and the BTG model, while we set it to 3 for Head-Finalization as their papers report.

We tune feature weights by the minimum error rate training (Och, 2003) to maximize the BLEU score using the development set. As an evaluation metric, we compute the BLEU score using the test set, and all the scores discussed in Sec. 6.4 are the test-set BLEU scores. Significance tests are conducted using bootstrap sampling (Koehn, 2004).

Method	EJ	JE
Proposed method ($\gamma = 10$)	**31.78**	**28.55**
BTG	28.82^{**}	26.98^{**}
HIERO	29.27^{**}	27.96^{*}
Tree-to-string	30.97^{**}	26.28^{**}
Head-Finalization	29.52^{**}	NA

Table 1: Test-set BLEU scores. The symbol ** represents a significant difference at the $p < .01$ level and * indicates a significant difference at the $p < .05$ level against our method.

6.4 Result and Discussion

In this section, we present experimental results and discuss them in detail.

Overall Performance Table 1 shows the BLEU scores, in which our method significantly outperforms all other models for both EJ and JE translation tasks. These results indicate that our method effectively incorporates syntactic information into the phrase-based model and improves the translation quality.

For EJ translation, our method outperforms the BTG model by 2.96, the HIERO by 2.51, the tree-to-string model by 0.81, and the Head-Finalization[3] by 2.26 in terms of BLEU score. When we compare our method to the Head-Finalization, both of them improve the BTG model by pre-processing the parallel corpus. Moreover, our method outperforms the Head-Finalization using richer syntactic information.

For JE translation, our method outperforms the BTG model by 1.57, the HIERO by 0.59, and the tree-to-string model by 2.27 in terms of BLEU score. Our method and the tree-to-string model, which depend on syntactic information, largely outperform the BTG model and HIERO in EJ translation. While the BTG model and HIERO, which are independent of syntactic information, outperform the tree-to-string model in JE translation. One reason for this phenomenon is that English is a strongly configurational language that has rigid word order while Japanese is an agglutinative language that has relatively free word order. A rigid syntactic structure provides solid clues for word reordering when translated into a flexible language, while a flexible structure provides weak clues for fitting it to a rigid structure.

[3]The BLEU score reported in this experiment differs from their papers. This may be because they use a phrase-based model in the Moses system, while we use the BTG model.

γ	EJ		JE	
	BLEU	height	BLEU	height
0	31.15	4.1 (1.5)	28.41	4.2 (1.4)
3	30.88	3.8 (1.7)	28.34	3.9 (1.6)
5	31.21	3.7 (1.5)	28.39	3.8 (1.5)
8	31.61	3.4 (1.4)	28.52	3.4 (1.4)
10	**31.78**	3.1 (1.3)	**28.55**	3.2 (1.3)
12	31.76	2.9 (1.3)	28.54	3.0 (1.3)
15	31.25	2.6 (1.2)	28.21	2.7 (1.2)
∞	28.82	1.0 (–)	26.98	1.0 (–)

Table 2: Effect of threshold γ

Effect of Flattening Threshold Table 2 shows BLEU scores when changing the flattening threshold γ in our method, and averages and standard deviations of the abstraction tree heights ($\gamma = \infty$ is equal to the BTG model). The performance improves as we increase the threshold, *i.e.*, increasing the level of abstraction. Our method achieves the best BLEU score when $\gamma = 10$ for both EJ and JE translation, with the performance degrading as we further increase the threshold.

This trend shows the trade-off between phrase-based and syntax-based approaches. When the threshold is too small, an abstraction tree becomes closer to the dependency tree and the tree-projection becomes difficult. In addition, context information becomes unavailable when conducting long-distance reordering with a deep tree. On the other hand, when setting the threshold too large, the abstraction tree becomes too abstracted and syntactic structures useful for long-distance word reordering are lost. We need to balance these effects by setting an appropriate threshold.

Effect of Non-Terminals and Fixed-Expressions We change the kinds of non-terminal labels in an abstraction tree to investigate their effect on the translation quality. When we merge the [P] label to the [X] label, *i.e.*, use only [N] and [X] labels, the BLEU score drops 0.40 in EJ translation while the score is unaffected in JE translation. This is because flexible Japanese syntax does not differentiate postpositional phrases with others, while English syntax prohibits such a flexibility.

When we merge all labels and only use the [X] label, the BLEU score drops 0.57 in EJ translation and 0.43 in JE translation. This result supports our design of the abstraction tree that distinguishes non-terminals according to their different functionalities in a sentence.

We also evaluate the effect of fixed-expressions as described in Sec. 5.2. Results show a significant change when over-splitting fixed-expressions; the BLEU score drops 1.13 for EJ and 0.36 for JE translation without reinserting fixed-expressions.

Method	acceptable ↑	global ↓	local ↓
Proposed	**52**	**30**	**4**
BTG	34	38	7
Tree-to-string	47	32	7

Table 3: Error distribution in 100 samples of EJ translation

Error Analysis We randomly sample 100 translation outputs per our method ($\gamma = 10$), BTG, and tree-to-string models for each EJ and JE translation tasks, and manually categorize errors based on (Vilar et al., 2006). We focus primarily on reordering errors and exclusively categorize the samples into acceptable translations, translations with only global or local reordering errors, as well as others that are complicated combinations of various errors. An acceptable translation correctly conveys the information in a source sentence even if it contains minor grammatical errors.

Table 3 shows the distribution of acceptable translations and those with global/local reordering errors in the EJ task (results of JE task are omitted due to the severe space limitation, but their trend is similar). It confirms that our method reduces reordering errors, not only for long-distance but for local reordering, and increases the ratio of acceptable translations compared to the BTG and tree-to-string models. We also find that long-distance reordering was attempted in 85, 66, and 70 sentences by our method, BTG, and tree-to-string, respectively, among these translations. The results show that our method performs long-distance reordering more frequently than others.

When we compare translations performed by our method to those performed by the tree-to-string model, we observe that their effectiveness depends on a range of reordering. Our method is effective in long-distance reordering like those of clauses, while the tree-to-string model performs middle-range reordering well. This is due to the trade-off regarding the level of abstraction as discussed in the flattening threshold experiment.

7 Conclusion and Future Work

We have proposed an abstraction tree for effectively conducting long-distance reordering using an off-the-shelf phrase-based model. Evaluation results show that our method outperforms conventional phrase-based and syntax-based models.

We plan to investigate the effect of translating language pairs and dependency grammars in abstraction tree generation. In addition, we will apply a structure-aware word aligner (Neubig et al., 2011) to improve the tree projection.

References

Alfred V. Aho and Jeffrey D. Ullman. 1972. *The theory of parsing, translation, and compiling*. Prentice-Hall Inc.

Masayuki Asahara and Yuji Matsumoto. 2003. ipadic version 2.7.0 user's manual. `http://sourceforge.jp/projects/ipadic/docs/ipadic-2.7.0-manual-en.pdf`.

David Burkett, John Blitzer, and Dan Klein. 2010. Joint parsing and alignment with weakly synchronized grammars. In *Proceedings of Conference of the North American Chapter of the Association for Computational Linguistics on Human Language Technology (NAACL-HLT 2010)*, pages 127–135.

David Chiang. 2007. Hierarchical phrase-based translation. *Computational Linguistics*, 33(2):201–228.

Michael Collins. 2002. Discriminative training methods for hidden Markov models: Theory and experiments with perceptron algorithms. In *Proceedings of Conference on Empirical Methods in Natural Language Processing (EMNLP 2002)*, pages 1–8.

Marie-Catherine de Marneffe, Bill MacCartney, and Christopher D. Manning. 2006. Generating typed dependency parses from phrase structure parses. In *Proceedings of International Conference on Language Resources and Evaluation (LREC 2006)*, pages 449–454.

Stefan Evert. 2008. Corpora and collocations. In Anke Lüdeling and Merja Kytö, editors, *Corpus Linguistics. An International Handbook*, volume 2, chapter 58. Mouton de Gruyter.

Yang Feng, Dongdong Zhang, Mu Li, Ming Zhou, and Qun Liu. 2012. Hierarchical chunk-to-string translation. In *Proceedings of Annual Meeting of the Association for Computational Linguistics (ACL 2012)*, pages 950–958.

Atsushi Fujii, Masao Utiyama, Mikio Yamamoto, and Takehito Utsuro. 2008. Overview of the patent translation task at the NTCIR-7 workshop. In *Proceedings of NTCIR-7 Workshop Meeting (NTCIR)*, pages 389–400.

Liang Huang and David Chiang. 2005. Better k-best parsing. In *Proceedings of International Workshop on Parsing Technology (IWPT 2005)*, pages 53–64.

Fei Huang and Cezar Pendus. 2013. Generalized reordering rules for improved SMT. In *Proceedings of Annual Meeting of the Association for Computational Linguistics (ACL 2013)*, pages 387–392.

Hideki Isozaki, Katsuhito Sudoh, Hajime Tsukada, and Kevin Duh. 2010. Head Finalization: A simple reordering rule for SOV languages. In *Proceedings of Joint Workshop on Statistical Machine Translation and Metrics MATR (WMT-MetricsMATR 2010)*, pages 244–251.

Hideki Isozaki, Katsuhito Sudoh, Hajime Tsukada, and Kevin Duh. 2012. HPSG-based preprocessing for English-to-Japanese translation. *ACM Transactions on Asian Language Information Processing (TALIP)*, 11(3):8:1–8:16.

Philipp Koehn, Franz J. Och, and Daniel Marcu. 2003. Statistical phrase-based translation. In *Proceedings of Conference of the North American Chapter of the Association for Computational Linguistics on Human Language Technology (NAACL-HLT 2003)*, pages 48–54.

Philipp Koehn, Hieu Hoang, Alexandra Birch, Chris Callison-Burch, Marcello Federico, Nicola Bertoldi, Brooke Cowan, Wade Shen, Christine Moran, Richard Zens, Chris Dyer, Ondrej Bojar, Alexandra Constantin, and Evan Herbst. 2007. Moses: Open source toolkit for statistical machine translation. In *Proceedings of Annual Meeting of the Association for Computational Linguistics (ACL 2007)*, pages 177–180.

Philipp Koehn. 2004. Statistical significance tests for machine translation evaluation. In *Proceedings of Conference on Empirical Methods in Natural Language Processing (EMNLP 2004)*, pages 388–395.

Taku Kudo and Yuji Matsumoto. 2002. Japanese dependency analysis using cascaded chunking. In *Proceedings of Conference on Natural Language Learning (CoNLL 2002)*, pages 1–7.

Taku Kudo, Kaoru Yamamoto, and Yuji Matsumoto. 2004. Applying conditional random fields to Japanese morphological analysis. In *Proceedings of Conference on Empirical Methods in Natural Language Processing (EMNLP 2004)*, pages 230–237.

Junhui Li, Zhaopeng Tu, Guodong Zhou, and Josef van Genabith. 2012. Head-driven hierarchical phrase-based translation. In *Proceedings of Annual Meeting of the Association for Computational Linguistics (ACL 2012)*, pages 33–37.

Yang Liu, Qun Liu, and Shouxun Lin. 2006. Tree-to-string alignment template for statistical machine translation. In *Proceedings of International Conference on Computational Linguistics and Annual Meeting of the Association for Computational Linguistics (COLING-ACL 2006)*, pages 609–616.

Yusuke Miyao and Jun'ichi Tsujii. 2005. Probabilistic disambiguation models for wide-coverage HPSG parsing. In *Proceedings of Annual Meeting on Association for Computational Linguistics (ACL 2005)*, pages 83–90.

Yusuke Miyao and Jun'ichi Tsujii. 2008. Feature forest models for probabilistic HPSG parsing. *Computational Linguistics*, 34(1):35–80.

Jiri Navratil, Karthik Visweswariah, and Ananthakrishnan Ramanathan. 2012. A comparison of syntactic reordering methods for English-German machine translation. In *Proceedings of International Conference on Computational Linguistics (COLING 2012)*, pages 2043–2058.

Graham Neubig, Taro Watanabe, Eiichiro Sumita, Shinsuke Mori, and Tatsuya Kawahara. 2011. An unsupervised model for joint phrase alignment and extraction. In *Proceedings of Annual Meeting of the Association for Computational Linguistics: Human Language Technologies (ACL-HLT 2011)*, pages 632–641.

Graham Neubig, Taro Watanabe, and Shinsuke Mori. 2012. Inducing a discriminative parser to optimize machine translation reordering. In *Proceedings of Joint Conference on Empirical Methods in Natural Language Processing and Computational Natural Language Learning (EMNLP-CoNLL 2012)*, pages 843–853.

Franz J. Och and Hermann Ney. 2003. A systematic comparison of various statistical alignment models. *Computational Linguistics*, 29(1):19–51.

Franz J. Och and Hermann Ney. 2004. The alignment template approach to statistical machine translation. *Computational Linguistics*, 30(4):417–449.

Franz J. Och. 2003. Minimum error rate training in statistical machine translation. In *Proceedings of Annual Meeting on Association for Computational Linguistics (ACL 2003)*, pages 160–167.

Kishore Papineni, Salim Roukos, Todd Ward, and Wei-Jing Zhu. 2002. BLEU: a method for automatic evaluation of machine translation. In *Proceedings of Annual Meeting on Association for Computational Linguistics (ACL 2002)*, pages 311–318.

Chris Quirk, Arul Menezes, and Colin Cherry. 2005. Dependency treelet translation: Syntactically informed phrasal SMT. In *Proceedings of Annual Meeting on Association for Computational Linguistics (ACL 2005)*, pages 271–279.

Andreas Stolcke. 2002. SRILM - An extensible language modeling toolkit. In *Proceedings of International Conference on Spoken Language Processing (ICSLP 2002)*, pages 901–904.

Katsuhito Sudoh, Kevin Duh, Hajime Tsukada, Tsutomu Hirao, and Masaaki Nagata. 2010. Divide and translate: Improving long distance reordering in statistical machine translation. In *Proceedings of Joint Workshop on Statistical Machine Translation and Metrics MATR (WMT-MetricsMATR 2010)*, pages 418–427.

David Vilar, Jia Xu, Luis Fernando d'Haro, and Hermann Ney. 2006. Error analysis of statistical machine translation output. In *Proceedings of International Conference on Language Resources and Evaluation (LREC 2006)*, pages 697–702.

Dekai Wu. 1997. Stochastic inversion transduction grammars and bilingual parsing of parallel corpora. *Computational Linguistics*, 23(3):377–403.

Jun Xie, Haitao Mi, and Qun Liu. 2011. A novel dependency-to-string model for statistical machine translation. In *Proceedings of Conference on Empirical Methods in Natural Language Processing (EMNLP 2011)*, pages 216–226.

Deyi Xiong, Qun Liu, and Shouxun Lin. 2006. Maximum entropy based phrase reordering model for statistical machine translation. In *Proceedings of International Conference on Computational Linguistics and Annual Meeting on Association for Computational Linguistics (COLING-ACL 2006)*, pages 521–528.

Jia Xu, Richard Zens, and Hermann Ney. 2005. Sentence segmentation using IBM word alignment model 1. In *Proceedings of Annual Conference of the European Association for Machine Translation (EAMT 2005)*, pages 280–287.

Peng Xu, Jaeho Kang, Michael Ringgaard, and Franz J. Och. 2009. Using a dependency parser to improve SMT for subject-object-verb languages. In *Proceedings of Conference of the North American Chapter of the Association for Computational Linguistics on Human Language Technology (NAACL-HLT 2009)*, pages 245–253.

Kenji Yamada and Kevin Knight. 2001. A syntax-based statistical translation model. In *Proceedings of Annual Meeting on Association for Computational Linguistics (ACL 2001)*, pages 523–530.

Jingbo Zhu and Tong Xiao. 2011. Improving decoding generalization for tree-to-string translation. In *Proceedings of Annual Meeting of the Association for Computational Linguistics: Human Language Technologies (ACL-HLT 2001)*, pages 418–423.

Improving the Lexical Function Composition Model with Pathwise Optimized Elastic-Net Regression

Jiming Li and **Marco Baroni** and **Georgiana Dinu**
Center for Mind/Brain Sciences
University of Trento, Italy
(jiming.li|marco.baroni|georgiana.dinu)@unitn.it

Abstract

In this paper, we show that the lexical function model for composition of distributional semantic vectors can be improved by adopting a more advanced regression technique. We use the pathwise coordinate-descent optimized elastic-net regression method to estimate the composition parameters, and compare the resulting model with several recent alternative approaches in the task of composing simple intransitive sentences, adjective-noun phrases and determiner phrases. Experimental results demonstrate that the lexical function model estimated by elastic-net regression achieves better performance, and it provides good qualitative interpretability through sparsity constraints on model parameters.

1 Introduction

Vector-based distributional semantic models of word meaning have gained increased attention in recent years (Turney and Pantel, 2010). Different from formal semantics, distributional semantics represents word meanings as vectors in a high-dimensional semantic space, where the dimensions are given by co-occurring contextual features. The intuition behind these models lies in the fact that words which are similar in meaning often occur in similar contexts, e.g., *moon* and *star* might both occur with *sky, night* and *bright*. This leads to convenient ways to measure similarity between different words using geometric methods (e.g., the cosine of the angle between two vectors that summarize their contextual distribution). Distributional semantic models have been successfully applied to many tasks in linguistics and cognitive science (Griffiths et al., 2007; Foltz et al., 1998; Laham, 1997; McDonald and Brew, 2004). However, most of these tasks only deal with isolated words, and there is a strong need to construct representations for longer linguistic structures such as phrases and sentences. In order to achieve this goal, the principle of compositionality of linguistic structures, which states that complex linguistic structures can be formed through composition of simple elements, is applied to distributional vectors. Therefore, in recent years, the problem of composition within distributional models has caught many researchers' attention (Clark, 2013; Erk, 2012).

A number of compositional frameworks have been proposed and tested. Mitchell and Lapata (2008) propose a set of simple component-wise operations, such as multiplication and addition. Later, Guevara (2010) and Baroni and Zamparelli (2010) proposed more elaborate methods, in which composition is modeled as matrix-vector multiplication operations. Particularly new to their approach is the proposal to estimate model parameters by minimizing the distance of the composed vectors to corpus-observed phrase vectors. For example, Baroni and Zamparelli (2010) consider the case of Adjective-Noun composition and model it as matrix-vector multiplication: adjective matrices are parameters to be estimated and nouns are co-occurrence vectors. The model parameter estimation procedure becomes a multiple response multivariate regression problem. This method, that, following Dinu et al. (2013) and others, we term the *lexical function* composition model, can also be generalized to more complex structures such as 3rd order tensors for modeling transitive verbs (Grefenstette et al., 2013).

Socher et al. (2012) proposed a more complex and flexible framework based on matrix-vector representations. Each word or lexical node in a parsing tree is assigned a vector (representing inherent meaning of the constituent) and a matrix (controlling the behavior to modify the meaning of

Model	Composition function	Parameters
Add	$w_1\vec{u} + w_2\vec{v}$	w_1, w_2
Mult	$\vec{u}^{w_1} \odot \vec{v}^{w_2}$	w_1, w_2
Dil	$\|\|\vec{u}\|\|_2^2\vec{v} + (\lambda - 1)\langle\vec{u}, \vec{v}\rangle\vec{u}$	λ
Fulladd	$W_1\vec{u} + W_2\vec{v}$	$W_1, W_2 \in \mathbf{R}^{m \times m}$
Lexfunc	$A_u\vec{v}$	$A_u \in \mathbf{R}^{m \times m}$
Fulllex	$\tanh([W_1, W_2]\begin{bmatrix} A_u\vec{v} \\ A_v\vec{u}\end{bmatrix})$	$W_1, W_2,$ $A_u, A_v \in \mathbf{R}^{m \times m}$

Table 1: Composition functions of inputs (u, v).

neighbor words or phrases) simultaneously. They use recursive neural networks to learn and construct the entire model and show that it reaches state-of-the-art performance in various evaluation experiments.

In this paper, we focus on the simpler, linear lexical function model proposed by Baroni and Zamparelli (2010) (see also Coecke et al. (2010)) and show that its performance can be further improved through more advanced regression techniques. We use the recently introduced elastic-net regularized linear regression method, which is solved by the pathwise coordinate descent optimization algorithm along a regularization parameter path. This new regression method can rapidly generate a sequence of solutions along the regularization path. Performing cross-validation on this parameter path should yield a much more accurate model for prediction. Besides better prediction accuracy, the elastic-net method also brings interpretability to the composition procedure through sparsity constraints on the model.

The rest of this paper is organized as follows: In Section 2, we give details on the above-mentioned composition models, which will be used for comparison in our experiments. In Section 3, we describe the pathwise optimized elastic-net regression algorithm. Experimental evaluation on three composition tasks is provided in Section 4. In Section 5 we conclude and suggest directions for future work.

2 Composition Models

Mitchell and Lapata (2008; 2010) present a set of simple but effective models in which each component of the output vector is a function of the corresponding components of the inputs. Given input vectors $\vec{u}$ and $\vec{v}$, the weighted additive model (**Add**) returns their weighted sum: $\vec{p} = w_1\vec{u} + w_2\vec{v}$. In the dilation model (**Dil**), the output vector is obtained by decomposing one of the input vectors, say $\vec{v}$, into a vector parallel to $\vec{u}$ and an orthogonal vector, and then dilating only the parallel vector by a factor λ before re-combining (formula in Table 1). Mitchell and Lapata also propose a simple multiplicative model in which the output components are obtained by component-wise multiplication of the corresponding input components. We use its natural *weighted* extension (**Mult**), introduced by Dinu et al. (2013), that takes w_1 and w_2 powers of the components before multiplying, such that each phrase component p_i is given by: $p_i = u_i^{w_1} v_i^{w_2}$.

Guevara (2010) and Zanzotto et al. (2010) explore a full form of the additive model (**Fulladd**), where the two vectors entering a composition process are pre-multiplied by weight matrices before being added, so that each output component is a weighted sum of *all* input components: $\vec{p} = W_1\vec{u} + W_2\vec{v}$.

Baroni and Zamparelli (2010) and Coecke et al. (2010), taking inspiration from formal semantics, characterize composition as *function application*. For example, Baroni and Zamparelli model adjective-noun phrases by treating the adjective as a regression function from nouns onto (modified) nouns. Given that linear functions can be expressed by matrices and their application by matrix-by-vector multiplication, a functor (such as the adjective) is represented by a matrix A_u to be composed with the argument vector $\vec{v}$ (e.g., the noun) by multiplication, returning the *lexical function* (**Lexfunc**) representation of the phrase: $\vec{p} = A_u\vec{v}$.

The method proposed by Socher et al. (2012) can be seen as a combination and non-linear extension of Fulladd and Lexfunc (that Dinu and colleagues thus called **Fulllex**) in which *both* phrase elements act as functors (matrices) *and* arguments (vectors). Given input terms *u* and *v* represented by $(\vec{u}, A_u)$ and $(\vec{v}, A_v)$, respectively, their composition vector is obtained by applying first a linear transformation and then the hyperbolic tangent function to the concatenation of the products $A_u\vec{v}$ and $A_v\vec{u}$ (see Table 1 for the equation). Socher and colleagues also present a way to construct matrix representations for specific phrases, needed to scale this composition method to larger constituents. We ignore it here since we focus on the two-word case.

Parameter estimation of the above composition models follows Dinu et al. (2013) by minimizing the distance to corpus-extracted phrase vectors. In

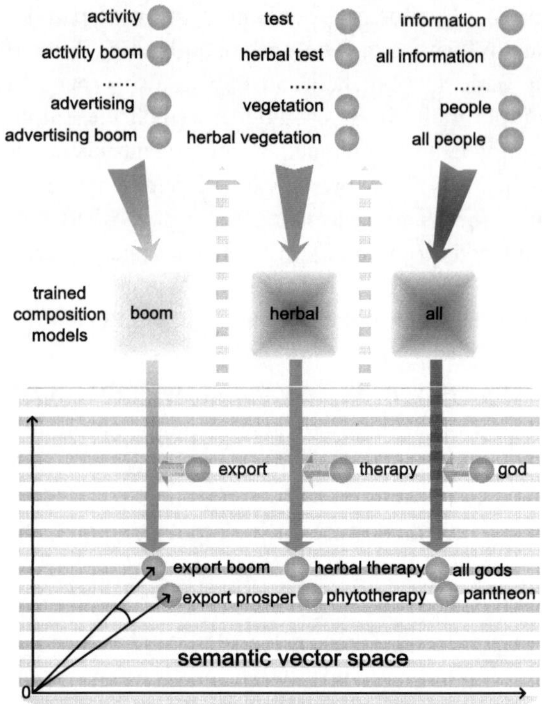

Figure 1: A sketch of the composition model training and composing procedure.

the case of the Fulladd and Lexfunc models this amounts to solving a multiple response multivariate regression problem.

The whole composition model training and phrase composition procedure is described with a sketch in Figure 1. To illustrate with an example, given an intransitive verb *boom*, we want to train a model for this intransitive verb so that we can use it for composition with a noun subject (e.g., *export*) to form an intransitive sentence (e.g., *export boom(s)*). We treat these steps as a composition model learning and predicting procedure. The training dataset is formed with pairs of input (e.g., *activity*) and output (e.g., *activity boom*) vectors. All composition models except Lexfunc also use the functor vector (*boom*) in the training data. Lexfunc does not use this functor vector, but it would rather like to encode the learning target's vector meaning in a different way (see experimental analysis in Section 4.3). Then, this dataset is used for parameter estimation of models. When a model (*boom*) is trained and given a new input semantic vector (e.g., *export*), it will output another vector representing the concept for *export boom*. And the concept *export boom* should be close to similar concepts (e.g., *export prosper*) in meaning under some distance metric in semantic vector space. The same training and composition scheme is applied for other types of functors (e.g., adjectives and determiners). All the above mentioned composition models are evaluated within this scheme, but note that in the case of Add, Dil, Mult and Fulladd, a single set of parameters is obtained across all functors of a certain syntactic category.

3 Pathwise Optimized Elastic-net Algorithm

The elastic-net regression method (Zou and Hastie, 2005) is proposed as a compromise between lasso (Tibshirani, 1996) and ridge regression (Hastie et al., 2009). Suppose there are N observation pairs (x_i, y_i), here $x_i \in \mathbb{R}^p$ is the ith training sample and $y_i \in \mathbb{R}$ is the corresponding response variable in the typical regression setting. For simplicity, assume the x_{ij} are standardized: $\sum_{i=1}^{N} x_{ij}^2 = 1$, for $j = 1, \ldots, p$. The elastic-net solves the following problem:

$$\min_{(\beta_0,\beta)\in\mathbb{R}^{p+1}} \left[\frac{1}{N} \sum_{i=1}^{N} (y_i - \beta_0 - x_i^T \beta)^2 + \lambda \mathbf{P}_\alpha(\beta) \right] \tag{1}$$

where

$$\begin{aligned} \mathbf{P}_\alpha(\beta) &= \lambda((1-\alpha)\frac{1}{2} \parallel \beta \parallel_{\ell_2}^2 + \alpha\beta_{\ell_1}) \\ &= \sum_{j=1}^{p} [\frac{1}{2}(1-\alpha)\beta_j^2 + \alpha|\beta_j|]. \end{aligned}$$

$\mathbf{P}$ is the elastic-net penalty, and it is a compromise between the ridge regression penalty and the lasso penalty. The merit of the elastic-net penalty depends on two facts: the first is that elastic-net inherits lasso's characteristic to shrink many of the regression coefficients to zero, a property called sparsity, which results in better interpretability of model; the second is that elastic-net inherits ridge regression's property of a grouping effect, which means important correlated features can be contained in the model simultaneously, and not be omitted as in lasso.

For these linear-type regression problem (ridge, lasso and elastic-net), the determination of the λ value is very important for prediction accuracy. Efron et al. (2004) developed an efficient algorithm to compute the entire regularization path for the lasso problem in 2004. Later, Friedman et al. (Friedman et al., 2007; Friedman et al., 2010) proposed a coordinate descent optimization method for the regularization parameter path, and they also provided a solution for elastic-net. The main idea of pathwise coordinate descent is to solve the penalized regression problem along an entire path of values for the regularization parameters λ, using the current estimates as warm starts. The idea turns out to be quite efficient for elastic-net regression. The procedure can be described as below: firstly establish an 100 λ value sequence in log scale, and for each of the 100 regularization parameters, use the following coordinate-wise updating rule to cycle around the features for estimating the corresponding regression coefficients until convergence.

$$\tilde{\beta}_j \leftarrow \frac{S\left(\frac{1}{N}\sum_{i=1}^{N} x_{ij}(y_i - \tilde{y}_i^{(j)}), \lambda\alpha\right)}{1 + \lambda(1-\alpha)} \quad (2)$$

where

- $\tilde{y}_i^{(j)} = \tilde{\beta}_0 + \sum_{\ell \neq j} x_{i\ell}\tilde{\beta}_\ell$ is the fitted value excluding the contribution from x_{ij}, and hence $y_i - \tilde{y}_i^{(j)}$ the partial residual for fitting β_j.
- $S(z, \gamma)$ is the soft-thresholding operator with value

$$\begin{aligned} S(z,\gamma) &= \text{sign}(z)(|z| - \gamma)_+ \\ &= \begin{cases} z - \gamma & \text{if } z > 0 \text{ and } \gamma < |z| \\ z + \gamma & \text{if } z < 0 \text{ and } \gamma < |z| \\ 0 & \text{if } \gamma \geq |z| \end{cases} \end{aligned}$$

Then solutions for a decreasing sequence of values for λ are computed in this way, starting at the smallest value $\lambda_{\max}$ for which the entire coefficient vector $\hat{\beta} = 0$. Then, 10-fold cross validation on this regularization path is used to determine the best model for prediction accuracy. The α parameter controls the model sparsity (the number of coefficients equal to zero) and grouping effect (shrinking highly correlated features simultaneously).

In what follows, we call the elastic-net regression lexical function model **EnetLex**. In Section 4, we will report the experiment results by EnetLex with $\alpha = 1$. It equals to pathwise coordinate descent optimized lasso, which favours sparser solutions and is often a better estimator when the number of training samples is far greater than the number of feature dimensions, as in our case. We also experimented with intermediate α values (e.g., $\alpha = 0.5$), that were, consistently, inferior or equal to the lasso setting.

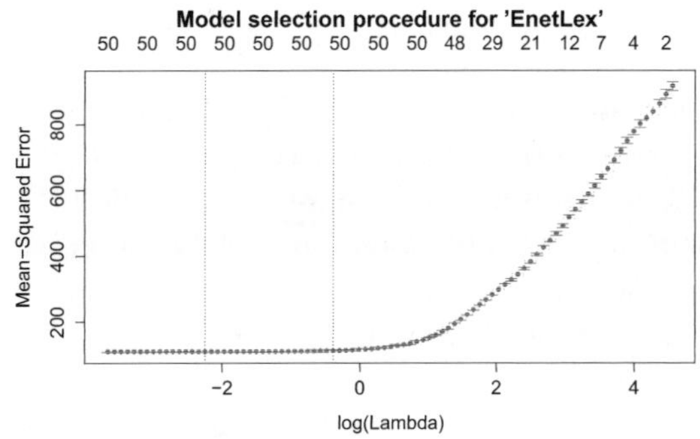

Figure 2: Example of model selection procedure for elastic-net regression (*"the"* model for determiner phrase experiment, SVD, 50 dimensions).

Figure 2 is an example of the model selection procedure between different regularization parameter λ values for determiner *"the"* (experimental details are described in section 4). When α is fixed, EnetLex first generates a λ sequence from $\lambda_{\max}$ to $\lambda_{\min}$ ($\lambda_{\max}$ is set to the smallest value which will shrink all the regression coefficients to zero, $\lambda_{\min} = 0.0001$) in log scale (rightmost point in the plot). The red points corresponding to each λ value in the plot represent mean cross-validated errors and their standard errors. To estimate a model corresponding to some λ value except $\lambda_{\max}$, we use the solution from previous λ value as the initial coefficients (the *warm starts* mentioned before) for iteration with coordinate descent. This will often generate a stable solution path for the whole λ sequence very fast. And we can choose the model with minimum cross-validation error on this path and use it for more accurate prediction. In Figure 2, the labels on the top are numbers of corresponding selected variables (features), the right vertical dotted line is the largest value of lambda such that error is within 1 standard error of the minimum, and the left vertical dotted line corresponds to the λ value which gives minimum cross-validated error. In this case, the λ value of minimum cross-validated error is 0.106, and its log is -2.244316. In all of our experiments, we will select models corresponding to minimum training-data cross-validated error.

4 Experiments

4.1 Datasets

We evaluate on the three data sets described below, that were also used by Dinu et al. (2013), our most direct point of comparison.

Intransitive sentences The first dataset, introduced by Mitchell and Lapata (2010), focuses on the composition of intransitive verbs and their noun subjects. It contains a total of 120 sentence pairs together with human similarity judgments on a 7-point scale. For example, *value slumps/value declines* is scored 7, *skin glows/skin burns* is scored 1. On average, each pair is rated by 30 participants. Rather than evaluating against mean scores, we use each rating as a separate data point, as done by Mitchell and Lapata. We report Spearman correlations between human-assigned scores and cosines of model-generated vector pairs.

Adjective-noun phrases Turney (2012) introduced a dataset including both noun-noun compounds and adjective-noun phrases (ANs). We focus on the latter, and we frame the task as in Dinu et al. (2013). The dataset contains 620 ANs, each paired with a single-noun paraphrase. Examples include: *upper side/upside*, *false belief/fallacy* and *electric refrigerator/fridge*. We evaluate a model by computing the cosine of all 20K nouns in our semantic space with the target AN, and looking at the rank of the correct paraphrase in this list. The lower the rank, the better the model. We report median rank across the test items.

Determiner phrases The third dataset, introduced in Bernardi et al. (2013), focuses on a class of determiner words. It is a multiple-choice test where target nouns (e.g., *omniscience*) must be matched with the most closely related determiner(-noun) phrases (DPs) (e.g., *all knowledge*). There are 173 target nouns in total, each paired with one correct DP response, as well as 5 foils, namely the determiner (*all*) and noun (*knowledge*) from the correct response and three more DPs, two of which contain the same noun as the correct phrase (*much knowledge, some knowledge*), the third the same determiner (*all preliminaries*). Other examples of targets/related-phrases are *quatrain/four lines* and *apathy/no emotion*. The models compute cosines between target noun and responses and are scored based on their accuracy at ranking the correct phrase first.

4.2 Setup

We use a concatenation of ukWaC, Wikipedia (2009 dump) and BNC as source corpus, totaling 2.8 billion tokens.[1] Word co-occurrences are collected within sentence boundaries (with a maximum of a 50-words window around the target word). Following Dinu et al. (2013), we use the top 10K most frequent content lemmas as context features, Pointwise Mutual Information as weighting method and we reduce the dimensionality of the data by both Non-negative Matrix Factorization (NMF, Lee and Seung (2000)) and Singular Value Decomposition (SVD). For both data dimensionality reduction techniques, we experiment with different numbers of dimension varying from 50 to 300 with a step of 50. Since the Mult model works very poorly when the input vectors contain negative values, as is the case with SVD, for this model we report result distributions across the 6 NMF variations only.

Model	Reduction	Dim	Correlation
Add	NMF	150	0.1349
Dil	NMF	300	0.1288
Mult	NMF	250	0.2246
Fulladd	SVD	300	0.0461
Lexfunc	SVD	250	0.2673
Fulllex	NMF	300	0.2682
EnetLex	SVD	250	**0.3239**

Table 2: Best performance comparison for intransitive verb sentence composition.

We use the DIStributional SEmantics Composition Toolkit (DISSECT)[2] which provides implementations for all models we use for comparison. Following Dinu and colleagues, we used ordinary least-squares to estimate Fulladd and ridge for Lexfunc. The EnetLex model is implemented in R with support from the glmnet package,[3] which implements pathwise coordinate descent elastic-net regression.

4.3 Experimental Results and Analysis

The experimental results are shown in Tables 2, 3, 4 and Figures 3, 4, 5. The best performances from each model on the three composition tasks are shown in the tables. The overall result distributions across reduction techniques and dimensionalities are displayed in the figure

[1] http://wacky.sslmit.unibo.it; http://www.natcorp.ox.ac.uk

[2] http://clic.cimec.unitn.it/composes/toolkit/

[3] http://cran.r-project.org/web/packages/glmnet/

Model	Reduction	Dim	Rank
Add	NMF	300	113
Dil	NMF	300	354.5
Mult	NMF	300	146.5
Fulladd	SVD	300	123
Lexfunc	SVD	150	117.5
Fulllex	SVD	50	394
EnetLex	SVD	300	**108.5**

Table 3: Best performance comparison for adjective noun composition (lower ranks mean better performance).

Model	Reduction	Dim	Rank
Add	NMF	100	0.3237
Dil	NMF	100	0.3584
Mult	NMF	300	0.2023
Fulladd	NMF	200	0.3642
Lexfunc	SVD	200	0.3699
Fulllex	SVD	100	0.3699
EnetLex	SVD	250	**0.4046**

Table 4: Best performance comparison for determiner phrase composition.

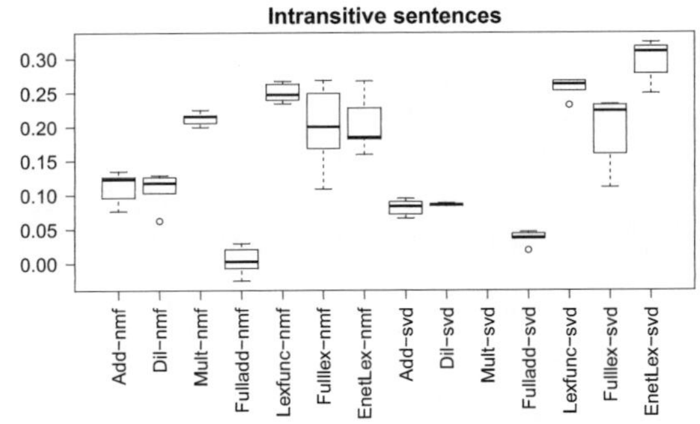

Figure 3: Intransitive verb sentence composition results.

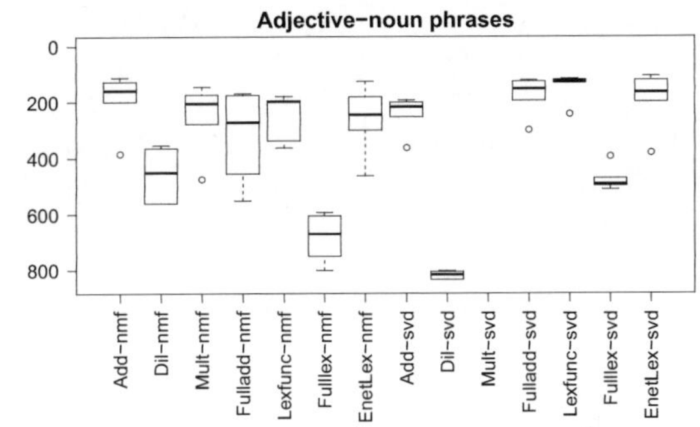

Figure 4: Adjective noun phrase composition results.

boxplots (NMF and SVD results are shown separately). From Tables 2, 3, 4, we can see that EnetLex consistently achieves the best composition performance overall, also outperforming the standard lexical function model. In the boxplot display, we can see that SVD is in general more stable across dimensionalities, yielding smaller variance in the results than NMF. We also observe, more specifically, larger variance in EnetLex performance on NMF than in Lexfunc, especially for determiner phrase composition. The large variance with EnetLex comes from the NMF low-dimensionality results, especially the 50 dimensions condition. The main reason for this lies in the fast-computing tricks of the coordinate descent algorithm when cycling around many features with zero values (as resulting from NMF), which cause fast convergence at the beginning of the regularization path, generating an inaccurate model. A subordinate reason might lie in the unstandardized larger values of the NMF features (causing large gaps between adjacent parameter values in the regularization path). Although data standardization or other feature scaling techniques are often adopted in statistical analysis, they are seldom used in semantic composition tasks due to the fact that they might negatively affect the semantic vector space. A reasonable way out of this problem would be to save the mean and standard deviation parameters used for data standardization and use them to project the composed phrase vector outputs back to the original vector space.

On the other hand, EnetLex obtained a stable good performance in SVD space, with the best results achieved with dimensions between 200 and 300. A set of Tukey's Honestly Significant Tests show that EnetLex significantly outperforms the other models across SVD settings for determiner phrases and intransitive sentences. The difference is not significant for most comparisons in the adjective phrases task.

For the simpler models for which it was computationally feasible, we repeated the experiments without dimensionality reduction. The results obtained with (unweighted) Add and Mult using full-space representations are reported in Table 5. Due to computational limitations, we tuned full-space weights for Add model only, obtaining similar results to those reported in the table. The full-space

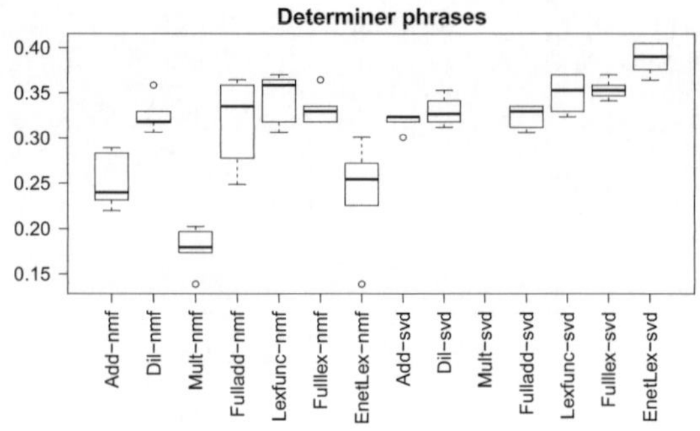

Figure 5: Determiner phrase composition results.

model	verb	adjective	determiner
Add	0.0259	957	0.2832
Mult	0.1796	298.5	0.0405

Table 5: Performance of Add and Mult models without dimensionality reduction.

results confirm that dimensionality reduction is not only a computational necessity when working with more complex models, but it is actually improving the quality of the underlying semantic space.

Another benefit that elastic-net has brought to us is the sparsity in coefficient matrices. Sparsity here means that many entries in the coefficient matrix are shrunk to 0. For the above three experiments, the mean adjective, verb and determiner models' sparsity ratios are 0.66, 0.55 and 0.18 respectively. Sparsity can greatly reduce the space needed to store the lexical function model, especially when we want to use higher orders of representation. Moreover, sparsity in the model is helpful to interpret the concept a specific functor word is conveying. For example, we show how to analyze the coefficient matrices for functor content words (verbs and adjectives). The verb *burst* and adjective *poisonous*, when estimated in the space projected to 100 dimensions with NMF, have percentages of sparsity 47% and 39% respectively, which means 47% of the entries in the *burst* matrix and 39% of the entries in the *poisonous* matrix are zeros.[4] Most of the (hopefully) irrelevant dimensions were discarded during model training. For visualization, we list the 6 most significant columns and rows from verb *burst* and adjective *poisonous* in Table 6. Each reduced NMF dimension is represented by the 3 largest original-context entries in the corresponding row of the NMF basis matrix. The top columns and rows are selected by ordering sums of row entries and sums of column entries (the 10 most common features across trained matrices are omitted). In the matrix-vector multiplication scenario, a larger column contributes more to all the features of the composed output phrase vector, while one large row corresponds to a large composition output feature. From these tables, we can see that the selected top columns and rows are mostly semantically relevant to the corresponding functor words (*burst* and *poisonous*, in the displayed examples).

A very interesting aspect of these experiments is the role of the intercept in our regression model. The path-wise optimization algorithm starts with a lambda value ($\lambda_{\max}$), which sets all the coefficients exactly to 0, and at that time the intercept is just the expected mean value of the training phrase vectors, which in turn is of course quite similar to the co-occurrence vector of the corresponding functor word (by averaging the *poisonous N* context distributions, we obtain a vector that approximates the *poisonous* distribution). And, although the intercept also changes with different lambda values, it still highly correlates with the co-occurrence vectors of the functor words in vector space. For adjectives and verbs, we compared the initial model's ($\lambda_{\max}$) intercept and the minimum cross-validation error model intercept with corpus-extracted vectors for the corresponding words. That is, we used the word co-occurrence vector for a verb or an adjective extracted from the corpus and projected onto the reduced feature space (e.g., NMF, 100 dimensions), then computed cosine similarity between this word meaning representation and its corresponding EnetLex matrix initial and minimum-error intercepts, respectively. Most of the similarities are still quite high after estimation: The mean cosine values for adjectives are 0.82 for the initial intercept and 0.72 for the minimum-error one. For verbs, the corresponding values are 0.75 and 0.69, respectively. Apparently, the sparsity constraint helps the intercept retaining information from training phrases.

Qualitatively, often the intercept encodes the representation of the original word meaning in

[4] We analyze NMF rather than the better-performing SVD features because the presence of negative values in the latter makes their interpretation very difficult. And NMF achieves comparably good performance for interpretation when dimension exceeds 100.

burst	*significant columns*	*significant rows*
	policeman, mob, guard Iraqi, Lebanese, Kurdish jealousy, anger, guilt hurricane, earthquake, disaster defender, keeper, striker volcanic, sediment, geological	hurricane, earthquake, disaster conquer, Byzantine, conquest policeman, mob, guard terminus, traffic, interchange convict, sentence, imprisonment boost, unveil, campaigner
poisonous	*significant columns*	*significant rows*
	bathroom, wc, shower ignite, emit, reactor reptile, mammal, predator ventilation, fluid, bacterium flowering, shrub, perennial sauce, onion, garlic	ventilation, fluid, bacterium ignite, emit, reactor infectious, infect, infected slay, pharaoh, tribe park, lorry, pavement knife, pierce, brass

Table 6: Interpretability for verbs and adjectives (exemplified by *burst* and *poisonous*).

vector space. For example, if we check the intercept for *poisonous*, the cosine between the original vector space representation (from corpus) and the minimum-error solution intercept (from training phrases) is at 0.7. The NMF dimensions corresponding with the largest intercept entries are rather intuitive for *poisonous*: $\langle$*ventilation, fluid, bacterium*$\rangle$, $\langle$*racist, racism, outrage*$\rangle$, $\langle$*reptile, mammal, predator*$\rangle$, $\langle$*flowering, shrub, perennial*$\rangle$, $\langle$*sceptical, accusation, credibility*$\rangle$, $\langle$*infectious, infect, infected*$\rangle$.

The mathematical reason for the above facts lies in the updating rule of the elastic-net's intercept:

$$\beta_0 = \bar{\mathbf{y}} - \sum_{j=1}^{p} \hat{\beta}_j \bar{\mathbf{x}}_j \tag{3}$$

Sparsity in the regression coefficients ($\hat{\beta}_j$) encourages intercept β_0 to stay as close to the mean value of response $\bar{\mathbf{y}}$ as possible. So the elastic-net lexical function composition model is *de facto* also capturing the inherent meaning of the functor word, learning it from the training word-phrase pairs. In future research, we would like to test if these lexical meaning representations are as good or even better than standard co-occurrence vectors for single-word similarity tasks.

5 Conclusion

In this paper, we have shown that the lexical function composition model can be improved by advanced regression techniques. We use pathwise coordinate descent optimized elastic-net, testing it on composing intransitive sentences, adjective-noun phrases and determiner phrases in comparison with other composition models, including lexical function estimated with ridge regression. The elastic-net method leads to performance gains on all three tasks. Through sparsity constraints on the model, elastic-net also introduces interpretability in the lexical function composition model. The regression coefficient matrices can often be easily interpreted by looking at large row and column sums, as many matrix entries are shrunk to zero. The intercept of elastic-net regression also plays an interesting role in the model. With the sparsity constraints, the intercept of the model tends to retain the inherent meaning of the word by averaging training phrase vectors.

Our approach naturally generalizes to similar composition tasks, in particular those involving higher-order tensors (Grefenstette et al., 2013), where sparseness might be crucial in producing compact representations of very large objects. Our results also suggest that the performance of the lexical function composition model might be further improved with even more advanced methods, such as nonlinear regression. In the future, we would also like to explore interpretability more in depth, by looking at grouping and interaction effects between features.

Acknowledgments

We acknowledge ERC 2011 Starting Independent Research Grant n. 283554 (COMPOSES), and we thank the reviewers for helpful feedback.

References

Marco Baroni and Roberto Zamparelli. 2010. Nouns are vectors, adjectives are matrices: Representing adjective-noun constructions in semantic space. In *Proceedings of EMNLP*, pages 1183–1193, Boston, MA.

Raffaella Bernardi, Georgiana Dinu, Marco Marelli, and Marco Baroni. 2013. A relatedness benchmark to test the role of determiners in compositional distributional semantics. In *Proceedings of ACL (Short Papers)*, pages 53–57, Sofia, Bulgaria.

Stephen Clark. 2013. Vector space models of lexical meaning. In Shalom Lappin and Chris Fox, editors, *Handbook of Contemporary Semantics, 2nd edition*. Blackwell, Malden, MA. In press.

Bob Coecke, Mehrnoosh Sadrzadeh, and Stephen Clark. 2010. Mathematical foundations for a compositional distributional model of meaning. *Linguistic Analysis*, 36:345–384.

Georgiana Dinu, Nghia The Pham, and Marco Baroni. 2013. General estimation and evaluation of compositional distributional semantic models. In *Proceedings of ACL Workshop on Continuous Vector Space Models and their Compositionality*, pages 50–58, Sofia, Bulgaria.

Bradley Efron, Trevor Hastie, Iain Johnstone, and Robert Tibshirani. 2004. Least angle regression. *The Annals of statistics*, 32(2):407–499.

Katrin Erk. 2012. Vector space models of word meaning and phrase meaning: A survey. *Language and Linguistics Compass*, 6(10):635–653.

Peter Foltz, Walter Kintsch, and Thomas Landauer. 1998. The measurement of textual coherence with Latent Semantic Analysis. *Discourse Processes*, 25:285–307.

Jerome Friedman, Trevor Hastie, Holger Höfling, and Robert Tibshirani. 2007. Pathwise coordinate optimization. *The Annals of Applied Statistics*, 1(2):302–332.

Jerome Friedman, Trevor Hastie, and Rob Tibshirani. 2010. Regularization paths for generalized linear models via coordinate descent. *Journal of statistical software*, 33(1):1.

Edward Grefenstette, Georgiana Dinu, Yao-Zhong Zhang, Mehrnoosh Sadrzadeh, and Marco Baroni. 2013. Multi-step regression learning for compositional distributional semantics. In *Proceedings of IWCS*, pages 131–142, Potsdam, Germany.

Tom Griffiths, Mark Steyvers, and Josh Tenenbaum. 2007. Topics in semantic representation. *Psychological Review*, 114:211–244.

Emiliano Guevara. 2010. A regression model of adjective-noun compositionality in distributional semantics. In *Proceedings of GEMS*, pages 33–37, Uppsala, Sweden.

Trevor Hastie, Robert Tibshirani, and Jerome Friedman. 2009. *The Elements of Statistical Learning, 2nd ed.* Springer, New York.

Darrell Laham. 1997. Latent Semantic Analysis approaches to categorization. In *Proceedings of CogSci*, page 979.

Daniel Lee and Sebastian Seung. 2000. Algorithms for Non-negative Matrix Factorization. In *Proceedings of NIPS*, pages 556–562.

Scott McDonald and Chris Brew. 2004. A distributional model of semantic context effects in lexical processing. In *Proceedings of ACL*, pages 17–24, Barcelona, Spain.

Jeff Mitchell and Mirella Lapata. 2008. Vector-based models of semantic composition. In *Proceedings of ACL*, pages 236–244, Columbus, OH.

Jeff Mitchell and Mirella Lapata. 2010. Composition in distributional models of semantics. *Cognitive Science*, 34(8):1388–1429.

Richard Socher, Brody Huval, Christopher Manning, and Andrew Ng. 2012. Semantic compositionality through recursive matrix-vector spaces. In *Proceedings of EMNLP*, pages 1201–1211, Jeju Island, Korea.

Rob Tibshirani. 1996. Regression shrinkage and selection via the lasso. *Journal of the Royal Statistical Society. Series B (Methodological)*, 58(1):267–288.

Peter Turney and Patrick Pantel. 2010. From frequency to meaning: Vector space models of semantics. *Journal of Artificial Intelligence Research*, 37:141–188.

Peter Turney. 2012. Domain and function: A dual-space model of semantic relations and compositions. *J. Artif. Intell. Res.(JAIR)*, 44:533–585.

Fabio Zanzotto, Ioannis Korkontzelos, Francesca Falucchi, and Suresh Manandhar. 2010. Estimating linear models for compositional distributional semantics. In *Proceedings of COLING*, pages 1263–1271, Beijing, China.

Hui Zou and Trevor Hastie. 2005. Regularization and variable selection via the elastic net. *Journal of the Royal Statistical Society: Series B (Statistical Methodology)*, 67(2):301–320.

Is Machine Translation Getting Better over Time?

Yvette Graham **Timothy Baldwin** **Alistair Moffat** **Justin Zobel**
Department of Computing and Information Systems
The University of Melbourne
{ygraham,tbaldwin,ammoffat,jzobel}@unimelb.edu.au

Abstract

Recent human evaluation of machine translation has focused on relative preference judgments of translation quality, making it difficult to track longitudinal improvements over time. We carry out a large-scale crowd-sourcing experiment to estimate the degree to which state-of-the-art performance in machine translation has increased over the past five years. To facilitate longitudinal evaluation, we move away from relative preference judgments and instead ask human judges to provide direct estimates of the quality of individual translations in isolation from alternate outputs. For seven European language pairs, our evaluation estimates an average 10-point improvement to state-of-the-art machine translation between 2007 and 2012, with Czech-to-English translation standing out as the language pair achieving most substantial gains. Our method of human evaluation offers an economically feasible and robust means of performing ongoing longitudinal evaluation of machine translation.

1 Introduction

Human evaluation provides the foundation for empirical machine translation (MT), whether human judges are employed directly to evaluate system output, or via the use of automatic metrics – validated through correlation with human judgments. Achieving consistent human evaluation is not easy, however. Annual evaluation campaigns conduct large-scale human assessment but report ever-decreasing levels of judge consistency – when given the same pair of translations to repeat-assess, even expert human judges will worryingly often contradict both the preference judgment of other judges and their own earlier preference (Bojar et al., 2013). For this reason, human evaluation has been targeted within the community as an area in need of attention, with increased efforts to develop more reliable methodologies.

One standard platform for human evaluation is WMT shared tasks, where assessments have (since 2007) taken the form of ranking five alternate system outputs from best to worst (Bojar et al., 2013). This method has been shown to produce more consistent judgments compared to fluency and adequacy judgments on a five-point scale (Callison-Burch et al., 2007). However, relative preference judgments have been criticized for being a simplification of the real differences between translations, not sufficiently taking into account the large number of different types of errors of varying severity that occur in translations (Birch et al., 2013). Relative preference judgments do not take into account the degree to which one translation is better than another – there is no way of knowing if a winning system produces far better translations than all other systems, or if that system would have ranked lower if the severity of its inferior translation outputs were taken into account.

Rather than directly aiming to increase human judge consistency, some methods instead increase the number of reference translations available to automatic metrics. HTER (Snover et al., 2006) employs humans to post-edit each system output, creating individual human-targeted reference translations which are then used as the basis for computing the translation error rate. HyTER, on the other hand, is a tool that facilitates creation of very large numbers of reference translations (Dreyer and Marcu, 2012). Although both approaches increase fairness compared to automatic metrics that use a single generic reference translation, even human post-editors will inevitably vary in the way they post-edit translations, and the process of creating even a single new reference translation for each system output is often too resource-intensive to be used in practice.

With each method of human evaluation, a trade-off exists between annotation time and the number of judgments collected. At one end of the spectrum, the WMT human evaluation collects large numbers of quick judgments (approximately 3.5 minutes per screen, or 20 seconds per label) (Bojar et al., 2013).[1] In contrast, HMEANT (Lo and Wu, 2011) uses a more time-consuming fine-grained semantic-role labeling analysis at a rate of approximately 10 sentences per hour (Birch et al., 2013). But even with this detailed evaluation methodology, human judges are inconsistent (Birch et al., 2013).

Although the trend appears to be toward more fine-grained human evaluation of MT output, it remains to be shown that this approach leads to more reliable system rankings – with a main reason to doubt this being that far fewer judgments will inevitably be possible. We take a counter-approach and aim to maintain the speed by which assessments are collected in shared task evaluations, but modify the evaluation set-up in two main ways: (1) we structure the judgments as monolingual tasks, reducing the cognitive load involved in assessing translation quality; and (2) we apply judge-intrinsic quality control and score standardization, to minimize noise introduced when crowd-sourcing is used to leverage numbers of assessments and to allow for the fact that human judges will vary in the way they assess translations. Assessors are regarded as reliable as long as they demonstrate consistent judgments across a range of different quality translations.

We elicit direct estimates of quality from judges, as a quantitative estimate of the magnitude of each attribute of interest (Steiner and Norman, 1989). Since we no longer look for relative preference judgments, we revert back to the original fluency and adequacy criteria last used in WMT 2007 shared task evaluation. Instead of five-point fluency/adequacy scales, however, we use a (100-point) continuous rating scale, as this facilitates more sophisticated statistical analyses of score distributions for judges, including worker-intrinsic quality control for crowd-sourcing. The latter does not depend on agreement with experts, and is made possible by the reduction in information-loss when a continuous scale is used. In addition, translations are assessed in isolation from alternate system outputs, so that judgments collected are no longer relative to a set of five translations. This has the added advantage of eliminating the criticism made of WMT evaluations that systems sometimes gain advantage from luck-of-the-draw comparison with low quality output, and vice-versa (Bojar et al., 2011).

Based on our proposed evaluation methodology, human judges are able to work quickly, on average spending 18 and 13 seconds per single segment adequacy and fluency judgment, respectively. Additionally, when sufficiently large volumes of such judgments are collected, mean scores reveal significant differences between systems. Furthermore, since human evaluation takes the form of direct estimates instead of relative preference judgments, our evaluation introduces the possibility of large-scale longitudinal human evaluation. We demonstrate the value of longitudinal evaluation by investigating the improvement made to state-of-the-art MT over a five year time period (between 2007 and 2012) using the best participating WMT shared task system output. Since it is likely that the test data used for shared tasks has varied in difficulty over this time period, we additionally propose a simple mechanism for scaling system scores relative to task difficulty.

Using the proposed methodology for measuring longitudinal change in MT, we conclude that, for the seven European language pairs we evaluate, MT has made an average 10% improvement over the past 5 years. Our method uses non-expert monolingual judges via a crowd-sourcing portal, with fast turnaround and at relatively modest cost.

2 Monolingual Human Evaluation

There are several reasons why the assessment of MT quality is difficult. Ideally, each judge should be a native speaker of the target language, while at the same time being highly competent in the source language. Genuinely bilingual people are rare, however. As a result, judges are often people with demonstrated skills in the target language, and a working knowledge – often self-assessed – of the source language. Adding to the complexity is the discipline that is required: the task is cognitively difficult and time-consuming when done properly. The judge is, in essence, being asked to decide if the supplied translations are what they

[1] WMT 2013 reports 361 hours of labor to collect 61,695 labels, with approximately one screen of five pairwise comparisons each yielding a set of 10 labels.

would have generated if they were asked to do the same translation.

The assessment task itself is typically structured as follows: the source segment (a sentence or a phrase), plus five alternative translations and a "reference" translation are displayed. The judge is then asked to assign a rank order to the five translations, from best to worst. A set of pairwise preferences are then inferred, and used to generate system rankings, without any explicit formation of stand-alone system "scores".

This structure introduces the risk that judges will only compare translations against the reference translation. Certainly, judges will vary in the degree they rely on the reference translation, which will in turn impact on inter-judge inconsistency. For instance, even when expert judges do assessments, it is possible that they use the reference translation as a substitute for reading the source input, or do not read the source input at all. And if crowd-sourcing is used, can we really expect high proportions of workers to put the additional effort into reading and understanding the source input when a reference translation (probably in their native language) is displayed? In response to this potential variability in how annotators go about the assessment task, we trial assessments of adequacy in which the source input is not displayed to human judges. We structure assessments as a monolingual task and pose them in such a way that the focus is on comparing the *meaning* of reference translations and system outputs.[2]

We therefore ask human judges to assess the degree to which the system output conveys the same meaning as the reference translation. In this way, we focus the human judge indirectly on the question we wish to answer when assessing MT: *does the translation convey the meaning of the source?* The fundamental assumption of this approach is that the reference translation accurately captures the meaning of the source; once that assumption is made, it is clear that the source is not required during the evaluation.

Benefits of this change are that the task is both easier to describe to novice judges, and easier to answer, and that it requires only monolingual speakers, opening up the evaluation to a vastly larger pool of genuinely qualified workers.

With this set-up in place for adequacy, we also re-introduce a fluency assessment. Fluency ratings can be carried out without the presence of a reference translation, reducing any remnant bias towards reference translations in the evaluation setup. That is, we propose a judgment regime in which each task is presented as a two-item fluency and adequacy judgment, evaluated separately, and with adequacy restructured into a monolingual "similarity of meaning" task.

When fluency and adequacy were originally used for human evaluation, each rating used a 5-point adjective scale (Callison-Burch et al., 2007). However, adjectival scale labels are problematic and ratings have been shown to be highly dependent on the exact wording of descriptors (Seymour et al., 1985). Alexandrov (2010) provides a summary of the extensive problems associated with the use of adjectival scale labels, including bias resulting from positively- and negatively-worded items not being true opposites of one another, and items intended to have neutral intensity in fact proving to have specific conceptual meanings.

It is often the case, however, that the question could be restructured so that the rating scale no longer requires adjectival labels, by posing the question as a statement such as *The text is fluent English* and asking the human assessor to specify how strongly they agree or disagree with that statement. The scale and labels can then be held constant across experimental set-ups for all attributes evaluated – meaning that if the scale is still biased in some way it will be equally so across all set-ups.

3 Assessor Consistency

One way of estimating the quality of a human evaluation regime is to measure its *consistency*: whether or not the same outcome is achieved if the same question is asked a second time. In MT, annotator consistency is commonly measured using Cohen's kappa coefficient, or some variant thereof (Artstein and Poesio, 2008). Originally developed as a means of establishing assessor independence, it is now commonly used in the reverse sense, with high numeric values being used as evidence of agreement. Two different measurements can be made – whether a judge is consistent with other judgments performed by themselves (intra-annotator agreement), and whether a judge is consistent with other judges (inter-annotator agreement).

Cohen's kappa is intended for use with categor-

[2]This dimension of the assessment is similar but not identical to the monolingual adequacy assessment in early NIST evaluation campaigns (NIST, 2002).

ical judgments, but is also commonly used with five-point adjectival-scale judgments, where the set of categories has an explicit ordering. One particular issue with five-point assessments is that score standardization cannot be applied. As such, a judge who assigns two neighboring intervals is awarded the same "penalty" for being "different" as the judge who chooses the extremities. The kappa coefficient cannot be directly applied to many-valued interval or continuous data.

This raises the question of how we should evaluate assessor consistency when a continuous rating scale is in place. No judge, when given the same translation to judge twice on a continuous rating scale, can be expected to give precisely the same score for each judgment (where repeat assessments are separated by a considerable number of intervening ones). A more flexible tool is thus required. We build such a tool by starting with two core assumptions:

***A*:** When a consistent assessor is presented with a set of repeat judgments, the mean of the initial set of assessments will not be significantly different from the mean score of repeat assessments.

***B*:** When a consistent judge is presented with a set of judgments for translations from two systems, one of which is known to produce better translations than the other, the mean score for the better system will be significantly higher than that of the inferior system.

Assumption B is the basis of our quality-control mechanism, and allows us to distinguish between Turkers who are working carefully and those who are merely going through the motions. We use a 100-judgment HIT structure to control same-judge repeat items and deliberately-degraded system outputs (*bad_reference* items) used for worker-intrinsic quality control (Graham et al., 2013). *bad_reference* translations for fluency judgments are created as follows: two words in the translation are randomly selected and randomly re-inserted elsewhere in the sentence (but not as the initial or final words of the sentence).

Since adding duplicate words will not degrade adequacy in the same way, we use an alternate method to create *bad_reference* items for adequacy judgments: we randomly delete a short sub-string of length proportional to the length of the original translation to emulate a missing phrase. Since this is effectively a new degradation scheme, we tested against experts. For low-quality translations, deleting just two words from a long sentence often made little difference. The method we eventually settled on removes a sequence of k words, as a function of sentence length n:

	total wrkrs	fltrd wrkrs	Assum A holds	total segs	fltrd segs
F	557	321 (58%)	314 (98.8%)	122k	78k (64%)
A	542	283 (52%)	282 (99.6%)	102k	62k (61%)

Table 1: Total quality control filtered workers and assessments (F = fluency; A = adequacy).

$$\begin{aligned} 2 \leq n \leq 3 &\rightarrow k = 1 \\ 4 \leq n \leq 5 &\rightarrow k = 2 \\ 6 \leq n \leq 8 &\rightarrow k = 3 \\ 9 \leq n \leq 15 &\rightarrow k = 4 \\ 16 \leq n \leq 20 &\rightarrow k = 5 \\ n > 20 &\rightarrow k = \lceil \frac{n}{5} \rceil \end{aligned}$$

To filter out careless workers, scores for *bad_reference* pairs are extracted, and a difference-of-means test is used to calculate a worker-reliability estimate in the form of a p-value. Paired tests are then employed using the raw scores for degraded and corresponding system outputs, using a reliability significance threshold of $p < 0.05$. If a worker does not demonstrate the ability to reliably distinguish between a bad system and a better one, the judgments from that worker are discarded. This methodology means that careless workers who habitually rate translations either high or low will be detected, as well as (with high probability) those that click (perhaps via robots) randomly. It also has the advantage of not filtering out workers who are internally consistent but whose scores happen not to correspond particularly well to a set of expert assessments.

Having filtered out users who are unable to reliably distinguish between better and worse sets of translations ($p \geq 0.05$), we can now examine how well Assumption A holds for the remaining users, i.e. the extent to which workers apply consistent scores to repeated translations. We compute mean scores for the initial and repeat items and look for even very small differences in the two distributions for each worker. Table 1 shows numbers of workers who passed quality control, and also that

S_i	S_{i+5}
1 bad reference	its corresponding system output
1 system output	a repeat of it
1 reference	its corresponding system output
Above in reverse for S_i and S_{i+5}	
4 system outputs	4 system outputs

Table 2: Control of repeat item pairs. S_i denotes the ith set of 10 translations assessed within a 100 translation HIT.

the vast majority (around 99%) of reliable workers have no significant difference between mean scores for repeat items.

4 Five Years of Machine Translation

To estimate the improvement in MT that took place between 2007 and 2012, we asked workers on Amazon's Mechanical Turk (MTurk) to rate the quality of translations produced by the best-reported participating system for each of WMT 2007 and WMT 2012 (Callison-Burch et al., 2007; Callison-Burch et al., 2012). Since it is likely that the test set has changed in difficulty over this time period, we also include in the evaluation the original test data for 2007 and 2012, translated by a single current MT system. We use the latter to calibrate the results for test set difficulty, by calculating the average difference in rating, Δ, between the 2007 and 2012 test sets. This is then added to the difference in rating for the best-reported systems in 2012 and 2007, to arrive at an overall evaluation of the 5-year gain in MT quality for a given language pair, separately for fluency and adequacy.

Experiments were carried out for each of German, French and Spanish into and out of English, and also for Czech-to-English. English-to-Czech was omitted because of a low response rate on MTurk. For language pairs where two systems tied for first place in the shared task, a random selection of translations from both systems was made.

HIT structure

To facilitate quality control, we construct each HIT on MTurk as an assessment of 100 translations. Each individual translation is rated in isolation from other translations with workers required to iterate through 100 translations without the opportunity to revisit earlier assessments. A 100-translation HIT contains the following items: 70 randomly selected system outputs made up of roughly equal proportions of translations for each evaluated system, 10 *bad_reference* translations (each based on one of the 70 system outputs), 10 exact repeats and 10 reference translations. We divide a 100-translation HIT into 10 sets of 10 translations. Table 2 shows how the content of each set is determined. Translations are then randomized only *within* each set (of 10 translations), with the original sequence order of the sets preserved. In this way, the order of quality control items is unpredictable but controlled so pairs are separated by a minimum of 40 intervening assessments (4 sets of translations). The HIT structure results in 80% of assessed translations corresponding to genuine outputs of a system (including exact repeat assessments), which is ultimately what we wish to obtain, with 20% of assessments belonging to quality control items (*bad_reference* or reference translations).

Assessment set-up

Separate HITs were provided for evaluation of fluency and adequacy. For fluency, a single system output was displayed per screen, with a worker required to rate the fluency of a translation on a 100-point visual analog scale with no displayed point scores. A similar set-up was used for adequacy but with the addition of a reference translation (displayed in gray font to distinguish it from the system output being assessed). The Likert-type statement that framed the judgment was *Read the text below and rate it by how much you agree that*:

- [for fluency] *the text is fluent English*
- [for adequacy] *the black text adequately expresses the meaning of the gray text.*

In neither case was the source language string provided to the workers.

Tasks were published on MTurk, with no region restriction but the stipulation that only native speakers of the target language should complete HITs, and with a qualification of an MTurk prior HIT-approval rate of at least 95%. Instructions were always presented in the target language. Workers were paid US$0.50 per fluency HIT, and US$0.60 per adequacy HIT.[3]

[3] Since insufficient assessments were collected for French and German evaluations in the initial run, a second and ultimately third set of HITs were needed for these languages with increased payment per HIT of US$1.0 per 100-judgment adequacy HIT, US$0.65 per 100-judgment fluency HIT and later again to US$1.00 per 100-judgment fluency HIT.

Close to one thousand individual Turkers contributed to this experiment (some did both fluency and adequacy assessments), providing a total of more than 220,000 translations, of which 140,000 were provided by workers meeting the quality threshold.

In general, it cost approximately US$30 to assess each system, with low-quality workers approximately doubling the cost of the annotation. We rejected HITs where it was clear that random-clicking had taken place, but did not reject solely on the basis of having not met the quality control threshold, to avoid penalizing well-intentioned but low-quality workers.

Overall change in performance

Table 3 shows the overall gain made in five years, from WMT 07 to WMT 12. Mean scores for the two top-performing systems from each shared task (BEST_{07}, BEST_{12}) are included, as well as scores for the benchmark current MT system on the two test sets (CURR_{07}, CURR_{12}). For each language pair, a 100-translation HIT was constructed by randomly selecting translations from the pool of $(3003 + 2007) \times 2$ that were available, and this results in apparently fewer assessments for the 2007 test set. In fact, numbers of evaluated translations are relative to the size of each test set. Average z scores for each system are also presented, based on the mean and standard deviation of all assessments provided by an individual worker, with positive values representing deviations above the mean of workers. In addition, we include mean BLEU (Papineni et al., 2001) and METEOR (Banerjee and Lavie, 2005) automatic scores for the same system outputs.

The CURR benchmark shows fluency scores that are 5.9 points higher on the 2007 data set than they are on the 2012 test data, with a larger difference in adequacy of 8.3 points. As such, the 2012 test data is more challenging than the 2007 test data. Despite this, both fluency and adequacy scores for the best system in 2012 have increased by 4.5 and 2.0 points respectively, amounting to estimated average gains of 10.4 points in fluency and 10.3 points in adequacy for state-of-the-art MT across the seven language pairs.

Looking at the standardized scores, it is apparent that the presence of the CURR translations for the 2007 test set pushes the mean score for the 2007 best systems below zero. The presence in the HITs of reference translations also shifts standardized system evaluations below zero, because they are not attributable to any of the systems being assessed.[4]

Results for automatic metrics lead to similar conclusions: that the test set has indeed increased in difficulty; and that, in spite of this, substantial improvements have been made according to automatic metrics, $+13.5$ using BLEU, and $+7.1$ on average using METEOR.

Language pairs

Table 4 shows mean fluency and adequacy scores by language pair for translation into English. Relative gains in both adequacy and fluency for the to-English language pairs are in agreement with the estimates generated through the use of the two automatic metrics. Most notably, Czech-to-English translation appears to have made substantial gains across the board, achieving more than double the gain made by some of the other language pairs; results for best participating 2007 systems show that this may in part be caused by the fact that Czech-to-English translation had a lower 2007 baseline to begin with (BEST_{07} F:40.8; A:41.7) in comparison to, for example, Spanish-to-English translation (BEST_{07} F:56.7; A:59.0).

Another notable result is that although the test data for each year's shared task is parallel across five languages, test set difficulty increases by different degrees according to human judges and automatic metrics, with BLEU scores showing substantial divergence across the to-English language pairs. Comparing BLEU scores achieved by the benchmark system for Spanish to English and Czech-to-English, for example, the benchmark system achieves close scores on the 2007 test data with a difference of only $|52.3 - 51.2| = 1.1$, compared to the score difference for the benchmark scores for translation of the 2012 test data of $|25.0 - 38.3| = 13.3$. This may indicate that the increase in test set difficulty that has taken place over the years has made the shared task disproportionately more difficult for some language pairs than for others. It does seem that some language pairs are harder to translate than others, and the differential change may be a consequence of the fact that increasing test set complexity for all languages in parallel has a greater impact on translation difficulty for language pairs that are intrinsically harder to translate between.

[4]Scores for reference translations can optionally be omitted for score standardization.

		CURR07	CURR12	Δ (CURR07 − CURR12)	BEST07	BEST12	5-Year Gain (BEST12 − BEST07 + Δ)
fluency	score	64.1	58.2	5.9	53.5	58.0 (+4.5)	10.4
	z	0.18	0.00	0.18	−0.16	0.00 (+0.16)	0.34
	n	12,334	18,654		12,513	18,579	
adequacy	score	65.0	56.7	8.3	54.0	56.0 (+2.0)	10.3
	z	0.18	−0.07	0.25	−0.16	−0.09 (+0.07)	0.32
	n	10,022	14,870		10,049	14,979	
metrics	BLEU	41.5	30.0	11.4	25.6	27.7 (+2.1)	13.5
	METEOR	49.2	41.1	8.1	41.1	40.1 (−1.0)	7.1

Table 3: Average human evaluation results for all language pairs; mean and standardized z scores are computed in each case for n translations. In this table, and in Tables 4 and 5, all reported fluency and adequacy values are in points relative to the 100-point assessment scale.

			CURR07	CURR12	Δ (CURR07 − CURR12)	BEST07	BEST12		5-Year Gain (BEST12 − BEST07 + Δ)
DE-EN	fluency	score	65.3***	57.9	7.4	52.8	55.0*	(+2.2)	9.6
		n	2,164	3,381		2,242	3,253		
	adequacy	score	63.8***	52.8	11.0	46.5	49.8**	(+3.3)	14.3
		n	1,458	2,175		1,454	2,193		
	metrics	BLEU	38.3	26.5	11.8	21.1	23.8	(+2.7)	14.5
		METEOR	40.3	32.7	7.6	33.4	31.7	(−1.7)	5.9
FR-EN	fluency	score	65.9***	58.0	7.9	57.8	60.2**	(+2.4)	10.3
		n	2,172	3,267		2,203	3,238		
	adequacy	score	61.0***	52.3	8.7	52.7	51.5	(−1.2)	7.5
		n	1,754	2,651		1,763	2,712		
	metrics	BLEU	39.4	32.0	7.4	28.6	31.5	(+2.9)	10.3
		METEOR	39.8	34.6	5.2	35.9	34.3	(−1.6)	3.6
ES-EN	fluency	score	68.4***	59.2	9.2	56.7	56.7	(+0.0)	9.2
		n	1,514	2,234		1,462	2,230		
	adequacy	score	68.0***	56.9	11.1	59.0***	55.7	(−3.3)	7.8
		n	1,495	2,193		1,492	2,180		
	metrics	BLEU	51.2	38.3	12.9	35.1	33.5	(−1.6)	11.3
		METEOR	45.4	37.0	8.4	39.9	36.0	(−3.9)	4.5
CS-EN	fluency	score	62.3***	49.9	12.4	40.8	50.5***	(+9.7)	22.1
		n	1,873	2,816		1,923	2,828		
	adequacy	score	62.4***	47.5	14.9	41.7	47.4***	(+5.7)	20.6
		n	1,218	1,830		1,257	1,855		
	metrics	BLEU	52.3	25.0	27.3	25.1	22.4	(−2.7)	24.6
		METEOR	44.7	31.6	13.1	34.3	30.8	(−3.5)	9.6

Table 4: Human evaluation of WMT 2007 and 2012 best systems for to-English language pairs. Mean scores are computed in each case for n translations. In this table and in Table 5, * denotes significance at $p < 0.05$; ** significance at $p < 0.01$; and *** significance at $p < 0.001$.

Table 5 shows results for translation out-of English, and once again human evaluation scores are in agreement with automatic metrics with English-to-Spanish translation achieving most substantial gains for the three out-of-English language pairs, an increase of 12.4 points for fluency, and 11.8 points with respect to adequacy, while English-to-French translation achieves a gain of 8.8 for

			CURR07	CURR12	Δ (CURR07 − CURR12)	BEST07	BEST12	5-Year Gain (BEST12 − BEST07 + Δ)
EN-ES	fluency	score	77.2***	73.4	3.8	63.3	71.9*** (+8.6)	12.4
		n	2,286	3,318		2,336	3,420	
	adequacy	score	75.2***	68.1	7.1	62.5	67.2 (+4.7)	11.8
		n	1,410	2,039		1,399	2,112	
	metrics	BLEU	48.2	38.7	9.5	29.1	35.3 (+6.2)	15.7
		METEOR	69.9	59.6	10.3	57.0	58.1 (+1.1)	11.4
EN-FR	fluency	score	57.1	55.2	1.9	49.5	56.4 (+6.9)	8.8
		n	1,008	1,645		1,039	1,588	
	adequacy	score	64.2*	61.9	2.3	57.2	62.3 (+5.1)	7.4
		n	1,234	1,877		1,274	1,775	
	metrics	BLEU	37.2	30.8	6.4	25.3	29.9 (+4.6)	11.0
		METEOR	59.4	52.9	6.5	50.4	52.0 (+1.6)	8.1
EN-DE	fluency	score	52.3	54.1*	−1.8	53.7	55.5 (+1.8)	0.0
		n	1,317	1,993		1,308	2,022	
	adequacy	score	60.3**	57.4	2.9	58.3	58.3 (+0.0)	2.9
		n	1,453	2,105		1,410	2,152	
	metrics	BLEU	23.6	18.7	4.9	14.6	17.2 (+2.6)	7.5
		METEOR	44.7	39.1	5.6	36.7	38.0 (+1.3)	6.9

Table 5: Human evaluation of WMT 2007 and 2012 best systems for out of English language pairs. Mean scores are computed in each case for n translations.

fluency and 7.4 points for adequacy. English-to-German translation achieves the lowest gain of all languages, with apparently no improvement in fluency, as the human fluency evaluation of the benchmark system on the supposedly easier 2007 data receives a substantially lower score than the same system over the 2012 data. This result demonstrates why fluency, evaluated without a reference translation, should not be used to evaluate MT systems without an adequacy assessment, since it is entirely possible for a low-adequacy translation to achieve a high fluency score.

For all language pairs, Figure 1 plots the net gain in fluency, adequacy and F_1 against increase in test data difficulty.

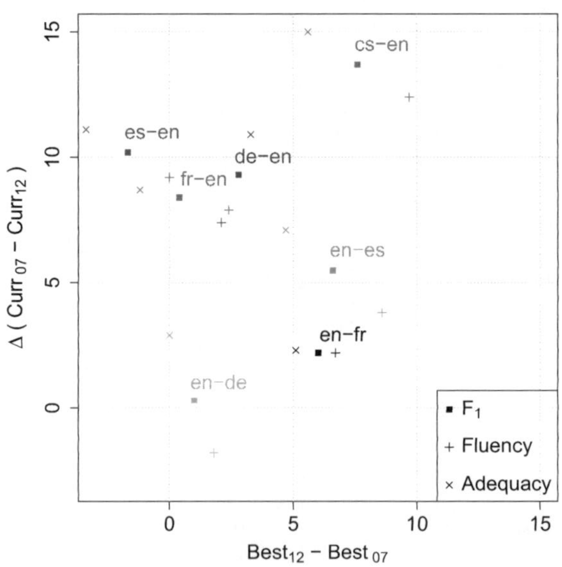

Figure 1: Mean fluency, adequacy and combined F_1 scores for language pairs.

5 Conclusion

We carried out a large-scale human evaluation of best-performing WMT 2007 and 2012 shared task systems in order to estimate the improvement made to state-of-the-art machine translation over this five year time period. Results show significant improvements have been made in machine translation of European language pairs, with Czech-to-English recording the greatest gains. It is also clear from our data that the difficulty of the task has risen over the same period, to varying degrees for individual language pairs.

Researchers interested in making use of the dataset are invited to contact the first author.

Acknowledgments This work was supported by the Australian Research Council.

References

A. Alexandrov. 2010. Characteristics of single-item measures in Likert scale format. *The Electronic Journal of Business Research Methods*, 8:1–12.

R. Artstein and M. Poesio. 2008. Inter-coder agreement for computational linguistics. *Computational Linguistics*, 34(4):555–596.

S. Banerjee and A. Lavie. 2005. METEOR: An automatic metric for mt evaluation with improved correlation with human judgements. In *Proc. Wkshp. Intrinsic and Extrinsic Evaluation Measures for Machine Translation and/or Summarization*, pages 65–73, Ann Arbor, MI.

A. Birch, B. Haddow, U. Germann, M. Nadejde, C. Buck, and P. Koehn. 2013. The feasibility of HMEANT as a human MT evaluation metric. In *Proc. 8th Wkshp. Statistical Machine Translation*, pages 52–61, Sofia, Bulgaria. ACL.

O. Bojar, M. Ercegovčevic, M. Popel, and O. Zaidan. 2011. A grain of salt for the WMT manual evaluation. In *Proc. 6th Wkshp. Statistical Machine Translation*, pages 1–11, Edinburgh, Scotland. ACL.

O. Bojar, C. Buck, C. Callison-Burch, C. Federmann, B. Haddow, P. Koehn, C. Monz, M. Post, R. Soricut, and L. Specia. 2013. Findings of the 2013 Workshop on Statistical Machine Translation. In *Proc. 8th Wkshp. Statistical Machine Translation*, pages 1–44, Sofia, Bulgaria. ACL.

C. Callison-Burch, C. Fordyce, P. Koehn, C. Monz, and J. Schroeder. 2007. (Meta-) evaluation of machine translation. In *Proc. 2nd Wkshp. Statistical Machine Translation*, pages 136–158, Prague, Czech Republic. ACL.

C. Callison-Burch, P. Koehn, C. Monz, M. Post, R. Soricut, and L. Specia. 2012. Findings of the 2012 Workshop on Statistical Machine Translation. In *Proc. 7th Wkshp. Statistical Machine Translation*, pages 10–51, Montreal, Canada. ACL.

M. Dreyer and D. Marcu. 2012. HyTER: Meaning-equivalent semantics for translation evaluation. In *Proc. 2012 Conf. North American Chapter of the ACL: Human Language Technologies*, pages 162–171, Montreal, Canada. ACL.

Y. Graham, T. Baldwin, A. Moffat, and J. Zobel. 2013. Continuous measurement scales in human evaluation of machine translation. In *Proc. 7th Linguistic Annotation Wkshp. & Interoperability with Discourse*, pages 33–41, Sofia, Bulgaria. ACL.

C. Lo and D. Wu. 2011. MEANT: An inexpensive, high-accuracy, semi-automatic metric for evaluating translation utility based on semantic roles. In *Proc. 49th Annual Meeting of the ACL: Human Language Techologies*, pages 220–229, Portland, OR. ACL.

NIST. 2002. The 2002 NIST machine translation evaluation plan. National Institute of Standards and Technology. `http://www.itl.nist.gov/iad/894.01/tests/mt/2003/doc/mt03_evalplan.v2.pdf`.

K. Papineni, S. Roukos, T. Ward, and W.-J. Zhu. 2001. BLEU: A method for automatic evaluation of machine translation. Technical Report RC22176 (W0109-022), IBM Research, Thomas J. Watson Research Center.

R. A. Seymour, J. M. Simpson, J. E. Charlton, and M. E. Phillips. 1985. An evaluation of length and end-phrase of visual analogue scales in dental pain. *Pain*, 21:177–185.

M. Snover, B. Dorr, R. Scwartz, J. Makhoul, and L. Micciula. 2006. A study of translation error rate with targeted human annotation. In *Proc. 7th Biennial Conf. of the Assoc. Machine Translaiton in the Americas*, pages 223–231, Boston, MA.

D. L. Steiner and G. R. Norman. 1989. *Health Measurement Scales, A Practical Guide to their Development and Use*. Oxford University Press, Oxford, UK, fourth edition.

Learning Dictionaries for Named Entity Recognition using Minimal Supervision

Arvind Neelakantan
Department of Computer Science
University of Massachusetts, Amherst
Amherst, MA, 01003
arvind@cs.umass.edu

Michael Collins
Department of Computer Science
Columbia University
New-York, NY 10027, USA
mcollins@cs.columbia.edu

Abstract

This paper describes an approach for automatic construction of dictionaries for Named Entity Recognition (NER) using large amounts of unlabeled data and a few seed examples. We use Canonical Correlation Analysis (CCA) to obtain lower dimensional embeddings (representations) for *candidate phrases* and classify these phrases using a small number of labeled examples. Our method achieves 16.5% and 11.3% F-1 score improvement over co-training on disease and virus NER respectively. We also show that by adding candidate phrase embeddings as features in a sequence tagger gives better performance compared to using word embeddings.

1 Introduction

Several works (e.g., Ratinov and Roth, 2009; Cohen and Sarawagi, 2004) have shown that injecting dictionary matches as features in a sequence tagger results in significant gains in NER performance. However, building these dictionaries requires a huge amount of human effort and it is often difficult to get good coverage for many named entity types. The problem is more severe when we consider named entity types such as gene, virus and disease, because of the large (and growing) number of names in use, the fact that the names are heavily abbreviated and multiple names are used to refer to the same entity (Leaman et al., 2010; Dogan and Lu, 2012). Also, these dictionaries can only be built by domain experts, making the process very expensive.

This paper describes an approach for automatic construction of dictionaries for NER using large amounts of unlabeled data and a small number of seed examples. Our approach consists of two steps. First, we collect a high recall, low precision list of *candidate phrases* from the large unlabeled data collection for every named entity type using simple rules. In the second step, we construct an accurate dictionary of named entities by removing the noisy candidates from the list obtained in the first step. This is done by learning a classifier using the lower dimensional, real-valued CCA (Hotelling, 1935) embeddings of the candidate phrases as features and training it using a small number of labeled examples. The classifier we use is a binary SVM which predicts whether a candidate phrase is a named entity or not.

We compare our method to a widely used semi-supervised algorithm based on co-training (Blum and Mitchell, 1998). The dictionaries are first evaluated on virus (GENIA, 2003) and disease (Dogan and Lu, 2012) NER by using them directly in dictionary based taggers. We also give results comparing the dictionaries produced by the two semi-supervised approaches with dictionaries that are compiled manually. The effectiveness of the dictionaries are also measured by injecting dictionary matches as features in a Conditional Random Field (CRF) based tagger. The results indicate that our approach with minimal supervision produces dictionaries that are comparable to dictionaries compiled manually. Finally, we also compare the quality of the candidate phrase embeddings with word embeddings (Dhillon et al., 2011) by adding them as features in a CRF based sequence tagger.

2 Background

We first give background on Canonical Correlation Analysis (CCA), and then give background on

Proceedings of the 14th Conference of the European Chapter of the Association for Computational Linguistics, pages 452–461,
Gothenburg, Sweden, April 26-30 2014.

CRFs for the NER problem.

2.1 Canonical Correlation Analysis (CCA)

The input to CCA consists of n paired observations $(x_1, z_1), \ldots, (x_n, z_n)$ where $x_i \in \mathbb{R}^{d_1}, z_i \in \mathbb{R}^{d_2}$ $(\forall i \in \{1, 2, \ldots, n\})$ are the feature representations for the two views of a data point. CCA simultaneously learns projection matrices $\Phi_1 \in \mathbb{R}^{d_1 \times k}, \Phi_2 \in \mathbb{R}^{d_2 \times k}$ (k is a small number) which are used to obtain the lower dimensional representations $(\bar{x}_1, \bar{z}_1), \ldots, (\bar{x}_n, \bar{z}_n)$ where $\bar{x}_i = \Phi_1^\top x_i \in \mathbb{R}^k, \bar{z}_i = \Phi_2^\top z_i \in \mathbb{R}^k$, $\forall i \in \{1, 2, \ldots, n\}$. Φ_1, Φ_2 are chosen to maximize the correlation between $\bar{x}_i$ and $\bar{z}_i$, $\forall i \in \{1, 2, \ldots, n\}$.

Consider the setting where we have a label for the data point along with it's two views and either view is sufficient to make accurate predictions. Kakade and Foster (2007) and Sridharan and Kakade (2008) give strong theoretical guarantees when the lower dimensional embeddings from CCA are used for predicting the label of the data point. This setting is similar to the one considered in co-training (Collins and Singer, 1999) but there is no assumption of independence between the two views of the data point. Also, it is an exact algorithm unlike the algorithm given in Collins and Singer (1999). Since we are using lower dimensional embeddings of the data point for prediction, we can learn a predictor with fewer labeled examples.

2.2 CRFs for Named Entity Recognition

CRF based sequence taggers have been used for a number of NER tasks (e.g., McCallum and Li, 2003) and in particular for biomedical NER (e.g., McDonald and Pereira, 2005; Burr Settles, 2004) because they allow a great deal of flexibility in the features which can be included. The input to a CRF tagger is a sentence $(w_1, w_2, \ldots, w_n)$ where w_i, $\forall i \in \{1, 2, \ldots, n\}$ are words in the sentence. The output is a sequence of tags $y_1, y_2, \ldots, y_n$ where $y_i \in \{\texttt{B}, \texttt{I}, \texttt{O}\}$, $\forall i \in \{1, 2, \ldots, n\}$. `B` is the tag given to the first word in a named entity, `I` is the tag given to all words except the first word in a named entity and `O` is the tag given to all other words. We used the standard NER baseline features (e.g., Dhillon et al., 2011; Ratinov and Roth, 2009) which include:

- Current Word w_i and its lexical features which include whether the word is capitalized and whether all the characters are capitalized. Prefix and suffixes of the word w_i were also added.
- Word tokens in window of size two around the current word which include $w_{i-2}, w_{i-1}, w_{i+1}, w_{i+2}$ and also the capitalization pattern in the window.
- Previous two predictions y_{i-1} and y_{i-2}.

The effectiveness of the dictionaries are evaluated by adding dictionary matches as features along with the baseline features (Ratinov and Roth, 2009; Cohen and Sarawagi, 2004) in the CRF tagger. We also compared the quality of the candidate phrase embeddings with the word-level embeddings by adding them as features (Dhillon et al., 2011) along with the baseline features in the CRF tagger.

3 Method

This section describes the two steps in our approach: obtaining candidate phrases and classifying them.

3.1 Obtaining Candidate Phrases

We used the full text of 110,369 biomedical publications in the BioMed Central corpus[1] to get the high recall, low precision list of candidate phrases. The advantages of using this huge collection of publications are obvious: almost all (including rare) named entities related to the biomedical domain will be mentioned and contains more recent developments than a structured resource like Wikipedia. The challenge however is that these publications are unstructured and hence it is a difficult task to construct accurate dictionaries using them with minimal supervision.

The list of virus candidate phrases were obtained by extracting phrases that occur between "the" and "virus" in the simple pattern "the ... virus" during a single pass over the unlabeled document collection. This noisy list had a lot of virus names such as *influenza*, *human immunodeficiency* and *Epstein-Barr* along with phrases that are not virus names, like *mutant*, *same*, *new*, and so on.

A similar rule like "the ... disease" did not give a good coverage of disease names since it is not the common way of how diseases are mentioned in publications. So we took a different approach

[1]The corpus can be downloaded at http://www.biomedcentral.com/about/datamining

to obtain the noisy list of disease names. We collected every sentence in the unlabeled data collection that has the word "disease" in it and extracted noun phrases[2] following the patterns "diseases like ....", "diseases such as ...." , "diseases including ...." , "diagnosed with ....", "patients with ...." and "suffering from ....".

3.2 Classification of Candidate Phrases

Having found the list of candidate phrases, we now describe how noisy words are filtered out from them. We gather (*spelling*, *context*) pairs for every instance of a candidate phrase in the unlabeled data collection. *spelling* refers to the candidate phrase itself while *context* includes three words each to the left and the right of the candidate phrase in the sentence. The *spelling* and the *context* of the candidate phrase provide a natural split into two views which multi-view algorithms like co-training and CCA can exploit. The only supervision in our method is to provide a few *spelling* seed examples (10 in the case of virus, 18 in the case of disease), for example, *human immunodeficiency* is a virus and *mutant* is not a virus.

3.2.1 Approach using CCA embeddings

We use CCA described in the previous section to obtain lower dimensional embeddings for the candidate phrases using the (*spelling*, *context*) views. Unlike previous works such as Dhillon et al. (2011) and Dhillon et al. (2012), we use CCA to learn embeddings for candidate phrases instead of all words in the vocabulary so that we don't miss named entities which have two or more words.

Let the number of (*spelling*, *context*) pairs be n (sum of total number of instances of every candidate phrase in the unlabeled data collection). First, we map the *spelling* and *context* to high-dimensional feature vectors. For the *spelling* view, we define a feature for every candidate phrase and also a boolean feature which indicates whether the phrase is capitalized or not. For the *context* view, we use features similar to Dhillon et al. (2011) where a feature for every word in the *context* in conjunction with its position is defined. Each of the n (*spelling*, *context*) pairs are mapped to a pair of high-dimensional feature vectors to get n paired observations $(x_1, z_1), \ldots, (x_n, z_n)$ with $x_i \in \mathbb{R}^{d_1}, z_i \in \mathbb{R}^{d_2}$, $\forall i \in \{1, 2, \ldots, n\}$ (d_1, d_2 are the feature space dimensions of the *spelling* and *context* view respectively). Using CCA[3], we learn the projection matrices $\Phi_1 \in \mathbb{R}^{d_1 \times k}, \Phi_2 \in \mathbb{R}^{d_2 \times k}$ ($k << d_1$ and $k << d_2$) and obtain *spelling* view projections $\bar{x}_i = \Phi_1^\top x_i \in \mathbb{R}^k, \forall i \in \{1, 2, \ldots, n\}$. The k-dimensional *spelling* view projection of any instance of a candidate phrase is used as it's embedding[4].

The k-dimensional candidate phrase embeddings are used as features to learn a binary SVM with the seed *spelling* examples given in figure 1 as training data. The binary SVM predicts whether a candidate phrase is a named entity or not. Since the value of k is small, a small number of labeled examples are sufficient to train an accurate classifier. The learned SVM is used to filter out the noisy phrases from the list of candidate phrases obtained in the previous step.

To summarize, our approach for classifying candidate phrases has the following steps:

- Input: n (*spelling*, *context*) pairs, *spelling* seed examples.
- Each of the n (*spelling*, *context*) pairs are mapped to a pair of high-dimensional feature vectors to get n paired observations $(x_1, z_1), \ldots, (x_n, z_n)$ with $x_i \in \mathbb{R}^{d_1}, z_i \in \mathbb{R}^{d_2}$, $\forall i \in \{1, 2, \ldots, n\}$.
- Using CCA, we learn the projection matrices $\Phi_1 \in \mathbb{R}^{d_1 \times k}, \Phi_2 \in \mathbb{R}^{d_2 \times k}$ and obtain *spelling* view projections $\bar{x}_i = \Phi_1^\top x_i \in \mathbb{R}^k, \forall i \in \{1, 2, \ldots, n\}$.
- The embedding of a candidate phrase is given by the k-dimensional *spelling* view projection of any instance of the candidate phrase.
- We learn a binary SVM with the candidate phrase embeddings as features and the *spelling* seed examples given in figure 1 as training data. Using this SVM, we predict whether a candidate phrase is a named entity or not.

3.2.2 Approach based on Co-training

We discuss here briefly the DL-CoTrain algorithm (Collins and Singer, 1999) which is based on co-training (Blum and Mitchell, 1998), to classify

[2]Noun phrases were obtained using http://www.umiacs.umd.edu/ hal/TagChunk/

[3]Similar to Dhillon et al. (2012) we used the method given in Halko et al. (2011) to perform the SVD computation in CCA for practical considerations.

[4]Note that a candidate phrase gets the same *spelling* view projection across it's different instances since the *spelling* features of a candidate phrase are identical across it's instances.

- Virus seed *spelling* examples
  - **Virus Names**: human immunodeficiency, hepatitis C, influenza, Epstein-Barr, hepatitis B
  - **Non-virus Names**: mutant, same, wild type, parental, recombinant
- Disease seed *spelling* examples
  - **Disease Names**: tumor, malaria, breast cancer, cancer, IDDM, DM, A-T, tumors, VHL
  - **Non-disease Names**: cells, patients, study, data, expression, breast, BRCA1, protein, mutant

Figure 1: Seed *spelling* examples

candidate phrases. We compare our approach using CCA embeddings with this approach. Here, two decision list of rules are learned simultaneously one using the *spelling* view and the other using the *context* view. The rules using the *spelling* view are of the form: full-string=human immunodeficiency → Virus, full-string=mutant → Not_a_virus and so on. In the *context* view, we used bigram[5] rules where we considered all possible bigrams using the *context*. The rules are of two types: one which gives a positive label, for example, full-string=human immunodeficiency → Virus and the other which gives a negative label, for example, full-string=mutant → Not_a_virus. The DL-CoTrain algorithm is as follows:

- Input: (*spelling*, *context*) pairs for every instance of a candidate phrase in the corpus, m specifying the number of rules to be added in every iteration, precision threshold ϵ, *spelling* seed examples.
- Algorithm:
  1. Initialize the *spelling* decision list using the *spelling* seed examples given in figure 1 and set $i = 1$.
  2. Label the entire input collection using the learned decision list of *spelling* rules.
  3. Add $i \times m$ new *context* rules of each type to the decision list of *context* rules using the current labeled data. The rules are added using the same criterion as given in Collins and Singer (1999), i.e., among the rules whose strength is greater than the precision threshold ϵ, the ones which are seen more often with the corresponding label in the input data collection are added.
  4. Label the entire input collection using the learned decision list of *context* rules.
  5. Add $i \times m$ new spelling rules of each type to the decision list of *spelling* rules using the current labeled data. The rules are added using the same criterion as in step 3. Set $i = i+1$. If rules were added in the previous iteration, return to step 2.

The algorithm is run until no new rules are left to be added. The *spelling* decision list along with its strength (Collins and Singer, 1999) is used to construct the dictionaries. The phrases present in the *spelling* rules which give a positive label and whose strength is greater than the precision threshold, were added to the dictionary of named entities. We found the parameters m and ϵ difficult to tune and they could significantly affect the performance of the algorithm. We give more details regarding this in the experiments section.

4 Related Work

Previously, Collins and Singer (1999) introduced a multi-view, semi-supervised algorithm based on co-training (Blum and Mitchell, 1998) for collecting names of people, organizations and locations. This algorithm makes a strong independence assumption about the data and employs many heuristics to greedily optimize an objective function. This greedy approach also introduces new parameters that are often difficult to tune.

In other works such as Toral and Muñoz (2006) and Kazama and Torisawa (2007) external structured resources like Wikipedia have been used to construct dictionaries. Even though these methods are fairly successful they suffer from a number of drawbacks especially in the biomedical domain. The main drawback of these approaches is that it is very difficult to accurately disambiguate ambiguous entities especially when the entities are

[5] We tried using unigram rules but they were very weak predictors and the performance of the algorithm was poor when they were considered.

abbreviations (Kazama and Torisawa, 2007). For example, *DM* is the abbreviation for the disease *Diabetes Mellitus* and the disambiguation page for *DM* in Wikipedia associates it to more than 50 categories since *DM* can be expanded to *Doctor of Management*, *Dichroic mirror*, and so on, each of it belonging to a different category. Due to the rapid growth of Wikipedia, the number of entities that have disambiguation pages is growing fast and it is increasingly difficult to retrieve the article we want. Also, it is tough to understand these approaches from a theoretical standpoint.

Dhillon et al. (2011) used CCA to learn word embeddings and added them as features in a sequence tagger. They show that CCA learns better word embeddings than CW embeddings (Collobert and Weston , 2008), Hierarchical log-linear (HLBL) embeddings (Mnih and Hinton, 2007) and embeddings learned from many other techniques for NER and chunking. Unlike PCA, a widely used dimensionality reduction technique, CCA is invariant to linear transformations of the data. Our approach is motivated by the theoretical result in Kakade and Foster (2007) which is developed in the co-training setting. We directly use the CCA embeddings to predict the label of a data point instead of using them as features in a sequence tagger. Also, we learn CCA embeddings for candidate phrases instead of all words in the vocabulary since named entities often contain more than one word. Dhillon et al. (2012) learn a multi-class SVM using the CCA word embeddings to predict the POS tag of a word type. We extend this technique to NER by learning a binary SVM using the CCA embeddings of a high recall, low precision list of candidate phrases to predict whether a candidate phrase is a named entity or not.

5 Experiments

In this section, we give experimental results on virus and disease NER.

5.1 Data

The noisy lists of both virus and disease names were obtained from the BioMed Central corpus. This corpus was also used to get the collection of (*spelling*, *context*) pairs which are the input to the CCA procedure and the DL-CoTrain algorithm described in the previous section. We obtained CCA embeddings for the $100,000$ most frequently occurring word types in this collection along with every word type present in the training and development data of the virus and the disease NER dataset. These word embeddings are similar to the ones described in Dhillon et al. (2011) and Dhillon et al. (2012).

We used the virus annotations in the GENIA corpus (GENIA, 2003) for our experiments. The dataset contains 18,546 annotated sentences. We randomly selected 8,546 sentences for training and the remaining sentences were randomly split equally into development and testing sentences. The training sentences are used only for experiments with the sequence taggers. Previously, Zhang et al. (2004) tested their HMM-based named entity recognizer on this data. For disease NER, we used the recent disease corpus (Dogan and Lu, 2012) and used the same training, development and test data split given by them. We used a sentence segmenter[6] to get sentence segmented data and Stanford Tokenizer[7] to tokenize the data. Similar to Dogan and Lu (2012), all the different disease categories were flattened into one single category of disease mentions. The development data was used to tune the hyperparameters and the methods were evaluated on the test data.

5.2 Results using a dictionary-based tagger

First, we compare the dictionaries compiled using different methods by using them directly in a dictionary-based tagger. This is a simple and informative way to understand the quality of the dictionaries before using them in a CRF-tagger. Since these taggers can be trained using a handful of training examples, we can use them to build NER systems even when there are no labeled sentences to train. The input to a dictionary tagger is a list of named entities and a sentence. If there is an exact match between a phrase in the input list to the words in the given sentence then it is tagged as a named entity. All other words are labeled as non-entities. We evaluated the performance of the following methods for building dictionaries:

- **Candidate List**: This dictionary contains all the candidate phrases that were obtained using the method described in Section 3.1. The noisy list of virus candidates and disease candidates had 3,100 and 60,080 entries respectively.

[6] https://pypi.python.org/pypi/text-sentence/0.13
[7] http://nlp.stanford.edu/software/tokenizer.shtml

Method	Virus NER			Disease NER		
	Precision	Recall	F-1 Score	Precision	Recall	F-1 Score
Candidate List	2.20	**69.58**	4.27	4.86	**60.32**	8.99
Manual	42.69	68.75	52.67	51.39	45.08	**48.03**
Co-Training	48.33	66.46	55.96	**58.87**	23.17	33.26
CCA	**57.24**	68.33	**62.30**	38.34	44.55	41.21

Table 1: Precision, recall, F- 1 scores of dictionary-based taggers

- **Manual**: Manually constructed dictionaries, which requires a large amount of human effort, are employed for the task. We used the list of virus names given in Wikipedia[8]. Unfortunately, abbreviations of virus names are not present in this list and we could not find any other more complete list of virus names. Hence, we constructed abbreviations by concatenating the first letters of all the strings in a virus name, for every virus name given in the Wikipedia list.

  For diseases, we used the list of disease names given in the Unified Medical Language System (UMLS) Metathesaurus. This dictionary has been widely used in disease NER (e.g., Dogan and Lu, 2012; Leaman et al., 2010)[9].

- **Co-Training**: The dictionaries are constructed using the DL-CoTrain algorithm described previously. The parameters used were $m = 5$ and $\epsilon = 0.95$ as given in Collins and Singer (1999). The phrases present in the *spelling* rules which give a positive label and whose strength is greater than the precision threshold, were added to the dictionary of named entities.

  In our experiment to construct a dictionary of virus names, the algorithm stopped after just 12 iterations and hence the dictionary had only 390 virus names. This was because there were no *spelling* rules with strength greater than 0.95 to be added. We tried varying both the parameters but in all cases, the algorithm did not progress after a few iterations. We adopted a simple heuristic to increase the coverage of virus names by using the strength of the *spelling* rules obtained after the 12th iteration. All *spelling* rules that give a positive label and which has a strength greater than θ were added to the decision list of *spelling* rules. The phrases present in these rules are added to the dictionary. We picked the θ parameter from the set [0.1, 0.2, 0.3, 0.4, 0.5, 0.6, 0.7, 0.8, 0.9] using the development data.

  The co-training algorithm for constructing the dictionary of disease names ran for close to 50 iterations and hence we obtained better coverage for disease names. We still used the same heuristic of adding more named entities using the strength of the rule since it performed better.

- **CCA**: Using the CCA embeddings of the candidate phrases[10] as features we learned a binary SVM[11] to predict whether a candidate phrase is a named entity or not. We considered using 10 to 30 dimensions of candidate phrase embeddings and the regularizer was picked from the set [0.0001, 0.001, 0.01, 0.1, 1, 10, 100]. Both the regularizer and the number of dimensions to be used were tuned using the development data.

Table 1 gives the results of the dictionary based taggers using the different methods described above. As expected, when the noisy list of candidate phrases are used as dictionaries the recall of the system is quite high but the precision is very low. The low precision of the Wikipedia virus lists was due to the heuristic used to obtain abbreviations which produced a few noisy abbreviations but this heuristic was crucial to get a high recall. The list of disease names from UMLS gives a low recall because the list does not contain many disease abbreviations and composite disease mentions such as *breast and ovarian cancer*. The pres-

[8]http://en.wikipedia.org/wiki/List_of_viruses

[9]The list of disease names from UMLS can be found at https://sites.google.com/site/fmchowdhury2/bioenex .

[10]The performance of the dictionaries learned from word embeddings was very poor and we do not report it's performance here.

[11]we used LIBSVM (http://www.csie.ntu.edu.tw/ cjlin/libsvm/) in our SVM experiments

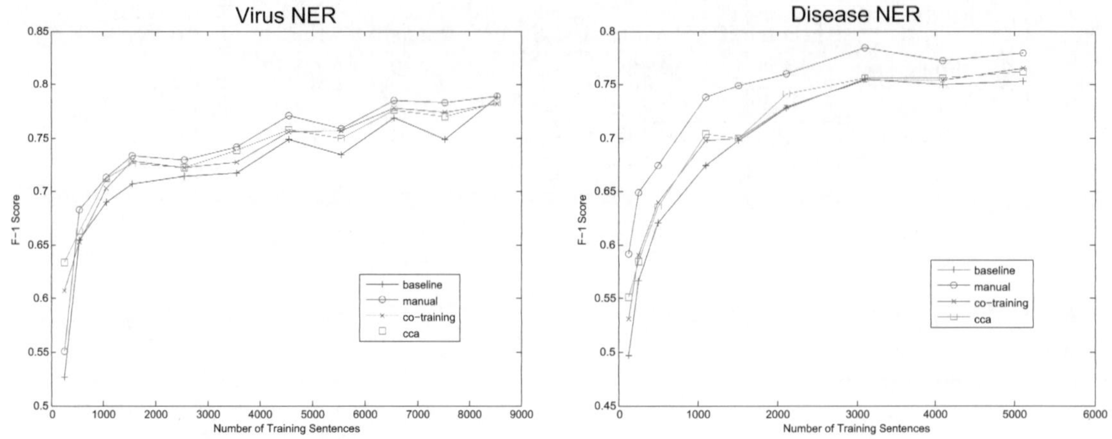

Figure 2: Virus and Disease NER F-1 scores for varying training data size when dictionaries obtained from different methods are injected

ence of ambiguous abbreviations affected the accuracy of this dictionary.

The virus dictionary constructed using the CCA embeddings was very accurate and the false positives were mainly due to ambiguous phrases, for example, in the phrase *HIV replication*, *HIV* which usually refers to the name of a virus is tagged as a RNA molecule. The accuracy of the disease dictionary produced using CCA embeddings was mainly affected by noisy abbreviations.

We can see that the dictionaries obtained using CCA embeddings perform better than the dictionaries obtained from co-training on both disease and virus NER even after improving the co-training algorithm's coverage using the heuristic described in this section. It is important to note that the dictionaries constructed using the CCA embeddings and a small number of labeled examples performs competitively with dictionaries that are entirely built by domain experts. These results show that by using the CCA based approach we can build NER systems that give reasonable performance even for difficult named entity types with almost no supervision.

5.3 Results using a CRF tagger

We did two sets of experiments using a CRF tagger. In the first experiment, we add dictionary features to the CRF tagger while in the second experiment we add the embeddings as features to the CRF tagger. The same baseline model is used in both the experiments whose features are described in Section 2.2. For both the CRF[12] experiments the regularizers from the set [0.0001, 0.001, 0.01, 0.1, 1.0, 10.0] were considered and it was tuned on the development set.

5.3.1 Dictionary Features

Here, we inject dictionary matches as features (e.g., Ratinov and Roth, 2009; Cohen and Sarawagi, 2004) in the CRF tagger. Given a dictionary of named entities, every word in the input sentence has a dictionary feature associated with it. When there is an exact match between a phrase in the dictionary with the words in the input sentence, the dictionary feature of the first word in the named entity is set to `B` and the dictionary feature of the remaining words in the named entity is set to `I`. The dictionary feature of all the other words in the input sentence which are not part of any named entity in the dictionary is set to `O`. The effectiveness of the dictionaries constructed from various methods are compared by adding dictionary match features to the CRF tagger. These dictionary match features were added along with the baseline features.

Figure 2 indicates that the dictionary features in general are helpful to the CRF model. We can see that the dictionaries produced from our approach using CCA are much more helpful than the dictionaries produced from co-training especially when there are fewer labeled sentences to train. Similar to the dictionary tagger experiments discussed

[12]We used CRFsuite (www.chokkan.org/software/crfsuite/) for our experiments with CRFs.

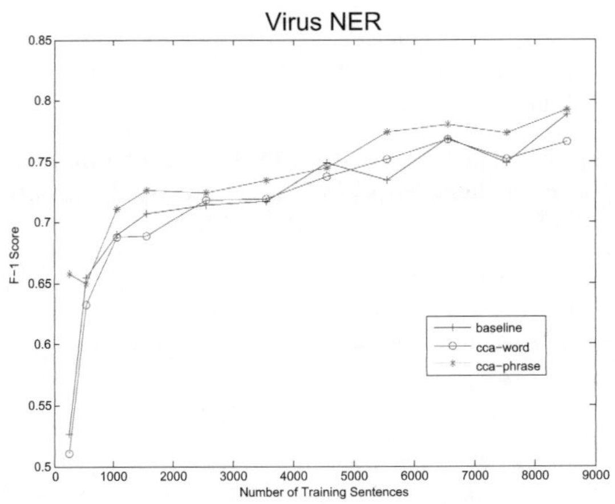

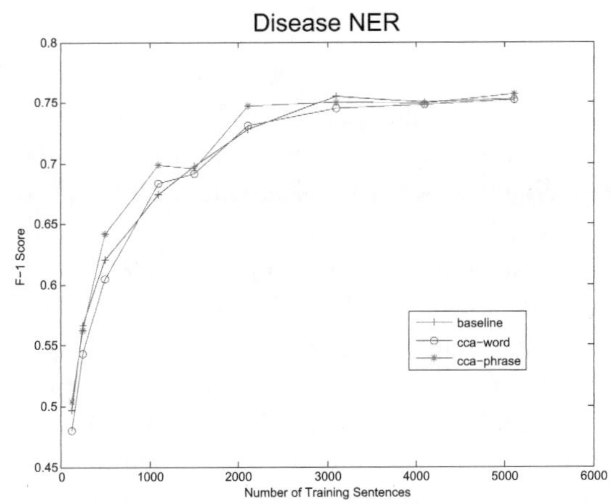

Figure 3: Virus and Disease NER F-1 scores for varying training data size when embeddings obtained from different methods are used as features

previously, the dictionaries produced from our approach performs competitively with dictionaries that are entirely built by domain experts.

5.3.2 Embedding Features

The quality of the candidate phrase embeddings are compared with word embeddings by adding the embeddings as features in the CRF tagger. Along with the baseline features, **CCA-word** model adds word embeddings as features while the **CCA-phrase** model adds candidate phrase embeddings as features. **CCA-word** model is similar to the one used in Dhillon et al. (2011).

We considered adding 10, 20, 30, 40 and 50 dimensional word embeddings as features for every training data size and the best performing model on the development data was picked for the experiments on the test data. For candidate phrase embeddings we used the same number of dimensions that was used for training the SVMs to construct the best dictionary.

When candidate phrase embeddings are obtained using CCA, we do not have embeddings for words which are not in the list of candidate phrases. Also, a candidate phrase having more than one word has a joint representation, i.e., the phrase "human immunodeficiency" has a lower dimensional representation while the words "human" and "immunodeficiency" do not have their own lower dimensional representations (assuming they are not part of the candidate list). To overcome this issue, we used a simple technique to differentiate between candidate phrases and the rest of the words. Let x be the highest real valued candidate phrase embedding and the candidate phrase embedding be a d dimensional real valued vector. If a candidate phrase occurs in a sentence, the embeddings of that candidate phrase are added as features to the first word of that candidate phrase. If the candidate phrase has more than one word, the other words in the candidate phrase are given an embedding of dimension d with each dimension having the value $2 \times x$. All the other words are given an embedding of dimension d with each dimension having the value $4 \times x$.

Figure 3 shows that almost always the candidate phrase embeddings help the CRF model. It is also interesting to note that sometimes the word-level embeddings have an adverse affect on the performance of the CRF model. The **CCA-phrase** model performs significantly better than the other two models when there are fewer labeled sentences to train and the separation of the candidate phrases from the other words seems to have helped the CRF model.

6 Conclusion

We described an approach for automatic construction of dictionaries for NER using minimal supervision. Compared to the previous approaches, our method is free from overly-stringent assumptions about the data, uses SVD that can be solved exactly and achieves better empirical performance. Our approach which uses a small number of seed examples performs competitively with dictionaries that are compiled manually.

Acknowledgments

We are grateful to Alexander Rush, Alexandre Passos and the anonymous reviewers for their useful feedback. This work was supported by the Intelligence Advanced Research Projects Activity (IARPA) via Department of Interior National Business Center (DoI/NBC) contract number D11PC20153. The U.S. Government is authorized to reproduce and distribute reprints for Governmental purposes notwithstanding any copyright annotation thereon. The views and conclusions contained herein are those of the authors and should not be interpreted as necessarily representing the official policies or endorsements, either expressed or implied, of IARPA, DoI/NBC, or the U.S. Government.

References

Andrew McCallum and Wei Li. *Early Results for Named Entity Recognition with Conditional Random Fields, Feature Induction and Web-Enhanced Lexicons.* 2003. Conference on Natural Language Learning (CoNLL).

Andriy Mnih and Geoffrey Hinton. *Three New Graphical Models for Statistical Language Modelling.* 2007. International Conference on Machine learning (ICML).

Antonio Toral and Rafael Muñoz. *A proposal to automatically build and maintain gazetteers for Named Entity Recognition by using Wikipedia.* 2006. Workshop On New Text Wikis And Blogs And Other Dynamic Text Sources.

Avrin Blum and Tom M. Mitchell. *Combining Labeled and Unlabeled Data with Co-Training.* 1998. Conference on Learning Theory (COLT).

Burr Settles. *Biomedical Named Entity Recognition Using Conditional Random Fields and Rich Feature Sets.* 2004. International Joint Workshop on Natural Language Processing in Biomedicine and its Applications (NLPBA).

H. Hotelling. *Canonical correlation analysis (cca)* 1935. Journal of Educational Psychology.

Jie Zhang, Dan Shen, Guodong Zhou, Jian Su and Chew-Lim Tan. *Enhancing HMM-based Biomedical Named Entity Recognition by Studying Special Phenomena.* 2004. Journal of Biomedical Informatics.

Jin-Dong Kim, Tomoko Ohta, Yuka Tateisi and Jun'ichi Tsujii. *GENIA corpus - a semantically annotated corpus for bio-textmining.* 2003. ISMB.

Junichi Kazama and Kentaro Torisawa. *Exploiting Wikipedia as External Knowledge for Named Entity Recognition.* 2007. Association for Computational Linguistics (ACL).

Karthik Sridharan and Sham M. Kakade. *An Information Theoretic Framework for Multi-view Learning.* 2008. Conference on Learning Theory (COLT).

Lev Ratinov and Dan Roth. *Design Challenges and Misconceptions in Named Entity Recognition.* 2009. Conference on Natural Language Learning (CoNLL).

Michael Collins and Yoram Singer. *Unsupervised Models for Named Entity Classification.* 1999. In Proceedings of the Joint SIGDAT Conference on Empirical Methods in Natural Language Processing and Very Large Corpora.

Nathan Halko, Per-Gunnar Martinsson, Joel A. Tropp. *Finding structure with randomness: Probabilistic algorithms for constructing approximate matrix decompositions.* 2011. Society for Industrial and Applied Mathematics.

Paramveer S. Dhillon, Dean Foster and Lyle Ungar. *Multi-View Learning of Word Embeddings via CCA.* 2011. Advances in Neural Information Processing Systems (NIPS).

Paramveer Dhillon, Jordan Rodu, Dean Foster and Lyle Ungar. *Two Step CCA: A new spectral method for estimating vector models of words.* 2012. International Conference on Machine learning (ICML).

Rezarta Islamaj Dogan and Zhiyong Lu. *An improved corpus of disease mentions in PubMed citations.* 2012. Workshop on Biomedical Natural Language Processing, Association for Computational Linguistics (ACL).

Robert Leaman, Christopher Miller and Graciela Gonzalez. *Enabling Recognition of Diseases in Biomedical Text with Machine Learning: Corpus and Benchmark.* 2010. Workshop on Biomedical Natural Language Processing, Association for Computational Linguistics (ACL).

Ronan Collobert and Jason Weston. *A unified architecture for natural language processing: deep neural networks with multitask learning.* 2008. International Conference on Machine learning (ICML).

Ryan McDonald and Fernando Pereira. *Identifying Gene and Protein Mentions in Text Using Conditional Random Fields.* 2005. BMC Bioinformatics.

Sham M. Kakade and Dean P. Foster. *Multi-view regression via canonical correlation analysis.* 2007. Conference on Learning Theory (COLT).

William W. Cohen and Sunita Sarawagi. *Exploiting Dictionaries in Named Entity Extraction: Combining Semi-Markov Extraction Processes and Data Integration Methods.* 2004. Semi-Markov Extraction

Processes and Data Integration Methods, Proceedings of KDD.

Improving Vector Space Word Representations Using Multilingual Correlation

Manaal Faruqui and **Chris Dyer**
Carnegie Mellon University
Pittsburgh, PA, 15213, USA
{mfaruqui, cdyer}@cs.cmu.edu

Abstract

The distributional hypothesis of Harris (1954), according to which the meaning of words is evidenced by the contexts they occur in, has motivated several effective techniques for obtaining vector space semantic representations of words using unannotated text corpora. This paper argues that lexico-semantic content should additionally be invariant across languages and proposes a simple technique based on canonical correlation analysis (CCA) for incorporating multilingual evidence into vectors generated monolingually. We evaluate the resulting word representations on standard lexical semantic evaluation tasks and show that our method produces substantially better semantic representations than monolingual techniques.

1 Introduction

Data-driven learning of vector-space word embeddings that capture lexico-semantic properties is a technique of central importance in natural language processing. Using cooccurrence statistics from a large corpus of text (Deerwester et al., 1990; Turney and Pantel, 2010),[1] it is possible to construct high-quality semantic vectors — as judged by both correlations with human judgements of semantic relatedness (Turney, 2006; Agirre et al., 2009) and as features for downstream applications (Turian et al., 2010).

The observation that vectors representing cooccurrence tendencies would capture meaning is expected according to the **distributional hypothesis** (Harris, 1954), famously articulated by Firth (1957) as *You shall know a word by the company it keeps.* Although there is much evidence in favor of the distributional hypothesis, in this paper we argue for incorporating *translational* context when constructing vector space semantic models (VSMs). Simply put: knowing how words translate is a valuable source of lexico-semantic information and should lead to better VSMs.

Parallel corpora have long been recognized as valuable for lexical semantic applications, including identifying word senses (Diab, 2003; Resnik and Yarowsky, 1999) and paraphrase and synonymy relationships (Bannard and Callison-Burch, 2005). The latter work (which we build on) shows that if different words or phrases in one language often translate into a single word or phrase type in a second language, this is good evidence that they are synonymous. To illustrate: the English word forms *aeroplane*, *airplane*, and *plane* are observed to translate into the same Hindi word: वायुयान (*vaayuyaan*). Thus, even if we did not know the relationship between the English words, this translation fact is evidence that they all have the same meaning.

How can we exploit information like this when constructing VSMs? We propose a technique that first constructs independent VSMs in two languages and then projects them onto a common vector space such that translation pairs (as determined by automatic word alignments) should be maximally correlated (§2). We review latent semantic analysis (LSA), which serves as our monolingual VSM baseline (§3), and a suite of standard evaluation tasks that we use to measure the quality of the embeddings (§4). We then turn to experiments. We first show that our technique leads to substantial improvements over monolingual LSA (§5), and then examine how our technique fares with vectors learned using two different neural networks, one that models word sequences and a second that models bags-of-context

[1]Related approaches use the internal representations from neural network models of word sequences (Collobert and Weston, 2008) or continuous bags-of-context wordsels (Mikolov et al., 2013a) to arrive at vector representations that likewise capture cooccurence tendencies and meanings.

Proceedings of the 14th Conference of the European Chapter of the Association for Computational Linguistics, pages 462–471,
Gothenburg, Sweden, April 26-30 2014.

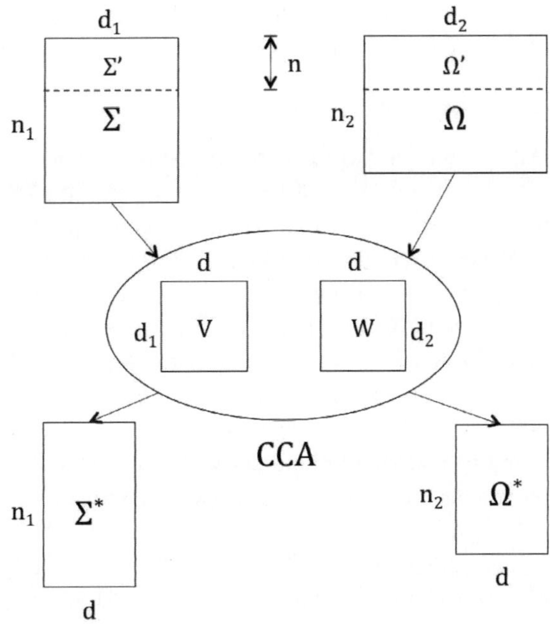

Figure 1: Cross-lingual word vector projection using CCA.

words. We observe substantial improvements over the sequential model using multilingual evidence but more mixed results relative to using the bags-of-contexts model (§6).

2 Multilingual Correlation with CCA

To gain information from the translation of a given word in other languages the most basic thing to do would be to just append the given word representation with the word representations of its translation in the other language. This has three drawbacks: first, it increases the number of dimensions in the vector; second, it can pull irrelevant information from the other language that doesn't generalize across languages and finally the given word might be out of vocabulary of the parallel corpus or dictionary.

To counter these problems we use CCA[2] which is a way of measuring the linear relationship between two multidimensional variables. It finds two projection vectors, one for each variable, that are optimal with respect to correlations. The dimensionality of these new projected vectors is equal to or less than the smaller dimensionality of the two variables.

Let $\boldsymbol{\Sigma} \in \mathbb{R}^{n_1 \times d_1}$ and $\boldsymbol{\Omega} \in \mathbb{R}^{n_2 \times d_2}$ be vector space embeddings of two different vocabularies where rows represent words. Since the two vocabularies are of different sizes (n_1 and n_2) and there might not exist translation for every word of $\boldsymbol{\Sigma}$ in $\boldsymbol{\Omega}$, let $\boldsymbol{\Sigma}' \subseteq \boldsymbol{\Sigma}$ where every word in $\boldsymbol{\Sigma}'$ is translated to one other word[3] in $\boldsymbol{\Omega}' \subseteq \boldsymbol{\Omega}$ and $\boldsymbol{\Sigma} \in \mathbb{R}^{n \times d_1}$ and $\boldsymbol{\Omega} \in \mathbb{R}^{n \times d_2}$.

Let $\boldsymbol{x}$ and $\boldsymbol{y}$ be two corresponding vectors from $\boldsymbol{\Sigma}'$ and $\boldsymbol{\Omega}'$, and $\boldsymbol{v}$ and $\boldsymbol{w}$ be two projection directions. Then, the projected vectors are:

$$\boldsymbol{x}' = \boldsymbol{x}\boldsymbol{v} \quad \boldsymbol{y}' = \boldsymbol{y}\boldsymbol{w} \tag{1}$$

and the correlation between the projected vectors can be written as:

$$\rho(\boldsymbol{x}', \boldsymbol{y}') = \frac{E[\boldsymbol{x}'\boldsymbol{y}']}{\sqrt{E[\boldsymbol{x}'^2]E[\boldsymbol{y}'^2]}} \tag{2}$$

CCA maximizes ρ for the given set of vectors $\boldsymbol{\Sigma}'$ and $\boldsymbol{\Omega}'$ and outputs two projection vectors $\boldsymbol{v}$ and $\boldsymbol{w}$:

$$\begin{aligned} \boldsymbol{v}, \boldsymbol{w} &= \mathrm{CCA}(\boldsymbol{x}, \boldsymbol{y}) \\ &= \arg\max_{\boldsymbol{v}, \boldsymbol{w}} \rho(\boldsymbol{x}\boldsymbol{v}, \boldsymbol{y}\boldsymbol{w}) \end{aligned} \tag{3}$$

Using these two projection vectors we can project the entire vocabulary of the two languages $\boldsymbol{\Sigma}$ and $\boldsymbol{\Omega}$ using equation 1. Summarizing:

$$\boldsymbol{V}, \boldsymbol{W} = \mathrm{CCA}(\boldsymbol{\Sigma}', \boldsymbol{\Omega}') \tag{4}$$

$$\Sigma^* = \boldsymbol{\Sigma}\boldsymbol{V} \quad \Omega^* = \boldsymbol{\Omega}\boldsymbol{W} \tag{5}$$

where, $\boldsymbol{V} \in \mathbb{R}^{d_1 \times d}$, $\boldsymbol{W} \in \mathbb{R}^{d_2 \times d}$ contain the projection vectors and $d = \min\{\mathrm{rank}(\boldsymbol{V}), \mathrm{rank}(\boldsymbol{W})\}$. Thus, the resulting vectors cannot be longer than the original vectors. Since $\boldsymbol{V}$ and $\boldsymbol{W}$ can be used to project the whole vocabulary, CCA also solves the problem of not having translations of a particular word in the dictionary. The schema of performing CCA on the monolingual word representations of two languages is shown in Figure 1.

Further Dimensionality Reduction: Since CCA gives us correlations and corresponding projection vectors across d dimensions which can be large, we perform experiments by taking projections of the original word vectors across only the top k correlated dimensions. This is trivial to implement as the projection vectors $\boldsymbol{V}$,

[2] We use the MATLAB module for CCA: `http://www.mathworks.com/help/stats/canoncorr.html`

[3] Further information on how these one-to-one translations are obtained in §5

$\boldsymbol{W}$ in equation 4 are already sorted in descending order of correlation. Therefore in,

$$\boldsymbol{\Sigma}_k^* = \boldsymbol{\Sigma}\boldsymbol{V}_k \quad \boldsymbol{\Omega}_k^* = \boldsymbol{\Omega}\boldsymbol{W}_k \tag{6}$$

$\boldsymbol{\Sigma}_k^*$ and $\boldsymbol{\Omega}_k^*$ are now word vector projections along the top k correlated dimensions, where, $\boldsymbol{V}_k$ and $\boldsymbol{W}_k$ are the column truncated matrices.

3 Latent Semantic Analysis

We perform latent semantic analysis (Deerwester et al., 1990) on a word-word co-occurrence matrix. We construct a word co-occurrence frequency matrix $\boldsymbol{F}$ for a given training corpus where each row $\boldsymbol{w}$, represents one word in the corpus and every column $\boldsymbol{c}$, is the context feature in which the word is observed. In our case, every column is a word which occurs in a given window length around the target word. For scalability reasons, we only select words with frequency greater than 10 as features. We also remove the top 100 most frequent words (mostly stop words) from the column features.

We then replace every entry in the sparse frequency matrix $\boldsymbol{F}$ by its pointwise mutual information (PMI) (Church and Hanks, 1990; Turney, 2001) resulting in $\boldsymbol{X}$. PMI is designed to give a high value to x_{ij} where there is a interesting relation between w_i and c_j, a small or negative value of x_{ij} indicates that the occurrence of w_i in c_j is uninformative. Finally, we factorize the matrix $\boldsymbol{X}$ using singular value decomposition (SVD). SVD decomposes $\boldsymbol{X}$ into the product of three matrices:

$$\boldsymbol{X} = \boldsymbol{U}\boldsymbol{\Psi}\boldsymbol{V}^\top \tag{7}$$

where, $\boldsymbol{U}$ and $\boldsymbol{V}$ are in column orthonormal form and $\boldsymbol{\Psi}$ is a diagonal matrix of singular values (Golub and Van Loan, 1996). We obtain a reduced dimensional representation of words from size $|\boldsymbol{V}|$ to k:

$$\boldsymbol{A} = \boldsymbol{U}_k\boldsymbol{\Psi}_k \tag{8}$$

where k can be controlled to trade off between reconstruction error and number of parameters, $\boldsymbol{\Psi}_k$ is the diagonal matrix containing the top k singular values, $\boldsymbol{U}_k$ is the matrix produced by selecting the corresponding columns from $\boldsymbol{U}$ and $\boldsymbol{A}$ represents the new matrix containing word vector representations in the reduced dimensional space.

4 Word Representation Evaluation

We evaluate the quality of our word vector representations on a number of tasks that test how well they capture both semantic and syntactic aspects of the representations.

4.1 Word Similarity

We evaluate our word representations on four different benchmarks that have been widely used to measure word similarity. The first one is the **WS-353** dataset (Finkelstein et al., 2001) containing 353 pairs of English words that have been assigned similarity ratings by humans. This data was further divided into two fragments by Agirre et al. (2009) who claimed that *similarity* (**WS-SIM**) and *relatedness* (**WS-REL**) are two different kinds of relations and should be dealt with separately. We present results on the whole set and on the individual fragments as well.

The second and third benchmarks are the **RG-65** (Rubenstein and Goodenough, 1965) and the **MC-30** (Miller and Charles, 1991) datasets that contain 65 and 30 pairs of nouns respectively and have been given similarity rankings by humans. These differ from **WS-353** in that it contains only nouns whereas the former contains all kinds of words. The fourth benchmark is the **MTurk-287** (Radinsky et al., 2011) dataset that constitutes of 287 pairs of words and is different from the above two benchmarks in that it has been constructed by crowdsourcing the human similarity ratings using Amazon Mechanical Turk.

We calculate similarity between a given pair of words by the *cosine* similarity between their corresponding vector representation. We then report Spearman's rank correlation coefficient (Myers and Well, 1995) between the rankings produced by our model against the human rankings.

4.2 Semantic Relations (SEM-REL)

Mikolov et al. (2013a) present a new semantic relation dataset composed of analogous word pairs. It contains pairs of tuples of word relations that follow a common semantic relation. For example, in *England : London :: France : Paris*, the two given pairs of words follow the country-capital relation. There are three other such kinds of relations: country-currency, man-woman, city-in-state and overall 8869 such pairs of words[4].

The task here is to find a word d that best fits the following relationship: $a : b :: c : d$ given a, b and c. We use the vector offset method described

[4]107 pairs were out of vocabulary for our vectors and were ignored.

in Mikolov et al. (2013a) that computes the vector $\boldsymbol{y} = \boldsymbol{x}_a - \boldsymbol{x}_b + \boldsymbol{x}_c$ where, $\boldsymbol{x}_a, \boldsymbol{x}_b$ and $\boldsymbol{x}_c$ are word vectors of a, b and c respectively and returns the vector $\boldsymbol{x}_w$ from the whole vocabulary which has the highest cosine similarity to $\boldsymbol{y}$:

$$\boldsymbol{x}_w = \arg\max_{\boldsymbol{x}_w} \frac{\boldsymbol{x}_w \cdot \boldsymbol{y}}{|\boldsymbol{x}_w| \cdot |\boldsymbol{y}|}$$

It is worth noting that this is a non-trivial $|V|$-way classification task where V is the size of the vocabulary.

4.3 Syntactic Relations (SYN-REL)

This dataset contains word pairs that are different syntactic forms of a given word and was prepared by Mikolov et al. (2013a). For example, in *walking* and *walked*, the second word is the past tense of the first word. There are nine such different kinds of relations: adjective-adverb, opposites, comaparative, superlative, present-participle, nation-nationality, past tense, plural nouns and plural verbs. Overall there are 10675 such syntactic pairs of word tuples. The task here again is identifying a word *d* that best fits the following relationship: *a : b :: c : d* and we solve it using the method described in §4.2.

5 Experiments

5.1 Data

For English, German and Spanish we used the WMT-2011[5] monolingual news corpora and for French we combined the WMT-2011 and 2012[6] monolingual news corpora so that we have around 300 million tokens for each language to train the word vectors.

For CCA, a one-to-one correspondence between the two sets of vectors is required. Obviously, the vocabulary of two languages are of different sizes and hence to obtain one-to-one mapping, for every English word we choose a word from the other language to which it has been aligned the maximum number of times[7] in a parallel corpus. We got these word alignment counts using cdec (Dyer et al., 2010) from the parallel news commentary corpora (WMT 2006-10) combined with the Europarl corpus for English-{German, French, Spanish}.

[5]http://www.statmt.org/wmt11/

[6]http://www.statmt.org/wmt12/

[7]We also tried weighted average of vectors across all aligned words and did not observe any significant difference in results.

5.2 Methodology

We construct LSA word vectors of length 640[8] for English, German, French and Spanish. We project the English word vectors using CCA by pairing them with German, French and Spanish vectors. For every language pair we take the top k correlated dimensions (cf. equation 6), where $k \in 10\%, 20\%, \ldots 100\%$ and tune the performance on **WS-353** task. We then select the k that gives us the best average performance across language pairs, which is $k = 80\%$, and evaluate the corresponding vectors on all other benchmarks. This prevents us from over-fitting k for every individual task.

5.3 Results

Table 1 shows the Spearman's correlation ratio obtained by using word vectors to compute the similarity between two given words and compare the ranked list against human rankings. The first row in the table shows the baseline scores obtained by using only the monolingual English vectors whereas the other rows correspond to the multilingual cases. The last row shows the average performance of the three language pairs. For all the tasks we get at least an absolute gain of 20 points over the baseline. These results are highly assuring of our hypothesis that multilingual context can help in improving the semantic similarity between similar words as described in the example in §1. Results across language pairs remain almost the same and the differences are most of the times statistically insignificant.

Table 1 also shows the accuracy obtained on predicting different kinds of relations between word pairs. For the **SEM-REL** task the average improvement in accuracy is an absolute 30 points over the baseline which is highly statistically significant ($p < 0.01$) according to the McNemar's test (Dietterich, 1998). The same holds true for the **SYN-REL** task where we get an average improvement of absolute 8 points over the baseline across the language pairs. Such an improvement in scores across these relation prediction tasks further enforces our claim that cross-lingual context can be exploited using the method described in §2 and it does help in encoding the meaning of a word better in a word vector than monolingual information alone.

[8]See section 5.5 for further discussion on vector length.

Lang	Dim	WS-353	WS-SIM	WS-REL	RG-65	MC-30	MTurk-287	SEM-REL	SYN-REL
En	640	46.7	56.2	36.5	50.7	42.3	51.2	14.5	36.8
De-En	512	68.0	**74.4**	64.6	**75.5**	**81.9**	53.6	43.9	**45.5**
Fr-En	512	**68.4**	73.3	**65.7**	73.5	81.3	**55.5**	43.9	44.3
Es-En	512	67.2	71.6	64.5	70.5	78.2	53.6	**44.2**	44.5
Average	–	56.6	64.5	51.0	62.0	65.5	60.8	44	44.7

Table 1: Spearman's correlation (left) and accuracy (right) on different tasks.

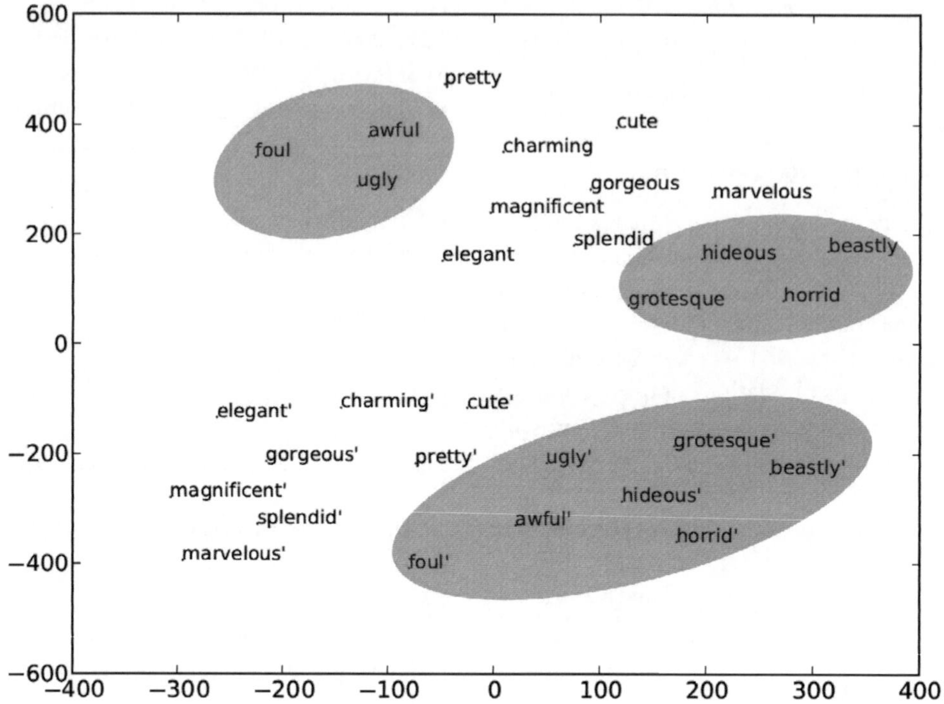

Figure 2: Monolingual (top) and multilingual (bottom; marked with apostrophe) word projections of the antonyms (shown in red) and synonyms of "beautiful".

5.4 Qualitative Example

To understand how multilingual evidence leads to better results in semantic evaluation tasks, we plot the word representations obtained in §3 of several synonyms and antonyms of the word "beautiful" by projecting both the transformed and untransformed vectors onto $\mathbb{R}^2$ using the t-SNE tool (van der Maaten and Hinton, 2008). The untransformed LSA vectors are in the upper part of Fig. 2, and the CCA-projected vectors are in the lower part. By comparing the two regions, we see that in the untransformed representations, the antonyms are in two clusters separated by the synonyms, whereas in the transformed representation, both the antonyms and synonyms are in their own cluster. Furthermore, the average intra-class distance between synonyms and antonyms is reduced.

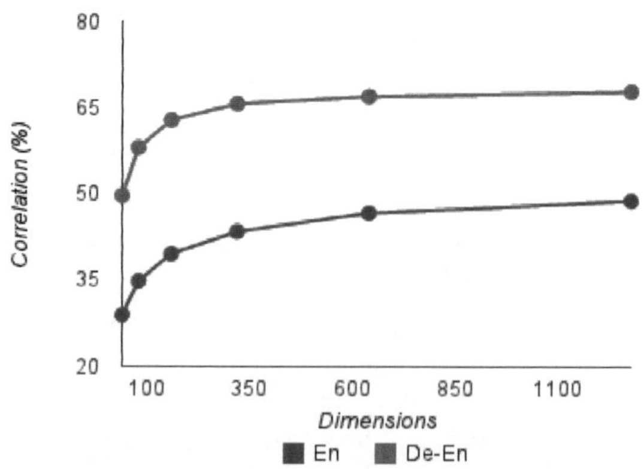

Figure 3: Performance of monolingual and multilingual vectors on **WS-353** for different vector lengths.

5.5 Variation in Vector Length

In order to demonstrate that the gains in performance by using multilingual correlation sustains for different number of dimensions, we compared the performance of the monolingual and (German-English) multilingual vectors with $k = 80\%$ (cf. §5.2). It can be see in figure 3 that the performance improvement for multilingual vectors remains almost the same for different vector lengths strengthening the reliability of our approach.

6 Neural Network Word Representations

Other kinds of vectors shown to be useful in many NLP tasks are word embeddings obtained from neural networks. These word embeddings capture more complex information than just co-occurrence counts as explained in the next section. We test our multilingual projection method on two types of such vectors by keeping the experimental setting exactly the same as in §5.2.

6.1 RNN Vectors

The recurrent neural network language model maximizes the log-likelihood of the training corpus. The architecture (Mikolov et al., 2013b) consists of an input layer, a hidden layer with recurrent connections to itself, an output layer and the corresponding weight matrices. The input vector $\boldsymbol{w}(t)$ represents input word at time t encoded using 1-of-N encoding and the output layer $\boldsymbol{y}(t)$ produces a probability distribution over words in the vocabulary V. The hidden layer maintains a representation of the sentence history in $\boldsymbol{s}(t)$. The values in the hidden and output layer are computed as follows:

$$\boldsymbol{s}(t) = f(\boldsymbol{U}\boldsymbol{w}(t) + \boldsymbol{W}\boldsymbol{s}(t-1)) \quad (9)$$

$$\boldsymbol{y}(t) = g(\boldsymbol{V}\boldsymbol{s}(t)) \quad (10)$$

where, f and g are the logistic and softmax functions respectively. $\boldsymbol{U}$ and $\boldsymbol{V}$ are weight matrices and the word representations are found in the columns of $\boldsymbol{U}$. The model is trained using backpropagation. Training such a purely lexical model will induce representations with syntactic and semantic properties. We use the RNNLM toolkit[9] to induce these word representations.

6.2 Skip Gram Vectors

In the RNN model (§6.1) most of the complexity is caused by the non-linear hidden layer. This is avoided in the new model proposed in Mikolov et al. (2013a) where they remove the non-linear hidden layer and there is a single projection layer for the input word. Precisely, each current word is used as an input to a log-linear classifier with continuous projection layer and words within a certain range before and after the word are predicted. These vectors are called the skip-gram (SG) vectors. We used the tool[10] for obtaining these word vectors with default settings.

6.3 Results

We compare the best results obtained by using different types of monolingual word representations across all language pairs. For brevity we do not show the results individually for all language pairs as they follow the same pattern when compared to the baseline for every vector type. We train word vectors of length 80 because it was computationally intractable to train the neural embeddings for higher dimensions. For multilingual vectors, we obtain $k = 60\%$ (cf. §5.2).

Table 2 shows the correlation ratio and the accuracies for the respective evaluation tasks. For the RNN vectors the performance improves upon inclusion of multilingual context for almost all tasks except for **SYN-REL** where the loss is statistically significant ($p < 0.01$). For **MC-30** and **SEM-REL** the small drop in performance is not statistically significant. Interestingly, the performance gain/loss for the SG vectors in most of the cases is not statistically significant, which means that inclusion of multilingual context is not very helpful. In fact, for **SYN-REL** the loss is statistically significant ($p < 0.05$) which is similar to the performance of RNN case. Overall, the best results are obtained by the SG vectors in six out of eight evaluation tasks whereas SVD vectors give the best performance in two tasks: **RG-65**, **MC-30**. This is an encouraging result as SVD vectors are the easiest and fastest to obtain as compared to the other two vector types.

To further understand why multilingual context is highly effective for SVD vectors and to a large extent for RNN vectors as well, we plot (Figure 4) the correlation ratio obtained by varying the length of word representations by using equation 6 for the three different vector types on two word similarity tasks: **WS-353** and **RG-65**.

SVD vectors improve performance upon the increase of the number of dimensions and tend to

[9] `http://www.fit.vutbr.cz/~imikolov/rnnlm/`

[10] `https://code.google.com/p/word2vec/`

Vectors	Dim	Lang	WS-353	WS-SIM	WS-REL	RG-65	MC-30	MTurk	SEM-REL	SYN-REL
SVD	80	Mono	34.8	45.5	23.4	30.8	21.0	46.6	13.5	24.4
	48	Multi	58.1	65.3	52.7	**62.7**	**67.7**	62.1	23.4	33.2
RNN	80	Mono	23.6	35.6	17.5	26.2	47.7	32.9	4.7	18.2
	48	Multi	35.4	47.3	29.8	36.6	46.5	43.8	4.1	12.2
SG	80	Mono	**63.9**	69.9	**60.9**	54.6	62.8	**66.9**	**47.8**	**47.8**
	48	Multi	63.1	**70.4**	57.6	54.9	64.7	58.7	46.5	44.2

Table 2: Spearman's correlation (left) and accuracy (right) on different tasks. Bold indicates best result across all vector types. Mono: monolingual and Multi: multilingual.

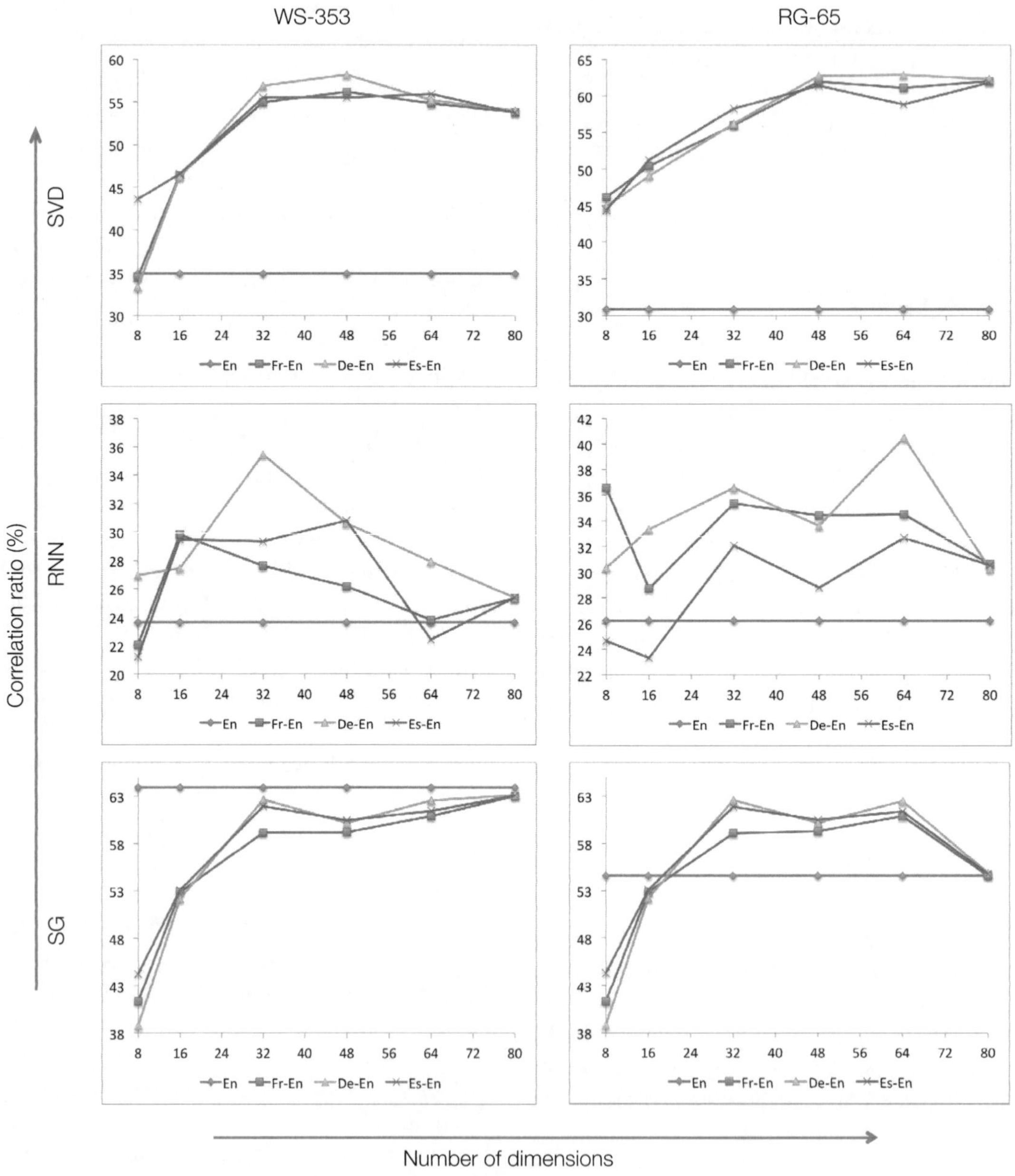

Figure 4: Performance as a function of vector length on word similarity tasks. The monolingual vectors always have a fixed length of 80, they are just shown in the plots for comparison.

saturate towards the end. For all the three language pairs the SVD vectors show uniform pattern of performance which gives us the liberty to use any language pair at hand. This is not true for the RNN vectors whose curves are significantly different for every language pair. SG vectors show a uniform pattern across different language pairs and the performance with multilingual context converges to the monolingual performance when the vector length becomes equal to the monolingual case ($k = 80$). The fact that both SG and SVD vectors have similar behavior across language pairs can be treated as evidence that semantics or information at a conceptual level (since both of them basically model word cooccurrence counts) transfers well across languages (Dyvik, 2004) although syntax has been projected across languages as well (Hwa et al., 2005; Yarowsky and Ngai, 2001). The pattern of results in the case of RNN vectors are indicative of the fact that these vectors encode syntactic information as explained in §6 which might not generalize well as compared to semantic information.

7 Related Work

Our method of learning multilingual word vectors is most closely associated to Zou et al. (2013) who learn bilingual word embeddings and show their utility in machine translation. They optimize the monolingual and the bilingual objective together whereas we do it in two separate steps and project to a common vector space to maximize correlation between the two. Vulić and Moens (2013) learn bilingual vector spaces from non parallel data induced using a seed lexicon. Our method can also be seen as an application of multi-view learning (Chang et al., 2013; Collobert and Weston, 2008), where one of the views can be used to capture cross-lingual information. Klementiev et al. (2012) use a multitask learning framework to encourage the word representations learned by neural language models to agree cross-lingually.

CCA can be used for dimension reduction and to draw correspondences between two sets of data.Haghighi et al. (2008) use CCA to draw translation lexicons between words of two different languages using only monolingual corpora. CCA has also been used for constructing monolingual word representations by correlating word vectors that capture aspects of word meaning and different types of distributional profile of the word (Dhillon et al., 2011). Although our primary experimental emphasis was on LSA based monolingual word representations, which we later generalized to two different neural network based word embeddings, these monolingual word vectors can also be obtained using other continuous models of language (Collobert and Weston, 2008; Mnih and Hinton, 2008; Morin and Bengio, 2005; Huang et al., 2012).

Bilingual representations have previously been explored with manually designed vector space models (Peirsman and Padó, 2010; Sumita, 2000) and with unsupervised algorithms like LDA and LSA (Boyd-Graber and Blei, 2012; Zhao and Xing, 2006). Bilingual evidence has also been exploited for word clustering which is yet another form of representation learning, using both spectral methods (Zhao et al., 2005) and structured prediction approaches (Täckström et al., 2012; Faruqui and Dyer, 2013).

8 Conclusion

We have presented a canonical correlation analysis based method for incorporating multilingual context into word representations generated using only monolingual information and shown its applicability across three different ways of generating monolingual vectors on a variety of evaluation benchmarks. These word representations obtained after using multilingual evidence perform significantly better on the evaluation tasks compared to the monolingual vectors. We have also shown that our method is more suitable for vectors that encode semantic information than those that encode syntactic information. Our work suggests that multilingual evidence is an important resource even for purely monolingual, semantically aware applications. The tool for projecting word vectors can be found at `http://cs.cmu.edu/~mfaruqui/soft.html`.

Acknowledgements

We thanks Kevin Gimpel, Noah Smith, and David Bamman for helpful comments on earlier drafts of this paper. This research was supported by the NSF through grant IIS-1352440.

References

Eneko Agirre, Enrique Alfonseca, Keith Hall, Jana Kravalova, Marius Paşca, and Aitor Soroa. 2009.

A study on similarity and relatedness using distributional and wordnet-based approaches. In *Proceedings of North American Chapter of the Association for Computational Linguistics*, NAACL '09, pages 19–27, Stroudsburg, PA, USA. Association for Computational Linguistics.

Colin Bannard and Chris Callison-Burch. 2005. Paraphrasing with bilingual parallel corpora. In *Proc. of ACL*.

Jordan L. Boyd-Graber and David M. Blei. 2012. Multilingual topic models for unaligned text. *CoRR*, abs/1205.2657.

Kai-Wei Chang, Wen-tau Yih, and Christopher Meek. 2013. Multi-relational latent semantic analysis. In *Proceedings of the 2013 Conference on Empirical Methods in Natural Language Processing*, pages 1602–1612, Seattle, Washington, USA, October. Association for Computational Linguistics.

Kenneth Ward Church and Patrick Hanks. 1990. Word association norms, mutual information, and lexicography. *Comput. Linguist.*, 16(1):22–29, March.

Ronan Collobert and Jason Weston. 2008. A unified architecture for natural language processing: deep neural networks with multitask learning. In *Proceedings of the 25th international conference on Machine learning*, ICML '08, pages 160–167, New York, NY, USA. ACM.

S. C. Deerwester, S. T. Dumais, T. K. Landauer, G. W. Furnas, and R. A. Harshman. 1990. Indexing by latent semantic analysis. *Journal of the American Society for Information Science*.

Paramveer S. Dhillon, Dean P. Foster, and Lyle H. Ungar. 2011. Multi-view learning of word embeddings via cca. In *NIPS*, pages 199–207.

Mona Talat Diab. 2003. *Word sense disambiguation within a multilingual framework*. Ph.D. thesis, University of Maryland at College Park, College Park, MD, USA. AAI3115805.

Thomas G. Dietterich. 1998. Approximate statistical tests for comparing supervised classification learning algorithms. *Neural Computation*, 10:1895–1923.

Chris Dyer, Adam Lopez, Juri Ganitkevitch, Jonathan Weese, Hendra Setiawan, Ferhan Ture, Vladimir Eidelman, Phil Blunsom, and Philip Resnik. 2010. cdec: A decoder, alignment, and learning framework for finite-state and context-free translation models. In *In Proceedings of ACL System Demonstrations*.

Helge Dyvik. 2004. Translations as semantic mirrors: from parallel corpus to wordnet. *Language and Computers*, 49(1):311–326.

Manaal Faruqui and Chris Dyer. 2013. An information theoretic approach to bilingual word clustering. In *Proceedings of the 51st Annual Meeting of the Association for Computational Linguistics (Volume 2: Short Papers)*, pages 777–783, Sofia, Bulgaria, August.

Lev Finkelstein, Evgeniy Gabrilovich, Yossi Matias, Ehud Rivlin, Zach Solan, Gadi Wolfman, and Eytan Ruppin. 2001. Placing search in context: the concept revisited. In *WWW '01: Proceedings of the 10th international conference on World Wide Web*, pages 406–414, New York, NY, USA. ACM Press.

J.R. Firth. 1957. A synopsis of linguistic theory 1930-1955. *Studies in linguistic analysis*, pages 1–32.

Gene H. Golub and Charles F. Van Loan. 1996. *Matrix computations (3rd ed.)*. Johns Hopkins University Press, Baltimore, MD, USA.

Aria Haghighi, Percy Liang, Taylor Berg-Kirkpatrick, and Dan Klein. 2008. Learning bilingual lexicons from monolingual corpora. In *Proc. of ACL*.

Zellig Harris. 1954. Distributional structure. *Word*, 10(23):146–162.

Eric H Huang, Richard Socher, Christopher D Manning, and Andrew Y Ng. 2012. Improving word representations via global context and multiple word prototypes. In *Proceedings of the 50th Annual Meeting of the Association for Computational Linguistics: Long Papers-Volume 1*, pages 873–882. Association for Computational Linguistics.

Rebecca Hwa, Philip Resnik, Amy Weinberg, Clara Cabezas, and Okan Kolak. 2005. Bootstrapping parsers via syntactic projection across parallel texts. *Natural Language Engineering*, 11:11–311.

Alexandre Klementiev, Ivan Titov, and Binod Bhattarai. 2012. Inducing crosslingual distributed representations of words. In *Proceedings of COLING*.

Tomas Mikolov, Kai Chen, Greg Corrado, and Jeffrey Dean. 2013a. Efficient estimation of word representations in vector space. *arXiv preprint arXiv:1301.3781*.

Tomas Mikolov, Wen-tau Yih, and Geoffrey Zweig. 2013b. Linguistic regularities in continuous space word representations. In *Proceedings of the 2013 Conference of the North American Chapter of the Association for Computational Linguistics: Human Language Technologies*, pages 746–751, Atlanta, Georgia, June. Association for Computational Linguistics.

George A. Miller and Walter G. Charles. 1991. Contextual correlates of semantic similarity. *Language and Cognitive Processes*, 6(1):1–28.

Andriy Mnih and Geoffrey Hinton. 2008. A scalable hierarchical distributed language model. In *In NIPS*.

Frederic Morin and Yoshua Bengio. 2005. Hierarchical probabilistic neural network language model. In *AISTATS05*, pages 246–252.

Jerome L. Myers and Arnold D. Well. 1995. *Research Design & Statistical Analysis*. Routledge, 1 edition, June.

Yves Peirsman and Sebastian Padó. 2010. Cross-lingual induction of selectional preferences with bilingual vector spaces. In *Human Language Technologies: The 2010 Annual Conference of the North American Chapter of the Association for Computational Linguistics*, HLT '10, pages 921–929, Stroudsburg, PA, USA. Association for Computational Linguistics.

Kira Radinsky, Eugene Agichtein, Evgeniy Gabrilovich, and Shaul Markovitch. 2011. A word at a time: computing word relatedness using temporal semantic analysis. In *Proceedings of the 20th international conference on World wide web*, WWW '11, pages 337–346, New York, NY, USA. ACM.

Philip Resnik and David Yarowsky. 1999. Distinguishing systems and distinguishing senses: new evaluation methods for word sense disambiguation. *Nat. Lang. Eng.*, 5(2):113–133, June.

Herbert Rubenstein and John B. Goodenough. 1965. Contextual correlates of synonymy. *Commun. ACM*, 8(10):627–633, October.

Eiichiro Sumita. 2000. Lexical transfer using a vector-space model. In *Proceedings of the 38th Annual Meeting on Association for Computational Linguistics*, ACL '00, pages 425–431, Stroudsburg, PA, USA. Association for Computational Linguistics.

Oscar Täckström, Ryan McDonald, and Jakob Uszkoreit. 2012. Cross-lingual word clusters for direct transfer of linguistic structure. In *The 2012 Conference of the North American Chapter of the Association for Computational Linguistics: Human Language Technologies*, volume 1, page 11. Association for Computational Linguistics.

Joseph Turian, Lev Ratinov, and Yoshua Bengio. 2010. Word representations: a simple and general method for semi-supervised learning. In *Proceedings of the 48th Annual Meeting of the Association for Computational Linguistics*, ACL '10, pages 384–394, Stroudsburg, PA, USA. Association for Computational Linguistics.

Peter D. Turney and Patrick Pantel. 2010. From frequency to meaning : Vector space models of semantics. *Journal of Artificial Intelligence Research*, pages 141–188.

Peter D. Turney. 2001. Mining the web for synonyms: Pmi-ir versus lsa on toefl. In *Proceedings of the 12th European Conference on Machine Learning*, EMCL '01, pages 491–502, London, UK, UK. Springer-Verlag.

Peter D. Turney. 2006. Similarity of semantic relations. *Comput. Linguist.*, 32(3):379–416, September.

Laurens van der Maaten and Geoffrey Hinton. 2008. Visualizing Data using t-SNE. *Journal of Machine Learning Research*, 9:2579–2605, November.

Ivan Vulić and Marie-Francine Moens. 2013. A study on bootstrapping bilingual vector spaces from non-parallel data (and nothing else). In *Proceedings of the 2013 Conference on Empirical Methods in Natural Language Processing*, pages 1613–1624, Seattle, Washington, USA, October. Association for Computational Linguistics.

David Yarowsky and Grace Ngai. 2001. Inducing multilingual pos taggers and np bracketers via robust projection across aligned corpora. In *Proceedings of the second meeting of the North American Chapter of the Association for Computational Linguistics on Language technologies*, NAACL '01, pages 1–8, Stroudsburg, PA, USA. Association for Computational Linguistics.

Bing Zhao and Eric P. Xing. 2006. Bitam: Bilingual topic admixture models for word alignment. In *In Proceedings of the 44th Annual Meeting of the Association for Computational Linguistics (ACL06*.

Bing Zhao, Eric P. Xing, and Alex Waibel. 2005. Bilingual word spectral clustering for statistical machine translation. In *Proceedings of the ACL Workshop on Building and Using Parallel Texts*, ParaText '05, pages 25–32, Stroudsburg, PA, USA. Association for Computational Linguistics.

Will Y. Zou, Richard Socher, Daniel Cer, and Christopher D. Manning. 2013. Bilingual word embeddings for phrase-based machine translation. In *Proceedings of the 2013 Conference on Empirical Methods in Natural Language Processing*, pages 1393–1398, Seattle, Washington, USA, October. Association for Computational Linguistics.

Using Distributional Similarity of Multi-way Translations to Predict Multiword Expression Compositionality

Bahar Salehi,♣♡ Paul Cook♡ and Timothy Baldwin♣♡
♣ NICTA Victoria Research Laboratory
♡ Department of Computing and Information Systems
The University of Melbourne
Victoria 3010, Australia
bsalehi@student.unimelb.edu.au, paulcook@unimelb.edu.au, tb@ldwin.net

Abstract

We predict the compositionality of multiword expressions using distributional similarity between each component word and the overall expression, based on translations into multiple languages. We evaluate the method over English noun compounds, English verb particle constructions and German noun compounds. We show that the estimation of compositionality is improved when using translations into multiple languages, as compared to simply using distributional similarity in the source language. We further find that string similarity complements distributional similarity.

1 Compositionality of MWEs

Multiword expressions (hereafter MWEs) are combinations of words which are lexically, syntactically, semantically or statistically idiosyncratic (Sag et al., 2002; Baldwin and Kim, 2009). Much research has been carried out on the extraction and identification of MWEs[1] in English (Schone and Jurafsky, 2001; Pecina, 2008; Fazly et al., 2009) and other languages (Dias, 2003; Evert and Krenn, 2005; Salehi et al., 2012). However, considerably less work has addressed the task of predicting the meaning of MWEs, especially in non-English languages. As a step in this direction, the focus of this study is on predicting the compositionality of MWEs.

An MWE is fully compositional if its meaning is predictable from its component words, and it is non-compositional (or idiomatic) if not. For example, *stand up* "rise to one's feet" is compositional, because its meaning is clear from the meaning of the components *stand* and *up*. However, the meaning of *strike up* "to start playing" is largely unpredictable from the component words *strike* and *up*.

In this study, following McCarthy et al. (2003) and Reddy et al. (2011), we consider compositionality to be graded, and aim to predict the *degree* of compositionality. For example, in the dataset of Reddy et al. (2011), *climate change* is judged to be 99% compositional, while *silver screen* is 48% compositional and *ivory tower* is 9% compositional. Formally, we model compositionality prediction as a regression task.

An explicit handling of MWEs has been shown to be useful in NLP applications (Ramisch, 2012). As an example, Carpuat and Diab (2010) proposed two strategies for integrating MWEs into statistical machine translation. They show that even a large scale bilingual corpus cannot capture all the necessary information to translate MWEs, and that in adding the facility to model the compositionality of MWEs into their system, they could improve translation quality. Acosta et al. (2011) showed that treating non-compositional MWEs as a single unit in information retrieval improves retrieval effectiveness. For example, while searching for documents related to *ivory tower*, we are almost certainly not interested in documents relating to elephant tusks.

Our approach is to use a large-scale multi-way translation lexicon to source translations of MWEs and their component words, and then model the relative similarity between each of the component words and the MWE, using distributional similarity based on monolingual corpora for the source language and each of the target languages. Our hypothesis is that using distributional similarity in more than one language will improve the prediction of compositionality. Importantly, in order to make the method as language-independent and

[1]In this paper, we follow Baldwin and Kim (2009) in considering MWE "identification" to be a token-level disambiguation task, and MWE "extraction" to be a type-level lexicon induction task.

Proceedings of the 14th Conference of the European Chapter of the Association for Computational Linguistics, pages 472–481,
Gothenburg, Sweden, April 26-30 2014.

broadly-applicable as possible, we make no use of corpus preprocessing such as lemmatisation, and rely only on the availability of a translation dictionary and monolingual corpora.

Our results confirm our hypothesis that distributional similarity over the source language in addition to multiple target languages improves the quality of compositionality prediction. We also show that our method can be complemented with string similarity (Salehi and Cook, 2013) to further improve compositionality prediction. We achieve state-of-the-art results over two datasets.

2 Related Work

Most recent work on predicting the compositionality of MWEs can be divided into two categories: language/construction-specific and general-purpose. This can be at either the token-level (over token occurrences of an MWE in a corpus) or type-level (over the MWE string, independent of usage). The bulk of work on compositionality has been language/construction-specific and operated at the token-level, using dedicated methods to identify instances of a given MWE, and specific properties of the MWE in that language to predict compositionality (Lin, 1999; Kim and Baldwin, 2007; Fazly et al., 2009).

General-purpose token-level approaches such as distributional similarity have been commonly applied to infer the semantics of a word/MWE (Schone and Jurafsky, 2001; Baldwin et al., 2003; Reddy et al., 2011). These techniques are based on the assumption that the meaning of a word is predictable from its context of use, via the neighbouring words of token-level occurrences of the MWE. In order to predict the compositionality of a given MWE using distributional similarity, the different contexts of the MWE are compared with the contexts of its components, and the MWE is considered to be compositional if the MWE and component words occur in similar contexts.

Identifying token instances of MWEs is not always easy, especially when the component words do not occur sequentially. For example consider *put on* in ***put*** *your jacket* ***on***, and ***put*** *your jacket* ***on*** *the chair*. In the first example *put on* is an MWE while in the second example, *put on* is a simple verb with prepositional phrase and not an instance of an MWE. Moreover, if we adopt a conservative identification method, the number of token occurrences will be limited and the distributional scores may not be reliable. Additionally, for morphologically-rich languages, it can be difficult to predict the different word forms a given MWE type will occur across, posing a challenge for our requirement of no language-specific preprocessing.

Pichotta and DeNero (2013) proposed a token-based method for identifying English phrasal verbs based on parallel corpora for 50 languages. They show that they can identify phrasal verbs better when they combine information from multiple languages, in addition to the information they get from a monolingual corpus. This finding lends weight to our hypothesis that using translation data and distributional similarity from each of a range of target languages, can improve compositionality prediction. Having said that, the general applicability of the method is questionable — there are many parallel corpora involving English, but for other languages, this tends not to be the case.

Salehi and Cook (2013) proposed a general-purpose type-based approach using translation data from multiple languages, and string similarity between the MWE and each of the component words. They use training data to identify the best-10 languages for a given family of MWEs, on which to base the string similarity, and once again find that translation data improves their results substantially. Among the four string similarity measures they experimented with, longest common substring was found to perform best. Their proposed method is general and applicable to different families of MWEs in different languages. In this paper, we reimplement the method of Salehi and Cook (2013) using longest common substring (LCS), and both benchmark against this method and combine it with our distributional similarity-based method.

3 Our Approach

To predict the compositionality of a given MWE, we first measure the semantic similarity between the MWE and each of its component words[2] using distributional similarity based on a monolingual corpus in the source language. We then repeat the process for translations of the MWE and its component words into each of a range of target languages, calculating distributional similarity using

[2]Note that we will always assume that there are two component words, but the method is easily generalisable to MWEs with more than two components.

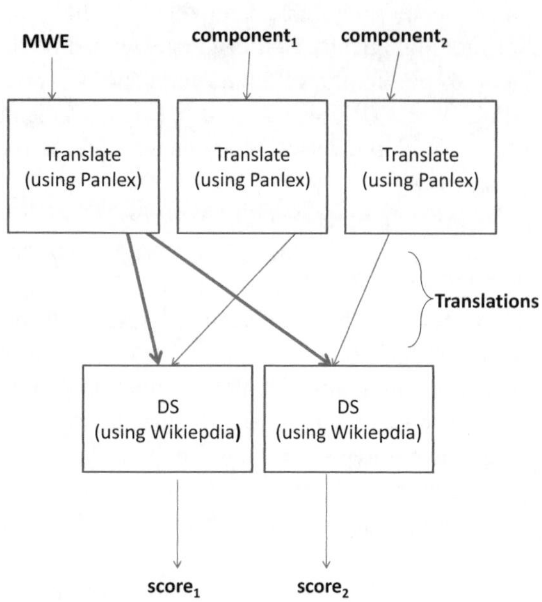

Figure 1: Outline of our approach to computing the distributional similarity (DS) of translations of an MWE with each of its component words, for a given target language. $score_1$ and $score_2$ are the similarity for the first and second components, respectively. We obtain translations from Panlex, and use Wikipedia as our corpus for each language.

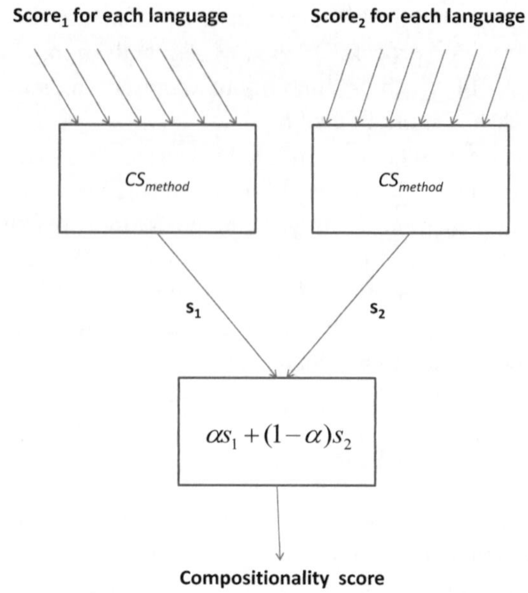

Figure 2: Outline of the method for combining distributional similarity scores from multiple languages, across the components of the MWE. CS_{method} refers to one of the methods described in Section 3.2 for calculating compositionality.

a monolingual corpus in the target language (Figure 1). We additionally use supervised learning to identify which target languages (or what weights for each language) optimise the prediction of compositionality (Figure 2). We hypothesise that by using multiple translations — rather than only information from the source language — we will be able to better predict compositionality.

We optionally combine our proposed approach with string similarity, calculated based on the method of Salehi and Cook (2013), using LCS.

Below, we detail our method for calculating distributional similarity in a given language, the different methods for combining distributional similarity scores into a single estimate of compositionality, and finally the method for selecting the target languages to use in calculating compositionality.

3.1 Calculating Distributional Similarity

In order to be consistent across all languages and be as language-independent as possible, we calculate distributional similarity in the following manner for a given language.

Tokenisation is based on whitespace delimiters and punctuation; no lemmatisation or case-folding is carried out. Token instances of a given MWE or component word are identified by full-token n-gram matching over the token stream. We assume that all full stops and equivalent characters for other orthographies are sentence boundaries, and chunk the corpora into (pseudo-)sentences on the basis of them. For each language, we identify the 51st–1050th most frequent words, and consider them to be content-bearing words, in the manner of Schütze (1997). This is based on the assumption that the top-50 most frequent words are stop words, and not a good choice of word for calculating distributional similarity over. That is not to say that we can't calculate the distributional similarity for stop words, however (as we will for the verb particle construction dataset — see Section 4.3.2) they are simply not used as the dimensions in our calculation of distributional similarity.

We form a vector of content-bearing words across all token occurrences of the target word, on the basis of these content-bearing words. Distributional similarity is calculated over these context vectors using cosine similarity. According to Weeds (2003), using dependency relations with the neighbouring words of the target word can better predict the meaning of the target word. However, in line with our assumption of no language-specific preprocessing, we just use word co-occurrence.

3.2 Calculating Compositionality

First, we need to calculate a combined compositionality score from the individual distributional similarities between each component word and the MWE. Following Reddy et al. (2011), we combine the component scores using the weighted mean (as shown in Figure 2):

$$\text{comp} = \alpha s_1 + (1 - \alpha) s_2 \qquad (1)$$

where s_1 and s_2 are the scores for the first and the second component, respectively. We use different α settings for each dataset, as detailed in Section 4.3.

We experiment with a range of methods for calculating compositionality, as follows:

CS_{L1}**:** calculate distributional similarity using only distributional similarity in the source language corpus (This is the approach used by Reddy et al. (2011), as discussed in Section 2).

CS_{L2N}**:** exclude the source language, and compute the mean of the distributional similarity scores for the best-N target languages. The value of N is selected according to training data, as detailed in Section 3.3.

CS_{L1+L2N}**:** calculate distributional similarity over both the source language (CS_{L1}) and the mean of the best-N languages (CS_{L2N}), and combine via the arithmetic mean.[3] This is to examine the hypothesis that using multiple target languages is better than just using the source language.

$CS_{SVR(L1+L2)}$**:** train a support vector regressor (SVR: Smola and Schölkopf (2004)) over the distributional similarities for all 52 languages (source and target languages).

CS_{string}**:** calculate string similarity using the LCS-based method of Salehi and Cook (2013).[4]

$CS_{string+L1}$**:** calculate the mean of the string similarity (CS_{string}) and distributional similarity in the source language (Salehi and Cook, 2013).

CS_{all}**:** calculate the mean of the string similarity (CS_{string}) and distributional similarity scores (CS_{L1} and CS_{L2N}).

3.3 Selecting Target Languages

We experiment with two approaches for combining the compositionality scores from multiple target languages.

First, in CS_{L2N} (and CS_{L1+L2N} and CS_{all} that build off it), we use training data to rank the target languages according to Pearson's correlation between the predicted compositionality scores and the gold-standard compositionality judgements. Based on this ranking, we take the best-N languages, and combine the individual compositionality scores by taking the arithmetic mean. We select N by determining the value that optimises the correlation over the training data. In other words, the selection of N and accordingly the best-N languages are based on nested cross-validation over training data, independently of the test data for that iteration of cross-validation.

Second in $CS_{SVR(L1+L2)}$, we combine the compositionality scores from the source and all 51 target languages into a feature vector, and train an SVR over the data using LIBSVM.[5]

4 Resources

In this section, we describe the resources required by our method, and also the datasets used to evaluate our method.

4.1 Monolingual Corpora for Different Languages

We collected monolingual corpora for each of 52 languages (51 target languages + 1 source language) from XML dumps of Wikipedia. These languages are based on the 54 target languages

[3] We also experimented with taking the mean over all the languages — target and source — but found it best to combine the scores for the target languages first, to give more weight to the source language.

[4] Due to differences in our random partitioning, our reported results over the two English datasets differ slightly over the results of Salehi and Cook (2013) using the same method.

[5] http://www.csie.ntu.edu.tw/~cjlin/libsvm

used by Salehi and Cook (2013), excluding Spanish because we happened not to have a dump of Spanish Wikipedia, and also Chinese and Japanese because of the need for a language-specific word tokeniser. The raw corpora were preprocessed using the WP2TXT toolbox[6] to eliminate XML tags, HTML tags and hyperlinks, and then tokenisation based on whitespace and punctuation was performed. The corpora vary in size from roughly 750M tokens for English, to roughly 640K tokens for Marathi.

4.2 Multilingual Dictionary

To translate the MWEs and their components, we follow Salehi and Cook (2013) in using Panlex (Baldwin et al., 2010). This online dictionary is massively multilingual, covering more than 1353 languages. For each MWE dataset (see Section 4.3), we translate the MWE and component words from the source language into each of the 51 languages.

In instances where there is no direct translation in a given language for a term, we use a pivot language to find translation(s) in the target language. For example, the English noun compound *silver screen* has direct translations in only 13 languages in Panlex, including Vietnamese (*màn bac*) but not French. There is, however, a translation of *màn bac* into French (*cinéma*), allowing us to infer an indirect translation between *silver screen* and *cinéma*. In this way, if there are no direct translations into a particular target language, we search for a single-pivot translation via each of our other target languages, and combine them all together as our set of translations for the target language of interest.

In the case that no translation (direct or indirect) can be found for a given source language term into a particular target language, the compositionality score for that target language is set to the average across all target languages for which scores can be calculated for the given term. If no translations are available for any target language (e.g. the term is not in Panlex) the compositionality score for each target language is set to the average score for that target language across all other source language terms.

[6] `http://wp2txt.rubyforge.org/`

4.3 Datasets

We evaluate our proposed method over three datasets (two English, one German), as described below.

4.3.1 English Noun Compounds (ENC)

Our first dataset is made up of 90 binary English noun compounds, from the work of Reddy et al. (2011). Each noun compound was annotated by multiple annotators using the integer scale 0 (fully non-compositional) to 5 (fully compositional). A final compositionality score was then calculated as the mean of the scores from the annotators. If we simplistically consider 2.5 as the threshold for compositionality, the dataset is relatively well balanced, containing 48% compositional and 52% non-compositional noun compounds. Following Reddy et al. (2011), in combining the component-wise distributional similarities for this dataset, we weight the first component in Equation 1 higher than the second ($\alpha = 0.7$).

4.3.2 English Verb Particle Constructions (EVPC)

The second dataset contains 160 English verb particle constructions (VPCs), from the work of Bannard (2006). In this dataset, a verb particle construction consists of a verb (the head) and a prepositional particle (e.g. *hand in*, *look up* or *battle on*).

For each component word (the verb and particle, respectively), multiple annotators were asked whether the VPC entails the component word. In order to translate the dataset into a regression task, we calculate the overall compositionality as the number of annotations of entailment for the verb, divided by the total number of verb annotations for that VPC. That is, following Bannard et al. (2003), we only consider the compositionality of the verb component in our experiments (and as such $\alpha = 1$ in Equation 1).

One area of particular interest with this dataset will be the robustness of the method to function words (the particles), both under translation and in terms of calculating distributional similarity, although the findings of Baldwin (2006) for English prepositions are at least encouraging in this respect. Additionally, English VPCs can occur in "split" form (e.g. ***put** your jacket **on***, from our earlier example), which will complicate identification, and the verb component will often be inflected and thus not match under our identification strategy (for both VPCs and the component verbs).

Dataset	Language	Frequency	Family
ENC	Italian	100	Romance
	French	99	Romance
	German	86	Germanic
	Vietnamese	83	Viet-Muong
	Portuguese	62	Romance
EVPC	Bulgarian	100	Slavic
	Breton	100	Celtic
	Occitan	100	Romance
	Indonesian	100	Indonesian
	Slovenian	100	Slavic
GNC	Polish	100	Slavic
	Lithuanian	99	Baltic
	Finnish	74	Uralic
	Bulgarian	72	Slavic
	Czech	40	Slavic

Table 1: The 5 best languages for the ENC, EVPC and GNC datasets. The language family is based on Voegelin and Voegelin (1977).

4.3.3 German Noun Compounds (GNC)

Our final dataset is made up of 246 German noun compounds (von der Heide and Borgwaldt, 2009; Schulte im Walde et al., 2013). Multiple annotators were asked to rate the compositionality of each German noun compound on an integer scale of 1 (non-compositional) to 7 (compositional). The overall compositionality score is then calculated as the mean across the annotators. Note that the component words are provided as part of the dataset, and that there is no need to perform decompounding. Following Schulte im Walde et al. (2013), we weight the first component higher in Equation 1 ($\alpha = 0.8$) when calculating the overall compositionality score.

This dataset is significant in being non-English, and also in that German has relatively rich morphology, which we expect to impact on the identification of both the MWE and the component words.

5 Results

All experiments are carried out using 10 iterations of 10-fold cross validation, randomly partitioning the data independently on each of the 10 iterations, and averaging across all 100 test partitions in our presented results. In the case of CS_{L2N} and other methods that make use of it (i.e. CS_{L1+L2N} and CS_{all}), the languages selected for a given training fold are then used to compute the compositionality scores for the instances in the test set. Figures 3a, 3b and 3c are histograms of the number of times each N is selected over 100 folds on ENC, EVPC and GNC datasets, respectively. From the histograms, $N = 6$, $N = 15$ and $N = 2$ are the most commonly selected settings for ENC, EVPC and GNC, respectively. That is, multiple languages are generally used, but more languages are used for English VPCs than either of the compound noun datasets. The 5 most-selected languages for ENC, EVPC and GNC are shown in Table 1. As we can see, there are some languages which are always selected for a given dataset, but equally the commonly-selected languages vary considerably between datasets.

Further analysis reveals that 32 (63%) target languages for ENC, 25 (49%) target languages for EVPC, and only 5 (10%) target languages for GNC have a correlation of $r \geq 0.1$ with gold-standard compositionality judgements. On the other hand, 8 (16%) target languages for ENC, 2 (4%) target languages for EVPC, and no target languages for GNC have a correlation of $r \leq -0.1$.

5.1 ENC Results

English noun compounds are relatively easy to identify in a corpus,[7] because the components occur sequentially, and the only morphological variation is in noun number (singular vs. plural). In other words, the precision for our token matching method is very high, and the recall is also acceptably high. Partly as a result of the ease of identification, we get a high correlation of $r = 0.700$ for CS_{L1} (using only source language data). Using only target languages (CS_{L2N}), the results drop to $r = 0.434$, but when we combine the two (CS_{L1+L2N}), the correlation is higher than using only source or target language data, at $r = 0.725$. When we combine all languages using SVR, the results rise slightly higher again to $r = 0.744$, which is slightly above the correlation of the state-of-the-art method of Salehi and Cook (2013), which combines their method with the method of Reddy et al. (2011) ($CS_{string+L1}$). These last two results support our hypothesis that using translation data can improve the prediction of compositionality. The results for string similarity on its own (CS_{string}, $r = 0.644$) are slightly lower than those using only source language distributional similarity, but when combined with

[7]Although see Lapata and Lascarides (2003) for discussion of the difficulty of reliably identifying low-frequency English noun compounds.

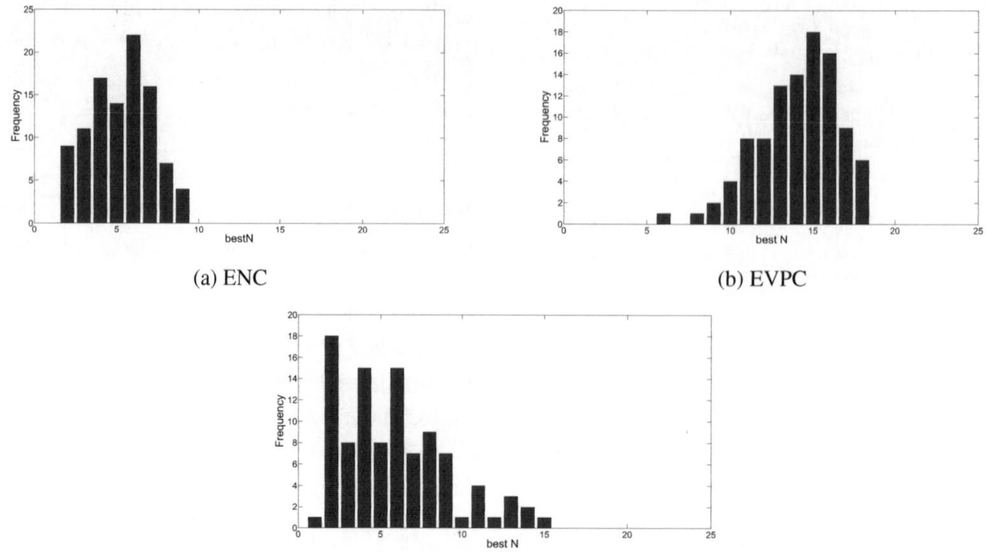

(a) ENC

(b) EVPC

(c) GNC

Figure 3: Histograms displaying how many times a given N is selected as the best number of languages over each dataset. For example, according to the GNC chart, there is a peak for $N = 2$, which shows that over 100 folds, the best-2 languages achieved the highest correlation on 18 folds.

Method	Summary of the Method	ENC	EVPC	GNC
CS_{L1}	Source language	0.700	0.177	0.141
CS_{L2N}	Best-N target languages	0.434	0.398	0.113
CS_{L1+L2N}	Source + best-N target languages	0.725	0.312	0.178
$CS_{SVR(L1+L2)}$	SVR (Source + all 51 target languages)	**0.744**	0.389	0.085
CS_{string}	String Similarity (Salehi and Cook, 2013)	0.644	0.385	**0.372**
$CS_{string+L1}$	CS_{string} +CS_{L1} (Salehi and Cook, 2013)	0.739	0.360	0.353
CS_{all}	CS_{L1} + CS_{L2N} + CS_{string}	0.732	**0.417**	0.364

Table 2: Pearson's correlation on the ENC, EVPC and GNC datasets

CS_{L1+L2N} (i.e. CS_{all}) there is a slight rise in correlation (from $r = 0.725$ to $r = 0.732$).

5.2 EVPC Results

English VPCs are hard to identify. As discussed in Section 2, VPC components may not occur sequentially, and even when they do occur sequentially, they may not be a VPC. As such, our simplistic identification method has low precision and recall (hand analysis of 927 identified VPC instances would suggest a precision of around 74%). There is no question that this is a contributor to the low correlation for the source language method (CS_{L1}; $r = 0.177$). When we use target languages instead of the source language (CS_{L2N}), the correlation jumps substantially to $r = 0.398$.

When we combine English and the target languages (CS_{L1+L2N}), the results are actually lower than just using the target languages, because of the high weight on the target language, which is not desirable for VPCs, based on the source language results. Even for $CS_{SVR(L1+L2)}$, the results ($r = 0.389$) are slightly below the target language-only results. This suggests that when predicting the compositionality of MWEs which are hard to identify in the source language, it may actually be better to use target languages only. The results for string similarity (CS_{string}: $r = 0.385$) are similar to those for CS_{L2N}. However, as with the ENC dataset, when we combine string similarity and distributional similarity (CS_{all}), the results improve, and we achieve the state-of-the-art for the dataset.

In Table 3, we present classification-based eval-

Method	Precision	Recall	F-score ($\beta = 1$)	Accuracy
Bannard et al. (2003)	60.8	66.6	63.6	60.0
Salehi and Cook (2013)	**86.2**	71.8	77.4	69.3
CS_{all}	79.5	**89.3**	**82.0**	**74.5**

Table 3: Results (%) for the binary compositionality prediction task on the EVPC dataset

uation over a subset of EVPC, binarising the compositionality judgements in the manner of Bannard et al. (2003). Our method achieves state-of-the-art results in terms of overall F-score and accuracy.

5.3 GNC Results

German is a morphologically-rich language, with marking of number and case on nouns. Given that we do not perform any lemmatization or other language-specific preprocessing, we inevitably achieve low recall for the identification of noun compound tokens, although the precision should be nearly 100%. Partly because of the resultant sparseness in the distributional similarity method, the results for CS_{L1} are low ($r = 0.141$), although they are lower again when using target languages ($r = 0.113$). However, when we combine the source and target languages (CS_{L1+L2N}) the results improve to $r = 0.178$. The results for $CS_{SVR(L1+L2)}$, on the other hand, are very low ($r = 0.085$). Ultimately, simple string similarity achieves the best results for the dataset ($r = 0.372$), and this result actually drops slightly when combined with the distributional similarities.

To better understand the reason for the lacklustre results using SVR, we carried out error analysis and found that, unlike the other two datasets, about half of the target languages return scores which correlate negatively with the human judgements. When we filter these languages from the data, the score for SVR improves appreciably. For example, over the best-3 languages overall, we get a correlation score of $r = 0.179$, which is slightly higher than CS_{L1+L2N}.

We further investigated the reason for getting very low and sometimes negative correlations with many of our target languages. We noted that about 24% of the German noun compounds in the dataset do not have entries in Panlex. This contrasts with ENC where only one instance does not have an entry in Panlex, and EVPC where all VPCs have translations in at least one language in Panlex. We experimented with using string similarity scores in the case of such missing translations, as opposed to the strategy described in Section 4.2. The results for $CS_{SVR(L1+L2)}$ rose to $r = 0.269$, although this is still below the correlation for just using string similarity.

Our results on the GNC dataset using string similarity are competitive with the state-of-the-art results ($r = 0.45$) using a window-based distributional similarity approach over monolingual German data (Schulte im Walde et al., 2013). Note, however, that their method used part-of-speech information and lemmatisation, where ours does not, in keeping with the language-independent philosophy of this research.

6 Conclusion and Future Work

In this study, we proposed a method to predict the compositionality of MWEs based on monolingual distributional similarity between the MWE and each of its component words, under translation into multiple target languages. We showed that using translation and multiple target languages enhances compositionality modelling, and also that there is strong complementarity between our approach and an approach based on string similarity.

In future work, we hope to address the question of translation sparseness, as observed for the GNC dataset. We also plan to experiment with unsupervised morphological analysis methods to improve identification recall, and explore the impact of tokenization. Furthermore, we would like to investigate the optimal number of stop words and content-bearing words for each language, and to look into the development of general unsupervised methods for compositionality prediction.

Acknowledgements

We thank the anonymous reviewers for their insightful comments and valuable suggestions. NICTA is funded by the Australian government as represented by Department of Broadband, Communication and Digital Economy, and the Australian Research Council through the ICT Centre of Excellence programme.

References

Otavio Acosta, Aline Villavicencio, and Viviane Moreira. 2011. Identification and treatment of multiword expressions applied to information retrieval. In *Proceedings of the Workshop on Multiword Expressions: from Parsing and Generation to the Real World*, pages 101–109, Portland, USA.

Timothy Baldwin and Su Nam Kim. 2009. Multiword expressions. In Nitin Indurkhya and Fred J. Damerau, editors, *Handbook of Natural Language Processing*. CRC Press, Boca Raton, USA, 2nd edition.

Timothy Baldwin, Colin Bannard, Takaaki Tanaka, and Dominic Widdows. 2003. An empirical model of multiword expression decomposability. In *Proceedings of the ACL-2003 Workshop on Multiword Expressions: Analysis, Acquisition and Treatment*, pages 89–96, Sapporo, Japan.

Timothy Baldwin, Jonathan Pool, and Susan M Colowick. 2010. Panlex and lextract: Translating all words of all languages of the world. In *Proceedings of the 23rd International Conference on Computational Linguistics: Demonstrations*, pages 37–40, Beijing, China.

Timothy Baldwin. 2006. Distributional similarity and preposition semantics. In Patrick Saint-Dizier, editor, *Computational Linguistics Dimensions of Syntax and Semantics of Prepositions*, pages 197–210. Springer, Dordrecht, Netherlands.

Colin Bannard, Timothy Baldwin, and Alex Lascarides. 2003. A statistical approach to the semantics of verb-particles. In *Proceedings of the ACL 2003 workshop on Multiword expressions: analysis, acquisition and treatment-Volume 18*, pages 65–72, Sapporo, Japan.

Colin James Bannard. 2006. *Acquiring Phrasal Lexicons from Corpora*. Ph.D. thesis, University of Edinburgh.

Marine Carpuat and Mona Diab. 2010. Task-based evaluation of multiword expressions: a pilot study in statistical machine translation. In *Human Language Technologies: The 2010 Annual Conference of the North American Chapter of the Association for Computational Linguistics*, pages 242–245, Los Angeles, USA.

Gaël Dias. 2003. Multiword unit hybrid extraction. In *Proceedings of the ACL 2003 Workshop on Multiword Expressions: Analysis, Acquisition and Treatment*, pages 41–48, Sapporo, Japan.

Stefan Evert and Brigitte Krenn. 2005. Using small random samples for the manual evaluation of statistical association measures. *Computer Speech and Language, Special Issue on Multiword Expressions*, 19(4):450–466.

Afsaneh Fazly, Paul Cook, and Suzanne Stevenson. 2009. Unsupervised type and token identification of idiomatic expressions. *Computational Linguistics*, 35(1):61–103.

Su Nam Kim and Timothy Baldwin. 2007. Detecting compositionality of English verb-particle constructions using semantic similarity. In *Proceedings of the 7th Meeting of the Pacific Association for Computational Linguistics (PACLING 2007)*, pages 40–48, Melbourne, Australia.

Mirella Lapata and Alex Lascarides. 2003. Detecting novel compounds: The role of distributional evidence. In *Proceedings of the 11th Conference of the European Chapter for the Association of Computational Linguistics (EACL-2003)*, pages 235–242, Budapest, Hungary.

Dekang Lin. 1999. Automatic identification of non-compositional phrases. In *Proceedings of the 37th annual meeting of the Association for Computational Linguistics on Computational Linguistics*, pages 317–324, College Park, USA.

Diana McCarthy, Bill Keller, and John Carroll. 2003. Detecting a continuum of compositionality in phrasal verbs. In *Proceedings of the ACL 2003 workshop on Multiword expressions: analysis, acquisition and treatment-Volume 18*, pages 73–80, Sapporo, Japan.

Pavel Pecina. 2008. *Lexical Association Measures: Collocation Extraction*. Ph.D. thesis, Faculty of Mathematics and Physics, Charles University in Prague, Prague, Czech Republic.

Karl Pichotta and John DeNero. 2013. Identifying phrasal verbs using many bilingual corpora. In *Proceedings of the 2013 Conference on Empirical Methods in Natural Language Processing (EMNLP 2013)*, Seattle, USA.

Carlos Ramisch. 2012. A generic framework for multiword expressions treatment: from acquisition to applications. In *Proceedings of ACL 2012 Student Research Workshop*, pages 61–66, Jeju Island, Korea.

Siva Reddy, Diana McCarthy, and Suresh Manandhar. 2011. An empirical study on compositionality in compound nouns. In *Proceedings of IJCNLP*, pages 210–218, Chiang Mai, Thailand.

Ivan Sag, Timothy Baldwin, Francis Bond, Ann Copestake, and Dan Flickinger. 2002. Multiword expressions: A pain in the neck for NLP. In *Proceedings of the 3rd International Conference on Intelligent Text Processing Computational Linguistics (CICLing-2002)*, pages 189–206, Mexico City, Mexico.

Bahar Salehi and Paul Cook. 2013. Predicting the compositionality of multiword expressions using translations in multiple languages. In *Proceedings of the Second Joint Conference on Lexical and Computational Semantics*, volume 1, pages 266–275, Atlanta, USA.

Bahar Salehi, Narjes Askarian, and Afsaneh Fazly. 2012. Automatic identification of Persian light verb constructions. In *Proceedings of the 13th International Conference on Intelligent Text Processing Computational Linguistics (CICLing-2012)*, pages 201–210, New Delhi, India.

Patrick Schone and Dan Jurafsky. 2001. Is knowledge-free induction of multiword unit dictionary headwords a solved problem. In *Proceedings of the 6th Conference on Empirical Methods in Natural Language Processing (EMNLP 2001)*, pages 100–108, Hong Kong, China.

Sabine Schulte im Walde, Stefan Müller, and Stephen Roller. 2013. Exploring vector space models to predict the compositionality of German noun-noun compounds. In *Proceedings of the Second Joint Conference on Lexical and Computational Semantics*, Atlanta, USA.

Hinrich Schütze. 1997. *Ambiguity Resolution in Language Learning*. CSLI Publications, Stanford, USA.

Alex J Smola and Bernhard Schölkopf. 2004. A tutorial on support vector regression. *Statistics and Computing*, 14(3):199–222.

Charles Frederick Voegelin and Florence Marie Voegelin. 1977. *Classification and index of the world's languages*, volume 4. New York: Elsevier.

Claudia von der Heide and Susanne Borgwaldt. 2009. Assoziationen zu Unter, Basis und Oberbegriffen. Eine explorative Studie. In *Proceedings of the 9th Norddeutsches Linguistisches Kolloquium*, pages 51–74.

Julie Elizabeth Weeds. 2003. *Measures and applications of lexical distributional similarity*. Ph.D. thesis, University of Sussex.

Word Embeddings through Hellinger PCA

Rémi Lebret
Idiap Research Institute
Rue Marconi 19, CP 592
1920 Martigny, Switzerland
remi@lebret.ch

Ronan Collobert
Idiap Research Institute
Rue Marconi 19, CP 592
1920 Martigny, Switzerland
ronan@collobert.com

Abstract

Word embeddings resulting from neural language models have been shown to be a great asset for a large variety of NLP tasks. However, such architecture might be difficult and time-consuming to train. Instead, we propose to drastically simplify the word embeddings computation through a Hellinger PCA of the word cooccurence matrix. We compare those new word embeddings with some well-known embeddings on named entity recognition and movie review tasks and show that we can reach similar or even better performance. Although deep learning is not really necessary for generating good word embeddings, we show that it can provide an easy way to adapt embeddings to specific tasks.

1 Introduction

Building word embeddings has always generated much interest for linguists. Popular approaches such as Brown clustering algorithm (Brown et al., 1992) have been used with success in a wide variety of NLP tasks (Schütze, 1995; Koo et al., 2008; Ratinov and Roth, 2009). Those word embeddings are often seen as a low dimensional-vector space where the dimensions are features potentially describing syntactic or semantic properties. Recently, distributed approaches based on neural network language models (NNLM) have revived the field of learning word embeddings (Collobert and Weston, 2008; Huang and Yates, 2009; Turian et al., 2010; Collobert et al., 2011). However, a neural network architecture can be hard to train. Finding the right parameters to tune the model is often a challenging task and the training phase is in general computationally expensive.

This paper aims to show that such good word embeddings can be obtained using simple (mostly linear) operations. We show that similar word embeddings can be computed using the word cooccurrence statistics and a well-known dimensionality reduction operation such as Principal Component Analysis (PCA). We then compare our embeddings with the CW (Collobert and Weston, 2008), Turian (Turian et al., 2010), HLBL (Mnih and Hinton, 2008) embeddings, which come from deep architectures and the LR-MVL (Dhillon et al., 2011) embeddings, which also come from a spectral method on several NLP tasks.

We claim that, assuming an appropriate metric, a simple spectral method as PCA can generate word embeddings as good as with deep-learning architectures. On the other hand, deep-learning architectures have shown their potential in several supervised NLP tasks, by using these word embeddings. As they are usually generated over large corpora of unlabeled data, words are represented in a generic manner. Having generic embeddings, good performance can be achieved on NLP tasks where the syntactic aspect is dominant such as Part-Of-Speech, chunking and NER (Turian et al., 2010; Collobert et al., 2011; Dhillon et al., 2011). For supervised tasks relying more on the semantic aspect as sentiment classification, it is usually helpful to adapt the existing embeddings to improve performance (Labutov and Lipson, 2013). We show in this paper that such embedding specialization can be easily done via neural network architectures and that helps to increase general performance.

2 Related Work

As 80% of the meaning of English text comes from word choice and the remaining 20% comes from word order (Landauer, 2002), it seems quite important to leverage word order to capture all the semantic information. Connectionist approaches have therefore been proposed to develop distributed representations which encode the struc-

Proceedings of the 14th Conference of the European Chapter of the Association for Computational Linguistics, pages 482–490,
Gothenburg, Sweden, April 26-30 2014.

tural relationships between words (Hinton, 1986; Pollack, 1990; Elman, 1991). More recently, a neural network language model was proposed in Bengio et al. (2003) where word vector representations are simultaneously learned along with a statistical language model. This architecture inspired other authors: Collobert and Weston (2008) designed a neural language model which eliminates the linear dependency on vocabulary size, Mnih and Hinton (2008) proposed a hierarchical linear neural model, Mikolov et al. (2010) investigated a recurrent neural network architecture for language modeling. Such architectures being trained over large corpora of unlabeled text with the aim to predict correct scores end up learning the co-occurence statistics.

Linguists assumed long ago that words occurring in similar contexts tend to have similar meanings (Wittgenstein, 1953). Using the word co-occurrence statistics is thus a natural choice to embed similar words into a common vector space (Turney and Pantel, 2010). Common approaches calculate the frequencies, apply some transformations (tf-idf, PPMI), reduce the dimensionality and calculate the similarities (Lowe, 2001). Considering a fixed-sized word vocabulary $\mathcal{D}$ and a set of words $\mathcal{W}$ to embed, the co-occurence matrix C is of size $|\mathcal{W}|\times|\mathcal{D}|$. C is then vocabulary size-dependent. One can apply a dimensionality reduction operation to C leading to $\bar{C} \in \mathbb{R}^{|\mathcal{W}|\times d}$, where $d \ll |\mathcal{D}|$. Dimensionality reduction techniques such as Singular Valued Decomposition (SVD) are widely used (e.g. LSA (Landauer and Dumais, 1997), ICA (Väyrynen and Honkela, 2004)). However, word co-occurence statistics are discrete distributions. An information theory measure such as the Hellinger distance seems to be more appropriate than the Euclidean distance over a discrete distribution space. In this paper we will compare the Hellinger PCA against the classical Euclidean PCA and the Low Rank Multi-View Learning (LR-MVL) method, which is another spectral method based on Canonical Correlation Analysis (CCA) to learn word embeddings (Dhillon et al., 2011).

It has been shown that using word embeddings as features helps to improve general performance on many NLP tasks (Turian et al., 2010). However these embeddings can be too generic to perform well on other tasks such as sentiment classification. For such task, word embeddings must capture the sentiment information. Maas et al. (2011) proposed a model for jointly capturing semantic and sentiment components of words into vector spaces. More recently, Labutov and Lipson (2013) presented a method which takes existing embeddings and, by using some labeled data, re-embed them in the same space. They showed that these new embeddings can be better predictors in a supervised task. In this paper, we consider word embedding-based linear and non-linear models for two NLP supervised tasks: Named Entity Recognition and IMDB movie review. We analyze the effect of fine-tuning existing embeddings over each task of interest.

3 Spectral Method for Word Embeddings

A NNLM learns which words among the vocabulary are likely to appear after a given sequence of words. More formally, it learns the next word probability distribution. Instead, simply counting words on a large corpus of unlabeled text can be performed to retrieve those word distributions and to represent words (Turney and Pantel, 2010).

3.1 Word co-occurence statistics

"You shall know a word by the company it keeps" (Firth, 1957). It is a natural choice to use the word co-occurence statistics to acquire representations of word meanings. Raw word co-occurence frequencies are computed by counting the number of times each context word $w \in \mathcal{D}$ occurs after a sequence of words T:

$$p(w|T) = \frac{p(w,T)}{p(T)} = \frac{n(w,T)}{\sum_w n(w,T)}, \quad (1)$$

where $n(w,T)$ is the number of times each context word w occurs after the sequence T. The size of T can go from 1 to t words. The next word probability distribution p for each word or sequence of words is thus obtained. It is a multinomial distribution of $|\mathcal{D}|$ classes (words). A co-occurence matrix of size $N \times |\mathcal{D}|$ is finally built by computing those frequencies over all the N possible sequences of words.

3.2 Hellinger distance

Similarities between words can be derived by computing a distance between their corresponding word distributions. Several distances (or metrics) over discrete distributions exist, such as the

Bhattacharyya distance, the Hellinger distance or Kullback-Leibler divergence. We chose here the Hellinger distance for its simplicity and symmetry property (as it is a true distance). Considering two discrete probability distributions $P = (p_1, \ldots, p_k)$ and $Q = (q_1, \ldots, q_k)$, the Hellinger distance is formally defined as:

$$H(P,Q) = \frac{1}{\sqrt{2}}\sqrt{\sum_{i=1}^{k}(\sqrt{p_i} - \sqrt{q_i})^2}\,, \quad (2)$$

which is directly related to the Euclidean norm of the difference of the square root vectors:

$$H(P,Q) = \frac{1}{\sqrt{2}}\|\sqrt{P} - \sqrt{Q}\|_2\,. \quad (3)$$

Note that it makes more sense to take the Hellinger distance rather than the Euclidean distance for comparing discrete distributions, as P and Q are unit vectors according to the Hellinger distance ($\sqrt{P}$ and $\sqrt{Q}$ are units vector according to the ℓ_2 norm).

3.3 Dimensionality Reduction

As discrete distributions are vocabulary size-dependent, using directly the distribution as a word embedding is not really tractable for large vocabulary. We propose to perform a principal component analysis (PCA) of the word co-occurence probability matrix to represent words in a lower dimensional space while minimizing the reconstruction error according to the Hellinger distance.

4 Architectures for NLP tasks

Traditional NLP approaches extract from documents a rich set of hand-designed features which are then fed to a standard classification algorithm. The choice of features is a task-specific empirical process. In contrast, we want to pre-process our features as little as possible. In that respect, a multilayer neural network architecture seems appropriate as it can be trained in an end-to-end fashion on the task of interest.

4.1 Sentence-level Approach

The sentence-level approach aims at tagging with a label each word in a given sentence. Embeddings of each word in a sentence are fed to linear and non-linear classification models followed by a CRF-type sentence tag inference. We chose here neural networks as classifiers.

Sliding window Context is crucial to characterize word meanings. We thus consider n context words around each word x_t to be tagged, leading to a window of $N = (2n+1)$ words $[x]^t = (x_{t-n}, \ldots, x_t, \ldots, x_{t+n})$. As each word is embedded into a d_{wrd}-dimensional vector, it results a $d_{wrd} \times N$ vector representing a window of N words, which aims at characterizing the middle word x_t in this window. Given a complete sentence of T words, we can obtain for each word a context-dependent representation by sliding over all the possible windows in the sentence. A same linear transformation is then applied on each window for each word to tag:

$$g([x]^t) = W[x]^t + b\,, \quad (4)$$

where $W \in \mathbb{R}^{M \times d_{wrd}N}$ and $b \in \mathbb{R}^M$ are the parameters, with M the number of classes. Alternatively, a one hidden layer non-linear network can be considered:

$$g([x]^t) = Wh(U[x]^t) + b\,, \quad (5)$$

where $U \in \mathbb{R}^{n_{hu} \times d_{wrd}N}$, with n_{hu} the number of hidden units and $h(.)$ a transfer function.

CRF-type inference There exists strong dependencies between tags in a sentence: some tags cannot follow other tags. To take the sentence structure into account, we want to encourage valid paths of tags during training, while discouraging all other paths. Considering the matrix of scores outputs by the network, we train a simple conditional random field (CRF). At inference time, given a sentence to tag, the best path which minimizes the sentence score is inferred with the Viterbi algorithm. More formally, we denote θ all the trainable parameters of the network and $f_\theta([x]_1^T)$ the matrix of scores. The element $[f_\theta]_{i,t}$ of the matrix is the score output by the network for the sentence $[x]_1^T$ and the ith tag, at the tth word. We introduce a transition score $[A]_{i,j}$ for jumping from i to j tags in successive words, and an initial score $[A]_{i,0}$ for starting from the ith tag. As the transition scores are going to be trained, we define $\tilde{\theta} = \theta \cup \{[A]_{i,j} \forall i, j\}$. The score of a sentence $[x]_1^T$ along a path of tags $[i]_1^T$ is then given by the sum of transition scores and networks scores:

$$s([x]_1^T, [i]_1^T, \tilde{\theta}) = \sum_{t=1}^{T}(A_{[i]_{t-1},[i]_t} + [f_\theta]_{[i]_t,t})\,. \quad (6)$$

We normalize this score over all possible tag paths $[j]_1^T$ using a softmax, and we interpret the resulting ratio as a conditional tag path probability. Taking the log, the conditional probability of the true path $[y]_1^T$ is therefore given by:

$$\log p([y]_1^T, [x]_1^T, \tilde{\theta}) = s([x]_1^T, [y]_1^T, \tilde{\theta}) - \underset{\forall [j]_1^T}{\text{logadd}}\, s([x]_1^T, [j]_1^T, \tilde{\theta}), \tag{7}$$

where we adopt the notation

$$\underset{i}{\text{logadd}}\, z_i = \log\left(\sum_i e^{z_i}\right). \tag{8}$$

Computing the log-likelihood efficiently is not straightforward, as the number of terms in the logadd grows exponentially with the length of the sentence. It can be computed in linear time with the Forward algorithm, which derives a recursion similar to the Viterbi algorithm (see Rabiner (1989)). We can thus maximize the log-likelihood over all the training pairs $([x]_1^T, [y]_1^T)$ to find, given a sentence $[x]_1^T$, the best tag path which minimizes the sentence score (6):

$$\underset{[j]_1^T}{\text{argmax}}\, s([x]_1^T, [j]_1^T, \tilde{\theta}). \tag{9}$$

In contrast to classical CRF, all parameters θ are trained in a end-to-end manner, by backpropagation through the Forward recursion, following Collobert et al. (2011).

4.2 Document-level Approach

The document-level approach is a document binary classifier, with classes $y \in \{-1, 1\}$. For each document, a set of (trained) filters is applied to the sliding window described in section 4.1. The maximum value obtained by the ith filter over the whole document is:

$$\max_t \left[w_i [x]^t + b_i \right]_{i,t} \quad 1 \leq i \leq n_{filter}. \tag{10}$$

It can be seen as a way to measure if the information represented by the filter has been captured in the document or not. We feed all these intermediate scores to a linear classifier, leading to the following simple model:

$$f_\theta(x) = \boldsymbol{\alpha} \max_t \left[W[x]^t + b \right]. \tag{11}$$

In the case of movie reviews, the ith filter might capture positive or negative sentiment depending on the sign of α_i. As in section 4.1, we will also consider a non-linear classifier in the experiments.

Training The neural network is trained using stochastic gradient ascent. We denote θ all the trainable parameters of the network. Using a training set $\mathcal{T}$, we minimize the following soft margin loss function with respect to θ:

$$\theta \leftarrow \sum_{(x,y)\in\mathcal{T}} \log\left(1 + e^{-y f_\theta(x)}\right). \tag{12}$$

4.3 Embedding Fine-Tuning

As seen in section 3, the process to compute generic word embedding is quite straightforward. These embeddings can then be used as features for supervised NLP systems and help to improve the general performance (Turian et al., 2010; Collobert et al., 2011; Chen et al., 2013). However, most of these systems cannot tune these embeddings as they are not structurally able to. By leveraging the deep architecture of our system, we can define a lookup-table layer initialized with existing embeddings as the first layer of the network.

Lookup-Table Layer We consider a fixed-sized word dictionary $\mathcal{D}$. Given a sequence of N words $w_1, w_2, \ldots, w_N$, each word $w_n \in W$ is first embedded into a d_{wrd}-dimensional vector space, by applying a lookup-table operation:

$$LT_W(w_n) = W \left(0, \ldots, \underset{\text{at index } w_n}{1}, \ldots, 0 \right) = \langle W \rangle_{w_n}, \tag{13}$$

where the matrix $W \in \mathbb{R}^{d_{wrd} \times |\mathcal{D}|}$ represents the embeddings to be tuned in this lookup layer. $\langle W \rangle_{w_n} \in \mathbb{R}^{d_{wrd}}$ is the wth column of W and d_{wrd} is the word vector size. Given any sequence of N words $[w]_1^N$ in $\mathcal{D}$, the lookup table layer applies the same operation for each word in the sequence, producing the following output matrix:

$$LT_W([w]_1^N) = \left(\langle W \rangle^1_{[w]_1} \;\; \ldots \;\; \langle W \rangle^1_{[w]_N} \right). \tag{14}$$

Training Given a task of interest, a relevant representation of each word is then given by the corresponding lookup table feature vector, which is trained by backpropagation. Word representations are initialized with existing embeddings.

5 Experimental Setup

We evaluate the quality of our embeddings obtained on a large corpora of unlabeled text by comparing their performance against the CW (Collobert and Weston, 2008), Turian (Turian et al., 2010), HLBL (Mnih and Hinton, 2008), and LR-MVL (Dhillon et al., 2011) embeddings on NER and movie review tasks. We also show that the general performance can be improved for these tasks by fine-tuning the word embeddings.

5.1 Building Word Representation over Large Corpora

Our English corpus is composed of the entire English Wikipedia[1] (where all MediaWiki markups have been removed), the Reuters corpus and the Wall Street Journal (WSJ) corpus. We consider lower case words to limit the number of words in the vocabulary. Additionally, all occurrences of sequences of numbers within a word are replaced with the string "NUMBER". The resulting text was tokenized using the Stanford tokenizer[2]. The data set contains about 1,652 million words. As vocabulary, we considered all the words within our corpus which appear at least one hundred times. This results in a 178,080 words vocabulary. To build the co-occurence matrix, we used only the 10,000 most frequent words within our vocabulary as context words. To get embeddings for words, we needed to only consider sequences T of $t = 1$ word. After PCA, each word can be represented in any n-dimensional vector (with $n \in \{1, \ldots, 10000\}$). We chose to embed words in a 50-dimensional vector, which is the common dimension among the other embeddings in the literature. The resulting embeddings will be referred as H-PCA in the following sections. To highlight the importance of the Hellinger distance, we also computed the PCA of the co-occurence probability matrix with respect to the Euclidean metric. The resulting embeddings are denoted E-PCA.

Computational cost The Hellinger PCA is very fast to compute. We report in Table 1 the time needed to compute the embeddings described above. For this benchmark we used Intel i7 3770K 3.5GHz CPUs. As the computation of the covariance matrix is highly parallelizable, we report results with 1, 100 and 500 CPUs. The Eigendecomposition of the C matrix has been computed with the SSYEVR LAPACK subroutine on one CPU. We compare completion times for 1,000 and 10,000 eigenvectors. Finally, we report completion times to generate the emdeddings by linear projection using 50, 100 and 200 eigenvectors. Although the linear projection is already quite fast on only one CPU, this operation can also be computed in parallel. Those results show that the Hellinger PCA can generate about 200,000 embeddings in about three minutes with a cluster of 100 CPUs.

	time (s)		
# of CPUs	1	100	500
Covariance matrix	9930	99	20
1,000 Eigenvectors	72	-	-
10,000 Eigenvectors	110	-	-
50D Embeddings	20	0.2	0.04
100D Embeddings	29	0.29	0.058
200D Embeddings	67	0.67	0.134
Total for 50D	10,022	171.2	92.04

Table 1: Benchmark of the experiment. Times are reported in seconds.

5.2 Existing Available Word Embeddings

We compare our H-PCA's embeddings with the following publicly available embeddings:

- **LR-MVL**[3]: it covers 300,000 words with 50 dimensions for each word. They were trained on the RCV1 corpus using the Low Rank Multi-View Learning method. We only used their context oblivious embeddings coming from the eigenfeature dictionary.
- **CW**[4]: it covers 130,000 words with 50 dimensions for each word. They were trained for about two months, over Wikipedia, using a neural network language model approach.
- **Turian**[5]: it covers 268,810 words with 25, 50, 100 or 200 dimensions for each word. They were trained on the RCV1 corpus using the same system as the CW embeddings but with different parameters. We used only the 50 dimensions.

[1] Available at http://download.wikimedia.org. We took the May 2012 version.

[2] Available at http://nlp.stanford.edu/software/tokenizer.shtml

[3] Available at http://www.cis.upenn.edu/ ungar/eigenwords/

[4] From SENNA: http://ml.nec-labs.com/senna/

[5] Available at http://metaoptimize.com/projects/wordreprs/

- **HLBL**[5] : it covers 246,122 words with 50 or 100 dimensions for each word. They were trained on the RCV1 corpus using a Hierarchical Log-Bilinear Model. We used only the 50 dimensions.

5.3 Supervised Evaluation Tasks

Using word embeddings as feature proved that it can improve the generalization performance on several NLP tasks (Turian et al., 2010; Collobert et al., 2011; Chen et al., 2013). Using our word embeddings, we thus trained the sentence-level architecture described in section 4.1 on a NER task.

Named Entity Recognition (NER) It labels atomic elements in the sentence into categories such as "PERSON" or "LOCATION". The CoNLL 2003 setup[6] is a NER benchmark data set based on Reuters data. The contest provides training, validation and testing sets. The networks are fed with two raw features: word embeddings and a capital letter feature. The "caps" feature tells if each word was in lowercase, was all uppercase, had first letter capital, or had at least one non-initial capital letter. No other feature has been used to tune the models. This is a main difference with other systems which usually use more features as POS tags, prefixes and suffixes or gazetteers. Hyper-parameters were tuned on the validation set. We selected $n = 2$ context words leading to a window of 5 words. We used a special "PADDING" word for context at the beginning and the end of each sentence. For the non-linear model, the number of hidden units was 300. As benchmark system, we report the system of Ando et al. (2005), which reached 89.31% F1 with a semi-supervised approach and less specialized features than CoNLL 2003 challengers.

The NER evaluation task is mainly syntactic. As we wish to evaluate whether our word embeddings can also capture semantic, we trained the document-level architecture described in section 4.2 over a movie review task.

IMDB Review Dataset We used a collection of 50,000 reviews from IMDB[7]. It allows no more than 30 reviews per movie. It contains an even number of positive and negative reviews, so randomly guessing yields 50% accuracy. Only highly polarized reviews have been considered. A negative review has a score ≤ 4 out of 10, and a positive review has a score ≥ 7 out of 10. It has been evenly divided into training and test sets (25,000 reviews each). For this task, we only used the word embeddings as features. We perform a simple cross-validation on the training set to choose the optimal hyper-parameters. The network had a window of 5 words and $n_{filter} = 1000$ filters. As benchmark system, we report the system of Maas et al. (2011), which reached 88.90% accuracy with a mix of unsupervised and supervised techniques to learn word vectors capturing semantic term-document information, as well as rich sentiment content.

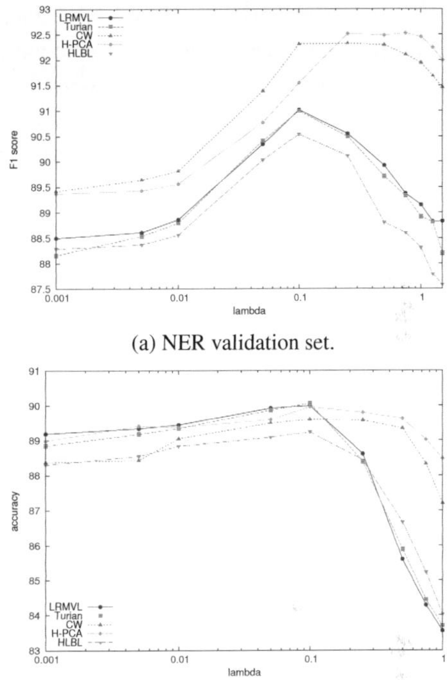

(a) NER validation set.

(b) IMDB review dataset.

Figure 1: Effect of varying the normalization factor λ with a non-linear approach and fine-tuning.

5.4 Embeddings Normalization

Word embeddings are continuous vector spaces that are not necessarily in a bounded range. To avoid saturation issues in the network architectures, embeddings need to be properly normalized. Considering the matrix of word embeddings E, the normalized embeddings are:

$$\tilde{E} = \frac{\lambda(E - \bar{E})}{\sigma(E)} \quad (15)$$

[6] http://www.cnts.ua.ac.be/conll2003/ner/

[7] Available at http://www.andrew-maas.net/data/sentiment

where $\bar{E}$ is the mean of the embeddings, $\sigma(E)$ is the standard deviation of the embeddings and λ is a normalization factor. Figure 1 shows the effect of λ on both supervised tasks. The embeddings normalization depends on the type of the network architecture. In the document-level approach, best results are obtained with $\lambda = 0.1$ for all embeddings, while a normalization factor set to 1 is better for H-PCA's embeddings in the sentence-level approach. These results show the importance of applying the right normalization for word embeddings.

5.5 Results

H-PCA's embeddings Results summarized in Table 2 reveal that performance on NER task can be as good with word embeddings from a word cooccurence matrix decomposition as with a neural network language model trained for weeks. The best F1 scores are indeed obtained using the H-PCA tuned embeddings. Results for the movie review task in Table 3 show that H-PCA's embeddings also perform as well as all the other embeddings on the movie review task. It is worth mentioning that on both tasks, H-PCA's embeddings outperform the E-PCA's embeddings, demonstrating the value of the Hellinger distance. When the embeddings are not tuned, the CW's embeddings slightly outperform the H-PCA's embeddings on NER task. The performance difference between both fixed embeddings on the movie review task is about 3%. Embeddings from the CW neural language model seems to capture more semantic information but we showed that this lack of semantic information can be offset by fine-tuning.

Embeddings fine-tuning We note that tuning the embeddings by backpropagation increases the general performance on both NER and movie review tasks. The increase is, in general, higher for the movie review task, which reveals the importance of embedding fine-tuning for NLP tasks with a high semantic component. We show in Table 4 that the embeddings after fine-tuning give a higher rank to words that are related to the task of interest which is movie-sentiment-based relations in this case.

Linear vs nonlinear model We also report results with a linear version of our neural networks. Having non-linearity helps for NER. It seems important to extract non-linear features for such a task. However, we note that the linear approach

Approach	**Fixed**	**Tuned**
Benchmark	89.31	
	Non-Linear Approach	
H-PCA	87.91 ± 0.17	89.16 ± 0.09
E-PCA	84.28 ± 0.15	87.09 ± 0.12
LR-MVL	86.83 ± 0.20	87.38 ± 0.07
CW	88.14 ± 0.21	88.69 ± 0.16
Turian	86.26 ± 0.13	87.35 ± 0.12
HLBL	83.87 ± 0.25	85.91 ± 0.17
	Linear Approach	
H-PCA	84.64 ± 0.11	87.97 ± 0.09
E-PCA	78.15 ± 0.15	85.99 ± 0.09
LR-MVL	82.27 ± 0.14	86.83 ± 0.17
CW	84.50 ± 0.19	86.84 ± 0.08
Turian	83.33 ± 0.07	86.79 ± 0.11
HLBL	80.31 ± 0.11	85.06 ± 0.13

Table 2: Performance comparison on NER task with different embeddings. The first column is results with the original embeddings. The second column is results with embeddings after fine-tuning for this task. Results are reported in F1 score (mean $\pm$ standard deviation of ten training runs with different initialization).

Approach	**Fixed**	**Tuned**
Benchmark	88.90	
	Non-Linear Approach	
H-PCA	84.20 ± 0.16	89.89 ± 0.09
E-PCA	74.85 ± 0.12	89.70 ± 0.06
LR-MVL	85.33 ± 0.14	90.06 ± 0.09
CW	87.54 ± 0.27	89.77 ± 0.05
Turian	85.33 ± 0.10	89.99 ± 0.05
HLBL	85.51 ± 0.14	89.58 ± 0.06
	Linear Approach	
H-PCA	84.11 ± 0.05	89.90 ± 0.10
E-PCA	73.27 ± 0.16	89.62 ± 0.05
LR-MVL	84.37 ± 0.16	89.77 ± 0.09
CW	87.62 ± 0.24	89.92 ± 0.07
Turian	84.44 ± 0.13	89.66 ± 0.10
HLBL	85.34 ± 0.10	89.64 ± 0.05

Table 3: Performance comparison on movie review task with different embeddings. The first column is results with the original embeddings. The second column is results with embeddings after fine-tuning for this task. Results are reported in classification accuracy (mean $\pm$ standard deviation of ten training runs with different initialization).

BORING		BAD		AWESOME	
before	*after*	*before*	*after*	*before*	*after*
SAD	CRAP	HORRIBLE	TERRIBLE	SPOOKY	TERRIFIC
SILLY	LAME	TERRIBLE	STUPID	AWFUL	TIMELESS
SUBLIME	MESS	DREADFUL	BORING	SILLY	FANTASTIC
FANCY	STUPID	UNFORTUNATE	DULL	SUMMERTIME	LOVELY
SOBER	DULL	AMAZING	CRAP	NASTY	FLAWLESS
TRASH	HORRIBLE	AWFUL	WRONG	MACABRE	MARVELOUS
LOUD	RUBBISH	MARVELOUS	TRASH	CRAZY	EERIE
RIDICULOUS	SHAME	WONDERFUL	SHAME	ROTTEN	LIVELY
RUDE	AWFUL	GOOD	KINDA	OUTRAGEOUS	FANTASY
MAGIC	ANNOYING	FANTASTIC	JOKE	SCARY	SURREAL

Table 4: Set of words with their 10 nearest neighbors before and after fine-tuning for the movie review task (using the Euclidean metric in the embedding space). H-PCA's embeddings are used here.

performs as well as the non-linear approach for the movie review task. Our linear approach captures all the necessary sentiment features to predict whether a review is positive or negative. It is thus not surprising that a bag-of-words based method can perform well on this task (Wang and Manning, 2012). However, as our method takes the whole review as input, we can extract *windows* of words having the most discriminative power: it is a major advantage of our method compared to conventional bag-of-words based methods. We report in Table 5 some examples of windows of words extracted from the most discriminative filters α_i (positive and negative). Note that there is about the same number of positive and negative filters after learning.

α_i	$[x]^t$
-	the worst film this year very worst film i 've very worst movie i 've
-	watch this unfunny stinker . , extremely unfunny drivel come , this ludicrous script gets
-	it was pointless and boring it is unfunny . unfunny film are awful and embarrassing
+	both really just wonderful . . a truly excellent film . a really great film
+	excellent film with great performances excellent film with a great excellent movie with a stellar
+	incredible . just incredible . performances and just amazing . one was really great .

Table 5: The top 3 positive and negative filters $\alpha_i w_i$ and their respective top 3 windows of words $[x]^t$ within the whole IMDB review dataset.

6 Conclusion

We have demonstrated that appealing word embeddings can be obtained by computing a *Hellinger PCA* of the word co-occurence matrix. While a neural network language model can be painful and long to train, we can get a word co-occurence matrix by simply counting words over a large corpus. The resulting embeddings give similar results on NLP tasks, even from a $N \times 10,000$ word co-occurence matrix computed with only one word of context. It reveals that having a significant, but not too large set of common words, seems sufficient for capturing most of the syntactic and semantic characteristics of words. As PCA of a $N \times 10,000$ matrix is really fast and not memory consuming, our method gives an interesting and practical alternative to neural language models for generating word embeddings. However, we showed that deep-learning is an interesting framework to fine-tune embeddings over specific NLP tasks. Our H-PCA's embeddings are available online, here: `http://www.lebret.ch/words/`.

Acknowledgments

This work was supported by the HASLER foundation through the grant "Information and Communication Technology for a Better World 2020" (SmartWorld).

References

R. K. Ando, T. Zhang, and P. Bartlett. 2005. A framework for learning predictive structures from multiple tasks and unlabeled data. *Journal of Machine Learning Research*, 6:1817–1853.

Y. Bengio, R. Ducharme, P. Vincent, and C. Janvin. 2003. A neural probabilistic language model. *J. Mach. Learn. Res.*, 3:1137–1155, March.

P. F. Brown, P. V. deSouza, R. L. Mercer, V. J. D. Pietra, and J C. Lai. 1992. Class-based n-gram models of natural language. *Computational Linguistics*, 18(4):467–479.

Y. Chen, B. Perozzi, R. Al-Rfou', and S. Skiena. 2013. The expressive power of word embeddings. *CoRR*, abs/1301.3226.

R. Collobert and J. Weston. 2008. A unified architecture for natural language processing: Deep neural networks with multitask learning. In *International Conference on Machine Learning, ICML*.

R. Collobert, J. Weston, L. Bottou, M. Karlen, K. Kavukcuoglu, and P. Kuksa. 2011. Natural language processing (almost) from scratch. *Journal of Machine Learning Research*, 12:2493–2537.

P. S. Dhillon, D. Foster, and L. Ungar. 2011. Multi-view learning of word embeddings via CCA. In *Advances in Neural Information Processing Systems (NIPS)*, volume 24.

J. L. Elman. 1991. Distributed representations, simple recurrent networks, and grammatical structure. *Machine Learning*, 7:195–225.

J. R. Firth. 1957. A synopsis of linguistic theory 1930-55. 1952-59:1–32.

G. E. Hinton. 1986. Learning distributed representations of concepts. In *Proceedings of the Eighth Annual Conference of the Cognitive Science Society*, pages 1–12. Hillsdale, NJ: Erlbaum.

F. Huang and A. Yates. 2009. Distributional representations for handling sparsity in supervised sequence-labeling. In *Proceedings of the Association for Computational Linguistics (ACL)*, pages 495–503. Association for Computational Linguistics.

T. Koo, X. Carreras, and M. Collins. 2008. Simple semi-supervised dependency parsing. In *Proceedings of the Association for Computational Linguistics (ACL)*, pages 595–603.

I. Labutov and H. Lipson. 2013. Re-embedding words. In *ACL*.

T. K. Landauer and S. T. Dumais. 1997. A solution to Plato's problem: The Latent Semantic Analysis theory of the acquisition, induction, and representation of knowledge. *Psychological Review*.

T. K. Landauer. 2002. On the computational basis of learning and cognition: Arguments from lsa. In N. Ross, editor, *The psychology of learning and motivation*, volume 41, pages 43–84. Academic Press, San Francisco, CA.

W. Lowe, 2001. *Towards a theory of semantic space*, pages 576–581.

A. L. Maas, R. E. Daly, P. T. Pham, D. Huang, A. Y. Ng, and C. Potts. 2011. Learning word vectors for sentiment analysis. In *ACL*, pages 142–150.

T. Mikolov, M. Karafiat, L. Burget, J. Cernocky, and Sanjeev Khudanpur. 2010. Recurrent neural network based language model.

A. Mnih and G. Hinton. 2008. A Scalable Hierarchical Distributed Language Model. In *Advances in Neural Information Processing Systems*, volume 21.

J. B. Pollack. 1990. Recursive distributed representations. *Artificial Intelligence*, 46:77–105.

L. R. Rabiner. 1989. A tutorial on hidden markov models and selected applications in speech recognition. In *Proceedings of the IEEE*, pages 257–286.

L. Ratinov and D. Roth. 2009. Design challenges and misconceptions in named entity recognition. In *Proceedings of the Thirteenth Conference on Computational Natural Language Learning (CoNLL)*, pages 147–155. Association for Computational Linguistics.

H. Schütze. 1995. Distributional part-of-speech tagging. In *Proceedings of the Association for Computational Linguistics (ACL)*, pages 141–148. Morgan Kaufmann Publishers Inc.

J. Turian, L. Ratinov, and Y. Bengio. 2010. Word representations: A simple and general method for semi-supervised learning. In *ACL*.

P. D. Turney and P. Pantel. 2010. From frequency to meaning: Vector space models of semantics. *J. Artif. Int. Res.*, 37(1):141–188, January.

J. J. Väyrynen and T. Honkela. 2004. Word category maps based on emergent features created by ICA. In *Proceedings of the STeP'2004 Cognition + Cybernetics Symposium*.

S Wang and C. D. Manning. 2012. Baselines and bigrams: Simple, good sentiment and topic classification. ACL '12.

L. Wittgenstein. 1953. *Philosophical Investigations*. Blackwell.

A Latent Variable Model for Discourse-aware Concept and Entity Disambiguation

Angela Fahrni and Michael Strube
Heidelberg Institute for Theoretical Studies gGmbH
Schloss-Wolfsbrunnenweg 35
69118 Heidelberg, Germany
(angela.fahrni|michael.strube)@h-its.org

Abstract

This paper takes a discourse-oriented perspective for disambiguating common and proper noun mentions with respect to Wikipedia. Our novel approach models the relationship between disambiguation and aspects of cohesion using Markov Logic Networks with latent variables. Considering cohesive aspects consistently improves the disambiguation results on various commonly used data sets.

1 Introduction

> *"I have to review a* ***paper****", the* ***supervisor*** *moaned from the* ***office****. "Please don't disturb me until I'm done with the* ***review****." His* ***student*** *nodded, went to the* ***cafeteria****, sat down in the* ***sunshine*** *and started to read yesterday's* ***paper****.*

This text snippet illustrates two aspects that have been neglected by previous disambiguation approaches. (1) The interpretation of different mentions, i.e. common and proper nouns, is determined by different notions of context: some mentions depend more on a local sentence-level context (*paper* in *read yesterday's paper*; the global context is misleading), some more on a global one (*review* in *I'm done with the review*; the local context is not discriminative), some on both global and local context (*paper* in *review a paper*). (2) The context relevant to disambiguate a mention depends on how it is embedded into discourse and is not bound to the surface form of a mention (*paper* in the first sentence vs. *paper* in the last one).

Starting from this observation, we argue that the context relevant to disambiguate a mention correlates with its cohesive scope, i.e. the text span within which a mention establishes cohesive relations. Therefore, we propose to disambiguate mentions differently depending on their cohesive scopes (Section 2). We distinguish between three different cohesive scopes of mentions and model them as latent variables using Markov Logic Networks (Section 3). The use of latent variables allows us to learn and predict the cohesive scope and the disambiguation of a mention jointly. This comes with the advantage that the learning of the scope assignment does not need annotated data by itself but is guided by the annotations available for the target prediction task, i.e. the disambiguation.

In this paper, we focus on concept and entity disambiguation[1] with respect to an inventory derived from Wikipedia and compare (1) to a state-of-the-art approach that treats all mentions alike and uses the same features for disambiguation, (2) to a pipeline-based approach, and (3) to other state-of-the-art approaches (Section 4).

While early work disambiguated concepts using the local context (Csomai and Mihalcea, 2008), current research focuses on exploiting the global document context (Milne and Witten, 2008; Kulkarni et al., 2009; Ratinov et al., 2011; Fahrni and Strube, 2012; Cheng and Roth, 2013). Although such global approaches try to balance between local and global context, they treat all mentions alike, i.e., they apply the same model and the same weighting of local and global context features for disambiguating all mentions (Section 5).

2 Motivation

Halliday and Hasan (1976) define *cohesion* as "relations of meaning that exist within the text, and that define it as a text" (p. 4). A *tie* is one instance of such a cohesive relation between two items. Cohesive ties occur on various linguistic levels, such as on the entity level (e.g. coreference and bridging relations) or on the concept level (e.g. lexical

[1] In the following, we use *concept* to refer to concepts and what is usually called entities (e.g. Ji et al. (2011)).

Proceedings of the 14th Conference of the European Chapter of the Association for Computational Linguistics, pages 491–500,
Gothenburg, Sweden, April 26-30 2014. ©2014 Association for Computational Linguistics

chains). In this paper, we focus on concept-level cohesion and assume that each concept referred to by a mention can exhibit cohesive ties with concepts from other lexical units. The *cohesive scope* of a mention is the text span within which a concept referred to by a mention shows such cohesive ties. We distinguish three broad categories of cohesive scopes: (1) Mentions with *local cohesive scope* exhibit cohesive ties with lexical units in the same sentence; (2) mentions with *intermediate cohesive scope* show cohesive ties both within the sentence and beyond; (3) mentions with *global cohesive scope* form cohesive ties with mentions across sentence boundaries.

The notion of scope is a means to define the appropriate context to disambiguate a mention. A mention of local scope does not exhibit relations with lexical units outside its sentence. Hence, the global context does not help to disambiguate it or can even lead to the wrong disambiguation. For a mention with global scope, the global context is crucial, while the local context is not discriminative or even misleading. For a mention with intermediate scope both local and global context are relevant. Hence, while the scope influences the appropriate disambiguation context, the disambiguation of a mention influences its scope. In the example (Section 1), *paper* in *read yesterday's paper* refers to the concept NEWSPAPER. Its scope is local, as it lacks some cohesive ties with mentions in other sentences. If it had been disambiguated to SCHOLARLY PAPER, its scope would be global. This reciprocal relationship between discourse structure and meaning has also been discussed by Asher and Lascarides (1995). They use rhetorical relations for structuring discourse while we rely on the notion of lexical cohesion and model scope assignment and disambiguation jointly.

Our notion of scope is related to work on lexical chains (Morris and Hirst, 1991; Nelken and Shieber, 2006; Mihalcea, 2006) and to work in content modeling, e.g. Haghighi and Vanderwende (2009) distinguish content vocabulary and document-specific vocabulary.

3 Approach

Given a set of features for disambiguation, we aim to weight them differently depending on the scope. To model the reciprocal relationship between scope assignment and disambiguation, we propose a latent variables based approach using Markov Logic Networks that allows us to learn the parameters for the scope assignment and the disambiguation tasks jointly and enables us to perform joint inference.

Our approach is *joint* as we assign the scope s and predict the concept c for a mention m simultaneously. As during learning training data is available for the disambiguation task but not for the scope assignment task, we face a problem with *latent variables*. Latent variables represent missing information in the input or a part of the output which is not relevant except for supporting the prediction of the target (Smith, 2011). In our approach, the different cohesive scopes are modeled by latent variables. Each mention to be disambiguated is assigned a scope s. All feature weights are parametrized by scope s. The parameters for the disambiguation and scope assignment tasks are learned jointly and are guided by the annotations available for the disambiguation task.

Markov Logic Networks can be represented as log-linear models, when grounded, and are therefore straightforward to extend with latent variables (Smith, 2011; Poon and Domingos, 2008). In addition, global features can be conveniently integrated.

3.1 Markov Logic Networks

Markov Logic (ML) incorporates first-order logic and probabilities (Domingos and Lowd, 2009). A Markov Logic Network (MLN) is a first-order knowledge base and consists of a set of pairs (F_i, w_i), where F_i is a first-order formula and $w_i \in \mathbb{R}$ is the weight of formula F_i. It is a template for constructing a Markov Network. This Markov Network has a binary node for each possible grounding for each predicate of the MLN. If the grounding of the predicate is true, the binary node's value is set to 1, otherwise to 0. Furthermore, it contains one feature[2] for each ground formula F_i. If a ground formula is true, its feature's value is set to 1, otherwise to 0. The feature's weight is provided by w_i.

The probability distribution in the ground Markov Network is given by

$$P(X = x) = \frac{1}{Z} \exp\left(\sum_i w_i n_i(x)\right)$$

[2]In this section *feature* is used differently than in the rest of the paper.

where $n_i(x)$ is the number of true groundings of F_i in x. The normalization factor Z is the partition function.

To perform MAP inference we use *thebeast*[3] which transforms the inference problem into an Integer Linear Program and solves it using cutting plane inference (Riedel, 2008).

3.1.1 Weight Learning with Latent Variables

Since no annotations are available for the scope distinction, we face a latent variable learning problem. For learning weights in this situation we follow Poon and Domingos (2008). We split our hidden predicates into two parts: V are the ones for which the ground truth is known (concepts) and U are the ones for which there is no annotation (scopes). Let O be the observed predicates. Let o and v be the values of O and V in the training data. u denotes values assigned to U. Weight learning finds a w that maximizes the conditional log-likelihood

$$\begin{aligned} L_w(o,v) &= \log P_w(V=v|O=o) \\ &= \log \sum_u P_w(V=v, U=u|O=o), \end{aligned}$$

where the sum is over all possible values of U.

Although $L_w(o,v)$ is not convex, a local optimum can be found via gradient descent by iteratively solving

$$w_{t+1} = w_t + \eta \nabla_w L_w(o,v),$$

where the gradient $\nabla_w L_w(o,v)$ is given by

$$\frac{\partial}{\partial w_i} L_w(o,v) = E_w[n_i(o,v,U)] - E_w[n_i(o,V,U)].$$

E_w denotes the expectation according to P_w and $n_i(o,v,u)$ is the number of true groundings of formula F_i under the assignment specified by (o,v,u). We use a voted perceptron (Lowd and Domingos, 2007) which approximates the expectations via computing the MAP solution with (o,v) fixed ($E_w[n_i(o,v,U)]$) and (o) fixed ($E_w[n_i(o,V,U)]$) respectively.

3.1.2 Scope-aware Concept Disambiguation

Both the scope assignment and the disambiguation task are performed jointly using Markov Logic Networks.

Table 1 shows the core of our proposed approach in terms of predicates and first-order logic formulas. We build upon our previous approach for joint concept disambiguation and clustering (Fahrni and Strube, 2012). For brevity, we only discuss the scope-aware extension of the disambiguation part. The extension for clustering is done analogously.

The purpose of assigning a scope to each mention m is to learn scope-specific weights for disambiguation to account for heterogenous scopes of mentions. The learned weights are parametrized by scopes. We indicate this parametrization of learned weights by $w(s)$ (cf. Table 1, $f8$, $f9$).

For each relation to predict, a hidden predicate is defined. We are interested in predicting two relations: a relation between a mention m and a concept c ($p1$: *hasConcept(m, c)*) and a relation between a mention m and a scope s ($p3$: *hasScope(m, s)*). To bridge between the disambiguation and the scope assignment task a third hidden predicate *relatesScopeToConcept(m, c, s)* ($p2$) models a relation between a mention m, a concept c and a scope s. This predicate together with Formulas $f4 - f7$ garantuees that the scope assignment and the selection of a concept for a mention influence each other and that the ground hidden predicates are in accordance.[4] Hard cardinality constraints (*f1*, *f2*, *f3*) enforce that each mention m is assigned exactly one scope s and at most one concept c.

The hidden predicates and formulas form the core. Features for the disambiguation and the scope assignment tasks are incorporated using local and global formulas with learned weights. The features are described in Section 3.2. Table 1 gives formula templates for both tasks (please note that these are templates not formulas (Section 3.2)): (1) a template for formulas that add information for scope assignment ($f8$) and (2) a template for formulas that add information for disambiguation ($f9$). All formulas with scope-parametrized weights that are relevant for the concept prediction task are defined for the predicate *relatesScopeToConcept*. This enables us to activate the relevant

[3] http://code.google.com/p/thebeast.

[4] We also run experiments with just two hidden predicates, i.e. *hasConcept(m, c)* and *hasScope(m, s)*. All formulas with learned weight were then defined in the following, less efficient way: $\forall m \in M, c \in C, s \in S$: $featureDisambiguation(m, c, q) \rightarrow hasConcept(m, c) \wedge hasScope(m, s)$. q is a score (Table 1).

Predicates	
Hidden predicates	
p1	$hasConcept(m, c)$
p2	$relatesScopeToConcept(m, c, s)$
p3	$hasScope(m, s)$
Predicate template for disambiguation features	
p4	$featureDisambiguation(m, c, q)$
Predicate template for scope assignment features	
p5	$featureScope(m, q)$
Formulas	
Hard cardinality constraints	
f1	$\forall m \in M: \ \lvert\{c \in C : hasConcept(m, c)\}\rvert \leq 1$
f2	$\forall m \in M: \ \lvert\{c \in C, s \in S : relatesScopeToConcept(m, c, s)\}\rvert \leq 1$
f3	$\forall m \in M: \ \lvert\{s \in S : hasScope(m, s)\}\rvert = 1$
Hard constraints	
f4	$\forall m \in M, c \in C, s \in S: \ relatesScopeToConcept(m, c, s) \rightarrow hasConcept(m, c)$
f5	$\forall m \in M, c \in C, s \in S: \ relatesScopeToConcept(m, c, s) \rightarrow hasScope(m, s)$
f6	$\forall m \in M, c \in C, s \in S: \ hasConcept(m, c) \wedge hasScope(m, s)$ $\rightarrow relatesScopeToConcept(m, c, s)$
f7	$\forall m \in M, c \in C: \ hasConcept(m, c) \rightarrow (\lvert\{s \in S : relatesScopeToConcept(m, c, s)\}\rvert = 1)$
Formula template with learned weights for scope assignment	
f8	$q \cdot w(s) \quad \forall m \in M, s \in S: \ featureScope(m, q) \rightarrow hasScope(m, s)$
Formula template with learned weights for disambiguation	
f9	$q \cdot w(s) \quad \forall m \in M, c \in C, s \in S: \ featureDisambiguation(m, c, q)$ $\rightarrow relatesScopeToConcept(m, c, s)$

Table 1: Predicates and formulas used for scope distinction and disambiguation (m represents a mention, M sets of mentions, c a concept, C sets of concepts, s a scope, S sets of scopes, q scores, w weights and $w(s)$ a weight which is parametrized by s). The two template predicates and formulas are generalized patterns to integrate the features for the scope assignment and disambiguation task (Section 3.2).

scope-specific weights $w(s)$ which depend on the chosen scope s. The final weight for a formula can also include a score q defined by the observed predicate.

3.2 Features

For disambiguation and clustering we build upon our previous work (Fahrni and Strube, 2012). We use the same features and formulas and adopt the latter to learn scope-specific weights. Given for example the local context similarity feature (predicate *hasContextSimilarity(m, c, q)* where q is the similarity score) and the corresponding formula

$$\forall m \in M, c \in C_m : \ hasContextSimilarity(m, c, q) \rightarrow hasConcept(m, c)$$

with weight $(q \cdot w)$ we adopt it in the following way (cf. Table 1, template $f9$):

$$\forall m \in M, s \in S, c \in C_m : hasContextSimilarity(m, c, q) \rightarrow relatesScopeToConcept(m, c, s)$$

with weight $(q \cdot w(s))$.

In order to distinguish between the three proposed scopes, we use the features described in Table 2. The first column shows the predicate which can be used for template $f8$ in Table 1.

4 Experiments

We compare our novel scope-aware approach to our previous scope-ignorant approach (Fahrni and Strube, 2012) – which has achieved good results in the English monolingual and Chinese and Spanish cross-lingual entity linking tasks at TAC 2012 and 2013 (Fahrni et al., 2014) – and a scope-aware pipeline-based approach using the same features and preprocessing to ensure a fair comparison. This allows us to identify the differences in the results that are due to scope-awareness and differences in the results that are due to different learning strategies (joint vs. pipeline-based). In addition, we compare our joint scope-aware approach to state-of-the-art approaches using various data sets.

4.1 Data

Table 3 summarizes our test sets (ACE 2005, ACE 2004, MSNBC and TAC 2011) and our training and development sets derived from Wikipedia (WP Training, WP Dev). For each data set we report the total number of annotated mentions, the number of mentions with a corresponding concept in Wikipedia (non-NILs) and the number of NILs (i.e. mentions that do not refer to a Wikipedia con-

Predicates	Description
	Mention-based Features
$\mathit{idfHead}(m, q)$	The more frequent a mention is, the more likely it is to exert a local scope. This is inspired by work on indexing for IR. We use the idf score of the head of a mention according the English Gigaword Corpus (Parker et al., 2011).
$\mathit{propernoun}(m)$	Proper nouns are usually more prominent than common nouns and are more likely to have an intermediate or global scope than common nouns.
$\mathit{singlewordNoun}(m)$	Single word NPs are often less prominent than multi-word NPs and are more likely to be of local scope.
$\mathit{abbrev}(m)$	Abbreviations with a terminal dot such as *Mr.* or *Ltd.* tend to have a local scope as they are usually local modifiers or specifications.
	Features Based on Modification
$\mathit{isPreModified}(m)$	If a mention is pre-modified, it tends to be more prominent than unmodified mentions. If a mention is more prominent, it is more likely to have a larger scope.
$\mathit{headOfRelClause}(m)$	Mentions that are the head of a relative clause are usually more prominent and are more likely to have an intermediate or global scope.
	Features Based on the Text Structure
$\mathit{inSubjPosition}(m)$	Mentions in theme position, which is in English often the subject, tend to pick up what has already been mentioned before (Daneš, 1974). Since this is not just the case on the reference-level, but also on the concept-level, the mention in theme position tends to be related to other mentions in the text and tends to have an intermediate or global scope.
$\mathit{posInSentence}(m, q)$	The earlier a mention appears in the sentence in English, the more thematic it is, and the more likely it has an intermediate or global scope.
$\mathit{focusingAdverb}(m)$	Focusing adverbs in the text pattern *<focusing adverb>* *<mention>* – e.g. "particularly *Jack*" – indicate that the mention is thematic and therefore has larger scope.
$\mathit{modifiesArgument}(m)$	A premodifier of a verbal argument is usually more likely to be of local scope.
$\mathit{passiveBy}(m)$	A passive construction – e.g. "the thief was catched by the police" – is a way to reduce the prominency of the agent (e.g. *police*). The agent tends to be of local scope.
$\mathit{inConjunction}(m)$	Conjunctions are often used for exemplifications. Therefore mentions in conjunctions are often less prominent.
$\mathit{inDepRelPP}(m_1, m_2)$ $\mathit{inDepRelGen}(m_1, m_2)$	In NPs with prepositional or genitive modifiers usually at most one part – either the modifying NP or the head – has intermediate or global scope.
$\mathit{morphoTiesHead}(m, q)$	The more frequent the head of a mention appears in the text – also as a derivation, e.g. a verb, according to CatVar (Habash and Dorr, 2003) –, the more prominent it is.
$\mathit{positionInText}(m, q)$	The earlier a mention appears in text, the more likely it is to exhibit global cohesive scope (cf. the hard-to-be-beat lead baseline in summarization (Radev et al., 2003)).

Table 2: Features for cohesive scope distinction. m, m_1, m_2 denote mentions, q a score. The predicates are plugged in the template formula $f8$ in Table 1.

Data set	No. of Mentions	Non-NILs	NILs	Avg. Ambiguity
WP Training	56,372	53,097	3,275	2.31
WP Dev	9,992	9,375	617	2.28
ACE 2005	29,300	27,184	2,116	6.52
ACE 2004	306	257	49	5.04
TAC 2011	2,250	1,124	1,126	6.32
MSNBC	756	629	127	5.29

Table 3: Statistics for data sets.

cept). The average ambiguity of mentions is given by our lexicon (see Section 4.2).

Our system is exclusively trained on the internal hyperlinks in Wikipedia with the advantage that no manual annotation effort is needed. We use 500 articles for training and 100 articles for development (Fahrni and Strube, 2012). Each internal hyperlink is considered as an annotated mention. The pointer to the Wikipedia article serves as the correct concept for this mention and all other candidate concepts we obtain from our lexicon as wrong concepts for this mention.

For the detailed analysis of our approach, we use a version of the ACE 2005 corpus which contains Wikipedia link annotations (Bentivogli et al., 2010). All ACE mentions, both common and proper nouns, are annotated with one or more links to the English Wikipedia or as NILs. If a mention is annotated with more than one link, we consider it as correctly disambiguated if one of the annotated concepts has been chosen by our system. ACE 2005 consists of 597 texts from newswire reports, broadcast news, internet sources and transcribed audio data and contains more annotations than the other data sets we use for comparison.

While ACE 2005 and ACE 2004 (Ratinov et al., 2011) fit our target scenario most (both common and proper nouns are annotated), MSNBC (Cucerzan, 2007) and TAC 2011 (Ji et al., 2011) are only annotated for proper nouns.

4.2 Preprocessing

The training, development and testing data are all preprocessed in the same way. We perform POS tagging, syntactic parsing and named entity recognition using the *Stanford CoreNLP* pipeline[5]. For identifying mentions we extract all noun phrases (excluding discontinuous phrases and determiners) and look them up in our lexicon. Our lexicon and also all other information we obtained from Wikipedia are extracted from the same English Wikipedia dump.[6] The lexicon consists of anchor texts, article titles and redirects.

4.3 Settings

Upper bound: The upper bound shows the maximum performance we can reach given our lexicon and preprocessing. If the correct concept is among the candidate concepts of a mention, it is considered as correct.

First Concept: The first concept baseline is a strong baseline in disambiguation. It chooses for each mention its most frequent concept.

Scope-ignorant (Disambig.): Our previous MLN-based approach for concept disambiguation (Fahrni and Strube, 2012).

Scope-ignorant (Disambig. & Clust.): Our previous MLN-based approach for joint disambiguation and clustering of concepts (Fahrni and Strube, 2012).

Pipeline-based Scope-aware (Disambig.): We compare our joint approach to a pipeline-based one in which the assignment of the cohesive scope is done before disambiguation. The features for the scope assignment and the disambiguation task are exactly the same as in the joint setting and implemented in Markov Logic. The weights for the scope assignment and disambiguation task are learned in a cascaded way. In contrast to the joint approach, the *hasScope(m, s)* predicate is observed during disambiguation.

Joint Scope-aware (Disambig.): This is our approach as described in Section 3 for concept disambiguation. As only local optimization is possible, initialization is crucial. We use the same initialization strategy as for the cascaded approach.

Joint Scope-aware (Disambig. & Clust.): This is our approach as described in Section 3 for disambiguation and clustering of concepts.

[5] http://nlp.stanford.edu/software/corenlp.shtml

[6] We use the English Wikipedia dump from Jan. 4, 2012.

4.4 Analysis of Scope-awareness on ACE 2005

In Table 4 we report precision (*P*), recall (*R*) and F-measure (*F*) for non-NILs and NILs for the ACE 2005 data. We also report overall accuracy (*Acc*) (aka micro-average) and calculate significance using a paired t-test.

Differences in the results can be exclusively traced back to differences in the modeling (scope-ignorant vs. scope-aware) and learning (pipeline-based vs. joint). Learning scope-specific models (pipeline-based or joint) significantly improves the result with $p < 0.01$ while using the same features for disambiguation. Scope-aware joint approaches significantly outperform the other corresponding approaches (pipeline-based and scope-ignorant) that use the same features for disambiguation (and clustering) with $p < 0.01$. While the pipeline-based approach suffers from error propagation, the joint approach also benefits from the learning strategy: learning weights for scope distinction can be guided by the training data available for the disambiguation task. Joint disambiguation and clustering of mentions improves the disambiguation results for both the scope-ignorant (Fahrni and Strube, 2012) and the scope-aware approach.

As Table 4 indicates, the gain of the joint scope-aware approach with respect to non-NILs is substantial in both precision and recall. For NILs the recall improves while the precision decreases. This leads to a slightly worse F-Measure for the NILs. As NILs are much rarer than non-NILs in the corpus, the overall accurracy for which we optimize is significantly higher for the scope-aware approaches.

As no gold annotations for cohesive scopes are available, we present statistics on the distribution of induced scopes. Table 5 shows the distribution of the mentions across induced scopes. Mentions with local scope are more frequent than mentions with intermediate scope followed by mentions with global scope. Table 5 compares the overall accurracy of the scope-ignorant joint disambiguation and clustering approach (Fahrni and Strube, 2012) with the accurracy of the corresponding joint scope-aware approach. The joint scope-aware approach improves the disambiguation results for mentions of all three scopes. The biggest gain (2.79) is achieved for mentions with induced global scope. The gain for mentions with local and intermediate scope is 1.27 and 0.3 re-

	Non-NILs			NILs			
	P	R	F	P	R	F	Acc
Upper bound	94.8	91.8	93.3	71.3	100.0	83.3	92.4
First Concept	68.6	70.0	69.3	55.3	40.3	46.6	67.9
Scope-ignorant (Disambig.) (Fahrni & Strube 2012)	77.3	76.0	76.6	44.7	54.2	49.0	74.4
Scope-ignorant (Disambig. & Clust.) (Fahrni & Strube 2012)	76.8	76.9	76.9	50.2	50.0	50.1	74.9
Pipeline-based Scope-aware (Disambig.)	80.1	75.8	77.9	37.3	63.4	47.0	74.9
Joint Scope-aware (Disambig.)	80.1	76.6	78.3	39.2	61.5	47.9	**75.5**
Joint Scope-aware (Disambig. & Clust.)	80.3	77.1	78.6	40.8	62.1	49.3	**76.0**

Table 4: Evaluation on ACE 2005 data

	Scope-ignorant Approach (Disambig. & Clust.) (Fahrni & Strube 2012) (Acc)	**Joint Scope-aware Approach (Disambig. & Clust.) (Acc)**	**Scope Distribution (%)**
Global Scope	73.20	75.99	8.54
Intermediate Scope	76.34	76.64	31.05
Local Scope	75.57	76.84	60.40
Total	75.61	76.71	100.00

Table 5: Evaluation on ACE 2005 data across induced scopes. The accurracy of the two compared systems is slightly higher than in Table 4 as we consider here only mentions that have been recognized by our mention identification strategy. In the evaluation in Table 4 mentions that have not been recognized are considered as wrong.

spectively. A comparison of the learned weights for the different scope-specific models shows that for mentions with local scope the local context has relatively more weight than for mentions with intermediate scope. For mentions with global scope, it is striking that candidiate concepts that are not related to the global context are relatively higher punished than in the other two models.

To obtain some insights on the behaviour of the joint scope-aware approach, we investigate some examples. In a text on the 2004 US elections, the mention *Kerry* in "*Kerry* was the clear winner, but victory was snatched from him" is wrongly disambiguated to KERRY GAA, a branch of the Gaelic football association, by the scope-ignorant approach, because the local context strongly prefers an interpretation in the domain of sports. In the joint scope-aware approach, *Kerry* is assigned global scope, and it is correctly disambiguated to JOHN KERRY, an American politician, as the global relatedness overrules the local context in this model. In another text on U.S. troops in Iraq, the scope-ignorant approach disambiguates *south* in "Monday's advances came one day after British forces in the *south* made their deepest push into Iraq's second largest city" to SOUTHERN UNITED STATES as concepts related to the USA are quite prominent in the text. In the scope-aware approach *south* is considered as being of local scope and is correctly disambiguated as SOUTH. In "we happen to be at a very nice *spot* by the beach where this is a chance for people to get away from cnn coverage" *spot* is disambiguated as SPOT (SATELLITE) in the scope-ignorant approach (misled by CNN), while it has been correctly recognized as NIL by the scope-aware approach in which it is considered as being of intermediate scope. The remaining disambiguation errors can be traced back to (1) scope assignment errors and (2) disambiguation errors (e.g. *Palmisano* (global scope) is disambiguated as SAMUEL J. PALMISANO, but the text refers to a different unknown Palmisano).

4.5 Comparison to State-of-the-art Approaches

Compared to the state-of-the-art for concept and entity disambiguation our approach performs favorably (Table 6). On ACE 2004 (Ratinov et al., 2011) – which contains annotations for common and proper nouns and fits our target scenario most – our scope-aware approach outperforms recent state-of-the-art approaches for concept and entity disambiguation, i.e. Ratinov et al. (2011) and Cheng and Roth (2013). We also ran Ratinov et al.'s (2011) sytem on ACE 2005, but it seems that its mention recognition is not designed for ACE 2005.

We also evaluate our system on the task of entity linking, i.e. the disambiguation of (selected) proper nouns (MSNBC and TAC 2011). Our system fails to beat the best systems, but still

System	ACE 2004	MSNBC	TAC 2011			
	BOC	BOC	Acc	B^3 P	B^3 R	B^3 F1
Ratinov et al. 2011; Cogcomp	77.3	74.9	78.7	75.7	76.5	76.1
Cheng & Roth 2013	85.3	81.2	86.1	82.9	84.5	83.7
Monahan et al. 2011 (Best System at TAC 2011)			86.1	84.4	84.7	84.6
Scope-ignorant (Disambig. & Clust.) (Fahrni & Strube 2012)	83.4	76.5	84.8	82.5	83.0	82.8
Joint Scope-aware (Disambig. & Clust.)	86.3	79.0	85.5	83.6	82.7	83.1

Table 6: Evaluation on various data sets using the respective standard evaluation metrics. *BOC* stands for Bag-of-Concepts. We use the code of Ratinov et al. (2011) to evaluate on ACE 2004 and MSNBC. For TAC 2011, we use the offical evaluation script and report the micro-average (*Acc*) and B^3 scores. Note that for TAC we use three additional disambiguation features – they measure the similarity of the article name to the context – both in the scope-ignorant and the scope-aware approach.

achieves competitive performance without training on TAC data. On all data sets, the joint scope-aware approach consistently outperforms the scope-ignorant approach ceteris paribus.

5 Related Work

Joint approaches have been successful in the past in NLP (e.g. Meza-Ruiz and Riedel (2009)). The idea of augmenting a model with additional latent variables to increase its expressiveness is known as *hidden* or *latent variable learning* (Smith, 2011) and is a promising research direction with successful applications in e.g. syntactic parsing (Petrov et al., 2006), statistical machine translation (Blunsom et al., 2008) and sentiment analysis (Yessenalina et al., 2010; Trivedi and Eisenstein, 2013). For latent variable learning generative approaches (Petrov et al., 2006), large margin methods (Smith, 2011) and conditional log-linear models have been proposed. We focus here on conditional log-linear models due to their flexibility and their previous success for many tasks. Blunsom et al. (2008) for instance use latent variables in the context of discriminative machine translation and model the derivation as a latent variable. Chang et al. (2010) is close to our approach, as their latent variable approach also uses ILP. Poon and Domingos (2008) also use latent variables with Markov Logic, although with a completely different aim, i.e. for unsupervised coreference resolution.

Most approaches that use Wikipedia as a resource for disambiguation focus on named entities (Bunescu and Paşca, 2006; Cucerzan, 2007; Dredze et al., 2010; Ji and Grishman, 2011; Hachey et al., 2013; Hoffart et al., 2011), while only a few disambiguate common and proper nouns like us (Csomai and Mihalcea, 2008; Milne and Witten, 2008; Zhou et al., 2010; Ratinov et al., 2011; Cheng and Roth, 2013). We build upon our previous Markov Logic based approach for joint concept disambiguation and clustering (Fahrni and Strube, 2012). In contrast to us, most approaches for lexical disambiguation use either one model for all mentions (Milne and Witten, 2008; Ratinov et al., 2011) or a separate model for each mention or concept which requires a lot of training data (e.g. Bryl et al. (2010)). Only a few approaches try to learn specific models for groups of mentions, although none of them is discourse-motivated as ours: Mihalcea and Csomai (2005) learn a specific model for each POS, Ando (2006) uses alternating structure optimization to simultantanously learn a number of WSD problems and Dhillon and Ungar (2009) improve feature selection for WSD by integrating knowledge from similar words.

6 Conclusions

In this paper, we discuss the relationship between cohesion and concept disambiguation and propose a cohesive scope-aware disambiguation approach. We distinguish between three different cohesive scopes (local, intermediate and global) and model the scope assignment and the disambiguation jointly using latent variables in the framework of MLN. The joint scope-aware approach significantly improves over both a state-of-the-art and a pipeline-based approach using the same features for the disambiguation task.

For future work, we are planning to investigate the relation between discourse structure and cohesive scope more deeply and to integrate scope-specific disambiguation features.

Acknowledgments

We would like to thank Sebastian Martschat for his valuable comments. This work has been partially funded by the Klaus Tschira Foundation.

References

Rie Kubota Ando. 2006. Applying alternating structure optimization to word sense disambiguation. In *Proceedings of the 10th Conference on Computational Natural Language Learning,* New York, N.Y., USA, 8–9 June 2006, pages 77–84.

Nicholas Asher and Alex Lascarides. 1995. Lexical disambiguation in a discourse context. *Journal of Semantics*, 12(1):69–108.

Luisa Bentivogli, Pamela Forner, Claudio Giuliano, Alessandro Marchetti, Emanuele Pianta, and Kateryna Tymoshenko. 2010. Extending English ACE 2005 corpus annotation with ground-truth links to Wikipedia. In *Proceedings of the 2nd Workshop on The People's Web: Colloboratively Constructed Semantic Resources,* Beijing, China, 28 August 2010, pages 19–27.

Phil Blunsom, Trevor Cohn, and Miles Osborne. 2008. A discriminative latent variable model for statistical machine translation. In *Proceedings of the 46th Annual Meeting of the Association for Computational Linguistics: Human Language Technologies,* Columbus, Ohio, 15–20 June 2008, pages 200–208.

Volha Bryl, Claudio Giuliano, Luciano Serafini, and Kateryna Tymoshenko. 2010. Supporting natural language processing with background knowledge: Coreference resolution case. In *Proceedings of the 9th International Semantic Web Conference, Revised Selected Papers, Part I,* Shanghai, China, 7-11 November 2010, pages 80–95.

Razvan Bunescu and Marius Paşca. 2006. Using encyclopedic knowledge for named entity disambiguation. In *Proceedings of the 11th Conference of the European Chapter of the Association for Computational Linguistics,* Trento, Italy, 3–7 April 2006, pages 9–16.

Ming-Wei Chang, Vivek Srikumar, Dan Goldwasser, and Dan Roth. 2010. Structured output learning with indirect supervision. In *Proceedings of the 27th International Conference on Machine Learning,* Haifa, Israel, 21–24 June 2010, pages 199–206.

Xiao Cheng and Dan Roth. 2013. Relational inference for Wikification. In *Proceedings of the 2013 Conference on Empirical Methods in Natural Language Processing,* Seattle, Wash., 18–21 October 2013, pages 1787–1796.

Andras Csomai and Rada Mihalcea. 2008. Linking documents to encyclopedic knowledge. *IEEE Intelligent Systems*, 23(5):34–41.

Silviu Cucerzan. 2007. Large-scale named entity disambiguation based on Wikipedia data. In *Proceedings of the 2007 Joint Conference on Empirical Methods in Natural Language Processing and Computational Language Learning,* Prague, Czech Republic, 28–30 June 2007, pages 708–716.

František Daneš. 1974. Functional sentence perspective and the organization of the text. In F. Daneš, editor, *Papers on Functional Sentence Perspective*, pages 106–128. Prague: Academia.

Paramveer S. Dhillon and Lyle H. Ungar. 2009. Transfer learning, feature selection and word sense disambguation. In *Proceedings of the ACL-IJCNLP 2009 Conference Short Papers,* Singapore, 2–7 August 2009, pages 257–260.

Pedro Domingos and Daniel Lowd. 2009. *Markov Logic: An Interface Layer for Artificial Intelligence.* Morgan Claypool Publishers.

Mark Dredze, Paul McNamee, Delip Rao, Adam Gerber, and Tim Finin. 2010. Entity disambiguation for knowledge base population. In *Proceedings of the 23rd International Conference on Computational Linguistics,* Beijing, China, 23–27 August 2010, pages 277–285.

Angela Fahrni and Michael Strube. 2012. Jointly disambiguating and clustering concepts and entities with Markov logic. In *Proceedings of the 24th International Conference on Computational Linguistics,* Mumbai, India, 8–15 December 2012, pages 815–832.

Angela Fahrni, Benjamin Heinzerling, Thierry Göckel, and Michael Strube. 2014. HITS' monolingual and cross-lingual entity linking system at TAC 2013. In *Proceedings of the Text Analysis Conference,* National Institute of Standards and Technology, Gaithersburg, Maryland, USA, 18–19 November 2013.

Nizar Habash and Bonnie Dorr. 2003. A categorial variation database for English. In *Proceedings of the Human Language Technology Conference of the North American Chapter of the Association for Computational Linguistics,* Edmonton, Alberta, Canada, 27 May -1 June 2003, pages 17–23.

Ben Hachey, Will Radford, Joel Nothman, Matthew Honnibal, and James R. Curran. 2013. Evaluating entity linking with Wikipedia. *Artificial Intelligence*, 194:130–150.

Aria Haghighi and Lucy Vanderwende. 2009. Exploring content models for multi-document summarization. In *Proceedings of Human Language Technologies 2009: The Conference of the North American Chapter of the Association for Computational Linguistics,* Boulder, Col., 31 May – 5 June 2009, pages 362–370.

M. A. K. Halliday and Ruqaiya Hasan. 1976. *Cohesion in English.* London, U.K.: Longman.

Johannes Hoffart, Mohamed Amir Yosef, Ilaria Bordino, Hagen Fürstenau, Manfred Pinkal, Marc Spaniol, Bilyana Taneva, Stefan Thater, and Gerhard Weikum. 2011. Robust disambiguation of named entities in text. In *Proceedings of the 2011 Conference on Empirical Methods in Natural Language*

Processing, Edinburgh, Scotland, U.K., 27–29 July 2011, pages 782–792.

Heng Ji and Ralph Grishman. 2011. Knowledge base population: Successful approaches and challenges. In *Proceedings of the 49th Annual Meeting of the Association for Computational Linguistics,* Portland, Oreg., 19–24 June 2011, pages 1148–1158.

Heng Ji, Ralph Grishman, and Hoa Dang. 2011. Overview of the TAC 2011 knowledge base population track. In *Proceedings of the Text Analysis Conference,* National Institute of Standards and Technology, Gaithersburg, Maryland, USA, 14–15 November 2011.

Sayali Kulkarni, Amit Singh, Ganesh Ramakrishnan, and Soumen Chakrabarti. 2009. Collective annotation of Wikipedia entities in web text. In *Proceedings of the 15th ACM SIGKDD Conference on Knowledge Discovery and Data Mining,* Paris, France, 28 June – 1 July 2009, pages 457–466.

Daniel Lowd and Pedro Domingos. 2007. Efficient weight learning for Markov logic networks. In *Proceedings of the 11th European Conference on Principles and Practices of Knowledge Discovery in Databases,* Warsaw, Poland, 17–21 September 2007, pages 200–211.

Ivan Meza-Ruiz and Sebastian Riedel. 2009. Jointly identifying predicates, arguments and senses using Markov logic. In *Proceedings of Human Language Technologies 2009: The Conference of the North American Chapter of the Association for Computational Linguistics,* Boulder, Col., 31 May – 5 June 2009, pages 155–163.

Rada Mihalcea and Andras Csomai. 2005. Sense-Learner: Word sense disambiguation for all words in unrestricted text. In *Proceedings of the Interactive Poster and Demonstrations Sessions at the 43rd Annual Meeting of the Association for Computational Linguistics,* Ann Arbor, Mich., 25–30 June 2005, pages 53–56.

Rada Mihalcea. 2006. Knowledge-based methods for WSD. In E. Agirre and P.G. Edmonds, editors, *Word Sense Disambiguation: Algorithms and Applications*, pages 107–131. Springer, Heidelberg, Germany.

David Milne and Ian H. Witten. 2008. Learning to link with Wikipedia. In *Proceedings of the ACM 17th Conference on Information and Knowledge Management (CIKM 2008),* Napa Valley, Cal., USA, 26–30 October 2008, pages 1046–1055.

Jane Morris and Graeme Hirst. 1991. Lexical cohesion computed by thesaural relations as an indicator of the structure of text. *Computational Linguistics,* 17(1):21–48.

Rani Nelken and Stuart Shieber. 2006. Lexical chaining and word-sense-disambiguation. Technical Report TR-06-07, Computer Science Group, Harvard University, Cambridge, Mass.

Robert Parker, David Graff, Junbo Kong, Ke Chen, and Kazuaki Maeda. 2011. English Gigaword Fifth Edition. LDC2011T07.

Slav Petrov, Leon Barrett, Romain Thibaux, and Dan Klein. 2006. Learning accurate, compact, and interpretable tree annotation. In *Proceedings of the 21st International Conference on Computational Linguistics and 44th Annual Meeting of the Association for Computational Linguistics,* Sydney, Australia, 17–21 July 2006, pages 433–440.

Hoifung Poon and Pedro Domingos. 2008. Joint unsupervised coreference resolution with Markov Logic. In *Proceedings of the 2008 Conference on Empirical Methods in Natural Language Processing,* Waikiki, Honolulu, Hawaii, 25–27 October 2008, pages 650–659.

Dragomir R. Radev, Simone Teufel, Horacio Saggion, Wai Lam, John Blitzer, Hong Qi, Arda Celebi, Danyu Liu, and Elliott Drabek. 2003. Evaluation challenges in large-scale document summarization. In *Proceedings of the 41st Annual Meeting of the Association for Computational Linguistics,* Sapporo, Japan, 7–12 July 2003, pages 375–382.

Lev Ratinov, Dan Roth, Doug Downey, and Mike Anderson. 2011. Local and global algorithms for disambiguation to Wikipedia. In *Proceedings of the 49th Annual Meeting of the Association for Computational Linguistics,* Portland, Oreg., 19–24 June 2011, pages 1375–1384.

Sebastian Riedel. 2008. Improving the accuracy and efficiency of MAP inference for Markov logic. In *Proceedings of the 24th Conference on Uncertainty in Artificial Intelligence,* Helsinki, Finland, 9–12 July 2008, pages 468–475.

Noah A. Smith. 2011. *Linguistic Structure Prediction.* Morgan & Claypool Publishers.

Rakshit Trivedi and Jacob Eisenstein. 2013. Discourse connectors for latent subjectivity in sentiment analysis. In *Proceedings of the 2013 Conference of the North American Chapter of the Association for Computational Linguistics: Human Language Technologies,* Atlanta, Georgia, 9–14 June 2013, pages 808–813.

Ainur Yessenalina, Yejin Choi, and Claire Cardie. 2010. Automatically generating annotator rationales to improve sentiment classification. In *Proceedings of the 48th Annual Meeting of the Association for Computational Linguistics,* Uppsala, Sweden, 11–16 July 2010, pages 336–341.

Yiping Zhou, Lan Nie, Omid Rouhani-Kalleh, Flavian Vasile, and Scott Gaffney. 2010. Resolving surface forms to Wikipedia topics. In *Proceedings of the 23rd International Conference on Computational Linguistics,* Beijing, China, 23–27 August 2010, pages 1335–1343.

Topical PageRank: A Model of Scientific Expertise for Bibliographic Search

James Jardine **Simone Teufel**
Natural Language and Information Processing Group
Computer Laboratory
Cambridge University, CB3 0FD, UK
{jgj29,sht25}@cam.ac.uk

Abstract

We model scientific expertise as a mixture of topics and authority. Authority is calculated based on the network properties of each topic network. ThemedPageRank, our combination of LDA-derived topics with PageRank differs from previous models in that topics influence both the bias and transition probabilities of PageRank. It also incorporates the age of documents. Our model is general in that it can be applied to all tasks which require an estimate of document–document, document–query, document–topic and topic–query similarities. We present two evaluations, one on the task of restoring the reference lists of 10,000 articles, the other on the task of automatically creating reading lists that mimic reading lists created by experts. In both evaluations, our system beats state-of-the-art, as well as Google Scholar and Google Search indexed againt the corpus. Our experiments also allow us to quantify the beneficial effect of our two proposed modifications to PageRank.

1 Introduction

For search, the presence of links in a document collection adds valuable information over that contained in the text of the documents alone. Each act of linking can be interpreted as a latent judgement of authority or trust which is bestowed onto the linked documents (Kleinberg, 1998). This makes authority an objective measure of how important that paper is to a community who confer that authority. The citation count is the simplest of these, which has been used successfully for decades for bibliometrics (Garfield, 1972) and for mapping out scientific fields via bibliometric coupling (Kessler, 1963) and co-citations (Small, 1978). More recently, citation counts have been shown to improve effectiveness of ad-hoc retrieval (Meij and De Rijke, 2007; Fujii, 2007).

In science, the peer review process ensures that the right to cite is hard-earned, but on the web, hyperlinking is infinitely cheap. This means that that the authority of webpages cannot simply be approximated as the number of incoming links. Algorithmically more complex authority such as the random-surfer model PageRank (Brin and Page, 1998) or the authorities/hub based algorithm HITS (Kleinberg, 1998)) have spectacularly improved search results in comparison to standard IR models relying on similarity calculations based on the words in the text and other text-internal informatioh.

Much recent work in bibliographic search has been driven by the intuition that what works for the web should also work for science, even though citations are more comparable to each other in weight than hyperlinks. Case studies comparing PageRank-based authority measures against citation counts alone report some cases where PageRank is superior (Chen et al., 2007; Ma et al., 2008), but experimental proof of standard PageRank outperforming citation counts in a large-scale bibliographic search experiment is still outstanding. In at least one such experiment, PageRank performed worse than citation count (Bethard and Jurafsky, 2010).

Straightforward PageRank calculations, when applied to the scientific literature, are hampered by two factors: on the one hand, the progression of time imposes a directional structure on the citation network. Therefore, PageRank values of older papers are systematically inflated as PageRank can only ever flow from newer to older papers (Walker et al., 2007).

Proceedings of the 14th Conference of the European Chapter of the Association for Computational Linguistics, pages 501–510,
Gothenburg, Sweden, April 26-30 2014.

Secondly, and more interestingly, researchers earn their expertise in particular, well-defined scientific fields. We propose that this requires a more fine-grained notion of specific – not global – expertise.

Our solution is to use LDA-derived topics (Blei et al., 2003) as approximations for scientific fields, and to model the importance of a paper as a mixture of its relative expertise in each of the topics it covers. The second aspect of our solution, somewhat more mundane but still necessary to adapt PageRank successfully to model scientific expertise, is to age-taper the resultant estimation.

In this paper, we present ThemedPageRank (TPR), our model of topic-specific scientific expertise, which incorporates the two modifications, and provide evidence that both are necessary for the adequate application of PageRank-style authority calculations to the scientific literature. In two evaluations, our model beats standard PageRank and citation counts by a large margin. Previous models exist which combine the idea of personalising PageRank by topics, but our manipulation of both PageRank's bias and transition probabilities differs from these. Our experiments also support the claim of our system's superiority over these models.

We use two tasks to evaluate the system's performance. The first is the reintroduction of an article's reference items that have been artificially removed. The assumption here is that a good model of document–document similarity should be able to guess which articles any given paper would have cited. The second task is the automatic creation of reading lists, of the kind that an expert might prepare for their students. We asked experts to create a gold standard of such reading lists, and compare our system against the current *de facto* state-of-the-art in such tasks, Google Scholar, and again find that our system beats it comfortably.

This article is structured as follows: the next section describes our model, which section 3 contrasts to related work. The evaluations are described in sections 4 and 5. Section 6 concludes.

2 Authority Model

Our model first determines an LDA space (Blei et al., 2003) representing the entire document collection, which results in a set of topics describing the entirety of the field. It then calculates an authority model for each topic based on a modification of Personalised PageRank (Page et al., 1998). Depending on the search need, the input (one or more keyword(s) or paper(s)) is converted into a topic distribution, which we then use to linearly combine the multiple topic-specific expertise scores of our model into a unique authority score representing the fit between search need and document.

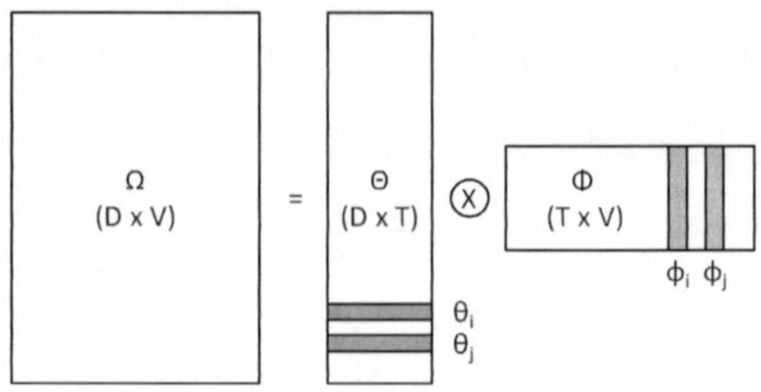

Figure 1: A High-level view of LDA.

Latent Dirichlet Allocation (LDA) (Blei et al., 2003) is a Bayesian generative probabilistic model for collections of discrete data, which has become popular for the modelling of scientific text corpora (Wei and Croft, 2006; He et al., 2009; Blei and Lafferty, 2006). In LDA, a document in the corpus is modelled and explicitly represented as a finite mixture over an underlying set of topics, while each topic is modelled as an infinite mixture over the underlying set of words in the corpus. We use LDA predominantly to produce the latent topics that form a foundation for the relationships between papers and technical terms in a corpus.

Technical terms act as the terms in our model (rather than words), because technical terms are important artefacts for formulating knowledge from scientific texts (Ananiadou, 1994; Justeson and Katz, 1995), because descriptions of topics are better understandable using technical terms rather than words (Wallach, 2006; Wang et al., 2007); and to make our model more scalable to large corpora. The method we use to find technical terms is light-weight and requires little infrastructure, but does not represent state-of-the-art in terminology detection (Lopez and Romary, 2010; Wang et al., 2007). We collect all n-grams of words which appear in 2 or more titles of all documents in the corpus, filter out all unigrams appearing in the Scrabble TWL98 word list, then all n-grams starting or ending in stop words. To decide whether a subsumed term should be removed if the subsuming term exists ("statistical machine translation" subsumes both "statistical machine" and "machine translation"), we remove those n-grams whose frequency is lower than 25% of their subsuming terms. Finally, only the most frequent 25% of the remaining unigrams and bigrams are retained.

We then build a $D \times V$ matrix Ω, which contains the counts of V technical-terms (the columns) in each of the D documents (the rows) in Fig. 1. Our own implementation of LDA (with LDA parameters $\alpha = \beta = 0.01$) is used to collapse matrix Ω into two denser, smaller matrices Θ (containing the distribution of documents over topics), and Φ (containing the distribution of topics over technical-terms).

To model topic-specific expertise in science, we modify the original PageRank calculation of Page at al. (1998) by adding a topic dimension to the score of both the bias and transition probabilities:

$$TPR(t,d,k+1) = \alpha B(t,d)$$
$$+(1-\alpha) \sum_{d' \in l_i(d)} T(t,d,d') TPR(t,d',k)$$

where $TPR(t,d,k)$ is the topic-specific PageRank of topic t for paper d at iteration k; $B(t,d)$ is the probability that paper d is chosen at random from the corpus, given topic t, and $T(t,d,d')$ is the transition probability of reaching page d from page d', given topic t. In our formula, the transition probability $T(t,d,d')$ takes into account the probabilities of topic t not only in documents d and d', but also in the other documents d'' referenced by document d':

$$B(t,d) = \frac{P(t|d)}{\sum_{d^* \in D} P(t|d^*)}$$

$$T^*(t,d,d') = \sqrt{\frac{P(t|d')}{\sum_{d^* \in D} P(t|d^*)} \frac{P(t|d)}{\sum_{d'' \in l_o(d')} P(t|d'')}}$$

$$T(t,d,d') = \frac{T^*(t,d,d')}{\sum_{d^* \in l_i(d)} T^*(t,d,d^*)}$$

Here d is a document whose TPR is being calculated, d' is a document that refers to document d and whose TPR score is being distributed during this iteration of the algorithm, and d'' is a document that is referred to by document d'. The first term in the transition function ensures that TPR scores are propagated only from citing documents that are highly relevant to topic t. The second term ensures that a larger proportion of a documents TPR score is propagated to cited documents that are highly relevant to topic t. The value $P(t|d)$ can be read directly from matrix Θ in Fig. 1.

In a final step, we age-taper TPR by dividing TPR values by the age of the citation concerned in years. Experimentally, this achieved the best model in comparison to more complex dampening methods (e.g., exponential).

3 Related Work

Others before us have observed that time effects bias PageRank if applied unmodified to the scientific literature (Walker et al., 2007). Walker et al.'s CiteRank algorithm modifies the bias probabilities of PageRank exponentially with age, favouring more recent publications.

We are also not the first to have combined a notion of topic-specification with Personalised PageRank. The idea goes back to the original PageRank paper by Page et al. (1998), who discuss the personalization of PageRank by introducing a bias towards only a set of trusted web sites W. Page et al. alter only the bias probability B, while leaving the transition probabilities T unchanged from global PageRank:

$$B(t,d) = \begin{cases} \frac{1}{|W|} & \text{if } d \in W \\ 0 & \text{if } d \notin W \end{cases}$$

$$T(t,d,d') = \frac{1}{|l_o(d')|}$$

Richardson and Domingos (2002) first used PageRank personalisation for specialisation at search time. For query q with corresponding topic $t = q$, they use the relevance of document d to query q as a bias. Haveliwalla (2003) calculates a Personalised PageRank for each of a set of 16 manually created topics t comprised of several documents by altering only the Bias term B, using Page et al.'s formula above. This solution avoids the computational scalability problem with Richardson and Domingos' approach, but is limited in applicability by requiring predefined topics. Several researchers followed Brin and Page and Haveliwala in altering only the bias probabilities, including Wu et al. (2006) and Gori and Pucci (2006).

In contrast, Narayan et al. (2003) and Pal and Narayan (2005) propose a model of personalisation that alters the transition probabilities instead of the bias probabilities. Under their model, the transition probability $T(t, d)$ is proportional to the number of words in document d that are strongly present in the documents contained in topic t. Nie et al. (2006) produce a more computationally scalable version of the ideas presented in Pal and Narayan (2005) by associating a context vector with each document, with a fixed set of topics (12 in their case), for which they learn these context vectors using a naive Bayes classifier. They then provide the possibility to alter both the bias and transition probabilities of each webpage as follows:

$$B(t, d) = \frac{1}{D} C_t(d)$$

$$T(t, d, d') = \gamma \frac{1}{|l_o(d')|} + (1 - \gamma) \sum_{t' \neq t} \frac{C_{t'}(d')}{l_o(d')}$$

where $C_t(d)$ is the context vector score for topic t associated with document d; the first term in $T(t, d, d')$ corresponds to the probability of arriving at page d from other pages in the *same* topic context; the second term is the probability of arriving at page d from other pages in a different context; and γ is a factor that weights the influence of same-topic jumps over other-topic jumps. Their results suggest that γ should be close to 1, indicating that distributing PageRank within topics generates better Personalised PageRank scores.

Other than the fact that they treat bias and transition probabilities differently to how we treat them, all personalisation methods discussed up to now have the disadvantage that they rely on a fixed list of manually selected topics, whereas our method offers adaptive specialisation to corpus or domain.

The previous work closest to ours is Yang et al. (2009), who were the first to use LDA to automatically discover abstract topic distributions in a corpus of scientific articles, and to combine them with Pagerank by – in principle – altering both the bias and transition probabilities according to the following model:

$$B(t, d) = \frac{1}{D} P(t|d)$$

$$T(t, d, d') = \gamma T_{s\_t}(t, d, d') + (1 - \gamma) T_{o\_t}(t, d, d')$$

$$T_{s\_t}(t, d, d') = P(d|d', t) \cong \frac{1}{|l_o(d')|}$$

where T is the number of LDA topics, $P(t|d)$ is a probability of topic t given document d, which can be read directly from the generated LDA probabilities, T_{s_t} is the probability of arriving at page d from other pages in the same topic context, whereas T_{o_t} treats the case of arriving at a different topic. Like Nie et al., they achieve best results with $\gamma = 1$, so they ultimately only use bias probabilities, like the models discussed above. Crucially, their decision that $P(d|d', t)$ does not to involve any of the LDA topic distributions is surprising. Under their model, as in ours, when the reader randomly jumps to a new paper, they will tend to favour papers that are closely associated with the topic. However, when they follow a citation in Yang et. al's model, one is picked with equal probability. In contrast, our model implements the obvious intuition that if one follows citations, one should also favour those that are closely associated with the topic.

Let us now turn to the task of reference list reintroduction (RLR), i.e., the prediction of which papers a target papers originally cited, given only some information about the paper which stands in as a search need – either its abstract, author names and other bibliometric information, and/or the full text of a paper (with citation information redacted). Evaluation of a search model by RLR is cheap because of the readily available gold standard, and it thus allows for experiments with large data sets.

State-of-the-art solutions to RLR combine lexical similarity (often via topic models), measures of authority over a citation graph, and information about social constructs and historic patterns of citation behaviour. Strohman et al. (2007) perform RLR with the paper text as a query to their recommendation system, using text similarity, citation counts, citation coupling, author information, and the citation graph. Their model achieves a mean-average precision of 0.102 against a corpus from the Rexa10 database. Bethard and Jurafsky (2010) improve on Strohman et al. by the use of a SVM with 19 features from 6 broad categories: similar terms; cited by others; recency; cited using similar terms; similar topics; and social habits. They achieve a MAP of

0.279 against the ACL Anthology Reference Corpus (Bird et al., 2008), with the following features performing best: publication age, citation counts, the terms in citation sentences, and the LDA topics of the citing documents. They also use (unchanged) PageRank authority counts as one of the features, but find that it provides little discriminative power to the SVM. A drawback of their method is the large amount of information that has to be provided to create their SVM features, and the expensive training routine, which is based on pairwise paper–paper comparisons in the corpus.

Variations of the RLR tasks exist, which additionally determine the position in the text of a paper where each recommended citation should occur (Tang and Zhang, 2009; He et al., 2011; Lu, 2011), a task which is typically solved by comparing a moving window in the query paper against millions of previously located citation contexts with. The drawback of this technique in contrast to ours is the fact that new papers, which have not collected sufficient contexts in the literature, are severely disadvantaged and will never be recommended.

We first create topics and then apply PageRank to find expertise within topical networks. It is however also possible to simultaneously model citations and terms (Cohn and Hofmann, 2001; Mann et al., 2006). Such models are not normally directly comparable to ours; for instance Bharat and Henzinger's (1998) model, a modified version of HITS (Kleinberg, 1998), is query-specific.

There are numerous extensions to LDA that incorporate external information in addition to the lexical information inside the documents in a corpus, via author-topic models and models of publication venues (Steyvers and Griffiths, 2007; Rosen-Zvi et al., 2010; Tang et al., 2008). Erosheva et al. (2004) model a corpus using a multinomial distribution simultaneously over the citations and terms in each document. Topics (which they call aspects) are associated with a list of the most likely words (interpretable as topics) and citations (interpretable as authorities) in that aspect. Extensions of the model exist (Nallapati and Cohen, 2008; Gruber et al., 2007; Chang and Blei, 2010; Kataria et al., 2010; Dietz et al., 2007).

We avoid the tight coupling of topic discovery and citation modeling that the above-mentioned works follow for several reasons. Firstly, such models only work for papers and citations that were present during the learning stage, and there is no mechanism for predicting influential citations for topics in general, or for combinations of topics. The tight coupling might also result in overlooking some authorities, namely those that are authoritative across several topics, which will be penalised via low joint distribution probabilities in combined methods because of the division of the probabilities across several topics. Secondly, and more disturbingly, such models will not locate topics that lack an authority because the authority component of the joint distribution will be near-zero. This rules out niches in a corpus where papers are equally relevant to each other, or where the niches are so young that they do not yet have an established citation network. There is also a scalability issue with joint models of topics and citations. The evaluation data used in coupled models is generally small, with the number of papers ranging under around 2,000, the number of citations ranging under 10,000, and the number of topics in their models ranging from eight to twenty. But LDA has been shown to scale to corpora of millions of terms (Newman et al., 2006), and PageRank to billions (Page et al., 1998) of documents. Our model, which advocates a pipelined approach, benefits from the fact that separate topic modelling is computationally tractable using LDA, and the fact that citation graph modelling is cheap using Personalised PageRank.

4 Evaluation 1: RLR

We evaluate our authority-based search model using the 2010 ACL Anthology Network (Radev et al., 2009). We removed from it corrupted documents, i.e., those of less than 100 characters or containing only control characters. The ACL Anthology Network provides external meta-data about the articles, which was manually curated. We do not use this meta-data because we wanted to build as system that can be applied to any large collection of articles, where external meta-data would not normally exist. We therefore build an approximate citation graph from the paper text itself, as a one-off task when constructing the LDA space. We extract titles, dates and full-text from every article and perform a search of each articles title in the full-text of all other

Model	MAP
800 test papers, as in B&J (2010)	
B&J; best model	0.287
TPR-NoDB	0.264
TPR-NoAge	0.267
TPR	**0.302**
10,000 test papers	
A: NFIDF Cosine	0.062
B: NFIDF + citation count	0.092
C: NFIDF + global PageRank	0.099
D: NFIDF LDA (KL divergence)	0.115
E: TPR-NoDB	0.233
F: TPR-NoAge	0.242
G: **TPR**	**0.268**

Figure 2: RLR results

articles (i.e., under the assumption that the reference list is the (only) place where we will find such titles).

Our system generates the RLR output (the recommended articles) for an article d by extracting technical terms as described in section 2, examining the topic distribution for that article $\theta_{d,t}$ (i.e. a θ_i in Fig. 1). We use the topic distribution of article d in place to generate the unique age-adjusted TPR tailored to the article, $TPR(d, d')$. The 100 articles d' with the highest ThemedPageRanks are recommend as citations for article d. Results are reported as mean average precision (MAP) of these 100 documents against the actual citations in the article.

We first compare our model to the state-of-the-art (Bethard and Jurafsky, 2010). We emulate their experimental setup by including only the pre-2004 articles in the corpus and testing only on the roughly 800 2005/6 articles with more than 5 intra-corpus citations in their reference list, for which we have per-paper average precision scores. The top part of Fig. 2 shows that our model (MAP=0.302) outperforms their best model (MAP=0.287; difference at 5% confidence with Wilcoxon Ranked Squares test), despite our model being a general, light-weight IR system, which relies on LDA and PageRank alone, and theirs is a specialised state-of-the art system, which relies on heavy-weight machine learning and on additional sociological features.

The lower part of Fig. 2 compares the influence of citation count, global PageRank, topic similarity, and combinations of topic similarity with citation counts or global PageRank, and our model (TPR). For these tests, we use the entire corpus of 10,000 papers with more than 5 citations. Over the baseline (**A**), n-gram-frequency-inverse-document-frequency (NFIDF), both citation counts (**B**) and global PageRank (**C**) make a small improvement. Global LDA similarity scores (**D**) fare little better.

As the performance of the full model (**G**; MAP=0.268) shows, the inclusion of topic models lead to a large improvement over any of the above. This is, as far as we are aware, the first time that a large-scale evaluation that finds significant improvements of a PageRank implementation over citation counts in scientific search.

We next consider our two modifications, age-adjusting **(E)** and double-biasing **(F)**, in isolation. We use two versions of our system where we switched off age-tapering and double-biasing (ie., we only work with a change in the bias probabilities, as do Nie etal. (2006), Havaliwala (2003) (although their models do not include automatically generated topics) and Yang et al. (2009)). Our model comfortably outperforms TPR-NoDB in both the 800 and 10,000 paper experiment. Similarly, the effect of age-tapering alone can be seen from the performance of TPR-NoAge (our model without age-adjusting), in the difference between 0.267 and 0.302 and that between 0.242 and 0.268 (significant at 99%). This confirms our claim that a topic-specific age-tapered PageRank is superior to global PageRank in scientific citation networks.

5 Evaluation 2: Reading Lists

The aim of the second experiment is to test our model against a much cleaner, albeit smaller gold standard: on the task of reconstructing the material of expert-created reading lists. We compare our system's performance to three standard, commonly used search engines: Lucene TFIDF, the Google-indexed ACL Anthology, and Google Scholar. We chose Google-index and Google Scholar because they represent commonly used state-of-the-art commercial search engines, and the Google-index is what is currently offered as the standard ACL Anthology search tool. In contrast, Lucene TFIDF was chosen to represent an easy-to-interpret, reproducible, out-of-the-box baseline implementing the simplest kind of lexical similarity search without any notion of authority. Of the three search engines, we would predict Google Scholar to be the toughest competitor to TPR, because it uses citation information directly and it is reasonable to expect that the Google Scholar algorithm employs some domain adaptation to the scientific domain.

We created gold standard expert-written reading lists using the following protocol. Eight experts were recruited from the computational linguistics groups of two universities (3 from one, 5 from the other). All experts had a PhD in computational linguistics and several years of research experience. They were asked to choose a subject for an (imaginary or existing) reading list for an MPhil student, concerning an area in which they know the literature well. We purposefully did not give them guidance as to the size of the reading list as we wanted to observe how experts create reading lists. During the interview, the experimenter documented the final list chosen by the expert and made sure all papers chosen were present in the 2010 version of the ACL Anthology Network.

This procedure resulted in reading lists of the following topics and sizes: statistical parsing (22 papers); parser evaluation (4); distributional semantics (14); domain adaptation for parsing (11); information extraction (9); lexical semantics (14); statistical machine translation models (5); and concept-to-text generation (16).

In our retrieval model, which topic distribution is chosen for a query depends on whether the query is an exact match to one of the technical terms found by our model. If it is, then the topic distribution of the technical term is used directly as the query topic distribution $\theta q, t$ (i.e. a transposed renormalized ψ in Fig. 1). If not, we perform a keyword-based search (using Lucene TFIDF), and use the average topic distribution of the top 20 documents returned as the query topic distribution (i.e. several θi in Fig. 1). The query topic distribution is then used to linearly combine the topic-specific TPRs into a unique TPR tailored to the query. The 20 documents with the highest TPR are recommended.

The three baselines are used as follows in the experiment: The experiment is performed by issuing the topic of the reading list (exactly as given to us by the experts) as a key-word based query to each system and recording the top 20 resulting papers answers. For Lucene TFIDF, we downloaded Lucene.NET v2.9.2 and indexed our 2010 snapshot of the ACL Anthology using standard Lucene parameters for the TFIDF model. For the Google-indexed ACL Anthology (AAN), we use the interface provided on the ACL Anthology website. In order to provide an identical search ground, we automatically exclude from the return lists papers added after the creation of the AAN snapshot. For Google Scholar (GS), we use the interface provided at `scholar.google.com`, and parse returns to exclude non-AAN material semi-automatically. In the case of Google Scholar, we restrict the search ground to the ACL Anthology by filtering the top 200 return sets (which may lead to fewer than 20 papers returned).

We report FCSC, RCSC and F-score for each algorithm. FCSC and RCSC are new metrics which address the problem that F-score, being binary, does not support the notion of a "close hit", combined with the fact that we require a fine-grained comparison of the quality of different systems retrieved lists despite the small size of our gold standard. Citation Substitution Coefficient (FCSC), a new metric for RLR, gives higher scores to papers closely related to the target papers by citation distance. The FCSC of each expert paper is the inverse of the number of nodes in the minimal citation graph connecting each expert paper to any system-retrieved paper (thus ranging between 0 and 1; non-connected expert papers receive a zero score). We also introduce Reverse Citation Substitution Coefficient (RCSC), which measures the inverse of the number of nodes in the minimal citation graph connecting each system-retrieved paper to any expert paper. RCSC makes sure that systems cannot simply increase their FCSC values by returning many irrelevant papers. RCSC thus corresponds to precision, while FCSC corresponds to recall. The system RCSC and FCSC scores we report are the average scores of all the system-retrieved and expert papers, respectively. Reporting both scores gives a good overall picture of system performance, particularly when read together with the F-score.

Fig. 3 shows that our model comfortably beats the competitor systems according to all metrics. In particular, our model > GS/AAN > Lucene TFIDF[1].

[1]For FCSC, the differences are statistically significant at

	FCSC	RCSC	F-score
AAN/Google	0.527	0.317	0.117
GS	0.519	0.364	0.112
Lucene TFIDF	0.412	0.330	0.040
TPR	**0.563**	**0.456**	**0.128**

Figure 3: Reading List Creation: Results.

Concerning simpler methods of estimating authority, Fig. 4 shows that a multiplication of TFIDF by citation count (as Fujii (2007) does) results in a FCSC/RCSC of 0.419/0.359 (reported as TF-CC), and age-tapering of citation-count by dividing the citation count by the age of the paper in years (reported as TF-CC-A) results in FCSC/RCSC of 0.491/0.442. We again compare different versions of PageRank. Global PageRank can be built into the system by simple multiplication of PR scores as above, with and without age-tapering (reported as TF-PR and TF-PR-A, respectively). We observe a similar effect to the one reported by Bethard and Jurafsky and seen in experiment 1, namely that global PageRank only performs similar to citation counts (0.450/0.360 vs 0.419/0.359). With respect to double-biasing and age-tapering we see the same effect as in experiment 2[2]. In fact, we can see from these results that global PageRank barely improves over standard TFIDF, while age-tapering even without topics already brings quite some improvement. Overall, these results confirms our claim of the superiority of a topic-specific PageRank over global PageRank in scientific citation networks.

6 Conclusions

We present here the first experiments that pinpoint which modifications to PageRank are necessary to adequately cater for the highly specialised situation we encounter in science. The modification we suggest are to use LDA-derived topics (Blei et al., 2003) as approximations for scientific fields, to calculate authority in a topic-specific way, and to age-taper the authority scores. We present formulae where topics personalise both the bias and the transition probabilities. This results in a general IR model for science incorporating a robust notion of authority. Our implementation requires only minimal resources and relies only on LDA and PageRank calculation, which means that it is efficient during training, retraining and at search time.

We perform two evaluations. In both, our model significantly outperforms not only state-of-the-art, but also standard PageRank, non-age-tapered (but topical) PageRank, and non-topical (but age-tapered) PageRank. Our model achieves its competitive performance by using only the raw text and citation links. It requires no external information, neither explicit sociological information such as past collaborations between authors, nor the expertise and cooperation of like-minded readers, as collaborative models do. While successful applications of collaborative filtering to bibliometric search are rife (Goldberg et al., 2001; Agarwal et al., 2005; McNee et al., 2006; Torres et al., 2004), including to reading list generation (Ekstrand et al., 2010), we wanted an entirely independent authority-based IR model similarity. CF also suffers from a cold-start phenomenon, where recommendations are generally poor where data is sparse, and has to wait for papers to be rated by a large number of authors (rather than cited) before it can rank them.

Should the reader wish to evaluate the performance of TPR on their own PDF papers, it has been incorporated into the Qiqqa reference management software [3].

	FCSC	RCSC
TF-CC	0.419	0.359
TF-CC-A	0.491	0.442
TF-PR	0.450	0.360
TF-PR-A	0.512	0.407
TPR-NoDB	0.541	0.440
TPR-NoAge	0.526	0.436

Figure 4: Citation counts and PageRank variants.

99% confidence via a two-tailed Wilcoxon Signed Ranks test, except that between GS and AAN (for which the confidence interval is only 96%) and that between Lucene and AAN, where it is 98%. Non-parametric paired tests such as the Wilcoxon Signed Ranks test can be used on FCSC, but not on RCSC, as there are different sets of underlying system-retrieved papers in each case. For RCSC, differences between our model and all others at 99% confidence interval, between GS and AAN/Lucene TFIDF at the 95% interval. F-score is reported for completeness.

[2]Wilcoxon Signed Rank test found all differences significant at the 99% level, except that between TF-PR and Lucene TFIDF (significant only at the 90% level), and the following equivalences: Lucene TFIDF = TF-CC; TF-PR = TF-CC; TF-CC-A = TF-PR-A; TF-CC-A = TF-PR.

[3]Available at http://www.qiqqa.com

References

N. Agarwal, E. Haque, H. Liu, and L. Parsons. 2005. Research paper recommender systems: A subspace clustering approach. *Advances in Web-Age Information Management.*

S. Ananiadou. 1994. A methodology for automatic term recognition. In *Proceedings of COLING.*

S.K. Pal B. Narayan, C. Murthy. 2003. Topic continuity for web document categorization and ranking. In *IEEE/WIC International Conference on Web Intelligence.*

B.D. Davison B. Wu, V. Goel. 2006. Topical trustrank: Using topicality to combat web spam. In *Proceedings of the 15th international conference on World Wide Web.*

S. Bethard and D. Jurafsky. 2010. Who should i cite: learning literature search models from citation behavior. In *Proceedings of the 19th ACM International Conference on Information and Knowledge Management.*

K. Bharat and M.R. Henzinger. 1998. Improved algorithms for topic distillation in a hyperlinked environment. In *Proceedings of SIGIR.*

S. Bird, R. Dale, B.J. Dorr, B. Gibson, M.T. Joseph, M.Y. Kan, D. Lee, B. Powley, D.R. Radev, and Y.F. Tan. 2008. The ACL anthology reference corpus: A reference dataset for bibliographic research in computational linguistics. In *Proc. of LREC08.*

D.M. Blei and J.D. Lafferty. 2006. Correlated Topic Models. In *Advances in Neural Information Processing Systems 18: Proceedings of the 2005 Conference*, page 147. Citeseer.

D.M. Blei, A.Y. Ng, and M.I. Jordan. 2003. Latent dirichlet allocation. *The Journal of Machine Learning Research*, 3:993–1022.

J. Boyd-Graber, D. Blei, and X. Zhu. 2007. A topic model for word sense disambiguation. In *Proceedings of EMNLP-CoNLL*, pages 1024–1033.

S. Brin and L. Page. 1998. The anatomy of a large-scale hypertextual web search engine. In *Proceedings of the 7th International World Wide Web Conference.*

J. Chang and D.M. Blei. 2010. Hierarchical relational models for document networks. *The Annals of Applied Statistics*, 4(1):124–150.

P. Chen, H. Xie, S. Maslov, and S. Redner. 2007. Finding scientific gems with google's pagerank algorithm. *Journal of Infometrics*, 1(1):8–15.

D. Cohn and T. Hofmann. 2001. The missing link-a probabilistic model of document content and hypertext connectivity. *Advances in neural information processing systems*, pages 430–436.

L. Dietz, S. Bickel, and T. Scheffer. 2007. Unsupervised prediction of citation influences. In *Proceedings of the 24th international conference on Machine learning*, page 240. ACM.

M.D. Ekstrand, P. Kannan, J.A. Stemper, J.T. Butler, J.A. Konstan, and J.T. Riedl. 2010. Automatically building research reading lists. In *Proceedings of the fourth ACM conference on Recommender systems*, pages 159–166. ACM.

E. Erosheva, S. Fienberg, and J. Lafferty. 2004. Mixed-membership models of scientific publications. *Proceedings of the National Academy of Sciences of the United States of America*, 101(Suppl 1):5220.

A. Fujii. 2007. Enhancing patent retrieval by citation analysis. In *Proceedings of SIGIR.*

E. Garfield. 1972. Citation analysis as a tool in journal evaluation. *American Association for the Advancement of Science.*

K. Goldberg, T. Roeder, D. Gupta, and C. Perkins. 2001. Eigentaste: A constant time collaborative filtering algorithm. *Information Retrieval*, 4(2):133–151.

M. Gori and A. Pucci. 2006. Research paper recommender systems: A random-walk based approach. *IEEE Computer Society.*

A. Gruber, M. Rosen-Zvi, and Y. Weiss. 2007. Hidden topic markov models. In *Proceedings of AISTATS.*

T.H. Haveliwala. 2003. Topic-sensitive pagerank: A context-sensitive ranking algorithm for web search. *IEEE transactions on knowledge and data engineering*, pages 784–796.

Q. He, B. Chen, J. Pei, B. Qiu, P. Mitra, and L. Giles. 2009. Detecting topic evolution in scientific literature: how can citations help? In *Proceeding of the 18th ACM conference on Information and knowledge management.*

Q. He, D. Kifer, J. Pei, P. Mitra, and C.L. Giles. 2011. Citation recommendation without author supervision. In *Proceedings of the fourth ACM international conference on Web search and data mining.*

J.S. Justeson and S.M. Katz. 1995. Technical terminology: some linguistic properties and an algorithm for identification in text. *Natural Language Engineering*, 1(01):9–27.

S. Kataria, P. Mitra, and S. Bhatia. 2010. Utilizing Context in Generative Bayesian Models for Linked Corpus. In *Proceedings of AAAI.*

M.M. Kessler. 1963. Bibliographic coupling between scientific papers. *American Documentation*, 14(1):10–25.

J. Kleinberg. 1998. Authoritative sources in a hyperlinked environment. In *Proceedings of the 9th ACM-SIAM Symposium on Discrete Algorithms.* Also available from `http://www.cs.cornell.edu/home/kleinber/`.

P. Lopez and L. Romary. 2010. HUMB: Automatic Key Term Extraction from Scientific Articles in GROBID. In *SemEval 2010 Workshop*.

Y. et al. Lu. 2011. Recommending citations with translation model. In *Proceedings of the 20th ACM international conference on Information and knowledge management*.

N. Ma, J. Guan, and Y. Zhao. 2008. Bringing pagerank to the citation analysis. *Information Processing and Management*, 44(2):800–810.

G.S. Mann, D. Mimno, and A. McCallum. 2006. Bibliometric impact measures leveraging topic analysis. In *Proceedings of the 6th ACM/IEEE-CS joint conference on Digital libraries*.

S.M. McNee, J. Riedl, and J.A. Konstan. 2006. Making recommendations better: an analytic model for human-recommender interaction. In *CHI'06 extended abstracts on Human factors in computing systems*.

E. Meij and M. De Rijke. 2007. Using prior information derived from citations in literature search. In *Large Scale Semantic Access to Content (Text, Image, Video, and Sound)*.

R. Nallapati and W. Cohen. 2008. Link-plsa-lda: A new unsupervised model for topics and influence of blogs. In *International Conference for Weblogs and Social Media*.

D. Newman, P. Smyth, and M. Steyvers. 2006. Scalable Parallel Topic Models. *Journal of Intelligence Community Research and Development*.

L. Nie, B.D. Davison, and X. Qi. 2006. Topical link analysis for web search. In *Proceedings of SIGIR*.

L. Page, S. Brin, R. Motwani, and T. Winograd. 1998. The pagerank citation ranking: Bringing order to the web. *Stanford Digital Library Technologies Project*.

D.R. Radev, P. Muthukrishnan, and V. Qazvinian. 2009. The ACL Anthology Network Corpus. In *Proceedings, ACL Workshop on NLP and IR for Digital Libraries*, Singapore.

M. Richardson and P Domingos. 2002. The intelligent surfer: Probabilistic combination of link and content information in pagerank. *Advances in neural information processing systems*, 14:1441–1448.

M. Rosen-Zvi, C. Chemudugunta, T. Griffiths, P. Smyth, and M. Steyvers. 2010. Learning author-topic models from text corpora. *ACM Transactions on Information Systems (TOIS)*, 28(1):1–38.

B. Narayan S.K. Pal. 2005. A web surfer model incorporating topic continuity. *IEEE Transactions on Knowledge and Data Engineering*, 17:726729.

H.G. Small. 1978. Cited documents as concept symbols. *Social Studies of Science*, 8:327–340.

M. Steyvers and T. Griffiths. 2007. Probabilistic topic models. In T. Landauer, D. S. McNamara, S. Dennis, and W. Kintsch, editors, *Handbook of latent semantic analysis*, page 427. Erlbaum, Hillsdale, NJ.

T. Strohman, W.B. Croft, and D. Jensen. 2007. Recommending citations for academic papers. In *Proceedings of SIGIR*.

J. Tang and J. Zhang. 2009. A discriminative approach to Topic-Based citation recommendation. *Advances in Knowledge Discovery and Data Mining*.

J. Tang, R. Jin, and J. Zhang. 2008. A topic modeling approach and its integration into the random walk framework for academic search. In *Eighth IEEE International Conference on Data Mining*.

R. Torres, S.M. McNee, M. Abel, J.A. Konstan, and J. Riedl. 2004. Enhancing digital libraries with TechLens+. In *Proceedings of the 4th ACM/IEEE-CS joint conference on Digital libraries*.

D. Walker, H. Xie, K.K. Yan, and S. Maslov. 2007. Ranking scientific publications using a model of network traffic. *Journal of Statistical Mechanics: Theory and Experiment*, 2007:P06010.

H.M. Wallach. 2006. Topic modeling: beyond bag-of-words (powerpoint). In *Proceedings of the 23rd international conference on Machine learning*.

X. Wang, A. McCallum, and X. Wei. 2007. Topical n-grams: Phrase and topic discovery, with an application to information retrieval. In *Proceedings of the 7th IEEE international conference on data mining*.

X. Wei and W.B. Croft. 2006. LDA-based document models for ad-hoc retrieval. In *Proceedings of SIGIR*.

W. Wong, W. Liu, and M. Bennamoun. 2009. A probabilistic framework for automatic term recognition. *Intelligent Data Analysis*, 13(4):499–539.

Z. Yang, J. Tang, J. Zhang, J. Li, and B. Gao. 2009. Topic-level random walk through probabilistic model. *Advances in Data and Web Management*.

D. Zhou, S. Zhu, K. Yu, X. Song, B.L. Tseng, H. Zha, and C.L. Giles. 2008. Learning multiple graphs for document recommendations. In *Proceeding of the 17th international conference on World Wide Web*.

Distributional Lexical Entailment by Topic Coherence

Laura Rimell
University of Cambridge
Computer Laboratory
laura.rimell@cl.cam.ac.uk

Abstract

Automatic detection of lexical entailment, or hypernym detection, is an important NLP task. Recent hypernym detection measures have been based on the Distributional Inclusion Hypothesis (DIH). This paper assumes that the DIH sometimes fails, and investigates other ways of quantifying the relationship between the co-occurrence contexts of two terms. We consider the top features in a context vector as a topic, and introduce a new entailment detection measure based on Topic Coherence (TC). Our measure successfully detects hypernyms, and a TC-based family of measures contributes to multi-way relation classification.

1 Introduction

Automatically detecting lexical entailment – for example, that *lion* entails *animal* or *guitar* entails *instrument*, also known as hypernym detection – is an important linguistic task in its own right, and is also a prerequisite for recognizing entailments between longer text segments such as phrases or sentences (Bos and Markert, 2005; Garrette et al., 2011; Baroni et al., 2012; Beltagy et al., 2013).

Several recent techniques for hypernym detection have made use of distributional semantics (Weeds and Weir, 2003; Weeds et al., 2004; Clarke, 2009; Kotlerman et al., 2010; Lenci and Benotto, 2012). These techniques are based on the Distributional Inclusion Hypothesis (Geffet and Dagan, 2005), hereafter DIH, which proposes that if term A entails term B (B is a hypernym of A), then the contexts in which A occurs are a subset of those in which B occurs. For example, all the contexts (co-occurrences) of *lion* – which might include *zoo, hunt, wild, food*, etc. – are also contexts of *animal*. Existing measures look at the *amount* of overlap between the co-occurrences of A and B, in order to judge whether B is a hypernym of A.

The motivation for the present paper is the well-known fact that the DIH is not fully correct. There are many reasons why a hyponym might occur in contexts where its hypernym does not. Some contexts are collocational, e.g. *lion king*. Other contexts are highly specific, e.g. *mane* applies uniquely to lions, horses, and zebras; it would be unusual to see text about *animals* with *manes*. The need to be informative is also relevant: *lion cub* will occur much more frequently than *animal cub*, since *animal* is of the wrong level of generality to pair with *cub*.

Moreover, the more general a hypernym becomes – up to the level of WordNet root elements, such as *entity* – its predominant sense ceases to correspond to the sense intended in hyponym-hypernym chains. Thus we never hear about going to visit an *entity* at the *zoo*.

This paper starts from the assumption that the DIH sometimes fails, and investigates not the *amount of containment* of A's features in B's features, but rather the *nature of the non-contained features*. We consider the top features of a distributional vector as a *topic*, and use recent measures for automatically measuring Topic Coherence (Newman et al., 2010; Mimno et al., 2011) to evaluate how the topics change under various conditions. Using a notion of vector negation, we investigate whether the distributional topic of e.g. *lion* becomes more or less coherent when we subtract the contexts of *animal*.

We introduce a new measure, Ratio of Change in Topic Coherence (RCTC), for detecting lexical entailment. The measure detects hypernyms with reasonable accuracy, and a family of Topic Coherence measures is used to perform a multi-way classification of tuples by relation class. Finally, we investigate how the level of generality of a hypernym affects entailment measures.

Proceedings of the 14th Conference of the European Chapter of the Association for Computational Linguistics, pages 511–519,
Gothenburg, Sweden, April 26-30 2014.

2 Related Work

Historically, manually developed resources such as WordNet (Miller, 1995) have been used to supply lexical entailment information to NLP applications (Bos and Markert, 2005). More recently, a number of techniques for detecting lexical entailment have been developed using distributional semantics (Weeds and Weir, 2003; Weeds et al., 2004; Geffet and Dagan, 2005; Clarke, 2009; Kotlerman et al., 2010; Lenci and Benotto, 2012). These measures quantify to what extent the co-occurrence features of a term A are included in those of another term B, by a direct comparison of the distributional vectors $\vec{A}$ and $\vec{B}$. Kotlerman et al. (2010) use the notion of Average Precision from Information Retrieval to weight the relative importance of the overlapping features. Lenci and Benotto (2012) also check the extent to which B's features are not a subset of A's, as a proxy for the more general character of B. The success of these feature inclusion measures has provided general support for the DIH. Following Szpektor and Dagan (2008), inclusion measures are also sometimes balanced with similarity measures such as LIN similarity (Lin, 1998), to ensure that A and B are semantically related, since unrelated pairs that differ in frequency can mimic feature inclusion.

Previous distributional approaches to hypernym detection have generally involved a single measure, designed to rank hypernyms above other relation classes. Evaluation has largely involved either ranking or binary classification tasks, and there has been little work on using a variety of measures to distinguish multiple relation classes. Lenci and Benotto (2012) perform a ranking task using the multi-class BLESS dataset (Baroni and Lenci, 2011), but not a classification. We perform a multi-way classification using a variety of Topic Coherence measures. Recent Semantic Relation Classification shared tasks (SemEval-2010 Task 8, SemEval-2012 Task 2) are also relevant, though the relation classes and approaches have differed.

3 Topic Coherence for Distributional Lexical Entailment

The intuition behind our approach is to investigate whether term A, the candidate hyponym, has a coherent topic reflected in its distributional features, which apply only to A and not to its hypernym B. Consider A=*beer*, B=*beverage*. They may share features such as *drink*, *cold*, and *party*. But if we minimize or exclude B's features and examine the remaining features of A (we discuss how to do this in Section 3.3), we might be left with more specific features such as *pint*, *lager*, and *brew*.

If A and B share almost all contexts, we would be left with a set of uninformative features, merely corpus noise. If A and B share few contexts, there would be little change to A's topic when excluding B's features. Between the extremes, a range of change in A's topic is possible; we seek to quantify this change and relate it to entailment.

To do this we need a way of treating a distributional context vector as a topic. We treat the N highest-weighted context features in $\vec{A}$ as the topic of A (topicA). If we represent the vector $\vec{A} \equiv \{f_{c_i,A}\}_i$, where $f_{c_i,A}$ is the weighted co-occurrence value of context feature c_i, then topicA is a set $\{c_j\}, j \in 1...N$, of the N highest-weighted context features c_j in $\vec{A}$.

3.1 Hypotheses

We consider two opposing hypotheses.

Hypothesis 1: Removing hypernym B's features from topicA will **decrease** the coherence of topicA. If being a B is very important to being an A, then the collection of remaining features may become more random. Hypothesis 1 is consistent with the DIH, since it implies that the important features of A are also features of B.

As a corollary, removing A's features from B may not change the coherence of topicB very much. Since A is just an instance of B, topicB retains coherence (i.e. there's a lot to being an *animal* besides what's involved in being a *lion*).

Hypothesis 2: Removing hypernym B's features from topicA will **increase** the coherence of topicA. Perhaps A, by virtue of being more specific, occurs in a highly coherent set of contexts where B does not. Hypothesis 2 is inconsistent with the DIH, since it imples that a hyponym always has specific features which the hypernym does not share.

As a corollary, removing hyponym A's features from hypernym B might decrease the coherence of topicB, if removing specific features leaves only more general, less informative features behind.

3.2 Topic Coherence Measure

We use a Topic Coherence (TC) measure from recent work on automatic evalution of topics generated from corpora by latent variable models (Newman et al., 2010; Mimno et al., 2011; Stevens et al., 2012). TC measures are applied to the top N words from a generated topic. They assign pairwise relatedness scores to the words, and return the mean or median from the word-pair scores.

We adopt the best method from Newman et al. (2010), equal to the median pairwise Pointwise Mutual Information (PMI) of the top N words, using Wikipedia as a background corpus for PMI.[1] The measure is given in Equation (1):

$$TC(\{c_j\}) = \text{median}(PMI(c_i, c_k), i, k \in 1...N, i < k) \quad (1)$$

where $\{c_j\}$ is the topic, and PMI is defined as:

$$PMI(c_i, c_k) = log \frac{p(c_i, c_k)}{p(c_i)p(c_k)} \quad (2)$$

We use intra-sentence co-occurrence in Wikipedia for calculating PMI.

Note that our definition of a topic, namely the top N features from a distributional vector, does not correspond to a topic generated by a latent variable model, because it does not have a probability distribution over words. However, the TC measures we adopt do not make use of such a probability distribution except for choosing the top N words from a topic, which are then treated as an unordered set for the pairwise operations. Newman et al. (2010) uses N=10, and Mimno et al. (2011) uses N=5...20; we investigate a range of N.

3.3 Vector Negation

For removing one topic from another, we draw on the concept of vector negation (Widdows and Peters, 2003; Widdows, 2003). Vector negation has proved useful for modeling word senses in Information Retrieval. For example, one might want to formulate a query for *suit* NOT *lawsuit*, which will retrieve terms such as *shirt* and *jacket* and exclude *plaintiff* and *damages*.

We test two versions of vector negation. The first, **Widdows** (Widdows, 2003), represents A NOT B as the projection of $\vec{A}$ onto $\vec{B}^{\perp}$, the subspace orthogonal to $\vec{B}$ in the vector space V. Specifically, $\vec{B}^{\perp} \equiv \{v \in V : v \cdot \vec{B} = 0\}$. The formula for Widdows A NOT B is:

$$\text{A NOT B} \equiv \vec{A} - \frac{\vec{A} \cdot \vec{B}}{|\vec{B}|^2}\vec{B} \quad (3)$$

The second, **Strict** negation, simply zeros out any context features of A that are non-zero in B:

$$f_{c_i,AnotB} \equiv \begin{cases} 0 & \text{if } f_{c_i,B} \neq 0 \\ f_{i,A} & \text{if } f_{c_i,B} = 0 \end{cases} \quad (4)$$

[1] In our case, Wikipedia is also the source corpus for our context vectors.

This measure is harsher than Widdows negation, which decreases the value of common features but does not remove them completely.

3.4 Generality Measure

Herbelot and Ganesalingam (2013) experiment with hypernym detection using a generality measure. They measure the Kullback-Leibler (KL) divergence (Eq. 5) between the probability distribution over context words for a term A, and the background probability distribution. The idea is that the greater the KL divergence, the more informative and therefore specific the term is, while hypernyms are likely to be more general.

$$D_{\text{KL}}(p(f_i|A)||p(f_i)) = \Sigma_i ln(\frac{p(f_i|A)}{p(f_i)})p(f_i) \quad (5)$$

Herbelot and Ganesalingam (2013) found that KL divergence on its own was not sufficient for successful hypernym detection. We experiment with it in combination with TC measures.

4 Methods

4.1 Context Vectors

We produced context vectors from a 2010 Wikipedia download, lemmatized using morpha (Minnen et al., 2001). The 10K most frequent lemmas in the corpus, minus common stop words and the 25 most frequent lemmas, served as the context features. Feature co-occurrences were counted in a 7-word window around the target lemma (three words each side of the target lemma), and limited to intra-sentence co-occurrences.

Co-occurrence counts were weighted using T-test. We chose T-test because it does not over-emphasize infrequent features; however, early experiments with Positive PMI weighting showed the overall performance of our measures to be similar with both weighting schemes.

We benchmarked our context vectors on the WS353 word similarity task (Finkelstein et al., 2002) and found them to be of comparable accuracy with previous literature.

Rel Class	Target	Related Word	Total
HYPER	*alligator*	*animal*	638
COORD	*alligator*	*lizard*	1,760
MERO	*alligator*	*mouth*	1,402
RAND-N	*alligator*	*message*	3,253

Table 1: Examples from the BLESS subset; number of tuples per relation in the development set.

	Macroaverage				Microaverage			
	Relation Class				Relation Class			
Coherence of	**HYPER**	**MERO**	**COORD**	**RAND-N**	**HYPER**	**MERO**	**COORD**	**RAND-N**
TopicA	5.14 ±1.63	5.16 ±1.66	5.13 ±1.63	5.16 ±1.66	5.14 ±1.59	5.37 ±1.56	5.22 ±1.63	5.28 ±1.62
TopicAnotB	3.82 ±1.27	3.86 ±1.02	3.49 ±0.94	5.07 ±1.50	3.88 ±1.73	4.07 ±1.42	3.58 ±1.51	5.17 ±1.64
TopicA-TopicAnotB	1.32 ±1.54	1.30 ±1.28	1.64 ±1.58	0.09 ±0.43	1.26 ±1.86	1.30 ±1.49	1.64 ±1.92	0.11 ±0.83
TopicB	4.97 ±0.58	4.51 ±0.52	5.02 ±0.73	4.49 ±0.24	5.01 ±1.15	4.53 ±1.44	5.07 ±1.63	4.50 ±1.30
TopicBnotA	4.36 ±0.55	3.92 ±0.53	3.33 ±0.67	4.45 ±0.27	4.37 ±1.15	3.89 ±1.32	3.35 ±1.61	4.46 ±1.41
TopicB-TopicBnotA	0.61 ±0.69	0.59 ±0.48	1.68 ±0.88	0.04 ±0.14	0.64 ±1.34	0.64 ±1.33	1.72 ±2.07	0.04 ±0.77

Table 2: Average Topic Coherence measures on the development set, using N=10, Strict negation.

4.2 Evaluation Dataset

We used a subset of the BLESS dataset (Baroni and Lenci, 2011) as defined by Lenci and Benotto (2012). The entire dataset consists of 200 concrete nouns in 17 broad noun classes (e.g. clothing, amphibian/reptile, vegetable, container), participating in a variety of relations. The subset contains the relation classes hypernym (HYPER), coordinate (COORD, i.e. co-hyponym), meronym (MERO, i.e. part-of), and random-noun (RAND-N, an unrelated noun). It consists of 14,547 tuples in total. Table 1 gives an example of each relation class, along with the total number of tuples per class in the development data.

Since there was no pre-defined development-test split for the BLESS subset, we randomly selected half of the data for development. For each of the 17 broad noun classes, we randomly chose half of the target nouns, and included all their HYPER, COORD, MERO, and RAND-N tuples. This resulted in a development set consisting of 96 target nouns and 7,053 tuples; and a test set consisting of 104 nouns and 7,494 tuples.

5 Topic Coherence Behavior

We first investigate how topic coherence behaves across the four relation classes. Table 2 shows the average values and standard deviation of TC-related measures on the development data. The left-hand side gives macro-averages, where values are first averaged per-class for each target word, then averaged across the 96 target words in the development set. The right-hand side gives micro-averages across all tuples in the development set. The micro- and macro-averages are similar, and we report macro-averages from now on.[2]

Row 1 of Table 2 shows the original coherence of topicA, and row 2 the coherence of topicAnotB. Row 3 is simply the difference between the two, showing the absolute change in coherence. Rows 4-6 are analogous. In general, coherence values for A and B ranged from the 3's to the 6's, with very high coherence of 7 or 8 and very low coherence of 1 or 2. We did not normalize TC values.

Comparing rows 1 and 4, we see that the B topics are slightly less coherent than the A topics, probably due to the makeup of the dataset (B terms include hypernyms and random words, while A terms are concrete nouns).

Column 1 shows that removing hypernym B from A results in a decrease in coherence, from 5.14 to 3.82. The difference in coherence, 1.32 in this case, is shown in row 3. Removing A from B also results in a coherence decrease, but a much smaller one: only a 0.61 average absolute decrease. Because the starting coherence values of A and B may be different, we focus on the amount of change in coherence when we perform the negation (rows 3 and 6), rather than the absolute coherence of the negated vectors (rows 2 and 5).

Interestingly, column 2 shows that the behaviour of meronyms is almost identical to hypernyms. This is surprising for two reasons: first, meronyms are intuitively more specific than their holonyms; and second, previous studies tended to conflate hypernyms with coordinates rather than meronyms (Lenci and Benotto, 2012).

Column 3, rows 3 and 6, show that coordinates behave differently from hypernyms and meronyms. Vector negation in both directions results in a similar loss of coherence (1.64 and 1.68), reflecting the fact that coordinates have a symmetrical relationship. The average change is also greater, although there is a wide variance. In column 4, the coherence differences for random nouns are again symmetrical, but in this case very small, since a randomly selected noun will not share many contexts with the target word.

We can also define a TC-based similarity mea-

[2]Lenci and Benotto (2012) also report macro-averages, but our figures are not comparable to theirs, which are based on a nearest-neighbor analysis.

	Relation Class			
Measure	HYPER	MERO	COORD	RAND-N
TC Meet	5.36	5.12	5.98	3.62
LIN	0.41	0.41	0.48	0.22
GenKLA	4.89	4.89	4.89	4.89
GenKLB	4.60	4.49	5.01	4.95
DiffGenKL	0.29	0.40	-0.12	-0.05

Table 3: Average similarity and generality measures on the dev. set, using N=10, Strict negation.

sure. We define $\vec{A}\,\text{MEET}\,\vec{B}$ as the intersection of two vectors, where each feature value $f_{c_i,A\text{ MEET }B} \equiv \min(f_{c_i,A}, f_{c_i,B})$. Table 3 shows TC(A MEET B), with LIN similarity (Lin, 1998) between A and B for comparison. We expect that if A and B are similar, their common features will form a coherent topic. Indeed hypernyms and meronyms have high values, with coordinates slightly higher and random nouns much lower.

Table 3 also shows the KL divergence-based generality measure from Section 3.4. Term B is slightly more general (lower score) than term A for hypernyms and meronyms. This may suggest that meronyms are more general distributionally than their holonyms, e.g. *leg* is a holonym of *alligator*, but also associated with many other animals.

Table 4 shows the topics for *owl* and its hypernym *creature*. Using Strict negation to create *owl* NOT *creature* causes a number of contexts to be removed from *owl*: *sized, owl, burrow, hawk, typical, medium, eagle, large, nest*. Instead, more idiosyncratic contexts rise to the top, including *northern, mexican, grouping*, and *bar* (as in an owl's markings). These idiosyncratic contexts are not mutually informative and cause a sizeable decrease in TC.

On the other hand, removing *owl* from *creature* does not decrease the coherence nearly as much. The contexts that are promoted – *fantastic, bizarre, fairy* – are mutually consistent with the other *creature* contexts.

So far our results support Hypothesis 1: removing B from A decreases its coherence. However, we hypothesize that this may not be the case for hypernyms at all levels of generality. Considering the pair *owl-chordate*, there is no change from topicA to topicAnotB. But *chordate* loses a sizeable amount of coherence when *owl* is removed; the topic changes from *primitive, ancestral, ancestor, evolution, lineage, basal, earliest, fossil, non-, neural* (TC 6.62), to *earliest, non-, neural, affinity, probable, genome, suspected, universally, group, approximation* (TC 3.60).

6 Hypernym Detection Measures

Since we use the same dataset as Lenci and Benotto (2012), we report the invCL measure introduced in that paper, which outperformed the other measures reported there, including those of Weeds and Weir (2003), Weeds et al. (2004), and Clarke (2009). Let f_A be the weight of feature f in $\vec{A}$, and let F_A be the set of features with non-zero weights in $\vec{A}$. Then we have:

$$\text{CL}(A,B) = \frac{\Sigma_{f\in F_A\cap F_b}\min(f_A, f_B)}{\Sigma_{f\in F_A} f_A} \quad (6)$$

$$\text{invCL}(A,B) = \sqrt{\text{CL}(A,B) * (1-\text{CL}(B,A))} \quad (7)$$

We also report the balAPinc measure of Kotlerman et al. (2010), which is not included in the Lenci and Benotto (2012) evaluation. This measure begins with APinc, in which the features of A are ranked by weight, highest to lowest:

$$\text{APinc}(A,B) = \frac{\Sigma_{r\in 1\ldots|F_A|} P(r) * rel(f_r)}{|F_A|} \quad (8)$$

where $P(r)$ is the "precision" at rank r, that is, how many of B's features are included at rank r in the features of A; and $rel(f_r)$ is a relevance feature reflecting how important f_r is in B (see Kotlerman et al. (2010) for details). The balanced version balAPinc is:

$$\text{balAPinc}(A,B) = \sqrt{LIN(A,B) * \text{APinc}(A,B)} \quad (9)$$

owl (5.19)	*owl* **not** *creature* (3.25)	*creature* (5.91)	*creature* **not** *owl* (5.09)	*owl* **meet** *creature* (4.14)
barn	barn	mythical	mythical	small
sized	grey	-like	supernatural	large
owl	northern	strange	alien	burrow
burrow	mexican	supernatural	legendary	night
hawk	falcon	magical	fantastic	elf
typical	creek	alien	bizarre	little
medium	mountains	evil	aquatic	giant
eagle	grouping	legendary	dangerous	prey
large	bar	giant	vicious	hunt
nest	california	resemble	fairy	purple

Table 4: Topics from the development data with Topic Coherence values.

	Widdows			
N =	5	10	15	20
HYPER	1.00	1.00	1.00	1.00
MERO	0.99	1.00	1.00	1.00
COORD	1.02	1.00	1.00	1.01
RAND-N	1.00	1.00	1.00	1.00
	Strict			
N =	5	10	15	20
HYPER	1.64	**1.42**	1.23	1.19
MERO	1.91	1.23	1.24	1.20
COORD	1.36	1.15	1.10	1.16
RAND-N	1.08	1.03	1.03	1.02

Table 5: RCTC with varying N and neg type.

We introduce a new measure, Ratio of Change in Topic Coherence (RCTC). Based on Section 5, we expect that for hypernyms the change in coherence from A to AnotB is greater than the change from B to BnotA. However, we cannot simply use the ratio (A-AnotB)/(B-BnotA), because the very small changes in the RAND-N class result in very small denominators and unstable values. Instead, we consider two ratios: the magnitude of TC(A) compared to TC(AnotB), and the magnitude of TC(B) compared to TC(BnotA). We take the ratio of these figures:

$$\mathrm{RCTC}(A, B) = \frac{\frac{TC(\mathrm{topicA})}{TC(\mathrm{topicAnotB})}}{\frac{TC(\mathrm{topicB})}{TC(\mathrm{topicBnotA})}} \quad (10)$$

If topicA is much more coherent than AnotB, the numerator will be relatively large. If topicB is not much more coherent than topicBnotA, the denominator will be relatively small. Both of these factors encourage RCTC to be larger.[3]

We also balanced RCTC with three different factors: LIN similarity, a generality ratio, and TC(MeetAB). In each case we calculated the balanced value as $\sqrt{RCTC * factor}$.

7 Experiments and Discussion

We first look at the effect of N (topic size) and negation type on RCTC on the development data (Table 5). It is clear that RCTC distinguishes relation types using Strict but not Widdows negation. We believe this is because, as the "harsher" version of negation, it allows less-related features to rise to the top of the topic and reveal greater differences in topic coherence. N=10 was the only value that ranked hypernyms the highest; we use N=10 for the remaining experiments.

	invCL	bal APinc	RCTC	RCTC bal LIN	RCTC bal GEN	RCTC bal MEET
HYPER	**0.41**	**0.23**	**1.37**	**0.72**	**1.09**	**2.62**
MERO	0.39	0.22	1.28	0.70	1.06	2.51
COORD	0.38	0.22	1.44	0.71	1.05	2.50
RAND-N	0.25	0.10	1.03	0.46	1.01	1.92

Table 6: Hypernym identification on full dataset: average value by relation.

We then proceed to hypernym identification on the full dataset (Table 6). All measures we tested assigned the highest average value to hypernyms (in bold) compared to the other relations.

7.1 Ranking Task

Lenci and Benotto (2012) introduced a ranking task for hypernym detection on the BLESS data, which we replicate here. In this task a measure is used to rank all tuples from the data. The accuracy of the ranking is assessed from the point of view of each relation class. The goal is for hypernyms to have the highest accuracy of all the classes.

We report the Information Retrieval (IR) measure Mean Average Precision (MAP) for each class, following Lenci and Benotto (2012). We also report Mean R-Precision (RPrec), equal to the precision at rank R where R is the number of elements in the class. None of the measures we evaluated achieves the highest result for hypernyms[4], though invCL consistently performs better for hypernyms than do the other measures (Table 7).

Both MAP and RPrec give more weight to correct rankings near the top of the list, as is suitable for IR applications. In the context of hypernym detection, they could test a system's ability to find one or two good-quality hypernyms quickly from a set of candidates. However, these measures are less appropriate for testing whether a system can, in general, rank hypernyms over other relations. Therefore, we also report Mean Area Under the ROC Curve, or Wilcoxon-Mann-Whitney statistic (AUC), which gives equal weight to correct rankings at the top and bottom of the list, and also compensates for unbalanced data. Table 7 shows that RCTCbalMEET performs identically to invCL on the AUC measure. This comparison suggests that invCL is better at placing hypernyms

[3]Although TC values are PMI values, which can be negative, in practice the median pairwise PMI is almost never negative, because there tend to be more positive than negative values among the pairwise comparisons. Therefore, we have not accounted for sign in the ratio. We have handled as special cases the few instances where TC(topicAnotB) or TC(topicBnotA) takes the value of −infinity due to zero co-occurrences between many of the features.

[4]Lenci and Benotto (2012) report a different result, possibly due to the use of different context vectors.

		invCL	balAPinc	RCTC	RCTC balLIN	RCTC balGEN	RCTC balMEET
RPrec	Hyper	**0.30**	0.25	0.17	0.20	0.12	0.19
	Mero	0.32	0.29	0.30	0.31	0.21	0.32
	Coord	0.39	0.43	0.27	0.42	0.27	0.40
	Rand-N	0.18	0.19	0.38	0.16	0.42	0.18
AUC	Hyper	**0.18**	0.17	0.16	0.17	0.14	**0.18**
	Mero	0.31	0.31	0.27	0.31	0.24	0.31
	Coord	0.38	0.39	0.25	0.39	0.28	0.37
	Rand-N	0.13	0.13	0.32	0.12	0.34	0.15
MAP	Hyper	**0.35**	0.30	0.22	0.24	0.17	0.24
	Mero	0.37	0.35	0.35	0.36	0.27	0.37
	Coord	0.41	0.46	0.30	0.45	0.32	0.43
	Rand-N	0.32	0.32	0.43	0.31	0.46	0.33

Table 7: Ranking results. Bold indicates best result for hypernyms by evaluation measure.

at the top of the ranking, but over the whole dataset the two measures rank hypernyms above other tuples equally.

7.2 Classification Task

We performed a four-way classification of tuples by relation class. We used LIBSVM (Chang and Lin, 2011). As described in Section 4.2, the BLESS data is unbalanced, with hypernyms – our target class – making up only about 9% of the data. To address this imbalance, we used LIBSVM's option to increase the cost associated with the smaller classes during parameter tuning and training. We based the weights on the development data only (HYPER: 9% of the data, weight factor 10; MERO: 20% of the data, weight factor 5; COORD: 25% of the data, weight factor 4).

We used LIBSVM's default Radial Basis Function kernel. On the development data we performed 10-fold cross-validation. We used LIBSVM's grid.py utility for tuning the parameters C and γ separately for each fold. We also tuned and trained models on the development data and tested them on the test data.

We used four sets of features (Table 8): (1) invCL on its own; (2) TC features; (3) all features (invCL, TC, plus additional similarity and generality measures); and (4) all except TC features.

The results of classification on the development data are shown in Table 9, and on the test data in Table 10. Although we report overall accuracy, this is a poor measure of classificaton quality for unbalanced data. The tables therefore provide the Precision, Recall, and F-score by relation class.

The overall accuracy is respectable, although it can be seen that the hypernym class was the most difficult to predict, despite weighting the cost function. Hypernyms may be particularly difficult

Feature	Description
invCL	Lenci's invCL(A, B) (Eq. 7)
topicA	$TC(A)$
topicAnotB	$TC(B)$
diffTopicA	$TC(A) - TC(A \text{ NOT } B)$
ratioTopicsA	$TC(A \text{ NOT } B)/TC(A)$
topicB	$TC(B)$
topicBnotA	$TC(B \text{ NOT } A)$
diffTopicB	$TC(B) - TC(B \text{ NOT } A)$
ratioTopicsB	$TC(B \text{ NOT } A)/TC(B)$
topicMeetAB	$TC(A \text{ MEET } B)$
ratioTopics1	$TC(A \text{ NOT } B)/TC(B \text{ NOT } A)$
ratioTopics2	diffTopicA / diffTopicB
DiffTopics1	diffTopicA - diffTopicB
DiffTopics2	diffTopicA + diffTopicB
RCTC	RCTC(A, B) (Eq. 10)
RCTCbalMEET	RCTCbalMEET(A, B)
APinc	Kotlerman's APinc(A, B) (Eq. 8)
balAPinc	Kotlerman's balAPinc(A, B) (Eq. 9)
LIN	LIN similarity
genKLA	$D_{\text{KL}}(p(f_i\|A)\|\|p(f_i))$ (Eq. 5)
genKLB	$D_{\text{KL}}(p(f_i\|B)\|\|p(f_i))$ (Eq. 5)
diffGenKL	genKLA - genKLB
ratioGenKL	genKLA / genKLB
RCTCbalLIN	RCTCbalLIN(A, B)
RCTCbalGEN	RCTCbalGEN(A, B)
RCTCbalInvCL	RCTC(A, B) bal. with invCL(A, B)

Table 8: Features used in classification experiment. InvCL; TC features; additional features.

to isolate given their similarity to meronyms and intermediate status between coordinates and random nouns on some of the features.

Importantly, while previous work has focused on single measures such as invCL, the classification task highlights a key aspect of the TC approach. Because we can measure the TC of several different vectors for any given tuple (original terms, negated topics, intersection, etc.) we can perform multi-way classification much more accurately than with the invCL measure alone. Moreover, the TC features make an important contribution to the multi-way classification over and above invCL and other previous similarity and generality

Feature Set	Acc	Class	P	R	F
invCL	39.2	Hyper	29.2	19.6	22.5
		Mero	25.5	51.7	34.0
		Coord	19.3	26.4	21.3
		Rand-N	73.5	44.9	55.6
TC Feats	56.7	Hyper	20.3	**41.4**	**27.1**
		Mero	36.5	48.4	41.4
		Coord	**66.5**	54.5	59.5
		Rand-N	**87.1**	64.7	74.2
All except TC	59.2	Hyper	28.7	19.7	22.9
		Mero	35.1	**56.2**	43.2
		Coord	58.2	54.5	56.2
		Rand-N	85.5	71.0	77.5
All	64.0	Hyper	**30.5**	24.4	26.7
		Mero	**44.9**	44.6	**44.6**
		Coord	60.3	**65.6**	**62.8**
		Rand-N	80.0	**79.6**	**79.7**

Table 9: Classification results on development data using 10-fold cross-validation.

Feature Set	Acc	Class	P	R	F
invCL	42.2	Hyper	31.1	19.3	23.8
		Mero	32.6	54.3	40.7
		Coord	23.1	29.3	25.8
		Rand-N	75.8	48.2	59.0
TC Feats	56.2	Hyper	20.0	**45.1**	27.7
		Mero	36.7	42.9	40.0
		Coord	**64.2**	56.5	60.1
		Rand-N	**88.6**	64.5	74.6
All except TC	60.6	Hyper	23.9	17.9	20.5
		Mero	38.1	**56.4**	**45.5**
		Coord	58.2	56.1	57.1
		Rand-N	86.5	73.8	79.6
All	63.1	Hyper	**33.9**	28.6	**31.0**
		Mero	**44.1**	36.9	40.2
		Coord	57.2	**64.3**	**60.6**
		Rand-N	78.2	**81.5**	**79.8**

Table 10: Classification results on test data using development data as training.

measures, with the set of all features yielding the highest overall accuracy.

Another interesting result is that classification with the TC features alone results in much higher recall (though lower precision) for hypernyms than any of the other feature sets, and on the development data (Table 9) results in the highest F-score for hypernyms.

8 Hypernym Depth

We performed a simple preliminary experiment to test the speculation that the interaction between topics depends on the level of generality of the hypernym. Using the WordNet::Similarity package (Pedersen et al., 2004), we divided the development data into bins according to the depth of the hypernym from the WordNet root node. Table 11 shows average values by hypernym depth.

D	Qty	diffA	diffB	RCTC	invCL	balAPinc
1	1	0.66	0.27	1.08	0.15	0.01
3	35	0.33	0.16	1.12	0.44	0.23
5	108	0.32	-0.65	1.32	0.33	0.16
6	41	1.21	0.24	1.50	0.44	0.21
7	160	1.45	0.64	1.34	0.44	0.27
8	136	1.30	0.90	1.25	0.35	0.19
9	71	1.37	1.09	1.26	0.41	0.23
10	51	1.90	2.10	2.08	0.41	0.24
11	15	1.85	1.50	1.23	0.48	0.31
12	13	2.08	1.45	1.24	0.28	0.17
13	3	2.49	0.97	1.67	0.27	0.12
14	4	2.02	1.97	1.05	0.27	0.09

Table 11: Average value by depth D of hypernym.

There is a striking result for diffA, i.e. TC(topicA) - TC(topicAnotB): the deeper the hypernym in the WordNet hierarchy, the greater the value. This suggests that more abstract hypernyms have less interaction with their hyponyms' topics. A similar, though less pronounced, effect is seen for diffB. However, the three measures RCTC, invCL, and balAPinc remain relatively stable as the hypernym depth changes. While this is somewhat reassuring, these averages clearly have not yet captured the difficulty which the DIH encounters in individual cases such as *owl–chordate*.

9 Conclusions

We have introduced a set of Topic Coherence measures, particularly the Ratio of Change in Topic Coherence, to identify hypernyms. These measures perform comparably to previous hypernym detection measures on many tasks, while providing a different view of the relationship between the distributional vectors of two terms, and contributing to a more accurate multi-way relation classification, especially higher recall for hypernyms.

The approach presented here provides a starting point for entailment measures that do not rely solely on the Distributional Inclusion Hypothesis. One issue with the current proposal is that it tests for a single coherent distributional topic, whereas multiple senses may be represented in a word's top context features. Future work will integrate Word Sense Disambiguation methods into the Topic Coherence based lexical entailment approach.

Acknowledgments

This work is supported by EPSRC grant EP/I037512/1. We gratefully acknowledge helpful discussion from Stephen Clark, Tamara Polajnar, Julie Weeds, Jeremy Reffin, David Weir, and the anonymous reviewers.

References

Marco Baroni and Alessandro Lenci. 2011. How we BLESSed distributional semantic evaluation. In *Proceedings of the EMNLP workshop on GEMS: GEometrical Models of natural language Semantics*, pages 1–10, Edinburgh.

Marco Baroni, Raffaella Bernardi, Ngoc-Quynh Do, and Chung chieh Shan. 2012. Entailment above the word level in distributional semantics. In *Proceedings of EACL*, pages 23–32.

Islam Beltagy, Cuong Chau, Gemma Boleda, Dan Garrette, Katrin Erk, and Raymond Mooney. 2013. Montague meets markov: Deep semantics with probabilistic logical form. In *Proceedings of *SEM*, pages 11–21, Atlanta, Georgia.

Johan Bos and Katja Markert. 2005. Recognising textual entailment with logical inference. In *Proceedings of HLT-EMNLP*, pages 628–635, Vancouver.

Chih-Chung Chang and Chih-Jen Lin. 2011. LIBSVM: A library for support vector machines. *ACM Transactions on Intelligent Systems and Technology*, 2:27:1–27:27. Software available at `http://www.csie.ntu.edu.tw/~cjlin/libsvm`.

Daoud Clarke. 2009. Context-theoretic semantics for natural language: an overview. In *Proceedings of the EACL workshop on GEMS: GEometrical Models of natural language Semantics*, pages 112–119, Athens.

Lev Finkelstein, Evgeniy Gabrilovich, Yossi Matias, Ehud Rivlin, Zach Solan, Gadi Wolfman, and Eytan Ruppin. 2002. Placing search in context: The concept revisited. *ACM Transactions on Information Systems*, 20:116–131.

Dan Garrette, Katrin Erk, and Raymond Mooney. 2011. Integrating logical representations with probabilistic information using Markov Logic. In *Proceedings of IWCS*, Oxford, UK.

M. Geffet and I. Dagan. 2005. The distributional inclusion hypotheses and lexical entailment. In *Proceedings of ACL*, Michigan.

Aurélie Herbelot and Mohan Ganesalingam. 2013. Measuring semantic content in distributional vectors. In *Proceedings of ACL*.

Lili Kotlerman, Ido Dagan, Idan Szpektor, and Maayan Zhitomirsky-Geffet. 2010. Directional distributional similarity for lexical inference. *Natural Language Engineering*, 16:359–389.

Alessandro Lenci and Giuli Benotto. 2012. Identifying hypernyms in distributional semantic spaces. In *Proceedings of *SEM*, pages 75–79, Montreal.

Dekang Lin. 1998. An information-theoretic definition of similarity. In *Proceedings of ICML*, Madison, Wisconson.

George A. Miller. 1995. WordNet: A lexical database for English. *Communications of the ACM*, 38(11):39–41.

David Mimno, Hanna M. Wallach, Edmund Talley, Miriam Leenders, and Andrew McCallum. 2011. Optimizing semantic coherence in topic models. In *Proceedings of EMNLP*, pages 262–272, Edinburgh.

Guido Minnen, John Carroll, and Darren Pearce. 2001. Applied morphological processing of English. *Natural Language Engineering*, 7(3):207–223.

David Newman, Jey Han Lau, Karl Grieser, and Timothy Baldwin. 2010. Automatic evaluation of topic coherence. In *Proceedings of NAACL*, pages 100–108, Los Angeles, California.

Ted Pedersen, Siddarth Patwardhan, and Jason Michelizzi. 2004. WordNet::Similarity - measuring the relatedness of concepts. In *Proceedings of NAACL (Demonstration System)*, pages 38–41, Boston, MA.

Keith Stevens, Philip Kegelmeyer, David Andrzejewski, and David Butler. 2012. Exploring topic coherence over many models and many topics. In *Proceedings of EMNLP*, pages 952–961, Jeju Island, Korea.

I. Szpektor and I. Dagan. 2008. Learning entailment rules for unary templates. In *Proceedings of COLING*, Manchester, UK.

Julie Weeds and David Weir. 2003. A general framework for distributional similarity. In *Proceedings of EMNLP*, pages 81–88, Sapporo, Japan.

Julie Weeds, David Weir, and Diana McCarthy. 2004. Characterising measures of lexical distributional similarity. In *Proceedings of COLING*, pages 1015–1021, Geneva.

Dominic Widdows and Stanley Peters. 2003. Word vectors and quantum logic. In *Proceedings of the Eight Mathematics of Language Conference*, Bloomington, Indiana.

Dominic Widdows. 2003. Orthogonal negation in vector spaces for modelling word-meanings and document retrieval. In *Proceedings of ACL*, pages 136–143, Sapporo, Japan.

Information Structure Prediction for Visual-world Referring Expressions

Micha Elsner
Department of Linguistics,
The Ohio State University
melsner@ling.osu.edu

Hannah Rohde
Linguistics & English Language,
University of Edinburgh
hannah.rohde@ed.ac.uk

Alasdair D. F. Clarke
School of Informatics,
University of Edinburgh
a.clarke@ed.ac.uk

Abstract

We investigate the order of mention for objects in relational descriptions in visual scenes. Existing work in the visual domain focuses on content selection for text generation and relies primarily on templates to generate surface realizations from underlying content choices. In contrast, we seek to clarify the influence of visual perception on the linguistic form (as opposed to the content) of descriptions, modeling the variation in and constraints on the surface orderings in a description. We find previously-unknown effects of the visual characteristics of objects; specifically, when a relational description involves a visually salient object, that object is more likely to be mentioned first. We conduct a detailed analysis of these patterns using logistic regression, and also train and evaluate a classifier. Our methods yield significant improvement in classification accuracy over a naive baseline.

1 Introduction

Visual-world referring expression generation (REG) is the task of instructing a listener how to find an object (the *target*) in a visual scene. In complicated scenes, people often produce relational descriptions, in which the target object is described relative to another (a *landmark*) (Viethen and Dale, 2008). While existing REG systems can generate relational descriptions, they tend to focus on content selection (that is, choosing an appropriate set of landmarks for each object). Surface realization (turning the selected content into a string of words) is handled by simple heuristics, such as sets of templates. Complex descriptions, however, have a non-trivial information structure— objects are not mentioned in an arbitrary order. Numerous studies in non-visual domains show that English speakers favor constructions that place familiar (given) information before unfamiliar (new) (Bresnan et al., 2007; Ward and Birner, 2001; Prince, 1981). We show that this pattern also holds for visual-world referring expressions (REs), and moreover, that objects with sufficient visual prominence are treated as given. Thus, we argue that the concept of salience used in surface realization should incorporate metrics from visual perception.

In this study, we create a model of information ordering in complex relational descriptions. Using a discriminative classifier, we learn to predict the information structuring strategies used in our corpus. We compare these strategies to the typical given/new pattern of English discourse. Experiments on a corpus of descriptions of cartoon people in the childrens' book "Where's Wally" (Handford, 1987), corpus described in (Clarke et al., 2013), show that our approach significantly outperforms a naive baseline, improving especially on prediction of non-canonical orderings.

This study has three main contributions. First, it demonstrates that humans use sophisticated information ordering strategies for REG, and therefore that the template strategies used in previous work do not adequately model human production. Second, it makes a practical proposal for an improved model which is capable of predicting these orderings; while this model is not a full-scale surface realizer, we view it as an important intermediate step towards one. Finally, it makes a theoretical contribution: By linking the information structures observed in the data to the existing re-

Proceedings of the 14th Conference of the European Chapter of the Association for Computational Linguistics, pages 520–529,
Gothenburg, Sweden, April 26-30 2014.

search on salience and information structure, we show that visually prominent objects are treated as part of common ground despite the lack of previous mention.

2 Related work

Computational models of REG (Krahmer and van Deemter, 2012) focus mainly on content selection: Given a list of objects in the scene and their visual attributes, such models decide what information to include in a description so as to specify the target object. Early systems (with the exception of Dale and Haddock (1991)) did not produce relational descriptions. Nor did these systems model the visual salience of the objects or attributes under discussion.

Later models (Kelleher et al., 2005; Kelleher and Kruijff, 2006; Duckham et al., 2010) introduce simple models of visual salience, prompted by psycholinguistic research which shows that objects are more likely to be selected as landmarks when they are easy for an observer to find (Beun and Cremers, 1998). Clarke et al. (2013) extend these results with a more complicated model of visual salience (Torralba et al., 2006). Fang et al. (2013) similarly note that generated REs should avoid information that is perceptually expensive to obtain. However, these results focus on content selection rather than surface realization.

In comparison to selection, surface realization for REG has received little attention. Many researchers do not even perform realization, but simply compare their systems' selected content with the gold standard under metrics like the Dice coefficient. The TUNA challenges (Gatt et al., 2008; Gatt et al., 2009; Gatt and Belz, 2010) are an exception; participants were required to provide surface realizations, which were evaluated via NIST, BLEU and string edit distance. Many participants used a template-based realizer written by Irene Langkilde-Geary, which imposes a fixed ordering on attributes like "size" and "color" but has no provisions for relational descriptions. A few participants created their own realizers. Brugman et al. (2009) describe a system with multiple hand-written templates. Di Fabbrizio et al. (2008) propose several learning-based systems; the most effective were a dependency-based approach which learned precedence relationships between pairs of words, and a template-based approach which learned global orderings over sets of attributes. Neither approach is designed to handle relational descriptions, nor do they incorporate visual information. Duan et al. (2013), also studying the Wally corpus, demonstrates that visual features affect determiner choice for NPs, but do not study information structure.

Several studies give basic principles for information structure in English discourse. Prince (1981) introduces the key distinctions between discourse-old and new entities (previously mentioned vs not mentioned) and hearer-old and new entities (familiar to the listener vs not familiar). Clark and Wilkes-Gibbs (1986) extends the latter distinction to a notion of common ground; entities in the common ground are familiar to both participants in the discourse, and each participant is in turn aware of the other's familiarity. As noted by Prince (1981) and expanded on by Ward and Birner (2001) and in Centering Theory (Grosz et al., 1995), the first element in an English sentence is generally reserved for old information, while new information is usually placed at the end. For instance, see these (contrived) examples:

(1) a. **Obama** adopted **a dog named Bo**.
b. **#A dog named Bo** was adopted by **Obama**.

Ex. (1-a) demonstrates the standard order (under the assumption that *Obama* is familiar to a reader of this paper while *Bo* may not be). (1-b) violates the ordering principles and is likely to be judged less felicitous. Importantly, *Obama* is hearer-old not because of a preceding discourse mention but due to (assumed) general knowledge; it is an *unused* (Prince, 1981), or *existential* (Bean and Riloff, 1999) entity. General knowledge shared by speakers of a community is one way in which an entity enters the common ground. Along with this shared socio-cultural background, speakers may also share physical co-presence and linguistic co-presence (Clark, 1996). They can indicate salient entities, individuals, or entire events by engaging their listener in joint attention via pointing or gaze cueing (Baldwin, 1995; Carpenter et al., 1998); in this paper, we demonstrate that visual prominence is also sufficient.

Maienborn (2001) explicitly suggests that this topic-comment structure principle is the motivation for the frequent appearance of locative modifiers in clause-initial position; however, she gives no felicity conditions on *when* this leftward movement is expected. Since most of the modifiers in this study are locatives, our data should be taken as endorsing this theoretical position, but supplying felicity conditions in terms of common ground.

These principles have been applied to computational surface realization in non-visual domains (Webber, 2004; Nakatsu and White, 2010, and others). Freer-word-order languages such as German also have predictable information structures which have been employed in surface realization systems, but these require a different structural analysis than in English (Zarrieß et al., 2012; Filippova and Strube, 2007).

3 Information structures in our corpus

In this section, we define the particular ordering strategies which we investigate in the rest of the paper. We begin by defining some terms: A relational description includes two objects, the *anchor*, which is the object being located, and the *landmark*, an object which is mentioned to make it easier to locate the anchor. The anchor may be the *target* of the entire expression, or it may in turn serve as a landmark in another relational description (as in "*the man* next to *the horse* next to *the building*" where "horse" serves as both a landmark for "man" and an anchor for "building".[1] The REs in this corpus reflect the variation in the way speakers constructed their descriptions: Some produced multiple complete sentences; others used abbreviated language and compacted their expression into a single sentence or phrase. In this paper we use the term "ordering" to refer to speakers' decisions of whether to precede or postpose a reference to one object relative to their reference to another. In this way, the "syntax" of the description is built out of references to particular objects (the noun phrases) and the relationships between those references. Note that the references may consist of a short phrase ("the man with the sword") or an entire clause ("he is standing and holding a sword")

In our corpus, speakers use three primary strategies to order anchors and landmarks, exemplified by the following REs from our corpus (shown with **bold** for text describing the anchor and *italics* for text for landmarks):

(2) Near the *hut that is burning*, there is a **man holding a lit torch in one hand, and a sword in the other**.

[1]In our examples below, the anchor is the target of the overall expression, i.e., the intended referent in the REG task.

(3) **Man** closest to *the rear tyre of the van*.

(4) There is **a person standing** in *the water* **wearing a blue shirt and yellow hat**

Ex. (2) places the landmark so that it precedes the anchor; Ex. (3) shows the landmark following it. Ex. (4) shows a more complex structure, which we refer to as *interleaved*, where information about the anchor is given in multiple phrases and the landmark phrase appears between them.[2] (These orders are determined with respect to the first mention of the landmark.) We denote these ordering strategies as PRECEDE, FOLLOW and INTER respectively.

We also distinguish between landmarks which are only mentioned in relation to an anchor and those which are first introduced in a non-relative construction such as "look at the X" or "there's an X":

(5) There is *a horse rearing up on its hind legs*. Behind *the horse* is **a man laying down on his back completely flat and straight.**

Since these constructions establish the existence of a landmark without immediately incorporating it into the description, we denote these as ESTABLISH constructions.

Finally, our annotation scheme distinguishes between genuine landmarks (visible objects or groups of objects in the scene) and image *regions* like "the left" or "bottom center":

(6) *Bottom center*, **man looking left**

4 Dataset

We use a collection of referring expressions elicited on Mechanical Turk, previously described in (Clarke et al., 2013).[3] The dataset contains descriptions of targets in 11 images from the childrens' book *Where's Wally*[4] (Handford, 1987; Handford, 1988); in each image, 16 people were designated as targets. Each participant saw each scene only once. An example scene is shown in Figure 1. The participant was instructed to type a description of the person in the red box so that another person viewing the same scene (but without the box) would be able to find them; to make sure

[2]This structure is not *syntactically* discontinuous, but visually it is; if the listener wants to confirm these details visually, they must first look at the person, then look away at the water and then look back at the person.

[3]Via `http://datashare.is.ed.ac.uk/handle/10283/336`

[4]Published in the USA as *Where's Waldo*.

this was clear, as part of the study instructions, they completed a few visual searches based on text descriptions. The image in the figure also contains a black box (not part of the initial stimulus), which the annotator has added to designate the landmark object "burning hut"). The dataset contains 1672 descriptions, contributed by 152 different participants (152 participants $\times$ 11 scenes).

The REs are annotated for visual and linguistic content. The annotation scheme indicates which substrings of the RE describe the target object, another mentioned object or an image region. References to parts or attributes of objects are not treated as separate objects; "a man holding torch and sword" in Figure 1 is a single object. The mentioned objects are linked to bounding boxes (or for very large objects, bounding polygons) in the image.

For each mention of a non-target object, the annotation indicates whether it is part of a relational description of a specific *anchor*, and if so which; if it is not, it receives an ESTABLISH tag. These annotations are used to determine the ordering strategies used in this study. In some cases, the linkage between objects is implicit:

(7) ...there are *4 men smoking*... the man you are looking for is **the one** [=of the 4 men] **leaning against a crate**

In the above RE, *4 men* is first introduced in an ESTABLISH construction. The word "one" refers implicitly to part of this set of men, so the annotator marks a relational link from "4 men" to "one". In our analysis in this study, we treat the entity "crates" as anchored to the target ("one") on the basis of this implicit link (so that this is an instance of the PRECEDE-ESTABLISH pattern), but we do not treat the hidden link itself as a mention or try to predict its nonexistent "position" in the string.

5 Distribution of ordering strategies

We first describe the distribution of these strategies across the corpus as a whole. As shown in Table 1, landmarks are ordered about equally to the FOLLOW or PRECEDE of the objects they help to locate. Regions, on the other hand, prefer the PRECEDE ordering. The INTER ordering is less common, but still quite well-represented. The ESTABLISH construction (initial "there is" or "look at") occurs only with PRECEDE ordering, and indeed can be viewed as a syntactic strategy for achieving such an order. We will explain these characteristic

`The <targ>man</targ> just to the left of the <lmark rel="targ" obj="imgID"> burning hut</lmark> <targ>holding a torch and a sword</targ>.`

Figure 1: Example scene (red box indicates target) with annotated referring expression. Words in `<targ>` tags describe the target. A single landmark (the burning hut, indicated by the `rel` attribute) is mentioned in a relational description whose anchor is the target; the annotator has marked it with a black box.

patterns in linguistic terms in Section 7.

As in most discourse tasks (Ford and Olson, 1975; Pechmann, 2009), speakers display a fair amount of variability. To measure this, we examine each anchor/landmark pair which is mentioned by more than one speaker, and compute how often these speakers use the same strategy. There are 664 such pairs,[5] appearing a total of 2361 times in the corpus.[6] Of these, 66% agree on the directional strategy.[7] Separately, 14% of the expressions use an ESTABLISH construction, and 43% of these are agreed on by the majority. (The remaining variation could in principle have two sources: The content of the expression as a whole could affect the realization of a particular pair of objects, or individual speakers might simply differ in their usage patterns.) Nonetheless, there is a good deal of regularity in speakers' decisions. In the rest of the paper, we attempt to model and predict this regularity.

[5]286 of these pairs are mentioned by exactly two speakers.

[6]This is more than the total number of referring expressions in the corpus, because many of the REs contain multiple pairs of entities.

[7]If strategies were assigned randomly using the overall marginals, we would expect only 34% agreement. Using this method of calculating chance agreement, we would obtain a Cohen's κ of .48.

	PRECEDE	INTER	FOLLOW
Region	60 (440)	21 (160)	19 (138)
L-mark	38 (977)	25 (632)	37 (945)

	ESTABLISH	NON-EST.
PRECEDE landmark	51 (495)	49 (482)

Table 1: Distribution of ordering strategies for all landmarks and regions in the corpus: *% (count)*. An additional 24 landmarks occur with no associated anchor (and therefore no discernible order).

6 Visual and non-visual information

Since visual properties are known to affect landmark selection (Kelleher et al., 2005; Viethen and Dale, 2008), we expect them to influence information structure as well. Our system uses three visual properties to predict information structure; we select properties that are known from previous work to help predict whether a landmark will be mentioned. These properties are the **area of the anchor and landmark**, the **distance** between them (Golland et al., 2010, among others) and their **centrality (centr.)** (distance from the center of the screen) (Kelleher et al., 2005).[8] These properties are all indicators of visual salience (Toet, 2011), the property which makes objects in a scene easy to find quickly (Wolfe, 2012) and tends to draw initial gaze fixations (Itti and Koch, 2000). We also include indicators for whether the anchor is the **target** object, and whether the landmark is an **image region (reg)** (see section 3).

In addition, we give a few non-visual features derived from the content structure. These include the **number of dependents** (landmarks which relate to each object in the description) and the **number of descendants** (the direct dependents, their dependents and so forth). When the speaker has to arrange a large number of landmarks, they tend to vary the ordering more, because of heavy-shift effects (White and Rajkumar, 2012) and the difficulty of preposing more than one constituent.

7 Regression analysis

To gain some insight into the influence of different features, we conduct a logistic regression analysis. For each pair of $(anchor, landmark)$ occurring in a relational description, we attempt to predict the manner of realization (direction and ESTABLISH). We performed a logistic regression for each class (one-vs-all); thus there are four regressors in total, making 0-1 predictions for PRECEDE, PRECEDE-ESTABLISH, INTER and FOLLOW.

Because their distributions are heavily skewed, area is transformed to square root area and distance/centrality values are log-transformed as in Clarke et al. (2013).[9] Features are scaled to zero mean and unit variance. Finally, centrality values are negated so that higher values indicate more central objects; this is for ease of interpretation. We fit models using random intercepts for speaker and image using the LME4 package (Bates et al., 2011), then removed all fixed effects which were never significant for any class and reran the analysis until a minimal model was reached (Crawley, 2007). This minimization removed the number of descendants features (but kept number of direct dependents). Table 2 shows the significant coefficients, standard deviations and Z-scores. (Note that as the regressions are separate, the coefficients are comparable reading down columns, but not across rows).

The regression analysis shows that as landmarks get larger, they are more likely to be realized with the PRECEDE ($\beta = 3.27$) or INTER ($\beta = 1.28$) strategies (but not PRECEDE-ESTABLISH) and less likely ($\beta = -3.76$) to be placed following. (This does not appear to be the case for landmarks that are central; these are slightly more likely to be ordered FOLLOW ($\beta = .81$).) The PRECEDE-ESTABLISH construction is neither favored nor disfavored by landmark area. It does, however, have a strong preference for landmarks with many dependents ($\beta = 2.38$), since these are more naturally realized in the clause-final position introduced by a "There is X"-type construction. In contrast, landmarks with many dependents disfavor the INTER strategy ($\beta = -1.07$), since this would require placing a heavy NP in a central rather than rightward position.

There are also a few effects of visual features of the anchor objects. Larger anchors (which are easier to see in their own right) prefer landmarks to FOLLOW ($\beta = .35$). This presumably reflects the fact that, since the listener is more likely to see them quickly, such anchors are more often re-

[8]Following Clarke et al. (2013), we attempted to also measuring distinctiveness from the background using a perceptual model of visual salience (Torralba et al., 2006). Although this measure is effective in predicting landmark selection, it proves uninformative here for predicting information structure, yielding no significant effects in any analyses.

[9]We use these continuous values in our analysis; our classifier model (below) uses discretized area, distance and centrality.

Feature	PRECEDE	Z	PREC.-EST.	Z	INTER	Z	FOLLOW	Z
intercept	-4.18 $\pm$ .37	-11.2	-2.66 $\pm$ .50	-5.3	-2.51 $\pm$ .32	-7.7	2.72 $\pm$ .32	8.5
anch area	-.27 $\pm$ .06	-4.6	-.19 $\pm$ .09	-2.2	-	-	.35 $\pm$ .05	6.9
anch centr	.11 $\pm$ .05	2.0	-	-	-	-	-	-
anch deps	-	-	-.74 $\pm$ .12	-6.2	.22 $\pm$ .06	3.6	-	-
anch=targ	.30 $\pm$ .13	2.3	-	-	.55 $\pm$ .14	4.0	-.71 $\pm$ .13	-5.7
distance	-	-	-.24 $\pm$ .09	-2.6	-	-	-	-
lmk=reg	11.46 $\pm$ 1.35	8.5	-	-	3.01 $\pm$ 1.19	2.5	-12.62 $\pm$ 1.17	-10.8
lmk area	3.27 $\pm$ .38	8.7	-	-	1.28 $\pm$ .32	4.0	-3.76 $\pm$ .32	-11.7
lmk centr	-	-	-	-	-	-	.81 $\pm$ .32	2.6
lmk deps	-	-	2.38 $\pm$ .14	16.9	-1.07 $\pm$ .13	-8.3	-1.37 $\pm$ .12	-11.5

Table 2: Regression coefficients, standard deviations and Z-scores from one-vs-all logistic regressions with direction/ESTABLISH status as output variable. Only effects significant at $p < .05$ level are shown; other effects are displayed as -.

alized at the start of an expression. (Clarke et al. (2013) show that they have fewer landmarks overall.) Again, the effect of centrality is counterintuitive, but weak ($\beta = .81$). Anchors with more dependents are slightly more likely to use the INTER slot ($\beta = .22$), suggesting that the various dependents are spread syntactically throughout the expression.

Although distance and centrality are weak indicators in this dataset, area shows strong effects which support our conclusion that visual salience behaves like discourse salience. The standard information order of English clauses places given information first and new information later (Prince, 1981). Thus, we observe that the non-right orders are used for larger objects, which is what we would expect if their visual perceptibility is sufficient to place them in common ground despite the lack of a previous mention.[10] On the other hand, the FOLLOW order is used for smaller objects that cannot be assumed to be part of common ground (and are therefore treated as new).

The use of ESTABLISH constructions for mid-sized objects also makes sense on theoretical grounds. ESTABLISH constructions are a way of achieving the PRECEDE information structure, which places the landmark first— and this makes sense primarily if the landmark is reasonably salient, since otherwise it will not be found any faster than the target. On the other hand, most of the constructions we discuss as ESTABLISH, such as existential "there is", require their object to be discourse-new (Ward and Birner, 1995); it would be infelicitous to start a description by stating the existence of something already in the common ground "there is a sky, and it is blue..." Thus, it makes sense that neither large or small objects favor the use of this construction; it can be used to foreground an object which is not salient enough to be assumed in common ground, but *is* salient enough to find without a great deal of visual search.

8 Information structure prediction

In this section, we experiment with an idealized version of the information structuring task. We provide our system with gold standard content selection— we know which objects will be mentioned, and if they serve as landmarks, we know the anchor they describe. However, we do not know which information strategies will be used to order them; our task is to predict this. In doing so, we are working with an idealized version of the standard generation pipeline, which often operates as a two-stage process, with content selection followed by surface realization. Information structure prediction is intermediate between these two stages; once we have decided which objects to mention (or in concert), we would like to decide what order to mention them in.

We set up the prediction task as in the previous section: Given an anchor/landmark pair, our system must decide what direction and ESTABLISH status to assign it. However, here we evaluate the system as a classifier. We treat anchor/landmark pair as independent from the others

[10]Prince (1981) discusses other discourse-new items that are nonetheless treated as familiar, like "The FBI", under the name *unused* (that is, available, but not previously in use in the discourse).

Feat type	# features
type (targ/lmark/region) of anchor	3
type (targ/lmark/region) of dep	3
quartile of anchor area	4
quartile of lmark area	4
quartile of anchor → lmark dist	4
quartile of dist anchor → screen ctr	4
quartile of dist lmark → screen ctr	4
# direct dependents of anchor	6
# descendents of anchor	6

Table 3: Feature templates and number of instantiations in our discriminative system.

(including other pairs from the same description); during development, we investigated a parser-like structured classifier based on (Socher et al., 2011; Salakhutdinov and Hinton, 2009) that jointly classified all the relational descriptions in a single utterance at once, but results did not improve over the classifier system, perhaps because on average the trees are fairly shallow.

8.1 Discriminative comparison

We train a discriminative multilabel classifier using maximum entropy.[11] We predict EST-DIR pairs given a set of discrete features shown in Table 3. This setup differs slightly from the previous section (which used one-vs-all); we are attempting to conform to the standard practices of psycholinguistics and computational linguistics respectively. Area, salience, distance to center and inter-object distance values are discretized by determining in which quartile of the training set each value falls (lowest 25%, mid-low, mid-high, highest 25%). Our initial model used continuous values as in the previous section, but results were somewhat poorer, suggesting some of these features may have nonlinear effects.

8.2 Experiments

We hold out three images (*vikings*, *airport*, *blackandwhite*) as a development set. In test, we exclude these 3 documents and use the other 8 for evaluation. In both development and test, we conduct experiments by crossvalidation, testing on one document at a time and training on the other ten.[12]

We report two trivial baseline strategies, all landmarks following (the best baseline for overall accuracy) and all landmarks preceding (the best baseline for predicting the direction, but not as good overall because the PRECEDE predictions are split between ESTABLISH and not ESTABLISH). Our preliminary analysis shows that regions have a strong tendency to precede their anchors, so we also report results for a baseline using this pattern (regions preceding, everything else following). We believe this baseline pattern is the one which would be learned as a template by previous systems like Di Fabbrizio et al. (2008), since this system can learn relationships between broad types of entities (target, landmark and region) but does not use visual features of the actual entities in the scene to make any finer distinctions.

We also provide two "inter-subject" oracle scores intended to estimate the performance ceiling imposed by human variability. This oracle assigns each anchor/landmark pair the direction and ESTABLISH status assigned by the majority of speakers who mentioned that pair. The "multiple mentions" estimate of agreement is the one mentioned in Section 5; it was based only on pairs mentioned by multiple speakers. The "all" estimate is based on all objects; it is higher because, for pairs mentioned by only one speaker, it is by definition perfect. Our system's use of the number of descendants feature is not captured by this oracle— these features capture information about a particular speaker's content plan beyond their decision to mention a particular pair— but we suspect that the oracle's performance will nonetheless be hard for any practical system to beat.

We report gross accuracy (correctly predicting both DIR and ESTABLISH) for relational pairs (Table 5), and also decompose by direction (Table 4) and ESTABLISH status (Table 6).

The baseline correctly predicts 43% of pairs, implying that this pattern (regions precede, landmarks follow) covers a bit under half the data. The classifier improves this to 52%. When predicting the direction alone, the best baseline (PRECEDE) scores 42%; the classifier scores 57%. All system scores are significantly better than the baseline (sign test on pairs, $p < 0.01$). In predictions of ESTABLISH tags, our result is a 60% f-score, which is indistinguishable from the lower bound

[11] Learned using the Theano neural-network package (Bergstra et al., 2010) and stochastic gradient descent code from `deeplearning.net/tutorial` (Bengio, 2009).

[12] This means we always use 10 of the 11 documents for training, whether in dev or test, but we didn't do error analysis on the training examples. Data size does appear to matter; training on 8 documents at a time and testing on 3 yields poorer results.

System	PRECEDE			INTER			FOLLOW			Dir Acc
	Prec	Rec	F	Prec	Rec	F	Prec	Rec	F	
Follow	0	0	0	0	0	0	32	100	49	32
Precede	44	100	62	0	0	0	0	0	0	44
Regions precede	61	32	42	0	0	0	37	87	52	42
Discr	66	69	68	39	23	29	53	65	58	57
Inter-subj (multiple mentions)	77	61	68	54	62	58	67	76	71	66
Inter-subj (all)	84	75	79	65	69	67	74	83	78	76

Table 4: Direction scores (p/r/f per direction and total pair directions correctly predicted) in 2382 pairs in test set. Overall accuracy differences between system and baselines are significant ($p < .01$).

System	Pair accuracy
Follow	36
Precede	29
Regions precede	43
Discr	52
Inter-subj (mult)	64
Inter-subj (all)	74

Table 5: Gross accuracy (%) for 2382 test pairs.

System	ESTABLISH		
	Prec	Rec	F
Follow	0	0	0
Precede	0	0	0
Regions precede	0	0	0
Discr	55	67	60
Inter-subj (mult)	68	43	53
Inter-subj (all)	82	66	73

Table 6: ESTABLISH scores (p/r/f for EST=TRUE) in 2382 pairs in test set.

estimate of interannotator agreement.

9 Conclusions

The results of this study show that the information structure of relational descriptions is highly variable, and depends on notions of salience and common ground that are difficult to capture with templates or simple case-based rules. This suggests that the question of realization for visual-word referring expressions may need to be reopened. A data-driven approach not only allows better prediction of which strategy will be used (reducing error by 9% absolute, 16% relative) but also enables us to analyze the pattern and conclude that the visual salience of an object acts in the same way as discourse salience.

Several open questions remain. One is the failure of the Torralba et al. (2006) visual distinctiveness model to make any difference: Is this actually a perceptual fact, or does it merely demonstrate that the model is not as predictive of human attentional patterns as we would like? More important is the question of what lies behind the substantial variations we observe across individuals. These may reflect truly different strategies; for instance, some speakers may generate REs incrementally as they scan the image (Pechmann, 2009) while others perform a more complete scan before beginning (Gatt et al., 2012). We suspect answering this question is beyond the scope of corpus studies, and intend to investigate via psycholinguistic experiments using an eyetracker.

Another question is to what extend the patterns we observe are intended to facilitate listeners' visual search (an audience design hypothesis) versus speakers' efficient construction of utterances. This study focused on predicting speaker behavior, while acknowledging that the utterances speakers produce are not always optimal for listeners (Belz and Gatt, 2008). However, we suspect that in this case, putting easy-to-see objects early really does help listeners; we are currently planning perception experiments to test this hypothesis.

Finally, we intend to incorporate the visual features used in this study into a full-scale realization system. This will enable us to create more human-like REs for visual domains. Such REs can be incorporated into natural language systems for a variety of interactive visual-world tasks.

Acknowledgements

The third author was supported by EPSRC grant EP/H050442/1 and ERC grant 203427 "Synchronous Linguistic and Visual Processing". We also thank Marie-Catherine de Marneffe, Craige Roberts, the OSU Pragmatics group and our anonymous reviewers for their helpful comments.

References

D. A. Baldwin. 1995. Understanding the link between joint attention and language. In *Joint attention: its origins and role in development*. Lawrence Erlbaum Assoc., Hillsdale, NJ.

D. Bates, M. Maechler, and B. Bolker. 2011. lme4: Linear mixed-effects models using s4 classes. Comprehensive R Archive Network: `cran.r-project.org`.

David L. Bean and Ellen Riloff. 1999. Corpus-based identification of non-anaphoric noun phrases. In *Proceedings of the 37th annual meeting of the Association for Computational Linguistics (ACL'99)*, pages 373–380, Morristown, NJ, USA. Association for Computational Linguistics.

Anja Belz and Albert Gatt. 2008. Intrinsic vs. extrinsic evaluation measures for referring expression generation. In *Proceedings of the 46th Annual Meeting of the Association for Computational Linguistics on Human Language Technologies: Short Papers*, pages 197–200. Association for Computational Linguistics.

Yoshua Bengio. 2009. Learning deep architectures for AI. *Foundations and Trends in Machine Learning*, 2(1):1–127. Also published as a book. Now Publishers, 2009.

James Bergstra, Olivier Breuleux, Frédéric Bastien, Pascal Lamblin, Razvan Pascanu, Guillaume Desjardins, Joseph Turian, David Warde-Farley, and Yoshua Bengio. 2010. Theano: a CPU and GPU math expression compiler. In *Proceedings of the Python for Scientific Computing Conference (SciPy)*, June. Oral Presentation.

Robbert-Jan Beun and Anita H.M. Cremers. 1998. Object reference in a shared domain of conversation. *Pragmatics and Cognition*, 6(1-2):121–152.

Joan Bresnan, Anna Cueni, Tatiana Nikitina, and R. Harald Baayen. 2007. Predicting the dative alternation. *Cognitive Foundations of Interpretation*, pages 69–94.

Ivo Brugman, Mariët Theune, Emiel Krahmer, and Jette Viethen. 2009. Realizing the costs: template-based surface realisation in the graph approach to referring expression generation. In *Proceedings of the 12th European Workshop on Natural Language Generation*, ENLG '09, pages 183–184, Stroudsburg, PA, USA. Association for Computational Linguistics.

M. Carpenter, K. Nagell, and M. Tomasello. 1998. Social cognition, joint attention, and communicative competence from 9 to 15 months of age. *Monographs of the Society for Research in Child Development*, 63(4).

Herbert H. Clark and Deanna Wilkes-Gibbs. 1986. Referring as a collaborative process. *Cognition*, 22(1):1–39.

Herbert H. Clark. 1996. *Using language*. Cambridge University Press, Cambridge.

Alasdair D. F. Clarke, Micha Elsner, and Hannah Rohde. 2013. Where's Wally: The influence of visual salience on referring expression generation. *Frontiers in Psychology (Perception Science)*, Issue on Scene Understanding: Behavioral and computational perspectives.

Michael Crawley. 2007. *The R Book*. Wiley-Blackwell, Hoboken, NJ.

Robert Dale and Nicholas J. Haddock. 1991. Generating referring expressions involving relations. In *EACL*, pages 161–166.

Giuseppe Di Fabbrizio, Amanda J. Stent, and Srinivas Bangalore. 2008. Referring expression generation using speaker-based attribute selection and trainable realization (ATTR). In *Proceedings of the 5th International Conference on Natural Language Generation (INLG)*, Salt Fork, OH.

Manjuan Duan, Micha Elsner, and Marie-Catherine de Marneffe. 2013. Visual and linguistic predictors for the definiteness of referring expressions. In *Proceedings of the 17th Workshop on the Semantics and Pragmatics of Dialogue (SemDial)*, Amsterdam.

Matt Duckham, Stephan Winter, and Michelle Robinson. 2010. Including landmarks in routing instructions. *Journal of Location Based Services*, 4(1):28–52.

Rui Fang, Changsong Liu, Lanbo She, and Joyce Y. Chai. 2013. Towards situated dialogue: Revisiting referring expression generation. In *Proceedings of the 2013 Conference on Empirical Methods in Natural Language Processing*, pages 392–402, Seattle, Washington, USA, October. Association for Computational Linguistics.

Katja Filippova and Michael Strube. 2007. Generating constituent order in German clauses. In *Proceedings of the 45th Annual Meeting of the Association of Computational Linguistics*, pages 320–327, Prague, Czech Republic, June. Association for Computational Linguistics.

William Ford and David Olson. 1975. The elaboration of the noun phrase in children's description of objects. *Journal of Experimental Child Psychology*, 19:371–382.

Albert Gatt and Anja Belz. 2010. Introducing shared task evaluation to NLG: The TUNA shared task evaluation challenges. In E. Krahmer and M. Theune, editors, *Empirical Methods in Natural Language Generation*. Springer, Berlin and Heidelberg.

Albert Gatt, Anja Belz, and Eric Kow. 2008. The TUNA-REG challenge 2008: Overview and evaluation results. In *Proceedings of the 5th International Conference on Natural Language Generation (INLG)*, Salt Fork, OH.

Albert Gatt, Anja Belz, and Eric Kow. 2009. The TUNA-REG challenge 2009: Overview and evaluation results. In *Proceedings of the 12th European Workshop on Natural Language Generation (ENLG)*, Athens.

A. Gatt, E. Krahmer, R. P. G. van Gompel, and K. van Deemter. 2012. Does domain size impact speech onset time during reference production? In *Proceedings of the 34th Annual Meeting of the Cognitive Science Society*, pages 1584–1589, Sapporo, Japan.

Dave Golland, Percy Liang, and Dan Klein. 2010. A game-theoretic approach to generating spatial descriptions. In *Proceedings of the 2010 Conference on Empirical Methods in Natural Language Processing*, pages 410–419, Cambridge, MA, October. Association for Computational Linguistics.

Barbara J. Grosz, Aravind K. Joshi, and Scott Weinstein. 1995. Centering: A framework for modeling the local coherence of discourse. *Computational Linguistics*, 21(2):203–225.

M. Handford. 1987. *Where's Wally?* Walker Books, London, 3 edition.

M. Handford. 1988. *Where's Wally Now?* Walker Books, London, 4 edition.

L. Itti and C. Koch. 2000. A saliency-based search mechanism for overt and covert shifts of visual attention. *Vision research*, 40(10-12):1489–1506.

John D. Kelleher and Geert-Jan M. Kruijff. 2006. Incremental generation of spatial referring expressions in situated dialog. In *ACL*.

J. Kelleher, F. Costello, and J. van Genabith. 2005. Dynamically structuring, updating and interrelating representations of visual and linguistic discourse context. *Artificial Intelligence*, 167(12):62 – 102. Connecting Language to the World.

Emiel Krahmer and Kees van Deemter. 2012. Computational generation of referring expressions: A survey. *Computational Linguistics*, 38(1):173–218, March.

Claudia Maienborn. 2001. On the position and interpretation of locative modifiers. *Natural Language Semantics*, 9(2):191–240.

Crystal Nakatsu and Michael White. 2010. Generating with discourse combinatory categorial grammar. *Linguistic Issues in Language Technology*, 4(1).

T. Pechmann. 2009. Incremental speech production and referential overspecification. *Linguistics*, 27(1):89–110.

Ellen Prince. 1981. Toward a taxonomy of given-new information. In Peter Cole, editor, *Radical Pragmatics*, pages 223–255. Academic Press, New York.

Ruslan Salakhutdinov and Geoffrey Hinton. 2009. Replicated softmax: an undirected topic model. In Y. Bengio, D. Schuurmans, J. Lafferty, C. K. I. Williams, and A. Culotta, editors, *Advances in Neural Information Processing Systems 22*, pages 1607–1614.

Richard Socher, Cliff C. Lin, Andrew Y. Ng, and Christopher D. Manning. 2011. Parsing natural scenes and natural language with recursive neural networks. In *Proceedings of the 26th International Conference on Machine Learning (ICML)*.

A. Toet. 2011. Computational versus psychophysical bottom-up image saliency: A comparative evaluation study. *Pattern Analysis and Machine Intelligence, IEEE Transactions on*, 33(11):2131 –2146.

A. Torralba, A. Oliva, M. Castelhano, and J. M. Henderson. 2006. Contextual guidance of attention in natural scenes: The role of global features on object search. *Psychological Review*, 113:766–786.

Jette Viethen and Robert Dale. 2008. The use of spatial relations in referring expressions. In *Proceedings of the 5th International Conference on Natural Language Generation*, Salt Fork, Ohio, USA.

Gregory Ward and Betty Birner. 1995. Definiteness and the English existential. *Language*, 71(4):722–742, December.

Gregory Ward and Betty Birner. 2001. Discourse and information structure. In Deborah Schiffrin, Deborah Tannen, and Heidi Hamilton, editors, *Handbook of discourse analysis*, pages 119–137. Basil Blackwell, Oxford.

Bonnie L. Webber. 2004. D-ltag: extending lexicalized tag to discourse. *Cognitive Science*, 28(5):751–779.

Michael White and Rajakrishnan Rajkumar. 2012. Minimal dependency length in realization ranking. In *Proceedings of the 2012 Joint Conference on Empirical Methods in Natural Language Processing and Computational Natural Language Learning*, pages 244–255, Jeju Island, Korea, July. Association for Computational Linguistics.

Jeremy M. Wolfe. 2012. Visual search. In P. Todd, T. Holls, and T. Robbins, editors, *Cognitive Search: Evolution, Algorithms and the Brain*, pages 159 – 175. MIT Press, Cambridge, MA, USA.

Sina Zarrieß, Aoife Cahill, and Jonas Kuhn. 2012. To what extent does sentence-internal realisation reflect discourse context? a study on word order. In *Proceedings of the 13th Conference of the European Chapter of the Association for Computational Linguistics*, pages 767–776, Avignon, France, April. Association for Computational Linguistics.

Machine Reading Tea Leaves: Automatically Evaluating Topic Coherence and Topic Model Quality

Jey Han Lau
Dept of Philosophy
King's College London
jeyhan.lau@gmail.com

David Newman
Google
dnewman@google.com

Timothy Baldwin
Dept of Computing and
Information Systems
The University of Melbourne
tb@ldwin.net

Abstract

Topic models based on latent Dirichlet allocation and related methods are used in a range of user-focused tasks including document navigation and trend analysis, but evaluation of the intrinsic quality of the topic model and topics remains an open research area. In this work, we explore the two tasks of automatic evaluation of single topics and automatic evaluation of whole topic models, and provide recommendations on the best strategy for performing the two tasks, in addition to providing an open-source toolkit for topic and topic model evaluation.

1 Introduction

Topic modelling based on Latent Dirichlet Allocation (LDA: Blei et al. (2003)) and related methods is increasingly being used in user-focused tasks, in contexts such as the evaluation of scientific impact (McCallum et al., 2006; Hall et al., 2008), trend analysis (Bolelli et al., 2009; Lau et al., 2012a) and document search (Wang et al., 2007). The LDA model is based on the assumption that document collections have latent topics, in the form of a multinomial distribution of words, which is typically presented to users via its top-N highest-probability words. In NLP, topic models are generally used as a means of preprocessing a document collection, and the topics and per-document topic allocations are fed into downstream applications such as document summarisation (Haghighi and Vanderwende, 2009), novel word sense detection methods (Lau et al., 2012b) and machine translation (Zhao and Xing, 2007). In fields such as the digital humanities, on the other hand, human users interact directly with the output of topic models. It is this context of topic modelling for direct human consumption that we target in this paper.

The topics produced by topic models have a varying degree of human-interpretability. To illustrate this, we present two topics automatically learnt from a collection of news articles:

1. ⟨*farmers, farm, food, rice, agriculture*⟩

2. ⟨*stories, undated, receive, scheduled, clients*⟩

The first topic is clearly related to agriculture. The subject of the second topic, however, is less clear, and may confuse users if presented to them as part of a larger topic model. Measuring the human-interpretability of topics and the overall topic model is the core topic of this paper.

Various methodologies have been proposed for measuring the semantic interpretability of topics. In Chang et al. (2009), the authors proposed an indirect approach based on word intrusion, where "intruder words" are randomly injected into topics and human users are asked to identify the intruder words. The word intrusion task builds on the assumption that the intruder words are more identifiable in coherent topics than in incoherent topics, and thus the interpretability of a topic can be estimated by measuring how readily the intruder words can be manually identified by annotators.

Since its inception, the method of Chang et al. (2009) has been used variously as a means of assessing topic models (Paul and Girju, 2010; Reisinger et al., 2010; Hall et al., 2012). Despite its wide acceptance, the method relies on manual annotation and has never been automated. This is one of the primary contributions of this work: the demonstration that we can automate the method of Chang et al. (2009) at near-human levels of accuracy, as a result of which we can perform automatic evaluation of the human-interpretability of topics, as well as topic models.

There has been prior work to directly estimate the human-interpretability of topics through automatic means. For example, Newman et al.

Proceedings of the 14th Conference of the European Chapter of the Association for Computational Linguistics, pages 530–539,
Gothenburg, Sweden, April 26-30 2014.

(2010) introduced the notion of topic "coherence", and proposed an automatic method for estimating topic coherence based on pairwise pointwise mutual information (PMI) between the topic words. Mimno et al. (2011) similarly introduced a methodology for computing coherence, replacing PMI with log conditional probability. Musat et al. (2011) incorporated the WordNet hierarchy to capture the relevance of topics, and in Aletras and Stevenson (2013a), the authors proposed the use of distributional similarity for computing the pairwise association of the topic words. One application of these methods has been to remove incoherent topics before generating labels for topics (Lau et al., 2011; Aletras and Stevenson, 2013b).

Ultimately, all these methodologies, and also the word intrusion approach, attempt to assess the same quality: the human-interpretability of topics. The relationship between these methodologies, however, is poorly understood, and there is no consensus on what is the best approach for computing the semantic interpretability of topic models. This is a second contribution of this paper: we perform a systematic empirical comparison of the different methods and find appreciable differences between them. We further go on to propose an improved formulation of Newman et al. (2010) based on normalised PMI. Finally, we release a toolkit which implements the topic interpretability measures described in this paper.

2 Related Work

Chang et al. (2009) challenged the conventional wisdom that held-out likelihood — often computed as the perplexity of test data or unseen documents — is the only way to evaluate topic models. To measure the human-interpretability of topics, the authors proposed a word intrusion task and conducted experiments using three topic models: Latent Dirichlet Allocation (LDA: Blei et al. (2003)), Probabilistic Latent Semantic Indexing (PLSI: Hofmann (1999)) and the Correlated Topic Model (CTM: Blei and Lafferty (2005)). Contrary to expectation, they found that perplexity correlates negatively with topic interpretability.

In the word intrusion task, each topic is presented as a list of six words — the five most probable topic words and a randomly-selected "intruder word", which has low probability in the topic of interest, but high probability in other topics — and human users are asked to identify the intruder word that does not belong to the topic in question.

Newman et al. (2010) capture topic interpretability using a more direct approach, by asking human users to rate topics (represented by their top-10 topic words) on a 3-point scale based on how coherent the topic words are (i.e. their observed coherence). They proposed several ways of automating the estimation of the observed coherence, and ultimately found that a simple method based on PMI term co-occurrence within a sliding context window over English Wikipedia produces the consistently best result, nearing levels of inter-annotator agreement over topics learnt from two distinct document collections.

Mimno et al. (2011) proposed a closely-related method for evaluating semantic coherence, replacing PMI with log conditional probability. Rather than using Wikipedia for sampling the word co-occurrence counts, Mimno et al. (2011) used the topic-modelled documents, and found that their measure correlates well with human judgements of observed coherence (where topics were rated in the same manner as Newman et al. (2010), based on a 3-point ordinal scale). To incorporate the evaluation of semantic coherence into the topic model, the authors proposed to record words that co-occur together frequently, and update the counts of all associated words before and after the sampling of a new topic assignment in the Gibbs sampler. This variant of topic model was shown to produce more coherent topics than LDA based on the log conditional probability coherence measure.

Aletras and Stevenson (2013a) introduced distributional semantic similarity methods for computing coherence, calculating the distributional similarity between semantic vectors for the top-N topic words using a range of distributional similarity measures such as cosine similarity and the Dice coefficient. To construct the semantic vector space for the topic words, they used English Wikipedia as the reference corpus, and collected words that co-occur in a window of ± 5 words. They showed that their method correlates well with the observed coherence rated by human judges.

3 Dataset

As one of the primary foci of this paper is the automation of the intruder word task of Chang et al. (2009), our primary dataset is that used in the original paper by Chang et al. (2009), which provides topics and human annotations for a range of domains and topic model types. In the dataset, two text collections were used: (1) 10,000 articles from English Wikipedia (WIKI); and (2) 8,447 articles from the New York Times dating from 1987 to 2007 (NEWS). For each document collection, topics were generated by three topic modelling methods: LDA, PLSI and CTM (see Section 2). For each topic model, three settings of T (the number of topics) were used: $T = 50$, $T = 100$ and $T = 150$. In total, there were 9 topic models (3 models $\times$ 3 T) and 900 topics (3 models $\times$ $(50 + 100 + 150)$) for each dataset.[1]

For some of topic interpretability estimation methods, we require a reference corpus to sample lexical probabilities. We use two reference corpora: (1) NEWS-FULL, which contains 1.2 million New York Times articles from 1994 to 2004 (from the English Gigaword); and (2) WIKI-FULL, which contains 3.3 million English Wikipedia articles (retrieved November 28th 2009).[2] The rationale for choosing the New York Times and English Wikipedia as the reference corpora is to ensure domain consistency with the word intrusion dataset; the full collections are used to more robustly estimate lexical probabilities.

4 Human-Interpretability at the Model Level

In this section, we evaluate measures for estimating human-interpretability at the *model* level. That is, for a measure — human-judged or automated — we first aggregate its coherence/interpretability scores for all topics from a given topic model to obtain the topic model's average coherence score. We then calculate the Pearson correlation coefficients between the two measures using the topic models' average coherence scores. In summary, the correlation is computed over nine sets of topics (3 topic modellers $\times$ 3 settings of T) for each of WIKI and NEWS.

4.1 Indirect Approach: Word Intrusion

The word intrusion task measures topic interpretability indirectly, by computing the fraction of annotators who successfully identify the intruder word. A limitation of the word intrusion task is that it requires human annotations, therefore preventing large-scale evaluation. We begin by proposing a methodology to fully automate the word intrusion task.

Lau et al. (2010) proposed a methodology that learns the *most representative* or *best* topic word that summarises the semantics of the topic. Observing that the word intrusion task — the task of detecting the *least representative* word — is the converse of the best topic word selection task, we adapt their methodology to automatically identify the intruder word for the word intrusion task, based on the knowledge that there is a unique intruder word per topic.

The methodology works as follows: given a set of topics (including intruder words), we compute the word association features for each of the top-N topic words of a topic,[3] and combine the features in a ranking support vector regression model (SVM^{rank}: Joachims (2006)) to learn the intruder words. Following Lau et al. (2010), we use three word association measures:

$$\text{PMI}(w_i) = \sum_{j}^{N-1} \log \frac{P(w_i, w_j)}{P(w_i)P(w_j)}$$

$$\text{CP1}(w_i) = \sum_{j}^{N-1} \frac{P(w_i, w_j)}{P(w_j)}$$

$$\text{CP2}(w_i) = \sum_{j}^{N-1} \frac{P(w_i, w_j)}{P(w_i)}$$

We additionally experiment with normalised pointwise mutual information (NPMI: Bouma (2009)):

$$\text{NPMI}(w_i) = \sum_{j}^{N-1} \frac{\log \frac{P(w_i, w_j)}{P(w_i)P(w_j)}}{-\log P(w_i, w_j)}$$

In the dataset of Chang et al. (2009) (see Section 3), each topic was presented to 8 annotators, with small variations in the displayed topic words (including the intruder word) for each annotator. That is, each topic has essentially 8 subtly different representations. To measure topic interpretability, the authors defined "model precision": the relative success of human annotators at identifying the intruder word, across all representations of the different topics. The model precision scores produced by human judges are henceforth referred to as WI-Human, and the scores produced by our

[1] In the WIKI topics there were corrupted symbols in the topic words for 24 topics. We removed these topics, reducing the total number of topics to 876.

[2] For both corpora we perform tokenisation and POS tagging using OpenNLP and lemmatisation using Morpha (Minnen et al., 2001).

[3] N is the number of topic words displayed to the human users in the word intrusion task, including the intruder word.

Topic Domain	Ref. Corpus	Pearson's r with WI-Human	
		WI-Auto-PMI	WI-Auto-NPMI
WIKI	WIKI-FULL	0.947	0.936
	NEWS-FULL	0.801	0.835
NEWS	NEWS-FULL	0.913	0.831
	WIKI-FULL	0.811	0.750

Table 1: Pearson correlation of WI-Human and WI-Auto-PMI/WI-Auto-NPMI at the model level.

automated method for the PMI and NPMI variants as WI-Auto-PMI and WI-Auto-NPMI respectively.[4]

The Pearson correlation coefficients between WI-Human and WI-Auto-PMI/WI-Auto-NPMI at the model level are presented in Table 1. Note that our two reference corpora are used to independently sample the lexical probabilities for the word association features.

We see very strong correlation for in-domain pairings (i.e. WIKI+WIKI-FULL and NEWS+NEWS-FULL), achieving $r > 0.9$ in most cases for both WI-Auto-PMI or WI-Auto-NPMI, demonstrating the effectiveness of our methodology at automating the word intrusion task for estimating human-interpretability at the model level. Overall, WI-Auto-PMI outperforms WI-Auto-NPMI.

Note that although our proposed methodology is supervised, as intruder words are synthetically generated and no annotation is needed for the supervised learning, the whole process of computing topic coherence via word intrusion is fully automatic, without the need for hand-labelled training data.

4.2 Direct Approach: Observed Coherence

Newman et al. (2010) defined topic interpretability based on a more direct approach, by asking human judges to rate topics based on the observed coherence of the top-N topic words, and various methodologies have since been proposed to automate the computation of the observed coherence. In this section, we present all these methods and compare them.

The word intrusion dataset is not annotated with human ratings of observed coherence. To create gold-standard coherence judgements, we used Amazon Mechanical Turk:[5] we presented the topics (with intruder words removed) to the Turkers and asked them to rate the topics using on a 3-point ordinal scale, following Newman et al. (2010). In total, we collected six to fourteen annotations per topic (an average of 8.4 annotations per topic). The observed coherence of a topic is computed as the arithmetic mean of the annotators' ratings, once again following Newman et al. (2010). The human-judged observed topic coherence is henceforth referred to as OC-Human.

For the automated methods, we experimented with the following methods for estimating the human-interpretability of a topic t:

1. **OC-Auto-PMI:** Pairwise PMI of top-N topic words (Newman et al., 2010):
$$\text{OC-Auto-PMI}(\mathbf{t}) = \sum_{j=2}^{N}\sum_{i=1}^{j-1} \log \frac{P(w_j, w_i)}{P(w_i)P(w_j)}$$
2. **OC-Auto-NPMI:** NPMI variant of OC-Auto-PMI:
$$\text{OC-Auto-NPMI}(\mathbf{t}) = \sum_{j=2}^{N}\sum_{i=1}^{j-1} \frac{\log \frac{P(w_j,w_i)}{P(w_i)P(w_j)}}{-\log P(w_i, w_j)}$$
3. **OC-Auto-LCP:** Pairwise log conditional probability of top-N topic words (Mimno et al., 2011):[6]
$$\text{OC-Auto-LCP}(\mathbf{t}) = \sum_{j=2}^{N}\sum_{i=1}^{j-1} \log \frac{P(w_j, w_i)}{P(w_i)}$$
4. **OC-Auto-DS:** Pairwise distributional similarity of the top-N topic words, as described in Aletras and Stevenson (2013a).

For OC-Auto-PMI, OC-Auto-NPMI and OC-Auto-LCP, all topics are lemmatised and intruder words are removed before coherence is computed.[7] In-domain and cross-domain pairings of

[4] Note that both variants use CP1 and CP2 features, i.e. WI-Auto-PMI uses PMI+CP1+C2 while WI-Auto-NPMI uses NPMI+CP1+C2 features.

[5] `https://www.mturk.com/mturk/`

[6] Although the original method uses the topic-modelled document collection and document co-occurrence for sampling word counts, for a fairer comparison we use log conditional probability only as a replacement to the PMI component of the coherence computation (i.e. words are still sampled using a reference corpus and a sliding window). For additional evidence that the original method performs at a subpar level, see Lau et al. (2013) and Aletras and Stevenson (2013a).

[7] We once again use Morpha to do the lemmatisation, and determine POS via the majority POS for a given word, aggregated over all its occurrences in English Wikipedia.

Topic Domain	Ref. Corpus	Pearson's r with OC-Human			
		OC-Auto-PMI	OC-Auto-NPMI	OC-Auto-LCP	OC-Auto-DS
WIKI	WIKI-FULL	0.490	0.903	0.959	0.859
	NEWS-FULL	0.696	0.844	0.913	
NEWS	NEWS-FULL	0.965	0.979	0.887	0.941
	WIKI-FULL	0.931	0.964	0.872	

Table 2: Pearson correlation of OC-Human and the automated methods — OC-Auto-PMI, OC-Auto-NPMI, OC-Auto-LCP and OC-Auto-DS — at the model level.

the topic domain and reference corpus are experimented with for these measures.

For OC-Auto-DS, all topics are lemmatised, intruder words are removed and English Wikipedia is used to generate the vector space for the topic words. The size of the context window is set to ± 5 word (i.e. 5 words to either side of the target word). We use PMI to weight the vectors, cosine similarity for measuring the distributional similarity between the top-N topic words, and the "Topic Word Space" approach to reduce the dimensionality of the vector space. A complete description of the parameters can be found in Aletras and Stevenson (2013a). Note that cross-domain pairings of the topic domain and reference corpus are not tested: in line with the original paper, we use only English Wikipedia to generate the vector space before distributional similarity.

We present the Pearson correlation coefficient of OC-Human and the four automated methods at the model level in Table 2. For OC-Auto-NPMI, OC-Auto-LCP and OC-Auto-DS, we see that they correlate strongly with the human-judged coherence. Overall, OC-Auto-NPMI has the best performance among the methods, and in-domain pairings generally produce the best results for OC-Auto-NPMI and OC-Auto-LCP. The results are comparable to those for the automated intruder word detection method in Section 4.1.

The non-normalised variant OC-Auto-PMI correlates well for NEWS but performs poorly for WIKI, producing a correlation of only 0.490 for the in-domain pairing. We revisit this in Section 6, and provide a qualitative analysis to explain the discrepancy in results between OC-Auto-PMI and OC-Auto-NPMI.

4.3 Word Intrusion vs. Observed Coherence

In the previous sections, we showed for both the direct and indirect approaches that the automated methods correlate strongly with the manually-annotated human-interpretability of topics at the model level (with the exception of OC-Auto-PMI). One question that remains unanswered, however, is whether word intrusion measures topic interpretability differently to observed coherence. This is the focus of this section.

From the results in Table 3 for the intruder word model vs. observed coherence, we see a strong correlation between WI-Human and OC-Human. This observation is insightful: it shows that the topic interpretability estimated by the two approaches is almost identical at the model level.

Between WI-Human and the observed coherence methods automated methods, overall we see a strong correlation for the OC-Auto-NPMI, OC-Auto-LCP and OC-Auto-DS methods. OC-Auto-PMI once again performs poorly over WIKI, but this is unsurprising given its previous results (i.e. its poor correlation with OC-Human). In-domain pairings tend to perform better, and the performance of OC-Auto-NPMI, OC-Auto-LCP and OC-Auto-DS is comparable, with no one clearly best method.

5 Human-Interpretability at the Topic Level

In this section, we evaluate the various methods at the *topic* level. We group together all topics for each dataset (without distinguishing the topic models that produce them) and calculate the correlation of one measure against another. That is, the correlation coefficient is computed for 900 topics/data points in the case of each of WIKI and NEWS.

5.1 Indirect Approach: Word Intrusion

In Section 4.1, we proposed a novel methodology to automate the word intrusion task (WI-Auto-PMI and WI-Auto-NPMI). We now evaluate its performance at the topic level, and present its correlation with the human gold standard (WI-Human) in Table 4.

The correlation of WI-Human and WI-Auto-PMI/WI-Auto-NPMI at the topic level is considerably worse, compared to its results at the model

Topic Domain	Ref. Corpus	Pearson's r with WI-Human				
		OC-Human	OC-Auto-PMI	OC-Auto-NPMI	OC-Auto-LCP	OC-Auto-DS
WIKI	WIKI-FULL	0.900	0.638	0.927	0.911	0.907
	NEWS-FULL		0.614	0.757	0.821	
NEWS	NEWS-FULL	0.915	0.865	0.866	0.867	0.925
	WIKI-FULL		0.838	0.874	0.893	

Table 3: Word intrusion vs. observed coherence: Pearson correlation coefficient at the model level.

Topic Domain	Ref. Corpus	Pearson's r with WI-Human		Human Agreement
		WI-Auto-PMI	WI-Auto-NPMI	
WIKI	WIKI-FULL	0.554	0.573	0.735
	NEWS-FULL	0.622	0.592	
NEWS	NEWS-FULL	0.602	0.612	0.770
	WIKI-FULL	0.638	0.648	

Table 4: Pearson correlation coefficient of WI-Human and WI-Auto-PMI/WI-Auto-NPMI at the topic level.

level (Table 1). The performance between WI-Auto-PMI and WI-Auto-NPMI is not very different, and the cross-domain pairing slightly outperforms the in-domain pairing.

To better understand the difficulty of the task, we compute the agreement between human annotators by calculating the Pearson correlation coefficient of model precisions produced by randomised sub-group pairs in the topics.[8] That is, for each topic, we randomly split the annotations into two sub-groups, and compute the Pearson correlation coefficient of the model precisions produced by the first sub-group and that of the second sub-group.

The original dataset has 8 annotations per topic. Splitting the annotations into two sub-groups reduces the number of annotations to 4 per group, which is not ideal for computing model precision. We thus chose to expand the number of annotations by sampling 300 random topics from each domain (for a total of 600 topics) and following the same process as Chang et al. (2009) to get intruder word annotations using Amazon Mechanical Turk. On average, we obtained 11.7 *additional* annotations per topic for these 600 topics. The human agreement scores (i.e. the Pearson correlation coefficient of randomised sub-group pairs) for the sampled 600 topics are presented in the last column of Table 4.

The sub-group correlation is around $r = 0.75$ for the topics from both datasets. As such, estimating topic interpretability at the topic level is a much harder task than model-level evaluation. Our automated methods perform at a highly credible $r = 0.6$, but there is certainly room for improvement. Note that the correlation values reported in Newman et al. (2010) are markedly higher than ours, as they evaluated based on Spearman rank correlation, which isn't attuned to the relative differences in coherence values and returns higher values for the task.

[8]To counter for the fact that annotators labelled varying numbers of topics.

5.2 Direct Approach: Observed Coherence

We repeat the experiments of observed coherence in Section 4.2, and evaluate the correlation of the automated methods (OC-Auto-PMI, OC-Auto-NPMI, OC-Auto-LCP and OC-Auto-DS) on the human gold standard (OC-Human) at the topic level. Results are summarised in Table 5.

OC-Auto-PMI performs poorly at the topic level in the WIKI domain, similar to what was seen at the model level in Section 4.2. Overall, both OC-Auto-NPMI and OC-Auto-DS are the most consistent methods. OC-Auto-LCP performs markedly worse than these two methods.

To get a better understanding of how well human annotators perform at the task, we compute the one-vs-rest Pearson correlation coefficient using the gold standard annotations. That is, for each topic, we single out each rating/annotation and compare it to the average of all other ratings/annotations. The one-vs-rest correlation result is displayed in the last column (titled "Human Agreement") in Table 5. The best automated methods surpass the single-annotator performance, indicating that they are able to perform the task as well as human annotators (unlike the topic-level results for the word intrusion task where humans were markedly better at the task than the automated methods).

Topic Domain	Ref. Corpus	Pearson's r with OC-Human				Human Agreement
		OC-Auto-PMI	OC-Auto-NPMI	OC-Auto-LCP	OC-Auto-DS	
WIKI	WIKI-FULL	0.533	0.638	0.579	0.682	0.624
	NEWS-FULL	0.582	0.667	0.496		
NEWS	NEWS-FULL	0.719	0.741	0.471	0.682	0.634
	WIKI-FULL	0.671	0.722	0.452		

Table 5: Pearson correlation of OC-Human and the automated methods at the topic level.

Topic Domain	Ref. Corpus	Pearson's r with WI-Human				
		OC-Human	OC-Auto-PMI	OC-Auto-NPMI	OC-Auto-LCP	OC-Auto-DS
WIKI	WIKI-FULL	0.665	0.472	0.557	0.547	0.639
	NEWS-FULL		0.504	0.571	0.455	
NEWS	NEWS-FULL	0.641	0.629	0.634	0.407	0.649
	WIKI-FULL		0.604	0.633	0.390	

Table 6: Word intrusion vs. observed coherence: pearson correlation results at the topic level.

5.3 Word Intrusion vs. Observed Coherence

In this section, we bring together the indirect approach of word intrusion and the direct approach of observed coherence, and evaluate them against each other at the topic level. Results are summarised in Table 6.

We see that the correlation between the human ratings of intruder words and observed coherence is only modest, implying that there are topic-level differences in the output of the two approaches. In Section 6, we provide a qualitative analysis and explanation as to what constitutes the differences between the approaches.

For the automated methods, OC-Auto-DS has the best performance, with OC-Auto-NPMI performing relatively well (in particularly in the NEWS domain).

6 Discussion

Normalised PMI (NPMI) was first introduced by Bouma (2009) as a means of reducing the bias for PMI towards words of lower frequency, in addition to providing a standardised range of $[-1, 1]$ for the calculated values.

We introduced NPMI to the automated methods of word intrusion (WI-Auto-NPMI) and observed coherence (OC-Auto-NPMI) to explore its suitability for the task. For the latter, we saw that NPMI achieves markedly higher correlation than OC-Human (in particular, at the model level). To better understand the impact of normalisation, we inspected a list of WIKI topics that have similar scores for OC-Human and OC-Auto-NPMI but very different OC-Auto-PMI scores. A sample of these topics is presented in Table 7. WIKI-FULL is used as the reference corpus for computing the scores. Note that the presented OC-Auto-NPMI* and OC-Auto-PMI* scores are post-normalised to the range $[0, 1]$ for ease of interpretation. To give a sense of how readily these topic words occur in the reference corpus, we additionally display the frequency of the first topic word in the reference corpus (last column).

All topics presented have an OC-Human score of 3.0 (i.e. these topics are rated as being very coherent by human judges) and similar OC-Auto-NPMI values. Their OC-Auto-PMI scores, however, are very different between the top-3 and bottom-3 topics. The bias of PMI towards lower frequency words is clear: topic words that occur frequently in the corpus receive a lower OC-Auto-PMI score compared to those that occur less frequently, even though the human-judged observed coherence is the same. OC-Auto-NPMI on the other hand, correctly estimates the coherence.

We observed, however, that the impact of normalising PMI is less in the word intrusion task. One possible explanation is that for the automated methods WI-Auto-PMI and WI-Auto-NPMI, the PMI/NPMI scores are used indirectly as a feature to a machine learning framework, and the bias could be reduced/compensated by other features.

On the subject of the difference between observed coherence and word intrusion in estimating topic interpretability, we observed that WI-Human and OC-Human correlate only moderately ($r \approx 0.6$) at the topic level (Table 6). To better understand this effect, we manually analysed topics that have differing WI-Human and OC-Human scores. A sample of topics with high divergence in estimated coherence score is given in Table 8. As before, the presented the OC-Human* and WI-

Topic	OC-Human	OC-Auto-NPMI*	OC-Auto-PMI*	Word Count
cell hormone insulin muscle receptor	3.0	0.59	0.61	#(cell) = 1.1M
electron laser magnetic voltage wavelength	3.0	0.52	0.54	#(electron) = 0.3M
magnetic neutrino particle quantum universe	3.0	0.55	0.55	#(magnetic) = 0.4M
album band music release song	3.0	0.56	0.37	#(album) = 12.5M
college education school student university	3.0	0.57	0.38	#(college) = 9.8M
city county district population town	3.0	0.52	0.34	#(city) = 22.0M

Table 7: A list of WIKI topics to illustrate the impact of NPMI.

Topic #	Topic	OC-Human*	WI-Human*
1	business company corporation **cluster** [loch] shareholder	0.94	0.25
2	**song** actor [clown] play role theatre	1.00	0.50
3	census [ethnic] female male population **village**	0.92	0.25
4	composer **singer** jazz music opera [piano]	1.00	0.63
5	choice count give i.e. simply [**unionist**]	0.14	1.00
6	[**digital**] clown friend love mother wife	0.17	1.00

Table 8: A list of WIKI topics to illustrate the difference between observed coherence and word intrusion. Boxes denote human chosen intruder words, and boldface denotes true intruder words.

Human* scores in the table are post-normalised to the range $[0, 1]$ for ease of comparison.

In general, there are two reasons for topics to have high OC-Human and low WI-Human scores. First, if a topic has an outlier word that is mildly related to the topic, users tend to choose this word as the intruder word in the word intrusion task, yielding a low WI-Human score. If they are asked to rate the observed coherence, however, the single outlier word often does not affect its overall coherence, resulting in a high OC-Human score. This is observed in topics 1 and 2 in Table 8, where *loch* and *clown* are chosen by annotators in the word intrusion task, as they detract from the semantics of the topic. This results in low WI-Human scores, but high observed coherence scores (OC-Human).

The second reason is the random selection of intruder words related to the original topic. We see this in topics 3 and 4, where related intruder words (*village* and *singer*) were selected.

For topics with low OC-Human and high WI-Human scores, the true intruder words are often very different to the domain/focus of other topic words. As such, annotators are consistently able to single them out to yield high WI-Human scores, even though the topic as a whole is not coherent. Topics 5 and 6 in Table 8 exhibit this.

All topic evaluation measures described in this paper are implemented in an open-source toolkit.[9]

[9] `https://github.com/jhlau/topic_interpretability`

7 Conclusion

In this paper, we examined various methodologies that estimate the semantic interpretability of topics, at two levels: the model level and the topic level. We looked first at the word intrusion task proposed by Chang et al. (2009), and proposed a method that fully automates the task. Next we turned to observed coherence, a more direct approach to estimate topic interpretability. At the model level, results were very positive for both the word intrusion and observed coherence methods. At the topic level, however, the results were more mixed. For observed coherence, our best methods (OC-Auto-NPMI and OC-Auto-DS) were able to emulate human performance. For word intrusion, the automated methods were slightly below human performance, with some room for improvement. We finally observed that there are systematic differences in the topic-level scores derived from the two task formulations.

Acknowledgements

This work was supported in part by the Australian Research Council, and for author JHL, also partly funded by grant ES/J022969/1 from the Economic and Social Research Council of the UK. The authors acknowledge the generosity of Nikos Aletras and Mark Stevenson in providing their code for OC-Auto-DS, and Jordan Boyd-Graber in providing the data used in Chang et al. (2009).

References

N. Aletras and M. Stevenson. 2013a. Evaluating topic coherence using distributional semantics. In *Proceedings of the Tenth International Workshop on Computational Semantics (IWCS-10)*, pages 13–22, Potsdam, Germany.

N. Aletras and M. Stevenson. 2013b. Representing topics using images. In *Proceedings of the 2013 Conference of the North American Chapter of the Association for Computational Linguistics: Human Language Technologies (NAACL HLT 2013)*, pages 158–167, Atlanta, USA.

D. Blei and J. Lafferty. 2005. Correlated topic models. In *Advances in Neural Information Processing Systems 17 (NIPS-05)*, pages 147–154, Vancouver, Canada.

D.M. Blei, A.Y. Ng, and M.I. Jordan. 2003. Latent Dirichlet allocation. *Journal of Machine Learning Research*, 3:993–1022.

L. Bolelli, Ş. Ertekin, and C.L. Giles. 2009. Topic and trend detection in text collections using Latent Dirichlet Allocation. In *Proceedings of ECIR 2009*, pages 776–780, Toulouse, France.

G. Bouma. 2009. Normalized (pointwise) mutual information in collocation extraction. In *Proceedings of the Biennial GSCL Conference*, pages 31–40, Potsdam, Germany.

J. Chang, J. Boyd-Graber, S. Gerrish, C. Wang, and D. Blei. 2009. Reading tea leaves: How humans interpret topic models. In *Advances in Neural Information Processing Systems 21 (NIPS-09)*, pages 288–296, Vancouver, Canada.

A. Haghighi and L. Vanderwende. 2009. Exploring content models for multi-document summarization. In *Proceedings of the North American Chapter of the Association for Computational Linguistics – Human Language Technologies 2009 (NAACL HLT 2009)*, pages 362–370.

D. Hall, D. Jurafsky, and C.D. Manning. 2008. Studying the history of ideas using topic models. In *Proceedings of the 2008 Conference on Empirical Methods in Natural Language Processing (EMNLP 2008)*, pages 363–371, Honolulu, USA.

M. Hall, P. Clough, and M. Stevenson. 2012. Evaluating the use of clustering for automatically organising digital library collections. In *Proceedings of the Second International Conference on Theory and Practice of Digital Libraries*, pages 323–334, Paphos, Cyprus.

T. Hofmann. 1999. Probabilistic latent semantic indexing. In *Proceedings of 22nd International ACM-SIGIR Conference on Research and Development in Information Retrieval (SIGIR'99)*, pages 50–57, Berkeley, USA.

T. Joachims. 2006. Training linear SVMs in linear time. In *Proceedings of the 12th ACM SIGKDD International Conference on Knowledge Discovery and Data Mining (KDD 2006)*, Philadelphia, USA.

J.H. Lau, D. Newman, S. Karimi, and T. Baldwin. 2010. Best topic word selection for topic labelling. In *Proceedings of the 23rd International Conference on Computational Linguistics (COLING 2010), Posters Volume*, pages 605–613, Beijing, China.

J.H. Lau, K. Grieser, D. Newman, and T. Baldwin. 2011. Automatic labelling of topic models. In *Proceedings of the 49th Annual Meeting of the Association for Computational Linguistics: Human Language Technologies (ACL HLT 2011)*, pages 1536–1545, Portland, USA.

J.H. Lau, N. Collier, and T. Baldwin. 2012a. Online trend analysis with topic models: #twitter trends detection topic model online. In *Proceedings of the 24th International Conference on Computational Linguistics (COLING 2012)*, pages 1519–1534, Mumbai, India.

J.H. Lau, P. Cook, D. McCarthy, D. Newman, and T. Baldwin. 2012b. Word sense induction for novel sense detection. In *Proceedings of the 13th Conference of the EACL (EACL 2012)*, pages 591–601, Avignon, France.

J.H. Lau, T. Baldwin, and D. Newman. 2013. On collocations and topic models. *ACM Transactions on Speech and Language Processing*, 10(3):10:1–10:14.

A McCallum, G.S. Mann, and D Mimno. 2006. Bibliometric impact measures leveraging topic analysis. In *Proceedings of the 6th ACM/IEEE-CS Joint Conference on Digital Libraries 2006 (JCDL'06)*, pages 65–74, Chapel Hill, USA.

D. Mimno, H. Wallach, E. Talley, M. Leenders, and A. McCallum. 2011. Optimizing semantic coherence in topic models. In *Proceedings of the 2011 Conference on Empirical Methods in Natural Language Processing (EMNLP 2011)*, pages 262–272, Edinburgh, UK.

G. Minnen, J. Carroll, and D. Pearce. 2001. Applied morphological processing of English. *Natural Language Engineering*, 7(3):207–223.

C. Musat, J. Velcin, S. Trausan-Matu, and M.A. Rizoiu. 2011. Improving topic evaluation using conceptual knowledge. In *Proceedings of the 22nd International Joint Conference on Artificial Intelligence (IJCAI-2011)*, pages 1866–1871, Barcelona, Spain.

D. Newman, J.H. Lau, K. Grieser, and T. Baldwin. 2010. Automatic evaluation of topic coherence. In *Proceedings of Human Language Technologies: The 11th Annual Conference of the North American Chapter of the Association for Computational Linguistics (NAACL HLT 2010)*, pages 100–108, Los Angeles, USA.

M. Paul and R. Girju. 2010. A two-dimensional topic-aspect model for discovering multi-faceted topics. In *Proceedings of the 24th Annual Conference on Artificial Intelligence (AAAI-10)*, Atlanta, USA.

J. Reisinger, A. Waters, B. Silverthorn, and R.J. Mooney. 2010. Spherical topic models. In *Proceedings of the 27th International Conference on Machine Learning (ICML 2010)*, pages 903–910, Haifa, Israel.

X. Wang, A. McCallum, and X. Wei. 2007. Topical n-grams: Phrase and topic discovery, with an application to information retrieval. In *Proceedings of the Seventh IEEE International Conference on Data Mining (ICDM 2007)*, pages 697–702, Omaha, USA.

B. Zhao and E.P. Xing. 2007. HM-BiTAM: Bilingual topic exploration, word alignment, and translation. In *Advances in Neural Information Processing Systems (NIPS 2007)*, pages 1689–1696, Vancouver, Canada.

What Substitutes Tell Us – Analysis of an "All-Words" Lexical Substitution Corpus

Gerhard Kremer
Institute for Computational Linguistics
University of Heidelberg, Germany
kremer@cl.uni-heidelberg.de

Katrin Erk
Dept. of Linguistics
University of Texas, Austin, U.S.A.
katrin.erk@utexas.edu

Sebastian Padó
Institute for Natural Language Processing
University of Stuttgart, Germany
pado@ims.uni-stuttgart.de

Stefan Thater
Dept. of Computational Linguistics
Saarland University, Saarbrücken, Germany
stth@coli.uni-sb.de

Abstract

We present the first large-scale English "all-words lexical substitution" corpus. The size of the corpus provides a rich resource for investigations into word meaning. We investigate the nature of lexical substitute sets, comparing them to WordNet synsets. We find them to be consistent with, but more fine-grained than, synsets. We also identify significant differences to results for paraphrase ranking in context reported for the SEMEVAL lexical substitution data. This highlights the influence of corpus construction approaches on evaluation results.

1 Introduction

Many, if not most, words have multiple meanings; for example, the word "bank" has a financial and a geographical sense. One common approach to deal with this *lexical ambiguity* is supervised *word sense disambiguation*, or WSD (McCarthy, 2008; Navigli, 2009), which frames the task as a lemma-level classification problem, to be solved by training classifiers on samples of lemma instances that are labelled with their correct senses.

This approach has its problems, however. First, it assumes a complete and consistent set of labels. WordNet, used in the majority of studies, does cover several 10,000 lemmas, but has been criticised for both its coverage and granularity. Second, WSD requires annotation for each sense and lemma, leading to an "annotation bottleneck". A number of technical solutions have been suggested regarding the second problem (Ando and Zhang, 2005; Navigli and Ponzetto, 2012), but not for the first.

In 2009, McCarthy and Navigli address both problems by proposing a fundamentally different approach, called *Lexical Substitution* (McCarthy and Navigli, 2009) which avoids capturing a word's meaning by a single label. Instead, annotators are asked to list, for each instance of a word, one or more alternative words or phrases to be substituted for the target in this particular context. This setup provides a number of benefits over WSD. It allows characterising word meaning without using an ontology and can be obtained easily from native speakers through crowdsourcing. Work on modelling Lexical Substitution data has also assumed a different focus from WSD. It tends to see the prediction of substitutes along the lines of compositional lexical semantics, concentrating on explaining how word meaning is modulated in context (Mitchell and Lapata, 2010).

There are, however, important shortcomings of the work in the Lexical Substitution paradigm. All existing datasets (McCarthy and Navigli, 2009; Sinha and Mihalcea, 2014; Biemann, 2013; McCarthy et al., 2013) are either comparatively small, are "lexical sample" datasets, or both. "Lexical sample" datasets consist of sample sentences for each target word drawn from large corpora, with just one target word substituted in each sentence. In WSD, "lexical sample" datasets contrast with "all-words" annotation, in which all content words in a text are annotated for sense (Palmer et al., 2001).

Proceedings of the 14th Conference of the European Chapter of the Association for Computational Linguistics, pages 540–549, Gothenburg, Sweden, April 26-30 2014.

In this paper, we present the first large "all-words" Lexical Substitution dataset for English. It provides substitutions for more than 30,000 words of running text from two domains of MASC (Ide et al., 2008; Ide et al., 2010), a subset of the American National Corpus (`http://www.anc.org`) that is freely available and has (partial) manual annotation. The main advantage of the all-words setting is that it provides a realistic frequency distribution of target words and their senses. We use this to empirically investigate (a) the nature of lexical substitution and (b) the nature of the corpus, seen through the lens of word meaning in context.

2 Related Work

2.1 Lexical Substitution: Data

The original "English Lexical Substitution" dataset (McCarthy and Navigli, 2009) comprises 200 target content words (balanced numbers of nouns, verbs, adjectives and adverbs). Targets were explicitly selected to exhibit interesting ambiguities. For each target, 10 sentences were chosen (mostly at random, but in part by hand) from the English Internet Corpus (Sharoff, 2006) and presented to 5 annotators to collect substitutes. Its total size is 2,000 target instances. Sinha and Mihalcea (2014) produced a small pilot dataset (500 target instances) for all-words substitution, asking three annotators to substitute all content words in presented sentences.

Biemann (2013) first investigated the use of crowdsourcing, developing a three-task bootstrapping design to control for noise. His study covers over 50,000 instances, but these correspond only to 397 targets, all of which are high-frequency nouns. Biemann clusters the resulting substitutes into word senses. McCarthy et al. (2013) applied lexical substitution in a cross-lingual setting, annotating 130 of the original McCarthy and Navigli targets with Spanish substitutions (i. e., translations).

2.2 Lexical Substitution: Models

The LexSub task at SEMEVAL 2007 (McCarthy and Navigli, 2009) required systems to both determine substitution candidates and choose contextual substitutions in each case. Erk and Padó (2008) treated the gold substitution candidates as given and focused on the context-specific ranking of those candidates. In this form, the task has been addressed through three types of (mostly unsupervised) approaches. The first group computes a single type representation and modifies it according to sentence context (Erk and Padó, 2008; Thater et al., 2010; Thater et al., 2011; Van de Cruys et al., 2011). The second group of approaches clusters instance representations (Reisinger and Mooney, 2010; Dinu and Lapata, 2010; Erk and Padó, 2010; O'Séaghdha and Korhonen, 2011). The third option is to use a language model (Moon and Erk, 2013). Recently, supervised models have emerged (Biemann 2013; Szarvas et al., 2013a,b).

3 COINCO – The MASC All-Words Lexical Substitution Corpus[1]

Compared to, e. g., WSD, there still is little gold-annotated data for lexical substitution. With the exception of the dataset created by Biemann (2013), all existing lexical substitution datasets are fairly small, covering at most several thousand instances and few targets which are manually selected. We aim to fill this gap, providing a dataset that mirrors the actual corpus distribution of targets in sentence context and is sufficiently large to enable a detailed, lexically specific analysis of substitution patterns.

3.1 Source Corpus Choice

For annotation, we chose a subset of the "Manually Annotated Sub-Corpus" MASC (Ide et al., 2008; Ide et al., 2010) which is "equally distributed across 19 genres, with manually produced or validated annotations for several layers of linguistic phenomena", created with the purpose of being "free of usage and redistribution restrictions". We chose this corpus because (a) our analyses can profit from the preexisting annotations and (b) we can release our annotations as part of MASC.

Since we could not annotate the complete MASC, we selected (complete) text documents from two prominent genres: *news* (18,942 tokens) and *fiction* (16,605 tokens). These two genres are both relevant for NLP and provide long, coherent documents that are appropriate for all-words annotation. We used the MASC part-of-speech annotation to identify all content words (verbs, nouns, adjectives, and adverbs), which resulted in a total of over 15,000 targets for annotation. This method differs from Navigli and McCarthy's (2009) in two crucial respects: we annotate all instances of each target, and include all targets regardless of frequency or level of lexical ambiguity. We believe that our corpus is considerably more representative of running text.

[1] Available as XML-formatted corpus "Concepts in Context" (COINCO) from `http://goo.gl/5C0jBH`. Also scheduled for release as part of MASC.

3.2 Crowdsourcing

We used the Amazon Mechanical Turk (AMT) platform to obtain substitutes by crowdsourcing. Inter-annotator variability and quality issues due to non-expert annotators are well-known difficulties (see, e. g., Fossati et al. (2013)). Our design choices were shaped by "best practices in AMT", including Mason and Suri (2012) and Biemann (2013).

Defining HITs. An AMT task consists of Human Intelligence Tasks (HITs), each of which is supposed to represent a minimal, self-contained task. In our case, potential HITs were annotations of (all target words in) one sentence, or just one target word. The two main advantages of annotating a complete sentence at a time are (a) less overhead, because the sentence has only to be read once; (b) higher reliability, since all words within a sentence will be annotated by the same person.

Unfortunately, presenting individual sentences as HITs also means that all sentences pay the same amount irrespective of their length. Since long sentences require more effort, they are likely to receive less attention. We therefore decided to generally present two random target words per HIT, and one word in the case of "leftover" singleton targets.

In the HITs, AMT workers ("turkers") saw the highlighted target word in context. Since one sentence was often insufficient to understand the target fully, we also showed the preceding and the following sentence. The task description asked turkers to provide (preferably single-word) substitutes for the target that "would not change the meaning". They were explicitly allowed to use a "more general term" in case a substitute was hard to find (e. g., *dog* for the target *dachshund*, cf. basic level effects: Rosch et al. (1976)). Turkers were encouraged to produce as many replacements as possible (up to 5). If they could not find a substitute, they had to check one of the following radio buttons: "proper name", "part of a fixed expression", "no replacement possible", "other problem (with description)".

Improving Reliability. Another major problem is reliability. Ideally, the complete dataset should be annotated by the same group of annotators, but turkers tend to work only on a few HITs before switching to other AMT jobs. Following an idea of Biemann and Nygaard (2010), we introduced a two-tier system of jobs aimed at boosting turker loyalty. A tier of "open tasks" served to identify reliable turkers by manually checking their given substitutes for plausibility. Such turkers were then invited to the second, "closed task" tier, with a higher payment. In both tiers, bonus payments were offered to those completing full HIT sets.

For each target, we asked 6 turkers to provide substitutions. In total, 847 turkers participated successfully. In the open tasks, 839 turkers submitted 12,158 HITs (an average of 14.5 HITs). In the closed tasks, 25 turkers submitted 42,827 HITs (an average of 1,713 HITs), indicating the substantial success of our turker retention scheme.

Cost. In the open task, each HIT was paid for with \$ 0.03, in the closed task the wage was \$ 0.05 per HIT. The bonus payment for completing a HIT set amounted to \$ 2 (\$ 1) in the open (closed) tasks. The average cost for annotations was \$ 0.22 for one target word instance and \$ 0.02 for one substitute. The total cost with fees was ~\$ 3,400.

3.3 CoInCo: Corpus and Paraset Statistics

We POS-tagged and lemmatised targets and substitutes in sentence context with TreeTagger (Schmid, 1994). We manually lemmatised unknown words. Our annotated dataset comprises a total of 167,336 responses by turkers for 15,629 target instances in 2,474 sentences (7,117 nouns, 4,617 verbs, 2,470 adjectives, and 1,425 adverbs). As outlined above, targets are roughly balanced across the two genres (news: 8,030 instances in 984 sentences; fiction: 7,599 instances in 1,490 sentences). There are 3,874 unique target lemmas; 1,963 of these occur more than once. On this subset, there is a mean of 6.99 instances per target lemma. To our knowledge, our corpus is the largest lexical substitution dataset in terms of lemma coverage.

Each target instance is associated with a *paraset* (i. e., the set of substitutions or paraphrases produced for a target in its context) with an average size of 10.71. Turkers produced an average of 1.68 substitutions per target instance.[2] Despite our instructions to provide single-word substitutes, 11,337 substitutions contain more than one word.

3.4 Inter-Annotator Agreement

McCarthy and Navigli (2009) introduced two inter-annotator agreement (IAA) measures for their dataset. The first one is *pairwise agreement* (PA),

[2]Note that a small portion of the corpus was annotated by more than 6 annotators.

dataset	# targets	PA	mode-%	PA_m
MN09	1,703	27.7	73.9	50.7
SM13	550	15.5	N/A	N/A
COINCO (complete)	15,400	19.3	70.9	44.7
COINCO (subset)	2,828	24.6	76.4	50.9

Table 1: Pairwise turker agreement (mode-%: percentage of target instances with a mode)

measuring the overlap of produced substitutions:

$$\mathrm{PA} = \sum_{t \in T} \sum_{\langle s_t, s'_t \rangle \in C_t} \frac{|s_t \cap s'_t|}{|s_t \cup s'_t|} \cdot \frac{1}{|C_t| \cdot |T|}$$

where t is a target in our target set T, s_t is the paraset provided by one turker for t, and C_t is the set comprising all pairs of turker-specific parasets for t. Only targets with non-empty parasets (i. e., not marked by turkers as a problematic target) from at least two turkers are included. The second one is *mode agreement* ($\mathrm{PA_m}$), the agreement of annotators' parasets with the *mode* (the unique most frequent substitute) for all targets where one exists:

$$\mathrm{PA_m} = \sum_{t \in T_m} \sum_{s_t \in S_t} [m \in s_t] \cdot \frac{1}{|s_t| \cdot |T_m|}$$

where T_m is the set of all targets with some mode m and S_t is the set of all parasets for target t. The Iverson bracket notation $[m \in s_t]$ denotes 1 if mode m is included in s_t (otherwise 0).

Table 1 compares our dataset to the results by McCarthy and Navigli (2009, MN09) and Sinha and Mihalcea (2014, SM13). The scores for our complete dataset (row 3) are lower than McCarthy and Navigli's both for PA (-8 %) and $\mathrm{PA_m}$ (-6 %), but higher than Sinha and Mihalcea's, who also note the apparent drop in agreement.[3]

We believe that this is a result of differences in the setup rather than an indicator of low quality: Note that PA will tend to decrease both in the face of more annotators and of more substitutes. Both of these factors are present in our setup. To test this interpretation, we extracted a subset of our data that is comparable to McCarthy and Navigli's regarding these factors. It comprises all target instances where (a) exactly 6 turkers gave responses (9,521 targets), and (b) every turker produced between one and three substitutes (5,734 targets). The results for this subset (row 4) are much more similar to those of McCarthy and Navigli: the pairwise agreement differs only by 3 %, and the mode agreement is almost identical. We take these figures as indication that crowdsourcing can serve as a sufficiently reliable way to create substitution data; note that Sinha and Mihalcea's annotation was carried out "traditionally" by three annotators.

Investigating IAA numbers by target POS and by genre, we found only small differences (≤ 2.6 %) among the various subsets, and no patterns.

[3]Please see McCarthy and Navigli (2009) for a possible explanation of the generally low IAA numbers in this field.

relation	all	verb	noun	adj	adv
syn	9.4	12.5	7.7	8.0	10.4
direct-hyper	6.6	9.3	7.6	N/A	N/A
direct-hypo	7.5	11.6	8.0	N/A	N/A
trans-hyper	3.2	2.8	4.7	N/A	N/A
trans-hypo	3.0	3.7	3.8	N/A	N/A
wn-other	68.9	60.7	66.5	88.5	85.4
not-in-wn	2.1	0.9	2.2	3.4	4.2

Table 2: Target–substitute relations in percentages, overall (*all*) and by POS. Note: WordNet contains no hypo-/hypernyms for adjectives and adverbs.

4 Characterising Lexical Substitutions

This section examines the collected lexical substitutions, both quantitatively and qualitatively. We explore three questions: (a) What lexical relations hold between targets and their substitutes? (b) Do parasets resemble word senses? (c) How similar are the parasets that correspond to the same word sense of a target? These questions have not been addressed before, and we would argue that they could not be addressed before, because previous corpora were either too small or were sampled in a way that was not conducive to this analysis.

We use WordNet (Fellbaum, 1998), release 3.1, as a source for both lexical relations and word senses. WordNet is the de facto standard in NLP and is used for both WSD and broader investigations of word meaning (Navigli and Ponzetto, 2012; Erk and McCarthy, 2009). Multi-word substitutes are excluded from all analyses.[4]

4.1 Relating Targets and Substitutes

We first look at the most canonical lexical relations between a target and its substitutes. Table 2 lists the percentage of substitutes that are synonyms (*syn*), direct/transitive (*direct-/trans-*) hypernyms (*hyper*)

[4]All automatic lexical substitution approaches, including Section 5, omit multi-word expressions. Also, they can be expected to have WordNet coverage and normalisation issues, which would constitute a source of noise for this analysis.

sentence	substitutes
Now, how can I help the elegantly mannered friend of my Nepthys and his surprising young charge?	dependent, person, *task, lass, protégé, effort, companion*
The distinctive whuffle of pleasure rippled through the betas on the bridge, and Rakal let loose a small growl, as if to caution his charges against false hope.	dependent, command, accusation, *private, companion, follower, subordinate, prisoner, teammate, ward, junior, underling, enemy, group, crew, squad, troop, team, kid*

Table 3: Context effects below the sense level: target noun "charge" (wn-other shown in italics)

and hyponyms (*hypo*) of the target. If a substitute had multiple relations to the target, the shortest path from any of its senses to any sense of the target was chosen. The table also lists the percentage of substitutes that are elsewhere in WordNet but not related to the target (*wn-other*) and substitutes that are not covered by WordNet (*not-in-wn*).

We make three main observations. First, WordNet shows very high coverage throughout – there are very few *not-in-wn* substitutes. Second, the percentages of synonyms, hypernyms and hyponyms are relatively similar (even though the annotation guidelines encouraged the annotation of hyponyms over hypernyms), but relatively small. Finally, and most surprisingly, the vast majority of substitutes across all parts of speech are *wn-other*.

A full analysis of *wn-other* is beyond the current paper. But a manual analysis of *wn-other* substitutes for 10 lemmas[5] showed that most of them were *context-specific* substitutes that can differ even when the sense of the target is the same. This is illustrated in Table 3, which features two occurrences of the noun "charge" in the sense of "person committed to your care". But because of the sentence context, the first occurrence got substitutes like "protégé", while the second one was paraphrased by words like "underling". We also see evidence of annotator error (e. g., "command" and "accusation" in the second sentence).[6] Discounting such instances still leaves a prominent role for correct *wn-other* cases.

But are these indeed contextual modulation effects below the sense level, or are parasets fundamentally different from word senses? We perform two quantitative analyses to explore this question.

4.2 Comparing Parasets to Synsets

To what extent do parasets follow the boundaries of WordNet senses? To address this question, we

paraset–sense mapping class	verb	noun	adj	adv
mappable	90.3	73.5	33.0	49.6
uniquely mappable	63.1	57.5	24.3	41.3

Table 4: Ratios of (uniquely) mappable parasets

establish a mapping between parasets and synsets. Since gold standard word senses in MASC are limited to high-frequency lemmas and cover only a small part of our data, we create a heuristic mapping that assigns each paraset to that synset of its target with which it has the largest intersection. We use *extended WordNet synsets* that include direct hypo- and hypernyms to achieve better matches with parasets. We call a paraset *uniquely mappable* if it has a unique best WordNet match, and *mappable* if one or more best matches exist. Table 4 shows that most parasets are mappable for nouns and verbs, but not for adjectives or adverbs.

We now focus on mappable parasets for nouns and verbs. To ensure that this does not lead to a confounding bias, we performed a small manual study on the 10 noun and verb targets mentioned above (247 parasets). We found 25 non-mappable parasets, which were due to several roughly equally important reasons: gaps in WordNet, multi-word expressions, metaphor, problems of sense granularity, and annotator error. We also found 66 parasets with multiple best matches. The two dominant sources were target occurrences that evoked more than one sense and WordNet synset pairs with very close meanings. We conclude that excluding non-mappable parasets does not invalidate our analysis.

To test whether parasets tend to map to a single synset, we use a cluster purity test that compares a set of clusters C to a set of gold standard classes C'. Purity measures the accuracy of each cluster with respect to its best matching gold class:

$$purity(C, C') = \frac{1}{N} \sum_{k=1}^{K} \max_{k'} |C_k \cap C'_{k'}|$$

where N is the total number of data points, K is the

[5]We used the nouns *business, charge, place, way* and the verbs *call, feel, keep, leave, show, stand.*

[6]A manual analysis of the same 10 lemmas showed only 38 out of 1,398 (0.027) of the substitutes to be erroneous.

measure	verbs	nouns
cluster purity (%)	75.1	81.2
common core size within sense	1.84	2.21
common core size across senses	0.39	0.41
paraset size	6.89	6.29

Table 5: Comparing uniquely mappable parasets to senses: overlap with best WordNet match as cluster purity (top), and intersection size of parasets with and without the same WordNet match (bottom)

number of clusters, and $C'_{k'}$ is the gold class that has the largest overlap with cluster C_k. In our case, C is the set of mappable parasets[7], C' the set of extended WordNet synsets, and we only consider substitutes that occur in one of the target's extended synsets (these are the data points). This makes the current analysis complementary to the relational analysis in Table 2.[8]

The result, listed in the first row of Table 5, shows that parasets for both verbs and nouns have a high purity, that is, substitutes tend to focus on a single sense. This can be interpreted as saying that annotators tend to agree on the general sense of a target. Roughly 20–25 % of substitutes, however, tend to stem from a synset of the target that is not the best WordNet match. This result comes with the caveat that it only applies to substitutes that are synonyms or direct hypo- and hypernyms of the target. So in the next section, we perform an analysis that also includes *wn-other* substitutes.

4.3 Similarity Between Same-Sense Parasets

We now use the WordNet mappings from the previous section to ask how (dis-)similar parasets are that represent the same word sense. We also try to identify the major sources for dissimilarity.

We quantify paraset similarity as the *common core*, that is, the intersection of *all* parasets for the same target that map onto the same extended WordNet synset. Surprisingly, the common core is mostly non-empty (in 85.6 % of all cases), and contains on average around two elements, as the second row in Table 5 shows. For this analysis, we only use uniquely mappable parasets. In relation to the average paraset size (see row 4), this means that one quarter to one third of the substitutes are shared among all instances of the same target–sense combination. In contrast, the common core for all parasets of targets that map onto two or more synsets contains only around 0.4 substitutes (see row 3) – that is, it is empty more often than not.

[7] For non-uniquely mappable parasets, the purity is the same for all best-matching synsets.

[8] Including *wn-other* substitutes would obscure whether low purity means substitutes from a mixture of senses (which we are currently interested in) or simply a large number of *wn-other* substitutes (which we have explored above).

set	elements
synset \ core	feel, perceive, comprehend
synset ∩ core	sense
core \ synset	notice
non-core substitutes	detect, recall, perceive, experience, note, realize, discern

Table 6: Target feel.v.03: synset and common core

At the same time, if about one quarter to one third of the substitutes are shared, this means that there are more non-shared than shared substitutes even for same-sense parasets. Some of these cases result from small samples: Even 6 annotators cannot always exhaust all possible substitutes. For example, the phrase "I'm starting to see more *business* transactions" occurs twice in the corpus. The two parasets for "business" share the same best WordNet sense match, but they have only 3 shared and 7 non-shared substitutes. This is even though the substitutes are all valid and apply to both instances. Other cases are instances of the context sensitivity of the Lexical Substitution task as discussed above. Table 6 illustrates on an example how the common core of a target sense relates to the corresponding synset; note the many context-specific substitutes outside the common core.

5 Ranking Paraphrases

While there are several studies on modelling lexical substitutes, almost all reported results use McCarthy and Navigli's SEMEVAL 2007 dataset. We now compare the results of three recent computational models on COINCO (our work) and on the SEMEVAL 2007 dataset to highlight similarities and differences between the two datasets.

Models. We consider the paraphrase ranking models of Erk and Padó (2008, EP08), Thater et al. (2010, TFP10) and Thater et al. (2011, TFP11). These models have been analysed by Dinu et al. (2012) as instances of the same general framework and have been shown to deliver state-of-the-art performance on the SEMEVAL 2007 dataset, with best results for Thater et al. (2011).

The three models share the idea to represent the meaning of a target word in a specific context by

corpus		syntactically structured			syntactically filtered		bag of words		random
		TFP11	TFP10	EP08	TFP11/EP08	TFP10	TFP11/EP08	TFP10	
COINCO	context	**47.8**	46.0	47.4	47.4	41.9	46.2	40.8	33.0
	baseline	46.2	44.6	46.2	45.8	38.8	44.7	37.5	
SEMEVAL 2007	context	**52.5**	48.6	49.4	50.1	44.7	48.0	42.6	30.0
	baseline	43.7	42.7	43.7	44.4	38.0	42.7	35.8	
COINCO Subset	context	**40.3**	37.7	39.0	39.2	34.1	37.7	32.5	23.7
	baseline	36.7	35.7	36.7	36.4	30.6	35.4	28.0	

Table 7: Corpus comparison in terms of paraphrase ranking quality (GAP percentage). SEMEVAL results from Thater et al. (2011). "Context": full models, "baseline": uncontextualised target-substitute similarity.

modifying the target's basic meaning vector with information from the vectors of the words in the target's direct syntactic context. For instance, the vector of "coach" in the phrase "the coach derailed" is obtained by modifying the basic vector representation of "coach" through the vector of "derail", so that the resulting contextualised vector reflects the train car sense of "coach".

We replicate the setup of Thater et al. (2011) to make our numbers directly comparable. We consider three versions of each model: (a) *syntactically structured* models use vectors which record co-occurrences based on dependency triples, explicitly recording syntactic role information within the vectors; (b) *syntactically filtered* models also use dependency-based co-occurrence information, but the syntactic role is not explicitly represented in the vector representations; (c) *bag-of-words* models use a window of ± 5 words. All co-occurrence counts are extracted from the English Gigaword corpus (`http://catalog.ldc.upenn.edu/LDC2003T05`), analysed with Stanford dependencies (de Marneffe et al., 2006).

We apply the models to our dataset as follows: We first collect all substitutes for all occurrences of a target word in the corpus. The task of our models for each target instance is then to rank the candidates so that the actual substitutes are ranked higher than the rest. We rank candidates according to the cosine similarity between the contextualised vector of the target and the vectors of the candidates. Like most previous approaches, we compare the resulting ranked list with the gold standard annotation (the paraset of the target instance), using generalised average precision (Kishida, 2005, GAP), and using substitution frequency as weights. GAP scores range between 0 and 1; a score of 1 indicates a perfect ranking in which all correct substitutes precede all incorrect ones, and correct high-weight substitutes precede low-weight substitutes.

Results. The upper part of Table 7 shows results for our COINCO corpus and the previous standard dataset, SEMEVAL 2007. "Context" refers to the full models, and "baseline" to global, context-unaware ranking based on the semantic similarity between target and substitute. Baselines are model-specific since they re-use the models' vector representations. Note that EP08 and TFP11 are identical unless syntactically structured vectors are used, and their baselines are identical.

The behaviour of the baselines on the two corpora is quite similar: random baselines have GAPs around 0.3, and uncontextualised baselines have GAPs between 0.35 and 0.46. The order of the models is also highly parallel: the syntactically structured TFP11 is the best model, followed by its syntactically filtered version and syntactically structured EP08. All differences between these models are significant ($p < 0.01$) for both corpora, as computed with bootstrap resampling (Efron and Tibshirani, 1993). That is, the model ranking on SEMEVAL is replicated on COINCO.

There are also substantial differences between the two corpora, though. Most notably, all models perform substantially worse on COINCO. This is true in absolute terms (we observe a loss of 2–5 % GAP) but even more dramatic expressed as the gain over the uninformed baselines (almost 9 % for TFP11 on SEMEVAL but only 1.2 % on COINCO). All differences between COINCO and SEMEVAL are again significant ($p < 0.01$).

We see three major possible reasons for these differences: variations in (a) the annotation setup (crowdsourcing, multiple substitutes); (b) the sense distribution; (c) frequency and POS distributions between the two corpora. We focus on (c) since it can be manipulated most easily. SEMEVAL contains exactly 10 instances for all targets, while COINCO reflects the Zipf distribution of "natural" corpora, with many targets occurring only once. Such corpora are easier to model in terms of absolute performance, because the paraphrase lists for rare targets contain less false positives for each instance. For hapax legomena, the set of substitution candidates is identical to the gold standard, and the only way to receive a GAP score lower than 1 for such targets is to rank low-weight substitutes ahead of high-weight substitutes. Not surprisingly, the mean GAP score of the syntactically structured TFP11 for hapax legomena is 0.863. At the same time, such corpora make it harder for full models to outperform uncontextualised baselines; the best model (TFP11) only outperforms the baseline by 1.6 %.

To neutralise this structural bias, we created "SEMEVAL-like" subsets of COINCO (collectively referred to as the COINCO Subset) by extracting all COINCO targets with at least 10 instances (141 nouns, 101 verbs, 50 adjectives, 36 adverbs) and building 5 random samples by drawing 10 instances for each target. These samples match SEMEVAL in the frequency distribution of its targets. To account for the unequal distribution of POS in the samples, we compute GAP scores for each POS separately and calculate these GAP scores' average.

The results for the various models on the COINCO Subset in the bottom part of Table 7 show that the differences between COINCO and SEMEVAL are not primarily due to the differences in target frequencies and POS distribution – the COINCO Subset is actually more different to SEMEVAL than the complete COINCO. Strikingly, the COINCO Subset is very difficult, with a random baseline of 24 % and model performances below 37 % (baselines) and up to 40 % (full models), which indicates that the set of substitutes in COINCO is more varied than in SEMEVAL as an effect of the annotation setup. Encouragingly, the margin between full models and baselines is larger than on the complete COINCO and generally amounts to 2–4 % (3.6 % for TFP11). That is, the full models are more useful on the COINCO corpus than they appeared at first glance; however, their effect still remains much smaller than on SEMEVAL.

6 Conclusion

This paper describes COINCO, the first large-scale "all-words" lexical substitution corpus for English. It was constructed through crowdsourcing on the basis of MASC, a corpus of American English.

The corpus has two major advantages over previous lexical substitution corpora. First, it covers contiguous documents rather than selected instances. We believe that analyses on our corpus generalise better to the application domain of lexical substitution models, namely random unseen text. In fact, we find substantial differences between the performances of paraphrase ranking models for COINCO and the original SEMEVAL 2007 LexSub dataset: the margin of informed methods over the baselines are much smaller, even when controlling for target frequencies and POS distribution. We attribute this divergence at least in part to the partially manual selection strategy of SEMEVAL 2007 (cf. Section 2.1) which favours a more uniform distribution across senses, while our whole-document annotation faces the "natural" distribution skewed towards predominant senses. This favours the non-contextualised baseline models, consistent with our observations. At the very least, our findings demonstrate the sensitivity of evaluation results on corpus properties.

The second benefit of our corpus is that its size enables more detailed analyses of lexical substitution data than previously possible. We are able to investigate the nature of the paraset, i. e., the set of lexical substitutes given for one target instance, finding that lexical substitution sets correspond fairly well to WordNet sense distinctions (parasets for the same synset show high similarity, while those for different senses do not). In addition, however, we observe a striking degree of context-dependent variation below the sense level: the majority of lexical substitutions picks up fine-grained, situation-specific meaning components that do not qualify as sense distinctions in WordNet.

Avenues for future work include a more detailed analysis of the substitution data to uncover genre- and domain-specific patterns and the development of lexical substitution models that take advantage of the all-words substitutes for global optimisation.

Acknowledgements

We are grateful to Jan Pawellek for implementing the AMT task, extracting MASC data, and preparing HITS. Furthermore, we thank Georgiana Dinu for her support with the word meaning models.

References

Rie Kubota Ando and Tong Zhang. 2005. A framework for learning predictive structures from multiple tasks and unlabeled data. *Journal of Machine Learning Research*, 6:1817–1853.

Chris Biemann and Valerie Nygaard. 2010. Crowdsourcing WordNet. In *Proceedings of the 5th Global WordNet conference*, Mumbai, India.

Chris Biemann. 2013. Creating a system for lexical substitutions from scratch using crowdsourcing. *Language Resources and Evaluation*, 47(1):97–122.

Marie-Catherine de Marneffe, Bill MacCartney, and Christopher D. Manning. 2006. Generating typed dependency parses from phrase structure parses. In *Proceedings of LREC*, pages 449–454, Genoa, Italy.

Georgiana Dinu and Mirella Lapata. 2010. Measuring distributional similarity in context. In *Proceedings of EMNLP*, pages 1162–1172, Cambridge, MA.

Georgiana Dinu, Stefan Thater, and Sören Laue. 2012. A comparison of models of word meaning in context. In *Proceedings of NAACL*, pages 611–615, Montréal, Canada.

Bradley Efron and Robert J. Tibshirani. 1993. *An Introduction to the Bootstrap*. Chapman and Hall, New York.

Katrin Erk and Diana McCarthy. 2009. Graded word sense assignment. In *Proceedings of EMNLP*, pages 440–449, Singapore.

Katrin Erk and Sebastian Padó. 2008. A structured vector space model for word meaning in context. In *Proceedings of EMNLP*, pages 897–906, Honolulu, HI.

Katrin Erk and Sebastian Padó. 2010. Exemplar-based models for word meaning in context. In *Proceedings of ACL*, pages 92–97, Uppsala, Sweden.

Christiane Fellbaum, editor. 1998. *WordNet: An electronic lexical database*. MIT Press, Cambridge, MA.

Marco Fossati, Claudio Giuliano, and Sara Tonelli. 2013. Outsourcing FrameNet to the crowd. In *Proceedings of ACL*, pages 742–747, Sofia, Bulgaria.

Nancy Ide, Collin F. Baker, Christiane Fellbaum, Charles Fillmore, and Rebecca Passonneau. 2008. MASC: The manually annotated sub-corpus of American English. In *Proceedings of LREC*, pages 2455–2461, Marrakech, Morocco.

Nancy Ide, Christiane Fellbaum, Collin Baker, and Rebecca Passonneau. 2010. The manually annotated sub-corpus: A community resource for and by the people. In *Proceedings of ACL*, pages 68–73, Uppsala, Sweden.

Kazuaki Kishida. 2005. Property of average precision and its generalization: An examination of evaluation indicator for information retrieval experiments. Technical Report NII-2005-014E, Japanese National Institute of Informatics.

Winter Mason and Siddharth Suri. 2012. Conducting behavioral research on Amazon's Mechanical Turk. *Behavior Research Methods*, 44(1):1–23.

Diana McCarthy and Roberto Navigli. 2009. The English lexical substitution task. *Language Resources and Evaluation*, 43(2):139–159.

Diana McCarthy, Ravi Sinha, and Rada Mihalcea. 2013. The cross-lingual lexical substitution task. *Language Resources and Evaluation*, 47(3):607–638.

Diana McCarthy. 2008. Word sense disambiguation. In *Linguistics and Language Compass*. Blackwell.

Jeff Mitchell and Mirella Lapata. 2010. Composition in distributional models of semantics. *Cognitive Science*, 34(8):1388–1429.

Taesun Moon and Katrin Erk. 2013. An inference-based model of word meaning in context as a paraphrase distribution. *ACM Transactions on Intelligent Systems and Technology*, 4(3).

Roberto Navigli and Simone Paolo Ponzetto. 2012. Babelnet: The automatic construction, evaluation and application of a wide-coverage multilingual semantic network. *Artificial Intelligence*, 193:217–250.

Roberto Navigli. 2009. Word sense disambiguation: A survey. *ACM Computing Surveys*, 41:1–69.

Diarmuid O'Séaghdha and Anna Korhonen. 2011. Probabilistic models of similarity in syntactic context. In *Proceedings of EMNLP*, pages 1047–1057, Edinburgh, UK.

Martha Palmer, Christiane Fellbaum, Scott Cotton, Lauren Delfs, and Hoa Trang Dang. 2001. English tasks: All-words and verb lexical sample. In *Proceedings of the SENSEVAL-2 workshop*, pages 21–24, Toulouse, France.

Joseph Reisinger and Raymond J. Mooney. 2010. Multi-prototype vector-space models of word meaning. In *Proceeding of NAACL*, pages 109–117, Los Angeles, CA.

Eleanor Rosch, Carolyn B. Mervis, Wayne D. Gray, David M. Johnson, and Penny Boyes-Braem. 1976. Basic objects in natural categories. *Cognitive Psychology*, 8(3):382–439.

Helmut Schmid. 1994. Probabilistic part-of-speech tagging using decision trees. In *Proceedings of NEMLAP*, pages 44–49, Manchester, UK.

Serge Sharoff. 2006. Open-source corpora: Using the net to fish for linguistic data. *International Journal of Corpus Linguistics*, 11(4):435–462.

Ravi Sinha and Rada Mihalcea. 2014. Explorations in lexical sample and all-words lexical substitution. *Natural Language Engineering*, 20(1):99–129.

György Szarvas, Chris Biemann, and Iryna Gurevych. 2013a. Supervised all-words lexical substitution using delexicalized features. In *Proceedings of NAACL-HLT*, pages 1131–1141, Atlanta, GA.

György Szarvas, Róbert Busa-Fekete, and Eyke Hüllermeier. 2013b. Learning to rank lexical substitutions. In *Proceedings of EMLNP*, pages 1926–1932, Seattle, WA.

Stefan Thater, Hagen Fürstenau, and Manfred Pinkal. 2010. Contextualizing semantic representations using syntactically enriched vector models. In *Proceedings of ACL*, pages 948–957, Uppsala, Sweden.

Stefan Thater, Hagen Fürstenau, and Manfred Pinkal. 2011. Word meaning in context: A simple and effective vector model. In *Proceedings of IJCNLP*, pages 1134–1143, Chiang Mai, Thailand.

Tim Van de Cruys, Thierry Poibeau, and Anna Korhonen. 2011. Latent vector weighting for word meaning in context. In *Proceedings of EMNLP*, pages 1012–1022, Edinburgh, Scotland.

Weighted Krippendorff's alpha is a more reliable metrics for multi-coders ordinal annotations: experimental studies on emotion, opinion and coreference annotation

Jean-Yves Antoine
Université François Rabelais de Tours, LI (EA 6300)
Blois, France
Jean-Yves.Antoine@univ-tours.fr

Jeanne Villaneau
Université Européenne de Bretagne, IRISA
Lorient, France
Jeanne.Villaneau@univ-ubs.fr

Anaïs Lefeuvre
Université François Rabelais de Tours, LI (EA 6300)
Blois, France
anais.lefeuvre@univ-tours.fr

Abstract

The question of data reliability is of first importance to assess the quality of manually annotated corpora. Although Cohen's κ is the prevailing reliability measure used in NLP, alternative statistics have been proposed. This paper presents an experimental study with four measures (Cohen's κ, Scott's π, binary and weighted Krippendorff's α) on three tasks: emotion, opinion and coreference annotation. The reported studies investigate the factors of influence (annotator bias, category prevalence, number of coders, number of categories) that should affect reliability estimation. Results show that the use of a weighted measure restricts this influence on ordinal annotations. They suggest that weighted α is the most reliable metrics for such an annotation scheme.

1 Introduction

The newly intensive use of machine learning techniques as well as the need of evaluation data has led Natural Language Processing (NLP) to develop large annotated corpora. The interest for such enriched language resources has reached domains (semantics, pragmatics, affective computing) where the annotation process is highly affected by the coders subjectivity. The reliability of the resulting annotations must be trusted by measures that assess the inter-coders agreement. While medecine, psychology, and more generally content analysis, have considered for years the issue of data reliability, NLP has only investigated this question from the mid 1990s. The influential work of Carletta (1996) has led the κ statistic (Cohen, 1960) to become the prevailing standard for measuring the reliability of corpus annotation. Many studies have however questioned the limitations of the κ statistic and have proposed alternative measures of reliability. Krippendorff claims that "*popularity of κ notwithstanding, Cohen's κ is simply unsuitable as a measure of the reliability of data*" in a paper presenting his α coefficient (Krippendorff, 2008).

Except for some rare but noticeable studies (Arstein and Poesio, 2005), most of these critical works restrict to theoretical issues about chance agreement estimation or limitations due to various statistical biases (Arstein and Poesio, 2008). On the opposite, this paper investigates experimentally these questions on three different tasks: emotion, opinion and coreference annotation. Four measures of reliability will be considered: Cohen's κ (Cohen, 1960), Scott's π (Scott, 1955) and two measures of Krippendorff's α (Krippendorff, 2004) with different distance.

Section 2 gives a comprehensive presentation of these metrics. Section 3 details the potential methodological biases that should affect the reliability estimation. In section 4, we explain the methodology we followed for this study. Lastly, experimental results are presented in section 5.

2 Reliability measures

Any reliability measure considers the most pertinent criterion to estimate data reliability to be reproducibility. Reproducibility can be estimated by observing the agreement among independent annotators (Krippendorff, 2004): the more the coders agree on the data they have produced, the more their annotations are likely to be reproduced by any other set of coders.

Pure observed agreement is not considered as a good estimator since it does not give any account to the amount of chance that yields to this agreement. For instance, a restricted number of coding categories should favor chance agreement. What must be estimated is the proportion of observed agreement beyond the one that is expected by chance:

(1) $$\text{Measure} = \frac{A_o - A_e}{1 - A_e}$$

Proceedings of the 14th Conference of the European Chapter of the Association for Computational Linguistics, pages 550–559,
Gothenburg, Sweden, April 26-30 2014. ©2014 Association for Computational Linguistics

where A_o is the observed agreement between coders and A_e is an estimation of the possible chance agreement. Reliability metrics differ by the way they estimate this chance agreement.

Cohen's κ (Cohen, 1960) defines chance as the statistical independence of the use of coding categories by the annotators. It postulates that chance annotation is governed by prior distributions that are specific to each coder (annotator bias). κ was originally developed for two coders and nominal data. (Davies and Fleiss, 1982) has proposed a generalization to any number of coders, while (Cohen, 1968) has defined a weighted version of the κ measure that fulfils better the need of reliability estimation for ordinal annotations: the disagreement between two ordinal annotations is no more binary, but depends on a Euclidian distance. This weighted generalization restricts however to a two coders scheme (Artstein and Poesio, 2008): a weighted version of the multi-coders κ statistics is still missing.

Unlike Cohen's κ, **Scott's π** (Scott, 1955) does not aim at modelling annotator bias. It defines chance as the statistical independence of the data and the set of coding categories, independently from the coders. It considers therefore the annotation process and not the behaviour of the annotators. Scott's original proposal concerned only two coders. (Fleiss 1971) gave a generalisation of the statistics to any number of coders through a measure of pairwise agreement.

Krippendorff's α (Krippendorff, 2004) considers chance independently from coders like Scott's π, but data reliability is estimated depending on disagreement instead of agreement:

$$\text{(2)} \qquad \text{Alpha} = \frac{D_e - D_o}{D_e}$$

where D_o is the observed disagreement between coders and D_e is an estimation of the possible chance disagreement. Another original aspect of this metrics is to allow disagreement estimation between two categories through any distance measure. This implies that α handles directly any number of coders and any kind of annotation (nominal or ordinal coding scheme). In this paper, we will consider the α statistics with a binary as well as a Euclidian distance, in order to assess separately the influence of the distance measure and the metrics by itself.

3 Quality criteria for reliability metrics

There is an abundant literature about the criteria of quality a reliability measure should satisfy (Hayes, 2007). These works emphasize on two important points:

- A trustworthy measure should provide stable results: measures must be reasonably independent of any factor of influence.
- The magnitude of the measure must be interpreted in terms of absolute level of reliability: the statistics must come up with trustworthy reliability thresholds.

These questions have mainly been investigated from a theoretical point of view. This section summarizes the main conclusions that should be drawn from these critical studies.

3.1 Annotator bias and number of coders

Annotator bias refers to the influence of the idiosyncratic behavior of the coders. It can be estimated by a bias index which measures the extent to which the distribution of categories differs from one coder's annotation to another (Sim and Wright, 2005). Annotator bias has an influence on the magnitude of the reliability measures (Feinstein and Cicchetti,1990). Besides, it concerns the invariance of the measures to the permutation or selection of annotators but also to the number of coders. A review of the literature shows that theoretical studies on annotator bias are not convergent. In particular, opposite arguments have been proposed concerning Cohen's κ (Di Eugenio and Glass 2004, Arstein and Poesio 2008, Hayes, 2007). This is why we have carried on experiments that investigate:

- to what extent measures depend on the selection of a specific set of coders (§ 5.3),
- to what extent the stability of the measures depends on the number of coders (§ 5.4). Arstein and Poesio (2005) have shown that the greater the number of coders is, the lower the annotator bias decreases. Our aim is to go further this conclusion: we will study whether one measure needs fewer coders than another one to converge towards an acceptable annotator bias.

3.2 Category prevalence

Prevalence refers to the influence on reliability estimation of a coding category under which a disproportionate amount of annotated data falls. It can be estimated by a prevalence index which measures the frequency differences of categories on cases where the coders agree (Sim and Wright, 2005). When the prevalence index is high, chance-corrected measures are spuriously reduced since chance agreement is higher in this situation (Brennan and Sliman, 1992; Di Eugenio and Glass, 2004). This yields some authors to propose corrected coefficients like the PABAK measure (Byrt and al., 1993), which is a prevalence adjusted and annotator bias adjusted version of Cohen's κ. The influence of prevalence will not be investigated here, since no category is significantly prevalent in our data.

3.3 Number of coding categories

The number of coding categories has an influence on the reliability measures magnitude: the larger the number of categories is, the less the coders have a chance to agree. Even if this decrease should concern chance agreement too, lower reliability estimations are observed with high numbers of categories (Brenner and Kliebsch, 1996). This paper investigates this influence by comparing reliability values obtained with a 3-categories and a 5-categories coding scheme applied on the same data (see § 5.1).

3.4 Interpreting the magnitude of measures in terms of effective reliability

One last question concerns the interpretation of the reliability measures magnitude. It has been particularly investigated with Cohen's κ. Carletta (1996) advocates 0.8 to be a threshold of good reliability, while a value between 0.67 and 0.8 is considered sufficient to allow tentative conclusion to be drawn. On the opposite, Krippendorff (2004b) claims that this 0.67 cutoff is a pretty low standard while Neuendorf (2002) supports an even more restrictive interpretation.

Thus, the definition of relevant levels of reliability remains an open problem. We will see how our experiments should draw a methodological framework to answer this crucial issue.

4 Experiments: methodology

4.1 Introduction

We have conducted experiments on three different annotation tasks in order to guarantee an appreciable generality of our findings. The first two experiments correspond to an ordinal annotation. They concern the affective dimension of language (emotion and opinion annotation). They have been conducted with naïve coders to preserve the spontaneity of judgment which is searched for in affective computing.

The third experiment concerns coreference annotation. It is a nominal annotation that has been designed to be used as a comparison with the previous ordinal annotations tasks.

The corresponding annotated corpora are available (TestAccord database) on the french Parole_Publique[1] corpus repository under a CC-BY-SA Creative Commons licence.

4.2 Emotion corpus

Emotion annotation consists in adding emotional information to written messages or speech transcripts. There is no real consensus about how an emotion has to be described in an annotation scheme. Two main approaches can be found in the literature. On the one hand, emotions are coded by affective modalities (Scherer, 2005), among which sadness, disgust, enjoyment, fear, surprise and anger are the most usual (Ekman, 1999; Cowie and Cornelius, 2003). On the other hand, an ordinal classification in a multidimensional space is considered. Several dimensions have been proposed among which three are prevailing (Russell, 1980): *valence*, *intensity* and *activation*. *Activation* distinguishes passive from active emotional states. *Valence* describes whether the emotional state conveyed by the text is positive, negative or neutral. Lastly, *intensity* describes the level of emotion conveyed.

Whatever the approach, low to moderate inter-annotator agreements are observed, what explains that reference annotation must be achieved through a majority vote with a significant number of coders (Schuller and al. 2009). Inter-coder agreement is particularly low when emotions are coded into modalities (Devillers and al., 2005; Callejas and Lopez-Cozar, 2008). This is why this study focuses on an ordinal annotation.

Our works on emotion detection (Le Tallec and al., 2011) deal with a specific context: affective robotics. We consider an affective multimodal interaction between hospitalized children and a companion robot. Consequently, this experiment will concern a child-dedicated corpus. Although many works already focused on child language (MacWhinney, 2000), no emotional child corpus is currently available in French, our studied language. We have decided to create a little corpus (230 sentences) of fairy tales, which are regularly used in works related to child affect analysis (Alm and al., 2005; Volkova and al., 2010). The selected texts come from modern fairy tales (Vassallo, 2004; Vanderheyden, 1995) which present the interest of being quite confidential. This guarantees that the coders discover

[1] www.info.univ-tours.fr/~antoine/parole_publique

the text during the annotation. We asked 25 subjects to characterize the emotional value conveyed by every sentence through a 5-items scale of values, ranging from *very negative* to *very positive*.

As shown on Table 1, this affective scale encompasses *valence* and *intensity* dimensions. It enables to compare without methodological bias an annotation with 3 coding categories (*valence*: negative, positive, neutral) and the original 5-categories (*valence+intensity*) annotation.

A preliminary experiment showed us that children meet difficulties to handle a 5-values emotional scale. This is why the annotation was conducted on the fairy tales corpus with adults (11 men/14 women; average age: 31.6 years). All the coders have a superior level of education (at least, high-school diploma), they did not know each other and worked separately during the annotation task. Only four of them had a prior experience in corpus annotation.

Value	Meaning	Valence / Polarity	Intensity / Strength
-2	very negative	negative	strong
-1	moderately negative	negative	moderate
0	no emotion	neutral	none
1	moderately positive	positive	moderate
2	very positive	positive	strong

Table 1. emotion or opinion annotation schemes

The coders were not trained but were given precise annotation guidelines providing some explanations and examples on the emotional values they had to use. They achieved the annotation once, without any restriction on time. They had to rely on their own judgment, without considering any additional information. Sentences were given in a random order to investigate an out-of-context perception of emotion. We conducted a second experiment where the order of the sentences followed the original fairy tale, in order to study the influence of the discourse context. The criterion of data significance – at least five chance agreements per category – proposed by (Krippendorff, 2004) is greatly satisfied for the valence annotation (3 categories). It is approached on the complete annotation where we can assure 4 chance agreements per category.

4.3 Opinion corpus

The second experiment concerns opinion annotation. Emotion detection can be related to a certain extent, with opinion mining (or sentiment analysis), whose aim is to detect the attitude of people in the texts they produce. A basic task in opinion mining consists in classifying the polarity of a given text, which should be either a sentence (Wilson and al., 2005), a speech turn or a complete document (Turney, 2002). *Polarity* plays the same role as valence does for affect analysis: it describes whether the expressed judgment is positive, negative, or neutral. One should also characterize the *sentiment strength* (Thelwall and al., 2010). This feature can be related to the notion of *intensity* used in emotional annotation. Both *polarity* and *sentiment strength* are considered in our annotation task.

This experiment has been carried out on a corpus of film reviews. The reviews were relatively short texts written by ordinary people on dedicated French websites (www.senscritique.com and www.allocine.fr). They concerned the same French movie. The corpus contains 183 sentences. Its annotation was conducted by the 25 previous subjects. The methodology is identical to the emotion annotation task. The subjects were asked to qualify the opinion that was conveyed by every sentence of the reviews by means of the same scale of values (Table 1). This scale encompasses this time the *polarity* and *sentiment strength* dimensions. Once again, the sentences were given in a random order and contextual order respectively. The criterion of data significance is satisfied here too.

On both annotations, experiments with the random or the contextual order give similar results. Results from the contextual annotation will be given only when necessary.

4.4 Coreference corpus

The last experiment concerns coreference annotation. We have developed an annotated corpus (ANCOR) which clusters various types of spontaneous and conversational speech. With a total of 488,000 lexical units, it is one of the largest coreference corpora dedicated to spoken language (Muzerelle and al. 2014). Its annotation was split into three successive phases:

- Entity mentions marking,
- Referential relations marking,
- Referential relations characterization

The experiment described in this paper concerns the characterization of the referential relations. This nominal annotation consists in classifying relations among five different types:

- *Direct coreference (DIR)* – Coreferent mentions are NPs with same lexical heads.
- *Indirect coreference (IND)* – These mentions are NPs with distinct lexical heads.
- *Pronominal anaphora (PRO)* – The subsequent coreferent mention is a pronoun.
- *Bridging anaphora (BRI)* – The subsequent mention does not refer to its antecedent but depends on it for its referential interpretation (example: meronymy).
- *Bridging pronominal anaphora (BPA)* – Bridging anaphora where the subsequent mention is a pronoun. This type emphasizes metonymies (example: *Avoid Central Hostel... they are unpleasant*)

The subjects (3 men / 6 women) were adult people (average age: 41.2 years) with a high proficiency in linguistics (researchers in NLP or corpus linguistics). They know each other but worked separately during the annotation, without any restriction on time. They are considered as experts since they participated to the definition of the annotation guide. The study was conducted on an extract of 10 dialogues, representing 384 relations. Krippendorff's (2004) criterion of significance is therefore satisfied here too.

4.5 Reliability measures

The experiments have been conducted with four chance-balanced reliability measures[2] :

- *Multi-κ*: multiple coders/binary distance Cohen's κ (Davies and Fleiss, 1982),
- *Multi-π*: multiple coders/binary distance Scott's π (Fleiss, 1971),
- α_b : Krippendorff's α with binary distance,
- α : standard Krippendorff's α with a 1-dimension Euclidian distance.

The use of Euclidian distance is unfounded on coreference which handles a nominal annotation. Thus, α will not be computed on this last corpus.

5 Results

5.1 Influence of the number of categories

Our affective coding scheme enables a direct comparison between a 3-classes (*valence* or *polarity*) and a 5-classes annotation. The 3-classes scheme clusters the coding categories with the same valence or polarity. For instance {-2,-1} negative values are clustered in the same category which receive the index 1. For the computation of the weighted α, the distance between negative (-1) and positive (1) classes will be equal to 2. Table 2 presents the reliability measures observed on all of the corpora.

Corpus	**Emotion (*fairy tales*)**			
Metric	**M-κ**	**M-π**	**α_b**	**α**
3-classes	0.41	0.41	0.41	0.57
5-classes	0.29	0.29	0.29	0.57
Abs. diff.	*0.12*	*0.12*	*0.12*	*0.0*
Corpus	**Opinion (*film reviews*)**			
Metric	**M-κ**	**M-π**	**α_b**	**α**
3-classes	0.58	0.58	0.58	0.75
5-classes	0.45	0.45	0.45	0.80
Abs. diff.	*0.13*	*0.13*	*0.13*	0.05
Corpus	**Coreference (*spoken dialogues*)**			
Metric	**M-κ**	**M-π**	**α_b**	**α**
5-classes	0.69	0.69	0.69	n.s.

Table 2. Reliability measures: emotion and opinion random annotation as well as coreference annotation

Several general conclusions can be drawn from these figures. At first, low inter-coder agreements are observed on affective annotation, which is coherent with many other studies (Devillers and al., 2005; Callejas and Lopez-Cozar, 2008). Non-weighted metrics (*multi-κ*; *multi-π*, α_b) range from 0.29 to 0.58, depending on the annotation scheme. This confirms that these annotation tasks are prone to high subjectivity. Higher levels of agreement may have been obtained if the annotators were trained with supervision. As said before, this would have reduced the spontaneity of judgment. Furthermore, a comprehensive meta-analysis (Bayerl and Paul, 2011) has shown that no difference may be found on data reliability between experts and novices.

The reliability measures given by the weighted version of Krippendorff's α on the two affective tasks are significantly higher: α values range from 0.57 to 0.80, which suggests a rather sufficient reliability. These results are not an artifact. They come from better disagreement estimation. For instance, the difference between a positive

[2] Experiments were also conducted with Cronbach'α_c (Cronbach, 1951). This metrics is based on a correlation measure. Krippendorff (2009) considers soundly that correlation coefficients are inappropriate to estimate reliability. Our results show that α_c is systematically outperformed by the other metrics. In particular, it is highly dependent to coder bias. For instance we observed a relative standard deviation of α_c measures higher than 22% when measuring the influence of coders set permuation (§ 5.3, table 5). This observation discards Cronbach'α_c as a trustworthy measure.

and a negative annotation is more serious than between the positive and the neutral emotion, what a weighted metrics accounts for.

Satisfactory measures are found on the contrary on the coreference task (0.69 with every metric). This result was expected, since a large part of the annotation decisions are based on objective (syntactic or semantic) considerations.

Whatever the experiment you consider, *multi-κ*, *multi-π* and α_b coefficients present very close values (identical until the 3rd decimal). A similar observation was made by (Arstein and Poesio, 2005) with 18 coders. This validates the theoretical hypothesis on the convergence of individual-distribution and single-distribution measures when the number of coders increases. Our experiments show that annotator bias is moderate with 25 coders when inter-coders agreement is rather low (affective tasks), while 9 coders are enough to guarantee a low annotator bias when data reliability is higher (coreference task).

Lastly, the comparison between the two annotation schemes (3 or 5 classes) in affective tasks provides some indications on the influence of the number of coding categories on reliability estimation[3]. As expected (see § 3.3), *multi-κ*, *multi-π* and α_b values increase significantly when the number of classes decreases.

On the contrary, weighted α is significantly less affected by the increase of the number of categories. The α value remains unchanged on the emotional corpus and its variation restricts to 0.05 on the opinion task. It seems that the use of a Euclidian distance counterbalances the higher risk of disagreement when the number of categories grows. Such an independence of the number of coding categories is an interesting property for a reliability measure, which has never been reported as far as we know.

Metric	M-κ	M-π	α_b	α
3-classes	0.61	0.61	0.61	0.78
5-classes	0.49	0.49	0.49	0.83
Abs. diff.	*0.12*	*0.12*	*0.12*	*0.05*

Table 3. Reliability measures with 3 and 5 annotation classes: opinion contextual annotation (film reviews).

Finally, Table 3 presents as an illustration the reliabilities measures we obtained with the contextual annotation of the opinion corpus. These results are fully coherent with the previous ones. One should note in addition that reliability measures are significantly higher on these contextual annotations: the context of discourse helps the coders to qualify opinions more objectively.

5.2 Influence of prevalence

Table 4 presents the distribution of the annotations on the three corpora. (Devillers and al., 2005; Callejas and Lopez-Cozar, 2008) reported that more than 80% of the speech turns are classified as neutral in their emotional corpora. This prevalence was not found on our affective corpora. Positive annotations are nearly as frequent as the neutral ones on the emotion task. This observation is due to the deliberate emotional nature of fairy tales. Likewise, the neutral opinion is minority among the film reviews, which aim frequently at expressing pronounced judgments. Positive opinions are slightly majority on the opinion corpus but this prevalence is limited: it represents an increase of only 50% of frequency, by comparison with a uniform distribution.

Corpus	Emotion (*fairy tales*)				
5-classes / *Distribution*	−2 / *8%*	−1 / *17%*	0 / *38%*	1 / *23%*	2 / *14%*
3-classes / *Distribution*	**Negative** / *25%*		**neutral** / *38%*	**Positive** / *37%*	
Corpus	**Opinion** (*film reviews*)				
5-classes / *Distribution*	-2 / *15%*	-1 / *21%*	0 / *14%*	1 / *26%*	2 / *25%*
3-classes / *Distribution*	**negative** / *36%*		**neutral** / *14%*	**positive** / *51%*	
Corpus	**Coreference** (*spoken dialogues*)				
5-classes / *Distribution*	DIR / *40%*	IND / *7%*	PRO / *42%*	BRI / *10%*	BPA / *1%*

Table 4. Distribution of the coding categories

In the coreference corpus, two classes are highly dominant, but they are not prevalent alone. There is no indication in the literature that the prevalence of two balanced categories has a bias on data reliability measure. For all these reasons, we didn't investigate the influence of prevalence. Besides, relevant works are questioning the importance of the influence of prevalence on inter-coders agreement measures (Vach, 2005).

5.3 Influence of coders set permutation

"*a coefficient for assessing the reliability of data must treat coders as interchangeable* (Krippendorff, 2004b). We have studied the stability of reliability measures computed on *any* combination of 10 coders (among 25) on the affective corpora, and 4 coders (among 9) on the corefer-

[3] The 3-classes coding scheme is a semantic reduction of the 5-classes one. One should wonder whether the same results can be observed with unrelated categories. (Chu-Ren *and al.*, 2002) shows indeed that expanding PoS tags with subcategories does not increase categorical ambiguity.

ence corpus. The influence of permutation is quantified by a measure of relative standard deviation (e.g. related to the average value) among the sets of coders (Table 5).

Corpus	Emotion (*fairy tales*)			
Metric	**M-κ**	**M-π**	**α_b**	**α**
3-classes	7.4%	7.7%	7.6%	6.2%
5-classes	9.0%	9.1%	9.1%	6.1%
Corpus	**Opinion (*film reviews*)**			
3-classes	3.4%	3.3%	3.3%	2.6%
5-classes	4.0%	4.0%	4.1%	1.7%
Corpus	**Coreference (*spoken dialogues*)**			
5-classes	4.6%	4.6%	4.6%	n.c.

Table 5. Relative standard deviation of measures on any independent sets of coders

Binary metrics do not differ on this criterion: *multi-κ*, *multi-π* and α_b present very similar results. On the opposite, the benefit of a Euclidian distance of agreement is clear: α is significantly less influenced by coders set permutation.

5.4 Influence of the number of coders

A good way to limit annotator bias is to enroll an important number of annotators. This need is unfortunately contradictory with a restriction of annotation costs. The estimation of data reliability must thereby remain trustworthy with a minimal number of coders. As far as we know, there is no clear indication in the literature about the definition of such a minimal size.

We have conducted an experiment which investigates the influence of the number of coders on the relevancy of reliability estimation. Considering N annotations (N=25 for affective annotation and N=9 for coreference annotation), we compute all the possible reliability values with any subsets of S coders, S varying from 2 to N. As an estimation of the trustworthiness of the coefficients, the relative standard deviation of the reliability values is computed for every size S (Figures 1 to 3). The influence of the number of coders is obvious: detrimental standard deviations are found with small coders set sizes. This finding concerns above all *multi-κ*, *multi-π* and α_b, which present very close behaviors on all annotations. One the opposite, the weighted α coefficient converges significantly faster to a trustworthy reliability measure The comparison between α_b and α is enlightening. It shows again that the main benefit of Krippendorff's proposal results from its accounting for a weighted distance in a multi-coders ordinal annotation.

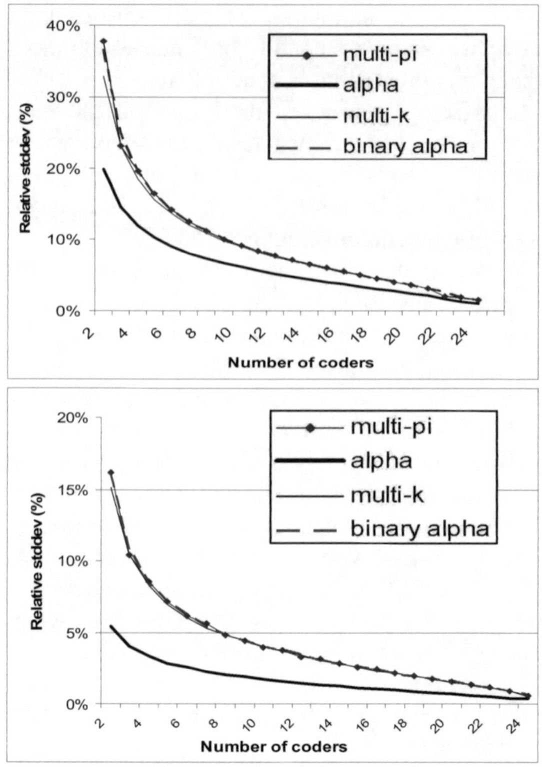

Figure 1. Relative standard deviation on any set of coders of a given size. 5-classes coding scheme. Emotion (top) and opinion (bottom) random annotation.

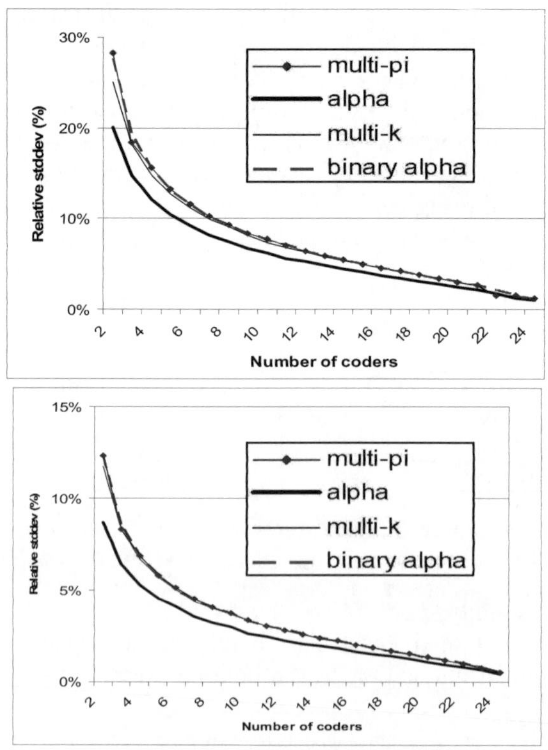

Figure 2. Relative standard deviation on any set of coders of a given size. 3-classes coding scheme. Emotion (top) and opinion (bottom) random annotation.

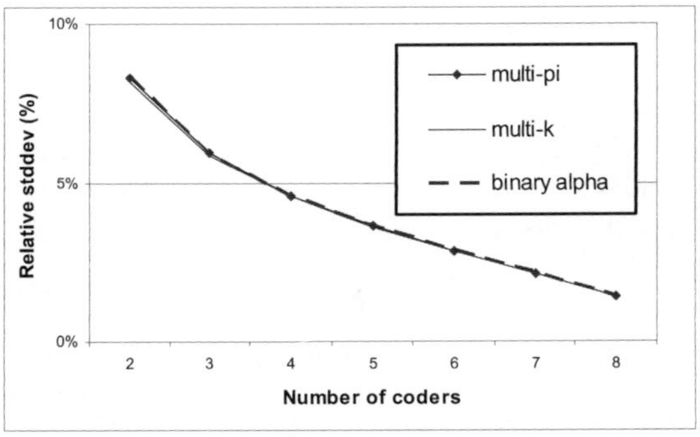

Figure 3. Relative st[d] deviation of measures on any sets of coders for a given coders set size: coreference

6 Conclusion and perspectives

Our experiments were conducted on various annotation tasks which assure a certain representativeness of our conclusions:

- Cohen's κ, Krippendorff's α and Scott's π provide close values when they use the same measure of disagreement.
- A convergence of these measures has been noticed in the literature when the number of coders is high. We observed it even on very restricted sets of annotators.
- The use of a weighted measure (Euclidian distance) has several benefits on ordinal data. It restricts the influence on reliability measure of both the number of categories and the number of coders. Unfortunately, Cohen's κ statistics cannot consider a weighted distance in a multi-coders framework contrary to Krippendorff's α.
- There is no benefit of using Krippendorff's α on nominal data, since a binary distance is mandatory on this situation.

To conclude, the main interest of Krippendorff's α is thus its ability to integrate any kind of distance. In light of our results, the weighted version of this coefficient must be preferred every time an ordinal annotation with multiple coders is considered.

Our experiments leave open an essential question: the objective definition of trustworthy thresholds of reliability. We propose to investigate this question in terms of expected modifications of the reference annotation. A majority vote is generally used as a gold standard to create this reference with multiple coders. As a preliminary experiment, we have compared our reference affective annotations (25 coders) with those obtained on any other included set of coders.

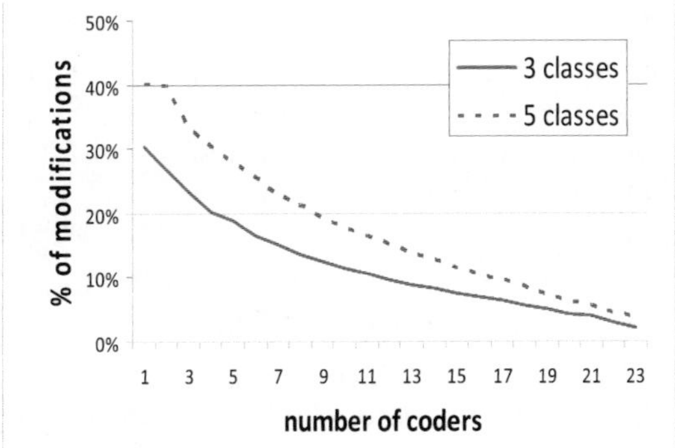

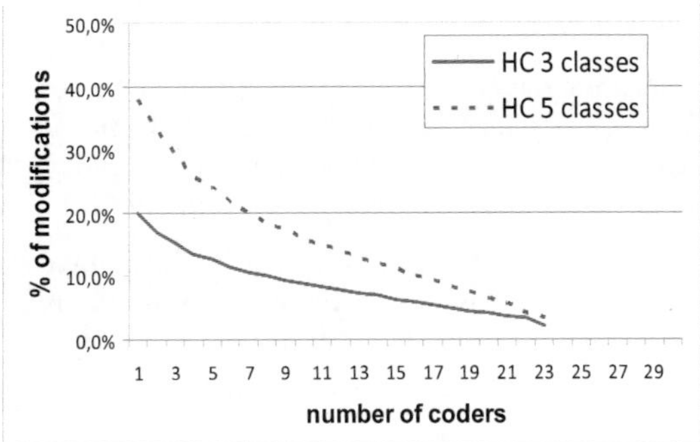

Figure 4. Average modifications of the reference according to the number of coders. Emotion annotation (top) and opinion annotation (bottom)

Figure 4 presents the average percentage of modifications of the reference according to the number of coders. We wonder to what extent these curves can be related to reliability measures. It seems indeed that the higher the measures are, the lower the modifications are too. For instance, almost all of the coefficients present higher or equal reliability values with 3 coding categories (Tables 2 & 3), which corresponds to lower levels of modifications on Figure 3. Likewise, reliability measures are higher on the opinion annotation, where we observe lower modifications of the reference.

As a result, we expect results like those presented on figure 4 to enable a direct interpretation of reliability measures. For instance, with a *multi-κ* values of 0.41, or a α_b value of 0.57 (Table 2, 3-classes emotion annotation), one should expect around 8% of errors on our reference annotation if 10 coders are considered. We plan to extend these experiments with simultated synthetic data to characterize precisely the relations between absolute reliability measures and expected confidence in the reference annotation. We expect to obtain with simulated annotation a sufficient variety of agreement to establish sound recommendations on data reliability thresholds. We intend to modify randomly human annotations to conduct this simulation.

References

Cecilia Alm, Dan Roth, Richard Sproat. 2005. Emotions from Text: Machine Learning for Text-based Emotion Prediction, In *Proc. HLT&EMNLP'2005*. Vancouver, Canada. 579-586

Ron Arstein and Masimo Poesio. 2008. Inter-Coder Agreement for Computational Linguistics. *Computational Linguistics*. 34(4):555-596.

Ron Artstein and Massimo Poesio. 2005. Bias decreases in proportion to the number of annotators. In *Proceedings FG-MoL'2005*, 141:150, Edinburgh, UK.

Petra Saskia Bayerl and Karsten Ingmar Paul, 2011. What Determines Inter-Coder Agreement in Manual Annotations? A Meta-Analytic Investigation . *Computational Linguistics*. 37(4), 699:725.

Paul Brennan and Alan Silman. 1992. Statistical methods for assessing observer variability in clinical measures. *BMJ*, 304:1491-1494.

Ted Byrt, Janet Bishop, John Carlin. 1993. Bias, prevalence and kappa. *Journal of Clinical Epidemiology*, 46:423-429.

Hermann Brenner and Ulrike Kliebsch. 1996. Dependance of weighted kappa coefficients on the number of categories. *Epidemiology*. 7:199-202.

Zoraida Callejas and Ramon Lopez-Cozar. 2008. Influence of contextual information in emotion annotation for spoken dialogue systems, *Speech Communication*, 50:416-433

Jean Carletta. 1996. Assessing agreement on classification tasks: the Kappa statistic. *Computational Linguistics*, 22(2):249-254

Jacob Cohen. 1960. A coefficient of agreement for nominal scales. *Educational and Psychological Measurement*, 20:37-46.

Jacob Cohen. 1968. Weighted kappa: nominal scale agreement with provision for scaled disagreement or partial credit. *Psychol. Bulletin*, 70(4):213–220

Roddy Cowie and Randolph Cornelius. 2003. Describing the emotional states that are expressed in speech. *Speech Communication.* 40 :5-32.

Lee J. Cronbach. 1951. Coefficient alpha and the internal structure of tests. *Psychometrica*. 16:297-334

Laurence Devillers, Laurence Vidrascu, Lori Lamel. 2005. Emotion detection in real-life spoken dialogs recorded in call center. *Journal of Neural Networks*, 18(4):407-422.

Paul Ekman. 1999. *Patterns of emotions: New Analysis of Anxiety and Emotion*. Plenum Press, New-York, NY.

Barbara Di Eugenio and Michael Glass. 2004. The kappa statistic: A second look. *Computational Linguistics*, 30(1):95–101

Mark Davies and Joseph Fleiss. 1982. Measuring agreement for multinomial data. *Biometrics*, 38(4):1047-1051.

Alvan Feinstein and Domenic Cicchetti. 1990. High agreement but low Kappa : the problem of two paradoxes. *J. of Clinical Epidemiology*, 43:543-549

Joseph L. Fleiss. 1971 Measuring nominal scale agreement among many raters. *Psychological Bulletin*, 76(5): 378–382

Andrew Hayes. 2007. Answering the call for a standard reliability measure for coding data. *Communication Methods and Measures 1*, 1:77-89.

Klaus Krippendorff. 2004. *Content Analysis: an Introduction to its Methodology*. Chapter 11. Sage: Thousand Oaks, CA.

Klaus Krippendorff. 2004b. Reliability in Content Analysis: Some Common Misconceptions and Recommendations. *Human Communication Research,* 30(3): 411-433, 2004

Klaus Krippendorff. 2008. Testing the reliability of content analysis data: what is involved and why. *In* Klaus Krippendorff, Mark Angela Bloch (Eds) *The content analysis reader*. Sage Publications. Thousand Oaks, CA.

Klaus Krippendorff. 2009. *Testing the reliability of content analysis data: what is involved and why*. In Klaus Krippendorff , Mary Angela Bock. *The Content Analysis Reader*. Sage: Thousand Oaks, CA

Marc Le Tallec, Jeanne Villaneau, Jean-Yves Antoine, Dominique Duhaut. 2011 Affective Interaction with a Companion Robot for vulnerable Children: a Linguistically based Model for Emotion Detection. In *Proc. Language Technology Conference 2011*, Poznan, Poland, 445-450.

Brian MacWhinney. 2000. *The CHILDES project : Tools for analyzing talk*. 3rd edition. Lawrence Erlbaum associates Mahwah, NJ.

Judith Muzerelle, Anaïs Lefeuvre, Emmanuel Schang, Jean-Yves Antoine, Aurore Pelletier, Denis Maurel, Iris Eshkol, Jeanne Villaneau. 2014. ANCOR_Centre, a large free spoken French coreference corpus: description of the resource and reliability measures. In Proc. *LREC'2014* (submitted).

Kimberly Neuendorf. 2002. *The Content Analysis Guidebook*. Sage Publications, Thousand Oaks, CA

James Russell. 1980. A Circumplex Model of Affect, *J. Personality and Social Psy.*, 39(6): 1161-1178.

Klaus Scherer. 2005. What are emotions? and how can they be measured? *Social Science Information*, 44 (4):694–729.

Björn Schuller, Stefan Steidl, Anto Batliner. 2009. The Interspeech'2009 emotion challenge. In *Proceedings Interspeech'2009*, Brighton, UK. 312:315.

William Scott. 1955. Reliability of content analysis: the case of nominal scale coding. *Public Opinions Quaterly*, 19:321-325.

Julius Sim and Chris Wright. 2005. The Kappa Statistic in Reliability Studies: Use, Interpretation, and Sample Size Requirements. *Physical Therapy*, 85(3):257:268.

Mike Thelwall, Kevan Buckley, Georgios Paltoglou, Di Cai, Arvid Kappas. 2010. Sentiment strength detection in short informal text. *Journal of the American Society for Information Science and Technology*, 61 (12): 2544–2558.

Peter Turney. 2002. Thumbs up or thumbs down? Semantic orientation applied to unsupervised classification of reviews, In *Proceedings ACL'02*, Philadelphia, Pennsylvania, 417-424.

Werner Vach, 2005. The dependence of Cohen's kappa on the prevalence does not matter, *Journal of Clinical Epidemiology*, 58, 655-661).

Rose-Marie Vassallo. 2004. *Comment le Grand Nord découvrit l'été*. Flammarion, Paris, France.

Kees Vanderheyden. 1995. *Le Noel des animaux de la montagne*. Fairy tale available at the URL : http://www.momes.net/histoiresillustrees/contesdemontagne/noelanimaux.html

Ekaterina Volkova, Betty Mohler, Detmar Meurers, Dale Gerdemann and Heinrich Bülthoff. 2010. Emotional perception of fairy tales: achieving agreement in emotion annotation of text, In *Proceedings NAACL HLT 2010.* Los Angeles, CA.

Theresa Wilson, Janyce Wiebe, Paul Hoffmann. 2005. Recognizing contextual polarity in phrase-level sentiment analysis. In *Proc. of HLT-EMNLP'2005*. 347-354.

Discriminating Rhetorical Analogies in Social Media

Christoph Lofi
National Inst. of Informatics
2-1-2 Hitotsubashi,
Chiyoda-ku, Tokyo
101-8430, Japan
lofi@nii.ac.jp

Christian Nieke
TU Braunschweig
Mühlenpfordtstr. 23
38106 Braunschweig
Germany
nieke@ifis.cs.tu-bs.de

Nigel Collier
National Inst. of Informatics
2-1-2 Hitotsubashi,
Chiyoda-ku, Tokyo
101-8430, Japan
collier@nii.ac.jp

Abstract

Analogies are considered to be one of the core concepts of human cognition and communication, and are very efficient at encoding complex information in a natural fashion. However, computational approaches towards large-scale analysis of the semantics of analogies are hampered by the lack of suitable corpora with real-life example of analogies. In this paper we therefore propose a workflow for discriminating and extracting natural-language analogy statements from the Web, focusing on analogies between locations mined from travel reports, blogs, and the Social Web. For realizing this goal, we employ feature-rich supervised learning models which we extensively evaluate. We also showcase a crowd-supported workflow for building a suitable Gold dataset used for this purpose. The resulting system is able to successfully learn to identify analogies to a high degree of accuracy (F-Score 0.9) by using a high-dimensional subsequence feature space.

1 Introduction

Analogies are one of the core concepts of human cognition (Hofstadter, 2001), and it has been suggested that analogical inference is the "thing that makes us smart" (Gentner, 2003). An analogy can be seen as a pattern of speech leading to a cognitive process that transfers some high-level meaning from one particular subject (often called the *analogue* or the *source*) to another subject, usually called the *target*. When using analogies, one emphasizes that the "*essence"* of source and target is similar, i.e. their most discriminating and prototypical processes and properties are perceived in a similar way.

The nature of analogies has been discussed and studied since the ancient Greeks, however computational approaches are still rather limited and in their infancy. One reason for this is that text corpora containing analogies are crucial to study the syntactic and semantic patterns of analogies in order to make progress on automated understanding techniques. For example, to learn about their distribution and the attribute-value pairs that are compared. However, to the best of our knowledge, no such corpus is freely available. We will therefore in this paper present a method for creating such a corpus in an efficient fashion, and make our corpus available for further research efforts.

As an example, consider this brief statement: "West Shinjuku (a Tokyo district) is like Lower Manhattan" It allows readers who know New York, but not Tokyo, to infer some of the more significant properties of the unknown district (e.g., it is an important business district, hosts the headquarters of many companies, features many skyscrapers, etc.). However, automatically understanding analogies is surprisingly hard due to the extensive domain knowledge required in order to perform analogical reasoning. For example, an *analogy repository* containing such domain knowledge has to provide information on which attributes of source and target are generally considered comparable. In contrast to Linked Open Data or typical ontologies, such analogical knowledge is *consensual*, i.e. there is no undisputable truth to analogical information, but a statement can be considered "good" analogical knowledge if its' semantics are perceived similarly by enough people (Lofi & Nieke, 2013). For example, while many properties of West Shinjuku and Lower Manhattan are dissimilar, nonetheless most people will immediately recognize dominant similarities.

In order to build an analogy repositories, a large number of actual analogy statements reflecting the diversity of people's opinions are required for analysis. In this paper, we make a start on this task by proposing a workflow for reliably extracting such statements by using feature-rich supervised learning models, and demonstrate its effectiveness for analogies between different places. Our contributions in this paper are as follows:

- First, we build a suitable *Gold corpus* for training and testing supervised learning models, focusing on *analogies between places*. This corpus will be based upon content mined from search engines and social media.
- We show the effectiveness, but also the challenges of *crowd-sourcing* as a technique for screening and refining potential Gold corpus documents. This process results in multi-sentence text snippets containing an analogy extracted from these documents.
- We design and evaluate supervised learning models with rich feature sets to *recognize analogy statements automatically*, allowing us to substitute crowd-sourcing with automated techniques for further expanding the corpus.
- We extensively *evaluate* our models, and discuss their strengths and shortcomings.

2 Processing Analogies

There exist several approaches for modeling and capturing the semantics of analogies, among them many formal ones relying, for example, on structural mapping (Gentner, 1983). These types of approaches aim at mapping characteristics and relationships of source and target, usually relying on factual domain knowledge given in propositional networks. One example typically used in this context is the Rutherford analogy "Atoms are like the Solar System", which can be derived by outlining similarities between the nucleus and the sun, which are both heavy masses in the center of their respective system, and electrons and planets, which revolve around the center attracted by a strong force (here, the coulomb force is analog to the gravitational force). This model resulted in several theoretical computational models (e.g. (Gentner & Gunn, 2001)).

The most extensively researched subset of analogies are 4-term analogies between two word pairs (mason, stone)::(carpenter, wood). Here, processing analogies boils down to measuring the *relational similarity* of the word pairs, i.e. a mason *works with* stone as a carpenter *works with* wood.

However, measuring the similarity between entities or relationships is a difficult task. While most structure-mapping approaches rely on processing facts, e.g. as extracted from ontologies or knowledge networks, supporters of *perceptual analogies* claim that this similarity has to be measured on a high perceptional level (Chalmers, French, & Hofstadter, 1992), i.e. there can be an analogy if people perceive or believe relations or properties to be as similar even if there are no hard facts supporting it (Kant, 1790), or even when facts oppose it. More formally, two entities A and B can be seen as being analogous (written as $A :: B$) when their relevant relationships and properties are *perceived sufficiently similar* (Lofi & Nieke, 2013). This type of *consensual* analogy is of high relevance in natural communication (in fact, most analogies we discovered in our data are of this type), but very hard to learn as there are no corpora for studying analogies readily available. Furthermore, this definition opens up other challenges: What are the relevant characteristics between two entities? When are they perceived as being similar? And when does an analogy hold true?

With this work, we aim at paving the way for future research on this challenging set of problems by providing a workflow for mining analogy examples from the Web and Social Media. To illustrate this, consider the following example extracted from our Gold corpus:

> "Tokyo, like Disneyland, is sterile. It's too clean and really safe, which are admirable traits, but also unrealistic. Tokyo is like a bubble where people can live their lives in a very naive and enchanted way because real problems do not exist." (No. 5310 in corpus)

This perceptual analogy between Tokyo and Disneyland is hard to explain when only relying on typical structured knowledge like Linked Open Data or ontologies, and thus requires specialized data repositories which can be built up using real-world examples as provided by our approach.

Unfortunately, actually detecting the use of an analogies in natural text, a requirement for building sufficiently large test corpora, is not an easy task, as there are only subtle syntactic and morphological differences between an analogy and a simple comparison. These differences cannot be grasped by simple classification models. For example, while many rhetorical analogies contain phrases as "is like" or ", like", as for example in "West Shinjuku is like Lower Manhattan" or "Tokyo is like Disneyland as it is very sterile" there is a plethora of very similar sentences which do not express an analogy ("Shinjuku is like this: ..." or "Tokyo, like the rest of Japan, ..."). These subtle differences, which are hard to grasp with handcrafted patterns and are often found in the surrounding context, can be modeled by our approach as outlined in section 5.

3 Related Work

There exist several works on the semantics of analogies from a cognitive, philosophical, or linguistic perspective, such as (Dedre Gentner, Keith J. Holyoak, & Boicho N. Kokinov, 2001), (Itkonen, 2005), or (Shelley, 2003).
Hearst-like patterns (Hearst, 1992), which we use as a first and very crude filter during the construction of the Gold dataset, have frequently been employed in recent years, especially in the area of extracting hyponyms, e.g., (Snow, Jurafsky, & Ng, 2004) which also aims at learning new extraction patterns based on word dependency trees. But also approaches for dealing with analogies are frequently based on patterns applied to text corpora. Most of these approaches are tailored for solving general analogy challenges given in a 4-term multiple-choice format, and are usually evaluated on the US-based SAT challenge dataset (part of the standardized aptitude test for college admission). SAT challenges are in 4-term analogy form, e.g. "ostrich is to bird AS a) cub is to bear OR b) lion is to cat", and the focus of those approaches is on heuristically assessing similarity of two given words pairs, to find the statistically more plausible answer. For example, (Bollegala, Matsuo, & Ishizuka, 2009), (Nakov & Hearst, 2008), or (Turney, 2008) approach this challenge by using pattern-based Web search and subsequent analysis of the resulting snippets. In contrast to these approaches, we do not focus on word pair similarity, but given one entity, we aim at finding other entities which are seen as analogous in a specific domain (in our case analogies between locations and places). Being focused on a special domain often renders approaches relying on thesauri like WordNet or CoreLex unusable, as many of the words relevant to the domain are simply not contained.
Closely related to analogy processing is the detection of metaphors or metonyms, which are a special form of analogy. Simplified, a metaphor is an analogy between two entities with the additional semantics that one entity can substitute the other and vice versa). While early approaches to metaphor identification relied on hand-crafted patterns (Wilks, 1978), newer ones therefore heavily exploit the interchangeability of the entities (Beust, Ferrari, & Perlerin, 2003) or (Shutova, 2010), and cannot be used for general analogy processing without extensive adoption. These approaches often also rely on some reasoning techniques based on thesauri, but also other approaches based on mining and corpus analysis became popular. For example in (Shutova, Sun, & Korhonen, 2010) a system is presented which, starting from a small seed set of manually annotated metaphorical expressions, is capable of harvesting a large number of metaphors of similar syntactic structure from a corpus.
Detecting analogies also has some similarities with relation extraction, e.g. (Bunescu & Mooney, 2006) using Subsequence Kernels. However, the task is slightly more difficult than simply mining for a "similar_to" relation, which is addressed by our approach in section 5.

4 Building the Gold Dataset

As the goal of this paper is to supply the tools for creating a large corpus of analogies from the Web, we require a reliable mechanism for automatically classifying if a text snippet contains an analogy or not. Such classification requires a Gold dataset which we construct in this section and which we make available to the community for download[1].
As we expect the number of analogies in a completely random collection of web documents to be extremely low, we first start by collecting a set of web documents that are likely to contain an analogy by applying some easy-to-implement but rather coarse techniques as follows:
In order to obtain a varied set of text snippets (i.e. short excerpts from larger Web documents), we first used a Web search engine (Google Search API) with simple Hearst-like patterns for crawling potentially relevant websites. These patterns were selected manually based on analysis of sample Web data by three experts. In contrast to other approaches relying on extraction patters, e.g. (Turney, 2008) or (Bollegala et al., 2009), our patterns are semi-open, e.g. "# * similar to * as", where # is replaced by one of 19 major cities we used for corpus extraction. * is a wildcard, therefore only one entity of the analogy is fixed by the pattern. Each pattern is created by combining one base part (in this case, "# * similar to *") with an extension part ("as"). We used 17 *different base* parts, and 14 different extensions, resulting in 238 different extraction patterns before inserting the city names. Using Web search, we initially obtained 109,121 search results and used them to crawl 22,360 documents, for which we extracted the text snippets surrounding the occurrence of the pattern (2 preceding and 2 succeeding sentences). The intention of our open Hearst-like patterns is to obtain a wide

[1] http://data.l3s.de/dataset/analogy-text-snippets

variety of text snippets which are not limited to simple analogy cases, so most snippets obtained will actually not be analogies at all. Therefore, additional filtering is required to find those which do actually contain an analogy between places. Unlike e.g. (Turney, 2008) where patterns of the form "[0..1] X [0..3] Y [0..1]", with X and Y two given entities, are used, we chose a more general approach and filtered out all snippets not containing at least two different locations (and hence no place analogy, locations provided by Stanford CoreNLP NER tagger), which left 14,141 snippets.

Since we lacked the means to manually classify all of these snippets as a Gold set, we randomly selected a subset of 8000 snippets, and performed a crowd-sourcing based filtering to detect potential analogies, as described in the following.

4.1 Crowd-Sourcing-Based Filtering

Under certain circumstances, crowd-sourcing can be very effective for handling large tasks requiring human intelligence without relying on expensive experts. In contrast to using expert annotators, crowd-workers are readily and cheaply available even for ad-hoc tasks. In this paper, we used micro-task crowd-sourcing, i.e. a central platform like for example Amazon Mechanical Turk[2] or CrowdFlower[3] assigns small tasks (called HITs, human-intelligence tasks) to workers for monetary compensation. HITs usually consist of multiple work units taking only a few minutes to process, and therefore pay few cents.

Crowd-sourcing has been shown to be effective for language processing related tasks, e.g. in (Snow, O'Connor, Jurafsky, & Ng, 2008) it was used to annotate text corpora, and the authors found that for this task, the combination of three crowd judgments roughly provides the quality of one expert worker. However, the quality can vary due to potential incompetence and maliciousness of workers, making quality control mandatory. The two basic tools for quality control in crowd-sourcing are majority votes and Gold units, which are both used in our process. Gold units are tasks for which the correct answer is known, and they are transparently mixed into normal HITs distributed to workers. If workers repeatedly provide an incorrect judgment for gold units, they are considered malicious, are not paid, and their judgments are excluded from the results.

Therefore, we continued to classify the selected 8,000 snippets using 90 gold units. 5 snippets are grouped within each HIT, for which we pay USD $0.04. For each snippet, 3 judgments are elicited. In total, 336 workers participated in categorizing 87 snippets on average (some top contributors categorized up to 1,975 snippets). As a result 895 snippets are classified as containing an analogy with a confidence of over 90% (confidence is computed as a weighted majority vote of worker judgments and worker reliability; with worker reliability resulting from workers failing or passing gold units in previous tasks).

A brief manual inspection showed that these results cannot be trusted blindly (a correctness of 78% compared to an expert judgment was measured in a small sample), so we performed an expert inspection on all potential analogy snippets, revising the crowd judgments where necessary. Furthermore, we manually tagged the names of the analogous locations. This resulted in 542 snippets which are now manually judged as analogies and 353 snippets that were manually judged as not being an analogy. For this task, worker performance is extremely asymmetrical as it is much easier for crowd-workers to reach an agreement for negative examples than for positive ones, and there were 3,023 snippets classified as no analogies with 100% confidence. This intuition was supported by a short evaluation in which we sampled 314 (10.3%) random snippets from this set and found none that had been misclassified. Therefore, the negative examples of our Gold set consist of the snippets manually re-classified by our expert annotators, and the snippets which had been classified with 100% confidence by the crowd-workers. This leaves out 4,082 snippets for which no clear consensus could be reached, and which are thus excluded from the Gold set.

5 Classifiers and Feature Extraction

Using crowd-sourcing for finding analogy statements is a tedious and still quite expensive task. Therefore, we aim at automating the processes of detecting analogies in a given text snippet by designing multiple rich feature sets for machine learning-based classification models, allowing us to discover new analogies quicker and cheaper.

5.1 Dataset Description

Our complete Gold dataset of 3,918 text snippets shows a ratio of positive to negative examples of roughly 1:8. For training and evaluation, we perform four stratified random selections on the Gold set to obtain 4 training sets with 2/3 of the overall

[2] https://www.mturk.com/

[3] http://crowdflower.com/

size (2,611), and respective test sets with 1/3 size (1,307). In each set, the original ratio between positive example (analogies) and negative examples (not analogies) is retained. We prefer this approach over n-fold cross-validation as some of our models are expensive to train.

All snippets in the Gold set consist of 5 sentences, with 105 words per snippet on average. This average does not significantly vary between positively and negatively classified snippets (94 vs. 106). The overall vocabulary contains 31,878 unique words, with 6,960 words in the positive and 30,234 in the negative subset. 5,316 of these words are shared between both sets (76% of those in the Gold set). This observation implies that the language in our snippets is highly varied and far from saturated (for the significantly smaller positive set, 12.84 new words per snippet are added to the vocabulary on average, while for the larger negative subset, this value only drops to 8.95). This situation looks similar for locations, which play a central role in this classification task: the overall number of different locations encountered in all snippets is 2,631, with 0.86 new locations per snippet in the positive set and 0.73 in the negative set. On average, there are 3.18 locations mentioned in a given snippet, again with no significant differences in the positive and negative subset (3.67 vs. 3.10). Please refer to Table 1 for exhaustive statistics.

5.2 Unigram (Bag-of-Word) Feature Model

As our evaluation baseline, we use a straight-forward unigram (bag-of-word) feature model for training a support vector machine. No stop words are removed, and the feature vectors are normalized to the average length of training snippets. Furthermore, we only retain the 5000 most frequent features, and skip any which occur only in a single snippet. For this experiments (and all other later experiments using a SVM), we used the LibSVM implementation (Chang & Lin, 2011) with a linear kernel due to the size of the feature space.

5.3 N-Gram-based Feature Model

Our first approach to increasing classification quality of the baseline is expanding the feature space to also include n-grams. We tested different versions of this model with *lexical* word-level n-grams, *part-of-speech* n-grams, and *both* of them simultaneously. In all cases, we include n-grams with a length of 1 to 4 words, and similar to the baseline, the top-5000 features are retained and values are normalized to the training snippet length, with a minimal frequency of 2. The required part-of-speech labels are obtained by using the Stanford CoreNLP library[4].The three resulting feature models have been trained and evaluated with three classification algorithms which are known to provide good performance in similar classification tasks: a *support vector machine* classifier (as in 5.2), a *Naïve Bayes* classifier (from the Weka library[5]), and Weka's *J48* implementation of the C4.5 classifier (Quinlan, 1993) (with pruning confidence 0.25 and min. leaf distance 2).

Table 1: Characteristics of Gold Data

characteristic	*all*	*positive*	*negative*
# of snippets	3,918	542	3,376
# of snippets in training set	2,611	361	2,250
# of snippets in test set	1,307	181	1,126
vocabulary size	31,878	6,960	30,234
voc. / #snippets	8.14	12.84	8.95
location vocabulary size	2,631	468	2,459
loc.voc. / #snipts.	0.67	0.86	0.73
# words / s. +	105	94	106
# locations / s.	3.18	3.67	3.10

+ #/s.: average count per snippet

5.4 Shortest Path Feature Model

In this subsection we design the Shortest Path feature model, a model aiming at exploiting some of the specific properties of place analogies. By definition, only text snippets featuring two different places can be a place analogy. The Shortest Path model furthermore assumes that both these locations occur in a single sentence (which is tested in 6.3), and that there is a meaningful lexical or grammatical dependency between these occurrences. For actually building our feature space, we rely on typed dependency parses (Marneffe, MacCartney, & Manning, 2006) of the snippets, and extract the shortest path in the resulting dependency tree between both locations (also using Stanford CoreNLP). This path represents the collapsed and propagated dependencies between both locations, i.e. basic tokens as "on" or "by" are integrated in the edge labels and don't appear as nodes. We considered three variations of this approach: paths built using *lexical* labels, path with *part-of-speech* labels, and a combination of *both.* During the construction of our Gold set, we manually annotated the two relevant places for all analogies. Therefore this approach can be applied

[4] http://nlp.stanford.edu/software/corenlp.shtml

[5] http://www.cs.waikato.ac.nz/ml/weka/

directly for positive training examples. However, for negative snippets, no relevant locations have been annotated. Hence, for all negative snippets in training and all snippets in the test set, we assume that all locations which appear in a snippet (as determined by a NER tagger) are relevant, and we extract all shortest paths between any of them. On average this results in 5.6 paths extracted from any given snippet. The extracted paths are generalized by replacing the locations with a generic, and the final feature model results from constructing a binary feature representing whether a given path occurs or not.

As with the n-gram-based feature model, we train and evaluate SVM, Naïve Bayes, and J48 classifiers with our feature vector (parameters as in 5.3). Please note that building this model is computationally significantly more expensive than the n-gram-based approach as it requires named entity recognition, and typed dependency parsing (we required roughly 30 minutes per training / test set on our Intel i7 laptop).

5.5 Subsequence Pattern Feature Model

Basically, this approach aims at creating something similar to the most common sub forests of all snippets, or skip-grams (Guthrie, Allison, Liu, Guthrie, & Wilks, 2006), i.e. results can be seen as a hybrid between "tree patterns" (as e.g. the Shortest Path) and n-grams. The intention is to avoid the problem of overly local patterns, allowing the patterns to work even in the presence of fill words and subsequences added to a sentence. For this, we utilize the PrefixSpan algorithm (Pei et al., 2001) to detect common, reappearing subsequence in the training set, i.e. sequences of words that appear in a given order, ignoring anything in-between. In contrast to the shortest path approach, this model focuses on multiple sentences simultaneously, and therefore is a significant contribution over state-of-the-art techniques.

As before, we used *lexical*, *part-of-speech*, and *combined* features. The general idea of this approach is to use the PrefixSpan algorithm to mine subsequence patterns from positive gold snippets (the *primitives*), and use these as binary features in a classification step, for which we trained three classifiers as described in 5.3.

In case of the lexical labels, we use the PrefixSpan algorithm to return all subsequences that appear at least 10 times (this value is dependent on characteristics of the dataset and has to be tuned manually) in the relevant part (i.e. the minimal set of consecutive sentences that include both locations) of the positive training set snippets. Depending on

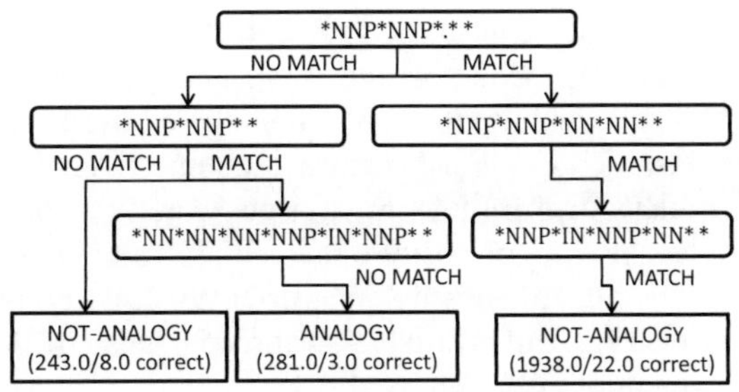

Figure 1: Example Classification Tree

the training set used, this resulted in about 40k common subsequences. To avoid unspecific patterns, we filtered out all sequences that did not contain both locations, which reduces the number to about 15k in average. We then replaced the actual locations with a generic, which allows building a regular expression from the pattern that allows any number of words in-between each part of the sequence. Before applying a pattern to an unknown snippet, we also replace all (NER tagged) locations with a generic. For example, "LOCATION * is * like * LOCATION" would match "Tokyo is also a lot like Seoul" using regular expressions.

The part-of-speech version is similar to the lexical one, but tries to create more generic and open patterns by mining subsequences from the POS representation of the relevant snippet part. For filtering, all patterns that do not contain two 'NNP' tags and appear less than 60 times are removed (the filter threshold is increased as POS patterns are more generic). We get around 60k to 80k patterns before, and ~10k to 20k primitive patterns after filtering which are used as binary features. Finally, we merged lexical and POS patterns and thus allowed the classifiers to use any of the features. A strongly truncated version of a rule tree created using J48 classification with POS subsequence primitives is shown in Figure 1. Please note that due to the open nature of the primitives and their independence, combining several of them in a feature vector will create extremely complex patterns quite easily. Even a vector that contains only the patterns *A*B* and *A*C* would create matches for ABC, ACB, ABAC, ACAB, AACB, AABC and allow any kind of additional fill words in between. However, this approach is computationally expensive (testing/training was around 6 hours on average).

6 Evaluation

In the following we evaluate the effectiveness of our analogy classifiers and models. We primarily rely on the *informedness* measure (Powers, 2007) for quantifying performance. In contrast to using only precision, recall, or F-Measure, it respects all error types, false positives (FP) and false negatives (FN), but also true positives (TP) and true negatives (TN), making it a fair and unbiased measure for classification. Furthermore, it compensates biased class distributions in datasets, e.g. as in our dataset the ratio of positive to negative snippets is 1:8, even an "always no" classifier has a correctness of 85%, but will have an informedness of 0. Informedness is given by:

$$informedness = recall + invRecall - 1$$

with: $recall = \frac{TP}{TP+FN}$ and $inverseRecall = \frac{TN}{TN+FP}$

In Table 2, we provide the average informedness, the percentage of correctly classified snippets, F-measure, precision, recall, and inverse recall (true negative rate) for all experiments. A discussion of these results follows in the next section.

6.1 Classifier Performance

Our straight-forward baseline approach, using unigrams and an SVM classifier results in a reasonable informedness of 0.5. Expanding the feature space to lexical n-grams slightly increases performance, while using more generic part-of-speech n-grams results in weaker results. Combining both, however, generally leads to better classification results. When comparing different classification algorithms, it shows that SVMs are most informed when classifying n-grams-based features, followed by J48. Both techniques will result in moderate recall values around 0.5 and precision around 0.6, with a rather high true negative (inv. Recall rate) of 0.9. This changes quite significantly for Naïve Bayes, which is more likely to classify a snippet as positive, therefore leading to higher recall values, but also much lower informedness, precision, and inverse recall. Consequently, the best approach is using SVM with a lexical-POS combined feature space, leading to an informedness of 0.55.

Shortest Path was intended to achieve higher precision results by exploiting additional semantic knowledge of the underlying problem. Unfortunately, it performs poorly if not used with a SVM, but even then it achieves inferior overall results than the best n-gram approach (informedness 0.4). This is due to some of its necessary assumptions not holding true (see section 6.4).

In contrast, our subsequence-based model achieves a higher informedness score of 0.85 and 0.87 in the best cases. While the lexical variants perform not as well, the more generic variants using POS allow for reliable classification. Combining the lexical and the POS features does unfortunately not increase the performance further (quite contrary, the scores generally decrease for combined features). A possible explanation is overfitting caused by the increased feature space.

6.2 Significance Tests

As our Gold set is of limited size, we performed statistical tests to investigate whether the differences reported in the last subsection are actually

Table 2: Classifier Result Comparison with respect to the Gold classification

Classifier		Informed.	% Correct	F-Measure	Precision	Recall	Inv. Recall
Always No		*0.00*	*0.85*	-	-	*0*	*1*
Unigram Lexical	*SVM*	*0.50*	*0.88*	*0.59*	*0.63*	*0.55*	*0.94*
n-Gram Lexical	SVM	0.53	0.89	0.63	0.68	0.58	0.95
n-Gram POS	SVM	0.42	0.87	0.52	0.58	0.48	0.94
n-Gram Lex & POS	**SVM**	**0.55**	**0.90**	**0.65**	**0.73**	**0.59**	**0.96**
n-Gram Lexical	Naïve Bayes	0.33	0.48	0.36	0.22	0.93	0.41
n-Gram POS	Naïve Bayes	0.38	0.61	0.39	0.26	0.81	0.58
n-Gram Lex & POS	Naïve Bayes	0.48	0.75	0.47	0.35	0.73	0.75
n-Gram Lexical	J48 (C4.5)	0.45	0.87	0.55	0.58	0.52	0.93
n-Gram POS	J48 (C4.5)	0.37	0.85	0.47	0.51	0.45	0.92
n-Gram Lex & POS	J48 (C4.5)	0.44	0.87	0.54	0.57	0.52	0.93
Shortest Path	**SVM**	**0.40**	**0.90**	**0.53**	**0.71**	**0.43**	**0.97**
Shortest Path	Naïve Bayes	0.27	0.87	0.40	0.55	0.32	0.96
Shortest Path	J48 (C4.5)	0.26	0.89	0.40	0.77	0.27	0.99
Subseq. Lexical	SVM	0.39	0.87	0.24	0.51	0.46	0.94
Subseq. Lexical	Naïve Bayes	0.53	0.79	0.49	0.36	0.73	0.80
Subseq. Lexical	J48 (C4.5)	0.34	0.86	0.44	0.47	0.41	0.93
Subseq. POS	SVM	0.84	0.97	0.87	0.89	0.85	0.98
Subseq. POS	Naïve Bayes	0.72	0.81	0.57	0.41	0.93	0.79
Subseq. POS	**J48 (C4.5)**	**0.85**	**0.97**	**0.90**	**0.93**	**0.86**	**0.99**
Subseq. Lex & POS	SVM	0.77	0.95	0.83	0.87	0.79	0.98
Subseq. Lex & POS	Naïve Bayes	0.70	0.80	0.56	0.41	0.91	0.79
Subseq. Lex & POS	**J48 (C4.5)**	**0.87**	**0.97**	**0.90**	**0.92**	**0.88**	**0.98**

significant or result from noise. We used an instance-based test relying on the theory of approximate randomization (Noreen, 1989)[6] to perform 100k iterations of randomized testing of the hypothesis that the pairwise performance differences of selected approaches are actually significant (excluding those pairs where the significance is obvious). First, we compared our baseline, lexical unigrams with SVM to using lexical n-grams to test whether using n-grams actually contributed to the quality, and found the difference to be significant (sign-test $p<0.024$). However, for SVM-based classification, the higher reported performance for also including POS features in addition to lexical n-grams could not be shown to be significant ($p>0.4$). Finally, we tested if the choice between SVM or J48 is significant for our two best subsequence-based approaches, and confirmed this clearly (sign-test: $p<0.006$). According to the reported subsequence results, combining lexical features with part-of-speech features counter-intuitively lowers the performance when using SVM or Naïve Bayes and the positive effect on J48 was shown to be insignificant ($p>0.68$). Therefore, we assume that lexical features don't make a substantial contribution when POS features are present.

6.3 Error Analysis

For only 2,845 of all 3,918 snippets, two different locations (regardless of their relevance to the analogy) are mentioned in the same sentence. This severely hampers the effectiveness of our *Shortest Path* approach, which is limited to cases where both locations appear in the same sentence. Those snippets (344 on average / test set) are then classified as "not analogy", decreasing the recall. The overall impact of this shortcoming is still low, as only 4% of these snippets are analogies. Our other approaches are unaffected.

Interestingly, we see what one might call the "inverse problem" when using the other two models (n-gram and subsequence) that search for the presence of certain terms or sequences, but do not explicitly connect them to the locations. They tend to create false positives by detecting statements that contain 2 locations and an analogy, but not between these locations. Consider:

> "They say New York is the City of Dreams. I say London is the theatre where it all happens" (No. 5627 in corpus).

Another source for false positives is when an analogy is not stated, but is requested:

> "What districts of Paris are similar to Shepherd's Bush or Ealing (both in West London..." (No. 8505 in corpus)

7 Summary and Outlook

We demonstrated approaches for discriminating analogy statements from the Web and Social Media. Our two major contributions are: a) We created a Gold dataset containing 3,918 example text snippets, of which 542 are positively identified as analogies. This dataset was extracted from 109k potential documents resulting from a Web search with manually crafted Hearst-like patterns. The dataset was consequently refined by using a combination of filters, crowd-sourcing, and expert judgments. We also discussed the challenges arising from a crowd-sourcing in such a setting.b) Using the Gold dataset, we designed and evaluated a set of machine learning models for classifying text snippets automatically with respect to containing place analogies. Besides more traditional n-gram based models, we also designed novel models relying on feature spaces resulting from shortest path analysis of the typed dependency tree, and high-dimensional feature spaces built from filtered subsequence patterns mined using the PrefixSpan algorithm. In an exhaustive evaluation, the latter approach, which bridges between lexical and structural features, could be shown to provide significantly superior performance with a maximal informedness of 0.87 compared to 0.55 for the next best approach.

In future work, classification performance can be further increased by better handling of current problem cases, e.g. analogies with out-of-domain targets (analogies between locations and other entity classes, analogies between other entities but unrelated locations nearby, etc.) or ambiguous sentence constructions. Also, our approach can be adopted to other domains relevant to Web-based information systems like movies, cars, books, or e-commerce products in general.

However, the more challenging next step is actually analyzing the semantics of the retrieved analogies, i.e. extracting the triggers of why people chose to compare the source and target. Achieving this challenge will allow building analogy repositories containing perceived similarities between entities and is a mandatory building block for actually implementing an analogy-enabled information system.

[6] Implementation at: http://www.clips.ua.ac.be/scripts/art

References

Beust, P., Ferrari, S., & Perlerin, V. (2003). NLP model and tools for detecting and interpreting metaphors in domain-specific corpora. In *Conf. on Corpus Linguistics*. Lancaster, UK.

Bollegala, D. T., Matsuo, Y., & Ishizuka, M. (2009). Measuring the similarity between implicit semantic relations from the web. In *18th Int. Conf. on World Wide Web (WWW)*. Madrid, Spain. doi:10.1145/1526709.1526797

Bunescu, R. C., & Mooney, R. J. (2006). Subsequence Kernels for Relation Extraction. In *Conf. on Advances in Neural Information Processing Systems (NIPS)*. Vancouver, Canada.

Chalmers, D. J., French, R. M., & Hofstadter, D. R. (1992). High-level perception, representation, and analogy: A critique of artificial intelligence methodology. *Journal of Experimental & Theoretical Artificial Intelligence*, *4*(3), 185–211. doi:10.1080/09528139208953747

Chang, C.-C., & Lin, C.-J. (2011). LIBSVM: A library for support vector machines. *ACM Transactions on Intelligent Systems and Technology (TIST)*, *2*(3).

Dedre Gentner, Keith J. Holyoak, & Boicho N. Kokinov (Eds.). (2001). *The analogical mind: perspectives from cognitive science* (Vol. 0, p. 541). MIT Press.

Gentner, D. (1983). Structure-mapping: A theoretical framework for analogy. *Cognitive science*, *7*, 155–170.

Gentner, D. (2003). Why We're So Smart. In *Language in Mind: Advances in the Study of Language and Thought* (pp. 195–235). MIT Press.

Gentner, D., & Gunn, V. (2001). Structural alignment facilitates the noticing of differences. *Memory & Cognition*, *29*(4), 565–77.

Guthrie, D., Allison, B., Liu, W., Guthrie, L., & Wilks, Y. (2006). A closer look at skip-gram modelling. In *Int. Conf. on Language Resources and Evaluation (LREC)*. Genoa, Italy.

Hearst, M. A. (1992). Automatic acquisition of hyponyms from large text corpora. In *Int. Conf. on Computational Linguistics (COLING)*. Nantes, France.

Hofstadter, D. R. (2001). Analogy as the Core of Cognition. In *The Analogical Mind* (pp. 499–538).

Itkonen, E. (2005). *Analogy as structure and process: Approaches in linguistics, cognitive psychology and philosophy of science*. John Benjamins Pub Co.

Kant, I. (1790). *Critique of Judgement*.

Lofi, C., & Nieke, C. (2013). Modeling Analogies for Human-Centered Information Systems. In *5th Int. Conf. On Social Informatics (SocInfo)*. Kyoto, Japan.

Marneffe, M.-C. de, MacCartney, B., & Manning, C. D. (2006). Generating typed dependency parses from phrase structure parses. In *Int. Conf. on Language Resources and Evaluation (LREC)*. Genoa, Italy.

Nakov, P., & Hearst, M. A. (2008). Solving relational similarity problems using the web as a corpus. In *Proc. of ACL:HLT*. Columbus, USA.

Noreen, E. W. (1989). *Computer-intensive Methods for Testing Hypotheses: An Introduction*. John Wiley & Sons, New York, NY, USA.

Pei, J., Han, J., Mortazavi-asl, B., Pinto, H., Chen, Q., Dayal, U., & Hsu, M. (2001). PrefixSpan: Mining Sequential Patterns Efficiently by Prefix-Projected Pattern Growth. *IEEE Computer Society*.

Powers, D. M. W. (2007). Evaluation: From Precision, Recall and F-Factor to ROC, Informedness, Markedness & Correlation. *Flinders University Adelaide Technical Report SIE07001*.

Quinlan, R. (1993). *C4.5: Programs for Machine Learning*. San Mateo, USA: Morgan Kaufmann Publishers, Inc.

Shelley, C. (2003). *Multiple Analogies In Science And Philosophy*. John Benjamins Pub.

Shutova, E. (2010). Models of metaphor in NLP. In *Annual Meeting of the Association for Computational Linguistics (ACL)*.

Shutova, E., Sun, L., & Korhonen, A. (2010). Metaphor identification using verb and noun clustering. In *Int. Conf. on Computational Linguistics (COLING)*. Beijing, China.

Snow, R., Jurafsky, D., & Ng, A. (2004). Learning syntactic patterns for automatic hypernym discovery. In *Advances in Neural Information Processing Systems (NIPS)*. Vancouver, Canada.

Snow, R., O'Connor, B., Jurafsky, D., & Ng, A. (2008). Cheap and fast---but is it good? Evaluating non-expert annotations for natural language tasks. In *Empirical Methods in Natural Language Processing (EMNLP)*. Honolulu, USA.

Turney, P. (2008). A uniform approach to analogies, synonyms, antonyms, and associations. In *Int. Conf. on Computational Linguistics (COLING)*. Manchester, UK.

Wilks, Y. (1978). Making preferences more active. *Artificial Intelligence*, *11*(3), 197–223.

Semi-supervised learning of morphological paradigms and lexicons

Malin Ahlberg
Språkbanken
University of Gothenburg
malin.ahlberg@gu.se

Markus Forsberg
Språkbanken
University of Gothenburg
markus.forsberg@gu.se

Mans Hulden
University of Helsinki
mans.hulden@helsinki.fi

Abstract

We present a semi-supervised approach to the problem of paradigm induction from inflection tables. Our system extracts generalizations from inflection tables, representing the resulting paradigms in an abstract form. The process is intended to be language-independent, and to provide human-readable generalizations of paradigms. The tools we provide can be used by linguists for the rapid creation of lexical resources. We evaluate the system through an inflection table reconstruction task using Wiktionary data for German, Spanish, and Finnish. With no additional corpus information available, the evaluation yields per word form accuracy scores on inflecting unseen base forms in different languages ranging from 87.81% (German nouns) to 99.52% (Spanish verbs); with additional unlabeled text corpora available for training the scores range from 91.81% (German nouns) to 99.58% (Spanish verbs). We separately evaluate the system in a simulated task of Swedish lexicon creation, and show that on the basis of a small number of inflection tables, the system can accurately collect from a list of noun forms a lexicon with inflection information ranging from 100.0% correct (collect 100 words), to 96.4% correct (collect 1000 words).

1 Introduction

Large scale morphologically accurate lexicon construction for natural language is a very time-consuming task, if done manually. Usually, the construction of large-scale lexical resources presupposes a linguist who constructs a detailed morphological grammar that models inflection, compounding, and other morphological and phonological phenomena, and additionally performs a manual classification of lemmas in the language according to their paradigmatic behavior.

In this paper we address the problem of lexicon construction by constructing a semi-supervised system that accepts concrete inflection tables as input, generalizes inflection paradigms from the tables provided, and subsequently allows the use of unannotated corpora to expand the inflection tables and the automatically generated paradigms.[1]

In contrast to many machine learning approaches that address the problem of paradigm extraction, the current method is intended to produce human-readable output of its generalizations. That is, the paradigms provided by the system can be inspected for errors by a linguist, and if necessary, corrected and improved. Decisions made by the extraction algorithms are intended to be transparent, permitting morphological system development in tandem with linguist-provided knowledge.

Some of the practical tasks tackled by the system include the following:

- Given a small number of known inflection tables, extract from a corpus a lexicon of those lemmas that behave like the examples provided by the linguist.
- Given a large number of inflection tables—such as those provided by the crowdsourced lexical resource, Wiktionary—generalize the tables into a smaller number of abstract paradigms.

2 Previous work

Automatic learning of morphology has long been a prominent research goal in computational linguistics. Recent studies have focused on unsupervised methods in particular—learning morphology from

[1] Our programs and the datasets used, including the evaluation procedure for this paper, are freely available at https://svn.spraakbanken.gu.se/clt/eacl/2014/extract

Proceedings of the 14th Conference of the European Chapter of the Association for Computational Linguistics, pages 569–578,
Gothenburg, Sweden, April 26-30 2014.

unlabeled data (Goldsmith, 2001; Schone and Jurafsky, 2001; Chan, 2006; Creutz and Lagus, 2007; Monson et al., 2008). Hammarström and Borin (2011) provides a current overview of unsupervised learning.

Previous work with similar semi-supervised goals as the ones in this paper include Yarowsky and Wicentowski (2000), Neuvel and Fulop (2002), Clément et al. (2004). Recent machine learning oriented work includes Dreyer and Eisner (2011) and Durrett and DeNero (2013), which documents a method to learn orthographic transformation rules to capture patterns across inflection tables. Part of our evaluation uses the same dataset as Durrett and DeNero (2013). Eskander et al. (2013) shares many of the goals in this paper, but is more supervised in that it focuses on learning inflectional classes from richer annotation.

A major departure from much previous work is that we do not attempt to encode variation as string-changing operations, say by string edits (Dreyer and Eisner, 2011) or transformation rules (Lindén, 2008; Durrett and DeNero, 2013) that perform mappings between forms. Rather, our goal is to encode all variation within paradigms by presenting them in a sufficiently generic fashion so as to allow affixation processes, phonological alternations as well as orthographic changes to naturally fall out of the paradigm specification itself. Also, we perform no explicit alignment of the various forms in an inflection table, as in e.g. Tchoukalov et al. (2010). Rather, we base our algorithm on extracting the longest common subsequence (LCS) shared by all forms in an inflection table, from which alignment of segments falls out naturally. Although our paradigm representation is similar to and inspired by that of Forsberg et al. (2006) and Détrez and Ranta (2012), our method of generalizing from inflection tables to paradigms is novel.

3 Paradigm learning

In what follows, we adopt the view that words and their inflection patterns can be organized into paradigms (Hockett, 1954; Robins, 1959; Matthews, 1972; Stump, 2001). We essentially treat a paradigm as an ordered set of functions $(f_1, \ldots, f_n)$, where $f_i\colon x_1, \ldots, x_n \mapsto \Sigma^*$, that is, where each entry in a paradigm is a function from variables to strings, and each function in a particular paradigm shares the same variables.

3.1 Paradigm representation

We represent the functions in what we call *abstract paradigm*. In our representation, an *abstract paradigm* is an ordered collection of strings, where each string may additionally contain interspersed variables denoted $x_1, x_2, \ldots, x_n$. The strings represent fixed, obligatory parts of a paradigm, while the variables represent mutable parts. These variables, when instantiated, must contain at least one segment, but may otherwise vary from word to word. A complete *abstract paradigm* captures some generalization where the mutable parts represented by variables are instantiated the same way for all forms in one particular inflection table. For example, the fairly simple paradigm

$$x_1 \quad x_1\textbf{+s} \quad x_1\textbf{+ed} \quad x_1\textbf{+ing}$$

could represent a set of English verb forms, where x_1 in this case would coincide with the infinitive form of the verb—**walk**, **climb**, **look**, etc.

For more complex patterns, several variable parts may be invoked, some of them discontinuous. For example, part of an inflection paradigm for German verbs of the type **schreiben** (to write) verbs may be described as:

x_1**+e+**x_2**+**x_3**+en**	INFINITIVE
x_1**+e+**x_2**+**x_3**+end**	PRESENT PARTICIPLE
ge+x_1**+**x_2**+e+**x_3**+en**	PAST PARTICIPLE
x_1**+e+**x_2**+**x_3**+e**	PRESENT 1P SG
x_1**+e+**x_2**+**x_3**+st**	PRESENT 2P SG
x_1**+e+**x_2**+**x_3**+t**	PRESENT 3P SG

If the variables are instantiated as x_1=**schr**, x_2=**i**, and x_3=**b**, the paradigm corresponds to the forms (**schreiben, schreibend, geschrieben, schreibe, schreibst, schreibt**). If, on the other hand, x_1=**l**, x_2=**i**, and x_3=**h**, the same paradigm reflects the conjugation of **leihen** (to lend/borrow)—(**leihen, leihend, geliehen, leihe, leihst, leiht**).

It is worth noting that in this representation, no particular form is privileged in the sense that all other forms can only be generated from some special form, say the infinitive. Rather, in the current representation, all forms can be derived from knowing the variable instantiations. Also, given only a particular word form and a hypothetical paradigm to fit it in, the variable instantiations can often be logically deduced unambiguously. For example, let us say we have a hypothetical form **steigend** and need to fit it in the above paradigm, without knowing which slot it should occupy. We may deduce that it must represent the present participle, and that x_1=**st**, x_2=**i**, and x_3=**g**. From this knowledge, all other forms can subsequently be derived.

Although we have provided grammatical information in the above table for illustrative purposes, our primary concern in the current work is the generalization from inflection tables—which for our purposes are simply an ordered set of word forms—to paradigms of the format discussed above.

3.2 Paradigm induction from inflection tables

The core component of our method consists of finding, given an inflection table, the *maximally general paradigm* that reflects the information in that table. To this end, we make the assumption that string subsequences that are shared by different forms in an inflection table are incidental and can be generalized over. For example, given the English verb **swim**, and a simple inflection table **swim#swam#swum**,[2] we make the assumption that the common sequences **sw** and **m** are irrelevant to the inflection, and that by disregarding these strings, we can focus on the segments that vary within the table—in this case the variation **i**∼**a**∼**u**. In other words, we can assume **sw** and **m** to be *variables* that vary from word to word and describe the table **swim#swam#swum** as x_1**+i+**x_2**#**x_1**+a+**x_2**#**x_1**+u+**x_2, where x_1=**sw** and x_2=**m** in the specific table.

3.2.1 Maximally general paradigms

In order to generalize as much as possible from an inflection table, we extract from it what we call the *maximally general paradigm* by:

1. Finding the longest common subsequence (LCS) to all the entries in the inflection table.

2. Finding the segmentation into variables of the LCS(s) (there may be several) in the inflection table that results in

   (a) The smallest number of variables. Two segments xy in the LCS must be part of the same variable if they always occur together in every form in the inflection table, otherwise they must be assigned separate variables.

   (b) The smallest total number of infixed non-variable segments in the inflection table (segments that occur between variables).

3. Replacing the discontinuous sequences that are part of the LCS with variables (every form in a paradigm will contain the same number of variables).

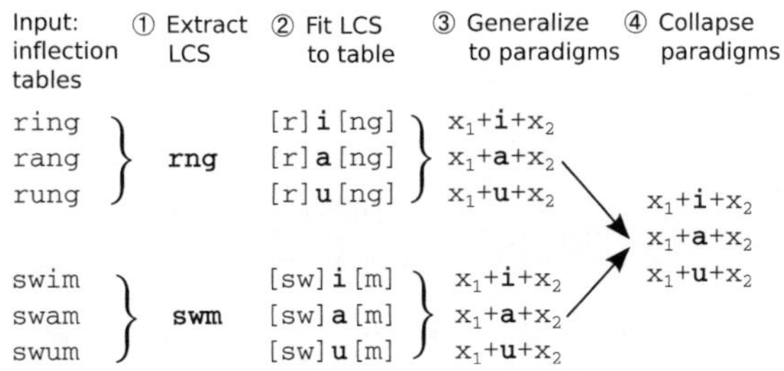

Figure 1: Illustration of our paradigm generalization algorithm. In step ① we extract the LCS separately for each inflection table, attempt to find a consistent fit between the LCS and the forms present in the table (step ②), and assign the segments that participate in the LCS variables (step ③). Finally, resulting paradigms that turn out to be identical may be collapsed (step ④) (section 3.3).

These steps are illustrated in figure 1. The first step, extracting the LCS from a collection of strings, is the well-known multiple longest common subsequence problem (MLCS). It is known to be NP-hard (Maier, 1978). Although the number of strings to find the LCS from may be rather large in real-world data, we find that a few sensible heuristic techniques allow us to solve this problem efficiently for practical linguistic material, i.e., inflection tables. We calculate the LCS by calculating intersections of finite-state machines that encode all subsequences of all words, using the *foma* finite-state toolkit (Hulden, 2009).[3]

While for most tables there is only one way to segment the LCS in the various forms, some ambiguous corner cases need to be resolved by imposing additional criteria for the segmentation, given in steps 2(a) and 2(b). As an example, consider a snippet of a small conjugation table for the Spanish verb **comprar** (to buy), **comprar#compra#compro**. Obviously the LCS is **compr**—however, this can be distributed in two different ways across the strings, as seen below.

[2] To save space, we will henceforth use the #-symbol as a delimiter between entries in an inflection table or paradigm.

[3] Steps 2 and 3 are implemented using more involved finite-state techniques that we plan to describe elsewhere.

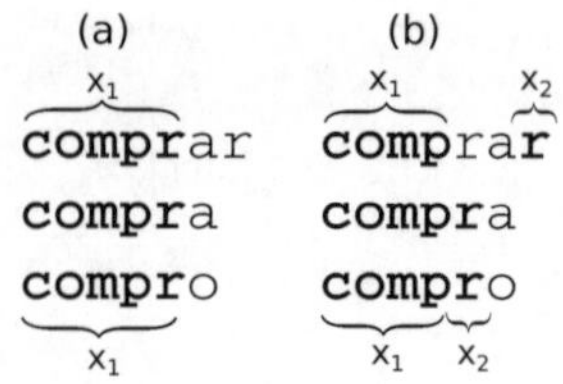

The obvious difference here is that in the first assignment, we only need to declare one variable x_1=**compr**, while in the second, we need two, x_1=**comp**, x_2=**r**. Such cases are resolved by choosing the segmentation with the smallest number of variables by step 2(a).

Remaining ambiguities are resolved by minimizing the total number of infixed segments. As an illustration of where this is necessary, consider a small extract from the Swedish noun table **segel** (sail): **segel#seglen#seglet**. Here, the LCS, of which there are two of equal length (**sege/segl**) must be assigned to two variables where either x_1=**seg** and x_2=**e**, or x_1=**seg** and x_2=**l**:

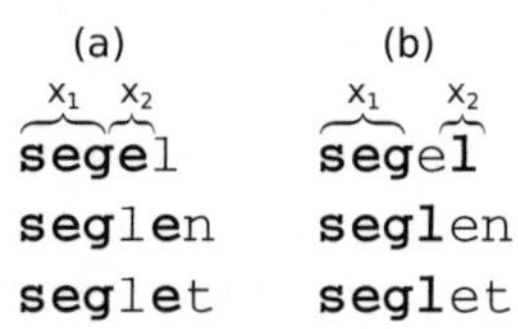

However, in case (a), the number of infixed segments—the **l**'s in the second and third form—total one more than in the distribution in (b), where only one **e** needs to be infixed in one form. Hence, the representation in (b) is chosen in step 2(b).

The need for this type of disambiguation strategy surfaces very rarely and the choice to minimize infix length is largely arbitrary—although it may be argued that some linguistic plausibility is encoded in the minimization of infixes. However, choosing a consistent strategy is important for the subsequent collapsing of paradigms.

3.3 Collapsing paradigms

If several tables are given as input, and we extract the *maximally general paradigm* from each, we may collapse resulting paradigms that are identical. This is also illustrated in figure 1.

As paradigms are collapsed, we record the information about how the various variables were interpreted prior to collapsing. That is, for the example in figure 1, we not only store the resulting single paradigm, but also the information that x_1=**r**, x_2=**ng** in one table and that x_1=**sw**, x_2=**m** in another. This allows us to potentially reconstruct all the inflection tables seen during learning. Storing this information is also crucial for paradigm table collection from text, fitting unseen word forms into paradigms, and reasoning about unseen paradigms, as will be discussed below.

Form	Input	Generalization
[Inf]	kaufen	x_1+**en**
[PresPart]	kaufend	x_1+**end**
[PastPart]	gekauft	**ge**+x_1+**t**
[Pres1pSg]	kaufe	x_1+**e**
[Pres1pPl]	kaufen	x_1+**en**
[Pres2pSg]	kaufst	x_1+**st**
[Pres2pPl]	kauft	x_1+**t**
[Pres3pSg]	kauft	x_1+**t**
[Pres3pPl]	kaufen	x_1+**en**
...	...	...
	x_1 = **kauf**	

Table 1: Generalization from a German example verb **kaufen** (to buy) exemplifying typical rendering of paradigms.

3.4 MLCS as a language-independent generalization strategy

There is very little language-specific information encoded in the strategy of paradigm generalization that focuses on the LCS in an inflection table. That is, we do not explicitly prioritize processes like prefixation, suffixation, or left-to-right writing systems. The resulting algorithm thus generalizes tables that reflect concatenative and non-concatenative morphological processes equally well. Tables 1 and 2 show the outputs of the method for German and Arabic verb conjugation reflecting the generalization of concatenative and non-concatenative patterns.

3.5 Instantiating paradigms

As mentioned above, given that the variable instantiations of a paradigm are known, we may generate the full inflection table. The variable instantiations are retrieved by matching a word form to one of the patterns in the paradigms. For example, the German word form **bücken** (to bend down) may be matched to three patterns in the paradigm exemplified in table 1, and all three matches yield the same variable instantiation, i.e., x_1=**bück**.

Paradigms with more than one variable may be sensitive to the matching strategy of the variables. To see this, consider the pattern x_1+**a**+x_2 and the word **banana**. Here, two matches are possible x_1=**b** and x_2=**nana** and x_1=**ban** and x_2 =**na**. In other words, there are three possible matching

Form	Input	Generalization
[Past1SG]	katabtu (كَتَبْتُ)	x_1+**a**+x_2+**a**+x_3+**tu**
[Past2SGM]	katabta (كَتَبْتَ)	x_1+**a**+x_2+**a**+x_3+**ta**
[Past2SGF]	katabti (كَتَبْتِ)	x_1+**a**+x_2+**a**+x_3+**ti**
[Past3SGM]	kataba (كَتَبَ)	x_1+**a**+x_2+**a**+x_3+**a**
[Past3SGF]	katabat (كَتَبَتْ)	x_1+**a**+x_2+**a**+x_3+**at**
...	...	...
[Pres1SG]	aktubu (أَكْتُبُ)	**a**+x_1+x_2+**u**+x_3+**u**
[Pres2SGM]	taktubu (تَكْتُبُ)	**ta**+x_1+x_2+**u**+x_3+**u**
[Pres2SGF]	taktubīna (تَكْتُبِينَ)	**ta**+x_1+x_2+**u**+x_3+**īna**
[Pres3SGM]	yaktubu (يَكْتُبُ)	**ya**+x_1+x_2+**u**+x_3+**u**
[Pres3SGF]	taktubu (تَكْتُبُ)	**ta**+x_1+x_2+**u**+x_3+**u**
...	...	...
x_1 = **k** (ك), x_2 = **t** (ت), x_3 = **b** (ب)		

Table 2: Generalization from an Arabic conjugation table involving the root **/k-t-b/** from which the stems **katab** (to write/past) and **ktub** (present/non-past) are formed, conjugated in Form I, past and present tenses. Extracting the longest common subsequence yields a paradigm where variables correspond to root radicals.

strategies:[4]

1. shortest match (x_1 =**b** and x_2 =**nana**)
2. longest match (x_1 =**ban** and x_2 =**na**)
3. try all matching combinations

The matching strategy that tends to be successful is somewhat language-dependent: for a language with a preference for suffixation, longest match is typically preferred, while for others shortest match or trying all combinations may be the best choice. All languages evaluated in this article have a preference for suffixation, so in our experiments we have opted for using the longest match for the sake of convenience. Our implementation allows for exploring all matches, however. Even though all matches were to be tried, 'bad' matches will likely result in implausible inflections that can be discarded using other cues.

4 Assigning paradigms automatically

The next problem we consider is assigning the correct paradigms to candidate words automatically. As a first step, we match the current word to a pattern. In the general case, all patterns are tried for a given candidate word. However, we usually have access to additional information about the candidate words—e.g., that they are in the base form of a certain part of speech—which we use to improve the results by only matching the relevant patterns.

From a candidate word, all possible inflection tables are generated. Following this, a decision procedure is applied that calculates a confidence score to determine which paradigm is the most probable. The score is a weighted combination of the following calculations:

1. Compute the longest common suffix for the generated base form (which may be the input form) with previously seen base forms. If of equal length, select the paradigm where the suffix occurs with higher frequency.
2. Compute frequency spread over the set of unique word forms according to the following formula: $\sum_{w \in set(W)} log(freq(w) + 1)$
3. Use the most frequent paradigm as a tie-breaker.

Step 1 is a simple memory-based approach, much in the same spirit as van den Bosch and Daelemans (1999), where we compare the current base form with what we have seen before.

For step 2, let us elaborate further why the frequency spread is computed on unique word forms. We do this to avoid favoring paradigms that have the same word forms for many or all inflected forms. For example, the German noun **Ananas** (pineapple) has a syncretic inflection with one repeated word form across all slots, **Ananas**. When trying to assign a paradigm to an unknown word form that matches x_1, it will surely fit the paradigm that **Ananas** has generated perfectly since we have encountered every word form in that paradigm, of which there is only one, namely x_1. Hence, we want to penalize low variation of word forms when assigning paradigms.

The confidence score calculated is not only applicable for selecting the most probable paradigm for a given word-form; it may also be used to rank a list of words so that the highest ranked paradigm is the most likely to be correct. Examples of such rankings are found in section 5.3.

[4]The number of matches may increase quickly for longer words and many variables in the worst case: e.g. **caravan** matches x_1+**a**+x_2 in three different ways.

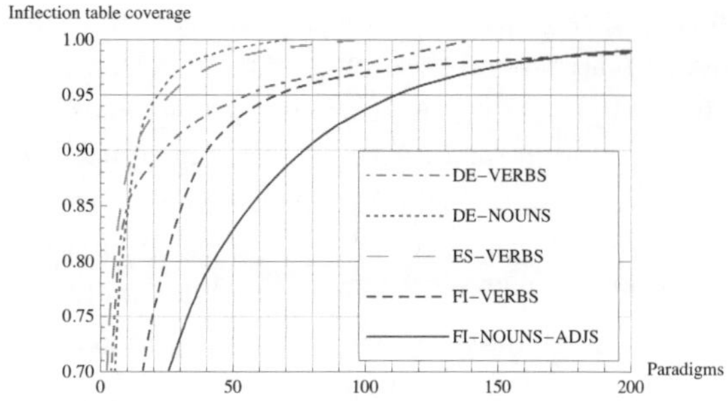

Figure 2: Degree of coverage with varying numbers of paradigms.

Data	Input: inflection tables	Output: abstract paradigms
DE-VERBS	1827	140
DE-NOUNS	2564	70
ES-VERBS	3855	97
FI-VERBS	7049	282
FI-NOUNS-ADJS	6200	258

Table 3: Generalization of paradigms. The number of paradigms produced from Wiktionary inflection tables by generalization and collapsing of abstract paradigms.

5 Evaluation

To evaluate the method, we have conducted three experiments. First we repeat an experiment presented in Durrett and DeNero (2013) using the same data and experiment setup, but with our generalization method. In this experiment, we are given a number of complete inflection tables scraped from Wiktionary. The task is to reconstruct complete inflection tables from 200 held-out base forms. For this task, we evaluate per form accuracy as well as per table accuracy for reconstruction. The second experiment is the same as the first, but with additional access to an unlabeled text dump for the language from Wikipedia.

In the last experiment we try to mimic the situation of a linguist starting out to describe a new language. The experiment uses a large-scale Swedish morphology as reference and evaluates how reliably a lexicon can be gathered from a word list using only a few manually specified inflection tables generalized into abstract paradigms by our system.

5.1 Experiment 1: Wiktionary

In our first experiment we start from the inflection tables in the development and test set from Durrett and DeNero (2013), henceforth D&DN13. Table 3 shows the number of input tables as well as the number of paradigms that they result in after generalization and collapsing. For all cases, the number of output paradigms are below 10% of the number of input inflection tables. Figure 2 shows the generalization rate achieved with the paradigms. For instance, the 20 most common resulting German noun paradigms are sufficient to model almost 95% of the 2,564 separate inflection tables given as input.

As described earlier, in the reconstruction task, the input base forms are compared to the abstract paradigms by measuring the longest common suffix length for each input base form compared to the ones seen during training. This approach is memory-based: it simply measures the similarity of a given lemma to the lemmas encountered during the learning phase. Table 4 presents our results juxtaposed with the ones reported by D&DN13. While scoring slightly below D&DN13 for the majority of the languages when measuring form accuracy, our method shows an advantage when measuring the accuracy of complete tables. Interestingly, the only case where we improve upon the form accuracy of D&DN13 is German verbs, where we get our lowest table accuracy.

Table 4 further shows an oracle score, giving an upper bound for our method that would be achieved if we were always able to pick the best fitting paradigm available. This upper bound ranges from 99% (Finnish verbs) to 100% (three out of five tests).

5.2 Experiment 2: Wiktionary and Wikipedia

In our second experiment, we extend the previous experiment by adding access to a corpus. Apart from measuring the longest common suffix length, we now also compute the frequency of the hypothetical candidate forms in every generated table and use this to favor paradigms that generate a large number of attested forms. For this, we use a Wikipedia dump, from which we have extracted word-form frequencies.[5] In total, the number of word types in the Wikipedia corpus was 8.9M (German), 3.4M (Spanish), 0.7M (Finnish), and 2.7M (Swedish). Table 5 presents the results,

[5]The corpora were downloaded and extracted as described at http://medialab.di.unipi.it/wiki/Wikipedia_Extractor

Data	Per table	D&DN13	Per form	D&DN13	Oracle accuracy per form (per table)
DE-VERBS	68.0	**85.0**	**97.04**	96.19	99.70 (198/200)
DE-NOUNS	76.5	**79.5**	87.81	**88.94**	100.00 (200/200)
ES-VERBS	**96.0**	95.0	99.52	**99.67**	100.00 (200/200)
FI-VERBS	**92.5**	87.5	96.36	**96.43**	99.00 (195/200)
FI-NOUNS-ADJS	**85.0**	83.5	91.91	**93.41**	100.00 (200/200)

Table 4: Experiment 1: Accuracy of reconstructing 200 inflection tables given only base forms from held-out data when paradigms are learned from the Wiktionary dataset. For comparison, figures from Durrett and DeNero (2013) are included (shown as D&DN13).

Data	Per table	Per form	Oracle acc. per form (table)
DE-VERBS	76.50	**97.87**	99.70 (198/200)
DE-NOUNS	**82.00**	**91.81**	100.00 (200/200)
ES-VERBS	**98.00**	99.58	100.00 (200/200)
FI-VERBS	**92.50**	**96.63**	99.00 (195/200)
FI-NOUNS-ADJS	**88.00**	**93.82**	100.00 (200/200)

Table 5: Experiment 2: Reconstructing 200 held-out inflection tables with paradigms induced from Wiktionary and further access to raw text from Wikipedia.

where an increased accuracy is noted for all languages, as is to be expected since we have added more knowledge to the system. The bold numbers mark the cases where we outperform the result in Durrett and DeNero (2013), which is now the case in four out of five tests for table accuracy, scoring between 76.50% for German verbs and 98.00% for Spanish verbs.

Measuring form accuracy, we achieve scores between 91.81% and 99.58%. The smallest improvement is noted for Finnish verbs, which has the largest number of paradigms, but also the smallest corpus.

5.3 Experiment 3: Ranking candidates

In this experiment we consider a task where we only have a small number of inflection tables, mimicking the situation where a linguist has manually entered a few inflection tables, allowed the system to generalize these into paradigms, and now faces the task of culling from a corpus—in this case labeled with basic POS information—the candidate words/lemmas that best fit the induced paradigms. This would be a typical task during lexicon creation.

We selected the 20 most frequent noun paradigms (from a total of 346), with one inflection table each, from our gold standard, the Swedish lexical resource SALDO (Borin et al., 2013). From this set, we discarded paradigms that lack plural forms.[6] We also removed from the paradigms special compounding forms that Swedish nouns have, since compound information is not taken into account in this experiment. The compounding forms are part of the original paradigm specification, and after a collapsing procedure after compound-form removal, we were left with a total of 11 paradigms.

Top-1000 rank	Correct/Incorrect
TOP 10%	100/0 (100.0%)
TOP 50%	489/11 (97.8%)
TOP 100%	964/36 (96.4%)

Table 6: Top-1000 rank for all nouns in SALDO

In the next step we ranked all nouns in SALDO (79.6k lemmas) according to our confidence score, which indicates how well a noun fits a given paradigm. We then evaluated the paradigm assignment for the top-1000 lemmas. Among these top-1000 words, we found 44 that were outside the 20 most frequent noun paradigms. These words were not necessarily incorrectly assigned, since they may only differ in their compound forms; as a heuristic, we considered them correct if they had the same declension and gender as the paradigm, and incorrect otherwise.

Table 6 displays the results, including a total accuracy of 96.4%.

Next, we investigated the top-1000 distribution for individual paradigms. This corresponds to the situation where a linguist has just entered a new inflection table and is looking for words that fit the resulting paradigm. The result is presented in two

[6] The paradigms that lack plural forms are subsets of other paradigms. In other words: when no plural forms are attested, we would need a procedure to decide if plural forms are even possible, which is currently beyond the scope of our method.

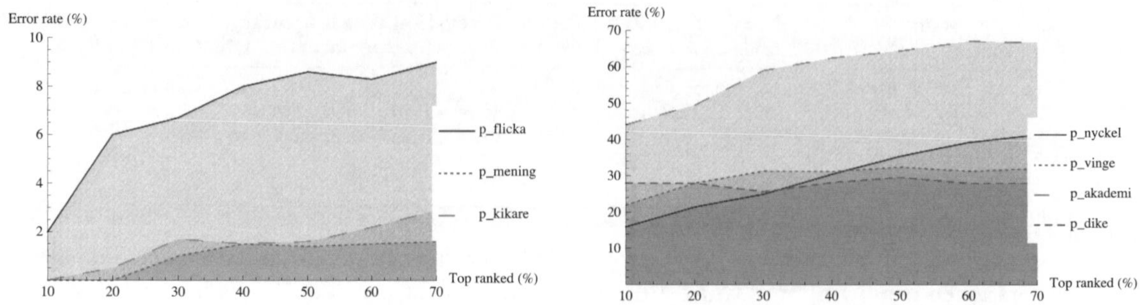

Figure 3: Top-1000: high and low precision paradigms.

error rate plots: figure 3 shows the low precision and high precision paradigms in two plots, where error rates range from 0-2% and 16-44% for the top 100 words.

We further investigated the worst-performing paradigm, **p_akademi** (academy), to determine the reason for the high error rate for this particular item. The main source of error (334 out of 1000) is confusion with **p_akribi** (accuracy), which has no plural. However, it is on semantic grounds that the paradigm has no plural; a native Swedish speaker would pluralize **akribi** like **akademi** (disregarding the fact that **akribi** is defective). The second main type of error (210 out of 1000) is confusion with the unseen paradigm of **parti** (party), which inflects similarly to **akademi**, but with a difference in gender—difficult to predict from surface forms—that manifests itself in two out of eight word forms.

6 Future work

The core method of abstract paradigm representation presented in this paper can readily be extended in various directions. One obvious topic of interest is to investigate the use of machine learning techniques to expand the method to completely unsupervised learning by first clustering similar words in raw text into hypothetical inflection tables. The plausibility of these tables could then be evaluated using similar techniques as in our experiment 2.

We also plan to explore ways to improve the techniques for paradigm selection and ranking. In our experiments we have, for the sake of transparency, used a fairly simple strategy of suffix matching to reconstruct tables from base forms. A more involved classifier may be trained for this purpose. An obvious extension is to use a classifier based on n-gram, capitalization, and other standard features to ascertain that word forms in hypothetical reconstructed inflection tables maintain similar shapes to ones seen during training.

One can also investigate ways to collapse paradigms further by generalizing over phonological alternations and by learning alternation rules from the induced paradigms (Koskenniemi, 1991; Theron and Cloete, 1997; Koskenniemi, 2013).

Finally, we are working on a separate interactive graphical morphological tool in which we plan to integrate the methods presented in this paper.

7 Conclusion

We have presented a language-independent method for extracting paradigms from inflection tables and for representing and generalizing the resulting paradigms.[7] Central to the process of paradigm extraction is the notion of *maximally general paradigm*, which we define as the inflection table, with all of the common string subsequences forms represented by variables.

The method is quite uncomplicated and outputs human-readable generalizations. Despite the relative simplicity, we obtain state-of-the art results in inflection table reconstruction tasks from base forms.

Because of the plain paradigm representation format, we believe the model can be used profitably in creating large-scale lexicons from a few linguist-provided inflection tables.

[7]The research presented here was supported by the Swedish Research Council (the projects *Towards a knowledge-based culturomics*, dnr 2012-5738, and *Swedish Framenet++*, dnr 2010-6013), the University of Gothenburg through its support of the Centre for Language Technology and its support of Språkbanken, and the Academy of Finland under the grant agreement 258373, *Machine learning of rules in natural language morphology and phonology*.

References

Lars Borin, Markus Forsberg, and Lennart Lönngren. 2013. SALDO: a touch of yin to WordNet's yang. *Language Resources and Evaluation*, May. Online first publication; DOI 10.1007/s10579-013-9233-4.

Erwin Chan. 2006. Learning probabilistic paradigms for morphology in a latent class model. In *Proceedings of the Eighth Meeting of the ACL Special Interest Group on Computational Phonology and Morphology*, pages 69–78. Association for Computational Linguistics.

Lionel Clément, Bernard Lang, Benoît Sagot, et al. 2004. Morphology based automatic acquisition of large-coverage lexica. In *LREC 04*, pages 1841–1844.

Mathias Creutz and Krista Lagus. 2007. Unsupervised models for morpheme segmentation and morphology learning. *ACM Transactions on Speech and Language Processing (TSLP)*, 4(1):3.

Grégoire Détrez and Aarne Ranta. 2012. Smart paradigms and the predictability and complexity of inflectional morphology. In *Proceedings of the 13th EACL*, pages 645–653. Association for Computational Linguistics.

Markus Dreyer and Jason Eisner. 2011. Discovering morphological paradigms from plain text using a Dirichlet process mixture model. In *Proceedings of the Conference on Empirical Methods in Natural Language Processing*, pages 616–627. Association for Computational Linguistics.

Greg Durrett and John DeNero. 2013. Supervised learning of complete morphological paradigms. In *Proceedings of NAACL-HLT*, pages 1185–1195.

Ramy Eskander, Nizar Habash, and Owen Rambow. 2013. Automatic extraction of morphological lexicons from morphologically annotated corpora. In *Proceedings of the 2013 Conference on Empirical Methods in Natural Language Processing*, pages 1032–1043. Association for Computational Linguistics.

Markus Forsberg, Harald Hammarström, and Aarne Ranta. 2006. Morphological lexicon extraction from raw text data. In *Advances in Natural Language Processing*, pages 488–499. Springer.

John Goldsmith. 2001. Unsupervised learning of the morphology of a natural language. *Computational linguistics*, 27(2):153–198.

Harald Hammarström and Lars Borin. 2011. Unsupervised learning of morphology. *Computational Linguistics*, 37(2):309–350.

Charles F Hockett. 1954. Two models of grammatical description. *Morphology: Critical Concepts in Linguistics*, 1:110–138.

Mans Hulden. 2009. Foma: a finite-state compiler and library. In *Proceedings of the 12th Conference of the European Chapter of the European Chapter of the Association for Computational Linguistics: Demonstrations Session*, pages 29–32, Athens, Greece. Association for Computational Linguistics.

Kimmo Koskenniemi. 1991. A discovery procedure for two-level phonology. *Computational Lexicology and Lexicography: A Special Issue Dedicated to Bernard Quemada*, 1:451–46.

Kimmo Koskenniemi. 2013. An informal discovery procedure for two-level rules. *Journal of Language Modelling*, 1(1):155–188.

Krister Lindén. 2008. A probabilistic model for guessing base forms of new words by analogy. In *Computational Linguistics and Intelligent Text Processing*, pages 106–116. Springer.

David Maier. 1978. The complexity of some problems on subsequences and supersequences. *Journal of the ACM (JACM)*, 25(2):322–336.

Peter H. Matthews. 1972. *Inflectional morphology: A theoretical study based on aspects of Latin verb conjugation.* Cambridge University Press.

Christian Monson, Jaime Carbonell, Alon Lavie, and Lori Levin. 2008. Paramor: finding paradigms across morphology. In *Advances in Multilingual and Multimodal Information Retrieval*, pages 900–907. Springer.

Sylvain Neuvel and Sean A Fulop. 2002. Unsupervised learning of morphology without morphemes. In *Proceedings of the ACL-02 workshop on Morphological and phonological learning-Volume 6*, pages 31–40. Association for Computational Linguistics.

Robert H Robins. 1959. In defence of WP. *Transactions of the Philological Society*, 58(1):116–144.

Patrick Schone and Daniel Jurafsky. 2001. Knowledge-free induction of inflectional morphologies. In *Proceedings of the second meeting of the North American Chapter of the Association for Computational Linguistics on Language technologies*, pages 1–9. Association for Computational Linguistics.

Gregory T. Stump. 2001. *A theory of paradigm structure.* Cambridge University Press.

Tzvetan Tchoukalov, Christian Monson, and Brian Roark. 2010. Morphological analysis by multiple sequence alignment. In *Multilingual Information Access Evaluation I. Text Retrieval Experiments*, pages 666–673. Springer.

Pieter Theron and Ian Cloete. 1997. Automatic acquisition of two-level morphological rules. In *Proceedings of the fifth conference on Applied natural language processing*, pages 103–110. Association for Computational Linguistics.

Antal van den Bosch and Walter Daelemans. 1999. Memory-based morphological analysis. In *Proceedings of the 37th Annual Meeting of the Association for Computational Linguistics*, pages 285–292. Association for Computational Linguistics.

David Yarowsky and Richard Wicentowski. 2000. Minimally supervised morphological analysis by multimodal alignment. In *Proceedings of the 38th Annual Meeting on Association for Computational Linguistics*, pages 207–216. Association for Computational Linguistics.

How to Produce Unseen Teddy Bears: Improved Morphological Processing of Compounds in SMT

Fabienne Cap, Alexander Fraser
CIS, University of Munich
{cap|fraser}@cis.uni-muenchen.de

Marion Weller
IMS, University of Stuttgart
wellermn@ims.uni-stuttgart.de

Aoife Cahill
Educational Testing Service
acahill@ets.org

Abstract

Compounding in morphologically rich languages is a highly productive process which often causes SMT approaches to fail because of unseen words. We present an approach for translation into a compounding language that splits compounds into simple words for training and, due to an underspecified representation, allows for free merging of simple words into compounds after translation. In contrast to previous approaches, we use features projected from the source language to predict compound mergings. We integrate our approach into end-to-end SMT and show that many compounds matching the reference translation are produced which did not appear in the training data. Additional manual evaluations support the usefulness of generalizing compound formation in SMT.

1 Introduction

Productive processes like compounding or inflection are problematic for traditional phrase-based statistical machine translation (SMT) approaches, because words can only be translated as they have occurred in the parallel training data. As parallel training data is limited, it is desirable to extract as much information from it as possible. We present an approach for compound processing in SMT, translating from English to German, that splits compounds prior to training (in order to access the individual words which together form the compound) and recombines them after translation. While compound splitting is a well-studied task, compound merging has not received as much attention in the past. We start from Stymne and Cancedda (2011), who used sequence models to predict compound merging and Fraser et al. (2012) who, in addition, generalise over German inflection. Our new contributions are: (i) We project features from the source language to support compound merging predictions. As the source language input is fluent, these features are more reliable than features derived from target language SMT output. (ii) We reduce compound parts to an underspecified representation which allows for maximal generalisation. (iii) We present a detailed manual evaluation methodology which shows that we obtain improved compound translations.

We evaluated compound processing both on held-out split data and in end-to-end SMT. We show that using source language features increases the accuracy of compound generation. Moreover, we find more correct compounds than the baselines, and a considerable number of these compounds are unseen in the training data. This is largely due to the underspecified representation we are using. Finally, we show that our approach improves upon the previous work.

We discuss compound processing in SMT in Section 2, and summarise related work in Section 3. In Section 4 we present our method for splitting compounds and reducing the component words to an underspecified representation. The merging to obtain German compounds is the subject of Section 5. We evaluate the accuracy of compound prediction on held-out data in Section 6 and in end-to-end SMT experiments in Section 7. We conclude in Section 8.

2 Dealing with Compounds in SMT

In German, two (or more) single words (usually nouns or adjectives) are combined to form a compound which is considered a semantic unit. The rightmost part is referred to as the *head* while all other parts are called *modifiers*. EXAMPLE (1) lists different ways of joining simple words into compounds: mostly, no modification is required (A) or a filler letter is introduced (B). More rarely, a letter is deleted (C), or transformed (D).

Proceedings of the 14th Conference of the European Chapter of the Association for Computational Linguistics, pages 579–587,
Gothenburg, Sweden, April 26-30 2014.

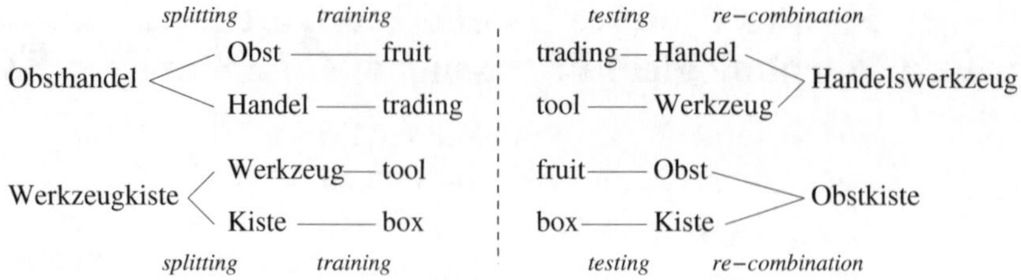

Figure 1: Compound processing in SMT allows the synthesis of compounds unseen in the training data.

EXAMPLE (1)

(A)	*Haus+Boot = Hausboot* ("house boat")
(B)	*Ort+****s****+Zeit = Ortszeit* ("local time")
(C)	*Kirch****e-e****+Turm = Kirchturm* ("church tower")
(D)	*Kriter****ium****+Liste = Kriter****ien****liste* ("criteria list")

German compounds are highly productive,[1] and traditional SMT approaches often fail in the face of such productivity. Therefore, special processing of compounds is required for translation into German, as many compounds will not (e.g. *Hausboot*, "house boat") or only rarely have been seen in the training data.[2] In contrast, most compounds consist of two (or more) simple words that occur more frequently in the data than the compound as a whole (e.g. *Haus* (7,975) and *Boot* (162)) and often, these compound parts can be translated 1-to-1 into simple English words. Figure 1 illustrates the basic idea of compound processing in SMT: imagine, *"Werkzeug"* ("tool") occurred only as a modifier of e.g. *"Kiste"* ("box") in the training data, but the test set contains "tool" as a simple word or as the head of a compound. Splitting compounds prior to translation model training enables better access to the component translations and allows for a high degree of generalisation. At testing time, the English text is translated into the split German representation, and only afterwards, some sequences of simple words are (re-)combined into (possibly unseen) compounds where appropriate. This merging of compounds is much more challenging than the splitting, as it has to be applied to disfluent MT output: i.e., compound parts may not occur in the correct word order and even if they do, not all sequences of German words that *could* form a compound *should* be merged.

3 Related Work

Compound processing for translation into a compounding language includes both compound splitting and merging, we thus report on previous approaches for both of these tasks.

In the past, there have been numerous attempts to split compounds, all improving translation quality when translating from a compounding to a non-compounding language. Several compound splitting approaches make use of substring corpus frequencies in order to find the optimal split points of a compound (e.g. Koehn and Knight (2003), who allowed only "(e)s" as filler letters). Stymne et al. (2008) use Koehn and Knight's technique, include a larger list of possible modifier transformations and apply POS restrictions on the substrings, while Fritzinger and Fraser (2010) use a morphological analyser to find only linguistically motivated substrings. In contrast, Dyer (2010) presents a lattice-based approach to encode different segmentations of words (instead of finding the one-best split). More recently, Macherey et al. (2011) presented a language-independent unsupervised approach in which filler letters and a list of words not to be split (e.g., named entities) are learned using phrase tables and Levenshtein distance.

In contrast to splitting, the merging of compounds has received much less attention in the past. An early approach by Popović et al. (2006) recombines compounds using a list of compounds and their parts. It thus never creates invalid German compounds, but on the other hand it is limited to the coverage of the list. Moreover, in some contexts a merging in the list may still be wrong, cf. EXAMPLE (3) in Section 5 below. The approach of Stymne (2009) makes use of a factored model, with a special POS-markup for compound modifiers, derived from the POS of the whole compound. This markup enables sound mergings of compound parts after translation if the POS of the candidate modifier (X-Part) matches the POS of the candidate compound head (X): *Inflations|N-Part + Rate|N = Inflationsrate|N* ("inflation rate"). In Stymne and Cancedda (2011) the factored ap-

[1]Most newly appearing words in German are compounds.

[2]~30% of the word types and ~77% of the compound types we identified in our training data occurred ≤ 3 times.

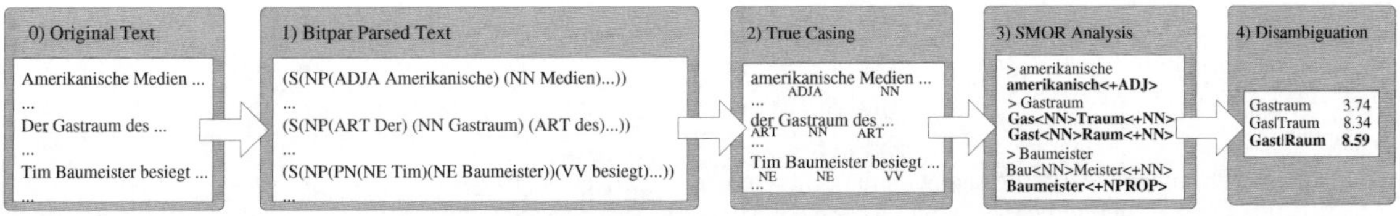

Figure 2: Compound splitting pipeline **1)** The original text is parsed with BITPAR to get unambiguous POS tags, **2)** The original text is then true-cased using the most frequent casing for each word and BITPAR tags are added, **3)** All words are analysed with SMOR, analyses are filtered using BITPAR tags (only **bold**-faced analyses are kept), **4)** If several splitting options remain, the geometric mean of the word (part) frequencies is used to disambiguate them.

proach was extended to make use of a CRF sequence labeller (Lafferty et al., 2001) in order to find reasonable merging points. Besides the words and their POS, many different target language frequency features were defined to train the CRF. This approach can even produce new compounds unseen in the training data, provided that the modifiers occurred in modifier position of a compound and heads occurred as heads or even as simple words with the same inflectional endings. However, as former compound modifiers were left with their filler letters (cf. *"Inflations"*), they can not be generalised to compound heads or simple words, nor can inflectional variants of compound heads or simple words be created (e.g. if *"Rate"* had only been observed in nominative form in the training data, the genitive *"Raten"* could not be produced). The underspecified representation we are using allows for maximal generalisation over word parts independent of their position of occurrence or inflectional realisations. Moreover, their experiments were limited to predicting compounds on held-out data; no results were reported for using their approach in translation. In Fraser et al. (2012) we re-implemented the approach of Stymne and Cancedda (2011), combined it with inflection prediction and applied it to a translation task. However, compound merging was restricted to a list of compounds and parts. Our present work facilitates more independent combination. Toutanova et al. (2008) and Weller et al. (2013) used source language features for target language inflection, but to our knowledge, none of these works applied source language features for compound merging.

4 Step 1: Underspecified Representation

In order to enhance translation model accuracy, it is reasonable to have similar degrees of morphological richness between source and target language. We thus reduce the German target language training data to an underspecified representation: we split compounds, and lemmatise all words (except verbs). All occurrences of simple words, former compound modifiers or heads have the same representation and can thus be freely merged into "old" and "new" compounds after translation, cf. Figure 1 above. So that we can later predict the merging of simple words into compounds and the inflection of the words, we store all of the morphological information stripped from the underspecified representation.

Note that erroneous over-splitting might make the correct merging of compounds difficult[3] (or even impossible), due to the number of correct decisions required. For example, it requires only 1 correct prediction to recombine *"Niederschlag|Menge"* into *"Niederschlagsmenge"* ("amount of precipitation") but 3 for the wrong split into *"nie|der|Schlag|Menge"* ("never|the|hit|amount"). We use the compound splitter of Fritzinger and Fraser (2010), who have shown that using a rule-based morphological analyser (SMOR, Schmid et al. (2004)) drastically reduced the number of erroneous splits when compared to the frequency-based approach of Koehn and Knight (2003). However, we adapted it to work on tokens: some words can, depending on their context, either be interpreted as named entities or common nouns, e.g., *"Dinkelacker"* (a German beer brand or "spelt|field").[4] We parsed the training data and use the parser's decisions to identify proper names, see *"Baumeister"* in Figure 2.

After splitting, we use SMOR to reduce words to lemmas, keeping morphological features like *gender* or *number*, and stripping features like *case*, as illustrated for *"Ölexporteure"* ("oil exporters"):

[3] In contrast, they may not hurt translation quality in the other direction, where phrase-based SMT is likely to learn the split words as a phrase and thus recover from that error.

[4] Note that Macherey et al. (2011) blocked splitting of words which can be used as named entities, independent of context, which is less general than our solution.

No.	Feature Description	Example	Experiment		
			Sc	T	Tr
1SC	surface form of the word	string: Arbeit<+NN><Fem><Sg>	X	X	
2SC	main part of speech of the word (from the parser)	string: +NN	X	X	
3SC	word occurs in a bigram with the next word	frequency: 0	X	X	
4SC	word combined to a compound with the next word	frequency: 10,000	X	X	X
5SC	word occurs in modifier position of a compound	frequency: 100,000	X	X	
6SC	word occurs in a head position of a compound	frequency: 10,000	X	X	
7SC	word occurs in modifier position vs. simplex	string: P>W (P= 5SC, W= 100,000)	X		
8SC	word occurs in head position vs. simplex	string: S<W (S= 6SC, W= 100,000)	X		
7SC+	word occurs in modifier position vs. simplex	ratio: 10 (10**ceil(log10(5SC/W)))		X	X
8SC+	word occurs in head position vs. simplex	ratio: 1 (10**ceil(log10(6SC/W)))		X	X
9N	different head types the word can combine with	number: 10,000		X	X

Table 1: Target language CRF features for compound merging. **SC** = features taken from Stymne and Cancedda (2011), **SC+** = improved versions, **N** = new feature. Experiments: **Sc** = re-implementation of Stymne and Cancedda (2011), **T**= use full **T**arget feature set, **Tr** = use **T**arget features, but only a **R**educed set.

EXAMPLE (2)

compound

Öl<NN>Exporteur<+NN><Masc><Nom><Pl>

Öl<+NN>**<Neut><Sg>** Exporteur<+NN> **<Masc><Pl>**

modifier *head*

While the former compound head (*"Exporteure"*) automatically inherits all morphological features of the compound as a whole, the features of the modifier need to be derived from SMOR in an additional step. We need to ensure that the representation of the modifier is identical to the same word when it occurs independently in order to obtain full generalisation over compound parts.

5 Step 2: Compound Merging

After translation from English into the underspecified German representation, post-processing is required to transform the output back into fluent, morphologically fully specified German. First, compounds need to be merged where appropriate, e.g., *"Hausboote"* ("house boats"):

Haus<+NN><Neut><Sg> + Boot<+NN><Neut><Pl>
→ Haus<NN>Boot<+NN><Neut><Pl> (merged)

and second, all words need to be inflected:

*Haus<NN>Boot<+NN><Neut><**Acc**><Pl>*
*→ Hausboot**en** (inflected)*

5.1 Target Language Features

To decide which words should be combined, we follow Stymne and Cancedda (2011) who used CRFs for this task. The features we derived from the target language to train CRF models are listed in Table 1. We adapted features No. 1-8 from Stymne and Cancedda (2011). Then, we modified two features (7+8) and created a new feature indicating the productivity of a modifier (9N).

5.2 Projecting Source Language Features

We also use new features derived from the English source language input, which is coherent and fluent. This makes features derived from it more reliable than the target language features derived from disfluent SMT output. Moreover, source language features might support or block merging decisions in unclear cases, i.e., where target language frequencies are not helpful, either because they are very low or they have roughly equal frequency distributions when occurring in a compound (as modifier or head) vs. as a simple word.

In Table 2, we list three types of features:

1. Syntactic features: different English noun phrase patterns that are aligned to German compound candidate words (cf. 10E-13E)
2. The POS tag of the English word (cf. 14E)
3. Alignment features, derived from word alignments (cf. 15E-18E)

The examples given in Table 2 (10E-13E) show that English compounds often have 1-to-1 correspondences to the parts of a German compound. Knowing that two consecutive German simple words are aligned to two English words of the same noun phrase is a strong indicator that the German words should be merged:

EXAMPLE (3)

should be merged:
ein erhöhtes **verkehrs aufkommen** sorgt für chaos
"an increased **traffic volume** causes chaos"
(S...(**NP**(DT An)(VN increased)**(NN traffic)(NN volume)**)..)))

should **not** be merged:
für die finanzierung des **verkehrs aufkommen**
"**pay** for the financing of **transport**"
(VP(**V pay**)(PP(IN for)(NP(NP(DT the)(NN financing))
(PP(IN of)(NP(**NN transport**)..))

In the compound reading of *"verkehr + aufkommen"*, the English parse structure indicates that the words aligned to *"verkehr"* ("traffic") and

No.	Feature Description	Type
10E	word and next word are aligned from a noun phrase in the English source sentence: (NP(NN traffic)(NN accident)) → *Verkehr* ("traffic") + *Unfall* ("accident")	true/false
11E	word and next word are aligned from a gerund construction in the English source sentence: (NP(VBG developing)(NNS nations)) → *Entwicklung* ("development") + *Länder* ("countries")	true/false
12E	word and next word are aligned from a genitive construction in the English source sentence: (NP(NP(DT the)(NN end))(PP(IN of)(NP(DT the)(NN year)) → *Jahr* ("year") + *Ende*("end")	true/false
13E	word and next word are aligned from an adjective noun construction in the English source sentence: (NP (ADJ protective)(NNS measures)) → *Schutz* ("protection") + *Maßnahmen* ("measures")	true/false
14E	print the POS of the corresponding aligned English word	string
15E	word and next word are aligned 1-to-1 from the same word in the English source sentence, e.g., $beef \begin{cases} Rind(\text{"cow"}) \\ Fleisch(\text{"meat"}) \end{cases}$	true/false
16E	like 15E, but the English word contains a dash, e.g., $Nobel-Prize \begin{cases} Nobel(\text{"Nobel"}) \\ Preis(\text{"prize"}) \end{cases}$	true/false
17E	like 15E, but also considering 1-to-n and n-to-1 links	true/false
18E	like 16E, but also considering 1-to-n and n-to-1 links	true/false

Table 2: List of new **source** language CRF features for compound merging.

"aufkommen" ("volume"), are both nouns and part of one common noun phrase, which is a strong indicator that the two words should be merged in German. In contrast, the syntactic relationship between "pay" (aligned to *"aufkommen"*) and "transport" (aligned to *"verkehr"*) is more distant[5]: merging is not indicated.

We also use the POS of the English words to learn (un)usual combinations of POS, independent of their exact syntactic structure (14E). Reconsider EXAMPLE (3): NN+NN is a more common POS pair for compounds than V+NN.

Finally, the alignment features (15E-18E) promote the merging into compounds whose alignments indicate that they should not have been split in the first place (e.g., *Rindfleisch*, 15E).

5.3 Compound Generation and Inflection

So far, we reported on how to decide **which** simple words are to be merged into compounds, but not **how** to recombine them. Recall from EXAMPLE (1) that the modifier of a compound sometimes needs to be transformed, before it can be combined with the head word (or next modifier), e.g., *"Ort"+"Zeit" = "Orts̲zeit"* ("local time").

We use SMOR to generate compounds from a combination of simple words. This allows us to create compounds with modifiers that never occurred as such in the training data. Imagine that *"Ort"* occurred only as compound head or as a single word in the training data. Using SMOR, we are still able to create the correct form of the modifier, including the required filler letter: *"Orts̲"*. This ability distinguishes our approach from previous approaches: Stymne and Cancedda (2011) do not reduce modifiers to their base forms[6] (they can only create new compounds when the modifier occurred as such in the training data) and Fraser et al. (2012) use a list for merging.

Finally, we use the system described in Fraser et al. (2012) to inflect the entire text.

6 Accuracy of Compound Prediction

We trained CRF models on the parallel training data (~40 million words)[7] of the EACL 2009 workshop on statistical machine translation[8] using different feature (sub)sets, cf. the "Experiment" column in Table 1 above. We examined the reliability of the CRF compound prediction models by applying them to held-out data:

1. split the German wmt2009 tuning data set
2. remember compound split points
3. predict merging with CRF models
4. combine predicted words into compounds
5. calculate f-scores on how properly the compounds were merged

Table 3 lists the CRF models we trained, together with their compound merging accuracies on held-out data. It can be seen that using more features (**SC→T→ST**) is favourable in terms of precision and overall accuracy and the positive impact of using source language features is clearer when only reduced feature sets are used (**TR** vs. **STR**).

However, these accuracies only somewhat correlate with SMT performance: while being trained and tested on clean, fluent German language, the

[5]Note that *"für etwas aufkommen"* (lit. "for sth. arise", idiom.: "to pay for sth.") is an idiomatic expression.

[6]They account for modifier transformations by using character n-gram features (cf.EXAMPLE (1)).

[7]However, target language feature frequencies are derived from the monolingual training data, ~146 million words.

[8]`http://www.statmt.org/wmt09`

exp	to be merged	all merged	correct merged	wrong merged	wrong not merged	merging wrong	precision	recall	f-score
SC	1,047	997	921	73	121	3	92.38%	88.13%	90.21%
T	1,047	979	916	59	128	4	93.56%	87.40%	90.38%
ST	1,047	976	917	55	126	4	93.95%	87.58%	90.66%
TR	1,047	893	836	52	204	5	93.62%	80.00%	86.27%
STR	1,047	930	866	58	172	6	93.12%	82.95%	87.74%

Table 3: Compound production accuracies of CRF models on held-out data: **SC**: re-implementation of Stymne and Cancedda (2011); **T**: all target language features, including a new one (cf. Table 1); **ST** = all **S**ource and **T**arget language features; **TR**: only a **r**educed set of target language features; **STR**: **TR**, plus all source language features given in Table 2.

exp	BLEU SCORES			#compounds found			
	mert.log	BLEU	RTS	all	ref	new	new*
RAW	14.88	14.25	1.0054	646	175	n.a.	n.a.
UNSPLIT	15.86	**14.74**	0.9964	661	185	n.a.	n.a.
SC	15.44	14.45	0.9870	882	241	47	8
T	15.56	14.32	0.9634	845	251	47	8
ST	15.33	14.51	0.9760	820	248	46	9
TR	15.24	14.26	0.9710	753	234	44	5
STR	15.37	**14.61**	0.9884	758	239	43	7
#compounds in reference text:				1,105	1,105	396	193

Table 4: SMT results. Tuning scores (mert.log) are on merged but uninflected data (except RAW). **RTS**: length ratio; **all**: #compounds produced; **ref**: reference matches; **new**: unknown to parallel data; **new***: unknown to target language data. **bold** face indicates statistical significance wrt. the RAW baseline, SC, T and TR.

models will later be applied to disfluent SMT output and might thus lead to different results there. Stymne and Cancedda (2011) dealt with this by *noisifying* the CRF training data: they translated the whole data set using an SMT system that was trained on the same data set. This way, the training data was less fluent than in its original format, but still of higher quality than SMT output of unseen data. In contrast, we left the training data as it was, but strongly reduced the feature set for CRF model training (e.g., no more use of surface words and POS tags, cf. **TR** and **STR** in Table 3) instead.

7 Translation Performance

We integrated our compound processing pipeline into an end-to-end SMT system. Models were trained with the default settings of the Moses SMT toolkit, v1.0 (Koehn et al., 2007) using the data from the EACL 2009 workshop on statistical machine translation. All compound processing systems are trained and tuned identically, except using different CRF models for compound prediction. All training data was split and reduced to the underspecified representation described in Section 4. We used KenLM (Heafield, 2011) with SRILM (Stolcke, 2002) to train a 5-gram language model based on all available target language training data. For tuning, we used batch-mira with '-safe-hope' (Cherry and Foster, 2012) and ran it separately for every experiment. We integrated the CRF-based merging of compounds into each iteration of tuning and scored each output with respect to an unsplit and lemmatised version of the tuning reference. Testing consists of:

1. translation into the split, underspecified German representation
2. compound merging using CRF models to predict recombination points
3. inflection of all words

7.1 SMT Results

We use 1,025 sentences for tuning and 1,026 sentences for testing. The results are given in Table 4. We calculate BLEU scores (Papineni et al., 2002) and compare our systems to a RAW baseline (built following the instructions of the shared task) and a baseline very similar to Fraser et al. (2012), using a lemmatised representation of words for decoding, re-inflecting them after translation, but without compound processing (UNSPLIT). Table 4 shows that only UNSPLIT and STR (source language and a reduced set of target language features) are significantly[9] improving over the RAW baseline. They also significantly outperform all other systems, except ST (full source and target language feature set). The difference between STR (14.61) and the UNSPLIT baseline (14.74) is **not** statistically significant.

[9]We used pair-wise bootstrap resampling with sample size 1000 and p-value 0.05, from: http://www.ark.cs.cmu.edu/MT

	group ID	example	reference	english	UNSPLIT	STR
lexically matches the reference	1a: perfect match	Inflationsrate	Inflationsrate	inflation rate	185	239
	1b: inflection wrong	Rohstoffpreisen	Rohstoffpreise	raw material prices	40	44
	2a: merging wrong	Anwaltsbewegung	Anwältebewegung	lawyers movement	5	9
	2b: no merging	Polizei Chef	Polizeichef	police chief	101	54
correct translation	3a: compound	Zentralbanken	Notenbank	central banks	92	171
	3b: no compound	pflanzliche Öle	Speiseöl	vegetable oils	345	291
wrong translation	4a: compound	Haushaltsdefizite	Staatshaushalts	state budget	12	42
	4b: no compound	Ansporn Linien	Nebenlinien	spur lines	325	255
Total number of compounds in reference text:					1,105	1,105

Table 5: Groups for detailed manual compound evaluation and results for **UNSPLIT** and **STR**.

reference	English source	UNSPLIT baseline		STR	
Teddybären	teddy bear	4b	Teddy tragen (Teddy, to bear)	1a	Teddybären (teddy bear)
Emissionsreduktion	emissions reduction	3b	Emissionen Reduzierung (emissions, reducing)	3a	Emissionsverringerung (emission decrease)
Geldstrafe	fine	4b	schönen (fine/nice)	3a	Bußgeld (monetary fine)
Tischtennis	table tennis	2b	Tisch Tennis (table, tennis)	4a	Spieltischtennis (play table tennis)
Kreditkartenmarkt	credit-card market	2b	Kreditkarte Markt (credit-card, market)	4a	Kreditmarkt (credit market)
Rotationstempo	rotation rate	2b	Tempo Rotation (rate, rotation)	4a	Temporotation (rate rotation)

Table 6: Examples of the detailed manual compound analysis for **UNSPLIT** and **STR**.

Compound processing leads to improvements at the level of unigrams and as BLEU is dominated by four-gram precision and length penalty, it does not adequately reflect compound related improvements. We thus calculated the number of compounds matching the reference for each experiment and verified whether these were known to the training data. The numbers in Table 4 show that all compound processing systems outperform both baselines in terms of finding more exact reference matches and also more compounds unknown to the training data. Note that STR finds less reference matches than e.g. T or ST, but it also produces less compounds overall, i.e. it is more precise when producing compounds.

However, as compounds that are correctly combined but poorly inflected are not counted, this is only a lower bound on true compounding performance. We thus performed two additional manual evaluations and show that the quality of the compounds (Section 7.2), and the human perception of translation quality is improving (Section 7.3).

7.2 Detailed Evaluation of Compounds

This evaluation focuses on how compounds in the the reference text have been translated.[10] We:

1. manually identify compounds in German reference text (1,105 found)
2. manually perform word alignment of these compounds to the English source text
3. project these English counterparts of compounds in the reference text to the decoded text using the "–print-alignment-info" flag
4. manually annotate the resulting tuples, using the categories given in Table 5

The results are given in the two rightmost columns of Table 5: besides a higher number of reference matches (cf. row 1a), STR overall produces more compounds than the UNSPLIT baseline, cf. rows 2a, 3a and 4a. Indirectly, this can also be seen from the low numbers of STR in category 2b), where the UNSPLIT baseline produces much more (101 vs. 54) translations that lexically match the reference without being a compound. While the 171 compounds of STR of category 3a) show that our system produces many compounds that are correct translations of the English, even though not matching the reference (and thus not credited by BLEU), the compounds of categories 2a) and 4a) contain examples where we either fail to reproduce the correct compound or over-generate compounds.

We give some examples in Table 6: for "teddy bear", the correct German word *"Teddybären"* is

[10] In another evaluation, we investigated the 519 compounds that our system produced but which did not match the reference: 367 were correct translations of the English, 87 contained erroneous lexemes and 65 were over-mergings.

missing in the parallel training data and instead of *"Bär"* ("bear"), the baseline selected *"tragen"* ("to bear"). Extracting all words containing the substring *"bär"* ("bear") from the original parallel training data and from its underspecified split version demonstrates that our approach is able to access all occurrences of the word. This leads to higher frequency counts and thus enhances the probabilities for correct translations. We can generalise over 18 different word types containing "bear" (e.g. "polar bears", "brown bears", "bear skin", "bear fur") to obtain only 2:

occurrences in raw training data: Bär (19), Bären (26), Bärendienst (42), Bärenfarmen (1), Bärenfell (2), Bärengalle(1), Bärenhaut (1), Bärenmarkt (1), Braunbär (1), Braunbären (3), Braunbärengebiete (1), Braunbär-Population (1), Eisbären(18), Eisbärenpopulation (2), Eisbärenpopulationen (1), Schwarzbär (1), Schwarzbären (1)

***"bär"* occurring in underspecified split data:**
Bär<+NN><Masc><Sg> (**94**)
Bär<+NN><Masc><Pl> (**29**)

"Emissionsverringerung" (cf. Table 6) is a typical example of group 3a): a correctly translated compound that does not lexically match the reference, but which is semantically very similar to the reference. The same applies for *"Bußgeld"*, a synonym of *"Geldstrafe"*, for which the UNSPLIT baseline selected *"schönen"* ("fine, nice") instead. Consider also the wrong compound productions, e.g. *"Tischtennis"* is combined with the verb *"spielen"* ("to play") into *"Spieltischtennis"*. In contrast, *"Kreditmarkt"* dropped the middle part *"Karte"* ("card"), and in the case of *"Temporotation"*, the head and modifier of the compound are switched.

7.3 Human perception of translation quality

We presented sentences of the UNSPLIT baseline and of STR in random order to two native speakers of German and asked them to rank the sentences according to preference. In order to prevent them from being biased towards compound-bearing sentences, we asked them to select sentences based on their native intuition, without revealing our focus on compound processing.

Sentences were selected based on source language sentence length: 10-15 words (178 sentences), of which either the reference or our system had to contain a compound (95 sentences). After removing duplicates, we ended up with 84 sentences to be annotated in two subsequent passes: first, without being given the reference sentence (approximating fluency), then, with the reference sentence (approximating adequacy). The results are given in Table 7. Both annotators preferred more sentences of our system overall, but the difference is clearer for the fluency task.

(a) Fluency: without reference sentence

$\kappa = 0.3631$		person 1			
		STR	UNSPLIT	equal	
person 2	STR	24	6	7	37
	UNSPLIT	5	16	9	30
	equal	6	2	9	17
		35	24	25	84

(b) Adequacy: with reference sentence

$\kappa = 0.4948$		person 1			
		STR	UNSPLIT	equal	
person 2	STR	23	4	5	32
	UNSPLIT	4	21	7	32
	equal	5	3	12	20
		32	28	24	84

Table 7: Human perception of translation quality.

8 Conclusion

Compounds require special attention in SMT, especially when translating into a compounding language. Compared with the baselines, all of our experiments that included compound processing produced not only many more compounds matching the reference exactly, but also many compounds that did not occur in the training data. Taking a closer look, we found that some of these new compounds could only be produced due to the underspecified representation we are using, which allows us to generalise over occurrences of simple words, compound modifiers and heads. Moreover, we demonstrated that features derived from the source language are a valuable source of information for compound prediction: experiments were significantly better compared with contrastive experiments without these features. Additional manual evaluations showed that compound processing leads to improved translations where the improvement is not captured by BLEU.

Acknowledgements

This work was supported by Deutsche Forschungsgemeinschaft grants Models of Morphosyntax for Statistical Machine Translation (Phase 2) and Distributional Approaches to Semantic Relatedness. We thank the anonymous reviewers for their comments and the annotators.

References

Colin Cherry and George Foster. 2012. Batch Tuning Strategies for Statistical Machine Translation. In *HLT-NAACL'12: Proceedings of the Human Language Technology Conference of the North American Chapter of the Association for Computational Linguistics*, volume 12, pages 34–35. Association for Computational Linguistics.

Chris Dyer. 2010. A Formal Model of Ambiguity and its Applications in Machine Translation. Phd dissertation, University of Maryland, USA.

Alexander Fraser, Marion Weller, Aoife Cahill, and Fabienne Cap. 2012. Modeling Inflection and Word Formation in SMT. In *EACL'12: Proceedings of the 13th Conference of the European Chapter of the Association for Computational Linguistics*, pages 664–674. Association for Computational Linguistics.

Fabienne Fritzinger and Alexander Fraser. 2010. How to Avoid Burning Ducks: Combining Linguistic Analysis and Corpus Statistics for German Compound Processing. In *Proceedings of the Fifth Workshop on Statistical Machine Translation*, pages 224–234. Association for Computational Linguistics.

Kenneth Heafield. 2011. KenLM: Faster and Smaller Language Model Queries. In *Proceedings of the Sixth Workshop on Statistical Machine Translation*, Edinburgh, UK, July. Association for Computational Linguistics.

Philipp Koehn and Kevin Knight. 2003. Empirical Methods for Compound Splitting. In *EACL '03: Proceedings of the 10th Conference of the European Chapter of the Association for Computational Linguistics*, pages 187–193, Morristown, NJ, USA. Association for Computational Linguistics.

Philipp Koehn, Hieu Hoang, Alexandra Birch, Chris Callison-Burch, Marcello Federico, Nicola Bertoldi, Brooke Cowan, Wade Shen, Christine Moran, Richard Zens, Chris Dyer, Ondrej Bojar, Alexandra Constantin, and Evan Herbst. 2007. Moses: Open Source Toolkit for Statistical Machine Translation. In *ACL'07: Proceedings of the 45th Annual Meeting of the Association for Computational Linguistics, Demonstration Session*, pages 177–180. Association for Computational Linguistics.

John Lafferty, Andrew McCallum, and Fernando Pereira. 2001. Conditional Random Fields: Probabilistic Models for Segmenting and Labeling Sequence Data. In *ICML'01: Proceedings of the 18th International Conference on Machine Learning*.

Klaus Macherey, Andrew M. Dai, David Talbot, Ashok C. Popat, and Franz Och. 2011. Language-independent Compound Splitting with Morphological Operations. In *ACL '11: Proceedings of the 49th annual meeting of the Association for Computational Linguistics*, pages 1395–1404. Association for Computational Linguistics.

Kishore Papineni, Salim Roukos, Todd Ward, and Wei-Jing Zhu. 2002. Bleu: A Method for Automatic Evaluation of Machine Translation. In *ACL'02: Proceedings of the 40th Annual Meeting of the Association for Computational Linguistics*, pages 311–318. Association for Computational Linguistics.

Maja Popović, Daniel Stein, and Hermann Ney. 2006. Statistical Machine Translation of German Compound Words. In *FinTAL'06: Proceedings of the 5th International Conference on Natural Language Processing*, pages 616–624. Springer Verlag.

Helmut Schmid, Arne Fitschen, and Ulrich Heid. 2004. SMOR: A German Computational Morphology Covering Derivation, Composition and Inflection. In *LREC '04: Proceedings of the 4th Conference on Language Resources and Evaluation*, pages 1263–1266.

Andreas Stolcke. 2002. SRILM – an Extensible Language Modelling Toolkit. In *ICSLN'02: Proceedings of the international conference on spoken language processing*, pages 901–904.

Sara Stymne and Nicola Cancedda. 2011. Productive Generation of Compound Words in Statistical Machine Translation. In *EMNLP'11: Proceedings of the 6th Workshop on Statistical Machine Translation and Metrics MATR of the conference on Empirical Methods in Natural Language Processing*, pages 250–260. Association for Computational Linguistics.

Sara Stymne, Maria Holmqvist, and Lars Ahrenberg. 2008. Effects of Morphological Analysis in Translation between German and English. In *ACL'08: Proceedings of the 3rd workshop on statistical machine translation of the 46th annual meeting of the Association for Compuational Linguistics*, pages 135–138. Association for Computational Linguistics,.

Sara Stymne. 2009. A Comparison of Merging Strategies for Translation of German Compounds. In *EACL '09: Proceedings of the Student Research Workshop of the 12th conference of the European Chapter of the Association for Computational Linguistics*, pages 61–69. Association for Computational Linguistics.

Kristina Toutanova, Hisami Suzuki, and Achim Ruopp. 2008. Applying Morphology Generation Models to Machine Translation. In *ACL'08: Proceedings of the 46th Annual Meeting of the Association for Computational Linguistics: Human Language Technologies*, pages 514–522. Association for Computational Linguistics.

Marion Weller, Alexander Fraser, and Sabine Schulte im Walde. 2013. Using Subcategorization Knowledge to Improve Case Prediction for Translation to German. In *ACL'13: Proceedings of the 51st Annual Meeting of the Association for Computational Linguistics*, pages 593–603. Association for Computational Linguistics.

Type-Supervised Domain Adaptation for Joint Segmentation and POS-Tagging

Meishan Zhang[†], **Yue Zhang**[‡], **Wanxiang Che**[†], **Ting Liu**[†*]
[†]Research Center for Social Computing and Information Retrieval
Harbin Institute of Technology, China
{mszhang, car, tliu}@ir.hit.edu.cn
[‡]Singapore University of Technology and Design
yue_zhang@sutd.edu.sg

Abstract

We report an empirical investigation on type-supervised domain adaptation for joint Chinese word segmentation and POS-tagging, making use of domain-specific tag dictionaries and only unlabeled target domain data to improve target-domain accuracies, given a set of annotated source domain sentences. Previous work on POS-tagging of other languages showed that type-supervision can be a competitive alternative to token-supervision, while semi-supervised techniques such as label propagation are important to the effectiveness of type-supervision. We report similar findings using a novel approach for joint Chinese segmentation and POS-tagging, under a cross-domain setting. With the help of unlabeled sentences and a lexicon of 3,000 words, we obtain 33% error reduction in target-domain tagging. In addition, combined type- and token-supervision can lead to improved cost-effectiveness.

1 Introduction

With accuracies of over 97%, POS-tagging of WSJ can be treated as a solved problem (Manning, 2011). However, performance is still well below satisfactory for many other languages and domains (Petrov et al., 2012; Christodoulopoulos et al., 2010). There has been a line of research on using a tag-dictionary for POS-tagging (Merialdo, 1994; Toutanova and Johnson, 2007; Ravi and Knight, 2009; Garrette and Baldridge, 2012). The idea is compelling: on the one hand, a list of lexicons is often available for special domains, such as bio-informatics; on the other hand, compiling a lexicon of word-tag pairs appears to be less time-consuming than annotating full sentences.

However, success in type-supervised POS-tagging turns out to depend on several subtle factors. For example, recent research has found that the quality of the tag-dictionary is crucial to the success of such methods (Banko and Moore, 2004; Goldberg et al., 2008; Garrette and Baldridge, 2012). Banko and Moore (2004) found that the accuracies can drop from 96% to 77% when a hand-crafted tag dictionary is replaced with a raw tag dictionary gleaned from data, without any human intervention. These facts indicate that careful considerations need to be given for effective type-supervision. In addition, significant manual work might be required to ensure the quality of lexicons.

To compare type- and token-supervised tagging, Garrette and Baldridge (2013) performed a set of experiments by conducting each type of annotation for two hours. They showed that for low-resource languages, a tag-dictionary can be reasonably effective if label propagation (Talukdar and Crammer, 2009) and model minimizations (Ravi and Knight, 2009) are applied to expand and filter the lexicons. Similar findings were reported in Garrette et al. (2013).

Do the above findings carry over to the Chinese language? In this paper, we perform an empirical study on the effects of tag-dictionaries for domain adaptation of Chinese POS-tagging. We aim to answer the following research questions: (a) Is domain adaptation feasible with only a target-domain lexicon? (b) Can we further improve type-supervised domain adaptation using unlabeled target-domain sentences? (c) Is crafting a tag dictionary for domain adaptation more effective than manually annotating target domain sentences, given similar efforts?

Our investigations are performed under two Chinese-specific settings. First, unlike low-resource languages, large amounts of annotation

*Corresponding author.

Proceedings of the 14th Conference of the European Chapter of the Association for Computational Linguistics, pages 588–597,
Gothenburg, Sweden, April 26-30 2014.

are available for Chinese. For example, the Chinese Treebank (CTB) (Xue et al., 2005) contains over 50,000 manually tagged news sentences. Hence rather than studying purely type-supervised POS-tagging, we make use of CTB as the source domain, and study domain adaptation to the Internet literature.

Second, one uniqueness of Chinese POS-tagging, in contrast to the POS-tagging of alphabetical languages, is that word segmentation can be performed jointly to avoid error propagation (Ng and Low, 2004; Zhang and Clark, 2008; Kruengkrai et al., 2009; Zhang and Clark, 2010). We adopt this approach for a strong baseline. Previous studies showed that unsupervised domain adaptation can give moderate improvements (Liu and Zhang, 2012). We show that accuracies can be much more significantly improved by using target-domain knowledge in the form of lexicons.

Both token-supervised and type-supervised domain adaptation rely on a set of source-domain annotations; while the former makes additional use of a small set of target annotations, the latter leverages a target-domain lexicon. We take a feature-based method, analogous to that of Daume III (2007), which tunes domain-dependent versions of features using domain-specific data. Our method tunes a set of lexicon-based features, so that domain-dependent models are derived from inserting domain-specific lexicons.

The conceptually simple method worked highly effectively on a test set of 1,394 sentences from the Internet novel "Zhuxian". Combined with the use of unlabeled data, a tag lexicon of 3,000 words gave a 33% error reduction when compared with a strong baseline system trained using CTB data. We observe that joint use of type- and token-supervised domain adaptation is more cost-effective than pure type- or token-supervision. With 10 hours of annotation, the best error reduction reaches 47%, with F-score increasing from 80.81% to 89.84%.

2 Baseline

We take as the baseline system a discriminative joint segmentation and tagging model, proposed by Zhang and Clark (2010), together with simple self-training (Liu and Zhang, 2012). While the baseline discriminative model gives state-of-the-art joint segmentation and tagging accuracies on CTB data, the baseline self-training makes use of unlabeled target domain data to find improved target domain accuracies over bare CTB training.

2.1 The Baseline Discriminative Chinese POS-Tagging Model

The baseline discriminative model performs segmentation and POS-tagging simultaneously. Given an input sentence $c_1 \cdots c_n$ (c_i refers to the ith character in the sentence), it operates incrementally, from left to right. At each step, the current character can either be appended to the last word of the existing partial output, or seperated as the start of a new word with tag p. A beam is used to maintain the *N-best* partial results at each step during decoding. At step i ($0 \leq i < n$), each item in the beam corresponds to a segmentation and POS-tagging hypothesis for the first $i-1$ characters, with the last word being associated with a POS, but marked as incomplete. When the next character c_i is processed, it is combined with all the partial results from the beam to generate new partial results, using two types of actions: (1) ***Append***, which appends c_i to the last (partial) word in a partial result; (2) ***Separate***$(\mathbf{p})$, which makes the last word in the partial result as completed and adds c_i as a new partial word with a POS tag $\mathbf{p}$.

Partial results in the beam are scored globally over all actions used to build them, so that the *N-best* can be put back to the agenda for the next step. For each action, features are extracted differently. We use the features from Zhang and Clark (2010). Discriminative learning with early-update (Collins and Roark, 2004; Zhang and Clark, 2011) is used to train the model with beam-search.

2.2 Baseline Unsupervised Adaptation by Self-Training

A simple unsupervised approach for POS-tagging with unlabeled data is EM. For a generative model such as HMM, EM can locally maximize the likelihood of training data. Given a good start, EM can result in a competitive HMM tagging model (Goldberg et al., 2008).

For discriminative models with source-domain training examples, an initial model can be trained using the source-domain data, and self-training can be applied to find a locally-optimized model using raw target domain sentences. The training process is sometimes associated with the EM algorithm. Liu and Zhang (2012) used perplexities of character trigrams to order unlabeled sentences, and applied self-training to achieve a 6.3% error

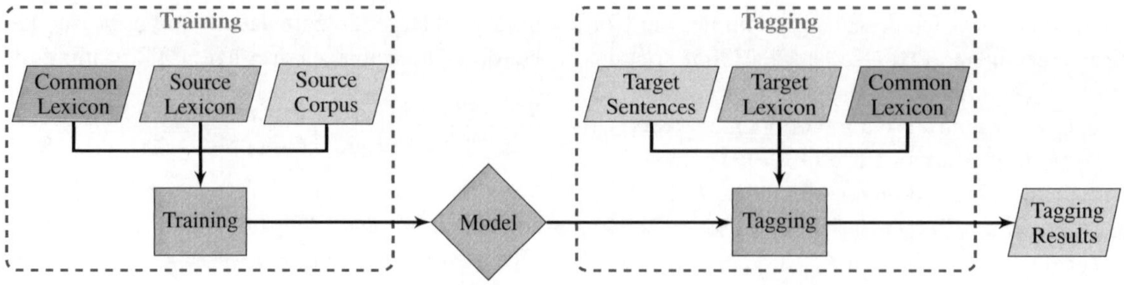

Figure 1: Architecture of our lexicon-based model for domain adaptation.

reduction on target-domain data when compared with source domain training. Their method is simple to implement, and we take it as our baseline.

3 Type-Supervised Domain Adaptation

To give a formal definition of the domain adaptation tasks, we denote by C_s a set of annotated source-domain sentences, C_t a set of annotated target-domain sentences, and $\mathfrak{L}_t$ an annotated target-domain lexicon. The form of $\mathfrak{L}_t$ is a list of target-domain words, each associated with a set of POS tags. *Token-supervised* domain adaptation is the task of making use of C_s and C_t to improve target-domain performances, while *type-supervised* domain adaptation is to make use of C_s and $\mathfrak{L}_t$ instead for the same purpose.

As described in the introduction, type-supervised domain adaptation is useful when annotated sentences are absent, but lexicons are available. In addition, it is an interesting question which type of annotation is more cost-effective when neither is available. We empirically compare the two approaches by proposing a novel method for type-supervised domain adaptation of a discriminate tagging model, showing that it can be a favourable choice in practical situation.

In particular, we split Chinese words into domain-independent and domain-specific categories, and define unlexicalized features for domain-specific words. We train lexicalized domain-independent and unlexicalized domain-specific features using the source domain annotated sentences and a source-domain lexicon, and then apply the resulting model to the target domain by replacing the source-domain lexicon with a target domain lexicon. Combined with unsupervised learning with unlabeled target-domain of sentences, the conceptually simple method worked highly effectively. Following Garrette and Baldridge (2013), we address practical questions on type-supervised domain adaptation by comparison with token-supervised methods under similar human annotation efforts.

3.1 System Architecture

Our method is based on the intuition that domain-specific words of certain types (e.g. proper names) can behave similarly across domains. For example, consider the source-domain sentence "江泽民|NR (Jiang Zemin) 随后|AD (afterwards) 访问|VV (visit) 上汽|NR (Shanghai Automobiles Corp.)" and the target-domain sentence "碧瑶|NR (Biyao) 随后|AD (afterwards) 来到|VV (arrive) 大竹峰|NR (the Bamboo Mountains)". "江泽民 (Jiang Zemin)" and "碧瑶 (Biyao)" are person names in the two domains, respectively, whereas "上汽 (Shanghai Automobiles Corp.)" and "大竹峰 (the Bamboo Mountains)" are location names in the two domains, respectively. If the four words are simply treated as domain-specific nouns, the two sentences both have the pattern "⟨domain-NR⟩ AD VV ⟨domain-NR⟩", and hence source domain training data can be useful in training the distributions of the lexicon-based features for both domains.

Further, we assume that the syntax structures and the usage of function words do not vary significantly across domains. For example, verbs, adjectives or proper nouns can be different from domain to domain, but the subject-verb-object sentence structure does not change. In addition, the usage of closed-set function words remains stable across different domains. In the CTB tagset, closed-set POS tags are the vast majority. Under this assumption, we introduce a set of unlexicalized features into the discriminative model, in order to capture the distributions of domain-specific dictionary words. Unlexicalized features trained for source domain words can carry over to the target domain. The overall architecture of our sys-

Action	Lexicon Feature templates
Separate	in-lex(w_{-1}), $l(w_{-1}) \circ$ in-lex(w_{-1}), in-lex(w_{-1}, t_{-1}), $l(w_{-1}) \circ$ in-lex(w_{-1}, t_{-1})

Table 1: Dictionary features of the type-supervised model, where w_{-1} and t_{-1} denote the last word and POS tag of a partial result, respectively; $l(w)$ denotes the length of the word w; in-lex(w, t) denotes whether the word-tag pair (w, t) is in the lexicon.

tem is shown in Figure 1, where lexicons can be treated as "plugins" to the model for different domains, and one model trained from the source domain can be applied to many different target domains, as long as a lexicon is available.

The method can be the most effective when there is a significant amount of domain-independent words in the data, which provide rich lexicalized contexts for estimating unlexicalized features for domain-specific words. For scientific domains (e.g. the biomedical domain) which share a significant proportion of common words with the news domain, and have most domain specific words being nouns (e.g. "糖尿病 (diabetes)"), the method can be the most effective. We choose a comparatively difficult domain pair (e.g. modern news v.s. ancient style novel), for which the use of many word types are quite different. Results on this data can be relatively more indicative of the usefulness of the method.

3.2 Lexicon-Based Features

Table 1 shows the set of new unlexicalized features for the domain-specific lexicons. In addition to words and POS tags, length information is also encoded in the features, to capture different distributions of different word sizes. For example, a one-character word in the dictionary might not be identified as confidently using the lexicon as a three-character word in the dictionary.

To acquire a domain-specific lexicon for the source domain, we use HowNet (Dong and Dong, 2006) to classify CTB words into domain-independent and domain-specific categories. Consisting of semantic information for nearly 100,000 common Chinese words, HowNet can serve as a resource of domain-independent Chinese words. We choose out of all words in the source domain training data those that also occur in HowNet for domain-independent words, and out of the remaining words those that occur more than 3 times for words specific to the source domain. We assume that the domain-independent lexicon applies to all target domains also. For some target domains, we can obtain domain-specific terminologies easily from the Internet. However, this can be a very small portion depending on the domain. Thus, it may still be necessary to obtain new lexicons by manual annotation.

3.3 Lexicon and Self-Training

The lexicon-based features can be combined with unsupervised learning to further improve target-domain accuracies. We apply self-training on top of the lexicon-based features in the following way: we train a lexicon-based model M using a lexicon $\mathfrak{L}_s$ of the source domain, and then apply M together with a target-domain lexicon $\mathfrak{L}_t$ to automatically label a set of target domain sentences. We combine the automatically labeled target sentences with the source-domain training data to obtain an extended set of training data, and train a final model M_{self}, using the lexicon $\mathfrak{L}_s$ and $\mathfrak{L}_t$ for source- and target-domain data, respectively.

Different numbers of target domain sentences can be used for self-training. Liu and Zhang (2012) showed that an increased amount of target sentences do not constantly lead to improved development accuracies. They use character perplexity to order target domain sentences, taking the top K sentences for self-training. They evaluate the optimal development accuracies using a range of different Kvalues, and select the best K for a final model. This method gave better results than using sentences in the internet novel in their original order (Liu and Zhang, 2012). We follow this method in ranking target domain sentences.

4 Experiments

4.1 Setting

We use annotated sentences from the CTB5 for source-domain training, splitting the corpus into training, development and test sections in the same way as previous work (Kruengkrai et al., 2009; Zhang and Clark, 2010; Sun, 2011).

Following Liu and Zhang (2012), we use the free Internet novel "Zhuxian" (henceforth referred to as ZX; also known as "Jade dynasty") as our target domain data. The writing style of the novel is in the literature genre, with the style of Ming and Qing novels, very different from news in CTB. Ex-

CTB sentences	ZX sentences
乔石会见俄罗斯议员团 (Qiaoshi meets the Russian delegates.) 李鹏强调要加快推行公务员制度 (Lipeng stressed on speeding the reform of official regulations.) 中国化学工业加快对外开放步伐 (Chinese chemistry industry increases the pace of opening up.)	天下之大，无奇不有，山川灵秀，亦多妖魔鬼怪。 (The world was big. It held everything. There were fascinating landscapes. There were haunting ghosts.) 时间无多，我去请出诛仙古剑。 (No time left. Let me call out Zhuxian, the ancient sword.) 忽听得狂笑风起，法宝异光闪动。(There came suddenly a gust of wind, out of which was laughters and magic flashes.)

Table 2: Example sentences from CTB and ZX to illustrate the differences between news and novel.

Data Set		Chap. IDs	# sents	# words
CTB5	Train	1-270, 400-931, 1001-1151	10,086	493,930
	Devel	301-325	350	6,821
	Test	271-300	348	8,008
ZX	Train	6.6-6.10, 7.6-7.10, 19	2,373	67,648
	Devel	6.1-6.5	788	20,393
	Test	7.1-7.5	1,394	34,355

Table 3: Corpus statistics.

ample sentences from the two corpora are shown in Table 2. Liu and Zhang (2012) manually annotated 385 sentences as development and test data, which we download from their website.[1] These data follow the same annotation guidelines as the Chinese Treebank (Xue et al., 2000).

To gain more reliable statistics in our results, we extend their annotation work to a total 4,555 sentences, covering the sections 6, 7 and 19 of the novel. The annotation work is based on the automatically labeled sentences by our baseline model trained with CTB5 corpus. It took an experienced native speaker 80 hours, about one minute on average to annotate one sentence. We use chapters 1-5 of section 6 as the development data, chapters 1-5 of section 7 as the test data, and the remaining data for target-domain training,[2] in order to compare type-supervised methods with token-supervised methods. Under permission from the author of the novel, we release our annotation for future reference. Statistics of both the source and the target domain data are shown in Table 3. The rest of the novel is treated as unlabeled sentences, used for type-annotation and self-training.

We perform the standard evaluation, using F-scores for both the segmentation accuracy and the overall segmentation and POS tagging accuracy.

4.2 Baseline Performances

The baseline discriminative model can achieve state-of-the-art performances on the CTB5, with a 97.62% segmentation accuracy and a 93.85% on overall segmentation and tagging accuracy. Using the CTB model, the performance on ZX drops significantly, to a 87.71% segmentation accuracy and a 80.81% overall accuracy. Applying self-training, the segmentation and overall F-scores can be improved to 88.62% and 81.94% respectively.

4.3 Development Experiments

In this section, we study type-supervised domain adaptation by conducting a series of experiments on the development data, addressing the following questions. First, what is the influence of tag-dictionaries through lexicon-based features? Second, what is the effect of type-supervised domain adaptation in contrast to token-supervised domain adaptation under the same annotation cost? Third, what is the interaction between tag-dictionary and self-training? Finally, what is the combined effect of type- and token-supervised domain adaptation?

4.3.1 The Influence of The Tag Dictionary

We investigate the effects of two different tag dictionaries. The first dictionary contains names of characters (e.g. 鬼厉 (Guili)) and artifacts (e.g. swords such as 斩龙 (Dragonslayer)) in the novel, which are obtained from an Internet Encyclopedia,[3] and requires little human effort. We extracted 159 words from this page, verified them, and put them into a tag dictionary. We associate every word in this tag dictionary with the POS "NR (proper noun)", and name the lexicon by ***NR***.

The second dictionary was constructed manually, by first employing our baseline tagger to tag the unlabeled ZX sentences automatically,

[1] http://faculty.sutd.edu.sg/~yue_zhang/emnlp12yang.zip

[2] We only use part of the training sentences in our experiments, and the remaining can be used for further research.

[3] http://baike.baidu.com/view/18277.htm

Model	Target-Domain Resources	Cost	Supervised		+Self-Training		
			SEG	POS	SEG	POS	ER
Baseline	—	0	89.77	82.92	90.35	83.95	6.03
Type-Supervision	NR(T)	0	89.84	83.91	91.18	85.22	8.14
	3K(T)	5h	91.93	86.53	92.86	87.67	8.46
	ORACLE(T)	∞	93.10	88.87	94.00	89.91	9.34
Token-Supervision	300(S)	5h	92.59	86.86	93.33	87.85	7.53
	600(S)	10h	93.19	88.13	93.81	89.01	7.41
	900(S)	15h	93.53	88.53	94.15	89.33	6.97
Combined Type- and Token-Supervision	3K(T) + 300(S)	10h	93.49	88.54	94.00	89.21	5.85
	3K(T) + 600(S)	15h	93.98	89.27	94.61	89.87	5.59

Table 4: Development test results, where **Cost** denotes the cost of type- or token-annotation measured by person hours, **ER** denotes the error reductions of overall performances brought by *self-training*, **T** denotes type-annotation and **S** denotes token-annotation.

and then randomly selecting the words that are not domain-independent for an experienced native speaker to annotate. To facilitate comparison with token-supervision, we spent about 5 person hours in annotating 3,000 word-tag pairs, at about the same cost as annotating 300 sentences. Finally we conjoined the 3,000 word-tag pairs with the ***NR*** lexicon, and name the resulting lexicon by ***3K***.

For the target domain, we mark the words from both ***NR*** and ***3K*** as the *domain-specific* lexicons. In all experiments, we use the same domain-independent lexicon, which is extracted from the source domain training data by HowNet matching.

The accuracies are shown in Table 4, where the ***NR*** lexicon improved the overall F-score slightly over the baseline, and the larger lexicon ***3K*** brought more significant improvements. These experiments agree with the intuition that the size and the coverage of the tag dictionary is important to the accuracies. To understand the extent to which a lexicon can improve the accuracies, we perform an oracle test, in which lexicons in the gold-standard test outputs are included in the dictionary. The accuracy is 88.87%.

4.3.2 Comparing Type-Supervised and Token-Supervised Domain Adaptation

Table 4 shows that the accuracy improvement by 3,000 annotated word-tag pairs (86.53%) is close to that by 300 annotated sentences (86.86%). This suggest that using our method, type-supervised domain adaptation can be a competitive choice to the token-supervised methods.

The fact that the token-supervised model gives slightly better results than our type-annotation method under similar efforts can probably be explained by the nature of domain differences. Texts in the Internet novel are different with CTB news in not only the vocabulary, but also POS n-gram distributions. The latter cannot be transferred from the source-domain training data directly. Texts from domains such as modern-style novels and scientific articles might have more similar POS distributions to the CTB data, and can potentially benefit more from pure lexicons. We leave the verification of this intuition to future work.

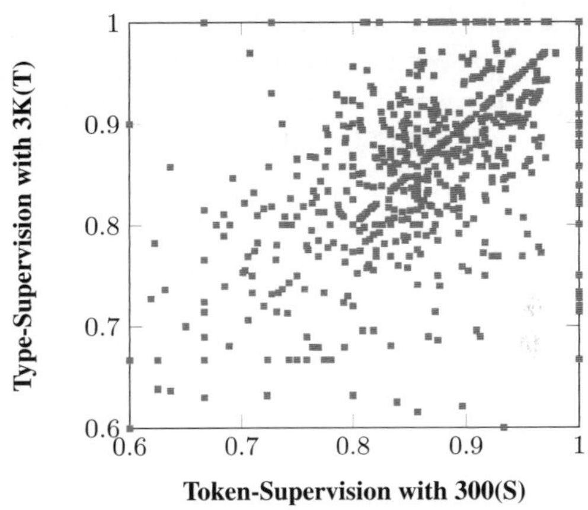

Figure 2: Sentence accuracy comparisons for type- and token-supervision with equal cost.

4.3.3 Making Use of Unlabeled Sentences

Both type- and token-supervised domain adaptation methods can be further improved via unlabeled target sentences. We apply self-training to both methods, and find improved results across the board in Table 4. The results indicate that unlabeled data is useful in further improving both type- and token-supervised domain adaptation.

Interestingly, the effects of the two methods on self-training are slightly different. The error reduction by self-training improves from 6.0% (baseline) to averaged 7.3% and 8.6% for token- and type-supervised adaptation, respectively. The better effect for the type-supervised method may result from comparatively more uniform coverage of the lexicon on sentences, since the target-domain lexicon is annotated by selecting words from much more than 300 sentences.

4.3.4 Combined Model of Type- and Token-Supervision

Figure 2 shows the F-scores of each development test sentence by type- and token-supervised domain adaptation with 5 person hours, respectively. It indicates that the two methods make different types of errors, and can potentially be used jointly for better improvements. We conduct a set of experiments as shown in Table 4, finding that the combined type- and token-supervised model with lexicon ***3K*** and 300 labeled sentences achieves an overall accuracy of 88.54%, exceeding the accuracies of both the type-supervised model with lexicon ***3K*** and the token-supervised model with 300 labeled sentences. Similar observation can be found for the combined model with lexicon ***3K*** and 600 labeled sentences. If combined with self-training, the same fact can be observed.

More interestingly, the combined model also exceeds pure type- and token-supervised models with the same annotation cost. For example, the combined model with ***3K*** and 300 labeled sentences gives a better accuracy than the token-supervised model with 600 sentences, with or without self-training. Similar observations hold between the combined model with ***3K*** and 600 labeled sentences and the token-supervised model with 900 sentences. The results suggest that the most cost-effective approach for domain adaptation can be combined type- and token-supervision: after annotating a set of raw sentences, one could stop to annotate some words, rather than continuing sentence annotation.

4.4 Final Results

Table 5 shows the final results on test corpus within ten person hours' annotation. With five person hours (lexicon ***3K***), the type-supervised model gave an error reduction of 32.99% compared with the baseline. The best result was obtained by the combined type- and token-supervised model, with

	SEG	POS	ER	Time
Baseline	87.71	80.81	0.00	0
Baseline+Self-Training	88.62	81.94	5.89	0
Type-Supervision				
NR(T)	88.34	82.54	9.02	0
NR(T)+ Self-Training	89.52	83.93	16.26	0
3K(T)	91.11	86.04	27.25	5h
3K(T)+Self-Training	92.11	87.14	32.99	5h
Token-Supervision				
300(S)	92.44	86.87	31.58	5h
300(S)+Self-Training	93.24	87.48	34.76	5h
600(S)	93.09	88.05	37.73	10h
600(S)+Self-Training	93.77	88.78	41.53	10h
Combined Type- and Token-Supervision				
3K(T)+300(S)	93.27	89.03	42.83	10h
3K(T)+300(S)+Self-Training	**93.98**	**89.84**	**47.06**	10h

Table 5: Final results on test set within ten person hours' annotation, where **ER** denotes the overall error reductions compared with *the baseline model*, **Time** denotes the cost of type- or token-annotation measured by person hours, **T** denotes type-annotation and **S** denotes token-annotation.

an error reduction of 47.06%, higher than that the token-supervised model with the same cost under the same setting (the model of 600 labeled sentences with an error reduction of 41.53%). The results confirm that the type-supervised model is a competitive alternative for joint segmentation and POS-tagging under the cross-domain setting. Combined type- and token-supervised model yields better results than single models.

5 Related Work

As mentioned in the introduction, tag dictionaries have been applied to type-supervised POS tagging of English (Toutanova and Johnson, 2007; Goldwater and Griffiths, 2007; Ravi and Knight, 2009; Garrette and Baldridge, 2012), Hebrew (Goldberg et al., 2008), Kinyarwanda and Malagasy (Garrette and Baldridge, 2013; Garrette et al., 2013), and other languages (Täckström et al., 2013). These methods assume that lexicon can be obtained by manual annotation or semi-supervised learning, and use the lexicon to induce tag sequences on unlabeled sentences. We study type-supervised Chinese POS-tagging, but under the setting of domain adaptation. The problem is how to leverage a target domain lexicon and an available annotated resources in a different source domain to improving POS-tagging. Consistent with Garrette et al. (2013), we also find that the type-supervised method is a competitive choice to token-supervised adaptation.

There has been a line of work on using graph-based label propagation to expand tag-lexicons for POS-tagging (Subramanya et al., 2010; Das and Petrov, 2011). Similar methods have been applied to character-level Chinese tagging (Zeng et al., 2013). We found that label propagation from neither the source domain nor auto-labeled target domain sentences can improve domain adaptation. The main reason could be significant domain differences. Due to space limitations, we omit this negative result in our experiments.

With respect to domain adaptation, existing methods can be classified into three categories. The first category does not explicitly model differences between the source and target domains, but use standard semi-supervised learning methods with labeled source domain data and unlabeled target domain data (Dai et al., 2007; Raina et al., 2007). The baseline self-training approach (Liu and Zhang, 2012) belongs to this category. The second considers the differences in the two domains in terms of features (Blitzer et al., 2006; Daume III, 2007), classifying features into domain-independent source domain and target domain groups and training these types consistently. The third considers differences between the distributions of instances in the two domains, treating them differently (Jiang and Zhai, 2007). Our type-supervised method is closer to the second category. However, rather than splitting features into domain-independent and domain-specific types, we use domain-specific dictionaries to capture domain differences, and train a model on the source domain only. Our method can be treated as an approach specific to the POS-tagging task.

With respect to Chinese lexical analysis, little previous work has been reported on using a tag dictionary to improve joint segmentation and POS-tagging. There has been work on using a lexicon in improving segmentation in a Chinese analysis pipeline. Peng et al. (2004) used features from a set of Chinese words and characters to improve CRF-based segmentation; Low et al. (2005) extracted features based on a Chinese lexicon from Peking University to help a maximum segmentor; Sun (2011) collected 12,992 idioms from Chinese dictionaries, and used them for rule-based pre-segmentation; Hatori et al. (2012) collected Chinese words from HowNet and the Chinese Wikipedia to enhance segmentation accuracies of their joint dependency parsing systems. In comparison with their work, our lexicon contain additional POS information, and are used for word segmentation and POS-tagging simultaneously. In addition, we separate domain-dependent lexicons for the source and target lexicons, and use a novel framework to perform domain adaptation.

Wang et al. (2011) collect word-tag statistics from automatically labeled texts, and use them as features to improve POS-tagging. Their word-tag statistics can be treated as a type of lexicon. However, their efforts differ from ours in several aspects: (1) they focus on in-domain POS-tagging, while our concern is cross-domain tagging; (2) they study POS-tagging on segmented sentences, while we investigate joint segmentation and POS-tagging for Chinese; (3) their tag-dictionaries are not tag-dictionaries literally, but statistics of word-tag associations.

6 Conclusions

We performed an empirical study on the use of tag-dictionaries for the domain adaptation of joint Chinese segmentation and POS-tagging, showing that type-supervised methods can be a competitive alternative to token-supervised methods in cost-effectiveness. In addition, combination of the two methods gives the best cost-effect. Finally, we release our annotation of over 4,000 sentences in the Internet literature domain online at `http://faculty.sutd.edu.sg/~yue_zhang/eacl14meishan.zip` as a free resource for Chinese POS-tagging.

Acknowledgments

We thank the anonymous reviewers for their constructive comments. We gratefully acknowledge the support of the National Key Basic Research Program (973 Program) of China via Grant 2014CB340503 and the National Natural Science Foundation of China (NSFC) via Grant 61133012 and 61370164, the National Basic Research Program (973 Program) of China via Grant 2014CB340503, the Singaporean Ministration of Education Tier 2 grant T2MOE201301 and SRG ISTD 2012 038 from Singapore University of Technology and Design.

References

Michele Banko and Robert C. Moore. 2004. Part-of-speech tagging in context. In *COLING*.

John Blitzer, Ryan McDonald, and Fernando Pereira. 2006. Domain adaptation with structural correspondence learning. In *Proceedings of the 2006 Conference on Empirical Methods in Natural Language Processing*, pages 120–128, Sydney, Australia, July. Association for Computational Linguistics.

Christos Christodoulopoulos, Sharon Goldwater, and Mark Steedman. 2010. Two decades of unsupervised POS induction: How far have we come? In *Proceedings of the 2010 Conference on Empirical Methods in Natural Language Processing*, pages 575–584, Cambridge, MA, October. Association for Computational Linguistics.

Michael Collins and Brian Roark. 2004. Incremental parsing with the perceptron algorithm. In *Proceedings of the 42nd Meeting of the Association for Computational Linguistics (ACL'04), Main Volume*, pages 111–118, Barcelona, Spain, July.

Wenyuan Dai, Gui-Rong Xue, Qiang Yang, and Yong Yu. 2007. Transferring Naive Bayes Classifiers for Text Classification. In *AAAI*, pages 540–545.

Dipanjan Das and Slav Petrov. 2011. Unsupervised part-of-speech tagging with bilingual graph-based projections. In *Proceedings of the 49th Annual Meeting of the Association for Computational Linguistics: Human Language Technologies*, pages 600–609, Portland, Oregon, USA, June. Association for Computational Linguistics.

Hal Daume III. 2007. Frustratingly easy domain adaptation. In *Proceedings of the 45th Annual Meeting of the Association of Computational Linguistics*, pages 256–263, Prague, Czech Republic, June. Association for Computational Linguistics.

Zhendong Dong and Qiang Dong. 2006. *Hownet And the Computation of Meaning*. World Scientific Publishing Co., Inc., River Edge, NJ, USA.

Dan Garrette and Jason Baldridge. 2012. Type-supervised hidden markov models for part-of-speech tagging with incomplete tag dictionaries. In *EMNLP-CoNLL*, pages 821–831.

Dan Garrette and Jason Baldridge. 2013. Learning a part-of-speech tagger from two hours of annotation. In *Proceedings of the 2013 Conference of the North American Chapter of the Association for Computational Linguistics: Human Language Technologies*, pages 138–147, Atlanta, Georgia, June. Association for Computational Linguistics.

Dan Garrette, Jason Mielens, and Jason Baldridge. 2013. Real-world semi-supervised learning of pos-taggers for low-resource languages. In *Proceedings of the 51st Annual Meeting of the Association for Computational Linguistics (Volume 1: Long Papers)*, pages 583–592, Sofia, Bulgaria, August. Association for Computational Linguistics.

Yoav Goldberg, Meni Adler, and Michael Elhadad. 2008. EM can find pretty good HMM POS-taggers (when given a good start). In *Proceedings of ACL-08: HLT*, pages 746–754, Columbus, Ohio, June. Association for Computational Linguistics.

Sharon Goldwater and Tom Griffiths. 2007. A fully bayesian approach to unsupervised part-of-speech tagging. In *Proceedings of the 45th Annual Meeting of the Association of Computational Linguistics*, pages 744–751, Prague, Czech Republic, June. Association for Computational Linguistics.

Jun Hatori, Takuya Matsuzaki, Yusuke Miyao, and Jun'ichi Tsujii. 2012. Incremental joint approach to word segmentation, pos tagging, and dependency parsing in chinese. In *Proceedings of the 50th Annual Meeting of the Association for Computational Linguistics (Volume 1: Long Papers)*, pages 1045–1053, Jeju Island, Korea, July. Association for Computational Linguistics.

Canasai Kruengkrai, Kiyotaka Uchimoto, Jun'ichi Kazama, Yiou Wang, Kentaro Torisawa, and Hitoshi Isahara. 2009. An error-driven word-character hybrid model for joint chinese word segmentation and pos tagging. In *Proceedings of the Joint Conference of the 47th Annual Meeting of the ACL and the 4th International Joint Conference on Natural Language Processing of the AFNLP*, pages 513–521, Suntec, Singapore, August. Association for Computational Linguistics.

Yang Liu and Yue Zhang. 2012. Unsupervised domain adaptation for joint segmentation and POS-tagging. In *Proceedings of COLING 2012: Posters*, pages 745–754, Mumbai, India, December. The COLING 2012 Organizing Committee.

Jin Kiat Low, Hwee Tou Ng, and Wenyuan Guo. 2005. A maximum entropy approach to chinese word segmentation. In *Proceedings of the Fourth SIGHAN Workshop on Chinese Language Processing*, pages 161–164.

Christopher D. Manning. 2011. Part-of-speech tagging from 97% to 100%: is it time for some linguistics? In *Proceeding of CICLing'11*.

Bernard Merialdo. 1994. Tagging english text with a probabilistic model. *Computational Linguistics*, 20(2).

Hwee Tou Ng and Jin Kiat Low. 2004. Chinese part-of-speech tagging: One-at-a-time or all-at-once? word-based or character-based? In Dekang Lin and Dekai Wu, editors, *Proceedings of EMNLP 2004*, pages 277–284, Barcelona, Spain, July. Association for Computational Linguistics.

Fuchun Peng, Fangfang Feng, and Andrew McCallum. 2004. Chinese segmentation and new word detection using conditional random fields. In *Proceedings of Coling 2004*, pages 562–568, Geneva, Switzerland, Aug 23–Aug 27. COLING.

Slav Petrov, Dipanjan Das, and Ryan McDonald. 2012. A universal part-of-speech tagset. In *Proceedings of LREC*, May.

Rajat Raina, Alexis Battle, Honglak Lee, Benjamin Packer, and Andrew Y. Ng. 2007. Self-taught learning: transfer learning from unlabeled data. In *ICML*, pages 759–766.

Sujith Ravi and Kevin Knight. 2009. Minimized models for unsupervised part-of-speech tagging. In *ACL/IJCNLP*, pages 504–512.

Amarnag Subramanya, Slav Petrov, and Fernando Pereira. 2010. Efficient graph-based semi-supervised learning of structured tagging models. In *Proceedings of the 2010 Conference on Empirical Methods in Natural Language Processing*, pages 167–176, Cambridge, MA, October. Association for Computational Linguistics.

Weiwei Sun. 2011. A stacked sub-word model for joint chinese word segmentation and part-of-speech tagging. In *Proceedings of the 49th Annual Meeting of the Association for Computational Linguistics: Human Language Technologies*, pages 1385–1394, Portland, Oregon, USA, June. Association for Computational Linguistics.

Oscar Täckström, Dipanjan Das, Slav Petrov, McDonald Ryan, and Joakim Nivre. 2013. Token and type constraints for cross-lingual part-of-speech tagging. In *Transactions of the ACL*. Association for Computational Linguistics, March.

Partha Pratim Talukdar and Koby Crammer. 2009. New regularized algorithms for transductive learning. In *ECML/PKDD (2)*, pages 442–457.

Kristina Toutanova and Mark Johnson. 2007. A bayesian lda-based model for semi-supervised part-of-speech tagging. In *NIPS*.

Yiou Wang, Jun'ichi Kazama, Yoshimasa Tsuruoka, Wenliang Chen, Yujie Zhang, and Kentaro Torisawa. 2011. Improving chinese word segmentation and pos tagging with semi-supervised methods using large auto-analyzed data. In *Proceedings of 5th International Joint Conference on Natural Language Processing*, pages 309–317, Chiang Mai, Thailand, November. Asian Federation of Natural Language Processing.

Nianwen Xue, Fei Xia, Shizhe Huang, and Tony Kroch. 2000. The bracketing guidelines for the chinese treebank. Technical report, University of Pennsylvania.

Nianwen Xue, Fei Xia, Fu-Dong Chiou, and Martha Palmer. 2005. The penn chinese treebank: Phrase structure annotation of a large corpus. *Natural Language Engineering*, 11(2):207–238.

Xiaodong Zeng, Derek F. Wong, Lidia S. Chao, and Isabel Trancoso. 2013. Graph-based semi-supervised model for joint chinese word segmentation and part-of-speech tagging. In *Proceedings of the 51st Annual Meeting of the Association for Computational Linguistics (Volume 1: Long Papers)*, pages 770–779, Sofia, Bulgaria, August. Association for Computational Linguistics.

Yue Zhang and Stephen Clark. 2008. Joint word segmentation and POS tagging using a single perceptron. In *Proceedings of ACL-08: HLT*, pages 888–896, Columbus, Ohio, June. Association for Computational Linguistics.

Yue Zhang and Stephen Clark. 2010. A fast decoder for joint word segmentation and POS-tagging using a single discriminative model. In *Proceedings of the 2010 Conference on Empirical Methods in Natural Language Processing*, pages 843–852, Cambridge, MA, October. Association for Computational Linguistics.

Yue Zhang and Stephen Clark. 2011. Syntactic processing using the generalized perceptron and beam search. *Computational Linguistics*, 37(1):105–151.

Applying the semantics of negation to SMT through n-best list re-ranking

Federico Fancellu
Centre for Global Intelligent Content
School of Computer Science and Statistics
Trinity College Dublin
ffancellu@cngl.ie

Bonnie Webber
School of Informatics
University of Edinburgh
Edinburgh, UK, EH8 9AB
bonnie@inf.ed.ac.uk

Abstract

Although the performance of SMT systems has improved over a range of different linguistic phenomena, negation has not yet received adequate treatment.
Previous works have considered the problem of translating negative data as one of data sparsity (Wetzel and Bond (2012)) or of structural differences between source and target language with respect to the placement of negation (Collins et al. (2005)). This work starts instead from the questions of *what is meant by negation* and *what makes a good translation of negation*. These questions have led us to explore the use of semantics of negation in SMT — specifically, identifying core semantic elements of negation (*cue, event* and *scope*) in a source-side dependency parse and re-ranking hypotheses on the n-best list produced after decoding according to the extent to which an hypothesis realises these elements.
The method shows considerable improvement over the baseline as measured by BLEU scores and Stanford's entailment-based MT evaluation metric (Padó et al. (2009)).

1 Introduction

Translating negation is a task that involves more than the correct rendering of a negation marker in the target sentence. For instance, translating *Italy did not defeat France in 1909* differs from translating *Italy defeated France in 1909*, or *France did not defeat Italy in 1909*, or *Italy did not conquer France in 1909*. These examples show that translating negation also involves placing in the right position the semantic arguments as well as the event directly negated. Moreover, if the source sentence was uttered in response to the statement *I think Italy defeated France in 1911*, where the focus is the temporal argument *in 1911*, one can see that the system should not lose track of the focus of negation when producing the hypothesis translation.

Although negation must be appropriately rendered to ensure correct representation of the semantics of the source sentence in the machine output, only some of the efforts to improve the translation of negation-bearing sentences in SMT address the problem.

Wetzel and Bond (2012) considered negation as a problem of data sparsity and so attempted to enrich the training data with negative paraphrases of positive sentences. Collins et al. (2005) and Li et al. (2009) both addressed differences in the placement of negation in source and target texts, by re-ordering negative elements in the source sentence to better resemble their position in the corresponding target text. Although these approaches show improvement over the baseline, neither considers negation as a linguistic phenomenon with specific characteristics.

This we do in the work presented here: We identify the elements of negation that an MT system has to reproduce and then devise a strategy to ensure that they are output correctly. These elements we take to be the *cue*, *event* and *scope* of negation[1]. Unlike previous works, we first validate the hypothesis that if the top-ranked translation in the n-best list does not replicate elements of negation from the source, there may be a more accurate translation after decoding, somewhere else on the n-best list. If the hypothesis is false, then problems in the translation of negation lie elsewhere.

[1]Due to its ambiguity and the fact that it is already included in the scope, we have ignored the *focus* of negation. That does not mean it may not be important to correctly reproduce the *focus*; there might be cases where, although not fully-capturing the *scope*, we want to translate correctly the part that is directly negated or emphasised.

Proceedings of the 14th Conference of the European Chapter of the Association for Computational Linguistics, pages 598–606,
Gothenburg, Sweden, April 26-30 2014.

We use dependency parsing as a basis for N-best list re-ranking. Dependencies between lexical elements appear to encode all elements of negation, offering a robust and easily-applicable way to extract negation-related information from a sentence. We carry out our exploration of N-best list re-ranking in two steps:

- First, an *oracle* translation is computed both to assess the validity of the approach and to understand the maximal extent to which it could possibly enhance performance. An oracle translation is obtained by performing n-best list re-ranking using reference translations as a gold-standard.
  To avoid the problem in Chinese-English Hierarchical Phrase-Based (HPB) translation of loss and/or misplacement of negation-related elements when hierarchical phrases are built, Chinese source sentences are first broken into sub-clauses Yang and Xue (2012), then translated and finally "stitched" back together for evaluation.

- Standard n-best list re-ranking is then performed using only *source-side* information. Hypotheses are re-ranked according to the degree of similarity between the negation-related elements in the hypotheses and those in the source sentence. Here the correspondence between source and target text is established through lexical translation probabilities output after training.

Results of this method show that n-best list reranking does lead to a significant improvement in BLEU score. However, BLEU says nothing about semantics, so we also evaluate the method using Stanford's entailment based MT metrics Padó et al. (2009), and also show improvement here. In the final section of the paper, we note the value of developing a custom metric that actually assesses the components of negation.

2 Related works

Negation has been a widely discussed topic outside the field of SMT, with recent works focused mainly on automatic detection of negation. Blanco and Moldovan (2011) have established the distribution of negative cues and the syntactic structures in which they appear in the WSJ section of the Penn Treebank, as a basis for automatically detecting scope and focus of negation using simple heuristics.

Machine-learning has been used by systems participating in the *SEM 2012 shared task on automatically detecting the scope and focus of negation. Those systems with the best F1 measures (Chowdhury and Mahbub (2012), Read et al. (2012) and Lapponi et al. (2012) all use a mixture of SVM (Support Vector Machines) and CRF. Their performance improves significantly when syntactic features are also considered. In particular, Lapponi et al. (2012) use features extracted from a dependency parse to guide their system to detect the correct scope boundary.

In translation, only few efforts have focussed on the problem of translating negation. Wetzel and Bond (2012) treat it as resulting from data sparsity. To remedy this, they enrich their Japanese-to-English training set with negative paraphrases of positive sentences, where negation is inserted as a 'handle' to the main verb after a sentence is parsed using MSR (Minimal Recursion Semantics Copestake et al. (2005)). Results show that BLEU score improves on a test sub-set containing *only negative sentences* when extra negative data is appended to the original training data and the language model is enriched as well. However, system performance deteriorates on both the original test set and on positive sentences. Moreover, generating paraphrases with negation expressed only on the main verb does not allow to fully capture the various ways negation can be expressed.

Other works considered negation in the framework of clause restructuring. Collins et al. (2005) pre-process the German source to resemble the structure of English while Li et al. (2009) tried to swap the order of the words in a Chinese sentence to resemble Korean. Rosa (2013) takes a post-processing approach to negation in English-Czech translation, "fixing" common errors such as the loss of a negation cue by either generating the morphologically negative form of the relevant verb (if the verb has such a form) or prefixing the verb with the negative prefix *ne*. Despite the improvements, these approaches do not really address what is special about negation.

3 Decomposing negation

Correctly translating negation involves more than placing a negative marker in the right position. We follow Blanco and Moldovan (2011) in decomposing negation into three main components:

- a *negation cue*, including negative markers, affixes and all the words or multiwords units that inherently express negation.
- a *negation event*, i.e. the event that is directly negated. Events can be either verbs (e.g. 'I do *not* **go** to the cinema) or adjectives (e.g. 'He is *not* **clever**').
- a *negation scope*, i.e. the part of the statement whose meaning is negated (Blanco and Moldovan, 2011, 229). The scope contains all those words that, if negated, would make the statement true. We follow here the guidelines for annotating negative data released during the *SEM 2012 Shared Task Morante et al. (2011) for a more detailed understanding on what to consider part of the negation scope.

In addition to these three components, formal semanticists identify a *negation focus*, i.e. the part of the scope that is directly negated or more emphasized. Focus is the most difficult part to detect since it is the most ambiguous. In the sentence 'he does not want to go to school by car' the speaker emphasized the fact that '**he** does not want to go to school by car' or that 'he does not want to go **to school** by car' (but he wants to go somewhere else) or that 'he does not want to go to school **by car**' (but by other means of transportation).

Translating negation is therefore a matter of ensuring that the *cue* is present, that its attachment to the corresponding *event* follows language-specific rules and that all the elements included in the scope are placed in the right order. Correctly reproducing the *focus* is left for future works.

4 Methodology

4.1 N-best list re-ranking

N-best list re-ranking is used in SMT to deal with sentence-level phenomena whose locality goes beyond n-grams or single hierarchical rules. It involves re-ranking the list of target-language hypotheses produced by decoding, using additional features extracted from the source sentence. In the case of negation, N-best list re-ranking allows us to assess whether a system is able to correctly translate the elements of negation, while failing to place the best hypothesis on these grounds at the top of the n-best list.

The current work follows the same approach as other n-best list re-rankers (Och et al. (2004); Specia et al. (2008); Apidianaki et al. (2012)) but using negation as the additional feature. Negation is here defined as the degree of overlap of *cue*, *event* and *scope* between the hypothesis translation and the source sentence.

Following Hasan et al. (2007), we use an n-best list of 10000 sentences but we do not initially tune the negation feature using MERT or interpolate it with other features. This is because in order to assess the degree of overlap between the scope in the source and the hypothesis sentence, a n-gram based score is used which conveys the same information as that of the *language model* score in the log-linear model. Moreover, our re-ranking exploits lexical translation probabilities, thereby resembling a simple *translation model*.

4.2 Extract negation using dependency parsing

The degree of overlap between the source sentence and the hypothesis translation is measured in terms of the overlap between their negation *cue*, *event* and *scope*. These must therefore be correctly extracted. Dependency parsing provides an efficient way to do so, with several advantages:

- Dependency parsing encodes the notions of *cue* and *event* as the dependant and the head respectively of a 'neg' relation. *Scope* can be approximated through *recursive retrieval of all the descendants of the verb-event*. The following example shows how these elements are extracted from the dependency parse:

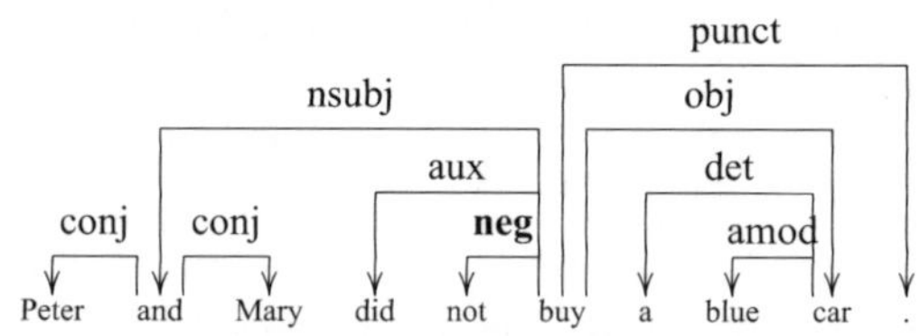

nsubj(buy-6, and-2) , conj(and-2, Peter-1), conj (and-2, Mary-3), aux(buy-6, did-4), **neg(buy-6, not-5)**, root(ROOT-0, buy-6), det(car-9, a-7), amod(car-9, blue-8) , dobj(buy-6, car-9)

The 'neg' dependency relation conveys both the negation *cue* (**not-5**) and the negation *event* (**buy-6**) of the sentence 'Peter and Mary did not buy a blue car'. An approximate scope can be recovered by following the path from the event (included) to the terminal nodes and collecting all the lexical elements along the way.

Also in the case of a sentence containing a subordinate clause, dependency parsing is

able to correctly capture the latter as part of the *scope* given that the relative pronoun depends directly on the *event* of the main clause. On the other hand, recursion from the negated event excludes coordinate clauses that are *not* considered part of the scope, given that the event is a dependant of the connective.
One problem with this method is that it is unable to capture the entire scope when the head is nominal. For instance, *'no reasons were given'*, the 'neg' dependency holds between *no* and *reasons* but it needs to climb the hierarchy further to get to the verbal head *given*. The same holds for negation on object nominals. We leave this to future work (along with affix-conveyed negation), needing to show first that the current approach is a good one.

- A dependency parser can be developed for any language for which a Treebank or Propbank is available for training. This extends the range of source languages to which the approach can be applied.

4.3 Computing an oracle translation

In order to test the validity of the method and to assess its maximum contribution, we first use it with an *oracle translation* in which n-best list re-ranking relies on a comparison with negation *cue*, *event* and *scope* extracted from the reference translation(s), here assumed to correctly contain all elements of negation.

Each hypothesis on the n-best list is assigned an overlap score with these reference-translation-derived elements, and the hypothesis with the highest score is re-ranked at the top and used for evaluation.

The overlap score is obtained by summing up three sub-scores: (i) the *cue overlap* score measures how many cues in reference are represented in the hypothesis, normalised by the number of cues in the reference; (ii) the *event overlap* score measures how many events in the reference are represented in the hypothesis, normalised by the number of the events in the reference; and (iii) the *scope overlap* score is a weighted n-gram overlap between hypothesis scope and reference scope, with higher weight for higher-order n-grams. Given less-than-perfect machine output, breaking down the score into subscores allows us to consider different degrees of correctness in translating negation. When multiple reference translations are available, the hypothesis is matched with each, and only the best score taken into consideration.

4.4 Re-ranking using lexical translation probabilities

After the oracle translation is computed, traditional n-best list re-ranking is performed relying on *source side information only*. We then bridge the gap between source and target language using *lexical translation probabilities* to render source-side *cue*, *event*, *scope* into the target language. Re-ranking involves three separate steps:

- The source sentence is parsed and dependencies extracted. Since the present work tackles Chinese-to-English translation, we had to enhance the representation of negative dependencies in the Chinese source, where only the adverb 不 *bu4* is flagged as 'neg' dependant. To do this, we follow the same intuition used to isolate negation-bearing sentences in the test set (see section 5).

- To obtain a rough translation of *cue*, *event* and *scope* in the target language, the top ten lexical translation probabilities for each lexical item, available in the lexical translations (in order of probability) table output after training, are considered.

- Hypotheses in the n-best list are re-scored taking into consideration the information above. Scoring *cue* and *event* is straightforward; the words for the *cue* and the *event* are assigned the lexical probability of being the translation of the *cue* and the *event* in the Chinese sentence by looking up the lexical translation table. If the *cue* or the *event* do not figure as translations of the negation *cue* and *event* in the Chinese sentence, a score of 0 is assigned to them.
The scope is instead scored by looping through the words in the hypothesis; for each such hypothesis word, the process identifies which source-side scope word it is most likely to be the translation of. If no *scope* can be retrieved, a score of 0 is given for scope matching. For each word the best translation probability is taken into account and these are then summed together to score how likely is the

scope in the hypothesis to be the translation of the scope in the source.

5 System

A hierarchical phrase based model (HPBM) was trained on a corpus of 625000 (~ 18.200.000 tokens) length-ratio filtered sentences. 56949 sentences (~ 9.11%) of the Chinese side and 48941 sentences (~ 7.83%) of the English side of the training set were found to include at least one instance of negation. 2500 sentences were instead included in the dev set to tune the log-linear model using the MERT algorithm. 3725 sentences from the Multiple-Translation Chinese Corpus 2.0 (LDC2002T01) were used as test set. The test set comes divided into four sub-sets; in this paper these sub-sets are referred as test set 1 to 4. The source side was tokenized using the Stanford Chinese Word Segmenter (Tseng et al. (2005)) and encoded in 'utf-8' so to serve as input to the system. In order to focus on the problem of translating negative data, the 563 sentence pairs containing negation were extracted from the original test set. This test set constitutes the true baseline improvements will be measured upon. Reducing the number of test sentences also eases the computation load when involved in dependency parsing on 10.000 sentences in each n-best list. Negated sentence were isolated by means of both regular expressions and dependency parsing; this is because, as pointed out above, the Chinese side does not flag all negative dependencies as such.[2]

6 Results

6.1 Baseline

BLEU scores for the baseline systems are given in Table 1, where the *negative* subset is compared to the *original* (all sentences) and *only positive sentences* conditions.

Table 2 shows instead the result for the negative baseline across three different metrics. Along with the BLEU scores, we also took into consideration an entailment-based MT evaluation metric, the RTE score[3] Padó et al. (2009). The RTE score assesses to what extent the hypothesis entails the reference translation across a wide variety of semantic and syntactic features. Another reason we chose this metric is because it contains a feature for polarity as well as features to check the degree of similarity between the syntactic tree and the dependencies between hypothesis and reference translation, the latter being what we used to recover the elements of negation. We expect this metric to give a further insight on the quality of the machine output.

Baseline results are in line with the results of Wetzel and Bond (2012), where there is a drop in BLEU scores between positive and negative sentences, and between the overall test set and the one containing negative data only.

When analysing the results from the baseline, we noticed that words were being deleted or moved inappropriately when the hierarchy of phrases was being built. This might be detrimental to the translation of negation since elements might end up outside the correct negation scope. The following example illustrates this problem.

(1) *Source* : 三 年 来 ， 这些 城市 累计 完成 固定 资产 投资 一百二十亿 元 ， 昔日 边境 城市 的 " 楼 不 高 ， 路 不 平 、 灯 不 明 、 水 不 清 、 通讯 不 畅 " 的 状 况 **已 得到 了 改变** 。
Baseline : Investment in fixed assets investment in the three years , 一百二十亿 yuan , **floor is not high** , " the former border city , road , and **communication conditions have not been completed** , **will not change .**

Due to unrestricted rule application, mainly guided by the language model, the underlined clauses containing negation on the source side have been deleted. Moreover, the polarity of the last clause, positive in the source, is changed into negative in the target translation, most probably because a negative cue is moved from somewhere else in the sentence.

In order to solve these two problems, we exploit the syntactic feature of the Chinese language of grouping clauses into a single sentence. We follow the intuition of Yang and Xue (2012) in using

[2]While the English dependency parser is able to identify almost all negative markers and their dependencies, the Chinese dependency parser here deployed (the Stanford Chinese Dependency parser) only captures sentences containing the adverb 不*bu4*. For this reason, we exploited the list of negation adverbs included in the Chinese Propbank (LDC2005T23) documentation and look for each of them via regular expressions. Moreover we also looked for words containing 不 as component since they are most likely to carry negative meaning (e.g. 不久, 'not-long').

[3]The entailment-based MT metric also outputs an RTE+MT score, where the RTE score is interpolated with traditional MT metrics (e.g. BLEU, NIST, TER, METEOR).

Test set	Original	Positive	Negative	Orig. → Neg.	Pos. → Neg.
Test 1	32.92	**32.95**	29.64	- 3.28	- 3.31
Test 2	25.88	**26.21**	24.31	- 1.57	- 1.9
Test 3	19.00	**19.78**	16.11	- 2.89	- 3.67
Test 4	28.64	**29.71**	27.14	- 1.5	- 2.57
Average	26.61	**27.16**	24.3	-2.31	- 2.96

Table 1: BLEU scores for the baseline system. The difference in BLEU scores between the *positive*, the *original* and the *negative* conditions is also reported.

Test set	BLEU	RTE	RTE+MT
Test 1	29.64	0.22	0.837
Test 2	24.31	0.307	0.732
Test 3	16.11	-0.603	-0.095
Test 4	27.14	-0.25	0.33
Average	24.3	-0.08	0.451

Table 2: BLEU, RTE and RTE+MT scores for the baseline system as tested on the sub-set only containing negative sentences.

commas to guide the segmentation of a sentence into constituent sub-clauses. Moreover, we also use other syntactic clues to segment the test sentences, including quotes in direct quotation, to reduce the size of the test sentences.
The constituent sub-clauses are then translated singularly and 'stitched' back together into the original sentence for evaluation.

6.2 Re-ranking results

Table 3 and 4 shows the performance of the system when n-best list re-ranking is performed. Table 3 shows the results for the oracle translation, while Table 4 the results for actual n-best list re-ranking. Two conditions are here compared: a *short* condition where test sentences are chunked into constituent sub-clauses prior to translation and a *original (orig.)* condition where no chunking is performed.

Results shows considerable improvements over the baseline when re-ranking is performed — an average BLEU score improvement of 1.75 points. As hypothesised, we get further improvement when Chinese source sentences are translated through their constituent sub-clauses — an average BLEU score improvement of 3.07 points. A similar improvement is shown in Table 5 where the original test sets comprising both positive and negative sentences are considered. This proves the validity of n-best list re-ranking using syntactic dependencies as a method to improve the quality of the translation of negative data. The following example shows the improvement in detail:

(2) *Source* : 关于 通货膨胀 ， 伊辛 说 ， 欧元区 通涨率 整体 呈 下降 态势 ,目前 没有 迹象 表明 在 经济 发展 的 中期 阶段 将 出现 物价 不 稳定 的 风险
Ex. reference : When asked about inflation, he said : "The overall inflation rate in the Euro area still exhibits a down trend. At present, there is no sign to show economic development in the medium term will create risks of price instability".
Baseline : on the inflation he said the euro dropped overall medium term economic development will in no signs of inflation risks .
Oracle : on inflation , said the euro dropped overall there is no signs of economic development in the medium term prices will not risks .
Source-only re-ranking : on inflation , said the euro dropped overall there is no signs of economic development in the medium term will price risks .

In (2) the baseline translation shows the problems mentioned earlier, where movement leaves negation with the wrong scope, changing the overall meaning of the sentence. Decomposing sentences into constituent clauses and then re-ranking the translations permits negation to retain its correct scope so that the meaning is the same as the reference sentence.

7 Conclusion

We have presented an approach to translating negative sentences that is based on the semantics of negation and applying it to n-best list re-ranking.

		BLEU	RTE	RTE+MT
1	Baseline	29.64	0.22	0.837
	Orig.	33.73 (+4.09)	0.64 (+0.42)	1.396 (+0.559)
	Short	**35.39 (+5.75)**	**0.74 (+ 0.52)**	**1.508 (+ 0.671)**
2	Baseline	24.31	0.307	0.732
	Orig.	27.43 (+3.12)	0.457 (+0.15)	1.12 (+0.388)
	Short	**27.29 (+3.18)**	**0.6 (+ 0.293)**	**1.175 (+ 0.443)**
3	Baseline	16.11	-0.603	-0.095
	Orig.	17.97 (+1.86)	**0.356 (+ 0.959)**	**0.958 (+ 1.053)**
	Short	**18.19 (+2.08)**	0.243 (+ 0.84)	0.78 (+ 0.875)
4	Baseline	27.14	-0.25	0.33
	Orig.	31.97 (+ 4.83)	0.42 (+ 0.67)	1.024 (+ 0.694)
	Short	**32.50 (+ 5.36)**	**0.57 (+ 0.82)**	**1.36 (+ 1.03)**
Avg.	Baseline	24.3	- 0.08	0.45
	Orig.	27.78 (+ 3.48)	0.47 (+ 0.55)	1.12 (+ 0.67)
	Short	**29.09 (+ 4.79)**	**0.52 (+ 0.60)**	**1.23 (+ 0.78)**

Table 3: BLEU, RTE and RTE+MT scores for the oracle translation. The test sets evaluated are marked from 1 to 4. Improvement over the baseline is reported.

		BLEU	RTE	RTE+MT
1	Baseline	29.64	0.22	0.837
	Orig.	31.96 (+ 2.32)	0.62 (+ 0.4)	1.382 (+ 0.545)
	Short	**34.20 (+ 4.56)**	**0.68 (+0.46)**	**1.452 (+ 0.615)**
2	Baseline	24.31	0.307	0.732
	Orig.	26.65 (+2.34)	0.48 (+ 0.173)	1.159 (+ 0.427)
	Short	**26.94 (+ 2.63)**	**0.49 (+0.183)**	**1.172 (+ 0.44)**
3	Baseline	16.11	-0.603	-0.095
	Orig.	17.20 (+ 1.09)	**0.35 (+ 0.953)**	**0.935 (+ 1.03)**
	Short	**17.41 (+ 1.3)**	0.226 (+0.829)	0.87 (+ 0.965)
4	Baseline	27.14	-0.25	0.33
	Orig.	28.42 (+ 1.28)	0.302 (+ 0.552)	1.01 (+ 0.68)
	Short	**30.96 (+ 3.82)**	**0.55 (+ 0.8)**	**1.36 (+ 1.03)**
Avg.	Baseline	24.3	-0.08	0.45
	Orig.	26.05 (+ 1.75)	0.438 (+ 0.518)	1.12 (+ 0.669)
	Short	**27.37 (+ 3.07)**	**0.51 (+ 0.59)**	**1.21 (+ 0.759)**

Table 4: BLEU, RTE and RTE+MT scores for the sentences re-ranked using source side information only. Improvement over the baseline is reported.

Dependency parsing and lexical translations are here considered as easily applicable methods to extract and translate negation related information across different language pairs. Improvements across different automatic evaluation metrics show that the above method is useful when translating negative data. In particular, the entailment-based RTE metric is here used as an alternative to the BLEU score given the semantic and syntactic features assessed, polarity included. Given the positive results, one can conclude that the problem is neither one of data sparsity nor syntactic mismatch.

We have also demonstrated that when dealing with sentences containing multiple sub-clauses, translating the constituent sub-clauses separately and then stitching them back together before evaluation avoids the loss or excessive movement of negation during decoding. This was evident in the case of Chinese and HPBMs but there is no reason why this does not hold also for other languages.

8 Future works

Given the validity of the present approach, future works should be focused in extending it to different language pairs. Also, it would be useful to research more in detail into language typology and try to devise a method which is language independent.

Although leading to an overall improvement, n-best list re-ranking does not always guarantee a perfect translation. It is therefore useful in the future to investigate ways of always ensuring that the n-best list contains a good translation of negation by, for instance, enriching the hypotheses list with paraphrases. Post-editing rules can also be considered to further correct the final output.

Finally, although we can show considerable improvement with respect to both n-gram overlap

		BLEU	RTE	RTE+MT
1	Baseline	32.92	-0.49	-0.073
	Orig.	33.54 (+ 0.62)	-0.38 (+ 0.11)	0.046 (+ 0.119)
	Short	**34.02 (+ 1.1)**	**-0.33 (+ 0.16)**	**0.057 (+ 0.13)**
2	Baseline	25.88	-2.173	-1.726
	Orig.	26.3 (+ 0.42)	-1.851 (+ 0.322)	-1.376 (+ 0.35)
	Short	**26.42 (+ 0.54)**	**-1.80 (+ 0.373)**	**-1.339 (+ 0.387)**
3	Baseline	19.00	-0.897	-0.644
	Orig.	19.20 (+ 0.20)	**-0.731 (+ 0.166)**	**-0.474 (+ 0.17)**
	Short	**19.23 (+ 0.23)**	-0.743 (+ 0.154)	-0.488 (+ 0.156)
4	Baseline	28.64	-3.43	-3.16
	Orig.	29.56 (+ 0.92)	-3.01 (+ 0.42)	-2.72 (+ 0.44)
	Short	**29.95 (+ 1.31)**	**-2.94 (+ 0.49)**	**-2.67 (+ 0.49)**
Avg.	Baseline	26.61	-1.747	-1.4
	Orig.	27.15(+ 0.54)	-1.488 (+ 0.259)	-1.131 (+ 0.269)
	Short	**27.41(+ 0.8)**	**-1.453 (+ 0.294)**	**-1.11 (+ 0.29)**

Table 5: BLEU, RTE and RTE+MT scores for the the original test set, containing both positive and negative sentences re-ranked using source side information only. Improvement over the baseline is reported.

with the reference translation (BLEU score) and overall semantic similarity, it remains to be determined the extent to which the machine output captures elements of negation present in the reference translation and on which system improvement depends. A more targeted metric is needed, that can effectively determine the extent to which cue, event and scope are captured in hypothesis translation as compared to the reference gold standard. That is the subject of current and future work (Fancellu (2013)), which should implement the new customized metric to include measures of precision, recall and a F1 measure.

References

Apidianaki, M., Wisniewski, G., Sokolov, A., Max, A., and Yvon, F. (2012). Wsd for n-best reranking and local language modeling in smt. In *Proceedings of the Sixth Workshop on Syntax, Semantics and Structure in Statistical Translation*, pages 1–9. Association for Computational Linguistics.

Blanco, E. and Moldovan, D. I. (2011). Some issues on detecting negation from text. In *FLAIRS Conference*.

Chowdhury, M. and Mahbub, F. (2012). Fbk: Exploiting phrasal and contextual clues for negation scope detection. In *Proceedings of the First Joint Conference on Lexical and Computational Semantics-Volume 1: Proceedings of the main conference and the shared task, and Volume 2: Proceedings of the Sixth International Workshop on Semantic Evaluation*, pages 340–346. Association for Computational Linguistics.

Collins, M., Koehn, P., and Kučerová, I. (2005). Clause restructuring for statistical machine translation. In *Proceedings of the 43rd annual meeting on association for computational linguistics*, pages 531–540. Association for Computational Linguistics.

Copestake, A., Flickinger, D., Pollard, C., and Sag, I. A. (2005). Minimal recursion semantics: An introduction. *Research on Language and Computation*, 3(2-3):281–332.

Fancellu, F. (2013). Improving the performance of chinese-to-english hierarchical phrase based models (hpbm) on negative data using n-best list re-ranking. Master's thesis, School of Informatics - University of Edinburgh.

Hasan, S., Zens, R., and Ney, H. (2007). Are very large n-best lists useful for smt? In *Human Language Technologies 2007: The Conference of the North American Chapter of the Association for Computational Linguistics; Companion Volume, Short Papers*, pages 57–60. Association for Computational Linguistics.

Lapponi, E., Velldal, E., Øvrelid, L., and Read, J. (2012). Uio 2: sequence-labeling negation using dependency features. In *Proceedings of the First Joint Conference on Lexical and Computational Semantics-Volume 1: Proceedings of the main conference and the shared task, and Volume 2: Proceedings of the Sixth International Workshop on Semantic Evaluation*, pages 319–327. Association for Computational Linguistics.

Li, J.-J., Kim, J., Kim, D.-I., and Lee, J.-H. (2009). Chinese syntactic reordering for adequate generation of korean verbal phrases in chinese-to-korean smt. In *Proceedings of the Fourth Workshop on Statistical Machine Translation*, pages 190–196. Association for Computational Linguistics.

Morante, R., Schrauwen, S., and Daelemans, W. (2011). Annotation of negation cues and their scope: Guidelines v1. Technical report, 0. Technical report, University of Antwerp. CLIPS: Computational Linguistics & Psycholinguistics technical report series.

Och, F. J., Gildea, D., Khudanpur, S., Sarkar, A., Yamada, K., Fraser, A., Kumar, S., Shen, L., Smith, D., Eng, K., et al. (2004). A smorgasbord of features for statistical machine translation. In *HLT-NAACL*, pages 161–168.

Padó, S., Galley, M., Jurafsky, D., and Manning, C. D. (2009). Textual entailment features for machine translation evaluation. In *Proceedings of the Fourth Workshop on Statistical Machine Translation*, pages 37–41. Association for Computational Linguistics.

Read, J., Velldal, E., Øvrelid, L., and Oepen, S. (2012). Uio 1: Constituent-based discriminative ranking for negation resolution. In *Proceedings of the First Joint Conference on Lexical and Computational Semantics-Volume 1: Proceedings of the main conference and the shared task, and Volume 2: Proceedings of the Sixth International Workshop on Semantic Evaluation*, pages 310–318. Association for Computational Linguistics.

Rosa, R. (2013). Automatic post-editing of phrase-based machine translation outputs. Master's thesis, Institute of Formal and Applied Linguistics, Charles University, Prague.

Specia, L., Sankaran, B., and Nunes, M. d. G. V. (2008). N-best reranking for the efficient integration of word sense disambiguation and statistical machine translation. In *Computational Linguistics and Intelligent Text Processing*, pages 399–410. Springer.

Tseng, H., Chang, P., Andrew, G., Jurafsky, D., and Manning, C. (2005). A conditional random field word segmenter for sighan bakeoff 2005. In *Proceedings of the Fourth SIGHAN Workshop on Chinese Language Processing*, volume 171. Jeju Island, Korea.

Wetzel, D. and Bond, F. (2012). Enriching parallel corpora for statistical machine translation with semantic negation rephrasing. In *Proceedings of the Sixth Workshop on Syntax, Semantics and Structure in Statistical Translation*, pages 20–29. Association for Computational Linguistics.

Yang, Y. and Xue, N. (2012). Chinese comma disambiguation for discourse analysis. In *Proceedings of the 50th Annual Meeting of the Association for Computational Linguistics: Long Papers-Volume 1*, pages 786–794. Association for Computational Linguistics.

Bilingual Sentiment Consistency for Statistical Machine Translation

Boxing Chen and **Xiaodan Zhu**
National Research Council Canada
1200 Montreal Road, Ottawa, Canada, K1A 0R6
{Boxing.Chen, Xiaodan.Zhu}@nrc-cnrc.gc.ca

Abstract

In this paper, we explore bilingual sentiment knowledge for statistical machine translation (SMT). We propose to explicitly model the consistency of sentiment between the source and target side with a lexicon-based approach. The experiments show that the proposed model significantly improves Chinese-to-English NIST translation over a competitive baseline.

1 Introduction

The expression of *sentiment* is an interesting and integral part of human languages. In written text sentiment is conveyed by *senses* and in speech also via *prosody*. Sentiment is associated with both *evaluative* (positive or negative) and *potency* (degree of sentiment) — involving two of the three major semantic differential categories identified by Osgood et al. (1957).

Automatically analyzing the sentiment of monolingual text has attracted a large bulk of research, which includes, but is not limited to, the early exploration of (Turney, 2002; Pang et al., 2002; Hatzivassiloglou & McKeown, 1997). Since then, research has involved a variety of approaches and been conducted on various type of data, e.g., product reviews, news, blogs, and the more recent social media text.

As sentiment has been an important concern in monolingual settings, better translation of such information between languages could be of interest to help better cross language barriers, particularly for sentiment-abundant data. Even when we randomly sampled a subset of sentence pairs from the NIST Open MT[1] training data, we found that about 48.2% pairs contain at least one sentiment word on both sides, and 22.4% pairs contain at least one intensifier word on both sides, which suggests a non-trivial percent of sentences may potentially involve sentiment in some degree[2].

# snt. pairs	% snt. with sentiment words	% snt. with intensifiers
103,369	48.2%	22.4%

Table 1. Percentages of sentence pairs that contain sentiment words on both sides or intensifiers[3] on both sides.

One expects that sentiment has been implicitly captured in SMT through the statistics learned from parallel corpus, e.g., the phrase tables in a phrase-based system. In this paper, we are interested in explicitly modeling sentiment knowledge for translation. We propose a lexicon-based approach that examines the consistency of bilingual subjectivity, sentiment polarity, intensity, and negation. The experiments show that the proposed approach improves the NIST Chinese-to-English translation over a strong baseline.

In general, we hope this line of work will help achieve better MT quality, especially for data with more abundant sentiment, such as social media text.

2 Related Work

Sentiment analysis and lexicon-based approaches Research on monolingual sentiment analysis can be found under different names such as *opinion*, *stance*, *appraisal*, and *semantic orientation,* among others. The overall goal is to label a span of text either as positive, negative, or neutral — sometimes the strength of sentiment is a concern too.

[1] http://www.nist.gov/speech/tests/mt

[2] The numbers give a rough idea of sentiment coverage; it would be more ideal if the estimation could be conducted on senses instead of words, which, however, requires reliable sense labeling and is not available at this stage. Also, according to our human evaluation on a smaller dataset, two thirds of such potentially sentimental sentences do convey sentiment.

[3] The sentiment and intensifier lexicons used to acquire these numbers are discussed in Section 3.2.

Proceedings of the 14th Conference of the European Chapter of the Association for Computational Linguistics, pages 607–615,
Gothenburg, Sweden, April 26-30 2014.

The granularities of text have spanned from words and phrases to passages and documents.

Sentiment analysis has been approached mainly as an unsupervised or supervised problem, although the middle ground, semi-supervised approaches, exists. In this paper, we take a lexicon-based, unsupervised approach to considering sentiment consistency for translation, although the translation system itself is supervised. The advantages of such an approach have been discussed in (Taboada et al., 2011). Briefly, it is good at capturing the basic sentiment expressions common to different domains, and certainly it requires no bilingual sentiment-annotated data for our study. It suits our purpose here of exploring the basic role of sentiment for translation. Also, such a method has been reported to achieve a good cross-domain performance (Taboada et al., 2011) comparable with that of other state-of-the-art models.

Translation for sentiment analysis A very interesting line of research has leveraged labeled data in a resource-rich language (e.g., English) to help sentiment analysis in a resource-poorer language. This includes the idea of constructing sentiment lexicons automatically by using a translation dictionary (Mihalcea et al., 2007), as well as the idea of utilizing parallel corpora or automatically translated documents to incorporate sentiment-labeled data from different languages (Wan, 2009; Mihalcea et al., 2007).

Our concern here is different — instead of utilizing translation for sentiment analysis; we are interested in the SMT quality itself, by modeling bilingual sentiment in translation. As mentioned above, while we expect that statistics learned from parallel corpora have implicitly captured sentiment in some degree, we are curious if better modeling is possible.

Considering semantic similarity in translation The literature has included interesting ideas of incorporating different types of semantic knowledge for SMT. A main stream of recent efforts have been leveraging semantic roles (Wu and Fung, 2009; Liu and Gildea, 2010; Li et al., 2013) to improve translation, e.g., through improving reordering. Also, Chen et al. (2010) have leveraged sense similarity between source and target side as additional features. In this work, we view a different dimension, i.e., semantic orientation, and show that incorporating such knowledge improves the translation performance. We hope this work would add more evidences to the existing literature of leveraging semantics for SMT, and shed some light on further exploration of semantic consistency, e.g., examining other semantic differential factors.

3 Problem & Approach

3.1 Consistency of sentiment

Ideally, sentiment should be properly preserved in high-quality translation. An interesting study conducted by Mihalcea et al. (2007) suggests that in most cases the sentence-level subjectivity is preserved by human translators. In their experiments, one English and two Romanian native speakers were asked to independently annotate the sentiment of English-Romanian sentence pairs from the SemCor corpus (Miller et al., 1993), a balanced corpus covering a number of topics in sports, politics, fashion, education, and others. These human subjects were restricted to only access and annotate the sentiment of their native-language side of sentence pairs. The sentiment consistency was observed by examining the annotation on both sides.

Automatic translation should conform to such a consistency too, which could be of interest for many applications, particularly for sentiment-abundant data. On the other hand, if consistency is not preserved for some reason, e.g., alignment noise, enforcing consistency may help improve the translation performance. In this paper, we explore bilingual sentiment consistency for translation.

3.2 Lexicon-based bilingual sentiment analysis

To capture bilingual sentiment consistency, we use a lexicon-based approach to sentiment analysis. Based on this, we design four groups of features to represent the consistency.

The basic idea of the lexicon-based approach is first identifying the sentiment words, intensifiers, and negation words with lexicons, and then calculating the sentiment value using manually designed formulas. To this end, we adapted the approaches of (Taboada et al., 2011) and (Zhang et al., 2012) so as to use the same formulas to analyze the sentiment on both the source and the target side.

The English and Chinese sentiment lexicons we used are from (Wilson et al. 2005) and (Xu and Lin, 2007), respectively. We further use 75 English intensifiers listed in (Benzinger, 1971; page 171) and 81 Chinese intensifiers from (Zhang et al., 2012). We use 17 English and 13 Chinese negation words.

Similar to (Taboada et al., 2011) and (Zhang et al., 2012), we assigned a numerical score to each sentiment word, intensifier, and negation word. More specifically, one of the five values: -0.8, -0.4, 0, 0.4, and 0.8, was assigned to each sentiment word in both the source and target sentiment lexicons, according to the strength information annotated in these lexicons. The scores indicate the strength of sentiment. Table 2 lists some examples. Similarly, one of the 4 values, i.e., -0.5, 0.5, 0.7 and 0.9, was manually assigned to each intensifier word, and a -0.8 or -0.6 to the negation words. All these scores will be used below to modify and shift the sentiment value of a sentiment unit.

Sentiment words	Intensifiers	Negation words
impressive (0.8)	extremely (0.9)	not (-0.8)
good (0.4)	very (0.7)	rarely (-0.6)
actually (0.0)	pretty (0.5)	
worn (-0.4)	slightly (-0.5)	
depressing (-0.8)		

Table 2: Examples of sentiment words and their sentiment strength; intensifiers and their modify rate; negation words and their negation degree.

Each sentiment word and its modifiers (negation words and intensifiers) form a sentiment unit. We first found all sentiment units by identifying sentiment words with the sentiment lexicons and their modifiers with the corresponding lexicon in a 7-word window. Then, for different patterns of sentiment unit, we calculated the sentiment values using the formulas listed in Table 3, where these formulas are adapted from (Taboada et al., 2011) and (Zhang et al., 2012) so as to be applied to both languages.

Sen. unit	Sen. value formula	Example	Sen. value
w_s	$S(w_s)$	good	0.40
$w_n w_s$	$D(w_n)S(w_s)$	not good	-0.32
$w_i w_s$	$(1+R(w_i))S(w_s)$	very good	0.68
$w_n w_i w_s$	$(1+D(w_n)R(w_i))S(w_s)$	not very good	0.176
$w_i w_n w_s$	$D(w_n)(1+R(w_i))S(w_s)$	very not good[4]	-0.544

Table 3: Heuristics used to compute the lexicon-based sentiment values for different types of sentiment units.

[4] The expression "very not good" is ungrammatical in English. However, in Chinese, it is possible to have this kind of expression, such as "很不漂亮", whose transliteration is "very not beautiful", meaning "very ugly".

For notation, $S(w_s)$ stands for the strength of sentiment word w_s, $R(w_i)$ is degree of the intensifier word w_i, and $D(w_n)$ is the negation degree of the negation word w_n.

Above, we have calculated the lexicon based sentiment value (LSV) for any given unit u_i, and we call it $lsv(u_i)$ below. If a sentence or phrase s contains multiple sentiment units, its *lsv*-score is a merge of the individual *lsv*-scores of all its sentiment units:

$$lsv(s) = merg_1^N(basis(lsv(u_i))) \qquad (1)$$

where the function *basis*(.) is a normalization function that performs on each $lsv(u_i)$. For example, the *basis*(.) function could be a standard *sign* function that just examines if a sentiment unit is positive or negative, or simply an identity function (using the *lsv*-scores directly). The *merg*(.) is a function that merge the *lsv*-scores of individual sentiment units, which may take several different forms below in our feature design. For example, it can be a *mean* function to take the average of the sentiment units' *lsv*-scores, or a logic OR function to examine if a sentence or phrase contains positive or negative units (depending on the basis function). It can also be a linear function that gives different weights to different units according to further knowledge, e.g., syntactic information. In this paper, we only leverage the basic, surface-level analysis[5].

In brief, our model here can be thought of as a unification and simplification of both (Taboada et al., 2011) and (Zhang et al., 2012), for our bilingual task. We suspect that better sentiment modeling may further improve the general translation performance or the quality of sentiment in translation. We will discuss some directions we think interesting in the future work section.

3.3 Incorporating sentiment consistency into phrase-based SMT

In this paper, we focus on exploring sentiment consistency for phrase-based SMT. However, the approach might be used in other translation framework. For example, consistency may be considered in the variables used in hierarchical translation rules (Chiang, 2005).

[5] Note that when sentiment-annotated training data are available, *merg*(.) can be trained, e.g., if assuming it to be the widely-used (log-) linear form.

We will examine the role of sentiment consistency in two ways: designing features for the translation model and using them for re-ranking. Before discussing the details of our features, we briefly recap phrase-based SMT for completeness.

Given a source sentence *f*, the goal of statistical machine translation is to select a target language string *e* which maximizes the posterior probability P(*e*|*f*). In a phrase-based SMT system, the translation unit is the phrases, where a "phrase" is a sequence of words. Phrase-based statistical machine translation systems are usually modeled through a log-linear framework (Och and Ney, 2002) by introducing the hidden word alignment variable *a* (Brown et al., 1993).

$$\tilde{e}^* = \arg\max_{e,a}(\sum_{m=1}^{M} \lambda_m H_m(\tilde{e}, \tilde{f}, a)) \quad (2)$$

where $\tilde{e}$ is a string of phrases in the target language, $\tilde{f}$ is the source language string, $H_m(\tilde{e}, \tilde{f}, a)$ are feature functions, and weights λ_m are typically optimized to maximize the scoring function (Och, 2003).

3.4 Feature design

In Section 3.2 above, we have discussed our lexicon-based approach, which leverages lexicon-based sentiment consistency. Below, we describe the specific features we designed for our experiments. For a phrase pair ($\tilde{f}, \tilde{e}$) or a sentence pair (*f*, *e*)[6], we propose the following four groups of consistency features.

Subjectivity The first group of features is designed to check the subjectivity of a phrase or a sentence pair (*f*, *e*). This set of features examines if the source or target side contains sentiment units. As the name suggests, these features only capture if *subjectivity* exists, but not if a sentiment is positive, negative, or neutral. We include four binary features that are triggered in the following conditions—satisfaction of each condition gives the corresponding feature a value of 1 and otherwise 0.

- F1: if neither side of the pair (f, e) contains at least one sentiment unit;
- F2: if only one side contains sentiment units;
- F3: if the source side contains sentiment units;
- F4: if the target side contains sentiment units.

Sentiment polarity The second group of features check the sentiment polarity. These features are still binary; they check if the polarities of the source and target side are the same.

- F5: if the two sides of the pair (f, e) have the same polarity;
- F6: if at least one side has a neutral sentiment;
- F7: if the polarity is opposite on the two sides, i.e., one is positive and one is negative.

Note that examining the polarity on each side can be regarded as a special case of applying Equation 1 above. For example, examining the positive sentiment corresponds to using an indicator function as the *basis* function: it takes a value of 1 if the *lsv*-score of a sentiment unit is positive or 0 otherwise, while the *merge* function is the logic OR function. The subjectivity features above can also be thought of similarly.

Sentiment intensity The third group of features is designed to capture the degree of sentiment and these features are numerical. We designed two types of features in this group.

Feature *F8* measures the difference of the LSV scores on the two sides. As shown in Equation (3), we use a *mean* function[7] as our *merge* function when computing the *lsv*-scores with Equation (1), where the *basis* function is simply the identity function.

$$lsv_1(s) = \frac{1}{n}\sum_{i=0}^{n} lsv(u_i) \quad (3)$$

Feature *F9, F10,* and *F11* are the second type in this group of features, which compute the ratio of sentiment units on each side and examine their difference.

- F8: $H_8(f,e) = |lsv_1(f) - lsv_1(e)|$
- F9: $H_9(f,e) = |lsv_+(f) - lsv_+(e)|$

[6] For simplicity, we hereafter use the same notation (*f*, *e*) to represent both a phrase pair and a sentence pair, when no confusion arises.

[7] We studied several different options but found the *average* function is better than others for our translation task here, e.g., better than giving more weight to the last unit.

- F10: $H_{10}(f,e) = | lsv_{-}(f) - lsv_{-}(e) |$
- F11: $H_{11}(f,e) = | lsv_{+-}(f) - lsv_{+-}(e) |$

$lsv_{+}(.)$ calculates the ratio of a positive sentiment units in a phrase or a sentence, i.e., the number of positive sentiment units divided by the total number of words of the phrase or the sentence. It corresponds to a special form of Equation 1, in which the *basis* function is an indicator function as discussed above, and the *merge* function adds up all the counts and normalizes the sum by the length of the phrase or the sentence concerned. Similarly, $lsv_{-}(.)$ calculates the ratio of negative units and $lsv_{+-}(.)$ calculates that for both types of units. The length of sentence here means the number of word tokens. We experimented with and without removing stop words when counting them, and found that decision has little impact on the performance. We also used the part-of-speech (POS) information in the sentiment lexicons to help decide if a word is a sentiment word or not, when we extract features; i.e., a word is considered to have sentiment only if its POS tag also matches what is specified in the lexicons[8]. Using POS tags, however, did not improve our translation performance.

Negation The fourth group of features checks the consistency of negation words on the source and target side. Note that negation words have already been considered in computing the *lsv*-scores of sentiment units. One motivation is that a negation word may appear far from the sentiment word it modifies, as mentioned in (Taboada et al., 2011) and may be outside the window we used to calculate the *lsv*-score above. The features here additionally check the counts of negation words. This group of features is binary and triggered by the following conditions.

- F12: if neither side of the pair (*f, e*) contain negation words;
- F13: if both sides have an odd number of negation words or both sides have an even number of them;
- F14: if both sides have an odd number of negation words not appearing outside any sentiment units, or if both sides have an even number of such negation words;
- F15: if both sides have an odd number of negation words appearing in all sentiment units, or if both sides have an even number of such negation words.

4 Experiments

4.1 Translation experimental settings

Experiments were carried out with an in-house phrase-based system similar to Moses (Koehn et al., 2007). Each corpus was word-aligned using IBM model 2, HMM, and IBM model 4, and the phrase table was the union of phrase pairs extracted from these separate alignments, with a length limit of 7. The translation model was smoothed in both directions with Kneser-Ney smoothing (Chen et al., 2011). We use the hierarchical lexicalized reordering model (Galley and Manning, 2008), with a distortion limit of 7. Other features include lexical weighting in both directions, word count, a distance-based RM, a 4-gram LM trained on the target side of the parallel data, and a 6-gram English *Gigaword* LM. The system was tuned with batch lattice MIRA (Cherry and Foster, 2012).

We conducted experiments on NIST Chinese-to-English translation task. The training data are from NIST Open MT 2012. All allowed bilingual corpora were used to train the translation model and reordering models. There are about 283M target word tokens. The development (dev) set comprised mainly data from the NIST 2005 test set, and also some balanced-genre web-text from NIST training data. Evaluation was performed on NIST 2006 and 2008, which have 1,664 and 1,357 sentences, 39.7K and 33.7K source words respectively. Four references were provided for all dev and test sets.

4.2 Results

Our evaluation metric is case-insensitive IBM BLEU (Papineni et al., 2002), which performs matching of n-grams up to n = 4; we report BLEU scores on two test sets NIST06 and NIST08. Following (Koehn, 2004), we use the bootstrap resampling test to do significance testing. In Table 4-6, the sign * and ** denote statistically significant gains over the baseline at the $p < 0.05$ and $p < 0.01$ level, respectively.

[8] The Stanford POS tagger (Toutanova et al., 2003) was used to tag phrase and sentence pairs for this purpose.

	NIST06	NIST08	Avg.
Baseline	35.1	28.4	31.7
+feat. group1	35.6**	29.0**	32.3
+feat. group2	35.3*	28.7*	32.0
+feat. group3	35.3	28.7*	32.0
+feat. group4	35.5*	28.8*	32.1
+feat. group1+2	35.8**	29.1**	32.5
+feat. group1+2+3	36.1**	29.3**	32.7
+feat. group1+2+3+4	**36.2****	**29.4****	**32.8**

Table 4: BLEU(%) scores on two original test sets for different feature combinations. The sign * and ** indicate statistically significant gains over the baseline at the $p < 0.05$ and $p < 0.01$ level, respectively.

Table 4 summarizes the results of the baseline and the results of adding each group of features and their combinations. We can see that each individual feature group improves the BLEU scores of the baseline, and most of these gains are significant. Among the feature groups, the largest improvement is associated with the first feature group, i.e., the subjectivity features, which suggests the significant role of modeling the basic subjectivity. Adding more features results in further improvement; the best performance was achieved when using all these sentiment consistency features, where we observed a 1.1 point improvement on the NIST06 set and a 1.0 point improvement on the NIST08 set, which yields an overall improvement of about 1.1 BLEU score.

To further observe the results, we split each of the two (i.e., the NIST06 and NIST08) test sets into three subsets according to the ratio of sentiment words in the reference. We call them low-sen, mid-sen and high-sen subsets, denoting lower, middle, and higher sentiment-word ratios, respectively. The three subsets contain roughly equal number of sentences. Then we merged the two low-sen subsets together, and similarly the two mid-sen and high-sen subsets together, respectively. Each subset has roughly 1007 sentences.

	low-sen	mid-sen	high-sen
baseline	33.4	32.3	29.3
+all feat.	34.4**	33.5**	30.4**
improvement	1.0	1.2	1.1

Table 5: BLEU(%) scores on three sub test sets with different sentiment ratios.

Table 5 shows the performance of baseline and the system with sentiment features (the last system of Table 4) on these subsets. First, we can see that both systems perform worse as the ratio of sentiment words increases. This probably indicates that text with more sentiment is harder to translate than text with less sentiment. Second, it is interesting that the largest improvement is seen on the mid-sen sub-set. The larger improvement on the mid-sen/high-sen subsets than on the low-sen may indicate the usefulness of the proposed features in capturing sentiment information. The lower improvement on high-sen than on mid-sen probably indicates that the high-sen subset is hard anyway and using simple lexicon-level features is not sufficient.

Sentence-level reranking Above, we have incorporated sentiment features into the phrase tables. To further confirm the usefulness of the sentiment consistency features, we explore their role for sentence-level reranking. To this end, we re-rank 1000-best hypotheses for each sentence that were generated with the baseline system. All the sentiment features were recalculated for each hypothesis. We then re-learned the weights for the decoding and sentiment features to select the best hypothesis. The results are shown in Table 6. We can see that sentiment features improve the performance via re-ranking. The improvement is statistically significant, although the absolute improvement is less than that obtained by incorporating the sentiment features in decoding. Not that as widely known, the limited variety of candidates in reranking may confine the improvement that could be achieved. Better models on the sentence level are possible. In addition, we feel that ensuring sentiment and its target to be correctly paired is of interest. Note that we have also combined the last system in Table 4 with the reranking system here; i.e., sentiment consistency was incorporated in both ways, but we did not see further improvement, which suggests that the benefit of the sentiment features has mainly been captured in the phrase tables already.

feature	NIST06	NIST08	Avg.
baseline	35.1	28.4	31.7
+ all feat.	35.4*	28.9**	32.1

Table 6: BLEU(%) scores on two original test sets on sentence-level sentiment features.

Human evaluation We conducted a human evaluation on the output of the baseline and the system that incorporates all the proposed sentiment features (the last system in Table 4). For this purpose, we randomly sampled 250 sentences from the two NIST test sets according to the following conditions. First, the selected sentences should contain at least one sentiment word—in this evaluation, we target the sentences that may convey some sentiment. Second, we do not consider sentences shorter than 5 words or longer than 50 words; or where outputs of the baseline system and the system with sentiment feature were identical. The 250 selected sentences were split into 9 subsets, as we have 9 human evaluators (none of the authors of this paper took part in this experiment). Each subset contains 26 randomly selected sentences, which are 234 sentences in total. The other 16 sentences are randomly selected to serve as a *common* data set: they are added to each of the 9 subsets in order to observe agreements between the 9 annotators. In short, each human evaluator was presented with 42 evaluation samples. Each sample is a tuple containing the output of the baseline system, that of the system considering sentiment, and the reference translation. The two automatic translations were presented in a random order to the evaluators.

As in (Callison-Burch *et al.*, 2012), we performed a pairwise comparison of the translations produced by the systems. We asked the annotators the following two questions Q1 and Q2:

- Q1(general preference): For any reason, which of the two translations do you prefer according to the provided references, otherwise mark "no preference"?
- Q2 (sentiment preference): Does the reference contains sentiment? If so, in terms of the translations of the sentiment, which of the two translations do you prefer, otherwise mark "no preference"?

We computed Fleiss's Kappa (Fleiss, 1971) on the common set to measure inter-annotator agreement, κ_{all}. Then, we excluded one and only one annotator at a time to compute κ^i (Kappa score without *i*-th annotator, *i.e.*, from the other eight). Finally, we removed the annotation of the two annotators whose answers were most different from the others': *i.e.*, annotators with the biggest $\kappa_{all} - \kappa^i$ values. As a result, we got a Kappa score 0.432 on question Q1 and 0.415 on question Q2, which both mean moderate agreement.

	base win	bsc win	equal	total
Translation	58 (31.86%)	82 (45.05%)	42 (23.09%)	182
Sentiment	30 (22.39%)	49 (36.57%)	55 (41.04%)	134

Table 7: Human evaluation preference for outputs from baseline *vs.* system with sentiment features.

This left 7 files from 7 evaluators. We threw away the common set in each file, leaving 182 pairwise comparisons. Table 6 shows that the evaluators preferred the output from the system with sentiment features 82 times, the output from the baseline system 58 times, and had no preference the other 42 times. This indicates that there is a human preference for the output from the system that incorporated the sentiment features over those from the baseline system at the $p<0.05$ significance level (in cases where people prefer one of them). For question Q2, the human annotators regarded 48 sentences as conveying no sentiment according to the provided reference, although each of them contains at least one sentiment word (a criterion we described above in constructing the evaluation set). Among the remaining 134 sentences, the human annotators preferred the proposed system 49 times and the baseline system 30 times, while they mark *no-preference* 55 times. The result shows a human preference for the proposed model that considers sentiment features at the $p<0.05$ significance level (in the cases where the evaluators did mark a preference).

4.3 Examples

We have also manually examined the translations generated by our best model (the last model of Table 4, named BSC below) and the baseline model (BSL), and we attribute the improvement to two main reasons: (1) checking sentiment consistency on a phrase pair helps punish low-quality phrase pairs caused by word alignment error, (2) such consistency checking also improves the sentiment of the translation to better match the sentiment of the source.

(1)	Phr. pairs	和谈 ||| *talks* vs. 和谈 ||| *peace talks*
	REF	… help the palestinians and the israelis to resume *peace talks* …
	BSL	… help the israelis and palestinians to resumption of the *talks* …
	BSC	… help the israelis and palestinians to resume *peace talks* …
(2)	Phr. pairs	备战 ||| *war* vs. 备战 ||| *preparing for*
	REF	… the national team is *preparing for* matches with palestine and Iraq …
	BSL	… the national team 's match with the palestinians and the iraq *war* …
	BSC	… the national team *preparing for* the match with the palestinian and iraq …
(3)	REF	… in china we have *top-quality people* , *ever-improving* facilities …
	BSL	… we have *talents* in china , an *increasing number of facilities* …
	BSC	… we have *outstanding talent* in china , *more and better* facilities …
(4)	REF	… continue to *strive* for that …
	BSL	… continue to *struggle* …
	BSC	… continue to *work hard to achieve* …

Table 8: Examples that show how sentiment helps improve our baseline model. REF is a reference translation, BSL stands for baseline model, and BSC (bilingual sentiment consistency) is the last model of Table 4.

In the first two examples of Table 8, the first line shows two phrase pairs that are finally chosen by the baseline and BSC system, respectively. The next three lines correspond to a reference (REF), translation from BSL, and that from the BSC system. The correct translations of "和谈" should be "peace negotiations" or "peace talks", which have a positive sentiment, while the word "talks" doesn't convey sentiment at all. By punishing the phrase pair "和谈 ||| talks", the BSC model was able to generate a better translation. In the second example, the correct translation of "备战" should be "prepare for", where neither side conveys sentiment. The incorrect phrase pair "备战 ||| war" is generated from incorrect word alignment. Since "war" is a negative word in our sentiment lexicon, checking sentiment consistency helps down-weight such incorrect translations. Note also that the incorrect phrase pair "备战 ||| war" is not totally irrational, as the literal translation of "备战" is "prepare for war".

Similarly, in the third example, "outstanding talent" is closer with respect to sentiment to the reference "top-quality people" than "talent" is; "more and better" is closer with respect to sentiment to the reference "ever-improving" than "an increasing number" is. These three examples also help us understand the benefit of the subjectivity features discussed in Section 3.4. In the fourth example, "work hard to achieve" has a positive sentiment, same as "strive", while "struggle" is negative. We can see that the BSC model is able to preserve the original sentiment better (the 9 human evaluators who were involved in our human evaluation (Section 4.3) all agreed with this).

5 Conclusions and future work

We explore lexicon-based sentiment consistency for statistical machine translation. By incorporating lexicon-based subjectivity, polarity, intensity, and negation features into the phrase-pair translation model, we observed a 1.1-point improvement of BLEU score on NIST Chinese-to-English translation. Among the four individual groups of features, subjectivity consistency yields the largest improvement. The usefulness of the sentiment features has also been confirmed when they are used for re-ranking, for which we observed a 0.4-point improvement on the BLEU score. In addition, human evaluation shows the preference of the human subjects towards the translations generated by the proposed model, in terms of both the general translation quality and the sentiment conveyed.

In the paper, we propose a lexicon-based approach to the problem. It is possible to employ more complicated models. For example, with the involvement of proper sentiment-annotated data, if available, one may train a better sentiment-analysis model even for the often-ungrammatical phrase pairs or sentence candidates. Another direction we feel interesting is ensuring that sentiment and its target are not only better translated but also better paired, i.e., their semantic relation is preserved. This is likely to need further syntactic or semantic analysis at the sentence level, and the semantic role labeling work reviewed in Section 2 is relevant.

References

C. Banea, R. Mihalcea, J. Wiebe and S. Hassan. 2008. Multilingual subjectivity analysis using machine translation. In Proc. of EMNLP.

E. M. Benzinger. 1971. Intensifiers in current English. PhD. Thesis. University of Florida.

P. F. Brown, S. Della Pietra, V. Della J. Pietra, and R. Mercer. 1993. The mathematics of Machine Translation: Parameter estimation. Computational Linguistics, 19(2): 263-312.

C. Callison-Burch, P. Koehn, C. Monz, R. Soricut, and L. Specia. 2012. Findings of the 2012 Workshop on Statistical Machine Translation. In Proc. of WMT.

D. Chiang. 2005. A hierarchical phrase-based model for statistical machine translation. In Proc. of ACL, 263–270.

B. Chen, G. Foster, and R. Kuhn. 2010. Bilingual Sense Similarity for Statistical Machine Translation. In Proc. of ACL, 834-843.

B. Chen, R. Kuhn, G. Foster, and H. Johnson. 2011. Unpacking and transforming feature functions: New ways to smooth phrase tables. In Proc. of MT Summit.

C. Cherry and G. Foster. 2012. Batch tuning strategies for statistical machine translation. In Proc. of NAACL.

J. L. Fleiss. 1971. Measuring nominal scale agreement among many raters. Psychological Bulletin, 76(5): 378–382.

M. Galley and C. D. Manning. 2008. A simple and effective hierarchical phrase reordering model. In Proc. of EMNLP: 848–856.

V. Hatzivassiloglou and K. McKeown. 1997. Predicting the semantic orientation of adjectives. In Proc. of EACL: 174-181.

P. Koehn. 2004. Statistical significance tests for machine translation evaluation. In Proc. of EMNLP: 388–395.

P. Koehn, H. Hoang, A. Birch, C. Callison-Burch, M. Federico, N. Bertoldi, B. Cowan, W. Shen, C. Moran, R. Zens, C. Dyer, O. Bojar, A. Constantin and E. Herbst. 2007. Moses: Open Source Toolkit for Statistical Machine Translation. In Proc. of ACL, 177-180.

J. Li, P. Resnik and H. Daume III. 2013. Modeling Syntactic and Semantic Structures in Hierarchical Phrase-based Translation. In Proc. of NAACL, 540-549.

D. Liu and D. Gildea. 2010. Semantic role features for machine translation. In Proc. of COLING, 716–724.

R. Mihalcea, C. Banea and J. Wiebe. 2007. Learning multilingual subjective language via cross-lingual projections. In Proc. of ACL.

F. J. Och and H. Ney. 2002. Discriminative Training and Maximum Entropy Models for Statistical Machine Translation. In Proc. of ACL.

F. J. Och. 2003. Minimum error rate training in statistical machine translation. In Proc. of ACL.

C. E. Osgood, G. J. Suci, and P. H. Tannenbaum. 1957. The measurement of meaning. University of Illinois Press.

B. Pang, L. Lee, S. Vaithyanathan. 2002. Thumbs up?: sentiment classification using machine learning techniques. In Proc. of EMNLP, 79-86.

K. Papineni, S. Roukos, T. Ward, and W. Zhu. 2002. Bleu: a method for automatic evaluation of ma-chine translation. In Proc. of ACL, 311–318.

M. Taboada, M. Tofiloski, J. Brooke, K. Voll, and M. Stede. 2011. Lexicon-Based Methods for Sentiment Analysis. Computational Linguistics. 37(2): 267-307.

K. Toutanova, D. Klein, C. Manning, and Y. Singer. 2003. Feature-Rich Part-of-Speech Tagging with a Cyclic Dependency Network. In Proc. of HLT-NAACL, 252-259.

P. Turney. 2002. Thumbs up or thumbs down? semantic orientation applied to unsupervised classification of reviews. In Proc. of ACL, 417-424.

S. Vogel, H. Ney, and C. Tillmann. 1996. HMM based word alignment in statistical translation. In Proc. of COLING.

X. Wan. 2009. Co-Training for Cross-Lingual Sentiment Classification. In proc. of ACL, 235-243.

T. Wilson, J. Wiebe, and P. Hoffmann. 2005. Recognizing Contextual Polarity in Phrase-Level Sentiment Analysis. In Proc. of EMNLP.

D. Wu and P. Fung. 2009. Semantic Roles for SMT: A Hybrid Two-Pass Model. In Proc. of NAACL, 13-16.

L. Xu and H. Lin. 2007. Ontology-Driven Affective Chinese Text Analysis and Evaluation Method. In Lecture Notes in Computer Science Vol. 4738, 723-724, Springer.

C. Zhang, P. Liu, Z. Zhu, and M. Fang. 2012. A Sentiment Analysis Method Based on a Polarity Lexicon. Journal of Shangdong University (Natural Science). 47(3): 47-50.

Augmenting Translation Models with Simulated Acoustic Confusions for Improved Spoken Language Translation

Yulia Tsvetkov **Florian Metze** **Chris Dyer**
Language Technologies Institute
Carnegie Mellon University
Pittsburgh, PA 15213; U.S.A.
{ytsvetko, fmetze, cdyer}@cs.cmu.edu

Abstract

We propose a novel technique for adapting text-based statistical machine translation to deal with input from automatic speech recognition in spoken language translation tasks. We simulate likely misrecognition errors using only a source language pronunciation dictionary and language model (i.e., without an acoustic model), and use these to augment the phrase table of a standard MT system. The augmented system can thus recover from recognition errors during decoding using synthesized phrases. Using the outputs of five different English ASR systems as input, we find consistent and significant improvements in translation quality. Our proposed technique can also be used in conjunction with lattices as ASR output, leading to further improvements.

1 Introduction

Spoken language translation (SLT) systems generally consist of two components: (i) an automatic speech recognition (ASR) system that transcribes source language utterances and (ii) a machine translation (MT) system that translates the transcriptions into the target language. These two components are usually developed independently and then combined and integrated (Ney, 1999; Matusov et al., 2006; Casacuberta et al., 2008; Zhou, 2013; He and Deng, 2013).

While this architecture is attractive since it relies only on components that are independently useful, such systems face several challenges. First, spoken language tends to be quite different from the highly edited parallel texts that are available to train translation systems. For example, disfluencies, such as repeated words or phrases, restarts, and revisions of content, are frequent in spontaneous speech,[1] while these are usually absent in written texts. In addition, ASR outputs typically lack explicit segmentation into sentences, as well as reliable casing and punctuation information, which are crucial for MT and other text-based language processing applications (Ostendorf et al., 2008). Second, ASR systems are imperfect and make recognition errors. Even high quality systems make recognition errors, especially in acoustically similar words with similar language model scores, for example morphological substitutions like confusing bare stem and past tense forms, and in high-frequency short words (function words) which often lack both disambiguating context and are subject to reduced pronunciations (Goldwater et al., 2010).

One would expect that training an MT system on ASR outputs (rather than the usual written-style texts) would improve matters. Unfortunately, there are few corpora of speech paired with text translations into a second language that could be used for this purpose. This has been an incentive to various MT adaptation approaches and development of speech-input MT systems. MT adaptation has been done via input text pre-processing, by transformation of spoken language (ASR output) into written language (MT input) (Peitz et al., 2012; Xu et al., 2012); via decoding ASR n-best lists (Quan et al., 2005), or confusion networks (Bertoldi et al., 2007; Casacuberta et al., 2008), or lattices (Dyer et al., 2008; Onishi et al., 2010); via additional translation features capturing acoustic information (Zhang et al., 2004); and with methods that follow a paradigm of unified decoding (Zhou et al., 2007; Zhou, 2013). In line with the previous research, we too adapt a standard MT system to a speech-input MT, but by altering the translation model itself so it is better able to

[1] Disfluencies constitute about 6% of word tokens in spontaneous speech, not including silent pauses (Tree, 1995; Kasl and Mahl, 1965)

Proceedings of the 14th Conference of the European Chapter of the Association for Computational Linguistics, pages 616–625, Gothenburg, Sweden, April 26-30 2014.

deal with ASR output (Callison-Burch et al., 2006; Tsvetkov et al., 2013a).

We address speech translation in a resource-deficient scenario, specifically, adapting MT systems to SLT when ASR is unavailable. We augment a discriminative set that translation models rescore with **synthetic translation options**. These automatically generated translation rules (henceforth synthetic phrases) are noisy variants of observed translation rules with simulated plausible speech recognition errors (§2). To simulate ASR errors we generate acoustically and distributionally similar phrases to a source (English) phrase with a phonologically-motivated algorithm (§4). Likely phonetic substitutions are learned with an unsupervised algorithm that produces clusters of similar phones (§3). We show that MT systems augmented with synthetic phrases increase the coverage of input sequences that can be translated, and yield significant improvement in the quality of translated speech (§6).

This work makes several contributions. Primary is our framework to adapt MT to SLT by populating translation models with synthetic phrases.[2] Second, we propose a novel method to generate acoustic confusions that are likely to be encountered in ASR transcription hypotheses. Third, we devise simple and effective phone clustering algorithm. All aforementioned algorithms work in a low-resource scenario, without recourse to audio data, speech transcripts, or ASR outputs: our method to predict likely recognition errors uses phonological rather than acoustic information and does not depend on a specific ASR system. Since our source language is English, we operate on a phone level and employ a pronunciation dictionary and a language model, but the algorithm can in principle be applied without pronunciation dictionary for languages with a phonemic orthography.

2 Methodology

We adopt a standard ASR-MT cascading approach and then augment translation models with synthetic phrases. Our proposed system architecture is depicted in Figure 1.

Synthetic phrases are generated from entries in the original translation model–phrase translation pairs acquired from parallel data. From a source side of an original phrase pair we generate list of its plausible misrecognition variants (pseudo-ASR outputs with recognition errors) and add them as a source side of a synthetic phrase. For k-best simulated ASR outputs we construct k synthetic phrases: a simulated ASR output in the source side is coupled with its translation–an original target phrase (identical for all k phrases). Synthetic phrases are annotated with five standard phrasal translation features (forward and reverse phrase and lexical translation probabilities and phrase penalty); these were found in the original phrase and remain unchanged. In addition, we add three new features to all phrase pairs, both synthetic and original. First, we add a boolean feature indicating the origin of a phrase: synthetic or original. Two other features correspond to an ASR language model score of the source side. One is LM score of the synthetic phrase, another is a score of a phrase from which the source side was generated. We then append synthetic phrases to a phrase table: k synthetic phrases for each original phrase pair, with eight features attached to each phrase. We show synthetic phrases example in Figure 2.

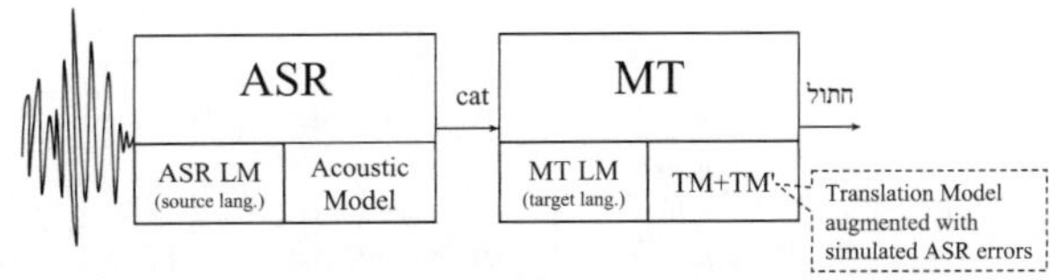

Figure 1: SLT architecture: ASR and MT are trained independently and then cascaded. We improve SLT by populating MT translation model with synthetic phrases. Each synthetic phrase is a variant of an original phrase pair with simulated ASR errors on the source side.

3 Acoustically confusable phones

The phonetic context of a given phone affects its acoustic realization, and a variability in a production of the same phone is possible depending on coarticulation with its neighboring phones.[3] In addition, there are phonotactic constraints that can restrict allowed sequences of phones. English has strong constraints on sequences of consonants; the sequence *[zdr]*, for example, cannot be a legal En-

[2] We augment phrase tables only with synthetic phrases that capture simulated ASR errors, the methodology that we advocate, however, is applicable to many problems in translation (Tsvetkov et al., 2013a; Ammar et al., 2013; Chahuneau et al., 2013).

[3] These are the reasons why in context-dependent acoustic modeling different HMM models are trained for different contexts.

Source phrase	Target phrase	Original phrase translation features	Synthetic indicator	Synthetic LM score	Original LM score
tells the story	*raconte l'histoire*	f_1, f_2, f_3, f_4, f_5	0	3.9×10^{-3}	3.9×10^{-3}
tell their story	raconte l'histoire	f_1, f_2, f_3, f_4, f_5	1	5.9×10^{-3}	3.9×10^{-3}
tells a story	raconte l'histoire	f_1, f_2, f_3, f_4, f_5	1	2.2×10^{-3}	3.9×10^{-3}
tell the story	raconte l'histoire	f_1, f_2, f_3, f_4, f_5	1	1.7×10^{-3}	3.9×10^{-3}
tell a story	raconte l'histoire	f_1, f_2, f_3, f_4, f_5	1	1.3×10^{-3}	3.9×10^{-3}
tell that story	raconte l'histoire	f_1, f_2, f_3, f_4, f_5	1	1.0×10^{-3}	3.9×10^{-3}
tell their stories	raconte l'histoire	f_1, f_2, f_3, f_4, f_5	1	0.9×10^{-3}	3.9×10^{-3}
tells the stories	raconte l'histoire	f_1, f_2, f_3, f_4, f_5	1	0.8×10^{-3}	3.9×10^{-3}
tells her story	raconte l'histoire	f_1, f_2, f_3, f_4, f_5	1	0.7×10^{-3}	3.9×10^{-3}
chelsea star	raconte l'histoire	f_1, f_2, f_3, f_4, f_5	1	0.5×10^{-3}	3.9×10^{-3}

Figure 2: Example of acoustically confusable synthetic phrases. Phrases were synthesized from the original phrase pair in Row 1 by generating acoustically similar phrases for the English phrase *tells the story*. All phrases have the same (target) French translation *me raconte l'histoire* and the same five basic phrase-based translation rule features. To these, three additional features are added: a synthetic phrase indicator, the source language LM score of the source phrase, and the source language LM score of a source phrase in the original phrase pair.

	T_{left}	T_{right}	TW_{left}	WIH_{right}	...
T				$P(T\|WIH)$	...
W	$P(W\|T)$				...
IH		$P(IH\|T)$	$P(IH\|TW)$		...
ER	$P(ER\|T)$				...
...	...	...	...	...	...

Figure 3: A fragment of the co-occurrence matrix for phone sequence [T W IH T ER]. Rows correspond to phones; columns correspond to left/right context phones of lengths one and two.

glish syllable onset (Jurafsky and Martin, 2000).

Motivated by the constraining effect of context on phonetic distribution, we cluster phones using a distance-based measure. To do so, we build a vector space model representation of each phone by creating a co-occurrence matrix from a corpus of phonetic forms where each row represents a phone and columns indicate the contextual phones. We take into account left/right context windows of lengths one and two. A cell $r_{p,c}$ in the vector space dictionary matrix represents phone p and context c using the empirical relative frequency $f(p \mid c)$, as estimated from a pronunciation dictionary. Figure 3 shows a fragment of the co-occurrence matrix constructed from a dictionary containing just the pronunciation of *Twitter* – [T W IH T ER].

Under this representation, the similarity of phones can be easily quantified by measuring their distance in the vector space, the cosine of the angle between them:

$$Sim(p_1, p_2) = \frac{p_1 \cdot p_2}{||p_1|| \cdot ||p_2||}$$

Armed with this similarity function, we apply the K-means algorithm[4] to partition the phones into disjoint sets.

4 Plausible misrecognition variants

For an input English sequence we generate top-k pseudo-ASR outputs, that are added as a source side of a synthetic phrase. Every ASR output that we simulate is a plausible misrecognition that has two distinguishing characteristics: it is **acoustically** and **linguistically** confusable with the input sequence. Former corresponds to phonetic similarity and latter to distributional similarity of these two phrases in corpus.

Given a reference string–a word or sequence of words $\mathbf{w}$ in the source language, we generate k-best hypotheses $\mathbf{v}$. This can be modeled as a weighted finite state transducer:

$$\{\mathbf{v}\} = G \circ D^{-1} \circ T \circ D \circ \{\mathbf{w}\} \quad (1)$$

where

- D maps from words to pronunciations
- T is a phone confusion transducer
- D^{-1} maps from pronunciations to words
- G is an ASR language model

D maps words to their phonetic representation[5], or multiple representations for words with several

[4]Value of K=12 was determined empirically.

[5]Using the CMU pronounciation dictionary http://www.speech.cs.cmu.edu/cgi-bin/cmudict

pronunciation variants. To create a phone confusion transducer T maps source to target phone sequences by performing a number of edit operations. Allowed edits are:

- Deletion of a consonant (mapping to ϵ).
- Doubling of a vowel.
- Insertion of one or two phones in the end of a sequence from the list of possible suffixes: S (*-s*), IX NG (*-ing*), D (*-ed*).
- Substitution of a phone by an acoustically similar phone. The clusters of the similar phones are {Z, S}, {XL, L, R}, {AA, AO, EY, UH}, {AXR, AX}, {XN, XM}, {P, B, F}, {DH, CH, ZH, T, SH}, {OY, AE}, {IY, AY, OW}, {EH, AH, IH, AW, ER, UW}. The phone clustering algorithm that produced these is detailed in the previous section.

After a series of edit operations, D^{-1} transducer maps new phonetic sequences from pronunciations to n-grams of words. The k-best variants resulting from the weighted composition are the k-best plausible misrecognitions.

One important property of this method is that it maps words in decoding vocabulary (41,487 types are possible inputs to transducer D) into CMU dictionary which is substantially larger (141,304 types are possible outputs of transducer D^{-1}). This allows to generate out-of-vocabulary (OOV) words and phrases, which are not only recognition errors, but also plausible variants of different source phrases that can be translated to one target phrase, e.g., verb past tense forms or function words.

Consider a bigram *tells the* from our synthetic phrase example in Figure 2. We first obtain its phonetic representation [T EH L Z] [DH IY], and then a sequence of possible edit operations is Substitute(T, CH), Substitute(Z, S), Delete(DH) and translation of phonetic sequence [CH EH L S IY] back to words brings us to *chelsea*. See Figure 4 for visualization.

5 Experimental setups

To establish the effectiveness and robustness of our approach, we conducted two sets of experiments—expASR and expMultilingual—with transcribed and translated TED talks (Cettolo et al., 2012b).[6] English is the source language in all the experiments.

```
tells the  T  EH L Z DH IY
           |       | |
chelsea    CH EH L S    IY
```

Figure 4: Pseudo-ASR output generation example for a bigram *tells the*. Phonetic edits are Substitute(T, CH), Substitute(Z, S), Delete(DH).

In expASR we used tst2011–the official test set of the SLT track of the IWSLT 2011 evaluation campaign on the English-French language pair (Federico et al., 2011).[7] This test set comprises reference transcriptions of 8 talks (approximately 1.1h of speech, segmented to 818 utterances), 1-best hypotheses from five different ASR systems, a ROVER combination of four systems (Fiscus, 1997), and three sets of lattices produced by the participants of the IWSLT 2011 ASR track.

In this set of experiments we compare baseline systems performance to a performance of systems augmented with synthetic phrases on (1) reference transcriptions, (2) 1-best hypotheses from all released ASR systems, and (3) a set of ASR lattices produced by FBK (Ruiz et al., 2011).[8] Experiments with individual systems are aimed to validate that MT augmented with synthetic phrases can better translate ASR outputs with recognition errors and sequences that were not observed in the MT training data. Consistency in performance across different ASRs is expected if our approach to generate plausible misrecognition variants is universal, rather than biased to a specific system. Comparison of 1-best system with synthetic phrases to lattice decoding setup without synthetic phrases should demonstrate whether n-best plausible misrecognition variants that we generate assemble multiple paths through a lattice.

The purpose of expMultilingual is to show that translation improvement is consistent across different target languages. This multilingual experiment is interesting because typologically different languages pose different challenges to translation (degree and locality of reordering, morphological richness, etc.). By showing that we improve results across languages (even with

[6] http://www.ted.com/

[7] http://iwslt2011.org/doku.php?id=06_evaluation#slt_track_english_to_french

[8] Pruning threshold for lattices is 0.08.

the same underlying ASR system), we show that our technique is robust to the different demands that languages place on the translation model. We could not find any publicly available multilingual data sets of the translated speech,[9] therefore we constructed a new test set.

We use our in-house speech recognizer and evaluate on locally crawled and pre-processed TED audio and text data. We build SLT systems for five target languages: French, German, Russian, Hebrew, and Hindi. Consequently, our test systems are diverse typologically and trained on corpora of different sizes. We sample a test set of seven talks, representing approximately two hours of English speech, for which we have translations to all five languages;[10] talks are listed in Table 1.

Due to segmentation differences in the released TED (text) corpora and then several automatic preprocessing stages, numbers of sentences for the same talks are not identical across languages. Therefore, we select English-French system as an oracle (this is the largest dataset), and first align it with the ASR output. Then, we filter out test sets for non-French MT systems, to retain only sentence pairs that are included in the English-French test set. Thus, our test sets for non-French MT systems are smaller, and source-side sentences in the English-French MT is a superset of source-side sentences in all five languages. Training, tuning, and test corpora sizes are listed in Table 2. Same training and development sets were used in both `expASR` and `expMultilingual` experiments.

	Training	Dev	Test
EN–FR	140,816	2,521	843
EN–DE	130,010	2,373	501
EN–RU	117,638	2,380	735
EN–HE	135,366	2,501	540
EN–HI	126,117	2,000	300

Table 2: Number of sentences in training, dev and `expMultilingual` test corpora.

5.1 ASR

In the `expMultilingual` set of experiments, we employ the JANUS Recognition Toolkit that features the IBIS single pass decoder (Soltau et al., 2001). The acoustic model is maximum likelihood system, no speaker adaptation or discriminative training applied. The acoustic model training data is 186h of Broadcast News-style data. 5-gram language model with modified Kneser-Ney smoothing is trained with the SRILM toolkit (Stolcke, 2002) on the EPPS, TED, News-Commentary, and the Gigaword corpora. The Broadcast News test set contains 4h of audio; we obtain 25.6% word error rate (WER) on this test set.

We segment the TED test audio by the timestamps of transcripts appearance on the screen. Then, we manually detect and discard noisy hypotheses around segmentation boundaries, and manually align the remaining hypotheses with the references which are the source side of the English-French MT test set. The resulting test set of 843 hypotheses, sentence aligned with transcripts, yields 30.7% WER. Higher error rates (relatively to the Broadcast News baseline) can be explained by the idiosyncratic nature of the TED genre, and the fact that our ASR system was not trained on the TED data.

For the `expASR` set of experiments the ASR outputs and lattices in standard lattice format (SLF) were produces by the participants of IWSLT 2011 evaluation campaign.

5.2 MT

We train and test MT using the TED corpora in all five languages. For French, German and Russian we use sentence-aligned training and development sets (without our test talks) released for the IWSLT 2012 evaluation campaign (Cettolo et al., 2012a); we split Hebrew and Hindi to training and development respectively.[11] We split Hebrew and Hindi to sentences with simple heuristics, and then sentence-align with the Microsoft Bilingual Sentence Aligner (Moore, 2002). Punctuation marks were removed, corpora were lowercased, and tokenized using the `cdec` scripts (Dyer et al., 2010).

In all MT experiments, both for sentence and lattice translation, we employ the Moses toolkit (Koehn et al., 2007), implementing the phrase-based statistical MT model (Koehn et al., 2003) and optimize parameters with MERT (Och, 2003). Target language 3-gram Kneser-Ney smoothed

[9]After we conducted our experiments, a new multilingual parallel corpus of translated speech was released for SLT track of IWSLT 2013 Evaluation Campaign, however, this data set does not include Russian, Hebrew and Hindi, which are a subject of this research.

[10]Since TED translation is a voluntary effort, not all talks are available in all languages.

[11]Since TED Hindi corpus is very small (only about 6K sentences) we augment it with additional parallel data (Bojar et al., 2010); however, this improved Hindi system quality only marginally, probably owing to domain mismatch.

TED id	TED talk
1	Al Gore, 15 Ways to Avert a Climate Crisis, 2006
39	Aubrey de Grey: A roadmap to end aging, 2005
142	Alan Russell: The potential of regenerative medicine, 2006
228	Alan Kay shares a powerful idea about ideas, 2007
248	Alisa Miller: The news about the news, 2008
451	Bill Gates: Mosquitos, malaria and education, 2009
535	Al Gore warns on latest climate trends, 2009

Table 1: Test set of TED talks.

language models are trained on the training part of each corpus. Results are reported using case-insensitive BLEU with a single reference and no punctuation (Papineni et al., 2002). To verify that our improvements are consistent and are not just an effect of optimizer instability (Clark et al., 2011), we train three systems for each MT setup. Statistical significance is measured with the MultEval toolkit.[12] Reported BLEU scores are averaged over three systems.

In MT adaptation experiments we augment baseline phrase tables with synthetic phrases. For each entry in the original phrase table we add (at most) five[13] best acoustic confusions, detailed in Section 4. Table 3 contains sizes of phrase tables, original and augmented with synthetic phrases.

	Original	Synthetic
EN–FR	4,118,702	24,140,004
EN–DE	2,531,556	14,807,308
EN–RU	1,835,553	10,743,818
EN–HE	2,169,397	12,692,641
EN–HI	478,281	2,674,025

Table 3: Sizes of phrase tables from the baseline systems, and phrase tables with synthetic phrases.

6 Experiments

6.1 expASR

We first measure the phrasal coverage of recognition errors that our technique is able to predict. We compute a number of 1- and 2-gram phrases in ASR hypotheses from the tst2011 that are not in the references: these are ASR errors. Then, we compare their OOV rate in the English-French phrase tables, original vs. synthetic. The purpose of synthetic phrases is to capture misrecognized sequences, ergo, reduction in OOV rate of ASR errors in synthetic phrase tables corresponds to the portion of errors that our method was able to predict. Table 4 shows that the OOV rate of n-grams in phrase tables augmented with synthetic phrases drops dramatically, up to 54%. Consistent reduction of recognized errors across outputs from five different ASR systems confirms that our error-prediction approach is ASR-independent.

tst2011	#1-grams	#2-grams
system0	29 (50.9%)	230 (20.3%)
system1	27 (41.5%)	234 (21.3%)
system2	36 (36.0%)	230 (20.1%)
system3	34 (44.1%)	275 (20.1%)
system4	46 (52.9%)	182 (16.8%)
ROVER	30 (54.5%)	183 (18.7%)

Table 4: Phrasal coverage of recognition errors that our technique is able to predict. These are raw counts of 1-gram and 2-gram types that are OOVs in the baseline system and are recovered by our method when we augment the system with plausible misrecognitions. Percentages in parentheses show OOV rate reduction due to recovered n-grams.

Next, we explore the effect of synthetic phrases on translation performance, across different (1-best) ASR outputs. For references, ASR hypotheses, and ROVERed hypotheses we compare translations produced by MT systems trained with and without synthetic phrases. We detail our findings in Table 5.

Improvements in translation are significant for all systems with synthetic phrases. This experiment corroborates the underlying assumption that simulated ASR errors are paired with correct target phrases. Moreover, this experiment supports the claim that incorporating noisier translations in the translation model successfully adapts MT to SLT scenario and has indeed a positive effect on speech translation. Interestingly, improvement of reference translations is also observed. We speculate that this stems from better lexical selection due to a smoothing effect that our technique may

[12] https://github.com/jhclark/multeval

[13] This threshold is of course rather arbitrary. In future experiments we are planning to conduct an in-depth investigation of the threshold value, based on ASR LM score and phonetic distance from the original phrase.

	WER	BLEU Baseline	BLEU Synthetic	p
references	-	30.8	31.2	0.05
system0	22.0	24.3	25.0	<0.01
system1	23.3	23.8	24.3	<0.01
system2	21.1	23.9	24.4	0.02
system3	32.4	20.8	21.3	<0.01
system4	19.5	24.5	25.0	0.01
ROVER	17.4	25.0	25.6	0.01

Table 5: Comparison of the baseline translation systems with the systems augmented with synthetic phrases. We measure EN–FR MT performance on the `tst2011` test set: reference transcripts and ASR outputs on from five systems and their ROVER combination. Improvements in translation of all ASR outputs are statistically significant. This confirms the claim that incorporating simulated ASR errors via synthetic phrases effectively adapts MT to SLT scenario.

have.

Finally, we contrast the proposed approach of translation models adaptation to a conventional method of lattice translation. We decode FBK lattices produced for IWSLT 2011 Evaluation Campaign, and compare results to FBK 1-best translation results, which correspond to system1 in Table 5. Table 6 summarizes our main finding: 1-best system with synthetic phrases significantly outperforms lattice decoding setup with baseline translation table.[14] The additional small improvement in lattice decoding with synthetic phrases suggests that lattice decoding and phrase table adaptation are two complementary strategies and their combination is beneficial.

6.2 `expMultilingual`

In the multilingual experiment we train ten MT setups: five baseline setups and five systems with synthetic phrases, three systems per setup. For each system we compare translations of the reference transcripts and ASR hypotheses on the multilingual test set described in Section 6. We evaluate translations produced by MT systems trained with and without synthetic phrases. Table 7 summarizes experimental results, along with the test set WER for each language.

[14]Automatic evaluation results (in terms of BLEU) published during the IWSLT 2011 Evaluation Campaign (Federico et al., 2011) (p. 21) are 26.1 for FBK systems. Unsurprisingly, performance of our systems is lower, as we focus only on translation table and do not optimize factors, such as LMs and others.

	BLEU Baseline	BLEU Synthetic
FBK 1-best	23.8	24.3
FBK lattices	24.0	24.4

Table 6: Comparison of the baseline EN–FR translation systems with the systems augmented with synthetic phrases, in 1-best and lattice decoding setups. 1-best synthetic system significantly outperforms baseline lattice decoding setup. Additional improvement in lattice decoding with synthetic phrases suggests that lattice decoding and phrase table adaptation are two complementary strategies.

	WER	Baseline		Synthetic	
		Ref	ASR	Ref	ASR
EN–FR	30.7	23.3	17.8	23.9	18.1
EN–DE	33.6	14.0	11.1	14.2	11.4
EN–RU	30.7	12.3	10.7	12.2	10.6
EN–HE	29.7	9.2	7.0	9.5	7.2
EN–HI	32.1	5.5	4.5	5.6	4.8

Table 7: Comparison of the baseline translation systems with the systems augmented with synthetic phrases. We measure MT performance on the reference transcripts and ASR outputs. Consistent improvements are observed in four out of five languages.

Modest but consistent improvements are observed in four out of five setups with synthetic phrases. Only French setup yielded statistically significant improvement ($p < .01$). However, if we concatenate the outputs of all languages, the improvement in translation of references with BLEU score averaged over all systems becomes statistically significant ($p = .03$), improving from 16.8 for the baseline system to 17.3 for the adapted MT outputs. While more careful evaluation is required in order to estimate the effect of acoustic confusions, the accumulated result show that synthetic phrases facilitate MT adaptation to SLT across languages.

7 Analysis

We conducted careful manual analysis of actual usages of synthetic phrases in translation. The purpose of this qualitative analysis is to verify that predicted ASR errors are paired with phrases that contribute to better translation to a target language. Table 8 shows some examples. In the first sentence from the `tst2011` test set (output from system 4) the word *area* was erroneously recognized as *airy*,

English ref	so what they do is they move into an **area**
ASR output	so what they do is they move into an **airy**
Baseline MT	donc ce qu'ils font c'est qu'ils se déplacer dans un **airy**
Synthetic MT	donc ce qu'ils font c'est qu'ils se déplacer dans une **zone**
French ref	donc ce qu'ils font c'est qu'ils emménagent dans une **zone**
English ref	so **i started thinking** and listing what all it was that i thought would make a perfect biennial
ASR output	so on **i started a thinking** and listing was all it was that i thought would make a pretty by neil
Baseline MT	donc **j'ai commencé à une pensée** et listing était tout c'était que je pensais ferait un assez par neil
Synthetic MT	donc **j'ai commencé à penser** et une liste était tout c'était que je pensais ferait un assez par neil
French ref	alors **j'ai commencé à penser** et à lister tout ce qui selon moi ferait une biennale parfaite

Table 8: Examples of translations improved with synthetic phrases.

which is an OOV word for the baseline system. Our confusion generation algorithm also produced the word *airy* as a plausible misrecognition variant for the word *area* and attached it to a correct target phrase *zone*, and this synthetic phrase was selected during decoding, yielding to a correct translation for the ASR error. Second example shows a similar behavior for an indefinite article *a*. Third example is taken from the English-Russian system in the multilingual test set. *Gauge* was produced as a plausible misrecognition variant to *age*, and therefore correctly translated (albeit incorrectly inflected) as возраста(age+sg+m+acc). Synthetic phrases were also used in translations containing misrecognized function words, segmentation-related examples, and longer n-grams.

8 Related work

Predicting ASR errors to improve speech recognition quality has been explored in several previous studies. Jyothi and Fosler-Lussier (2009) develop weighted finite-state transducer framework for error prediction. They build a confusion matrix FST between phones to model acoustic errors made by the recognizer. Costs in the confusion matrix combine acoustic variations in the HMM representations of the phones (information from the acoustic model) and word-based phone confusions (information from the pronunciation model). In their follow-up work, Jyothi and Fosler-Lussier (2010) employ this error-predicting framework to train the parameters of a global linear discriminative language model that improves ASR.

Sagae et al. (2012) examined three protocols for 'hallucinating' ASR n-best lists. First approach generates confusions on the phone level, with a phone-based finite-state transducer that employs real n-best lists produced by the ASR system. Second is generating confusions at the word level with a MT-based approach. Third is a phrasal cohorts approach, in which acoustically confusable phrases are extracted from ASR n-best lists, based on *pivots*–identical left and right contexts of a phrase. All three methods were evaluated on the task of ASR improvement through decoding with discriminative language models. Discriminative language models trained on simulated n-best lists produced with phrasal cohorts method yielded the largest WER reduction on the telephone speech recognition task.

Our approach to generating plausible ASR misrecognitions is similar to previously explored FST-based methods. The fundamental difference, however, is in speech-free phonetic confusion transducer that does not employ any data extracted from acoustic models or ASR outputs. Simulated ASR errors are typically used to improve ASR applications. To the best of our knowledge no prior work has been done on integrating ASR errors directly in the translation models.

9 Conclusion

The idea behind the novel ASR error-prediction algorithm that we devise is to identify phonological neighbors with similar distributional properties, i.e. similar sounding words for which language model probabilities are insufficient for their disambiguation. These sequences have been identified as significant contributors to ASR errors (Goldwater et al., 2010). Additional and even more important factors that cause recognition errors are disfluencies in speech (Tsvetkov et al., 2013b). In the task of adapting MT to SLT these and other irregularities can effectively be incorporated in a useful general framework: *synthetic phrases* that augment phrase tables. Our experiments show that simulated acoustic confusions capture real ASR errors and that proposed framework effectively exploits them to improve translation.

Acknowledgments

We are grateful to João Miranda and Alan Black for providing us the TED audio with transcriptions, and to Zaid Sheikh for his help with ASR decoding. This work was supported in part by the U. S. Army Research Laboratory and the U. S. Army Research Office under contract/grant number W911NF-10-1-0533.

References

Waleed Ammar, Victor Chahuneau, Michael Denkowski, Greg Hanneman, Wang Ling, Austin Matthews, Kenton Murray, Nicola Segall, Yulia Tsvetkov, Alon Lavie, and Chris Dyer. 2013. The CMU machine translation systems at WMT 2013: Syntax, synthetic translation options, and pseudo-references.

Nicola Bertoldi, Richard Zens, and Marcello Federico. 2007. Speech translation by confusion network decoding. In *Proc. ICASSP*, pages 1297–1300. IEEE.

Ondrej Bojar, Pavel Stranak, and Daniel Zeman. 2010. Data issues in English-to-Hindi machine translation. In *Proceedings of LREC*.

Chris Callison-Burch, Philipp Koehn, and Miles Osborne. 2006. Improved statistical machine translation using paraphrases. In *Proceedings of HLT/NAACL*, pages 17–24. Association for Computational Linguistics.

Francisco Casacuberta, Marcello Federico, Hermann Ney, and Enrique Vidal. 2008. Recent efforts in spoken language translation. *Signal Processing Magazine, IEEE*, 25(3):80–88.

Mauro Cettolo, Marcello Federico, Luisa Bentivogli, Michael Paul, and Sebastian Stüker. 2012a. Overview of the IWSLT 2012 evaluation campaign.

Mauro Cettolo, Christian Girardi, and Marcello Federico. 2012b. WIT^3: Web inventory of transcribed and translated talks. In *Proceedings of EAMT*, pages 261–268, Trento, Italy.

Victor Chahuneau, Eva Schlinger, Noah A. Smith, and Chris Dyer. 2013. Translating into morphologically rich languages with synthetic phrases. In *Proceedings of EMNLP*.

Jonathan H. Clark, Chris Dyer, Alon Lavie, and Noah A. Smith. 2011. Better hypothesis testing for statistical machine translation: Controlling for optimizer instability. In *Proceedings of ACL*, pages 176–181. Association for Computational Linguistics.

Chris Dyer, Smaranda Muresan, and Philip Resnik. 2008. Generalizing word lattice translation. In *Proceedings of ACL-08: HLT*, pages 1012–1020. Association for Computational Linguistics.

Chris Dyer, Adam Lopez, Juri Ganitkevitch, Johnathan Weese, Ferhan Ture, Phil Blunsom, Hendra Setiawan, Vladimir Eidelman, and Philip Resnik. 2010. cdec: A decoder, alignment, and learning framework for finite-state and context-free translation models. In *Proceedings of ACL*.

Marcello Federico, Luisa Bentivogli, Michael Paul, and Sebastian Stüker. 2011. Overview of the IWSLT 2011 evaluation campaign. In *Proc. IWSLT*, pages 8–9.

Jonathan G. Fiscus. 1997. A post-processing system to yield reduced word error rates: Recognizer output voting error reduction (ROVER). In *Proc. ASRU*, pages 347–352. IEEE.

Sharon Goldwater, Dan Jurafsky, and Christopher D Manning. 2010. Which words are hard to recognize? prosodic, lexical, and disfluency factors that increase speech recognition error rates. *Speech Communication*, 52(3):181–200.

Xiaodong He and Li Deng. 2013. Speech-centric information processing: An optimization-oriented approach. *IEEE*, 101(5):1116–1135.

Dan Jurafsky and James H Martin. 2000. *Speech & Language Processing*. Pearson Education India.

Preethi Jyothi and Eric Fosler-Lussier. 2009. A comparison of audio-free speech recognition error prediction methods. In *Proc. INTERSPEECH*, pages 1211–1214.

Preethi Jyothi and Eric Fosler-Lussier. 2010. Discriminative language modeling using simulated asr errors. In *Proc. INTERSPEECH*, pages 1049–1052.

Stanislav V Kasl and George F Mahl. 1965. The relationship of disturbances and hesitations in spontaneous speech to anxiety. In *Journal of Personality and Social Psychology*, volume 1(5), pages 425–433.

Philipp Koehn, Franz Josef Och, and Daniel Marcu. 2003. Statistical phrase-based translation. In *Proceedings of HLT/NAACL*, pages 48–54. Association for Computational Linguistics.

Philipp Koehn, Hieu Hoang, Alexandra Birch, Chris Callison-Burch, Marcello Federico, Nicola Bertoldi, Brooke Cowan, Wade Shen, Christine Moran, Richard Zens, Chris Dyer, Ondrej Bojar, Alexandra Constantin, and Evan Herbst. 2007. Moses: Open source toolkit for statistical machine translation. In *Proceedings of ACL*, pages 177–180. Association for Computational Linguistics.

Evgeny Matusov, Stephan Kanthak, and Hermann Ney. 2006. Integrating speech recognition and machine translation: Where do we stand? In *Proc. ICASSP*, pages V–1217–V–1220. IEEE.

Robert C. Moore. 2002. Fast and accurate sentence alignment of bilingual corpora. In *Proceedings of AMTA*, pages 135–144, London, UK. Springer-Verlag.

Hermann Ney. 1999. Speech translation: Coupling of recognition and translation. In *Proc. ICASSP*, volume 1, pages 517–520. IEEE.

Franz Josef Och. 2003. Minimum error rate training in statistical machine translation. In *Proceedings of ACL*, pages 160–167, Morristown, NJ, USA. Association for Computational Linguistics.

Takashi Onishi, Masao Utiyama, and Eiichiro Sumita. 2010. Paraphrase lattice for statistical machine translation. In *Proceedings of ACL*.

Mari Ostendorf, Benoît Favre, Ralph Grishman, Dilek Hakkani-Tur, Mary Harper, Dustin Hillard, Julia Hirschberg, Heng Ji, Jeremy G Kahn, Yang Liu, Sameer Maskey, Evgeny Matusov, Hermann Ney, Andrew Rosenberg, Elizabeth Shriberg, Wen Wang, and Chuck Wooters. 2008. Speech segmentation and spoken document processing. *Signal Processing Magazine, IEEE*, 25(3):59–69.

Kishore Papineni, Salim Roukos, Todd Ward, and Wei-Jing Zhu. 2002. BLEU: a method for automatic evaluation of machine translation. In *Proceedings of ACL*, pages 311–318. Association for Computational Linguistics.

Stephan Peitz, Simon Wiesler, Markus Nußbaum-Thom, and Hermann Ney. 2012. Spoken language translation using automatically transcribed text in training. In *Proc. IWSLT*.

Vu H Quan, Marcello Federico, and Mauro Cettolo. 2005. Integrated n-best re-ranking for spoken language translation. In *Proc. INTERSPEECH*, pages 3181–3184. IEEE.

Nick Ruiz, Arianna Bisazza, Fabio Brugnara, Daniele Falavigna, Diego Giuliani, Suhel Jaber, Roberto Gretter, and Marcello Federico. 2011. FBK@ IWSLT 2011. In *Proc. IWSLT*.

Kenji Sagae, M. Lehr, E. Prud'hommeaux, P. Xu, N. Glenn, D. Karakos, S. Khudanpur, B. Roark, M. Saraçlar, I. Shafran, D. Bikel, C. Callison-Burch, Y. Cao, K. Hall, E. Hasler, P. Koehn, A. Lopez, M. Post, and D. Riley. 2012. Hallucinated n-best lists for discriminative language modeling. In *Proc. ICASSP*. IEEE.

H. Soltau, F. Metze, C. Fügen, and A. Waibel. 2001. A one-pass decoder based on polymorphic linguistic context assignment. In *Proc. ASRU*.

Andreas Stolcke. 2002. SRILM—an extensible language modeling toolkit. In *Proc. ICSLP*, pages 901–904.

Jean E Fox Tree. 1995. The effects of false starts and repetitions on the processing of subsequent words in spontaneous speech. *Journal of memory and language*, 34(6):709–738.

Yulia Tsvetkov, Chris Dyer, Lori Levin, and Archna Bhatia. 2013a. Generating English determiners in phrase-based translation with synthetic translation options. In *Proceedings of WMT*. Association for Computational Linguistics.

Yulia Tsvetkov, Zaid Sheikh, and Florian Metze. 2013b. Identification and modeling of word fragments in spontaneous speech. In *Proc. ICASSP*. IEEE.

Ping Xu, Pascale Fung, and Ricky Chan. 2012. Phrase-level transduction model with reordering for spoken to written language transformation. In *Proc. ICASSP*, pages 4965–4968. IEEE.

Ruiqiang Zhang, Genichiro Kikui, Hirofumi Yamamoto, Taro Watanabe, Frank Soong, and Wai Kit Lo. 2004. A unified approach in speech-to-speech translation: integrating features of speech recognition and machine translation. In *Proceedings of COLING*, page 1168. Association for Computational Linguistics.

Bowen Zhou, Laurent Besacier, and Yuqing Gao. 2007. On efficient coupling of ASR and SMT for speech translation. In *Proc. ICASSP*, volume 4, pages IV–101. IEEE.

Bowen Zhou. 2013. Statistical machine translation for speech: A perspective on structures, learning, and decoding. *IEEE*, 101(5):1180–1202.

A Generative Model for User Simulation in a Spatial Navigation Domain

Aciel Eshky[1], **Ben Allison**[2], **Subramanian Ramamoorthy**[1], and **Mark Steedman**[1]
[1]School of Informatics, University of Edinburgh, UK
[2]Actual Analytics Ltd., Edinburgh, UK
{a.eshky,s.ramamoorthy,steedman}@ed.ac.uk
ballison@actualanalytics.com

Abstract

We propose the use of a generative model to simulate user behaviour in a novel task-oriented dialog domain, where user goals are spatial routes across artificial landscapes. We show how to derive an efficient feature-based representation of spatial goals, admitting exact inference and generalising to new routes. The use of a generative model allows us to capture a range of plausible behaviour given the same underlying goal. We evaluate intrinsically using held-out probability and perplexity, and find a substantial reduction in uncertainty brought by our spatial representation. We evaluate extrinsically in a human judgement task and find that our model's behaviour does not differ significantly from the behaviour of real users.

1 Introduction

Automated dialog management is an area of research that has undergone rapid advancement in the last decade. The driving force of this innovation has been the rise of the statistical paradigm for monitoring dialog state, reasoning about the effects of possible dialog moves, and planning future actions (Young et al., 2013). Statistical dialog management treats conversations as Markov Decision Processes, where dialog moves are associated with a utility, estimated online by interacting with a simulated user (Levin et al., 1998; Roy et al., 2000; Singh et al., 2002; Williams and Young, 2007; Henderson and Lemon, 2008). Slot-filling domains have been the subject of most of this research, with the exception of work on troubleshooting domains (Williams, 2007) and relational domains (Lison, 2013).

Although navigational dialogs have received much attention in studies of human conversational behaviour (Anderson et al., 1991; Thompson et al., 1993; Reitter and Moore, 2007), they have not been the subject of statistical dialog management research, and existing systems addressing navigational domains remain largely hand crafted (Janarthanam et al., 2013). Navigational domains present an interesting challenge, due to the disparity between the spatial goals and their grounding as utterances. This disparity renders much of the statistical management literature inapplicable. In this paper, we address this deficiency.

We focus on the task of simulating user behaviour, both because of the important role simulators plays in the induction of dialog managers, and because it provides a self-contained means of developing the domain representations which facilitate dialog reasoning. We show how a generative model of user behaviour can be induced from data, alleviating the manual effort typically involved in the development of simulators, and providing an elegant mechanism for reproducing the natural variability observed in human behaviour.

1.1 Spatial Goals of Users

Users in task-oriented domains are goal-directed, with a persistent notion of what they wish to accomplish from the dialog. In slot-filling domains, goals are comprised of a group of categorical entities, represented as slot-value pairs. These entities can be placed directly into the user's utterance. For example, in a flight booking domain, if a user's goal is to fly to London from New York on the 3rd of November, then the goal takes the form: {origin="New York", dest="London", depart_date="03-11-13"}, and expressing the destination takes the form: *Provide* dest="London".

In contrast, consider the task of navigating somebody across a landscape. Figure 1 shows a pair of maps taken from a spatial navigation domain, the Map Task. Because the Giver aims to communicate their route, one can view the route

Proceedings of the 14th Conference of the European Chapter of the Association for Computational Linguistics, pages 626–635, Gothenburg, Sweden, April 26-30 2014.

Natural Language	Semantic Representation
G: you are above the camera shop	*Instruct* POSITION(ABOVE, LM)
F: yeah	*Acknowledge*
G: go left jus– just to the side of the paper, $\star$ then south, under the parked van $\diamond$ you have a parked van?	*Instruct* MOVE(TO, PAGE_LEFT) $\star$ *Instruct* MOVE(TOWARDS, ABSOLUTE_SOUTH) *Instruct* MOVE(UNDER, LM) $\diamond$ *Query-yn*
F: a parked van no	*Reply-n*
G: you go– you just go west, $\star$ and down, and then you go along to the– you go east $\diamond$	*Clarify* MOVE(TOWARDS, ABSOLUTE_WEST) $\star$ *Clarify* MOVE(TOWARDS, ABSOLUTE_SOUTH) *Clarify* MOVE(TOWARDS, ABSOLUTE_EAST) $\diamond$
F: south then east	*Check*
G: yeah	*Reply-y*

Table 1: A Giver (G) and a Follower (F) alternating turns in a dialog concerning the maps in Figure 1. The utterances are shown in natural language (left), and the semantic equivalent (right), which is composed of *Dialog Acts* and SEMANTIC UNITS. Utterances marked $\star$ demonstrate a plausible variability in expressing the same part of the route on the Giver's map, and similarly those marked $\diamond$. We model the Giver's behaviour, conditioned on the Follower's, at the semantic level.

as the Giver's goal for the dialog. However, unlike goals in slot-filling domains, it is unclear whether the route can be represented categorically in a form that would allow the giver to communicate it by placing it directly into an utterance. As raw data, a specific route is represented numerically as a series of pixel coordinates. Before modelling interlocutors in this domain, we must derive a meaningful representation for the spatial goals, and then devise a mechanism that takes us from the spatial goals to the utterances which express them.

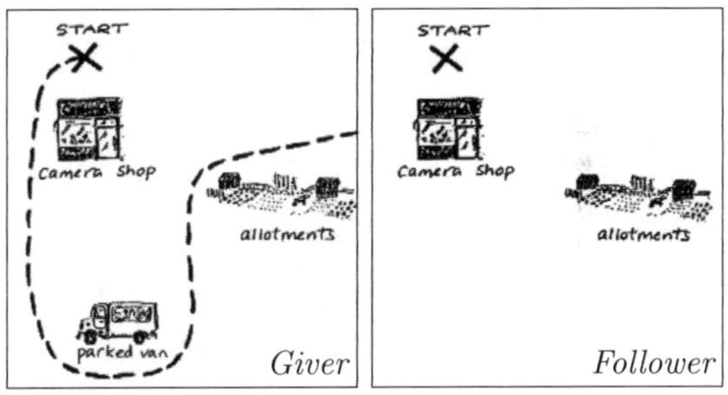

Figure 1: In the Map Task, the instruction Giver's task is to communicate a route to a Follower, whose map may differ. The route can be seen as the Giver's goal which the Follower tries to infer. A corresponding dialog is shown in Table 1.

1.2 Utterance Variability for the Same Goal

In addition to making sensible utterances, a concern for user simulation is providing plausible variability in utterances, to provide dialog managers with realistic training scenarios. Consider the dialog in Table 1, resulting from the maps in Figure 1. Utterances marked $\star$ (and similarly those marked $\diamond$) illustrate how the same route can be described in different ways, not only at the natural language level, but also at the semantic level[1]. A model providing a 1-to-1 mapping from spatial routes to semantic utterances would fail to capture this phenomenon. Instead, we need to be able to account for plausible variability in expressing the underlying spatial route as semantic utterances.

[1]Route descriptor TOWARDS indicates a movement in the direction of the referent ABS_WEST, whereas TO indicates a movement until the referent is reached.

1.3 Overview of Approach

In order to perform efficient reasoning, we propose a new feature-based representation of spatial goals, transforming them from coordinate space to a low-dimensional feature space. This groups similar routes together intelligently, permitting exact inference, and generalising to new routes. To address the problem of variability of utterances given the same underlying route, we learn a distribution over possible utterances given the feature vector derived from a route, with probability proportional to the plausibility of the utterance.

Because this domain has not been previously addressed in the context of dialog management or user simulation, there is no directly comparable prior work. We thus conduct several novel evaluations to validate our model. We first use intrinsic information theoretic measures, which compute the extent of the reduction in uncertainty brought by our feature-based representation of the spatial goals. We then evaluate extrinsically by generating utterances from our model, and comparing them to held-out utterance of real humans in the test data. We also utilise human judgements for the task, where the judges score the output of the different models and the human utterances based on their suitability to a particular route.

2 Related Work

2.1 Related Work on the Map Task

To our knowledge, there are no attempts to model instruction Givers as users in the Map Task domain. Two studies model the Follower, in the context of understanding natural language instructions and interpreting them by drawing a route (Levit and Roy, 2007; Vogel and Jurafsky, 2010). Both studies exclude dialog from their modelling. Although their work is not directly comparable to ours, they provide a corpus suitable for our task.

2.2 Related Work on User Simulation

Early user simulation techniques are based on N-grams (Eckert et al., 1997; Levin and Pieraccini, 2000; Georgila et al., 2005; Georgila et al., 2006), ensuring that simulator responses to a machine utterance are sensible locally. However, they do not enforce user consistency throughout the dialog.

Deterministic simulators with trainable parameters mitigate the lack of consistency using rules in conjunction with explicit goals or agendas (Scheffler and Young, 2002; Rieser and Lemon, 2006; Pietquin, 2006; Ai and Litman, 2007; Schatzmann and Young, 2009). However, they require large amounts of hand crafting and restrict the variability in user responses, which by extension restricts the access of the dialog manager to potentially interesting states. An alternative approach to dealing with the lack of consistency is to extend N-grams to explicitly model user goals and condition utterances on them (Pietquin, 2004; Cuayáhuitl et al., 2005; Pietquin and Dutoit, 2006; Rossignol et al., 2010; Rossignol et al., 2011; Eshky et al., 2012).

3 The Model

Our task is to model the Giver's utterances in response to the Follower's, at the semantic level. A Giver's utterance takes the form:

$$g = \mathit{Instruct},\ u = \textsc{Move}\,(\textsc{Under}, \mathrm{LM})$$

consisting of a dialog act g and a semantic unit u[2]. Aligned with u, is an ordered set of waypoints W, corresponding only to part of the route u describes. Figure 2(a) shows an example of such a sub-route. The point-set W can be seen as the Giver's current goal on which they base their behaviour. Because the routes are drawn on the Giver's maps, we treat W as observed.

To model some of the interaction between the Giver and the Follower, we additionally consider in our model the previous dialog act of the Follower, which could for example be:

$$f = \mathit{Acknowledge}$$

Given point-set W and preceding Follower act f, as the giver, we need to determine a procedure for choosing which dialog act g and semantic unit u to produce. In other words, we are interested in the following distribution:

$$p\,(g, u|f, W) \tag{1}$$

which says that, as the Giver, we select our utterances on the basis of what the Follower says, and on the set of waypoints we next wish to describe.

To formalise this idea into a generative model, we assume that the Giver act g depends only on the Follower act f. We further assume that the semantic unit u depends on the set of waypoints W which it describes, and on the Giver's choice of dialog act g. Thus, u and f are conditionally independent given g. This provides a simple way of incorporating the different sources of information into a complete generative model[3]. Using Bayes' theorem, we can rewrite Equation (1) as:

$$p\,(g, u|f, W) = \frac{p(u)\; p(g|u)\; p(f|g)\; p(W|u)}{\sum_{g'u'} p(u')\; p(g'|u')\; p(f|g')\; p(W|u')} \tag{2}$$

requiring four distributions: $p(u)$, $p(g|u)$, $p(f|g)$, and $p(W|u)$. The first three become the semantic component of our model, to which we dedicate Section 3.1. The fourth is the spatio-semantic component, to which we dedicate Sections 3.2–3.4.

[2] We align g and u in a preprocessing step, and store the names of landmarks which the units abstract away from.

[3] Further advancements to this work would investigate the effects of relaxing the conditional independence assumption.

3.1 The Semantic Component

The semantic component concerns only the categorical variables, f, g, and u, and addresses how the Giver selects their semantic utterances based on what the Follower says. We model the distributions u, $g|u$, and $f|g$ from Equation (2) as categorical distributions with uniform Dirichlet priors:

$$u \sim Cat(\alpha) \qquad \alpha \sim Dir(\epsilon) \tag{3a}$$

$$g|u \sim Cat(\beta) \qquad \beta \sim Dir(\kappa) \tag{3b}$$

$$f|g \sim Cat(\gamma) \qquad \gamma \sim Dir(\lambda) \tag{3c}$$

We use point estimates for α, β and γ, fixing them at their posterior means in the following manner:

$$\hat{\beta_{gu}} = p(g|u) = \frac{Count(g,u)+1}{\sum_{g'} Count(g',u)+L} \tag{4}$$

and similarly for $\hat{\alpha}$ and $\hat{\gamma}$ (L = size of vector β).

3.2 Spatial Goal Abstraction

Each ordered point-set W on some given map can be seen as the Giver's current goal, on which they base their behaviour. Let $W = \{w_i; 0 \leq i < n\}$, where $w_i = (x_i, y_i)$ is a waypoint, and x_i, y_i are pixel coordinates on the map, typically obtained through a vision processing step.

Given this goal formulation, from Equation (2) we require $p(W|u)$, i.e. the probability of a set of waypoints given a semantic unit. However, there are two problems with deriving a generative model directly over W. Firstly, the length of W varies from one point-set to the next, making it hard to compare probabilities with different numbers of observations. Secondly, deriving a model directly over x, y coordinates introduces sparsity problems, as we are highly unlikely to encounter the same set of coordinates multiple times. We thus require an abstraction away from the space of pixel coordinates.

Our approach is to extract feature vectors of fixed length from the point-sets, and then derive a generative model over the feature vectors instead of the point-sets. Feature extraction allows point-sets with similar characteristics, rather than exact pixel values, to give rise to similar distributions over units, thus enabling the model to reason given previously unseen point-sets. The features we extract are detailed in Section 3.4.

3.3 The Multivariate Normal Distribution

Let M be an unordered point-set describing map elements, such as landmark locations and map boundary information. $M = \{m_j; 0 \leq j < k\}$, where $m_j = (x_j, y_j)$ is a map element with pixel coordinates x_j and y_j. We define a spatial feature function $\psi : W, M \rightarrow \mathbb{R}^n$ which captures, as feature values, the characteristics of the point-set W in relation to elements in M. Let the spatial feature vector, extracted from the point-set W and the map elements M, be:

$$v = \psi(W, M) \tag{5}$$

Figure 2(b) illustrates the feature extraction process. We now define a distribution over the feature vector v given the semantic unit u. We model $v|u$ as a multivariate normal distribution (recall that v is in $\mathbb{R}^n$):

$$v|u \sim N(\mu_u, \Sigma_u) \tag{6}$$

where μ and Σ are the mean vectors and covariance matrices respectively. Subscript $_u$ indicates that there is one such parameter for each unit u.

Since the alignments between units u and point-sets W are fully observed, parameter estimation is a question of estimating the mean vectors $\mu_{u'}$ and the covariance matrices $\Sigma_{u'}$ from the point-sets co-occuring with unit u'. We use maximum likelihood estimators. To avoid issues with degenerate covariance matrices resulting from small amounts of data, we consider diagonal covariance matrices. Because $v|u$ is normally distributed, inference, both for parameters and conditional distributions over units, can be performed exactly, and so the model is exceptionally quick to learn and perform inference.

3.4 The Spatial Feature Sets

We derive four feature sets from the ordered point-set W, while considering the map elements in the unordered point-set M:

1. **Absolute features** capture directions and distances of movement. We compute the distance between the first and last points in W, and compute the angle between unit vector $<0,-1>$ and the line connecting first and last points in W

2. **Polynomial features** capture shapes of movements as straight lines or curves. We compute the mean residual of a degree one polynomial fit to the points in W (linear), and a degree two polynomial (quadratic)[4]

[4]These features are computed quickly and efficiently, requiring only the solution to a least squares problem.

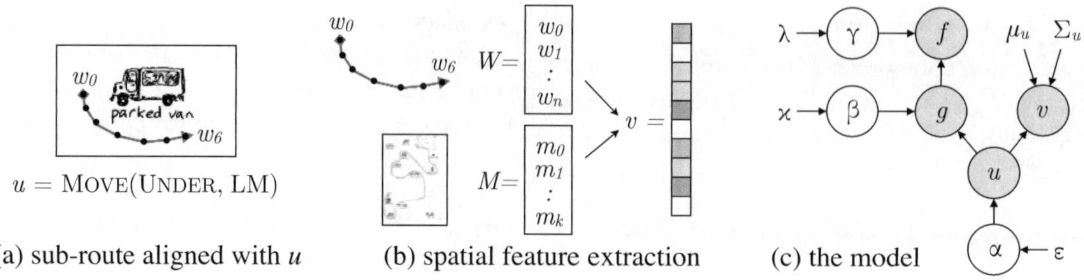

(a) sub-route aligned with *u* (b) spatial feature extraction (c) the model

Figure 2: (a) At training time, a Giver's semantic unit u is aligned with an ordered point-set W, representing a sub-route. (b) We extract a spatial feature vector v of fixed length, from point-sets W and M of varying lengths. (c) We define a generative model of the Giver, over Giver act g and semantic unit u, preceding Follower act f, and spatial feature vector v. Latent parameters and priors are shown.

3. **Landmark features** capture how close the route takes the Follower to the nearest landmark. We compute the distance between the end-point in W and the nearest landmark in M, and compute the angle between the route taken in W and the line connecting the start point in to the nearest landmark

4. **Edge features** capture the relationship between the movement and the map edges. We compute the distance from the start-point in W to the nearest edge and corner in M, and similarly for the end-point in W

3.5 The Complete Generative Model

Our complete generative model of the Giver is a distribution over Giver act g and semantic unit u, given the preceding Follower act f and the spatial feature vector v. Vector v is the result of applying the feature extraction function ψ over W and M, where W is the ordered point-set describing the sub-route aligned with u, and M is the point-set describing landmark locations and map edge information. We rewrite Equation (2) as:

$$p(g, u|f, v) = \frac{p(u)\, p(g|u)\, p(f|g)\, p(v|u)}{\sum_{g'u'} p(u')\, p(g'|u')\, p(f|g')\, p(v|u')} \quad (7)$$

We call our model the Spatio-Semantic Model, **SSM**, and depict it in Figure 2(c).

4 Corpus Statistics and State Space

We conduct our experiments on the Map Task corpus (Anderson et al., 1991), a collection of cooperative human-human dialogs arising from the task explained in Figure 1 and Table 1. The original corpus was labelled with dialog acts, such as *Acknowledge* and *Instruct*. The semantic units can be obtained through a semantic parse of the natural language utterances, while the spatial information can be obtained through vision processing of the maps. We use an existing extension of the corpus by Levit and Roy (2007), which is semantically and spatially annotated. The spatial annotation are x, y pixel coordinates of landmark locations and evenly spaces points on the routes. All 15 maps were annotated. The semantic units take the predicates MOVE, TURN, POSITION, or ORIENTATION, and two arguments: a route descriptor and a referent. The semantic annotations were restricted to the Giver's *Instruct*, *Clarify*, and *Explain* acts. Out of the original 128 dialogs, 25 were semantically annotated.

For our experiments, we use all 15 pairs of maps, and all 25 semantically annotated dialogs. A dialog on average contain 57.5 instances, where an instance is an occurrence of f, g, u, and W. We find 87 unique semantic units u in our data, however, according to the semantic representation, there can be 456 distinct possible values for u[5]. As for the rest of the variables, f takes 15 values, g takes 4, and v is a real-valued vector of length 10, extracted from the real valued sets W and M of varying lengths. We thus reason in a semantic state space of $87 \times 15 \times 4 = 5220$, and an infinite spatial state space.

5 Intrinsic Evaluation

Our first evaluation metric is an information theoretic one, based on notion that better models find new instances of data (not used to train them) to be more predictable. One such metric is the probability a model assigns to the data, (higher is better). A

[5] 20×2 for TURN and ORIENTATION, + 208×2 for MOVE and POSITION.

second metric is perplexity, which computes how surprising a model finds the data (lower is better). Both metrics have been used to evaluate user simulators in the literature (Georgila et al., 2005; Eshky et al., 2012; Pietquin and Hastie, 2013). We compute the per-utterance probability of held-out data, instead of the per-dialog probability, since the latter was deemed incompatible across dialogs of different lengths by Pietquin and Hastie (2013). Perplexity is $2^{-log_2(d)}$ where d is the probability of the instance in question. We evaluate using leave-one-out validation, which estimates the model from all but one dialog, then evaluates the probability of that dialog. We repeat this process until all dialogs have been evaluated as the unseen dialog.

Because we evaluate on held-out dialogs, we need to be able to assign probabilities to previously unseen instances. We therefore smooth our models (at training time) by learning a **background model** which we estimate from all the training data. This results in high variance in the distribution over features and a flat overall distribution. Where no model can be estimated for a particular semantic unit, we use that semantic unit's smoothed prior probability combined with the background model for its likelihood.

We first consider the suitability of the different feature sets for predicting utterances. Figure 4 shows the mean per-utterance probability our model assigns to held-out data when using different sets. The more predictable the model finds the data, the higher the probability. Note that the target metric here is *not* 1, as there is no single correct answer. It can be seen that the most successful features in order of predictiveness are: Absolute, then Polynomial, then Landmark, and finally Edge. The combination of all buys us further improvement. Perplexity is shown in Table 2.

Secondly, we consider two baselines inspired by similar approaches of comparison in the literature (Eckert et al., 1997; Levin and Pieraccini, 2000; Georgila et al., 2005). Both are variants of our model that lack the spatial component, i.e. they are not goal-based. Although the baselines are weak, they allow us to measure the reduction in uncertainty brought by the introduction of the spatial componenet to our model, which is the purpose of this comparison. **Baseline 1** is $p(g, u)$ while **Baseline 2** is $(g, u|f)$. The first tells us how predictable giver utterances are (in the held-out data), based only on the normalised frequencies. The

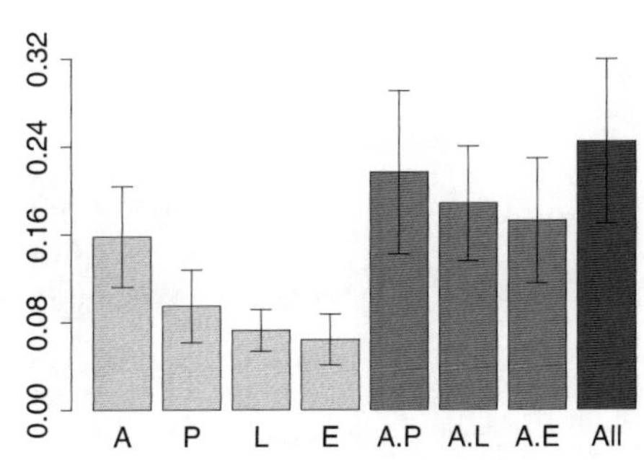

Figure 3: Mean per-utterance probability, assigned to held-out data by our model, when defined over the four feature sets and their combinations, estimated through leave-one-out validation. A=Absolute, P=Polynomial, L=Landmark, and E=Edge. Error bars are standard deviations.

Feature Set	Perplexity
Absolute (A)	7.26 ± 4.08
Polynomial (P)	12.86 ± 8.39
Landmark (L)	15.16 ± 6.27
Edge (E)	17.92 ± 8.47
All	4.66 ± 2.22

Table 2: Perplexity scores (and standard deviations) of our model, computed over the four feature sets and their combination, estimated through leave-one-out validation. (A) outperforms all individual sets, while the combination performs best.

second tells us how predictable they become when we condition on the previous follower act. Details of the baselines are similar to Section 3.1.

Figure 4 shows the mean per-utterance probability our model assigns to held-out data when compared to the two baselines. Baseline 2 slightly improves our predictions over Baseline 1, although not reliably so, when considering the small increase in perplexity in Table 3. SSM demonstrates a much larger relative improvement across both metrics. The results demonstrate that our spatial component enables substantial reduction in uncertainty, brought by the transfer of information from the maps to the utterances.

Intrinsic metrics, such as the probability of held-out data and perplexity, provide us with an elegant way of evaluating probabilistic models in a setting where there is no single correct answer, but a range of plausible answers, because they exploit the model's inherit ability to assign probability to behaviour. However, the metrics can be hard to interpret in an absolute sense, providing much better

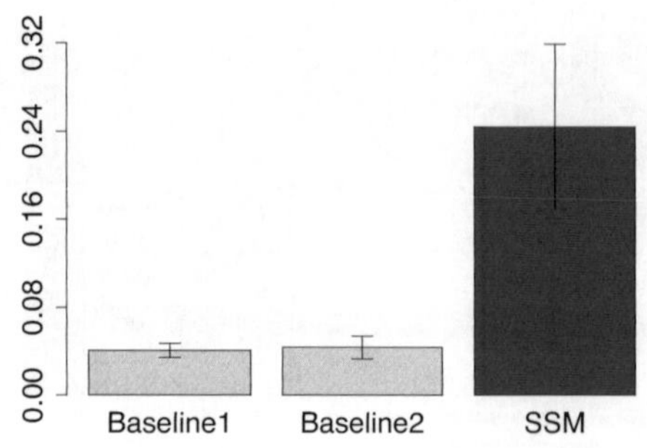

Figure 4: Mean per-utterance probability, assigned to held-out data by our model (SSM), compared to two baselines which lack the spatial componenet, estimated through leave-one-out validation. Error bars are standard deviations.

Model	Perplexity
Baseline1	24.95 ± 4.05
Baseline2	25.06 ± 12.02
SSM	4.66 ± 2.22

Table 3: Perplexity scores of our model (SSM), compared to the two baselines, estimated through leave-one-out validation. SSM finds the held-out data to be least surprising.

information about the relative strengths of different models rather than their absolute utility. In the next section, we explore methods for determining the utility of the models when applied to tasks.

6 Extrinsic Evaluation

In this section, we undertake a task-based evaluation of model output. We train on 22 of the dialogs, holding out 3 at random for testing. The task is to then generate, for each sub-route in the test dialogs, the most probable unit to describe it[6]. Figure 5 shows some examples of sub-routes taken from the test dialogs, and shows the the most probable unit to describe each under our model, **SSM**.

We first explore a naive notion of accuracy: the percentage of model-generated units matching **Real Giver** units observed in the test dialogs. We compute the same for **Baseline** 1 from Section 5 as a lower bound. A quick glance at the results in Table 4 might suggest that both models have little utility: SSM is "correct" only 33% of the time. However, the extent to which this conclusion follows depends on the suitability of accuracy as a

[6]The models can generate 1 of the 87 units observed in the training set, but are made to output the most probable in this experiment.

	Baseline	SSM
Match to Real Giver	7.69%	33.08%

Table 4: Percentage of model-generated units that match Real Giver units in the test set. The models output the most probable unit to describe a given sub-route. We argue that this metric is unsuitable as it assumes one correct answer.

Mismatch	Baseline	SSM	Real Giver
1.45	3.04	5.27	5.11

Table 5: Average scores assigned by human judges to model-generated units on a 7-level Likert scale. Mismatch is judged to be the worst, followed by Baseline. SSM and Real Giver are scored well, and are judged to be of similar quality.

means of evaluating dialog. In most situations, there is not a single correct description and a host of incorrect ones, but rather a gradient of descriptions from the highly informative and appropriate to the nonsensical and confusing. Such subtleties are not captured by an accuracy test (or the closely related recall and precision). In demonstration of this point, we next conduct qualitative evaluation of model output.

We ask humans to rate, on a Likert scale of 7, the degree to which a given unit provides a suitable description of a given sub-route. Sub-routes are taken from the test dialogs, and are marked similarly to Figure 5 but on the complete map. Units are generated from SSM, Baseline, Real Giver, and a control condition: a deliberate **Mismatch** to the sub-route. The Mismatch is generated automatically by taking the least probable unit under SSM, of the form MOVE(TOWARD, x) where x is one of the four compass directions. We collect 5 judgements for each sub-route-unit combinations on Mechanical Turk, and randomise so that no judge sees the same order of pairs. Test dialogs contained 94 distinct sub-routes.

We analyse the results with a two-way ANOVA, with the first factor being model, and the second being the sub-route, for a 4×94 design. The *means* of the "model" factor are shown in Table 5. It can be seen that Mismatch and Baseline are scored sensibly poorly, while SSM and Real Giver are scored reasonably well, and are judged to be of a similar quality. We thus proceed with a more rigorous analysis. The ANOVA summary is shown in Table 6. A significant effect of the model fac-

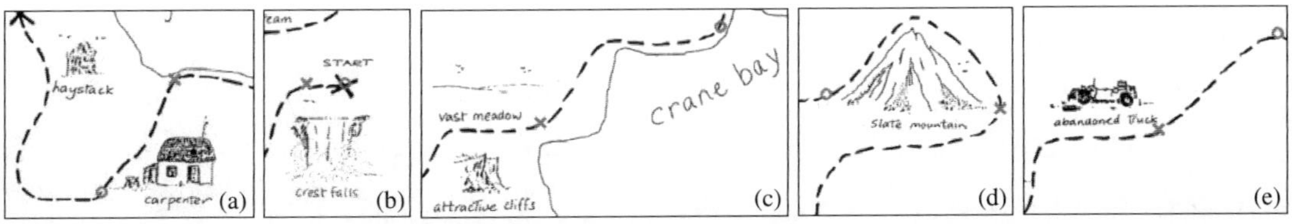

Figure 5: Given a sub-route marked with start-point ○ and end-point × (in red), SSM generates the following u: (a) MOVE(TOWARDS, ABS_NORTHEAST) (b) TURN(ABS_WEST) (c) MOVE(FOLLOW-BOUNDARY, LM) (d) MOVE(AROUND, LM) (e) MOVE(TOWARDS, ABS_SOUTHWEST)

Factor	**S Sq**	**Df**	**F**	**Pr(>F)**
Model	**4845.3**	3	783.93	**<0.001**
Sub-route	1140.0	93	5.95	<0.001
M:S	2208.7	279	3.84	<0.001
Residuals	3263.5	1584		

Table 6: Two way ANOVA with factors model (4 possibilities), and sub-route (94 possibilities). Results show a model effect accounting for most of the variance. Meaning that the scores assigned to the units by human judges are significantly influenced by the model used to generate the units.

Model Comparison	**t value**	**Pr(>|t|)**
Mismatch : Baseline	-16.974	<0.001
SSM : Baseline	23.882	<0.001
Real Giver : Baseline	23.192	<0.001
SSM : Mismatch	40.857	<0.001
Real Giver : Mismatch	40.507	<0.001
SSM : Real Giver	1.171	**0.646**

Table 7: Tukey HSD shows that all models are assigned significantly different scores by judges, apart from SSM and Real Giver. This asserts that, although only 33% of SSM units match Real Giver units (as shown in Table 4), the quality of the units are not judged to be significantly different.

tor is present, meaning that the scores assigned by human judges to the units are significantly influenced by which model was used to generate the units. Additionally, a significant effect for the sub-route factor can be seen, which is due to some sub-routes being harder to describe than others. An interaction effect is also present, which is expected given such a large number of examples. Note how the model factor accounts for the largest amount of variance of all the factors.

Having confirmed the presence of a model effect, we conduct a post-hoc analysis of the model factors. Table 7 shows a Tukey HSD test, demonstrating that all models are significantly different from one another, except Real Giver and SSM. Results show that, despite the large number of judgements collected, we are unable to separate the quality of our model's unit from that in the original data, against which accuracy was being judged in Table 4. This demonstrates that when many answers are feasible, scoring correctness against the original human units is unsuitable. It also firmly demonstrates the suitability of our spatial representation, and the strength of the generative model we have induced for the task.

7 Conclusion and Discussion

We have shown how to represent spatial goals in a navigational domain, and have validated our representation by inducing (fully from data) a generative model of the Giver's semantic utterances conditioned on the spatial goal and the previous Follower act. Intrinsic and extrinsic evaluation demonstrate the strength of our model.

A direct application of this work is robot guidance, by using the Giver's simulator to induce an optimal Follower: an MDP-based dialog manager that interprets and follows navigational instructions. Another variation would be to learn a generative model of the Follower, by extracting features from Follower maps (labelled with routes drawn by real Followers). Finally, this work has broader applications beyond simulation, in particular for systems that describe routes to users (spatial goal representation and model dependencies would hold). Decisions about which part of the route to describe next is one extension to that end.

Acknowledgements

We thank Ioannis Konstas, Johanna Moore, Robin Hill, S. M. Ali Eslami, and the anonymous reviewers for valuable feedback. This work is funded by King Saud University. Mark Steedman is supported by EC-PF7-270273 Xperience and ERC Advanced Fellowship 249520 GRAMPLUS.

References

Hua Ai and Diane J. Litman. 2007. Knowledge consistent user simulations for dialog systems. In *InterSpeech 2007*, pages 2697–2700.

Anne H. Anderson, Miles Bader, Ellen Gurman Bard, Elizabeth Boyle, Gwyneth Doherty, Simon Garrod, Stephen Isard, Jacqueline Kowtko, Jan McAllister, Jim Miller, Catherine Sotillo, Henry S. Thompson, and Regina Weinert. 1991. The hcrc map task corpus. *Language and Speech*, 34(4):351–366.

Heriberto Cuayáhuitl, Steve Renals, Oliver Lemon, and Hiroshi Shimodaira. 2005. Human-computer dialogue simulation using hidden markov models. In *ASRU 2005*, pages 290–295.

Wieland Eckert, Esther Levin, and Roberto Pieraccini. 1997. User modeling for spoken dialogue system evaluation. In *Proceedings of IEEE Workshop on Automatic Speech Recognition and Understanding*.

Aciel Eshky, Ben Allison, and Mark Steedman. 2012. Generative goal-driven user simulation for dialog management. In *EMNLP-CoNLL 2012*, pages 71–81, Jeju Island, Korea, July. Association for Computational Linguistics.

Kallirroi Georgila, James Henderson, and Oliver Lemon. 2005. Learning user simulations for information state update dialogue systems. In *InterSpeech 2005*.

Kallirroi Georgila, James Henderson, and Oliver Lemon. 2006. User Simulation for Spoken Dialogue Systems: Learning and Evaluation. In *InterSpeech 2006*.

James Henderson and Oliver Lemon. 2008. Mixture model pomdps for efficient handling of uncertainty in dialogue management. In *ACL*, HLT-Short '08, pages 73–76, Stroudsburg, PA, USA. Association for Computational Linguistics.

Srinivasan Janarthanam, Oliver Lemon, Phil Bartie, Tiphaine Dalmas, Anna Dickinson, Xingkun Liu, William Mackaness, and Bonnie Webber. 2013. Evaluating a city exploration dialogue system with integrated question-answering and pedestrian navigation. In *ACL*.

Esther Levin and Roberto Pieraccini. 2000. A stochastic model of human-machine interaction for learning dialog strategies. In *IEEE Transactions on Speech and Audio Processing*.

Esther Levin, Roberto Pieraccini, and Wieland Eckert. 1998. Using markov decision process for learning dialogue strategies. In *Proc. ICASSP*, pages 201–204.

M. Levit and D. Roy. 2007. Interpretation of spatial language in a map navigation task. *IEEE Transactions on Systems, Man, and Cybernetics, Part A*, 37(3):667–679.

Pierre Lison. 2013. Model-based bayesian reinforcement learning for dialogue management. In *Interspeech 2013*.

Olivier Pietquin and Thierry Dutoit. 2006. A probabilistic framework for dialog simulation and optimal strategy learning. *Audio, Speech, and Language Processing, IEEE Transactions on*, 14(2):589–599, march.

Olivier Pietquin and Helen Hastie. 2013. A survey on metrics for the evaluation of user simulations. *Knowledge Eng. Review*, 28(1):59–73.

Olivier Pietquin. 2004. *A Framework for Unsupervised Learning of Dialogue Strategies*. Ph.D. thesis, Faculté Polytechnique de Mons, TCTS Lab (Belgique), apr.

Olivier Pietquin. 2006. Consistent goal-directed user model for realisitc man-machine task-oriented spoken dialogue simulation. In *Multimedia and Expo, 2006 IEEE International Conference on*, pages 425–428. IEEE.

David Reitter and Johanna D. Moore. 2007. Predicting success in dialogue. In *ACL*.

Verena Rieser and Oliver Lemon. 2006. Cluster-based user simulations for learning dialogue strategies. In *INTERSPEECH 2006 - ICSLP, Ninth International Conference on Spoken Language Processing*, September.

Stéphane Rossignol, Olivier Pietquin, and Michel Ianotto. 2010. Simulation of the grounding process in spoken dialog systems with bayesian networks. In *IWSDS*, pages 110–121.

Stéphane Rossignol, Olivier Pietquin, and Michel Ianotto. 2011. Training a bn-based user model for dialogue simulation with missing data. In *IJCNLP*, pages 598–604.

Nicholas Roy, Joelle Pineau, and Sebastian Thrun. 2000. Spoken dialogue management using probabilistic reasoning. In *Proceedings of the 38th Annual Meeting on Association for Computational Linguistics*, ACL '00, pages 93–100, Stroudsburg, PA, USA. Association for Computational Linguistics.

Jost Schatzmann and Steve Young. 2009. The hidden agenda user simulation model. *Audio, Speech, and Language Processing, IEEE Transactions on*, 17(4):733–747.

Konrad Scheffler and Steve Young. 2002. Automatic learning of dialogue strategy using dialogue simulation and reinforcement learning. In *Proceedings of HLT 2002*.

Satinder Singh, Diane J. Litman, Michael Kearns, and Marilyn A. Walker. 2002. Optimizing dialogue management with reinforcement learning: Experiments with the njfun system. *Journal of Artificial Intelligence Research*, 16:105–133.

Henry S. Thompson, Anne Anderson, Ellen G. Bard, Gwyneth D. Sneddon, Alison Newlands, and Cathy Sotillo. 1993. The HCRC Map Task corpus: natural dialogue for speech recognition. In *Proceedings of the workshop on Human Language Technology*, HLT '93, pages 25–30, Stroudsburg, PA, USA. Association for Computational Linguistics.

Adam Vogel and Daniel Jurafsky. 2010. Learning to follow navigational directions. In *ACL 2010, Proceedings of the 48th Annual Meeting of the Association for Computational Linguistics, July 11-16, 2010, Uppsala, Sweden*, pages 806–814. The Association for Computer Linguistics.

Jason D. Williams and Steve Young. 2007. Partially observable markov decision processes for spoken dialog systems. *Computer Speech and Language*, 21(2):393–422.

Jason D. Williams. 2007. Applying pomdps to dialog systems in the troubleshooting domain. In *Proceedings of the Workshop on Bridging the Gap: Academic and Industrial Research in Dialog Technologies*, NAACL-HLT '07, pages 1–8, Morristown, NJ, USA. Association for Computational Linguistics.

Steve Young, Milica Gasic, Blaise Thomson, and Jason D. Williams. 2013. Pomdp-based statistical spoken dialog systems: A review. *Proceedings of the IEEE*, 101(5):1160–1179.

Verbose, Laconic or Just Right: A Simple Computational Model of Content Appropriateness under Length Constraints

Annie Louis*
School of Infomatics
University of Edinburgh
Edinburgh EH8 9AB
alouis@inf.ed.ac.uk

Ani Nenkova
Computer and Information Science
University of Pennsylvania
Philadelphia, PA 19103
nenkova@seas.upenn.edu

Abstract

Length constraints impose implicit requirements on the type of content that can be included in a text. Here we propose the first model to computationally assess if a text deviates from these requirements. Specifically, our model predicts the appropriate length for texts based on content types present in a snippet of constant length. We consider a range of features to approximate content type, including syntactic phrasing, constituent compression probability, presence of named entities, sentence specificity and intersentence continuity. Weights for these features are learned using a corpus of summaries written by experts and on high quality journalistic writing. During test time, the difference between actual and predicted length allows us to quantify text verbosity. We use data from manual evaluation of summarization systems to assess the verbosity scores produced by our model. We show that the automatic verbosity scores are significantly negatively correlated with manual content quality scores given to the summaries.

1 Introduction

In dialog, the appropriate length of a speaker turn and the amount of detail in it are hugely influenced by the pragmatic context. For example what constitutes an appropriate answer to the question "How was your vacation?" would be very different when the question is asked as two acquaintances pass each other in the corridor or right after two friends have ordered dinner at a restaurant. Similarly in writing, content is tailored to explicitly defined or implicitly inferred constraints on the appropriate length of text. Many academics have experienced the frustration of needing to adjust their writing when they need to write a short abstract of two hundred words or an answer to reviewer in no more than five hundred words.

50 word summary:
The De Beers cartel has kept the diamond market stable by matching supply to demand. African nations have recently demanded better terms from the cartel. After the Soviet breakup, De Beers contracted for diamonds with the Yukutian Republic. The US remains the largest diamond market, followed by Japan.
100 word summary:
The De Beers cartel, controlled by the Oppenheimer family controls 80% of the uncut diamond market through its Central Selling Organization. The cartel has kept the diamond market stable by maintaining a buffer pool of diamonds for matching supply to demand. De Beers opened a new mine in 1992 and extended the life of two others through underground mining. Innovations have included automated processing and bussing workers in daily from their homes. African nations have recently demanded better terms. After the Soviet breakup, De Beers contracted for diamonds with the Yukutian Republic. The US remains the largest diamond market, followed by Japan.

Table 1: 50 and 100 word summaries written by the same person for the same set of documents

For a specific application-related example consider the texts in Table 1. These are summaries of a set of news articles discussing the De Beers diamond cartel, written by the same person.[1] The first text is written with the instruction to produce a summary of about 50 words while the latter is in response to a request for a 100 word summary. Obviously the longer summary contains more details. It doesn't however simply extend the shorter summary with more sentences; additional details

*Work done while at University of Pennsylvania.

[1]These summaries come from the Document Understanding Conference dataset (year 2001).

Proceedings of the 14th Conference of the European Chapter of the Association for Computational Linguistics, pages 636–644, Gothenburg, Sweden, April 26-30 2014. ©2014 Association for Computational Linguistics are interspersed with the original shorter summary.

The performance of a range of human-machine applications can be enhanced if they had the ability to predict the appropriate length of a system contribution and the type of content appropriate for that length. Such applications include document generation (O'Donnell, 1997), soccer commentator (Chen and Mooney, 2008) and question answering with different compression rates for different types of questions (Kaisser et al., 2008). Predicting the type of content appropriate for the given length alone would be highly desirable, for example in automatic essay grading, summarization and even in information retrieval, in which verbose writing is particularly undesirable. In this respect, our work supplements recent computational methods to predict varied aspects of writing quality, such as popular writing style and phrasing in novels (Ganjigunte Ashok et al., 2013), science journalism (Louis and Nenkova, 2013), and social media content (Danescu-Niculescu-Mizil et al., 2012; Lakkaraju et al., 2013).

Our work is the first to explore text verbosity. We introduce a simple application-oriented definition of verbosity and a model to automatically predict verbosity scores. We start with a brief overview of our approach in the next section.

2 Text length and content appropriateness

In this first model of verbosity, we do not carry out an elaborate annotation experiment to create labels for verbosity. There are two main reasons for this choice: a) People find it hard to distinguish between individual aspects of quality and often the ratings for different aspects are highly correlated (Conroy and Dang, 2008; Pitler et al., 2010) b) Moreover, for verbosity in particular, the most appropriate data for annotation would be concise and verbose versions of the same text (possibly of similar lengths). It is more likely that people can distinguish between verbosity of these controlled pairs compared to ratings on an individual article. Such writing samples are not easily available. So we have avoided the uncertainties in annotation in this first work by adopting a simpler approach based on three key ideas.

(i) We define a concise article of length l as "an article that has the appropriate types of content expected in an article of length l". Note that length is not equal to verbosity in our model. Our definition allows for articles of different lengths to be considered concise. Verbosity depends on the appropriateness of content for the article length.

(ii) We model this appropriateness of content for the given length restriction via a set of easily computable features that serve as proxies for (a) type of content and level of detail (syntactic features and sentence specificity) (b) sentence complexity (simple readability-related features), (c) secondary details (syntactic structures with high compression probability) and (d) structure (discourse relations and inter-sentence continuity).

(iii) Forgoing any explicit annotation, we simply train the model on professionally written text in which we assume content is appropriately tailored to the length requirements. We train a regression model on the well-written texts to predict the length of an article based on a single snippet of fixed (short) length from the article. For a new test article, we can obtain a predicted length from this model (length supposing the article is written concisely) based on a short snippet. We use the mismatch between the predicted and actual text length of the article to determine if it is verbose.

We believe that this definition of verbosity has natural uses in applications such as summarization. For example, current systems do not distinguish the task of summary creation for different target lengths. They simply try to maximize estimated sentence importance and to minimize repetitive information. They pay no attention to the fact that the same type of sentences are unlikely to be an optimal selection for both a 50 word and a 400 word summary.

We now briefly present the formal definition of the problem of content appropriateness for a specified text length. Let $T = (t_1, t_2, ...t_n)$ be a collection of concisely-written texts and let $l(t_i)$ denote the length of text t_i. The learning task is to obtain a function based on the content type properties of t_i which helps to predict $l(t_i)$. More specifically, we are given a snippet from t_i, called s_{t_i}, of a constant length k where k is a parameter of our model and $k < \min_{t_j} l(t_j)$. The mapping f is learned based on the constant length snippet only and the aim is to predict the original text length.

$$f(s_{t_i}) \rightarrow \hat{l}(t_i)$$

In our work we choose to work with topical segments from documents rather than the complete documents themselves.

Once the model is trained, we identify the verbosity for a test article as follows: Let us consider a new topic segment t_x during test time. Let the length of the segment be l. We obtain a snippet s_{t_x} of size k from t_x. Now assume that our model predicts $f(s_{t_x}) = \hat{l}$.

Case 1: $\hat{l} \simeq l$, the content type in t_x matches the content types generally present in articles of length l. We consider such articles as concise.

Case 2: $\hat{l} \gg l$, the type of content included in t_x is really suitable for longer and detailed topic segments. Thus t_x is likely conveying too much detail given its length i.e. it is verbose.

Case 3: $\hat{l} \ll l$, the content in t_x is of the type that a skillful writer would include in a much shorter and less detail-oriented text. Thus t_x is likely lacking appropriate details (laconic).

We compute the following scores to quantify verbosity:

Predicted length. is the model prediction $\hat{l}$.

Verbosity degree. This score is the difference between the predicted length and the actual length of the text, $\hat{l} - l$. Positive values of the score indicate the degree of verbosity, negative values indicate that the text is laconic.

Deviation score. Since both being verbose and being laconic is potentially problematic for text, we define a score which does not differentiate the type of mismatch. This score is given by the absolute magnitude $|\hat{l} - l|$.

The next section describes the features used for indicating the content type of a snippet. In Section 4, we test the features on a four-way classification task to predict the length of a human-written summary based on a snippet of the summary. In Section 5, we extend our model to a regression setting by learning feature weights on news articles of varied lengths from the New York Times (NYT), which we consider to be a sample in which content is chosen appropriately for each article length. Finally in Section 6 we evaluate the model trained on NYT articles on machine-produced summaries and confirm that summaries scored with higher verbosity by our model also receive poor content quality scores during manual evaluation.

3 Features mapping content type to appropriate length

We propose a diverse set of 87 features for characterizing content type. These features are computed over the constant length snippet sampled from an article. All the syntax based features are computed from the constituency trees produced from the Stanford Parser (Klein and Manning, 2003).

Length of units (10 features).

This set of features captures basic word and sentence length, and redundancy properties of the snippet. It includes number of sentences, average sentence length in words, average word length in characters, and type to token ratio. We also include the counts of noun phrases, verb phrases and prepositional phrases and the average length in words of these three phrase types.

Syntactic realization (30 features).

We compute the grammatical productions in a set of around 47,000 sentences taken from the AQUAINT corpus (Graff, 2002) We select the most frequent 15 productions in this set that involve a description of entities, i.e the LHS (left-hand side) of the production is a noun phrase. The count of each of these productions is added as a feature allowing us to track what type of information about the entities is conveyed in the snippet. We also add features for the most frequent 15 productions whose LHS is not a noun phrase.

Discourse relations (5 features).

These features are based on the hypothesis that different discourse relations would vary in their appropriateness for articles of different lengths. For example causal information may be included only in more detailed texts.

We use a tool (Pitler and Nenkova, 2009) to identify all explicit discourse connectives in our snippets, along with the general semantic class of the connective (temporal, comparison, contingency and expansion). We use the number of discourse connectives of each of the four types as features, as well as the total number of connectives.

Continuity (6 features).

These features capture the degree to which adjacent sentences in the snippet are related and continue the topic. The amount of continuity for subtopics is likely to vary for long and short texts.

We add the number of pronouns and determiners as two features. Another feature is the average word overlap value between adjacent sentences. For computing the overlap measure, we represent every sentence as a vector where each dimension represents a word. The number of times the word appears in the sentence is the value for that dimension. Cosine similarity is computed between the vectors of adjacent sentences and the average value of the similarity across all pairs of adjacent sentences is the feature value.

We also run the Stanford Coreference tool (Raghunathan et al., 2010) to identity pronoun and entity coreference links within the snippet. The number of total coreference links, and the number of intra- and inter-sentence links are added as three separate features.

Amount of detail (7 features).

To indicate descriptive words, we compute the number of adjectives and adverbs (two features). We also include the total number of named entities (NEs), average length of NEs in words and the number of sentences that do not have any NEs. The named entities were identified using the Stanford NER recognition tool (Finkel et al., 2005).

We also use the predictions of a classifier trained to identify general versus specific sentences. We use a data set of general and specific sentences and features described in Louis and Nenkova (2011) to implement a sentence specificity model. The classifier produces a binary prediction and also a graded score for specificity. We add two features—the percentage of specific sentences and the average specificity score of words.

Compression likelihood (29 features).

These features use an external source of information about content importance. Specifically, we use data commonly employed to develop statistical models for sentence compression (Knight and Marcu, 2002; McDonald, 2006; Galley and McKeown, 2007). It consists of pairs of sentences in an original text and a professional summary of that text. In every pair, one of the sentences (source) appeared in the original text and the other is a shorter version with the superfluous details deleted. Both sentences were produced by people.

We use the dataset created by Galley and McKeown (2007). The sentences are taken from the Ziff Davis Corpus which contains articles about technology products. This data also contains alignment between the constituency parse nodes of the source and summary sentence pair. Through the alignment it is possible to track nodes that where preserved during compression.

On this data, we identify for every production in the source sentence whether it undergoes deletion in the compressed sentence. A production (LHS $\rightarrow$ RHS) is said to undergo deletion when either the LHS node or any of the nodes in the RHS do not appear in the compressed sentence. Only productions which involve non-terminals in the RHS are used for this analysis as lexical items could be rather corpus-specific. The proportion of times a production undergoes deletion is called the *deletion probability*. We also incorporate frequency of the production with the deletion probability to obtain a representative set of 25 productions which are frequently deleted and also occur commonly. This *deletion score* is computed as: *deletion probability* * log(*frequency of production in source sentences*)

Parentheticals appear in the list as would be expected and also productions involving conjunctions, prepositional phrases and subordinate clauses. We expect that such productions will indicate the presence of details that are only appropriate for longer texts.

To compute the compression-related features for a snippet, we first obtain the set of all productions in the sentences from the snippet. We add features that indicate the number of times each of the top 25 'most deleted' productions was used in the snippet. We also use the sum, average and product of deletion probabilities for set of snippet productions as features. The product feature gives the likelihood of the text being deleted. We also add the perplexity value based on this likelihood, $P^{-1/n}$ where P is the likelihood and n is the number of productions from the snippet for which we have deletion information in our data.[2]

For training a model, we need texts which we can assume are written in a concise manner. We use two sources of data—summaries written by people and high quality news articles.

4 A classification model on expert summaries

Here we use a collection of news summaries written by expert analysts for four different lengths and build a classification model to predict given a snippet what is the length of the summary from which the snippet was taken. This task only differentiates four lengths but is a useful first approach for testing our assumptions and features.

4.1 Data

We use human written summaries from the Document Understanding Conference (DUC[3]) evalua-

[2]Some productions may not have appeared in the Ziff Davis Corpus.

[3]http://duc.nist.gov

tion workshops conducted in 2001 and 2002. An input given for summarization contains 10 to 15 documents on a topic. The person had to create 50, 100, 200 and 400 word summaries for each of the inputs. These summary writers are retired information analysts and we can assume that their summaries are of high quality and concise nature. Further, the four different length summaries for an input are produced by the same person.[4] Therefore differences in length are not confounded by differences in writing style of different people.

The 2001 dataset has 90 summaries for each of the four lengths. In 2002, there are 116 summaries for each length. All of the summaries are abstracts, i.e. people wrote the summary in their own words, with the exception of one set. In 2002, abstracts were only created for 50, 100 and 200 lengths. However, extracts created by people are available for 400 words. In extracts, the summary writer is only allowed to choose complete sentences (no edits can be done), however, the sentences can be ordered in the summary and people tend to create coherent extractive summaries as well. Since it is desirable to have data for another length, we also include the 400-word extracts from the 2002 data.

4.2 Snippet selection

We choose 50 words as the snippet length for our experiment since the length of the shortest summaries is 50. We experiment with multiple ways to select a snippet: the first 50 words of the summary (START), the last 50 words (END) and 50 words starting at a randomly chosen sentence (RANDOM). However, we do not truncate any sentence in the middle to meet the constraint for 50 words. We allow a leeway of 20 words so that snippets can range from 30 to 70 words. When a snippet could not be created within this word limit (eg. the summary has one sentence which is longer than 70 words), we ignore the example.

4.3 Classification results

The task is to predict the length of the summary from which the fixed length snippet was taken, i.e. 4-way classification—50, 100, 200 or a 400 word summary. We trained an SVM classifier with a radial basis kernel on the 2001 data. The regularization and kernel parameters were tuned using 10-fold cross validation on the training set. The accuracies of classification on the 2002 data are shown

[4] Different inputs however may be summarized by different assessors.

snippet position	accuracy
START	38.4
RANDOM	34.4
END	39.3

Table 2: Length prediction results on DUC summaries

in Table 2. Since there are four equal classes, the random baseline performance is 25%.

The START and END position snippets gave the best accuracies, 38% and 39% which are 13-14% absolute improvement above the baseline. At the same time, there is much scope for improvement. The confusion matrices showed that 50 and 400 word lengths, the extreme ones in this dataset, were the easiest to predict. Most of the confusions occur with the 100 and 200 word summaries.

The overall accuracy is slightly better when snippets from the END of the summary are chosen compared to those from the START. However, with START snippets, better prediction of different length summaries was obtained, whereas the accuracy in the END case comes mainly from correct prediction of 50 and 400 word summaries. So we use the START selection for further experiments.

5 A regression approach based on New York Times editorials

We next build a model where we predict a wider range of lengths compared to just the four classes we had before. Here our training set comprises news articles from the New York Times (NYT) based on the assumption that edited news from a good source would be of high quality overall.

5.1 Data

We obtain the text of the articles from the NYT Annotated Corpus (Sandhaus, 2008). We choose the articles from the opinion section of the newspaper since they are likely to have good topic continuity and related content compared to general news which often contain lists of facts. We further use only the editorial articles to ensure that the articles are of high quality.

We collect 10,724 opinion articles from years 2000 to 2007 of the NYT. We divide each article into topic segments using the unsupervised topic segmentation method developed by Eisenstein and Barzilay (2008). We use the following heuristic to decide on the number of topic segments for each article. If the article has fewer than 50 sentences, we create segments such that the expected length of a segment is 10 sentences, i.e, we assign the number of segments as number of sentences divided by 10. When the article is longer, we create 5 segments. This step gives us 18,167 topic segments, ranging in length from 14 to 773 words.

We use a stratified sampling method to select training and test examples. Starting from 90 words and upto a maximum length of 500 words, we divide the range into bins in increments of 30 words. From each bin we select 100 texts for training and around 35 for testing. There are 2,100 topic segments in the training set and 681 for testing.

5.2 Training approach

We use 100 word snippets for our experiments. We learn a linear regression model on the training data using *lm* function in R (R Development Core Team, 2011). The features which turned out significant in the model are shown in Table 3. The significance value shown is associated with a t-test to determine if the feature can be ignored from the model. We report the coefficients for the significant features under column 'Beta'. The R-squared value of the model is 0.219.

Many of the most significant features are related to entities. Longer texts are associated with larger number of noun phrases but they tend not to be proper names. Average word and sentence length also increase with article length, at the same time, longer articles have shorter verb phrases. Specific sentences and determiners are also positively related to article length. At the discourse level, comparison relations increase with length.

5.3 Accuracy of predictions

On the test data, the lengths predicted by the model have a Pearson correlation of 0.44 with the true length of the topic segment. The correlation is highly significant (p-value $< 2.2e\text{-}16$). The Spearman correlation value is 0.43 and the Kendall Tau is 0.29, both also highly significant. These results show that our model can distinguish content types for a range of article lengths.

6 Text quality assessment for automatic summaries

In the models above, we learned weights which relate the features to the length of concisely written human summaries and NYT articles. Now we use the model to compute verbosity scores and assess how well they correlate with text quality scores assigned by people.

Feature	**Beta**	**p-value**
Positive coefficients		
total noun phrases	6.052e+00	***
avg. word length	3.201e+01	***
avg. sent. length	3.430e+00	**
avg. NP length	6.557e+00	*
no. of adverbs	4.244e+00	**
% specific sentences	4.773e+01	**
comparison relations	9.296e+00	.
determiners	2.955e+00	*
NP → NP PP	4.305e+00	*
NP → NP NP	1.174e+01	*
PP → IN S	7.268e+00	.
WHNP → WDT	1.196e+01	**
Negative coefficients		
NP → NNP	-8.630e+00	***
no. of sentences	-2.498e+01	**
no. of relations	-1.128e+01	**
avg. VP length	-2.982e+00	**
type token ratio	-1.784e+02	*
NP → NP , SBAR	-1.567e+01	*
NP → NP , NP	-9.582e+00	*
NP → DT NN	-3.423e+00	.
VP → VBD	-1.189e+01	.
S → S : S .	-1.951e+01	.
ADVP → RB	-4.198e+00	.

Table 3: Significant regression coefficients in the length prediction model on NYT editorials. '***' indicates p-value < 0.001, '**' is p-value < 0.01, '*' is < 0.05 and '.' is < 0.1

We perform this evaluation for the system summaries produced during the 2006 DUC evaluation workshop. There are 22 automatic systems in that evaluation.[5] Each system produced 250 word summaries for each of 20 multidocument inputs. Each summary was evaluated by DUC assessors for multiple dimensions of quality. We examine how the verbosity predictions from our model are related to these summary scores. In this experiment, we use automatic summaries only.

6.1 Gold-standard summary scores

Two kinds of manual scores—content and linguistic quality—are available for each summary from the DUC dataset. One type of content score, the 'pyramid score' (Nenkova et al., 2007) computes the overlap of semantic units of the system summary with that present in human-written summaries for the same input. For the other content score, called 'content responsiveness', assessors directly provide a rating to summaries on a scale from 1 (very poor) to 5 (very good) without using any reference human summaries.

[5] We use only the set of systems for which pyramid scores are also available.

Verbosity scores	Corr. with actual length
predicted length	-0.01
verbosity degree	-0.29
deviation score	-0.27

Table 4: Relationship between verbosity scores and summary length

Linguistic quality is evaluated separately from content for different aspects. Manually assigned scores are available for *non-redundancy* (absence of repetitive information), *focus* (well-established topic), and *coherence* (good flow from sentence to sentence). For each aspect, the summary is rated on a scale from 1 (very poor) to 5 (very good).

This dataset is less ideal for our task in some ways as system summaries often lack coherent arrangement of sentences. Some of our features which rely on coreference and adjacent sentence overlaps when computed on these summaries could be misleading. However, this data contains large scale quality ratings for different quality aspects which allow us to examine our verbosity predictions across multiple dimensions.

6.2 Verbosity scores and summary quality

We choose the first 100 words of each summary as the snippet. No topic segmentation was done on the summary data. We use the NYT regression model to predict the expected lengths of these summaries and compute its verbosity and deviation scores as defined in Section 2.

We also compute two other measures for comparison.

Actual length. To understand how the verbosity scores are related to the length of the summary, we also keep track of the actual number of words present in the summary.

Redundancy score: We also add a simple score to our analysis to indicate redundancy between adjacent sentences in the summary. It is simple measure of verbosity since repetitive information leads to lower informativeness overall. The score is the cosine similarity based sentence overlap measure described in Section 3.

For each of the 22 automatic systems, the scores of its 20 summaries (one for each input) are averaged. (We ignore empty summaries and those which are much smaller than the 100 word snippet that we require). We find the average values for both our verbosity based scores above and the gold-standard scores (pyramid, content responsiveness, focus, non-redundancy and coherence). We also compute the average value of the summary lengths for each system.

	Content quality	
scores	Pyramid	Resp.
actual length	0.64*	0.43*
predicted length	-0.29	-0.11
verbosity degree	-0.47*	-0.23
deviation score	-0.44*	-0.29
redundancy score	-0.01	-0.06

	Linguistic quality		
scores	Non-red	Focus	Coher.
actual length	-0.32	-0.25	-0.32
predicted length	0.48*	0.39·	0.38·
verbosity degree	0.55*	0.44*	0.46*
deviation score	0.53*	0.40·	0.42·
redundancy score	0.06	0.32	0.23

Table 5: Pearson correlations between verbosity scores and gold standard summary quality scores

First we examine the relationship between verbosity scores and the actual summary lengths. The Pearson correlations between the three verbosity measures and true length of the summaries are reported in Table 4. The verbosity scores are not significantly related to summary length. They seem to have an inverse relationship but the correlations are not significant even at 90% confidence level. This result supports our hypothesis that verbosity scores based on expected length are different from the actual summary length.

Next Table 5 presents the Pearson correlations of the verbosity measures with gold standard summary quality scores. Since the number of points (systems) is only 22, we indicate whether the correlations are significant at two levels, 0.05 (marked by a '*' superscript) and 0.1 (a '.' superscript).

The first line of the table indicates that longer summaries are associated with higher content scores both according to pyramid and content responsiveness evaluations. This result also supports our hypothesis that length alone does not indicate verbosity. Longer summaries on average have better content quality. The length is not significantly related to linguistic quality scores but there is a negative relationship in general.

On the other hand, all the three verbosity scores have a negative correlation with content scores. The verbosity degree score is the strongest indicator of summary quality with -0.47 (significant) correlation with pyramid score. At the same time however, verbosity is preferred for linguistic quality. This effect could arise due to the fact these summaries are bags of unordered sentences. Therefore verbose style could be perceived as hav-

System 23's summary: Actual length = 253 words, Predicted length = 343 words, Verbosity degree = 90
A senior Scotland Yard police officer apologized to the parents of a black teenager slain five years ago in a race killing that has become the focus of debate over relations between police and ethnic minorities. Black teenager Stephen Lawrence was stabbed to death at a bus-stop in Eltham, south London by five white youngsters six years ago. The parents of the murdered black teenager Stephen Lawrence began legal action against the men suspected of his killing. Two suspects in the Stephen Lawrence murder case and one other man were arrested on suspicion of theft by Kent Police. The five men suspected of killing Stephen Lawrence were thumped and pelted with bottles by an enraged crowd Tuesday after a day of evasive and implausible evidence that made a mockery of their appearance before the public inquiry. The dawn raids came as police questioned three men in connection with the country's most notorious racist crime: the unsolved 1993 murder of black teenager Stephen Lawrence. A public inquiry after the Lawrence case found London police institutionally racist, prompting a government pledge to take a more active role in combating racial intolerance. The report, commissioned after police botched the investigation into the 1993 racially motivated murder of a black teenager, Stephen Lawrence has put pressure on Sir Paul Condon, the Metropolitan Police chief, to resign. British authorities and police have learned from the 1993 murder of black teen-ager Stephen Lawrence by a gang of white youths and the failure of the police to
System 18's summary: Actual length = 244 words, Predicted length = 597 words, Verbosity degree = 353
The government, which has received praise from backers of the Lawrence family for its pursuit of the case, came in for criticism on Monday for actions it took this weekend to prevent publication of a leaked version of the report, which is due to be made public on Wednesday. Sir William Macpherson, a retired High Court justice who was the author of the report and chairman of the eight-month government inquiry, defined institutional racism as 'the collective failure of an organization to provide an appropriate professional service to people because of their color, culture or ethnic origin' reflected, he said, in 'processes, attitudes and behavior which amounts to discrimination through unwitting prejudice ignorance, thoughtlessness and racist stereotyping.' Richard Norton-Taylor, whose play about Lawrence's killing, 'The Color of Justice,' has been playing to rave reviews in London, said that the attention paid to the Lawrence case and others was a sign that British attitudes toward the overarching authority of the police and other institutions were finally being called into question. She said British authorities and police have learned from the 1993 murder of black teenager Stephen Lawrence by a gang of white youths and the failure of the police to investigate his death adequately A senior Scotland Yard police officer Wednesday apologized to the parents of a black teenager slain five years ago in a race killing that has become the focus of debate over relations between police and ethnic minorities.

Table 6: Summaries produced by two systems for input D0624 (DUC 2006) shown with the verbosity scores from our model

ing greater coherence compared to short and succinct sentences which are jumbled such that it is hard to decipher the full story.

The simple redundancy score (last row of the table) does not have any significant relationship to quality scores. One reason could be that most summarization systems make an effort to reduce redundant information (Carbonell and Goldstein, 1998) and therefore a simple measure of word overlap is not helpful for distinguishing quality.

As examples of the predictions from our model, Table 6 shows two summaries produced for the same input by two different systems. They both have almost the same actual length but the first received a prediction close to its actual length while the other is predicted with a much higher verbosity degree score. Intuitively, the second example is more verbose compared to the first one. According to the manual evaluations as well, the first summary receives a higher score of 0.4062 (pyramid) compared to 0.2969 for the second summary.

7 Conclusions

There are several ways in which our approach can be improved. In this first work, we have avoided the complexities of manual annotation. In future, we will explore the feasibility of human annotations of verbosity on a suitable corpus, such as news articles on the same topic from different sources. In addition, our current approach only considers a snippet of the text or topic segment during prediction but ignores the writing in the remaining text. In future work, we plan to use a sliding window to obtain and aggregate length predictions while considering the full text.

Acknowledgements

This work was partially supported by a NSF CAREER 0953445 award. We also thank the anonymous reviewers for their comments.

References

J. Carbonell and J. Goldstein. 1998. The use of mmr, diversity-based reranking for reordering documents and producing summaries. In *Proceedings of SIGIR*, pages 335–336.

D. L. Chen and R. J. Mooney. 2008. Learning to sportscast: a test of grounded language acquisition. In *Proceedings of ICML*, pages 128–135.

J. M. Conroy and H. T. Dang. 2008. Mind the gap: Dangers of divorcing evaluations of summary content from linguistic quality. In *Proceedings of COLING*, pages 145–152.

C. Danescu-Niculescu-Mizil, J. Cheng, J. Kleinberg, and L. Lee. 2012. You had me at hello: How phrasing affects memorability. In *Proceedings of ACL*, pages 892–901.

J. Eisenstein and R. Barzilay. 2008. Bayesian unsupervised topic segmentation. In *Proceedings of EMNLP*, pages 334–343.

J. R. Finkel, T. Grenager, and C. Manning. 2005. Incorporating non-local information into information extraction systems by gibbs sampling. In *Proceedings of ACL*, pages 363–370.

M. Galley and K. McKeown. 2007. Lexicalized markov grammars for sentence compression. In *Proceedings of HLT-NAACL*.

V. Ganjigunte Ashok, S. Feng, and Y. Choi. 2013. Success with style: Using writing style to predict the success of novels. In *Proceedings of EMNLP*, pages 1753–1764.

D. Graff. 2002. The AQUAINT Corpus of English News Text. *Corpus number LDC2002T31, Linguistic Data Consortium, Philadelphia*.

M. Kaisser, M. A. Hearst, and J. B. Lowe. 2008. Improving search results quality by customizing summary lengths. In *Proceedings of ACL-HLT*, pages 701–709.

D. Klein and C.D. Manning. 2003. Accurate unlexicalized parsing. In *Proceedings of ACL*, pages 423–430.

K. Knight and D. Marcu. 2002. Summarization beyond sentence extraction: A probabilistic approach to sentence compression. *Artificial Intelligence*, 139(1).

H. Lakkaraju, J. J. McAuley, and J. Leskovec. 2013. What's in a name? understanding the interplay between titles, content, and communities in social media. In *ICWSM*.

A. Louis and A. Nenkova. 2011. Automatic identification of general and specific sentences by leveraging discourse annotations. In *Proceedings of IJCNLP*, pages 605–613.

A. Louis and A. Nenkova. 2013. What makes writing great? first experiments on article quality prediction in the science journalism domain. *TACL*, 1:341–352.

R. McDonald. 2006. Discriminative sentence compression with soft syntactic evidence. In *Proceedings of EACL*.

A. Nenkova, R. Passonneau, and K. McKeown. 2007. The pyramid method: Incorporating human content selection variation in summarization evaluation. *ACM Trans. Speech Lang. Process.*, 4(2):4.

M. O'Donnell. 1997. Variable-length on-line document generation. In *Proceedings of the 6th European Workshop on Natural Language Generation*.

E. Pitler and A. Nenkova. 2009. Using syntax to disambiguate explicit discourse connectives in text. In *Proceedings of ACL-IJCNLP*, pages 13–16.

E. Pitler, A. Louis, and A. Nenkova. 2010. Automatic evaluation of linguistic quality in multi-document summarization. In *Proceedings of ACL*.

R Development Core Team, 2011. *R: A Language and Environment for Statistical Computing*. R Foundation for Statistical Computing.

K. Raghunathan, H. Lee, S. Rangarajan, N. Chambers, M. Surdeanu, D. Jurafsky, and C. Manning. 2010. A multi-pass sieve for coreference resolution. In *Proceedings of EMNLP*, pages 492–501.

E. Sandhaus. 2008. The New York Times Annotated Corpus. *Corpus number LDC2008T19, Linguistic Data Consortium, Philadelphia*.

Discovering Implicit Discourse Relations Through Brown Cluster Pair Representation and Coreference Patterns

Attapol T. Rutherford
Department of Computer Science
Brandeis University
Waltham, MA 02453, USA
tet@brandeis.edu

Nianwen Xue
Department of Computer Science
Brandeis University
Waltham, MA 02453, USA
xuen@brandeis.edu

Abstract

Sentences form coherent relations in a discourse without discourse connectives more frequently than with connectives. Senses of these implicit discourse relations that hold between a sentence pair, however, are challenging to infer. Here, we employ Brown cluster pairs to represent discourse relation and incorporate coreference patterns to identify senses of implicit discourse relations in naturally occurring text. Our system improves the baseline performance by as much as 25%. Feature analyses suggest that Brown cluster pairs and coreference patterns can reveal many key linguistic characteristics of each type of discourse relation.

1 Introduction

Sentences must be pieced together logically in a discourse to form coherent text. Many discourse relations in the text are signaled explicitly through a closed set of discourse connectives. Simply disambiguating the meaning of discourse connectives can determine whether adjacent clauses are temporally or causally related (Pitler et al., 2008; Wellner et al., 2009). Discourse relations and their senses, however, can also be inferred by the reader even without discourse connectives. These implicit discourse relations in fact outnumber explicit discourse relations in naturally occurring text. Inferring types or senses of implicit discourse relations remains a key challenge in automatic discourse analysis.

A discourse parser requires many subcomponents which form a long pipeline. The implicit discourse relation discovery has been shown to be the main performance bottleneck of an end-to-end parser (Lin et al., 2010). It is also central to many applications such as automatic summarization and question-answering systems.

Existing systems, which make heavy use of word pairs, suffer from data sparsity problem as a word pair in the training data may not appear in the test data. A better representation of two adjacent sentences beyond word pairs could have a significant impact on predicting the sense of the discourse relation that holds between them. Data-driven theory-independent word classification such as Brown clustering should be able to provide a more compact word representation (Brown et al., 1992). Brown clustering algorithm induces a hierarchy of words in a large unannotated corpus based on word co-occurrences within the window. The induced hierarchy might give rise to features that we would otherwise miss. In this paper, we propose to use the cartesian product of Brown cluster assignment of the sentence pair as an alternative abstract word representation for building an implicit discourse relation classifier.

Through word-level semantic commonalities revealed by Brown clusters and entity-level relations revealed by coreference resolution, we might be able to paint a more complete picture of the discourse relation in question. Coreference resolution unveils the patterns of entity realization within the discourse, which might provide clues for the types of the discourse relations. The information about certain entities or mentions in one sentence should be carried over to the next sentence to form a coherent relation. It is possible that coreference chains and semantically-related predicates in the local context might show some patterns that characterize types of discourse relations. We hypothesize that coreferential rates and coreference patterns created by Brown clusters should help characterize different types of discourse relations.

Here, we introduce two novel sets of features for implicit discourse relation classification. Further, we investigate the effects of using Brown clusters as an alternative word representation and analyze the impactful features that arise from

Proceedings of the 14th Conference of the European Chapter of the Association for Computational Linguistics, pages 645–654,
Gothenburg, Sweden, April 26-30 2014.

	Number of instances	
	Implicit	Explicit
COMPARISON	2503 (15.11%)	5589 (33.73%)
CONTINGENCY	4255 (25.68%)	3741 (22.58%)
EXPANSION	8861 (53.48%)	72 (0.43%)
TEMPORAL	950 (5.73%)	3684 (33.73%)
Total	16569 (100%)	13086 (100%)

Table 1: The distribution of senses of implicit discourse relations is imbalanced.

Brown cluster pairs. We also study coreferential patterns in different types of discourse relations in addition to using them to boost the performance of our classifier. These two sets of features along with previously used features outperform the baseline systems by approximately 5% absolute across all categories and reveal many important characteristics of implicit discourse relations.

2 Sense annotation in Penn Discourse Treebank

The Penn Discourse Treebank (PDTB) is the largest corpus richly annotated with explicit and implicit discourse relations and their senses (Prasad et al., 2008). PDTB is drawn from Wall Street Journal articles with overlapping annotations with the Penn Treebank (Marcus et al., 1993). Each discourse relation contains the information about the extent of the arguments, which can be a sentence, a constituent, or an incontiguous span of text. Each discourse relation is also annotated with the sense of the relation that holds between the two arguments. In the case of implicit discourse relations, where the discourse connectives are absent, the most appropriate connective is annotated.

The senses are organized hierarchically. Our focus is on the top level senses because they are the four fundamental discourse relations that various discourse analytic theories seem to converge on (Mann and Thompson, 1988). The top level senses are COMPARISON, CONTINGENCY, EXPANSION, and TEMPORAL.

The explicit and implicit discourse relations almost orthogonally differ in their distributions of senses (Table 1). This difference has a few implications for studying implicit discourse relations and uses of discourse connectives (Patterson and Kehler, 2013). For example, TEMPORAL relations constitute only 5% of the implicit relations but 33% of the explicit relations because they might not be as natural to create without discourse connectives. On the other hand, EXPANSION relations might be more cleanly achieved without ones as indicated by its dominance in the implicit discourse relations. This imbalance in class distribution requires greater care in building statistical classifiers (Wang et al., 2012).

3 Experiment setup

We followed the setup of the previous studies for a fair comparison with the two baseline systems by Pitler et al. (2009) and Park and Cardie (2012). The task is formulated as four separate one-against-all binary classification problems: one for each top level sense of implicit discourse relations. In addition, we add one more classification task with which to test the system. We merge ENTREL with EXPANSION relations to follow the setup used by the two baseline systems. An argument pair is annotated with ENTREL in PDTB if an entity-based coherence and no other type of relation can be identified between the two arguments in the pair. In this study, we assume that the gold standard argument pairs are provided for each relation. Most argument pairs for implicit discourse relations are a pair of adjacent sentences or adjacent clauses separated by a semicolon and should be easily extracted.

The PDTB corpus is split into a training set, development set, and test set the same way as in the baseline systems. Sections 2 to 20 are used to train classifiers. Sections 0–1 are used for developing feature sets and tuning models. Section 21–22 are used for testing the systems.

The statistical models in the following experiments are from MALLET implementation (McCallum, 2002) and libSVM (Chang and Lin, 2011). For all five binary classification tasks, we try Balanced Winnow (Littlestone, 1988), Maximum Entropy, Naive Bayes, and Support Vector Machine. The parameters and the hyperparameters of each classifier are set to their default values. The code for our model along with the data matrices is available at `github.com/attapol/brown_coref_implicit`.

4 Features

Unlike the baseline systems, all of the features in the experiments use the output from automatic natural language processing tools. We use the Stanford CoreNLP suite to lemmatize and part-of-speech tag each word (Toutanova et al., 2003;

Toutanova and Manning, 2000), obtain the phrase structure and dependency parses for each sentence (De Marneffe et al., 2006; Klein and Manning, 2003), identify all named entities (Finkel et al., 2005), and resolve coreference (Raghunathan et al., 2010; Lee et al., 2011; Lee et al., 2013).

4.1 Features used in previous work

The baseline features consist of the following: First, last, and first 3 words, numerical expressions, time expressions, average verb phrase length, modality, General Inquirer tags, polarity, Levin verb classes, and production rules. These features are described in greater detail by Pitler et al. (2009).

4.2 Brown cluster pair features

To generate Brown cluster assignment pair features, we replace each word with its hard Brown cluster assignment. We used the Brown word clusters provided by MetaOptimize (Turian et al., 2010). 3,200 clusters were induced from RCV1 corpus, which contains about 63 million tokens from Reuters English newswire. Then we take the Cartesian product of the Brown cluster assignments of the words in Arg1 and the ones of the words in Arg2. For example, suppose Arg1 has two words $w_{1,1}, w_{1,2}$, Arg2 has three words $w_{2,1}, w_{2,2}, w_{2,3}$, and then $B(.)$ maps a word to its Brown cluster assignment. A word w_{ij} is replaced by its corresponding Brown cluster assignment $b_{ij} = B(w_{ij})$. The resulting word pair features are $(b_{1,1}, b_{2,1})$, $(b_{1,1}, b_{2,2})$, $(b_{1,1}, b_{2,3})$, $(b_{1,2}, b_{2,1})$, $(b_{1,2}, b_{2,2})$, and $(b_{1,2}, b_{2,3})$.

Therefore, this feature set can generate $O(3200^2)$ binary features. The feature set size is orders of magnitude smaller than using the actual words, which can generate $O(V^2)$ distinct binary features where V is the size of the vocabulary.

4.3 Coreference-based features

We want to take advantage of the semantics of the sentence pairs even more by considering how coreferential entities play out in the sentence pairs. We consider various inter-sentential coreference patterns to include as features and also to better describe each type of discourse relation with respect to its place in the coreference chain.

For compactness in explaining the following features, we define *similar words* to be the words assigned to the same Brown cluster.

Number of coreferential pairs: We count the number of inter-sentential coreferential pairs. We expect that EXPANSION relations should be more likely to have coreferential pairs because the detail or information about an entity mentioned in Arg1 should be expanded in Arg2. Therefore, entity sharing might be difficult to avoid.

Similar nouns and verbs: A binary feature indicating whether similar or coreferential nouns are the arguments of the similar predicates. Predicates and arguments are identified by dependency parses. We notice that sometimes the author uses synonyms while trying to expand on the previous predicates or entities. The words that indicate the common topics might be paraphrased, so exact string matching cannot detect whether the two arguments still focus on the same topic. This might be useful for identifying CONTINGENCY relations as they usually discuss two causally-related events that involve two seemingly unrelated agents and/or predicates.

Similar subject or main predicates: A binary feature indicating whether the main verbs of the two arguments have the same subjects or not and another binary feature indicating whether the main verbs are similar or not. For our purposes, the two subjects are said to be the same if they are coreferential or assigned to the same Brown cluster. We notice that COMPARISON relations usually have different subjects for the same main verbs and that TEMPORAL relations usually have the same subjects but different main verbs.

4.4 Feature selection and training sample reweighting

The nature of the task and the dataset poses at least two problems in creating a classifier. First, the classification task requires a large number of features, some of which are too rare and inconducive to parameter estimation. Second, the label distribution is highly imbalanced (Table 1) and this might degrade the performance of the classifiers (Japkowicz, 2000). Recently, Park and Cardie (2012) and Wang et al. (2012) addressed these problems directly by optimally select a subset of features and training samples. Unlike previous work, we do not discard any of data in the training set to balance the label distribution. Instead, we reweight the training samples in each class during parameter estimation such that the performance on the development set is maximized. In addition, the

	Current			Park and Cardie (2012)	Pitler et al. (2009)
	P	R	F_1	F_1	F_1
COMPARISON vs others	27.34	72.41	**39.70**	31.32	21.96
CONTINGENCY vs others	44.52	69.96	**54.42**	49.82	47.13
EXPANSION vs others	59.59	85.50	70.23	-	-
EXP+ENTREL vs others	69.26	95.92	**80.44**	79.22	76.42
TEMPORAL vs others	18.52	63.64	**28.69**	26.57	16.76

Table 2: Our classifier outperform the previous systems across all four tasks without the use of gold-standard parses and coreference resolution.

COMPARISON		
Feature set	F_1	% change
All features	39.70	-
All excluding Brown cluster pairs	35.71	-10.05%
All excluding Production rules	37.27	-6.80%
All excluding First, last, and First 3	39.18	-1.40%
All excluding Polarity	39.39	-0.79%

CONTINGENCY		
Feature set	F_1	% change
All	54.42	-
All excluding Brown cluster pairs	51.50	-5.37%
All excluding First, last, and First 3	53.56	-1.58%
All excluding Polarity	53.82	-1.10%
All excluding Coreference	53.92	-0.92%

EXPANSION		
Feature set	F_1	% change
All	70.23	-
All excluding Brown cluster pairs	67.48	-3.92%
All excluding First, last, and First 3	69.43	-1.14%
All excluding Inquirer tags	69.73	-0.71%
All excluding Polarity	69.92	-0.44%

TEMPORAL		
Feature set	F_1	% change
All	28.69	-
All excluding Brown cluster pairs	24.53	-14.50%
All excluding Production rules	26.51	-7.60%
All excluding First, last, and First 3	26.56	-7.42%
All excluding Polarity	27.42	-4.43%

Table 3: Ablation study: The four most impactful feature classes and their relative percentage changes are shown. Brown cluster pair features are the most impactful across all relation types.

number of occurrences for each feature must be greater than a cut-off, which is also tuned on the development set to yield the highest performance on the development set.

5 Results

Our experiments show that the Brown cluster and coreference features along with the features from the baseline systems improve the performance for all discourse relations (Table 2). Consistent with the results from previous work, the Naive Bayes classifier outperforms MaxEnt, Balanced Winnow, and Support Vector Machine across all tasks regardless of feature pruning criteria and training sample reweighting. A possible explanation is that the small dataset size in comparison with the large number of features might favor a generative model like Naive Bayes (Jordan and Ng, 2002). So we only report the performance from the Naive Bayes classifiers.

It is noteworthy that the baseline systems use the gold standard parses provided by the Penn Treebank, but ours does not because we would like to see how our system performs realistically in conjunction with other pre-processing tasks such as lemmatization, parsing, and coreference resolution. Nevertheless, our system still manages to outperform the baseline systems in all relations by a sizable margin.

Our preliminary results on implicit sense classification suggest that the Brown cluster word representation and coreference patterns might be indicative of the senses of the discourse relations, but we would like to know the extent of the impact of these novel feature sets when used in conjunction with other features. To this aim, we conduct an ablation study, where we exclude one of the feature sets at a time and then test the resulting classifier on the test set. We then rank each feature set by the relative percentage change in F_1 score when excluded from the classifier. The data split and experimental setup are identical to the ones described in the previous section but only with Naive Bayes classifiers.

The ablation study results imply that Brown cluster features are the most impactful feature set across all four types of implicit discourse relations. When ablated, Brown cluster features degrade the performance by the largest percentage compared to the other feature sets regardless of the relation types(Table 3). TEMPORAL relations benefit the most from Brown cluster features. Without them, the F_1 score drops by 4.12 absolute or 14.50% relative to the system that uses all of the features.

6 Feature analysis

6.1 Brown cluster features

This feature set is inspired by the word pair features, which are known for its effectiveness in predicting senses of discourse relations between the two arguments. Marcu et al (2002), for instance, artificially generated the implicit discourse relations and used word pair features to perform the classification tasks. Those word pair features work well in this case because their artificially generated dataset is an order of magnitude larger than PDTB. Ideally, we would want to use the word pair features instead of word cluster features if we have enough data to fit the parameters. Consequently, other less sparse handcrafted features prove to be more effective than word pair features for the PDTB data (Pitler et al., 2009). We remedy the sparsity problem by clustering the words that are distributionally similar together and greatly reduce the number of features.

Since the ablation study is not fine-grained enough to spotlight the effectiveness of the individual features, we quantify the predictiveness of each feature by its mutual information. Under Naive Bayes conditional independence assumption, the mutual information between the features and the labels can be efficiently computed in a pairwise fashion. The mutual information between a binary feature X_i and class label Y is defined as:

$$I(X_i, Y) = \sum_{y} \sum_{x=0,1} \hat{p}(x, y) \log \frac{\hat{p}(x, y)}{\hat{p}(x)\hat{p}(y)}$$

$\hat{p}(\cdot)$ is the probability distribution function whose parameters are maximum likelihood estimates from the training set. We compute mutual information for all four one-vs-all classification tasks. The computation is done as part of the training pipeline in MALLET to ensure consistency in parameter estimation and smoothing techniques. We then rank the cluster pair features by mutual information. The results are compactly summarized in bipartite graphs shown in Figure 1, where each edge represents a cluster pair. Since mutual information itself does not indicate whether a feature is favored by one or the other label, we also verify the direction of the effects of each of the features included in the following analysis by comparing the class conditional parameters in the Naive Bayes model.

The most dominant features for COMPARISON classification are the pairs whose members are from the same Brown clusters. We can distinctly see this pattern from the bipartite graph because the nodes on each side are sorted alphabetically. The graph shows many parallel short edges, which suggest that many informative pairs consist of the same clusters. Some of the clusters that participate in such pair consist of named-entities from various categories such as airlines (*King, Bell, Virgin, Continental, ...*), and companies (*Thomson, Volkswagen, Telstra, Siemens*). Some of the pairs form a broad category such as political agents (*citizens, pilots, nationals, taxpayers*) and industries (*power, insurance, mining*). These parallel patterns in the graph demonstrate that implicit COMPARISON relations might be mainly characterized by juxtaposing and explicitly contrasting two different entities in two adjacent sentences.

Without the use of a named-entity recognition system, these Brown cluster pair features effectively act as features that detect whether the two arguments in the relation contain named-entities or nouns from the same categories or not. These more subtle named-entity-related features are cleanly discovered through replacing words with their data-driven Brown clusters without the need for additional layers of pre-processing.

If the words in one cluster semantically relates to the words in another cluster, the two clusters are more likely to become informative features for CONTINGENCY classification. For instance, technical terms in stock and trading (*weighted, Nikkei, composite, diffusion*) pair up with economic terms (*Trading, Interest, Demand, Production*). The cluster with *analysts* and *pundits* pairs up with the one that predominantly contains quantifiers (*actual, exact, ultimate, aggregate*). In addition to this pattern, we observed the same parallel pair pattern we found in COMPARISON classification. These results suggest that in establishing a CONTINGENCY relation implicitly the author might shape the sentences such that they have semantically related words if they do not mention named-entities of the same category.

Through Brown cluster pairs, we obtain features that detect a shift between generality and speci-

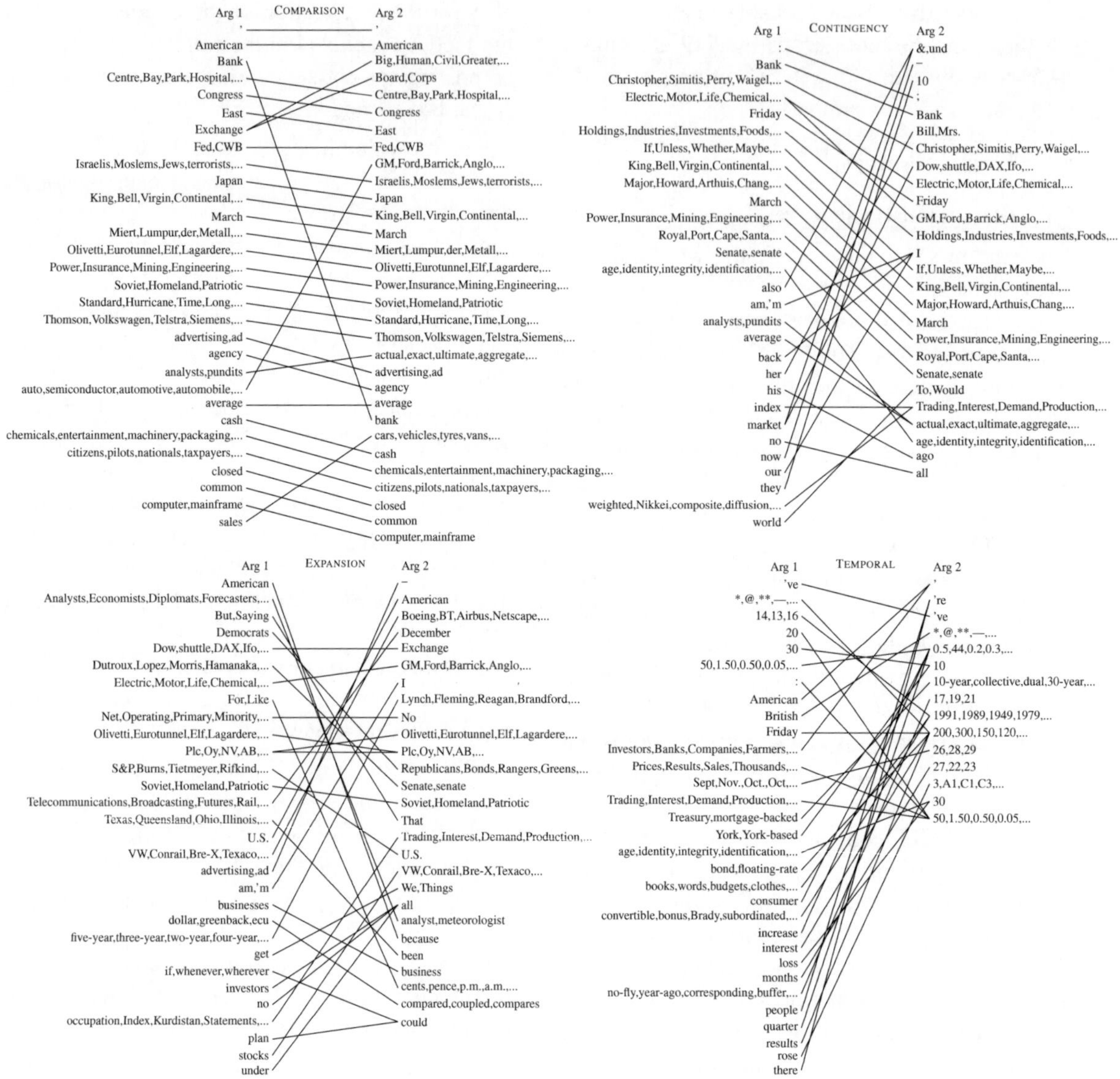

Figure 1: The bipartite graphs show the top 40 non-stopword Brown cluster pair features for all four classification tasks. Each node on the left and on the right represents word cluster from Arg1 and Arg2 respectively. We only show the clusters that appear fewer than six times in the top 3,000 pairs to exclude stopwords. Although the four tasks are interrelated, some of the highest mutual information features vary substantially across tasks.

ficity within the scope of the relation. For example, a cluster with industrial categories (*Electric, Motor, Life, Chemical, Automotive*) couples with specific brands or companies (*GM, Ford, Barrick, Anglo*). Or such a pair might simply reflects a shift in plurality e.g. *businesses - business* and *Analysts -analyst*. EXPANSION relations capture relations in which one argument provides a specification of the previous and relations in which one argument provides a generalization of the other. Thus, these shift detection features could help distinguish EXPANSION relations.

We found a few common coreference patterns of names in written English to be useful. First and last name are used in the first sentence to refer to a person who just enters the discourse. That person is referred to just by his/her title and last name in the following sentence. This pattern is found to be

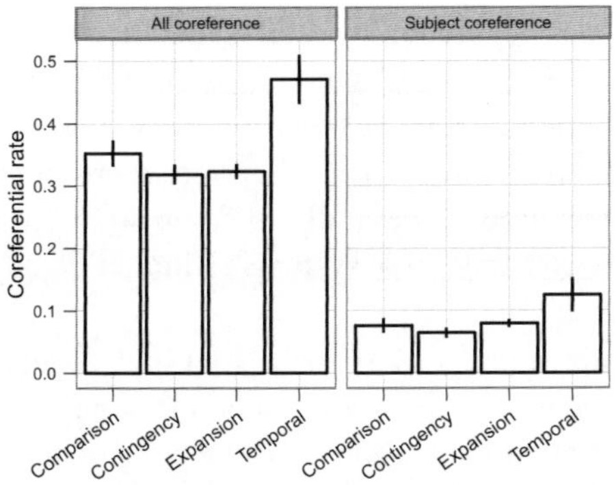

Figure 2: The coreferential rate for TEMPORAL relations is significantly higher than the other three relations ($p < 0.05$, corrected for multiple comparison).

informative for EXPANSION relations. For example, the edges (not shown in the graph due to lack of space) from the first name clusters to the title (*Mr, Mother, Judge, Dr*) cluster.

Time expressions constitutes the majority of the nodes in the bipartite graph for TEMPORAL relations. More strikingly, the specific dates (e.g. clusters that have positive integers smaller than 31) are more frequently found in Arg2 than Arg1 in implicit TEMPORAL relations. It is possible that TEMPORAL relations are more naturally expressed without a discourse connective if a time point is clearly specified in Arg2 but not in Arg1.

TEMPORAL relations might also be implicitly inferred through detecting a shift in quantities. We notice that clusters whose words indicate changes e.g. *increase, rose, loss* pair with number clusters. Sentences in which such pairs participate might be part of a narrative or a report where one expects a change over time. These changes conveyed by the sentences constitute a natural sequence of events that are temporally related but might not need explicit temporal expressions.

6.2 Coreference features

Coreference features are very effective given that they constitute a very small set compared to the other feature sets. In particular, excluding them from the model reduces F_1 scores for TEMPORAL and CONTINGENCY relations by approximately 1% relative to the system that uses all of the features. We found that the sentence pairs in these two types of relations have distinctive coreference patterns.

We count the number of pairs of arguments that are linked by a coreference chain for each type of relation. The coreference chains used in this study are detected automatically from the training set through Stanford CoreNLP suite (Raghunathan et al., 2010; Lee et al., 2011; Lee et al., 2013). TEMPORAL relations have a significantly higher coreferential rate than the other three relations ($p < 0.05$, pair-wise t-test corrected for multiple comparisons). The differences between COMPARISON, CONTINGENCY, and EXPANSION, however, are not statistically significant (Figure 2).

The choice to use or not to use a discourse connective is strongly motivated by linguistic features at the discourse levels (Patterson and Kehler, 2013). Additionally, it is very uncommon to have temporally-related sentences without using explicit discourse connectives. The difference in coreference patterns might be one of the factors that influence the choice of using a discourse connective to signal a TEMPORAL relation. If sentences are coreferentially linked, then it might be more natural to drop a discourse connective because the temporal ordering can be easily inferred without it. For example,

(1) Her story is partly one of personal downfall. [*previously*] She was an unstinting teacher who won laurels and inspired students... (WSJ0044)

The coreference chain between the two temporally-related sentences in (1) can easily be detected. Inserting *previously* as suggested by the annotation from the PDTB corpus does not add to the temporal coherence of the sentences and may be deemed unnecessary. But the presence of coreferential link alone might bias the inference toward TEMPORAL relation while CONTINGENCY might also be inferred.

Additionally, we count the number of pairs of arguments whose grammatical subjects are linked by a coreference chain to reveal the syntactic-coreferential patterns in different relation types. Although this specific pattern seems rare, more than eight percent of all relations have coreferential grammatical subjects. We observe the same statistically significant differences between TEMPORAL relations and the other three types of relations. More interestingly, the subject coreferential rate for CONTINGENCY relations is the lowest among the three categories ($p < 0.05$, pair-wise t-test corrected for multiple comparisons).

It is possible that coreferential subject patterns suggest temporal coherence between the two sentences without using an explicit discourse connective. CONTINGENCY relations, which can only indicate causal relationships when realized implicitly, impose the temporal ordering of events in the arguments; i.e. if Arg1 is causally related to Arg2, then the event described in Arg1 must temporally precede the one in Arg2. Therefore, CONTINGENCY and TEMPORAL can be highly confusable. To understand why this pattern might help distinguish these two types of relations, consider these examples:

(2) He also asserted that exact questions weren't replicated. [*Then*] When referred to the questions that match, he said it was coincidental. (WSJ0045)

(3) He also asserted that exact questions weren't replicated. When referred to the questions that match, she said it was coincidental.

When we switch out the coreferential subject for an arbitrary uncoreferential pronoun as we do in (3), we are more inclined to classify the relation as CONTINGENCY.

7 Related work

Word-pair features are known to work very well in predicting senses of discourse relations in an artificially generated corpus (Marcu and Echihabi, 2002). But when used with a realistic corpus, model parameter estimation suffers from data sparsity problem due to the small dataset size. Biran and McKeown (2013) attempts to solve this problem by aggregating word pairs and estimating weights from an unannotated corpus but only with limited success.

Recent efforts have focused on introducing meaning abstraction and semantic representation between the words in the sentence pair. Pitler et al. (2009) uses external lexicons to replace the one-hot word representation with semantic information such as word polarity and various verb classification based on specific theories (Stone et al., 1968; Levin, 1993). Park and Cardie (2012) selects an optimal subset of these features and establishes the strongest baseline to best of our knowledge.

Brown word clusters are hierarchical clusters induced by frequency of co-occurrences with other words (Brown et al., 1992). The strength of this word class induction method is that the words that are classified to the same clusters usually make an interpretable lexical class by the virtue of their distributional properties. This word representation has been used successfully to augment the performance of many NLP systems (Ritter et al., 2011; Turian et al., 2010).

Louis et al. (2010) uses multiple aspects of coreference as features to classify implicit discourse relations without much success while suggesting many aspects that are worth exploring. In a corpus study by Louis and Nenkova (2010), coreferential rates alone cannot explain all of the relations, and more complex coreference patterns have to be considered.

8 Conclusions

We present statistical classifiers for identifying senses of implicit discourse relations and introduce novel feature sets that exploit distributional similarity and coreference information. Our classifiers outperform the classifiers from previous work in all types of implicit discourse relations. Altogether these results present a stronger baseline for the future research endeavors in implicit discourse relations.

In addition to enhancing the performance of the classifier, Brown word cluster pair features disclose some of the new aspects of implicit discourse relations. The feature analysis confirms our hypothesis that cluster pair features work well because they encapsulate relevant word classes which constitute more complex informative features such as named-entity pairs of the same categories, semantically-related pairs, and pairs that indicate specificity-generality shift. At the discourse level, Brown clustering is superior to a one-hot word representation for identifying inter-sentential patterns and the interactions between words.

Coreference chains that traverse through the discourse in the text shed the light on different types of relations. The preliminary analysis shows that TEMPORAL relations have much higher inter-argument coreferential rates than the other three senses of relations. Focusing on only subject-coreferential rates, we observe that CONTINGENCY relations show the lowest coreferential rate. The coreference patterns differ substantially and meaningfully across discourse relations and deserve further exploration.

References

Or Biran and Kathleen McKeown. 2013. Aggregated word pair features for implicit discourse relation disambiguation. In *Proceedings of the 51st Annual Meeting of the Association for Computational Linguistics*, pages 69–73. The Association for Computational Linguistics.

Peter F Brown, Peter V deSouza, Robert L Mercer, Vincent J Della Pietra, and Jenifer C Lai. 1992. Class-based n -gram models of natural language. *Computational Linguistics*, 18(4):467–479, December.

Chih-Chung Chang and Chih-Jen Lin. 2011. LIBSVM: A library for support vector machines. *ACM Transactions on Intelligent Systems and Technology*, 2:27:1–27:27. Software available at `http://www.csie.ntu.edu.tw/~cjlin/libsvm`.

Marie-Catherine De Marneffe, Bill MacCartney, Christopher D Manning, et al. 2006. Generating typed dependency parses from phrase structure parses. In *Proceedings of LREC*, volume 6, pages 449–454.

Jenny Rose Finkel, Trond Grenager, and Christopher Manning. 2005. Incorporating non-local information into information extraction systems by gibbs sampling. In *Proceedings of the 43rd Annual Meeting on Association for Computational Linguistics*, pages 363–370. Association for Computational Linguistics.

Nathalie Japkowicz. 2000. Learning from imbalanced data sets: a comparison of various strategies. In *AAAI workshop on learning from imbalanced data sets*, volume 68.

Michael Jordan and Andrew Ng. 2002. On discriminative vs. generative classifiers: A comparison of logistic regression and naive bayes. *Advances in neural information processing systems*, 14:841.

Dan Klein and Christopher D Manning. 2003. Accurate unlexicalized parsing. In *the 41st Annual Meeting*, pages 423–430, Morristown, NJ, USA. Association for Computational Linguistics.

Heeyoung Lee, Yves Peirsman, Angel Chang, Nathanael Chambers, Mihai Surdeanu, and Dan Jurafsky. 2011. Stanford's multi-pass sieve coreference resolution system at the conll-2011 shared task. In *Proceedings of the Fifteenth Conference on Computational Natural Language Learning: Shared Task*, pages 28–34. Association for Computational Linguistics.

Heeyoung Lee, Angel Chang, Yves Peirsman, Nathanael Chambers, Mihai Surdeanu, and Dan Jurafsky. 2013. Deterministic coreference resolution based on entity-centric, precision-ranked rules. *Computational Linguistics*.

Beth Levin. 1993. *English verb classes and alternations: A preliminary investigation*, volume 348. University of Chicago press Chicago.

Ziheng Lin, Hwee Tou Ng, and Min-Yen Kan. 2010. A PDTB-Styled End-to-End Discourse Parser. *arXiv.org*, November.

Nick Littlestone. 1988. Learning quickly when irrelevant attributes abound: A new linear-threshold algorithm. *Machine learning*, 2(4):285–318.

Annie Louis and Ani Nenkova. 2010. Creating local coherence: An empirical assessment. In *Human Language Technologies: The 2010 Annual Conference of the North American Chapter of the Association for Computational Linguistics*, pages 313–316. Association for Computational Linguistics.

Annie Louis, Aravind Joshi, Rashmi Prasad, and Ani Nenkova. 2010. Using entity features to classify implicit discourse relations. In *Proceedings of the 11th Annual Meeting of the Special Interest Group on Discourse and Dialogue*, pages 59–62. Association for Computational Linguistics.

William C Mann and Sandra A Thompson. 1988. Rhetorical structure theory: Toward a functional theory of text organization. *Text*, 8(3):243–281.

Daniel Marcu and Abdessamad Echihabi. 2002. An unsupervised approach to recognizing discourse relations. In *Proceedings of the 40th Annual Meeting on Association for Computational Linguistics*, pages 368–375. Association for Computational Linguistics.

Mitchell P Marcus, Mary Ann Marcinkiewicz, and Beatrice Santorini. 1993. Building a large annotated corpus of english: The penn treebank. *Computational linguistics*, 19(2):313–330.

Andrew Kachites McCallum. 2002. Mallet: A machine learning for language toolkit. http://www.cs.umass.edu/ mccallum/mallet.

Joonsuk Park and Claire Cardie. 2012. Improving implicit discourse relation recognition through feature set optimization. In *Proceedings of the 13th Annual Meeting of the Special Interest Group on Discourse and Dialogue*, pages 108–112. Association for Computational Linguistics.

Gary Patterson and Andrew Kehler. 2013. Predicting the presence of discourse connectives. In *Proceedings of the Conference on Empirical Methods in Natural Language Processing*. Association for Computational Linguistics.

Emily Pitler, Mridhula Raghupathy, Hena Mehta, Ani Nenkova, Alan Lee, and Aravind K Joshi. 2008. Easily identifiable discourse relations. *Technical Reports (CIS)*, page 884.

Emily Pitler, Annie Louis, and Ani Nenkova. 2009. Automatic sense prediction for implicit discourse relations in text. In *Proceedings of the Joint Conference of the 47th Annual Meeting of the ACL and the 4th International Joint Conference on Natural Language Processing of the AFNLP: Volume 2-Volume 2*, pages 683–691. Association for Computational Linguistics.

Rashmi Prasad, Nikhil Dinesh, Alan Lee, Eleni Miltsakaki, Livio Robaldo, Aravind K Joshi, and Bonnie L Webber. 2008. The penn discourse treebank 2.0. In *LREC*. Citeseer.

Karthik Raghunathan, Heeyoung Lee, Sudarshan Rangarajan, Nathanael Chambers, Mihai Surdeanu, Dan Jurafsky, and Christopher Manning. 2010. A multi-pass sieve for coreference resolution. In *Proceedings of the 2010 Conference on Empirical Methods in Natural Language Processing*, EMNLP '10, pages 492–501, Stroudsburg, PA, USA. Association for Computational Linguistics.

Alan Ritter, Sam Clark, Oren Etzioni, et al. 2011. Named entity recognition in tweets: an experimental study. In *Proceedings of the Conference on Empirical Methods in Natural Language Processing*, pages 1524–1534. Association for Computational Linguistics.

Philip Stone, Dexter C Dunphy, Marshall S Smith, and DM Ogilvie. 1968. The general inquirer: A computer approach to content analysis. *Journal of Regional Science*, 8(1).

Kristina Toutanova and Christopher D Manning. 2000. Enriching the knowledge sources used in a maximum entropy part-of-speech tagger. In *Proceedings of the 2000 Joint SIGDAT conference on Empirical methods in natural language processing and very large corpora: held in conjunction with the 38th Annual Meeting of the Association for Computational Linguistics-Volume 13*, pages 63–70. Association for Computational Linguistics.

Kristina Toutanova, Dan Klein, Christopher D Manning, and Yoram Singer. 2003. Feature-rich part-of-speech tagging with a cyclic dependency network. In *Proceedings of the 2003 Conference of the North American Chapter of the Association for Computational Linguistics on Human Language Technology-Volume 1*, pages 173–180. Association for Computational Linguistics.

Joseph Turian, Lev Ratinov, and Yoshua Bengio. 2010. Word representations: a simple and general method for semi-supervised learning. In *Proceedings of the 48th Annual Meeting of the Association for Computational Linguistics*, pages 384–394. Association for Computational Linguistics.

Xun Wang, Sujian Li, Jiwei Li, and Wenjie Li. 2012. Implicit discourse relation recognition by selecting typical training examples. In *Proceedings of COLING 2012*, pages 2757–2772, Mumbai, India, December. The COLING 2012 Organizing Committee.

Ben Wellner, James Pustejovsky, Catherine Havasi, Anna Rumshisky, and Roser Sauri. 2009. Classification of discourse coherence relations: An exploratory study using multiple knowledge sources. In *Proceedings of the 7th SIGdial Workshop on Discourse and Dialogue*, pages 117–125. Association for Computational Linguistics.

"I Object!" Modeling Latent Pragmatic Effects in Courtroom Dialogues

Dan Goldwasser
University of Maryland
Institute for Advanced Computer Studies
College Park, MD , USA
goldwas1@umiacs.edu

Hal Daumé III
Department of Computer Science
University of Maryland
College Park, MD , USA
hal@cs.umd.edu

Abstract

Understanding the actionable outcomes of a dialogue requires effectively modeling situational roles of dialogue participants, the structure of the dialogue and the relevance of each utterance to an eventual action. We develop a latent-variable model that can capture these notions and apply it in the context of courtroom dialogues, in which the *objection* speech act is used as binary supervision to drive the learning process. We demonstrate quantitatively and qualitatively that our model is able to uncover natural discourse structure from this distant supervision.

1 Introduction

Many dialogues lead to decisions and actions. The participants in such dialogues each come with their own goals and agendas, their own perspectives on dialogue topics, and their own ways of interacting with others. Understanding the actionable results of a dialogue requires accurately modeling both the content of dialogue utterances, as well as the relevant features of its participants.

In this work, we devise a discriminative latent variable model that is able to capture the overall structure of a dialogue as relevant to specific acts that occur as a result of that dialogue. We aim to model both the *relevance* of preceding dialogue to particular action, as well as a binary structured relationship among utterances, while taking into account the pragmatic effect introduced by the different speakers' perspectives.

We focus on a particular domain of dialogue: courtroom transcripts. This domain has the advantage that while its range of topics can be broad, the roles of participants are relatively well-defined. Courtroom dialogues also contain a specialized speech act: **the objection**.

In real court settings (as opposed to fictionalized courts), an objection is a decision made by the party opposing the side holding the floor, to *interrupt* the flow of the courtroom discussion. While motivation behind taking this decision can stem from different reasons, it is typically an indication that a particular pragmatic *rule* has been broken. The key insight is that objections are sustained when a nuanced rule of court is being violated: for instance, the *argumentative* objection is "raised in response to a question which prompts a witness to *draw inferences* from facts of the case"[1], as opposed to the witness stating concrete facts.

The objectionable aspects of the preceding dialogue can be identified by a well-trained person; however these aspects are quite subtle to a computational model. In this work we take a first step toward addressing this problem computationally, and focus on identifying the key properties of dialogue interactions relevant for learning to identify and classify courtroom objections.

Our technical goal is to drive latent learning of dialogue structure based on a combination of raw input and pragmatic binary supervision. The binary supervision we use is derived from *objection* speech acts appearing in the dialogue (described in Section 2.1).

We are primarily interested in constructing a representation suitable for learning the challenging task of identifying objections in courtroom proceedings (Figure 1 provides an example).

In order to make classifications reliably, a deeper representation of the dialogue is required.

[1]Source: Wikipedia, July 2011, http://en.wikipedia.org/wiki/Argumentative.

Proceedings of the 14th Conference of the European Chapter of the Association for Computational Linguistics, pages 655–663, Gothenburg, Sweden, April 26-30 2014.

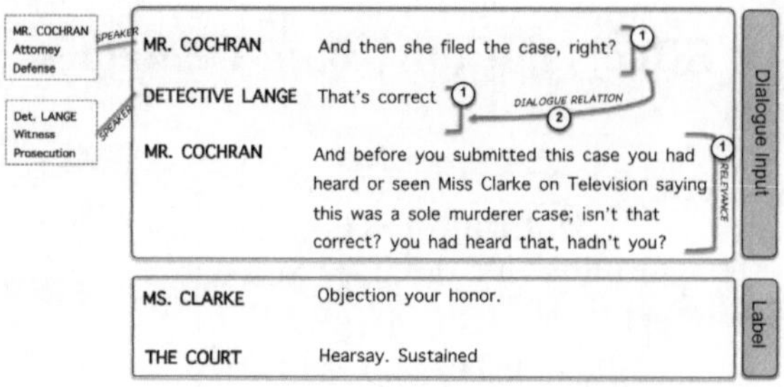

Figure 1: **Moving from raw text to a meaningful representation.** The raw textual representation hides complex interactions, relevant for understanding the dialogue flow and making decisions over it. We break the text into dialogue turns, each associated with a *speaker*, explicitly annotated with their role and side in the court case. Judgements of the relevance of each dialogue component for the classification task, produce a more accurate representation of the dialogue which is easier to learn. These judgments can be over individual sentences ((1)) or over pairs of sentences across different turns ((2)), which represent relevant information flow. The parameters required for making these judgements are obtained via interaction with the learning process. We explain these consideration and the construction stages in Section 2.

Notation	Explanation
$\mathbf{x}$	Input dialogue
$\mathbf{x}_{Sit}$	Situated dialogue
$\mathbf{h}$	Latent structure variables
t	Dialogue turn
$t.speaker.\{name, role, side\}$	Speaker information
$t.text$	Text in a dialogue turn
$t.s_i.\{text, type, subj, entities\}$	Sentence level information

Table 1: Notation Summary

Our model makes use of three conceptually different components capturing linguistic and pragmatic considerations and their relevance in the context of the dialogue structure.

Our linguistic model focuses on enriching a lexical representation of the dialogue utterances using linguistic resources capturing biased language use, such as subjective speech, expressions of sentiment, intensifiers and hedges. For example, the phrase *"So he was driving negligently?"* is an *argumentative* expression, as it requires the witness to draw inferences, rather than describe facts. Identifying the use of biased language in this phrase can help capture this objectionable aspect. In addition, we use a named entity recognizer, as we observe that relevant entity mentions provide a good indication of the dialogue focus. We refer the reader to Section 2.2 for further explanations.

The surface representation of dialogue turns hides the complex interactions between its participants. These interactions are driven by their agendas and roles in the trial. Understanding the lexical cues in this context requires *situating* the dialogue in the context of the court case. We condition the lexical representation of a turn on its speaker, the speaker's role and side in the trial, thus allowing the model to capture the relevant pragmatic influences introduced by the different speakers.

Next, a discriminative latent variable model learns a structured representation of the dialogue that is useful in making high-level semantic/pragmatic predictions (section 2.3). The latent variable model consists of two types of variables.

The first type of latent variable aims to identify content relevant for the objection identification decision. To this end, it determines the relevance of individual sentences to the classification decision, based on properties such as the lexical items appearing in the sentence, the sentence type, and expressions of subjectivity. *The second latent variable type focuses on the information flow* between speakers. It identifies relevant dialogue relations between turns. This decision is made by constructing a joint representation of two sentences, across different dialogue turns, capturing responses to questions and joining lexical items appearing in factual sentences across different turns.

Both dialogue aspects are formalized as latent variables, trained jointly with the final classification task using automatically extracted supervision. In Sec. 3 we describe the learning process.

We evaluate our approach over short dialogue snippets extracted from the O.J. Simpson murder trial. Our experiments evaluate the contribution of the different aspects of our system, showing that the dialogue representation determined by our latent model results in considerable improvements.

Our evaluation process considers several different views of the extracted data. Interestingly, despite the formal definitions of objections, the majority of objections are raised without justification (and are subsequently overruled), typically for the purpose of interrupting the opposing side when controversial topics are touched upon. Our experiments analyze the differences between sustained and overruled objections and show that sustained objections are easier to detect. We describe our experiments in section 4.

2 Dialogue Structure Modeling

Making predictions in such a complex domain requires a rich representation, capturing the interactions between different participants, the tone of conversation, understanding of controversial issues presented during the trial, and their different interpretations by either side in the trial. Obtaining this information manually is a labor intensive task, furthermore, its subjective nature allows for many different interpretations of the interactions leading to the objection.

Our approach, therefore, tries to avoid this difficulty by using a data-driven approach to learn the correct representation for the input, jointly with learning to classify correctly. Our representation transforms the raw input, dialogue snippets extracted automatically from court proceedings, into meaningful interactions between dialogue participants using a set of variables to determine the relevant parts of the dialogue and the relations between them. We inform these decisions using generic resources providing *linguistic* knowledge and *pragmatic* information, situating the dialogue in the context of the trial.

In this section we explain this process, starting from the automatic process of extracting examples (Section 2.1), the linguistic knowledge resources and pragmatic information used (Section 2.2), we summarize the notation used to describe the dialogue and its properties in Table 1. We formulate the inference process, identifying the meaningful interactions for prediction as an Integer Linear Programming (ILP) optimization problem (Section 2.3). The objective function used when solving this optimization problem is learned from data, by treating these decisions as latent variables during learning. We explain the learning process and its interaction with inference in Section 3.

2.1 Mining Courtroom Proceedings

The first step in forming our dataset consists of collecting a large set of relevant courtroom dialogue snippets. First, we look for textual occurrences of *objections* in the trial transcript by looking for *sustain* or *overrule* word lemma patterns, attributed to the judge. We treat the judge ruling turn and the one preceding it as sources of supervision, from which an indication of an objection, its type and sustained/overruled ruling, can be extracted. [2]

We treat the preceding dialogue as the cause for the objection, which could appear in any of the previous turns (or sequence of several turns intervening).We consider the previous $n{=}6$ turns as the context potentially relevant for the decision and let the latent variable model *learn* which aspects of the context are actually relevant.

2.2 Linguistic and Pragmatic Information

Objection decisions often rely on semantic and pragmatic patterns which are not explicitly encoded. Rather than annotating these manually, we use generic resources to enrich our representation.

We make a conceptual distinction between two types of resources. The first, an array of linguistic resources, which provides us an indication of structure, topics of controversy, and the sentiment and tone of language used in the dialogue.

The second captures pragmatic considerations by situating the dialogue utterances in the context of the courtroom. Each utterance is attributed to a speaker, thus capturing meaningful patterns specific to individual speakers.

Linguistic Resources (1) **Named Entities** provide strong indications of the topics discussed in the dialogue and help uncover relevant utterances, such as ones making claims associating individuals with locations. We use the Named Entity Recognizer (NER) described in (Finkel et al., 2005) to identify this information.

(2) **Subjective and Biased Language** Equally important to understanding the topics of conversation is the way they are discussed. Expressions of subjectivity and sentiment are useful linguistic tools for changing the tone of the dialogue and are likely to attract opposition. We use several resources to capture this information. We use a lexicon of subjective and positive/negative sentiment expressions (Riloff and Wiebe, 2003). This resource can help identify subjective statements attempting to bias the discussion (e.g., *"So he was driving* ***negligently?****"*)

We use a list of hedges and boosters (Hyland, 2005). This resource can potentially allow the model to identify evasive (*"I* ***might*** *have seen him"*) and (overly) confident responses (*"I am* ***absolutely sure*** *that I have seen him"*).

We use a lexicon of biased language provided by (Recasens et al., 2013), this lexicon extracted from Wikipedia edits consists of words indicative of bias, for example in an attempt to *frame* the facts raised in the discussion according to one of the viewpoints (*"The* ***death*** *of Nicolle Simposon"* vs. *"The* ***murder*** *of Nicolle Simposon"*).

Finally we use a Patient Polarity Verbs lexicon (Goyal et al., 2010). This lexicon consists

[2]In 4 we provide details about the extracted dataset and its distribution according to types.

of verbs in which the agent performs an action with a positive (*"He **donated** money to the foundation"*) or negative (*"He **stole** money from the foundation"*) consequence to the patient.

(3) **Sentence Segmentation** Many turns discuss multiple topics, some more relevant than others. In order to accommodate a finer-grained analysis, we segment each turn into its sentences. Each sentence is associated with a label, taken from a small set of generic labels. Labels include FORMALITY (e.g., a witness being sworn in), QUESTION, RESPONSE (which could be either POSITIVE or NEGATIVE) and a general STATEMENT[3].

Capturing Pragmatic Effects We observe that in the context of a courtroom discussion, utterance interpretation (and subsequent dialogue actions) is conditioned to a large extent on the speaker's motivation and goals rather than in isolation. We capture this information by explicitly associating relevant characteristics of the speakers involved in the dialogue with their utterances. We use the list of *actors* which appear in the trial transcripts, and associate each turn with a speaker, their role in the trial and the side they represent. We augment the lexical turn representation with this information (see Sec. 2.3.4).

2.3 Identifying Relevant Interactions using Constrained Optimization

In this section we take the next step towards a meaningful representation by trying to identify dialogue content and information flow relevant for objection identification. Since this information is not pre-annotated, we allow it to be learned as latent variables. These latent variables act as boolean indicator variables, which determine how each dialogue input example will be represented.

This process consists of two conceptual stages, corresponding to two types of boolean variables: (1) relevant utterances are identified; (2) meaningful connections between them, across dialogue turns, are identified. This information is exemplified as ① and ② in Figure 1. These decisions are taken jointly by formalizing this process as an optimization problem over the space of possible binary relations between dialogue turns and sentences.

[3]Determined by lexical information (question marks, dis/agreement indications and sentence length)

2.3.1 Relevance Decisions

Our raw representation allows as many as six previous turns to be relevant to the classification decision, however not all turns are indeed relevant, and even relevant turns may consist only of a handful of relevant sentences. Given a dialogue consisting of $(t_1, .., t_n)$ turns, each consisting of $(t_i.s_1, .., t_i.s_k)$ sentences, we associate with each sentence.

- **Relevance** variables, denoted by $h^r_{i,j}$, indicating the relevance of the j-th sentence in the i-th turn, for the classification decision.
- **Irrelevance** variables, denoted by $h^i_{i,j}$, indicating that the j-th sentence in the i-th turn is not relevant for the classification decision.
- **Variable pair activation constraints** Given a sentence the activation of these variables should be mutually exclusive. We encode this fact by constraining the decision with a linear constraint.

$$\forall i, j, \quad h^r_{i,j} + h^i_{i,j} = 1 \tag{1}$$

2.3.2 Dialogue Structure Decisions

In many cases the information required to make the classification is not contained in a single dialogue turn, but rather is the product of the information flow between dialogue participants. Given a dialogue consisting of $(t_1, .., t_n)$ turns, each consisting of $(t_i.s_1, .., t_i.s_k)$ sentences, we associate with every two sentences, $s_j \in t_i$, $s_k \in t_l$, such that $(i \neq l)$:

- **Sentences-Connected** variables, denoted by $h^c_{(i,j),(k,l)}$, indicating that the combination of the two sentences is relevant for the classification decision.
- **Sentences-not-Connected** variables, denoted by $h^n_{(i,j),(k,l)}$, indicating that the combination of the two sentences is not relevant for the classification decision.
- **Variable pair activation constraints** Given a sentence pair the activation of these variables should be mutually exclusive. We encode this fact by constraining the decision with a linear constraint.

$$\forall i, j, k, l \quad h^c_{(i,j),(k,l)} + h^n_{(i,j),(k,l)} = 1 \tag{2}$$

- **Decision Consistency constraints** Given a sentence pair, the activation of the variable indicating the relevance of the sentence pair entails the activation of the variables indicating the relevance of the individual sentences.

$$\forall i,j,k,l, (h^c_{(i,j),(k,l)}) \implies (h^r_{i,j} \wedge h^r_{k,l}) \tag{3}$$

2.3.3 Overall Optimization Function

The boolean variables described in the previous section define a space of competing dialogue representations, each representation considers different parts of the dialogue as relevant for the objection classification decision. When making this decision a single representation is selected, by quantifying the decisions and looking for the optimal set of decisions maximizing the overall sum of decision scores. We construct this objective function by associating each decision with a feature vector, obtained using a feature function ϕ (described in Section 2.3.4), mapping the relevant part of the input to a feature set.

More formally, given an input $\mathbf{x}$, we denote the space of all possible dialogue entities (i.e., sentences and sentence pairs) as $\Gamma(\mathbf{x})$. Assuming that $\Gamma(\mathbf{x})$ is of size N, we denote latent representation decisions as $\mathbf{h} \in \{0,1\}^N$, a set of indicator variables, that selects a subset of the possible dialogue entities that constitute the dialogue representation. For a given dialogue input $\mathbf{x}$ and a dialog entity $s \in \Gamma(\mathbf{x})$, we denote $\phi_s(\mathbf{x})$ as the feature vector of s. Given a fixed weight vector $\mathbf{w}$ that scores intermediate representations for the final classification task, our decision function (for predicting "objectionable or not") becomes:

$$f_{\mathbf{w}}(\mathbf{x}) = \max_{\mathbf{h}} \sum_s h_s \mathbf{w}^T \phi_s(\mathbf{x})$$
$$\text{subject to} \quad \text{(1)-(3)}; \;\; \forall s; h_s \in \{0,1\} \tag{4}$$

In our experiments, we formalize Eq. (4) as an ILP instance, which we solve using the highly optimized Gurobi toolkit[4].

2.3.4 Features

In this section we describe the features used in each of the different decision types.

Relevance (h^r) :

Bag-of-words: $\{(w, t.speaker.*^5) | \forall w \in t.s.text\}$

Biased-Language: $\{(w, resourceContains(w), t.speaker.*) | \forall w \in t.s.text\}$ [6]

Irrelevance (h^i) :

SentType: $(t.s.type)$

ContainsNamedEntity $(t.s.entities \neq \emptyset)$

Sentences-(not)-Connected (h^c,h^n) :

SentTypes: $(t_i.s_j.type, t_k.s_l.type)$

QA pair: $(t_i.s_j.type = Question) \wedge (t_k.s_l.type = Response)$
$\times \{qa | \forall w \in t_i.s_j.text, qa = (w, t_k.s_l.type)\}$

FactPair: $(t_i.s_j.type = Statement) \wedge (t_k.s_l.type = Statement)$
$\times \{qa | \forall w \in t_i.s_j.text, qa = (w, t_k.s_l.type)\}$

SpeakerPair: $(t_i.speaker.*, t_k.speaker.*)$

3 Learning and Inference

Unlike the traditional classification settings, in which learning is done over a fixed representation of the input, we define the learning process over a set of latent variables. The process of choosing a good representation is formalized as an optimization problem that selects the elements and associated features that best contribute to successful classification. In the rest of this section we explain the learning process for the parameters of the model needed both for the representation decision and the final classification decision.

3.1 Learning

Similar to the traditional formalization of support vector machines (Boser et al., 1992), learning is formulated as the following margin-based optimization problem, where λ is a regularization parameter, and ℓ is the squared-hinge loss function:

$$\min_{\mathbf{w}} \frac{\lambda}{2}\|\mathbf{w}\|^2 + \sum_i \ell\left(-y_i f_{\mathbf{w}}(\mathbf{x}_i)\right) \tag{5}$$

Unlike standard support vector machines, our decision function $f_{\mathbf{w}}(\mathbf{x}_i)$ is defined over a set of latent variables. We substitute Eq. (4) into Eq.(5), and obtain the following formulation for a latent structure classifier:

$$\min_{\mathbf{w}} \frac{\lambda}{2}\|\mathbf{w}\|^2 + \sum_i \ell\left(-y_i \max_{\mathbf{h}\in\mathcal{C}} \mathbf{w}^T \sum_{s\in\Gamma(\mathbf{x})} h_s \phi_s(\mathbf{x}_i)\right) \tag{6}$$

[4] http://www.gurobi.com/

[5] "*" denotes all properties

[6] refers to all linguistic resources used. We also included a +/-1 word window around words appearing in these resources

This formulation is not a convex optimization problem and care must be taken to find a good optimum. In our experiments, we use the algorithm presented in (Chang et al., 2010) to solve this problem. The algorithm solves this non-convex optimization function iteratively, decreasing the value of the objective in each iteration until convergence. In each iteration, the algorithm determines the values of the latent variables of positive examples, and optimizes the modified objective function using a cutting plane algorithm. This algorithmic approach is conceptually (and algorithmically) related to the algorithm suggested by (Yu and Joachims, 2009).

As standard, we classify $\mathbf{x}$ as positive iff $f_{\mathbf{w}}(\mathbf{x}) \geq 0$. In Eq. (4), $\mathbf{w}^T\phi_s(\mathbf{x})$ is the score associated with the substructure s, and $f_{\mathbf{w}}(\mathbf{x})$ is the score for the entire intermediate representation. Therefore, our decision function $f_{\mathbf{w}}(\mathbf{x}) \geq 0$ makes use of the intermediate representation and its score to classify the input.

4 Empirical Study

Our experiments were designed with two objectives in mind. Since this work is the first to tackle the challenging task of objection prediction, we are interested in understanding the scope and feasibility of finding learning-based solutions.

Our second goal is to examine the individual aspects of our model and how they impact the overall decision and the latent structure it imposes. In particular, we are interested in understanding the effect that modeling the situated context (pragmatics) of the dialogue has on objection prediction.

4.1 Experimental Setup

Evaluated Systems In order to understand the different components of our system, we construct several variations, which differ according to the resources used during learning (see Section 2.2 for details), and the latent variable formulation used (see Section 2.3). We compare our latent model with and without using pragmatic information (denoted DIAL($\mathbf{x}_{Sit}$) and DIAL($\mathbf{x}$), respectively). We also compare two baseline systems, which do not use the latent variable formulation, these systems are trained, using linear SVM, directly over all the features activated by the h^r decisions for all the turns in the dialogue. Again, we consider two variations, with and without pragmatic information (denoted ALL($\mathbf{x}_{Sit}$) and ALL($\mathbf{x}$), respectively).

4.2 Datasets

Our dataset consists of dialogue snippets collected from the transcripts of the famous O.J. Simpson murder trial[7], collected between January of 1995 to September of that year. We also extracted from the same resource a list of all trial participants, their roles in the murder case. Section 2.1 describes the technical details concerned with mining these examples. The collected dataset consists of 4981 dialogue snippets resulting in an objection being raised, out of which 2153 were *sustained*. In addition, we also mined the trial transcript for negative examples, collecting 6269 of those examples. Negative examples are dialogue snippets which do not result in an objection. To ensure fair evaluation, we mined negative examples from each hearing, proportionally to the number of positive examples identified in the same hearing. These examples were mined randomly, by selecting dialogue snippets that were not followed by an objection in any of the three subsequent turns.

We constructed several datasets, each capturing different characteristics of courtroom interaction.

All Objections Our first dataset consists of all the objections (both sustained and overruled). The objection might not be justified, but the corresponding dialogue either has the characteristics of a justified objection, or it touches upon points of controversy. In order to simulate this scenario, we use all the examples, treating all examples resulting in an objection as positive examples. We randomly select 20% as test data. We refer to this dataset as ALLOBJ. In addition, to examine the different properties of sustained and overruled objections we create two additional dataset, consisting only of sustained/overruled objections and negative examples. We denote the dataset consisting only of sustained/overruled objections as SUSTAINEDOBJ and OVERRULEDOBJ, respectively.

Objections by Type Our final dataset breaks the objections down by type. Unfortunately, most objections are not raised with an explanation of their type. We therefore can only use subsets of the larger ALLOBJ dataset. We use the occurrences of each objection type as the test dataset and match it with negative examples, proportional to the size of the typed dataset. For training, we use all the positive examples marked with an UNKNOWN type. The size of each typed dataset appears in Table 3.

[7] http://en.wikipedia.org/wiki/O._J._Simpson_murder_case

Objection Type	#Pos/#Neg	DIAL($\mathbf{x}_{Sit}$)	DIAL($\mathbf{x}$)	ALL($\mathbf{x}_{Sit}$)	ALL($\mathbf{x}$)
CALLS FOR SPECULATION	304 / 364	59.4	58.6	58	58
IRRELEVANT	275 / 330	58.5	58.6	55.2	56.6
LACK OF FOUNDATION	238 / 285	60.6	55	57	52.1
HEARSAY	164 / 196	60.3	57.2	60	55
ARGUMENTATIVE	153 / 183	68.8	65.8	64.8	64.8
FACTS NOT IN EVIDENCE	120 / 144	64.7	65.5	59.8	59.4
LEADING QUESTION	116 / 139	56.7	58.4	56.8	58

Table 3: **Accuracy results by objection type**. Note that the dataset size varies according to the objection type.

System	ALLOBJ	OVERRULEDOBJ	SUSTAINEDOBJ
ALL($\mathbf{x}$)	64.9	63.7	66.9
ALL($\mathbf{x}_{Sit}$)	65.1	63.7	67.9
DIAL($\mathbf{x}$)	65.4	65.1	66.7
DIAL($\mathbf{x}_{Sit}$)	**69.1**	**66.3**	**70.2**

Table 2: **Overall Accuracy results**. Results show considerable improvement when using our latent learning framework with pragmatic information.

4.3 Empirical Analysis

Overall results We begin our discussion with the experiments conducted over the three larger datasets (ALLOBJ, SUSTAINEDOBJ, OVERRULEDOBJ). Table 2 summarizes the results obtained by the different variations of our systems over these datasets.

The most striking observation emerging from these results is the combined contribution of capturing relevant dialogue content and interaction (using latent variables), combined with pragmatic information. For example in the ALLOBJ, when used in conjunction, their joint contribution pushed performance to 69.1 accuracy, a considerable improvement over using each one in isolation - 65.1 for the deterministic system using pragmatic information, and 65.4 of the latent-variable formulation which does not use this information. These results are consistent in all of our experiments.

We also observe that sustained objections are easier to predict than overruled objections. This is not surprising since objections raised for unjustified reasons are harder to detect.

Pragmatic Considerations Pragmatic information in our system is modeled by using the $\mathbf{x}_{Sit}$ representation, which conditions all decisions on the speaker identity and role. The results in Table 2 show that this information typically results in better quality predictions.

An interesting side effect of using pragmatic information is its impact on the dialogue structure predictions learned as latent variables during learning. We can quantify the effect by looking at the number of latent variables activated for each model. When pragmatic information is used, 5.6 relevance variables are used on average (per dialogue snipped). In contrast, when pragmatic information is not used, this number rises to 6.3[8]. In addition, the average number of sentence-connection variables active when pragmatic information is used is 3.44. This number drops to 2.53 when it is not. These scores suggest that information about the dialogue pragmatics allows the model to take advantage of the dialogue structure at the level of the latent information, focusing the learner of higher level information, such as the relation between turns, and less on low level, lexical information. The effect of using the pragmatic information can be observed qualitatively as exemplified in Figure 2, where the latent decisions, when pragmatic information is available, construct a more topically centered representation of the dialogue for the classification decision.

Typed Objections The results over the different objection types are summarized in Table 3. These results provide some intuition on which of the objection types are harder to predict, and the contribution of each aspect of our system for that objection type.[9] We can see that across the objection types, using latent variables modeling typically results in a considerable improvement in performance. The most striking example of the importance of using pragmatic information is the LACK OF FOUNDATION objection type. This objection definition as "the evidence lacks testimony as to its authenticity or source."[10] can explain this fact, as information about the side in the trial introducing specific evidence in testimony is very likely to impact the objection decision.

5 Related Work and Discussion

Our work applies latent variable learning to the problem of uncovering pragmatic effects in court-

[8]The average number of sentences per dialogue is 8.6

[9]Since these datasets vary in size, their results are neither directly comparable to each other nor to the results in Table 2.

[10]http://en.wikipedia.org/wiki/Foundation_(evidence)

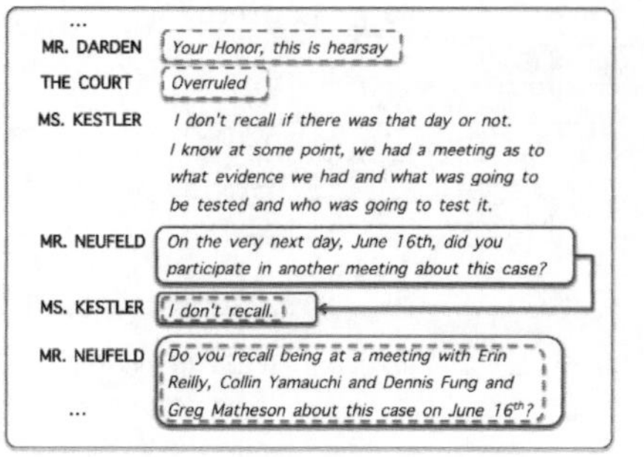

Figure 2: **Example of the pragmatic effect on latent dialogue structure.** Constructing the latent dialogue structure over situated text marks unrelated sentences as irrelevant, while marking topically related sentences and identifying the connection between the question-answer pair (decisions marked in solid blue lines). When trained *without* situated information, the latent output structure marks topically unrelated sentences as relevant for objection classification. Note that in this case all the edge variables are turned off (marked with dashed red lines).

room dialogues. We adopted the structured latent variable model defined in (Chang et al., 2010), and use ILP to solve the structure prediction inference problem (Roth and Yih, 2007).

Our prediction task, identifying the actionable result of a dialogue, requires capturing the dialogue and discourse relations. While we view these relations as latent variables in the context of action prediction, studying these relations independently has been the focus of significant research efforts, such as discourse relations (Prasad et al., 2008), rhetorical structure (Marcu, 1997) and dialogue act modeling (Stolcke et al., 2000). Fully supervised approaches for learning to predict dialogue and discourse relations (such as (Baldridge and Lascarides, 2005)) typically requires heavy supervision and has been applied only to limited domains.

Moving away from full supervision, the work of (Golland et al., 2010) uses a game-theoretic model to explicitly model the roles of dialogue participants. In the context of dialogue and situated language understanding, the work of (Artzi and Zettlemoyer, 2011) shows how to derive supervision for dialogue processing from its structure.

Discriminative latent variables models have seen a surge of interest in recent years, both in the machine learning community (Yu and Joachims, 2009; Quattoni et al., 2007) as well as various application domains such as NLP (Täckström and McDonald, 2011) and computer vision (Felzenszwalb et al., 2010). In NLP, one of the most well-known applications of discriminative latent structured classification is to the Textual Entailment (TE) task (Chang et al., 2010; Wang and Manning, 2010). The TE task bears some resemblances ours, as both tasks require making a binary decision on the basis of a complex input object (i.e., the history of dialogue, pairs of paragraphs), creating the need for a learning framework that is flexible enough to model the complex latent structure that exists in the input. Another popular application domain is sentiment analysis (Yessenalina et al., 2010; Täckström and McDonald, 2011; Trivedi and Eisenstein, 2013). The latent variable model allows the learner to identify finer grained sentiment expression than annotated in the data.

A related area of work with different motivations and different technical approaches has focused on attempting to understand narrative structure. For instance, Chambers and Jurafsky (Chambers and Jurafsky, 2008; Chambers and Jurafsky, 2009) model narrative flow in the style of Schankian scripts (Schank and Abelson, 1977). Their focus is on common sequences of actions, not specifically related to dialogue. Somewhat more related is recent work (Goyal et al., 2010) that aimed to build a computational model of Lehnert's Plot Units (Lehnert, 1981) model. That work focused primarily on actions and not on dialogue: in fact, their results showed that the lack of dialogue understanding was a significant detriment to their ability to model plot structure.

Instead of focusing on actions, like the above work, we focus on dialogue content and relationships between utterances. Furthermore, unlike most of the relevant work in NLP, our approach requires only very lightweight annotation coming for "free" in the form of courtroom objections, and use a latent variable model to provide judgements of relevant linguistic and dialogue relations, rather than annotating it manually. We enhance this model using pragmatic information, capturing speakers' identity and role in the dialogue, and show empirically the relevance of this information when making predictions.

It is important to recognize that courtroom objections are not the only actionable result of dialogues. Many discussions that occur on online forums, in social media, and by email result in measurable *real-world* outcomes. We have shown that one particular type of outcome, realized as a speech-act, can drive dialogue interpretation; the field is wide open to investigate others.

References

Adam Vogel and Christopher Potts and Dan Jurafsky. 2011. Implicatures and Nested Beliefs in Approximate Decentralized-POMDPs. In *EMNLP*.

Yoav Artzi and Luke S. Zettlemoyer. 2011. Bootstrapping semantic parsers from conversations. In *EMNLP*.

Jason Baldridge and Alex Lascarides. 2005. Probabilistic head-driven parsing for discourse structure. In *CoNLL*.

B. E. Boser, I. M. Guyon, and V. N. Vapnik. 1992. A training algorithm for optimal margin classifiers. In *Proc. 5th Annu. Workshop on Comput. Learning Theory*, pages 144–152.

Nathanael Chambers and Dan Jurafsky. 2008. Unsupervised learning of narrative event chains. In *Proceedings of ACL-08: HLT*, June.

Nathanael Chambers and Dan Jurafsky. 2009. Unsupervised learning of narrative schemas and their participants. In *ACL/IJCNLP*, pages 602–610.

Ming-Wei Chang, Dan Goldwasser, Dan Roth, and Vivek Srikumar. 2010. Discriminative learning over constrained latent representations. In *NAACL*.

Pedro F. Felzenszwalb, Ross B. Girshick, David A. McAllester, and Deva Ramanan. 2010. Object detection with discriminatively trained part-based models. *IEEE Trans. Pattern Anal. Mach. Intell.*

Jenny Rose Finkel, Trond Grenager, and Christopher Manning. 2005. Incorporating non-local information into information extraction systems by gibbs sampling. In *ACL*.

Dave Golland, Percy Liang, and Dan Klein. 2010. A game-theoretic approach to generating spatial descriptions. In *EMNLP*.

Amit Goyal, Ellen Riloff, and Hal Daumé III. 2010. Automatically producing plot unit representations for narrative text. In *Empirical Methods in Natural Language Processing (EMNLP)*.

K. Hyland. 2005. Metadiscourse: Exploring interaction in writing. In *Continuum, London and New York*.

W. G. Lehnert. 1981. Plot units and narrative summarization. In *Cognitive Science*.

Daniel Marcu. 1997. The rhetorical parsing of natural language texts. In *ACL*.

R. Prasad, N. Dinesh, A. Lee, E. Miltsakaki, L Robaldo, A. Joshi, and B. Webber. 2008. The penn discourse treebank 2.0. In *LREC*.

Ariadna Quattoni, Sybor Wang, L-P Morency, Michael Collins, and Trevor Darrell. 2007. Hidden conditional random fields. *Pattern Analysis and Machine Intelligence, IEEE Transactions on*.

Marta Recasens, Cristian Danescu-Niculescu-Mizil, and Dan Jurafsky. 2013. Linguistic models for analyzing and detecting biased language. In *Proceedings of ACL*.

E. Riloff and J. Wiebe. 2003. Learning extraction patterns for subjective expressions. In *NAACL*.

D. Roth and W. Yih. 2007. Global inference for entity and relation identification via a linear programming formulation. In Lise Getoor and Ben Taskar, editors, *Introduction to Statistical Relational Learning*. MIT Press.

Roger C. Schank and Robert P. Abelson. 1977. Scripts, plans, goals and understanding. In *ACL/IJCNLP*.

Andreas Stolcke, Klaus Ries, Noah Coccaro, Elizabeth Shriberg, Rebecca Bates, Daniel Jurafsky, Paul Taylor, Rachel Martin, Carol Van Ess-Dykema, and Marie Meteer. 2000. Dialogue act modeling for automatic tagging and recognition of conversational speech. *COMPUTATIONAL LINGUISTICS*, 26:339–373.

Oscar Täckström and Ryan T. McDonald. 2011. Discovering fine-grained sentiment with latent variable structured prediction models. In *ECIR*.

Rakshit Trivedi and Jacob Eisenstein. 2013. Discourse connectors for latent subjectivity in sentiment analysis. classification. In *NAACL*.

Mengqiu Wang and Christopher D. Manning. 2010. Probabilistic tree-edit models with structured latent variables for textual entailment and question answering. In *Proceedings of the 23rd International Conference on Computational Linguistics (COLING 2010)*.

Ainur Yessenalina, Yisong Yue, and Claire Cardie. 2010. Multi-level structured models for document-level sentiment classification. In *EMNLP*.

C. Yu and T. Joachims. 2009. Learning structural svms with latent variables. In *Proc. of the International Conference on Machine Learning (ICML)*.

Encoding Semantic Resources in Syntactic Structures for Passage Reranking

Kateryna Tymoshenko
Trento RISE
38123 Povo (TN), Italy
k.tymoshenko@trentorise.eu

Alessandro Moschitti
Qatar Computing Research Instit.
5825 Doha, Qatar
amoschitti@qf.org.qa

Aliaksei Severyn
University of Trento
38123 Povo (TN), Italy
severyn@disi.unitn.it

Abstract

In this paper, we propose to use semantic knowledge from Wikipedia and large-scale structured knowledge datasets available as Linked Open Data (LOD) for the answer passage reranking task. We represent question and candidate answer passages with pairs of shallow syntactic/semantic trees, whose constituents are connected using LOD. The trees are processed by SVMs and tree kernels, which can automatically exploit tree fragments. The experiments with our SVM rank algorithm on the TREC Question Answering (QA) corpus show that the added relational information highly improves over the state of the art, e.g., about 15.4% of relative improvement in P@1.

1 Introduction

Past work in TREC QA, e.g. (Voorhees, 2001), and more recent work (Ferrucci et al., 2010) in QA has shown that, to achieve human performance, semantic resources, e.g., Wikipedia[1], must be utilized by QA systems. This requires the design of rules or machine learning features that exploit such knowledge by also satisfying syntactic constraints, e.g., the semantic type of the answer must match the question focus words. The engineering of such rules for *open domain* QA is typically very costly. For instance, for automatically deriving the correctness of the answer passage in the following question/answer passage (Q/AP) pair (from the TREC corpus[2]):

Q: *What company owns the soft drink brand "Gatorade"?*

A: *Stokely-Van Camp bought the formula and started marketing the drink as Gatorade in 1967. Quaker Oats Co. took over Stokely-Van Camp in 1983.*

[1]http://www.wikipedia.org

[2]It will be our a running example for the rest of the paper.

we would need to write the following complex rules:

```
is(Quaker Oats Co.,company),
own(Stokely-Van Camp,Gatorade),
took_over(Quaker Oats Co.,Stokely-Van Camp),
took_over(Y, Z)→own(Z,Y),
```

and carry out logic unification and resolution. Therefore, approaches that can automatically generate patterns (i.e., features) from syntactic and semantic representations of the Q/AP are needed. In this respect, our previous work, e.g., (Moschitti et al., 2007; Moschitti and Quarteroni, 2008; Moschitti, 2009), has shown that tree kernels for NLP, e.g., (Moschitti, 2006), can exploit syntactic patterns for *answer passage reranking* significantly improving search engine baselines. Our more recent work, (Severyn and Moschitti, 2012; Severyn et al., 2013b; Severyn et al., 2013a), has shown that using automatically produced semantic labels in shallow syntactic trees, such as question category and question focus, can further improve passage reranking and answer extraction (Severyn and Moschitti, 2013).

However, such methods cannot solve the class of examples above as they do not use background knowledge, which is essential to answer complex questions. On the other hand, Kalyanpur et al. (2011) and Murdock et al. (2012) showed that semantic match features extracted from large-scale background knowledge sources, including the LOD ones, are beneficial for answer reranking.

In this paper, we tackle the candidate answer passage reranking task. We define kernel functions that can automatically learn structural patterns enriched by semantic knowledge, e.g., from LOD. For this purpose, we carry out the following steps: first, we design a representation for the Q/AP pair by engineering a pair of shallow syntactic trees connected with relational nodes (i.e.,

Proceedings of the 14th Conference of the European Chapter of the Association for Computational Linguistics, pages 664–672, Gothenburg, Sweden, April 26-30 2014.

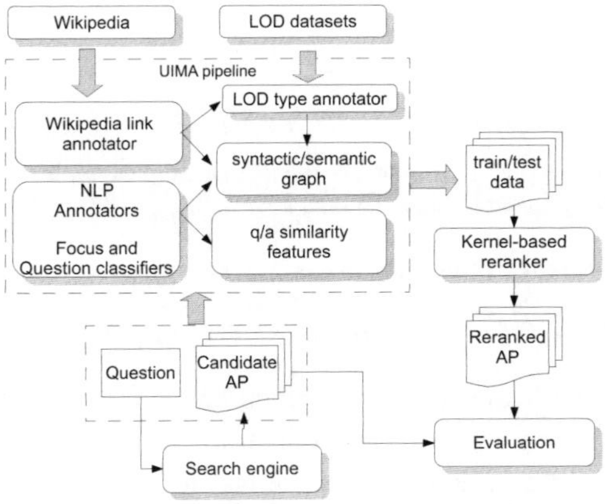

Figure 1: Kernel-based Answer Passage Reranking System

those matching the same words in the question and in the answer passages).

Secondly, we use YAGO (Suchanek et al., 2007), DBpedia (Bizer et al., 2009) and WordNet (Fellbaum, 1998) to match constituents from Q/AP pairs and use their generalizations in our syntactic/semantic structures. We employ word sense disambiguation to match the right entities in YAGO and DBpedia, and consider all senses of an ambiguous word from WordNet.

Finally, we experiment with TREC QA and several models combining traditional feature vectors with automatic semantic labels derived by statistical classifiers and relational structures enriched with LOD relations. The results show that our methods greatly improve over strong IR baseline, e.g., BM25, by 96%, and on our previous state-of-the-art reranking models, up to 15.4% (relative improvement) in P@1.

2 Reranking with Tree Kernels

In contrast to ad-hoc document retrieval, structured representation of sentences and paragraphs helps to improve question answering (Bilotti et al., 2010). Typically, rules considering syntactic and semantic properties of the question and its candidate answer are handcrafted. Their modeling is in general time-consuming and costly. In contrast, we rely on machine learning and automatic feature engineering with tree kernels. We used our state-of-the-art reranking models, i.e., (Severyn et al., 2013b; Severyn et al., 2013a) as a baseline. Our major difference with such approach is that we encode knowledge and semantics in different ways, using knowledge from LOD. The next sections outline our new kernel-based framework, although the detailed descriptions of the most innovative aspects such as new LOD-based representations are reported in Section 3.

2.1 Framework Overview

Our QA system is based on a rather simple reranking framework as displayed in Figure 1: given a question Q, a search engine retrieves a list of candidate APs ranked by their relevancy. Next, the question together with its APs are processed by a rich NLP pipeline, which performs basic tokenization, sentence splitting, lemmatization, stopword removal. Various NLP components, embedded in the pipeline as UIMA[3] annotators, perform more involved linguistic analysis, e.g., POS-tagging, chunking, NE recognition, constituency and dependency parsing, etc.

Each Q/AP pair is processed by a Wikipedia link annotator. It automatically recognizes n-grams in plain text, which may be linked to Wikipedia and disambiguates them to Wikipedia URLs. Given that question passages are typically short, we concatenate them with the candidate answers to provide a larger disambiguation context to the annotator.

These annotations are then used to produce computational structures (see Sec. 2.2) input to the reranker. The semantics of such relational structures can be further enriched by adding links between Q/AP constituents. Such relational links can be also generated by: (i) matching lemmas as in (Severyn and Moschitti, 2012); (ii) matching the question focus type derived by the question classifiers with the type of the target NE as in (Severyn et al., 2013a); or (iii) by matching the constituent types based on LOD (proposed in this paper). The resulting pairs of trees connected by semantic links are then used to train a kernel-based reranker, which is used to re-order the retrieved answer passages.

2.2 Relational Q/AP structures

We use the shallow tree representation that we proposed in (Severyn and Moschitti, 2012) as a baseline structural model. More in detail, each Q and its candidate AP are encoded into two trees, where lemmas constitute the leaf level, the part-of-speech (POS) tags are at the pre-terminal level and the sequences of POS tags are organized into the third level of chunk nodes. We encoded structural relations using the **REL** tag, which links the related structures in Q/AP, when there is a match

[3]http://uima.apache.org/

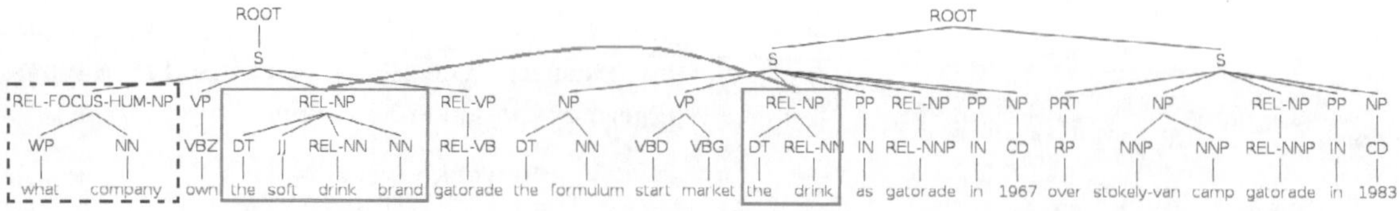

Figure 2: Basic structural representations using a shallow chunk tree structure for the Q/AP in the running example. Curved line indicates the tree fragments in the question and its answer passage linked by the relational **REL** tag.

between the lemmas in Q and AP. We marked the parent (POS tags) and grand parent (chunk) nodes of such lemmas by prepending a **REL** tag.

However, more general semantic relations, e.g., derived from the question focus and category, can be encoded using the **REL-FOCUS-<QC>** tag, where **<QC>** stands for the question class. In (Severyn et al., 2013b; Severyn et al., 2013a), we used statistical classifiers to derive question focus and categories of the question and of the named entities in the AP. We again mark (i) the focus chunk in the question and (ii) the AP chunks containing named entities of type compatible with the question class, by prepending the above tags to their labels. The compatibility between the categories of named entities and questions is evaluated with a lookup to a manually predefined mapping (see Table 1 in (Severyn et al., 2013b)). We also prune the trees by removing the nodes beyond a certain distance (in terms of chunk nodes) from the **REL** and *REL-FOCUS* nodes. This removes irrelevant information and speeds up learning and classification. We showed that such model outperforms bag-of-words and POS-tag sequence models (Severyn et al., 2013a).

An example of a Q/AP pair encoded using shallow chunk trees is given in Figure 2. Here, for example, the lemma "drink" occurs in both Q and AP (we highlighted it with a solid line box in the figure). "Company" was correctly recognized as a focus[4], however it was misclassified as "HUMAN" ("HUM"). As no entities of the matching type "PERSON" were found in the answer by a NER system, no chunks were marked as **REL-FOCUS** on the answer passage side.

We slightly modify the **REL-FOCUS** encoding into the tree. Instead of prepending **REL-FOCUS-<QC>**, we only prepend **REL-FOCUS** to the target chunk node, and add a new node QC as the rightmost child of the chunk node, e.g, in Figure 2, the focus node would be marked as **REL-FOCUS** and the sequence of its children would be *[WP NN HUM]*. This modification intends to reduce the feature sparsity.

[4]We used the same approach to focus detection and question classification used in (Severyn et al., 2013b)

3 LOD for Semantic Structures

We aim at exploiting semantic resources for building more powerful rerankers. More specifically, we use structured knowledge about properties of the objects referred to in a Q/AP pair. A large amount of knowledge has been made available as LOD datasets, which can be used for finding additional semantic links between Q/AP passages.

In the next sections, we (i) formally define novel semantic links between Q/AP structures that we introduce in this paper; (ii) provide basic notions of Linked Open Data along with three of its most widely used datasets, YAGO, DBpedia and WordNet; and, finally, (iii) describe our algorithm to generate linked Q/AP structures.

3.1 Matching Q/AP Structures: Type Match

We look for token sequences (e.g., complex nominal groups) in Q/AP pairs that refer to entities and entity classes related by *isa* (Eq. 1) and *isSubclassOf* (Eq. 2) relations and then link them in the structural Q/AP representations.

$$isa : entity \times class \rightarrow \{true, false\} \quad (1)$$

$$isSubclassOf : class \times class \rightarrow \{true, false\} \quad (2)$$

Here, entities are all the objects in the world both real or abstract, while classes are sets of entities that share some common features. Information about entities, classes and their relations can be obtained from the external knowledge sources such as the LOD resources. *isa* returns *true* if an entity is an element of a class (*false* otherwise), while *isSubclassOf(class1,class2)* returns *true* if all elements of *class1* belong also to *class2*.

We refer to the token sequences introduced above as to *anchors* and the entities/classes they refer to as *references*. We define anchors to be in a Type Match (TM) relation if the entities/classes they refer to are in *isa* or *isSubclassOf* relation. More formally, given two anchors a_1 and a_2 belonging to two text passages, p_1 and p_2, respectively, and given an $R(a, p)$ function, which returns a reference of an anchor a in passage p, we define $TM\ (r_1, r_2)$ as

$$\begin{cases} isa\,(r_1, r_2) : if\ isEntity\,(r_1) \wedge isClass\,(r_2) \\ subClassOf\,(r_1, r_2) : if\ isClass\,(r_1) \wedge isClass\,(r_2) \end{cases} \quad (3)$$

where $r_1 = R(a_1, p_1)$, $r_2 = R(a_2, p_2)$ and *isEntity(r)* and *isClass(r)* return true if *r* is an entity or a class, respectively, and *false* otherwise. It should be noted that, due to the ambiguity of natural language, the same anchor may have different references depending on the context.

3.2 LOD for linking Q/A structures

LOD consists of datasets published online according to the Linked Data (LD) principles[5] and available in open access. LOD knowledge is represented following the Resource Description Framework (RDF)[6] specification as a set of *statements*. A statement is a *subject-predicate-object* triple, where predicate denotes the directed relation, e.g., *hasSurname* or *owns*, between subject and object. Each object described by RDF, e.g., a class or an entity, is called a resource and is assigned a Unique Resource Identifier (URI).

LOD includes a number of common schemas, i.e., sets of classes and predicates to be reused when describing knowledge. For example, one of them is RDF Schema (RDFS)[7], which contains predicates `rdf:type` and `rdfs:SubClassOf` similar to the *isa* and *subClassOf* functions above. LOD contains a number of large-scale cross-domain datasets, e.g., YAGO (Suchanek et al., 2007) and DBpedia (Bizer et al., 2009). Datasets created before the emergence of LD, e.g., WordNet, are brought into correspondence with the LD principles and added to the LOD as well.

3.2.1 Algorithm for detecting TM

Algorithm 1 detects n-grams in the Q/AP structures that are in TM relation and encodes TM knowledge in the shallow chunk tree representations of Q/AP pairs. It takes two text passages, P_1 and P_2, and a LOD knowledge source, LOD_{KS}, as input. We run the algorithm twice, first with AP as P_1 and Q as P_2 and then vice versa. For example, P_1 and P_2 in the first run could be, according to our running example, Q and AP candidate, respectively, and LOD_{KS} could be YAGO, DBpedia or WordNet.

Detecting anchors. $getAnchors(P_2, LOD_{KS})$ in line 1 of Algorithm 1 returns all anchors in the given text passage, P_2. Depending on LOD_{KS} one may have various implementations of this procedure. For example, when LOD_{KS} is WordNet, *getAnchor* returns token subsequences of the chunks in P_2 of lengths *n-k*, where n is the number of tokens in the chunk and $k = [1, .., n-1)$.

Algorithm 1 Type Match algorithm

Input: P_1, P_2 - text passages; LOD_{KS} - LOD knowledge source.

1: **for all** $anchor \in$ getAnchors(P_2,LOD_{KS}) **do**
2:   **for all** uri $\in$ getURIs($anchor$,P_2,LOD_{KS}) **do**
3:     **for all** $type \in$ getTypes(uri,LOD_{KS}) **do**
4:       **for all** ch $\in$ getChunks(P_1) **do**
5:         $matchedTokens \leftarrow$ checkMatch(ch, type.labels)
6:         **if** $matchedTokens \neq \emptyset$ **then**
7:           markAsTM($anchor$,$P_2.parseTree$)
8:           markAsTM($matchedTokens$, $P_1.parseTree$)

In case when LOD_{KS} is YAGO or DBpedia, we benefit from the fact that both YAGO and DBpedia are aligned with Wikipedia on entity level by construction and we can use the so-called *wikification* tools, e.g., (Milne and Witten, 2009), to detect the anchors. The *wikification* tools recognize n-grams that may denote Wikipedia pages in plain text and disambiguate them to obtain a unique Wikipedia page. Such tools determine whether a certain n-gram may denote a Wikipedia page(s) by looking it up in a precomputed vocabulary created using Wikipedia page titles and internal link network (Csomai and Mihalcea, 2008; Milne and Witten, 2009).

Obtaining references. In line 2 of Algorithm 1 for each anchor, we determine the URIs of entities/classes it refers to in LOD_{KS}. Here again, we have different strategies for different LOD_{KS}. In case of WordNet, we use the all-senses strategy, i.e., getURI procedure returns a set of URIs of synsets that contain the anchor lemma.

In case when LOD_{KS} is YAGO or DBpedia, we use *wikification* tools to correctly disambiguate an anchor to a Wikipedia page. Then, Wikipedia page URLs may be converted to DBpedia URIs by substituting the `en.wikipedia.org/wiki/` prefix to the `dbpedia.org/resource/`; and YAGO URIs by querying it for subjects of the RDF triples with `yago:hasWikipediaUrl`[8] as a predicate and Wikipedia URL as an object.

For instance, one of the anchors detected in the running example AP would be "Quaker oats",

[5] `http://www.w3.org/DesignIssues/LinkedData.html`

[6] `http://www.w3.org/TR/rdf-concepts/`

[7] `http://www.w3.org/TR/rdf-schema/`

[8] `yago:` is a shorthand for the http prefix `http://yago-knowledge.org/resource/`

a wikification tool would map it to `wiki:Quaker_Oats_Company`[9], and the respective YAGO URI would be `yago:Quaker_Oats_Company`.

Obtaining type information. Given a *uri*, if it is an entity, we look for all the classes it belongs to, or if it is a class, we look for all classes for which it is a subclass. This process is incorporated in the *getTypes* procedure in line 3 of Algorithm 1. We call such classes *types*. If LOD_{KS} is WordNet, then our types are simply the URIs of the hypernyms of *uri*. If LOD_{KS} is DBpedia or YAGO, we query these datasets for the values of the `rdf:type` and `rdfs:subClassOf` properties of the *uri* (i.e., objects of the triples with *uri* as subject and *type/subClassOf* as predicates) and add their values (which are also URIs) to the *types* set. Then, we recursively repeat the same queries for each retrieved type URI and add their results to the *types*. Finally, the *getTypes* procedure returns the resulting *types* set.

The extracted URIs returned by *getTypes* are HTTP ids, however, frequently they have human-readable names, or labels, specified by the `rdfs:label` property. If no label information for a URI is available, we can create the label by removing the technical information from the type URI, e.g., *http* prefix and underscores. *type.labels* denotes a set of type human-readable labels for a specific *type*. For example, one of the types extracted for `yago:Quaker_Oats_Company` would have label "company".

Checking for TM. Further, the *checkMatch* procedure checks whether any of the labels in the *type.labels* matches any of the chunks in P_1 returned by *getChunks*, fully or partially (line 5 of Algorithm 1). Here, *getChunks* procedure returns a list of chunks recognized in P_1 by an external chunker.

More specifically, given a chunk, ch, and a type label, $type.label$, *checkMatch* checks whether the ch string matches[10] $type.label$ or its last word(s). If no match is observed, we remove the first token from ch and repeat the procedure. We stop when the match is observed or when no tokens in ch are left. If the match is observed, *checkMatch* returns all the tokens remaining in ch as $matchedTokens$. Otherwise, it returns an empty set. For example, the question of the running example contains the chunk "what company", which partially matches the human readable "company" label of one of the types retrieved for the "Quaker oats" anchor from the answer. Our implementation of the $checkMatch$ procedure would return "company" from the question as one of the *matchedTokens*.

If the $matchedTokens$ set is not empty, this means that $TM(R(anchor, P_2), R(matchedTokens, P_1))$ in Eq. 3 returns *true*. Indeed, a_1 is an $anchor$ and a_2 is the *matchedTokens* sequence (see Eq. 3), and their respective references, i.e., URI assigned to the anchor and URI of one of its types, are either in *subClassOf* or in *isa* relation by construction. Naturally, this is only one of the possible ways to evaluate the TM function, and it may be noise-prone.

Marking TM in tree structures. Finally, if the TM match is observed, i.e., *matchedTokens* is not an empty set, we mark tree substructures corresponding to the anchor in the structural representation of P_2 ($P_2.parseTree$) and those corresponding to *matchedTokens* in that of P_1 ($P_1.parseTree$) as being in a TM relation. In our running example, we would mark the substructures corresponding to "Quaker oats" anchor in the answer (our P_2) and the "company" *matchedToken* in the question (our P_1) shallow syntactic tree representations. We can encode TM match information into a tree in a variety of ways, which we describe below.

3.2.2 Encoding TM knowledge in the trees

a_1 and a_2 from Eq. 3 are n-grams, therefore they correspond to the leaf nodes in the shallow syntactic trees of p_1 and p_2. We denote the set of their preterminal parents as N_{TM}. We considered the following strategies of encoding TM relation in the trees: (i) **TM node (TM_N).** Add leaf sibling tagged with *TM* to all the nodes in N_{TM}. (ii) **Directed TM node (TM_{ND}).** Add leaf sibling tagged with **TM-CHILD** to all the nodes in N_{TM} corresponding to the anchor, and leaf siblings tagged with **TM-PARENT** to the nodes corresponding to *matchedTokens*. (iii) **Focus** TM (TM_{NF}). Add leaf siblings to all the nodes in N_{TM}. If *matchedTokens* is a part of a question focus label them as **TM-FOCUS**. Otherwise, label them as **TM**. (iv) **Combo** TM_{NDF}. Encode using the TM_{ND} strategy. If *matchedTokens* is a part of a question focus label then also add a child labeled *FOCUS* to each of the TM labels. Intu-

[9] `wiki:` is a shorthand for the http prefix `http://en.wikipedia.org/wiki/`

[10] case-insensitive exact string match

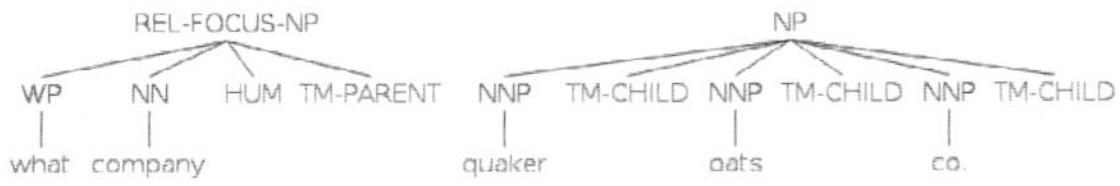

Figure 3: Fragments of a shallow chunk parse tree annotated in TM_{ND} mode.

itively, TM_{ND}, TM_{NF}, TM_{NDF} are likely to result in more expressive patterns. Fig. 3 shows an example of the TM_{ND} annotation.

3.3 Wikipedia-based matching

Lemma matching for detecting **REL** may result in low coverage, e.g., it is not able to match different variants for the same name. We remedy this by using Wikipedia link annotation. We consider two word sequences (in Q and AP, respectively) that are annotated with the same Wikipedia link to be in a matching relation. Thus, we add new **REL** tags to Q/AP structural representations as described in Sec. 2.2.

4 Experiments

We evaluated our different rerankers encoding several semantic structures on passage retrieval task, using a factoid open-domain TREC QA corpus.

4.1 Experimental Setup

TREC QA 2002/2003. In our experiments, we opted for questions from years 2002 and 2003, which totals to 824 factoid questions. The AQUAINT corpus[11] is used for searching the supporting passages.

Pruning. Following (Severyn and Moschitti, 2012) we prune the shallow trees by removing the nodes beyond distance of 2 from the **REL**, **REL-FOCUS** or **TM** nodes.

LOD datasets. We used the core RDF distribution of YAGO2[12], WordNet 3.0 in RDF[13], and the datasets from the 3.9 DBpedia distribution[14].

Feature Vectors. We used a subset of the similarity functions between Q and AP described in (Severyn et al., 2013b). These are used along with the structural models. More explicitly: *Term-overlap features:* i.e., a cosine similarity over question/answer, $sim_{COS}(Q, AP)$, where the input vectors are composed of lemma or POS-tag n-grams with $n = 1, .., 4$. *PTK score:* i.e., output of the Partial Tree Kernel (PTK), defined in (Moschitti, 2006), when applied to the structural representations of Q and AP, $sim_{PTK}(Q, AP) = PTK(Q, AP)$ (note that, this is computed within a pair). PTK defines similarity in terms of the number of substructures shared by two trees. *Search engine ranking score:* the ranking score of our search engine assigned to AP divided by a normalizing factor.

SVM re-ranker. To train our models, we use SVM-light-TK[15], which enables the use of structural kernels (Moschitti, 2006) in SVM-light (Joachims, 2002). We use default parameters and the preference reranking model described in (Severyn and Moschitti, 2012; Severyn et al., 2013b). We used PTK and the polynomial kernel of degree 3 on standard features.

Pipeline. We built the entire processing pipeline on top of the UIMA framework.We included many off-the-shelf NLP tools wrapping them as UIMA annotators to perform sentence detection, tokenization, NE Recognition, parsing, chunking and lemmatization. Moreover, we used annotators for building new sentence representations starting from tools' annotations and classifiers for question focus and question class.

Search engines. We adopted Terrier[16] using the accurate BM25 scoring model with default parameters. We trained it on the TREC corpus (3Gb), containing about 1 million documents. We performed indexing at the paragraph level by splitting each document into a set of paragraphs, which are then added to the search index. We retrieve a list of 50 candidate answer passages for each question.

Wikipedia link annotators. We use the Wikipedia Miner (WM) (Milne and Witten, 2009)[17] tool and the Machine Linking (ML)[18] web-service to annotate Q/AP pairs with links to Wikipedia. Both tools output annotation confidence. We use all WM and ML annotations with confidence exceeding 0.2 and 0.05, respectively. We obtained these figures heuristically, they are low because we aimed to maximize the Recall of the Wikipedia link annotators in order to maxi-

[11] `http://catalog.ldc.upenn.edu/LDC2002T31`

[12] `http://www.mpi-inf.mpg.de/yago-naga/yago1_yago2/download/yago2/yago2core_20120109.rdfs.7z`

[13] `http://semanticweb.cs.vu.nl/lod/wn30/`

[14] `http://dbpedia.org/Downloads39`

[15] `http://disi.unitn.it/moschitti/Tree-Kernel.htm`

[16] `http://terrier.org`

[17] `http://sourceforge.net/projects/wikipedia-miner/files/wikipedia-miner/wikipedia-miner_1.1`, we use only topic detector module which detects and disambiguates anchors

[18] `http://www.machinelinking.com/wp`

System	MRR	MAP	P@1
BM25	28.02±2.94	0.22±0.02	18.17±3.79
CH+V (CoNLL, 2013)	37.45	0.3	27.91
CH+V+QC+TFC (CoNLL, 2013)	39.49	0.32	30
CH + V	36.82±2.68	0.30±0.02	26.34±2.17
CH + V+ QC+TFC	40.20±1.84	0.33±0.01	30.85±2.35
CH+V+QC+TFC*	40.50±2.32	0.33±0.02	31.46±2.42

Table 1: Baseline systems

mize the number of TMs. In all the experiments, we used a union of the sets of the annotations provided by WM and ML.

Metrics. We used common QA metrics: Precision at rank 1 (P@1), i.e., the percentage of questions with a correct answer ranked at the first position, and Mean Reciprocal Rank (MRR). We also report the Mean Average Precision (MAP). We perform 5-fold cross-validation and report the metrics averaged across all the folds together with the std.dev.

4.2 Baseline Structural Reranking

In these experiments, we evaluated the accuracy of the following baseline models: **BM25** is the BM25 scoring model, which also provides the initial ranking; **CH+V** is a combination of tree structures encoding Q/AP pairs using relational links with the feature vector; and **CH+V+QC+TFC** is **CH+V** extended with the semantic categorial links introduced in (Severyn et al., 2013b).

Table 1 reports the performance of our baseline systems. The lines marked with *(CoNLL, 2013)* contain the results we reported in (Severyn et al., 2013b). Lines four and five report the performance of the same systems, i.e., **CH+V** and **CH+V+QC+TFC**, after small improvement and changes. Note that in our last version, we have a different set of **V** features than in *(CoNLL, 2013)*. Finally, **CH+V+QC+TFC*** refers to the performance of **CH+V+QC+TFC** with question type information of semantic **REL-FOCUS** links represented as a distinct node (see Section 2.2). The results show that this modification yields a slight improvement over the baseline, thus, in the next experiments, we add LOD knowledge to **CH+V+QC+TFC***.

4.3 Impact of LOD in Semantic Structures

These experiments evaluated the accuracy of the following models (described in the previous sections): (i) a system using Wikipedia to establish the REL links; and (ii) systems which use LOD knowledge to find type matches (TM).

The first header line of the Table 2 shows which baseline system was enriched with the TM knowledge. *Type* column reports the TM encoding strategy employed (see Section 3.2.2). *Dataset* column reports which knowledge source was employed to find TM relations. Here, *yago* is YAGO2, *db* is DBpedia, and *wn* is WordNet 3.0. The first result line in Table 2 reports the performance of the strong **CH+V** and **CH+V+QC+TFC*** baseline systems. Line with the "wiki" dataset reports on **CH+V** and **CH+V+QC+TFC*** using both Wikipedia link annotations provided by ML and MW and hard lemma matching to find the related structures to be marked by **REL** (see Section 3.3 for details of the Wikipedia-based REL matching). The remainder of the systems is built on top of the baselines using both hard lemma and Wikipedia-based matching. We used bold font to mark the top scores for each encoding strategy.

The tables show that all the systems exploiting LOD knowledge, excluding those using DBpedia only, outperform the strong **CH+V** and **CH+V+QC+TFC*** baselines. Note that **CH+V** enriched with TM tags performs comparably to, and in some cases even outperforms, **CH+V+QC+TFC***. Compare, for example, the outputs of **CH+V+**TM_{NDF} using YAGO, WordNet and DBpedia knowledge and those of **CH+V+QC+TFC*** with no LOD knowledge.

Adding TM tags to the top-performing baseline system, **CH+V+QC+TFC***, typically results in further increase in performance. The best-performing system in terms of MRR and P@1 is **CH+V+QC+TFC*+**TM_{NF} system using the combination of WordNet and YAGO2 as source of TM knowledge and Wikipedia for REL-matching. It outperforms the **CH+V+QC+TFC*** baseline by 3.82% and 4.15% in terms of MRR and P@1, respectively. Regarding MAP, a number of systems employing YAGO2 in combination with WordNet and Wikipedia-based REL-matching obtain 0.37 MAP score thus outperforming the **CH+V+QC+TFC*** baseline by 4%.

We used paired two-tailed t-test for evaluating the statistical significance of the results reported in Table 2. ‡ and † correspond to the significance levels of 0.05 and 0.1, respectively. We compared (i) the results in the *wiki* line to those in the *none* line; and (ii) the results for the *TM* systems to those in the *wiki* line.

The table shows that we typically obtain better results when using YAGO2 and/or WordNet. In our intuition this is due to the fact that these resources are large-scale, have fine-grained class

Type	Dataset	CH + V			CH + V + QC + TFC*		
		MRR	**MAP**	**P@1**	**MRR**	**MAP**	**P@1**
-	none	36.82±2.68	0.30±0.02	26.34±2.17	40.50±2.32	0.33±0.02	31.46±2.42
-	wiki	39.17±1.29‡	0.31±0.01‡	28.66±1.43‡	41.33±1.17	0.34±0.01	31.46±1.40
TM_N	db	40.60±1.88	0.33±0.01‡	31.10±2.99†	40.80±1.01	0.34±0.01	30.37±1.90
TM_N	wn	41.39±1.96‡	0.33±0.01‡	31.34±2.94	42.43±0.56	0.35±0.01	32.80±0.67
TM_N	wn+db	40.85±1.52‡	0.33±0.01‡	30.37±2.34	42.37±1.12	0.35±0.01	32.44±2.64
TM_N	yago	40.71±2.07	0.33±0.03†	30.24±2.09‡	43.28±1.91†	**0.36±0.01**†	33.90±2.75
TM_N	yago+db	41.25±1.57‡	0.34±0.02‡	31.10±1.88‡	42.39±1.83	0.35±0.01	32.93±3.14
TM_N	yago+wn	**42.01±2.26**‡	**0.34±0.02**‡	**32.07±3.04**‡	**43.98±1.08**‡	**0.36±0.01**‡	**35.24±1.46**‡
TM_N	yago+wn+db	41.52±1.85‡	**0.34±0.02**‡	30.98±2.71‡	43.13±1.38	**0.36±0.01**	33.66±2.77
TM_{NF}	db	40.67±1.94†	0.33±0.01‡	30.85±2.22†	41.43±0.70	0.35±0.01	31.22±1.09
TM_{NF}	wn	40.95±2.27‡	0.33±0.01‡	30.98±3.74	42.37±0.98	0.35±0.01	32.56±1.76
TM_{NF}	wn+db	40.84±2.18†	**0.34±0.01**‡	30.73±3.04	43.08±0.83†	0.36±0.01†	33.54±1.29†
TM_{NF}	yago	**42.01±2.44**†	**0.34±0.02**‡	**32.07±3.01**‡	43.82±2.36†	0.36±0.02‡	34.88±3.35
TM_{NF}	yago+db	41.32±1.70†	**0.34±0.02**‡	31.10±2.48‡	43.19±1.17†	0.36±0.01†	33.90±1.86
TM_{NF}	yago+wn	41.69±1.66‡	**0.34±0.02**‡	31.10±2.44‡	**44.32±0.70**‡	0.36±0.01‡	**35.61±1.11**‡
TM_{NF}	yago+wn+db	41.56±1.41‡	**0.34±0.02**‡	30.85±2.22†	43.79±0.73‡	**0.37±0.01**†	34.88±1.69‡
TM_{ND}	db	40.37±1.87	0.33±0.01‡	30.37±2.17	41.58±1.02	0.35±0.01†	31.46±1.59
TM_{ND}	wn	41.13±2.14‡	0.33±0.01‡	30.73±2.75	42.19±1.39	0.35±0.01	32.32±1.36
TM_{ND}	wn+db	41.28±1.03‡	0.34±0.01‡	30.73±0.82‡	42.37±1.16	0.36±0.01	32.44±2.71
TM_{ND}	yago	42.11±3.24‡	0.34±0.02‡	32.07±4.06†	44.04±2.05‡	0.36±0.01‡	34.63±2.17‡
TM_{ND}	yago+db	42.28±2.01‡	**0.35±0.01**‡	32.44±1.99‡	43.77±2.02†	**0.37±0.01**†	34.27±2.42
TM_{ND}	yago+wn	**42.96±1.45**‡	**0.35±0.01**‡	**33.05±2.04**‡	**44.25±1.32**‡	**0.37±0.00**‡	**34.76±1.61**‡
TM_{ND}	yago+wn+db	42.56±1.25‡	**0.35±0.01**‡	32.56±1.91‡	43.91±1.01‡	**0.37±0.01**†	34.63±1.32‡
TM_{NDF}	db	40.40±1.93†	0.33±0.01‡	30.49±1.78‡	41.85±1.05	0.35±0.01‡	31.83±0.80
TM_{NDF}	wn	40.84±1.69‡	0.33±0.01‡	30.49±2.24	41.89±0.99	0.35±0.01	31.71±0.86
TM_{NDF}	wn+db	41.14±1.29‡	0.34±0.01‡	30.73±1.40‡	42.31±0.92	0.36±0.01	32.32±2.36
TM_{NDF}	yago	42.31±2.57‡	**0.35±0.02**‡	32.68±3.01‡	**44.22±2.38**‡	**0.37±0.02**‡	**35.00±2.88**‡
TM_{NDF}	yago+db	41.96±1.82‡	**0.35±0.01**‡	32.32±2.24‡	43.82±1.95‡	**0.37±0.01**‡	34.51±2.39†
TM_{NDF}	yago+wn	42.80±1.19‡	**0.35±0.01**‡	33.17±1.86‡	43.91±0.98‡	**0.37±0.01**‡	34.63±0.90‡
TM_{NDF}	yago+wn+db	**43.15±0.93**‡	**0.35±0.01**‡	**33.78±1.59**‡	43.96±0.94‡	**0.37±0.01**‡	34.88±1.69‡

Table 2: Results in 5-fold cross-validation on TREC QA corpus

taxonomy and contain many synonymous labels per class/entity thus allowing us to have a good coverage with TM-links. DBpedia ontology that we employed in the *db* experiments is more shallow and contains fewer labels for classes, therefore the amount of discovered TM matches is not always sufficient for increasing performance. YAGO2 provides better coverage for TM relations between entities and their classes, while WordNet contains more relations between classes[19]. Note that in (Severyn and Moschitti, 2012), we also used supersenses of WordNet (unsuccessfully) whereas here we use hypernymy relations and a different technique to incorporate semantic match into the tree structures.

Different TM-knowledge encoding strategies, TM_N, TM_{ND}, TM_{NF}, TM_{NDF} produce small changes in accuracy. We believe, that the difference between them would become more significant when experimenting with larger corpora.

5 Conclusions

This paper proposes syntactic structures whose nodes are enriched with semantic information from statistical classifiers and knowledge from LOD. In particular, YAGO, DBpedia and WordNet are used to match and generalize constituents from QA pairs: such matches are then used in syntactic/semantic structures. The experiments with TREC QA and the above representations also combined with traditional features greatly improve over a strong IR baseline, e.g., 96% on BM25, and on previous state-of-the-art reranking models, up to 15.4% (relative improvement) in P@1. In particular, differently from previous work, our models can effectively use semantic knowledge in statistical learning to rank methods. These promising results open interesting future directions in designing novel semantic structures and using innovative semantic representations in learning algorithms.

[19]We consider the WordNet synsets to be classes in the scope of our experiments

Acknowledgments

This research is partially supported by the EU's 7th Framework Program (FP7/2007-2013) (#288024 LiMoSINe project) and by a Shared University Research award from the IBM Watson Research Center - Yorktown Heights, USA and the IBM Center for Advanced Studies of Trento, Italy. The third author is supported by the Google Europe Fellowship 2013 award in Machine Learning.

References

Matthew W. Bilotti, Jonathan L. Elsas, Jaime Carbonell, and Eric Nyberg. 2010. Rank learning for factoid question answering with linguistic and semantic constraints. In *Proceedings of the 19th*

ACM international Conference on Information and Knowledge Management (CIKM), pages 459–468.

Christian Bizer, Jens Lehmann, Georgi Kobilarov, Sören Auer, Christian Becker, Richard Cyganiak, and Sebastian Hellmann. 2009. Dbpedia - a crystallization point for the web of data. *Web Semantics: Science, Services and Agents on the World Wide Web*, 7(3):154–165, September.

Andras Csomai and Rada Mihalcea. 2008. Linking documents to encyclopedic knowledge. *IEEE Intelligent Systems*, 23(5):34–41.

Christiane Fellbaum, editor. 1998. *WordNet: An Electronic Lexical Database*. MIT Press.

David Ferrucci, Eric Brown, Jennifer Chu-Carroll, James Fan, David Gondek, Aditya Kalyanpur, Adam Lally, J. William Murdock, Eric Nyberg, John Prager, Nico Schlaefer, and Chris Welty. 2010. Building watson: An overview of the deepqa project. *AI Magazine*, 31(3).

Thorsten Joachims. 2002. Optimizing search engines using clickthrough data. In *ACM SIGKDD Conference on Knowledge Discovery and Data Mining (KDD)*, pages 133–142. ACM.

Aditya Kalyanpur, J William Murdock, James Fan, and Christopher Welty. 2011. Leveraging community-built knowledge for type coercion in question answering. In *The Semantic Web–ISWC 2011*, pages 144–156. Springer.

David Milne and Ian H Witten. 2009. An open-source toolkit for mining wikipedia. In *New Zealand Computer Science Research Student Conference (NZCSRSC)*.

Alessandro Moschitti and Silvia Quarteroni. 2008. Kernels on linguistic structures for answer extraction. In *Proceedings of the 46th Annual Meeting of the Association for Computational Linguistics on Human Language Technologies: Short Papers (ACL)*, pages 113–116.

Alessandro Moschitti, Silvia Quarteroni, Roberto Basili, and Suresh Manandhar. 2007. Exploiting syntactic and shallow semantic kernels for question/answer classification. In *Proceedings of the 45th Annual Meeting of the Association of Computational Linguistics (ACL)*, pages 776–783.

Alessandro Moschitti. 2006. Efficient convolution kernels for dependency and constituent syntactic trees. In *Proceedings of the 17th European Conference on Machine Learning (ECML)*, pages 318–329. Springer.

Alessandro Moschitti. 2009. Syntactic and semantic kernels for short text pair categorization. In *Proceedings of the 12th Conference of the European Chapter of the Association for Computational Linguistics (EACL)*, pages 576–584. Association for Computational Linguistics.

J William Murdock, Aditya Kalyanpur, Chris Welty, James Fan, David A Ferrucci, DC Gondek, Lei Zhang, and Hiroshi Kanayama. 2012. Typing candidate answers using type coercion. *IBM Journal of Research and Development*, 56(3.4):7–1.

Aliaksei Severyn and Alessandro Moschitti. 2012. Structural relationships for large-scale learning of answer re-ranking. In *Proceedings of the 35th international ACM SIGIR conference on Research and development in information retrieval (SIGIR)*, pages 741–750. ACM.

Aliaksei Severyn and Alessandro Moschitti. 2013. Automatic feature engineering for answer selection and extraction. In *Proceedings of the 2013 Conference on Empirical Methods in Natural Language Processing (EMNLP)*, pages 458–467.

Aliaksei Severyn, Massimo Nicosia, and Alessandro Moschitti. 2013a. Building structures from classifiers for passage reranking. In *Proceedings of the 22nd ACM international conference on Conference on information & knowledge management (CIKM)*, pages 969–978. ACM.

Aliaksei Severyn, Massimo Nicosia, and Alessandro Moschitti. 2013b. Learning adaptable patterns for passage reranking. In *Proceedings of the Seventeenth Conference on Computational Natural Language Learning (CoNLL)*.

Fabian M. Suchanek, Gjergji Kasneci, and Gerhard Weikum. 2007. Yago: a core of semantic knowledge. In *Proceedings of the 16th international conference on World Wide Web (WWW)*, pages 697–706. ACM Press.

Ellen M Voorhees. 2001. Overview of the TREC 2001 Question Answering Track. In *Proceedings of TREC*, pages 42–51.

Automatic Food Categorization from Large Unlabeled Corpora and Its Impact on Relation Extraction

Michael Wiegand and **Benjamin Roth** and **Dietrich Klakow**
Spoken Language Systems
Saarland University
D-66123 Saarbrücken, Germany
{Michael.Wiegand|Benjamin.Roth|Dietrich.Klakow}@lsv.uni-saarland.de

Abstract

We present a weakly-supervised induction method to assign semantic information to food items. We consider two tasks of categorizations being food-type classification and the distinction of whether a food item is composite or not. The categorizations are induced by a graph-based algorithm applied on a large unlabeled domain-specific corpus. We show that the usage of a domain-specific corpus is vital. We do not only outperform a manually designed open-domain ontology but also prove the usefulness of these categorizations in relation extraction, outperforming state-of-the-art features that include syntactic information and Brown clustering.

1 Introduction

In view of the large interest in food in many parts of the population and the ever increasing amount of new dishes/food items, there is a need of automatic knowledge acquisition. We approach this task with the help of natural language processing.

We investigate different methods to assign categories to food items. We focus on two categorizations, being a classification of food items to categories of the *Food Guide Pyramid* (U.S. Department of Agriculture, 1992) and a categorization of whether a food item is composite or not.

We present a semi-supervised graph-based approach to induce these food categorizations from an unlabeled domain-specific text corpus crawled from the Web. The method only requires minimal manual guidance for the initialization of the algorithm with seed terms. It depends, however, on an automatically constructed high-quality similarity graph. For that we choose a pattern-based representation that outperforms a distributional-based representation. For initialization, we examine some manually compiled seed words and a very few simple surface patterns to automatically induce such expressions. As a hard baseline, we compare the effectiveness of using a general-purpose ontology for the same types of categorizations. Apart from an intrinsic evaluation, we also examine the categories in relation extraction.

The contributions of this paper are a method requiring minimal supervision for a comprehensive classification of food items and a proof of concept that the knowledge that can thus be gained is beneficial for relation extraction. Even though we focus on a specific domain, the induction method can be easily translated to other domains. In particular, other life-style domains, such as fashion, cosmetics or home & gardening, show parallels since comparable textual web data are available and similar relation types (e.g. that two items fit together or can be substituted by each other) exist.

Our experiments are carried out on German data but our findings should carry over to other languages since the issues we address are (mostly) language universal. For general accessibility, all examples are given as English translations.

2 Data & Annotation

2.1 Domain-Specific Text Corpus

In order to generate a dataset for our experiments, we used a crawl of *chefkoch.de*[1] (Wiegand et al., 2012b) consisting of $418,558$ webpages of food-related forum entries. *chefkoch.de* is the largest German web portal for food-related issues.

2.2 Food Categorization

As a food vocabulary, we employ a list of 1888 food items: 1104 items were directly extracted from GermaNet (Hamp and Feldweg, 1997), the German version of WordNet (Miller et al., 1990). The items were identified by extracting all hyponyms of the synset *Nahrung* (English: *food*). By

[1] www.chefkoch.de

Proceedings of the 14th Conference of the European Chapter of the Association for Computational Linguistics, pages 673–682, Gothenburg, Sweden, April 26-30 2014.

Class	Description	Size	Perc.
MEAT	meat and fish (products)	394	20.87
BEVERAGE	beverages (incl. alcoholic drinks)	298	15.78
VEGE	vegetables (incl. salads)	231	12.24
SWEET	sweets, pastries and snack mixes	228	12.08
SPICE	spices and sauces	216	11.44
STARCH	starch-based side dishes	185	9.80
MILK	milk products	104	5.51
FRUIT	fruits	94	4.98
GRAIN	grains, nuts and seeds	77	4.08
FAT	fat	41	2.18
EGG	eggs	20	1.06

Table 1: The different food types (*gold standard*).

Class	Description	Examples	Perc.
DISH	composite food items	*cake, falafel, meat loaf*	32.10
ATOM	non-composite food items	*apple, steak, potato*	67.90

Table 2: Distribution of dishes and atomic food items among the food vocabulary (*gold standard*).

consulting the relation tuples from Wiegand et al. (2012c) a further 784 items were added. We manually annotated this vocabulary w.r.t. two tasks:

2.2.1 Task I: Food Types

The food type categories we chose are mainly inspired by the *Food Guide Pyramid* (U.S. Department of Agriculture, 1992) that divides food items into categories with similar nutritional properties. This categorization scheme not only divides the set of food items in many intuitive homogeneous classes but it is also the scheme that is most commonly agreed upon. Table 1 lists the specific categories we use. For category assignment of complex dishes comprising different food items we applied a heuristics: we always assign the category that dominates the dish. A *meat sauce*, for example, would thus be assigned MEAT (even though there may be other ingredients than meat).

2.2.2 Task II: Dishes vs. Atomic Food Items

In addition to Task I, we include another categorization that divides food items into dishes and atomic food items (Table 2). By dish, we mainly understand food items that are composite food items made of other (*atomic*) food items. This categorization is orthogonal to the previous classification of food items. We refrained from adding dishes as a further category of food types in §2.2.1, as we would have ended up with a very heterogeneous class in the set of homogeneous food type categories. Thus, dishes that differ greatly in nutrient content, such as *Waldorf salad* and *chocolate cake*, would have been subsumed by one class.

3 Method

3.1 Graph-based Induction

We propose a semi-supervised graph-based approach to label food items with their respective food categories. The underlying data structure is a similarity graph connecting different food items. Food items that belong to the same category should be connected by highly weighted edges. In order to infer the labels for each respective food item, one first needs to specify a small set of seeds for each category and then apply a graph-based clustering method that divides the graph into clusters that represent distinct food categories. Our method is a low-resource approach that can also be easily adapted to other domains. The only domain-specific information required are an unlabeled corpus and a set of seeds.

3.1.1 Construction of the Similarity Graph

To enable a graph-based induction, we generate a similarity graph that connects similar food items. For that purpose, a list of *domain-independent* similarity-patterns was compiled. Each pattern is a lexical sequence that connects the mention of two food items (Table 3). Each pair of food items observed with any of those patterns is connected via a weighted edge (the different patterns are treated equally). The weight is the total frequency of all patterns co-occurring with a particular food pair.

Due to the high precision of our patterns, with one or a few prototypical seeds we cannot expect to find all items of a food category within the set of items to which the seeds are *directly* connected. Instead, one also needs to consider transitive connectedness within the graph. For example, in Figure 1 *banana* and *redberry* are not directly connected but they can be reached via *pear* or *raspberry*. However, by considering mediate relationships it becomes more difficult to determine the most appropriate category for each food item since most food items are connected to food items of different categories (in Figure 1, there are not only edges between *banana* and other types of fruits but there is also some edge to some sweet, i.e. *chocolate*). For a unique class assignment, we apply a robust graph-based clustering algorithm. (It will figure out that *banana*, *pear*, *raspberry* and *redberry* belong to the same category and *chocolate* belongs to another category, since it is mostly

Patterns	food_item$_1$ (*or*|*or rather*|*instead of*|"(") food_item$_2$
Example	{*apple*: *pineapple, pear, fruit, strawberry, kiwi*} {*steak*: *schnitzel, sausage, roast, meat loaf, cutlet*}

Table 3: *Domain-independent* patterns for building the similarity graph.

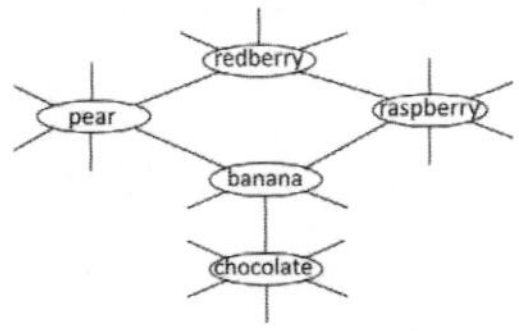

Figure 1: Illustration of the similarity graph.

linked to many other food items not being fruits.)

3.1.2 Semi-Supervised Graph Optimization

Our semi-supervised graph optimization (Belkin and Niyogi, 2004) is a robust algorithm that was primarily chosen since it only contains few free parameters to adjust. It is based on two principles: First, similar data points should be assigned similar labels, as expressed by a similarity graph of labeled and unlabeled data. Second, for labeled data points the prediction of the learnt classifier should be consistent with the (actual) gold labels.

We construct a weighted transition matrix W of the graph by normalization of the matrix with co-occurrence counts C which we obtain from the similarity graph (§3.1.1). We use the common normalization by a power of the degree function $d_i = \sum_j C_{ij}$: it defines $W_{ij} = \frac{C_{ij}}{d_i^\lambda d_j^\lambda}$ if $i \neq j$, and $W_{ii} = 0$. The normalization weight λ is the first of two parameters used in our experiments for semi-supervised graph optimization. For learning the semi-supervised classifier, we use the method of Zhou et al. (2004) to find a classifying function which is sufficiently smooth with respect to both the structure of unlabeled and labeled points.

Given a set of data points $\mathcal{X} = \{x_1, \ldots, x_n\}$ and label set $\mathcal{L} = \{1, \ldots, c\}$, with $x_{i:1 \leq i \leq l}$ labeled as $y_i \in \mathcal{L}$ and $x_{i:l+1 \leq i \leq n}$ unlabeled. For prediction, a vectorial function $F : \mathcal{X} \to \mathbb{R}^c$ is estimated assigning a vector F_i of label scores to every x_i. The predicted labeling follows from these scores as $\hat{y}_i = \arg\max_{j \leq c} F_{ij}$. Conversely, the gold labeling matrix Y is a $n \times c$ matrix with $Y_{ij} = 1$ if x_i is labeled as $y_i = j$ and $Y_{ij} = 0$ otherwise.

Minimizing the cost function $\mathcal{Q}$ aims at a trade-off between information from neighbours and initial labeling information, controlled by parameter μ (the second parameter used in our experiments):

$$\mathcal{Q} = \frac{1}{2}\left(\sum_{i,j=1}^{n} W_{ij} \left\| \frac{1}{\sqrt{\delta_i}} F_i - \frac{1}{\sqrt{\delta_j}} F_j \right\| + \mu \sum_{i=1}^{n} \|F_i - Y_i\|\right)$$

where δ_i is the degree function of W.

The first term in $\mathcal{Q}$ is the smoothness constraint, its minimization leads to adjacent edges having similar labels. The second term is the fitting constraint, its minimization leads to consistency of the function F with the labeling of the data. The solution to the above cost function is found by solving a system of linear equations (Zhou et al., 2004).

As we do not possess development data for this work, we set the two free parameters $\lambda = 0.5$ and $\mu = 0.01$. This setting is used for both induction tasks and all configurations. It is a setting that provided reasonable results without any notable bias for any particular configuration we examine.

Patterns	Categorization	Examples
patt$_{hearst}$	Food Types	food_item *is some* food_type, food_type *such as* food_item, ...
patt$_{dishes}$	Dishes	*recipe for* food_item
patt$_{atom}$	Atomic Food Items	*made of*|*contains* food_item

Table 4: List of patterns to extract seeds.

3.1.3 Manually vs. Automatically Extracted Seeds

We explore two types of seed initializations: (a) a manually compiled list of seed food items and (b) a small set of patterns (Table 4) by the help of which such seeds are automatically extracted.

In order to extract seeds for Task I with the pattern-based approach, we apply the patterns from Hearst (1992). These patterns have been designed for the acquisition of hyponyms. Task I can also be regarded as some type of hyponym extraction. The food types (*fruit*, *meat*, *sweets*) represent the hypernyms for which we extract seed hyponyms (*banana*, *beef*, *chocolate*).

In order to extract seeds for Task II, we apply two domain-specific sets of patterns (*patt$_{dish}$* and *patt$_{atom}$*). We rank the food items according to the frequency of occurring with the respective pattern set. Since food items may occur in both rankings, we merge the two rankings in the following way:

$$score(food\,item) = \#patt_{dish}(food\,it.) - \#patt_{atom}(food\,it.)$$

The top end of this ranking represents dishes while the bottom end represents atoms.

3.2 Using a General-Purpose Ontology

As a hard baseline, we also make use of the semantic relationships encoded in GermaNet. Our two types of food categorization schemes can be approximated with the hypernymy graph in that ontology: We manually identify nodes that resemble our food categories (e.g. *fruit*, *meat* or *dish*) and label any food item that is an immediate or a mediate hyponym of these nodes (e.g. *apple* for *fruit*) with the respective category label. The downside of this method is that a large amount of food items is missing from the GermaNet-database (§2.2).

3.3 Other Baselines & Post-Processing

In addition to the previous methods we implement a heuristic baseline (**HEUR**) that rests on the observation that German food items of the same food category often share the same suffix, e.g. *Schokoladenkuchen* (English: *chocolate cake*) and *Apfelkuchen* (English: *apple pie*). For HEUR, we manually compiled a set of few typical suffixes for each food type/dish category (ranging from 3 to 8 suffixes per category). For classification of a food item, we assign the food item the category label whose suffix matched with the food item.[2]

We also examine an *unsupervised* baseline (**UNSUP**) that applies spectral clustering on the similarity graph following von Luxburg (2007):

- Input: a similarity matrix W and the number of categories to detect k.
- The laplacian L is constructed from W. It is the symmetric laplacian $L = I - D^{1/2}WD^{1/2}$, where D is a diagonal degree matrix.[3]
- A matrix $U \in \mathbb{R}^{n \times k}$ is constructed that contains as columns the first k eigenvectors $u_1, \ldots, u_k$ of L.
- The rows of U are interpreted as the new data points. The final clustering is obtained by k-means clustering of the rows of U.

UNSUP (which is completely parameter-free) gives some indication about the intrinsic expressiveness of the similarity graph as it lacks any guidance towards the categories to be predicted.

In graph-based food categorization, one can only make predictions for food items that are connected (be it directly or indirectly) to seed food items within the similarity graph. To expand labels to unconnected food items, we apply some post-processing (**POSTP**). Similarly to HEUR, it exploits the suffix-similarity of food items. It assigns each unconnected food item the label of the food item (that could be labeled by the graph optimization) that shares the longest suffix. Due to their similar nature, we refrain from applying POSTP on HEUR as it would produce no changes.

[2]Unlike German food items, English food items are often multi-word expressions. Therefore, we assume that for English, instead of analyzing suffixes the usage of the head of a multiword expression (i.e. *chocolate cake*) would be an appropriate basis for a similar heuristic.

[3]That is, D_{ii} equals to the sum of the ith row.

		PLAIN				+POSTP			
Configuration	**graph**	**Acc**	**Prec**	**Rec**	**F1**	**Acc**	**Prec**	**Rec**	**F1**
UNSUP	✓	46.2	43.1	35.7	36.0	56.1	41.0	42.5	38.4
HEUR (plain)		25.5	87.9	32.2	42.9	*N/A*	*N/A*	*N/A*	*N/A*
HEUR	✓	56.4	73.6	52.1	54.7	68.7	72.3	64.3	60.7
PAT-Top1	✓	52.4	60.2	51.2	52.5	64.5	58.2	62.9	57.4
PAT-Top5	✓	61.1	70.7	61.9	64.4	74.5	67.9	76.0	69.7
PAT-Top10	✓	60.2	69.6	60.5	62.2	73.4	66.7	74.2	67.3
1-PROTO	✓	58.0	68.0	58.0	59.5	70.2	64.1	71.0	63.8
5-PROTO	✓	64.5	76.6	63.7	68.6	78.6	73.8	78.5	75.2
10-PROTO	✓	65.8	79.0	**65.5**	71.0	80.2	75.9	**80.6**	77.7
GermaNet (plain)		52.1	**94.0**	52.0	65.7	75.4	73.2	75.0	72.4
GermaNet	✓	**68.3**	84.7	63.4	**71.6**	**82.7**	**81.8**	77.7	**79.1**

Table 5: Comparison of different food-type classifiers (*graph* indicates graph-based optimization).

4 Experiments

We report precision, recall and F-score and accuracy.[4] For precision, recall and F-score, we list the macro-averaged score.

4.1 Evaluation of Food Categorization

4.1.1 Detection of Food Types

Table 5 compares different classifiers and configurations for the prediction of food types (against the gold standard from Table 1). Apart from the previously described baselines, we consider n manually selected prototypes (***n*-PROTO**) and the top n food items produced by Hearst-patterns (**PAT-Top*n***) as seeds for graph-based optimization. The table shows that the semi-supervised graph-based approach with these seeds outperforms the baselines UNSUP and HEUR. Only as few as 5 prototypical seeds (per category) are required to obtain performance that is even better than using plain GermaNet. The table also shows that post-processing (with our suffix-heuristics) consistently improves performance. Manually choosing prototypes is more effective than instantiating seeds via Hearst-patterns. The quality of the output of Hearst-patterns degrades from top 10 onwards. However, considering that PAT-Top*n* does not include any manual intervention, it already produces decent results. Finally, even GermaNet can be effectively used as seeds.

4.1.2 Detection of Dishes

Table 6 compares different classifiers for the detection of dishes (against the gold standard from Table 2). Dishes and atomic food items are very

[4]All manually labeled resources are available at: `www.lsv.uni-saarland.de/personalPages/michael/relFood.html`

		PLAIN				+POSTP			
Configuration	graph	Acc	Prec	Rec	F1	Acc	Prec	Rec	F1
UNSUP	✓	54.5	59.6	40.2	37.3	67.9	59.0	50.0	40.6
HEUR (plain)		**74.1**	**84.3**	59.9	58.6	*N/A*	*N/A*	*N/A*	*N/A*
PAT-Top25	✓	59.7	72.2	54.6	61.9	74.1	70.1	67.6	68.4
PAT-Top50	✓	60.9	74.4	55.6	63.1	75.9	72.7	69.2	70.3
PAT-Top100	✓	62.7	77.6	57.2	65.2	78.4	76.5	71.5	73.0
PAT-Top250	✓	59.6	71.8	55.1	62.2	74.2	70.3	68.7	69.3
RAND-25	✓	61.4	77.1	54.3	61.8	76.1	74.4	67.1	68.4
RAND-50	✓	62.6	76.3	60.1	67.2	77.2	74.0	76.8	74.4
RAND-100	✓	66.5	82.7	**63.0**	**71.3**	**83.0**	**80.8**	**79.5**	**80.1**
GermaNet (plain)		49.5	81.3	46.5	59.3	79.0	75.9	75.5	75.7
GermaNet	✓	60.8	79.4	51.3	57.6	75.9	78.2	64.4	65.4

Table 6: Comparison of different classifiers distinguishing between dishes and atomic food items (*graph* indicates graph-based optimization).

		PLAIN				+POSTP			
Configuration	graph	Acc	Prec	Rec	F1	Acc	Prec	Rec	F1
PAT-Top100 (plain)		9.5	89.5	10.5	18.6	63.6	61.5	63.5	61.3
PAT-Top100	✓	62.7	77.6	57.2	65.2	78.4	76.5	71.5	73.0
RAND-100 (plain)		10.6	**100.0**	12.2	21.4	70.2	69.7	69.0	69.0
RAND-100	✓	**66.5**	82.7	**63.0**	**71.3**	**83.0**	**80.8**	**79.5**	**80.1**

Table 7: Impact of graph-based optimization (*graph*) for the detection of dishes.

heterogeneous classes which is why more seeds are required for initialization. This means that we cannot look for *prototypes*. For simplicity, we resorted to randomly sample seeds from our gold standard (**RAND-*n***). For HEUR, we could not find a small and intuitive set of suffixes that are shared by *many* atomic food types, therefore we considered all food types from our vocabulary whose suffix did not match a typical dish suffix as atomic. As this leaves no unspecified food items in our vocabulary, we cannot use the output of HEUR as seeds for graph-based optimization.

In contrast to the previous experiment, HEUR is a more robust baseline. But again, post-processing mostly improves performance, and patterns are not as good as manual (random) seeds yet the former are notably better than HEUR w.r.t. F-Score. Unlike in the food-type classification, graph-based optimization applied on GermaNet does not result in some improvement. We assume that the precision of plain GermaNet with 81.3% is too low.[5]

Since GermaNet cannot effectively be used as seeds for the graph-based optimization and post-processing has already a strong positive effect, we may wonder how effective the actual graph-based optimization is for this classification task. After all, significantly more seeds are required for this classification task than for the previous task, so we need to show that it is not the mere seeds (+post-processing) that are required for a reasonable categorization. Table 7 examines two key configurations *with* and *without* graph-based optimization. It shows that also for this classification task, graph-based optimization produces a categorization superior to the mere seeds. Moreover, the suffix-based post-processing is complementary to the improvement by the graph-based optimization.

4.1.3 Comparison of Initialization Methods

Table 8 compares for each food type 5 manually selected prototypical seeds (i.e. 5-PROTO) and the 5 food items most frequently been observed with patt_{hearst} (Table 4). While the manually chosen seeds represent the spectrum of food items within each particular class (e.g. for STARCH, some type of pasta, rice and potato was chosen), it is not possible to enforce such diversity with the automatically extracted seeds. However, most food items are correct. Table 9 displays the 10 most highly ranked dishes and atomic food items extracted with patt_{dish} and patt_{atom} (Table 4). Unlike the previous task (Table 8), we obtain more heterogeneous seeds within the same class.

4.1.4 Distributional Similarity

Since many recent methods for related tasks, such as noun classification, are based on so-called *distributional similarity* (Riloff and Shepherd, 1997; Lin, 1998; Snow et al., 2004; Weeds et al., 2004; Yamada et al., 2009; Huang and Riloff, 2010; Lenci and Benotto, 2012), we also examine this as an alternative representation to the pattern-based similarity graph (Table 3). We represent each food item as a vector which itself is an aggregate of the contexts of all mentions of a particular food item. We weighted the individual (context) words co-occurring with the food item at a fixed window size of 5 words with *tf-idf*. We can now apply graph-based optimization on the similarity matrix encoding the cosine similarities between any possible pair of vectors representing two food items. As seeds, we use the best configuration (not employing GermaNet), i.e. *10-PROTO* for food type classification and *RAND-100* for the dish classification. Since, however, the graph clustering is not actually necessary, as we have a full similarity matrix (rather than a sparse graph) that also al-

[5]For other seeds for which it worked, we usually measured a precision of 90% or higher.

Class	5 Manually Chosen Seeds (5-PROTO)	5 Hearst-Pattern Seeds (PAT-Top5)
MEAT	*schnitzel, rissole, bologna, redfish, trout*	*salmon, beef, chicken, turkey hen, poultry*
BEVERAGE	*coffee, tea, water, beer, coke*	*coffee, beer, mineral water, lemonade, tea*
VEGE	*peas, green salad, tomato, cauliflower, carrot*	*zucchini, lamb's salad, broccoli, leek, cauliflower*
SWEET	*chocolate, torte, popcorn, apple pie, potato crisps*	*wine gum, marzipan, custard, pancake, biscuits*
SPICE	*pepper, cinnamon, salt, gravy, remoulade*	*cinnamon, laurel, clove, tomato sauce, basil*
STARCH	*spaghetti, basmati rice, white bread, potato, french fries*	*au gratin potatoes, jacket potato, potato, pita, jam*
MILK	*yoghurt, gouda, cream cheese, cream, butter milk*	*butter milk, bovine milk, soured milk, goat cheese, sour cream*
FRUIT	*banana, apple, strawberries, apricot, orange*	*banana, strawberries, pear, melon, kiwi*
GRAIN	*hazelnut, pumpkin seed, rye flour, semolina, wheat*	*sesame, spelt, wheat, millet, barley*
FAT	*margarine, lard, colza oil, spread, butter*	*margarine, lard, resolidified butter, coconut oil, tartar*
EGG	*scrambled eggs, fried eggs, chicken egg, omelette, pickled egg*	*yolk, fried eggs, albumen, offal, easter egg*

Table 8: Comparison of different seed initializations for the food type categorization task (underlined food items represent erroneously extracted food items).

lows us to compare any arbitrary pair of food items *directly*, we also employ a second classifier (for comparison) based on the *nearest neighbour* principle. We assign each food item the label of the most similar seed food item.

Table 10 compares these two classifiers with the best previous result. It shows that the pattern-based representation consistently outperforms the distributional representation. The former may be sparse but it produces high-precision similarity links.[6] The vector representation, on the other hand, may not be sparse but it contains a high degree of noise. The major problem is that not only vectors of similar food items, such as *chips* (*fries*), *potatoes* and *rice*, are similar to each other, but also vectors of different food items that are typically consumed with each other (e.g. *fish* and *chips*). This is because of their frequent co-occurrence (as in collocations like *fish & chips*). Unfortunately, these pairs belong to different food types. For the dish classification, however, the vector representation is less of a problem.[7]

The distributional representation works better with the simple nearest neighbour classifier. We assume that graph-based optimization adds further noise to the classification since, unlike the nearest neighbour which only calculates the *direct* similarity between two vectors, it also incorporates indirect relationships (which may be more error-prone than the direct relationships) between food items.

4.1.5 Do we need a domain-specific corpus?

In this section, we want to provide evidence that apart from the similarity graph and seeds the textual source for the graph, i.e. our domain-specific

Class	10 Seeds Extracted with Patterns (PAT-Top10)
DISH	*cookies, cake, praline, bread dumpling, jam, biscuit, cheese cake, black-and-whites, onion tart, pasta salad*
ATOM	*marzipan, flour, potato, olive oil, water, sugar, cream, chocolate, milk, tomato*

Table 9: Illustration of seed initialization for the distinction between dishes and atomic food items.

Task	Similarity	Classifier	Acc	F1
Food Type	distributional	nearest neighbour	53.4	51.1
	distributional	graph	25.6	25.6
	pattern-based	graph	**80.2**	**77.7**
Dish	distributional	nearest neighbour	76.8	75.2
	distributional	graph	71.5	71.2
	pattern-based	graph	**83.0**	**80.1**

Table 10: Impact of the similarity representation.

corpus (*chefkoch.de*), is also important. For that purpose, we compare our current corpus against an open-domain corpus. We consider the German version of *Wikipedia* since this resource also contains encyclopedic knowledge about food items. Table 11 compares the graph-based induction. As in the previous section, we only consider the best previous configuration. The table clearly shows that our domain-specific text corpus is a more effective resource for our purpose than *Wikipedia*.

4.2 Evaluation for Relation Extraction

We now examine whether automatic food categorization can be harnessed for relation extraction. The task is to detect instances of the relation types *SuitsTo*, *SubstitutedBy* and *IngredientOf* introduced Wiegand et al. (2012b) (repeated in Table 12) and motivated in Wiegand et al. (2012a). These relation types are highly relevant for customer advice/product recommendation. In particular, *SuitsTo* and *SubstitutedBy* are fairly domain-independent relation types. Customers want to

[6]By the label propagation within the graph-based optimization, the sparsity problem is also mitigated.

[7]*Fish* and *chips* are both atoms, so in the dish classification, it is no mistake to consider them similar food items.

know which items can be used together (*SuitsTo*), be it two food items that can be used as a meal or two fashion items that can be worn together. Substitutes are also relevant for situations in which item A is out of stock but item B can be offered as an alternative. Therefore, insights from this work should carry over to other domains.

We randomly extracted 1500 sentences from our text corpus (§2.1) in which (at least) two food items co-occur. Each food pair mention was manually assigned one label. In addition to the three relation types from above, we introduce the label *Other* for cases in which either another relation between the target food items is expressed or the co-occurrence is co-incidental. On a subset of 200 sentences, we measured a *substantial* inter-annotation agreement of Cohen's $\kappa = 0.67$ (Landis and Koch, 1977).

We train a supervised classifier and incorporate the knowledge induced from our domain-specific corpus as features. We chose Support Vector Machines with 5-fold cross-validation using *SVM^light-multi-class* (Joachims, 1999).

Table 13 displays all features that we examine for supervised classification. Most features are widely used throughout different NLP tasks. One special feature *brown* takes into consideration the output of *Brown clustering* (Brown et al., 1992) which like our graph-based optimization produces a corpus-driven categorization of words. Similar to *UNSUP*, this method is unsupervised but it considers the entire vocabulary of our text corpus rather than only food items. Therefore, this information can be considered as a generalization of all contextual words. Such type of information has been shown to be useful for named-entity recognition (Turian et al., 2010) and relation extraction (Plank and Moschitti, 2013).

For syntactic parsing, Stanford Parser (Rafferty and Manning, 2008) was used. For Brown clustering, the SRILM-toolkit (Stolcke, 2002) was used. Following Turian et al. (2010), we induced 1000 clusters (from our domain-specific corpus §2.1).

4.2.1 Why should food categories be helpful for relation extraction?

All relation types we consider comprise pairs of two food items which makes these relation types likely to be confused. Contextual information may be used for disambiguation but there may also be frequent contexts that are not sufficiently informative. For example, 25% of the instances of *IngredientOf* follow the lexical pattern *food_item*$_1$ *with food_item*$_2$ (1). However, the same pattern also covers 15% of the instances of *SuitsTo* (2).

			PLAIN		+POSTP	
Task	**Corpus**	**graph**	**Acc**	**F1**	**Acc**	**F1**
Food Type	Wikipedia	✓	40.3	49.4	61.4	59.8
	chefkoch.de	✓	65.8	**71.0**	80.2	**77.7**
Dish	Wikipedia	✓	50.4	53.1	75.4	71.1
	chefkoch.de	✓	66.5	**71.3**	83.0	**80.1**

Table 11: Comparison of Wikipedia and domain-specific corpus as a source for the similarity graph.

(1) We had a stew with red lentils. *(Relation: IngredientOf)*
(2) We had salmon with broccoli. *(Relation: SuitsTo)*

The food type information we learned from our text corpus might tell us which of the food items are dishes. Only in (1), there is a dish, i.e. *stew*. So, one may infer that the presence of dishes is indicative of *IngredientOf* rather than *SuitsTo*.

food_item$_1$ *and food_item*$_2$ is another ambiguous context. It cannot only be observed with the relation *SuitsTo*, as in (3) (66% of all instantiations of that pattern), but also *SubstitutedBy* (20% of all mentions of that relation match that pattern), as in (4). For *SuitsTo*, two food items that belong to two different classes (e.g. *MEAT* and *STARCH* or *MEAT* and *VEGE*) are quite characteristic. For *SubstitutedBy*, the two food items are very often of the same category of the *Food Guide Pyramid*.

(3) I very often eat fish and chips. *(Relation: SuitsTo)*
(4) For these types of dishes you can offer both Burgundy wine and Champagne. *(Relation: SubstitutedBy)*

Since the second ambiguous context involves the two general relation types *SuitsTo* and *SubstitutedBy*, resolving this ambiguity with automatically induced type information has some significance for other domains. In particular, for other life-style domains, domain-specific type information could be obtained following our method from §3.1. The disambiguation rule that two entities of the same type imply *SubstitutedBy* otherwise they imply *SuitsTo* should also be widely applicable.

4.2.2 Results

Table 14 displays the performance of the different feature sets for relation extraction. The features designed from graph-based induction (i.e. *graph*) work slightly better than GermaNet. The performance of *patt* is not impressively high. However, one should consider that *patt* can be used directly without a supervised classifier (as each pattern is

Relation	Description	Example	Freq.	Perc.
SuitsTo	food items that are typically consumed together	My kids love the simple combination of fish fingers with mashed potatoes.	633	42.20
SubstitutedBy	similar food items commonly consumed in the same situations	We usually buy margarine instead of butter.	336	22.40
IngredientOf	ingredient of a particular dish	Falafel is made of chickpeas.	246	16.40
Other	other relation *or* co-occurrence of food items are co-incidental	On my shopping list, I've got bread, cauliflower, ...	285	19.00

Table 12: The different relation types and their respective frequency on our dataset.

Features	Description
patt	lexical surface patterns used in Wiegand et al. (2012b)
word	bag-of-words features: all words within the sentence
brown	features using Brown clustering: all features from *word* but words are replaced by induced clusters
pos	part-of-speech sequence between target food items and tags of the words immediately preceding and following them
synt	path from syntactic parse tree from first target food item to second target food item
conj	conjunctive features: *patt* with brown classes of target food items; *pos* sequence with brown classes of target food items; *synt* with brown classes of target food items
graph	semantic food information induced by graph optimization (config.: *10-PROTO(+POSTP)* and *RAND-100(+POSTP)*)
germanet	semantic food information derived from (plain) GermaNet

Table 13: Description of the feature set.

Features	Acc	Prec	Rec	F1
germanet	45.3	41.3	37.2	37.3
graph	46.0	39.4	39.7	38.6
patt	59.8	49.8	41.1	38.7
word	60.1	56.9	54.5	55.1
word+patt	60.3	57.3	54.9	55.5
word+brown	59.5	56.1	54.6	54.9
word+synt	60.3	57.7	55.4	56.0
word+pos	59.8	56.6	54.6	55.1
word+germanet	61.3	58.6	56.0	56.7
word+graph	62.9	59.2	57.6	58.1°
word+patt+brown+synt+pos	60.4	57.3	56.2	56.5
word+patt+brown+synt+pos+conj	61.7	59.0	57.8	58.2*
word+patt+brown+synt+pos+conj+germanet	63.1	60.2	58.6	59.1°
word+patt+brown+synt+pos+conj+graph	**64.7**	**62.1**	**60.3**	**60.9°†**

statistical significance testing (paired t-test): better than *word* * at $p < 0.1$/ ° at $p < 0.05$; † better than *word+patt+brown+synt+pos+conj* at $p < 0.05$

Table 14: Comparison of various features (Table 13) for (unrestricted) relation extraction.

designed for a particular relation type, one can read off from the matching pattern which class is predicted). *word* is slightly better but, unlike *patt*, it is dependent on supervised learning.

The only feature that individually manages to significantly outperform *word* is *graph*. The traditional features (i.e. *pos*, *synt* and *brown*) only produce some mild improvement when added jointly to *word* along some conjunctive features. When *graph* is added to this feature set (i.e. *word+patt+pos+synt+brown+conj*), we obtain another significant improvement. In conclusion, the information we induced from our domain-specific corpus cannot be obtained by other NLP-features, including other state-of-the-art induction methods such as Brown clustering.

5 Related Work

While many of the previous works on noun categorization also address the task of hypernym classification (Hearst, 1992; Caraballo, 1999; Widdows, 2003; Kozareva et al., 2008; Huang and Riloff, 2010; Lenci and Benotto, 2012) and some include examples involving food items (Widdows and Dorow, 2002; Cederberg and Widdows, 2003), only van Hage et al. (2005) and van Hage et al. (2006) specifically focus on the classification of food items. van Hage et al. (2005) deal with ontology mapping whereas van Hage et al. (2006) explore part-whole relations.

The task of data-driven lexicon expansion has also been explored before (Kanayama and Nasukawa, 2006; Das and Smith, 2012), however, our paper presents the first attempt to carry out a *comprehensive* categorization for the food domain. For the first time, we also show that type information can effectively improve the extraction of very common relations. For the twitter domain, the usage of type information based on clustering has already been found effective for supervised learning (Bergsma et al., 2013).

6 Conclusion

We presented an induction method to assign semantic information to food items. We considered two types of categorizations being food-type information and information about whether a food item is composite or not. The categorization is induced by graph-based optimization applied on a large unlabeled domain-specific text corpus. We produce categorizations that outperform a manually compiled resource. The usage of such a domain-specific corpus based on a pattern-based representation is vital and largely outperforms other text corpora or a distributional representation. The induced knowledge improves relation extraction.

Acknowledgements

This work was performed in the context of the Software-Cluster project SINNODIUM. Michael Wiegand was funded by the German Federal Ministry of Education and Research (BMBF) under grant no. 01IC12SO1X. Benjamin Roth is a recipient of the Google Europe Fellowship in Natural Language Processing, and this research is supported in part by this Google Fellowship. The authors would like to thank Stephanie Köser for annotating the dataset presented in this paper.

References

Mikhail Belkin and Partha Niyogi. 2004. Semi-supervised learning on Riemannian manifolds. *Machine Learning*, 56(1-3):209–239.

Shane Bergsma, Mark Dredze, Benjamin Van Durme, Theresa Wilson, and David Yarowsky. 2013. Broadly Improving User Classification via Communication-Based Name and Location Clustering on Twitter. In *Proceedings of the Human Language Technology Conference of the North American Chapter of the ACL (HLT/NAACL)*, pages 1010–1019, Atlanta, GA, USA.

Peter F. Brown, Peter V. deSouza, Robert L. Mercer, Vincent J. Della Pietra, and Jenifer C. Lai. 1992. Class-based n-gram models of natural language. *Computational Linguistics*, 18:467–479.

Sharon A. Caraballo. 1999. Automatic construction of a hypernym-labeled noun hierarchy from text. In *Proceedings of the Annual Meeting of the Association for Computational Linguistics (ACL)*, pages 120–126, College Park, MD, USA.

Scott Cederberg and Dominic Widdows. 2003. Using LSA and Noun Coordination Information to Improve the Precision and Recall of Automatic Hyponymy Extraction. In *Proceedings of the Conference on Computational Natural Language Learning (CoNLL)*, pages 111–118, Edmonton, Alberta, Canada.

Dipanjan Das and Noah A. Smith. 2012. Graph-Based Lexicon Expansion with Sparsity-Inducing Penalties. In *Proceedings of the Human Language Technology Conference of the North American Chapter of the ACL (HLT/NAACL)*, pages 677–687, Montréal, Quebec, Canada.

Birgit Hamp and Helmut Feldweg. 1997. GermaNet - a Lexical-Semantic Net for German. In *Proceedings of ACL workshop Automatic Information Extraction and Building of Lexical Semantic Resources for NLP Applications*, pages 9–15, Madrid, Spain.

Marti A. Hearst. 1992. Automatic Acquisition of Hyponyms from Large Text Corpora. In *Proceedings of the International Conference on Computational Linguistics (COLING)*, pages 539–545, Nantes, France.

Ruihong Huang and Ellen Riloff. 2010. Inducing Domain-specific Semantic Class Taggers from (almost) Nothing. In *Proceedings of the Annual Meeting of the Association for Computational Linguistics (ACL)*, pages 275–285, Uppsala, Sweden.

Thorsten Joachims. 1999. Making Large-Scale SVM Learning Practical. In B. Schölkopf, C. Burges, and A. Smola, editors, *Advances in Kernel Methods - Support Vector Learning*, pages 169–184. MIT Press.

Hiroshi Kanayama and Tetsuya Nasukawa. 2006. Fully Automatic Lexicon Expansion for Domain-oriented Sentiment Analysis. In *Proceedings of the Conference on Empirical Methods in Natural Language Processing (EMNLP)*, pages 355–363, Sydney, Australia.

Zornitsa Kozareva, Ellen Riloff, and Eduard Hovy. 2008. Semantic Class Learning from the Web with Hyponym Pattern Linkage Graphs. In *Proceedings of the Annual Meeting of the Association for Computational Linguistics (ACL)*, pages 1048–1056, Columbus, OH, USA.

J. Richard Landis and Gary G. Koch. 1977. The Measurement of Observer Agreement for Categorical Data. *Biometrics*, 33(1):159–174.

Alessandro Lenci and Guilia Benotto. 2012. Identifying hypernyms in distributional semantic spaces. In *Proceedings of the Joint Conference on Lexical and Computational Semantics (*SEM)*, pages 75–79, Montréal, Quebec, Canada.

Dekang Lin. 1998. Automatic Retrieval and Clustering of Similar Words. In *Proceedings of the Annual Meeting of the Association for Computational Linguistics and International Conference on Computational Linguistics (ACL/COLING)*, pages 768–774, Montreal, Quebec, Canada.

George Miller, Richard Beckwith, Christiane Fellbaum, Derek Gross, and Katherine Miller. 1990. Introduction to WordNet: An On-line Lexical Database. *International Journal of Lexicography*, 3:235–244.

Barbara Plank and Alessandro Moschitti. 2013. Embedding Semantic Similarity in Tree Kernels for Domain Adapation of Relation Extraction. In *Proceedings of the Annual Meeting of the Association for Computational Linguistics (ACL)*, pages 1498–1507, Sofia, Bulgaria.

Anna Rafferty and Christopher D. Manning. 2008. Parsing Three German Treebanks: Lexicalized and Unlexicalized Baselines. In *Proceedings of the ACL Workshop on Parsing German (PaGe)*, pages 40–46, Columbus, OH, USA.

Ellen Riloff and Jessica Shepherd. 1997. A Corpus-Based Approach for Building Semantic Lexicons. In *Proceedings of the Conference on Empirical Methods in Natural Language Processing (EMNLP)*, pages 117–124, Providence, RI, USA.

Rion Snow, Daniel Jurafsky, and Andrew Y. Ng. 2004. Learning Syntactic Patterns for Automatic Hypernym Discovery. In *Advances in Neural Information Processing Systems (NIPS)*, Vancouver, British Columbia, Canada.

Andreas Stolcke. 2002. SRILM - An Extensible Language Modeling Toolkit. In *Proceedings of the International Conference on Spoken Language Processing (ICSLP)*, pages 901–904, Denver, CO, USA.

Joseph Turian, Lev Ratinov, and Yoshua Bengio. 2010. Word Representations: A Simple and General Method for Semi-supervised Learning. In *Proceedings of the Annual Meeting of the Association for Computational Linguistics (ACL)*, pages 384–394, Uppsala, Sweden.

Human Nutrition Information Service U.S. Department of Agriculture. 1992. The Food Guide Pyramid. Home and Garden Bulletin 252, Washington, D.C., USA.

Willem Robert van Hage, Sophia Katrenko, and Guus Schreiber. 2005. A Method to Combine Linguistic Ontology-Mapping Techniques. In *Proceedings of International Semantic Web Conference (ISWC)*, pages 732 – 744, Galway, Ireland. Springer.

Willem Robert van Hage, Hap Kolb, and Guus Schreiber. 2006. A Method for Learning Part-Whole Relations. In *Proceedings of International Semantic Web Conference (ISWC)*, pages 723 – 735, Athens, GA, USA. Springer.

Ulrike von Luxburg. 2007. A Tutorial on Spectral Clustering. *Statistics and Computing*, 17:395–416.

Julie Weeds, David Weir, and Diana McCarthy. 2004. Characterising Measures of Lexical Distributional Similarity. In *Proceedings of the International Conference on Computational Linguistics (COLING)*, pages 1015–1021, Geneva, Switzerland.

Dominic Widdows and Beate Dorow. 2002. A Graph Model for Unsupervised Lexical Acquisition. In *Proceedings of the International Conference on Computational Linguistics (COLING)*, pages 1093–1099, Taipei, Taiwan.

Dominic Widdows. 2003. Unsupervised methods for developing taxonomies by combining syntactic and statistical information. In *Proceedings of the Human Language Technology Conference of the North American Chapter of the ACL (HLT/NAACL)*, pages 197–204, Edmonton, Alberta, Canada.

Michael Wiegand, Benjamin Roth, and Dietrich Klakow. 2012a. Knowledge Acquisition with Natural Language Processing in the Food Domain: Potential and Challenges. In *Proceedings of the ECAI-Workshop on Cooking with Computers (CWC)*, pages 46–51, Montpellier, France.

Michael Wiegand, Benjamin Roth, and Dietrich Klakow. 2012b. Web-based Relation Extraction for the Food Domain. In *Proceedings of the International Conference on Applications of Natural Language Processing to Information Systems (NLDB)*, pages 222–227, Groningen, the Netherlands. Springer.

Michael Wiegand, Benjamin Roth, Eva Lasarcyk, Stephanie Köser, and Dietrich Klakow. 2012c. A Gold Standard for Relation Extraction in the Food Domain. In *Proceedings of the Conference on Language Resources and Evaluation (LREC)*, pages 507–514, Istanbul, Turkey.

Ichiro Yamada, Kentaro Torisawa, Jun'ichi Kazama, Kow Kuroda, Masaki Murata, Stijn De Saeger, Francis Bond, and Asuka Sumida. 2009. Hypernym Discovery Based on Distributional Similarity and Hierarchical Structures. In *Proceedings of the Conference on Empirical Methods in Natural Language Processing (EMNLP)*, pages 929–927, Singapore.

Dengyong Zhou, Olivier Bousquet, Thomas Navin Lal, Jason Weston, and Bernhard Schölkopf. 2004. Learning with Local and Global Consistency. In *Advances in Neural Information Processing Systems (NIPS)*, Vancouver and Whistler, British Columbia, Canada.

Redundancy Detection in ESL Writings

Huichao Xue and **Rebecca Hwa**
Department of Computer Science,
University of Pittsburgh,
210 S Bouquet St, Pittsburgh, PA 15260, USA
{hux10,hwa}@cs.pitt.edu

Abstract

This paper investigates *redundancy detection* in ESL writings. We propose a measure that assigns high scores to words and phrases that are likely to be redundant within a given sentence. The measure is composed of two components: one captures *fluency* with a language model; the other captures *meaning preservation* based on analyzing alignments between words and their translations. Experiments show that the proposed measure is five times more accurate than the random baseline.

1 Introduction

Writing concisely is challenging. It is especially the case when writing in a foreign language that one is still learning. As a non-native speaker, it is more difficult to judge whether a word or a phrase is redundant. This study focuses on automatically detecting redundancies in English as a Second Language learners' writings.

Redundancies occur when the writer includes some extraneous word or phrase that do not add to the meaning of the sentence but possibly make the sentence more awkward to read. Upon removal of the unnecessary words or phrases, the sentence should improve in its fluency while maintaining the original meaning. In the NUCLE corpus (Dahlmeier and Ng, 2011), an annotated learner corpus comprised of essays written by primarily Singaporean students, 13.71% errors are tagged as "local redundancy errors", making redundancy error the second most frequent problem.[1]

Although redundancies occur frequently, it has not been studied as widely as other ESL errors. A major challenge is that, unlike mistakes that violate the grammaticality of a sentence, redundancies do not necessarily "break" the sentence. Determining which word or phrase is redundant is more of a stylistic question; it is more subjective, and sometimes difficult even for a native speaker.

To the best of our knowledge, this paper reports a first study on redundancy detection. In particular, we focus on the task of defining a redundancy measure that estimates the likelihood that a given word or phrase within a sentence might be extraneous. We propose a measure that takes into account each word's contribution to fluency and meaning. The fluency component computes the language model score of the sentence after the deletion of a word or a phrase. The meaning preservation component makes use of the sentence's translation into another language as pivot, then it applies a statistical machine translation (SMT) alignment model to infer the contribution of each word/phrase to the meaning of the sentence. As a first experiment, we evaluate our measures on their abilities in picking the most redundant phrase of a given length. We show that our measure is five times more accurate than a random baseline.

2 Redundancies in ESL Writings

According to *The Elements of Style* (Strunk, 1918): concise writing requires that *"every word tell."* In that sense, words that "do not tell" are redundant. Determining whether a certain word/phrase is redundant is a stylistic question, which is difficult to quantify. As a result, most annotation resources do not explicitly identify redundancies. One exception is the NUCLE corpus. Below are some examples from the NUCLE corpus, where the bold-faced words/phrases are marked as redundant.

> $\mathbf{Ex_1}$: First of all , there should be a careful consideration about what **are the things that** governments should pay for.

[1] The most frequent error type is *Wrong collocation/idiom preposition*, which comprises 15.69% of the total errors.

Proceedings of the 14th Conference of the European Chapter of the Association for Computational Linguistics, pages 683–691,
Gothenburg, Sweden, April 26-30 2014.

$\mathbf{Ex_2}$: GM wishes to reposition itself as an innovative company **to the public**.
$\mathbf{Ex_3}$: These findings are often unpredictable **and uncertain**.
$\mathbf{Ex_4}$: ...the cost incurred is not **only** just large sum of money ...

These words/phrases are considered redundant because they are unnecessary (e.g. $\mathbf{Ex_1}$, $\mathbf{Ex_2}$) or repetitive (e.g. $\mathbf{Ex_3}$, $\mathbf{Ex_4}$).

However, in NUCLE's annotation scheme, some words that were marked redundant are really words that carry undesirable meanings. For example:

$\mathbf{Ex_5}$: ...through which they **can** insert a special ...
$\mathbf{Ex_6}$: ...the analysis and **therefore** selection of a single solution for adaptation...

Note that unlike redundancies, these undesirable words/phrases change the sentences' meanings. Despite the difference in definitions, our experimental work uses the NUCLE corpus because it provides many real world examples of redundancy.

While redundancy detection has not yet been widely studied, it is related to several areas of active research, such as grammatical error correction (GEC), sentence simplification and sentence compression.

Work in GEC attempts to build automatic systems to detect/correct grammatical errors (Leacock et al., 2010; Liu et al., 2010; Tetreault et al., 2010; Dahlmeier and Ng, 2011; Rozovskaya and Roth, 2010). Both redundancy detection and GEC aim to improve students' writings. However, because redundancies do not necessarily break grammaticality, they have received little attention in GEC.

Sentence compression and sentence simplification also consider deleting words from input sentences. However, these tasks have different goals.

Automated sentence simplification (Coster and Kauchak, 2011) systems aim at reducing the grammatical complexity of an input sentence. To illustrate the difference, consider the phrase "critical reception." A sentence simplification system might rewrite it into "reviews"; but a system that removes redundancy should leave it unchanged because neither "critical" nor "reception" is extraneous. Moreover, consider the redundant phrase "had once before" in $\mathbf{Ex_4}$. A simplification system does not need to change it because these words do not add complexity to the sentence.

... and [the] cost incurred is [not] only [just] large sum of money ...

Figure 1: Among the three circled words, "just" is more redundant because deleting it hurts nether fluency nor meaning.

Sentence compression systems (Jing, 2000; Knight and Marcu, 2000; McDonald, 2006; Clarke and Lapata, 2007) aim at shortening a sentence while retaining the most important information and keeping it grammatically correct. This goal distinguishes these systems from ours in two major aspects. First, sentence compression systems assume that the original sentence is well-written; therefore retaining words specific to the sentence (e.g. "uncertain" in $\mathbf{Ex_3}$) can be a good strategy (Clarke and Lapata, 2007). In the ESL context, however, even specific words could still be redundant. For example, although "uncertain" is specific to $\mathbf{Ex_3}$, it is redundant, because its meaning is already implied by "unpredictable". Second, sentence compression systems try to shorten a sentence as much as possible, but an ESL redundancy detector should leave as much of the input sentences unchanged, if possible.

One challenge involved in redundancy detection is that it often involves open class words ($\mathbf{Ex_3}$), as well as multi-word expressions ($\mathbf{Ex_1}$, $\mathbf{Ex_4}$). Current GEC systems dealing with such error types are mostly MT based. MT systems tend to either require large training corpora (Brockett et al., 2006; Liu et al., 2010), or provide whole sentence rewritings (Madnani et al., 2012). Hermet and Désilets (2009) attempted to extract single preposition corrections from whole sentence rewritings. Our work incorporates alignments information to handle complex changes on both word and phrase levels.

In our approximation, we consider MT output as an approximation of word/phrase meanings. Using words in other languages to represent meanings has been explored in Carpuat and Wu (2007), where the focus is the aligned words' identities. Our work instead focuses more on how many words each word is aligned to.

3 A Probabilistic Model of Redundancy

We consider a word or a phrase to be redundant if deleting it results in a fluent English sentence that conveys the same meaning as before. For example, "not" and "the" are not considered re-

(a) Unaligned English words are considered redundant.

(b) Multiple English words aligned to the same meaning unit. These words are considered redundant.

Figure 2: Configurations our system consider as redundant. In each figure, the shaded squares are the words considered to be more redundant than other words in the same figure.

dundant in Figure 1. This is because discarding "not" would flip the sentence's meaning; discarding "the" would lose a necessary determiner before a noun. In contrast, discarding "just" would hurt neither fluency nor meaning. It is thus considered to be more redundant.

Therefore, our computational model needs to consider words' contributions to both fluency and meaning. Figure 2 illustrates words' contribution to meaning. In those two examples, each subgraph visualizes a sentence: English words correspond to squares in the top row, while their meanings correspond to circles in the bottom row. The knowledge of which word represents what meaning helps in evaluating its contribution. In particular, if a word does not connote any significant meaning, deleting it would not affect the overall sentence; if several words express the same meaning, then deleting some of them might not affect the overall sentence either. Also, deleting a more semantically meaningful word (or phrase) is more likely to cause a loss of meaning of the overall sentence (e.g. *uncertain* v.s. *the*).

Our model computes a single probabilistic value for both fluency judgment and meaning preservation – the log-likelihood that after deleting a certain word or phrase of a sentence, the new sentence is still fluent and conveys the same meaning as before. This value reflects our definition of redundancy – the higher this probability, the more redundant the given word/phrase is.

More formally, suppose an English sentence e contains l_e words: $e = e_1 e_2 \dots e_{l_e}$; after some sub-string $e^{s,t} = e_s \dots e_t (1 \leq s \leq t \leq l_e)$ is deleted from e, we obtain a shorter sentence, denoted as $e_{-}^{s,t}$. We wish to compute the quantity $R(s,t;e)$, the chance that the sub-string $e^{s,t}$ is redundant in sentence e. We propose a probabilistic model to formalize this notion.

Let M be a random variable over some meaning representation; $\Pr(M|e)$ is the likelihood that M carries the meaning of e. If the sub-string $e^{s,t}$ is redundant, then the new sentence $e_{-}^{s,t}$ should still express the same meaning; $\Pr(e_{-}^{s,t}|M)$ computes the likelihood that the after-deletion sentence can be generated from meaning M.

$$
\begin{aligned}
& R(s,t;e) \\
= \;& \log \sum_{M=m} \Pr(m|e) \Pr(e_{-}^{s,t}|m) \\
= \;& \log \sum_{M=m} \frac{\Pr(m|e) \Pr(e_{-}^{s,t}) \Pr(m|e_{-}^{s,t})}{\Pr(m)} \\
= \;& \log \Pr(e_{-}^{s,t}) + \log \sum_{M=m} \frac{\Pr(m|e_{-}^{s,t}) \Pr(m|e)}{\Pr(m)} \\
= \;& \mathrm{LM}(e_{-}^{s,t}) + \mathrm{AGR}(M|e_{-}^{s,t}, e) \qquad (1)
\end{aligned}
$$

The first term $\mathrm{LM}(e_{-}^{s,t})$ is the after-deletion sentence's log-likelihood, which reflects its fluency. We calculate the first term with a trigram language model (LM).

The second term $\mathrm{AGR}(M|e_{-}^{s,t}, e)$ can be interpreted as the chance that e and $e_{-}^{s,t}$ carry the same meaning, discounted by "chance agreement". This term captures meaning preservation.

The two terms above are complementary to each other. Intuitively, LM prefers keeping common words in $e_{-}^{s,t}$ (e.g. *the, to*) while AGR prefers keeping words specific to e (e.g. *disease, hypertension*).

To make the calculation of the second term practical, we make two simplifying assumptions.

Assumption 1 A sentence's meaning can be represented by its translations in another language; its words' contributions to the meaning of the sentence can be represented by the mapping between the words in the original sentence and its translations (Figure 3).

Note that the choice of translation language may impact the interpretation of words' contributions. We will discuss about this issue in our experiments (Section 5).

Assumption 2 Instead of considering all possible translations f for e, our computation will make use of the most likely translation, f_*.

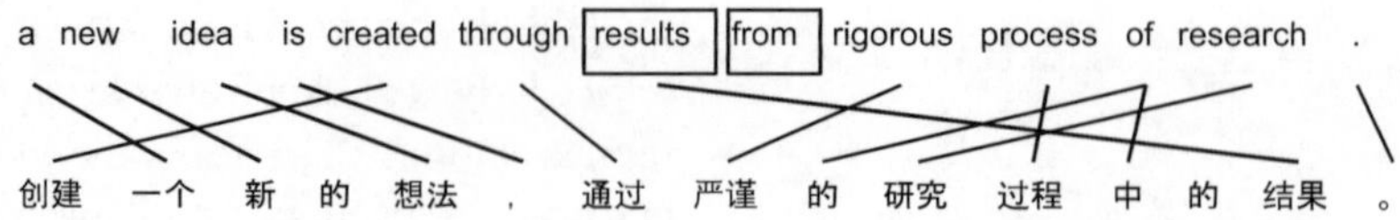

Figure 3: Illustration of Assumption 1 and Approximation 1. An English sentence's meaning is presented as a Chinese translation. Meanwhile, each (English) word's contribution to the sentence meaning is realized as a word alignment. For Approximation 1, note that sentence alignments normally won't be affected before/after deleting words (e.g. "results from") from the source sentence.

With the two approximations:

$$\begin{aligned}\text{AGR}(M|e_-^{s,t}, e) &\approx \log \frac{\Pr(f_*|e_-^{s,t}) \Pr(f_*|e)}{\Pr(f_*)} \\ &= \log \Pr(f_*|e_-^{s,t}) + C_1(e)\end{aligned}$$

(We use $C_i(e)$ to denote constant numbers within sentence e throughout the paper.)

We now rely on a statistical machine translation model to approximate the translation probability $\log \Pr(f_*|e_-^{s,t})$.

One naive way of calculating this probability measure is to consult the MT system. This method, however, is too computationally expensive for one single input sentence. For a sentence of length n, calculating the redundancy measure for all chunks in it would require issuing $O(n^2)$ translation queries. We propose an approximation that instead calculates the difference of translation probability caused by discarding $e^{s,t}$, based on an analysis on the alignment structure between e and f_*. We show the measure boils down to summing the expected number of aligned words for each $e_i (s \leq i \leq t)$, and possibly weighting these numbers by e_i's unigram probability. This method requires one translation query, and $O(n^2)$ queries into a language model, which is much more suitable for practical applications. Our method also sheds light on the role of alignment structures in the redundancy detection context.

3.1 Alignments Approximation

One key insight in our approximation is that the alignment structure a between $e_-^{s,t}$ and f_* would be largely similar with the alignment structure between e and f_*. We illustrate this notion in Figure 3. Note that after deleting two words "results from" from the source sentence in Figure 3, the alignment structure remains unchanged elsewhere. Also, "结果", the word once connected with "results", can now be seen as connected to blanks.

We hence approximate $\log \Pr(f_*|e_-^{s,t})$ by reusing the alignment structure between e and f_*. To make the alignment structures compatible, we start with redefining $e_-^{s,t}$ as $e_1, e_2, \ldots, e_{s-1}, \square, \ldots, \square, e_{t+1}, \ldots, e_{l_e}$, where the deleted words are left blank.

Let $\Pr(a|f, e)$ be the posterior distribution of alignment structure between sentence pair (f, e).

Approximation 1 We formalize the similarity between the alignment structures by assuming the KL-divergence between their alignment distributions to be small.

$$D_{\text{KL}}(a|f_*, e; a|f_*, e_-^{s,t}) \approx 0$$

This allows using $\Pr(a|f_*, e)$ to help approximate $\log \Pr(f_*|e_-^{s,t})$:

$$\begin{aligned}&\log \Pr(f_*|e_-^{s,t}) \\ =\ & \log \sum_a \Pr(a|f_*, e) \frac{\Pr(f_*, a|e_-^{s,t})}{\Pr(a|f_*, e)} \\ =\ & \sum_a \Pr(a|f_*, e) \log \frac{\Pr(f_*, a|e_-^{s,t})}{\Pr(a|f_*, e)} \\ & \underbrace{+ \sum_a \Pr(a|f_*, e) \log \left(\Pr(f_*|e_-^{s,t}) / \frac{\Pr(f_*, a|e_-^{s,t})}{\Pr(a|f_*, e)} \right)}_{D_{\text{KL}}(a|f_*, e; a|f_*, e_-^{s,t}) \approx 0} \\ \approx\ & \sum_a \Pr(a|f_*, e) \log \Pr(f_*|e_-^{s,t}, a) + C_2(e)\end{aligned}$$

We then use an SMT model to calculate $\log \Pr(f_*|e_-^{s,t}, a)$, the translation probability under a given alignment structure.

3.2 The Translation Model

Approximation 2 We will use IBM Model 1 (Brown et al., 1993) to calculate $\log \Pr(f_*|e_-^{s,t}, a)$

IBM Model 1 is one of the earliest statistical translation models. It helps us to compute

$\log \Pr(f_*|e_{-}^{s,t}, a)$ by making explicit how each word contributes to words it aligns with. In particular, to compute the probability that f is a translation of e, $\Pr(f|e)$, IBM Model 1 defined a generative alignment model where every word f_i in f is aligned with exactly one word e_{a_i} in e, so that f_i and e_{a_i} are word level translations of each other.

$$\begin{aligned}&\sum_a \Pr(a|f_*, e) \log \Pr(f_*|e_{-}^{s,t}, a)\\ =& \sum_a \Pr(a|f_*, e) \sum_{1\le i\le l_{f_*}} \log \Pr(f_*^i|e_{-a_i}^{s,t})\\ =& \sum_a \Pr(a|f_*, e) \sum_{1\le i\le l_{f_*}} \log \frac{\Pr(f_*^i|e_{-a_i}^{s,t})}{\Pr(f_*^i|e_{a_i})} + C_3(e)\end{aligned}$$

Note that

$$\log \frac{\Pr(f_*^i|e_{-a_i}^{s,t})}{\Pr(f_*^i|e_{a_i})} = \begin{cases} 0 & \text{, for } a_i \notin \{s \ldots t\} \\ \log \frac{\Pr(f_*^i|\Box)}{\Pr(f_*^i|e_{a_i})} & \text{, otherwise} \end{cases}$$

$$\begin{aligned}&\sum_a \Pr(a|f_*, e) \sum_{1\le i\le l_{f_*}} \log \frac{\Pr(f_*^i|e_{-a_i}^{s,t})}{\Pr(f_*^i|e_{a_i})}\\ =& \sum_a \Pr(a|f_*, e) \sum_{1\le i\le l_{f_*}} \sum_{s\le j\le t} I_{a_i=j} \log \frac{\Pr(f_*^i|\Box)}{\Pr(f_*^i|e_j)}\\ =& \underbrace{\sum_{s\le j\le t} \sum_{1\le i\le l_{f_*}} \underbrace{\Pr(a_i = j|f_*, e)}_{A_{i,j}} \log \frac{\Pr(f_*^i|\Box)}{\Pr(f_*^i|e_j)}}_{\mathrm{DIFF}(e_{-}^{s,t}, e)}\end{aligned}$$

Here $A_{i,j} = \Pr(a_i = j \mid f_*, e)$, which is the probability of the i-th word in the translation being aligned to the j-th word in the original sentence.

3.3 Per-word Contribution

Through deductions,

$$\begin{aligned} R(s, t; e) &= \mathrm{LM}(e_{-}^{s,t}) + \mathrm{DIFF}(e_{-}^{s,t}, e) \\ &\quad + C_1(e) + C_2(e) + C_3(e) \end{aligned}$$

the redundancy measure boils down to how we define $\Pr(f_*^i|\Box_j)$, which is: when we discard e_j, how do we generate the word it aligns f_*^i with in its translation. This value reflects e_j's contribution in generating f_*^i.

We approximate $\Pr(f_*^i|\Box_j)$ in two ways.

1. Suppose that all words in the translation are of equal importance. We assume $\log \frac{\Pr(f_*^i|\Box)}{\Pr(f_*^i|e_j)} = -C_c$, where C_c is a constant number. A larger C_c value indicates a higher importance of e_j during the translation.

$$\begin{aligned} \mathrm{DIFF}(e_{-}^{s,t}, e) &= -C_c \sum_{s\le j\le t} \sum_{1\le i\le l_{f_*}} A_{i,j} \\ &= -C_c \sum_{s\le j\le t} A(j) \end{aligned} \quad (2)$$

Here $A(j)$ is the expected number of alignments to e_j. This metric demonstrates the intuition that words aligned to more words in the translation are less redundant.

2. We note that rare words are often more important, and therefore harder to be generated. We assume $\Pr(f_*^i|\Box) = \Pr(e_j|\Box)\Pr(f_*^i|e_j)$.

$$\begin{aligned} &\mathrm{DIFF}(e_{-}^{s,t}, e) \\ =& \sum_{s\le j\le t} \sum_{1\le i\le l_{f_*}} A_{i,j} \log \frac{\Pr(e_j|\Box)\Pr(f_*^i|e_j)}{\Pr(f_*^i|e_j)} \\ =& \sum_{s\le j\le t} A(j) \log \Pr(e_j|\Box) \end{aligned} \quad (3)$$

This gives us counts on how likely each word is aligned with Chinese words according to $\Pr(a|f_*, e)$, where each word is weighted by its importance $\log \Pr(e_j|\Box)$. We use e_j's unigram probability to approximate $\log \Pr(e_j|\Box)$.

When estimating the alignment probabilities $A_{i,j}$, we smooth the alignment result from Google translation using Dirichlet-smoothing, where we set $\alpha = 0.1$ empirically based on experiments in the development dataset.

4 Experimental Setup

A fully automated redundancy detector has to decide (1) whether a given sentence contains any redundancy errors; (2) how many words constitute the redundant part; and (3) which exact words are redundant. In this paper, we focus on the third part while assuming the first two are given. Thus, our experimental task is: given a sentence known to contain a redundant phrase of a particular length, can that redundant phrase be accurately identified? For most sentences in our study, this results in choosing one from around 20 words/phrases.

While the task has a somewhat limited scope, it allows us to see how we could formally measure the difference between redundant words/phrases and non-redundant ones. For each measure, we observe whether it has assigned the highest score to the redundant part of the sentence. We compare the proposed redundancy model described in Section 3 against a set of baselines and other potential redundancy measures (to be described shortly).

To better understand different measures' performance on function words vs. content words, we also calculate the percentage of redundant function/content words that are detected successfully – accuracy in both categories. In our experiments, we consider prepositions and determiners as function words; and we consider other words/phrases as content words/phrases.

4.1 Redundancy Measures

To gain insight into redundancy error detection's difficulty, we first consider a random baseline.

random The random baseline assigns a random score to each word/phrase. The resulting system will pick one word/phrase of the given length at random.

We consider relying on large scale language models to decide redundancy.

trigram We use a trigram language model to capture fluency, by calculating the log-likelihood of the whole sentence after discarding the given word/phrase. A higher probability indicates a higher fluency.

round-trip Inspired by Madnani et al. (2012; Hermet and Désilets (2009), an MT system may eliminate grammar errors with the help of large scale language models. In this method, we analyze which parts are considered redundant by an MT system by comparing the original sentence with its round-trip translation. We use Google translate to first translate one sentence into a pivot language, and then back to English. We measure one phrase's redundancy by the number of words that disappeared after the round-trip. We determine if one word disappeared in two ways:

extract word match: one word is considered disappeared if the same word does not occur in the round-trip.

aligned word: we use the Berkeley aligner (DeNero and Klein, 2007) to align original sentences with their round-trip translations. Unaligned words are considered to have disappeared.

We consider measures for words/phrases' contributions to sentence meaning.

sig-score This measure accounts for whether one word w_i is capturing the gist of a sentence (Clarke and Lapata, 2007)[2]. It was shown to help decide whether one part should be discarded during sentence compression.

$$I(w_i) = -\frac{l}{N} \cdot f_i \log \frac{F_a}{F_i}$$

f_i and F_i are the frequencies of w_i in the current document and a large corpus respectively; F_a is the number of all word occurrences in the corpus; l is the number of clause constituents above w_i; N is the deepest level of clause embeddings. This measure assigns low scores to document specific words occurring at deep syntax levels.

align # We use the number of alignments that a word/phrase has in the translation to measure its redundancy, as deducted in Equation 2.

contrib We compute the word/phrase's contribution to meaning, according to Equation 3.

We consider the combinations of measures.

trigram + $C_c$align # We use a linear combination between language model and align # (Equation 2). We tune C_c on development data.

trigram+contrib This measure (as we proposed in Section 3) is the sum of the *trigram* language model component and the *contrib* component which represents the phrase's contribution to meaning.

trigram+α round-trip/sig-score We combine language model with **round-trip** and **sig-score** linearly (McDonald, 2006; Clarke and Lapata, 2007). To obtain baselines that are as strong as possible, we tune the weight α on evaluation data for best accuracy.

4.2 Pivot Languages

Our proposed model uses machine translation outputs from different pivot languages. To see which language helps measuring redundancy, we compare 52 pivot languages available at Google translate[3] for meaning representation[4].

[2]We extend this measure, which was only defined for content words in Clarke and Lapata (2007), to include all English words.

[3]http://translate.google.com

[4]These languages include Albanian (sq), Arabic (ar), Azerbaijani (az), Irish (ga), Estonian (et), Basque (eu),

length	count	percentage
1	356	67.55%
2	80	15.18%
3	40	7.59%
4	18	3.42%
other	33	6.26%

Table 1: Length distribution of redundant chunks' lengths in the evaluation data.

4.3 Data and Tools

We extract instances from the NUCLE corpus (Dahlmeier and Ng, 2011), an error annotated corpus mainly written by Singaporean students, to conduct this study. The corpus is composed of 1,414 student essays on various topics. Annotations in NUCLE include error locations, error types, and suggested corrections. Redundancy errors are marked by annotators as *Rloc*. In this study, we only consider the cases where the suggested correction is to delete the redundant part (97.09% among all *Rloc* errors).

To construct our evaluation dataset, we pick sentences with exactly one redundant word/phrase. This is the most common case (81.18%) among sentences containing redundant words/phrases. We use 10% of the essays (336 sentences) for development purposes, and another 200 essays as the evaluation corpus (527 sentences). A distribution of redundant chunks' lengths in evaluation corpus is shown in Table 1.

We train a trigram language model using the SRILM toolkit (Stolcke, 2002) on the Agence France-Presse (afp) portion of the English Gigawords corpus.

5 Experiments

The experiment aims to address the following questions: (1) Does a sentence's translation serve as a reasonable approximation for its meaning? (2) If so, does the choice of the pivot language matter? (3) How do the potentially conflicting goals of preserving fluency versus preserving meaning impact the definition of a redundancy measure?

Our experimental results are presented in Figure 4 and Table 2. In Figure 4 we compare using different pivot languages in our proposed model; in Table 2 we compare using different redundancy metrics for the same pivot language – French.

Metrics	overall	function words	content words
random	4.44%	4.62%	4.36%
trigram	8.06%	3.95%	9.73%
sig-score	10.71%	22.16%	6.07%
round-trip (aligned word)	10.69%	12.72%	9.87%
round-trip (exact word match)	5.75%	4.27%	6.35%
trigram + α round-trip (aligned word)	14.80%	11.84%	16.00%
trigram + α round-trip (exact word match)	9.49%	4.61%	11.47%
trigram + α sig-score	11.01%	22.68%	6.28%
align #	5.04%	3.36%	5.72%
trigram + $C_c \times$align #	9.58%	4.61%	11.60%
contrib	8.59%	20.23%	3.87%
trigram + contrib	21.63%	38.16%	14.93%

Table 2: Redundancy part identification accuracies for different redundancy metrics on NUCLE corpus, using French as the pivot language.

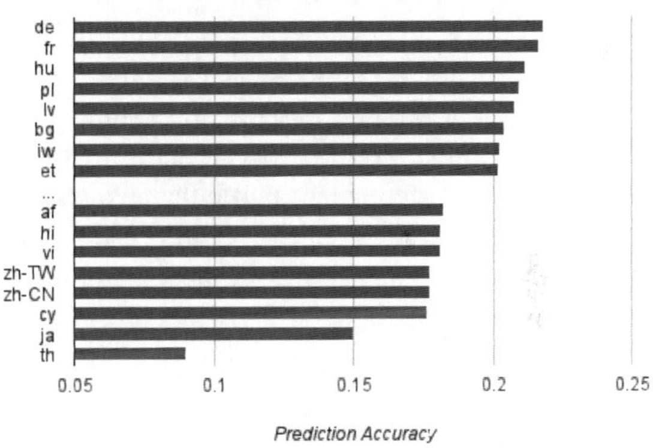

Figure 4: Using different pivot languages for redundancy measurement.

First, compared to other measures, our proposed model best captures redundancy. In particular, our model picks the correct redundant chunk 21.63% of the time, which is five times higher than the random baseline. This suggests that using translation to approximate sentence meanings is a plausible option. Note that one partial reason for the low figures is the limitation of data resources. During error analysis, we found linkers/connectors (e.g. moreover, however) and modal auxiliaries (e.g.

Byelorussian (be), Bulgarian (bg), Icelandic (is), Polish (pl), Persian (fa), Boolean (language ((Afrikaans) (af), Danish (da), German (de), Russian (ru), French (fr), Tagalog (tl), Finnish (fi), Khmer (km), Georgian (ka), Gujarati (gu), Haitian (Creole (ht), Korean (ko), Dutch (nl), Galician (gl), Catalan (ca), Czech (cs), Kannada (kn), Croatian (hr), Latin (la), Latvian (lv), Lao (lo), Lithuanian (lt), Romanian (ro), Maltese (mt), Malay (ms), Macedonian (mk), Bengali (bn), Norwegian (no), Portuguese (pt), Japanese (ja), Swedish (sv), Serbian (sr), Esperanto (eo), Slovak (sk), Slovenian (sl), Swahili (sw), Telugu (te), Tamil (ta), Thai (th), Turkish (tr), Welsh (cy), Urdu (ur), Ukrainian (uk), Hebrew (iw), Greek (el), Spanish (es), Hungarian (hu), Armenian (hy), Italian (it), Yiddish (yi), Hindi (hi), Indonesian (id), English (en), Vietnamese (vi), Simplified Chinese (zh-CN), Traditional Chinese (zh-TW).

can, had) are often marked redundant when they actually carry undesirable meanings ($\mathbf{Ex_6}$, $\mathbf{Ex_5}$). These cases comprise a 16% portion among our model's failures. Despite this limitation, the evaluation still suggests that current approaches are not ready for a full redundancy detection pipeline.

Second, we find that the choice of pivot language does make a difference. Experimental result suggests that the system tends to achieve higher redundancy detection accuracy when using translations of a language more similar to English. In particular, when using European languages (e.g. German (de), French (fr), Hungarian (hu) etc.) as pivot, the system performs much better than using Asian languages (e.g. Chinese (zh-CN), Japanese (ja), Thai (th) etc.). One reason for this phenomenon is that the default Google translation output in Asian languages (as well as the alignment between English and these languages) are organized into characters, while characters are not the minimum meaning component. For example, in Chinese, "解释" is the translation of "explanation", but the two characters "解" and "释" mean "to solve" and "to release" respectively. In the alignment output, this will cause certain words being associated with more or less alignments than others. In this case, the number of alignments no longer directly reflect how many meaning units a certain word helps to express. To confirm this phenomenon, we tried improving the system using Simplified Chinese as the pivot language by merging characters together. In particular, we applied Chinese tokenization (Chang et al., 2008), and then merged alignments accordingly. This raised the system's accuracy from 17.74% to 20.11%.

Third, to better understand the salient features of a successful redundancy measure, we experimented with using different components in isolation. We find that the language model component is better at detecting redundant content words, while the alignment analysis component is better at detecting redundant function words. The language model detects the function word redundancies with a worse accuracy than the random baseline; the alignment analysis component also has a worse accuracy than the random baseline on content words. However, the English language model and the alignment analysis result can build on top of each other when we analyze the redundancies.

We also found that alignments help us to better account for each word's contribution to the "meaning" of the sentence. A linear combination of a language model score and our proposed measure based on analysis of alignments best captures redundancy. However, as our experimental results suggest, it is necessary both to use alignments in translation outputs, and to use them in a good way. Alignments help isolating fluency from the meaning component – making them easy to integrate. As our experiments demonstrated, although methods comparing Google round-trip translation's output with the original sentence could lead to a 10.69% prediction accuracy, it is harder to combine it with the English language model. This is partly because of the non-orthogonality of these two measures – the English language model has already been used in the round-trip translation result. Also, an information theoretical interpretation of alignments is essential for the model's success. For example, a more naive way of using alignment results, **align #,** which counts the number of alignments, leads to a much lower accuracy.

6 Conclusions

Despite the prevalence of redundant phrases in ESL writings, there has not been much work in the automatic detection of these problems. We conduct a first study on developing a computational model of redundancies. We propose to account for words/phrases redundancies by comparing an ESL sentence with outputs from off-the-shelf machine translation systems. We propose a redundancy measure based on this comparison. We show that by interpreting the translation outputs with IBM Models, redundancies can be measured by a linear combination of a language model score and the words' contribution to the sentence's meaning. This measure accounts for both the fluency and completeness of a sentence after removing one chunk. The proposed measure outperforms the direct round-trip translation and a random baseline by a large margin.

Acknowledgements

This work is supported by U.S. National Science Foundation Grant IIS-0745914. We thank the anonymous reviewers for their suggestions; we also thank Joel Tetreault, Janyce Wiebe, Wencan Luo, Fan Zhang, Lingjia Deng, Jiahe Qian, Nitin Madnani and Yafei Wei for helpful discussions.

References

Chris Brockett, William B. Dolan, and Michael Gamon. 2006. Correcting ESL errors using phrasal smt techniques. In *Proceedings of the 21st International Conference on Computational Linguistics and the 44th annual meeting of the Association for Computational Linguistics*, ACL-44, pages 249–256, Sydney, Australia. Association for Computational Linguistics.

P.F. Brown, V.J.D. Pietra, S.A.D. Pietra, and R.L. Mercer. 1993. The mathematics of statistical machine translation: Parameter estimation. *Computational linguistics*, 19(2):263–311.

M. Carpuat and D. Wu. 2007. Improving statistical machine translation using word sense disambiguation. In *Proceedings of the 2007 Joint Conference on Empirical Methods in Natural Language Processing and Computational Natural Language Learning (EMNLP-CoNLL)*, pages 61–72.

Pi-Chuan Chang, Michel Galley, and Christopher D Manning. 2008. Optimizing chinese word segmentation for machine translation performance. In *Proceedings of the Third Workshop on Statistical Machine Translation*, pages 224–232. Association for Computational Linguistics.

James Clarke and Mirella Lapata. 2007. Modelling compression with discourse constraints. In *Proceedings of the 2007 Joint Conference on Empirical Methods in Natural Language Processing and Computational Natural Language Learning (EMNLP-CoNLL)*, pages 1–11.

Will Coster and David Kauchak. 2011. Learning to simplify sentences using wikipedia. In *Proceedings of the Workshop on Monolingual Text-To-Text Generation*, pages 1–9, Portland, Oregon, June. Association for Computational Linguistics.

Daniel Dahlmeier and Hwee Tou Ng. 2011. Grammatical error correction with alternating structure optimization. In *Proceedings of the 49th Annual Meeting of the Association for Computational Linguistics: Human Language Technologies - Volume 1*, HLT '11, pages 915–923, Portland, Oregon, USA. Association for Computational Linguistics.

John DeNero and Dan Klein. 2007. Tailoring word alignments to syntactic machine translation. In *Proceedings of the 45th Annual Meeting of the Association of Computational Linguistics*, pages 17–24, Prague, Czech Republic, June. Association for Computational Linguistics.

Matthieu Hermet and Alain Désilets. 2009. Using first and second language models to correct preposition errors in second language authoring. In *Proceedings of the Fourth Workshop on Innovative Use of NLP for Building Educational Applications*, pages 64–72. Association for Computational Linguistics.

Hongyan Jing. 2000. Sentence reduction for automatic text summarization. In *Proceedings of the sixth conference on Applied natural language processing*, pages 310–315. Association for Computational Linguistics.

Kevin Knight and Daniel Marcu. 2000. Statistics-based summarization - step one: Sentence compression. In *Proceedings of the Seventeenth National Conference on Artificial Intelligence and Twelfth Conference on Innovative Applications of Artificial Intelligence*, pages 703–710. AAAI Press.

C. Leacock, M. Chodorow, M. Gamon, and J. Tetreault. 2010. Automated grammatical error detection for language learners. *Synthesis lectures on human language technologies*, 3(1):1–134.

Xiaohua Liu, Bo Han, Kuan Li, Stephan Hyeonjun Stiller, and Ming Zhou. 2010. SRL-based verb selection for ESL. In *Proceedings of the 2010 Conference on Empirical Methods in Natural Language Processing*, EMNLP '10, pages 1068–1076, Cambridge, Massachusetts. Association for Computational Linguistics.

Nitin Madnani, Joel Tetreault, and Martin Chodorow. 2012. Re-examining machine translation metrics for paraphrase identification. In *Proceedings of the 2012 Conference of the North American Chapter of the Association for Computational Linguistics: Human Language Technologies*, pages 182–190, Montréal, Canada, June. Association for Computational Linguistics.

Ryan McDonald. 2006. Discriminative sentence compression with soft syntactic evidence. In *Proceedings of the 11th Conference of the European Chapter of the Association for Computational Linguistics*, volume 6, pages 297–304. Association for Computational Linguistics.

Alla Rozovskaya and Dan Roth. 2010. Generating confusion sets for context-sensitive error correction. In *Proceedings of the 2010 Conference on Empirical Methods in Natural Language Processing*, EMNLP '10, pages 961–970, Cambridge, Massachusetts. Association for Computational Linguistics.

Andreas Stolcke. 2002. Srilm-an extensible language modeling toolkit. In *Proceedings of the international conference on spoken language processing*, volume 2, pages 901–904.

William Strunk. 1918. *The elements of style / by William Strunk, Jr.*

Joel Tetreault, Jennifer Foster, and Martin Chodorow. 2010. Using parse features for preposition selection and error detection. In *Proceedings of the ACL 2010 Conference Short Papers*, ACLShort '10, pages 353–358, Uppsala, Sweden. Association for Computational Linguistics.

Fast Recursive Multi-class Classification of Pairs of Text Entities for Biomedical Event Extraction

Xiao Liu, Antoine Bordes, Yves Grandvalet
Université de Technologie de Compiègne & CNRS
Heudiasyc UMR 7253
60200 Compiègne Cedex, France
firstname.lastname@hds.utc.fr

Abstract

Biomedical event extraction from articles has become a popular research topic driven by important applications, such as the automatic update of dedicated knowledge base. Most existing approaches are either pipeline models of specific classifiers, usually subject to cascading errors, or joint structured models, more efficient but also more costly and more involved to train. We propose here a system based on a pairwise model that transforms event extraction into a simple multi-class problem of classifying pairs of text entities. Such pairs are recursively provided to the classifier, so as to extract events involving other events as arguments. Our model is more direct than the usual pipeline approaches, and speeds up inference compared to joint models. We report here the best results reported so far on the BioNLP 2011 and 2013 Genia tasks.

1 Introduction

Huge amounts of biomedical documents, such as molecular biology reports or genomic papers are generated daily. Automatically organizing their content in dedicated databases enables advanced search and eases information retrieval for researchers in biology, medicine or other related fields. Nowadays, these data sources are mostly in the form of unstructured free text, which is complex to incorporate into databases. Hence, many text-mining research initiatives are organized around the issue of automatically extracting information from biomedical text. Efforts specifically dedicated to biomedical text are necessary because standard Natural Language Processing tools cannot be readily applied to extract biomedical events since such texts, articles or reports involve highly domain-specific jargon, syntax and dependencies (Kim et al., 2011a).

This paper tackles the problem of event extraction from biomedical documents. Building on previous advances in named entity recognition (for detecting gene or protein mentions for instance), this task consists in associating to these entities the related events expressed in the text. Such events are of multiple types and involve at least one text entity as *argument* and another one as *trigger*; they can be quite complex since some events have several arguments, and recursive in the sense that arguments can themselves be events. An example of event is given in Figure 1.

Biomedical event extraction is attracting more and more attention, especially thanks to the organization of recurrent dedicated BioNLP challenges (Kim et al., 2009; Kim et al., 2011b; Kim et al., 2013). We propose here a new approach which relies on a single multi-class classifier for recursively detecting events from (*trigger*, *argument*) pairs. Compared to standard pipeline approaches based on sequences of classifiers (Björne and Salakoski, 2013; Hakala et al., 2013), we avoid the intermediate problem of associating isolated triggers to event types, relying on a tricky multi-label classification problem. Instead, we directly extract compounds of events in the form of (*trigger*, *argument*) pairs, simply relying on a multi-class problem, whereby (*trigger*, *argument*) pairs are associated to event types. Considering pairs of words also allows us to characterize examples by sophisticated joint features such as shortest path in the dependency parse tree, and hence to achieve much accurate trigger detection than pipeline models. Besides, compared to Markov random fields (Riedel and McCallum, 2011a), our discriminant model does not represent the full joint distribution of words and events. We thus have a simpler inference process, which results into drastically reduced training times (15

Proceedings of the 14th Conference of the European Chapter of the Association for Computational Linguistics, pages 692–701,
Gothenburg, Sweden, April 26-30 2014.

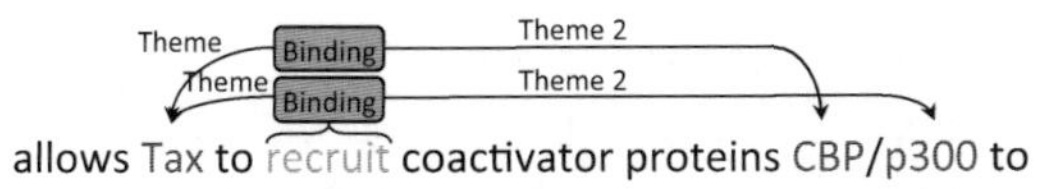

Figure 1: Part of a sentence and corresponding extracted events for the BioNLP 2013 Genia task.

times faster for processing about 800 training documents). In short, we propose in this work a *happy medium* between pipeline and joint models. Our approach builds on our previous proposal (Liu et al., 2013), where we detected triggers directly from (*trigger*, *argument*) pairs. Here, we upgrade our scheme by adding a recursive classification process that considerably improves the detection of complex events.

This paper is organized as follows: Section 2 introduces the problem of biomedical event extraction and discusses related works. Section 3 describes our recursive model and its training process. The post-processing procedures and the features used are detailed in Sections 4 and 5. Section 6 shows that our method achieves excellent empirical results, with the best performance reported so far on the BioNLP 2011 and 2013 Genia tasks, and a reduced training duration compared to the previously state-of-the-art models.

2 Context and Related Works

Biomedical event extraction aims at extracting *event formulas* from sentences, defined as sequences of *tokens* (words, numbers, or symbols).

2.1 Task Definition

Terminology regarding biomedical events, triggers, etc. varies from one task or data set to another; in the following, we use the definitions used by the Genia (GE) task 1 of the BioNLP challenges. An event is constituted of two kinds of elements: an event *trigger* and one or several *arguments*. The event trigger is an *entity*, that is, a sequence of consecutive tokens which indicates that an event is mentioned in the text. The arguments of an event are participants, which can be proteins, genes or other biomedical events.

In the data settings of the GE task, protein mentions are already annotated in the text. Figure 1 illustrates biomedical event extraction in the GE task framework: given 3 proteins "*Tax*", "*CBP*" and "*p300*", one must detect "*recruit*" as an event trigger for two events of the *Binding* category , encoded by the formulas: ("*recruit*", theme:"*Tax*", theme_2:"*CBP*") and ("*recruit*", theme:"*Tax*", theme_2:"*p300*").

Class	*Type*	*Principal arg*	*Optional arg*
SVT	Gene_expression	theme (P)	
	Transcription	theme (P)	
	Protein_catabolism	theme (P)	
	Phosphorylation	theme (P)	
	Localization	theme (P)	
BIN	Binding	theme (P)	theme_2 (P)
REG	Regulation	theme (P/E)	cause (P/E)
	Positive_regulation	theme (P/E)	cause (P/E)
	Negative_regulation	theme (P/E)	cause (P/E)

Table 1: Classes and types of events with their arguments (P stands for *Protein*, E for *Event*).

A key part of the task is to detect the trigger entities among the candidates sequences of tokens. The BioNLP GE task considers 9 types of events.[1] Table 1 lists these events. The 9 event types may be merged into three broader categories: the first 5 (termed SVT) have a single *theme* argument; the *Binding* event (or BIN) can accept up to two theme arguments; the last 3 types (termed REG) also accept up to two arguments, a theme and an optional *cause*. REG events can be recursive because their arguments can be proteins or events.

2.2 Related Works

Current approaches fall into two main categories: pipeline incremental models and global joint methods. Pipeline approaches (Sætre et al., 2009; Cohen et al., 2009; Quirk et al., 2011) are the simplest way to tackle the problem of event extraction. A sequence of specific classifiers are ran on the text to successively (P_1) detect event triggers, (P_2) assign them arguments, (P_3) detect event triggers whose arguments can be events, and (P_4) assign them arguments (steps (P_3) and (P_4) can be ran multiple times). Such systems are relatively easy to set up and experienced many successes: the TEES system (Björne et al., 2009; Bj[Pleaseinsertintopreamble]rne et al., 2012; Björne and Salakoski, 2013) won the BioNLP GE task in 2009 and ranked 2nd in 2013, whereas the EVEX system won in 2013 (Van Landeghem et al., 2011; Hakala et al., 2013). However, all these methods suffer from error cascading. Besides, prediction must be formalized as

[1]The BioNLP 2013 challenge considered 13 types of events, but we only dealt with the 9 types defined in the previous challenges, because there was not enough data on the newly defined types for proper training or model selection.

a multi-label classification problem because some words can participate in the definition of several events of different types. Detecting triggers in isolation of their arguments in steps (P_1) and (P_3) are ill-posed intermediate problems, since the notion of trigger is intrinsically tied to its argument. The latter brings contextual information that is indisputably relevant for detection. Besides, rich features coding for (trigger, argument) pairs (Miwa et al., 2010) are only used by pipeline models for assigning arguments, whereas they could be useful for trigger detection as well.

Global joint approaches (Riedel et al., 2009; McClosky et al., 2011) aim at solving the event extraction task at once, so as to resolve the drawbacks of pipeline models. In (McClosky et al., 2011), event annotations are converted into pseudo-syntactic representations and the task is solved as a syntactic extraction problem by traditional parsing methods. In (Riedel et al., 2009; Riedel and McCallum, 2011a; Riedel et al., 2011; Riedel and McCallum, 2011b), some models are proposed based on the maximization of a global score taking into account the annotations of nodes and edges in a graph representing each sentence. This maximization problem is formalized as an integer linear program with consistency constraints, and solved via dual decomposition. Such joint models perform very well (winner of the BioNLP 2011 GE task), but suffer from consequential computing costs, as all possible combinations of words are considered as potential events. In the following, we show that our model is able to reach better accuracies than joint models while being computationally much cheaper.

A method based on the search-based structured prediction paradigm (Vlachos and Craven, 2012) has been proposed as an intermediate step between joint and pipeline approaches, by turning the structured prediction problem into a sequence of multiclass classification tasks. Our experiments demonstrate that, despite being conceptually simpler, our recursive pairwise model outperforms it.

3 Recursive Pairwise Model

In this section, we present our recursive pairwise model. It directly extracts pairwise interactions between entities, thereby contrasting with the usual pipeline approaches, which require detecting triggers as an intermediate problem. Our approach proceeds in two steps:

1. **Main (trigger, theme) pair extraction**: main event extraction step that detects the triggers with one of their arguments;

2. **Post-processing**: step that adds extra-arguments to BIN and REG events.

Step 1 is the main innovative part of our system, and is detailed in the remainder of this section. Step 2, which relies on more established techniques, is described in Section 4.

3.1 Direct Extraction of Simple Events

We process entities differently depending on whether they are marked as proteins in the annotation or not; the latter are termed *candidate* entities. We denote $\mathcal{C}_S = \{c_i\}_i$ the set of candidate entities, which is built from the sentence tokens (see Section 5 for details on its construction), $\mathcal{A}_S = \{a_j\}_j$ the set of candidate arguments (that is, the proteins identified by a named-entity recognizer beforehand) in a given sentence S, and the set of event types (augmented by *None*) is $\mathcal{Y}$.

The first steps of a pipeline model consist in predicting whether candidate entities $c_i \in \mathcal{C}_S$ are triggers or not and then, whether arguments $a_j \in \mathcal{A}_S$ can participate to a subset of events from $\mathcal{Y}$. Instead, our pairwise model directly addresses the problem of classifying the (candidate, argument) pairs $p_{ij} = (c_i, a_j)$ as events of type from $\mathcal{Y}$.

This classification is based on Support Vector Machines (SVMs), where the multi-class problem is broken down in a series of one-vs-rest binary problems, one for each event type. The final decision associated to each pair p_{ij} is simply taken as the event (including *None*) whose score is maximal. Classifying a pair p_{ij} as not-*None* jointly detects the event trigger c_i and its argument a_j.

3.2 Recursive Extraction of Complex Events

For simple SVT and BIN events, the set $\mathcal{A}_S$ of possible arguments is restricted to proteins, but the events of class REG may have other events as arguments, thus $\mathcal{A}_S$ has to be enriched. Considering all possible events would be intractable, so that the set of possible arguments is updated dynamically in the process of extracting events. As here possible arguments are exclusive to event types, in practice it is simpler to update the set of pairs that remain to be assessed.

Assume that an event has been actually predicted, that is, that $p_{\alpha\beta} = (c_\alpha, a_\beta)$ has been clas-

Algorithm 1 Recursive pairwise event extraction

```
input sentence S, candidate entities C_S = {c_i}_i
    and labeled proteins A_S = {a_j}_j
initialize candidate pairs
    P_S = {(c_i, a_j), c_i ∈ C_S, a_j ∈ A_S}
initialize extracted events E_S = ∅
score and label the pairs in P_S
while P_S ≠ ∅ do
    select the pair p_αβ ∈ P_S with highest score
    update P_S ← P_S − {p_αβ}
    if ŷ_αβ ≠ None then
        create event ê_αβ = (c_α, a_β, ŷ_αβ)
        update E_S ← E_S ∪ {ê_αβ}
        update P_S ← P_S ∪ {(c_i, ê_αβ) | c_i ∈ C_S}
        censor pairs P_S to avoid cycles
        score and label the new {(c_i, ê_αβ)} pairs
    end if
end while
return extracted events E_S
```

sified as $\hat{y}_{\alpha\beta} \neq None$; the predicted event is denoted $\hat{e}_{\alpha\beta} = (c_\alpha, a_\beta, \hat{y}_{\alpha\beta})$. We create all pairs with it as argument, $\{(c_i, \hat{e}_{\alpha\beta}) | c_i \in \mathcal{C}_S\}$, and add them to $\mathcal{P}_S$, so as to allow for the detection of recursive events. We assume that recursive events constitute a directed acyclic graph, where the ancestor of a candidate entity cannot be used as its argument. The dynamic updating process is thus constrained to prevent the creation of cycles.

Algorithm 1 summaries our event extraction algorithm. For all events with a single argument, predicting $\hat{y}$ variables directly responds to the event extraction problem. When appropriate, additional optional arguments are added after all pairwise events have been extracted, by the post-processing described in Section 4.

3.3 Fitting the Pairwise Model

The prediction process described above relies on a multi-class classifier. We stress again that, since pairs are assigned to a single class, there is no need to address the more difficult multi-label problem encountered in standard pipeline approaches. An entity may still be assigned to several events, possibly of different types, through the allocation of labels to several pairs comprising this entity.

Training SVMs For each event type, a series of binary linear SVMs is fitted to the available training data, using the implementation from `scikit-learn.org`. As events are rare, each binary classification problem is highly unbalanced. We thus use different losses for positive and negative examples (Morik et al., 1999; Veropoulos et al., 1999), resulting in two hyperparameters that are set by cross-validation, so as to maximize the F-score of the corresponding event type taken in isolation.

For the SVT and BIN events, the training sets are all composed of the possible (candidate, argument) pairs $\mathcal{P}_S = \{p_{ij} = (c_i, a_j) | c_i \in \mathcal{C}_S,\ a_j \in \mathcal{A}_S\}$ readily extracted from all training sentences, and they only differ in the definition of the positive and negative class, according to the true label associated to each pair.

Creating the training sets for REG events is more complicated: since they can take events as arguments, new pairs are added to $\mathcal{P}_S$ by considering all the events already detected, as sketched in Algorithm 1. Hence, the sets of training examples are not deterministically known before training, but depend on predictions of all other classifiers. Training directly on them requires to use either online algorithms or complex search-based structured prediction procedures as in (Vlachos and Craven, 2012). In this paper, we prefer to use instead the true labels $y_{\alpha\beta}$ during the training phase of REG and *None* classifiers: the training sets are then the enriched sets of possible (candidate, argument) pairs $\mathcal{P}_S = \{p_{ij} = (c_i, a_j) | c_i \in \mathcal{C}_S,\ a_j \in \mathcal{A}_S\} \cup \{p_{i\alpha} = (c_i, e_{\alpha\beta}) | c_i \in \mathcal{C}_S, \exists\beta : y_{\alpha\beta} \neq None\}$. This allows to know all training examples beforehand and hence to use standard batch SVM algorithms. The drawback is that, since extracted events in test are imperfect, this creates a divergence between training and testing scenarios, which can lead to degraded performance. However, as our experiments show, this effect is marginal compared to the advantages of using fast reliable batch training algorithms.

Score Combination As said earlier, the decision rule simply consists in predicting the class corresponding to the highest SVM score. This simple scheme could be improved, either by using multi-class classifiers or by using more refined combinations optimizing a global criterion as proposed in (Liu et al., 2013). Though this route deserves to be thoroughly tested, we conjecture that only marginal gains should be expected since the vast majority of errors are due to the detection of an event when there is none or to the absence of detection of an existing event: when an event is detected, its correct type is predominantly predicted.

3.4 Computational Considerations

The pairwise structure leads to a simple inference procedure, with a slight increase in computational complexity compared to pipeline models. We denote $m = \text{card}(\mathcal{C}_S)$, the number of candidate entities, $n = \text{card}(\mathcal{A}_S)$, the number of annotated proteins and m' the number of detected triggers. The complexity of a pipeline model is $\mathcal{O}(m'(n+m'))$, whereas that of our approach is $\mathcal{O}(m(n+m'))$. This implies more calls to the classifying mechanism, but this is not too penalizing, since SVM-based classification scales well with the number of examples. Besides, this is still cheaper than joint models such as (Riedel and McCallum, 2011a), whose complexity is $\mathcal{O}(m(n^2+m))$.

4 Post-Processing

This section describes the post-processing carried out once the (trigger, theme) pairs are detected and labeled as events. The goal is to look whether extra-arguments should be added to these extracted events.

4.1 Binding Theme Fusion

This step attempts to merge several pairs labeled as *Binding* to create multiple arguments events. We take the set of extracted *Binding* events $\{(c_\alpha, a_\beta)\}$ that share the same trigger c_α, and all combinations $\{(c_\alpha, a_\beta, a_\gamma) | \gamma \neq \beta\}$ are classified by a binary SVM. Once a combination $(c_\alpha, a_\beta, a_\gamma)$ is predicted as a correct merge, it is added to predicted events while both pairs (c_α, a_β) and (c_α, a_γ) are removed.

4.2 Regulation Cause Assignment

This step looks for optional *cause* arguments that may be added to the extracted REG events. Given an extracted event (c_α, a_β) and a candidate argument set $\mathcal{A}_S = \{a_\gamma\}$ containing all the proteins of the sentence S as well as all events extracted by the classifier, all combinations $\{(c_\alpha, a_\beta, a_\gamma) | \gamma \neq \beta\}$ are classified by a binary SVM. Since *cause* argument could be another event, we extract them incrementally in a dynamic process alike (trigger, theme) pair extraction, also with constraints avoiding the creation of cycles.

5 Features

This section details our features as well as the data preprocessing used by our system.

Pre-processing Tokenization and sentence splitting have an important impact on the quality of the dependency parse trees as well as the way we handle compound words that contain protein names. Data is split in sentences using both the `nltk` toolkit (`nltk.org`) and the sentence splitting provided for the BioNLP GE task. High quality dependency parse trees require a fine grained tokenization, whereas coarse tokenization conserves some biomedical jargon that could also provide essential information. Hence, two tokenizations are used for different features. *Tokenization1*, provided by the organizers of the BioNLP GE task, is a coarse tokenization that is used to characterize when a candidate entity and a protein are in the same token. *Tokenization2* is fined grained, based on the Stanford parser (McClosky et al., 2011) that is slightly modified for primary tokenization. It supplies the dependency parse, candidate entity match and most of our features. The dependency parse trees are finally obtained using a phrase structure parser (McClosky et al., 2010), using the post-processing of the Stanford `corenlp` package (De Marneffe et al., 2006). We used stems (obtained by Snowball stemmer provided in `nltk`) as base forms for the tokens.

Candidate set For each sentence S, the set $\mathcal{C}_S$ is built with a gazetteer: candidate entities are recursively added by searching first the longest token sequences (from Tokenization2) from the gazetteer. For entities with several tokens, a representative *head* token is selected by a heuristic based on the dependency parse.

Candidate entities Three types of tokens are considered: the head token, its parent and child nodes in the dependency tree, and the tokens belonging to a neighboring window of the entity. The size k of the word window is a hyper-parameter of our model. Table 2 lists all features which include stems, part-of-speech (POS) tags, etc. Special care was taken to design the feature for head token since it plays an extremely important role in candidate entities. We hence employed features and heuristics to deal with compound-words, hyphens and prefixes, inspired by such tools developed in the code of the UCLEED system (based on Tok-

Candidate entity features	Base form (stem) of the head token.
	Base form of the head token without '-' or '/' before of after.
	Sub-string after '-' in the head token.
	POS of the head token.
	First token of the entity is after '-' or '/'.
	Last token of the entity is before '-' or '/'.
	Head token has a special prefix: "over", "up", "down", "co"
	Concat. of base form and POS of parents of the head token in dependency parse.
	Concat. of base form and POS of children of the head token in dependency parse.
	Base forms of k neighboring tokens around the entity.
	POS of k neighboring tokens around the entity.
	Neighborhood of the entity has '-' or '/'.
	Sentence has "mRNA".
	Entity is connected with another string using Tokenization1.
Argument features	Argument is a protein.
	POS of the head token.
	Features extracted from IntAct when the argument is a protein.
	Base forms of k neighboring tokens around the argument.
	POS of k neighboring tokens around the argument.
	Concat. of base form and POS of children of the head token in dependency parse.
Pairwise features	Token sequence between candidate and argument has proteins.
	V-walk features between candidate and argument with base forms.
	E-walk features between candidate and argument with base forms.
	V-walk features between candidate and argument with POS.
	E-walk features between candidate and argument with POS.
	Candidate and the argument share a token using Tokenization1.

Table 2: Features used by our system. Most are based on Tokenization2 except when specified.

enization2).[2] Protein names and POS in tokens are substituted by the token PROT, e.g. transforming "LPS-activated" into "PROT-activated". There is total of a 35,365 candidate features.

Arguments Table 2 also lists the argument features, which are a subset of those for candidate entities. Most head word features are removed, but base forms and POS of the neighboring tokens and of the parent node in the dependency tree are still included. Assigning label from SVT or BIN event classes to a $(c_i, e_{\alpha\beta})$ pair should never occur, because only regulation events could have another event as argument. Therefore, we add a feature that indicates whether the argument is a protein

[2]See github.com/riedelcastro/ucleed.

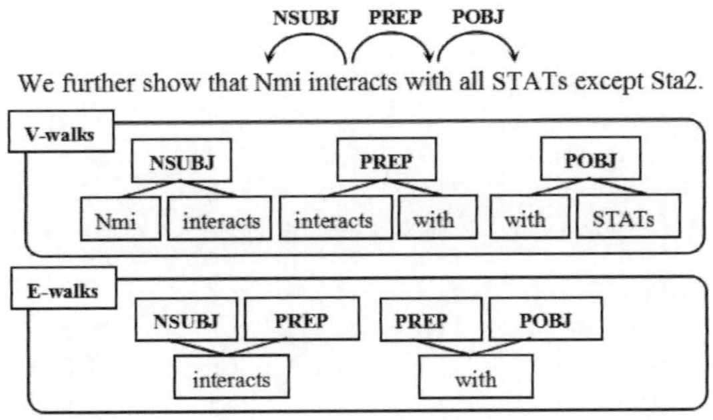

Figure 2: Example of E-walks and V-walks features for encoding a dependency parse tree.

or a trigger entity. Proteins are also described using features extracted from the Uniprot knowledge base (uniprot.org). There is total of 4,349 argument features.

Pairwise relations Our pairwise approach is able to take advantage of features that code interactions between candidate triggers and arguments, such as those listed in Table 2. Hence, we have a feature indicating if both elements of a pair belong to the same token (based on Tokenization1).

But the most important pairwise features come from the shortest path linking two candidate and arguments in the dependency parse tree of the sentence. Incorporating such dependency information into the pairwise model relies on the process encoding the path into feature vectors. Many formatting methods have been proposed in previous works. Following (Miwa et al., 2010), our system use a combination of *E-walks*, that encode the path into triplets (*dep-tag*, *token*, *dep-tag*), and *V-walks* that encode it into triplets (*token*, *dep-tag*, *token*), where *tokens* are encoded via stem and POS tags, and *dep-tags* are the dependency labels. Figure 2 illustrates this formatting: from the dependency parse given on top, three *V-walk* and two *E-walk* features are defined. These are inserted in the feature vector using a bag-of-words process, thus losing any relative ordering information. These imperfect representations lose a lot of information and can even add noise, especially when the path is long. Therefore, we applied heuristics from the UCLEED system to remove some uninformative edges from the dependency parse. Moreover, dependency parse features are added only for pairs for which the (candidate, argument) path length is below a threshold whose value is a hyper-parameter. There is a total of 176,106 pairwise features.

Event Type or Class	TEES 2.1	EVEX	Pipeline counterpart	Our approach
Gene_expression	82.7	82.7	83.9	**85.1**
Transcription	55.0	55.0	61.7	**62.8**
Protein_catabol	56.3	56.3	66.7	**68.8**
Phosphorylation	72.6	71.5	**81.8**	**81.8**
Localization	**63.3**	60.7	56.9	57.7
SVT TOTAL	74.9	74.5	79.0	**79.6**
BIN TOTAL	**43.3**	42.9	41.6	42.4
Regulation	23.0	23.4	23.1	**31.8**
Positive_regul	38.7	39.2	36.5	**46.3**
Negative_regul	43.7	**43.9**	38.1	43.6
REG TOTAL	38.1	38.4	35.1	**43.2**
ALL TOTAL	50.7	51.0	50.8	**54.4**

Table 3: F-scores on the test set of the BioNLP 2013 GE task.

6 Experiments

In this section, we evaluate empirically our system in the framework (data, annotations and evaluation) of biomedical event extraction defined in the GE tasks of the BioNLP challenges. More precisely, we present results on the test sets of the fresh 2013 GE task, and of the 2011 edition to compare to joint methods.

In order to assess the efficiency of our modeling choices, we also implemented a pipeline counterpart system, following the structure of the TEES approach (Björne et al., 2009; Bj[Pleaseinsertintopreamble]rne et al., 2012; Björne and Salakoski, 2013) but using the same feature set, pre-processing and a similar post-processing as our system. This pipeline system comprises four steps: (1) *trigger classification*, which assigns event types from $\mathcal{Y}$ to candidate entities $c_i \in \mathcal{C}_S$ using a multi-class SVM classifier; (2) *edge detection*, which identifies the edges between extracted triggers and proteins and between REG triggers and all the triggers; labels from $\mathcal{Y}_{edge} = \{theme, cause, None\}$ are assigned to those pairs; (3) *binding theme fusion*, identical to as in Section 4.1; (4) *theme-cause fusion*, as in Section 4.2, given two predicted pairs $(c_i, theme : a_\beta)$, $(c_i, cause : a_\gamma)$, this step decides whether they should be merged into a single event $(c_i, theme : a_\beta, cause : a_\gamma)$.

6.1 Genia Shared Task 2013

For the BioNLP 2013 GE task, the hyper-parameters of our system have been optimized on the GE task development set (except for the regularization parameters of the SVMs, which are selected by cross-validation), after training on the corresponding training sets: token window size is 2 for candidate entities and 1 for arguments, the threshold for dependency path is 4. Using these hyper-parameter values, the final model submitted for test evaluation on the GE task server has been trained on all documents from training and development sets of BioNLP 2011 and 2013 GE tasks. Detailed descriptions of the BioNLP 2011 and 2013 GE data are respectively given in (Kim et al., 2011b) and (Kim et al., 2013).

Table 3 lists the detailed test F-scores, as returned by the official challenge test server (using the default *approximate span & recursive matching* evaluation setting). We compare our model to the winner of the challenge, EVEX (Hakala et al., 2013), and of the best runner-up, TEES 2.1 (Björne and Salakoski, 2013), which are both pipeline approaches.

Our approach is slightly below TEES 2.1 on BIN events, but overall, it outperforms all competitors significantly (by more than 3%), with a wide margin on REG events. Our pipeline counterpart has an overall performance similar to EVEX and TEES 2.1, while being better for SVT and worse for BIN and REG events. These disparities are due to the differences in features and in processing details. The benefits of the pairwise structure and the recursive process are demonstrated by the considerable improvement upon the pipeline counterpart (using the same features, pre- and post-processing). In particular, the recursive prediction process run on REG events brings about a very substantial improvement (more than 8%).

6.2 Genia Shared Task 2011

The best performing methods on the BioNLP 2013 GE task were pipeline approaches, but the joint models that were performing better in the previous challenge were not competing in 2013. As these joint models are quite tricky to train, we compare our system with joint models on the BioNLP 2011 GE task, where trustworthy performances have been publicly released. We train our model using the training and development sets available at the time of the challenge and we then get an evaluation on the same test data using the official test server maintained online by BioNLP organizers. Table 4 lists the results of our approach, its pipeline counterpart, and those of UCLEED (Riedel and McCallum, 2011a) and TEES (Bj[Pleaseinsertintopreamble]rne et al.,

Event Class	UCLEED	SEARN	TEES	Pipeline counterpart	Our approach
SVT	73.5	71.8	n/a	71.8	**74.0**
BIN	48.8	45.8	n/a	40.0	**50.5**
REG	43.8	43.0	n/a	35.7	**45.1**
ALL	55.2	53.5	53.3	50.0	**55.6**

Table 4: F-scores on the test set of the BioNLP 2011 GE task.

2012), which are respectively the best performing joint model and best pipeline on this task. We also added SEARN (Vlachos and Craven, 2012), which is a hybrid between them.[3]

As for 2013 data, our system achieves a higher F-score on all event classes compared to its pipeline counterpart. The benefits of the pairwise structure and the recursive process are larger here, thereby outperforming the overall F-score of TEES (no detailed results available), which itself performs better than our pipeline counterpart. Systematic improvements on all event classes are also observed compared to the joint model UCLEED and to the search-based structured prediction approach of SEARN. To our knowledge, our model thus reaches the best overall performance reported so far on this data set for a single model.[4]

By combining the use of the simple pair structure between triggers and arguments with a recursive prediction process, our approach is able to outperform pipeline models and to be at least at par with models relying on much more sophisticated structures. For this task, it is thus highly beneficial to consider pairwise interactions from beginning to end, but more complex dependencies seem not to be essential, especially since they come at a higher computational cost.

6.3 Training Durations

In this last section, we propose to illustrate the lower complexity of our approach compared to UCLEED by providing durations for training both systems on BioNLP 2011 GE. These timings do not involve preprocessing but only running cross-validation on the training set and evaluation on the development and test sets. For UCLEED, we used the code (in java & scala) provided by the authors[5] and we chose BioNLP 2011 GE because this code was primarily designed to run on it. Our code, in python, is publicly available from `github.com/XiaoLiuAI/RUPEE`. Experiments were conducted on the same computer, with a quad-core Intel Xeon CPU and 16GB of RAM. Both codes are multi-threaded and used all 4 threads simultaneously. Under these conditions, UCLEED requires around *8h30min* to run its 10 epochs,[6] while our code completes training in about *30min*. Some of these differences may be due to implementation choices, but we believe that the 15 fold speed increase (for around 800 training documents) is at least partially due to the lower complexity of our approach.

7 Conclusion

We introduced a recursive pairwise model designed for biomedical event extraction. This pairwise model improves on the best current approaches of the BioNLP 2013 and 2011 GE tasks. Our system breaks down the overall event extraction task into the classification of (trigger, theme) pairs, assigned to event types. These (trigger, theme) pairs enable to use joint features in off-the-shelf classifiers, without resorting to costly global inference models. We also implemented a recursive procedure that deals with regulation events, which may include other events in their definition. All operations are run in a unified framework, using a single event classifier.

Our system is fast and more accurate than the available pipeline models or joint models. Given its simplicity and scalability, we believe that our model is a strong basis for large-scale event extraction projects. Several refinements are possible, for example by exploring other types features, or by enabling the direct processing of triplets that may be encountered in binding or regulation events.

Acknowledgments

This work was carried out in the framework of the Labex MS2T funded by the French National Agency for Research through the program "Investments for the future" (ANR-11-IDEX-0004-02), and supported by the "young researchers" program (EVEREST-12-JS02-005-01).

[3]The results for UCLEED, TEES and SEARN models are reproduced from (Riedel and McCallum, 2011a; Bj[Pleaseinsertintopreamble]rne et al., 2012; Vlachos and Craven, 2012) respectively.

[4]We do not compare with the results of FAUST (Riedel et al., 2011), which achieved the best F-score on this task (56.0) because this is an ensemble of various models of UCLEED and of the Stanford system (McClosky et al., 2011), which makes it an unfair comparison.

[5]See `github.com/riedelcastro/ucleed`.

[6]UCLEED might be faster by using feature caching, but we had to disable it because it was taking up too much RAM.

References

J. Björne and T. Salakoski. 2013. TEES 2.1: Automated annotation scheme learning in the BioNLP 2013 shared task. In *Proceedings of BioNLP Shared Task 2013 Workshop*, Sofia, Bulgaria, August. Association for Computational Linguistics.

J. Björne, J. Heimonen, F. Ginter, A. Airola, T. Pahikkala, and T. Salakoski. 2009. Extracting complex biological events with rich graph-based feature sets. In *Proceedings of the BioNLP 2009 Workshop Companion Volume for Shared Task*, pages 10–18, Boulder, Colorado, June. Association for Computational Linguistics.

J. Björne, F. Ginter, and T. Salakoski. 2012. University of turku in the bionlp'11 shared task. *BMC Bioinformatics*, 13(Suppl 11):S4.

K. B. Cohen, K. Verspoor, H. Johnson, C. Roeder, P. Ogren, W. Baumgartner, E. White, and L. Hunter. 2009. High-precision biological event extraction with a concept recognizer. In *Proceedings of the BioNLP 2009 Workshop Companion Volume for Shared Task*, pages 50–58, Boulder, Colorado, June. Association for Computational Linguistics.

M.-C. De Marneffe, B. MacCartney, and C. D. Manning. 2006. Generating typed dependency parses from phrase structure parses. In *Proceedings of LREC*, volume 6, pages 449–454.

K. Hakala, S. Van Landeghem, T. Salakoski, Y. Van de Peer, and F. Ginter. 2013. EVEX in ST'13: Application of a large-scale text mining resource to event extraction and network construction. In *Proceedings of BioNLP Shared Task 2013 Workshop*, Sofia, Bulgaria, August. Association for Computational Linguistics.

J.-D. Kim, T. Ohta, S. Pyysalo, Y. Kano, and J. Tsujii. 2009. Overview of BioNLP'09 shared task on event extraction. In *Proceedings of the BioNLP 2009 Workshop Companion Volume for Shared Task*, pages 1–9, Boulder, Colorado, June. Association for Computational Linguistics.

J.-D. Kim, T. Ohta, S. Pyysalo, Y. Kano, and J. Tsujii. 2011a. Extracting bio-molecular events from literature. *Computational Intelligence*, 27(4):513–540.

J.-D. Kim, Y. Wang, T. Takagi, and A. Yonezawa. 2011b. Overview of genia event task in bionlp shared task 2011. In *Proceedings of BioNLP Shared Task 2011 Workshop*, pages 7–15, Portland, Oregon, USA, June. Association for Computational Linguistics.

J.-D. Kim, Y. Wang, and Y. Yasunori. 2013. The genia event extraction shared task, 2013 edition - overview. In *Proceedings of the BioNLP Shared Task 2013 Workshop*, pages 8–15, Sofia, Bulgaria, August. Association for Computational Linguistics.

X. Liu, A. Bordes, and Y. Grandvalet. 2013. Biomedical event extraction by multi-class classification of pairs of text entities. In *Proceedings of the BioNLP Shared Task 2013 Workshop*, pages 45–49, Sofia, Bulgaria, August. Association for Computational Linguistics.

D. McClosky, E. Charniak, and M. Johnson. 2010. Automatic domain adaptation for parsing. In *Human Language Technologies: The 2010 Annual Conference of the North American Chapter of the Association for Computational Linguistics*, HLT '10, pages 28–36, Stroudsburg, PA, USA. Association for Computational Linguistics.

D. McClosky, M. Surdeanu, and C. D. Manning. 2011. Event extraction as dependency parsing. In *Proceedings of the 49th Annual Meeting of the Association for Computational Linguistics: Human Language Technologies - Volume 1*, HLT '11, pages 1626–1635, Stroudsburg, PA, USA. Association for Computational Linguistics.

M. Miwa, R. Sætre, J.-D. Kim, and J. Tsujii. 2010. Event extraction with complex event classification using rich features. *J. Bioinformatics and Computational Biology*, 8(1):131–146.

K. Morik, P. Brockhausen, and T. Joachims. 1999. Combining statistical learning with a knowledge-based approach - a case study in intensive care monitoring. In *Proceedings of the Sixteenth International Conference on Machine Learning (ICML 1999)*.

C. Quirk, P. Choudhury, M. Gamon, and L. Vanderwende. 2011. MSR-NLP entry in BioNLP shared task 2011. In *Proceedings of BioNLP Shared Task 2011 Workshop*, pages 155–163, Portland, Oregon, USA, June. Association for Computational Linguistics.

S. Riedel and A. McCallum. 2011a. Fast and robust joint models for biomedical event extraction. In *Proceedings of the 2011 Conference on Empirical Methods in Natural Language Processing*, pages 1–12, Edinburgh, Scotland, UK., July. Association for Computational Linguistics.

S. Riedel and A. McCallum. 2011b. Robust biomedical event extraction with dual decomposition and minimal domain adaptation. In *Proceedings of BioNLP Shared Task 2011 Workshop*, pages 46–50, Portland, Oregon, USA, June. Association for Computational Linguistics.

S. Riedel, H.-W. Chun, T. Takagi, and J. Tsujii. 2009. A Markov logic approach to bio-molecular event extraction. In *Proceedings of the BioNLP 2009 Workshop Companion Volume for Shared Task*, pages 41–49, Boulder, Colorado, June. Association for Computational Linguistics.

S. Riedel, D. McClosky, M. Surdeanu, A. McCallum, and C. D. Manning. 2011. Model combination for event extraction in BioNLP 2011. In *Proceedings of BioNLP Shared Task 2011 Workshop*, pages 51–55, Portland, Oregon, USA, June. Association for Computational Linguistics.

R. Sætre, M. Miwa, K. Yoshida, and J. Tsujii. 2009. From protein-protein interaction to molecular event extraction. In *Proceedings of the BioNLP 2009 Workshop Companion Volume for Shared Task*, pages 103–106, Boulder, Colorado, June. Association for Computational Linguistics.

S. Van Landeghem, F. Ginter, Y. Van de Peer, and T. Salakoski. 2011. Evex: A pubmed-scale resource for homology-based generalization of text mining predictions. In *Proceedings of BioNLP 2011 Workshop*, pages 28–37, Portland, Oregon, USA, June. Association for Computational Linguistics.

K. Veropoulos, C. Campbell, and N. Cristianini. 1999. Controlling the sensitivity of support vector machines. In T. Dean, editor, *Proceedings of the International Joint Conference on Artificial Intelligence*, pages 55–60.

A. Vlachos and M. Craven. 2012. Biomedical event extraction from abstracts and full papers using search-based structured prediction. *BMC bioinformatics*, 13(Suppl 11):S5.

Cluster-based Prediction of User Ratings for Stylistic Surface Realisation

Nina Dethlefs, Heriberto Cuayáhuitl, Helen Hastie, Verena Rieser and Oliver Lemon
Heriot-Watt University, Mathematical and Computer Sciences, Edinburgh
n.s.dethlefs@hw.ac.uk

Abstract

Surface realisations typically depend on their target style and audience. A challenge in estimating a stylistic realiser from data is that humans vary significantly in their subjective perceptions of linguistic forms and styles, leading to almost no correlation between ratings of the same utterance. We address this problem in two steps. First, we estimate a mapping function between the linguistic features of a corpus of utterances and their human style ratings. Users are partitioned into clusters based on the similarity of their ratings, so that ratings for new utterances can be estimated, even for new, *unknown* users. In a second step, the estimated model is used to re-rank the outputs of a number of surface realisers to produce stylistically adaptive output. Results confirm that the generated styles are recognisable to human judges and that predictive models based on clusters of users lead to better rating predictions than models based on an average population of users.

1 Introduction

Stylistic surface realisation aims not only to find the best realisation candidate for a semantic input based on some underlying trained model, but also aims to adapt its output to properties of the user, such as their age, social group, or location, among others. One of the first systems to address stylistic variation in generation was Hovy (1988)'s PAULINE, which generated texts that reflect different speaker attitudes towards events based on multiple, adjustable features. Stylistic variation in such contexts can often be modelled systematically as a *multidimensional variation space* with several continuous dimensions, so that varying stylistic scores indicate the strength of each dimension in a realisation candidate. Here, we focus on the dimensions of *colloquialism, politeness* and *naturalness*. Assuming a target score on one or more dimensions, candidate outputs of a data-driven realiser can then be ranked according to their predicted affinity with the target scores.

In this paper, we aim for an approach to stylistic surface realisation which is on the one hand based on natural human data so as to reflect stylistic variation that is as natural as possible. On the other hand, we aim to minimise the amount of annotation and human engineering that informs the design of the system. To this end, we estimate a mapping function between automatically identifiable shallow linguistic features characteristic of an utterance and its human-assigned style ratings. In addition, we aim to address the high degree of variability that is often encountered in subjective rating studies, such as assessments of recommender systems (O'Mahony et al., 2006; Amatriain et al., 2009), sentiment analysis (Pang and Lee, 2005), or surface realisations, where user ratings have been shown to differ significantly ($p<0.001$) for the same utterance (Walker et al., 2007). Such high variability can affect the performance of systems which are trained from an average population of user ratings. However, we are not aware of any work that has addressed this problem principally by estimating ratings for both *known* users, for whom ratings exists, and *unknown* users, for whom no prior ratings exist. To achieve this, we propose to partition users into clusters of individuals who assign similar ratings to linguistically similar utterances, so that their ratings can be estimated more accurately than

Proceedings of the 14th Conference of the European Chapter of the Association for Computational Linguistics, pages 702–711,
Gothenburg, Sweden, April 26-30 2014.

based on an average population of users. This is similar to Janarthanam and Lemon (2014), who show that clustering users and adapting to their level of domain expertise can significantly improve task success and user ratings. Our resulting model is evaluated with realisers not originally built to deal with stylistic variation, and produces natural variation recognisable by humans.

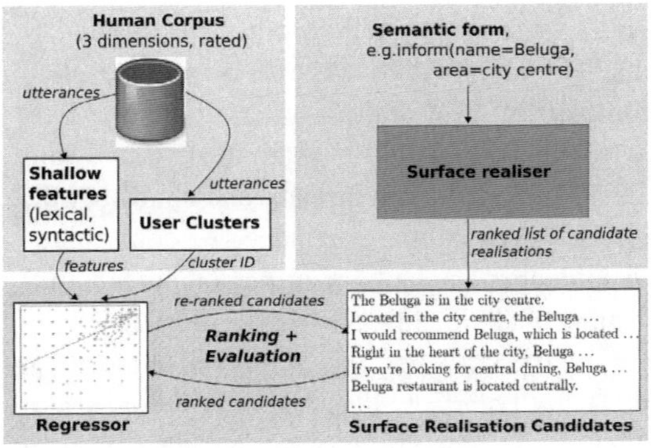

Figure 1: Architecture of stylistic realisation model. Top left: user clusters are estimated from corpus utterances described by linguistic features and ratings. Top right: surface realisation ranks a list of output candidates based on a semantic input. These are ranked stylistically given a trained regressor.

2 Architecture and Domain

We aim to with generating restaurant recommendations as part of an interactive system. To do this, we assume that a generator input is provided by a preceding module, e.g. the interaction manager, and that the task of the surface realiser is to find a suitable stylistically appropriate realisation. An example input is *inform(food=Italian, name=Roma)*, which could be expressed as *The restaurant Roma serves Italian food.* A further aspect is that users are initially *unknown* to the system, but that it should adapt to them over time by discovering their stylistic preferences. Future work involves integrating the surface realiser into the PARLANCE[1] (Hastie et al., 2013) spoken dialogue system with a method for triggering the different styles. Here, we leave the question of when different styles are appropriate as future work and focus on being able to generate them.

The architecture of our model is shown in Figure 1. Training of the regression model from stylistically-rated human corpora is shown in the top-left box (grey). Utterance ratings from human judges are used to extract shallow linguistic features as well as to estimate user clusters. Both types of information inform the resulting stylistic regression model. For surface realisation (top-right box, blue), a semantic input from a preceding model is given as input to a surface realiser. Any realiser is suitable that returns a ranked list of output candidates. The resulting list is re-ranked according to stylistic scores estimated by the regressor, so that the utterance which most closely reflects the target score is ranked highest. The re-ranking process is shown in the lower box (red).

3 Related Work

3.1 Stylistic Variation in Surface Realisation

Our approach is most closely related to work by Paiva and Evans (2005) and Mairesse and Walker (2011), discussed in turn here. Paiva and Evans (2005) present an approach that uses multivariate linear regression to map individual linguistic features to distinguishable styles of text. The approach works in three steps. First, a factor analysis is used to determine the relevant stylistic dimensions from a corpus of human text using shallow linguistic features. Second, a hand-crafted generator is used to produce a large set of utterances, keeping traces of each generator decision, and obtaining style scores for each output based on the estimated factor model. The result is a dataset of *<generator decision, style score>* pairs which can be used in a correlation analysis to identify the predictors of particular output styles. During generation, the correlation equations inform the generator at each choice point so as to best express the desired style. Unfortunately, no human evaluation of the model is presented so that it remains unclear to what extent the generated styles are perceivable by humans.

Closely related is work by Mairesse and Walker (2011) who present the PERSONAGE system, which aims to generate language reflecting particular personalities. Instead of choosing generator decisions by considering their predicted style scores, however, Mairesse and Walker (2011) directly predict generator decisions based on target personality scores. To obtain the generator, the authors first generate a corpus of utterances which differ randomly in their linguistic choices. All utterances are rated by humans indicating the

[1] http://parlance-project.eu

extent to which they reflect different personality traits. The best predictive model is then chosen in a comparison of several classifiers and regressors. Mairesse and Walker (2011) are the first to evaluate their generator with humans and show that the generated personalities are indeed recognisable.

Approaches on replicating personalities in realisations include Gill and Oberlander (2002) and Isard et al. (2006). Porayska-Pomsta and Mellish (2004) and Gupta et al. (2007) are approaches to politeness in generation, based on the notion of face and politeness theory, respectively.

3.2 User Preferences in Surface Realisation

Taking users' individual content preferences into account for training generation systems can positively affect their performance (Jordan and Walker, 2005; Dale and Viethen, 2009). We are interested in individual user perceptions concerning the *surface realisation* of system output and the way they relate to different stylistic dimensions. Walker et al. (2007) were the first to show that individual preferences exist for the perceived *quality* of realisations and that these can be modelled in trainable generation. They train two versions of a rank-and-boost generator, a first version of which is trained on the average population of user ratings, whereas a second one is trained on the ratings of individual users. The authors show statistically that ratings from different users are drawn from different distributions ($p<0.001$) and that significantly better performance is achieved when training and testing on data of individual users. In fact, training a model on one user's ratings and testing it on another's performs as badly as a random baseline. However, no previous work has modelled the individual preferences of *unseen* users–for whom no training data exists.

4 Estimation of Style Prediction Models

4.1 Corpora and Style Dimensions

Our domain of interest is the automatic generation of restaurant recommendations that differ with respect to their *colloquialism* and *politeness* and are as *natural* as possible. All three stylistic dimension were identified from a qualitative analysis of human domain data. To estimate the strength of each of them in a single utterance, we collect user ratings for three data sets that were collected under different conditions and are freely available.

Corpus	Colloquial	Natural	Polite
LIST	3.38 ± 1.5	4.06 ± 1.2	4.35 ± 0.8
MAI	3.95 ± 1.2	4.32 ± 1.0	4.27 ± 0.8
CLASSIC	4.29 ± 1.1	4.20 ± 1.2	3.64 ± 1.3

Table 1: Average ratings with standard deviations. Ratings between datasets (except one) differ significantly at $p<0.01$, using the Wilcoxon signed-rank test.

- LIST is a corpus of restaurant recommendations from the website The List.[2] It consists of professionally written reviews. An example is *"Located in the heart of Barnwell, Beluga is an excellent restaurant with a smart menu of modern Italian cuisine."*
- MAI is a dataset collected by Mairesse et al. (2010),[3] using Amazon Mechanical Turk. Turkers typed in recommendations for various specified semantics; e.g. *"I recommend the restaurant Beluga near the cathedral."*
- CLASSIC is a dataset of transcribed spoken user utterances from the CLASSiC project.[4] The utterances consist of user queries for restaurants, such as *"I need an Italian restaurant with a moderate price range."*

Our joint dataset consists of $1,361$ human utterances, 450 from the LIST, 334 from MAI, and 577 from CLASSIC. We asked users on the CrowdFlower crowdsourcing platform[5] to read utterances and rate their colloquialism, politeness and naturalness on a 1-5 scale (the higher the better). The following questions were asked.

- **Colloquialism:** The utterance is colloquial, i.e. could have been spoken.
- **Politeness:** The utterance is polite / friendly.
- **Naturalness:** The utterance is natural, i.e. could have been produced by a human.

The question on naturalness can be seen as a general quality check for our training set. We do not aim to generate unnatural utterances. 167 users took part in our rating study leading to a rated dataset of altogether $3,849$ utterances. All users were from the USA. The average ratings per dataset and stylistic dimension are summarised in Table 1. From this, we can see that LIST utterances were perceived as the least natural and

[2] http://www.list.co.uk/

[3] http://people.csail.mit.edu/francois/research/bagel/

[4] http://www.classic-project.org/

[5] http://crowdflower.com/

colloquial, but as the most polite. CLASSIC utterances were perceived as the most colloquial, but the least polite, and MAI utterances were rated as the most natural. Differences between ratings for each dimension and dataset are significant at p<0.01, using the Wilcoxon signed-rank test, except the naturalness for MAI and CLASSIC.

Since we are mainly interested in the lexical and syntactic features of utterances here, the fact that CLASSIC utterances are spoken, whereas the other two corpora are written, should not affect the quality of the resulting model. Similarly, some stylistic categories may seem closely related, such as *colloquialism* and *naturalness*, or orthogonal to each other, such as *politeness* and *colloquialism*. However, while ratings for *colloquialism* and *naturalness* are very close for the CLASSIC dataset, they vary significantly for the two other datasets (p<0.01). Also, the ratings for *colloquialim* and *politeness* show a weak positive correlation of 0.23, i.e. are not perceived as orthogonal by users. These results suggest that all in all our three stylistic categories are perceived as sufficiently different from each other and suitable for training to predict a spectrum of different styles.

Another interesting aspect is that individual user ratings vary significantly, leading to a high degree of variability for identical utterances. This will be the focus of the following sections.

4.2 Feature Estimation

Table 2 shows the feature set we will use in our regression experiments. We started from a larger subset including 45 lexical and syntactic features as well as unigrams and bigrams, all of which could be identified from the corpus without manual annotation. The only analysis tool we used was the Stanford Parser,[6] which identified certain types of words (pronouns, wh-words) or the depth of syntactic embedding. A step-wise regression analysis was then carried out to identify those features that contributed significantly (at p<0.01) to the overall regression equation obtained per stylistic dimension. Of all lexical features (unigrams and bigrams), the word *with* was the only contributor. A related feature was the average *tf-idf* score of the content words in an utterance.

[6]http://nlp.stanford.edu/software/lex-parser.shtml

Feature	Type
Length of utterance	num
Presence of personal pronouns	bool
Presence of WH words	bool
with cue word	bool
Presence of negation	bool
Average length of content words	num
Ave *tf-idf* score of content words	num
Depth of syntactic embedding	num

Table 2: Features used for regression, which were identified as significant contributors (p<0.01) from a larger feature set in a step-wise regression analysis.

4.3 Regression Experiments

Based on the features identified in Section 4.2, we train a separate regressor for each stylistic dimension. The task of the regressor is to predict, based on the extracted linguistic features of an utterance, a score in the range of 1-5 for colloquialism, politeness and naturalness. We compare: (1) a multivariate multiple regressor (MMR), (2) an M5P decision tree regressor, (3) a support vector machine (SVM) with linear kernel, and (4) a ZeroR classifier, which serves as a majority baseline. We used the *R* statistics toolkit[7] for the MMR and the Weka toolkit[8] for the remaining models.

Average User Ratings The regressors were first trained to predict the average user ratings of an utterance and evaluated in a 10-fold cross validation experiment. Table 3 shows the results. Here, r denotes the Pearson correlation coefficient, which indicates the correlation between the predicted and the actual user scores; R^2 is the coefficient of determination, which provides a measure of how well the learnt model fits the data; and $RMSE$ refers to the Root Mean Squared Error, the error between the predicted and actual user ratings.

We can observe that MMR achieves the best performance for predicting colloquialism and naturalness, whereas M5P best predicts politeness. Unfortunately, all regressors achieve at best a moderate correlation with human ratings. Based on these results, we ran a correlation analysis for all utterances for which more than 20 original user ratings were available. The purpose was to find out to what extent human raters agree with each other. The results showed that user agreement in fact ranges from a high positive corre-

[7]http://www.r-project.org/

[8]http://www.cs.waikato.ac.nz/ml/weka/

	Model	r	R^2	$RMSE$
Colloquial	MMR	**0.50**	**0.25**	**0.85**
	SVM	0.47	0.22	0.86
	M5P	0.48	0.23	0.85
	ZeroR	-0.08	0.006	0.97
Natural	MMR	**0.30**	**0.09**	**0.78**
	SVM	0.24	0.06	0.81
	M5P	0.27	0.07	0.78
	ZeroR	-0.09	0.008	0.81
Polite	MMR	0.33	0.11	0.71
	SVM	0.31	0.09	0.73
	M5P	**0.42**	**0.18**	**0.69**
	ZeroR	-0.09	0.008	0.76

Table 3: Comparison of regression models per dimension *using average user ratings*. The best model is indicated in bold-face for the correlation coefficient.

	Model	r	R^2	$RMSE$
Colloquial	MMR	**0.61**	**0.37**	**1.05**
	SVM	0.36	0.13	1.3
	M5P	0.56	0.31	1.07
	ZeroR	-0.06	0.004	1.3
Natural	MMR	**0.55**	**0.30**	**0.96**
	SVM	0.36	0.13	1.13
	M5P	0.49	0.24	0.99
	ZeroR	-0.08	0.06	1.13
Polite	MMR	0.69	0.48	0.76
	SVM	0.54	0.30	0.92
	M5P	**0.71**	**0.50**	**0.73**
	ZeroR	-0.04	0.002	1.04

Table 4: Comparison of regression models per dimension *using individual user ratings*. The best model is indicated in bold-face for the correlation coefficient.

lation of 0.79 to a moderate negative correlation of -0.55. The average is 0.04 (SD=0.95), i.e. indicating *no correlation between user ratings*, even for the same utterance. This observation is partially in line with related work that has found high diversity in subjective user ratings. Yeh and Mellish (1997) report only 70% agreement of human judges on the best choice of referring expression. Amatriain et al. (2009) report inconsistencies in user ratings in recommender systems with an RMSE range of 0.55 to 0.81 and argue that this constitutes a lower bound for system performance. This inconsistency is exacerbated by raters recruited via crowdsourcing platforms as in our study (Koller et al., 2010; Rieser et al., 2011). However, while crowdsourced data have been shown to contain substantially more noise than data collected in a lab environment, they do tend to reflect the general tendency of their more controlled counterparts (Gosling et al., 2004).

Individual User Ratings Given that individual preferences exist for surface realisation (Walker et al., 2007), we included the *user's ID* as a regression feature and re-ran the experiments. The hypothesis was that if users differ in their preferences for realisation candidates, they may also differ in terms of their perceptions of linguistic styles. The results shown in Table 4 support this: the obtained correlations are significantly higher ($p<0.001$, using the Fisher r-to-z transformation) than those without the user's ID (though we are still not able to model the full variation observed in ratings). Importantly, this shows that user ratings are *intrinsically coherent* (not random) and that variation exists mainly for inter-user agreement. This model performs satisfactorily for a known population of users. However, it does not allow the prediction of ratings of *unknown* users, who we mostly encounter in generation.

5 Clustering User Rating Behaviour

5.1 Spectral Clustering

The goal of this section is to find a number of k clusters which partition our data set of user ratings in a way that users in one cluster rate utterances with particular linguistic properties most similarly to each other, while rating them most dissimilarly to users in other clusters. We assume a set of n data points $x_1 \ldots x_n$, which in our case correspond to an individual user or group of users, characterised in terms of word bigrams, POS tag bigrams, and assigned ratings of the utterance they rated. An example is *Beluga*_NNP *serves*_VBZ *Italian*_JJ *food*_NN*; [col=5.0, nat=5.0, pol=4.0]*. Features were chosen as a subset of relevant features from the larger set used for regression above.

Using spectral clustering (von Luxburg, 2007), clusters can be identified from a set of eigenvectors of an affinity matrix S derived from pair-wise similarities between data points $s_{ij} = s(x_i, x_j)$ using a symmetric and non-negative similarity function. To do that, we use a cumulative similarity based on the Kullback-Leibler divergence,

$$D(P,Q) = \frac{\sum_i p_i log_2(\frac{p_i}{q_i}) + \sum_j q_j log_2(\frac{q_j}{p_j})}{2},$$

where P is a distribution of words, POS tags or ratings in data point x_i; and Q a similar distribution in data point x_j. The lower the cumulative di-

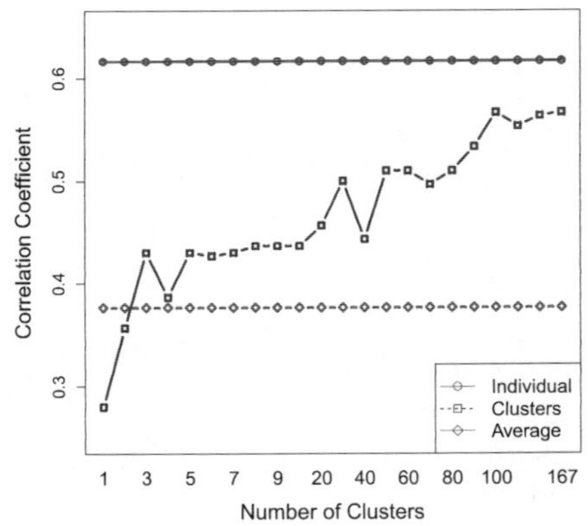

Figure 2: Average correlation coefficient for different numbers of clusters. For comparison, results from *average* and *individual* user ratings are also shown.

vergence between two data sets, the more similar they are. To find clusters of similar users from the affinity matrix S, we use the algorithm described in Ng et al. (2001). It derives clusters by choosing the k largest eigenvectors $u_1, u_2, \ldots, u_k$ from the Laplacian matrix $L = D^{1/2} - SD^{1/2}$ (where D is a diagonal matrix), arranging them into columns in a matrix $U = [u_1 u_2 \ldots u_k]$ and then normalising them for length. The result is a new matrix T, obtained through $t_{ij} = u_{ij}/(\sum_k u_{ik}^2)^{1/2}$. The set of clusters $C_1, \ldots C_k$ can then be obtained from T using the K-means algorithm, where each row in T serves as an individual data point. Finally, each original data point x_i (row i of T) is assigned to a cluster C_j. In comparison to other clustering algorithms, experiments by Ng et al. (2001) show that spectral clustering is robust for convex and non-convex data sets. The authors also demonstrate why using K-means only is often not sufficient.

The main clusters obtained describe surface realisation preferences by particular groups of users. An example is the realisation of the location of a restaurant as a prepositional phrase or as a relative clause as in *restaurant in the city centre* vs. *restaurant located in the city centre*; or the realisation of the food type as an adjective, *an Italian restaurant*, vs. a clause, *this restaurant serves Italian food*. Clusters can then be characterised as different combinations of such preferences.

5.2 Results: Predicting Stylistic Ratings

Figure 2 shows the average correlation coefficient r across dimensions in relation to the number of clusters, in comparison to the results obtained with *average* and *individual* user ratings. We can see that the baseline without user information is outperformed with as few as three clusters. From 30 clusters on, a medium correlation is obtained until another performance jump occurs around 90 clusters. Evidently, the best performance would be achieved by obtaining one cluster per user, i.e. 167 clusters, but nothing would be gained in this way, and we can see that useful generalisations can be made from much fewer clusters. Based on the clusters found, we will now predict the ratings of known and unknown users.

Known Users For known users, first of all, Figure 3 shows the correlations between the predicted and actual ratings for colloquialism, politeness and naturalness based on 90 user clusters. Correlation coefficients were obtained using an MMR regressor. We can see that a medium correlation is achieved for naturalness and (nearly) strong correlations are achieved for politeness and colloquialism. This confirms that clustering users can help to better predict their ratings than based on shallow linguistic features alone, but that more generalisation is achieved than based on individual user ratings that include the user's ID as a regression feature. The performance gain in comparison to predicting average ratings is significant ($p<0.01$) from as few as three clusters onwards.

Unknown Users We initially sort unknown users into the majority cluster and then aim to make more accurate cluster allocations as more information becomes available. For example, after a user has assigned their first rating, we can take it into account to re-estimate their cluster more accurately. Clusters are re-estimated with each new rating, based on our trained regression model. While estimating a user cluster based on linguistic features alone yields an average correlation of 0.38, an estimation based on linguistic features and a single rating alone already yields an average correlation of 0.45. From around 30 ratings, the average correlation coefficients achieved are as good as for known users. More importantly, though, estimations based on a single rating alone significantly outperform ratings based on the av-

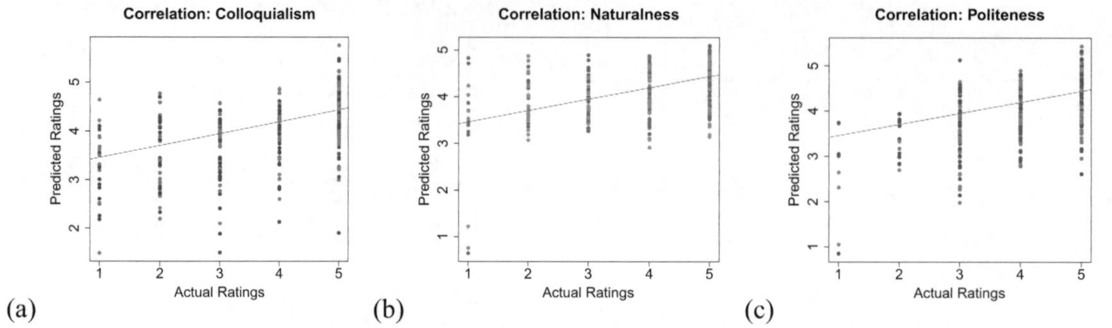

Figure 3: Correlations per dimension between actual and predicted user ratings based on 90 user clusters: (a) Colloquialism ($r = 0.57$, p<0.001), (b) Naturalness ($r = 0.49$, p<0.001) and (c) Politeness ($r = 0.59$, p<0.001).

erage population of users (p<0.001). Fig. 4 shows this process. It shows the correlation between predicted and actual user ratings for unknown users over time. This is useful in interactive scenarios, where system behaviour is refined as more information becomes available (Cuayáhuitl and Dethlefs, 2011; Gašić et al., 2011), or for incremental systems (Skantze and Hjalmarsson, 2010; Dethlefs et al., 2012b; Dethlefs et al., 2012a).

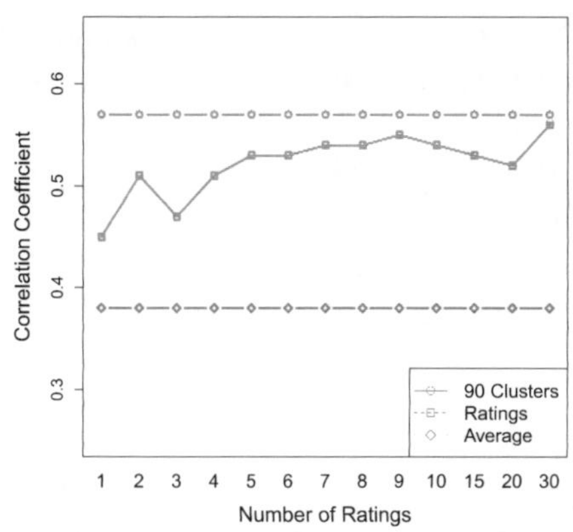

Figure 4: Average correlation coefficient for *unknown* users with an increasing number of ratings. Results from *90 clusters* and *average* ratings are also shown.

6 Evaluation: Stylistically-Aware Surface Realisation

To evaluate the applicability of our regression model for stylistically-adaptive surface realisation, this section describes work that compares four different surface realisers, which were not originally developed to produce stylistic variation. To do that, we first obtain the cluster for each input sentence s: $c^* = \arg\min_{c \in C} \sum_x D(P_s^x | Q_c^x)$, where x refers to n-grams, POS tags or ratings (see Section 5.1); P refers to a discrete probability distribution of sentence s; and Q refers to a discrete probability distribution of cluster c. The best cluster is used to compute the style score of sentence s using: $score(s) = \sum_i^n \theta_i f_i(s), c^* \in F$, where θ_i are the weights estimated by the regressor, and f_i are the features of sentence s; see Table 2. The idea is that if well-phrased utterances can be generated, whose stylistic variation is recognisable to human judges, then our regressor can be used in combination with any statistical surface realiser. Note however that the stylistic variation observed depends on the stylistic spectrum that each realiser covers. Here, our goal is mainly to show that whatever stylistic variation exists in a realiser can be recognised by our model.

6.1 Overview of Surface Realisers

In a human rating study, we compare four surface realisers (ordered alphabetically), all of which are able to return a ranked list of candidate realisations for a semantic input. Please refer to the references given for details of each system. The BAGEL and SPaRKy realisers were compared based on published ranked output lists.[9]

- **BAGEL** is a surface realiser based on dynamic Bayes Nets originally trained using Active Learning by Mairesse et al. (2010). It was shown to generate well-phrased utterances from unseen semantic inputs.
- **CRF (global)** treats surface realisation as a

[9]Available from `http://people.csail.mit.edu/francois/research/bagel` and `http://users.soe.ucsc.edu/~maw/downloads.html`.

System	Utterance
BAGEL	*Beluga is a moderately priced restaurant in the city centre area.* **Col** = 4.0, **Pol** = 4.0, **Nat** = 4.0
CRF (global)	*Set in the city centre, Beluga is a moderately priced location for the celebration of the Italian spirit.* **Col** = 2.0, **Pol** = 5.0, **Nat** = 2.0
p**CRU**	*Beluga is located in the city centre and serves cheap Italian food.* **Col** = 4.0, **Pol** = 3.0, **Nat** = 5.0
SPaRKy	*Beluga has the best overall quality among the selected restaurants since this Italian restaurant has good decor, with good service.* **Col** = 3.0, **Pol** = 4.0, **Nat** = 5.0

Table 5: Example utterances for the BAGEL, **CRF (global)**, ***p*****CRU** and **SPaRKy** realisers shown to users. Sample ratings from individual users are also shown.

sequence labelling task: given a set of (observed) linguistic features, it aims to find the best (hidden) sequence of phrases realising a semantic input (Dethlefs et al., 2013).

- ***p*****CRU** is based on probabilistic context-free grammars and generation is done using Viterbi search, sampling (used here), or random search. It is based on Belz (2008).
- **SPaRKy** is based on a rank-and-boost approach. It learns a mapping between the linguistic features of a target utterance and its predicted user ratings and ranks candidates accordingly (Walker et al., 2007).

6.2 Results: Recognising Stylistic Variation

242 users from the USA took part in a rating study on the CrowdFlower platform and rated altogether 1,702 utterances, from among the highest-ranked surface realisations above. For each utterance they read, they rated the *colloquialism, naturaless* and *politeness* based on the same questions as in Section 4.1, used to obtain the training data. Based on this, we compare the perceived strength of each stylistic dimension in an utterance to the one predicted by the regressor. Example utterances and ratings are shown in Table 5. Results are shown in Table 6 and confirm our observations: ratings for *known* users can be estimated with a medium (or high) correlation based on clusters of users who assign similar ratings to utterances with similar linguistic features. We can also see that such estimations do not depend on a particular data set or realiser.

System	Colloquial	Polite	Natural
BAGEL	0.78	0.66	0.69
CRF global	0.58	0.63	0.63
*p*CRU	0.67	0.42	0.77
SPaRKy	0.87	0.56	0.81

Table 6: Correlation coefficients between subjective user ratings and ratings predicted by the regressor for *known* users across data-driven surface realisers.

A novel aspect of our technique in comparison to previous work on stylistic realisation is that it does not depend on the time- and resource-intensive design of a hand-coded generator, as in Paiva and Evans (2005) and Mairesse and Walker (2011). Instead, it can be applied in conjunction with any system designer's favourite realiser and preserves the realiser's original features by re-ranking only its top n (e.g. 10) output candidates. Our method is therefore able to strike a balance between highly-ranked and well-phrased utterances and stylistic adaptation. A current limitation of our model is that some ratings can still not be predicted with a high correlation with human judgements. However, even the medium correlations achieved have been shown to be significantly better than estimations based on the average population of users (Section 5.2).

7 Conclusion and Future Work

We have presented a model of stylistic realisation that is able to adapt its output along several stylistic dimensions. Results show that the variation is recognisable by humans and that user ratings can be predicted for *known* as well as *unknown* users. A model which clusters individual users based on their ratings of linguistically similar utterances achieves significantly higher performance than a model trained on the average population of ratings. These results may also play a role in other domains in which users display variability in their subjective ratings, e.g. recommender systems, sentiment analysis, or emotion generation. Future work may explore the use of additional clustering features as a more scalable alternative to re-ranking. It also needs to determine how user feedback can be obtained during an interaction, where asking users for ratings may be disruptive. Possibilities include to infer user ratings from their next dialogue move, or from multimodal information such as hesitations or eye-tracking.

Acknowledgements This research was funded by the EC FP7 programme FP7/2011-14 under grant agreements no. 270019 (SPACEBOOK) and no. 287615 (PARLANCE).

References

Xavier Amatriain, Josep M. Pujol, and Nuria Oliver. 2009. I like It... I Like It Not: Evaluating User Ratings Noise in Recommender Systems. In *In the 17th International Conference on User Modelling, Adaptation, and Personalisation (UMAP)*, pages 247–258, Trento, Italy. Springer-Verlag.

Anja Belz. 2008. Automatic Generation of Weather Forecast Texts Using Comprehensive Probabilistic Generation-Space Models. *Natural Language Engineering*, 14(4):431–455.

Penelope Brown and Stephen Levinson. 1987. *Some Universals in Language Usage*. Cambridge University Press, Cambridge, UK.

Heriberto Cuayáhuitl and Nina Dethlefs. 2011. Optimizing Situated Dialogue Management in Unknown Environments. In *INTERSPEECH*, pages 1009–1012.

Robert Dale and Jette Viethen. 2009. Referring Expression Generation Through Attribute-Based Heuristics. In *Proceedings of the 12th European Workshop on Natural Language Generation (ENLG)*, Athens, Greece.

Nina Dethlefs, Helen Hastie, Verena Rieser, and Oliver Lemon. 2012a. Optimising Incremental Dialogue Decisions Using Information Density for Interactive Systems. In *Proceedings of the Conference on Empirical Methods in Natural Language Processing (EMNLP-CoNLL)*, Jeju, South Korea.

Nina Dethlefs, Helen Hastie, Verena Rieser, and Oliver Lemon. 2012b. Optimising Incremental Generation for Spoken Dialogue Systems: Reducing the Need for Fillers. In *Proceedings of the International Conference on Natural Language Generation (INLG)*, Chicago, Illinois, USA.

Nina Dethlefs, Helen Hastie, Heriberto Cuayáhuitl, and Oliver Lemon. 2013. Conditional Random Fields for Responsive Surface Realisation Using Global Features. In *Proceedings of the 51st Annual Meeting of the Association for Computational Linguistics (ACL)*, Sofia, Bulgaria.

Michael Fleischman and Eduard Hovy. 2002. Emotional Variation in Speech-Based Natural Language Generation. In *Proceedings of the 2nd International Natural Language Generation Conference*.

Milica Gašić, Filip Jurčíček, Blaise Thomson, Kai Yu, and Steve Young. 2011. On-Line Policy Optimisation of Spoken Dialogue Systems via Interaction with Human Subjects. In *Proceedings of the IEEE Automatic Speech Recognition and Understanding (ASRU) Workshop*.

Alastair Gill and Jon Oberlander. 2002. Taking Care of the Linguistic Features of Extraversion. In *Proceedings of the 24th Annual Conference of the Cognitive Science Society*, pages 363–368, Fairfax, VA.

Samuel Gosling, Simine Vazire, Sanjay Srivastava, and Oliver John. 2004. Should We Trust Web-Based Studies? A Comparative Analysis of Six Preconceptions About Internet Questionnaires. *American Psychologist*, 59(2):93–104.

Swati Gupta, Marilyn Walker, and Daniela Romano. 2007. How Rude Are You? Evaluating Politeness and Affect in Interaction. In *Proceedings of the 2nd International Conference on Affective Computing and Intelligent Interaction*.

Helen Hastie, Marie-Aude Aufaure, Panos Alexopoulos, Heriberto Cuayhuitl, Nina Dethlefs, James Henderson Milica Gasic, Oliver Lemon, Xingkun Liu, Peter Mika, Nesrine Ben Mustapha, Verena Rieser, Blaise Thomson, Pirros Tsiakoulis, Yves Vanrompay, Boris Villazon-Terrazas, and Steve Young. 2013. Demonstration of the PARLANCE System: A Data-Driven, Incremental, Spoken Dialogue System for Interactive Search. In *Proceedings of the 14th Annual Meeting of the Special Interest Group on Discourse and Dialogue (SIGdial)*.

Eduard Hovy. 1988. *Generating Natural Language under Pragmatic Constraints*. Lawrence Erlbaum Associates, Hillsdale, NJ.

Amy Isard, Carsten Brockmann, and Jon Oberlander. 2006. Individuality and Alignment in Generated Dialogues. In *Proceedings of the 4th International Natural Language Generation Conference (INLG)*, Sydney, Australia.

Srini Janarthanam and Oliver Lemon. 2014. Adaptive generation in dialogue systems using dynamic user modeling. *Computational Linguistics*. (in press).

Pamela Jordan and Marilyn Walker. 2005. Learning Content Selection Rules for Generating Object Descriptions in Dialogue. *Journal of Artificial Intelligence Research*, 24:157–194.

Alexander Koller, Kristina Striegnitz, Donna Byron, Justine Cassell, Robert Dale, and Johanna Moore. 2010. The First Challenge on Generating Instructions in Virtual Environments. In M. Theune and E. Krahmer, editors, *Empirical Methods in Natural Language Generation*, pages 337–361. Springer Verlag, Berlin/Heidelberg.

François Mairesse and Marilyn Walker. 2011. Controlling User Perceptions of Linguistic Style: Trainable Generation of Personality Traits. *Computational Linguistics*, 37(3):455–488, September.

François Mairesse, Milica Gašić, Filip Jurčíček, Simon Keizer, Blaise Thomson, Kai Yu, and Steve Young. 2010. Phrase-based statistical language generation using graphical models and active learning. In *Proceedings of the Annual Meeting of the*

Association for Computational Linguistics (ACL), pages 1552–1561.

Andrew Ng, Michael Jordan, and Yair Weiss. 2001. On Spectral Clustering: Analysis and an Algorithm. In *Advances in Neural Information Processing Systems*, pages 849–856. MIT Press.

Michael O'Mahony, Neil Hurley, and Guénolé Silvestre. 2006. Detecting Noise in Recommender System Databases. In *Proceedings of the International Conference on Intelligent User Interfaces (IUI)s*. ACM Press.

Daniel Paiva and Roger Evans. 2005. Empirically-Based Control of Natural Language Generation. In *Proceedings of the 43rd Annual Meeting of the Association for Computational Linguistics (ACL)*, Ann Arbor, Michigan, USA.

Bo Pang and Lillian Lee. 2005. Seeing Stars: Exploiting Class Relationships for Sentiment Categorization with Respect to Rating Scales. In *Proceedings of the 43rd Annual Meeting of the Association for Computational Linguistics (ACL)*.

Kaska Porayska-Pomsta and Chris Mellish. 2004. Modelling Politness in Natural Language Generation. In *Proceedings of the 3rd International Natural Language Generation Conference (INLG)*, Brighton, UK.

Verena Rieser, Simon Keizer, Xingkun Liu, and Oliver Lemon. 2011. Adaptive Information Presentation for Spoken Dialogue Systems: Evaluation with Human Subjects. In *Proceedings of the 13th European Workshop on Natural Language Generation (ENLG)*, Nancy, France.

Gabriel Skantze and Anna Hjalmarsson. 2010. Towards Incremental Speech Generation in Dialogue Systems. In *Proceedings of the 11th Annual SigDial Meeting on Discourse and Dialogue*, Tokyo, Japan.

Ulrike von Luxburg. 2007. A Tutorial on Spectral Clustering. *Statistics and Computing*, 17(4).

Marilyn Walker, Amanda Stent, François Mairesse, and Rashmi Prasad. 2007. Individual and Domain Adaptation in Sentence Planning for Dialogue. *Journal of Artificial Intelligence Research*, 30(1):413–456.

Ching-long Yeh and Chris Mellish. 1997. An Empirical Study on the Generation of Anaphora in Chinese. *Computational Linguistics*, 23:169–190.

Improving the Estimation of Word Importance for News Multi-Document Summarization

Kai Hong
University of Pennsylvania
Philadelphia, PA, 19104
hongkai1@seas.upenn.edu

Ani Nenkova
University of Pennsylvania
Philadelphia, PA, 19104
nenkova@seas.upenn.edu

Abstract

We introduce a supervised model for predicting word importance that incorporates a rich set of features. Our model is superior to prior approaches for identifying words used in human summaries. Moreover we show that an extractive summarizer using these estimates of word importance is comparable in automatic evaluation with the state-of-the-art.

1 Introduction

In automatic extractive summarization, sentence importance is calculated by taking into account, among possibly other features, the importance of words that appear in the sentence. In this paper, we describe experiments on identifying words from the input that are also included in human summaries; we call such words **summary keywords**. We review several unsupervised approaches for summary keyword identification and further combine these, along with features including position, part-of-speech, subjectivity, topic categories, context and intrinsic importance, in a superior supervised model for predicting word importance.

One of the novel features we develop aims to determine the intrinsic importance of words. To this end, we analyze abstract-article pairs in the New York Times corpus (Sandhaus, 2008) to identify words that tend to be preserved in the abstracts. We demonstrate that judging word importance just based on this criterion leads to significantly higher performance than selecting sentences at random. Identifying intrinsically important words allows us to generate summaries without doing any feature computation on the input, equivalent in quality to the standard baseline of extracting the first 100 words from the latest article in the input. Finally, we integrate the schemes for assignment of word importance into a summarizer which greedily optimizes for the presence of important words. We show that our better estimation of word importance leads to better extractive summaries.

2 Prior work

The idea of identifying words that are descriptive of the input can be dated back to Luhn's earliest work in automatic summarization (Luhn, 1958). There keywords were identified based on the number of times they appeared in the input, and words that appeared most and least often were excluded. Then the sentences in which keywords appeared near each other, presumably better conveying the relationship between the keywords, were selected to form a summary.

Many successful recent systems also estimate word importance. The simplest but competitive way to do this task is to estimate the word probability from the input (Nenkova and Vanderwende, 2005). Another powerful method is log-likelihood ratio test (Lin and Hovy, 2000), which identifies the set of words that appear in the input more often than in a background corpus (Conroy et al., 2006; Harabagiu and Lacatusu, 2005).

In contrast to selecting a set of keywords, weights are assigned to all words in the input in the majority of summarization methods. Approaches based on (approximately) optimizing the coverage of these words have become widely popular. Earliest such work relied on TF*IDF weights (Filatova and Hatzivassiloglou, 2004), later approaches included heuristics to identify summary-worthy bigrams (Riedhammer et al., 2010). Most optimization approaches, however, use TF*IDF or word probability in the input as word weights (McDonald, 2007; Shen and Li, 2010; Berg-Kirkpatrick et al., 2011).

Proceedings of the 14th Conference of the European Chapter of the Association for Computational Linguistics, pages 712–721,
Gothenburg, Sweden, April 26-30 2014.

Word weights have also been estimated by supervised approaches, with word probability and location of occurrence as typical features (Yih et al., 2007; Takamura and Okumura, 2009; Sipos et al., 2012).

A handful of investigations have productively explored the mutually reinforcing relationship between word and sentence importance, iteratively re-estimating each in either supervised or unsupervised framework (Zha, 2002; Wan et al., 2007; Wei et al., 2008; Liu et al., 2011). Most existing work directly focuses on predicting sentence importance, with emphasis on the formalization of the problem (Kupiec et al., 1995; Celikyilmaz and Hakkani-Tur, 2010; Litvak et al., 2010). There has been little work directly focused on predicting keywords from the input that will appear in human summaries. Also there has been only a few investigations of suitable features for estimating word importance and identifying keywords in summaries; we address this issue by exploring a range of possible indicators of word importance in our model.

3 Data and Planned Experiments

We carry out our experiments on two datasets from the Document Understanding Conference (DUC) (Over et al., 2007). DUC 2003 is used for training and development, DUC 2004 is used for testing. These are the last two years in which generic summarization was evaluated at DUC workshops.

There are 30 multi-document clusters in DUC 2003 and 50 in DUC 2004, each with about 10 news articles on a related topic. The task is to produce a 100-word generic summary. Four human abstractive summaries are available for each cluster.

We compare different keyword extraction methods by the F-measure[1] they achieve against the gold-standard summary keywords. We do not use stemming when calculating these scores.

In our work, keywords for an input are defined as those words that appear in *at least* i of the human abstracts, yielding four gold-standard sets of keywords, denoted by G_i. $|G_i|$ is thus the cardinality of the set for the input. We only consider the words in the summary that also appear in the original input[2], with stopwords excluded[3]. Table 1 shows the average number of unique content words for the respective keyword gold-standard.

i	1	2	3	4
Mean $\|G_i\|$	102	32	15	6

Table 1: Average number of words in G_i

For the summarization task, we compare results using ROUGE (Lin, 2004). We report ROUGE-1, -2, -4 recall, with stemming and without removing stopwords. We consider ROUGE-2 recall as the main metric for this comparison due to its effectiveness in comparing machine summaries (Owczarzak et al., 2012). All of the summaries were truncated to the first 100 words by ROUGE[4].

We use Wilcoxon signed-rank test to examine the statistical significance as advocated by Rankel et al. (2011) for both tasks, and consider differences to be significant if the p-value is less than 0.05.

4 Unsupervised Word Weighting

In this section we describe three unsupervised approaches of assigning importance weights to words. The first two are probability and log-likelihood ratio, which have been extensively used in prior work. We also apply a markov random walk model for keyword ranking, similar to Mihalcea and Tarau (2004). In the next section we describe a summarizer that uses these weights to form a summary and then describe our regression approach to combine these and other predictors in order to achieve more accurate predictions for the word importance in Section 7.

The task is to assign a score to each word in the input. The keywords extracted are thus the content words with highest scores.

4.1 Word Probability (Prob)

The frequency with which a word occurs in the input is often considered as an indicator of its importance. The weight for a word is computed as $p(w) = \frac{c(w)}{N}$, where $c(w)$ is the number of times word w appears in the input and N is the total number of word tokens in the input.

[1] 2*precision*recall/(precision+recall)

[2] On average 26.3% (15.0% with stemming) of the words in the four abstracts never appear in the input.

[3] We use the stopword list from the SMART system (Salton, 1971), augmented with punctuation and symbols.

[4] ROUGE version 1.5.5 with parameters: -c 95 -r 1000 -n 4 -m -a -l 100 -x

4.2 Log-likelihood Ratio (LLR)

The log-likelihood ratio test (Lin and Hovy, 2000) compares the distribution of a word in the input with that in a large background corpus to identify topic words. We use the Gigaword corpus (Graff et al., 2007) for background counts. The test statistic has a χ^2 distribution, so a desired confidence level can be chosen to find a small set of topic words.

4.3 Markov Random Walk Model (MRW)

Graph methods have been successfully applied to weighting sentences for generic (Wan and Yang, 2008; Mihalcea and Tarau, 2004; Erkan and Radev, 2004) and query-focused summarization (Otterbacher et al., 2009).

Here instead of constructing a graph with sentences as nodes and edges weighted by sentence similarity, we treat the words as vertices, similar to Mihalcea and Tarau (2004). The difference in our approach is that the edges between the words are defined by syntactic dependencies rather than depending on the co-occurrence of words within a window of k. We use the Stanford dependency parser (Marneffe et al., 2006). In our approach, we consider a word w more likely to be included in a human summary when it is syntactically related to other (important) words, even if w itself is not mentioned often. The edge weight between two vertices is equal to the number of syntactic dependencies of any type between two words within the same sentence in the input. The weights are then normalized by summing up the weights of edges linked to one node.

We apply the Pagerank algorithm (Lawrence et al., 1998) on the resulting graph. We set the probability of performing random jump between nodes λ=0.15. The algorithm terminates when the change of node weight between iterations is smaller than 10^{-4} for all nodes. Word importance is equal to the final weight of its corresponding node in the graph.

5 Summary Generation Process

In this section, we outline how summaries are generated by a greedy optimization system which selects the sentence with highest weight iteratively. This is the main process we use in all our summarization systems. For comparison we also use a summarization algorithm based on KL divergence.

5.1 Greedy Optimization Approach

Our algorithm extracts sentences by weighting them based on word importance. The approach is similar to the standard word probability baseline (Nenkova et al., 2006) but we explore a range of possibilities for assigning weights to individual words. For each sentence, we calculate the sentence weight by summing up the weights of all words, normalized by the number of words in the sentence. We sort the sentences in descending order of their scores into a queue. To create a summary, we iteratively dequeue one sentence, check if the sentence is more than 8 words (as in Erkan and Radev (2004)), then append it to the current summary if it is non-redundant. A sentence is considered non-redundant if it is not similar to any sentences already in the summary, measured by cosine similarity on binary vector representations with stopwords excluded. We use the cut-off of 0.5 for cosine similarity. This value was tuned on the DUC 2003 dataset, by testing the impact of the cut-off value on the ROUGE scores for the final summary. Possible values ranged from 0.1 to 0.9 with step of 0.1.

5.2 KL Divergence Summarizer

The KLSUM summarizer (Haghighi and Vanderwende, 2009) aims at minimizing the KL divergence between the probability distribution over words estimated from the summary and the input respectively. This summarizer is a component of the popular topic model approaches (Daumé and Marcu, 2006; Celikyilmaz and Hakkani-Tür, 2011; Mason and Charniak, 2011) and achieves competitive performance with minimal differences compared to a full-blown topic model system.

6 Global Indicators from NYT

Some words evoke topics that are of intrinsic interest to people. Here we search for global indicators of word importance regardless of particular input.

6.1 Global Indicators of Word Importance

We analyze a large corpus of original documents and corresponding summaries in order to identify words that consistently get included in or excluded from the summary. In the 2004-2007 NYT corpus, many news articles have abstracts along with the original article, which makes it an appropriate

Metric	Top-30 words
$KL(A \parallel G)(w)$	photo(s), pres, article, column, reviews, letter, York, Sen, NY, discusses, drawing, op-ed, holds, Bush correction, editorial, dept, city, NJ, map, corp, graph, contends, Iraq, John, dies, sec, state, comments
$KL(G \parallel A)(w)$	Mr, Ms, p.m., lot, Tuesday, CA, Wednesday, Friday, told, Monday, time, a.m., added, thing, Sunday things, asked, good, night, Saturday, nyt, back, senator, wanted, kind, Jr., Mrs, bit, looked, wrote
$Pr_A(w)$	photo, photos, article, York, column, letter, Bush, state, reviews, million, American pres, percent, Iraq, year, people, government, John, years, company, correction national, federal, officials, city, drawing, billion, public, world, administration

Table 2: Top 30 words by three metrics from NYT corpus

resource to do such analysis. We identified $160,001$ abstract-original pairs in the corpus. From these, we generate two language models, one estimated from the text of all abstracts (LM_A), the other estimated from the corpus of original articles (LM_G). We use *SRILM* (Stolcke, 2002) with Ney smoothing.

We denote the probability of word w in LM_A as $Pr_A(w)$, the probability in LM_G as $Pr_G(w)$, and calculate the difference $Pr_A(w) - Pr_G(w)$ and the ratio $Pr_A(w)/Pr_G(w)$ to capture the change of probability. In addition, we calculate KL-like weighted scores for words which reflect both the change of probabilities between the two samples and the overall frequency of the word. Here we calculate both $KL(A \parallel G)$ and $KL(G \parallel A)$. Words with high values for the former score are favored in the summaries because they have higher probability in the abstracts than in the originals and have relatively high probability in the abstracts. The later score is high for words that are often not included in summaries.

$$KL(A \parallel G)(w) = Pr_A(w) \cdot \ln \frac{Pr_A(w)}{Pr_G(w)}$$

$$KL(G \parallel A)(w) = Pr_G(w) \cdot \ln \frac{Pr_G(w)}{Pr_A(w)}$$

Table 2 shows examples of the global information captured from the three types of scores—$KL(A \parallel G)$, $KL(G \parallel A)$ and $Pr_A(w)$—listing the 30 content words with highest scores for each type. Words that tend to be used in the summaries, characterized by high $KL(A \parallel G)$ scores, include locations *(York, NJ, Iraq)*, people's names and titles *(Bush, Sen, John)*, some abbreviations *(pres, corp, dept)* and verbs of conflict *(contends, dies)*. On the other hand, from $KL(G \parallel A)$, we can see that it is unlikely for writers to include courtesy titles *(Mr, Ms, Jr.)* and relative time reference in summaries. The words with high $Pr_A(w)$ scores overlaps with those ranked highly by $KL(A \parallel G)$ to some extent, but also includes a number of generally frequent words which appeared often both in the abstracts and original texts, such as *million* and *percent*.

6.2 Blind Sentence Extraction

In later sections we include the measures of global word importance as a feature of our regression model for predicting word weights for summarization. Before turning to that, however, we report the results of an experiment aimed to confirm the usefulness of these features. We present a system, BLIND, which uses only weights assigned to words by $KL(A \parallel G)$ from NYT, without doing any analysis of the original input. We rank all non-stopword words from the input according to this score. The top k words are given weight 1, while the others are given weight 0. The summaries are produced following the greedy procedure described in Section 5.1.

Systems	R-1	R-2	R-4
RANDOM	30.32	4.42	0.36
BLIND (80 keywords)	30.77	5.18	0.53
BLIND (300 keywords)	32.91	5.94	0.61
LASTESTLEAD	31.39	6.11	0.63
FIRST-SENTENCE	34.26	7.22	1.21

Table 3: Blind sentence extraction system, compared with three baseline systems (%)

Table 3 shows that the BLIND system has R-2 recall of 0.0594 using the top 300 keywords, significantly better than picking sentences from the input randomly. It also achieves comparable performance with the baseline in DUC 2004, formed by selecting the first 100 words from the latest article in the input (LASTESTLEAD). However it is significantly worse than another baseline of selecting the first sentences from the input. Table 4 gives sample summaries generated by these three approaches. These results confirm that the information gleaned from the analysis

Random Summary
It was sunny and about 14 degrees C(57 degrees F) in Tashkent on Sunday. The president is a strong person, and he has been through far more difficult political situations, Mityukov said, according to Interfax. But Yeltsin's aides say his first term, from 1991 to 1996, does not count because it began six months before the Soviet Union collapsed and before the current constitution took effect. He must stay in bed like any other person, Yakushkin said. The issue was controversial earlier this year when Yeltsin refused to spell out his intentions and his aides insisted he had the legal right to seek re-election.

NYT Summary from global keyword selection, $KL(A \parallel G)$, k = 300
Russia's constitutional court opened hearings Thursday on whether Boris Yeltsin can seek a third term. Yeltsin's growing health problems would also seem to rule out another election campaign. The Russian constitution has a two-term limit for presidents. Russian president Boris Yeltsin cut short a trip to Central Asia on Monday due to a respiratory infection that revived questions about his overall health and ability to lead Russia through a sustained economic crisis. The upper house of parliament was busy voting on a motion saying he should resign. The start of the meeting was shown on Russian television.

First Sentence Generated Summary
President Boris Yeltsin has suffered minor burns on his right hand, his press office said Thursday. President Boris Yeltsin's doctors have pronounced his health more or less normal, his wife Naina said in an interview published Wednesday. President Boris Yeltsin, on his first trip out of Russia since this spring, canceled a welcoming ceremony in Uzbekistan on Sunday because he wasn't feeling well, his spokesman said. Doctors ordered Russian President Boris Yeltsin to cut short his Central Asian trip because of a respiratory infection and he agreed to return home Monday, a day earlier than planned, officials said.

Table 4: Summary comparison by Random, Blind Extraction and First Sentence systems

of NYT abstract-original pairs encodes highly relevant information about important content independent of the actual text of the input.

7 Regression-Based Keyword Extraction

Here we introduce a logistic regression model for assigning importance weights to words in the input. Crucially, this model combines evidence from multiple indicators of importance. We have at our disposal abundant data for learning because each content word in the input can be treated as a labeled instance. There are in total $32,052$ samples from the 30 inputs of DUC 2003 for training, $54,591$ samples from the 50 inputs of DUC 2004 for testing. For a word in the input, we assign label 1 if the word appears in at least one of the four human summaries for this input. Otherwise we assign label 0.

In the rest of this section, we describe the rich variety of features included in our system. We also analyze and discuss the predictive power of those features by performing Wilcoxon signed-rank test on the DUC 2003 dataset. There are in total $9,261$ features used, among them $1,625$ are significant (p-value < 0.05). We rank these features in increasing p-values derived from Wilcoxon test. Apart from the widely used features of word frequency and positions, some other less explored features are highly significant.

7.1 Frequency Features

We use the Probability, LLR chi-square statistic value and MRW scores as features. Since prior work has demonstrated that for LLR weights in particular, it is useful to identify a small set of important words and ignore all other words in summary selection (Gupta et al., 2007), we use a number of keyword indicators as features. For these indicators, the value of feature is 1 if the word is ranked within top k_i, 0 otherwise. Here k_i are preset cutoffs[5]. These cutoffs capture different possibilities for defining the keywords in the input. We also add the number of input documents that contain the word as a feature. There are a total of 100 features in this group, all of which are highly significant, ranked among the top 200.

7.2 Standard features

We now describe some standard features which have been applied in prior work on summarization.

Word Locations: Especially in news articles, sentences that occur at the beginning are often the most important ones. In line with this observation, we calculate several features related to the position in which a word appears. We first compute the relative positions for word tokens, where the tokens are numbered sequentially in order of appearance in each document in the input. The relative position for one word token is therefore its corresponding number, divided by total number of tokens minus one in the document, e.g., 0 for the first token, 1 for the last token. For each word, we calculate its *earliest first location*, *latest last location*, *average location* and *average first location* for tokens of this word across all documents in the input. In addition we have a binary feature indicating if the word appears in the

[5] 10, 15, 20, 30, 40, ···, 190, 200, 220, 240, 260, 280, 300, 350, 400, 450, 500, 600, 700 (in total 33 values)

first sentence and the number of times it appears in a first sentence among documents in one input. There are 6 features in this group. All of them are very significant, ranked within the top 100.

Word type: These features include Part of Speech (POS) tags, Name Entity (NE) labels and capitalization information. We use the Stanford POS-Tagger (Toutanova et al., 2003) and Name Entity Recognizer (Finkel et al., 2005). We have one feature corresponding to each possible POS and NE tag. The value of this feature is the proportion of occurrences of the word with this tag; in most cases only one feature gets a non-zero value. We have two features which indicate if one word has been capitalized and the ratio of its capitalized occurrences.

Most of the NE features (6 out of 8) are significant: there are more *Organizations* and *Locations* but fewer *Time* and *Date* words in the human summaries. Of the POS tags, 11 out of 41 are significant: there are more nouns (*NN, NNS, NNPS*); fewer verbs (*VBG, VBP, VB*) and fewer cardinal numbers in the abstracts compared to the input. Capitalized words also tend to be included in human summaries.

KL: Prior work has shown that having estimates of sentence importance can also help in estimating word importance (Wan et al., 2007; Liu et al., 2011; Wei et al., 2008). The summarizer based on KL-divergence assigns importance to sentences directly, in a complex function according to the word distribution in the sentence. Therefore, we use these summaries as potential indicators of word importance. We include two features here, the first one indicates if the word appears in a KLSUM summary of the input, as well as a feature corresponding to the number of times the word appeared in that summary. Both of the features are highly significant, ranked within the top 200.

7.3 NYT-weights as Features

We include features from the relative rank of a word according to $KL(A \parallel G)$, $KL(G \parallel A)$, $Pr_A(w) - Pr_G(w)$, $Pr_A(w)/Pr_G(w)$ and $Pr_A(w)$, derived from the NYT as described in Section 6. If the rank of a word is within top-k or bottom-k by one metric, we would label it as 1, where k is selected from a set of pre-defined values[6]. We have in total 70 features in this category, of which 56 are significant, 47 having a p-value less than 10^{-7}. The predictive power of those global indicators are only behind the features which indicates frequency and word positions.

[6] 100, 200, 500, 1000, 2000, 5000, 10000 in this case.

7.4 Unigrams

This is a binary feature corresponding to each of the words that appeared at least twice in the training data. The idea is to learn which words from the input tend to be mentioned in the human summaries. There are in total $8,691$ unigrams, among which $1,290$ are significant. Despite the high number of significant unigram features, most of them are not as significant as the more general ones we described so far. It is interesting to compare the significant unigrams identified in the DUC abstract/input data with those derived from the NYT corpus. Unigrams that tend to appear in DUC summaries include *president*, *government*, *political*. We also find the same unigrams among the top words from NYT corpus according to $KL(A \parallel G)$. As for words unlikely to appear in summaries, we see *Wednesday*, *added*, *thing*, etc, which again rank high according to $KL(G \parallel A)$.

7.5 Dictionary Features: MPQA and LIWC

Unigram features are notoriously sparse. To mitigate the sparsity problem, we resort to more general groupings to words according to salient semantic and functional categories. We employ two hand-crafted dictionaries, MPQA for subjectivity analysis and LIWC for topic analysis.

The MPQA dictionary (Wiebe and Cardie, 2005) contains words with different polarities (positive, neutral, negative) and intensities (strong, weak). The combinations correspond to six features. It turns out that words with strong polarity, either positive or negative, are seldomly included in the summaries. Most strikingly, the p-value from significance test for the strong negative words is less than 10^{-4}—these words are rarely included in summaries. There is no significant difference on weak polarity categories.

Another dictionary we use is LIWC (Tausczik and Pennebaker, 2007), which contains manually constructed dictionaries for multiple categories of words. The value of the feature is 1 for one word if the word appears in the particular dictionary for the category. 34 out of 64 LIWC features are significant. Interesting categories which appear at higher rate in summaries include events about death, anger, achievements, money and negative emotions. Those that appear at lower rate in the summaries include auxiliary verbs, hear, pronouns, negation, function words, social words, swear, adverbs, words related to families, etc.

7.6 Context Features

We use context features here, based on the assumption that context importance around a word affects the importance of this word. For context we consider the words before and after the target word. We extend our feature space by calculating the weighted average of the feature values of the context words. For word w, we denote L_w as the set of words before w, R_w as the set of words after w. We denote the feature for one word as $w.f_i$, the way of calculating the newly extended word-before feature $w.l_{f_i}$ could be written as:

$$w.l_{f_i} = \sum_i p(w_l) \cdot w_l.f_i, \; \forall w_l \in L_w$$

Here $p(w_l)$ is the probability word w_l appears before w among all words in L_w.

For context features, we calculate the weighted average of the most widely used basic features, including frequency, location and capitalization for surrounding contexts. There are in total 220 features of this kind, among which 117 are significant, 74 having a p-value less than 10^{-4}.

8 Experiments

The performance of our logistic regression model is evaluated on two tasks: keyword identification and extractive summarization. We name our system REGSUM.

8.1 Regression for Keyword Identification

For each input, we define the set of keywords as the top k words according to the scores generated from different models. We compare our regression system with three unsupervised systems: PROB, LLR, MRW. To show the effectiveness of new features, we compare our results with a regression system trained only on word frequency and location related features described in Section 7. Those features are the ones standardly used for ranking the importance of words in recent summarization works (Yih et al., 2007; Takamura and Okumura, 2009; Sipos et al., 2012), and we name this system REGBASIC.

Figure 1 shows the performance of systems when selecting the 100 words with highest weights

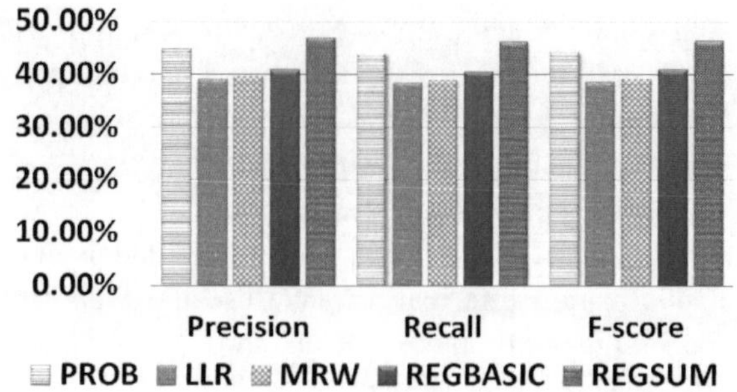

Figure 1: Precision, Recall and F-score of keyword identification, 100 words selected, G_1 as gold-standard

as keywords. Each word from the input that appeared in any of the four human summaries is considered as a gold-standard keyword. Among the unsupervised approaches, word probability identifies keywords better than LLR and MRW by at least 4% on F-score. REGBASIC does not give better performance at keyword identification compared with PROB, even though it includes location information. Our system gets 2.2% F-score improvement over PROB, 5.2% over REGBASIC, and more improvement over the other approaches. All of these improvements are statistically significant by Wilcoxon test.

Table 5 shows the performance of keyword identification for different G_i and different number of keywords selected. The regression system has no advantage over PROB when identifying keywords that appeared in all of the four human summaries. However our system achieves significant improvement for predicting words that appeared in more than one or two human summaries.[7]

8.2 Regression for Summarization

We now show that the performance of extractive summarization can be improved by better estimation of word weights. We compare our regression system with the four models introduced in Section 8.1. We also include PEER-65, the best system in DUC-2004, as well as KLSUM for comparison. Apart from these, we compare our model with two state-of-the-art systems, including the submodular approach (SUBMOD) (Lin and

[7]We also apply a weighted keyword evaluation approach, similar to the pyramid method for summarization. Still our system shows significant improvement over the others. See https://www.seas.upenn.edu/~hongkai1/regsum.html for details.

G_i	#words	PROB	LLR	MRW	REGBASIC	**REGSUM**
G_1	80	43.6	37.9	38.9	39.9	45.7
G_1	100	44.3	38.7	39.2	41.0	46.5
G_1	120	44.6	38.5	39.2	40.9	46.4
G_2	30	47.8	44.0	42.4	47.4	50.2
G_2	35	47.1	43.3	42.1	47.0	49.5
G_2	40	46.5	42.4	41.8	46.4	49.2
G_3	10	51.2	46.2	43.8	46.9	50.2
G_3	15	51.4	47.5	43.7	49.8	52.9
G_3	20	49.7	47.6	42.5	49.3	51.5
G_4	5	50.0	48.8	44.9	43.6	45.1
G_4	6	51.4	46.9	43.7	45.2	47.6
G_4	7	50.9	48.2	43.7	45.8	47.8

Table 5: Keyword identification F-score (%) for different G_i and different number of words selected.

Bilmes, 2012) and the determinantal point process (DPP) summarizer (Kulesza and Taskar, 2012). The summaries were kindly provided by the authors of these systems (Hong et al., 2014).

As can been seen in Table 6, our system outperforms PROB, LLR, MRW, PEER-65, KLSUM and REGBASIC. These improvements are significant on ROUGE-2 recall. Interestingly, although the supervised system REGBASIC which uses only frequency and positions achieve low performance in keyword identification, the summaries it generates are of high quality. The inclusion of position features negatively affects the performance in summary keyword identification but boosts the weights for the words which appear close to the beginning of the documents, which is helpful for identifying informative sentences. By including other features we greatly improve over REGBASIC in keyword identification. Similarly here the richer set of features results in better quality summaries.

We also examined the ROUGE-1, -2, -4 recall compared with the SUBMOD and DPP summarizers[8]. There is no significant difference on R-2 and R-4 recall compared with these two state-of-the-art systems. DPP performed significantly better than our system on R-1 recall, but that system is optimizing on R-1 F-score in training. Overall, our conceptually simple system is on par with the state of the art summarizers and points to the need for better models for estimating word importance.

System	R-1	R-2	R-4
PROB	35.14	8.17	1.06
LLR	34.60	7.56	0.83
MRW	35.78	8.15	0.99
REGBASIC	37.56	9.28	1.49
KL	37.97	8.53	1.26
PEER-65	37.62	8.96	1.51
SUBMOD	39.18	9.35	1.39
DPP	39.79	9.62	1.57
REGSUM	**38.57**	**9.75**	**1.60**

Table 6: System performance comparison (%)

9 Conclusion

We presented a series of experiments which show that keyword identification can be improved in a supervised framework which incorporates a rich set of indicators of importance. We also show that the better estimation of word importance leads to better extractive summaries. Our analysis of features related to global importance, sentiment and topical categories reveals rather unexpected results and confirms that word importance estimation is a worthy research direction. Success in the task is likely to improve sophisticated summarization approaches too, as well as sentence compression systems which use only crude frequency related measures to decide which words should be deleted from a sentence.[9]

[8]The results are slightly different from the ones reported in the original papers due to the fact that we truncated to 100 words, while they truncated to 665 bytes.

[9]The work is partially funded by NSF CAREER award IIS 0953445.

References

Taylor Berg-Kirkpatrick, Dan Gillick, and Dan Klein. 2011. Jointly learning to extract and compress. In *Proceedings of ACL-HLT*, pages 481–490.

Asli Celikyilmaz and Dilek Hakkani-Tur. 2010. A hybrid hierarchical model for multi-document summarization. In *Proceedings of ACL*, pages 815–824.

Asli Celikyilmaz and Dilek Hakkani-Tür. 2011. Discovery of topically coherent sentences for extractive summarization. In *Proceedings of ACL-HLT*, pages 491–499.

John M. Conroy, Judith D. Schlesinger, and Dianne P. O'Leary. 2006. Topic-focused multi-document summarization using an approximate oracle score. In *Proceedings of COLING/ACL*, pages 152–159.

Hal Daumé, III and Daniel Marcu. 2006. Bayesian query-focused summarization. In *Proceedings of ACL*, pages 305–312.

Gunes Erkan and Dragomir R. Radev. 2004. Lexrank: graph-based lexical centrality as salience in text summarization. *Journal of Artificial Intelligence Research*, 22(1):457–479.

Elena Filatova and Vasileios Hatzivassiloglou. 2004. A formal model for information selection in multi-sentence text extraction. In *Proceedings of COLING*.

Jenny Rose Finkel, Trond Grenager, and Christopher Manning. 2005. Incorporating non-local information into information extraction systems by gibbs sampling. In *Proceedings of ACL*, pages 363–370.

D. Graff, J. Kong, K. Chen, and K. Maeda. 2007. English gigaword third edition. *Linguistic Data Consortium, Philadelphia, PA*.

Surabhi Gupta, Ani Nenkova, and Dan Jurafsky. 2007. Measuring importance and query relevance in topic-focused multi-document summarization. In *Proceedings of ACL*, pages 193–196.

Aria Haghighi and Lucy Vanderwende. 2009. Exploring content models for multi-document summarization. In *Proceedings of HLT-NAACL*, pages 362–370.

Sanda Harabagiu and Finley Lacatusu. 2005. Topic themes for multi-document summarization. In *Proceedings of SIGIR 2005*, pages 202–209.

Kai Hong, John M. Conroy, Benoit Favre, Alex Kulesza, Hui Lin, and Ani Nenkova. 2014. A repositary of state of the art and competitive baseline summaries for generic news summarization. In *Proceedings of LREC*, May.

Alex Kulesza and Ben Taskar. 2012. Determinantal point processes for machine learning. *Foundations and Trends in Machine Learning*, 5(2–3).

Julian Kupiec, Jan Pedersen, and Francine Chen. 1995. A trainable document summarizer. In *Proceedings of SIGIR*, pages 68–73.

Page Lawrence, Brin Sergey, Rajeev Motwani, and Terry Winograd. 1998. The pagerank citation ranking: Bringing order to the web. Technical report, Stanford University.

Hui Lin and Jeff Bilmes. 2012. Learning mixtures of submodular shells with application to document summarization. In *UAI*, pages 479–490.

Chin-Yew Lin and Eduard Hovy. 2000. The automated acquisition of topic signatures for text summarization. In *Proceedgins of COLING*, pages 495–501.

Chin-Yew Lin. 2004. Rouge: A package for automatic evaluation of summaries. In *Text Summarization Branches Out: Proceedings of the ACL-04 Workshop*, pages 74–81.

Marina Litvak, Mark Last, and Menahem Friedman. 2010. A new approach to improving multilingual summarization using a genetic algorithm. In *Proceedings of ACL*, pages 927–936.

Fei Liu, Feifan Liu, and Yang Liu. 2011. A supervised framework for keyword extraction from meeting transcripts. *Transactions on Audio Speech and Language Processing*, 19(3):538–548.

H. P. Luhn. 1958. The automatic creation of literature abstracts. *IBM Journal of Research and Development*, 2(2):159–165, April.

M. Marneffe, B. Maccartney, and C. Manning. 2006. Generating Typed Dependency Parses from Phrase Structure Parses. In *Proceedings of LREC-06*, pages 449–454.

Rebecca Mason and Eugene Charniak. 2011. Extractive multi-document summaries should explicitly not contain document-specific content. In *Proceedings of the Workshop on Automatic Summarization for Different Genres, Media, and Languages*, pages 49–54.

Ryan McDonald. 2007. A study of global inference algorithms in multi-document summarization. In *Proceedings of ECIR*, pages 557–564.

Rada Mihalcea and Paul Tarau. 2004. Textrank: Bringing order into text. In *Proceedings of EMNLP*, pages 404–411.

Ani Nenkova and Lucy Vanderwende. 2005. The impact of frequency on summarization. Technical report, Microsoft Research.

Ani Nenkova, Lucy Vanderwende, and Kathleen McKeown. 2006. A compositional context sensitive multi-document summarizer: exploring the factors that influence summarization. In *Proceedings of SIGIR*, pages 573–580.

Jahna Otterbacher, Günes Erkan, and Dragomir R. Radev. 2009. Biased lexrank: Passage retrieval using random walks with question-based priors. *Information Processing and Management*, 45(1):42–54.

Paul Over, Hoa Dang, and Donna Harman. 2007. Duc in context. *Inf. Process. Manage.*, 43(6):1506–1520.

Karolina Owczarzak, John M. Conroy, Hoa Trang Dang, and Ani Nenkova. 2012. An assessment of the accuracy of automatic evaluation in summarization. In *NAACL-HLT 2012: Workshop on Evaluation Metrics and System Comparison for Automatic Summarization*, pages 1–9.

Peter Rankel, John Conroy, Eric Slud, and Dianne O'Leary. 2011. Ranking human and machine summarization systems. In *Proceedings of EMNLP*, pages 467–473.

Korbinian Riedhammer, Benoît Favre, and Dilek Hakkani-Tür. 2010. Long story short - global unsupervised models for keyphrase based meeting summarization. *Speech Communication*, 52(10):801–815.

G. Salton. 1971. *The SMART Retrieval System: Experiments in Automatic Document Processing*. Prentice-Hall, Inc., Upper Saddle River, NJ, USA.

Evan Sandhaus. 2008. The new york times annotated corpus. *Linguistic Data Consortium, Philadelphia, PA*.

Chao Shen and Tao Li. 2010. Multi-document summarization via the minimum dominating set. In *Proceedings of Coling*, pages 984–992.

Ruben Sipos, Pannaga Shivaswamy, and Thorsten Joachims. 2012. Large-margin learning of submodular summarization models. In *Proceedings of EACL*, pages 224–233.

Andreas Stolcke. 2002. SRILM – an extensible language modeling toolkit. In *Proceedings of ICSLP*, volume 2, pages 901–904.

Hiroya Takamura and Manabu Okumura. 2009. Text summarization model based on maximum coverage problem and its variant. In *Proceedings of EACL*, pages 781–789.

Yla R Tausczik and James W Pennebaker. 2007. The Psychological Meaning of Words: LIWC and Computerized Text Analysis Methods. *Journal of Language and Social Psychology*, 29:24–54.

Kristina Toutanova, Dan Klein, Christopher D. Manning, and Yoram Singer. 2003. Feature-rich part-of-speech tagging with a cyclic dependency network. In *Proceedings of the NAACL-HLT*, pages 173–180.

Xiaojun Wan and Jianwu Yang. 2008. Multi-document summarization using cluster-based link analysis. In *Proceedings of SIGIR*, pages 299–306.

Xiaojun Wan, Jianwu Yang, and Jianguo Xiao. 2007. Towards an iterative reinforcement approach for simultaneous document summarization and keyword extraction. In *Proceedings of ACL*, pages 552–559.

Furu Wei, Wenjie Li, Qin Lu, and Yanxiang He. 2008. Query-sensitive mutual reinforcement chain and its application in query-oriented multi-document summarization. In *Proceedings of SIGIR*, pages 283–290.

Janyce Wiebe and Claire Cardie. 2005. Annotating expressions of opinions and emotions in language. language resources and evaluation. In *Language Resources and Evaluation (formerly Computers and the Humanities)*, page 1(2).

Wen-tau Yih, Joshua Goodman, Lucy Vanderwende, and Hisami Suzuki. 2007. Multi-document summarization by maximizing informative content-words. In *Proceedings of IJCAI*, pages 1776–1782.

Hongyuan Zha. 2002. Generic summarization and keyphrase extraction using mutual reinforcement principle and sentence clustering. In *Proceedings of SIGIR*, pages 113–120.

Hybrid text simplification using synchronous dependency grammars with hand-written and automatically harvested rules

Advaith Siddharthan
Computing Science
University of Aberdeen
UK
advaith@abdn.ac.uk

M. A. Angrosh
Computing Science
University of Aberdeen
UK
angroshmandya@abdn.ac.uk

Abstract

We present an approach to text simplification based on synchronous dependency grammars. The higher level of abstraction afforded by dependency representations allows for a linguistically sound treatment of complex constructs requiring reordering and morphological change, such as conversion of passive voice to active. We present a synchronous grammar formalism in which it is easy to write rules by hand and also acquire them automatically from dependency parses of aligned English and Simple English sentences. The grammar formalism is optimised for monolingual translation in that it reuses ordering information from the source sentence where appropriate. We demonstrate the superiority of our approach over a leading contemporary system based on quasi-synchronous tree substitution grammars, both in terms of expressivity and performance.

1 Introduction

Text simplification is sometimes defined as the process of reducing the grammatical and lexical complexity of a text, while still retaining the original information content and meaning. The main goal of simplification is to make information more accessible to the large numbers of people with reduced literacy. The National Literacy Trust (http://www.literacytrust.org.uk) estimates that one in six adults in the UK have poor literacy skills. The situation is often worse in developing countries. Aluísio et al. (2008) report that 68% of Brazilians between 15 and 64 years who have studied up to 4 years only reach the rudimentary level of literacy, and even among those who have studied for 8 years, only a quarter can be considered fully literate. While there is a large body of evidence that manual text simplification is an effective intervention (Anderson and Freebody, 1981; L'Allier, 1980; Beck et al., 1991; Anderson and Davison, 1988; Linderholm et al., 2000; Kamalski et al., 2008), there has till recently been little work on automatic simplification. The pace of research has picked up in recent years though, with many teams applying machine translation approaches to perform "monolingual translation" from English to simplified English. The goals of this paper are to (1) identify the limitations of recently published approaches to text simplification with regard to their coverage of linguistic constructs, (2) to describe an approach based on synchronous grammars operating on typed dependency representations that permits a more sophisticated handling of many linguistic constructs, and (3) to present a hybrid system that combines a small set of hand written grammar rules for purely syntactic constructs with a much larger set of automatically acquired rules for lexicalised constructs in one synchronous formalism.

We summarise work on text simplification in Section 2, before describing our method in Section 3 and presenting our results in Section 4.

2 Related work

There are two largely distinct bodies of work on automatic text simplification – those that use hand-crafted rules, and those that apply machine translation approaches.

2.1 Hand-crafted text simplification systems

The first body of work uses hand-crafted rules to perform syntactic simplification operations (e.g., splitting coordinated and subordinated clauses, and disembedding apposition and relative clauses). Some early systems (Chandrasekar et al., 1996; Siddharthan, 2002) used flat representations (chunked and part-of-speech tagged text). More commonly, text simplification systems use

Proceedings of the 14th Conference of the European Chapter of the Association for Computational Linguistics, pages 722–731,
Gothenburg, Sweden, April 26-30 2014.

hand crafted rules that apply to hierarchical representations, including constituency-based parses (Canning, 2002; Candido Jr et al., 2009; De Belder and Moens, 2010) and dependency parses (Bott et al., 2012; Siddharthan, 2010; Siddharthan, 2011). For languages without corpora of simplified texts, hand crafted systems are typically the only available alternative.

2.2 Text simplification as monolingual translation

Recent years have seen the increased application of machine translation approaches to text simplification, often referred to as "monolingual translation", and driven by the new availability of corpora of simplified texts such as Simple English Wikipedia (SEW).

Wubben et al. (2012) and Coster and Kauchak (2011) apply Phrase Based Machine Translation (PBMT) to the task of text simplification. PMBT can only perform a small set of simplification operations, such as lexical substitution, deletion and simple paraphrase. They are not well suited for reordering or splitting operations. Specifically, the syntactic simplification operations that hand-crafted systems focus on are out of scope.

Zhu et al. (2010) in contrast present an approach based on syntax-based SMT (Yamada and Knight, 2001). Their translation model encodes probabilities for four specific rewrite operations on the parse trees of the input sentences: substitution, reordering, splitting, and deletion. Splitting is encoded as two probabilities: A segmentation table stores probabilities of sentence splitting at particular words (e.g., *which*). A completion table stores probabilities of the splitting word to be deleted from the translation, and for the governing phrase to be inserted to complete the sentence. This allows the translation model to handle constructs such as relative clauses and apposition.

Dras (1999) was the first to apply synchronous grammars to monolingual tasks. His approach is to map between two TAG grammars using a Generalised Synchronous TAG formalism, and to use Integer Programming to generate a text that satisfies the externally imposed constraints (such as length or readability) using minimal paraphrasing. Woodsend and Lapata (2011) further develop this line of research. Their model is based on quasi-synchronous grammar (Smith and Eisner, 2006) and integer linear programming. Quasi-synchronous grammars, like the Generalised Synchronous TAGs of Dras (1999), aims to relax the isomorphism constraints of synchronous grammars, in this case by generating a loose alignment between parse trees. The Woodsend and Lapata (2011) model is trained on two different datasets: one containing alignments between sentences in Wikipedia and English Simple Wikipedia, and one containing alignments between edits in the revision history of Simple Wikipedia. The latter performs best in their study, and also achieves better scores than the Zhu et al. (2010) system, both when evaluated using BLEU, and on human evaluations of simplicity, grammaticality and meaning preservation. We will directly compare our approach to Woodsend and Lapata (2011), as this is the best performing contemporary system that has the same linguistic scope as ours.

2.3 Formalisms and linguistic coverage

The systems summarised above differ primarily in the level of linguistic knowledge they encode. PBMT systems use the least knowledge, and as such are ill equipped to to handle simplifications that require morphological changes, syntactic reordering or sentence splitting.

Syntax based approaches use syntactic knowledge. However, both Zhu et al. (2010) and Woodsend and Lapata (2011) use the Stanford Parser (Klein and Manning, 2003) for syntactic structure, and this representation lacks morphological information. This means that some simplification operations such as voice conversion are not handled well. For example, to simplify "trains are liked by John" to "John likes trains", besides deleting auxiliaries and reordering the arguments of the verb "like", the verb also needs to agree in number with the new subject ("John"), and take the tense of the auxiliary verb ("are").

The grammar acquisition process leads to further problems. From an aligned pair "John, who was tired, went to sleep." and "John was tired. He went to sleep.", systems would learn a simplification rule that introduces the pronoun "He". The governing syntax for this rule is the verb "went"; hence, "Susan, who was tired, went to sleep." might later get simplified as "Susan was tired. He went to sleep.".

Hand-crafted systems have an advantage here. Such systems would typically use rules that duplicate the noun phrase, generating "John was tired. John went to sleep." and "Susan was tired. Susan went to sleep." Systems such as Siddharthan (2011) use transformation rules that encode morphological changes as well as deletions, re-orderings, substitutions and sentence splitting, and are well suited to handle the voice conversion example above. On the other hand, hand-crafted systems are limited in scope to syntactic simplification. While purely syntactic rules can be written manually, there are too many lexico-syntactic and lexical simplifications to enumerate by hand.

In this paper, we present a hybrid text simplification system that combines manually written synchronous grammars for common syntactic simplifications with a much larger automatically acquired synchronous grammar for lexicalised constructs. Our framework, using dependency representations, is better suited to text simplification. We demonstrate that the higher level of abstraction in dependency parses allows for linguistically correct rules for complex operations such as voice conversion, while also providing a better model of context for lexical simplification.

3 Method

We describe a text simplification system that uses a synchronous grammar defined over typed dependencies. We demonstrate that this has specific advantages over previous work on text simplification: (1) it allows for better linguistic modelling of simplification operations that require morphological changes, (2) the higher level of abstraction makes it easy to write and read grammar rules; thus common syntactic operations (such as conversion of passive to active voice) can be handled in this framework through accurate hand-written rules, and (3) It is easier and more elegant to automatically acquire a synchronous grammar from data, compared to synchronous grammars based on constituency-parses. In this section we describe our framework and text simplification system in more detail; then, in section 4, we report an evaluation that compares our system against a human simplification and the Woodsend and Lapata (2011) system.

3.1 Synchronous dependency insertion grammars

Ding and Palmer (2005) introduce the notion of a Synchronous Dependency Insertion Grammar (SDIG) as a tree substitution grammar defined on dependency trees. They define elementary trees (ETs) to be sub-sentential dependency structures containing one or more lexical items. The SDIG formalism assumes that the isomorphism of the two syntactic structures is at the ET level, thus allowing for non-isomorphic tree to tree mapping at the sentence level. We base our approach to text simplification on SDIGs, but the formalism is adapted for the monolingual task, and the rules are written in a formalism that is suited to writing rules by hand as well as automatically acquiring rules from aligned sentences. Our system follows the architecture proposed in Ding and Palmer (2005), reproduced in Fig. 1. In this paper, we will present the ET Transfer component as a set of transformation rules. The rest of Section 3 will focus on the linguistic knowledge we need to encode in these rules, the method for automatic acquisition of rules from a corpus of aligned sentences, and the generation process.

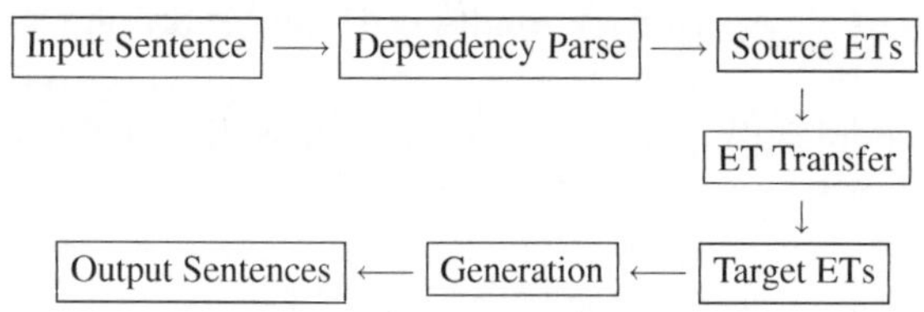

Figure 1: System Architecture

3.2 Extracting synchronous grammars from aligned sentences

To acquire a synchronous grammar from dependency parses of aligned English and simple English sentences, we just need to identify the differences. For example, consider two aligned sentences from the aligned corpus described in Woodsend and Lapata (2011):

1. (a) Also, lichen fungi can reproduce sexually, producing spores.
   (b) Also, lichen fungi can reproduce sexually by producing spores.

An automatic comparison of the dependency parses for the two sentences (using the Stanford Parser, and ignoring punctuation for ease of presentation) reveals that there are two typed dependencies that occur only in the parse of the first sentence, and two that occur only in the parse of the second sentence (in italics):

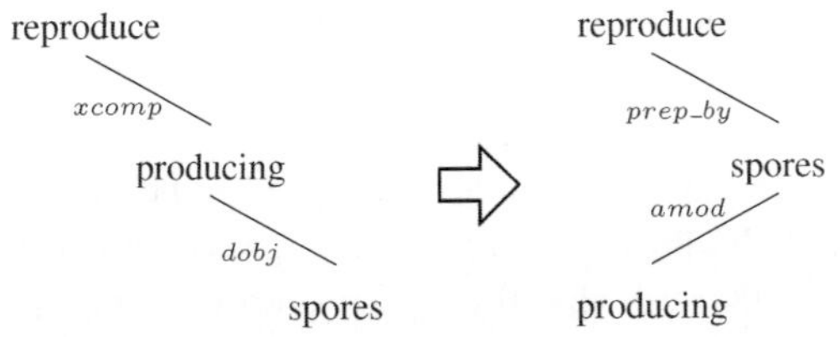

Figure 2: Transduction of Elementary Trees (ETs)

1. (a)	**1. (b)**
advmod(reproduce, Also)	advmod(reproduce, Also)
nn(fungi, lichen)	nn(fungi, lichen)
nsubj(reproduce, fungi)	nsubj(reproduce, fungi)
aux(reproduce, can)	aux(reproduce, can)
advmod(reproduce,sexually)	advmod(reproduce,sexually)
xcomp(reproduce,producing)	*amod(spores,producing)*
dobj(producing, spores)	*prep_by(reproduce, spores)*

Thus, to convert the first sentence into the second, we need to delete two dependencies and introduce two others. The rule contains variables (?Xn), which can be forced to match certain words in square brackets:

RULE: PRODUCING2BY_PRODUCING

1. DELETE
   (a) xcomp(?X0[reproduce], ?X1[producing])
   (b) dobj(?X1[producing], ?X2[spores])
2. INSERT
   (a) amod(?X2, ?X1)
   (b) prep_by(?X0, ?X2)

By collecting such rules, we can produce a meta-grammar that can translate dependency parses in one language (English) into the other (simplified English). The rule above will translate "reproduce, producing spores" to "reproduce by producing spores". This rule is alternatively shown as a transduction of elementary trees in Fig. 2. Such deletion and insertion operations are central to text simplification, but a few other operations are also needed to avoid broken dependency links in the Target ETs (cf. Fig. 1).

Consider lexical simplification; for example, where the word "extensive" is replaced by "big", resulting in one *amod* relation being deleted and a new one inserted. Now, a third list is automatically created when a variable (?X1) is present in the DELETE list but not the INSERT list. This is a command to move any other relations (edges) involving the node ?X1 to the newly created node ?X2, and ensures correct rule application in new contexts where there might be additional relations involving the deleted word.

RULE: EXTENSIVE2BIG

1. DELETE
   (a) amod(?X0[network], ?X1[extensive])
2. INSERT
   (a) amod(?X0, ?X2[big])
3. NODE OPERATION
   (a) MOVE: ?X1 $\longrightarrow$?X2

We also apply a process of generalisation, so that a single rule can be created from multiple instances in the training data. For example, if the modifier "extensive" has been simplified to "big" in the context of a variety of words in the ?X0 position, this can be represented succinctly as "?X0[networks, avalanches, blizzard, controversy]". Note that this list provides valid lexical contexts for application of the rule. If the word is seen in sufficient contexts, we make it universal by removing the list. An example of a generalised rule follows:

RULE: *2BIG

1. DELETE
   (a) amod(?X0, ?X1[extensive, large, massive, sizable, major, powerful, unprecedented, developed, giant])
2. INSERT
   (a) amod(?X0, ?X2[big])
3. NODE OPERATION
   (a) MOVE: ?X1 $\longrightarrow$?X2

This rule states that any of the words in "[extensive, large, massive, sizable, major, powerful, unprecedented, developed, giant]" can be replaced by "big" in any lexical context ?X0; i.e., these words are not ambiguous. We acquire rules such as the above automatically, filtering out rules that involve syntactic constructs that we require manually-written rules for (relative clauses, apposition, coordination and subordination). We have extracted 3180 rules from SEW revision histories and aligned SEW-EW sentence pairs. From the same data, Woodsend and Lapata (2011) extract 1431 rules, but these include rules for deletion, as well as for purely syntactic sentence splitting. The 3180 rules we derive are only lexical simplifications or simple paraphrases. We do not perform deletion operations, and use manually written rules for sentence splitting rules

Our approach allows for the encoding of local lexico-syntactic context for lexical simplification. Only if a simplification is seen in many contexts do we generalise the rule by relaxing the lexical context. We consider this a better solution to that implemented in Woodsend and Lapata (2011), who have to discard lexical rules that are only seen once, because they do not model lexical context.

3.3 Manual grammars for common syntactic cases

In addition to the automatically acquired grammar as described above, our system uses a small hand crafted grammar for common syntactic simplifications. As discussed earlier, these rules are difficult to learn from corpora, as difficult morphology and tense manipulations would have to be learnt from specific instances seen in a corpus. In practice, it is easy enough to code these rules correctly. We have 26 hand-crafted rules for apposition, relative clauses, and combinations of the two. A further 85 rules handle subordination and coordination. These are greater in number because they are lexicalised on the conjunction. 11 further rules cover voice conversion from passive to active. Finally, we include 14 rules to standardise quotations; i.e., reduce various constructs for attribution to the form "X said: Y." Performing this step allows us to simplify constructs embedded within quotations - another case that is not handled well by existing systems. One of the rules for converting passive to active voice is shown below:

RULE: PASSIVE2ACTIVE

1. DELETE
   (a) nsubjpass(?X0, ?X1)
   (b) auxpass(?X0, ?X2)
   (c) agent(?X0, ?X3)
2. INSERT
   (a) nsubj(?X0, ?X3)
   (b) dobj(?X0, ?X1)
3. NODE OPERATIONS
   (a) AGR-TENSE: ?X0 ⟵ ?X2
   (b) AGR-NUMBER: ?X0 ⟵ ?X3

The rule specifies that the node ?X0 should inherit the tense of ?X2 and agree in number with ?X3. This rule correctly captures the morphological changes required for the verb, something not achieved by the other systems discussed in Section 2. The dependency representation makes such linguistic constraints easy to write by hand. However, we are not yet in a position to learn such constraints automatically. Our argument is that a small number of grammar rules need to be coded carefully by hand to allow us to express the difficult syntactic constructions, while we can harvest large grammars for local paraphrase operations including lexical substitution.

3.4 Elementary tree transfer

In this work we apply the simplification rules exhaustively to the dependency parse; i.e., every rule for which the DELETE list is matched is applied iteratively. As an illustration, consider:

> The cat was chased by a dog that was barking.

det(cat-2, The-1)
nsubjpass(chased-4, cat-2)
auxpass(chased-4, was-3)
det(dog-7, a-6)
agent(chased-4, dog-7)
nsubj(barking-10, dog-7)
aux(barking-10, was-9)
rcmod(dog-7, barking-10)

Two rules match; the first simplifies relative clauses:

RULE: RELATIVECLAUSE

1. DELETE
   (a) rcmod(??X0, ??X1)
   (b) nsubj(??X1, ??X0)
2. INSERT
   (a) nsubj(??X1, ??X0)

This rule removes the embedding "rcmod" relation, when there is a subject available for the verb in the relative clause. Then we apply the rule to convert passive to active voice, as described in Section 3.3. Following these two rule applications, we are left with the following list of dependencies:

det(cat-2, The-1)
dobj(chased-4, cat-2)
det(dog-7, a-6)
nsubj(chased-4, dog-7)
aux(barking-10, was-9)
nsubj(barking-10, dog-7)

This list now represents two trees with *chased* and *barking* as root nodes:

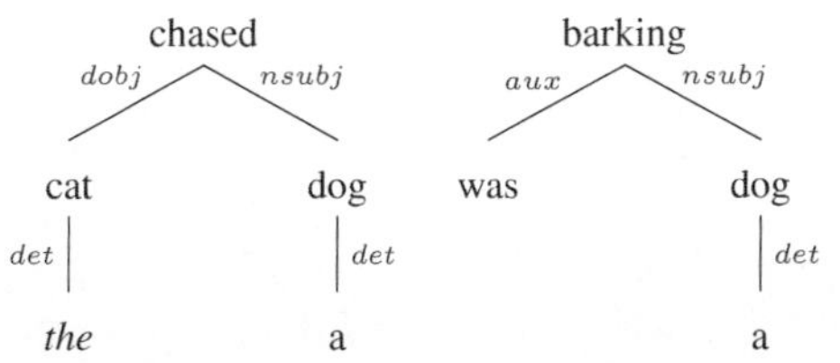

3.5 Generating from typed dependency representations

Generating from constituency-based parse trees is trivial, in that leaf nodes need to be output in the order processed by a depth first LR search. The higher level of abstraction of dependency representations makes generation more complicated, as the dependencies abstract away from constituent ordering and word morphology. One option is to use an off the shelf generator; however, this does not work well in practice; e.g., Siddharthan (2011) found that misanalyses by the parser can result in unacceptable word and constituent orders in the generated texts. In the system described here, we follow the generation-light approach adopted by Siddharthan (2011). We reuse the word order from the input sentence as a default, and the synchronous grammar encodes any changes in ordering. For example, in Rule PASSIVE2ACTIVE above, we include a further specification:

4 Traversal Order Specifications

(a) Node ?X0: [?X3, ?X0, ?X1]

This states that for node ?X0, the traversal order should be subtree ?X3 followed by current node ?X0 followed by subtree ?X1. Using this specification would allow us to traverse the tree using the original word order for nodes with no order specification, and the specified order where a specification exists. In the above instance, this would lead us to simplify "*The cat is chased by the dogs*" to "*the dogs chase the cat*". Details of the generation process can be found elsewhere (Siddharthan, 2011, for example), but to summarise, the gen-light approach implemented here uses four lists:

1. DELETE: List of relations to delete.
2. INSERT: List of relations to insert.
3. ORDERING: List of nodes with subtree order specified
4. NODE-OPERATIONS: List of morphological changes and deletion operations on nodes.

At present the automatically harvested rules do not encode morphological changes. They do however encode reordering information, which is automatically detected from the relative word positions in the original and simplified training sentences.

4 Evaluation

We performed a manual evaluation of how fluent and simple the text produced by our simplification system is, and the extent to which it preserves meaning. We use the evaluation set previously used by Woodsend and Lapata (2011), Zhu et al. (2010) and Wubben et al. (2012). This consists of 100 sentences from English Wikipedia, aligned with Simple English Wikipedia (SEW) sentences. Previous work report various automatic measures, including BLEU and readability metrics such as the Flesch-Kincaid Grade Level Index (FKGL). None of these have been validated for the automatic text simplification task, however, and we prefer to conduct an evaluation with human raters.

Our system (henceforth, HYBRID) is compared to QTSG (the system by Woodsend and Lapata (2011) that learns a quasi-synchronous grammar from the same data as the automated component of HYBRID), and the manual gold standard SEW. We selected the first 25 sentences from the evaluation set for which both QTSG and HYBRID had performed at least one simplification[1]. Five human raters[2] were shown sets containing the original Wikipedia sentence, followed by QTSG, HYBRID and SEW in a randomised order. For each such set, they were asked to rate each simplified version for fluency, simplicity and the extent to which it preserved the meaning of the original, using a Likert scale of 1–5, where 1 is totally unusable output, and 5 is output that is perfectly usable. The results are shown in Table 1. Our HYBRID system outperforms QTSG on all three metrics, and is comparable to the SEW version. Raters R1–3 provide very similar ratings, while R4–5 demonstrate a greater preference for the HYBRID system relative to the SEW. The HYBRID system performs best on meaning preservation (in

[1]36 sentences were considered and 11 sentences were excluded in this process. QTSG did not simplify 3 sentences and HYBRID as many as 9, as it does not perform compression operations. One sentence was left unchanged by both systems.

[2]R1–R4 are Computational Linguists, while R5 is a doctoral student in Public Health Communication. None of them are connected with this research, and none of them have previously seen the output of text simplification systems.

Rater	FLUENCY			SIMPLICITY			MEANING PRESERVATION		
	QTSG	HYBRID	SEW	QTSG	HYBRID	SEW	QTSG	HYBRID	SEW
R1	2.60	4.44	4.60	3.04	3.88	4.36	3.16	4.68	4.24
R2	3.08	4.24	4.52	3.20	4.08	4.48	3.28	4.76	4.36
R3	2.40	4.20	4.68	3.12	3.80	4.44	2.96	4.52	3.80
R4	2.32	3.88	3.48	2.92	3.44	3.44	2.72	4.52	3.56
R5	2.00	3.44	3.48	2.00	3.52	3.56	2.48	4.52	3.84
Mean	2.48	4.04	4.15	2.85	3.74	4.05	2.92	4.60	3.96
Median	2	4	4	3	4	4	3	5	4

Table 1: Results of human evaluation with five raters R1–R5. QTSG is the system by Woodsend and Lapata (2011). HYBRID is the system described in this paper, with manual and automatically acquired rules. SEW is the human generated simplification from Simple English Wikipedia. All differences in means for Simplicity and Meaning Preservation are significant ($p < 0.001$; t-test). For Fluency, HYBRID and SEW are significantly better than QTSG ($p < 0.001$; t-test).

large part because it is the only version that does not delete information through sentence compression).

Table 2 shows some examples of simplifications from the evaluation dataset, along with their average scores for fluency, simplicity and meaning preservation. These examples have been selected to help interpret the results in Table 1. QTSG frequently generates fragments ("Komiyama is a.", etc.), likely through incorrect splitting rules in the grammar; this is penalised heavily by the raters. The HYBRID system uses manually written rules for sentence splitting and is more robust in this regard. This is confirmed by looking at standard deviations of ratings. For fluency, QTSG has $sd = 1.41$, almost twice that of HYBRID ($sd = .76$). A similar trend is observed for meaning preservation, where QTSG has $sd = 1.29$, compared to $sd = .68$ for HYBRID.

QTSG does perform very elegant compressions in some cases; this is a strength of that system. Our system aims to preserve meaning, which it does rather well. However, this is is not necessarily a valid objective. Perhaps future evaluations should distinguish between modifying information in misleading ways (undesirable) and removing peripheral information (desirable). It is clear that the latter, done well, is useful and will be addressed in future work.

An error analysis shows that the main cause of errorful output for our system is parser errors, particularly mistakes in relative clause attachment and clause boundary identificaton. Methods such as those in Siddharthan (2003b) can be used to improve parser performance on these tasks.

Finally, this work and the cited related work only investigate sentence-level text simplification. There are various discourse level effects that also need to be considered when simplifying larger texts, including sentence ordering (Barzilay et al., 2002; Siddharthan, 2003a; Barzilay and Lapata, 2008), discourse connectives (Siddharthan and Katsos, 2010) and anaphora choice (Nenkova et al., 2005; Siddharthan et al., 2011).

5 Conclusions

We have presented a framework for text simplification based on synchronous grammars over typed dependency representations. Our HYBRID system, that uses hand-written rules for common syntactic simplifications, and automatically harvested rules for a much larger set of lexicalised simplifications is more robust than a similar system based on quasi-synchronous tree substitution grammars, outperforming it in terms of fluency, simplicity and meaning preservation. By abstracting away from constituent ordering and morphological variations, our approach allows for linguistically sound rules to be written for complex lexico-syntactic transformations, including passive to active voice. In the version of the system described and evaluated here, changes to morphology and constituent ordering are specified within the rules. Alternately, an off the shelf surface realiser could be used to generate from the dependency representation.

Acknowledgements

This research is supported by an award made by the EPSRC; award reference: EP/J018805/1.

ORIGINAL	QTSG	HYBRID	SEW
Takanobu Komiyama (born October 3, 1984 in Chiba, Japan) is a Japanese football player who currently plays for the J-league team Kawasaki Frontale.	His father. Komiyama is a. F=1, S=1.4, M=1	Takanobu Komiyama (born October 3, 1984 in Chiba, Japan) is a Japanese football player. Takanobu Komiyama at present plays for the J-league team Kawasaki Frontale. F=4, S=3.8, M=4.8	Takanobu Komiyama (born 3 October 1984) is a Japanese football player. He plays for Kawasaki Frontale. F=4.6, S=4.4, M=4.2
The occupants of Swadlincote often shorten its name to simply 'Swad'.	Swadlincote watch. The occupants often shorten its name to simply 'Swad'. F=2.6, S=2.6, M=3.2	The occupants of Swadlincote often shorten its name to just 'Swad'. F=4.4, S=4, M=5	People from Swadlincote often shorten its name to simply Swad. F=4.6, S=4.6, M=4.8
Today the nearest railway station is Burton upon Trent, about five miles away, as the railway between Burton and Leicester lost its passenger service under the Beeching Plan in the 1960s and now carries only freight.	Today the nearest railway station is Burton upon Trent, about five miles away, as the railway between Burton and Leicester lost service under the Beeching Plan in the 1960s. It now carries freight. F=4.2, S=3.6, M=4.6	The closest railway station is now Burton upon Trent, about five miles away. This is because the railway between Burton and Leicester now carries only freight. The railway lost its passenger service under the Beeching Plan in the 1960s. F=4.4, S=3.8, M=5	The nearest railway station is Burton upon Trent which is five miles away. F=4, S=4, M=2.2
Since December 2005 it has also been a candidate for joining the European Union and has applied for NATO membership.	Since December 2005, it is a candidate for joining the European Union. F=4, S=4.2, M=3.6	Since December 2005 it has also been a candidate for joining the European Union. And it has applied for NATO membership. F=4.2, S=4, M=4.8	Since December 2005 it has also been a candidate for joining the European Union. It has applied for NATO membership. F=4.2, S=4, M=4.8
Although most Irish political parties recognize his contribution to the foundation of the modern Irish state, supporters of Fine Gael hold his memory in particular esteem, regarding him as their movement's founding father, through his link to their precursor Cumann na nGaedhael.	The modern Irish state watch. Most Irish political parties recognize his contribution to foundation. Supporters of Gael hold his memory in particular esteem, regarding him as their movement's founding father, through his link to their precursor Cumann na nGaedhael. F=2.6, S=3.2, M=3.8	Supporters of Fine Gael hold his memory in very esteem, regarding him as their movement's founding father, through his link to their precursor Cumann na nGaedhael. But, all Irish political parties recognize his contribution to the foundation of the modern Irish state. F=3.4, S=3.6, M=4.2	Most Irish political parties think his contributions were important to make the modern Irish state. Members and supporters of Fine Gael remember him in particular as one of the founders of their movement, or its predecessor Cumann na nGaedhael. F=3.6, S=3.4, M=4.6

Table 2: Examples of simplifications from the test set, along with average scores for (F)luency, (S)implicity and (M)eaning Preservation.

References

Sandra M Aluísio, Lucia Specia, Thiago AS Pardo, Erick G Maziero, and Renata PM Fortes. 2008. Towards brazilian portuguese automatic text simplification systems. In *Proceedings of the eighth ACM symposium on Document engineering*, pages 240–248. ACM.

Richard C. Anderson and Alice Davison. 1988. Conceptual and empirical bases of readibility formulas. In Alice Davison and G. M. Green, editors, *Linguistic Complexity and Text Comprehension: Readability Issues Reconsidered*. Lawrence Erlbaum Associates, Hillsdale, NJ.

Richard Anderson and Peter Freebody. 1981. Vocabulary knowledge. In John Guthrie, editor, *Comprehension and Teaching: Research Reviews*, pages 77–117. International Reading Association, Newark, DE.

R. Barzilay and M. Lapata. 2008. Modeling Local Coherence: An Entity-Based Approach. *Computational Linguistics*, 34(1):1–34.

R. Barzilay, N. Elhadad, and K. McKeown. 2002. Inferring Strategies for Sentence Ordering in Multidocument News Summarization. *Journal of Artificial Intelligence Research*, 17(3):35–55.

Isabel L. Beck, Margaret G. McKeown, Gale M. Sinatra, and Jane A. Loxterman. 1991. Revising social studies text from a text-processing perspective: Evidence of improved comprehensibility. *Reading Research Quarterly*, pages 251–276.

Stefan Bott, Horacio Saggion, and Simon Mille. 2012. Text simplification tools for spanish. In *LREC*, pages 1665–1671.

Arnaldo Candido Jr, Erick Maziero, Caroline Gasperin, Thiago AS Pardo, Lucia Specia, and Sandra M Aluisio. 2009. Supporting the adaptation of texts for poor literacy readers: a text simplification editor for brazilian portuguese. In *Proceedings of the Fourth Workshop on Innovative Use of NLP for Building Educational Applications*, pages 34–42. Association for Computational Linguistics.

Yvonne Canning. 2002. *Syntactic simplification of Text*. Ph.D. thesis, University of Sunderland, UK.

Raman Chandrasekar, Christine Doran, and Bangalore Srinivas. 1996. Motivations and methods for text simplification. In *Proceedings of the 16th International Conference on Computational Linguistics (COLING '96)*, pages 1041–1044, Copenhagen, Denmark.

William Coster and David Kauchak. 2011. Learning to simplify sentences using wikipedia. In *Proceedings of the Workshop on Monolingual Text-To-Text Generation*, pages 1–9. Association for Computational Linguistics.

Jan De Belder and Marie-Francine Moens. 2010. Text simplification for children. In *Prroceedings of the SIGIR workshop on accessible search systems*, pages 19–26.

Yuan Ding and Martha Palmer. 2005. Machine translation using probabilistic synchronous dependency insertion grammars. In *Proceedings of the 43rd Annual Meeting on Association for Computational Linguistics*, pages 541–548. Association for Computational Linguistics.

Mark Dras. 1999. *Tree adjoining grammar and the reluctant paraphrasing of text*. Ph.D. thesis, Macquarie University NSW 2109 Australia.

J. Kamalski, T. Sanders, and L. Lentz. 2008. Coherence marking, prior knowledge, and comprehension of informative and persuasive texts: Sorting things out. *Discourse Processes*, 45(4):323–345.

D. Klein and C.D. Manning. 2003. Accurate unlexicalized parsing. In *Proceedings of the 41st Annual Meeting on Association for Computational Linguistics-Volume 1*, pages 423–430. Association for Computational Linguistics.

J.J. L'Allier. 1980. *An evaluation study of a computer-based lesson that adjusts reading level by monitoring on task reader characteristics*. Ph.D. thesis, University of Minnesota, Minneapolis, MN.

T. Linderholm, M.G. Everson, P. van den Broek, M. Mischinski, A. Crittenden, and J. Samuels. 2000. Effects of Causal Text Revisions on More-and Less-Skilled Readers' Comprehension of Easy and Difficult Texts. *Cognition and Instruction*, 18(4):525–556.

Ani Nenkova, Advaith Siddharthan, and Kathleen McKeown. 2005. Automatically learning cognitive status for multi-document summarization of newswire. In *Proceedings of HLT/EMNLP 2005*, pages 241–248, Vancouver, Canada.

Advaith Siddharthan and Napoleon Katsos. 2010. Reformulating discourse connectives for non-expert readers. In *Proceedings of the 11th Annual Conference of the North American Chapter of the Association for Computational Linguistics (NAACL-HLT 2010)*, Los Angeles, CA.

Advaith Siddharthan, Ani Nenkova, and Kathleen McKeown. 2011. Information status distinctions and referring expressions: An empirical study of references to people in news summaries. *Computational Linguistics*, 37(4):811–842.

Advaith Siddharthan. 2002. An architecture for a text simplification system. In *Proceedings of the Language Engineering Conference (LEC'02)*, pages 64–71, Hyderabad, India.

Advaith Siddharthan. 2003a. Preserving discourse structure when simplifying text. In *Proceedings of the European Natural Language Generation Workshop (ENLG), 11th Conference of the European Chapter of the Association for Computational Linguistics (EACL'03)*, pages 103–110, Budapest, Hungary.

Advaith Siddharthan. 2003b. Resolving pronouns robustly: Plumbing the depths of shallowness. In *Proceedings of the Workshop on Computational Treatments of Anaphora, 11th Conference of the European Chapter of the Association for Computational Linguistics (EACL'03)*, pages 7–14, Budapest, Hungary.

Advaith Siddharthan. 2010. Complex lexico-syntactic reformulation of sentences using typed dependency representations. In *Proceedings of the 6th International Natural Language Generation Conference (INLG 2010)*, Dublin Ireland.

Advaith Siddharthan. 2011. Text simplification using typed dependencies: a comparison of the robustness of different generation strategies. In *Proceedings of the 13th European Workshop on Natural Language Generation*, pages 2–11. Association for Computational Linguistics.

David A Smith and Jason Eisner. 2006. Quasi-synchronous grammars: Alignment by soft projection of syntactic dependencies. In *Proceedings of the Workshop on Statistical Machine Translation*, pages 23–30. Association for Computational Linguistics.

Kristian Woodsend and Mirella Lapata. 2011. Learning to simplify sentences with quasi-synchronous grammar and integer programming. In *Proceedings of the Conference on Empirical Methods in Natural Language Processing*, pages 409–420. Association for Computational Linguistics.

Sander Wubben, Antal van den Bosch, and Emiel Krahmer. 2012. Sentence simplification by monolingual machine translation. In *Proceedings of the 50th Annual Meeting of the Association for Computational Linguistics: Long Papers-Volume 1*, pages 1015–1024. Association for Computational Linguistics.

Kenji Yamada and Kevin Knight. 2001. A syntax-based statistical translation model. In *Proceedings of the 39th Annual Meeting on Association for Computational Linguistics*, pages 523–530. Association for Computational Linguistics.

Zhemin Zhu, Delphine Bernhard, and Iryna Gurevych. 2010. A monolingual tree-based translation model for sentence simplification. In *Proceedings of the 23rd international conference on computational linguistics*, pages 1353–1361. Association for Computational Linguistics.

A Summariser based on Human Memory Limitations and Lexical Competition

Yimai Fang
Computer Laboratory
University of Cambridge
15 JJ Thomson Avenue, CB3 0FD, UK
Yimai.Fang@cl.cam.ac.uk

Simone Teufel
Computer Laboratory
University of Cambridge
15 JJ Thomson Avenue, CB3 0FD, UK
Simone.Teufel@cl.cam.ac.uk

Abstract

Kintsch and van Dijk proposed a model of human comprehension and summarisation which is based on the idea of processing propositions on a sentence-by-sentence basis, detecting argument overlap, and creating a summary on the basis of the best connected propositions. We present an implementation of that model, which gets around the problem of identifying concepts in text by applying coreference resolution, named entity detection, and semantic similarity detection, implemented as a two-step competition. We evaluate the resulting summariser against two commonly used extractive summarisers using ROUGE, with encouraging results.

1 Introduction

Kintsch and van Dijk (1978) (henceforth KvD) present a model of human comprehension and memory retention which is based on research in artificial intelligence, experimental psychology and discourse linguistics. It models the processing of incoming text or speech by human memory limitations, and makes verifiable predictions about which propositions in a text will be recalled by subjects later. It has been very influential, particularly in the 1980 and 1990s in educational (Palinscar and Brown, 1984; King, 1992) and cognitive (Paivio, 1990) psychology, and is still today used as a theoretical model of reading and comprehension (Baddeley, 2007; Zwaan, 2003; DeLong et al., 2005; Smith, 2004). It has also been used for improving education, particularly for the production of better instructional text (Britton and Gulgoz, 1991; Pressley, 2006), and for teaching humans how to read for deep comprehension (Coiro and Dobler, 2007; Duke and Pearson, 2002; Koda, 2005; Driscoll, 2005) and to summarise (Hidi, 1986; Brown et al., 1983).

In the summarisation community, the model has been commended for its elegant and explanatory "deep" treatment of the summarisation process (Lehnert, 1981; Spärck Jones, 1993; Endres-Niggemeyer, 1998), but has not lead to any practical prototypes, mainly due the impossibility of implementing the knowledge- and inference-based aspects the model relies on.

We present here an implementation of the model, which attempts to circumvent some of these problems by the application of distributional semantics, and by modelling the construction of the coherence tree as a double competition (firstly of concept partners for word forms, secondly of attachment sites for propositions).

In the KvD model, a text (e.g. Figure 1) is converted into propositions (see Table 1) which have one functor and one or more arguments. The functor can be taken either from a fixed list of grammatical relations (e.g. IS A; AT; BETWEEN; OR) or an open class-set of so-called concepts, (e.g. BLOODY; TEACH). Arguments can be concepts or proposition numbers. Proposition numbers express embedded semantic structures (e.g. #9 in Table 1). Kintsch et al. (1979) assumed that this tranformation is performed manually; they were able to train humans to do so consistently.

> A series of violent, bloody encounters between police and Black Panther members punctuated the early summer days of 1969. Soon after, a group of black students I teach at California State College, Los Angeles, who were members of the Panther Party, began to complain of continuous harassment by law enforcement officers.

Figure 1: First two sentences from the example paragraph *Bumperstickers* by KvD (1978).

Proceedings of the 14th Conference of the European Chapter of the Association for Computational Linguistics, pages 732–741,
Gothenburg, Sweden, April 26-30 2014.

No.	Proposition
Cycle 1	
1	SERIES (ENCOUNTER)
2	VIOLENT (ENCOUNTER)
3	BLOODY (ENCOUNTER)
4	BETWEEN (ENCOUNTER, POLICE, BLACK PANTHER)
5	TIME: IN (ENCOUNTER, SUMMER)
6	EARLY (SUMMER)
7	TIME: IN (SUMMER, 1969)
Cycle 2	
8	SOON (#9)
9	AFTER (#4, #16)
10	GROUP (STUDENT)
11	BLACK (STUDENT)
12	TEACH (SPEAKER, STUDENT)
13	LOCATION: AT (#12, CAL STATE COLLEGE)
14	LOCATION: AT (CAL STATE COLLEGE, LOS ANGELES)
15	IS A (STUDENT, BLACK PANTHER)
16	BEGIN (#17)
17	COMPLAIN (STUDENT, #19)
18	CONTINUOUS (#19)
19	HARASS (POLICE, STUDENT)

Table 1: Propositions for Figure 1.

The KvD algorithm is manually simulated in their work, but is described in a mechanistic manner that should in principle lend itself to implementation, once propositions are created. Propositions form a tree where a proposition is attached to another proposition with which they share at least one argument; attachment higher in the tree is preferred. The tree is built incrementally; blocks of propositions, each of which roughly corresponding to one sentence, are processed in cycles. After each cycle, a process of "forgetting" is simulated by copying only the most salient propositions to the short-term memory (STM). This selection is performed by the so-called leading edge strategy (LES), which prefers propositions that are attached more recently and those attached at higher positions. This algorithms mirrors van Dijk's (1977) model of textual coherence.

When choosing an attachment site for proposition, arguments which are currently in STM are preferred. A resource-consuming search in long-term memory (LTM) is only triggered if a proposition cannot be attached in STM; in that case a bridging proposition is reintroduced into the tree.

The KvD model can be used to explain human recall of stories, and can also to create a summary of a text. The most natural way for a human to summarise from scratch is to replace propositions with so-called macropropositions, and the KvD model prefers this style of summary creation. An example for macroproposition is a statement that generalises over other propositions. This results in a more abstract version of the text. However if for any reason it is not possible to create macropropositions (for instance due to lack of deep knowledge representation), a summary can also be created in a simpler way based only on the propositions contained in the text. In that case, the selection criterion is the number of cycles a proposition has remained in STM.

There are three main stumbling blocks in the way of an implementation of the KvD model:

1. The automatic creation of propositions from text, and of summary text from summary propositions;
2. The automatic creation of concepts from words (including coreference resolution);
3. The creation of macropropositions, which would require sophisticated knowledge representation and reasoning.

We present a fully automatic version of the KvD model based on the following assumptions:

1. Current parser technology allows us to reconstruct the compositional semantics of the text well enough to make the KvD model operational, both in terms of creating propositions from text, and in terms of creating reasonably understandable output text from propositions (even if not fully grammatical).
2. We model the lexical variation of how a concept is expressed in a text probabilistically by semantic similarity and coreference resolution. This creates a competition between plausible expressions for argument overlap.
3. Our core algorithm is modelled as two competitions: (a) the competition between concept matches as mentioned in the point above; and (b) the competition between possible positions in a tree where a proposition could attach.
4. We also observed that KvD's method of choosing the tree root in the first processing cycle, and to never change it afterwards unless texts are truly incoherent (resorting to multiple trees), is too limiting, in particular in combination with their LES. Texts can have topic changes and still be perfectly co-

herent, particularly if they are longer and less linearly structured than the examples used by KvD. We therefore experiment with more flexible root choice strategies.

We have nothing to say on the third and biggest obstacle, the creation of macropropositions. Nevertheless, the experiments presented here test whether our hypotheses 1 – 4 are strong enough to provide our summariser with useful information concerning the discourse structure of the texts. We test this by comparing its performance to that of two current state-of-the-art summarisers, which instead rely on the sole use of lexical information. A psychologically-motivated summariser such as ours should be evaluated by comparison to abstractive, i.e., reformulated human summaries, rather than by comparison to extractive summaries. We do so using ROUGE, an evaluation framework that supports such comparisons (Lin and Hovy, 2003).

The structure of the paper is as follows. In the next section, we will detail our implementation of the KvD model, with particular emphasis on the creation of propositions, probabilistic concepts, proposition attachment, and root choice. In Section 4, we will present experiments comparing our summariser against two research extractive summarisers, MEAD and LexRank. We also test how our inventions including similarity-based concept matching and root choice strategy contribute to performance. We compare to related work in Section 3, and draw our conclusions in Section 5.

2 Our implementation of KvD

Figure 2 shows the structure of our summariser. The *Proposition Creation* module transforms surface text to propositions with the aid of a grammatical parser. Recall that in the original KvD model (shown as "Human (KvD)"), propositions are generated manually. Apart from such, our implementation follows the KvD algorithm as closely as possible. The core of this algorithm is the *Memory Retention Cycle* in the centre of the figure.

A cycle begins with the detection of coherence between the new propositions and the current STM content. This results in a hierarchy of all so-far processed propositions called the *Coherence Tree*. Propositions are attached to the tree by a variety of strategies, as explained in Subsection 2.2.

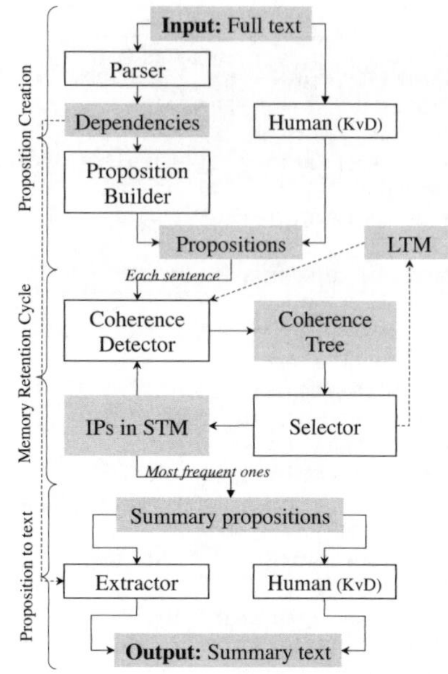

Figure 2: Framework of the summariser.

At the end of each cycle, important propositions (IPs) are selected by the *Selector*, stored in STM, and thus retained for the next cycle, where they are available for new incoming propositions to attach to. The selector is a full implementation of KvD's LES, which also updates the recency of propositions reinstantiated from the LTM.[1] Less important propositions leave the cycle and go into the LTM, which is conceptually a secondary repository of propositions to provide the "missing links" when no coherence between the STM and the incoming propositions can be established.

After the text is consumed, a propositional representation of the summary is created by recalling the propositions that were retained in STM most frequently. The summary text is then either created manually (in the KvD model), or in our implementation, as a prototype, automatically by extracting words from the parser's dependencies.

2.1 Proposition builder

We aim to create propositions of comparable semantic weight to each other. This is a consequence of our decision to recast KvD as a competition model (as will become clear in subsection 2.2), because by defining propositions as blocks of arguments they should contain a similar number of

[1] KvD implied this in the last cycle of the *Bumperstickers* paragraph, by placing the two reinstantiated propositions below #37, though they are older than #37.

meaningful arguments to ensure similar potential for overlap.

To achieve suitable granularity of propositions, we aggregate information spread out over several grammatical dependencies, and exclude semantically empty words from participating in argument overlap. We use Stanford Parser (Klein and Manning, 2003), and aggregate subjects and complements of a predicate into a single proposition. Active and passive voices are unified; clauses are treated as embedded propositions; controlling subjects of open clausal complements are recovered.

Some predicates are not verbs, but nominalised verbs or coordination. For instance, KvD model the phrase " *encounters between police and Black Panther Party members* " as BETWEEN (ENCOUNTER, POLICE, BLACK PANTHER). Producing such a proposition instead of two separate ones BETWEEN (ENCOUNTER, POLICE) and BETWEEN (ENCOUNTER, BLACK PANTHER) is advantageous, because this single proposition provides a strong connection between POLICE and BLACK PANTHER which cannot be derived from other dependencies.

However we lack a subcategorisation lexicon that provides information about how many arguments a preposition like "*between*" takes. Therefore we scan conjoined prepositional phrases, aggregate the objects, and attach them to the governors of the prepositional phrases. In this example, the resulting preposition is ENCOUNTER (POLICE, MEMBER). The word "*between*" is excluded because it is semantically empty and may interfere with overlap detection.

We take care to detect and exclude semantically empty material. For instance, the *empty semantic heads* in noun phrases such as "a series of" and "a group of" are detected using a list of of 21 words we collected, and treated by redirecting the dependencies involving the empty heads to the corresponding content heads. In this treatment, the relation between an empty head and its content head is not entirely erased, but encoded as a general modifier relation.

2.2 Probabilistic concept matching

The notion of argument overlap in KvD's model is sophisticated in that it "knows" which surface expressions (pronouns, synonyms, etc) in text refer to the same concept. Concept mapping is the task of forming equivalence classes of surface expressions; each concept then corresponds to one such equivalence class. The KvD model, because it simulates concept mapping and proposition attachment in parallel, conceals some of the choices that a fully automatic model has to make.

Given current technology, concept mapping can only be performed probabilistically. We use the Stanford coreference resolution, named-entity detection (to extend coreference detection to non-same-head references, e.g. mapping "*the tech giant*" to "*Apple Inc.*"[2]); and to find synonymy or at least semantic relatedness, we use a well-known measure of semantic similarity, namely Lin's Dependency-Based Thesaurus (Lin, 1998). We are not committed to this particular measure, but it empirically performed best out of the 11 we tried; especially it outperformed WordNet path-based measures. Note however that only the 200 most similar words for each word are provided by this tool. The similarity measure is normalised by relative ranking to provide the probability that an expression refers to the same concept as another expression. We use WordNet (Miller, 1995) for derivationally related forms (to solve e.g. nominalisation). This establishes the first competition, the one between concept matches.

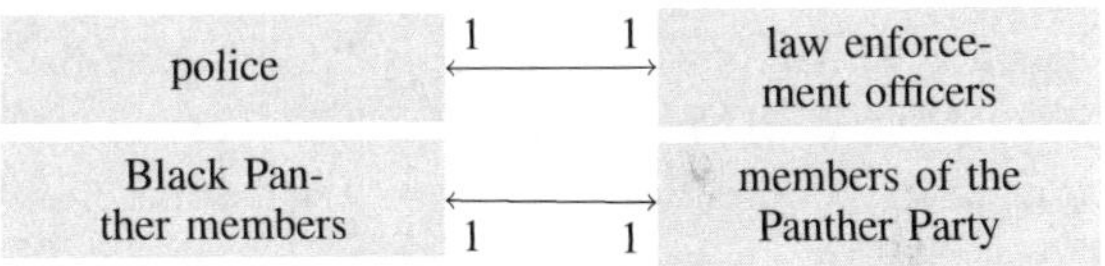

Figure 3: KvD's concept matching.

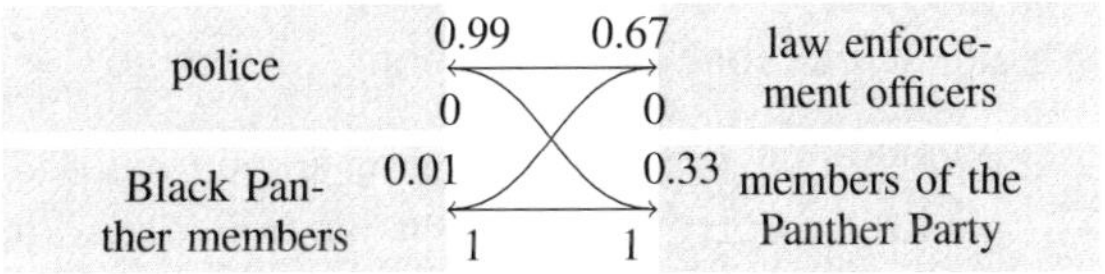

Figure 4: Probabilistic concept matching.

Modelling concepts probabilistically has its implication for the next task: finding the best attachment site for a proposition. Let us explain this with an example. Notice that in the example text in Figure 1, "*police*" (from #4, in the first sentence) and

[2]A WordNet synset is defined for each named-entity type; here "*giant*" is connected to its hypernym "*organization*" via "*enterprise*".

"*law enforcement officer*" (from #19, in the second sentence) refer to the same concept POLICE. Figure 3 illustrates how this is handled in KvD's model, where intelligent concept matching establishes with 100% certainty that the two strings refer to the same concept. Certainty about the argument overlap then enables them to later attach #19 to #4. In their model it is important whether a matching proposition is found in STM or LTM: If the only proposition that mentions "*police*" (#4) is no longer in STM when the proposition containing "*law enforcement officer*" (#19) is processed, and for any reason the other arguments in #19 (i.e. STUDENT) cannot find overlaps either, KvD find no concept match in STM and know therefore, again with full certainty, that an LTM search must be triggered[3], which in this case leads to the successful recall of #19 for #4 to attach to.

Figure 4 illustrates the corresponding situation in our model, where #4 with "*police*" is in LTM, the probability of a concept match between "*law enforcement officer*" and "*police*" is 66.7%, whereas that of a match with "*members*", which is in STM, is 33.3%. The probabilistic concept matching cannot provide enough certainty to single out #4 because of full argument overlap. The probabilities of concept match have to act as a much weaker filter in our model, and all previous propositions have to be considered as potential landing sites for #19. In particular, we do not know whether a concept match within STM is "good enough", or whether a LTM search is needed. There is, in this case, a competition between a weak match in STM (the direct vicinity) and a strong match in LTM (further away), which will hopefully result in a successful match between "*police*" and "*law enforcement officer*". In other words, we always have to search for matches in both repositories.

After obtaining the graph of interrelated expressions, the competition between landing sites for each proposition takes place, whereby higher positions are preferred. This double competition is a core aspect of our model.

2.3 Choice of root

The KvD model almost always maintains the root determined in the first cycle (either by overlap with title concepts or by coverage of the main clause of the first sentence). The model introduces multiple roots if a text is totally incoherent, namely when propositions cannot be attached anywhere and therefore a forest of disjoint trees has to be developed. This strategy does not generalise well to longer texts with topic changes, for example newspaper texts with anecdotal leads. Although these texts are perfectly coherent, KvD cannot treat them appropriately.[4]

Our more flexible rooting strategy is run once in each cycle, assessing whether any of the current root's children in the working memory would make a better root. In case of a root change, the edge between the old and the new root is reversed, and the old root becomes a child of the new root. Then we perform the same strategy on the new tree until no root change is needed.

We denote the current root as i, and a new root candidate (a child of i) j. J is the set of descendants of j (inclusive of j), and I the set of all nodes V excluding J, i.e. $I = V \setminus J$. Then nodes in J will be promoted after the root change, while those in I will go one level deeper. Since edge weights, i.e. attachment strengths, are asymmetric, we denote the weight for j being a child of i as $w_{i,j}$, and $w_{j,i}$ for the reversed attachment. Each node v also carries a weight $x_v = m_v \cdot a^{d_v}$, where m_v is a memory status factor (e.g. $m_v = 1$ if v is in STM, 0.5 if otherwise), $0 < a \leq 1$ is an attenuation factor, and d_v is depth of v in the tree. To decide, we evaluate

$$s = w_{j,i} \sum_{v \in J} x_v - w_{i,j} \sum_{v \in I} x_v \qquad (1)$$

If $s > 0$, the root change is permitted.[5] This evaluation makes root change easier if the edge in question favours i being a child of j, or there are more important nodes that can benefit from the change, and vice versa.

An example of such a root change taken from the *Bumperstickers* is given in Figure 5 (refer to Table 1 for proposition contents). As the central topic of the text changes from the encounters to

[3]KvD only mentioned retrieving embedded propositions as LTM search rarely happens, but the goal is the same as here: to establish overlap.

[4]In our scenario the situation can barely ever arise where absolutely no proposition attachment is possible, as the probabilistic concept mapping is usually able suggest some concept match, albeit with small probability.

[5]In case when multiple candidates are permitted, the one with the highest s is chosen.

that the identity of Panther Party members are actually the author's students, the summariser recognises this change after reading one more sentence, by flipping the edge connecting #3 and #14.

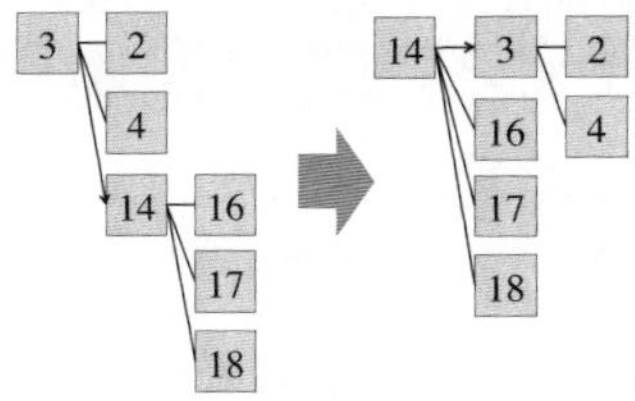

Figure 5: Tree before and after a root change.

3 Related Work

One of the dilemmas in summarisation research is how "deep", i.e. semantics-oriented, a summariser should be. Shallow analysis of lexical similarity between sentences and/or the keywords contained in sentences has lead to summarisers that are robust and perform very well for most texts (Radev et al., 2004; Dorr and Zajic, 2003; Carbonell and Goldstein, 1998). The methods applied include a random-surfer model (Mihalcea and Tarau, 2004; Radev, 2004), a model of attraction and repulsion of similar summary sentences (Carbonell and Goldstein, 1998). There are statistical models of sentence shortening (Knight and Marcu, 2002). While much work in summarisation has concentrated on multi-document summarisation, where the main challenge is the detection of redundant information, the summariser presented here is a single-document summariser.

However, researchers have been attracted by deeper, more symbolic and thus more explanatory summarisation models that use semantic representations of some form (Radev and McKeown, 1998) and often rely on explicit discourse modelling (Lehnert, 1981; Kintsch and van Dijk, 1978; Cohen, 1984). The problem with template-based summarisers is that they tend to be domain-dependent; the problem with discourse structure-based summarisers is in general that they require knowledge modelling and reasoning far beyond the capability of today's state of the art in artificial intelligence. Rhetorical Structure Theory (Mann and Thompson, 1987) provides a domain-independent framework that takes local discourse structure into account, which has lead to a successful prototype summariser (Marcu, 2000). This summarisation strategy does not however look at the lexical content of the propositions or clause-like units it connects, only at the way how the connection is performed.

The summariser presented here is a hybrid: its core algorithm is symbolic, but its limited powers of generalisation come from a semantic similarity metric that is defined via distributionally derived probabilities. Because its core processing is symbolic and based on a simple semantic representation, it is possible to derive an explanation based on the coherence tree and the propositions selected from it. There are some similarities to the idea of summarisation via lexical chains (Barzilay and Elhadad, 1997), as both methods trace concepts (as representatives of topics) across a document. The KvD model arguably uses more informative meaning units, as it is based on the combination of concepts within propositions, rather than on concept repetition alone.

A different, related stream of research looked at the automatic detection of coherence in text. Graesser et al (2004) present a coherence checker based on over 200 coherence metrics, including argument overlap as in KvD. Barzilay and Lapata (2008) use a profiling of texts akin to Centering theory to rank texts according to their coherence. It would be interesting to combine their notion of entity-based coherence with KvD's notion of argument overlap.

4 Experiments

We now perform two experiments. The first tests the contribution of our concept matcher and root change strategy on a small document set we have collected, and compares against two research summarisers. In the second experiment, we test the performance of our summariser on a much larger and standard dataset.

We will use the intrinsic evaluation strategy of comparison to a gold standard. Human judgements would be the most credible, but as a cheap alternative, we use ROUGE-L (Lin, 2004), which has been shown to correlate well to human judgements. For each sentence, ROUGE-L treats it as a sequence of words, and finds the longest common subsequences (LCSs) with any sentence in a gold standard summary. The score is defined as the F-measure of the precision and recall of the LCSs.

The next question is how the gold standard summaries used in ROUGE are defined. Because our summariser is deep and has a fine granularity, it should be compared against human-written summaries on a variety of texts.

For the first experiment, we have collected from volunteers 8 human abstractive summaries for each of the 4 short scientific articles or stories we found in Kintsch and Vipond (1979) (average length: 120 words), and 4 for each of 2 longer political news texts (average length: 523 words). The volunteers were instructed to condense the text to 1/3 of its length for the short texts, and to 100 words for the longer ones. They were also instructed not to paraphrase, but to use the words in the text as much as possible. This was because no summariser in this experiment has a paraphrasing ability. Nevertheless, not all subjects followed this instruction strictly.

For the second experiment, we use the DUC 2002 dataset (Over and Liggett, 2002). There are 827 texts from news media, of a variety of topics and lengths, among which our script is able to extract titles and contents of 822 documents. We use the provided single document abstractive summaries, which are of 100 words in length each, as gold standard summaries. A few of the documents are selected in multiple clusters and therefore have multiple summaries; all of them are used in evaluation.

We compare our summariser against a baseline constructed with the first n words from the original text, where n is the summary length as defined above, and two summarisers: MEAD (Radev et al., 2004) is a research summariser which uses a centroid-based paradigm and is known to perform generally well over a range of texts. LexRank (Radev, 2004) uses lexically derived similarities in its similarity graph of sentences, sharing the same idea of sentence similarity with MEAD. Note that both summarisers are extractive.

We illustrate what our summaries look like in Table 2, where we asked the summariser to give us summaries as close to 20 and 50 word summaries as possible, with Table 3 showing the underlying propositions. In contrast, MEAD can only extract sentences as-is (thus not as flexible in length), and does not have meaning blocks like our propositions.

Encounters between police and Black Panther members. Students to complain of harassment. Automobiles Panther Party signs glued to bumpers.
Bloody encounters between police and Black Panther members punctuated the summer days of 1969. Students to complain of continuous harassment by law enforcement officers. They receiving many traffic citations. Automobiles with Panther Party signs glued to their bumpers. I to determine whether we were hearing the voice of paranoia or reality.

Table 2: Summaries produced by our summariser.

3	encounters (between: police; between: Black Panther members)
16	to complain (students; of: harassment)
34	with: Panther Party signs (automobiles)
35	glued (#34; to: bumpers)

Table 3: Summary propositions for the first summary above.

We create summaries for all three summarisers following this procedure: We provide sentence-split texts and their headlines (not needed by LexRank), and run the summarisers in such a way as to produce a summary of the same length as stipulated for the standard summaries. Our summariser controls word count precisely; we require MEAD to produce summaries close to the length (allowing variations), and for LexRank we allow it to go beyond the limit by less than one sentence and then discard the exceeding part in the sentence with the lowest salience.

The results of Experiment 1 are summarised in Table 4. As is well-known from similar experiments, it is hard beating the first n baseline due to the fact that journalistic style (in the long texts) already puts a summary of each text first. It is slightly surprising that this effect also holds for the short texts (literary style). It is of note that our KvD summariser beats both MEAD and LexRank on this dataset, which is shelved away during development, with statistical significance on the long texts: the 95%-confidence interval of ours is 0.403 – 0.432, and that of MEAD is 0.370 – 0.411.

	Long Texts	Short Texts
Ours	**0.418**	0.333
Ours – without similarity	0.396	0.271
Ours – without word info	0.319	0.185
Ours – without root change	0.388	**0.348**
MEAD	0.391	0.343
LexRank	0.378	0.326
First n words	**0.460**	**0.368**

Table 4: ROUGE-L F-measures for Experiment 1.

	Precision	Recall	F-measure
Our summariser	0.361	0.332	0.344
MEAD	0.366	0.355	0.358
First n words	**0.403**	**0.395**	**0.399**

Table 5: ROUGE-L scores for Experiment 2.

We test whether concept matching is beneficial by switching off similarity derived from distributional semantics, or switching off all "word information" which includes distributional semantics, lemmatisation, and coreference detection, i.e. to consider matching only for the same word. Performance deteriorates when concept matching is switched off, substantially if all word information is off. This confirms our hypothesis that one of the cornerstones of KvD, concept matching, can be at least partially simulated using today's distributional semantics methods. As for root change, turning it off seems to hurt performance on the longer texts, but not so on the shorter ones, which matches our speculation that root change is useful for longer texts, which have some focus shifts.

The result of Experiment 2 is shown in Table 5. This experiment on a large dataset demonstrates that our summariser performs in the ballpark of typical results of extractive summarisers, although it is still statistically a little worse than the state-of-the-art MEAD (whose F-measure 95%-confidence interval is 0.349 – 0.367). Our summariser is good at precision because many summaries produced have not used up the 100-word limit, making the average summary length smaller than that of MEAD's. This indicates that our summariser might be good at very short summaries, or we could improve the memory selection to allow for a more diversified important proposition set. Considering this, and the fact that we have many parameters not tuned for the task, and we have not utilised the structural / positional features (whose importance is shown in the first-n baseline), the result is still encouraging.

5 Conclusions

We present here a first prototype of the feasibility of basing a summarisation algorithm on Kintsch and van Dijk's (1978) model. Our implementation successfully creates flexible-length summaries, highly compressed if desired, and provides some explanation for why certain meaning units appear in the summary. We have avoided some of the hardest aspects of KvD's model, which have to do with the generation of macropropositions and with keeping closer track of larger discourse structures, but we show that some core aspects of the model can be approximated with today's parsing and lexical semantics technology. Although the output summaries are not yet in all cases grammatical, we show that our system performs comparably with extractive state-of-the-art summarisers.

During the implementation, we had to solve several practical problems that the KvD did not give enough procedural detail about, or skipped over in their manual simulation. For instance, we have turned the distinction between LTM and STM to two parallel salience levels from KvD's two disjoint stages, formalised the tree building process and improved KvD's root choice strategy.

The KvD model does not keep track of unique events, but would profit from doing so, for instance in texts where more than one event of the same type is referred to. It has no explicit model of time, but would profit from one. It does not even use information about which entities in a text form the same concept or individual, for selecting all information about that concept into the summary. There are also many interesting ways how the memory cycle could be modified by giving more weight to particular events, concepts and individuals.

On the implementational side, much remains to be tried. Anything that improves the proposition builder should bear direct fruit in the quality of the summaries. The limitations of our proposition builder come from the limitations of parsing technology as well as the fact that semantics is not entirely determined by syntax. For instance, we noticed some problems caused by incorrect prepositional phrase attachment. A better coreference system would also improve this summariser immensely, reducing much uncertainty in the concept matching. The deep nature of the summariser also enables natural language generation to improve the readability of our textual summary.

Acknowledgement

Joint scholarship from the Cambridge Commonwealth, European & International Trust and the China Scholarship Council is gratefully acknowledged.

References

A Baddeley. 2007. *Working memory, thought, and action*. Oxford University Press.

Regina Barzilay and Michael Elhadad. 1997. Using lexical chains for text summarization. In Inderjeet Mani and Mark T. Maybury, editors, *Proceedings of the ACL/EACL-97 Workshop on Intelligent Scalable Text Summarization*.

Regina Barzilay and Mirella Lapata. 2008. Modeling local coherence: An entity-based approach. *Computational Linguistics*, 34(1):1–34.

BK Britton and S Gulgoz. 1991. Using kintsch's computational model to improve instructional text: Effects of repairing inference calls on recall and cognitive structures. *Journal of Educational Psychology*.

Ann L. Brown, Jeanne D. Day, and Jones R. S. 1983. The development of plans for summarizing text. *Child development*. was in press in 1983.

Jaime Carbonell and Jade Goldstein. 1998. The use of MMR, diversity-based reranking for reordering documents and producing summaries. In *Proceedings of the 21th (SIGIR-98)*, pages 335–336, Melbourne, Australia.

Robin Cohen. 1984. A computational theory of the function of clue words in argument understanding. In *Proceedings of the 10th (COLING-84)*, pages 251–255.

J Coiro and E Dobler. 2007. Exploring the online reading comprehension strategies used by sixthgrade skilled readers to search for and locate information on the internet. *Reading research quarterly*.

KA DeLong, TP Urbach, and M Kutas. 2005. Probabilistic word pre-activation during language comprehension inferred from electrical brain activity. *Nature neuroscience*.

Bonnie Dorr and David Zajic. 2003. Hedge trimmer: A parse-and-trim approach to headline generation. In *in Proceedings of Workshop on Automatic Summarization*, pages 1–8.

MP Driscoll. 2005. *Psychology of learning for instruction*. Allyn and Bacon.

NK Duke and PD Pearson. 2002. Effective practices for developing reading comprehension. In Alan E. Farstrup and S. Jay Samuels, editors, *What research has to say about reading instruction*.

Brigitte Endres-Niggemeyer. 1998. *Summarizing Information*. Springer-Verlag, New York, NY.

Arthur C. Graesser, Danielle S. McNamara, Max M. Louwerse, and Zhiqiang Cai. 2004. Coh-metrix: Analysis of text on cohesion and language. *Behavior Research Methods, Instruments, & Computers*, 36(2):193–202.

V Anderson Hidi. 1986. Producing written summaries: Task demands, cognitive operations, and implications for instruction. *Review of educational research*.

A King. 1992. Comparison of self-questioning, summarizing, and notetaking-review as strategies for learning from lectures. *American Educational Research Journal*.

Walter Kintsch and Teun A. van Dijk. 1978. Toward a model of text comprehension and production. *Psychological review*, 85(5):363–394.

Walter Kintsch and Douglas Vipond. 1979. Reading comprehension and readability in educational practice and psychological theory. In Lars-Göran Nilsson, editor, *Perspectives on Memory Research: Essays in Honor of Uppsala's 500th Anniversary*, pages 329–365. Erlbaum Associates.

Dan Klein and Christopher D Manning. 2003. Accurate unlexicalized parsing. In *Proceedings of the 41st Annual Meeting on Association for Computational Linguistics-Volume 1*, pages 423–430. Association for Computational Linguistics.

Kevin Knight and Daniel Marcu. 2002. Summarization beyond sentence extraction: A probabilistic approach to sentence compression. *Artificial Intelligence*, 139(1).

Keiko Koda. 2005. *Insights into second language reading: A cross-linguistic approach*. Cambridge Univeristy Press.

Wendy G Lehnert. 1981. Plot units and narrative summarization. *Cognitive Science*, 5(4):293–331.

Chin-Yew Lin and Eduard Hovy. 2003. Automatic evaluation of summaries using n-gram co-occurrence statistics. In *Proceedings of the 2003 Conference of the North American Chapter of the Association for Computational Linguistics on Human Language Technology-Volume 1*, pages 71–78. Association for Computational Linguistics.

Dekang Lin. 1998. Automatic retrieval and clustering of similar words. In *Proceedings of the 17th international conference on Computational linguistics-Volume 2*, pages 768–774. Association for Computational Linguistics.

Chin-Yew Lin. 2004. ROUGE: A package for automatic evaluation of summaries. In *Text Summarization Branches Out: Proceedings of the ACL-04 Workshop*, pages 74–81.

William C. Mann and Sandra A. Thompson. 1987. Rhetorical Structure Theory: Description and construction of text structures. In Gerard Kempen, editor, *Natural Language Generation: New Results in Artificial Intelligence, Psychology, and Linguistics*, pages 85–95. Marinus Nijhoff Publishers, Dordrecht, NL.

Daniel Marcu. 2000. *The Theory and Practice of Discourse Parsing and Summarization*. MIT Press.

R Mihalcea and P Tarau. 2004. Textrank: Bringing order into texts. In *Proceedings of the EMLNP*.

George A Miller. 1995. Wordnet: a lexical database

for english. *Communications of the ACM*, 38(11):39–41.

Paul Over and W Liggett. 2002. Introduction to duc: An intrinsic evaluation of generic news text summarization systems. In *Proc. DUC*. http://www-nlpir.nist.gov/projects/duc/guidelines/2002.html.

A Paivio. 1990. *Mental representations*. Oxford Science Publications.

Aannemarie Sullivan Palinscar and Ann L. Brown. 1984. Reciprocal teaching of comprehension-fostering and comprehension-monitoring activities. *Cognition and Instruction*, 1:117–175.

Michael Pressley. 2006. *Reading instruction that works: The case for balanced teaching*. Guildford Press.

Dragomir R. Radev and Kathleen R. McKeown. 1998. Generating natural language summaries from multiple on-line sources. 24(3):469–500.

Dragomir Radev, Timothy Allison, Sasha Blair-Goldensohn, John Blitzer, Arda Celebi, Stanko Dimitrov, Elliott Drabek, Ali Hakim, Wai Lam, Danyu Liu, Jahna Otterbacher, Hong Qi, Horacio Saggion, Simone Teufel, Michael Topper, Adam Winkel, and Zhu Zhang. 2004. Mead – a platform for multidocument multilingual text summarization. In *Proceedings of LREC-04*.

Dragomir R. Radev. 2004. Lexrank: Graph-based lexical centrality as salience in text summarization. *Journal of Artificial Intelligence Research*.

F Smith. 2004. *Understanding reading: A psycholinguistic analysis of reading and learning to read*. Lawrence Erlbaum.

Karen Spärck Jones. 1993. What might be in a summary? Technical report, Computer Laboratory, University of Cambridge.

Teun A. van Dijk. 1977. *Text and Context: Explorations in the Semantics and Pragmatics of Discourse*. Longman, London, UK.

RA Zwaan. 2003. The immersed experiencer: Toward an embodied theory of language comprehension. *Psychology of learning and motivation*.

Learning part-of-speech taggers with inter-annotator agreement loss

Barbara Plank, Dirk Hovy, Anders Søgaard
Center for Language Technology
University of Copenhagen, Denmark
Njalsgade 140, DK-2300 Copenhagen S
bplank@cst.dk,dirk@cst.dk,soegaard@hum.ku.dk

Abstract

In natural language processing (NLP) annotation projects, we use inter-annotator agreement measures and annotation guidelines to ensure consistent annotations. However, annotation guidelines often make linguistically debatable and even somewhat arbitrary decisions, and inter-annotator agreement is often less than perfect. While annotation projects usually specify how to deal with linguistically debatable phenomena, annotator disagreements typically still stem from these "hard" cases. This indicates that some errors are more debatable than others. In this paper, we use small samples of doubly-annotated part-of-speech (POS) data for Twitter to estimate annotation reliability and show how those metrics of *likely* inter-annotator agreement can be implemented in the loss functions of POS taggers. We find that these cost-sensitive algorithms perform better across annotation projects and, more surprisingly, even on data annotated according to the same guidelines. Finally, we show that POS tagging models sensitive to inter-annotator agreement perform better on the downstream task of chunking.

1 Introduction

POS-annotated corpora and treebanks are collections of sentences analyzed by linguists according to some linguistic theory. The specific choice of linguistic theory has dramatic effects on downstream performance in NLP tasks that rely on syntactic features (Elming et al., 2013). Variation across annotated corpora in linguistic theory also poses challenges to intrinsic evaluation (Schwartz et al., 2011; Tsarfaty et al., 2012), as well as for languages where available resources are mutually inconsistent (Johansson, 2013). Unfortunately, there is no grand unifying linguistic theory of how to analyze the structure of sentences. While linguists agree on certain things, there is still a wide range of unresolved questions. Consider the following sentence:

(1) @GaryMurphyDCU of @DemMattersIRL will take part in a panel discussion on October 10th re the aftermath of #seanref ...

While linguists will agree that *in* is a preposition, and *panel discussion* a compound noun, they are likely to disagree whether *will* is heading the main verb *take* or vice versa. Even at a more basic level of analysis, it is not completely clear how to assign POS tags to each word in this sentence: is *part* a particle or a noun; is *10th* a numeral or a noun?

Some linguistic controversies may be resolved by changing the vocabulary of linguistic theory, e.g., by leaving out numerals or introducing *ad hoc* parts of speech, e.g. for English *to* (Marcus et al., 1993) or words ending in *-ing* (Manning, 2011). However, standardized label sets have practical advantages in NLP (Zeman and Resnik, 2008; Zeman, 2010; Das and Petrov, 2011; Petrov et al., 2012; McDonald et al., 2013).

For these and other reasons, our annotators (even when they are trained linguists) often disagree on how to analyze sentences. The strategy in most previous work in NLP has been to monitor and later resolve disagreements, so that the final labels are assumed to be reliable when used as input to machine learning models.

Our approach

Instead of glossing over those annotation disagreements, we consider what happens if we embrace the uncertainty exhibited by human annotators when learning predictive models from the annotated data.

To achieve this, we incorporate the uncertainty exhibited by annotators in the training of our model. We measure inter-annotator agreement on small samples of data, then incorporate this in the loss function of a structured learner to reflect the confidence we can put in the annotations. This provides us with cost-sensitive online learning algorithms for inducing models from annotated data that take inter-annotator agreement into consideration.

Specifically, we use online structured perceptron with drop-out, which has previously been applied to POS tagging and is known to be robust across samples and domains (Søgaard, 2013a). We incorporate the inter-annotator agreement in the loss function either as inter-annotator $F1$-scores or as the confusion probability between annotators (see Section 3 below for a more detailed description). We use a small amounts of doubly-annotated Twitter data to estimate $F1$-scores and confusion probabilities, and incorporate them during training via a modified loss function. Specifically, we use POS annotations made by two annotators on a set of 500 newly sampled tweets to estimate our agreement scores, and train models on existing Twitter data sets (described below). We evaluate the effect of our modified training by measuring intrinsic as well as downstream performance of the resulting models on two tasks, namely named entity recognition (NER) and chunking, which both use POS tags as input features.

2 POS-annotated Twitter data sets

The vast majority of POS-annotated resources across languages contain mostly newswire text. Some annotated Twitter data sets do exist for English. Ritter et al. (2011) present a manually annotated data set of 16 thousand tokens. They do not report inter-annotator agreement. Gimpel et al. (2011) annotated about 26 thousand tokens and report a raw agreement of 92%. Foster et al. (2011) annotated smaller portions of data for cross-domain evaluation purposes. We refer to the data as RITTER, GIMPEL and FOSTER below.

In our experiments, we use the RITTER splits provided by Derczynski et al. (2013), and the October splits of the GIMPEL data set, version 0.3. We train our models on the concatenation of RITTER-TRAIN and GIMPEL-TRAIN and evaluate them on the remaining data, the dev and test set provided by Foster et al. (2011) as well as an in-house annotated data set of 3k tokens (see below).

The three annotation efforts (Ritter et al., 2011; Gimpel et al., 2011; Foster et al., 2011) all used different tagsets, however, and they also differ in tokenization, as well as a wide range of linguistic decisions. We mapped all the three corpora to the universal tagset provided by Petrov et al. (2012) and used the same dummy symbols for numbers, URLs, etc., in all the data sets. Following (Foster et al., 2011), we consider URLs, usernames and hashtags as NOUN. We did not change the tokenization.

The data sets differ in how they analyze many of the linguistically hard cases. Consider, for example, the analysis of *will you come out to* in GIMPEL and RITTER (Figure 1, top). While Gimpel et al. (2011) tag *out* and *to* as adpositions, Ritter et al. (2011) consider them particles. What is the right analysis depends on the compositionality of the construction and the linguistic theory one subscribes to.

Other differences include the analysis of abbreviations (PRT in GIMPEL; X in RITTER and FOSTER), colon (X in GIMPEL; punctuation in RITTER and FOSTER), and emoticons, which can take multiple parts of speech in GIMPEL, but are always X in RITTER, while they are absent in FOSTER. GIMPEL-TRAIN and RITTER-TRAIN are also internally inconsistent. See the bottom of Figure 1 for examples and Hovy et al. (2014) for a more detailed discussion on differences between the data sets.

Since the mapping to universal tags could potentially introduce errors, we also annotated a data set directly using universal tags. We randomly selected 200 tweets collected over the span of one day, and had three annotators tag this set. We split the data in such a way that each annotator had 100 tweets: two annotators had disjoint sets, the third overlapped 50 items with each of the two others. In this way, we obtained an initial set of 100 doubly-annotated tweets. The annotators were *not* provided with annotation guidelines. After the first round of annotations, we achieved a raw agreement of 0.9, a Cohen's κ of 0.87, and a Krippendorff's α of 0.87. We did one pass over the data to adjudicate the cases where annotators disagreed,

		will	you	come	out	to	the	
GIMPEL	...	VERB	PRON	VERB	**ADP**	**ADP**	DET	...
RITTER		VERB	PRON	VERB	**PRT**	**PRT**	DET	

RITTER

...	you/PRON	**come/VERB**	**out/PRT**	to/PRT	...
	it/PRON	**comes/VERB**	**out/ADP**	nov/NOUN	

GIMPEL

...	Advances/NOUN	and/CONJ	**Social/NOUN**	**Media/NOUN**	.../X	...
	Journalists/NOUN	and/CONJ	**Social/ADJ**	**Media/NOUN**	experts/NOUN	

Figure 1: Annotation differences between (top) and within (bottom) two available Twitter POS data sets.

or where they had flagged their choice as debatable. The final data set (`lowlands.test`), referred below to as INHOUSE, contained 3,064 tokens (200 tweets) and is publicly available at `http://bitbucket.org/lowlands/costsensitive-data/`, along with the data used to compute inter-annotator agreement scores for learning cost-sensitive taggers, described in the next section.

3 Computing agreement scores

Gimpel et al. (2011) used 72 doubly-annotated tweets to estimate inter-annotator agreement, and we also use doubly-annotated data to compute agreement scores. We randomly sampled 500 tweets for this purpose. Each tweet was annotated by two annotators, again using the universal tag set (Petrov et al., 2012). All annotators were encouraged to use their own best judgment rather than following guidelines or discussing difficult cases with each other. This is in contrast to Gimpel et al. (2011), who used annotation guidelines. The average inter-annotator agreement was 0.88 for raw agreement, and 0.84 for Cohen's κ. Gimpel et al. (2011) report a raw agreement of 0.92.

We use two metrics to provide a more detailed picture of inter-annotator agreement, namely *$F1$-scores* between annotators on individual parts of speech, and *tag confusion probabilities*, which we derive from confusion matrices.

The $F1$-score relates to precision and recall in the usual way, i.e, as the harmonic mean between those two measure. In more detail, given two annotators A_1 and A_2, we say the precision of A_1 relative to A_2 with respect to POS tag T in some data set X, denoted $Prec_T(A_1(X), A_2(X))$, is the number of tokens both A_1 and A_2 predict to be T over the number of times A_1 predicts a token to be T. Similarly, we define the recall with respect to some tag T, i.e., $Rec_T(A_1(X), A_2(X))$, as the number of tokens both A_1 and A_2 predict to be T over the number of times A_2 predicts a token to be T. The only difference with respect to standard precision and recall is that the gold standard is replaced by a second annotator, A_2. Note that $Prec_T(A_1(X), A_2(X)) = Rec_T(A_2(X), A_1(X))$. It follows from all of the above that the $F1$-score is symmetrical, i.e., $F1_T(A_1(X), A_2(X)) = F1_T(A_2(X), A_1(X))$.

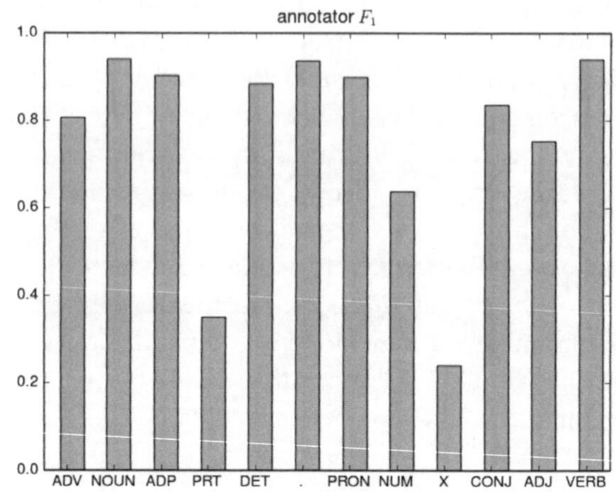

Figure 2: Inter-annotator $F1$-scores estimated from 500 tweets.

The inter-annotator $F1$-scores over the 12 POS tags in the universal tagset are presented in Figure 2. It shows that there is a high agreement for nouns, verbs and punctuation, while the agree-

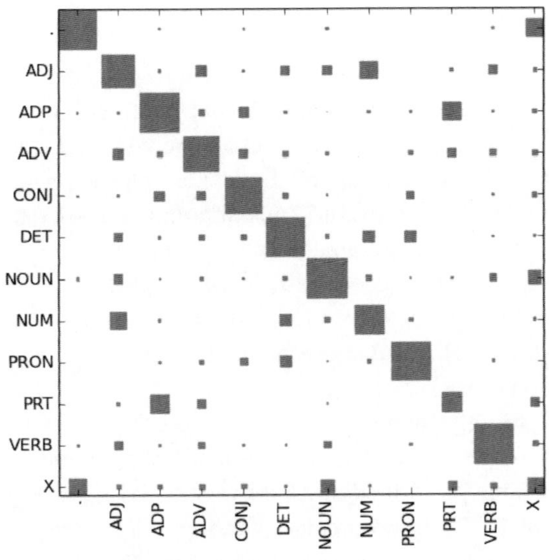

Figure 3: Confusion matrix of POS tags obtained from 500 doubly-annotated tweets.

ment is low, for instance, for particles, numerals and the X tag.

We compute tag confusion probabilities from a confusion matrix over POS tags like the one in Figure 3. From such a matrix, we compute the probability of confusing two tags t_1 and t_2 for some data point $\mathbf{x}$, i.e. $P(\{A_1(\mathbf{x}), A_2(\mathbf{x})\} = \{t_1, t_2\})$ as the mean of $P(A_1(\mathbf{x}) = t_1, A_2(\mathbf{x}) = t_2)$ and $P(A_1(\mathbf{x}) = t_2, A_2(\mathbf{x}) = t_1)$, e.g., the confusion probability of two tags is the mean of the probability that annotator A_1 assigns one tag and A_2 another, and vice versa.

We experiment with both agreement scores ($F1$ and confusion matrix probabilities) to augment the loss function in our learner. The next section describes this modification in detail.

4 Inter-annotator agreement loss

We briefly introduce the cost-sensitive perceptron classifier. Consider the weighted perceptron loss on our ith example $\langle \mathbf{x}_i, y_i \rangle$ (with learning rate $\alpha = 1$), $L_{\mathbf{w}}(\langle \mathbf{x}_i, y_i \rangle)$:

$$\gamma(\text{sign}(\mathbf{w} \cdot \mathbf{x}_i), y_i) \max(0, -y_i \mathbf{w} \cdot \mathbf{x}_i)$$

In a non-cost-sensitive classifier, the weight function $\gamma(y_j, y_i) = 1$ for $1 \leq i \leq N$. The two cost-sensitive systems proposed only differ in how we formulate $\gamma(\cdot, \cdot)$. In one model, the loss is weighted by the inter-annotator $F1$ of the gold tag in question. This boils down to

$$\gamma(y_j, y_i) = F1_{y_i}(A_1(X), A_2(X))$$

where X is the small sample of held-out data used to estimate inter-annotator agreement. Note that in this formulation, the predicted label is not taken into consideration.

The second model is slightly more expressive and takes *both* the gold and predicted tags into account. It basically weights the loss by how likely the gold and predicted tag are to be mistaken for each other, i.e., (the inverse of) their confusion probability:

$$\gamma(y_j, y_i)) = 1 - P(\{A_1(X), A_2(X)\} = \{y_j, y_i\})$$

In both loss functions, a lower gamma value means that the tags are more likely to be confused by a pair of annotators. In this case, the update is smaller. In contrast, the learner incurs greater loss when easy tags are confused.

It is straight-forward to extend these cost-sensitive loss functions to the structured perceptron (Collins, 2002). In Figure 4, we provide the pseudocode for the cost-sensitive structured online learning algorithm. We refer to the cost-sensitive structured learners as $F1$- and *CM-weighted* below.

$X = \{\langle \mathbf{x}_i, y_i \rangle\}_{i=1}^{N}$ with $\mathbf{x}_i = \langle x_i^1, \ldots, x_i^m \rangle$
I iterations
$\mathbf{w} = \langle 0 \rangle^m$
for *iter* $\in I$ **do**
  for $1 \leq i \leq N$ **do**
    $\hat{y} = \arg\max_{y \in \mathcal{Y}} \mathbf{w} \cdot \Phi(\mathbf{x}_i, y)$
    $\mathbf{w} \leftarrow \mathbf{w} + \gamma(\hat{y}, y_i)[\Phi(\mathbf{x}_i, y_i) - \Phi(\mathbf{x}_i, \hat{y})]$
    $\mathbf{w}^* += \mathbf{w}$
  end for
end for
return $\mathbf{w}^* / = (N \times I)$

Figure 4: Cost-sensitive structured perceptron (see Section 3 for weight functions γ).

5 Experiments

In our main experiments, we use structured perceptron (Collins, 2002) with random corruptions using a drop-out rate of 0.1 for regularization, following Søgaard (2013a). We use the LXMLS toolkit implementation[1] with default parameters. We present learning curves across iterations, and only set parameters using held-out data for our downstream experiments.[2]

5.1 Results

Our results are presented in Figure 5. The top left graph plots accuracy on the training data per iteration. We see that CM-weighting does not hurt training data accuracy. The reason may be that the cost-sensitive learner does not try (as hard) to optimize performance on inconsistent annotations. The next two plots (upper mid and upper right) show accuracy over epochs on in-sample evaluation data, i.e., GIMPEL-DEV and RITTER-TEST. Again, the CM-weighted learner performs better than our baseline model, while the $F1$-weighted learner performs much worse.

The interesting results are the evaluations on out-of-sample evaluation data sets (FOSTER and IN-HOUSE) - lower part of Figure 5. Here, both our learners are competitive, but overall it is clear that the CM-weighted learner performs best. It consistently improves over the baseline and $F1$-weighting. The former is much more expressive as it takes confusion probabilities into account and does not only update based on gold-label uncertainty, as is the case with the $F1$-weighted learner.

5.2 Robustness across regularizers

Discriminative learning typically benefits from regularization to prevent overfitting. The simplest is the averaged perceptron, but various other methods have been suggested in the literature.

We use structured perceptron with drop-out, but results are relatively robust across other regularization methods. Drop-out works by randomly dropping a fraction of the active features in each iteration, thus preventing overfitting. Table 1 shows the results for using different regularizers, in particular, Zipfian corruptions (Søgaard, 2013b) and averaging. While there are minor differences across data sets and regularizers, we observe that the corresponding cell using the loss function suggested in this paper (CM) always performs better than the baseline method.

[1] `https://github.com/gracaninja/lxmls-toolkit/`

[2] In this case, we use FOSTER-DEV as our development data to avoid in-sample bias.

6 Downstream evaluation

We have seen that our POS tagging model improves over the baseline model on three out-of-sample test sets. The question remains whether training a POS tagger that takes inter-annotator agreement scores into consideration is also effective on downstream tasks. Therefore, we evaluate our best model, the CM-weighted learner, in two downstream tasks: shallow parsing—also known as chunking—and named entity recognition (NER).

For the downstream evaluation, we used the baseline and CM models trained over 13 epochs, as they performed best on FOSTER-DEV (cf. Figure 5). Thus, parameters were optimized only on POS tagging data, not on the downstream evaluation tasks. We use a publicly available implementation of conditional random fields (Lafferty et al., 2001)[3] for the chunking and NER experiments, and provide the POS tags from our CM learner as features.

6.1 Chunking

The set of features for chunking include information from tokens and POS tags, following Sha and Pereira (2003).

We train the chunker on Twitter data (Ritter et al., 2011), more specifically, the 70/30 train/test split provided by Derczynski et al. (2013) for POS tagging, as the original authors performed cross validation. We train on the 70% Twitter data (11k tokens) and evaluate on the remaining 30%, as well as on the test data from Foster et al. (2011). The FOSTER data was originally annotated for POS and constituency tree information. We converted it to chunks using publicly available conversion software.[4] Part-of-speech tags are the ones assigned by our cost-sensitive (CM) POS model trained on Twitter data, the concatenation of Gimpel and 70% Ritter training data. We did not include the CoNLL 2000 training data (newswire text), since adding it did not substantially improve chunking performance on tweets, as also shown in (Ritter et al., 2011).

The results for chunking are given in Table 2. They show that using the POS tagging model (CM) trained to be more sensitive to inter-annotator agreement improves performance over

[3] `http://crfpp.googlecode.com`

[4] `http://ilk.uvt.nl/team/sabine/homepage/software.html`

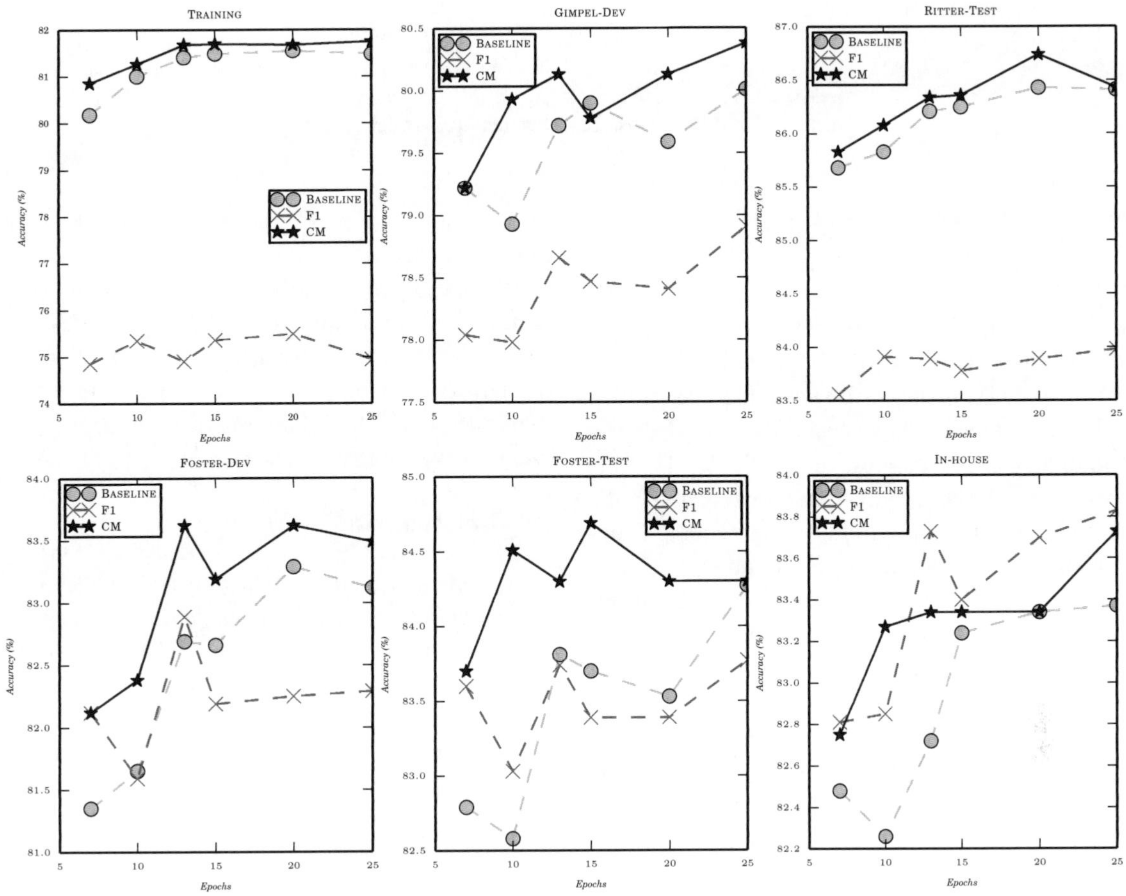

Figure 5: POS accuracy for the three models: baseline, confusion matrix loss (CM) and $F1$-weighted ($F1$) loss for increased number of training epochs. Top row: in-sample accuracy on training (left) and in-sample evaluation datasets (center, right). Bottom row: out-of-sample accuracy on various data sets. CM is robust on both in-sample and out-of-sample data.

	RITTER-TEST			
F1:	All	NP	VP	PP
BL	76.20	78.61	74.25	86.79
CM	76.42	79.07	74.98	86.19
	FOSTER-TEST			
F1:	All	NP	VP	PP
BL	68.49	70.73	60.56	86.50
CM	68.97	71.25	61.97	87.24

Table 2: Downstream results on chunking. Overall F1 score (All) as well as F1 for NP, VP and PP.

the baseline (BL) for the downstream task of chunking. Overall chunking F1 score improves. More importantly, we report on individual scores for NP, VP and PP chunks, where we see consistent improvements for NPs and VPs (since both nouns and verbs have high inter-annotator agreement), while results on PP are mixed. This is to be expected, since PP phrases involve adpositionals (ADP) that are often confused with particles (PRT), cf. Figure 3. Our tagger has been trained to deliberately abstract away from such uncertain cases. The results show that taking uncertainty in POS annotations into consideration during training has a positive effect in downstream results. It is thus better if we do not try to urge our models to make a firm decision on phenomena that neither

	BASELINE			CM		
Regularizer	FOSTER-DEV	FOSTER-TEST	IN-HOUSE	FOSTER-DEV	FOSTER-TEST	IN-HOUSE
Averaging	0.827	0.837	0.830	0.831	0.844	0.833
Drop-out	0.827	0.838	0.827	0.836	0.843	0.833
Zipfian	0.821	0.835	0.833	0.825	0.838	0.836

Table 1: Results across regularizers (after 13 epochs).

linguistic theories nor annotators do agree upon.

6.2 NER

In the previous section, we saw positive effects of cost-sensitive POS tagging for chunking, and here we evaluate it on another downstream task, NER.

For the named entity recognition setup, we use commonly used features, in particular features for word tokens, orthographic features like the presence of hyphens, digits, single quotes, upper/lowercase, 3 character prefix and suffix information. Moreover, we add Brown word cluster features that use 2,4,6,8,..,16 bitstring prefixes estimated from a large Twitter corpus (Owoputi et al., 2013).[5]

For NER, we do not have access to carefully annotated Twitter data for training, but rely on the crowdsourced annotations described in Finin et al. (2010). We use the concatenation of the CoNLL 2003 training split of annotated data from the Reuters corpus and the Finin data for training, as in this case training on the union resulted in a model that is substantially better than training on any of the individual data sets. For evaluation, we have three Twitter data set. We use the recently published data set from the MSM 2013 challenge (29k tokens)[6], the data set of Ritter et al. (2011) used also by Fromheide et al. (2014) (46k tokens), as well as an in-house annotated data set (20k tokens) (Fromheide et al., 2014).

F1:	RITTER	MSM	IN-HOUSE
BL	78.20	82.25	82.58
CM	78.30	82.00	82.77

Table 3: Downstream results for named entity recognition (F1 scores).

Table 3 shows the result of using our POS models in downstream NER evaluation. Here we observe mixed results. The cost-sensitive model is able to improve performance on two out of the three test sets, while being slightly below baseline performance on the MSM challenge data. Note that in contrast to chunking, POS tags are just one of the many features used for NER (albeit an important one), which might be part of the reason why the picture looks slightly different from what we observed above on chunking.

7 Related work

Cost-sensitive learning takes costs, such as misclassification cost, into consideration. That is, each instance that is not classified correctly during the learning process may contribute differently to the overall error. Geibel and Wysotzki (2003) introduce instance-dependent cost values for the perceptron algorithm and apply it to a set of binary classification problems. We focus here on structured problems and propose cost-sensitive learning for POS tagging using the structured perceptron algorithm. In a similar spirit, Higashiyama et al. (2013) applied cost-sensitive learning to the structured perceptron for an entity recognition task in the medical domain. They consider the distance between the predicted and true label sequence smoothed by a parameter that they estimate on a development set. This means that the entire sequence is scored at once, while we update on a per-label basis.

The work most related to ours is the recent study of Song et al. (2012). They suggest that some errors made by a POS tagger are more serious than others, especially for downstream tasks. They devise a hierarchy of POS tags for the Penn treebank tag set (e.g. the class NOUN contains NN, NNS, NNP, NNPS and CD) and use that in an SVM learner. They modify the Hinge loss that can take on three values: $0, \sigma, 1$. If an error occurred and the predicted tag is in the same class as the gold tag, a loss σ occurred, otherwise it counts as full cost. In contrast to our approach, they let the learner focus on the more difficult cases by occurring a bigger loss when the predicted POS tag

[5] http://www.ark.cs.cmu.edu/TweetNLP/

[6] http://oak.dcs.shef.ac.uk/msm2013/ie_challenge/

is in a different category. Their approach is thus suitable for a fine-grained tagging scheme and requires tuning of the cost parameter σ. We tackle the problem from a different angle by letting the learner abstract away from difficult, inconsistent cases as estimated from inter-annotator scores.

Our approach is also related to the literature on regularization, since our cost-sensitive loss functions are aimed at preventing over-fitting to low-confidence annotations. Søgaard (2013b; 2013a) presented two theories of linguistic variation and perceptron learning algorithms that regularize models to minimize loss under expected variation. Our work is related, but models variations in annotation rather than variations in input.

There is a large literature related to the issue of learning from annotator bias. Reidsma and op den Akker (2008) show that differences between annotators are not random slips of attention but rather different biases annotators might have, i.e. different mental conceptions. They show that a classifier trained on data from one annotator performed much better on in-sample (same annotator) data than on data of any other annotator. They propose two ways to address this problem: i) to identify subsets of the data that show higher inter-annotator agreement and use only that for training (e.g. for speaker address identification they restrict the data to instances where at least one person is in the focus of attention); ii) if available, to train separate models on data annotated by different annotators and combine them through voting. The latter comes at the cost of recall, because they deliberately chose the classifier to abstain in non-consensus cases.

In a similar vein, Klebanov and Beigman (2009) divide the instance space into easy and hard cases, i.e. easy cases are reliably annotated, whereas items that are hard show confusion and disagreement. Hard cases are assumed to be annotated by individual annotator's coin-flips, and thus cannot be assumed to be uniformly distributed (Klebanov and Beigman, 2009). They show that learning with annotator noise can have deteriorating effect at test time, and thus propose to remove hard cases, both at test time (Klebanov and Beigman, 2009) and training time (Beigman and Klebanov, 2009).

In general, it is important to analyze the data and check for label biases, as a machine learner is greatly affected by annotator noise that is not random but systematic (Reidsma and Carletta, 2008). However, rather than training on subsets of data or training separate models – which all implicitly assume that there is a large amount of training data available – we propose to integrate inter-annotator biases directly into the loss function.

Regarding measurements for agreements, several scores have been suggested in the literature. Apart from the simple agreement measure, which records how often annotators choose the same value for an item, there are several statistics that qualify this measure by adjusting for other factors, such as Cohen's κ (Cohen and others, 1960), the G-index score (Holley and Guilford, 1964), or Krippendorff's α (Krippendorf, 2004). However, most of these scores are sensitive to the label distribution, missing values, and other circumstances. The measure used in this paper is less affected by these factors, but manages to give us a good understanding of the agreement.

8 Conclusion

In NLP, we use a variety of measures to assess and control annotator disagreement to produce homogenous final annotations. This masks the fact that some annotations are more reliable than others, and which is thus not reflected in learned predictors. We incorporate the annotator uncertainty on certain labels by measuring annotator agreement and use it in the modified loss function of a structured perceptron. We show that this approach works well independent of regularization, both on in-sample and out-of-sample data. Moreover, when evaluating the models trained with our loss function on downstream tasks, we observe improvements on two different tasks. Our results suggest that we need to pay more attention to annotator confidence when training predictors.

Acknowledgements

We would like to thank the anonymous reviewers and Nathan Schneider for valuable comments and feedback. This research is funded by the ERC Starting Grant LOWLANDS No. 313695.

References

Eyal Beigman and Beata Klebanov. 2009. Learning with annotation noise. In *ACL*.

Jacob Cohen et al. 1960. A coefficient of agreement

for nominal scales. *Educational and psychological measurement*, 20(1):37–46.

Michael Collins. 2002. Discriminative training methods for hidden markov models: Theory and experiments with perceptron algorithms. In *EMNLP*.

Dipanjan Das and Slav Petrov. 2011. Unsupervised part-of-speech tagging with bilingual graph-based projections. In *ACL*.

Leon Derczynski, Alan Ritter, Sam Clark, and Kalina Bontcheva. 2013. Twitter part-of-speech tagging for all: overcoming sparse and noisy data. In *RANLP*.

Jakob Elming, Anders Johannsen, Sigrid Klerke, Emanuele Lapponi, Hector Martinez, and Anders Søgaard. 2013. Down-stream effects of tree-to-dependency conversions. In *NAACL*.

Tim Finin, Will Murnane, Anand Karandikar, Nicholas Keller, Justin Martineau, and Mark Dredze. 2010. Annotating named entities in Twitter data with crowdsourcing. In *NAACL-HLT 2010 Workshop on Creating Speech and Language Data with Amazon's Mechanical Turk*.

Jennifer Foster, Ozlem Cetinoglu, Joachim Wagner, Josef Le Roux, Joakim Nivre, Deirde Hogan, and Josef van Genabith. 2011. From news to comments: Resources and benchmarks for parsing the language of Web 2.0. In *IJCNLP*.

Hege Fromheide, Dirk Hovy, and Anders Søgaard. 2014. Crowdsourcing and annotating NER for Twitter #drift. In *Proceedings of LREC 2014*.

Peter Geibel and Fritz Wysotzki. 2003. Perceptron based learning with example dependent and noisy costs. In *ICML*.

Kevin Gimpel, Nathan Schneider, Brendan O'Connor, Dipanjan Das, Daniel Mills, Jacob Eisenstein, Michael Heilman, Dani Yogatama, Jeffrey Flanigan, and Noah A. Smith. 2011. Part-of-speech tagging for twitter: Annotation, features, and experiments. In *ACL*.

Shohei Higashiyama, Kazuhiro Seki, and Kuniaki Uehara. 2013. Clinical entity recognition using cost-sensitive structured perceptron for NTCIR-10 MedNLP. In *NTCIR*.

Jasper Wilson Holley and Joy Paul Guilford. 1964. A Note on the G-Index of Agreement. *Educational and Psychological Measurement*, 24(4):749.

Dirk Hovy, Barbara Plank, and Anders Søgaard. 2014. When POS datasets don't add up: Combatting sample bias. In *Proceedings of LREC 2014*.

Richard Johansson. 2013. Training parsers on incompatible treebanks. In *NAACL*.

Beata Klebanov and Eyal Beigman. 2009. From annotator agreement to noise models. *Computational Linguistics*, 35(4):495–503.

Klaus Krippendorf, 2004. *Content Analysis: An Introduction to Its Methodology, second edition*, chapter 11. Sage, Thousand Oaks, CA.

John Lafferty, Andrew McCallum, and Fernando Pereira. 2001. Conditional random fields: probabilistic models for segmenting and labeling sequence data. In *ICML*.

Christopher D Manning. 2011. Part-of-speech tagging from 97% to 100%: is it time for some linguistics? In *Computational Linguistics and Intelligent Text Processing*, pages 171–189. Springer.

Mitchell Marcus, Mary Marcinkiewicz, and Beatrice Santorini. 1993. Building a large annotated corpus of English: the Penn Treebank. *Computational Linguistics*, 19(2):313–330.

Ryan McDonald, Joakim Nivre, Yvonne Quirmbach-Brundage, Yoav Goldberg, Dipanjan Das, Kuzman Ganchev, Keith Hall, Slav Petrov, Hao Zhang, Oscar Täckström, Claudia Bedini, Núria Bertomeu Castelló, and Jungmee Lee. 2013. Universal dependency annotation for multilingual parsing. In *ACL*.

Olutobi Owoputi, Brendan O'Connor, Chris Dyer, Kevin Gimpel, Nathan Schneider, and Noah A Smith. 2013. Improved part-of-speech tagging for online conversational text with word clusters. In *NAACL*.

Slav Petrov, Dipanjan Das, and Ryan McDonald. 2012. A universal part-of-speech tagset. In *LREC*.

Dennis Reidsma and Jean Carletta. 2008. Reliability measurement without limits. *Computational Linguistics*, 34(3):319–326.

Dennis Reidsma and Rieks op den Akker. 2008. Exploiting 'subjective' annotations. In *Workshop on Human Judgements in Computational Linguistics, COLING*.

Alan Ritter, Sam Clark, Oren Etzioni, et al. 2011. Named entity recognition in tweets: an experimental study. In *EMNLP*.

Roy Schwartz, Omri Abend, Roi Reichart, and Ari Rappoport. 2011. Neutralizing linguistically problematic annotations in unsupervised dependency parsing evaluation. In *ACL*.

Fei Sha and Fernando Pereira. 2003. Shallow parsing with conditional random fields. In *NAACL*.

Anders Søgaard. 2013a. Part-of-speech tagging with antagonistic adversaries. In *ACL*.

Anders Søgaard. 2013b. Zipfian corruptions for robust pos tagging. In *NAACL*.

Hyun-Je Song, Jeong-Woo Son, Tae-Gil Noh, Seong-Bae Park, and Sang-Jo Lee. 2012. A cost sensitive part-of-speech tagging: differentiating serious errors from minor errors. In *ACL*.

Reut Tsarfaty, Joakim Nivre, and Evelina Andersson. 2012. Cross-framework evaluation for statistical parsing. In *EACL*.

Daniel Zeman and Philip Resnik. 2008. Cross-language parser adaptation between related languages. In *IJCNLP*.

Daniel Zeman. 2010. Hard problems of tagset conversion. In *Proceedings of the Second International Conference on Global Interoperability for Language Resources*.

Author Index

Association for Computational Linguistics
209 N. Eighth Street
Stroudsburg, Pennsylvania 18360

CURRAN ASSOCIATES INC
proceedings.com

16th International Conference on Interfaces and Human Computer Interaction (IHCI2022) and 15th International Conference on Game and Entertainment Technologies (GET2022)

Held at the 16th Multi-Conference on Computer Science and Information Systems (MCCSIS 2022)

Lisbon, Portugal
19-22 July 2022

iadis